THE SHORT OXFORD HISTORY OF
ENGLISH LITERATURE

THE SHORT OXFORD HISTORY OF
ENGLISH LITERATURE

THIRD EDITION

Andrew Sanders

OXFORD
UNIVERSITY PRESS

OXFORD

UNIVERSITY PRESS

Great Clarendon Street, Oxford OX2 6DP

Oxford University Press is a department of the University of Oxford.
It furthers the University's objective of excellence in research, scholarship,
and education by publishing worldwide in

Oxford New York

Auckland Bangkok Buenos Aires Cape Town Chennai
Dar es Salaam Delhi Hong Kong Istanbul Karachi Kolkata
Kuala Lumpur Madrid Melbourne Mexico City Mumbai Nairobi
São Paulo Shanghai Taipei Tokyo Toronto

Oxford is a registered trade mark of Oxford University Press
in the UK and in certain other countries

Published in the United States
by Oxford University Press Inc., New York

© Andrew Sanders 1994, 1996, 1999, 2004

First published 1994
Revised edition 1996
Second edition 1999
Third edition 2004

British Library Cataloguing in Publication Data

Data available

Library of Congress Cataloging in Publication Data

Data applied for

ISBN 0-19-926338-8

10 9 8 7 6 5 4 3 2 1

Typeset by SNP Best-set Typesetter Ltd., Hong Kong
Printed in Great Britain
on acid-free paper by
Ashford Colour Press Limited, Gosport, Hampshire

For Agnes and Cecilia

ACKNOWLEDGEMENTS

I AM most grateful to the following friends and colleagues who made close, helpful, encouraging, and often indispensable comments on various aspects in this *History*: Isobel Armstrong, Sandra Clark, Robert Inglesfield, Peter Mudford, Graham Parry, Jan Jedrzejewski (formerly of the University of Lodz, now of the University of Ulster), Chantal Cornut-Gentille D'Arcy (of the University of Zaragoza), Mihaela Irimia (of the University of Bucharest), and Anita Weston-Bilardello (of the University of Perugia). I am also, if less directly, grateful to the many anonymous readers of sections of the manuscript whose detailed comments were generally most helpful. Above all, I would like to thank my patient wife, Edwina Porter, for bearing the strains of composition and for offering immediate critical comment on pages thrust in front of her. Shirley Levy provided what I needed when I was most out of my depth: carefully considered direction and notes for the chapter on medieval literature. I am also grateful to my colleagues in the English department at Birkbeck College for two terms of 'light teaching' over a four-year period which enabled me to complete certain parts of the text without significant interruption (except for examination scripts!). My final thanks are due to Kim Scott Walwyn who flattered me into writing this book, to Andrew Lockett who coaxed and encouraged it into its present existence, to Jason Freeman who oversaw its progress through the press and to Michael Rogers who so patiently and scrupulously helped to proof-read it.

Andrew Sanders

Sophie Goldsworthy's invitation to revise this book for the Oxford University Press has given me the opportunity to add sections to it concerning authors and topics which I had, for various reasons (mostly ignorance), omitted from the first edition. I have also had the welcome opportunity to substantially revise the closing chapter. I am most grateful to the many people who have generously praised my earlier efforts and to those who prompted me to rethink or who helped shape my ideas. My particular gratitude is due to Ian Doyle, Michael O'Neill, Will Wootten, Alison Shell, Arnold Hunt, and James Birkett. My thanks too, to the same James Birkett for his help in revising the Guide to Further Reading.

London—Durham
February—March 1999

A call for a third edition of this book has enabled me to make further additions and to emend certain sections of the text. I am most grateful to those anonymous readers sought out by the Oxford University Press and to those amongst my friends who have suggested certain expansions or the inclusion of writers whom I had previously omitted. My especial thanks are due again to Anita Weston and James Birkett, to Corinne Saunders and David Fuller for encouragement and technical assistance, and to Andrew Rudd, who helped me in revising and updating the bibliography.

London—Durham
October 2003

CONTENTS

A NOTE ON THE TEXT

IN the case of quotations I have endeavoured to cite the best scholarly texts available. In most instances this has meant that the spellings have not been brought into line with modern usage, though where I have quoted from the plays and certain poems of Shakespeare and his contemporaries I have followed the common editorial practice of accepting a modernized spelling. I apologize if these anomalies offend certain readers. I hope that the quotations in the text give some sense of the development of the English language and English usage over the centuries.

INTRODUCTION

Poets' Corners: The Development of a Canon of English Literature

Soon after his death in October 1400 the body of Geoffrey Chaucer was placed in a modest tomb in the eastern aisle of the north transept of Westminster Abbey, the coronation church of the English kings. He was so honoured not because he was the author of *The Canterbury Tales*, but because he had formerly held the post of Clerk of the King's Works and because he had been living in the precincts of the Abbey at the time of his death. He was, moreover, distantly connected to the royal family through his wife Philippa. When John Gower died some eight years later he was interred in the Priory Church of St Mary Overie in Southwark (now Southwark Cathedral). Gower, who had retired to the Priory in his old age, received a far more elaborate tomb, one which proclaimed him to be *Anglorum Poeta celeberrimus* ('the most famous poet of the English nation') and one which showed him in effigy somewhat uncomfortably resting his head on his three great works, the *Vox Clamantis*, the *Speculum Meditantis*, and the *Confessio Amantis*.

The respective fortunes of the burial sites of these two 'dead, white, male poets' is to a significant degree indicative of how a distinct canon of English literature has emerged over the centuries. Although St Mary Overie's, renamed St Saviour's in the sixteenth century, later housed the tombs of the playwrights John Fletcher (d. 1625) and Philip Massinger (d. 1640) and of Bishop Lancelot Andrewes (who died at the nearby Winchester House in 1626), it never proved as prestigious a church as the distinctly aristocratic Westminster Abbey. Nor did the body of Gower prove to be as powerful an object of poetic veneration as that of Chaucer. In 1556 Nicholas Brigham, a government official with antiquarian tastes, erected a new, but conservatively Gothic, monument over Chaucer's bones. His act of national piety was a tribute to Chaucer's acknowledged status as, to use Edmund Spenser's term, the 'pure well head of Poesie'. It was within feet of Chaucer's grave that Spenser himself was buried in 1599, his mural monument, erected some twenty years later, pronouncing him to be 'the Prince of Poets in his Tyme'. Thus specially consecrated to the Muses, this corner of a royal church later contained the ashes of Michael Drayton, who 'exchanged his Laurell for a Crowne of Glorye' in 1631, of 'rare' Ben Jonson who died in 1637, and of Abraham Cowley who died in 1667. Its prestige was firmly established with the burial of John Dryden in 1700 and by the subsequent construction of an elegant funerary monument which seems to guard the entrance to the aisle.

Writing in *The Spectator* in 1711, Joseph Addison referred to this already celebrated part of the Abbey as 'the poetical Quarter'. Its name was gradually transmogrified into the familiar 'Poets' Corner'. The seal was set on its function as a place where English poets might, and indeed ought, to be commemorated, regardless of their actual place of interment, in the middle years of the eighteenth century. Here, in what was rapidly becoming less like an exclusively royal church and more like a national pantheon, was an area largely devoted to the posthumous celebration of writers. Here distinguished citizens, and not the state, decreed that, with the Dean of Westminster's permission, men of letters might rest or be sculpturally remembered in the ancient Roman manner. In 1721 the architect James Gibbs designed a fine mural tablet in memory of Matthew Prior. In 1737 William Benson, a connoisseur of literature and the Surveyer-General of Works, paid for the setting-up of Rysbrack's posthumous bust of John Milton (d. 1674) and, three years later, a spectacular mural cenotaph, carved by Peter Scheemakers, was erected to the honour of William Shakespeare (who had been buried in provincial Stratford 124 years earlier). The monument, proudly inscribed with the words *Amor Publicus Posuit* ('The public's love placed it here'), was the outcome of an appeal for funds made by a committee which included Lord Burlington and Alexander Pope. Although Pope himself contributed notably to the Abbey's expanding collection of poetic epitaphs, he never received even the most modest of memorials in Poets' Corner. The honour was, however, accorded to James Thomson in 1762, to Thomas Gray in 1771, and to Oliver Goldsmith in 1774. In 1784, to affirm the Abbey's status as a national pantheon, the much respected Samuel Johnson was interred in the floor of the south transept at the foot of the monument to Shakespeare.

Edmund Spenser's conscious construction of a literary tradition, in which he was associated in life and death with the poetic example of Chaucer, had therefore been instrumental in establishing the significance of Poets' Corner in the minds of those who sought to define a line of succession in national literature. In common with many other self-appointed arbiters of public taste, however, the Abbey authorities were singularly behindhand in recognizing the marked shift in literary fashions in the first two decades of the nineteenth century. While relatively minor poets such as William Mason (d. 1797) and the author of the once celebrated *New Bath Guide*, Christopher Anstey (d. 1805), were commemorated in wall-tablets, the new generation of poets, many of whom died young, were initially conspicuous for their absence. Notoriously, in 1824 the 'immoral' Lord Byron was refused a tomb by the Dean of Westminster, a refusal compounded seven years later by the rejection of

Thorvaldsen's marble statue of the pensive poet specially commissioned by a group of Byron's friends. A memorial slab to Byron was somewhat shame-facedly installed only in 1969. Keats and Shelley, both buried in Rome, equally had to wait until the mid-twentieth century for an Abbey monument. By the early Victorian period, however, both public and ecclesiastical opinion deemed it proper to erect posthumous busts of Coleridge (d. 1834) and Southey (d. 1843) and a statue of the seated Wordsworth (d. 1850), all of them significantly clustered in the protective shadow of Shakespeare.

The enlightened Victorian Dean of Westminster, Arthur Stanley (1815–81), a former pupil of Dr Arnold's at Rugby, was instrumental in allotting the already over-occupied south transept its most visited grave, that of Charles Dickens (d. 1870). Stanley's decision to bury Dickens in the Abbey is notable for two reasons: he overrode Dickens's express desire to be buried in Rochester, and he also, for the first time, included a novelist amongst its eminent literary dead. The privilege had already been denied to Thackeray (d. 1863) and Elizabeth Gaskell (d. 1865) and was not extended to the agnostic George Eliot (d. 1880) (though it had been suggested to Stanley that she was 'a woman whose achievements were without parallel in the previous history of womankind') or to the singularly 'churchy' Anthony Trollope (d. 1882). After Stanley's time, however, the niceties of religious belief and unbelief were largely set aside as the graves of Browning, Tennyson, Hardy, and Kipling virtually filled the available space and gave the entire transept its popular, if narrow, character as a Who was Who of English letters. When one says 'English' letters, it should be remembered that Victorian inclusiveness insisted on the addition of busts of Sir Walter Scott and Robert Burns, on the commemoration of the American Longfellow and of Adam Lindsay Gordon, the 'Poet of Australia'. Since the nineteenth century, literary societies and informal pressure groups have sys-tematically brought about the canonization by tablet of the particular objects of their admiration. Thus women writers (Jane Austen, the Brontës, and George Eliot) have received belated notice. The once overlooked or notably absent now have their busts (Thackeray by Marochetti, Blake by Epstein), their mural tablets (Ruskin, Matthew Arnold, Clare), or their engraved floor slabs (Cædmon, Hopkins, Edward Lear, Lewis Carroll, Anthony Trollope, Henry James, D. H. Lawrence, Dylan Thomas, John Masefield, T. S. Eliot, W. H. Auden, and an *omnium gatherum* of poets who served in the First World War).

Poets' Corner has always commemorated a surprisingly arbitrary selection of writers and, like any parallel attempt to draw up a canon or a list, generally represents the opinions of what a certain group of influential people have wanted to believe mattered to them and to their times. What the memorials in Poets' Corner represent is a loose series of decisions, all of them, in their time, considered decisions, which have subsequently been interpreted as categorical and canonical. This is how most canons come into being. The trouble with canons is that they not only become hallowed by tradition, they also enforce tradition.

In its original sense, the idea of a canon included not just the biblical books approved as a source of doctrine by the Church, but also the list of saints whose names could be invoked in prayer and to whom a degree of devotion could be directed. There have always been writers who have sought to associate themselves with a secular canon and a secular apostolic succession as earnestly as the Christian Church hallowed its Scriptures and looked to its history in order to justify its continued existence. Chaucer was anxious to prove his credentials as an innovative English poet by appealing to ancient authority and by displaying his knowledge of modern French and Italian writers. Some 150 years later, Spenser insisted not only that he had drunk deeply at the well of Italian poetry, but also that he was nourished by a vernacular tradition that he dated back to Chaucer. Milton, in his turn, claimed to be the heir to the 'sage and serious' Spenser. In the nineteenth century such invocations of a tradition were supplemented by a reverence only marginally this side of idolatry. In the third book of *The Prelude*, William Wordsworth described his sense of intimacy as a Cambridge undergraduate, with the spirits of Chaucer, Spenser, and Milton, and the dizzy 'libations' drunk to the memory of the sober Milton in the poet's former 'lodge and oratory'. Later in life Wordsworth insisted to his nephew that he had always seen himself as standing in an apostolic line: 'When I began to give myself up to the profession of a poet for life, I was impressed with a conviction, that there were four English poets whom I must have continually before me as examples—Chaucer, Shakespeare, Spenser and Milton.' These four poets he claimed to have systematically studied and attempted to equal '*if I could*'. John Keats treasured an engraving of Shakespeare and fancied that the Bard was a 'good Genius' presiding over his work. He posed in front of the Shakespeare for his own portrait, and, when composing, was apt to imagine 'in what position Shakespeare sat when he began "To be or not to be"'. Sir Walter Scott had a cast of Shakespeare's Stratford monument placed in a niche in his library at Abbotsford and hung an engraving of Thomas Stothard's painting of Chaucer's Canterbury Pilgrims over the fireplace in his study. In 1844 Charles Dickens had a copy of the same engraving hung in the entrance hall at 1 Devonshire Terrace and gilt-framed portraits of his friends, Carlyle and Tennyson, prominently displayed in his library. When he acquired Gad's Hill Place in Kent in 1856 he was so proud of its loose Shakespearian connection that he had a framed inscription proclaiming the fact placed in his hallway. Before the privations of his career as a Jesuit began, the undergraduate Gerard Manley Hopkins asked for portraits of Tennyson, Shelley, Keats, Shakespeare, Milton, and Dante to decorate his rooms at Oxford. The grace of the literary tradition stretched even to the death-bed. Tennyson, who had been rereading Shakespeare's plays in his last illness, was buried clasping a copy of *Cymbeline* and crowned with a wreath of laurel plucked from Virgil's tomb. Even in the anti-heroic twentieth century this yearning to be associated with an established tradition seems not to have diminished. Amidst the plethora of his own images which decorate George Bernard Shaw's house at Ayot St Lawrence is a

Staffordshire pottery figure of Shakespeare; behind Vita Sackville-West's writing table in her sitting-room at Sissinghurst hang portraits of the Brontë sisters and Virginia Woolf; according to one of his recent biographers, T. S. Eliot acquired a photograph of Poets' Corner, with Dryden's monument prominent in the foreground, soon after his arrival in England.

An awareness of the significance, as well as the decorative value, of the English literary tradition was by no means confined to literary aspirants to that tradition. By the mid-eighteenth century English porcelain manufacturers were marketing paired statuettes of Shakespeare and Milton, designed to stand like household gods on refined middle-class chimney-pieces. The Shakespeare was modelled on the Scheemakers statue in Westminster Abbey, the Milton being given a similar half-column on which to rest a pile of books and his elegant left elbow. These models, with variations, remained current until well into the Victorian era, being imitated in cheap Staffordshire pottery (such as seems later to have appealed to Shaw) and in more up-market *biscuit* and Parian ware. The phenomenal popularity of high-quality Parian china in the mid-nineteenth century meant that there were at least 11 different versions of busts or statuettes of Shakespeare on sale to a mass public from various manufacturers. There were also some 6 distinct models available of Milton, 7 of Scott, 6 of Burns, 5 of Byron, 4 of Dickens, 3 of Tennyson, and one each of Bunyan, Johnson, Wordsworth, Shelley, Browning, Thackeray, and Ruskin. The pairing of Shakespeare and Milton as chimney-ornaments, in Parian china and in other cheaper materials, was reflected for Scots and Scotophiles by parallel figures representing Scott and Burns. It is interesting to note, despite political arguments to the contrary, how easily a popular view of the literary tradition seems to have assimilated both establishment and antiestablishment figures. Much as it balanced the 'classical' Milton against that 'Gothic' warbler of native woodnotes wild, Shakespeare, so it seems to have accepted the counterpoise of the (we assume) royalist Shakespeare and the republican Milton. So too, it balanced the Tory Scott and the radical Burns. Although this decorative art may have sprung from a hero-worshipping impulse, it was scarcely confrontational. The idea of possessing representations of famous writers (or, still nowadays, of composers) may have been stimulated by a desire to show off an aspiration to, or an acquisition of, an 'élite' culture, but it cannot properly be seen as a fashion imposed exclusively from above.

The desire to commemorate a line of development and to dignify certain representative writers did, however, have a distinctly gentlemanly precedent, one that went with the possession of a library, or rather with the luxury of a room set aside for books and private study. One of the most remarkable collections of English literary portraits to survive outside the National Portrait Gallery is that assembled in the 1740s by the fourth Earl of Chesterfield (1694–1773) and now in the possession of the University of London Library. Chesterfield bought pictures from the sales of two earlier collectors and patrons of literature—Edward Harley, second Earl of Oxford and Charles Montagu,

Earl of Halifax—and also commissioned new images of his own. The paintings were installed in the library of his grand house in Mayfair in 1750 with the portrait of Shakespeare (now in Stratford-upon-Avon) in pride of place over the mantelpiece. Chesterfield's selection of authors may have largely depended on what painted images were available to him, but the series of portraits still represents a sound guide to what his contemporaries would have regarded as the major figures in English writing up to their own day. Apart from Shakespeare, the collection included images of Chaucer, Sidney, Spenser, Jonson, Denham, Prior, Cowley, Butler, Otway, Dryden, Wycherley, Rowe, Congreve, Swift, Addison, and Pope (the last two painted expressly for his library). Chesterfield also owned two portraits once mistakenly assumed to be of Milton (one is now believed to show Edmund Waller, the other the minor dramatist, William Cartwright). Chesterfield's canonical selection would probably not coincide exactly with a list drawn up by a classically-minded modern scholar of pre-eighteenth-century literature. Given its exclusion of most medieval poets, most Elizabethan and Jacobean dramatists, and all the disciples of Donne, it would almost certainly clash with how most other twentieth-century readers would choose to view the literary history of the same period.

The drawing up of canons and the making of lists is always a fraught business, one conditioned not only by private tastes and transient public fashions but also by what successors are likely to see as ancestral myopia. But then, the present is always inclined to read the past proleptically as a means of justifying its own prejudices and emphases. The late twentieth century has not proved able to liberate itself from an inherited inclination to catalogue, calibrate, and categorize, let alone from an insistently progressivist view of history. When modern publishers·periodically draw up lists of the 'Twenty Best Young British Novelists', or of the 'Ten Best Modern Writers', or when newspapers absurdly attempt to determine who have been the 'Thousand Makers of the Twentieth Century', they are only following pseudo-scientific habits of mind formed in the eighteenth and nineteenth centuries. We are more conditioned by Linnaean systems of thought than we often choose to recognize. The nineteenth-century European habit of inscribing famous names on public buildings, of placing busts in architectural niches, and of enhancing cornices with the statues of the great is a case in point. The habit followed from the idea that buildings could be *read* and it represented an attempt to petrify a particular view of cultural history. It was probably killed not by a wholesale revision of cultural history but by a reaction against representation and symbolic art in the 1920s and by the virtual abolition of architectural sculpture in the 1950s. If the names of half-forgotten composers still decorate the façades of opera-houses and the walls of concert-halls throughout Europe, certain prominent British buildings also proclaim the significance of 'national' literature. When, for example, a Royal Commission was established in 1841 to oversee the decorative scheme of the new Houses of Parliament, they determined that the subjects for frescos for the interiors should be drawn exclusively from British history and from the works of three English poets: Spenser, Shakespeare, and Milton. None of the designs originally proposed came to fruition, though, in the early 1850s, a series of literary frescos was executed in the Upper Waiting Hall, the subjects being taken from the works of eight writers: Chaucer, Spenser, Shakespeare, Milton, Dryden, Pope, Byron, and Scott. This stress on national poetry in a building ostensibly dedicated to the workings of Victorian democracy is not really surprising. Literature was seen not only as an identifiable achievement of the British nation, but also as an expression of the unity and of the continuity of the institutions of that same nation (the inclusion of Scott amongst these eight poets was, in part, an acknowledgement of Scotland's place in the union; an Irish equivalent was evidently difficult to find). Only three English writers, Chaucer, Shakespeare, and Milton, appeared on the south front of the plinth of the Albert Memorial, finished in 1867, but then they had to jostle for eminence in the select company of thirty-six other European poets and musicians. Where one might have expected international, or at least European reference, in the domed Reading-Room of the British Museum, a list of names of exclusively British writers was chosen in 1907 to be inscribed in the empty panels above the cornice. Having faded, they were obliterated in 1952. Here in temporary gilt splendour the names of Chaucer, Caxton, Tyndale, Spenser, Shakespeare, Bacon, Milton, Locke, Addison, Swift, Pope, Gibbon, Wordsworth, Scott, Byron, Carlyle, Macaulay, Tennyson, and Browning overshadowed the labours of the latterday readers and scribblers below. The fact that the names were not replaced is a further illustration, if one were needed, of the very contentiousness of all attempts to formulate a canon.

Several distinguished modern commentators have argued that the most important attempt to fix a canon of English literature was that made in the late nineteenth century by those who introduced English as a university subject. As D. J. Palmer, Chris Baldick, Terry Eagleton, Brian Doyle, Peter Brooker, and Peter Widdowson have variously suggested, in England, at least, 'English' arrived belatedly and with an ulterior motive.[1] This, as Robert Crawford has recently observed, was England's anomaly.[2] In Scotland, it seems things had been ordered differently, or at least ordered so as to direct the attention of aspirant Scots to their proper place within a United Kingdom and a substantially united literature. The tradition of teaching rhetoric and *belles-lettres*, established at the universities of Edinburgh and Glasgow in the mid-eighteenth century, was designed to introduce students to the supposed refinements of the classics *and* to the superior felicities of modern English stylists as a means of

---

[1] See D. J. Palmer, *The Rise of English Studies* (London: Oxford University Press, 1965); Chris Baldick, *The Social Mission of English Criticism 1848–1932* (Oxford: Oxford University Press, 1983); Terry Eagleton, *Literary Theory: An Introduction* (Oxford: Blackwell, 1983); Brian Doyle, 'The Invention of English', and Peter Brooker and Peter Widdowson, 'A Literature for England', in Robert Collis and Philip Dodd (eds.), *Englishness, Politics and Culture 1880–1920* (London: Croom Helm, 1986), 89–115, 116–63. See also Ian Michael, *The Teaching of English from the Sixteenth Century to 1870* (Cambridge: Cambridge University Press, 1987).

[2] Robert Crawford, *Devolving English Literature* (Oxford: Clarendon Press, 1992).

weaning them away from narrowly provincial preoccupations. The teaching of
English began, therefore, with some clear ideological intent. In attempting
to suppress a certain 'Scottishness' this programme remained distinctively
Scottish by the very fact of its aim of shaping Scottish intellectuals in an
enlightened European mould. Contemporary Edinburgh was reconstructed as
an Athens, and not a London, of the North.

The English language as used by British, and not exclusively English, stylists, was seen in Scotland as an essentially unifying and progressivist force.
When the teaching of English literature and history was introduced to the colleges of the new University of London in the 1830s it had a distinctly Scottish
bias. Although the first Professor of English at both University and King's
College, the Reverend Thomas Dale, was a Cambridge graduate, the pattern
of lectures and undergraduate study that he devised bore a marked resemblance to the courses in rhetoric already established in Scotland. By the late
1850s, when the first part of the London BA examinations included an obligatory paper in English language, literature, and history, the teaching of
English had evidently become a moral as well as an ideological exercise. As the
emphatically Christian *Handbook of English Literature* published in 1865 by
Joseph Angus, MA DD, 'Examiner in English Language, Literature and
History to the University of London', stresses, however, the grandly imperial
idea of England and its culture had come to embrace all aspects of the written
literature of the island of Britain. English literature, Angus writes, was 'the
reflection of the national life, an exhibition of the principles to which we owe
our freedom and progress: a voice of experience speaking for all time, to any
who are willing to hear'. 'No nation', he adds, somewhat chauvinistically, 'could
have originated it but in circumstances like those of England, and no nation
can receive and welcome it without reproducing in its life the image of our
own.' Although Angus warns his readers of the dangers of much modern prose
fiction (*'mentally*, habitual novel reading is destructive of real vigour; and
morally, it is destructive of real kindness'), his book is generally thorough,
broad-minded, and wide-ranging. He deals with early literature, with poetry,
drama, and prose from the mid-fourteenth to the mid-nineteenth century, and
he includes subsections on historical, philosophical, theological and, somewhat
more warily, rationalist writing. His main fault lies in his largely unrelieved
dullness, a dullness which very probably derived from his and his university's
strictly factual and chronological approach to the new subject. Angus defines
no restrictive canons, no patterns of saving literary grace, and no theories of
literature. All he can do at the end of his *Handbook is* draw the lame conclusions that study broadens the mind, that a student's style could be improved
with reference to established models, that history has a tendency to repeat itself,
and that literature ideally ought to be 'studied under the guidance of Christian
truth'.

A more restrictive and prescriptive line of argument is evident in Thomas
Arnold junior's *Manual of English Literature* (1862, expanded and reprinted in

1868 as *Chaucer to Wordsworth: A Short History of English Literature, From the Earliest Times to the Present Day*). Arnold (1823–1900) had been appointed Professor of English Literature at Newman's Catholic University in Dublin in 1862; he later held the chair at its successor institution, University College, Dublin. His *Manual* manages to proclaim both the liberally progressivist virtues insisted on by his firmly Protestant father and, to a lesser degree, the Catholic sensibility that he himself had espoused (and which his university embodied). Nevertheless, Arnold's study is both lively and engaging. He sees Elizabethan England, with its imposed Protestantism, as still managing to enjoy 'a joyous, sanguine, bustling time'; it was an age 'in which the movement was all forward, and the cold shade of reaction had not as yet appeared'. He finds the late eighteenth century, by contrast, a period of 'dim and dismal twilight', a twilight relieved only by the blazing lights of the emergent Romantic poets, 'young men full of hope and trust, and fresh untried vigour, whose hearts and imaginations were most powerfully acted upon by the great moral and political eruption in France'. Although Arnold ends his survey with these same poets, and although he warns in his Preface of the dangers of 'confounding the perishable with the enduring' in judging all modern writing, he firmly believes in the future potential of both English literature and of the study of English literature. The last sentence of his *Short History* refers prophetically back to Oxford, his own Alma Mater: 'A century hence, Englishmen will scarcely believe that England's most ancient and important university was still without a chair devoted to the systematic study of the national literature, in the year of grace 1868.'

If the tendency to view English literature as if it were a historical progression of worthy authors determined the University of London syllabus until well into the twentieth century, the ancient English universities, once they got round to establishing chairs and then courses of study, felt obliged to make English acceptable by rendering it dry, demanding, and difficult. The problem began with the idea that English was a parvenu subject largely suited to social and intellectual upstarts (a category which it was assumed included women). In order to appear 'respectable' in the company of gentlemanly disciplines such as classics and history, it had to require hard labour of its students. In the University of Oxford in particular, the axis of what was taken to be the received body of English literature was shifted drastically backwards. The popular perception of a loose canon, like Arnold's, which stretched from Chaucer to Wordsworth (or later Tennyson), was countered by a new, and far less arbitrary, choice of texts with a dominant stress on the close study of Old and Middle English literature. Beyond this insistence on a grasp of the earliest written forms of the English language, the Oxford syllabus virtually dragooned its students into a systematic consideration of a series of monumental poetic texts, all of which were written before the start of the Victorian age. In the heyday of the unreformed syllabus, in the 1940s, the undergraduate Philip Larkin was, according to his friend Kingsley Amis, driven to the kind of protest unbecoming to a future university librarian. Amis recalls working his own way resentfully through Spenser's *Faerie Queene* in an edition owned by his college library. At the foot of the last page he discovered an unsigned pencil note in Larkin's hand which read: 'First I thought Troilus and Criseyde was the most *boring* poem in English. Then I thought Beowulf was. Then I thought Paradise Lost was. Now I *know* that The Faerie Queene is the *dullest thing out. Blast* it.'

It was in reaction against syllabuses such as those devised by the universities of London and Oxford, and against the well-bred vacuousness of the first King Edward VII Professor of English Literature at Cambridge, Sir Arthur Quiller-Couch (1863–1944), that F. R. Leavis (1895–1978) defined his own ideas and his own canon. Although Quiller-Couch had defended the study of English against charge of 'easiness' and against the narrow oppressions of a strict and particular sect of medievalists, his published lectures suggest the extent to which he merely cited favourite books rather than interrogated or scrutinized them. Amid his classical tags and his elegant blandness he attempted to offer candidates for the new English degree (introduced in 1917) a grand overview of the subject, suggesting at one point that students might 'fasten on the great authors' whom he lists in select little groups (Shakespeare; Chaucer and Henryson; Spenser, Marlowe, Donne; Bacon, Milton, Dryden, Pope; Samuel Johnson, Burke; Coleridge, Wordsworth, Keats, Byron, Shelley; Dickens, Browning, Carlyle). With the reform of the Cambridge English Tripos in 1926, and with the appointment of Leavis as a probationary lecturer a year later, a far more rigorous approach to the study of English began to emerge. In his own lectures, Leavis took a malicious delight in citing examples of what he considered 'bad' poetry, extracted from Quiller-Couch's once standard anthology, *The Oxford Book of English Verse* (1900), expatiating on them as reflections of the anthologizer's standards and taste.

Leavis's influence was not, however, confined to Cambridge lecture halls or to his intense tutorial interaction with his personal students. In 1932 he founded the journal *Scrutiny* as a vehicle for the wider dissemination of his ideas and it was through *Scrutiny* that he and his disciples systematically explored a series of provocative critical judgements based on what he deemed to be life-enhancing principles. From this moral basis, established by Leavis and his approved contributors, there evolved a new canon of writers who were seen as part of a tradition that was 'alive in so far as it is alive to us'. Out went the non-critical, annalist, historical approach that Leavis associated with the Victorian critic, George Saintsbury (1845–1933); in came a dogmatically defined series of 'lines of development'. In *Revaluation: Tradition and Development in English Poetry* (1936), derived from essays first published in *Scrutiny*, the influence of T. S. Eliot's radical protest against Milton's style led Leavis to an alternative stress on a 'line of wit' stretching from Donne to Marvell. Shelley too was to be disparaged as one who handed poetry over to 'a sensibility that has no more dealings with intelligence than it can help'. *The*

Great Tradition (1948, also derived from *Scrutiny* essays) opens with the unequivocal statement: 'The great English novelists are Jane Austen, George Eliot, Henry James and Joseph Conrad . . .'. It barely pauses to reflect upon the fact that James was an American novelist or that Conrad's roots were distinctly un-English; it relegates Richardson, the Brontës, and Dickens to relatively minor roles; it ignores Thackeray, Gaskell, and Trollope; it insists that although Fielding deserved the place of importance given him in the despised Saintsburian literary histories, 'he hasn't the kind of classical distinction we are also invited to credit him with'; and it sees Scott as primarily 'a kind of inspired folk-lorist, qualified to have done in fiction something analogous to the ballad-opera'. Leavis's new canon was in some significant ways defined retrospectively. If, as he seems to suggest elsewhere, all 'lines of development' culminated in the work of D. H. Lawrence and Eliot, and not in that of Joyce or Woolf, so, reading back from Lawrence and Eliot, a new tradition was established, one that included Donne and Bunyan while excluding Spenser and Milton, one that added James while subtracting Sterne, one that praised Blake while remaining silent about Tennyson. It was only in 1970 that Dickens was allotted his place in a 'great tradition' that seemed formerly to have got on well enough without him (though, as Leavis's apologists were quick to point out, an 'analytic note' of 1948 had proclaimed that the then neglected *Hard Times* was a masterpiece).

As Lawrence's self-appointed mediator and advocate, Leavis made his critical readings of English literature central to a moral mission to redeem England from the consequences of its empty secularism. It was a mission which, like missions before and since, depended on dividing sheep from goats and distinguishing 'them' from 'us'. 'They', the goats, were confusingly various. 'They' controlled both the popular press and the academic journals; 'they' were upper middle-class dilettantes and Bloomsburyite intellectuals; 'they' were the demagogues of the right and the would-be tribunes of the people; latterly, 'they' were the underminers of civilization through television and all those who had failed to respond to Leavis's prophetic voice. 'We' (his readers) were, by contrast, a small élite who recognized the saving grace of the life-enhancers named in the select canon. To dismiss Leavis for his lack of a theoretical basis to his criticism, as certain Marxist critics have always done, is to miss the point of his mission. He suspected theory as much as he disliked historical criticism, because he considered it irrelevant to the real business of critical debate and irrelevant to the kind of careful textual analysis that he advocated. The narrowness of his insistence on 'close readings'—hermetically sealing texts from reference to the biographical, historical, social, political, and cultural circumstances which moulded them—has some parallels to the methods employed by Structuralists. Both now seem time-locked. More significantly, Leavis's determination to straighten and redefine the canon of English literature in the name of civilization looks like an attempt to halt both civilization and redefinition in their tracks.

Leavis and the Scrutineers had a profound impact on the teaching of English literature in Britain and its former Empire. Their influence waned not simply as a result of the challenges consistently presented to that influence by its enemies nor as a consequence of the advent of theoretical criticism in the 1970s and 1980s, but because of self-evident changes in the circumstances in which literature is produced and discussed in the late twentieth century. The ideas of 'tradition and development' and of a fixed set of values that Leavis sought to establish are no longer acceptable in a plural culture which encourages multiple ways of thinking, reading, and dissenting. The peremptory reform of an already restrictive canon matters less than the opening up of that canon. English literature can no longer be seen as expressive of the values of a self-perpetuating ruling class or as the exclusive inheritance of an educated élite. Nor can it be seen as some broad, classless social panacea or as a substitute for religion and politics. Alternatively, to dismiss it as inattentive to the class struggle or as a body of work produced by a line of dead, white, middle-class, English men scarcely helps to move any worthwhile debate forward. The long-established centrality of certain texts and selected authors, first advocated by eighteenth-century critics, has had to give way to the idea of decentralization, much as long centralized nations, including the United Kingdom, have been obliged to consider the implications of devolution and federal association.

In some significant ways the study of 'English literature' has had to return to basic historical principles. The long-standing international success of Émile Legouis's *A Short History of English Literature* (which this present *History* is intended to replace) suggests that in some circles these basic principles remained unchallenged. Legouis published his larger *History of English Literature* in 1929, in collaboration with his distinguished colleague Louis Cazamian, largely to answer the demand for such a text from the students he taught at the Sorbonne. His vastly slimmed-down *Short History* first appeared in an English translation in 1934 and managed to hold its own for nearly sixty years (despite the fact that its last entries dealt with Galsworthy, Conrad, and Shaw). Legouis's approach is straightforward and non-theoretical. 'Abstraction had to be avoided', he affirms in his Preface, 'and concreteness must be aimed at'. His overall theme stresses that both the language and the literature of the British Isles were expansive and inclusive. If his closing statements seem bland to some modern readers they cannot be dismissed out of hand. English literature shows 'a greater capacity than any other literature for combining a love of concrete statement with a tendency to dream, a sense of reality with lyrical rapture'. It is also characterized by 'loving observation of Nature, by a talent for depicting strongly-marked character, and by a humour that is the amused and sympathetic noting of the contradictions of human nature and the odd aspects of life'.

Although the tidy-minded Legouis could not quite bring himself to admit it, literature written in English has consistently been marked by even greater contradictions and contradistinctions: it has always been both multiple and polarized, both popular and élite. Decisions taken by certain generations to favour the example of Chaucer over Langland, Surrey over Skelton, Waller over Donne, Wordsworth over Cowper, or Eliot over Masefield, have had long-term ramifications, but they have never fully precluded the study and appreciation of the work of Langland, Skelton, Donne, Cowper, and Masefield. Periodic revivals of interest and reversals of taste have dramatically altered twentieth-century perceptions of, for example, the poetry and prose of the seventeenth century. Since the eighteenth century, when the teaching of 'English' had its tentative beginnings, the canonical balance of Shakespeare and Milton has been crucial to how 'English literature' was understood by a wide range of readers and critics (though, ironically, for the Scrutineers the 'dislodging' of Milton seemed to offer an expansion, rather than a deprivation of the canon). Certain readers and critics continue to make up their own canons—political, feminist, internationalist, mystical, whimsical, or simply (and most happily) for reasons of personal pleasure. Given the fertility of writing in English and the goodwill and commercial sense of publishers, choices remain multiple. As the huge international sales of Austen's, Dickens's, and Hardy's novels testify, the writing of the past often seems more vivid and satisfying, though never less disconcerting, than that of the present.

The decentralization of English literature has inevitably had to follow the advance of English as a world language, spoken and written by millions of men and women who have no other connection with England. No twentieth-century commentator could share the imperial presumption of Joseph Angus's sentiment that 'no nation can receive and welcome [English literature] without reproducing in its life the image of our own'. Even in Angus's time, Scottish writing continued to flourish as an alternative tradition to that of England (or, in some cases, of Britain), and the United States had begun to evolve its own distinctively American expression. If American literature is now generally accepted as quite independent of that of England, so increasingly is the literature of Scotland. Scotland, long partly subsumed in the idea of Britain and often confused with England by outsiders who ought to know better, is only following where the far less willingly 'British' Ireland led. Anglo-Scottish literature now has as many claims to be regarded as distinct from 'English' literature as Anglo-Irish literature (the unmilitant shelves of Scottish bookshops at least suggest that this is the case). The far smaller corpus of Anglo-Welsh literature, which is quite as expressive of cultural alternatives as parallel writing from Scotland and Ireland, is already acknowledged as a sub-discipline in most Welsh universities. The distinctive English-language literatures of Canada, Australia, New Zealand, Africa, India, and the Caribbean have equally and inevitably flourished by exploring a mature sense of identity quite separate from that of what was once fondly referred to as the 'mother country'.

Perhaps the most significant of the new disciplines that have destabilized and decentralized the old concept of English literature has been the development of women's studies. Long-overdue scholarship has not merely reconsidered the reputations of established women writers, but has also rescued the work of others from near oblivion. Feminist criticism, feminist history, and broader feminist discourses have also been crucial in changing inherited assumptions about how the literature of the past and the present can be read. Absences have become presences, some of them, as in the rewriting of the history of the novel, forceful presences. The long silences, which it was once patronizingly assumed marked the history of women's poetry, have been filled by the discovery of a neglected articulacy. The study of the drama, too, has been transformed by a critical insistence that women's voices should be heard and that women's roles, or the fact of the lack of them, should be re-explored. Where Leavis and other critics looked to a tradition that was 'alive in so far as it is alive to us', so women's studies have breathed a new life into a tradition which is at once central and 'alternative'. The restrictive, largely male 'canon', as it was once received, no longer has its old validity.

This present *History* has attempted to look at the range of English literature from the Anglo-Saxon period to the present day. Its definitions of what is 'English' and what is 'literature' have remained, as far as is feasible, open. It will inevitably offend certain readers by what it has included and what it has excluded. It has dealt, for the most part, with named authors rather than with the body of anonymous work which has existed in all historical periods and which forms a particularly noteworthy part of what survives of the literature of the Middle Ages. Problems of space, and the non-existence of *standard* anthologies of such anonymous work, have precluded all but the most cursory and unsatisfactory reference to it. The *History* has, however, included a good deal of reference to what other critics and historians might automatically take to be Anglo-Irish, Anglo-Scottish, and Anglo-Welsh literature and as inappropriate to a history of 'English' literature. I have included Irish, Scottish, and Welsh writers not out of imperial arrogance or ignorance but because certain Irish, Scottish, and Welsh writers cannot easily be separated from the English tradition or from the broad sense of an English literature which once embraced regional, provincial, and other national traditions within the British Isles. It is proper, for example, to see Yeats as an Anglo-Irish poet, but to what extent can we see Shaw exclusively as an Anglo-Irish dramatist? Joyce and Beckett, it is true, deliberately avoided England as a place of exile from Ireland, but how readily can Burke, Goldsmith, Wilde, George Moore, Bram Stoker, or Louis MacNeice be taken out of the English contexts they chose for themselves? And how could the history of *English* literature in the eighteenth century be written without due reference to Swift? It is right to abandon the term 'Scottish Chaucerian' to describe Henryson and Dunbar and to allow that both should be seen as distinctive Scots poets working in Scotland in a loose Chaucerian tradition. But how far can we take the idea that James Thomson is a distinctively Scottish poet who happened to work in England in a loose Miltonic tradition? It is essential to recognize the Welshness of Dylan Thomas, but it is rather harder to put one's finger on the Welshness of Henry Vaughan.

This *History* has also included certain English writers who wrote in Latin and others whose origins were not English, let alone British or Irish, whose work seems to have been primarily intended to associate them with a British market and with an English literary tradition. Conrad and T. S. Eliot, who are included, took British citizenship in mid-career and accepted that their writing was 'English' in the narrow sense of the term. On the other hand, Henry James, who is excluded, took British citizenship only at the close of his life and when his writing career was effectively over. Both Auden and Isherwood, who became citizens of the United States in the 1940s, have been included simply because it seems impossible to separate their most distinctive work from the British context in which it was written. The situations of Conrad, Eliot, James, Auden, and Isherwood are in certain ways exemplary of what has happened to English literature in the twentieth century. It is both English and it is not. It is both British and it is not. What really matters is that English literature, rather than being confined to an insular Poets' Corner, now belongs in and to a wider world.

1

Old English Literature

THE term 'Old English' was invented as a patriotic and philological convenience. The more familiar term 'Anglo-Saxon' has a far older pedigree. 'Old English' implied that there was a cultural continuity between the England of the sixth century and the England of the nineteenth century (when German, and later British, philologists determined that there had been phases in the development of the English language which they described as 'Old', 'Middle', and 'Modern'). 'Anglo-Saxon' had, on the other hand, come to suggest a culture distinct from that of modern England, one which might be pejoratively linked to the overtones of 'Sassenach' (Saxon), a word long thrown back by angry Celts at English invaders and English cultural imperialists. In 1871 Henry Sweet, the pioneer Oxford phonetician and Anglicist, insisted in his edition of one of King Alfred's translations that he was going to use 'Old English' to denote 'the unmixed, inflectional state of the English language, commonly known by the barbarous and unmeaning title of "Anglo-Saxon" '. A thousand years earlier, King Alfred himself had referred to the tongue which he spoke and in which he wrote as 'englisc'. It was the language of the people he ruled, the inhabitants of Wessex who formed part of a larger English nation. That nation, which occupied most of the fertile arable land in the southern part of the island of Britain, was united by its Christian religion, by its traditions, and by a form of speech which, despite wide regional varieties of dialect, was already distinct from the 'Saxon' of the continental Germans. From the thirteenth century onwards, however, Alfred's 'English' gradually became incomprehensible to the vast majority of the English-speaking descendants of those same Anglo-Saxons. Scholars and divines of the Renaissance period may have revived interest in the study of Old English texts in the hope of proving that England had traditions in Church and State which distinguished it from the rest of Europe. Nineteenth-century philologists, like Sweet, may have helped to lay the foundations of all modern textual and linguistic research, and most British students of English literature may have been obliged, until relatively recently, to acquire some kind of mastery of the earliest written form of their language, but there remains a general and almost ineradicable prejudice that the culture of early England was severed from all that came after it by the Norman Conquest of 1066. 1066 is still the most familiar date in the history of the island of Britain, and, despite Henry Sweet's Victorian protest, many latter-day 'barbarians' have persisted in seeing pre-Conquest England, and its wide and complex civilization, as somehow that of a lost tribe of 'Anglo-Saxons'.

The Germanic peoples known as the Angles, the Saxons, and the Jutes, who had successfully invaded the former Roman colony of Britain in the fifth and sixth centuries, brought with them their language, their paganism, and their distinctive warrior traditions. They had also driven the Christianized Celtic inhabitants of Britain westwards to the confines of Wales and Cornwall and northwards into the Highlands of Scotland. The radical success of their colo-nization is evident in the new place-names that they imposed on their areas of settlement, emphatically English place-names which proclaim their ownership of homesteads and cultivated land (the main exceptions to this nomenclature generally pertain to the residually Celtic names of rivers, hills, and forests or to the remains of fortified Roman towns which were delineated by the Latin-derived suffixes *-chester* and *-cester*). The fate of the old Celtic inhabitants who were not able to remove themselves is announced in the English word *Wealh* (from which the term 'Welsh' is derived), a word once applied both to a native Briton and to a slave. The old Roman order had utterly disintegrated under pressure from the new invaders, though stories of determined Celtic resistance to the Saxons in the sixth century, a resistance directed by a prince claiming imperial authority, were later associated with the largely mythological exploits of the fabled King Arthur.

The process of re-Christianization began in the late sixth century. The mis-sionary work was undertaken in the north and in Scotland by Celtic monks, but in the south the mission was entrusted to a group of Benedictines sent from Rome in AD 596 by Pope Gregory the Great. This mission, led by Augustine, the first Archbishop of Canterbury, was of incalculable importance to the future development of English culture. The organizational zeal of the Benedictines and the chain of monasteries eventually established by them served to link Britain both to the Latin civilization of the Roman Church and to the newly germinating Christian national cultures of Western Europe. By the end of the seventh century all the kingdoms of Anglo-Saxon England had accepted the discipline and order of Roman Christianity. A century after Augustine's arrival from Rome, the English Church had confidently begun to send out its own missionaries in order to convert its pagan kinsmen on the Continent. The most spectacularly successful of these missionaries were the Northumbrian priest, Willibrord (658–739), the founder of the Dutch see of Utrecht and of the great abbey at Echternach, and Boniface (680–754), the so-called 'Apostle of Germany', who famously felled the oak tree sacred to the god Thor at Geismar, who was consecrated as the first Archbishop of Mainz in 747 and who, having enthusiastically returned to the mission field, met a martyr's death in Frisia.

According to Bede (673–735), the first great English historian, Augustine's mission to England was reinforced, four years after his arrival, by new clergy from Rome bringing with them 'everything necessary for the worship and service of the Church'. Bede stresses that these pastoral requisites included 'many books'. The written word was of crucial importance to the Church, for its services depended upon the reading of the Holy Scriptures and its spirituality steadily drew on glosses on those Scriptures, on sermons, and on meditations. This emphasis on the written and read word must, however, have been a considerable novelty to the generally unlettered new converts. The old runic alphabet of the Germanic tribes, which seems to have been used largely for inscriptions, was gradually replaced by Roman letters (though, as certain distinctly Christian artefacts show, both alphabets coexisted until well into the eighth century, and in some parts of the country runes were used for inscriptions until the twelfth century). All this newly imposed written literature was in Latin, the language that the Roman Church had directly inherited from the defunct Roman *imperium*. England was thus brought into the mainstream of Western European culture, a Christian culture which tenaciously clung to its roots in the fragmented ancient civilizations of Greece, Rome, and Israel, while proclaiming the advent of its own new age. It was through the medium of Latin that a highly distinguished pattern of teaching and scholarship was steadily developed at English monastic and cathedral schools, an intellectual discipline which fostered the achievements of such men as Aldhelm, Bishop of Sherborne (*c*.639–709) (the master of an ornate, and once much admired, Latin style in both verse and prose) and Alcuin (*c*.735–804), the most respected and widely accomplished scholar at the influential court of Charlemagne. It was in Latin, and for an international audience, that Bede wrote his great *Historia Ecclesiastica Gentis Anglorum* (*The Ecclesiastical History of the English People*, completed in 731). Bede's *History*, of which more than 150 medieval manuscripts survive, remains an indispensable record of the advance of Christianity in England. It is also a work which bears the imprint of the distinctive intellectual energy, the scholarly coherence, and the wide-ranging sympathies of its author.

Literacy in early England may well have been limited to those in holy orders, but literature in a broader, oral form appears to have remained a more general possession. In this, the first of the Germanic lands to have been brought into the sphere of the Western Church, Latin never seems to have precluded the survival and development of a vigorous, vernacular literary tradition. Certain aspects of religious instruction, notably those based on the sermon and the homily, naturally used English. The most important of the surviving sermons date from late in the Anglo-Saxon era. The great monastery of Winchester in the royal capital of Wessex (and later of all England) is credited with a series of educational reforms in the late tenth century which may have influenced the lucid, alliterative prose written for the benefit of the faithful by clerics such as Wulfstan (d. 1023), Bishop of Worcester and Archbishop of York (the author of the *Sermo Lupi ad Anglos*, 'Wolf's Sermon to the English'), and Ælfric (*c*.955–*c*.1010), formerly a monk at Winchester and later Abbot of Eynsham (whose two series *Catholic Homilies* and *Lives of the Saints* suggest a familiarity with the idioms of Old English poetry). The Scriptures, generally available only in St Jerome's fourth-century Latin translation (the so-called Vulgate version), were also subject to determined attempts to render them into English for the benefit of those who were deficient in Latin. Bede was engaged on an English translation of the Gospel of St John at the time of his death and a vernacular gloss in Northumbrian English was added in the tenth century to the superbly illuminated seventh-century manuscript known as the Lindisfarne Gospels. A West Saxon version of the four Gospels has survived in six manuscripts, the formal, expressive, liturgical rhythms of which found a muted echo in every subsequent translation until superseded by the flat, functional English of the mid-twentieth century.

The religious and cultural life of the great, and increasingly well-endowed, Anglo-Saxon abbeys did not remain settled. In 793—some sixty-two years after Bede had concluded his *History* at the monastery at Jarrow with the optimistic sentiment that 'peace and prosperity' blessed the English Church and people—the neighbouring abbey at Lindisfarne was sacked and devastated by Viking sea-raiders. A similar fate befell Jarrow in the following year. For a century the ordered and influential culture fostered by the English monasteries was severely disrupted, even extinguished. Libraries were scattered or destroyed and monastic schools deserted. It was not until the reign of the determined and cultured Alfred, King of Wessex (848–99), that English learning was again purposefully encouraged. A thorough revival of the monasteries took place in the tenth century under the aegis of Dunstan, Archbishop of Canterbury (*c*.910–88), Æthelwold, Bishop of Winchester (?908–84), and Oswald, Bishop of Worcester (d. 992). From this period date the four most significant surviving volumes of Old English verse, the so-called Junius manuscript, the Beowulf manuscript, the Vercelli Book, and the Exeter Book. These collections were almost certainly the products of monastic *scriptoria* (writing-rooms) although the anonymous authors of the poems may not necessarily have been monks themselves. Many of the poems are presumed to date from a much earlier period, but their presence in these tenth-century anthologies indicates not just the survival, acceptability, and consistency of an older tradition; it also amply suggests how wide-ranging, complex, and sophisticated the poetry of the Anglo-Saxon period was. While allowing that the surviving poems are representative of the tradition, many modern scholars none the less allow that what has survived was probably subject to two distinct processes of selection: one an arbitrary selection imposed by time, by casual destruction, or by the natural decay of written records; the other a process of editing, exclusion, excision, or suppression by monastic scribes. This latter process of anonymous censorship has left us with a generally elevated, elevating, and male-centred literature, one which lays a stress on the virtues of a tribal community, on the ties of loyalty between lord and liegeman, on the significance of individual heroism, and on the powerful sway of *wyrd*, or fate. The earliest dated poem that we have is ascribed by Bede to a writer named Cædmon, an unskilled servant employed at the monastery at Whitby in the late seventh century. Cædmon, who had once been afraid to take the harp and sing to its accompaniment at secular feasts, was divinely granted the gift of poetry in a dream and, on waking, composed a short hymn to God the Creator. Such was the quality of his divine inspiration that the new poet was admitted to the monastic community and is said to have written a series of now lost poems on Scriptural subjects, including accounts of Christ's Incarnation, Passion, and Resurrection. Bede's mention of Cædmon's early fear of being a guest 'invited to sing and entertain the company' at a feast suggests something of the extent to which poetry was a public and communal art. It also suggests that a specifically religious poetry both derived from, and could be distinct from, established secular modes of composition. Bede's story clearly indicates that the poetry of his day followed rules of diction and versification which were readily recognized by its audience. That audience, it is also implied, accepted that poetry was designed for public repetition, recitation and, indeed, artful improvisation. The elaborate, conventional language of Old English poetry probably derived from a Germanic bardic tradition which also accepted the vital initiatory role of a professional poet, or *scop*, the original improviser of a song on heroic themes. This *scop*, drawing from a 'word-hoard' of elevated language and terminology, would be expected to perform his verses at celebratory gatherings in the royal, lordly, and even monastic halls which figure so prominently in the literature of the period. The writer of *Beowulf* speaks, for example, of 'the clear song of the *scop*' ('swutol sang scopes') (l. 90) and of a poet, 'a thane of the king's . . . who remembered many traditional stories and improvised new verses' (ll. 867–71). The vitality of the relationship of a *scop* to his lord, and the dire social misfortune attendant on the loss of such patronage, also feature in the elegiac poem known as *Deor*, a poem which dwells purposefully, and somewhat mournfully, on the importance of the poet's memorializing. The *scop*'s inherited pattern of poetry-making derived from an art which was essentially oral in its origins and development. Old English verse uses a complex pattern of alliteration as the basis of its form. Elaborately constructed sentences, and interweaving words and phrases are shaped into two-stressed half-lines of a varying number of syllables; the half-lines are then linked into full-lines by means of alliteration borne on the first stress of the second half-line. The dying speech of Beowulf, commanding the construction of a barrow to his memory, suggests something of the steady majesty this verse can carry:

Hatað heaðomære   hlæw gewyrcean
beorhtne æfter bæle   æt brimes nosan;
se scel to gemyndum   minum leodum
heah hlifian   on Hronesnæsse,
þæt hit sæliðend   syððan hatan
Biowulfes biorh,   ða ðe brentingas
ofer floda genipu   feorran drifað.

(Command the warriors famed in battle build a bright mound after my burning at the sea headland. It shall tower high on Whale Ness, a reminder to my people, so that sea-farers may afterwards call it Beowulf's barrow when they drive their ships from afar over the dark waves.)

Beowulf

It was long held that the most substantial surviving Old English poem, *Beowulf*, was a pre-Christian composition which had somehow been tampered with by monastic scribes in order to give it an acceptably Christian frame of reference. This argument is no longer tenable, though some scholars hold that the tenth-century manuscript of the poem may postdate its composition by as much as three or even four hundred years. The anonymous poet-narrator recognizes that his story is a pagan one and that his characters hold to pagan virtues and to a pre-Christian world-view, but he is also aware that older concepts of heroism and heroic action can be viewed as compatible with his own religious and moral values. *Beowulf* refers back to an age of monster slayings in Scandinavia, but it interprets them as struggles between good and evil, between humanity and the destructive forces which undo human order. Grendel, the first monster of the poem, is seen as 'Godes andsaca', the enemy of God (l. 1682) and as a descendant of the biblical Cain, the first murderer (l. 107). The poem's original audience must have shared this mixed culture, one which readily responded to references to an ancestral world and one which also recognized the relevance of primitive heroism to a Christian society. As other surviving Old English poems suggest, Christ's acts in redeeming the world, and the missions and martyrdoms of his saints, could be interpreted according to supra-biblical concepts of the hero. In a sense, a poem like *Beowulf* mediates between a settled and an unsettled culture, between one which enjoys the benefits of a stable, ordered, agricultural society and one which relished the restlessness of the wandering warrior hero. Despite the fact that the bards of the royal hall at Heorot sing of God's Creation much as Cædmon sang of it, *Beowulf* springs from a religious culture which saw infinite mystery in the natural world, and the world itself as if hidden by a veil. It saw in nature a mass of confused signs, portents, and meanings. Marvels and horrors, such as Grendel, his kin, and the dragon, suggested that there was a multiplicity in divine purposes. By properly understanding God's marvels, his will could also be understood; by battling against manifestations of evil, his purposes could be realized.

Beowulf can properly be called an 'epic' poem in the sense that it celebrates the achievements of a hero in narrative verse. Although it may strike some readers as casually episodic when compared to the ostensibly tighter narrative structures of Homer or Virgil, the poem is in fact constructed around three encounters with the other-worldly, with monsters who seem to interrupt the narrative by literally intruding themselves into accounts of human celebration and community. Around these stories others are woven, stories which serve to broaden the context to a larger civilization and tradition. While the humans gather in the warmth and comradeship of the mead-hall, the monsters come from a bleak and unfriendly outside, contrasts which suggest starkly alternating phases of the social and the alien. Human society is seen as being bound together by ties of loyalty—the lord providing protection, nourishment, and a place in an accepted hierarchy for which his warriors return service. The lord is the bountiful 'ring-giver', the 'gold-friend', the rewarder of Beowulf's bravery, and the founder of feasts. Beyond this predominantly masculine hierarchy of acknowledged ties and obligations, centred at the beginning of the poem on King Hrothgar's court at Heorot, there lies another order, or rather disorder, of creatures intent on destroying both king and court. Grendel the predator stalks at night, dwelling apart from men and from faith. It is Beowulf who challenges the intruder, who drives the wounded monster back to his lair in the wilderness and kills him. When Grendel's enraged mother mounts a new attack on Heorot, and Beowulf and his companions pursue her to her watery retreat, there follows a further evocation of uninhabitable deserts, of empty fens and bleak sea-cliffs. It is in such passages that the poet suggests the gulf still fixed between the social world of humankind and the insecure, cold, untamed world of the beasts, the inheritance of the outcast, the exile, and the outsider.

Beowulf's victory over Grendel in the wastes of Denmark is compared by King Hrothgar's *scop* to those of the great dragon-slayer of Teutonic legend, Sigemund. To the poem's original audience such a comparison would probably have suggested that Beowulf's heroic progress would lead, just as inexorably as Sigemund's, to new encounters with monsters and, ultimately, to his undoing by death. The parallel carried with it a grand and tragic irony appropriate to epic. When Beowulf enters what will prove to be his final struggle with a dragon, he seems to be a more troubled man, one haunted by an awareness of fate, the looming sense of destiny that the Anglo-Saxons referred to as *wyrd*. He who has lived by his determining ancestral inheritance, the sword, must now die by it. Beowulf, betrayed by those of his liegemen who have feared the fight, leaves a realm threatened by neighbouring princes anxious to exploit the political vacuum left by the death of so effective a hero. The poem ends in mourning and with the hero's ashes paganly interred in a barrow surrounded by splendidly wrought treasures of the kind that were discovered at Sutton Hoo in Suffolk in 1939. The last lines of *Beowulf* evoke a pre-Christian spectacle, but the poem's insistent stress on mortality and on the determining nature of *wyrd* might equally have conveyed to a Christian audience a message of heroic submission to the just commands of a benevolent but almighty God.

The Battle of Maldon and the Elegies

The system of social and military loyalties evoked throughout *Beowulf* is reflected elsewhere in Old English literature. In the fragmentary poem known as *The Battle of Maldon* (written *c*.1000) a fatal skirmish between the Essex nobleman, Byrhtnoth, and a raiding party of Vikings is celebrated. The 'battle', which took place in 991, seems to have stirred its latter-day poet, possibly a monastic one, into echoing an older heroic style and into exploring the tensions inherent in the heroic code of action. Byrhtnoth is seen as something more than a brave, if rash, warrior. In some senses he is a martyr, generously throwing away his life, and those of his loyal vassals, for the sake of his liege-lord (King Ethelred) and for his nation ('folc and foldan'). Yet his 'martyrdom' is ambiguous. His rashness in allowing the Danes to cross the river which should have formed his best line of defence, and his consequent defeat at their hands, may be viewed by the poet as a sacrifice for Christian culture against a pagan enemy, but there are also suggestions that the spirit of loyalty and fraternity amongst Byrhtnoth's men particularly matters because God is potentially indifferent to their fate. *Deor* offers a complete contrast, albeit one which illuminates a similarly pervasive stress on loyalty and on the mutual relationship of a lordly patron and his vassal. The poem, spoken in the first person, purports to be the lament of a *scop* who has been supplanted by a rival. Deor's self-consolation takes the form of a meditation on five instances of misfortune, all of them drawn from Germanic legend and history; in each case, he assures himself, the sorrow passed away, so likewise may the pain of his rejection pass. Each meditation ends with an echoed refrain, with its concluding section moving beyond a broadly pagan endurance of the rule of fate into a Christian assertion of faith in divine providence.

Widsith also takes the form of a soliloquy spoken by an imaginary *scop*, here a 'far-wanderer' who 'unlocks his word-hoard' in order to describe the peoples and princes amongst whom he has journeyed. His catalogue of nations is predominantly Teutonic, but the peripatetic poet, proudly manifesting his knowledge of the Bible, also includes the Jews, the Egyptians, the Assyrians, the Medes, and the Persians. He also carefully emphasizes the rewards given to him by discerning patrons, both a reference to past generosity and to the traditional interdependence of poet and patron, and a public reminder of present obligations. The *scop* 'Widsith' has prospered in his journeyings; the narrator of the poem known as *The Wanderer*, who is not necessarily a minstrel, claims to have lost his lord and patron and is now confronted with a bitterly alienating vision of frozen waves, sea-birds, and winter cold. His is a wasteland of exile evoked through the use of precise metaphors and carefully placed adjectives. Here the sea, so significant to the ancestral history of settlers on an island, has become the disconnecter; its emptiness and its winter violence are rendered as the embodiment of the failure of human relationships, of loneliness, of severance and exile. The 'wanderer', like other Old English narrators, comforts himself with a wisdom which has been shaped by patience in the face of a divine fate. In *The Seafarer* the contrast between the comforts of a settled life on land and the hardships and dangers of the sea is at once more poignant and more ambiguous. The narrator tells us that he has endured 'bitre breostceare' ('bitter breast-sorrow'), that he has laboured and has heard nothing but 'the pounding of the sea and the ice-cold wave' ('hlimman sæ, | iscaldne wæg'), but his experiences seem to thrill him. His exile is self-imposed, not forced upon him by rejection, by loss of patronage, or by fate. Somewhat disconcertingly, the poem gradually establishes that though the Seafarer delights in the security of life on shore, he also distrusts it. For him, the cuckoo, the harbinger of summer on land, merely reminds him of the passage of the seasons, while the cry of a sea-bird urges a return to the exhilaration of the waves. At the end of the poem the narrator establishes a new opposition towards which his whole argument has been moving: the shore comes to represent the transitory and uncertain nature of the world against which heaven, the truly secure home of the peregrinatory soul, can properly be defined.

The insecure nature of earth's joys and achievements, and an implied longing for heavenly resolution, also figure in the short fragmentary poem known as *The Ruin*. The poem muses over the crumbling stones of a ruined city (probably the wreck of the Roman city of Aquae Sulis, the modern Bath), ruins which cause its narrator to wonder that there could ever have been a race of such mighty builders (most ambitious Anglo-Saxon structures were of wood, not stone, and the earliest English colonizers seem, perhaps superstitiously, to have avoided old Roman settlements). The narrator of *The Ruin* does not, however, seek to evoke a sense of alienation; rather, he speaks of an exile from vanished wonders, an awareness reinforced by the ravages of time and *wyrd*. *The Wife's Lament*, which, along with *The Wanderer*, *The Seafarer*, *Deor*, *Widsith*, and *The Ruin*, has survived in the great anthology known as the Exeter Book, offers a further, but quite distinct, variation on the common themes of banishment, displacement, and social disgrace. In *The Wife's Lament* a rare woman's voice is heard mourning the absence of her banished husband, though the precise situation is left unclear and many of the allusions are cryptic. The poem has sometimes been linked to the verses known as *The Husband's Message*. They may also be associated with the short poetic Riddles (also preserved in the Exeter Book), dense little poems which suggest the degree to which Anglo-Saxon audiences indulged a fascination with the operations of metaphor. Given the clear ecclesiastical pedigree of the Exeter anthology, *The Wife's Complaint* has sometimes been explained as a paraphrase of the Song of Songs, a book traditionally interpreted by the Christian Church as the soul's yearning for its heavenly lover. All these elegiac poems, with their stress on loss, estrangement, and exile, also recall the potency of the famous image of the transience of earthly pleasure employed by Bede in his *History*. When, according to Bede's narrative, King Edwin of Northumbria summoned a council in 627 to discuss whether or not to accept Christianity, one of the King's chief courtiers compares human life to the flight of a sparrow through a warm, thronged, royal hall, a short period of security compared to the winter storms raging outside the hall. The sparrow's origins and his destination are as mysterious as are the destinies of humankind. Only a religious perspective, the counsellor insists, allows the Christian to understand the surrounding darkness and to cope with the emptiness of a world where companionship, loyalty, and order falter and decay.

The Biblical Poems and *The Dream of the Rood*

A substantial body of Old English religious poetry is based directly on Scriptural sources and on Latin saints' lives. We know from Bede's *History* that Cædmon is supposed to have written verses with subjects drawn from Genesis, Exodus, and the Gospels, but none of the surviving poems on these subjects can now be safely ascribed to a named poet. The verses known as *Genesis*, *Exodus*, *Daniel*, and *Judith* are much more than straightforward paraphrases of Scripture. *Genesis*, for example, opens with a grand justification of the propriety of praising the Lord of Hosts and moves to a lengthy, and non-Scriptural, account of the fall of the angels. Much of the poem is framed around the idea of a vast struggle between the principles of good and evil. The most effective sections of the interpolation (known awkwardly as *Genesis B*) treat the fall of Adam as a betrayal of the trust of his Almighty liege-lord, a betrayal punished by exile from the benevolent protection of his Creator. Military metaphors also run through *Exodus* which treats the struggle of the Jews and the Egyptians as an armed conflict in which the departing Jews triumph. Its apparent poetic sequel, *Daniel*, emphasizes the force of divine intervention in human affairs and perhaps reflects the prominent use of Old Testament stories of deliverance in the ceremonies and liturgies of Holy Week and Easter. Christ himself is portrayed as a warrior battling against the forces of darkness in *Christ and Satan*, a poem which ranges from a further rehearsal of the story of the fall of the angels, through a description of the Harrowing of Hell, to the Saviour's Resurrection and Ascension (though the story of the gradual victory over Satan reaches its climax in an account of the temptation in the wilderness). *Judith*, a fragmentary poem which survives in the *Beowulf* manuscript, has a valiant female warrior as its protagonist. Judith, the chaste defender of Israel, struggles as much against a monster of depravity (in the form of the invader, Holofernes) as does Beowulf against Grendel and his kin. The poems based on apocryphal saints' lives also suggest the degree to which the modes, metaphors, and language of secular heroic verse could be adapted to the

purposes of Christian epic. In *Andreas*, a decidedly militant St Andrew journeys across the sea to rescue his fellow apostle St Matthew from imprisonment
and, somewhat more extraordinarily, from the threat of being eaten by the
anthropophagi of Mermedonia. *The Fates of the Apostles*, which is signed at
the end in runic fashion by a poet known as Cynewulf, recounts the missionary journeys and martyrdoms of the 'twelve men of noble heart', Christ's disciples being cast in the roles of hardy Nordic heroes. This same Cynewulf is
also credited with the authorship of *Elene*, the story of St Helena's discovery
of the True Cross, and of *Juliana*, the history of a Roman virgin martyr.

   Much Old English religious poetry commands more respect (albeit, sometimes grudging) than it does affection and admiration. To many modern
readers, unaccustomed to the stately piety of the saints' life tradition, by far
the most profound, moving, and intellectually sophisticated of the specifically
Christian poems is *The Dream of the Rood*. The shape of the poem, which
describes a vision of Christ's cross (the Rood), has a fluid daring which is, at
times, almost surreal in its play with paradox and its fascination with metamorphosis. What appears to be a quotation from it in a runic inscription on
the margins of the eighth-century Ruthwell cross (a stone monument sited just
over the present Scottish border) suggests a relatively early date for the poem.
Its subject, for which several earlier analogues exist (most notable amongst
them being the familiar Passiontide Office hymns *Pange Lingua* and *Vexilla
Regis* by the sixth-century French bishop Venantius Fortunatus), concerns the
shift in the narrator's perceptions of Christ's cross. *The Dream of the Rood*
opens with a dreamer's vision of a gilded and bejewelled cross of victory ('sige
beam'), worshipped by the angels. Its supernatural effulgence seems, none the
less, to inspire a deep sense of unworthiness and sin in the earthbound
beholder, and the troubled narrator begins to understand that the outward
appearance of the cross is paradoxical. The Rood is both glorious and moist
with blood:

> Hwæðre ic þurh þæt gold   ongytan meahte
> earmra ærgewin,   þæt hit ærest ongan
> swætan on þa swiðran healfe.   Eall ic wæs mid sorgum gedrefed.

(Yet through that gold I could perceive the former strife of wretched men, that it had
once bled on the right side. I was greatly troubled with sorrows.)

The cross itself then begins to speak, describing how a tree was felled and fashioned into a gallows which a 'young hero' embraced. Both cross and hero have
been pierced by the same nails, both have been scorned and both bloodied.
Having thus been obliged to be a partaker in the Passion of Christ, the cross
is discarded, buried, and later discovered by the 'Lord's thanes' who recognize
it as the instrument of salvation. At one with its Lord, the Rood has been
miraculously transformed by his Resurrection and Ascension, and it is now
glorified in Heaven as 'the best of signs' ('beacna selest'). When the rood ceases

to speak and the dreamer resumes, his words are transfused with a sense of joy, worship, and wonder. Like the narrators of *The Wanderer* and *The Seafarer* he is torn between the contemplation of heavenly serenity and his attachment to the uncertainties and limitations of life on earth. The dreamer longs for the heaven which he glimpses as a glorified royal mead-hall, the focus of Lordly bounty and the fitting setting for the eternal communion of saints. *The Dream of the Rood* plays with the great paradoxes of the Christian religion, but its play is more profound and more concrete than that of the elusive quizzicality of a riddle. It presents its readers with an icon, a paradoxical sign which requires interpretation and which is finally merged with the meaning that it signifies. There are few more impressive religious poems in English.

2

Medieval Literature
1066–1510

STRICTLY speaking, the Bayeux Tapestry, which provides the most vivid pictorial record of the events leading up to the conquest of England by the Normans, is not a tapestry at all. The 70-metre long embroidery, known in the Norman cathedral city of Bayeux as 'the tapestry of Queen Matilda', is equally unlikely to be the painstaking work of the wife of William the Conqueror. Long before the Conquest, and long after it, England was famed for the intricacy and brilliance of its needlework. The great narrative hanging was probably the result of a celebratory, and possibly enforced, commission to English needle-women to mark both the Norman victory of 1066 and the consecration of the cathedral at Bayeux in 1077 by its bishop, William's half-brother Odo. After the conquest Odo had been rewarded by William with large estates in England and with the title Earl of Kent. He later acted, with some ruthlessness, as the King's viceroy in the north of England. Odo's periodic and prominent appear-ances on the tapestry as William's counsellor, as the blesser of food at a banquet on English soil before the battle of Hastings, and as the armed wielder of a great wooden staff in the battle itself (clerics were forbidden to carry swords), suggest that he at least would not have found it inappropriate to decorate his new cathedral with an embroidered commemoration of his brother's famous victory.

As so often in medieval art, the Bayeux Tapestry interconnects the sacred and the secular, the military and the miraculous, the humanly determined and the divinely destined. The embroidery is an ideological statement which is both narrative and didactic; it would have proved a propagandist point to those already acquainted with events and it would have enforced a distinctly Norman interpretation of the justice of Duke William's campaign to the ignorant and the unlettered. It shows the English Earl Harold, as William's companion in arms and as his guest, swearing an oath of fealty to him by emphatically placing outspread hands on a pair of reliquaries; when the saintly King Edward the Confessor is buried in his new abbey at Westminster, the hand of God appears in a cloud in order to reinforce the idea of divine blessing and of a heavenly control of human affairs; when Harold, having broken his oath, is crowned as Edward's successor by the excommunicated Archbishop Stigand, his perturbed subjects are seen marvelling at the appearance of a blazing star (in fact Halley's comet). William's involvement in English affairs is presented as part of a providential scheme by which a holy English king is rightfully succeeded by an appointed Norman heir, one who has perforce to claim his rights in the face of a faithless and perjured usurper. The tapestry represents the major characters and their supporters in action. It complements this narrative with a terse running commentary in Latin and with figures of winged beasts and with working men and women in the upper and lower borders. The now damaged end of the embroidery shows bloody scenes of the battle of Hastings and the disorder of the English army in defeat. In the lower border there are vivid pictures of severed limbs and dishonoured corpses while the Latin text baldly reports: HIC HAROLD REX INTERFECTUS EST, 'Here King Harold is Killed'.

The Bayeux Tapestry does more than show how and why William the Bastard, Duke of Normandy, succeeded to the royal dignity of King of England. It suggests a continuity of the kingdom of England and of English kingship under a new monarch (one from whom all subsequent sovereigns have claimed descent and due rights of succession). This continuity may well have been more evident to the conquerors who commissioned the embroidery than to the newly conquered needlewomen who made it. William found England a feudal land, ruled by a native aristocracy and ordered by a rich and influential Church. When he died in 1087 he left his new kingdom with an ordered feudal system reinforced by a powerful Norman aristocracy and a zealous Norman episcopate. He conquered an England where king, nobleman, and peasant spoke English and where an educated English clergy employed Latin in both their worship and their study. He left England trilingual, with a literate clergy still refined by Latin, but with Norman French defining the new ruling class and with English now largely confined to the ruled. Although William, at the age of 43, endeavoured to learn the language of his new subjects he did not persevere. No English king would speak English as his native language for some three hundred years and although the Norman aristocracy and administration were gradually, and of necessity, obliged to become bilingual, it was only in the mid-fourteenth century that English was permitted to be used in petitions to Parliament, in legal procedure, and in legal documents such as wills and deeds.

The Conquest resulted in the supplanting of an English-speaking upper class by a French-speaking one. It otherwise did little to alter the existing social structure of the kingdom. Old place-names were retained, if occasionally distorted by French tongues and Latinate scribes, and the only Norman names to take permanent hold were those of newly built castles and newly founded abbeys (Belvoir, Richmond, and Montgomery; Rievaulx, Fountains, Jervaulx and, above all, Battle) or of estates that passed into Norman hands and took the family names of their owners. The new King was generally inclined to

respect established English institutions and customs and his French knights
were conspicuously elevated to the title of earl rather than to the continental
dignity of 'count'. Although senior churchmen of European extraction and
European education had been prominent in Edward the Confessor's reign,
William accelerated the introduction of a new clerical élite into England.
Within ten years of the Conquest only one English bishop, Wulfstan of
Worcester, remained in his see and only two major monasteries, Bath and
Ramsey, remained under the control of English abbots. The errant Stigand was
deprived and replaced as Archbishop of Canterbury in 1070 by Lanfranc
(*c*.1015–89), the Italian-born scholar-prior of the great Norman abbey of Bec.
When a vacancy occurred in York in 1069 on the death of Archbishop Ealdred
a further eminent Norman, Thomas of Bayeux, was appointed to the see. The
temporal wealth of the Church which these imported prelates now controlled
was recorded in Domesday Book, the great survey of English landownership
commissioned by the King in 1086. This same Domesday Book also exactly
catalogued the material and territorial possessions of a newly imported secular
aristocracy. Immediately after the Conquest the Norman, French, and
Flemish adventurers who had brought about the success of William's invasion
were rewarded with estates confiscated from those English landowners who had
taken up arms against the new King or who had refused to acknowledge
his suzerainty. The process of confiscation and acquisition continued as all
gestures of armed English resistance to the new order were vigorously
suppressed.

    In terms of its long-term effect on English culture, William's achievement
was fourfold. He and his Norman, Angevin, and Plantagenet successors forced
the English language into a subservient position from which it only gradually
re-emerged as a tongue simplified in structure and with its spelling, vocabulary, and literary expression strongly influenced by the impact of Norman
French. The political, economic, and geographical importance of London, and
not Winchester, as the administrative centre of the kingdom also helped to
determine the future written and spoken forms of 'standard' English. Thirdly,
an exclusive aristocratic taste for the forms, tropes, and subjects of contemporary French literature shifted the subjects of writing in English away from its
old Germanic insularity towards a broader, shared Western European pattern.
Fourthly, there is a somewhat more tendentious claim, periodically voiced by
those wedded to a conspiratorial theory of cultural history, that the Norman
Conquest fixed a social and cultural gulf between a privileged ruling caste and
the alienated mass of the population. The theory, sometimes linked to the idea
of a 'Norman Yoke' or to popular stories of Robin Hood's merry outlaws, had
a particular impact in subsequent periods of social change or upheaval (notably
during the Peasants' Revolt of 1381, in the years following the trial and execution of Charles I in 1648/9 and, with the help of Sir Walter Scott's *Ivanhoe*,
in the period of the Industrial Revolution in the late eighteenth and early nineteenth centuries). Reinterpreted in terms of class-consciousness, this eleventh-

century gulf between 'them' and 'us' has been seen as beginning the process by which an imported, feudal nobility, which spoke a different language and which responded to alien literary forms, steadily transformed itself into a self-perpetuating ruling class which continued to use élitist cultural values as a means of enforcing its influence. Whatever the truth of such claims, it can be demonstrated that the Conquest effectively eliminated upper-class patronage of Old English secular poetry and prose and gradually supplanted it with a new literary culture, responsive to wider influences, international in outlook, and truly European in its authority.

The invasion of England by the Normans forced the island of Britain into the orbit of an aggressive, confident, militaristic culture, one which controlled a loose empire which stretched from Sicily and Apulia in the south to the Scottish Lowlands in the north. The conquered English scarcely needed reminding either of their own 'colonial' advances into Britain or of the more recent Viking settlements in the north and east of the island. Nor had their francophone conquerors forgotten their own origins as restlessly ambitious Scandinavian 'Northmen' intent on settling richer lands in France. As the Bayeux Tapestry serves to suggest, these Christianized Normans chose to see their arrival in Britain as part of a civilizing mission and as a proper extension of their superior cultural achievement. Although they defiantly bore Norman-French names and although they might not have mastered the language of the natives that they ruled, those who settled permanently in England would soon be calling themselves English. When in the early twelfth century the Norman hegemony was extended westwards to include Ireland, the Lordship of the western island was, with papal blessing, exercised in the name of the King of England. It was an act of imperial expansion for which the 'English' have not been readily pardoned.

The Church, Church Building, and Clerical Historians

When the Conqueror died in Normandy in September 1087 he was buried, in the midst of a conflagration, in the abbey he had founded at Caen. The version of the Anglo-Saxon Chronicle, to which the monks at Peterborough long continued to add entries in English, recorded his passing with a mixture of apprehension and adulation. The anonymous chronicler, who claimed to have spent time at court, recognized that William had been a king of 'great wisdom and power' who 'surpassed in honour and in strength all those who had gone before him'; though 'stern beyond measure to those who opposed his will', he was kind 'to those good men who loved God'. As the chronicler is at pains to point out, William was no saint but he was a strong, just, and rightful sovereign who loved the Church and honoured the monastic life in particular. Not only had he endowed a new abbey at Battle in Sussex on the site of his victory over the usurping Harold, but 'such was the state of religion in his time that every man that wished to, whatever considerations there might be with regard to his rank, could follow the profession of a monk'. William and his clerical appointees may have forced the English Church into line with an essentially Norman view of administrative efficiency, piety, and scholarship, but they also opened it up to full participation in the French-centred renaissance of Christian discipline, learning, and design which marked Western Europe in the twelfth century.

The prelates promoted by the Norman and Angevin sovereigns of England were not merely seen as intellectual ornaments to the English Church; they were also useful administrative servants of the feudal state into which they were incorporated as Lords Spiritual. When Lanfranc ('the venerable father and consolation of monks' as the Peterborough Chronicle described him) died in 1089, he was succeeded as Archbishop of Canterbury by a yet greater Italian-born scholar and administrator, Anselm (1033–1109, informally canonized after his death and declared a Doctor of the Church in 1720). Anselm, the author of a celebrated Latin treatise on the Atonement (*Cur Deus Homo*, 'Why did God become Man?'), offered a defence of the Christian faith which insisted on the exercise of God-given human reason rather than merely on appeals to Scriptural or inherited theological authority. Despite the royal patronage which had brought him to Canterbury, Anselm did not have an easy political relationship with the kings he served and his particularly fraught relationship with the scholarly King Henry I (reigned 1100–35) in many ways prefigures the yet more tempestuous conflict between the claims of the supranational Catholic Church and the insistent demands of a feudal kingship in the reign of Henry II (1154–89), a conflict which culminated in the murder of Archbishop Thomas Becket (?1118–70). Becket, the son of Norman settlers in England and a former student at Paris and Bologna, was appointed to the see of Canterbury at the instigation of his former friend and political ally, the King, in 1162. The interests of sovereign and primate were subsequently diametrically opposed. When the Archbishop provocatively returned to England from exile in France in the winter of 1170 he was assassinated by four of the King's knights as he prepared to say mass at an altar in his cathedral. The event provoked indignation throughout Europe, miracles were reported at Becket's tomb, and in February 1173 he was formally canonized by Pope Alexander III (who recognized the spiritual and political value of martyrs like Becket to the independent temporal influence of the Church). Eighteen months later the humbled King was obliged to do public penance before the new saint's shrine.

Becket's murder and the subsequent stream of pilgrims to his tomb at Canterbury did more than enhance the already considerable status of the Church militant; both gave a further boost to the creation of an architecturally splendid setting for worship and for pilgrimage. In the years following the conquest the advent of senior clerics from Normandy had provided an incentive for the rebuilding of English cathedral and abbey churches on a previously unrivalled scale. These vast Romanesque buildings, notably the new cathedrals at Canterbury (begun 1070), Ely (begun 1083), London (begun 1087) and, most spectacularly, Durham (begun 1093) and the abbeys at St Albans (begun 1077) and Peterborough (begun 1118), were rendered somewhat old-fashioned by the emergence of the new Gothic style in the Île de France in the 1140s.

When the eastern arm of the cathedral at Canterbury was gutted by fire in 1174 the monks of the priory readily seized the opportunity of rebuilding the church in the innovative French Gothic style. The new choir was a direct tribute to St Thomas Becket and a reflection of the wealth that his cult was already bringing to Canterbury. The work was entrusted to a French architect, William of Sens, but on his retirement, the rebuilding was completed by a second designer, William the Englishman. The choir and the Trinity Chapel, its spectacularly raised eastward extension built to contain Becket's sumptuous shrine, proved to be influential over the subsequent development of ecclesiastical architecture in England. They reveal a sophisticated adaptation of the most advanced French Gothic to the particular needs of a monastic cathedral, and they mark the point from which a distinctive English architectural style separated itself and began to go its own, sometimes highly innovative, way.

Becket's gilded and bejewelled shrine, raised above the high altar and above the heads of pilgrims alike, dominated the interior of Canterbury Cathedral much as the Cathedral itself dominated the medieval city of Canterbury. Both were beacons, irradiating spiritual light and drawing the faithful towards them for the healing of mind and body. In *c*.1188 a monk of Canterbury, Gervase, was commissioned by his brethren to write a history of his monastery in which was offered a particularly careful account of the rebuilding and furnishing of the choir and the martyr's chapel. Gervase's pride in this achievement is very evident. If he does not attempt to offer a symbolic interpretation of the architecture, he is well aware of the impact of the new work on any pious observer and of how a gradual, ascending progress through the building towards the saint's relics accentuated a pilgrim's sense of awe. Gervase's history, written in part to assert the dignity of his monastery in the face of archiepiscopal interference, was not a unique literary enterprise. It is one of several surviving contemporary Latin histories which served to draw attention to the historic origins of a particular community or which stressed the cultural influence of that community in national and international life. The Shrewsbury-born Anglo-Norman monk, Ordericus Vitalis (1075–?1142), a member of a Benedictine house in Normandy, gave over a good deal of his voluminous, moralizing *Ecclesiastical History* to a history of his own abbey, though the majority of his latter-day readers are more likely to be drawn to his lengthy digressions concerning the conquest of England, the motives and personality of the Conqueror, and the subsequent relationship of Normandy and England. Ordericus, who proudly insisted on his English origins, reveals himself to be considerably indebted to the precedent, method, and example of Bede (whose *History* he had copied out as a novice monk). William of Malmesbury (*c*.1090–*c*.1143), the librarian of Malmesbury Abbey in Wiltshire, produced two complementary histories of England, the secular *Gesta Regum Anglorum* (1120) and the ecclesiastical *Gesta Pontificum Anglorum* (1125). Both deal with events from the fifth and sixth centuries down to the author's present, placing particular emphasis on the western part of England and, incidentally, on the figure of King Arthur (on whose fabled prowess William casts historical doubts). Yet more partisan is the *Chronicle* of Bury St Edmunds Abbey in Suffolk written by the abbey's hospitaller Jocelin de Brakelond (*fl.*1200). Jocelin's history deals with the vigorous reform of the monastic community, its lands, and its buildings in the years 1173–1202 under the determined leadership of Abbot Samson, a man Jocelin begins by admiring, though his admiration is tempered when Samson brazenly promotes a protégé to the dignity of Prior (on which occasion Jocelin expresses 'stupefaction'). Equally lively is Matthew Paris's *Chronica Maiora* produced at the Abbey of St Albans between 1235 and 1259. Matthew (*c.*1199–1259), an expert scribe, illuminator, and biographer of the abbots of St Albans, attempted in his *Chronica* to describe the history of the world from the Creation to his own times. His most distinctive passages deal not with what he piously imagines but with events that he has witnessed. He is, for example, particularly critical of papal venality and comments sourly on King Henry III's tendency to promote foreigners over native Englishmen (though neither king nor chronicler would necessarily have spoken English).

For Ordericus, William of Malmesbury, Jocelin de Brakelond, and their equally remarkable contemporary, Henry, Archdeacon of Huntingdon (?1084–1155), history was manifestly a moral process in which the mysterious purposes of God were revealed to humankind. When each of these historians stands back from merely recording, he tends to reflect on the wondrous way in which God has imprinted his will on his creature, nature, on how tempests, shipwrecks, and disasters testify to his wrath, and how miraculous cessations of disease or fire exemplify his mercy. God's saints express their displeasure in dreams and visions and show their benediction in miraculous acts of healing wrought at their intercession. However scrupulous the early medieval historian was in sifting through his sources, human records were generally interpreted as a temporal manifestation of an eternal verity and as a monument to human aspiration in an uncertain and mysterious world.

For one particularly popular and hugely influential historian, however, history was more than a providential or moral process, it was a magical and imaginative one. For Geoffrey of Monmouth (*c.*1100–55), a Welsh monk latterly promoted to the bishopric of St Asaph, the Welsh nation still held the key to the future destinies of Britain. Geoffrey claimed that his *Historia Regum Britanniae* (*The History of the Kings of Britain*, *c.*1130–8) had been translated from 'a very old book in the British tongue'. It is more likely that he adapted oral traditions, amplifying them with a great deal of material from his own singularly fertile imagination (a notable factor in his fanciful expositions of the origins of place-names). Geoffrey's *History*, of which some 190 manuscripts survive scattered over Europe, is not only the prime written source for many of the legends of King Arthur and his Round Table; it also served to popularize the fond notion that the British had derived their ancestry from the Trojan prince Brutus, the son of Sylvius and great-grandson of Aeneas. This Brutus, having fled from Troy, had supposedly landed at Totnes in Devon, had vanquished a breed of giants (including the 12-foot-high Gogmagog), and had gone on to found Troynovant (the future London). From Brutus had stemmed the ancient line of British kings whose stories (including those of Gorboduc, Lear, and Cymbeline) so fascinated Elizabethan writers. Geoffrey's assertively 'British' narrative, which reveals a venomous antipathy to the Saxon invaders, also repeats the story of Vortigern, the British king who had enlisted the help of the Saxon mercenaries, Hengist and Horsa, in his struggles against the Picts, though it is embroidered with the addition of an unfortunate marriage between Vortigern and Hengist's daughter Rowena, and an insistent sense of the subsequent doom of Romano-Celtic Britain. Untrustworthy and chronologically incredible Geoffrey's narrative may have seemed to more serious historians, both ancient and modern, but it long continued to serve as a rich quarry for generations of poets, story-tellers, and national propagandists.

Early Middle English Literature

Amongst the writers who first recognized the political and literary potential of material quarried from Geoffrey of Monmouth's *Historia Regum Britanniae* were the Anglo-Norman poets Geoffrey Gaimar (*fl.* 1140) and Wace (*c.*1100–after 1171) and Wace's English-speaking imitator, Laȝamon (*fl.*1200). Geoffrey Gaimar's poem, the *Estorie des Engles* (the 'history of the English'), began with a (now lost) reiteration of the mythical origins of the Britons before describing the Saxon invasions and the more recent exploits of the Conqueror and his son William Rufus. The Jersey-born Wace, an equally ready apologist for the Norman hegemony in England, celebrated the achievements and conquests of the dukes of Normandy in his *Roman de Rou* (or the *Geste des Normands*). He also translated and transformed a good deal of Geoffrey of Monmouth's Latin history into French octosyllabics as the verse chronicle the *Roman de Brut*. Although Laȝamon, a Worcestershire parish priest nourished in Old English rather than Norman–French literary traditions, based much of his own voluminous poem *Brut* on Wace's *Roman de Brut*, he was writing not for a cosmopolitan court but for an obscurer, if scarcely less discriminating, audience in the English provinces. The 16,000 lines of *Brut* open with a patriotic statement of intent. Writing in the third person, Laȝamon declares that his mind and his imagination were stimulated by the idea of writing of 'the noble origins of the English, what they were called and whence those who first possessed England came'. Here, and throughout his poem, the words 'English' and 'British', 'England' and 'Britain', are interchangeable. The destinies of the island of which Laȝamon writes are seen as having been historically forged by invasions and conflicts and even the Britain once guarded by the glorious Arthur had finally succumbed to Saxon conquest. With his inherited alertness to the Anglo-Saxon concept of *wyrd*, Laȝamon seems to recognize that Britain, first colonized by refugees from a devastated Troy, continues to derive a certain moral authority from its acceptance of the processes of change and decay. Its future, like its past, will reflect the uncertainties, reversals, and restorations which mark all human experience, but a providentially inspired continuity will determine its survival. Stories of Arthur are central to the text both physically and morally. Despite the fact that his greatest battles are fought against invading, pagan Saxons, Laȝamon's Arthur is the kind of generous, splendidly nonchalant and unswervingly mighty warrior familiar to the audiences of Old English poetry. The poem's imagery, unlike that of Laȝamon's more circumspect sources, equally hearkens back to a wilder heroic world. In the most famous of Laȝamon's similes, Arthur comes down on his foes like a swift wolf of the woods, his fur hung with snow ('bihonged mid snawe'), intent on devouring whatever animals he chooses ('swule deor swa him likeð'). His enemy, Childric, is hunted through a forest like a fox driven to ground and in the culminating battle at Bath the fleeing, armed Saxons lie drowned in the river Avon like steel fish girt with swords, their scales gleaming like gold-plated shields, their fins floating as if they were spears ('heore scalen wleoteð swulc gold-faȝe sceldes | þer fleoteð heore spiten swulc hit spaeren weoren').

One version of Laȝamon's *Brut* survives in a manuscript compendium with a very different poem, the anonymous *The Owl and the Nightingale* (probably written in the opening years of the thirteenth century). Where *Brut* takes the broad sweep of national history as its subject, *The Owl and the Nightingale* takes the form of an overheard debate between two birds. Where Laȝamon seems to hanker for the syllabically irregular, alliterative verse of his ancestors, the author of *The Owl and the Nightingale* writes spirited, even jocular, four-stressed rhyming couplets. Despite his debts to a Latin tradition of debate poetry, to vernacular beast fables, and to the kind of popular bestiary which drew out a moral *significatio* from the description of an animal, his poem is more of an intellectual *jeu d'esprit* than a moral or didactic exercise. *The Owl and the Nightingale* presents the birds as birds, while endowing them with a human intelligence and a human articulacy. The fastidious nightingale opens the debate by insulting the owl's deficient personal hygiene and by suggesting that her song is distinctly miserable. The owl, stung into response, insists that her voice is bold and musical and likely to be misunderstood by one who merely chatters 'like an Irish priest'. As they argue, personal abuse gives way to more subtle charges and countercharges; they score intellectual points off one another and they twist in and out of complex issues, capped aspersions, and temporary advantages. Both birds establish themselves in irreconcilable philosophical opposition to one another. The nightingale sees the owl as dirty, dismal, pompous, perverse, and life-denying; the owl looks down on the nightingale as flighty, frivolous, libidinous, and self-indulgent. The arguments, like the kind of contemporary legal, philosophical, or theological debates on which the poem may be based, need an arbiter, and it is solely on the choice of this human arbiter that the birds agree. They finally resolve to fly off to Portisham in Dorset to submit themselves to the judgement of an underpaid clerk, one Master Nicholas of Guildford. Such is the emphasis placed by the birds on this provincial priest's wisdom and discrimination that some commentators have claimed that the poem must be the work of the otherwise unknown Nicholas (and, moreover, a covert plea for his professional advancement). Whether or not *The Owl and the Nightingale* bears Master Nicholas's personal imprint, it conspicuously ends with his distinguished arbitration unrealized. The disputants wing their way to Dorset while the narrator abruptly resorts to silence: 'As to how their case went, I can tell you nothing more. There is no more to this tale' ('Her nis na more of þis spelle').

It has been suggested that *The Owl and the Nightingale* may have been written for the edification and amusement of a literate, but not necessarily highly Latinate, community of English nuns. Such communities, and their stricter alternatives—women recluses who had chosen the solitary life—were of considerable importance to the intense religious culture of twelfth- and thirteenth-century England. The prose-texts in the so-called Katherine-group—which concentrate on the lives of heroic virgin saints (Katherine, Margaret, and Juliana), on the person of Christ, and on his mystical relationship with his contemplative and chaste brides—seem to have been written specifically for a group of women in Herefordshire who did not possess the command of Latin expected of their male equivalents. The same would seem to be true of the most substantial devotional text of the early thirteenth century, the *Ancrene Riwle* ('the Anchoresses' Rule or Guide'). The work was originally composed in English by a male confessor for the instruction and comfort of three young sisters of good family who had elected to withdraw into a life of solitary prayer, penance, and contemplation (it was reworked, for more general devotional use, as the *Ancrene Wisse*). The *Ancrene Riwle* is divided into eight books which give detailed, practical, personal advice to the solitaries and recommend regular reading and meditation as well as formal spiritual discipline and religious observance (such as the increasingly popular practices of self-examination, private confession, and penance). While the writer does not shy away from the spiritual benefits of humiliation and mortification, he offers counsel against the dangers inherent in excessive introspection. Although the women are separated from the world and obliged to explore their inner resources of spiritual strength, they are recommended to see Christ as a mystical wooer, as a knight, and as a king and to respond actively and exuberantly to his proffered love and honour. God comes in love to those who pine for him with a pure heart and Love is his chamberlain, his counsellor, and his wife from whom he can hide nothing. The first and last sections of the *Ancrene Riwle* govern the outer life while its middle sections explore the promised joys of the inner life. At the end, the writer returns to more mundane affairs, offering advice on diet, dress, and hygiene and on how to cope with illness. The sisters are advised to keep a cat rather than a cow (they are likely to become too concerned for the cow and be tempted into worldliness) and, in order that they should be well provided for without having to shop and cook, to confine themselves to two maidservants each. The writer ends with the hope that his book will be profitably read and then, somewhat disarmingly, adds the thought that he would rather take the arduous journey to Rome than have to write it all over again.

Chivalry and 'Courtly' Love

As the word 'chevalier' suggests, a medieval knight was in origin a soldier rich enough to possess a horse and to be able to equip himself with the armour and weapons appropriate to a mounted warrior. That England insistently clung to the term 'knight' (from the Old English *cniht*, a youth and, by extension, a military servant) rather than to the French word, offers further evidence of the fact that the Conquest merely developed an existing kind of feudal service prevalent amongst the ruling classes. By the beginning of the twelfth century the ancient Germanic military system which entailed the apprenticeship of a young warrior to an older man had been refined and formalized by a complex pattern of rituals blessed by the Church. These rituals and the code of conduct developed from them employed a vocabulary which was largely French in origin. According to the chivalric code observed throughout Western Europe, a squire, who had served his term of apprenticeship to a knight, was himself able to rise by degrees to the formal dignity of knighthood. The new knight, after a ritual bath, a night's vigil, and sacramental confession, was ceremonially dubbed by his liege-lord (most often his king). The knight swore a binding oath of loyalty to his lord and pledged himself to protect the weak (a group deemed to include all women), to right wrongs (a category usually defined by his liege), and to defend the Christian faith (especially against the advances of Muslim infidels). At its most elevated level this system of aristocratic male bonding inspired the creation of the three great European crusading Military Orders, the Order of the Hospital of St John of Jerusalem or the Hospitallers (founded *c.*1099), the Order of the Poor Knights of Christ and the Temple of Solomon or the Templars (founded *c.*1119), and the Teutonic Knights of St Mary's Hospital at Jerusalem (founded *c.*1143). These tightly knit bodies of celibate gentlemen soldiers were originally formed to protect the pilgrim routes to Jerusalem following the brutal European capture of the Holy City from the Saracens in 1099. Although gradually forced into an inglorious westward retreat by the resurgence of the Saracens, the great wealth and prestige acquired by these international Military Orders allowed them to continue to exercise considerable authority throughout Western Christendom.

Despite the zealous suppression of the Templars by the kings of France and

England in the early fourteenth century, the idea of knighthood, if not exactly its crusading enterprise, continued to flourish under new royal patronage. Looking back nostalgically to the reign of the largely mythical Arthur rather than to the days of the First Crusade, King Edward III of England founded the Order of the Garter in *c*.1344. This new military confraternity, which dispensed with the arcane lore and the semi-monastic vows of bodies like the Templars, was restricted to twenty-five members including the monarch himself. Edward presided as a pseudo-Arthur at a mock Round Table, genially participating in ceremonials and festivities and watching over tournaments designed to show off the valour of his knights. Ornamental pageantry had triumphed over organized pugnacity. The motto Edward chose for his new Order none the less threw down a challenge to anyone who might oppose either his chivalric ideal or his assertive claim to the throne of France: *Honi soit qui mal y pense*—'Shame to him who thinks evil of it'.

King Edward III's fascination with the idea of Arthur was no mere whim. His new order of chivalry was a belated realization of long cherished military ideals and long fostered literary images. Since the time of the inventive Geoffrey of Monmouth, Arthur had emerged as the type and mirror of all Christian kings. Arthur's fabled court became not merely the focus of chivalric enterprise; it was consistently reinvented as a fixed point to which a whole variety of legends, Celtic myths, and religious, literary, and moral concepts could be loosely attached. The knights of the Round Table acquired names, ancestries, coats of arms, and quests from extraordinarily diverse sources. They also became the literary beneficiaries of a new-found concern with amatory relationships. Aided by the cosmopolitan influence of Eleanor of Aquitaine, in succession the Queen first of Louis VII of France and then of Henry II of England in the mid- to late twelfth century, the culture of the troubadours of Provence had spread north to two relatively sober, French-speaking courts. Eleanor, the granddaughter of the first troubadour poet and the dedicatee of Wace's *Brut*, exercised her patronage in favour of a new kind of poetry which linked the elevated view of sexual love first cultivated by the troubadours with stories associated with the exploits of Arthurian knights. This new concern with *fin'amors* (sometimes described as 'courtly love') recognized a parallel between the feudal service of a knight to his liege-lord and the service of a lover to an adored and honoured lady. Whether or not this cultivated literary pattern was based on a courtly reality is much disputed; what is certain is that the culture of the twelfth century began to place a new emphasis on the dignity and distinctiveness of women in what remained a male-dominated, clerical, and military civilization. In the Latin treatise *De Amore* written *c*.1184–6 by Andreas Capellanus, the chaplain to Eleanor's daughter Marie de Champagne, woman emerges as the dominant partner in a love-affair, and sexual love itself as integral to the composition and practice of a chivalric court (as they were, Andreas insists, in Arthur's day). Andreas, in common with the poetic celebrators of *fin'amors*, saw the true vassalage of lover to lady as an ideal which functioned beyond or outside marriage; despite the precepts of the Church, few writers seem to have assumed that such relationships were chaste, but the shared passion of the often adulterous lovers was recognized as ennobling and semi-religious in its intensity, if ultimately unfulfilled and unfulfilling.

Two influential French poets, both of whom are likely to have worked in England—Marie de France (*fl.* 1160–90) and Chrétien de Troyes (*fl.* 1170–90)—made particularly effective literary capital out of such *fin'amors*. Marie's twelve brief *Lais*, adapted, she claims, from Breton stories, draw on a wide range of settings and geographic references (Norway, Brabant, Ireland, Normandy, Britain). Only one, *Lanval*, refers to Arthur by name but most of the other stories deal with the amatory encounters of knights and ladies in a world informed by both chivalrous action and supernatural influence. Like Marie, Chrétien wrote a (now lost) version of the Tristan legend, but his five surviving romances reveal a more deliberate interest in stories centred on Camelot. His *Yvain*, his *Chevalier de la Charrette* (or *Lancelot*), and his incomplete *Perceval* or *Le Conte du Graal* all treat legends which were later considered central to the Arthurian canon. The works of both poets seem to have circulated both widely and over a long period in England, *Yvain* being translated, and somewhat simplified, as *Ywain and Gawain* (*c.*1400) and Marie's *Lanval* providing the base for several late fourteenth-century versions of the same story (*Sir Landeval*, *Sir Lambewell*, *Sir Lamwell*, and Thomas Chestre's *Sir Launfal*). Equally significantly, the forms perfected in French by Marie and Chrétien were to exercise a considerable influence over later English poets either as translators or as confident vernacular practitioners. Marie's short rhymed 'Breton' *lais* provided models for Chaucer's Franklin's Tale and for Gower's 'Tale of Rosiphilee', while the romances of Chrétien and his contemporaries (essentially courtly stories concerned with classical or knightly heroes and written in 'romance' or the modern French vernacular) helped determine the subjects and style of anonymous Middle English poems such as *Sir Orfeo* and *Sir Gawain and the Green Knight*.

The shift in thirteenth-century French poetry away from exclusively military or heroic subjects is especially evident in the compendious *Roman de la rose* begun by Guillaume de Lorris (d. 1237) and completed *c.*1275 by a distinctively different poet, Jean de Meun (d. 1305). The very title of the poem, 'The Romance of the Rose', suggests the degree to which fashionable romance had swung away from a concentration on knightly prowess to an allegorical and philosophical treatment of *fin'amors* centred on a richly symbolic flower. In a dream or vision the courtly poet-narrator discovers a delicately planted, walled garden on a bright May morning. In the midst of the garden a well reflects the image of a rose, a rose which at first can neither be plucked nor embraced but which serves to represent the perfection of his love. The body of the poem is concerned with the dreamer's quest to achieve the rose, a quest which is variously assisted or opposed by allegorical figures who embody aspects of his beloved. It proved a vastly popular poem. A manuscript copy is listed amongst the books in King Richard II's library in 1384–5; Chaucer, clearly steeped in the poem, translated a long section of it into English as *The Romaunt of the Rose* (a translation which earned him the fulsome praise of his French contemporary, Eustache Deschamps); above all, it proved profoundly influential over a succession of English fourteenth-century poems which employ the device of a dream-allegory, whether as a modified love-vision such as Chaucer's own *Book of the Duchess,* or as a religious revealing such as *Pearl,* a poem generally ascribed to the so-called *Gawain*-poet.

English Romances and the *Gawain*-Poet

Although most French and English romances tend to be secular in subject-matter, most express a pious confidence in the values of an explicitly Christian society (as opposed to a pagan or Muslim one). Most tend to present their heroes as knights pursuing a lonely quest, but they also stress the importance of the shared, communal values of a chivalric world. The romance genre nevertheless remains a defined one. In general, English translations, naturalizations, imitations, and reflections of French romances tend to be simpler in form and more direct in address than their originals. *King Horn,* the earliest surviving English poem to have been categorized as a romance by latter-day scholars, dates from *c.*1225. It tells the story of a prince who, driven out of his homeland by invading Saracens, takes refuge in the kingdom of Westernesse where he falls in love with the King's daughter, the high-spirited Rymenhild. When the lovers are betrayed, Horn is banished to Ireland where he proves the quality of his knightly heroism by performing spectacular deeds of valour. Having recovered his kingdom, he finally claims Rymenhild as his queen. *King Horn* presents its protagonist as matured both by adventure and by love and happily matched by a woman equal to him in fidelity, wit, and courage. The pattern of exile and return is followed in *The Lay of Havelok the Dane* (written in Lincolnshire *c.*1300). The poem traces the fortunes of the dispossessed Prince Havelok who seeks refuge in England. He is at first obliged to eek out a humble existence at Grimsby but his noble origins are twice revealed by a mystical light that shines over his head. Havelok returns to Denmark with his bride, Princess Goldborough, kills his usurping guardian and regains his rightful throne. Although the story stresses Havelok's inborn royalty, it also dwells on details of ordinary life and labour and shows a hero who is prepared to defend himself with his fists and a wooden club as much as with his sword.

The subjects of English romances can, like their French models, be broadly categorized as dealing with three types of historical material: the 'matter' of Rome (that is, classical legend); the 'matter' of France (often tales of Charlemagne and his knights, or stories concerned with the struggle against the advancing Saracens); and the 'matter' of Britain (Arthurian stories, or tales

dealing with later knightly heroes). *Sir Orfeo* (written in the early fourteenth
century) proclaims itself to be a story of Breton origin, though it is in fact an
embroidered retelling of the legend of Orpheus and Eurydice (with a Celtic
fairyland supplanting Hades and with a happy denouement replacing the tragic
ending of the Greek story). *Floris and Blancheflour* (written in the first half of
the thirteenth century) deals with the adventures of two precocious children
at the court of a Saracen Emir, one of them a magically endowed Muslim
prince, the other the daughter of a Christian lady. The conventionally Christian
ending somewhat incongruously requires the Emir to overcome his religious
scruples and to bless their union. Saracens are shown in a less benign light in
Otuel and Roland (*c.*1330) which traces the knightly career of a formerly
Muslim knight at the court of Charlemagne who is miraculously converted
when the Holy Ghost alights on his helmet in the form of a dove, and in *The
Sege of Melayne* (*c.*1400) which deals with the defence of Christianity in
Lombardy. In two particularly popular late thirteenth-century English
romances, both of them designed to celebrate the putative ancestors of prominent aristocratic families, the eponymous heroes face a series of dire challenges
during their respective quests to prove themselves and the quality of their love.
However, where the hero of *Bevis of Hampton is* finally content to accept the
rewards of his international labours, Sir Guy in *Guy of Warwick* feels compelled to atone for his worldly pride by embarking on a new series of exploits
solely for the glory of God. He ends his life as a hermit unrecognized by his
wife who brings food to his obscure retreat.

Despite the verve and the variety of subject, setting, and treatment of many
earlier English romances, none seriously challenges the sustained energy, the
effective patterning, and the superb detailing of *Sir Gawain and the Green
Knight*. Although the poem's author is anonymous—like many other medieval
writers, painters, and architects—his language indicates that he was born in the
northwest Midlands of England and that he was writing in the second half of
the fourteenth century. He is known as 'the *Gawain*-poet' after the longest of
four poems preserved in a single, crudely illustrated manuscript in the British
Library. None of the poems has a title in the manuscript, but it is generally
assumed that they share a common author if not a common subject, theme, or
line of development. *Pearl*, *Cleanness* (or *Purity*), *Patience*, and *Sir Gawain and
the Green Knight* are also central to what has been seen as an 'alliterative revival'
which took place in the literature produced in northern and north-western
England from *c.*1350 (though it may be that this 'revival' is more of a survival
of a pre-Conquest interest in alliterative verse made newly manifest by the
patronage of English-speaking noblemen). *Sir Gawain and the Green Knight* and
its companion poems cannot properly be seen as the written climax of a largely
provincial, oral, and unrecorded tradition. They are the work of a highly sophisticated narrative artist, well-versed in the Holy Scriptures and in devotional literature and possessed of an easy familiarity with the French and English
romances which continued to divert his contemporaries.

Gawain opens with reference to the line of British kings, sprung from Brutus, which has culminated in the glorious reign of Arthur. Into Arthur's festive court on New Year's Day rides an armed challenger (Arthur, it appears, always relishes some kind of adventure before he feasts at New Year), but this challenger is highly distinctive: rider, armour, and horse are all bright green in hue. The knight's real ambivalence is, however, signified by his bearing both of a holly branch and an axe 'huge and monstrous' ('hoge and unmete'). Whereas the green branch betokens life, an appropriate and familiar enough aspiration for the northern Christmas season, the axe threatens death. The pagan, Celtic origins of this Green Knight become obvious in the 'beheading game' he proposes to the King, a challenge taken up by Arthur's champion, his nephew Gawain. Rolling his eyes, knitting his green brows, and waving his green beard, the mysterious challenger suggests that a knight may cut off his head provided that the knight agrees to submit to the same bloody rite in a year's time. When Gawain cleanly severs the neck bone, the unabashed Green Knight strides up to his missing head, picks it up, bows to the King, disembodiedly repeats his dire condition, and rides out of Camelot with fire sparking from his horse's hooves ('his hed in his handes | þat þe fyr of þe flint flaȝe for fole houes'). The *Gawain*-poet has not only fused a Celtic beheading myth with an Arthurian adventure; he goes on to interpret Gawain's subsequent quest to find the Green Knight and his Green Chapel, and his resistance to temptation, in terms of Christian knighthood.

Gawain sets out on his mission on All Saints' Day (1 November) when the optimism of new beginnings at New Year seems to have melted into the unease of the season of dying. Nevertheless, he prepares himself ceremoniously and splendidly:

> He dowellez þer al þat day, and dressez on þe morn,
> Askez erly hys armez, and alle were þey broȝt.
> Fyrst a tulé tapit tyȝt over þe flet,
> And miche watz þe gyld gere þat glent þeralofte;
> þe stif mon steppez þeron, and þe stel hondelez,
> Dubbed in a dublet of a dere tars,
> And syþen a crafty capados, closed aloft,
> þat with a bryȝt blaunner was bounden withinne.
> þenne set þay þe sabatounz upon þe segge fotez,
> His legez lapped in stel with luflych grevez,
> With polaynez piched perto, policed ful clene,
> Aboute his knez knaged wyth knotez of golde;
> Queme quyssewes þen, þat coyntlych closed
> His thik prawen þyȝez, with þwonges to tachched;
> And syþen þe brawden bryné of bryȝt stel ryngez
> Unbeweved þat wyȝ upon wlonk stuffe,
> And wel bornyst brace upon his boþe armes,
> With gode cowterz and gay, and glovez of plate,

And alle þe godlych gere þat hym gayn schulde þat tyde:
> Wyth ryche cote-armure,
> His gold sporez spend with pryde,
> Gurde wyth a bront ful sure
> With silk sayn unmbe his syde.

(He stays there all that day, and dresses in the morning, asks for his arms early and they were all brought. First a carpet of red silk [*tulé*] was spread over the floor, and much gilded armour gleamed upon it. The strong man steps on it, and takes hold of the steel, clad in a doublet made of costly oriental silk [tars], and then in a skilfully made hood [*capados*], fastened at the neck and trimmed with ermine [*blaunner*]. Then they put steel shoes [*sabatounz*] on the knight's feet, his legs were wrapped in steel with handsome greaves, with knee-pieces [*polaynez*] attached to them, polished clean, fastened to his knees with knots of gold; then fine thigh-pieces [*quyssewes*], which cunningly enclosed his thick muscular thighs, were secured with thongs; and then the linked coat of mail [*bryné*] of bright steel rings enveloped the warrior, over a tunic made of glorious material; and well-burnished arm-pieces [*brace*] upon both his arms, with good, fair elbow-pieces [*cowterz*] and gloves of steel-plate, and all the goodly gear that should be an advantage to him at that time; with rich coat armour, his gold spurs splendidly fastened, girt with a stout sword and a silk girdle at his side.)

Thus accoutred, and with an image of the Virgin Mary on the inside of his shield and mystical pentangle on the outside (the symbol of the virtues central to his pure knighthood), Gawain rides out into filthy weather and empty land-scapes. The rain freezes as it falls, the waterfalls are ice-bound, and the nights are bitter. He fights, the narrator tells us almost offhandedly, with dragons, wolves, and wild men of the woods, but his spirits are kept up by prayers to Christ and to his holy mother. Gawain's real test comes when neither he nor the reader expects it. Having come across a castle in the wilderness (it appears by happy accident) he is warmly received for yet another round of Christmas rituals and festivities. He is as strict in his religious observance as he is warm in his responses to his host's courtesy, readily agreeing to exchange 'winnings' with him. On the third day, however, he fails to give up a girdle presented to him by his hostess (it is supposed to protect its wearer from death). When Gawain is finally directed to the Green Chapel he honourably kneels to receive three blows from the beheading axe; two are feints, aborted by the seeming skill of the Green Knight; the third lightly cuts his neck. The Knight then reveals himself as the lord of the castle and explains that Gawain has received an exact punishment for his failure to render the girdle up to his host. The whole affair has been a plot against Arthur and the Round Table magically contrived by Morgan le Fay. Despite such explanations, Gawain is distraught at the expo-sure of his fallibility and condemns his lapse in a torrent of self-disgust. It is only in the generous, knightly world of Camelot that his imperfection can finally be excused as human folly, not condemned as a crime against chivalry.

Sir Gawain and the Green Knight identifies Gawain's quest as a trial not of his valour (which remains undoubted) but of his chastity. But the morality explored throughout the poem is not merely sexual. In his poem the *Gawain* poet offers a series of contrasts which help to call into question not just the value of knighthood but the idea of value itself. He allows an already old-fashioned chivalric, gentlemanly ideal, in which personal integrity is linked to feudal and communal loyalties, to co-exist with what can be seen as a mercantile notion of barter and exchange (merchants, and Lord Mayors of London in particular, were already beginning to rise to the dignity of knighthood). He suggests that the codes of Christian chivalry can help define the true path of human advance towards spiritual integrity. Gawain is required to attempt to live up to the symbolic pentangle that he bears on his shield, a mysterious Solomonic emblem of perfection. It is drawn as one unending line, an 'endless knot' of five intersecting points which are interpreted within the narrative as standing for the five wits, the five fingers, the five wounds of Christ, the five joys of Mary, and the fivefold practice of generosity, fellowship, cleanness, courtesy, and pity. When Gawain slips, his fault lies in accepting a girdle, a broken line but one that can be joined end to end to make a circle. It is the token of his fear and of his loss of fidelity to the codes he holds most dear. It is, however, in this act of failure that Gawain discovers his fullest humanity and the truest test of his knightly integrity. When he is ultimately received back into the fellowship of another emblem of perfection, the *Round* Table, his fellow-knights join him in wearing the green girdle not simply as a sign of shame, but as a public avowal of the 'renoun of þe Rounde Table'. In the manuscript the poem triumphantly ends with a statement of the motto of the new Order of the Garter: 'Shame to him who thinks evil of it'. The humble garter, we recall, like the practical girdle, can be fastened into the shape of a circle and both can be elevated by the knights that wear them into a sign of honour.

The high ideals of Christian knighthood, human lapses from uprightness, and the suggestive power of numbers are all to some degree reflected in the other poems ascribed to the *Gawain*-poet. *Patience* is largely taken up with a somewhat idiosyncratic retelling of the story of Jonah, the prophet himself being associated not with the divine virtue of patience but with its contrary, human impatience. Jonah accepts nothing with equanimity, neither God's checks nor signs of God's mercy. When the Almighty forgives the people of Nineveh, his chosen prophet is vexed enough to reproach him for his excess of 'cortaysye', the tolerant generosity which the fourteenth century would most readily have associated with Arthurian ideals of knightly conduct. The poet takes a decidedly different view of divine providence in *Cleanness*, an exploration of three defective societies described in the Old Testament as having justly provoked the wrath and indignation of God. Where Jonah bemoans the proffered chance of repentance at Nineveh, the narrator of *Cleanness* sees punishment as the proper reward for the sacrilegious and 'unnatural' defilement of God's image evident in the time of Noah, at Sodom, and in Belshazzar's Babylon.

Pearl is at once a more delicate, compassionate and, to many twentieth-century readers, sympathetic work of art. It purports to describe the dream of a distraught father, bereaved of his 2-year-old daughter, who seeks for her in the image of a pearl. The poem's subject may well be gently shaped around a punning reference to the common medieval name Margaret (Latin, *margarita*, a pearl); it certainly makes play with Christ's parable of the pearl of great price, itself cipher for the kingdom of heaven (Matthew 13: 46). At the opening of the poem, the narrator seeks for his lost gem ('so smal, so smoþe') in an arbour (perhaps at the site of her grave) in the 'high season' of August (the month in which the feast of the heavenly Assumption of the Virgin Mary is celebrated). He falls asleep on the mound and is granted a dream of a land bright with imperishable jewels, a land recognizably that of the vision of St John (who saw each of the twelve gates of the heavenly Jerusalem as formed from a pearl). The white-clad maiden the dreamer meets is barely recognizable; she is glorious but he is struck both by hesitancy and by wonder. The two then engage in a dialogue in which the pearl-maiden both reproaches the dreamer's tendency to disbelief and carefully answers his often dazed questions. She, it emerges, is now a bride of Christ and, like all other saints, is now through God's 'courtesy' a monarch in heaven ('So fare we all wyth luf and lyste | To kyng and quene by cortaysye'). When asked why she, who was too young to know even the simplest of the Church's prayers on earth, can now be a queen, she replies by repeating Christ's parable of the vineyard in which all workers are treated equally. With each answer the dreamer's own rapture seems to increase and he finally plunges into the stream that separates his transformed daughter only to awaken in the arbour with his head lying on the mound where he had lost his pearl. Despite the ostensible simplicity of its subject and its dream structure, *Pearl* is a theologically profound and psychologically probing poem. It is also extraordinarily complex in terms of its metrical and numerological form. Its 101 stanzas perhaps refer to the perfection of God (101 being classed as a 'perfect' number). These stanzas are grouped into twenty sections, and within each section the last line of a stanza is not only repeated, with minor variations as a kind of refrain, but is also used to provide a link into the next section (by being echoed in the new first line). The poem's alliterative opening line ('Perle, pleasaunte to princes paye', 'Pearl, pleasing to the delight of prince') is also half-echoed in the very last line ('Ande precious perles unto his pay', 'And precious pearls for his delight'). The twelve-line stanzas, the poem's 1,212 lines, and the procession of 144,000 virgins all serve as symbolic representations of the dimensions and structure of the heavenly Jerusalem that the poet describes.

English Lyrics of the Middle Ages

Much of the wide and impressive range of medieval lyric poetry written in the thirteenth, fourteenth, and fifteenth centuries remains anonymous. Like the contemporary romances, the earliest surviving love-lyrics suggest a marked, and French-inspired, shift away from heroic and assertively male and military subjects to a new fascination with service to a fair, and sometimes fickle, lady rather than to a feudal lord. This love poetry expresses an urgent and often unhappy longing, a longing frequently stirred by early spring and related to ideas of a lusty but fleeting youth. One fine poem, contained in the British Library MS Harley 2253, opens with insistent linking of the beloved to a regenerate nature:

> Bitwenë March and Avëril, [April]
> When spray [the twig] biginneth to springe,
> The litel foul [bird] hath hire wil,
> On hyrë lede [her language] to synge.
> Ich live in love-longinge,
> For semeliest [the fairest] of allë thynge,
> She may me blissë bringe,
> Ich am in hire baundoun [power].
>   An hendy hap Ichave y-hent [good fortune I have received]
>   Ichot [I know] from hevene it is me sent,
>   From alle wommen my love is lent [has gone]
>   And light [alighted] on Alysoun.

A related, unrestrained, but somewhat more chaste longing also haunts the considerable body of surviving religious lyrics of the period, and particularly those of the fourteenth century. The fair lady is now identified with the Virgin Mary and the liege lord is a Christ bound up with human suffering. In the lyric 'As I lay upon a night' (which appears in a variety of MSS) a sleepless Christian seems to hear the Virgin rocking her child to sleep on Christmas Day:

> *Lullay, lullay, lay, lay lullay:*
> *Mi dere moder* [mother], *sing lullay.*
>
> As I lay upon a night
>   Alone in my longing,
> Me thoughte I saw a wonder sight,
>   A maiden child rokking.
>   *Lullay, lullay,* etc.
>
> The maiden wolde withouten song
>   Hire child o slepë bringe [to put her child to sleep];
> The child thoughtë she dide him wrong,
>   And bad his moder singe.
>   *Lullay, lullay,* etc.
>
> 'Sing now, moder,' seide that child,
>   'What me shal befalle
> Here after when I come to ild [maturity],
>   So don modrës alle.
>   *Lullay, lullay,* etc.

The Virgin recounts what she knows of Gabriel's salutation, and the child's birth at Bethlehem, but she can say no more. It is left for the dreamer, and the faithful reader, to extrapolate from the joyful mysteries the meaning of the sorrowful and the glorious mysteries to come.

Fourteenth-Century England: Death, Disruption, and Change

Much has been made recently of a 'Ricardian' resurgence in English writing. Though King Richard II cannot be personally credited with encouraging this resurgence, his twenty-year reign (1377–99) was to prove remarkable for the quality, quantity, variety, and energy of its literary enterprise in English. It was equally remarkable for the steady consolidation of the last stylistic phase of English Gothic architecture, the so-called Perpendicular Style, a development which a recent architectural historian has described as 'much the most important phenomenon in English art'. However much that architectural judgement might be open to dispute or qualification, the phenomenal *literary* achievements of Richard II's reign, and particularly that of Geoffrey Chaucer, have exercised a profound influence over the subsequent history of British culture. Chaucer and Gower, as influential and well-connected London-based poets, were aware both of internationally based court styles and fashions and of one another's work (Chaucer dedicated his *Troilus and Criseyde* to the 'moral Gower'), but it is probable that both remained largely unresponsive to the alliterative enterprise of more essentially provincial and insular writers such as the *Gawain*-poet. There is equally no reason to assume that the *Gawain*-poet or his fellow alliterative poet, Langland, were unsympathetic to those internationally shaped, metropolitan tastes and styles that determined the nature and subjects of Gower's and Chaucer's poetry. Langland, educated in the west of England but working in London on the fringes of the ecclesiastical establishment, was almost certainly addressing the urgent social and theological vision of *Piers Plowman* not to a provincial aristocratic circle but to a broad national audience which embraced both churchmen and laity, both connoisseurs of continental poetic mannerisms and admirers of plainer and localized English forms. The literary resurgence of Richard II's reign is almost certainly related to the emphatic shift towards the use of English as the pre-eminent medium of communication, government, and entertainment amongst the ruling élite. Whereas Gower elected to write his *Misour de l'Omme* (the *Speculum Meditantis, c.*1376–8) in French, his *Vox Clamantis* (*c.*1379–81) in Latin, and his *Confessio Amantis* (*c.*1390) in English, Chaucer was notable in helping to raise the literary status of English by writing exclusively in his native tongue. Richard II's equally bilingual successor, Henry IV (reigned 1399–1413), conducted all his government business in English. Henry's son Henry V, who was intent on pressing home his claim to the throne of France throughout his reign

(1413–22), went further by making a conspicuous point of preferring the use of English to French both at court and in all his official transactions.

This notable shift in favour of the English language accompanied more gradual but equally noteworthy changes in English society. For John Gower, society was still constituted of 'three estates of men'. According to this commonly held medieval political theory, the clergy fostered the spiritual well-being of the state, a warrior-aristocracy defended both Church and people, and the third estate supported the other two by the fruits of its labour. This traditional tripartite division of society was sanctioned by theological speculation and political theory alike. By the early fourteenth century the theory was, however, becoming somewhat divorced from social reality. If England remained an overwhelmingly rural society, it was none the less a society in which, as elsewhere in northern Europe, cities exercised an increasing influence as centres both of population and of economic power. By *c.*1370 London probably had a population of around 40,000, York and Bristol each contained over 10,000 people, and six other cities (Coventry, Norwich, Lincoln, Salisbury, King's Lynn, and Colchester) are estimated to have held upwards of 6,000. In York during Richard II's reign, poll-tax returns suggest that there were over one thousand men with identifiable occupations, some 850 of them working as their own masters in close on a hundred defined crafts. The growth of literacy, and of vernacular literacy in particular, had also substantially diminished the old clerical monopoly of administrative posts and consequently of administrative power. These changes are evident enough in Chaucer's *Canterbury Tales* where the diversity of occupation, outlook, culture, profession, and class of his Canterbury pilgrims suggests a real difficulty in exactly assigning characters such as the Man of Law, the Franklin, the Host, the Reeve, the Shipman, and the Wife of Bath to his or her 'estate'. Chaucer's prosperous London guildsmen—the Haberdasher, the Carpenter, the Weaver, the Dyer, and the Tapicer—are deemed to be 'ech of hem a fair burgeys' and sufficiently distinguished, at least in their own eyes, for their wives to be addressed as 'madame'.

The most dramatic change was, however, demographic. The most devastating of the great fourteenth-century plagues, the Black Death, first appeared in Dorset in 1348 and reached its height in the summer of 1349 (killing some two hundred people a day in London). If the precise medical analysis of the causes and consequences of this European pandemic remains indeterminate, and if contemporary estimates of the death-toll were wildly exaggerated, even sober-minded modern historians concede that England may have lost as much as one-third of its population. The effects of this devastation were long term. The parish clergy, professionally intimate with the circumstances of the dead and dying, were particularly affected. Not only were their numbers severely depleted, so were their financial resources. Nearly forty years later in the Prologue to *The Vision of Piers Plowman* Langland reports that 'Persons [parsons] and parisshe prestes pleyned [complained] hem to the bisshop | That hire parisshes weren povere sith the pestilence tyme'. In one manor owned by the Bishop of Winchester it has been estimated that some 66 per cent of tenants died of the plague in 1348 alone. The Black Death placed a very considerable strain on both the rural labour-market and on the towns. As late as the mid-fifteenth century the citizens of Lincoln and York were still complaining of the consequent decline in their cities' trade, population, and manufactures. At the time, the pestilence seemed like a visitation from a wrathful God—sudden, inexplicable, unstoppable and, to the survivors, profoundly shocking. Reason preaches the message that 'thise pestilences were for pure synne' in Passus V of *Piers Plowman*, while the chronicler of Louth Park Abbey in Lincolnshire mournfully records that 'so great a multitude was not swept away, it was believed, even by the flood in the days of Noah'. Into the soft stone of the tower of the parish church at Ashwell in Hertfordshire in 1350 some despairing, unknown hand scratched the Latin words: 'Penta miseranda ferox violenta pestis superest plebs pessima testis' ('Wretched, wild, distracted, the dregs of the common people alone survive to tell the tale').

The Black Death and the labour shortages that followed it served to exacerbate the long-standing social tensions between those who profited from the land and those who actually worked it. When in the revision of his Latin poem *Vox Clamantis* Gower introduced an allegorical description of a wild peasant rabble rampaging through the land in the guise of beasts, his socially privileged first readers would readily have recognized his pointed and antipathetic reference to the traumatic Peasants' Revolt of the summer of 1381. This, the most concerted and disruptive popular revolt in English medieval history, had insistently and disconcertingly pressed home the question first raised by popular preachers: 'When Adam dalf [delved] and Eve span | Who was then a gentilman?' The imposition of a vastly unpopular poll-tax on the labouring classes may have been the immediate provocation for the revolt, but its often articulate leaders were also able to identify misgovernment and exploitation as its deeper causes. Unpopular senior representatives of Church and State were dragged from the Tower and summarily executed when the rebels briefly held London in June, and the radical priest, John Ball, preached to the assembled crowd at Blackheath on the social justice of laying aside 'the yoke of serfdom'. This same John Ball saw support for his arguments not simply in the primitive communism practised by early Christians but also in the teachings of modern clerical dissidents and even in the speculative social theology of Langland's *Piers Plowman*. When the Peasants' Revolt collapsed at the end of June its ordinary adherents dispersed and its leaders, including Ball, were pursued by royal justice, tried and executed. The poll-tax, however, was not revived nor were the commons of England (unlike the commons of France) ever again made the objects of the kind of direct taxation that left the first and second estates unburdened. It has also been argued that the decimation of the population through the plague, coupled with the fear of a repetition of the great fourteenth-century revolt, brought about a longer-term political consequence: the gradual introduction of a greater social mobility. As the century developed, the English nobility, unlike their continental equivalents, increasingly proved to be unwilling to define themselves as a closed, separate, and uniquely privileged order. England did not hereafter lack a distinct ruling class, but it was a class open to new recruitment from below and relatively responsive to social and ideological change.

The Church was also deeply affected by the unstable nature of society and its beliefs in the late fourteenth century. The parish clergy, thinned out by the Black Death, seems to have suffered from a decline not only in numbers but also in quality. The moral and intellectual shortcomings of the clergy, though scarcely novel as causes for literary complaint, struck certain English observers with particular force. If the worldliness of monks, friars, and religious hangers-on was a butt of Chaucer's satire, the more worrying inadequacy of the parish clergy proved a recurrent theme in Langland's poetry. Relatively few educated Englishmen and women expressed doubts concerning the basic truths of Christianity as they were defined by the Church, but many more were prepared to question the standing, authority, and behaviour of the Church's ordained representatives. Central to the questioning of religious institutions, practices, and hierarchies in the late fourteenth and early fifteenth centuries are the writings of the theologian and would-be reformer, John Wyclif (or Wycliffe, *c*.1330–84). Wyclif's attacks on the misuse of papal powers and revenues, and his criticism of the sale of indulgences and of the parasitism of monks and friars, seem to have struck a sympathetic chord in many otherwise orthodox believers. His questioning of more basic theological assumptions (such as the status, authority, and special dignity of the Catholic Church and its ministers), however, brought him into direct conflict with the Pope and the English ecclesiastical hierarchy. Wyclif's later forthright denunciation of the doctrine of transubstantiation as both philosophically unsound and likely to encourage superstition revealed him to be skating on the thinnest possible theological ice. At the Blackfriars Council of 1382, he and his followers were formally abominated and it was only the vigorous protection offered by King Richard's uncle, John of Gaunt, that shielded him from the dire secular consequences of religious displeasure. Although he died peacefully in retirement at his rectory at Lutterworth in Leicestershire, in 1415 Wyclif's remains were exhumed, burned, and sprinkled in the river Swift after the Council of Constance had declared his teachings heretical. However, his English disciples, popularly known as Lollards, continued to propagate his emphatic belief that the Holy Scriptures were the sole authority in religion, despite powerful attempts to eliminate their teachings in the fifteenth century.

Although he was once popularly (if mistakenly) viewed by his contemporaries as an inspirer of the Peasants' Revolt, and although he has often been subsequently lauded as the most important English precursor of the sixteenth-century Reformation, Wyclif himself was no real popularist. His surviving writings, virtually all of which are in Latin, convey the impression of a dissident academic, not of a man intent on stirring up a premature reformation or mounting a concerted popular attack on received notions of religious orthodoxy. In one significant area, however, he did exercise a profound and long-term influence over national life. This was his call (in Latin) for a translation of the Scriptures into English. The translation of the (corrupt) text of the Latin Vulgate was undertaken in the 1380s by Wyclif's disciples, Nicholas of Hereford (d. *c*.1420) and John Purvey (*c*.1353–*c*.1428). Though this considerable enterprise was sufficient to win the wholehearted praise of the great Czech reformer, Jan Hus (who could not speak English), and of one contemporary English chronicler (who recognized the significance of opening the Bible 'to the laity, and even to those women who know how to read'), the translation none the less awkwardly echoed both the inaccuracies and the Latinate rhythms of the Vulgate. Despite its historical significance, the 'Wycliffite' translation has justly been criticized as 'a version of a version'. Its real importance lay not simply in its implicit assertion of the status of the English language as the proper medium for Holy Scripture but also in the incentive it provided to the equally determined, but more scholarly, translators of the sixteenth and early seventeenth centuries.

Langland and *Piers Plowman*

William Langland (*c*.1330–*c*.1386), an unbeneficed clerk in minor orders, knew his Vulgate Bible well; as his poem suggests, he used it, and the Book of Psalms in particular, exactly and receptively. As a man intimate with the private and public offices of the Church that he served he might properly have been expected to have read, marked, learned, and expounded the Scriptures. For Langland the writer, however, these same Scriptures provided both a theological framework within which to work out the implications of his poetic allegory and a series of moral ideas with which his poem makes profound and sometimes radical play. If he was neither a professional scholar nor the kind of overnice academic exegete who for the most part dominated the teaching of medieval universities, he was none the less an advanced, adept, and devout theological explorer. *The Vision of Piers Plowman*, on which he worked from the 1360s to the early 1380s, is one of the most searching Christian narratives in the English language.

In common with his educated contemporaries, Langland would have read the Christian Scriptures both literally and speculatively. While recognizing that the Old and New Testaments told a divinely inspired historical truth, he would also have accepted that human readers could discern other layers of meaning— notably analogical, moral, typological, and allegorical ones—which co-existed, intertwined, and overlapped one with another. Much as the Old Testament was read as a grandly patterned parallel to the New, with the events of Christ's birth, mission, and passion variously prefigured in the historic and prophetic annals of the Jews, so Langland's *Piers Plowman* would have been readily recognized by its first readers as variously exploring and demonstrating the active involvement of God in his physical Creation. Where the Christian Scriptures were interpreted as revealing the incarnation of God in human form as the fulfilment of ancient prophecy and as the enactment of a new covenant, and where the medieval Church had come to view the Mass as a symbolic acting out of the life and death of Christ in which Christ's body and blood became physically present on the altar, so Langland's poem represents a continuing, covenanted incarnation in which God involves himself with humankind. Throughout the poem there is a sense of expectation and latter-day fulfilment as if God's ultimate purposes were being imminently realized. At certain crucial points readers are bidden to recognize Christ himself in the representative human figure of Piers (or Peter), the humble ploughman and the bearer of a familiar form of the name of the greatest of Christ's Apostles, the rock on which the Church was built. In Passus XIII, for example, Dowel insists that *'Petrus, id est, Christus'* ('Peter, that is, Christ') and at the opening of the climactic Passus XVIII the dreaming narrator sees the meek Christ who enters Jerusalem in triumph on Palm Sunday as 'semblable to the Samaritan, and somdeel to Piers the Plowman'. The Son of God humbles himself by taking the form of a country workman, but this same workman is in turn elevated through his association with a glorious, ineffable, and eternal God. In Passus XIX Piers is seen ploughing with 'foure grete oxen' given him by Grace, oxen named after the four evangelists ('oon was Luk, a large beest and a lowe chered [meek-looking], | And Mark, and Matthew the thridde—myghty beestes bothe; | And joyned to hem oon Johan, moost gentil of alle'). Piers's ploughing is further assisted by harrows (formed by the Old and New Testaments), by four more sturdy beasts (named for the great Latin Fathers, Augustine, Ambrose, Gregory, and Jerome), and by seeds which are the cardinal virtues (Prudence, Temperance, Fortitude, Justice). Piers is thus the supereffective earthly ploughman, one supernaturally endowed by Grace, but he is also, and at the same time, the enactor of one of Christ's agricultural parables, and an actual embodiment of Christ and his Apostles, speeding the advance of the kingdom of heaven.

Langland appears to have developed the shape of his poem gradually. Not only does each section open up new and enigmatic vistas into what is to follow, in an appropriately dreamlike manner, but the three distinct surviving versions of the narrative (traditionally known as the A-, B-, and C-texts) also suggest shifting approaches to an expanding and would-be universal subject. The unfinished A-text, dating from the 1360s, contains only twelve sections, or as Langland styles them, *passus* (Latin, 'steps'). The so-called B-text, probably of the late 1370s, offers a complete revision of the earlier work, adding to it a further eight passus. The C-text, which may or may not represent Langland's final version, suggests a date of composition in the early 1380s, and offers a further scrupulous verbal revision and a new rearrangement of the narrative (now into a Prologue and twenty-two passus). Langland's central figure, the dreamer/narrator of all three versions, is neither a courtly lover contained in the cultivated world of a walled garden, nor an entranced Dantesque wanderer caught up in the affairs of worlds beyond worlds. His vision presents readers with the open, working landscape of England 'in a somer seven', but a landscape variously shot through with human confusion and divine wonder. From a broad point of vantage on the Malvern Hills in Worcestershire there opens up to him an animated vision of a 'fair feeld ful of folk . . . alle manere of men, the meene and the riche'.

The early passus of the poem seem to represent an attempt to come to terms with the confusions, corruptions, and innate contradictions within the religious and social life of contemporary England. Throughout the narrative, however, Langland deliberately intermixes genres and adds an element of ambiguity to what might otherwise have emerged as conventionally monitory figures (such as the personified female representations of Holy Church, Truth, Repentance and, above all, Lady Meed—in part fair reward, in part financial corruption). Unlike the distressed dreamer of a poem such as *Pearl*, Langland's visionary is offered little direct or transcendental consolation for the evident ills of the world; instead, he passes through a succession of dreams interspersed with periods of waking and contemplation. He is variously preached at, prophesied to, and illuminated by theological, moral, or ritual demonstration. In Passus V, for example, the Seven Deadly Sins lumberingly attempt to make their confessions at the bidding of Lady Repentance in scenes rendered particularly immediate by satirical observation (Sloth, 'with two slymy eighen [eyes]', falls asleep in mid-shrift, while Gluttony is waylaid into an ale-house and stays there until he 'had y-glubbed [swallowed] a galon and a gille'). Perhaps the most ambiguous figure of all is that of the dreamer himself, at once detached from the author and intimately associated with him. Like the writer, he is called Will, a name which can be taken both literally and (as Shakespeare was later to do in his Sonnets) as an abstract quality or allegorical name. The name of 'William Langland' can be played with in Passus XV when Will cryptically announces: 'I have lyved in londe . . . my name is Longe Wille' (B-text, l. 152). Alternatively, some sixty lines later we are told by the figure of Anima (the soul) that Piers Plowman 'parceyveth moore depper | What is the wille, and wherefore that many wight suffreth' and only 'thorugh wil alone' can we recognize the associative fusion of the figure of Christ with that of Piers. 'Will' is moral will, the will to act well, and the less admirable human quality of wilfulness. Langland is both the judge and the penitent, at times exhibiting the significance of discriminating perception, at others offering passages of autobiographical self-examination (such as the opening of Passus VI in the C-text).

In the B- and C-texts the poem takes on a climactic and visionary resolution in the description of Christ's passion and his descent into hell in order to redeem the virtuous who had died before him. These sections show Langland's narrative, lexical, and imaginative fusion at its most powerful. In Passus XVIII in the B-text the poet's imaginative recall, the Church's ceremonial enactments of Holy Week, the literal and historical representation, and the moral allegory are all inextricably bound up. The section opens on Palm Sunday as the world-weary narrator dreams of children bearing palm branches into church and of the people singing their Hosannas as a ceremonial remembrance of Christ's ride into Jerusalem. The historical Jesus who rides the ass may be vitally glimpsed as the humble servant (the Samaritan and the Plowman), but he is also a timeless representative of humanity and, in particularly significant terms for fourteenth-century readers, a knightly champion who, armed in human flesh, is ready to joust 'in his helm and his haubergeon [coat of mail]—*humana natura*'. Throughout the passus Langland also plays with the potential implications of a verse from Psalm 84 (Psalm 85 in the Anglican tradition) in which 'Mercy and truth are met together; righteousness and peace have kissed each other'. Once Christ achieves his hard-fought victory over the realm of darkness, the verse is used to suggest that the four daughters of God, the embodiments of complimentary virtues, have found a proper cause for their joyous embrace:

> 'After sharpest shoures,' quod Pees [Peace], 'most shene is the sonne;
> Is no weder warmer than after watry cloudes;
> Ne no love levere [more precious], ne lever [dearer] frendes
> Than after werre [war] and wo, whan love and pees ben maistres.
> Was nevere werre in this world, ne wikkednesse so kene,
> That Love, and hym liste, to laughynge ne broughte,
> And Pees, thorough pacience, alle perils stoppede.'
>   'Trewes!' [Truce] quod Truthe; 'thow tellest us sooth, by Jesus!
> Clippe we in covenaunt, and ech of us kisse oother.'
>   'And lete no peple,' quod Pees, 'parceyve that we chidde [argued];
> For inpossible is no thyng to Hym that is almighty.'
>   'Thow seist sooth,' seide Rightwisnesse, and reverentliche hire kiste,
> Pees, and Pees hire [her], *per secula seculorum.*
> *Misericordia et Veritas obviaverunt sibi; Justicia et Pax osculate sunt.*
>   Truthe trumpede tho and song *Te Deum laudamus*;
> And thanne lutede [sang to the lute] Love in a loude note,
> '*Ecce quam bonum et quam iocundum &c*'.

The build-up to a second citation of the Latin Psalter (here Psalm 132 (133): 'Behold, how good and how pleasant it is for brethren to dwell together in unity!') allows the Latin words to emerge as a ritual affirmation. Rarely have the two languages, the one largely sacred in its usage, the other largely secular, been juxtaposed so tellingly as the animated English narrative line coincides with three, more static, quotations from the Latin ceremonial of the Church. Speculative vernacular poetry meets and embraces the ritually dignified fixed point on its own terms, as if in demonstration of the contextual and sacramental confluence of the human and the divine, the quotidian and the numinous, the world and the Church. Rather than confusing matters, the specific resonance of the Latin phrases serves to amplify and condition a reading of the English. The fourteenth-century poet's device, readily acceptable to those of his educated contemporaries who were attuned to a bilingual religious culture, indirectly looks forward to the verbal games and surprises of the far more secular and rootless poetry of early twentieth-century Modernism. In Langland's case, a poet self-evidently steeped in the Church's doctrine, one familiar with the methods of its preachers and teachers, and one perhaps influenced by Wyclif's insistence on the centrality of the Scriptures in the development of the Christian life, may be attempting to demonstrate the creative power of the *Logos*, the Word of God which has become the instrument of salvation for all nations.

Geoffrey Chaucer

Despite the manifest political and social disruptions of his age, Geoffrey Chaucer's poetry both expresses and embodies a firm sense of order. This is true as much of his twin masterpieces, *Troilus and Criseyde* (probably written in the mid-1380s) and *The Canterbury Tales* (planned *c*.1387), as of his more modestly conceived 'minor' poems and surviving prose works. This sense of order is evident not simply in his reflections on the nature and workings of the cosmos (such as his prose treatise on the use of the astrolabe, written to instruct his little son Lewis) and in his frequent allusions to Boethius's highly esteemed disquisition *De consolatione philosophiae* (which Chaucer himself translated into English prose in *c*.1380) but also in his steady affirmations of an orthodox Christian belief in divine involvement in human affairs. In *Troilus and Criseyde*, at the end of his evocation of incidents supposed to have taken place at the time of the Trojan War, Chaucer turns from his account of 'payens corsed olde rytes' ('the accursed old rites of the pagans') to a vision of Troilus translated from this world to the next and able to laugh serenely at the woe of those who mourn his death. If tragedy is here transformed into a divine comedy, so the 'olde rytes' are effectively blotted out in the pious concluding address to the Holy Trinity. This exultant prayer, in part derived from Dante, sees the Triune God as reigning eternally over all things and setting his mystical seal on human aspiration.

Chaucer (*c*.1343–1400), in common with most of his European contemporaries, also recognized that the natural and the human worlds could be seen as interrelated in the divine scheme of things, and, like the kingdom of heaven, ordered in hierarchies. In the witty, elegantly formed *The Parlement of Foulys*, written, it has been argued, to compliment the marriage of King Richard II to Anne of Bohemia in 1382, he presents a vision of birds assembled on St Valentine's Day in order to choose their proper mates. The birds have gathered before the goddess of Nature, and, in accordance with 'natural' law, they pay court, dispute, and pair off in a strictly stratified way. The royal eagles, seated in the highest places, take precedence, followed in descending order by other birds of prey until we reach the humblest and smallest seed-eaters. The debate in this avian parliament about how properly to secure a mate may remain unresolved, but it is clear that the nobler the bird the more formal are the rituals of courtship accorded to it. Ducks may prove pragmatic when snubbed by particular drakes ('"Ye quek [quack]!" yit seyde the doke, ful well and feyre, | "There been mo sterres [stars], God wot, than a payre!"') but eagles seek for higher things in defining and exploring love and look down on such churlish common sense ('"Thy kynde is of so low a wrechednesse | That what love is, thow canst net seen ne gesse"').

The question of degree, and of the social perceptions conditioned by rank, also determines the human world that Chaucer variously delineates in *The Canterbury Tales*. The General Prologue, which sets out the circumstances which bring the pilgrims together at the Tabard Inn before they set off for Canterbury to pray at the tomb of the martyred St Thomas Becket, also presents them to us, as far as it is feasible, according to their estate ('Me thynketh it accordaunt to resoun | To telle yow al the condicioun | Of ech of hem, so as it semed me, | And whiche they weren, and of what degree'). The Knight is naturally placed first, followed by his son the Squire, and by his attendant Yeoman. The Knight is duly succeeded by representatives of the Church: the fastidious Prioress with an accompanying Nun, personal chaplain, and three other priests; the Monk who holds the office of outrider in his monastery (and who therefore appears to enjoy extra-mural luxuries more than the disciplined life of his order); and the equally worldly and mercenary Friar. The third estate is represented by a greater variety of figures, rich, middling, and poor, beginning with a somewhat shifty Merchant, a bookish Oxford Clerk, a Sergeant of the Law, and a Franklin. We move downwards socially to the urban guildsmen (Haberdasher, Carpenter, Weaver, Dyer, and Tapicer), to the skilled tradesmen (Cook, Shipman, Doctor of Physic), and to a well-off widow with a trade of her own (the Wife of Bath). Chaucer relegates his Parson, his Ploughman, his Manciple, and his reprobates (the Reeve, the Miller, the Summoner, and the Pardoner) to the end of his troupe (though he also modestly includes himself, a high-ranking royal official, at the end of the list). It is with this last group that he seems to want to surprise his readers by contrasting paragons of virtue with those whose very calling prompts periodic falls from grace (the Reeve strikes fear into his master's tenants while feathering his own nest; the Miller steals corn and overcharges his clients; the lecherous Summoner makes a parade of his limited learning; and the Pardoner trades profitably in patently false relics). Where the Manciple's native wit and acquired administrative skills seem to render him worthy of better things, Chaucer's stress on the due humility of the Parson and the Ploughman proclaims their exemplary fitness for their modest but essential social roles. If the Knight at the top of the social scale had seemed 'a worthy man', loyal to his knightly vows and embodying the spirit of chivalry, so, in their respective callings, the Parson stands for the true mission of the Church to the poor, and the Ploughman for the blessedness of holy poverty. When Chaucer describes the two as brothers, it is likely that he sees their fraternity as rooted in Christian meekness and closeness to God. Both, in the manner of Langland's Piers, act out the gospel: the Parson by offering a 'noble ensample to his sheep' and the Ploughman by 'lyvynge in pees and parfit charitee'.

Although it has been suggested that the Knight's professional career has been marked by a series of military disasters and that both his portrait and his tale can be read ironically, it would seem likely that the overall scheme of *The Canterbury Tales*, had it ever been completed, would have served to enhance his dignity rather than to undermine it. The Host of the Tabard proposes that each of the pilgrims should tell two tales on the way to Canterbury and two on the return journey. Even in the fragmentary and unfinished form in which the poem has come down to us (only twenty-four tales are told), it is clear that the Knight's taking precedence as the first story-teller is not merely a matter of chance. The narrator comments that although he cannot tell whether it was a matter of 'aventure, or sort, or cas [chance]' that the luck of the draw fell to such a natural leader, the fact that it did so both pleases the other pilgrims and satisfies the demands of social decorum. The Knight's Tale, an abbreviated version of Boccaccio's *Teseida*, is an appropriately high-minded history of the rivalry of two noble cousins for the love of a princess, a history elegantly complemented by accounts of supernatural intervention in human affairs and equally elegant and decisive human ceremonial. If the Ploughman is not allotted a tale, the Parson's, with which *The Canterbury Tales* concludes, is a long prose treatise on the seven deadly sins, less a tale than a careful sermon expressive of devout *gravitas* and earnest learning. Sandwiched between these two tales Chaucer arranges stories loosely fitted to their tellers' tastes and professions and tailored to fit into the overarching narrative shape by prologues, interjections, or disputes between characters. The Parson's singularly worthy discourse is complemented by that of the otherwise shadowy Nun's Priest who offers a lively story of a wily cock caught by a fox, a story which he rounds off with the clerical insistence that listeners grasp 'the moralite'. The Pardoner too tells a tidy moral tale, though its carefully shaped warning of the mortal dangers of covetousness can be seen reflecting back on the personal avarice to which its teller spiritedly and frankly confesses in his prologue: 'I preche of no thyng but for coveityse | . . . Thus kan I preche agayn that same vice | Which that I use, and that is avarice. | But though myself be gilty in that synne, | Yet kan I maken oother folk to twynne [turn] | From avarice, and soore to repente.' The Prioress also tells a short, devotional tale of a pious Christian child whose throat is cut by Jews but who miraculously manages to continue singing a Marian hymn after his death. Its pathos, if not to the taste of more morally squeamish ages, is evidently well received by its devout fourteenth-century hearers.

Elsewhere in *The Canterbury Tales* tellers seem to have far less inclination to wear their hearts and consciences on their sleeves. The Merchant, prompted by the Clerk's adaptation of Boccaccio's story of the trials of patient Griselda, offers the salutary tale of an old husband (January) and his 'fresshe' young bride (May), an impatiently frisky wife who, exploiting her husband's sudden blindness, is seduced in a pear tree by her lover. When January's sight is mischievously restored by the god Pluto, Proserpine equally mischievously inspires May to claim that she was acting in her husband's best interests: 'Up peril of my soule, I shal not lyen, | As me was taught, to heele with youre eyen, Was no thyng bet, to make yow see, | Than strugle with a man upon a tree. God woot, I dide it in ful good entente.' At the lower end of the social, and perhaps moral, scale Chaucer allots still earthier stories to the Miller, the Reeve, the Friar, and the Summoner. When the Host proposes that the Knight's 'noble storie' should be succeeded by something equally decorous from the Monk, the Miller drunkenly intrudes himself and, somewhat improbably, tells the beautifully plotted tale of a dull-witted carpenter, his tricksy wife, and her two suitors. The Miller's Tale presents a diametrically opposed view of courtship to that offered by the Knight. It also serves to provoke the Reeve (who is a carpenter by profession) into recounting an anecdote about a cuckolded miller. In like manner, the Friar tells a story about an extortionate summoner who is carried off to hell by the Devil, and the enraged Summoner ('lyk an aspen leef he quoke for ire') responds with the history of an ingenious friar obliged to share out the unexpected legacy of 'the rumblynge of a fart' amongst his brethren.

The Chaucer who so modestly placed himself last in the list of the pilgrims also casts himself in the role of an incompetent story-teller. His irony is nowhere more pointed than in this cleverly extended and self-deprecatory ruse which opens with a direct challenge to his assumed shyness from the Host. 'What man artow [art thou]?', 'Chaucer' is asked, 'Thou lookest as thou woldest find an hare, | For evere on the ground I see thee stare'. The response is the tale of Sir Thopas, a parody of contemporary romance told in awkward, singsong, six-line stanzas. The parody may always have served to amuse sophisticated readers, but the Host, who rudely interrupts its progress, claims that its teller's evident ineptness is boring the company. The pilgrim 'Chaucer' is therefore obliged to begin another tale, this time a long and weighty prose homily which retells the story of imprudent Melibeus and his wife, the aptly named Prudence. At its conclusion the Host somewhat over-politely compensates for his earlier rudeness by unenthusiastically confessing that he would have liked his own wife to have heard the tale ('for she nys no thyng of swich pacience'). Despite such soothing politeness, Chaucer's pretence of incompetence in the company of such accomplished story-tellers as his fellow-pilgrims is a highly effective device. He had indirectly prepared for this device by insisting on the virtues of 'truthful' narrative representation at the end of the General Prologue. He had also attempted to justify his realism by citing the highest authorities:

Whoso shal telle a tale after a man,
He moot reherce as ny as evere he kan
Everich a word, if it be in his charge,
Al speke he never so rudeliche and large,
Or ellis he moot telle his tae untrewe,
Or feyne thyng, or fynde wordes newe.
He may nat spare, althogh he were his brother;
He moot as wel seye o [one] word as another.
Crist spak hymself ful brode [plainly] in hooly writ,
And wel ye woot no vileynye is it.
Eek Plato seith, whoso that kan hym rede,
The wordes moote be cosyn [akin] to the dede.
Also I prey yow to foryeve [forgive] it me.
Al have I nat set folk in hir degree
Heere in this tale, as that they sholde stonde.
My wit is short, ye may wel understonde.

Here is the pretence of modesty and incompetence, but here too is the insistence on frankness and proper representation, albeit justified with reference to Christ and to Plato (beyond whose authority few medieval readers would feel the need to refer). Chaucer neutralizes and diminishes himself as a narrator in order that his narrative representation of others' words and narratives might shine with a greater 'truth' to God's nature. In a way that his theologically minded contemporaries might readily understand, he is posing as the servant of the servants of Christ, having become, like St Paul before him, 'all things to all men' ('omnibus factus sum omnia'). The Christian poet of *The Canterbury Tales*, one variously influenced by both Boccaccio and Dante, endeavours to show us a broad spectrum of sinful humanity on an earthly journey, a journey which original readers would readily have recognized as a prevision of, and a preparation for, a heavenly one.

Despite his intellectual delight in the concept of cosmic, natural, and human order, Chaucer the poet and the truth-teller of necessity subverts certain received ideas of degree. Most crucially, he effectively undermines the commonly held medieval idea of the natural inferiority of women to men by representing articulate and intelligent women at the centre of human affairs rather than on the periphery. If the well-born ladies of antiquity are allowed to become norms against which human behaviour can be measured in *The Legend of Good Women* (*c.*1372–86), *Troilus and Criseyde*, and certain of *The Canterbury Tales*, the Wife of Bath asserts a distinctly ungenteel opposition to antifeminist stereotypes. Although some readers may have interpreted the Wife's 856-line prologue as evidence of a woman protesting too much (and therefore confirming, or at the very least endorsing, many of the male prejudices against which she loudly complains), Chaucer's adoption of a strident woman's voice ought also to be seen as opening up an alternative polemic. Her very stridency, we also realize, is a direct consequence of over-rigid patriarchal ways of thinking and acting. The Wife of Bath is certainly no model of meekness, patience, and chastity. She opens her discourse with the word 'experience', and from that experience of living with five husbands (three of them good men, she observes, because they were 'riche, and olde') she builds up a spirited case against conventional, theoretical, clerically inspired antifeminism. Celibacy and virginity are all very well, she insists, but Christ's stricter demands were addressed 'to hem that wolde lyve parfitly', and, as she adds for the benefit of her male listeners, 'lordynges, by youre leve, that am nat I'. Moreover, if God gave her her sexuality, she has been determined to enjoy it, albeit within the bounds of marriage ('In wyfhod I wol use myn instrument | As frely as my Makere hath it sent'). Having learned by experience and native wit how to manage her first partners ('Atte ende I hadde the bettre in ech degree, | By sleighte, or force, or by som maner thyng, | As by continueel murmur or grucchyng') she seems to have met her match in the clerk Jankyn, her junior by twenty years. Jankyn had the particularly irritating habit of reading learned tracts against women in her presence, quoting choice items aloud in order to demonstrate the superiority of his own sex. Provoked into decisive action, she ripped three pages out of the book and dealt Jankyn a blow with her fist, only to be floored herself by a retaliatory blow. Nevertheless, her consequent unconsciousness (perhaps feigned) has worked its proper effect: the shocked Jankyn is brought to sudden repentance and thereafter she has ruled the domestic roost ('He yaf [gave] me al the bridel in my hond, | To han the governance of hous and lond, | And of his tonge, and of his hond also; | And made hym brenne [burn] his book anon right tho').

The Wife of Bath achieves mastery in what can be seen as an essentially bourgeois domestic comedy, albeit one informed with partially disgraced academic theories about women's limited marital and social roles. Elsewhere in his work, Chaucer stresses a distinctive self-assurance and dignity in women of the ancient and modern ruling classes, qualities which are more vital than the special honour accorded to the sex by the male-defined code of chivalry. In the early dream-poem, *The Book of the Duchess* (probably written *c*.1369 as an allegorical lament on the death of Blanche of Lancaster, the first wife of John of Gaunt), the narrator encounters a desolate knight, clad in black. The knight is mourning the death of a wife not, as in so much contemporary love-poetry, the absence, the fickleness, or the coldness of a mistress. Theirs has been more than a courtly liaison and more than the amorous vassalage of him to her. Mutual respect has made for a marriage of minds, and as far as was possible, a partnership in love. She was, the knight confesses, 'that swete wif, | My suffisaunce, my lust, my lyf, | Myn hap, myn hele, and al my blesse'. The knight's therapeutic account of his long courtship, happy marriage, and unhappy bereavement is prefaced by a retelling of Ovid's story of the widowed Queen Alcyone, who, faithful to the memory of the dead King Ceyx, is granted a vision of him. The pattern of re-exploring classical instances and Ovidian exempla is repeated on a far grander scale in the unfinished *The Legend of Good*

Women. Here ancient history is ransacked for appropriate subjects because, Chaucer's narrator insists, it had traditionally provided his predecessors with approved stories 'of holynesse, or regnes, of victoryes, | Of love, of hate'. It is on women's holiness and steadfastness in love that the narrator dwells, he having been rebuked in a dream by the god of Love for the former 'heresies' of speaking ill of women in *The Romaunt of the Rose* and *Troilus and Criseyde*. The nine legends he retells as a penance speak of heroines who suffered, and sometimes died, as a consequence of their devout love for faithless men. Instances of male violence and treachery are monotonously heaped one on another as Antony abandons Cleopatra, Aeneas Dido, Tarquin Lucrece, and Theseus Ariadne. By frequently appealing to sources, to named authors, and to what was commonly acknowledged to be the authority of 'olde bokes', Chaucer attempts to turn an equally derivative clerical tradition of unrelenting misogyny on its head. He also shapes the legends to emphasize what he sees as the feminine virtue of 'pitee'. It is pity which renders women susceptible to male deceit, but it is also seen as an aspect of the highly esteemed human quality of generosity of spirit. As the legends demonstrate, this same aspect of generosity, to which men seem to be impervious, allows women to respond so fully to love, to grow in love and, through tragedy, to find the emotional strength which enables them to explore the depths of suffering.

In the Prologue to *The Legend of Good Women* the dapper god of Love seems to disparage Chaucer's most carefully wrought and self-consciously achieved single poem by referring to it simply as the story of 'how that Crisseyde Troylus forsok'. The god appears to have been persuaded that *Troilus and Criseyde* had taken up the traditional misogynist theme that throughout history 'wemen han don mis' in their dealings with men. The god may not have been alone in his prejudiced reading of the story, but to many latter-day readers it seems to be a narrow and ungenerous one. The poem is less the story of a man betrayed by a woman than the account of how a woman, having been pressured into responding to a man's over enthusiastic love for her, is driven from one relationship to another. Instead of being portrayed as contrasted representatives of faith and betrayal, both Troilus and Criseyde are observed as victims of circumstances, at once humanly and divinely contrived, and beyond their direct control. Although Chaucer drew heavily on Boethius for his consolatory explorations of the ideas of free will, predestination, mutability, and fortune throughout *Troilus and Criseyde*, his immediate and principal source for the poem was contemporary. In no sense, however, was Chaucer merely translating Boccaccio's familiar and admired Trojan story, *Il Filostrato*, into English. His distinctive shifts in emphasis, narrative shape, and characterization clearly indicate that this is more a deliberate reinterpretation than a translation. Boccaccio's Criseida is, for example, willingly persuaded by her cousin Pandaro into accepting Troilo as a lover. In Chaucer's version the characters of Criseyde and Pandarus possess both a new dramatic energy and a new blood-relationship. Pandarus is transformed into Criseyde's sensible, sentimental, but none the less manipulative uncle, one who acts as her guardian and counsellor in the absence of her father. His task of persuading his niece to look favourably on Troilus's love is rendered one of subtle negotiation, mediation, suggestion, and emotional conditioning. She, rather than being fickle by nature, is seen as tender, sensitive, ingenuous, and open to change. Chaucer's narrative carefully balances the length of the process by which she is persuaded to accept Troilus against the time she takes over agonizing about abandoning him. When the lovers are forced apart by her removal to join her father in the Greek camp outside Troy, Criseyde's grief is intense. Her avowals are as extravagant as they are agonized:

> 'And Troilus, my clothes everychon
> Shul blake ben in tokenyng, herte swete,
> That I am as out of this world agon,
> That wont was yow to setten in quiete;
> And of myn ordre, ay til deth me mete,
> The observance evere, in youre absence,
> Shal sorwe ben, compleynt and abstinence.

> 'Myn herte and ek the woful goost therinne
> Byquethe I, with youre spirit to compleyne
> Eternaly, for they shal nevere twynne.
> For though in erthe ytwynned be we tweyne,
> Yet in the feld of pite, out of peyne,
> That highte Elisos [Elysium], shal we ben yfeere [together],
> As Orpheus with Euridice, his fere [companion, wife].

Her ambiguously optimistic interpretation of the Orpheus/Eurydice story may well lead us to perceive how uneasily tragic are the undertones of her avowal. For Criseyde, lovers symbolically pass through Hades to reach Elysium, or, in medieval Christian terms, they suffer penitentially in Purgatory as a preparation for Paradise. Criseyde's descent to Hades/Purgatory, a place where the only certainty is uncertainty, will be metaphoric. Separated from Troilus, from her friends, and from her roots she in fact discovers the advantages of Lethean forgetfulness in shoring up the determinants of her life and her heart. When the narrator reaches the issue of her final denial of her vows to Troilus, a new element of ambiguity enters the narrative. The narrator himself purports to consult his source to find an exaggeratedly clear statement of her treachery; Criseyde, however, is painfully conscious that hers is indeed a world-without-end decision, one which will render her infamous in subsequent human annals:

> But trewely, the storie telleth us,
> Ther made nevere woman moore wo
> Than she, whan that she falsed Troilus.
> She seyde, 'Allas! for now is clene ago [gone]
> My name of trouthe in love, for everemo!

For I have falsed oon the gentileste
That evere was, and oon the worthieste!

'Allas! of me, unto the worldes ende,
Shal neyther ben ywriten nor ysonge
No good word, for thise bokes wol me shende [reproach].
O, rolled shal I ben on many a tonge!
Thourghout the world my belle shal be ronge!
And wommen moost wol haten me of alle.
Allas, that swich a cas me sholde falle!'

Faced with such agonized self-awareness, the narrator retreats into pity, reluctant to blame her more than his historic predecessors have done but willing to concede that her penitence impresses him ('For she so sory was for hire untrouthe, | Iwis, I wolde excuse hire yet for routhe [pity]').

If the narrator of *Troilus and Criseyde* is neither the gentle incompetent 'Chaucer' of *The Canterbury Tales* nor the incomprehending innocent of the dream-poems, he nevertheless shares something of their generous susceptibility. Like them, he suggests a tense, shifting relationship between the poet and his persona, and consequently between the poet and his poem. He moves around his characters, allowing them to express their respective points of view, at times ruminating on the iron laws of fate and divinely imposed predestination, at others both suggesting and withdrawing from judgement. He allows the story a certain autonomy while varying his commentary by deferring both to his sources and to his audience. In *Troilus and Criseyde* at least, he seems to insist that history is steady and needs to be retold, while allowing that *his* history is reshaped in the very act of telling it. Essentially, he remains ambivalent, or, perhaps, given his evident sympathy with women and his admiration for what he seems to have identified as feminine generosity of spirit, he assumes a deliberate androgyny. He is certainly the least egocentric of poets. Although Chaucer is in every sense a writer of his time, he was also the first poet in English both to display and to make a particular narrative issue of the quality which John Keats later so memorably defined as 'negative capability'.

Gower, Lydgate, and Hoccleve

For some two hundred years after their respective deaths, Chaucer's contemporary and friend, John Gower (?1330–1408), was considered to be his rival in English eloquence, richness of style, and narrative artistry. The honour originally accorded to Gower's English poem, the *Confessio Amantis* (c.1386), is witnessed by the survival of over fifty manuscript copies (three times as many as *Troilus and Criseyde*, though some eighty manuscripts of *The Canterbury Tales* are extant) and by the elegant illuminations provided for certain copies by the prestigious court painter, Herman Scheerre (a mark of status rarely accorded to Chaucer). The poems of both were amongst the earliest vernacular works to be issued by the prodigiously busy printer, publisher, and translator, William Caxton, in the late fifteenth century (Chaucer's *Canterbury Tales* in 1478, Gower's *Confessio Amantis* in 1483). Patriotic pride dictated that editions of both poets were to be formally dedicated to King Henry VIII in 1532 and it was to Gower that Shakespeare respectfully turned for a source for *Pericles, Prince of Tyre* (1608) (though it must be admitted that his tribute to 'the worthy and ancient' poet begins to look condescending once a superannuated Gower is pressed into service to act as his dusty choric narrator).

Despite distinct signs of a revival in interest in Gower's narrative art in the late twentieth century, since Shakespeare's day his reputation has been almost totally, and somewhat unjustly, eclipsed by Chaucer's. The latter's tribute to the 'moral Gower', generous though it was in its day, has not exactly helped to win him a broad and sympathetic modern audience. Nevertheless, it seems to have been the didactic earnestness of Gower's earlier poems, the *Mirour de l'Omme* written in French and the *Vox Clamantis* in Latin, which had won him the profound appreciation of his contemporaries. The *Mirour de l'Omme* had offered a lengthy critical survey of the corrupt state of sinful humankind and had recommended amendment through a universal repentance aided by the prayers of the Virgin Mary. The apocalyptic *Vox Clamantis* (the 'voice calling to account', a voice which echoes Isaiah's 'voice of him that crieth in the wilderness') more specifically extends these concerns to a judgement of English society and its royal government. It sees England's modern prostration in the contexts of history and Scripture; it offers an exposure of the chronic moral diseases of each of the estates of the realm; and it prophetically asserts that unless there is a radical change of heart the nation will continue its headlong rush towards doom. When Gower recast his poem in the 1390s he must have felt some uneasy satisfaction in adding to it metamorphosed accounts of the Peasants' Revolt and the deposition of Richard II as evidence that his prophecies were being fulfilled.

The *Confessio Amantis* (the 'Lover's Confession', written in the late 1380s) suggests a purposeful relaxation of Gower's earlier moral strenuousness. Its subject is a divinely 'comic' admixture of pleasure and instruction, not undiluted prophetic admonishment. The relaxed tone of the poem—Gower declared in the opening lines of his first version—had been inspired by King Richard's personal request for 'some newe thing'; when he revised it after Richard's fall, he felt obliged to insist that he had composed a poem containing 'somewhat of lust, somewhat of lore' of the kind 'that fewe men endite | In oure englissh' and, moreover, one written not for the King's but 'for Engelondes sake'. The *Confessio Amantis* fuses the modes of a manual of penitence and a codification of the religion of love. In playing with Christian modes he none the less uses the broad idea of love, including sexual love, to reinforce rather than to undermine Christian morality. Gower represents

himself as an unsuccessful but hopeful lover (Amans) making his formal confession to Genius, the priest of the goddess Venus (her 'oghne [own] clerk' as
she describes him). In hearing his confession, and in responding with spiritual
counsel, Genius tells a series of exemplary stories illustrative of the seven
deadly sins and their equally mortal sub-species. Each of these miscellaneous
tales can be read as a demonstration of the moral importance of self-discipline,
a mastering of blind passion in order to discover the elevated virtue of 'fyn
lovynge'. In many ways Gower's investigation of love and its laws parallels his
concern elsewhere in his work with the proper regulation of the medieval state
and its hierarchical pattern of rule. A spiritual awareness of pattern, harmony,
and order stems from a disciplined balance within the individual, a balance
partly achieved through the exercise of penance. The individual, whether that
individual be king, lord, priest, or commoner, is seen as a social being allotted
his or her degree by God and divinely called to act according to the God-given
principle or universal harmony. The grace which flows from the sacramental
act of confession (albeit to a venerean priest) is thus both politicized and socialized. At the end of his poem Gower, supposedly purged of his amatory
affectations, prays on his knees that God 'this land in siker weye [in like
manner] | Wole sette uppon good governance' and that its citizens will remember 'what it is to live in unite'.

The *Confessio Amantis* reveals that Gower is far from being an insistently
hard and dispiriting ethical teacher. Although, compared to Chaucer, his narrative style eschews elaboration, his merits as 'plain' story-teller lie in his
melodic precision, his sense of literary decorum, his steady flow of argument,
and his imaginative sympathy (particularly with wronged women such as
his Phillis and his Lucrece). He readily acknowledges that, as the stories
recounted in his narrative reveal, the passions are unruly, the heart unsteady,
the will unready, and history itself is inconsistent. He is especially wry in
portraying himself as a slow, sometimes slothful, and unfulfilled lover, one
acutely aware of the refined feelings required of a knight, but one who tends
to recognize nobility or generosity of spirit in others rather than in himself.
In the eighth book of his poem Gower moves towards a kind of epilogue in
which the lover retires from the service of love, aware that he is a tired old
man. Cupid puts forth his hand and pulls out 'a firy lancegay' ('a fiery dart')
which he had once thrust into the younger lover's heart. All passion appears
to be spent and Venus firmly recommends the blessings of retirement, presenting Gower with a necklace of black beads inscribed with the words *'Por
reposer'* ('for your rest'):

> And thus thenkende thoghtes fele [many],
> I was out of my swoune affrayed,
> Whereof I sih my wittes strayed,
> And gan to clepe [call] hem hom ayein.
> And whan Resoun it herde sein [said]
> That Loves rage was aweye,

He came to me the rihte weye,
And hath remued the sotye [folly]
Of thilke unwise fantasye,
Whereof that I was wont to pleigne,
So that of thilke firy peine
I was mad sobre and hol inowh [enough].

At the end of Gower's poem it is evident that an old man has dreamed dreams. When he awakes from his distraction he tells his beads and soothes the rashly acquired wounds of his youth with the balm, not of forgetfulness, but of wisdom.

Gower was not alone in having his name coupled with that of Chaucer by their literary successors. The Scots poet William Dunbar, for example, looked back in his poem *The Golden Targe* to three, not two, exemplary English writers: to Chaucer, 'rose of rhetoris [rhetoric] all', to 'morall Gower', and to 'Ludgate laureate'. Few readers since the early sixteenth century have esteemed the work of John Lydgate (?1370–1449) quite so highly. In his own day, Lydgate, a Benedictine monk at the powerful abbey at Bury St Edmunds, had found ready and influential patrons at court, patrons who, like Dunbar, happily conceded to him the honour of a poet's laurels. He was also one of the most prolix and productive poets in the English language. As Lydgate became older and more honour-laden, so his poems appear to have grown longer and to have lapsed more easily into the leaden mode. His three most substantial works, the *Troy Book* (1412–20), *The Siege of Thebes* (1420–2), and the once highly esteemed *The Fall of Princes* (1431–8), all of them versions of Italian or French originals, run respectively to 30,000, 24,000, and 36,000 lines. Despite its obvious ponderousness, Lydgate's achievement ought to be considered in the light of its contemporary popular impact. The poet who saw his role as the consolidator of Chaucer's innovations in style, versification, and vocabulary was, by virtue of his influence, responsible for the firm establishment of the elder writer's literary and lexical authority in the fifteenth century. Although he lacked Chaucer's subtlety, delicacy, and discrimination, Lydgate successfully continued the process of rendering English a universally acceptable vehicle for the practical and flexible expression of elevated thought in poetry. Chaucer's creative influence is particularly recognizable in Lydgate's variations on *Troilus and Criseyde*, *The Book of the Duchess*, and *The House of Fame—The Floure of Curtesy*, *The Complaint of the Black Knight*, and *The Temple of Glas* (all of them written in the early 1400s). Even in his later work, where his emphatic gravity and deliberate parades of learning tend to preclude Chaucerian whimsy, he can still aspire to moments of irony (particularly when he deals with women). As *The Siege of Thebes* and the encyclopaedic catalogue of human ills delineated in *The Fall of Princes* suggest, Lydgate saw history as offering a lurid series of warnings against excessive ambition in princes and in the upper nobility. His imaginative exploration of the threats to civil peace and of the consequences of national discord was doubtless seen as uncomfortably prophetic by those readers who turned to his works during the period of the profoundly contentious civil and dynastic upheavals of the Wars of the Roses (1455–85).

The poetry of Thomas Hoccleve (?1369–1426) suggests a very different kind of unease. Hoccleve, a scrivener in the office of the Privy Seal at Westminster, certainly never enjoyed the degree of influential patronage accorded to Lydgate, though *The Regement of Princes* (1411–12), written for the future King Henry V when he was Prince of Wales, was clearly intended to recommend both moral virtue and the poet's talents to the heir to the throne. Despite this and other claims to public attention (such as his *Balade after King Richard II's bones were brought to Westminster*), Hoccleve emerges as the most self-consciously autobiographical of the poets of the immediately post-Chaucerian decades. He was one of the first writers to use the often fraught events of his own life as a subject for his verse. This is especially true of the Prologue to the *Regement*, a 2,000-line complaint cast in the form of a dialogue with a beggar whom the poet meets as he wanders the streets on a sleepless night ('So long a nyght ne felte I never non'). Earlier poets had described restless lovers, but for Hoccleve it is thought itself, not thoughts of love, that determines his mental distress:

> The smert [pain] of Thought I by experience
> Knowe as wel as any man doth lyvynge;
> Hys frosty swoot [sweat] and fyry hote fervence,
> And troubly dremes, drempt al in wakynge,
> My mazyd hed sleplees han of konnyng
> And wyt despoylyd, and me so bejapyd,
> That after deth ful often have I gapyd.

The narrator's nervous melancholy here is quite distinct from the generous resilience of the kind of persona employed by Hoccleve's 'dere mayster . . . and fadir [father]', Chaucer. His private and professional dejection has, he claims, been determined by the tedium of his job, the tyranny of his employers, the failure of his eyesight due to poring over scraps of parchment, and the paucity of his remuneration. As a young man about town he pursued women, but had little success with them; now, as an old man, all he has to look forward to is penury. His complaint is more than a conventional diatribe against the moral distortions and abuses of the age (though, as the listening beggar is obliged to hear, those abuses are distressing too); rather, he is dramatically representing a private and unanswerable dilemma (though the beggar does attempt to offer some consolatory reflections on the universal fickleness of fortune). Hoccleve endured a severe mental breakdown in the years 1415–20, a distressing period which he recalled in the linked series of poems written in the early 1420s. The sequence opens with the gloomy *Complaint* (set in 'the broun sesoun of Myhelmesse [Michaelmas]') and continues with the more optimistic *Dialogue with a Friend,* an account of a friend's efforts to coax and cajole the poet back into a self-confidence and back to the consolations of poetry.

Poetry in Scotland in the Fifteenth Century

The Kingdom of Scotland, or to put it more precisely the independent realm ruled by the King of Scots, witnessed a distinctive flowering of literature in English in the fifteenth and early sixteenth centuries. The significance of this efflorescence lay not simply in the fact that the literature was written in the English language as it was spoken in the Lowlands of Scotland, and therefore not in the Gaelic of the Celtic-dominated Highlands, but also in its receptiveness to the vernacular traditions evolved south of the border with England by Chaucer, Gower, and Lydgate. The Scots poets of the period readily acknowledged their affinities with English writing, and especially their debts to the example of Chaucer, but they were well aware of their distinctive Scots identity and of the cultural and political independence of their nation from the imperial pretensions of the South. Although Lowland Scotland had fallen under the sway of an Anglo-Norman aristocracy in the eleventh century, and although the kingdom as a whole had consistently maintained close cultural and political ties with France as a security against English interference, Scots writers of the post-Chaucerian era proved to be no less and no more indebted to French literary precedent than their English contemporaries.

The continuing, unsophisticated vigour of an existing tradition of poetic composition in the 'Inglis' language in Scotland is witnessed by the work ascribed to John Barbour, Archdeacon of Aberdeen (?1320–95), and to Henry the Minstrel, more popularly known as 'Blind Harry' (?1440–?1492). Barbour's 13,000-line chronicle poem, *The Bruce* or *The Actes and Life of the Most Victorious Conqueror, Robert the Bruce King of Scotland* (written *c*.1376), celebrates the feats of the hero of what Scotland had rightly come to regard as its long war of independence against England, a struggle which had culminated in the routing of the army of King Edward II at Bannockburn in 1314. Barbour's fiercely patriotic enterprise had been taken up, yet more aggressively, by Harry in his 12,000-line *Schir William Wallace* of *c*.1460. The poem, which gleefully and bloodcurdlingly describes incidents in the military campaigns of the great inspirer of the first phase of the war against the Plantagenets—the 'martyred' Sir William Wallace (?1272–1305)—also claims the historic 'authority' of being based on the work of Wallace's chaplain, John Blair.

A key figure in the fostering of the flowering of a post-Chaucerian literature in Scotland was James Stewart who reigned as James I, King of Scots (1394–1437). As a boy of 11, James had been captured on his way to France

by an English ship and had been obliged to spend nineteen years as a prisoner
in the Tower of London and other royal fortresses (though he was occasionally paraded at court for state festivities). As a captive, apart from having ample
leisure to continue his education and to acquire an easy familiarity with the
new advances in vernacular poetry, he may also have made the acquaintance of
a fellow-hostage to the English Crown, the great French poet, Charles, duc
d'Orléans (1394–1465). Nevertheless, it was the precedents set by the work of
Chaucer and Gower which served to inspire James's most significant poem,
The Kingis Quair ('the King's Book') of *c*.1435. The poem looks back to his
period of imprisonment, and its subject, the sudden enrapturing of a prisoner
by the sight of a beautiful lady walking in a garden, may well relate to the
King's espousal to Lady Jane Beaufort in 1424. Selectively autobiographical or
not, *The Kingis Quair* certainly seeks to parallel the situation of the lovesick
royal prisoners of Chaucer's Knight's Tale and to echo the afflictions of
Troilus and Gower's Amans. The story begins with the sleepless prisoner pon-
dering the workings of destiny and taking up Boethius's *De consolatione*
philosophiae as a means of finding studious comfort. When the early matins bell
stirs him, he looks down from the tower window to an enclosed garden where
a juniper tree shelters an arbour, and it is here that he espies the lady, 'the
fairest or the freschest yonge floure | That ever I sawe', a sight that utterly rav-
ishes him ('For quhich sodayn abate [shock] anone astert | The blude of all
my body to my hert'). This sudden capitulation to love brings home to him
more painfully than ever the fact of his enforced restraint:

> I may nought ellis done bot wepe and waile,
> Within thir calde wallis thus ilokin [locked].
> From hennesfurth my rest is my travaile,
> My drye thrist with teris [tears] sall I slokin [slake],
> And on my self bene all my harmys wrokin [avenged].
> Thus bute [help] is none, bot Venus of hir grace
> Will schape remede [contrive a remedy], or do my spirit pace.

Venus does indeed come to his aid, whisking him up into the heavens by unseen
hands and showing him the kingdoms of Love and Reason. This brief apo-
theosis serves to instruct the dreamer in the true relation of mortal to heavenly love and he returns, still dreaming, to earth to expatiate on the goodness
of God evidenced in his creation. Thus fortified by divine hope, he seeks out
Fortune in her strong tower and is shown that his own destiny is about to take
an upward turn, from which happy vision he is awoken by Fortune striking
him smartly on the ear. The last stanzas of the poem delicately suggest the
prisoner musing on the consolations of his newly acquired philosophy and
coming to terms with his new-found blessings. He also piously hopes that his
hymn to love might find a place beside those of his masters, the Gower and
Chaucer whom he acknowledges to be 'superlative as poetis laureate'.

We cannot tell precisely what impact James's poetry and his generally Anglicized literary taste had on contemporary Scotland. Certainly, none of his Stewart successors showed much interest in, or patronage of, literature. What is clear, however, is that the fifteenth century saw a considerable opening up of the kingdom to wider European influences, an opening up matched by an insistent and accentuated national self-consciousness which largely defined itself against the threat of English imperialism. The century was marked by the establishment of the first Scottish universities at St Andrews in 1411, at Glasgow in 1451, and at Aberdeen in 1495, and by the Pope's raising the bishoprics of St Andrews and Glasgow to archiepiscopal status in 1472 and 1492 respectively. These moves asserted a freeing of the upper areas of educational and ecclesiastical life from English claims to suzerainty (the Archbishop of York had long claimed metropolitan authority over Scotland, and the much older universities of Oxford and Cambridge had generally assumed that they had the unique privilege of serving the whole island of Britain). The success of this new enterprise is evident in the educational and professional careers of the three most prominent Scots poets of the late fifteenth and early sixteenth centuries: Gavin Douglas (?1475–1522), a graduate of St Andrews who was briefly, but unsuccessfully, named as the city's Archbishop before being nominated to the bishopric of Dunkeld in 1515; Robert Henryson (?1424–?1506), probably a Glasgow graduate who later served as a schoolmaster attached to Dunfermline Abbey; and William Dunbar (?1456–?1513), who appears to have received the degree of MA from St Andrews in 1479 and who was variously employed by the court of James IV.

Douglas, who patriotically insisted that he wrote in the 'Scottis' language, was none the less, as his learned early poem *The Palice of Honour* (1501) suggests, a distant disciple of Chaucer's. His reputation is, however, firmly based on the extraordinary vigour of the translation of Virgil's *Aeneid* into rhymed heroic couplets. The translation, completed in *c.*1513, conscientiously follows the original Latin while managing to possess a quite distinct verve of its own. Each of the books is provided with a prologue, the first of which complains, with due scholarly disdain, of William Caxton's translation of a French retelling of Virgil's story, dismissing it as 'na mair lyke Virgill, dar I lay, | Na the owle resemblis the papyngay [parrot]'. The prologue to Book VII is notable for its keenly observed picture of a bleak northern winter: 'Mountayne toppis sleikit with snaw ourheildis [covers], | On raggit rolkis [ragged rocks] of hard harsk quhyne stane [whinstone], | . . . | Bewtie was lost, and barrand schew the landis, | With frostis haire ourfret the feldis standis.' Where Virgil speaks out, he perforce expresses himself in what Douglas accepts are 'hamely playn termys', that is with a modern, emphatically Scots, currency. Douglas remakes the Latin text while profoundly respecting its original integrity. Virgil's concision may be stifled by Douglas's vivid adjectival energy, but his rhetorical figures are part echoed, part literally translated, part transfigured into something rich and strange, albeit a strangeness related to what the translator half-apologetically saw as his 'harsk spech and lewit barbour [ignorant and barbarous] tong'.

When Robert Henryson refers modestly to his 'hamelie language' and his 'termis rude' in the 'Prolog' to *The Morall Fabillis of Esope the Phrygian* (written in the last quarter of the fifteenth century) he sees himself not only as a translator, but also as a popular educator seeking for a rough and ready equivalent to the 'polite termes of sweit rhetore [rhetoric]' which were 'richt pleasand' to the discriminating ear. He was doing more than rendering the fables traditionally ascribed to Æsop (and other writers) into the Scots vernacular; he was attempting to make 'brutal beistis' speak both naturally and to 'gude purpois'. Henryson's thirteen *Morall Fabillis* expand the often terse original stories into highly observant, carefully shaped poetic narratives which move inexorably to their moral denouements. They expose not fussy and improbable animal pretensions to human qualities, but human pride, human vanity, and human inconsistency. In the extended *moralitas* which explores the meaning of the 'The Taill of the Wolf and the Lamb', for instance, he suggests that the lamb can be taken to represent the poor whose life is 'half ane purgatorie', while the wolf betokens 'fals extortioneris | And oppressouris of pure [poor] men'. These oppressors are perverted lawyers who are out for their own gain, rich men 'quhilk ar sa gredie and sa covetous' and tyrannous landowners who attempt to ignore the fact that their crimes against the poor cry for 'vengeance unto the hevennis hie'. Elsewhere, Henryson seems more inclined to sport with human folly rather than with economic crime. In 'The Taill of the Uponlandis Mous, and the Burges Mous' he delightfully exposes the snobbery of a well-off urban ('burges') mouse on a social visit to a country cousin. Dissatisfied with homely, and decidedly Scottish, rural fare (food, the burges mouse insists, that 'will brek my teith, and mak my wame [stomach] fful sklender') the two mice resort to the town. Here the opinions of what constitutes discomfort are reversed and the country mouse, terrified by cats and butlers, quickly returns to her den 'als warme as woll' and to her plain diet of beans, nuts, peas, rye, and wheat. The *moralitas* points to the ancient conclusion, much beloved of non-aspirant contemporary humanists, that 'of eirthly joy it beiris maist degre, | Blyithnes in hart, with small possessioun'.

Henryson's explorations of, and extrapolations from, purely human relationships equally attempt to intermix what his original readers would have readily recognized as 'earnest' and 'game'. At one extreme, *The Bludy Serk* interprets the story of a knight killed by a giant as he rescues a princess from his thrall as a parable of Christ's salvation of the human soul ('godis dochtir deir'). In a far more relaxed moral vein, *Robene and Makyne* takes the form of a spirited pastoral dialogue between a shepherd and a country girl in which he first spurns her, changes his mind, and then finds that she has, quite properly, lost interest in him. Henryson's most moving poem, *The Testament of Cresseid*, shifts us into a very different aspect of 'game', this time a 'play' with the idea of a continuation of Chaucer's *Troilus and Criseyde*. Right from the beginning of the poem it is obvious that the 'game' is very much in earnest. In a 'doolie [mournful] sessoun', the poet makes himself a drink ('my spreitis to comfort'), stirs his fire to keep warm, and takes up Chaucer's poem to read 'to cut the winter nicht and make it schort'. As he insists, the 'careful dyte'—the melancholy poem—and the season 'correspond' and are 'equivalent'. Images of cold and human misery haunt his own poem which describes Cresseid's unhappy life after the end of Chaucer's narrative and after her desertion by the feckless Diomeid. When Cresseid curses Venus and Cupid for betraying her, she sees a vision of the planetary gods led by a miserably frosty Saturn ('His teith chatterit and cheverit [shivered] with the Chin, | His Ene drowpit, how sonkin [sunken] his heid, | Out of his Nois [nose] the meldrop [mucus] fast can rin'). The gods curse her impiety and Saturn afflicts her with a disfiguring leprosy. When Cynthia, the moon goddess, declares, 'Fra heit of bodie I the now deprive', we appreciate how, her passion spent, she too has been given over to the cold. The most painful section of the poem, that in which Henryson's Chaucerian 'pitee' for his subject is most evident, describes the brief encounter of Troilus and Cresseid. Neither recognizes the other:

> Then upon him scho kest up baith hir ene,
> And with ane blenk it came into his thocht
> That he sumtime hir face befoir had sene.
> Bot scho was in sic plye [plight] he knew hir nocht;
> Yit than hir luik into his mynd it brocht
> The sweit visage and amorous blenking
> Of fair Cresseid, sumtyme his awin darling.

He passes by, giving the unknown leper a purse of gold 'for knichtlie pietie and memoriall'. When she learns the identity of her distant benefactor, she can only agonize over her desertion of a lost and noble lover. Henryson may end his poem with an insistence that his women readers should not ruin themselves by an indulgence in 'fals deceptioun' but it is plain that his sympathy for the desperately miserable Cresseid is grounded in the fact of her painful and self-accusatory discovery of herself. Unlike the April with which Chaucer optimistically begins his *Canterbury Tales* or the bright May of a whole succession of garden-based courtly lovers, the 'doolie sessoun' has found its 'cairfull' subject.

The gnawing cold of the 'dirk [dark] and drublie [cloudy] dayis' of a northern winter is also pointedly recalled in William Dunbar's lyric 'In Winter'. Dunbar is a far more various, far more obviously 'courtly' and generally less consistently impressive poet than Henryson. He consciously identified himself with the upper areas of the Scottish court and its 'nobles off bluid' and he was happy both to provide the right poem for the right official occasion (such as his allegorical celebration of the marriage of James IV to Margaret Tudor in 1503, *The Thrissill and the Rose*) and to throw off versified complaints about the non-payment of his royal salary (such as the gently mocking *Respontio regis*). Dunbar's variety is evident in his range of subjects and metres. He could, for example, turn his hand to the splendidly witty account of a meeting of gossips, *The Tua Mariit Wemen and the Wedo*, and allow his merry widow (who owes something to the Wife of Bath) to confess that she wears colourful and fashionable clothes under her weeds and that she can impress her late husband's friends by finding ready tears in a conveniently hidden sponge ('Than wring I it full wylely and wetis my chekis | . . . Than say thai all that sittis about, "Se ye nought, allace [alas] | Yone lustlese led [unhappy woman], so leleley [loyally] scho luffit hir husband"'). He could also debunk the fraudulent claims of an alchemical friar to be able to fly by calling all the birds of the air to witness against him in *Ane Ballat of the Fenyeit Frier of Tungland*. Nevertheless, the same poet could address a devout, and far more lexically and metrically challenging, 'ballat' to the Blessed Virgin Mary and celebrate the resurrection of Christ with a triumphant and sonorous paean of joy:

> Done is a battel on the dragon blak;
> Our campioun Chryst confoundit hes his force:
> The yettis [gates] of hell ar brokin with a crak,
> The signe triumphall rasit is of the croce,
> The divillis trymmillis [tremble] with hiddous voce,
> The saulis ar borrowit [redeemed] and to the blis can go
> Chryst with his blud our ransonis dois indoce [endorse]:
> *Surrexit Dominus de sepulchro.*

The vitality of Dunbar's religious lyrics is balanced by the resignation which informs his meditation on human mortality, the *Lament for the Makaris*. The poet, 'trublit now with gret seiknes', and seemingly haunted by the reiterated refrain with which he closes each of his twenty-five four-line stanzas (*'Timor mortis conturbat me'*, 'the fear of death troubles me'), links himself to a line of dead English and Scots poets ('makars' or 'makers'). The poem is both a muted celebration of his art and a preparation for a death which he sees as rendering negative the pretensions of princes, prelates, potentates, physicians, and poets alike. It would not have been lost on Dunbar's first readers that he heads his list of names of distinguished poets with those of 'noble Chaucer, of makeris flour', of Lydgate, and of Gower. The poem may end with the suggestion that the hope of heaven may raise the eyes of the believer from a contemplation of dust, but the *Lament* itself seems to raise the more earthly hope that poetry can be instrumental in alerting the human soul to its potential.

Late Medieval Drama

'I am sent from God: Deth is my name', the figure of Mors announces as he ominously intrudes into King Herod's feast and prepares to strike the over-confident king: 'To hym wyl I go and geve hym such an hete | That all the lechis [doctors] of the londe his lyf xul [shall] nevyr restore'. Mors's unwelcome intrusion probably delighted certain members of the original audiences of the cycle of English mystery plays in which the incident occurs (Herod had been portrayed as a ranting villain and his sudden demise may have stimulated a certain sense of satisfaction). To other observers, the entry of the figure of death may have provoked an acute and chilling unease. At the end of the cycle of plays, God proclaims the Day of Judgement. A virtuous soul welcomes the event and the opening prospect of heaven; the sinful souls, by contrast, dread the 'hydous horne' that summons them to judgement: 'Allas! for drede sore may we quake, | Oure dedis [deeds] beis oure dampnacioune'. The texts of the four surviving cycles of religious dramas are none of them earlier than the mid-fifteenth century, though all four would seem to have originated in the late fourteenth century when vivid memories of the Black Death must have rendered the idea of the four last things—death, judgement, heaven, and hell—perilously familiar. The cycles stress the goodness and the grace of God, but they also point to his awesome power and the justice of his purposes. They trace the history of the divine will from the fall of Lucifer, through the creation of the world and the fall of Adam, to Christ's acts of redemption. They end with a calculated bang as God's 'for-thoght' is fulfilled in the ending of 'all erthely thyng'.

English theatre had its formal beginnings in the Latin liturgical enactments of the Church, certain of which were dramatized for particular effect on major feast-days. On Palm Sunday, for example, the faithful processed bearing palms in imitation of the people of Jerusalem and they heard the great passion narrative chanted by various voices, each playing a distinctive role (as Jesus, Pilate, Peter, etc.). On the greatest of all feasts, Easter, an instructive prelude to the main Mass of the day acted out the visit of the three Maries to the empty tomb of Christ (though the Maries were decorously played by men vested in albs and copes). It would seem that the greatest stimulus to non-liturgical religious drama was provided by the institution of the feast of Corpus Christi in the Western Church in 1264. The new feast, generally observed in England from 1318, required that the Blessed Sacrament be ceremoniously carried round the streets of the parish. In greater towns the procession would have been accompanied by guildsmen, representative of various established trades, dressed in livery and bearing the banners of their craft. In England, as in other European countries, this summer feast-day also became the focus of urban street theatre organized under the auspices of these same, largely secular, guilds. The guilds added to their prestige not only by commissioning and maintaining the texts of the plays that they engaged to perform, but also by making and storing the costumes, the stage-properties and, above all, the movable platforms which the performances required. Records survive of the annual productions of the cycles in many British cities, from Aberdeen to Canterbury, but the complete texts of the plays exist only for York (consisting of 48 plays), Chester (24 plays),

Wakefield (32 plays), and for an unknown Midlands town (42 plays). There are also surviving fragments from Coventry (plays once celebrated throughout England), Norwich, Northampton, and Newcastle as well as cycles in the Cornish language of the mineral-rich far south-west of the island. In some instances particular guilds would perform a play appropriate to their trade or mystery. At Chester, for example, the scene of Noah's flood was presented by the 'Water-leaders and Drawers in Dee' (that is, those who supplied the city with water drawn from the river Dee); the Crucifixion was re-enacted by the Ironmongers (men who sold nails) and, somewhat less appositely, the Harrowing of Hell was performed through the good offices of the Cooks and Innkeepers (men certainly used to the virtues of a good fire). At York the Fishers and Mariners presented the story of Noah, the Pinners and Painters the Crucifixion, and the Bakers the Last Supper. Although the majority of the actors were amateurs it would seem that they were supported both by fine stage effects (the records of the Coventry Drapers Company list a 'Hell-mouth', a barrel designed to produce the sound of an earthquake, and 'a link to set the world on fire') and by seasoned performers (the clerk, Absolon, in Chaucer's Miller's Tale delights to 'shewe his lightnesse and maistrye' in playing Herod 'upon a scaffold hye').

The surviving cycles suggest that the major centres of performance were cities in the North and the Midlands of England where the trade guilds could proudly demonstrate their independence from the jurisdiction of the Church. Though no 'original' survives, there is evidence that certain plays directly parallel others in shape, language, and style. Six plays from the so-called Towneley cycle (probably performed at Wakefield) closely resemble their York equivalents. The work of the anonymous fifteenth-century writer known as 'the Wakefield Master', to whom are ascribed the two Shepherds' plays which accompany the representation of the Nativity, is particularly remarkable for its extensive use of a distinctive Yorkshire dialect and local reference. The two Shepherds' plays, written perhaps for performance in alternate years or for different guilds, reveal a close understanding of the hardships endured by northern shepherds whose labour sustained the local wool-trade. The two plays also suggest a greater awareness of the realities of rural life than does the more emphatically urban York cycle. The shepherds complain frankly of the cold weather and of oppressive landlords in what at first seems to be a harshly comic farce. With the appearance of the angel, however, their coarseness is transformed into an instructive humility before the miracle of the birth that they have been privileged to witness. It is as if the old covenant of wrath melts away with the establishment of the new covenant of love. The Wakefield Master was no mere secular proto-realist; he had a mind carefully attuned by theology and symbolism (as his use of a stolen sheep swaddled in a cradle as a witty parallel to the birth of the Lamb of God serves to suggest). The comedy which relieves the agonies of human and divine history in the other cycles also suggests a devout intermixture of game and earnest rooted in popular storytelling and performance. King Herod's rampaging almost topples over into the pantomimic ('I wot not where I may sit for anger and for teen [rage]') and the truculence of Noah's wife, when she refuses to go into the ark, threatens the future of the entire human race. In the Chester play she is finally forced aboard by her sons, while in the Wakefield version she has to wait for the flood to touch her toes ('Yei, water nyghes so nere that I sit not dry') before she grudgingly assents to be saved.

In none of the cycles is comedy or individual characterization allowed to detract from the central theme of the unity of human history and its perceived pattern of salvation. Characters from the Old Testament are seen as archetypes of the suffering, triumphant Christ while God's hand is seen prompting patriarchs and prophets to help realize the pre-ordained scheme of redemption. Far more so than the stained-glass windows of the great medieval churches (many of which were barely decipherable to the myopic or the uninformed), these plays were genuinely the 'books of the illiterate'. Like the graphic doom-paintings which featured so prominently in many parish churches during the period, they also brought home to the faithful the mighty workings of God and the fearfulness of falling unprepared into his hands. The urgency of the call to repentance, and the necessary response to divine mercy in the face of the advances of death, are also evident in the 'morality' plays which have survived from the fifteenth and early sixteenth centuries. These moralities seem, for the most part, to have been tailored to suit the needs of groups of travelling actors who were prepared to perform in the more intimate and contained spaces of inn-yards and halls. *Everyman* (c.1495), which derives from a Flemish original, shows a representative figure of the human race summoned unexpectedly by death ('O Deth, thou comest when I had the leest in mynde') and made acutely aware that his erstwhile friends, Fellowship, Kindred, Cousin, and Goods, will not go with him. It is Good Deeds who finally supports him and who offers to justify him before the throne of God. The East Anglian play *Mankind* (written c.1465), which opens with a sermon delivered by Mercy, shows its title character, an ostensibly upright countryman who is prepared to defend himself with his spade, variously tempted by the vices and the grotesquely comic devil, Titivillus. Mankind is increasingly drawn by spiritual sloth to despair of his salvation ('A rope, a rope, a rope! I am not worthy') but, having learned to be wary of his 'ghostly enemies'—the world, the flesh, and the devil—he is ultimately delivered up to God's justice by Mercy. The most elaborate, and the earliest, of the surviving morality plays, *The Castle of Perseverance* (c.1405) demands a cast of 36 actors and a grand, diagrammatic open-air staging in order to dramatize the life of Humanum Genus (Humankind) from birth, via a staged tournament between vices and virtues, to a concluding pageant of death and judgement.

The popular significance of the performances of religious drama is witnessed by their relatively long survival. Although the texts of the plays were systematically revised, excised, and amplified long before the impact of the Reformation was felt, certain plays which grated on new Protestant sensibilities in the 1540s and 1550s (notably those representing the posthumous triumphs of the Virgin Mary) were quietly suppressed. By the 1560s the civil and ecclesiastical authorities were clearly intent on a wholesale extinction of the plays, regarding their performance as offensive to the dignity of God and his saints. The York cycle was last performed in 1569, the Chester cycle in 1575, and the Coventry plays in 1580. It is theoretically possible, therefore, that Shakespeare (born in nearby Stratford in 1564) could have had his first experience of the theatre by seeing the far-famed Coventry mysteries before their texts were consigned to a Protestant dustbin. The powerful emotional impact of performances of the surviving cycles and morality plays had otherwise to wait to be released by their revival in the less religiously susceptible, but infinitely more secular, twentieth century.

Late Medieval Religious Writing

The texts of the mystery and morality plays provide firm evidence of a flourishing religious dramatic literature written in English for the instruction and entertainment of a wide, largely uneducated though discriminating audience. The writings of Richard Rolle, of the author of *The Cloud of Unknowing*, of Walter Hilton, and of Julian of Norwich are, by contrast, an expression of an intensely private religious experience. All four writers were, at some point in their lives, recluses. At the age of 18, Rolle (*c.*1300–49) had abruptly broken off his studies at Oxford and, appalled by the vanity of the world, retreated to a hermitage in his native Yorkshire. He ended his days living in seclusion near a convent of Cistercian nuns at Hampole in the West Riding. It was probably for the spiritual guidance of certain of these nuns, women who were ignorant of Latin, that Rolle wrote the short English epistles now known as *Ego Dormio*, *The Commandment*, and *The Form of Living*. Rolle consistently lays stress on a combustive passion for God. In *The Form of Living*, for example, he defines love as 'byrnand [burning] yernyng in God' and God himself as 'lyght & byrning'. God's light 'clarifies oure skyll [reason]'; his burning kindles 'oure covayties that we desyre noght bot hym' ('our desire to know nothing but him'). Where secular poets such as Chaucer and Gower, and before them Dante, had sought to relate human love to its divine origin and had seen earthly passion as ultimately subsumed in an all-enveloping heavenly love, Rolle yearns exclusively for God, rapturously concentrating his heart and mind on the divine wooer of his soul. 'I sytt and syng of luf langyng that in my breste es bredde', he writes in one of the love-poems interpolated into the text of *Ego Dormio*, 'Jhesu, Jhesu, Jhesu, when war I to the ledde?' ('when shall I come to thee?'). Elsewhere in his work, as the incantatory lyrics 'A Song of Love-longing to

Jesus' and 'A Salutation to Jesus' suggest, he seems to repeat the sacred name almost as a comfortingly amorous mantra.

It is possible that the unnamed author of *The Cloud of Unknowing* (written *c*.1380) deliberately chose anonymity as a self-abnegatory statement. Working in a mystical tradition derived from the sixth-century theologian known as Dionysius the Pseudo-Areopagite, and pointedly suspicious of what he calls the 'curiouste of ymaginacion', he begins with the negative proposition that the reason can never 'know' God. Neither meditative evocations of the Passion nor ideas of a divine light clarifying human reason seem to him to have the force of the 'blinde steryng [stirring] of love' which wondrously enlightens the contemplative. It is, he indicates, essentially to the affective quality of the soul rather than to the intellect that God reveals himself. The darkness or the 'cloud of unknowing' that lies between the human and the divine can, the writer implies, be pierced only by 'a sharp dart' of love from heaven. This dart, which he otherwise pictures as a 'beme of goostly light', mystically links the contemplative soul to the godhead. In this blessed state, God unveils his secrets to the 'enflaumid' ('enflamed') soul, showing a 'privete' of which 'man may not, ne kan not, speke'. A similar sense of pierced darkness and intensified spiritual experience marks the work of Walter Hilton (d. 1396). Hilton, who spent a period as a hermit before becoming an Augustinian canon at Thurgarton in Nottinghamshire, is best known for his *Scala Perfectionis* or *The Scale of Perfection*. The treatise, written for a woman recluse, advises moral reform, humility, and asceticism as a way of preparing for a life of contemplative prayer. God's image, Hilton suggests, can be restored in the soul only by this strict preparation and by an endurance of a 'dark night' in which the soul is detached from earthly things while still yearning for the divine fulfilment of the things of the spirit ('soothly the murkier that this night is, the nearer is the true day of the love of Jhesu').

Hilton's work enjoyed a considerable currency in fifteenth-century England, the *Scala Perfectionis* being printed in 1494. Partly thanks to T. S. Eliot's quotations from it in 'Little Gidding', it is, however, Julian of Norwich's *Revelations of Divine Love* that appears to have attracted most sympathetic interest in the twentieth century. In her careful and detailed account of her mystical experience, Julian (*c*.1342–*post* 1416) recounts that on 8 May 1373, when she was some 30 years old and lying sick of what was presumed to be a mortal illness, she was vouchsafed a series of visions or 'showings'. Two separate versions survive of her account of her 'showings'; the first was possibly set down shortly after her experience; the second, written 'twenty yere after the tyme of the shewyng save thre monthys', is far longer and suggests an intervening period of reflection on the nature of the mysteries revealed to her (she mentions that her account had been 'renewde by lyghtenynges and touchynges'). From echoes of their work in her own, Julian would seem to have had a close knowledge of the treatises of Rolle, Hilton, and the author of *The Cloud of Unknowing*. Where Rolle and Hilton had offered spiritual counsel to devout contemplative women, however, Julian shows us the fruits of her own, supremely distinguished, female spirituality. If she modestly insists that she was a 'symple creature unlet-tyrde' and a woman 'leued, febille, & freyle' ('ignorant, feeble and frail'), her style suggests that, though she may not have known Latin, she was a writer of real sophistication, tact, and expressiveness. Like her mystic predecessors, but with a yet greater emphasis, she sees divine love as providing the answer to all the problems of human existence. In the account of her first 'showing' she describes Christ directing her to look at her hand: 'And in this he schewyd me a lyttle thynge, the qwantyte of a haselle nutte [hazelnut] lyggande [lying] in the palme of my hande . . . I lokede ther oponn and thought, "Whate may this be?" And I was annsweredde generaly thus, "It is alle that ys made".' The universe is miraculously contracted, contained, comprehended for the benefit of the wondering soul. Julian's vision is sustained by the spiritual presence of another woman, the Virgin Mary, who is revealed as 'a sympille maydene and a meeke, yonge of age, in stature that scho [she] was when scho conceyvede'. The account of the showing presents readers with two vast divine mysteries in which women play vital roles: Julian holds the contracted universe in the palm of her hand just as Mary bore God in her womb. As the showings continue, Julian is confronted with a series of visions of Christ. He appears at his most glorious in the twelfth of her revelations and here, uncomprehendingly, she questions the Lord about the place of evil in the scheme of redemption. Christ's reply is tender, firmly measured, and utterly reassuring to her: 'I maye make alle thynge wele, I can make alle thynge wele, I wille make alle thynge wele, and I schalle make alle thynge wele, and thowe schalle se thyselfe that alle thynge schalle be wele.' If Julian seems to pause at the end of this section of her text, it is to ponder on the vast consequences of what she has heard. Her pause allows for the expression of a second reassurance, one that must be seen as supplementing, rather than contradicting, the teachings of the Church: 'It is goddys wille that we witte [know] that alle schalle be wele in generalle; botte it is nought goddys wille that we schulde witte it nowe, botte as it langes to us for the tyme [except what is proper for the time]: & that is the techynge of haly kyrke [holy Church]'. Julian, having been made privy to a spiritually explosive message, seems to retreat into the protective bosom of theological speculation as safely defined by the Church.

Julian's tact is equally evident in the advice she gave to a devout woman of a quite different disposition, Marjorie Kempe (?1373–*post* 1433). Kempe, who left a detailed account of her 'conversion', her visions, her anguish, her extensive travels, and her almost pathological religiosity in *The Book of Marjorie Kempe* (*c*.1432, revised 1436–8), was told by Julian that she should fulfil whatever God had put into her soul, provided 'it wer not a-geyn the worshep of God' and the well-being of her fellow Christians. Nevertheless, Marjorie felt an uncommon pressure on her to speak out rather than suffer fools gladly and quietly. She was convinced she had a mission and it was not a mission that led her to the confines of a convent or to an anchorite's cell of her own. She was frequently overwhelmed with floods of tears, tears inspired both by a contemplation of the Divine Mysteries and by her frustration with the state of the sinful world that so oppressed and often rejected her. 'The more despyte, schame, & repryf that ye have in the world', she was advised, 'the mor is yowr meryte in the sygth of God.' Marjorie sought out and cherished models of womanly piety and womanly action. While Julian's counsel to her was of a passive acceptance of her lot, she also cultivated a particular devotion to the singularly energetic St Bridget (Birgitta) of Sweden (1303–73, canonized 1391). Bridget, who had married young and had borne eight children, was widowed in 1343. Thereafter, she gave over all her energies to the establishment of a new religious order (the 'Bridgettines') a foundation that included men and women under the rule of an abbess. She ended her life in Rome, proffering often unwelcome advice to the Pope and his Court concerning contemporary corruptions of Church and State. Like Marjorie, Bridget was a determined pilgrim and claimed to have visions which determined both her vocation and her mission. These she recorded in her *Revelations* (which date from the 1340s and had a considerable currency in England, particularly, it would seem, amongst women readers). Marjorie clearly identified with Bridget's inner assurance and her espousal of the active spiritual life. She travelled widely as a pilgrim (Jerusalem, Rome, Compostela, Norway, Germany) and was much given to arguing openly with those by whom she was affronted or offended (be they bishop, heretic, or backslider). Although her forthrightness offended some in high places, and many of her fellow pilgrims, she was also able to find crucial support for her mission and for a written record of her vision. She was cautious, however, when it came to the timing of that very personal record:

Summe of these worthy & worshepful clerkys tokyn it in perel of her [their] sowle and as thei wold answer to God that this creatur was inspyred wyth the Holy Gost and bodyn [bade] hyr that sche schuld don hym wryten [have them write] & maken a booke of hyr felyngs & hir reuelacyons. Sum proferyd [offered] hir to wryten hyr felyngs wyth her [their] owen handys, & sche wold not consentyn in no wey, for sche was comawndyd in hir sowle that sche schuld not wrytyn so soone.

It was some twenty years after her first mystical experience that she was sufficiently confident that God had ordained that the time was right for her to proclaim the divine nature of her 'revelations' so that 'hys goodnesse myth [might] be knowyn to alle the world'. In order to do so Marjorie, who was possibly illiterate, dictated her narrative to two male scribes, both of them sympathetic clerics. The record she and her scribes have left us is of an often fraught and overwrought spiritual quest which can fascinate and infuriate modern readers, much as it did her ecclesiastical contemporaries. She is none the less a deeply impressive figure: a woman who offers an account of an unconventional vocation, one that entailed leaving her husband, her home, and her household in determined pursuit of her calling. Marjorie dramatically renounced human sexual relations in order to proclaim her intimate spiritual union with a new beloved: Christ. Often overwhelmed by the privileges and emotional demands of this intimacy, she is frequently reduced to tears, 'roaring' and weeping both spontaneously and inconsolably. Marjorie's record is one of the earliest and most revealing autobiographies in English.

Malory and Caxton

In October 1471 Margaret Paston, the wife of a Norfolk gentleman, wrote to her husband in London to describe the violent incursions of armed men employed by the Duke of Norfolk on their property. The Duke's men had not simply ransacked the Pastons' estate and other manors in the area, but they also desecrated the local parish church by standing on the altar, pillaging the images, and taking away anything of value that they found. The Pastons' troubles were scarcely unique, given the multiple uncertainties of political and social life in medieval England and the frequent intimidations of the less by the great. Nevertheless, their difficulties were compounded, and national uncertainties accentuated, by the manifold disruption of England by what subsequent generations have known as the 'Wars of the Roses'. The Pastons, a large number of whose family letters have been preserved for posterity (a selection was first published in 1787), played a relatively insignificant part in the highly divisive national politics of their day. Their social position nevertheless rendered them first-hand witnesses to much of the turbulence of the fifteenth century, intent as they were on preserving what they could of their estates and their domestic security while cautiously advancing the prestige of their family.

By the 1450s the English Crown's hopes of establishing a permanent hegemony over France were ending in ignominy. The battle of Castillon, fought in July 1453, finally extinguished the grand ambitions which had fired the notable triumph of Henry V at Agincourt some thirty-eight years earlier. England's once extensive territorial possessions were steadily reduced to a mere foothold at Calais. Parallel to these disasters in France was the gradual disintegration of the domestic political order established by the Lancastrian kings, Henry IV and Henry V. The latter's untimely death in 1422 left the realm under the nominal rule of his heir, a 9-month-old child. The reign of King Henry VI was the most disrupted of any in English history, marked not only by a grave disillusion with French affairs but also by a slow but inexorable slide into civil war. Once he attained his majority in 1437, it became evident to his friends and potential enemies alike that the devout Henry VI believed more in the power of prayer than in the advantages of policy. His conspicuous piety, which took concrete form in royal educational foundations at Eton and Cambridge, belatedly earned him a reputation for saintliness (the formal claims to which were pursued at Rome by certain of his royal successors, and, latterly, by Old Etonians). His political impotence, which was accentuated by a brief lapse into insanity in 1453 and a more serious collapse in 1455, led inevitably to a series of power struggles between factions led by aristocratic magnates. These bitter struggles centred on the legitimacy of Henry's claim to the throne through descent from Edward III's son, John of Gaunt, Duke of Lancaster, and the rival claims of Richard, Duke of York (descended from an elder brother of Gaunt's). The 'Wars of the Roses', which erupted into armed conflict at the battle of St Albans in May 1455, take their name from the fabled adoption of a red rose as an emblem by the Lancastrian faction, a white by the Yorkist. The long-drawn-out wars, which involved the deposition of Henry VI in 1461, his replacement by the Yorkist King Edward IV, his restoration in 1470, and his murder under the restored Edward IV in 1471, also finally claimed the lives of some 12 princes of the blood, some 200 noblemen, and some 100,000 gentry and commoners. When Edward IV died in April 1483, the effective usurpation of the throne by his brother Richard III brought a further period of extreme political instability. This instability was only eliminated by the invasion, success in battle, and subsequent political skill of Henry Tudor, who claimed the throne as Henry VII in August 1485. Henry's somewhat specious ancestral claim to the crown of the Plantagenets was purposefully brushed aside by Tudor propagandists who preferred to lay stress on his Welsh blood and his somewhat improbable line of descent from King Arthur.

From a literary point of view, the 'matter' of Britain—the accounts of the legendary exploits of Arthur and his knights—reached its apogee in the work of Sir Thomas Malory (d. 1471) and William Caxton (?1422–91), men of quite different social class and outlook. Malory appears to have finished the composition of his *Le Morte Darthur* in 1469–70 during a period of imprisonment on charges of violence, theft, extortion, and felonious rape. It was printed and published in July 1485 by the adventurous Caxton who had not only edited and excised Malory's text but also reordered it into twenty-one books. The text of the original version (in eight sections) was rediscovered only in 1934. If the Sir Thomas Malory, to whom the authorship of the *Morte Darthur is* generally accredited, was indeed the Malory held in prison on a charge of decidedly unknightly violence, it is but one of several profound ironies which attach themselves to the book. Rape and robbery scarcely sit well with the high chivalric principles which are extolled in the text. If this Malory was also the faithful liegeman of successive earls of Warwick, he saw service under commanders notably deficient in their respect for knightly codes of behaviour. Though the account of Arthur's European military triumphs and his imperial coronation by the Pope in section 2 of the *Morte Darthur* seems deliberately to shadow the famous victories of Henry V, there must have seemed scant parallels between the courteous actions of Arthur's knights and the conduct of those responsible for the military and civil disasters of the reign of Henry VI. Malory looked back to the first establishment and the glorious realization of the ideals of knighthood while the England of his own age was witnessing the bloody decline of the authority of a military aristocracy. Finally, though Malory's text was transmitted to posterity by Caxton, it is perhaps ironic that this same Caxton should be a merchant alert to the profits to be made from courtly literature, rather than a soldier and a courtier.

Despite his benign tampering with the text, Caxton recognized the extent to which Malory had managed to centre his narrative on 'the byrth, lyf, and actes of the sayd kyng Arthur [and] of his noble knyghtes of the Round Table'. He also acknowledged that the book gave its readers an encompassing view of a range of moral experience: 'Herein may be seen noble chivalrye, curtosye, humanyte, frendlynesse, hardynesse, love, frendshyp, cowardyse, murdre, hate, vertue, and synne.' Malory worked from a considerable variety of English and French sources in both verse and prose. He translated them all into a prose epic written in a vigorous, alliterative, formal, supple and often hauntingly rhythmical English (he also possessed an extraordinary gift for vivid verbal exchange and for ceremonious dialogue). His Arthur rules a kingdom which is at once a never-never land and a palpable Christian England of Winchester, Salisbury, Canterbury, and Carlisle, of medieval counties, castles, and chantries. Malory traces the Arthurian story from the King's begetting, birth, education, and assumption of power to his and his court's tragic decay. Between these determining poles he gives over long sections to the careers of Lancelot, Gareth, and Tristram, to the pursuit of the Holy Grail, and to the adulterous love of Lancelot and Guinevere. We begin with the optimism associated with the unknown prince who 'lightly and fiersly' pulls the sword out of the stone; we end with the fearful decline of Arthur's greatness and his terrible dream of falling into 'an hydeous depe blak watir' which contains 'all maner of serpentis and wormes and wilde bestis fowle and orryble'. The end of the narrative is haunted by the recurring phrase 'the noble felyshyp of the Rounde Table is brokyn for ever' and by a sense of the mutability of all human affairs. Knowingly reflecting the anomalies in his sources, Malory's defeated king is both carried off in a barge 'into the vale of Avylyon to hele [him] of [his] grevous wounds' and buried in a tomb at Glastonbury inscribed: 'HIC IACET ARTHURUS, REX QUONDAM REXQUE FUTURUS'. The ambiguity of a once and future king, a deliverer who would rise from his tomb to save endangered England, may well have offered political comfort to a prisoner in the perilous days of King Edward IV. The idea was certainly to prove of political use to the fanciful mythologizers of the Tudors and the early Stuarts.

Malory's *Morte Darthur* exercised a profound influence over English writers from the age of Spenser (a poet who saw himself as the heir to the last chivalrous enchantments of the Middle Ages) to that of Tennyson (a poet much inclined to echo Malory's melancholy cadences). With historical hindsight it could be said that Malory, the greatest prose writer of the fifteenth century, was composing a prose elegy to the dying age of aristocratic chivalry. It was, however, Caxton, the middle-class entrepreneur who first brought his work to public attention, who emerges, with the benefit of the same hindsight, as the real harbinger of a new age in which the printed word was to play an indispensable and revolutionary role.

3

Renaissance and Reformation: Literature 1510–1620

ALTHOUGH not one of them spoke Welsh, the five English monarchs of the Tudor dynasty were inclined to insist on the significance of their Welsh origins. For propaganda purposes they were pronounced to be princes of ancient British descent who had returned to claim King Arthur's throne and to restore the promised dignity and prestige of Camelot. It was, however, under the Tudor dynasty (1485–1603) that the modern English language emerged and with it a firm sense of England as a nation state. With the accession of James VI of Scotland as James I of England in 1603 that sense of national consciousness was extended to embrace the entire island of Britain. When Calais, the last relic of English domination of France and the symbol of Edward III's victory at Crecy and Henry V's at Agincourt, fell in January 1558 its loss finally exposed the hollowness of the Plantagenet claim to the French Crown. It also, willynilly, enforced the idea of the insular sovereignty of the Tudors and of their Stuart successors.

King Henry VIII's 'imperial' sovereignty, his declaration of independence from papal overlordship, had been asserted in 1533 in the preamble to the Act of Parliament which announced the advent of the English Reformation. By this 'Act in Restraint of Appeals', Parliament cut off future legal reference to the superior authority of Rome and proclaimed that England was ruled by 'one supreme head and king' who governed without interference from 'any foreign princes or potentates'. Given the assertion that the islands of Britain and Ireland represented a law unto themselves, and given the claims of the Tudor monarchs to an imperial sovereignty, the process of extending the political influence of the kings of England was pursued with a particular reforming vigour by the ministers and servants of the Crown. Hand in hand with this process went the imposition of the English language as it was spoken and written at court. In 1536, for example, the reform of Welsh legal procedure culminated in what was effectively an act of union between England and Wales. In 1543 the union was reinforced when Wales was organized into twelve counties on the English model, English common law was introduced, and seats in the Westminster Parliament allocated. By these Acts of Parliament the status of Wales changed from that of an occupied province to that of an integral part of a single (English) realm. The privileges accorded to English customs and to the English language in Wales were even more emphatically enforced in the linguistically and culturally divided Ireland. Gaelic Ireland, stretching beyond the Pale of Dublin and its seaboard, was gradually coerced into submission to English concepts of good manners and good government. An Act of 1537 ordered all the inhabitants of the island to speak the language of its rulers and to adopt English styles of dress. For much of the rest of the century English 'civilization' was to be imposed by armies rather than by laws and by attempts to extirpate Gaelic society rather than to transform it.

The would-be 'imperial' dynastic relations of the Tudor monarchs with the still independent Kingdom of Scotland proved as fraught as their attempts to subdue Ireland. King Henry VII's bid for a lasting peace with his northern neighbour, cemented by the marriage of his daughter to James IV, floundered when Scotland reaffirmed its useful 'auld alliance' with France, and suffered a crushing defeat at the battle of Flodden in 1513. When in 1542 Henry VIII attempted to forge a Protestant alliance by marrying his son Edward to the infant Mary, Queen of Scots, his ambition was effectively countered by the opposition of a Francophile party in Scotland. This same Mary, as a direct descendant of the first of the Tudors and as the prime Catholic claimant to the English throne, proved to be a thorn in the side of the ministers of the last Tudor, the childless upholder of a new Protestant order, Elizabeth I. It was, however, Mary Stuart's Protestant son and Elizabeth's godson, James VI, who was ultimately to unite the Crowns of England and Scotland as Elizabeth's approved successor in 1603.

For James VI and I and his often imaginative panegyrists, the emergence of what the King was proud to style 'Great Britain' seemed to be the fulfilment of an Arthurian dream of an independent and unified island. 'Great Britain' was also viewed as a restoration of the lost order originally given to the nation by its mythical founders, the followers of the Trojan refugee prince, Brutus. As King James entered his English capital in state in March 1604 he was greeted by specially erected triumphal arches, whose iconography reminded him of his supposed Trojan ancestry and fancifully welcomed him to a new Troy ('Troynovant'). The entertainments and pageants written for the same occasion by the playwrights Thomas Dekker and Ben Jonson reinforced these elaborate fancies with a series of scholarly parallels and intellectual conceits. One of the speeches in Dekker's *Magnificent Entertainment* spoke of James and his realm as

> so rich an Empyre, whose fayre brest,
> Contaynes foure Kingdomes by your entrance blest
> By Brute divided, but by you alone,
> All are againe united and made One,
> Whose fruitfull glories shine so far and even,
> They touch not onely earth, but they kisse heaven.

The myth of a restored, integral, and independent Britain, first fostered by the usurping and expansionist Tudor dynasty, continued to sustain the optimistic but increasingly unsteadily based pageantry of the early Stuarts. 'Great Britain' was an ideological convenience, one which expressed a humanly engineered and divinely blessed unity, conformity, and order. The union of kingdoms was also taken to imply the existence of united customs, creeds, and modes of expression.

The truth was not always as uniform and impressive as the contrived fiction. The sixteenth century witnessed changes in national life as radical as any since the Norman Conquest. Henry VIII's break with the Pope, his removal of the English Church from its ancient allegiance to Rome, and his suppression of some eight hundred monastic foundations began a process of religious reform which was later rigorously extended in the reigns of Edward VI and Elizabeth. Although the reshaping of what was proclaimed to be a national Church in England was relatively conservative (the parallel reform in Scotland proved far more radical), the process left the Church both impoverished and subservient to its new royal Supreme Head. If the changes forced on the English Church in the sixteenth century were by no means unique in northern Europe, Henry VIII's reformation deprived the old Catholic order in Europe of one of its major pillars and temporarily cut England off, politically, artistically, and religiously, from a European mainstream. The state, outwardly a happy and harmonious union of the secular and the ecclesiastical, had in fact been given a uniformity imposed from above, not gradually determined by multi-lateral consensus. Dissent from the new status quo was at best rigorously discouraged, at worst bloodily suppressed. Although to some modern commentators the ideology and machinery of the Tudor state seem to re-semble those of a twentieth-century dictatorship, such parallels are often based on loose and uncoordinated historical assumptions. Nevertheless, the literature which sprang from, or was influenced by, the culture of the English court in the sixteenth and early seventeenth centuries necessarily reflected the political and religious inclinations of a ruling élite. Much of the officially approved, propagandist culture of Renaissance England can now be seen as a calculated attempt to create an illusion of ordered compliance and national unity as a means of discountenancing internal and external opposition.

Poetry at the Court of Henry VIII

English culture was in a state of conspicuous flux in the early sixteenth century. It was actively and experimentally coming to terms with imported novelties which were as much religious and intellectual as they were linguistic. The advances in printing made since the establishment of Caxton's first press at Westminster in 1476 had assisted in the circulation of the pan-European 'new' learning but they had also stimulated a fresh interest in established vernacular classics. Though Latin remained the prime medium of educated communication and the essential acquirement of any man or woman who pretended to learning, the inherited tradition of poetry in English was increasingly viewed with nationalistic pride. That pride was, however, diluted by the awareness that the language, the conditions of writing, and the very fabric of poetry were changing. In 1532 William Thynne, a gentleman in Henry VIII's service, produced a full edition of Chaucer's works which he dedicated to his royal master. In the Preface to this edition a fellow-courtier, Sir Brian Tuke (d. 1545), directs the attention of readers to the significance of human expression through 'speche or language' and singles out for praise those Englishmen who had 'notably endevoyred and employed them selves to the beautifyeng and bettryng of thenglysh tonge'. For Tuke, 'that noble and famous clerke Chaucer' was the supreme national poet, a writer possessed of 'suche frutefulnesse in wordes . . . so swete and plesaunt sentences . . . suche sensyble and open style lackyng neither maieste ne mediocrite [moderation]'; he was also the eloquent master of a language which now deserved an honoured place amongst other, generally more Latinate, Western European languages. In the same year the printer Thomas Berthelet (or Berthelette) produced an edition of Gower's *Confessio Amantis*, also solemnly dedicated to the King. Crucial to his dedication was Berthelet's patriotic stress on the importance of the continued use of an established poetic vocabulary: 'olde englysshe wordes and vulgars', he insists, 'no wyse man because of theyr antiquite wyll throwe asyde'. Modern writers, he complains, had begun to play with neologisms and to introduce 'newe termes . . . whiche they borrowed out of latyne frenche and other langages', an unhappy process which might be reversed by a renewed interest in the study of Gower, a lantern who could provide any true English poet with light 'to wryte counyngly and to garnysshe his sentences in our vulgar tonge'.

To the most prominent and most senior of the early Tudor poets, John Skelton (?1460–1529), the language used by Chaucer, Gower, and Lydgate now had self-evident disadvantages. In the character of Dame Margery, the narrator of his poem *Phyllyp Sparrowe* (c.1505), he complains of the impossibility of writing eloquently in his native tongue. When Margery attempts to compose an epitaph for the dead pet sparrow, she is forced to admit that 'Our naturall tong is rude, | And hard to be ennuede [made fresh]'. It is a language 'so rusty, | So cankered and so full | Of forwardes [awkward words] and so dul' that if she attempted to 'write ornatly' no terms existed to serve her mind. Dame Margery finds Gower's English 'olde | And of no value' and that of Lydgate 'diffuse'. Even Chaucer, whose matter is 'delectable' and whose language is 'well alowed . . . pleasaunt, easy and playne', fails the test of true modern expressiveness, and her elegy is finally written in Latin 'playne and lyght'. As his self-laudatory poem *The Garlande or Chapelet of Laurell* suggests, Skelton himself was happy to balance the mass of his English works against a body of internationally acceptable poems in Latin. He was also inordinately proud of the tributes accorded to him by the universities of Cambridge, Oxford, and Louvain for his command of classical rhetoric, and tended to sign himself as 'Poete Laureate'. As a priest and as a former tutor to Prince Henry it was proper that he should have sought to express himself in the language of learning and elevated international communication, yet he remained confident enough of certain residual qualities in his native tongue to employ it for his extraordinarily direct, abusive, and rumbustious satires on contemporary manners.

Despite the vividness of his art, Skelton is a poet who found it difficult to be succinct in his structures and chaste in his choice of words, deficiencies which did not endear him to later sixteenth-century critics. He rejoices in scurrility and in the rhythmic immediacy of ballads and folk-poetry. In *Agaynst the Scottes* (1513), for example, he abuses Scotland for its challenge to the authority of Henry VIII and rubs Scottish noses in their signal defeat at Flodden ('Jemmy is ded | And closyd in led | That was theyr owne kynge. | Fy on that wynnyng!', 'Are nat these Scottys | Folys [fools] and sottys | Such boste to make, | To prate and crake [boast], | To face, to brace, | All voyde of grace'). Closer to home, in *Speke Parrott*, he adopts the persona of a polyglot parrot, a 'byrde of Paradyse, | By Nature devysed of a wonderowus kynde', and turns finally to an attack on the paltriness of an English court over which the King towers nobly like some kind of moral colossus ('So manye bolde barons, there hertes as dull as lede; | So many nobyll bodyes, undyr on dawys [simpleton's] hedd; | So royall a kyng, as reynythe uppon us all— | Syns Dewcalions flodde, was nevyr sene nor shall'). Skelton's intensest bile was, however, reserved for attacks on Henry VIII's powerful minister, Cardinal Wolsey, notably in Why *Come Ye Nat to Courte?* (1522). Not only does the narrator famously suggest an improper contemporary confusion between 'the kynges courte' and Wolsey's more sumptuous palace at Hampton Court, he also directly warns of the dangers of the Cardinal's political presumption: 'he wyll play checke mate | With ryall [royal] majeste | Counte himselfe as good as he; | A prelate potencyall | To rule under Bellyall [Belial]'.

The so-called 'Skeltonic metre' (if it is indeed metric) takes its name from Skelton's clever repetitions of tumblingly breathless short lines with two or three accents and an indefinite number of syllables. At times these recurring rhymes seem little better than mere doggerel; at others, readers are faced with a popular verbal and rhythmic energy which could be described as a kind of proto-rap. In the case of *Phyllyp Sparrowe* Skelton can suggest a series of hopping, twittering bird-like jerks. In *The Tunnyng of Elynour Rummynge* (*c*.1520) the irregularity of his metre playfully evokes the atmosphere of an untidy inn, the effects of an unsavoury but potent beer, and the quarrelling, tumbling rush of Elynour's customers. In *Collyn Clout* (*c*.1522), a poem narrated by an unsophisticated pauper, Skelton seeks to typify his own verbal art:

> For though my rhyme be ragged,
> Tattered and jagged,
> Rudely rayne-beaten,
> Rusty and mothe-eaten,

> Yf ye take well therwith
> It hath in it some pyth.

Collyn Clout speaks roughly, vividly, indelicately, old-fashionedly, but by no means unlearnedly. His eloquence has little to do with the established rules of rhetoric or the supposed courtliness of Latinate lyricism. He attacks the abuses, vices, and hypocrisies of the secular clergy as Langland and Chaucer had before him, but he also deliberately heightens certain specific modern circumstances (including reference to the 'brennynge sparke | Of Luthers warke [work]'). Despite his often radical alertness to the problems inherent in the early Tudor Church and commonwealth, and despite his delight in the resources of the English language, Skelton remained a literary conservative, a poet content with agile variations on established vernacular traditions rather than one who opened his art to the challenge of extraneous influence.

It is a somewhat over-simplified reading of literary history to see Skelton merely as a dogged upholder of a tradition that was rapidly becoming defunct and his younger contemporaries, Sir Thomas Wyatt (1503–42) and Henry Howard, Earl of Surrey (?1517–47) as the genteel leaders of an imported, progressive avant-garde. All three poets were innovators in their distinctive ways; all three were bred in a similar Latinate, as opposed to Italianate culture; all three cultivated plain words and a plain English style and drew on a popular English tradition. Nevertheless, it was to the work of Wyatt and Surrey that later sixteenth-century poets admiringly returned and to the poems of Skelton that they condescendingly looked back as a relic of semi-barbarity.

Relatively few of Wyatt's poems appeared in print in his lifetime, but his work, together with that of Surrey, was effectively canonized in 1557 with the appearance of the influential anthology *Songes and Sonettes, written by the right honorable Lorde Henry Haward late Earle of Surrey and other*, a collection familiarly known as *Tottel's Miscellany*. Richard Tottel's Preface to the collection proclaimed that 'the honorable stile' of Surrey and the 'weightinesse' of the work of the 'depewitted' Wyatt offered proof that English poetry could now stand proper comparison with the ancient Latin and the modern Italian. Tottel told his readers that his volume had been published 'to the honor of the English tong, and for the profit of the studious of Englishe eloquence'. With the aid of the nine editions of the *Miscellany* published between 1557 and 1587 a generation of Elizabethan poets and would-be poets (including Shakespeare's Abraham Slender in *The Merry Wives of Windsor*) schooled themselves in the courtly expression of love and in the proper verbal posturing of a lover. They were also introduced to the novelty of the Italianate discipline of the fourteen-line sonnet, to *ottava rima*, to *terza rima*, and to unrhymed iambic pentameter. To successive critics, historians, and anthologists the poetry of Wyatt and Surrey was deemed to stand at the fountain-head of a developing lyric tradition, while that of Skelton was presumed to have fed into some kind of literary slough of despond.

Wyatt, the well-travelled and sophisticated courtier-diplomat, introduced a full-blooded Petrarchanism to England. He was well read in the tradition of Tuscan lyric poetry that stemmed from Petrarch's *Rime Sparse* and he translated, and freely adapted into English, verses by Petrarch himself and by several of his fifteenth-century disciples, most notably poems by Serafino d'Aquilano (1466–1500). Wyatt's 'epigrams', often eight-line poems modelled on the *strambotti* of Serafino, also suggest a response to the kind of pithy moral observation cultivated at the French court by Clement Marot (1496–1544) rather than to the comparatively prolix tirades of Skelton. Most of these 'epigrams' reflect on the uncertainties and ambiguities of power and on the process of negotiating a way through the thickets of contemporary politics. If, it is optimistically suggested in one of these poems, venomous thorns sometimes bear flowers, so, by a devout analogy, 'every wo is joynid with some welth'; elsewhere, more sanguinely, an enigmatic pistol informs its owner that 'if I be thine enemy I may thy life ende'; in another, a wretched prisoner, whose life seems to be worn away by the 'stynke and close ayer' of his cell, proclaims that his only hope is 'innocencie' while recognizing that although 'this wound shall heale agayne . . . the scarre shall styll remayne'; in yet another, a man conspicuously out of favour at court bitterly sees his former acquaintance crawling from him 'like lyse [lice] awaye from ded bodies'. In lines based on a translation of a section of Seneca's play *Thyestes*, the speaker sees jockeying for power at court as akin to standing on a 'slipper [slippery] toppe', and the potential for redemptive self-knowledge as lying well beyond its narrow and dangerous confines. As Wyatt's satires and certain of his bleaker lyrics (such as 'Who lyst his welthe and eas Retayne') indicate, heavenly thunder rolls around kings' thrones ('*circa Regna tonat*'), bloody days break hearts, and severed heads serve as dire warnings of the force of royal displeasure. In the epistolary address to his friend, 'Myne owne John Poyntz', he purports to 'fle the presse of courtes . . . | Rather then to lyve thrall under the awe | Of lordly lookes' and he proclaims that he cannot honour those that 'settes their part | With Venus and Baccus all ther lyf long'. One of his most anxious poems ('In mornyng [mourning] wyse') pays tribute to the five men beheaded in 1536 for alleged sexual relations with the disgraced Queen Anne Boleyn (a disgrace in which Wyatt himself was also implicated, though his arrest led merely to a spell in the Tower). Few poems of the period convey as vividly the arbitrary shifts in fate and in the exercise of royal power:

> And thus ffarwell eche one in hartye wyse!
> The Axe ys home, your hedys be in the stret;
> The trykklyngge tearys dothe ffall so from my yes [eyes]
> I skarse may wryt, my paper ys so wet.
> But what can hepe [help] when dethe hath playd his part,
> Thoughe naturs cours wyll thus lament and mone?
> Leve sobes therffor, and every crestyn [Christian] hart
> Pray ffor the sowlis [souls] of thos be dead and goone.

Wyatt's poem is ostensibly a Christian valediction which indulges in, rather than forbids, mourning, but it is also a poem which edgily acknowledges the political danger of mourning traitors.

Wyatt's love-poetry suggests an equally intimate acquaintance with the whims and moods of those who possess and manipulate power, though here the power dealt with is both political and erotic. It is essentially a courtly poetry; it assumes an acquaintance with codes of manners and formal approaches, withdrawals and responses; it reads signs and interprets codes; it indulges in elaborate displays of both loyalty and affliction and it plays lyrical surfaces against insecure and often perplexed subtexts. Throughout, the poet casts himself in the role of the unfulfilled Petrarchan lover, albeit one who tends to view his mistresses as fickle rather than as chastely detached and one who cultivates an air of melancholic self-pity. Much of the finest verse has a directness and an immediacy of address. Wyatt poses direct questions ('And wylt thow leve me thus?', 'Ys yt possyble | That hye debate, | So sharpe, so sore, and off suche rate | Shuld end so sone and was begone so late? | Is it possible?', 'What shulde I saye | Sinns [since] faithe is dede | And truthe awaye | From you ys fled?') and he throws down challenges or issues for debate ('Unstable dreme according to the place | Be stedfast ons [once]: or els at leist be true', 'Wythe servyng styll | This have I wonne, | Ffor my good wyll | To be undonne'). He is the self-conscious poet singing the role of the defeated lover in 'My lute, awake!' but in 'They fle from me' and 'Who so list to hunt' he is the courtly male stalker, wooer, and pursuer of female animals, both tame and wild. The domesticated animals that once took bread from the narrator's hand in 'They fle from me' desert him when his fortune shifts and 'all is torned thorough my gentilnes | Into a straunge fasshion of forsaking'.

In what was probably his own first appearance in print in 1542, Surrey, Wyatt's junior by fourteen years, paid posthumous tribute to a poet whose innovations were 'wrought to turne to Britaines gayne'. Wyatt had possessed a head 'where wisdom misteries did frame' and a hand 'that taught what might be sayd in ryme'. If Surrey's poem makes only oblique reference to Wyatt's 'witnesse of faith'—his interlinked paraphrases of the seven Penitential Psalms (Psalms 6, 32, 38, 51, 102, 130, and 143)—it does so as part of an explicitly Christian epitaph in which piety counts for more than courtship. Surrey had, however, clearly been deeply impressed by the novelty and shapeliness of the older poet's borrowings from the Italian and by his recasting of the form of lyrical, amorous verse in English. His own sonnets, which were much admired as pioneer expressions of neo-classical propriety by critics from the sixteenth to the eighteenth century, have an assured regularity which smoothes out Wyatt's occasional metrical awkwardness. They also have a certain glibness which suggests a poet writing to a formula rather than evolving a personal mode of expression. Surrey is at his most expressive when he allows a persona to particularize emotion. His stanzaic poem on the Windsor where he was imprisoned in 1537 ('So crewell prison'), for example, looks back on the lost joys of adolescent friendship, on entertainments, hunts, and tournaments ('On fominge horse with swordes and friendly hertes'), without any need for the traditional moral resort to a reflection on the whims of Fate. The complaint of a grieving wife in 'O happy dames' is also transformed from a public plea for sympathy into a precise evocation of an acute and restless private passion:

> When other lovers in armes acrosse
> Rejoyce their chief delight,
> Drowned in teares to mourne my losse
> I stand the bitter night
> In my window, where I may see
> Before the windes how the cloudes flee.
> Lo, what a mariner love hath made me!

Where Wyatt adapted Petrarch and Petrarchanism to English sounds and into English metres, a good deal of Surrey's verse tends to look back beyond Petrarch to the Latin culture which had informed the development of Tuscan poetry. His debt to Latin verse is most evident in his attempts to echo the syntax and the rhetoric of Virgil in his translations of Books II and IV of the *Aeneid*. An admiration for the sonority of Virgil's poetry was scarcely a new discovery in European humanist circles; the desire to explore a vernacular equivalent to Virgil's formal eloquence was, however, part of a general campaign to reform modern European verse according to Latinate principles. Surrey had before him the pioneer translation of the *Aeneid* by Gavin Douglas who had rendered Virgil's hexameters into lively heroic couplets (or, as he patriotically preferred to call it, 'Scottish metre'). Though Surrey was prepared to lift words, phrases, and even whole lines from Douglas, he made a significant move to unrhymed verse. His choice of an unrhymed pentameter of more or less ten syllables, rather than an approximation to Latin hexameter, had a lasting effect on English poetry.

An Educated Élite: More, Elyot, and Ascham

Wyatt's professed, but unrealized, desire to 'fle the presse of courtes' in order to attain a philosophic calm would probably have been recognized by its first readers as a commonplace which reflected the culture of the Platonic academies of the Renaissance rather than that of a medieval hermitage. The revival of classical learning which had taken place in fifteenth-century Italy had put a particular stress on self-knowledge and on the cultivation of the reasoning faculty through the study of the *literae humaniores*, the body of ancient literature and thought which was regarded as the essential inheritance of modern civilization. A close knowledge of classical Greek and of the philosophy of Plato had come to be particularly esteemed as a means of countering the reductive Aristotelian scholasticism which had dominated the curricula of medieval universities and seminaries. The study of ancient Greek literature, philosophy, and science had been belatedly introduced to England in the 1490s by the priest-scholars William Grocyn (1449–1519) and Thomas Linacre (?1460–1524), both of whom had extended a conventional enough Oxford education by studying Greek in humanist circles in Italy, notably under the Platonist scholar, Angelo Poliziano (1454–94). When in 1516 Richard Fox, Bishop of Winchester, founded Corpus Christi College at Oxford, he made special provision for a lectureship in Greek as a complement to the study of Latin and Divinity. A desire to reform the secular education of boys according to the principles of the new learning also lay behind the foundation of St Paul's School in London by the Cathedral's Dean, John Colet (1466–1519). The English disciples of the Florentine humanists saw the advance of Greek studies as a means of purging both the textual and the spiritual corruptions of the Middle Ages; they were also Platonists to a man. They sought to reinvigorate Church and State alike by impressing on a new ruling élite the importance of the ideals of spiritual integrity and of a commonwealth as free as possible from depravity.

When the great Dutch scholar, Desiderius Erasmus (?1467–1536), paid his extended visits to England in 1499 and in 1509–14, he absorbed the Platonic enthusiasm of the English humanists. Apart from the scholarly rewards of his working relationships with Grocyn, Linacre, and Colet, Erasmus was particularly taken with the mind, character, and company of a younger man, Thomas More (?1477–1535). The contrast between the public careers of Erasmus and More, both of whom were acknowledged to be intellectuals of European renown by the 1520s, serves to illuminate a crisis in humanist thought. It was not a matter of deciding between the alternative claims of the *vita activa* and the *vita contemplativa*, for both men had already determined that their vocation to serve God and the God-given human intellect lay in the sphere of public life. For Erasmus the world was best improved by writing, by education, and by a scholar's freedom of action, not by a direct involvement in state politics; for More, however, the highest duty of a man learned in the theory and practice of ancient government was to serve his king. There were ample precedents in Greek and Roman history to justify both courses of action, though to the majority of humanists Erasmus's scrupulous avoidance of court patronage, court promotion, and court corruption seemed the nobler way. A prince was best counselled against tyranny from a safe distance, ideally through a literature which increasingly took on the nature of an extended political discourse. When More was convicted of high treason against the person and dignity of the tyrannical Henry VIII in 1535 he may have seemed to many of his fellow-humanists to have provided yet another salutary example of the perils and deceptions of public service.

More was himself acutely aware of this humanist dilemma. It was he who in 1505 had issued a translation of the *Lyfe of Johan Picus, erle of Myrandula*, a biography of the leading Platonist, Pico della Mirandola (1463–94), a

Florentine aristocrat who had eschewed both the cloister and the court and who had ended his life as a disciple of the reformist Dominican friar, Savonarola. The distinction between the indirect and general counsel of a philosopher and the active and particular work of a royal counsellor surfaces again at the end of the first book of More's Latin masterpiece, *Utopia* (published in Louvain in 1516 under Erasmus's supervision, but not translated into English until 1551). When Raphael Hythlodaeus (whose surname means 'learned in nonsense') argues with a fictional 'Thomas More' (whose surname Erasmus had playfully rendered into Greek as 'moros'—'a fool'), he takes the purely Platonic view that a sensible man ought to steer clear of state politics. 'If I proposed beneficial measures to some king and tried to uproot from his soul the seeds of evil and corruption', Hythlodaeus insists, 'do you not suppose that I should be forthwith banished or treated with ridicule?' 'More', however, advocates not deserting the immediate needs of the commonwealth. Public life, he proposes, is akin to a ship in a storm which a man should not abandon because he cannot control the winds.

The ambiguity of this dialogue is characteristic of *Utopia* as a whole. It is in every sense the book of a writer playing the role of a sophisticated and elusive 'fool'. It is both an experimental intellectual exegesis in the manner of Plato and a *ballon d'essai*, which has since managed to appeal to an extraordinarily wide range of political opinion (always excepting the Machiavellian). It functions on the principle of juxtaposed and often antithetical ideas, not as a blueprint for future social experiment. During the years 1514–18, when More was at work on *Utopia*, he was also engaged on what proved to be an unfinished *History of King Richard III* (a text which after its belated publication in 1557 helped shape the prejudices of Shakespeare's play). This *History*, written in parallel English and Latin texts, suggests that More was a careful student of the techniques of ancient Roman historians as well as an assembler of anecdotes drawn from contemporary witnesses, prominent amongst whom was his boyhood patron, Cardinal Morton. For More, Richard III is the type of the tyrant, a man physically and mentally corrupted, 'close and secrete, a deepe dissimuler, lowlye of counteynaunce, arrogant of heart, outwardly coumpinable [friendly] where he inwardely hated, not letting to kisse whome he thoughte to kyll'. Richard embodies the shortcomings of a monarchic government and twists the web of loyalties centred on the person of the king for his own benefit. *Utopia*, initially set in the semi-autonomous cities of the Netherlands, speculates about a form of government alien to most other European states of the early sixteenth century. The island which Hythlodaeus describes is a loosely decentralized kingdom ruled by a shadowy, elected monarch who governs with the consent of a council of the great and good. Personal property, money, and vice have been effectively abolished and the root-causes of crime, ambition, and political conflict have been eliminated. It has several religions, all of them officially tolerated, and all of them dominated by the principle of a benevolent Supreme Being. Its priesthood, which includes some women, is limited in numbers because it is open only to the exceptionally pious, 'which means there are very few'. It is a proto-Welfare State in which the old are honoured and the young are taught to be conformist and respectful; dress is uniform and meals are served in communal canteens. The more we know of it, the more Utopia emerges as a society of improbable virtue and equally improbable high-mindedness. It is in fact controlled by a self-perpetuating oligarchy which ultimately functions with the consent of the acquiescent mass of the population and with the forced labour of slaves, disfranchised dissidents, and convicts. Utopia's political and social blessings are countered by its uniformity and its timelessness. It is a place which has abolished original sin, the prospect of redemption, and the idea of history. Nothing changes because its ideology insists that it has fulfilled all human aspirations. For a Christian reader of More's own historical period this 'ideal' must have lain in the realm of the purest and most secular fantasy. *Utopia* should in fact be considered in terms of its exclusive address to a highly educated Renaissance élite. More's 'folly' ended bloodily when he attempted to define Europe according to historically Roman and Catholic boundaries and his King according to the frontiers of national sovereignty; by 1535 the un-placed *Utopia* must have seemed little more than whimsical speculation.

Although More personally fostered the education of his daughter Margaret, he saw the constitution of Utopia as founded on the rule of the oldest male in each household and on the due submission of wives to their husbands. Few humanists were prepared to contemplate the removal of social and educational discrimination against women. Certain well-placed women, notably Henry VIII's daughters Mary and Elizabeth, and their cousin, the brief pretender to Mary's throne, Lady Jane Grey, were given broad and sophisticated educations as a preparation for their public lives, but relatively few other women, even those born into aristocratic households, progressed beyond the acquisition of literacy and the rudiments of Latin. A challenge, led by Erasmus, to older aristocratic prejudices about the instruction of boys, and a desire to extend learning beyond the confines of the clergy, remained, however, one of the central pillars of humanist, and later both Protestant and Jesuit, educational thought. In a society which, with the exception of the persons of the two Tudor Queens, was exclusively dominated by men, the attention of humanist educators was focused on the creation of a cultivated male élite, a ruling class mentally equipped to rule.

The literate and moderately well-educated Henry VIII was the first king of England to write and publish a book—a Latin attack on Luther, known as the *Assertio septem sacramentorum*—which earned him and his successors the papal title of 'Defender of the Faith'. Henry was also, in a self-consciously political way, a patron of literature, which was recognized and honoured in the formal dedications to him of reprinted English classics, of geographical and topographical treatises, and of certain offshoots of the new learning, such as Sir Thomas Elyot's pioneer Latin–English *Dictionary* of 1538. In 1531 Elyot

(?1490–1546) had also inscribed the 'Proheme' of his most influential work, *The Boke named the Governour*, to a King noted for his 'benevolent inclination towards the universall weale' of his subjects. The chief concern of Elyot's book was to demonstrate to a ruling aristocracy that the common good of the realm depended on the proper education of a male upper class. He did not dispute the inherited principle of a single 'soveraigne governour' from whom stemmed order in the state, but he sought to determine that those placed in authority under that sovereign should truly be 'noble wits', trained for public service and capable of broadly advancing the public good. In the twelfth and thirteenth sections of his first book he catalogues examples of well-educated rulers of the past and bemoans the fact that 'noble men be nat as excellent in lernyng as they were in olde tyme amonge the Romanes and grekes'. Although his stress is on the importance of a modern boy's grasp of the grammar of the classical tongues, and on his later advances into the study of rhetoric, cosmography, history, and philosophy, Elyot shows an equal interest in the acquisition of skills in drawing, sculpture, swimming, riding, hunting, music, and dancing. His book is a summary of the broad humanist ideal of aristocratic cultivation tailored to a court and a nobility which looked back nostalgically to fanciful Arthurian codes of chivalry and which attempted to enhance that vision with reference to the modern values embodied in Baldassare Castiglione's *Il libro del cortegiano* (translated into English as *The Courtyer* in 1552–3 by Sir Thomas Hoby (1530–66)).

In one vital sense, however, Elyot was aware that he was writing in and for an age which delighted in scholarly novelty. He was one of the most deliberate and assiduous neologizers of the sixteenth century, a man as proud of his learning as he was of his application of it to the enlargement of his native tongue. In addressing his prospective audience in English and not Latin he acknowledged the need to borrow words 'publicke and commune' from Latin in order to make up for what he saw as the 'insufficiencie of our owne language'. In his *Of the Knowledg whiche maketh a wise man* of 1533 he proudly describes the King himself remarking on the fact that *The Boke named the Governour* contained 'no terme new made by me of a latine or frenche worde, but it is there declared so playnly by one mene or other to a diligent reader that no sentence is therby made derke or hard to understande'. What Elyot referred to as the 'necessary augmentation' of the English language was to include the introduction of such adapted borrowings as 'maturity', 'discretion' and 'industry', though others amongst his new words (such as 'illecebrous', 'pristinate', and 'levigate') failed to establish themselves as indispensable.

In the dedication of his dialogue on the pleasures of archery, *Toxophilus* (1545), to the 'Gentlemen of England', Roger Ascham (1515–68) half apologized for, and half defended, his use of the English language. His gentlemanly dedicatees, he acknowledges, may not share his command of Latin and Greek, but in using the vernacular as his medium he professes to regret the relative inelegance of his native tongue ('every thinge in a maner so meanly, bothe for the matter and handelynge that no man can do worse'). Ascham is assertively nationalistic in his pride in the longbows which had gained the victory at Agincourt, but he maintains an apologetic stance about what he sees as the clumsiness of the native language of the bowman. In *The Scholemaster* (written *c.*1563 and published posthumously in 1570) he returns to the premiss that only Latin and Greek provide 'the trew preceptes, and perfite examples of eloquence' though later in his text he will allow that 'the rudenes of common and mother tonges, is no bar for wise speaking'. Unlike Elyot, he was no great cultivator of Latinate neologisms. *The Scholemaster* attempts to set out, in plain and unfussy English, the advantages and uses of a classical education. It recommends kindness not coercion as the wisest course for a teacher and it recognizes the dangers and limitations of flashy intelligence in a boy ('Quicke wittes commonlie, be apte to take, unapte to keepe ... in most part of all their doinges, over quicke, hastie, rashe, headie, and brainsicke'). His book began, he tells us, with a discussion over dinner at Windsor; it develops as a chatty and discursive series of observations, examples, and anecdotes. He admires Italian culture and the Italian language, but worries about the corruptions of Roman religion and Venetian morals, prejudices he bases on Protestant theology, xenophobia, and a nine days' visit to Venice ('I sawe in that litle tyme, in one Citie, more libertie to sinne, than ever I hard tell of in our noble Citie of London in ix yeare'). If women are notable for their absence from Elyot's *The Governour*, they are conspicuous for their presence in *The Scholemaster*. The book's Preface pointedly refers to Ascham's reading Demosthenes in Greek with Queen Elizabeth as an after-dinner relaxation, and its most famous anecdote, an account of his encounter with Lady Jane Grey (discovered studiously reading Plato while her family was out hunting), is introduced to demonstrate the true pleasures of learning. When Ascham later returns to the praise of Queen Elizabeth's command of ancient and modern languages he flatteringly compares her achievement to that of the cream of her academic male subjects: 'She hath obteyned that excellencie of learnyng, to understand, speake, and write, both wittely with head, and faire with hand, as scarce one or two rare wittes in both the Universities have in many yeares reached unto.' For Ascham, a scholar steeped in liberal humanist concepts and in the experimental theology of the Reformation, knowledge meant freedom. For all its eccentricities, *The Scholemaster* attempts to establish the bases of a discourse on the nature of education in a society. Ascham was also well aware that he was writing for a society which was inclined to accept that the Platonic ideal of a philosopher-king had been realized in the person of a Protestant philosopher-queen.

The Literature of the English Reformation

The English Reformation was alternately initiated, delayed, fostered, reversed, and reshaped by four Tudor monarchs and their ministers. It began with violent severance and ended with an uneasy compromise. When Henry VIII appointed Thomas Cranmer (1489–1556) to the archbishopric of Canterbury in 1532, he promoted a man known to be sympathetic to reform. Cranmer was to become the chief instrument of the King's policy for the removal of papal supremacy in England. When the Pope's long-sought sanction for the King's divorce was denied, it was Cranmer who annulled Henry's marriage to Catherine of Aragon, and he who crowned Anne Boleyn queen in her stead in 1533. It was Cranmer who was chiefly responsible for the promulgation of the 'Ten Articles' in 1536, the first statement of faith issued by the independent English Church, and he who took responsibility for the first official dissemination of the Bible in the English language. It was, however, the King and his Vicar-General, Thomas Cromwell, who set in motion the wholesale dissolution of the monasteries between 1536 and 1539, who created six new bishoprics with cathedrals in defunct abbey churches, and who determined on the destruction of those saints' shrines which had long been centres of pilgrimage (notably, in 1538, that of the early medieval champion of the rights of the Church against the Crown, Thomas Becket).

The dissolution of the monasteries led not only to the extinction of traditional religious communities, to the wholesale destruction of their buildings, and to the dispersal of their historic libraries, but also to vast changes in the ownership of land. The Crown may have felt itself more secure with the power and morale of the Church reduced in proportion to its income, but those who benefited most from the confiscation of monastic, diocesan, and chantry land were laymen, and noblemen and gentlemen in particular. Some seven thousand monks, nuns, and friars were dispossessed in the mid-1530s. A sizeable number of the male religious took on the duties of the secular clergy; some ex-abbots were appointed to bishoprics or became the heads of new cathedral chapters, others lived comfortably in retirement as country squires. The disappearance of the women's communities did, however, leave a hiatus in the development of women's consciousness and culture in England. Despite the traumas occasioned by the destruction of the greater abbeys and the sporadic local attempts to restore the old order, such as the ruthlessly suppressed Pilgrimage of Grace of 1536, later Protestant propaganda fostered a deep and often prurient suspicion of the monastic life which endured until well into the nineteenth century. There was little official mourning for the passing of the religious houses and the culture which had sustained them.

Regardless of the revolutionary nature of his ecclesiastical policies, Henry VIII, who had so stoutly defended the Catholic sacraments against Luther in 1521, remained theologically and liturgically conservative. Under his 'Whip with Six Strings', the Act of Six Articles of 1539, denial of transubstantiation became automatically punishable with burning, communion remained in one kind only, and a reinforcement of the principle of clerical celibacy obliged even Archbishop Cranmer to send his secretly acquired wife back to Germany. When Henry died in January 1547, however, his earlier decision to entrust the education of his son to convinced Protestants meant that in the new reign the pace of Church reform rapidly accelerated. Edward VI, a precocious 9-year-old at the time of his accession, remained under the influence of the powerful Protestant aristocrats, some might even say gangster barons, who served as counsellors during his turbulent six years as king. By order of the Privy Council, images were forcibly removed from churches, clerical marriages were recognized, and further substantial ecclesiastical endowments confiscated by the Crown; the Acts of Parliament against Lollardy and the Act of Six Articles were repealed and in 1549 an Act of Uniformity imposed the English liturgy, as set forth in the new Book of Common Prayer, on all parish churches and cathedrals. In 1552 this relatively conservative liturgy was revised in order to meet the criticisms of prominent continental Protestants who had found a temporary welcome in England. Neither this second Prayer Book nor its major English promoters endured for long. When the sickly Edward died in 1553, his devoutly Catholic sister and successor, Mary, attempted to undo systematically the reforming zeal of the two previous reigns (though the question of the restoration of church land was left in abeyance). Churchmen and -women who opposed her attempts to stamp out what she unequivocally saw as heresy either suffered for their faith at the stake or took refuge abroad. In safe Protestant enclaves in Germany and Switzerland, English exiles imbibed a yet more heady spirit of religious reform, while at home in 1555–6 Archbishop Cranmer, and the former bishops of London, Worcester, and Gloucester— Nicholas Ridley, Hugh Latimer, and John Hooper—became the most prominent victims of a wave of persecution. Mary's short-lived attempt to reconcile England to Rome died with her in November 1558. She left a legacy of bitterness and bigotry which subsequent Protestant historians and propagandists exploited avidly.

The religious and political negatives of Mary's reign were assiduously reversed by Henry VIII's third surviving child, Elizabeth. Largely devoid of particular conviction, though never short of forcefully expressed opinions, Elizabeth chose religious and political expediency, striving throughout her reign to shape and consolidate a national Church which eschewed both Roman excess and Genevan severity. The second Prayer Book of Edward VI's reign was reissued in 1559, with some significantly 'Protestant' nuances removed, and in 1562 the often ambiguous set of doctrinal formulas, known subsequently as the 'Thirty-Nine Articles', was approved by Convocation after Elizabeth had personally interfered with the wording and expression of two of them. The *via media*, the middle way of the Church of England, became the established norm of Elizabethan religious life, imposed by law and generally accepted by the mass of the population. The Anglican settlement was, however, anathematized both by recusant Catholics (especially after Pope Pius V's excommunication of the Queen in 1570) and by an influential number of extreme Protestants who viewed an episcopal Church with a fixed liturgy, calendar, ceremonies, and vestments as unscriptural and corrupt. 'Puritanism', often allied to and inspired by the radical Presbyterian example of John Knox's Scotland, became increasingly vociferous and contentious from the 1570s onwards. It also left its own distinctive mark on the religious and literary history of Britain.

The Reformers of the English Church placed a consistent stress on the use of the vernacular in worship and on the importance of the Holy Scriptures in a scholarly translation which freed them from the distortions and inaccuracies of the Latin Vulgate. The twenty-fourth of Elizabeth's Articles of Religion insisted that 'it is a thing plainly repugnant to the Word of God, and the custom of the Primitive Church' that services should be conducted 'in a tongue not understanded of the people'. Before the principle of a vernacular liturgy had been established, it was already felt, in both conservative and radical circles, that there was a need for an English Bible translated directly from its Hebrew and Greek originals. When Cranmer instructed all parish priests to provide and display an English Bible in their churches in 1538, the text sponsored by the Archbishop and by Thomas Cromwell was that of the lavishly printed 'Great Bible', revised and reissued, under Cromwell's patronage, in 1540. This 'Great Bible' was a revision of the work of several distinct translators, the most important of whom was William Tyndale (?1494–1536). Tyndale's influence on the text of the volume was both covert and posthumous. Having failed to gain official support for his work, he had gone into exile in Germany in 1524. When copies of his translation of the New Testament arrived in England two years later, the Bishop of London, Thomas More's friend and ally, Cuthbert Tunstall, made desperate attempts both to suppress and to discredit them as Lutheran infections. From his new base in Antwerp Tyndale issued translations of the Pentateuch in 1530 and of the Book of Jonah in 1531; he also left a text of the Books of Joshua, Judges, Ruth, Samuel, Kings, and Chronicles in manuscript when he was arrested in 1535. He was executed as a heretic by strangling and burning near Brussels in the October of the following year.

Tyndale expressed a steady confidence both in the 'grace' of the English language and in the potential propriety of, as he put it, a ploughboy's knowing the Scriptures better than a learned bishop. He pre-empted the charge that his native tongue was an unfit vehicle for a translation of the Bible by insisting in his tract *The Obedience of a Christen man* of 1528 that not only did the Greek language agree 'more with the englysh then with the latyne', but the properties of Hebrew agreed 'a thousande tymes moare'. The Hebrew texts, he claimed, could be translated word for word into English 'when thou must seke a compasse in the latyne and yet shalt have moch worke to translate in welfaveredly'. Tyndale's English version is straightforward, homely, unsolemn, and often monosyllabic. His serpent assures Eve with the words 'Tush ye shall not dye' rather than with the more formal 'Ye shall not surely die' of the now familiar 1611 version. He speaks of 'shyre-towns' in Roman Palestine and translates 'centurion' as 'under-captain', but to him are due the coinings of such significant Hebrew-based terms as 'passover' and 'scapegoat'. When

Tyndale renders the Greek words 'ekklesia' and 'presbyteros' into English he opts, however, for the fresh, but accurate, translations 'congregation' and 'senior' rather than for 'church' and 'priest' in order to avoid terms which might have implied that the modern ecclesiastical hierarchy was continuous with that of the age of St Paul. A great deal of Tyndale's pioneer translation survived largely intact, but unacknowledged, as the base from which the English texts of the so-called 'Geneva Bible' of 1560 and of the 'Authorized Version' of 1611 were developed.

The first complete printed English Bible of 1535 was the work of a translator who appears to have been the master of little Greek and distinctly less Hebrew. Miles Coverdale (1488–1568) who, like most of his sixteenth-century successors, took over those books already translated by Tyndale for his edition, added versions of others derived mostly from the Latin text of the Vulgate supplemented by reference to Martin Luther's German Bible. His most lasting impact on English letters was the result of the incorporation of his revised version of the Book of Psalms (1539) into the Book of Common Prayer. As such, Coverdale's Psalter became an integral part of the formal daily worship of the Church of England, ingrained in generations of worshippers through its daily recitation in parish churches and in what the Prayer Book refers to as 'Quires and Places where they sing'. The distinctive 'yeas', 'evens', and 'neithers', which indicate emphases within the original texts, serve to give the English versions a regular and dignified pace which echoes between Psalms expressive of quite different moods. Coverdale's gift for phrasing manages to retain both the solemnity of the Latin Psalter, so long familiar in the worship of the Western Church, and the vivid imagery of the original Hebrew poetry. Mountains skip 'like rammes' in Psalm 114 and in Psalm 65 the valleys 'stand so thicke with corne, that they shall laugh and sing'. The Lord makes 'darknesse his secret place' and 'his pavilion round him, with darke water' in Psalm 18; in Psalm 19, in which 'the heavens declare the glory of God', he comes forth 'as a bridegroome out of his chamber, and rejoyceth as a giant to run his course', while in Psalm 104 he decks himself 'with light as it were with a garment: and spreadest out the heavens like a curtaine'. Certain of Coverdale's most carefully blended phrases (such as the famous 'valley of the shadow of death' of Psalm 23, the description of mariners in Psalm 107 as 'they that goe downe to the Sea in ships', or the haunting mistranslation 'the yron entred into his soule' of Psalm 105) have become so assimilated into spoken English as almost to seem detached from their precise Biblical and liturgical source.

The Book of Common Prayer, to which Coverdale's Psalter was attached, is the statement of one of the most influential liturgical reforms of the sixteenth century, paralleling those of the more conservative Lutheran churches of Germany and those of the Roman Catholic Church set in motion by the Council of Trent. In 1548 Archbishop Cranmer, supported by a committee of scholars, completed the draft of a single, comprehensive and authoritative guide to the future worship of both priest and people in the English Church.

It was designed as a vernacular replacement for the multiple and often purely local Latin rites in use in pre-Reformation England and Wales (notably those of Salisbury, York, Hereford, and Bangor) and for private devotional volumes, breviaries, and prayer books ('Common Prayer' implied public and corporate worship). It was also to serve as a further significant element in the Tudor policy of bringing a degree of uniformity to national life. The 1549 Book of Common Prayer was deliberately open-ended in its eucharistic theology, deliberately conservative in its retention of Mass vestments and in prayers for the dead. As revised in 1552 its emphasis became more Protestant, with, for example, the words 'Mass' and 'altar' omitted from the recast Communion rite. As revised again on the accession of Elizabeth, a certain theological ambiguity crept back into its formulas and expression, much to the subsequent offence of Puritan dissenters. Most of the original wording determined on by Cranmer and his committee remained unaltered despite efforts to curtail, move, or break up certain fixed prayers, addresses, or responses. Cranmer's tact in adapting and simplifying is perhaps best observed in the shapes he evolved for the Morning and Evening Offices, both of them fluent structural developments from the Hours of Prayer used in medieval collegiate and monastic churches and now adapted for use in parish and cathedral alike. The Collects, the short prayers appointed for the major feast-days and Sundays of the Christian year, are, for the most part, careful translations of Latin texts, though Cranmer himself probably added the two first Advent Collects (the second of which famously asks that God might assist the faithful as they 'hear . . . read, marke, learne, and inwardly digest' the Holy Scriptures). The effect of these Collects frequently depends on a balance of synonyms and on a suggestive development of concepts through series of complementary phrases. The second Collect for peace in the 'order for Morning prayer', for example, opens with an address to God as 'the author of peace, and lover of concord, in knowledge of whom standeth our eternal life, whose service is perfect freedom' and the third Evening Collect ('for ayde against all perils') petitions: 'Lighten our darknesse, wee beseech thee, O Lord, and by thy great mercy defend us from all perils and dangers of this night, for the love of thy onely Sonne our Saviour Jesus Christ.' The Book of Common Prayer is distinctive for its general (some might say typically English) avoidance of emotional language and imagery. Though scrupulously Christocentric in its piety, it eschews dwelling on the passion, the wounded body, the saving blood, and the bloody sweat of the Saviour; though insistent on the particular dignity accorded to the Virgin Mary and on 'the one communion and fellowship' of the saints, it refuses to drift towards Mariolatry or to contemplate the agonies of the martyrs; though sure and certain of the Resurrection of the Dead and of the 'unspeakable joyes' of the Heavenly City, it declines to indulge in rapturous previews of Heaven; though it recognizes the 'manifold sinnes and wickednesse' of humanity, it generally abstains from the expression of morbid self-abasement and from threatening sinners with an eternity in hell. The 'middle way' pursued by the Church of England, and later by its imperial daughter Churches, was, from the beginning, significantly defined by the sober beauty and the prescriptive chastity of its liturgy.

Emotionalism and a highly charged description of the sufferings of martyrs were, however, the key to the success of John Foxe's great survey of the persecution of the faithful, the so-called *Book of Martyrs*, first published in English in 1563. His book, approved and officially publicized by Elizabethan bishops, went through four editions in its author's lifetime and was placed next to the Bible on lecterns in many parish churches. Foxe (1516–87), ordained deacon by Bishop Ridley in 1550 according to the form of the new Ordinal, and driven into exile in 1554, was determined to relate the sufferings of English Protestants under Queen Mary to what he saw as the tradition of Christian martyrdom in and by the Western Church. The ambitious full title stressed the urgency of his mission: *Actes and Monuments of these latter and perilous dayes, touching matters of the Church, wherein ar comprehended and described the great persecutions & horrible troubles, that have bene wrought and practised by the Romishe Prelates, speciallye in this Realme of England and Scotlande, from the yeare of our Lorde a thousande, unto the tyme nowe present. Gathered and collected according to the true copies & wrytinges certificatorie as wel of the parties them selves that suffered, as also out of the Bishops Registers, which wer the doers thereof.* Foxe's martyrology attempted to outclass the old legends of the saints by countering them with modern instances of pious resolution. In his first edition he even included a contentiously Protestant Calendar in celebration of the new generation of champions of true Christendom, but, as the new research included in his subsequent editions suggests, he also attempted to undo old superstitions by presenting testimony derived from documentary and oral sources. As a historian he had, however, no use for impartiality. His vigorous side-notes or glosses ('Marke the apish pageants of these popelings', 'This answer smelleth of forging and crafty packing', 'A wholesome company of caterpillars') provide pointers as to how he hopes this text will be read, and his gory wood-block illustrations (showing, for example, a naked Tyndale being strangled, a venerable Cranmer placing his right hand in the flames, and Bishop Bonner clearly enjoying himself as he beats a prisoner in his orchard) serve to underline the theme of the corruption of those who persecute the righteous. For the next two hundred years Foxe's continually reprinted, revised, and vulgarly amplified volume helped to shape the popular myth of the working out of a special providence in the destinies of an elect nation. It presented a series of sensational pictures which suggested that history was a nightmare from which Elizabethan England seemed blessedly to have awoken.

Early and Mid-Sixteenth-Century Drama

The most important effect of the Tudor Reformation on contemporary writing was in many ways the result of its increasingly secular, as opposed to devotional, emphases. The official ideology that preached that Church and Nation were constitutionally linked in the sovereign state and that God was best served in the world and not in the cloister was echoed, parroted, or merely tacitly accepted in a broad range of the literature of the period. The stress on the secular is particularly evident in the prolific development of vernacular drama during the sixteenth century. Protestant suspicion, allied to the disappearance of its old sponsors—the monasteries, the chantries, and the guilds—gradually suppressed local traditions of popular religious drama (though in some towns morality cycles flourished until the 1570s). In London, civic intolerance and government censorship, banning plays which conflicted with authorized religion or which suggested any degree of profanity, steadily determined a shift away from a drama based on sacred subjects. Even given the number of play-texts that survives, any attempt to chart the rise of a secular theatre in the period is hampered by the often random selection of printed volumes, manuscripts, and records which have come down to us. Certain plays or interludes, written to commission or for specific festivities in royal, noble, or institutional halls, were probably regarded as ephemeral pieces while others which circulated as printed texts were neglected or destroyed as theatrical and literary fashions changed.

Skelton's only surviving play, the 'goodly interlude' *Magnyfycence*, was probably written at some point between 1515 and 1523. Although it is an entertainment ostensibly shaped, like the earlier *Mankind*, as an externalized battle between Virtues and Vices for the human soul, its moral concerns seem to be specific rather than general. *Magnyfycence* treats the importance of moderation in the affairs of a great Someone, not the general virtue of circumspection in the life of an Everyman. Very much in the manner of the humanists, it offers indirect advice to a princely figure by warning against pride, corruption, profligacy, and folly. If, as some commentators suppose, the protagonist's situation offers an allegorical reflection of Cardinal Wolsey's extravagant splendour, the play proceeds to represent the stages of a political and moral collapse. 'Magnificence', laudable enough in itself, here is distorted by pride; pride leads to false magnificence, and the decline into false values provokes a fall from both grace and prosperity.

In the hands of John Foxe's friend and ally, the former Carmelite friar, John Bale (1495–1563), the moral interlude was severed from its increasingly weak Catholic doctrinal roots to become a vehicle for Protestant polemic. Bale, an early protégé of Archbishop Cranmer's, was the author of some twenty-one plays, all of them written in the years 1533–43. His *Kyng Johan* of *c.*1536 is often claimed as the first English drama to be based on national history, though it uses that history exclusively to make narrow propagandist points and it balances its gestures towards presenting historically based characters with traditional enough embodiments of virtue and vice. King John, the victim of papal displeasure in the early thirteenth century, is shown as a brave precursor of Henry VIII trying to free 'Widow England' from the oppressive grip of 'the wild boar of Rome'. Bale's *Three Lawes*, and the plays that stem from it, *God's Promises, John the Baptist*, and *The Temptation of Our Lord*, all consider the human corruption of the divine scheme of redemption. All four plays equate the distortion of the pure Law of Christ with the former triumphs of the papal Antichrist, and all four look to individual repentance and general reformation as a means of restoring humankind to grace. When, for example, Christ is tempted by Satan in the fourth play, his adversary approaches in the guise of a dim-witted hermit who at first pretends not to recognize biblical quotations ('We religious men live all in contemplation: | Scriptures to study is not our occupation'). Once exposed for what he really is, he gleefully proclaims to Jesus that his prime allies in his scheme to corrupt the Church will in future be popes.

Very little that indicates a particularly vigorous Catholic response to Protestant dramatic propaganda has survived. Much of the acceptable drama performed or revived in Queen Mary's reign suggests a tactful avoidance of contentious issues. John Heywood (1497–?1579), a loyal Catholic who claimed to have achieved the difficult feat of making the Queen smile, was prepared to expose the long-familiar peccadilloes of hypocritical pardoners and friars, but he chose to do so in the form of untidy farces with tidily orthodox conclusions, such as *The playe called the foure PP* (which ends with a declaration of loyalty to the 'Church Universal') and *The Pardoner and the Friar* (which arbitrarily concludes with attempts by the parson and the constable to drive the hypocrites away). Nicholas Udall (1504–56), a schoolmaster who, despite his earlier unconcealed Protestant sympathies, managed to find favour in the palaces of Queen Mary and of her Lord Chancellor, Bishop Gardiner, concentrated on writing plays for the boys in his charge. The comedies ascribed to Udall, most notably *Ralph Roister Doister* (*c.*1552), suggest a writer, well versed in the work of Plautus and Terence, who possessed a modest talent for finding English equivalents to the stock characters of the ancients. The text of *Ralph Roister Doister* is divided, on the ancient model, into acts and scenes, but its boisterous language, its songs, and its tediously rhymed doggerel are confidently those of modern London and not just a dim reflection of ancient Rome. The influence of Terence also shows in the five-act structure of the anonymous *Gammer Gurtons Nedle*, a comedy first performed at Christ's College, Cambridge, probably in the early 1560s (it was printed in 1575). The play's 'low', rustic, and somewhat slight subject (the loss of Gammer Gurton's needle during the mending of a pair of leather breeches and its painful rediscovery when the owner of the breeches is kicked in the backside) is decidedly unacademic (at least in the narrow sense of that term). Although its author was determined to squeeze what entertainment value he could out of a series of trivial domestic crises, the very shapeliness of the play suggests a degree of subtlety and structural sophistication new in English comedy.

English universities and many of the schools that fed them with literate students shared the pan-European vogue for reviving and performing classical

plays and for sponsoring new entertainments which would show off the
proficiency of their authors and actors. Children's companies, and notably
the boys of the Chapel Royal in London, remained a significant feature in the
development of Elizabethan drama, but it was the revival of interest in classical tragedy that proved decisive in the evolution of a distinctive national mode.
Native English tragedy was distinctly marked by the bloody, high-flown,
and sombre influence of Seneca. Between 1559 and 1561 Jasper Heywood
(1535–98), the younger son of the author of *The playe called the foure PP*, published English translations of Seneca's *Troas*, *Thyestes*, and *Hercules Furens*.
His enterprise was matched in the mid-1560s by workmanlike English versions
of four further tragedies, all by young graduates determined to demonstrate
that the art of the heathen Seneca could provide Christian England with a
lesson in moral gravity and, equally importantly, with a salutary example of
dramatic decorum. His plays were seen as model structures, suggesting the
serene workings out of divine justice and revealing the effects of human
vengeance; they dwelt on the vicissitudes of earthly fortune and they traced
the tragic falls of men of high degree; above all, they expressed pithy moral
sentiments with an exaggeratedly rhetorical flourish.

When Sir Philip Sidney claimed in his *Defence of Poesie* that Thomas Norton
and Thomas Sackville's *Gorboduc* was 'full of stately speeches and well sounding Phrases, clyming to the height of *Seneca* his stile, and as full of notable
moralitie', he was offering what would have struck his contemporaries as
the zenith of praise. *Gorboduc*, sometimes known by its alternative title *The
Tragidie of Ferrex and Porrex*, remains perhaps the most striking and novel of
the dramas produced in the opening years of Queen Elizabeth's reign. It does
more than naturalize Seneca for an educated English audience; it attempts to
harness the potential of national history and myth as a dramatic contribution
to an extended political discourse. The play, first acted by the gentlemen students of the Inner Temple in the January of 1562, was performed again at
court some days later before the Queen herself. Norton (1532–84) is believed
to have contributed the first three acts, Sackville (1536–1608) the last two, but
what particularly marks the play is its consistently high-toned exploration of
the roots of political decay. Its story, derived from Geoffrey of Monmouth's
fanciful history of the descendants of the Trojan Brutus, considers the end of
the dynasty brought about by the follies of the old and the jealousies of the
young (its parallels to *King Lear*, written some forty years later, would have
been evident to Shakespeare's first audiences). As the play's chorus preempt-
ively insists at the end of its first act, its action could provide 'A myrrour . . .
to princes all | To learne to shunne the cause of suche a fall'. At its end, the
dead King Gorboduc's counsellor, Eubulus, is given a speech of some ninety-
nine lines which mourns the loss of national unity and civil order and insists,
with unashamed anachronism, that a proper way forward should have been the
summons of a Parliament that would have appointed royal heirs 'To stay the
title of established right, | And in the people plant obedience | While yet

the prince did live'. It was a warning that was doubtless clear both to an audience of lawyers and to the court of an unmarried Queen. The achievement of *Gorboduc* is not merely political and monitory. The play's effects depend on the steady, intelligent, and dramatic development of its theme and on its spectacle. Each of the acts is introduced by a dumb-show; in the first, accompanied by 'the musicke of violence', six wild men act out a demonstration of the dangers of disunity; in the fourth, the 'musicke of howboies' introduces three Furies in black who drive before them a king and a queen 'who had slaine their owne children'; in the last, 'drommes and fluites' are succeeded by armed men 'in order of battaile' who march about and (again anachronistically) noisily discharge their firearms. Despite the presence of what might strike a twentieth-century reader as an excess of both pomp and pomposity, the text of *Gorboduc* can be seen as setting a standard against which later Elizabethan dramatists had to measure their theatrical ambitions.

The Defence and the Practice of Poetry: Puttenham and the Sidneys

The two most articulate and acute Elizabethan critics of poetry, George Puttenham (?1529–91) and Sir Philip Sidney (1554–86), recognized that they were confronting a crisis in English writing. Puttenham's *The Arte of English Poesie* (1589) and Sidney's *The Defence of Poesie* (1595) endeavour to trace a poetic tradition which embraces the work of the ancient and of selected vernacular poets and they attempt to define a way forward by offering prescriptive definitions. Both men confidently press the case for poetry as the foremost of the human arts and they suggest that its new European refinement ought to be taken as the gauge of true civilization. For Sidney, taking a broad retrospect, 'neyther Phylosopher nor Historiographer coulde at the first have entred into the gates of populer judgements, if they had not taken a great Pasport of Poetry, which in all Nations at this day, wher learning florisheth not, is plaine to be seene, in all which they have some feeling of Poetry'. Poetry, even amongst the marginalized cultures on the fringes of Europe, had always, he insists, acted as the great communicator, and it was, from the first, the encourager of learning. In glancing at those lands where 'learning florisheth not', Sidney notes that in benighted Turkey 'besides their lawe-giving Divines, they have no other Writers but Poets' and that even in Ireland ('where truelie learning goeth very bare') poets are held 'in a devoute reverence' (though he also later recalls the story that Irish bards could rhyme their victims to death by placing poetical curses on them). For modern England, laying claim to membership of the exclusive club of 'learned' nations, the honour it accorded to its poets should be seen as the touchstone of its modern sophistication, even though, as Sidney feels constrained to admit, 'since our erected wit maketh us know what perfection is . . . yet our infected will keepeth us from reaching it'.

Like Sidney's *Defence*, Puttenham's *The Arte of English Poesie* is generally assumed to have been circulated in manuscript for some time before it finally appeared in print. Puttenham, a nephew of Sir Thomas Elyot, shared with his uncle a conviction of the cultural centrality and proper eminence of the cultivated courtier. His treatise, in three books, returns again and again to the notion of the enhancement of the dignity of the modern gentleman poet by the values and social standing of a princely court. The 'courtly makers' of Henry VIII's reign, 'of whom Sir *Thomas Wyat . . . & Henry* Earle of Surrey were the two chieftaines', had been succeeded by 'Noble men and Gentlemen of her Majesties owne servantes, who have written excellently well' (among whom he includes the conspicuously gentlemanly figures of Sidney, Sir Walter Ralegh, and Sir Fulke Greville). Puttenham's carefully developed and scholarly thesis is consequently steeped in the adulatory oils which lubricated the machinery of the Elizabethan state. In the past, he asserts, it was proper that 'all good and vertuous persons should for their great well doings be rewarded with commendation, and the great Princes above all others with honors and praises'. If the ancient poets were 'the trumpeters of all fame', so Puttenham, as the definer of the nature of poetry and an aspirant poet himself, takes the figure of Queen Elizabeth as the focus of his modern enterprise. When he lists 'the most commended writers in our English Poesie' he concludes by trumpeting forth the writerly talents of 'our soveraigne Lady, whose learned, delicate, noble Muse, easily surmounteth all the rest that have written before her time or since, for sense, sweetnesse and subtilltie'. Not only does the Queen exceed 'all the rest of her most humble vassalls' as a practitioner, she is also the subject of his model anagrams and of three of the examples of the pictogrammatic poems, or 'figures', that he prints in his second book ('Of Proportion'). The Queen's 'most noble and vertuous nature' is seen as resembling a spire in a tapershaped lyric; she is compared to a crowned pillar in a columnar poem; and the shape of a 'Roundell or Spheare' is discovered to reflect essential qualities of the nature of God, the World, and the Virgin Monarch ('All and whole and ever alone, | Single sans peere, simple, and one').

In addition to its insistent and sometimes over-ingenious courtliness, Puttenham's *The Arte of English Poesie* also attempts to establish codes of literary good manners. It offers a definition of a canon of acceptable poets: Chaucer and Gower ('both of them I suppose Knightes') provisionally pass muster, but Skelton, 'a rude rayling rimer' and a 'buffon', is banished from the respectable ranks of those more recent 'courtly makers' whose work Puttenham holds up for admiration. The main emphasis of the second and third books of his treatise falls upon attempts to define and explain genre, form, metre, and imagery. Like many later prescriptive literary theorists, he reveals little actual sensitivity to the material with which he deals, and, while making a pretence of disliking 'schollerly affectation' and the 'peevish affectation of words out of the primative languages', he attempts to dazzle his readers with displays of cleverness, with illustrative diagrams, and with a plethora of Greek definitions.

The overall tone of Sidney's *The Defence of Poesie* seems easy and conversational in comparison to Puttenham's portentousness. Sidney begins, offhand-edly enough, with an anecdote derived from his embassy to Germany during which he encountered one of the Emperor's Italian courtiers. This anecdote allows him to make play both with his Christian name (Philip, the 'lover of horses') and with his knightly profession ('Hee sayd, Souldiours were the noblest estate of mankinde, and horsemen the noblest of Souldiours . . . I think he would have perswaded mee to wishe my selfe a horse'). This witty opening gambit serves to alert us to Sidney's fascination with words and to his unpre-tentious projection of himself into his writings. As he gradually develops the strands of his argument in *The Defence of Poesie*, he avoids confronting his readers with what might pass as proofs delivered *de haut en bas* by instead bidding them to question the authority of those practitioners who have allowed poetry to descend to 'the laughing-stocke of children'. His treatise is shaped both by a need to reply to the case put by Plato and his fellow *mysomousoi* or Poet-haters, and by an evident pleasure in displaying his own enthusiasms and observations. If Sidney seems prepared to admit that Plato's intolerance has a validity when directed against sacred and philosophical verse—the poetry most likely to corrode or misrepresent ideas—he is at his most relaxed and eloquent when he expounds the counterbalancing virtues of a form of writing which he sees as primarily offering 'delight'. The philosopher, Sidney argues, teaches obscurely because he addresses himself to 'them that are already taught'; the poet, by contrast, is 'the foode for the tenderest stomacks'. When poetry, and lyric poetry above all, gives delight it also breeds virtue. To illustrate his point he variously cites examples of men finding 'their harts mooved to the exercise of courtesie' by reading medieval romances and of Hungarian soldiers rejoi-cing in 'songes of their Auncestours valour'. He also freely admits how much he was touched by a military ballad sung by a blind fiddler 'with no rougher voyce then rude stile'. When, however, he turns to bemoaning the relative dearth of refined modern love-poetry in English, he speaks as feelingly of amorous verse as he had of the martial, significantly beginning with a chival-ric image: 'But truely many of such writings as come under the banner of unre-sistable love, if I were a Mistres, would never perswade mee they were in love; so coldely they apply fiery speeches, as men that had rather read Lovers writ-ings . . . then that in truth they feele those passions.' For Sidney, despite his merriment and the calculated gentlemanly nonchalance of his final address to his readers as those that have had 'the evill lucke to read this incke-wasting toy of mine', poetry has to be taken seriously because it releases the earthbound mind by elevating and inspiriting it. True poetry draws from the experience of sinful humankind, but it ultimately offers both a vision of freedom and an injection of herculean strength, both a celebration of mortal love and the hope of immortality.

In many ways, the arguments posited in *The Defence of Poesie* are qualified, amplified, and justified by the body of Sidney's work in prose and verse, most of it unpublished at the time of his death in 1586. When he died at Arnhem of wounds received during one of Queen Elizabeth's half-hearted campaigns in support of Dutch independence, he was accorded a hero's funeral in St Paul's Cathedral, 200-odd formal elegies and, some twenty years later, an adulatory biography by Fulke Greville which helped provide the strands from which national myths about suave soldiers and patriotic decorum were woven. The memory of Sidney the courtier, the diplomat, and the soldier became public property; his writings, circulated privately in his lifetime, emerged as crucial to the political, literary, and sexual discourses of the late sixteenth century. The *Arcadia*, his long prose romance interspersed with poems and pastoral elegies, his royal entertainment *The Lady of May*, and his sonnet sequence *Astrophil and Stella* all suggest processes of negotiation, persuasion, self-projection, and self-fashioning which interrelate affairs of state with affairs of the heart. *The Lady of May*, performed before the Queen at Wanstead in 1578 or 1579, takes the form of a dignified dispute between a shepherd and a forester for the hand of the Lady of the title. Having seen the masque the Queen was called upon to act as the judge between the suitors, though, misreading the entertainment's subtext, she is said to have chosen the wrong candidate.

Although the formal speechifying of *The Lady of May* is relieved by the comic Latinate pedantry of the schoolmaster, Rombus ('I am gravidated with child, till I have indoctrinated your plumbeous cerebrosities'), it is the innovative variety, mastery of register, and narrative shaping of *Astrophil and Stella* (written *c*.1582 and published in 1591) that most clearly distinguishes it from Sidney's earlier treatment of the interaction of courtship with the courtly graces. The 108 sonnets, and the eleven songs which diversify the sequence, describe the development of the unrequited love of a star-lover (Gk. *astrophil*) for a distant star (Lat. *stella*). The difference between the two classical tongues from which the names of the lovers are derived itself suggests the irreconcilable nature of the relationship, but Sidney's poems do not merely play with the idea of distance and unattainability nor do they slavishly follow the pattern of amatory frustration and exultation first established in the fourteenth century by Petrarch. Sidney readily acknowledges that he is working in a well-tried Petrarchan tradition, but he rejects the 'phrases fine' and the 'pale dispaire' of earlier love-poets in the third and sixth of his own sonnets and he is prepared to play ironically with the decorative imagery of the Italian imitators of 'poore *Petrarch*'s long deceased woes' in sonnet 15. Where Petrarch's Laura remains coolly unresponsive, Sidney's Astrophil holds to the hope that his Stella might still favour him, and he ends his long campaign aware of his failure, not with Petrarch's expressions of having passed through a purifying spiritual experience. *Astrophil and Stella* is both an extended dialogue with the conventions of the Italian sonneteers and a varied Elizabethan narrative which, by means of a constantly changing viewpoint, considers the developing conflict between private and public obligation. Stella is from the first the ungiving beloved and the generous inspirer of poetry, the object of the poem and the provoker of it, the dumbfounder and the giver of eloquence. The opening sonnet proclaims the ambiguities of the sequence as a whole; the frustrated lover at first searches for the words which 'came halting forth, wanting Invention's stay', but as he nervously bites his 'truant' pen the responsive voice of the Muse (who is also the unresponsive Stella) directs him to 'looke in thy heart and write'. In sonnet 34 the potential confusions and conflicts between public statement and private silence are expressed in the form of an internal dialogue:

> Come let me write, 'And to what end?' To ease
>   A burthned hart, 'How can words ease, which are
>   The glasses of thy dayly vexing care?'
> Oft cruell fights well pictured forth do please.
> 'Art not asham'd to publish thy disease?'
>   Nay, that may breed my fame, it is so rare:
>   'But will not wise men thinke thy words fond ware?'
> Then be they close, and so none shall displease.
>   'What idler thing, then speake and not be hard?'
> What harder thing then smart, and not to speake?
> Peace, foolish wit, with wit my wit is mard.
> Thus write I while I doubt to write, and wreake
>   My harmes on Ink's poore losse, perhaps some find
>   *Stella's* great pow'rs, that so confuse my mind.

Although Stella is portrayed as the enabler of poetry, she is also the star, 'the onely Planet of my light', who in sonnet 68 seeks to quench the star-lover's 'noble fire'. Throughout the sequence, the 'noble' concerns of a soldier and courtier intrude only to be frustrated by a woman who commands chivalric service and who exercises a sometime whimsical authority over those who willingly give her service. She who elevates by virtue of her heavenly nature also degrades. That Stella's star-like authority seems at times to parallel that of the Queen, of whose enigmatic political behaviour Sidney complained in his letters, is scarcely coincidental. The imagery of war moulds the urgent sonnet 20 ('Flie, fly, my friends, I have my death wound; fly'), while the jouster and the knight figure in sonnets 41, 49, and 53; the state of contemporary European politics gives an edge to sonnets 8, 29, and 30 ('Whether the Turkish new-moone minded be | To fill his hornes this yeare on Christian coast'), but as Stella asserts her royal command over Astrophil she effectively distracts and confounds alternative enterprise, interposing her imperial presence and her sovereign will even in the face of courtly debate ('These questions busie wits to me do frame; | I, cumbred with good maners, answer do, | But know not how, for still I thinke of you'). Her face is 'Queen *Vertue*'s court in sonnet 9; her heart is a citadel 'fortified with wit, stor'd with disdaine' in sonnet 12; she seems to allow her lover the 'monarchie' of her heart in sonnet 69, though, as he recognizes at the end of the poem, 'No kings be crown'd but they some covenants make'; in the penultimate sonnet, 107, she emerges as a 'Princesse' and a 'Queene, who from her presence sends | Whom she imployes' and who provokes fools to comment scornfully on the absolute demands of her rule.

The influence of *Astrophil and Stella* on later English sonneteers was profound. Within Sidney's own circle of family and sympathetic friends his sonnets exercised a particular authority over the poetry of his younger brother Robert (1563–1626). Sir Robert Sidney (created Viscount L'Isle in 1605, and Earl of Leicester in 1618) left his surviving poems in a manuscript collection which was edited and published in its entirety only in 1984. His sonnets, like his brother's, are interspersed with longer songs and, though they tend to lack the range, the wit, and the carefully modulated shifts of mood of *Astrophil and Stella*, they too project an often ambiguous picture of a self-fashioning, self-indulging male lover. The sixth song ('Yonder comes a sad pilgrim'), for example, is shaped as a pseudo-medieval dialogue between a pilgrim returning from the East and the Lady to whom he narrates the circumstances of her melancholy and frustrated lover's death ('Near unto the sea this knight | Was brought to his last will; | Present cares were his delight, | Absent joys did him kill'). His most striking poems are characterized by their vividly dark, almost obsessive meditations on what are so often the poetic commonplaces of transience, decay, and dissolution. The brief seventeenth song broods pessimistically on the approach of night and ponders 'what trust is there to a light | that so swift flyes', while the thirty-first sonnet ('Forsaken woods, trees with sharp storms oppressed') considers a devastated winter landscape and contrasts two perceptions of Time: 'they who knew Time, Time will find again: | I that fair times lost, on Time call in vain'. The twenty-sixth sonnet ('Ah dearest limbs, my life's best joy and stay') opens with the complaint of a wounded man contemplating the amputation of his gangrenous limbs, and draws out a parallel between desperate diseases and the state of the crippled and emotionally corrupted lover:

> My love, more dear to me than hands or eyes,
> Nearer to me than what with me was born,
> Delayed, betrayed, cast under change and scorn,
> Sick past all help or hope, or kills or dies;
> While all the blood it sheds my heart doth bleed
> And with my bowels I his cancers feed.

Philip Sidney's fatally, but cleanly wounded, lover of 'Flie, fly, my friends' was the victim of Cupid's darts; his brother's lover is threatened with a lingering, painful, and probably terminal infection.

Mary Sidney (1561–1621), who married Henry, second Earl of Pembroke in 1577, provided a centre for the Sidney circle at her home at Wilton House. At Wilton Philip Sidney wrote the *Arcadia* for her and there she gathered around her a distinguished group of poets, intellectuals, and Calvinistically-inclined theologians all intent on continuing her brother's cultural mission after his untimely death. It was Mary who approved the posthumous publication of Philip Sidney's works and she who made her own quite distinct contribution to English poetry by revising and continuing her brother's verse translation of the Psalms (first published in 1823). This enterprise, essentially in keeping with the devoutly Protestant tone of the little court at Wilton, reveals Mary Sidney as a remarkably resourceful experimenter with words and sounds. Where Philip Sidney had aimed at a dextrous solidity of expression in the versions of the first forty-three Psalms that he had completed, Mary's free translations of the remaining 107 suggest a metrical, lexical, phrasal, and metaphorical variety which is quite her own. In Psalm 58, for example, she rejoices in the justification of the faithful and appeals for wrath to descend on the heads of the un-Godly:

> Lord, crack their teeth: Lord, crush these lions' jaws,
>   So let them sink as water in the sand.
> When deadly bow their aiming fury draws,
>   Shiver the shaft ere past the shooter's hand.
> So make them melt as the dis-housed snail
>   Or as the embryo, whose vital band
> Breaks ere it holds, and formless eyes do fail
>   To see the sun, though brought to lightful land.

In the urgent plea for delivery from those that persecute 'poor me, Poor inno-cent' in Psalm 59 she presents a vivid picture of her foes prating and babbling 'void of fear, | For, tush, say they, who now can hear?'. She expands her version of the terse Psalm 134 into an hour-glass-shaped hymn of praise which opens up finally to a vision of an all-creating God 'Whom Sion holds embow-ered, | Who heaven and earth of nought hath raised'. Where Coverdale speaks of taking 'the wings of the morning' in Psalm 139, Sidney asks the sun to lend 'thy lightful flightful wings'. Where Coverdale had soberly declared that he was 'fearfully and wonderfully made' and that 'though I be made secretly and fash-ioned beneath in the earth, Thine eyes did see my substance', she delights in the idea of God as a careful craftsman knowing 'how my back was beam-wise laid', seeing the 'raft'ring of my ribs' and the covering human flesh in 'brave embroid'ry fair arrayed' like a divine couturier working away 'in shop both dark and low'. Mary Sidney's is one of the most precise, eloquent, and unsolemn Protestant voices of the sixteenth century.

Sixteenth- and Early Seventeeth-Century Prose Fiction

To argue that the English novel, as it was developed in the eighteenth and nine-teenth centuries, grew directly from the native saplings of the prose fiction of the sixteenth century is as unhelpful a historical judgement as to insist that Elizabethan and Jacobean fiction should be judged according to the realist norms evolved by the Victorians. What is significant is that the last quarter of the sixteenth century saw a vast increase in the amount of prose fiction avail-able to the reading public (it has been estimated that three times more fiction was published in the 45-year reign of Queen Elizabeth than had appeared in the eighty preceding years). This explosion of vernacular fiction appears to have established new patterns of reading and writing which have been interpreted all too narrowly as evidence of the rise of 'bourgeois' tastes or seen merely as raw prologues to the imperial theme of the mature English novel. A handful of sixteenth-century texts, most notably Sir Philip Sidney's *Arcadia*, continued to be popular, however, with a wide range of English readers long after the age and the audience for which they were originally written. Sidney's *Arcadia*, first printed in its unfinished, revised form in 1590, and in 1593 published in a new version cobbled together with additions from an earlier manuscript, remained a standard favourite. The university teacher and critic, Gabriel Harvey (*c.*1550–1631), recommended it to readers in 1593 as 'a written Pallace of Pleasure, or rather a printed Court of Honour'; it diverted and inspirited King Charles I during his confinement; and, as late as the early nineteenth century, it delighted Charles Lamb, who, in spite of what he recognized as a certain 'stiffness and encumberment' in the narrative, rejoiced in 'the noble images, passions, sentiments and poetical delicacies of character, scattered all over the Arcadia'.

The ancient, medieval, and modern sources of Sidney's *Arcadia* serve to suggest something of the complexity of its origins and its essentially aristocratic reference. Jacopo Sannazaro's *Arcadia* of 1504, a series of Italian verse eclogues connected by a prose narrative, gave Sidney his structural cue and shaped his conception of the modern pastoral set amid idealized ancient landscapes. Sidney's perspective on the Greek world was, however, probably determined by the third-century account of the miscellaneous adventures of thwarted and separated lovers, Heliodorus's *Aethiopica*. Sidney's replay of European chivalric norms also reveals a debt to medieval romances and particularly to *Amadis of Gaul*, the fifteenth-century story of Spanish origin which, he had noted in his *Defence*, had retained its power to move men's hearts 'to the exercise of courtesie, liberalitie, and especially courage'. Both the so-called *Old Arcadia* (composed *c.*1577–80) and the revised work of *c.*1581–4 consist of complex narrative patterns built around expressions of conflicting attitudes and codes. King Basilius's impulse to withdraw himself and his family into an Arcadian retreat ostensibly represents a vain attempt to escape the fulfilment of a curse. It also suggests an espousal of passivity and inaction which is to be negated by the active series of intrigues indulged in by the two princes, Musidorus and Pyrocles, who intrude themselves into Basilius's pastoral refuge. Sidney seeks to draw out contrasted themes of honour and deception, calmness of mind and discordant passion, cultivated courtesy and rough wooing, gentility and seduction, ordered ceremonial and violence. The first version of his story culminates in a trial for murder and in the meting out of a savage justice (though the situation is happily resolved by the reawakening of the supposedly poisoned king). In the revised text, where Sidney attempted to expunge the offences of seduction and attempted rape, the insertion of new characters and of fresh adventures for existing ones serves to add to the multiple oppositions of behaviour and emotion. His narrative shape is as much clogged with moral reflection and circuitous demonstration as his longer sentences are loaded with simile, metaphor, and conceit. The second 'Book or Act' of the *Old Arcadia* opens, for example, with a description of the feverish disruption brought about by the 'poison' of love: 'In these pastoral pastimes a great number of days were sent to follow their flying predecessors, while the cup of poison, which was deeply tasted of all this noble company, had left no sinew of theirs without mortally searching into it; yet never manifesting his venomous work till once that, having drawn out the evening to his longest line, no sooner had the night given place to the breaking out of the morning's light and the sun bestowed his beams upon the tops of the mountains but that the woeful Gynecia (to whom rest was no ease) had left her loathed lodging and gotten herself into the solitary places those deserts were full of, going up and down with such unquiet motions as the grieved and hopeless mind is wont to bring forth.' The *Arcadia* resembles nothing so much as an elaborate Renaissance pleasure-garden, endlessly and symbolically varied with floral knots and mazes, lodges and bowers, topiary and trellis, the familiar and the rare. It serves as a vital key to the dense interweaving of novelty and tradition in English culture in the late sixteenth century, but the very intensity and scale of its artifice have tended to dispirit those modern readers predisposed to prefer the kinship of the wilder touches of nature to the arts of formal cultivation.

Sidney's *Arcadia* exhibits the sophistication to which much courtly Elizabethan prose fiction aspired. A very different display of narrative sophistication is, however, evident in George Gascoigne's *The Adventures of Master F. J.*, first published in Gascoigne's anthology of his own poetry, prose, and drama, *A Hundreth Sundrie Flowres*, in 1573. Gascoigne (*c.*1534–77) later relegated an emasculated revision of the story to the 'Weedes' section of his later collection *The Posies of George Gascoigne* (1575) where he was at pains to insist in his Preface that his fiction was purely imaginary and that 'there is no living creature touched or to be noted therby'. This Preface may well have been intended to add a new ironic dimension to an already complex narration and to place a fresh emphasis on a fictionality which had failed to impress some literal-minded readers. In the original version of *Master F. J.* Gascoigne comments generally on the amatory affectations of his time and he debunks the posturings of courtly love, but the very structure of his story indicates that he was also a careful craftsman. F. J.'s amorous adventures are recounted by two intermediary narrators, G. T. and his friend H. W. The often comic presentation of a triangle of lovers, subtly framed by H. W. and G. T., effectively counters G. T.'s self-deprecating protestation that he has merely presented his readers with a 'thriftless history'.

A triangular relationship, though a far less interesting one, also figures in John Lyly's *Euphues: The Triumph of Wyt* (1578). The thin plot of *Euphues* is more a vehicle for Lyly's elaborately poised style than an experiment in narrative playfulness or an examination of manners and motives. Lyly (?1554–1606) was essentially more interested in the art of speaking than in the art of telling. His book and its sequel *Euphues and his England* (published in 1580 when the much admired *Euphues* was already in its fourth edition) provided a witty, courtly, rhetorical, and learned *divertissement* fit 'for all gentlemen to read, and most necessary to remember'. Lyly presents his readers with character types (Euphues—'well endowed with natural gifts' or 'witty'; Eubulus—'good counsellor'; Philautus—'selfish man') and moves his narrative forward, like a debate, by means of shapely oppositional discourses. If both books purport to preach the virtues of experience married to wit, they do so by exposing readers to moral and intellectual choice. Lyly's once celebrated sentences, principally shaped by balanced antitheses, insist on a reader's grasp of the effect of contrasted perceptions and of extremes. When, for example, Eubulus attempts to explain the dangers which threaten an inexperienced and 'high climbing' intelligence, he offers Euphues a string of examples: 'The fine crystal is sooner crazed than the hard marble, the greenest beech burneth faster than the driest oak, the fairest silk is soonest soiled, and the sweetest wine turneth to the sharpest vinegar. The pestilence doth most rifest infect the clearest complexion, and the caterpillar cleaveth unto the ripest fruit. The most delicate wit is allured with small enticement unto vice and most subject to yield unto vanity.' Although the structure of *Euphues and his England* is marginally less dependent on formal speechifying, it too attempts to elucidate the educational ideas contained in treatises such as Ascham's *The Scholemaster*. Like Ascham, Lyly flatters the learning of Queen Elizabeth and her chief courtiers and even allows the infatuated Euphues to write back to Naples, describing England as 'a place in my opinion (if any such may be in the earth) not inferior to a Paradise'. It is, however, a paradise peopled exclusively by gentlemen and ordered by the demands of gentlemanly behaviour.

The fiction of Thomas Nashe (1567–1601) tends to exhibit less confidence in the traditional standing, values, and authority of an aristocratic élite. Like Lyly, Nashe was fascinated by the potential of a learned, innovative, allusive, and polemical English prose; unlike him, he delighted in a precarious virtuosity and he plays with a style which experiments with the effects of lexical novelty, violence, and disconnection. He allows his various narrators to express themselves in styles appropriate both to their condition and to the often disorienting circumstances in which they find themselves. Even when Nashe purports to speak *in propria persona*, as he does in the burlesque encomium of herrings in *Nashes Lenten Stuffe* (1599), his style can veer towards the carnivalesque. When, for example, he glances at the instance of the English ambassador to the Ottoman Sultan ('the *Behemoth* of *Constantinople*') pleading for the release of certain captives, he refers his readers to documentary sources with a neologistic flourish: 'How impetrable [successful] hee was in mollyfying the adamantinest tiranny of mankinde, and hourely crucifier of *Jesus*

Christ crucified, and wrooter up of *Pallestine*, those that be scrutinus to pry into, let them resolve the *Digests* of our English discoveries cited up in the precedence, and be documentized most locupeatley [richly].' Alternatively, when he meditates on the sins of modern London in the extravagant tract *Christs Teares over Jerusalem* (1593), he attacks the 'gorgeous' ladies of the court by evoking horrors of the grave where funereal toads steal 'orient teeth' and engender their young in 'the jelly of . . . decayed eyes' while the hollow eye-sockets ('theyr transplendent juyce so pollutionately employd') are left to become houses for 'shelly snails'. Nashe's various and episodic fictional works have proved difficult to classify. Both *Pierce Pennilesse his Supplication to the Divell* (1592) and *The Unfortunate Traveller. Or The Life of Jacke Wilton* (1594) have been seen anachronistically as a species of 'journalism', as precursors of the picaresque novel, and as experiments in 'realism'. *Pierce Pennilesse*, the complaint of an impoverished professional writer in search of patronage, takes the form of a satirical diatribe against the 'lamentable condition of our times', times which oblige 'men of Arte' to 'seeke almes of Cormorantes'. Pierce desperately bemoans the decline of aristocratic patronage, but in addressing himself to gentlemen whose circumstances parallel his own he seems both to regret the advent of a market economy for literature and also to acquiesce to a necessary evil. Pierce emerges as an Elizabethan malcontent but not as a displaced Romantic outsider or as the self-proclaimed representative of an alienated intelligentsia; he supports the social system as it is, but regrets that it does not work more directly to his benefit. *The Unfortunate Traveller* (dedicated in its first edition to the Earl of Southampton) is equally sanguine in its view of the shortcomings of the ruling class. Jack Wilton's account of his adventures as 'a Gentleman at least . . . a certain kind of an appendix or page belonging or appertaining in or unto the confines of the English court' looks back to the reign of Henry VIII, 'the onely true subject of Chronicles', the patron of chivalry, and the promoter of military enterprise (most of it, we realize, vainglorious). A reader's view of manners and events is controlled by Jack's vigorous and various first-person narration and by his generally unflattering observation. It is not just *what* Jack sees, but *how* he sees. He sharply 'particularizes' the singularly inelegant performances of the noble jousters in Surrey's tournament at Florence; he voyeuristically watches a sordid rape 'thorough a crannie of my upper chamber unseeled', and he makes a point of exactly recording the revolting details of two executions at Rome after disarmingly proclaiming, 'Ile make short worke, for I am sure I have wearyed all my readers'.

Thomas Deloney's four short, best-selling novels, *Jack of Newberie*, the two parts of *The gentle craft*, and *Thomas of Reading*, were all published in the three closing years of the sixteenth century. Each is informed by the values of a hard-working and successful tradesman rather than by those of a gentleman and courtier. Deloney (?1560–1600), the author of ballads on, amongst other things, the defeat of the Spanish Armada, was able to adapt the simple

directness of popular ballad narrative to shape what he described in the address
to shoemakers prefaced to the first part of *The gentle craft* as 'a quaint and
plain discourse . . . seeing we have no cause herein to talk of Courtiers or
Scholars'. *Jack of Newberie* (or *Newbury*) is particularly forthright in its proclamation of the sturdy and independent virtues of a Berkshire clothier in the
reign of 'that most noble and victorious prince', Henry VIII. Its hero, 'a poore
Clothier, whose lands are his looms', ostentatiously shows off both his wealth
and his loyalty to the throne by providing a troop of fifty mounted men clad
in white coats and red caps for the royal campaign against Scotland, and he
later proudly demonstrates to King Henry that he himself is a prince of ants
intent on warding off the assaults of idle, gilded butterflies (doubtless a barbed
reference to the gentlemen of the court). Having feasted his monarch and
impressed him with a pageant performed by local children, Jack emphatically
declines the offer of a knighthood by proclaiming that 'honour and worship
may be compared to the lake of Lethe, which makes men forget themselves
that taste thereof'. This forgetfulness seems to be the vice that separates the
careers of the worthy Jack and the proud Cardinal Wolsey who accompanies
the King; both are poor boys who have made good, but Jack alone emerges as
the possessor of the qualities which make for true social worth. Deloney's
clothiers, shoemakers, and merchants can in some ways be seen as the fore-
runners of the self-confident tradesmen and industrialists of Defoe, Holcroft,
Disraeli, Gaskell, and Shaw; more significantly perhaps, none of them are pictured as social-revolutionaries or as a threat to the stratified class-system of
Tudor England.

The fiction of Robert Greene (1558–92) was clearly calculated to appeal to
a broad audience. Having begun his career with variations on the style, theme,
and shape of Lyly's *Euphues* (such as *Mamillia* of 1583 and *Euphues his Censure
to Philautus* of 1587), Greene experimented with romances which intermix
Sidneian pastoral with Greek romance and proved to be a prolific writer of
pamphlets concerned with low life and urban criminality (such as *A Notable
Discovery of Coosnage* of 1592 and the three animated studies of 'cony-
catching' of the same year). It was, however, with his pastoral romances,
Pandosto. The Triumph of Time (1588) and *Menaphon* (1589), that he most
influenced the developing art of story-telling in prose. Both stories successfully forge together elements of adventure, intrigue, disaster, disguise, malevolent fortune, and relatively happy resolution; both contrast the courtly and
the bucolic and both make significant play with cross-class marriage. The
popular appeal of Greene's abrupt changes of fortune, shifts of mood, and contrasts of tragic and comic elements in *Pandosto* proved sufficiently attractive to
Shakespeare for him to take the plot as the basis of *The Winter's Tale* (*c.*1611).
Where Shakespeare allows all to resolve itself happily, Greene kills off his first
heroine (Bellaria) at the time of her trial and abruptly 'closes up' his comedy
'with a tragical stratagem'—the suicide of King Pandosto. For Greene, a story
describing the irrational behaviour of an enraged king, the trial of a queen, and

the pronouncement of her daughter's bastardy may well have contained too many painful echoes of recent English history for every element in the plot to be blessedly transformed as destiny is fulfilled.

Shakespeare also used the finest of Thomas Lodge's stories, *Rosalynde*, *Euphues golden legacie*, as a quarry for his *As You Like It*. Lodge (1558–1625) pursued a various career as a sailor, physician, translator, critic, and playwright (he collaborated with Greene on the play *A Looking Glasse for London and England* in 1594), but it is as the author of the subtle, delicately observant, pastoral romance *Rosalynde* (1590) that he is best remembered (and not purely for the novel's Shakespearian ramifications). Lodge's other fiction, especially his forays into the historical (*Robert Second Duke of Normandie* of 1591) and the exotic (*A Margarite of America* of 1596), is untidy and restless; *Rosalynde* is by contrast both shapely and equable. As his full title implies, Lodge nods towards the example of Lyly and sprinkles the soliloquies, or 'meditations', of his characters with choice moral observation in the manner of the supposed author, Euphues. More effectively, Lodge also uses these meditations to explore his characters' feelings and motives and to externalize their inner debates. He varies his texture by including a series of songs, sonnets, and eclogues by means of which characters display both their passions and their technical skills. Rosalynde and her cousin Alinda, her admirer Rosader, and his once oppressive brother Saladyne retreat to an Arden which is already the refuge of the deposed King Gerismond. Arden is an untroubled Arcadia, peopled by poetic shepherds and unvexed by winter, rough weather, and man's ingratitude; its lawns are 'diapred with *Floras* riches' and its trees open to form an Amphitheatre 'interseamed with Limons and Citrons'. It is a garden in which the disguised Rosalynde comes to recognize 'that Peasaunts have theyr passions, as well as Princes, that Swaynes as they have their labours, so they have theyr amours, and Love lurkes assoone about a Sheepcoate as a Pallaice'. Lodge's forest lacks the innate contradictions and contradistinctions of Shakespeare's. Instead, it comes to represent an idealized refuge from the jealousies, the enmities, and the cruelties of the outside world. After a necessary period of withdrawal and realignment, it ultimately forms the base from which King Gerismond and his new knights, Rosader and Saladyne, launch their successful military campaign to restore the lost rights of the kingdom.

The intermixture of love and politics, chivalry and philosophy in Lodge's *Rosalynde* complements the more intricate investigation of those themes in Sidney's *Arcadia*. The powerful influence of Sidney's work can, however, be most directly felt in the moulding of the multiple interconnected narratives which make up Lady Mary Wroth's *The Countesse of Montgomeries Urania* (1621). Both the title and the opening line of *Urania* nod respectfully to its distinguished predecessor, and its decorative title-page was specifically designed to remind readers of a genteel derivation which was as much aristocratic as it was literary. The *Urania* is almost certainly the first work of fiction published by an English woman writer and its title-page emphatically lays out her respectable credentials: 'written by the right honourable the Lady Mary Wroath. Daughter to the right Noble Robert Earle of Leicester. And Neere to the ever famous, and renowned Sir Philip Sidney knight. And to ye most exalt[ed] Lady Mary Countesse of Pembroke late deceased.' Mary Wroth (*c.*1586–*post* 1640) adds a decidedly feminine perspective to the Sidneian base from which she worked. Although the *Urania* reveals a pleasure in the rituals of chivalry, in knightly quests, and in the refined pursuit of a love which is both earthly and heavenly, Wroth emerges as a master of character and discourse and as a determined champion of the dignity of her many women characters. Her fictional world may have struck contemporaries as containing a somewhat too exact and offensive transcription of the scandals, traits, shortcomings, and fads of the court of James I (Wroth was obliged to withdraw the book from sale soon after its publication), but to modern readers her interfusion of romance and realism suggests a questioning of the increasingly outmoded codes by which aristocratic society functioned. Wroth's accumulation of story upon story, narrative upon narrative, catalogues a pattern of unhappiness and unfulfilment: love sets traps for the unwary and the vulnerable (particularly women), mistresses are abandoned by bored questors, faithful lovers are spurned and wives oppressed by jealous husbands. In Book I Pamphilia complains that she has been 'tyrannically tortured by love': 'Had I wronged his name, scorned his power or his might, then I had been justly censured to punishment; but ill kings, the more they see obedience, tread the more upon their subjects—so doth this all-conquering king. O love, look on me, my heart is thy prey, my self thy slave. Then take some pity on me.' The *Urania* looks back to medieval romance and to the manner in which those romances were adapted by Elizabethan writers; it also looks forward, albeit stiffly, to the kind of fiction which has little room for conventional and idealized patterns of courtship and emotional fulfilment.

This Island and the Wider World: History, Chorography, and Geography

Although the English Reformation was an emphatic assertion of national independence and mature nationhood, its progress in the reigns of Henry VIII and Edward VI had been marked by an officially sanctioned attack on what later centuries loosely interpreted as the 'national heritage'. The habits, rituals, ceremonies, and religious language of centuries were all subjected to a rigorous process of reform. Monastic foundations, and the pilgrimages to the shrines often associated with them, were suppressed, their buildings demolished or left to decay, and their libraries dispersed. Churches were 'purged' of much of their imagery and even of their secular memorials by the purposeful zeal of often ill-informed iconoclasts. The Church which had once been the chief patron of godliness and good learning and the keeper of a national historical memory found itself deprived of much of its wealth and of many of its traditional educational resources. By the time the tides of destruction, expurgation, experiment, and Roman reaction were stemmed in the reign of Queen Elizabeth a new sense of national tradition had begun to emerge. It was a tradition informed by a generally Protestant and secular spirit, but it was one that inspired a generation of antiquaries to attempt to conserve the evidence of the past and to shape it into a coherent and avowedly propagandist picture of the history and development of the English nation. The antiquaries of the late sixteenth century found ready enough patrons in Matthew Parker (1504–75) and William Cecil, Lord Burghley (1520–98), respectively Elizabeth's first Archbishop of Canterbury and the Queen's chief minister. Both were patrons well aware of the political convenience of historical arguments which stressed the continuing lines of development of Church and Nation alike. Both also recognized that a selective presentation of the materials of the Roman, British, Saxon, Norman, and Plantagenet history of the island could effectively prop up the unsteady Elizabethan religious and political compromise.

John Leland (*c.*1503–52), granted the grand title 'Antiquary Royal' by Henry VIII in 1533, was the founder of this new school of historical and topographical research. Between 1536 and 1542 Leland travelled the length and breadth of England and Wales in an attempt to gather information from the rapidly disappearing records hitherto preserved in monastic libraries. Not only did he avidly snap up what were all too often unconsidered trifles, he also proudly claimed to have visited almost every bay, river, lake, mountain, valley, moor, heath, wood, city, castle, manor-house, monastery, and college in the kingdom. His learning was prodigious, his experience unsurpassed, his notes voluminous, but his projected 'History and Antiquities of this Nation' remained unwritten. Unhinged either by the scope of his 'History' or by the continued threat to the records on which it was to be based, Leland was declared insane in 1550. His surviving manuscript accounts of his journeys and researches, however, proved an invaluable source from which his Elizabethan disciples drew both inspiration and data. They were eventually published in nine volumes as *The Itinerary of John Leland* between 1710 and 1712.

Chief amongst Leland's disciples were the pioneer antiquaries John Stow (1525–1605) and William Camden (1551–1623). Camden followed his master's example and 'perambulated' the island of Britain; Stow, a tailor by profession, concentrated on the single city of whose history and traditions he was inordinately proud, his native London. Stow's *A Survay of London. Conteyning the Originall, Antiquity, Increase, Moderne estate and description of that City* first appeared in 1598 and was reissued in an expanded form in 1603. Its first edition opens with an insistent affirmation of London's honourable antiquity: 'As Rome, the chiefe citie of the world, to glorifie it selfe, drew her originall from the gods, goddesses, and demy gods, by the Trojan progeny, so this famous citie of London for greater glorie, and in emulation of Rome, deriveth itselfe from the very same originall.' For Stow, London's real distinction lay in its actual rather than its legendary history. His account of how the modern city had come into being was based both on a systematic study of written public records and on his own and other people's memories of how things were. He remembers that in his youth 'devout people, as well men as women of this citie' would walk out to give alms to the 'poore bed-rid people' who occupied cottages at Houndsditch, but he adds that the area is now the property of Magdalene College in Cambridge and that the cottages and the charity are gone for ever. When he records details of the 520-foot high steeple of St Paul's Cathedral which was destroyed by lightning in 1561, he intrudes an abruptly inconclusive sentence concerning the failure of the City and its Bishop to rebuild the once famous spire: 'divers models were devysed and made, but little else was done, through whose default, God knoweth; it was said that the money appointed for the new building of the steeple was collected and brought to the hands of Edmond Grendall, then Bishop of London.' This innuendo (dropped in the 1603 edition) is probably an attempt to settle a score with the intolerantly Puritanical Bishop Grindal who in 1569 had sent his chaplain to snoop into Stow's library of 'unlawful . . . old fantastical popish books printed in the old time'. As Stow's *Survay* consistently suggests, however, although historians may discover no pressing reasons to forgive, they have a profound obligation not to forget.

William Camden's great Latin history of Britain and Ireland, *Britannia sive . . . Angliae, Scotiae, Hiberniae . . . ex antiquitate . . . descriptio* (first published in 1587, and amplified in its sixth edition of 1607), is considerably more ambitious in scope than Stow's *Survay*. Camden's aim was both to provide a scholarly 'chorography' (a historical delineation which combined aspects of geography, topography, and archaeology) of the entire British Isles and also to present a case for the distinctive nature of Britain to a European audience (hence his choice of Latin as a medium). Throughout the *Britannia*, Camden argues for the continuity of British traditions while reminding his readers of the European dimension within which British history might be properly studied. He sees both the lineal descent of the English monarchy and the apostolic descent of the English Church as central to his thesis that the island's institutions had developed consistently, organically, and independently since pre-Roman times. The argument was supplemented and reiterated in Camden's chronicle of the reign of Queen Elizabeth, the *Annales Rerum Anglicarum et Hibernicarum regnante Elizabetha* (1615, 1625) and in his delightfully miscellaneous English supplement to the *Britannia*, the frequently reprinted *Remaines of a greater worke concerning Britaine* (1605). The concerns of the *Remaines* range from studies of the origins and development of the English language, through the derivations of names and surnames and the histories of clothes and coins, to examples of rhetorical and proverbial wisdom. Britain, he tells his readers at the outset, is 'the most flourishing and excellent, most renowned and famous isle of the whole world'; it takes 'honour and precedence' over other realms because its 'true Christian religion' was first planted by Joseph of Arimathea, Simon Zelotes, and even (he allows) by the Apostles Peter and Paul. Its ancient line of kings held their throne from God alone, 'acknowledging no superiors, in no vassalage to emperour or Pope'. Camden's *Elizabeth* is described as living up both to her Hebrew name as a fosterer of the 'Peace of the Lord' and to her personal motto, *semper eadem* ('always the same'). In his section on anagrams he is even prepared to assert the justice of the rearrangement of the letters of King James's full name (Charles James Stuart) into the patriotic phrase 'Claims Arthurs seat'.

A similar patriotic assurance informs the two volumes of Raphael Holinshed's *Chronicles* (1577, reissued and posthumously expanded in three volumes, 1586–7). Holinshed (d.?1580) was often a plagiarist and 'his' text, in its expanded form, is semi-original material enhanced by a series of borrowings from earlier historians and contributions from contemporaries. Despite this multiple authorship and the enforced deletion of certain passages which offended Queen Elizabeth's censors, the *Chronicles* possessed sufficient authority and consistent narrative vigour to attract the attention of most of the Elizabethan and Jacobean dramatists who adapted incidents from national history for the stage. 'Holinshed' became an especially important quarry for Shakespeare who drew on it for his two Plantagenet tetralogies as well as for *King John*, *Henry VIII*, *Macbeth*, *King Lear*, and *Cymbeline*. Though Shakespeare substantially altered the story of Lear's misfortunes to suit his particular tragic predilection (in Holinshed's account the King both retains his sanity and regains his throne), in his English history plays he tended to remain faithful to his source as a record of received opinions of character, motive, and political consequence. The King John of the *Chronicles* is the victim of 'the pride and pretended authoritie of the cleargie', and the 'greatlie unfortunate' Richard II is a man 'rather coveting to live in pleasure, than to deale with much businesse, and the weightie affaires of the realme' (though Shakespeare chose to ignore the claim that 'there reigned abundantlie the filthie sinne of leacherie and fornication, with abhominable adulterie, speciallie in the king'). Holinshed's Henry V is a paragon ('a capteine against whom fortune never frowned, nor mischance once spurned . . . his vertues notable, his qualities most praiseworthie'), while his Richard III is a shifty basilisk ('When he stood musing, he would bite and chaw busilie his nether lip . . . the dagger which he ware, he would (when he studied) with his hands plucke up & downe in the sheath to the midst, never drawing it fullie out . . . he was of a readie, pregnant, and quicke wit, wilie to feine, and apt to dissemble'). Despite the aberrant behaviour, the deficient morality, and the frequent sins of usurpation which stain the careers of certain kings, the line of monarchs which marches through the pages of the *Chronicles* effectively stretches out to the crack of doom. England and Scotland are seen as sharing a common history of royal government and destiny, if not as yet a common dynasty. Holinshed's volumes view history from a narrowly monarchic perspective, but if on one level they see the weight of national history and royal tradition as justifying the new emphases of Tudor and Stuart policy, on another they treat the past as a series of dramatic, occasionally tragic, occasionally bathetic, conflicts between personalities.

Patriotic and propagandist zeal was not the exclusive preserve of antiquarians who saw the present as an organic development of patterns implicit in the national past. An emphasis on divine providence, on the providential movement of history, and on the special destinies of Britain also marks the accounts of the often unlearned men engaged in expanding the frontiers of British influence in the world beyond Western Europe. Richard Hakluyt's enterprise in collecting the testimonies and celebrating the exploits of contemporary sailors, traders, adventurers, and explorers in his *Principall Navigations, Voiages, and Discoveries of the English Nation* (1589) enabled both relatively commonplace and quite extraordinary men to speak out plainly and proudly. Hakluyt (1552–1616) expanded his collection into a three-volume work in 1598–1600 (adding the mercantile word 'Traffiques' to his title). It was further supplemented in 1625 by Samuel Purchas's *Hakluytus Posthumus, or Purchas his Pilgrimes, contayning a History of the World in Sea Voyages and Land Travell by Englishmen and others*, a work partly based on data acquired but left unpublished by his predecessor. Samuel Purchas (?1557–1626), a London parish priest, chose his title carefully. His heroes, like Hakluyt's, are pilgrims seeking future promises rather than historic shrines. Their secular quests are both blessed and inspired by God. The voyages described by Hakluyt's and Purchas's explorers are beset by storms, fevers, famines, and enemies to the body and the soul; they are rewarded, as the overall editorial structure implies, by the knowledge that something momentous has been achieved for the good of God's Englishmen. Sailors are enslaved by Pagans and Christians alike and they are menaced both by the determined natives whose cultures they threaten and by the Spanish Inquisition ('that rakehell order') whose principles they defy. English travellers are variously fascinated by the sumptuous entertainment at the Czar's table on Christmas Day ('they were served in vessels of gold, and that as much as could stand one by another upon the tables'), by the Emperor Akbar's ménage ('The King hath in Agra and Fatehpur as they do credibly report 1000 elephants, thirtie thousand horses, 1400 tame deer, 800 concubines; such store of ounces, tigers, buffaloes, cocks and hawks that is very strange to see'), and by the 'great reverence' accorded to the King of Benin ('it is such that if we would give as much to Our Saviour Christ we should remove from our heads many plagues which we daily deserve for our contempt and impiety'). Openings for trade are paramount in the Old World; seizures of Spanish Gold, Anglican missionizing, and advantageous English settlement in the New. Hakluyt's and Purchas's economic pilgrims stumble upon the exotic and the wondrous and they react either with amazement or with an insular intolerance of cultural otherness, struggling to articulate the import of their epiphanies.

Perhaps the most sophisticated of Hakluyt's narrators was Sir Walter Ralegh (?1554–1618). Ralegh, one of Queen Elizabeth's most gifted and arrogantly

assertive courtiers, remained preoccupied with the idea of an English settlement in Guiana to the unhappy end of his career (indeed, his unsubstantiated
insistence on the wonders of this Eldorado contributed to the charges of
treason brought against him by the intransigent and pro-Spanish James I). In
his *The Discoverie of the Large, Rich and Beautiful Empire of Guiana* (published
by Hakluyt) Ralegh stresses that he had come to a paradisal land as its liberator. He tells the Indian chiefs that he represents something finer than their
Spanish oppressors: 'I made them understand that I was the servant of a Queen
who was the great *cacique* [chieftain] of the north, and a virgin, and had more
caciqui under her than there were trees in that island; that she was an enemy
to the *Castellani* [Spaniards] in respect of their tyranny and oppression, and
that she delivered all such nations about her, as were by them oppressed, and
having freed all the coast of the northern world from their servitude, had sent
me to free them also, and withal to defend the country of Guiana from their
invasion and conquest.' Ralegh was a passionate and arrogant Elizabethan but
a less than sympathetic subject of her Stuart successor. He continued to
promote, with equal fervency, the virtues of his Virgin Queen and the divinely
inspired civilizing mission of the English nation.

In Ralegh's first published prose work, *A Report of the Truth of the Fight
About the Isles of the Azores . . . Betwixt the Revenge . . . and an Armada of the
King of Spain* (1591), even the gallantly foolish Sir Richard Grenville's crushing defeat in a naval skirmish with Spanish forces could be safely interpreted
as a victory for the undying English spirit. His ambitious *The History of the
World* (1614), written during the long period of his imprisonment in the Tower
as a convicted traitor, is, by contrast, an extended elegiac reflection on disappointment and defeat. The body of the *History* deals with the negatives of the
rise and fall of the empires of the ancient world but in the Preface Ralegh meditates both on English politics and on human mutability, the 'tide of man's life'
which 'after it turneth and declineth, ever runneth, with a perpetuall ebbe and
falling streame, but never floweth againe'. 'Who hath not observed', he asks
with some bitterness, 'what labour, practice, peril, bloodshed, and crueltie, the
Kings and Princes of the world have undergone, exercised, taken on them, and
committed.' It was a question prompted both by the wealth of the historical
justification at hand and, it would seem likely, by his own King's vindictiveness (James later condemned the *History* as 'too saucy in censuring princes').
In his *History*, as much as in his poem 'What is our life', Ralegh has recourse
to theatrical metaphors ('We are all . . . Comedians in religion', 'God, who is
the Author of all our tragedies, hath written out for us, and appointed us all
the parts we are to play'). Life, seen in a vast historical context or perilously
played out as a versifying courtier, a navigator, and an adventurer, revealed
manifold changes of scene. In its last act it also had a tragic earnestness imposed
by the inevitability of death.

Ralegh, Spenser, and the Cult of Elizabeth

The forty-odd lyric poems attributed to Ralegh often suggest a man self-consciously playing out a role, or, more precisely, a series of roles as the formal knightly lover, as the courtly poet, or as the bold actor in a drama of passion, adventure, and mortality. Many of the fragmentary translations from classical writers included in *The History of the Word*, as well as the later meditations on impending death ('What is our Life?', 'Even such is Time', and the couplet 'On the snuff of a candle, the night before he died'), reinforce the idea of a latter-day stoic whose morale is buttressed by his learning and by the hope of a Christian resurrection. In the case of the haunting pilgrim lyric, 'Give me my scallop shell of quiet' (first published in 1604), he both imagines a heavenly transformation of the earthly body and sports the playfully striking metaphors ('. . . then to test those nectar suckets | At the cleare wells | Where sweetenes dwells. | Drawne up by saints in Christall buckets'). In his ostensibly amorous verse Ralegh revised Petrarchan conventions by the beams of a distinctly Elizabethan moon. Diana's 'faire and harmles light' is praised by association with the Virgin Queen, a Queen whose majesty was evident in the sway she exercised over dedicated nymphs and knights and whose eternal beauty remained unwithered by sublunary changes. For Ralegh at his most blandiloquent the Queen, rather than any mere beloved, is the woman set apart, the inaccessible ideal, the paragon untouched by human mortality, and the mistress who commands love and service. Elizabeth is the 'dear empresse of my heart' and 'a saint of such perfection', but she is also the absent, distant, and chaste lover of Ralegh's adaptation of the ballad 'As You Came from the Holy Land of Walsinghame'. The poem, shaped as a dialogue between a despairing lover and a pilgrim returning from the Marian shrine at Walsingham, links Elizabeth both to the Virgin Queen of Heaven (whose cult had been so diminished in Protestant England) and to a now distant but eternally youthful and queenly 'nymph' who 'sometymes did me lead with her selfe, | And me lovde as her owne'.

Although Ralegh's powerful lyric 'The Lie' erupts with bitterness against a court which glows and shines 'like rotten wood', the body of his poetry is overtly supportive of the Queen-centred courtly culture which Elizabeth's propagandists presented as an ideal. According to the devout fancies of her semi-official panegyrists, the Queen ruled a court which embodied the idea of unchanging perfection. Her person was to be compared to that of the chaste moon-goddesses Diana and Cynthia and her reign likened to the promised return of heavenly justice and peace under the virgin Astraea (who had been translated skywards as the constellation Virgo at the close of the Golden Age). Less paganly, the fact that Elizabeth's birthday fell on the Christian feast of the Nativity of the Blessed Virgin Mary was regarded as a sign of her partaking both of the grace and of the honour accorded to the second Eve. The threat of political weakness implicit in the rule of a woman who had been declared illegitimate by her father's Parliament, and who had been formally excommunicated by the Pope in 1570, was countered by an orchestrated revival of the pomps and principles of medieval chivalry and by annual Accession Day jousts in celebration of Elizabeth as the queen of romance and the fount of honour. Even the inevitable process of human ageing was ignored not simply by poets who professed to see an eternally youthful nymph, but by a royal Council that in 1563 drafted a proclamation forbidding further portraits of the monarch until an approved pattern of representation had been evolved. That pattern was to exhibit the splendour of the Virgin Queen in a series of hieratic painted images showing a sumptuous but depersonalized figure triumphing as a jewel-encrusted imperial artefact.

Elizabeth fashioned herself in her chosen roles as brilliantly and as self-consciously as her faithful courtier Ralegh acted out his. As an astute, wary, and wily Renaissance politician she readily recognized the intermediary influence of secular icons. She accepted the flattering addresses of courtly poets and ideologically approved painters as assiduously as she submitted herself to the equally flattering arts of her maids of honour, her cosmeticians, her wig-makers, and her dress-designers. She showed herself to her people ostentatiously and theatrically and, when occasion demanded, she was a master of emphatic assertions of royal dignity, velvet-gloved menaces, golden promises, and fine words. When, for example, in 1563 uncertainties about the succession to the throne troubled Parliament, she maternally assured members that 'though after my death you may have many stepdames, yet shall you never have a more natural mother than I mean to be unto you all'. The Queen, who liked to dwell on the convenient idea that she was 'married' to England, proclaimed to the Commons towards the end of her reign that 'there will never Queen sit in my seat with more zeal to my country, care to my subjects, and that will sooner with willingness yield and venture her life for your good and safety than myself. And though you have had and may have many princes more mighty and wise sitting in this seat, yet you never had or shall have any that will be more careful and loving'. Perhaps her supreme moment of calculated theatrical bravura was her appropriately costumed address to her troops at Tilbury in 1588 as the Spanish Armada threatened the shores of her kingdom. Elizabeth appeared on horseback armed in a steel breastplate and attended by a page bearing a white-plumed helmet. As she announced in her speech, though she knew she had 'the body but of a weak and feeble Woman', she had 'the heart and stomach of a King, and of a King of England too, and I think foul scorn that Parma or Spain, or any Prince of Europe should dare invade the Borders of my Realm'.

The image of the eloquent and armour-plated Elizabeth of 1588 may well have contributed to the most conspicuous of many tributes to the Queen in Edmund Spenser's *The Faerie Queene*, that of the figure of the warrior virgin, Britomart. Although Spenser (c.1552–99) had modelled Britomart on a parallel figure in Ariosto's *Orlando Furioso* and had adapted her name from that of a character in a poem by Virgil, he was also anxious to suggest to his readers that here was a truly British heroine who had actively assumed the port of Mars. Elizabeth is effectively present in each of the six massive books of *The Faerie Queene*. She is the 'Magnificent Empresse' to whom the poem is dedicated (or, rather, 'consecrated'); she is Gloriana, 'that greatest Glorious Quene of *Faerie* lond', who is the fount of chivalry, the 'flowre of grace and chastitie', and the ultimate focus of each of the knightly quests that Spenser sets out to describe; she is the chaste Belphoebe who puts Braggadocchio to flight in Book II and who rescues Amoret from Corflambo in Book IV; above all, her qualities are to be recognized as informing and inspiring the complex expositions of 'morall vertue' pursued as the poem develops towards its intended (but unrealized) climax. In the first three books, published in 1590 (the thirty-first year of the Queen's reign), her dual dignity as Head of State and as Supreme Governor of the Church of England is honoured in allegorical explorations of Holiness, Temperance, and Chastity. The second three books, published in 1596, treat the virtues of Friendship, Justice, and Courtesy, while the incomplete seventh book (represented only by the two so-called 'Mutabilitie Cantos') would have dealt with Constancy, probably as a reflection on the Queen's personal motto, *semper eadem*.

Spenser's grand original scheme for a vast poem in twelve books, each of which was to describe the 'severall adventures' undertaken by knights and knightly dames in honour of the twelve days of Gloriana's annual feast, had been outlined in a letter of January 1589 addressed to Ralegh and published as a Preface to the poem. Gloriana was to be identified with 'the most excellent and glorious person of our sovereine', and the living Queen's virtues were also to be 'shadowed' in the thoughts, words, and deeds of the imagined heroes and heroines who sought the faerie court. Spenser stressed to Ralegh that his poem stood in the epic tradition forged anciently by Homer and Virgil and latterly in Italy by Ariosto and Tasso. Like Virgil, the martial opening lines of whose *Aeneid* were echoed in his own first canto, Spenser was determined to suggest that a modern political settlement was to be seen as legitimized by reference to the mythical 'Trojan' past. His Britomart is descended from 'noble *Britons* sprong from *Trojans* bold' and in canto x of Book II his Sir Guyon discovers volumes concerned with the *'Antiquitie* of *Faerie* lond' and is enthralled by the long account of the historical derivation of Gloriana's royal title from her ancestor, Brutus. Guyon, 'quite ravisht with delight', ends his study by exclaiming with patriotic fervour, 'Deare countrey, o how dearely deare | Ought thy remembraunce, and perpetuall band | Be to thy foster Childe' As was anciently true of the *Aeneid*, Spenser implies that his own poem should be open to interpretation according to a prevalent ideology. Aeneas, the 'goode governour and a vertuous man', had been identified with Augustus; so Elizabeth could be recognized as a Faerie Queene, as a succession of faerie knights and as the descendant of the peripatetic hero whose adventures run like a thread through the various narratives, the 'magnificent' Arthur.

More pervasive than Spenser's debt of honour to Virgil is the influence on *The Faerie Queene* of Ariosto's *Orlando Furioso* (finished 1532 and impressively translated into English by Sir John Harington in 1591) and Tasso's *Gerusalemme Liberata* (1580, 1581; partially translated into English by Richard Carew in 1594). Spenser imitated phrases, verbal patterns, and knightly images from both texts (which he knew in Italian), and he directly borrowed characters, encounters, and incidents, absorptions which would have been taken as laudable examples of intertextuality by a Renaissance audience. Ariosto's and Tasso's lengthy, digressive poems are belated monuments to the revival, or possibly the reinvention of chivalry in Italy. The subjects of both poets stem from a deep fascination at the court of the d'Este family in Ferrara with the north-European Arthurian romance tradition and with the related codes of knightly behaviour. Spenser may have dispensed with Ariosto's specific references to Charlemagne's campaigns against the Saracens and with the setting of Tasso's epic at the time of the First Crusade, but, despite the deliberate vagueness of time and place in his own poem, he was to prove himself equally responsive to the themes, codes, and landscapes of medieval chivalric romance.

Though Spenser looked back on the past from an essentially Renaissance perspective, and with modern Italian models in mind, his allegory and his language suggest a more immediate response to native literary traditions. As with the dense literary allegories of the English Middle Ages, the 'darke conceit' of Spenser's poem requires that its readers be alert to distinct levels of meaning and interpretation, to extended metaphors, to relatively simple comparisons, and to sophisticated rhetorical parallels. A reading of *The Faerie Queene* demands a response both to a literal meaning and to a series of allegorical constructions (historical, moral, mystical, socio–political). Much as his characters face moral choices and dilemmas, so Spenser's readers need both to deconstruct his metaphors and to discriminate between a variety of possible 'meanings'. It is vital to the adventure of reading the poem that its audience should participate in the process of evaluation by throwing a various light on the darkness of the conceit.

Spenser's acknowledgements of a Chaucerian precedent (he not only derives his description of the forest trees in Book I from a passage in the *Parlement of Foules*, but also makes direct reference to the poem in the third canto of Book VI) suggest that he was fully aware of the methods employed by a major medieval allegorist. The Chaucer who is so appreciatively cited as the 'well of English undefyled' and as the 'pure well head of Poesie' was also a major influence on Spenser's style. Although he was acutely aware of the changes in English since the fifteenth century, Spenser's own poetic language was neither a close imitation of the old, nor an assertively modern one. It was an artificial language which served to draw attention to the very artifice of his poem. It recalled the romance through its often archaic terminology, its heraldic adjectives, and its stock comparisons, but it also served to alert readers to the anti-naturalistic tenor of the narratives. When he describes Chaucer's English as 'undefyled' Spenser is also hinting at the nature of his own elevated and formal expression, one which eschews glossy modern neologisms as much as it veers away from the colloquial and the quotidian. The imagined world of Spenser's poem is at once an unlocated never-never land ravaged by beasts and giants and a land of lost content, but his language seeks to affirm a historic sturdiness and a tradition of solid specification. The very stateliness of his lament for the decline of chivalric virtue in the first canto of Book III, though closely modelled on a stanza of Ariosto's, completely lacks the ironic twist of the original:

> O goodly usage of those antique times,
>   In which the sword was servant unto right;
> When not for malice and contentious crimes,
>   But all for praise, and proofe of manly might,
>   The martiall brood accustomed to fight:
> Then honour was the meed of victorie,
>   And yet the vanquished had no despight:
>   Let later age that noble use envie,
> Vile rancour to avoid, and cruell surquedrie [pride or arrogance].

Spenser's English style, for all its historicizing and its artificiality, was to exert a profound influence on those eighteenth- and nineteenth-century poets who sought either to escape from the Latinate conventions and circumlocutions recommended by neo-classical critics or to test their own technical skills against those of an admired master of stanza form and of a distinct 'poetic' language.

The imaginative pictorialism of *The Faerie Queene* also held a special appeal for those who looked back at it through lenses ground by Romantic, Pre-Raphaelite, and neo-Gothic prejudices. All proleptic and anachronistic perspectives have tended to distort the fact that *The Faerie Queene* is emphatically the work of an artist of the international Renaissance. Spenser's epic syncretically blends and antithetically opposes aspects of the old and the new, the Pagan and the Christian, the revived Roman and the residual Gothic, the pastoral and the courtly. Like the allegorical paintings of Mantegna or Botticelli, or the Titian *poesie* produced for the d'Estes and for Philip II of Spain, Spenser's poem incorporates elements of classical philosophy and biblical lore, radical theological redefinition and obstinately conservative mythopoeia, playful frivolity and ponderously learned reference. Like the great Elizabethan country houses built for show by pushily ambitious English noble families in the closing decades of the sixteenth century (for example, Longleat 1568–80, Wollaton 1580–8, and Hardwick 1590–7), *The Faerie Queene* elaborates the setting of courtly ceremonial and lordly entertainment within the context of architectural regularity, ordered display, and shapely structural cross-reference. It is likely that when Spenser foregrounded accounts of buildings, gardens, and pageants in his narrative he intended them to be seen as reflections of Renaissance pictorial and architectural display. His architecture and his horticulture are presented precisely and symbolically while his untamed forests, his thickets, plains, and pastures remain vague (if no less symbolic). Acrasia's Bower of Blisse in Book II, for example, is 'a place pickt out by choice of best alive, | That natures worke by art can imitate'; it has a gate that is 'a worke of admirable wit' and a porch fashioned 'with rare device'. The house of Busyrane in canto xi of Book III is hung with 'goodly arras of great majesty', tapestries 'woven with gold and silke' which graphically represent the 'lusty-hed' of the gods. The Temple of Venus, described by Scudamour in canto x of Book IV, is squarely

> . . . seated in an Island strong,
> Abounding all with delices most rare,
> And wall'd by nature gainst invaders wrong,
> That none might have accesse, nor inward fare,
> But by one way, that passage did prepare.
> It was a bridge ybuilt in goodly wize,
> With curious Corbes [corbels] and pendants graven faire,
> And arched all with porches, did arize
> On stately pillours, fram'd after Doric guize.

Where Spenser's landscapes tend to be generalized, his buildings are solid and spatially imagined and his formal gardens are ordered and ornamentally planted. Each is the occasion of a knightly sojourn, temptation, distraction, or recuperation, but each also helps to stabilize the foundations from which the poem's allegory rises.

Nevertheless, to represent Spenser exclusively as a poet of order, solidity, and stasis is to misconstrue him. Where, on the one hand, he idealized the principles of royal government, gentle blood, and the 'great difference | Betweene the vulgar and the noble seed' (Book II, canto iv), on the other he sees his own political present as marked by signs of decay. The modern world has in Book V run 'quite out of square, | From the first point of his appointed sourse, | And being once amisse growe[s] daily wourse and wourse'. There is a real distinction between the confident optimism of the first three books and the increasing sense of things falling apart in the second three. At the end of Book VI, for example, the rampaging Blatant Beast, who has defamed men with his 'vile tongue' and 'many causelesse caused to be blamed', is temporarily tamed by Sir Calidore. In the closing stanzas, however, the Beast breaks free again and threatens in the present tense as he grows 'so great and strong of late, | Barking and biting all that him doe bate, | Albe they worthy blame, or cleare of crime'. Although the Blatant Beast may be only the embodied spirit of slander, he threatens the untarnished ideals of Gloriana's court as much as the wiles of Duessa, Archimago, or Acrasia have done. Moreover, in the 'Mutabilitie Cantos' the timelessness of Gloriana's rule, and even her seemingly ageless beauty, are challenged by the force of inexorable change.

Neither history nor the image of the perfected earthly kingdom presented in the poem can be held in permanent fixity. In a sense, the contradictions within the allegorical and lexical structure of *The Faerie Queene* seem ultimately to claim an equal status with the poem's representations of harmony and its shadowings of perfection. Some commentators have sought an explanation of this troubling awareness of corruption in Spenser's growing disquiet with the state of Ireland (he had acted as secretary to the Lord Deputy and as one of the 'undertakers' for the English settlement of Munster but he was abruptly driven out in 1598 by the sacking of his country house during the rebellion of the O'Neills). If his *View of the Present State of Ireland* (published posthumously in 1633) proclaims the superiority of modern English government, society, and enterprise over the older patterns of Irish clan loyalty, it also suggests an imperial incomprehension of otherness typical enough of the 'civilized' European colonizer of his time (for W. B. Yeats, writing in 1902 Spenser 'never pictured the true countenance of Irish scenery . . . nor did he ever understand the people he lived among or the historical events that were changing all things about him'). Unsubdued, feudal, rebellious Ireland may well have presented a challenge to any extended idealization of the moral virtues of an imagined chivalric past, but it is also possible that the root of Spenser's disquiet lay in England in the court of the ageing Elizabeth. In *Prosopopoia, or Mother Hubberds Tale*, a couplet satire in the Chaucerian manner, probably written in the late 1570s, he had expressed an old-fashioned distaste for the 'newfangleness', the affectation, and the 'inconstant mutabilitie' of court manners. After the successful publication of the first three books of *The Faerie Queene*, however, Spenser had revisited London under the friendly patronage of Ralegh. His reaction to his visit is most clearly indicated in the allegorical pastoral he wrote when he returned to Ireland, *Colin Clouts come home again* (1595). Although the poetic swain, Colin, adulates the 'presence faultlesse' of the great 'shepheardesse, that *Cynthia* hight' (yet another virginal stand-in for the Queen) and although he admires Cynthia's beauty, power, mercy, and divinity, when he is asked why he has abandoned the court of this paragon he is forced to admit that he has witnessed 'enormities' during his stay:

> Where each one seeks with malice and with strife,
> To thrust downe other into foule disgrace,
> Himselfe to raise: and he doth soonest rise
> That best can handle his deceitfull wit,
> In subtil shifts, and finest sleights devise,
> Either by slaundring his well deemed name,
> Through leasings lewd, and fained forgerie.

This is the culture of the Blatant Beast rather than of Arthurian gentility and under its dire influence even the chastely wise Cynthia seems to falter and lapse into misjudgement.

Late Sixteenth-Century Verse

Some readers, predisposed by a post-Romantic preference for lyric poetry, have tended to regard the epic ambitions of *The Faerie Queene* as something of a distraction from the miscellaneous body of verse that Spenser might have written if he had so chosen. As the thirty-third sonnet of the *Amoretti* (printed 1595) suggests, however, Spenser himself thought the reverse. 'Great wrong I doe, I can it not deny | To that most sacred Empresse my dear dred', he announces by way of apology to his Queen rather than to his Muse, for 'not finishing her Queene of faery'. Both the love-affair that occasioned the sonnets, and the writing of the poems themselves, are later referred to in sonnet 80 as a 'pleasant . . . sport' and as an opportunity to take 'new breath' before returning to a higher vocation. If, as is probable, he began work on his epic in *c.*1579, most of his poetry in other forms seems to have struck Spenser as an intrusion between his grand idea and the proper fulfilment of his project. His earlier work, most notably the twelve eclogues which make up *The Shepheardes Calender* (published in 1579), reveals a poet experimenting with Virgilian pastoral conventions and with a variety of metrical forms, subjects, and voices (ten of the poems are presented as dialogues). It was, however, with the eighty-nine *Amoretti* and the marriage hymn *Epithalamion* which was printed with them that Spenser's lyrical distinction became most evident. The sonnets substantially readjust the Petrarchan model by seeing the mistress not as an unattainable image of perfection, but as a creature reflecting, and sometimes clouding, the glory of her Divine Creator. The sonnets chart the passage of time from the spring of one year to the Lent and Easter of the next (sonnet 68 opens with a direct address to the risen Christ and ends with a pious reminder to the beloved that 'love is the lesson which the Lord us taught'). In some senses *Epithalamion* can be seen as the climactic celebration of the courtship pursued in the sonnets. With its echoes of the Song of Solomon ('Wake, now my love, awake; for it is time') and of the Psalms ('Open the temple gates unto my love') the poem re-enacts the ceremonial and festivities of a marriage, albeit a Christian celebration shot through with pagan reference. Its twenty-four 18-line stanzas, each of which closes with a variation on the same refrain, trace the progress of the bridal couple from a summer dawn to a consummation at nightfall. It delights both in excess (the wine at the banquet is sprinkled on the walls 'that they may sweat, and drunken be withall') and in a counterbalancing decorum (the marriage-bed, from which Puck and 'other evill sprights' are conjured to depart, is chastely illuminated by the moon-goddess, Cynthia, and blessed by Juno, the heavenly patron of 'the laws of wedlock'). Spenser's other nuptial ode, *Prothalamion* (1596), written in honour of the marriage of the two daughters of the Earl of Worcester, is both more formal and more public in tone. It commemorates the journey of the noble brides along a nymph-lined rural Thames to 'merry London', but, on observing certain of the sights of the capital, it also sees fit to introduce a personal complaint about 'old woes' and to nod obsequiously to the Earl of Essex (probably in the hope of redress).

The range of Spenser's poetic achievement is in some important ways representative of the larger ambitions of late sixteenth-century poets and of a general determination not to confine experiment in English verse to one form or type. Although the poetry of the last decades of the century is often marked by an assertive nationalism and by a concern to establish a sophisticated philosophical and political discourse in English, it has more often been seen as notable for the smaller-scale triumphs of a strong, post-Sidneian, lyric impulse. 'Let others sing of Knights and Palladines, | In aged accents and untimely words', Samuel Daniel remarked with obvious reference to *The Faerie Queene* in the forty-sixth sonnet of his *Delia*, 'But I must sing of thee and those faire eyes'. For Daniel (1563–1619) the English model to follow was Sidney, not Spenser. Some twenty-eight of the *Delia* sonnets had originally been published in 1591 as a supplement to an edition of *Astrophil and Stella*. When the fifty sonnets appeared in a separate volume a year later they bore a dedicatory epistle to Mary Sidney which also expressed high-flown admiration for Sir Philip's example. But despite the Sidneian precedent and Daniel's clear debts to Petrarch and to recent Italian and French sonneteers, what most characterizes his poems is an intense delight in the potential richness of English rhythms and the echoing of English speech in English verse (he published *A Defence of Ryme* in 1603 partly as an attempt to refute the 'tyrannicall Rules of idle Rhetorique' which recommended unrhymed verse in the classical manner). In his sonnets he repeats words and, on occasion, re-employs the last line of one poem as the first of another as a means of squeezing meaning, or alternative meanings, from them. Daniel also makes play with inventive verbal and intellectual conceits. 'Swift speedy Time', in sonnet 31, is 'feathred with flying howers [hours]'; winter 'snowes upon thy golden heares [hairs]' in sonnet 33 and sonnet 45 opens with an address to 'Care-charmer sleepe, sonne of the Sable night, | Brother to death, in silent darknes borne'. In several of the most striking sonnets he also recasts situations from classical legend as modern instances: Pygmalion carved 'his proper griefe upon a stone', but the modern poet has to work with Delia's flint (sonnet 13); Delia's self-centredness is exemplified with reference to the fates of Narcissus and Hyacinth (29); the poet is a floundering Leander begging Hero for rescue from the waves (38) and in sonnet 39 his face, 'a volume of despayres', is compared to 'the wayling Iliades of my tragicke wo'. In sonnet 43, Daniel attempts to detach himself from a myopic preoccupation with his frustrated love by patriotically turning his thoughts to the island that bore his mistress. 'Faire *Albion*', victorious over the Armada, is now the 'glory of the North' and has amorously become '*Neptunes* darling helde betweene his arms: | Devided from the world as better worth, | Kept for himselfe, defended from all harmes'. This patriotic urgency later translated itself into a poetic concern with national history, national destiny, and national identity. Daniel's eight books of *The Civil Wars between the two Houses of Lancaster and York* (published between 1595 and 1609) is both a stanzaic exploration of the pre-Tudor crisis in English affairs to which so many of his contemporaries returned for instructive political lessons, and a study of historic character in the manner of the ancient Roman historians. He also pursued a successful career as a court poet and as a deviser of aptly flattering masques for the eminently flatterable King James.

The political developments which marked the often uneasy transition from the sixteenth to the seventeenth century, and from the ebbing optimism of the reign of Queen Elizabeth to the challenges posed by a new dynasty, are commemorated in the twenty-sixth poem of Michael Drayton's sonnet sequence, *Idea* (published in its final version in 1619):

> Calling to minde since first my love begun,
> Th'incertaine times oft varying in their course,
> How things still unexpectedly have runne,
> As't please the fates, by their resistlesse force:
> Lastly, mine eyes amazedly have seene
> Essex great fall, Tyrone his peace to gaine,
> The quiet end of that long-living Queene,
> This Kings faire entrance, and our peace with Spaine,
> We and the Dutch at length our selves to sever;
> Thus the world doth, and evermore shall reele:
> Yet to my goddesse am I constant ever;
> How e'er blind fortune turne her giddie wheele:
> > Though heaven and earth, prove both to me untrue,
> > Yet I am still inviolate to you.

Drayton (1563–1631) ends with the comfort of a Petrarchan commonplace, but his poem charts a series of rifts, rebellions, and revisions which had determined contemporary English civil, Irish, and foreign policy. A parallel series of rifts and revisions determined how Drayton's readers received his work. He tended to despise those gentleman poets 'whose verses are deduced to chambers . . . kept in cabinets, and must only pass by transcription'. Perhaps because of his own relatively humble origins, he proved himself to be a writer determined to secure his own public reputation by continually rearranging, rethinking, and reworking his steadily growing body of verse. *Idea*, first published as *Ideas Mirror* in 1594, was systematically pruned and expanded during the subsequent twenty-five years. It charts a relationship between lovers which is characterized not by distant adoration but by disruptions, absences, squabbles, and protests. The thirty-first sonnet opens with a conversational shrug ('Since ther's no helpe, come let us kisse and part, | Nay I have done'), while the thirty-third employs the imagery of a battle with Eros ('Truce, gentle love, a parly now I crave, | Me thinkes 'tis long since first these warres begun, | Nor thou, nor I, the better yet can have'). Elsewhere the poet parades his intellectual sparrings with this same 'gentle' Eros. In one of the most striking poems (published in the 1599 arrangement), Love 'in a humour', plays the prodigal and, having invited the poet's senses 'to a solemn feast', regales them with drink distilled from tears; at the height of the feast, a drunken Eros 'plays a swagg'ring ruffins part' and, Alexander-like, slays 'his dear friend, my kind and truest heart'. In the twenty-fifth sonnet he insists to the god that he hates him ('which I'de have thee know') and in the twenty-ninth he and Love, like wits in an inn, bandy proverbs but end by learning nothing ('having thus awhile each other thwarted, | Fooles as we met, so fooles againe we parted').

The opening sonnet of *Idea* (addressed 'To the reader') seeks to indicate how that reader might seek to view Drayton's *œuvre*: his verse, he suggests, is 'the true image of my mind | Ever in motion, still desiring change' and his muse is 'rightly of the English straine, | That cannot long one fashion intertaine'. By the final 1619 version of the sonnets Drayton had amply demonstrated the versatility required by this inconstant English muse by publishing in a variety of forms and on a variety of subjects. His *The Shepheards Garland* (1593, revised 1606 and 1619), which takes the form of 'eglogs' (eclogues) in the Spenserian pastoral manner, indulges in praise for Queen Elizabeth (Eglog III) and mourning for Sidney (Eglog IV); *Endimion and Phoebe* of 1595 (which was rewritten as *The Man on the Moone* in 1606) experiments with an Ovidian mythological form; the 'legends' of *Pierce Gaveston* (*c.*1593), *Matilda* (1594), and *Robert Duke of Normandie* (1596) and the ambitiously weighty *Mortimeriados* of 1596 all attempt to deal with subjects from national history. *Mortimeriados*, a study of the turmoil of the reign of Edward II, was expanded with yet more epic pretensions and its seven-line stanzas remoulded as *ottava rima* in imitation of Ariosto, as *The Barons Warres* in 1603. Drayton's determined quarrying of medieval and modern English history for instructive subjects was also evident in two of the more jingoistic *Odes* of 1606, the celebration of new colonial enterprise in 'To the Virginian Voyage' ('You brave heroique minds, | Worthy your countries name, | That honour still pursue, | Goe, and subdue') and the celebrated 'To the Cambro-Britans, and their harpe, his ballad of Agincourt' ('Faire stood the wind for *France*, | When we our sayles advance'). If these two poems contain pre-echoes of the imperial balladry of the late Victorians, *Englands Heroicall Epistles* (1597), twelve pairs of verse-letters supposedly exchanged by historic lovers and modelled on Ovid's *Heroides*, occasionally serves to suggest prefigurations of the static costumed tableaux beloved of early Romantic painters and imitated in wax by Madame Tussaud. Drayton's patriotic ambitions reached a climax in the 30,000 worthy lines of *Poly-Olbion*, a vast topographical study of England and Wales published in two parts in 1612 and 1622. The title, which partly puns on the name 'Albion', is translatable from the Greek as 'having many blessings'. The island described in the thirty 'songs' into which the poem is divided is explored with the chorographic enthusiasm of Camden (from whose research Drayton borrowed). Its rivers teem with fish, its valleys stand thick with corn, and its hills are haunted by shepherds and fairies. Its often legendary Celtic bedrock is overlaid with fertile Roman, Saxon, and Norman soils and is amply watered by streams each of which has its tutelary nymph.

Poly-Olbion, which was dedicated to King James's eldest son Henry, Prince of Wales, perpetually finds occasions for sermons in stones and, thanks to the Arthurian pretensions of the Stuart dynasty, seeks to discover evidence of present good in all historical precedent.

Placed beside the self-assertion, the ebullience, and the nationalism of much of Drayton's work, the poetry of Fulke Greville, first Lord Brooke (1554–1628), seems, to use Drayton's phrase, 'deduced to chambers', excessively private, even despondent. Greville, who published little in his lifetime, made clear how he wished posterity to remember him in the epitaph he composed for his tomb: 'servant to Queen Elizabeth, councillor to King James, and friend to Sir Philip Sidney. Trophaeum Peccati [the trophy or the spoils of sin].' Greville's friendship with, and profound reverence for, Sidney conditioned not simply the flattering biography he wrote of his upright friend but also the censorious remarks that the *Life* contains concerning the reign of Elizabeth and the comparative moral turpitude of the court of King James. Sidney's religious opinions and the example of *Astrophil and Stella* also helped to determine the themes and patterns of Greville's own verse. The earliest lyrics in the posthumously published miscellany, *Caelica* (printed as part of *Certaine Learned and Elegant Workes* in 1633), appear to have circulated in the Sidney circles in the 1580s; the later poems probably date from the early seventeenth century. Taken as a whole, however, the 109 lyrics (41 of them sonnets) radically re-explore Sidneian models and charge them with a distinctive intellectual earnestness and, increasingly, with a Calvinistic gloom. Where Astrophil addresses a single, distant Stella within the developing narrative of a sonnet sequence, Greville's lover focuses his emotional and mental energy on a variety of situations and mistresses (variously named Caelica, Myra, and Cynthia), and interweaves his randomly placed sonnets with other lyrical forms. Love may be, as he describes it in the first of the poems, 'the delight of all well-thinking minds', but throughout the early part of the miscellany he returns again and again to the ideas of impermanence and insecurity in the world, in the individual, and in human relationships. If, as he grants in poem 7, the world is ever moving and the beloved Myra alone seems constant, even she carries in her eyes 'the doome of all Change'. In poem 18 he allows that Caelica finds him changeable but he then turns the accusation round by insisting that it is she who is dominated by ideas of change and contempt. In poem 30 Myra's inconstancy is boldly compared to that of the shifting systems of government in ancient Rome and the sonnet concludes with the reflection that by 'acting many parts' both Rome and Myra have managed to lose their 'commanding arts'. What relates these ostensibly amorous poems to the later religious meditations on the corruption of all human aspiration is the insistent idea that the only unchanging reality is that of a stern, unsmiling, judgmental God. When Greville contemplates the finality of death in poem 87 he is also haunted by the embarrassed exposure of human frailty before the throne of a perfect and sinless Creator:

When as Mans life, the light of humane lust,
In socket of his earthly lanthorne burnes,
That all this glory unto ashes must,
And generation to corruption turnes;
   Then fond desires that onely feare their end,
   Doe vainly wish for life, but to emend.

But when this life is from the body fled,
To see it selfe in that *eternall Glasse*,
Where time doth end, and thoughts accuse the dead,
Where all to come, is one with all that was;
   Then living men aske how he left his breath,
   That while he lived never thought of death.

The poem's shivers of horror at the prospect of eternal condemnation are to some extent conditioned by the intellectual control of the theological drama. Where he had once argued with and on behalf of his mistresses, Greville ends by debating the niceties of the human condition before the tribunal of the last and universal Judge. In poem 98 he sees himself 'wrapt up . . . in mans degeneration' and only released from 'this depth of sinne, this hellish grave' by the mercy of God; in poem 99 he is pinioned and condemned on a 'sp'rtuall Crosse' from which only the sacrifice of Christ will deliver him, and in poem 109 he looks to a 'God unknowne' to redeem 'that sensuall unsatiable vaste wombe | Of thy seene Churche' (the flawed body of believers) from the consequences of the Fall. If, like Donne, Greville attempts to confront God with metaphors which express the paradoxes implicit in theological definition, in certain of his late poems (most notably poem 102, 'The Serpent, Sinne, by showing humane lust | Visions and dreames inticed man to doe | Follies . . .') he attempts, like Milton, to explore the central issues, the contradictions, and even the rational absurdities in the Christian myth of the Fall.

Greville's discursive poems, or 'Treaties' (treatises), on Monarchy, Human Learning, and Wars, are lengthy and somewhat unadventurous extensions of this process of cerebration in verse. A similar didacticism marks Sir John Davies's meditation in quatrains on the nature of man and the immortality of the soul, *Nosce Teipsum* (1599). Davies (1569–1626) is, however, chiefly remembered for his inventive exploration of the signification of dance in *Orchestra Or a Poeme of Dauncing* (1596). The poem, which purports to represent the ingenious arguments put by the suitor Antinous to Penelope in order to 'woo the Queene to dance', relates the plotted movement of formal dance to the rhythms and patterns of a divinely created Nature. Dancing began, Antinous insists, 'when the first seedes whereof the world did spring, | The Fire, Ayre, Earth and Water did agree, | By Loves perswasion, Natures mighty King, | To leave their first disordered combating'. It asserts the regular harmony of the terrestrial order and it mirrors the tidy concert of the cosmos:

Behold the *World* how it is *whirled round*,
And for it is so *whirl'd*, is named so;

> In whose large volume many rules are found
> Of this new Art, which it doth fairely show:
> For your quick eyes in wandring too and fro
>> From East to West, on no one thing can glaunce,
>> But if you marke it well, it seemes to daunce.

The poem takes us through the distinctly un-Homeric steps, turns, and leaps of the court dances of the sixteenth century (the galliard, the coranto, and the lavolta) and, like many early twentieth-century theorists of dance, it attempts to intertwine metaphysical, natural, mythological, moral, and ritualistic arguments as a means of justifying the art of the choreographer.

The concern with celestial harmony and earthly concord which runs through Davies's *Orchestra* ought properly to be seen in the context of the ceremonial, the formal entertainments, and the masques which had increasingly determined the prestige of the courts of Europe in the late Renaissance period. Whether through the employment of professional performers and composers, such as the lutenist John Dowland (1563–1626), or through the active involvement of courtiers themselves (some of whom provided Dowland with lyrics), music, dance, and song formed a vital part in proclaiming the cultural standing of a ruling class. Thomas Campion (1567–1620), poet, critic of poetry, musician, and doctor of medicine, wrote 150 lyrics, many of them with instrumental settings provided by the poet himself. In the early years of the seventeenth century Campion also emerged as an especially prominent composer of masques for the court and for influential noble families. When King James's son Henry Frederick died in 1612, Campion published an elegy which paid tribute to a particularly versatile patron of the arts who had been as adept a performer on the stage and the dance-floor as he had been in the tiltyard ('When Court and Musicke call'd him, off fell armes, | And, as hee had beene shap't for loves alarmes, | In harmony hee spake, and trod the ground | In more proportion then the measur'd sound'). It is, however, as a writer of intense, delicately shaped lyrics, collected as the five *Books of Airs* published between 1601 and 1617, that Campion's own mastery of melodic and metrical proportion becomes most evident. These songs not only suggest the keenness of a musician's ear which delighted in modulation, variation, and repetition, but also fulfil much of Campion's determination to re-create in English the effects of the Latin lyrics of Catullus and Tibullus (his version of Catullus' 'My sweetest Lesbia, let us live and love' is particularly successful). Although his *Observations in the Art of English Poesie* (1602) argues for the primacy of quantitative metres over 'the vulgar and unartificiall custome of riming', and although the poem 'Rose-cheekt *Lawra*, come' exemplifies his sensitive command of a scansion based on the duration of syllables, the majority of his lyrics reveal a mastery of rhyme and varied stanza form. The deftness of many of Campion's adaptations of conventional erotic sentiments, and his fondness for words such as 'bright', 'sun', 'beams', and 'glitter', sometimes serve to conceal the strain of melancholy that lurks in the shadows beyond the sunlit gardens and groves frequented by courtly lovers. He can, at times, use a lyric to suggest, with some cynicism, that both scorn and death can sting:

> When thou must home to shades of underground,
>   And there arriv'd, a new admired guest,
> The beauteous spirits do engirt thee round,
>   White Iope, blithe Helen and the rest,
> To hear the stories of thy finish'd love
> From that smooth tongue, whose music hell can move:
>
> Then wilt thou speak of banqueting delights,
>   Of masks and revels which sweet youth did make,
> Of tourneys and great challenges of knights,
>   And all these triumphs for thy beauties sake.
> When thou hast told these honours done to thee,
> Then tell, O tell, how thou didst murder mee.

Campion's work, for all its miniature delicacy, testifies not simply to the broad sophistication of English secular music in the reigns of Elizabeth and James, but also to the coming of age of the modern English language as an appropriate vehicle for lyrical emotion.

Marlowe and Shakespeare as non-Dramatic Poets

Christopher Marlowe's 'The Passionate Shepherd to His Love' ('Come live with me, and be my love, | And we will all the pleasures prove') was probably the most popular of all Elizabethan lyrics. Marlowe (1564–93) himself quoted it, with a nod and a wink to his audience, in the fourth act of *The Jew of Malta*; Sir Hugh Evans sings a snatch of it in the third act of *The Merry Wives of Windsor*; Ralegh provided a response ('The Nimphs reply to the Sheepheard') and Donne composed the best known of the many parodies of it in his poem 'The Baite'. The body of Marlowe's surviving verse, none of it printed under his name in his lifetime, suggests, however, that his poetic ambitions lay elsewhere than in the lyric. As a student at Cambridge he produced an uneven, and sometimes carelessly offhand, translation of Ovid's *Elegies* into English couplets. At some point later in his career he turned to a Latin poet with whose rhetoric and spleen he evidently sympathized, translating the first book of Lucan's *De Bello Civili* into unrhymed English pentameters (published posthumously in 1600). This account of the war between Caesar and Pompey, with its opening stress on the miseries of civil strife, held an obvious interest for an England periodically reminded by Tudor propagandists of the disruptions of its own earlier civil wars. Lucan's portrait of a reckless Caesar, who declares on crossing the Rubicon 'Here, here, . . . | An end of peace; here end polluted laws; | Hence leagues and covenants; Fortune thee I follow', also doubtless appealed to the author of *Tamburlaine*.

Despite the occasional fire which shoots from Marlowe's version of *Lucans First Booke*, his most substantial achievement in non-dramatic verse remains the 818 lines of the unfinished *Hero and Leander*. The poem, divided into two parts and somewhat stodgily completed with the addition of four further 'sestiads' by George Chapman, was published in 1598. Marlowe turned once again to Ovid for inspiration though he supplemented his reading with a Latin translation of a narrative poem on the fates of Hero and Leander by the fifth-century Greek poet, Musaeus. The tone, the eroticism, and the wry observation of the poem are, however, emphatically Marlowe's. The story of the meeting, the embracing, and the parting of the lovers is told with an amused detachment which systematically undercuts any suggestion of high tragedy in their situation. Marlowe's prim, meticulously dressed Hero, 'whom young Apollo courted for her hair', is contradictorily described as 'Venus' nun'; his hirsute Leander is possessed of an effeminate beauty which serves to make 'the rudest peasants melt' and men in general to swear 'he was a maid in man's attire'. This sexual ambiguity is set to determine both the 'tragedy' and the poem's overall frame of reference. The temple of Venus is decorated with images of 'the gods in sundry shapes, | Committing heady riots, incest, rapes' which are both hetero- and homosexual. When Leander swims naked across the Hellespont, Neptune, mistaking him for Jove's catamite, Ganymede, caresses him in the waves:

> He clapp'd his plump cheeks, with his tresses play'd,
> And smiling wantonly, his love bewray'd.
> He watch'd his arms, and as they open'd wide
> At every stroke, betwixt them would he slide
> And steal a kiss, and then run out and dance,
> And as he turn'd, cast many a lustful glance,
> And threw him gaudy toys to please his eye,
> And dive into the water, and there pry
> Upon his breast, his thighs and every limb
> And up again, and close behind him swim,
> And talk of love.

Here both the god and the youth are denied due tragic dignity. The threat of drowning is confused with that of sexual assault and divine passion is diluted to little more than liquid philandery. Even Leander's protest 'You are deceiv'd, I am no woman, I' sounds the tinkling note of the *faux naif* rather than a sonorous chord of high seriousness.

William Shakespeare's *Venus and Adonis* (1593) shares the Ovidian reference, the irony, and the amused irreverence of *Hero and Leander*. Although Shakespeare (1564–1616) probably lacked the breadth of Marlowe's reading of Greek and Latin literature, and although he had also missed out on the social and intellectual cachet of a university education, his poem suggests that he was measuring himself against the standards set by a rival both on the public stage and in the more private realm of neo-classical narrative verse. *Venus and Adonis*, conspicuously dedicated to the much-wooed bachelor Henry Wriothesley, Earl of Southampton, describes the courtship of a recalcitrant young man by a mature, 'sick-thoughted' goddess. When we first meet the lovers in the early morning of the opening of the poem, Venus has already pounced on her prey; she is leading his horse by one arm, while under the other she grasps the unwilling object of her attentions 'who blush'd and pouted in a dull disdain, | With leaden appetite, unapt to toy; | She red and hot as coals of glowing fire, | He red for shame, but frosty in desire'. Having established these contrasts of red and white, hot and cold, fire and ice, Shakespeare proceeds to build upon them. Their first encounter reaches a preposterous climax when Adonis falls on top of the buxom goddess who has hung so heavily round his neck, but, when Adonis escapes from her to pursue his adolescent fascination with hunting, the poem modulates between comedy and tragedy before lurching towards a bloody denouement. The goddess of love, aware of the mortal threat to Adonis, has the paradoxes of loving and losing, possessing and parting, pleasure and pain, brought home to her. When she catches sight of the gored body she is as flamboyant in her grief as she once was in her wooing. At first, like a snail, she shrinks back in pain; then 'dumbly she passions, franticly she doeth'; finally, when she articulates her agony, she concocts an erotic fantasy of Adonis's fatal embrace:

> But this foul, grim, and urchin-snouted boar,
> Whose downward eye still looketh for a grave,
> Ne'er saw the beauteous livery that he wore;
> Witness the entertainment that he gave.
>   If he did see his face, why then I know
>   He thought to kiss him, and hath kill'd him so.
>
> 'Tis true, 'tis true, thus was Adonis slain:
> He ran upon the boar with his sharp spear,
> Who did not whet his teeth at him again,
> But by a kiss thought to persuade him there;
>   And nuzzling in his flank, the loving swine
>   Sheath'd unaware the tusk in his soft groin.

'Had I been tooth'd like him', Venus confesses as she lovingly expands on the idea of a porcine *Liebestod*, 'with kissing him I should have kill'd him first'.

The 'graver labour' promised in honour of the Earl of Southampton in Shakespeare's dedication to *Venus and Adonis* was probably the far darker, far more conventionally 'tragic' *Lucrece* of 1594. Where the earlier poem had contrasted a passive male sexuality with an active female one, *Lucrece* retells the instructive story of the rape of a virtuous Roman noblewoman by the libidinous Sextus Tarquinius, son of King Tarquin. As Shakespeare reminded his readers in the Argument prefixed to the poem, public reaction to the incident had been instrumental in securing the banishment of the Tarquins and the change of Roman government from a monarchy to a republic. Thus both the labour and the subject demanded *gravitas*. Although the rapist, the victim, and the rape itself are presented dramatically, the poem relies far more on formal soliloquy, static declamation, and rhetorical complaint than did *Venus and Adonis*. Its narrative movement from Tarquin's plotting of his assault through its realization to Lucrece's exemplary death is purposefully staggered by sections which offer analyses of, and metaphors for, characters' motives, pangs, and passions.

Lucrece's resolute response to her violation follows the high Roman fashion of an assertion of personal integrity in the face of disaster: having eloquently denounced her ravisher, she commits suicide. The no less dignified lament of the unnamed female narrator of 'A Lover's Complaint', however, looks less to Roman models than to the late medieval and Tudor tradition of the 'complaint'. The poem, published as an addendum to Shakespeare's *Sonnets* in 1609, represents the confession of a straw-hatted country girl who has come to recognize 'the patterns of [her former lover's] foul beguiling'. She has been taken in by his protests of love, his presents, his 'deep-brained sonnets', and, above all, by his tears; now, in the agony of her desertion she is throwing his lovetokens and the torn remains of his letters into a river. In one sense she resembles the 'poor soul' of Desdemona's 'song of willow'; in another, she is a refiguration of the suicidal Ophelia. More crucially, Shakespeare's original readers would probably have recognized that in placing the poem at the end of his *Sonnets* he was reflecting on the shape of Daniel's *Delia* which had been published in 1592 with the addition of 'The Complaint of Rosamond', an account of the seduction and destruction of Henry II's mistress, 'the Fair Rosamond'. 'A Lover's Complaint' can also be taken as a particularly bitter coda to the *Sonnets*, one which provides a poignant trans-sexual echo of the concern in some of the most striking of the later poems with confusion, frustration, sexual betrayal, and seduction.

Shakespeare's 154 *Sonnets* have generally been recognized as falling into three distinct groups. The first 126 are addressed to a 'fair youth'; the next 26 refer to a new association with the 'Dark Lady'; the last two give a new twist to the erotic theme by playing fancifully with stories of Cupid and the loss of his (phallic) 'brand'. These unmarked divisions contain within them subgroups (sonnets 1–17, for example, encourage the youth to marry, while sonnets 76–86 are disturbed by the threat posed by a rival poet). In the later poems the ambiguous relationship between the narrator, the young man, and the Dark Lady takes on the nature of an emotional triangle in which, as sonnet 144 suggests, the narrator is torn not only between 'Two loves . . . of comfort and despair' but also between the love for the young man and the love for the woman who appears to have seduced him. If these later poems suggest a confusion of motive and an emotional turmoil, they also serve to remind readers that the overall sequence of the *Sonnets* neither traces an autobiographical pattern nor implies a line of narrative development. Although the 'Dark Lady' poems clearly imply a series of dislocated reactions and shifting viewpoints, the ostensibly adulatory poems addressed to the young man ought also to be seen as heterogeneous, and occasionally fraught interrogations of the language and perception of love. Shakespeare both reorders and confounds Petrarchan conventions. In two sonnets, addressed respectively to the man and to the woman—numbers 21 ('So is it not with me as with that Muse, | Stirred by a painted beauty to his verse') and 130 ('My mistress' eyes are nothing like the sun')—the old hyperboles applied to human beauty are qualified and questioned. Elsewhere the poet transfers exaggerated praise from the 'mistress' of earlier sonnet sequences to a 'master'. The 'lovely boy' is famously compared to a summer's day (18); he, the ambiguous 'master-mistress' of the poet's passion, has a woman's face, 'with Nature's own hand painted' (20); he is the 'Lord of my love' to whom the poet is a vassal (26); he is the Muse 'that pour'st into my verse | Thine own sweet argument' (38), and he ennobles the humble poet with a love that is 'better than high birth . . . | Richer than wealth, prouder than garments cost' (91). Where sonnet 54 sees poetry as the distiller of truth, sonnet 55 proudly claims that 'Not marble nor the gilded monuments | Of princes shall outlive this powerful rhyme', and sonnet 81 announces that his name 'from hence immortal life shall have', we neither learn the boy's name nor do we have a precise idea of what he looks like.

Nevertheless, time and mortality haunt the first 126 poems. In sonnet 12 ('When I do count the clock that tells the time') the poet relates arbitrary human measurements of time to those of the biological clock before resorting, almost in desperation, to a plea for procreation as the only defence against death. In the superbly controlled sonnet 64, however, love itself has to be defined against the steady pressure of individual, political, and geographical change:

> When I have seen by Time's fell hand defaced
> The rich proud cost of outworn buried age,
> When sometime lofty towers I see down-razed,
> And brass eternal slave to mortal rage;
> When I have seen the hungry ocean gain
> Advantage on the kingdom of the shore,
> And the firm soil win of the wat'ry main,
> Increasing store with loss and loss with store;
> When I have seen such interchange of state,
> Or state itself confounded to decay,
> Ruin hath taught me thus to ruminate—
> That Time will come and take my love away.
>   This thought is as a death, which cannot choose
>   But weep to have that which it fears to lose.

The assurance of the boy's love may pierce the poet's gloom with an intense joy in sonnets 29 and 30, their courtship may be accompanied with feelings of exhilaration and poetic triumphalism, but the relationship remains chaste and non-sensual. Compared to Marlowe's thrilled imaginings of the naked

Leander, Shakespeare's young man remains as purely aesthetic as he is anonymous. As many of the earlier sonnets suggest, however, all hopes of human perfection and human union are riven by uncertainties and doubts and glancingly overshadowed by guilt and restlessness (lilies fester in sonnet 94, sonnets 109–112 fret about falseness and scandal, and sonnets 118–120 are marked by metaphors of drugs and disease). Insecurity, sexual vulnerability, and self-loathing burst out with an uncommon violence in sonnet 129, the account of an unspecified, but traumatic, spiritual disturbance. The old idealized love has now been swept away by a torrent of revulsion:

> The expense of spirit in a waste of shame
> Is lust in action, and, till action, lust
> Is perjur'd, murd'rous, bloody, full of blame,
> Savage, extreme, rude, cruel, not to trust . . .

As this poem suggests, Shakespeare's *Sonnets* do more than revise the conventions and then reject the courtliness or the mythological paraphernalia of the sonnet sequences of the 1590s. They throb with a new metrical energy, they explore a new emotional range, they wrestle with the implications of a new language, and they enact new dramas within their exact, fourteen-line structures. Above all, they suggest that the faults which make and mar human buoyancy lie not in the stars, nor in a particular unattainable star, but in ourselves.

Theatre in the 1590s: Kyd and Marlowe

The widespread prejudice, which has held sway since at least the middle of the eighteenth century, that Elizabethan literature was dominated by the drama would not have been one that was shared by Shakespeare's educated contemporaries. If the fiction of the period was systematically marginalized by subsequent generations of readers and critics, and if perceptions of its poetry were clouded by a predisposition for lyric verse, the work of its playwrights has long been seen as reflecting something of the glory of the steadily read, readily performed, and much eulogized Shakespeare. To the select, but substantial, audiences who first saw Elizabethan and Jacobean plays performed on the London stage, or perhaps acted outside town during provincial tours by the London companies, Shakespeare himself must have seemed one gifted metropolitan dramatist amongst many, while his dramatic enterprise, like that of his rivals, would probably have been viewed more as entertainment than as high art. Published play-texts purchased for domestic study or private diversion were sometimes pirated from illicit copies or, as was the case of the 'bad' Quarto of *Hamlet* of 1603, clumsily assembled with the aid of the erratic memories of members of the cast. In most cases, the title-pages of published plays bear the name of the acting company for whom they were written rather than the name of the author. The relatively prolific Shakespeare, who prepared his narrative poems for publication in the early 1590s and who probably authorized the appearance of his *Sonnets* in 1609, may well have sought to protect the rights of the companies with which he was associated by reserving the majority of his play-texts for their exclusive use. The first Folio, published posthumously in 1623 by two fellow 'actor-sharers' (shareholders) in the company known as the King's Men, contains thirty-six plays of which eighteen appeared in print for the first time. Ben Jonson, who boldly printed his poems, plays, and masques in 1616 as his *Works*, went to considerable lengths to demonstrate that his plays were to be considered as serious literature and that the actable word deserved the distinction of being transmitted as the readable word. Nevertheless, when Sir Thomas Bodley established his Library at the University of Oxford in 1602, he insisted that it should exclude the kind of ephemera that he referred to as 'idle books and riff raffs' (by which he meant 'almanacks, plays and proclamations'). Modern drama, as Bodley appears to be recognizing, was as transient as it was popular. It was also likely to distract the scholar from more fulfilling demands on his time.

In late sixteenth-century London, however, suburban theatres, outside the control of less than sympathetic City magistrates, had begun to establish themselves as an essential, and internationally acknowledged, part of popular metropolitan culture. They were visited and (fortunately for theatre historians) described and sketched by European visitors; companies of English actors were, in turn, to perform plays on the Continent (Kyd's *The Spanish Tragedy*, for example, was acted at Frankfurt in 1601 and at Dresden in 1626 when its popularity at home was waning). Such prestige, even if qualified by an incomprehension of the English language as a medium, is testimony to the flourish and flexibility of the public theatres and theatre companies of late sixteenth-century London. Both were relatively new creations. A Royal Patent was granted to the Earl of Leicester's men in 1574 and by 1576 James Burbage, a joiner turned actor turned entrepreneur, had recognized the opening presented by royal and aristocratic favour and established a permanent playhouse in Shoreditch. This playhouse, trumpeting its classical pretensions by calling itself the Theatre, signalled the end of the rudimentary performances by actors in inn-yards. The Theatre was followed in 1577 by Burbage's second purpose-built playhouse, the Curtain (also in Shoreditch), and by the more celebrated structures on the south bank of the Thames, the Rose (1587), the Swan (1595), the Globe (1599), and the Hope (1613). From what is known of these theatres, each probably followed a related, pragmatic, but rapidly evolving plan. These wooden, unroofed amphitheatres were either polygonal or so shaped as to allow a polygon to pass itself off as a circle (the 'wooden O' of the Globe referred to in Shakespeare's *Henry V*). It is possible that, both in shape and in orientation, the later playhouses, such as the Globe, contained echoes of the principles of theatre design established by Greek and Roman architects, though the vagaries of the London weather required a roofed stage and unbanked tiers of covered galleries in which richer spectators were seated. In 1597

Burbage attempted a new venture by leasing the remains of the domestic buildings of the disused Dominican Friary at Blackfriars and requesting permission
to convert it into an indoor commercial theatre. Although the move was temporarily blocked by local residents, it was to the new Blackfriars Theatre that
Shakespeare's company, the King's Men, moved in 1609.

A Dutch visitor to Bankside in 1596 claimed that the Swan Theatre held as
many as 3,000 people, a figure which has been recently justified by estimates
that the smaller Rose (the remains of which were excavated in 1989) could hold
some 1,937 spectators, a capacity which was increased to an uncomfortable
maximum of 2,395 when the theatre was rebuilt in 1592. Given London's population of between 150,000 and 200,000 people, this implies that by 1620
perhaps as many as 25,000 theatre-goers per week visited the six playhouses
then working. In 1624 the Spanish ambassador complained that 12,000 people
had seen Thomas Middleton's anti-Spanish political satire *A Game at Chess*.
The theatres that these large audiences patronized were likely to have been
richly decorated according to current English interpretations of Renaissance
ornament. Given the substantial income that these audiences brought in, the
professional actors they saw were expensively, even extravagantly, costumed.
Surviving records indicate, for example, that the wardrobe for Marlowe's
Tamburlaine contained scarlet and purple satin cloaks, white satin and cloth-
of-gold gowns for women characters and, for Tamburlaine himself, a particularly sumptuous doublet in copper lace and carnation velvet; in 1613 the
management of the Globe paid no less than £38 for a costume for Cardinal
Wolsey in Shakespeare's *Henry VIII* (Shakespeare himself had paid £60 for
his large house in Stratford). These costumes may have set the actors apart
from their audiences. They worked without sets but in close physical proximity to a mass of spectators referred to by Jonson as 'a rude, barbarous crew'.
They would scarcely have expected the reverential atmosphere of a modern
auditorium. A company would initially have performed a new play a mere
handful of times, reviving it or adapting it only as occasion, public demand, or
a wide repertory determined. Finally, it should be remembered that the professional companies were composed exclusively of male actors, with boys or,
as seems more likely given the demands of certain parts, young men playing
women's roles.

The evolution of theatre buildings and companies in the last years of Queen
Elizabeth's reign was to some degree paralleled by the rapid development of a
newly expressive blank-verse tragedy. The key figures in this evolution were
Thomas Kyd (1558–94) and his close associate Christopher Marlowe. Kyd's
The Spanish Tragedy: or, Hieronimo is Mad Again, presented at the Rose
Theatre in the early months of 1592 and published anonymously later in the
same year, proved amongst the most popular and influential of all the plays of
the period. It introduced a new kind of central character, an obsessive, brooding, mistrustful and alienated plotter, and it set a pattern from which a line of
dramatic explorations of the theme of revenge developed. Prominent in this

line of 'revenge plays' are Marston's *The Malcontent* of 1604, Middleton's *The Revenger's Tragedy* of 1607, and, above all, Shakespeare's *Hamlet* published in 1603 (though Kyd himself is believed to have written an earlier, now lost, play on the same subject). Although it continued to be revived into the early years of the seventeenth century, *The Spanish Tragedy* ultimately proved to be a play as parodied and ridiculed by other dramatists (notably Jonson) as it had once been flattered by imitation. What particularly established its reputation was its intermixture of dense plotting, intense action, swiftly moving dialogue, and long, strategically placed, rhetorically shaped speeches. The soliloquies of Hieronimo, a father determined to revenge the murder of his son, both gave prominence to an inward drama of private disillusion and created an impression of an agonized soul writhing as it debated with itself. Unsubtle and declamatory these speeches may often seem ('O eyes, no eyes, but fountains fraught with tears; | O life, no life, but lively form of death; | O world, no world, but mass of public wrongs, | Confus'd and fill'd with murder and misdeeds'), but they were integral to the fusion of violent action, exaggerated gesture, and boisterous rhetoric which mark Kyd's theatrical style.

Calculated exaggeration, coupled with a far greater control of metrical pace and inventive poetic effect, help to determine the often startling and disconcerting quality of Marlowe's dramatic verse, verse that brought English iambic pentameter to its first maturity. If we can trust the evidence wrung from Kyd by the Privy Council in 1593, the 'atheistical' disputations found in the lodgings that he shared with his fellow playwright were Marlowe's, not his. If this is indeed so, the 'atheistical' speculations of Marlowe's plays probably stem from a private fascination with 'forbidden' knowledge, with ambition, and with the disruptive leaps of the human imagination which the Elizabethan political and religious establishment would readily have interpreted as seditious. What also emerges from his plays, however, is the equally disruptive awareness that imaginative ambition must, for good or ill, confront its own limits. In Marlowe's first great theatrical success, *Tamburlaine the Great* (published 1590), for example, Tamburlaine sets out to demonstrate that, though he was born a shepherd, his deeds will prove him a lord. Nature, he claims, teaches us all to have aspiring minds, and he, the aspirer *par excellence* will seek to hold 'the Fates bound fast in iron chains, | And with my hand turn Fortune's wheel about'. But Marlowe does not allow such naked military and political ambition to parade itself unchallenged. In the fifth scene of Act II Tamburlaine relishes the prospect of sway in Persia by revealing a commensurate relish for the rolling rhythm of words, names, and reiterations:

> And ride in triumph through Persepolis!—
> Is it not brave to be a king, Techelles!—
> Usumcasane and Theridamas,
> Is it not passing brave to be a king,
> And ride in triumph through Persepolis?

Tamburlaine's subsequent question to his companion, 'Why say, Theridamas, wilt thou be a king?' receives the disenchanted answer, 'Nay, though I praise it, I can live without it'.

Marlowe impels his dramas forwards by evoking the power of dreams and then deflating them. His deflations can be hard-headed refusals to believe in dreams or, sometimes comic, disinclinations to indulge in the fantasies enjoyed by others. Both are equally subversive of pretensions to power. The two parts of *Tamburlaine the Great* (the second written in response to the popularity of the first) confront audiences with a picture of a conquering 'hero', a breaker of moulds and a forger of new orders. Nevertheless, somewhat like those nineteenth-century European writers who belatedly attempted to come to terms with the phenomenon of Napoleon, Marlowe seeks to expose the concept of heroism as well as to praise it. His Tamburlaine is not so much unheroic as hollow. He may not be presented as an unwitting slave to historical or social circumstance, but he is shown as susceptible to the beauty and to the pleas of the beloved Zenocrate and he is finally defeated by Time and Death. Although his aspiration is limitless, his ability to obtain fulfilment is shown as being restricted by forces beyond his control.

A similar pattern can be observed in Marlowe's other tragedies. Although God may seem to be an indifferent observer and although his religion may be mocked as ineffective, his instruments continue to wreak havoc on those who challenge his authority. If some commentators have chosen to see Marlowe as finally retreating from the consequences of the freedom of thought and action that his plays begin to proclaim, the punishments he brings down upon his protagonists in fact derive from their own unbending Promethean daring. In a significant way, each is obliged to confront his own self-indulgence. In *The Jew of Malta* (performed *c.*1592 though not published till 1633) the situation of the overreacher is presented with the kind of exaggerated gusto which threatens to topple over into black comedy. Barabas, whose very name is likely to grate on Christian sensibilities, is glorious in his cupidity, extravagant in his selfishness, and splendid in his ingenuity. His energy is directed to his advancement in the face of his enemies and he glories in the kind of illicit manipulation spoken of in the play's prologue by 'Machiavel'. Barabas himself acknowledges the importance of 'policy' at the point when his attempts to pit one side against another reach their zenith: 'Since by wrong thou got'st authority, | Maintain it bravely by firm policy; | At least, unprofitably lose it not'. It is ultimately by a miscalculation in his 'policy' that he fails, outwitted and sent screaming to his death by a double-crosser far less spirited in his malevolence than is Barabas himself. The tragedy of *The Tragical History of Doctor Faustus* (performed at the Rose in the early 1590s and belatedly published in 1604) hangs on an even greater miscalculation. Faustus's intellectual world is one in which humanist new learning has broken free of the strait-jackets of medieval science and divinity. For Faustus himself, restlessly moving from book to book and discipline to discipline in his opening speech, knowledge is power. As with Tamburlaine, the humbly born man aspires to the realization of his proper natural authority; as with Barabas, the outsider seeks to demonstrate that he is at liberty to reject the imposed restrictions that he despises. Like both, when Faustus sets himself against convention he slips into an arrogant self-justifying fantasy of his invincibility. Marlowe also allows him to confuse opposites and blur distinctions (he sees his necromantic books as 'heavenly' and, more damnably, he signs away his soul to Mephistophilis with Christ's last words on the cross: '*Consummatum est*, 'It is finished' or 'completed'). Before this fatal contract reaches its term, Faustus has frittered away the large opportunities that it has opened to him. He may have gloriously welcomed the spirit of Helen of Troy with an impassioned desire to share her eternity ('Was this the face that launched a thousand ships? | And burnt the topless towers of Ilium? | Sweet Helen, make me immortal with a kiss'), but he has also played silly practical jokes on popes and innkeepers and dumbfounded dukes with unseasonal bunches of grapes. His final speeches, uttered as a clock chimes away his last hours, do, however, force on us an awareness of quite how horridly he has corrupted his genius and ignored' the implications of Christian redemption:

> Now hast thou but one bare hour to live.
> And then thou must be damn'd perpetually.
> Stand still, you ever-moving spheres of heaven,
> That time may cease, and midnight never come;
> Fair Nature's eye, rise, rise again, and make
> A year, a month, a week a natural day,
> That Faustus may repent and save his soul.
> *O lente, lente currite, noctis equi.*
> The stars move still, time runs, the clock will strike,
> The devil will come, and Faustus must be damn'd.
> O, I'll leap up to my God—Who pulls me down?—
> See, see, where Christ's blood streams in the firmament.
> One drop would save my soul, half a drop: ah, my Christ—

Here Faustus both clings to his cleverness by quoting, out of context, an amorous line from Ovid ('run slowly, slowly, horses of the night') and desperately attempts to reverse his old dismissal of the scheme of salvation as he claims to see the sacrificial streams of blood and to claim Christ for his own. Yet still, as any orthodox member of Marlowe's audience would recognize, neither will his arrogance admit true repentance nor will his intellect fully accept service to the God he has so spectacularly rejected.

Edward II (published in 1592) differs from Marlowe's other tragedies in that it exploits a far greater equilibrium between its central character and those surrounding him. Where the other plays insistently celebrate the dangerous detachment of the hero from the limiting restraints of society, *Edward II* explores the problem of moral conflict within an established society. Unlike the megalomaniac seekers after military, political, or intellectual power, Edward is born into an inheritance of royal government but effectively throws it away in favour of another mastery, that of a homosexual love unacceptable to the weighty historical world in which he is obliged to move. Edward is a king without command, a lover denied fulfilment, a lion transformed into 'a lamb encompassed by wolves' and a man finally reduced by his enemies (including his wife and son) to the depths of human misery. He is Marlowe's most conventionally 'tragic' character in what is perhaps also his most deeply unconventional tragedy.

Shakespeare's Plays

Politics and History

For some 250 years after the deaths of the dramatists the plays of Shakespeare completely eclipsed those of Kyd and Marlowe. As has become increasingly evident, however, Shakespeare's early tragedies and histories existed, and continue to exist, in a symbiotic relationship with those of his contemporaries. Kyd's revenge dramas stimulated a public appetite to which Shakespeare responded with a sensational replay of Kyd's themes and echoes of his rhetoric in *Titus Andronicus* (*c*.1587, published 1594). Shakespeare's professional rivalry with Marlowe was to be more intense and to prove more fertile. Some of Aaron's speeches in *Titus Andronicus* distantly echo the cadences of *Tamburlaine* and, far less distantly, the malevolent gusto of Barabas. It was, however, with the first sequence of plays based on English history that Shakespeare found a distinctive voice and presented a considered riposte to the radical challenge posed by Marlowe. The 'tiger-hearted' Queen Margaret of the three parts of *Henry VI* (*c*.1588–91) who learns to spit curses, to wheedle, and to fight, is also the mistress of the kind of flamboyant gesture that audiences might readily have associated with Marlowe's male protagonists. It is she who so extravagantly insults the royal pretences of the captured Duke of York and his 'mess of sons' by putting a paper crown on his head and then knocking it off again to the words 'Off with the crown and with the crown his head'. But it is one of these sons, the Gloucester whom she has characterized to his father as 'that valiant crookback prodigy . . . that with his grumbling voice | Was wont to cheer his dad in mutinies', who as Richard III most menacingly outcapers Marlowe's Machiavellian villains. If, as some critics believe, *Edward II* was Marlowe's reply in historical kind, its moodiness and its exploration of the tragic dimension in the fall of a king were in turn to stimulate both the new departures and the plangency of Shakespeare's *Richard II* (*c*.1595, published 1597).

Shakespeare's two sequences of English historical plays (the three parts of *Henry VI* and *Richard III*; and *Richard II*, the two parts of *Henry IV* of *c*.1596 and *c*.1597, and *Henry V* of 1599) plus *King John* of *c*.1595 and

Henry VIII of *c*.1612–13, reinvent the myths, memories, and constructions of recent history which had so preoccupied Tudor historians. They explored divisions, depositions, usurpations, and civil wars, but they also bolstered the concept of secure monarchic government propagated by officially approved apologists for the Tudor dynasty. If the subject-matter of *Richard II* proved to be sufficiently contentious for the deposition scene to be omitted in the three editions published in the lifetime of Queen Elizabeth, and if in 1601 the Earl of Essex and his fellow conspirators recognized that a performance of the play might arouse support for their proposed *coup d'état*, such susceptibility served to prove how well Shakespeare had understood affairs of state. His history plays have continued to shape British perceptions of the national past and of nationhood. They remain political and patriotic statements of some potency (as Laurence Olivier's cinematic reworking of *Henry V* proved at a crucial phase of the Second World War). The ten history plays are central to the conception of Shakespeare as a, perhaps *the*, national poet which began to emerge in the late seventeenth century. To Samuel Johnson, writing in the mid-1760s, the *Henry IV* plays seemed to mark the apogee of a certain kind of dramatic art ('Perhaps no author has ever in two plays afforded so much delight'). To English and European Romantic poets, from Keats, Browning, and Tennyson to Goethe, Hugo, and Pushkin, Shakespeare emerged as the key figure in the moulding of a particular national consciousness and the deviser of the model from which future national historical dramas could develop.

In all, Shakespeare refers to England 247 times in his plays and to the English 143 times. It is scarcely surprising that the vast majority of these references should occur in the history plays (the intensely nationalistic *King John*, for example, mentions England no less than 43 times, *Henry V* 49 times, and *Henry VIII* 12 times). To many fond anthologists, the central statement of Shakespeare's feeling for his homeland occurs in *Richard II* as the dying John of Gaunt feels himself 'a prophet new-inspired':

> This royal throne of kings, this sceptred isle,
> This earth of majesty, this seat of Mars,
> This other Eden, demi-paradise,
> This fortress built by nature for herself
> Against infection and the hand of war,
> This happy breed of men, this little world,
> This precious stone set in the silver sea
> Which serves it in the office of a wall,
> Or as a moat defensive to a house
> Against the envy of less happier lands;
> This blessed plot, this earth, this realm, this England, . . .

This statement of an ideal, separate, secure, peaceful, kingly, little island is frequently truncated by those who cite it before the prophetic Gaunt gets to his point: the ideal does not exist and the England of Richard II 'hath made a shameful conquest of itself'. Gaunt's idealized vision is used in the play, and, by means of echoes, in the three dramas that follow it, to expose the reality of a realm descending into disunity and war. The 'other Eden' and the 'demi-paradise' are, if they ever existed, now lost. If, on one level, *Richard II* and its successors explore the consequences of the disruption of the direct line of royal descent from the Conqueror, on another they demonstrate that power struggles and conflicts of interest are not exclusively concerned with dynastic rights nor does civil peace automatically stem from the legitimate rule of divinely appointed kings. The Earl of Essex would not have been alone in 1601 in recognizing that history was ramified in the guts and minds of the living.

The historical play entitled *The Reign of Edward III*, which was once loosely ascribed to Shakespeare, was published in 1596 (it was registered for publication a year earlier). In its first two acts it is concerned not with showing us a golden age basking in the glory of a chivalrous warrior King, but with that King's dishonourable pursuit of the Countess of Salisbury. Edward emerges as a flawed hero who redeems his 'honour' by chasing the chimera of his supposed rights in France (the same chimera to be pursued, as Shakespeare himself showed, by another 'hero King', Henry V). *The Reign of Edward III* provided the context from which *Richard II* and its successors developed. The memory of Edward III and his foreign wars served to show up the domestic disasters of the reign of Edward's grandson Richard (whose only military campaign is a failed one in Ireland). In turn, the deposition of Richard leads to the disorders which so shake Henry Bolingbroke and which persuade the sleepless king to acknowledge that the crown has sat 'troublesome' upon his head. Even though Henry V attempts to distract minds at home from civil ills by taking up Edward III's claims in France, he too is obliged to muse sleeplessly in the night before the battle of Agincourt on 'the fault | My father made in compassing the crown'. Despite Henry's military triumph and despite his French marriage, Chorus reminds us at the end of the play that his heir's inheritance will be bitter; France will be lost and England will bleed, an event 'which oft our stage hath shown'. *Henry V* returns us, therefore, to the historical point at which Shakespeare began to explore the civil disasters of late medieval history, the first of the three *Henry VI* plays.

What distinguishes *I* and *II Henry IV* from the history plays that Shakespeare wrote both before and after it is his presentation of an England which prospers and suffers beyond the King's court and the circle of the King's aristocratic enemies. In a sense, the cue for this celebration of a wider, popular England lay in the traditional interpretation of the transformation of the scapegrace Prince Hal into the gracious and honourable King Harry. Where Holinshed excused the former as some kind of adolescent prelude to the famous victories of the King, Shakespeare sought to show us a Prince who carefully calculates in all that he does. He is both prig and prodigal son, but in his prodigality he encounters a world which is more than an alternative to his father's troubled court. Hal does not simply drop *out* from a fraught ruling class, he drops in to the society of the ruled. Through Falstaff, he learns the intense delights of irresponsibility and experiences the exercise of an elastic morality, but he has to teach himself the significance of responsibility and the law. Where Falstaff discounts honour as 'a mere scutcheon', Hal has to outface his father's enemy, Hotspur, who once rejoiced in the idea of plucking 'bright honour from the pale-faced moon'. Where Falstaff claims to have misused the King's press 'damnably' in Part I and cynically demonstrates his scandalous methods of recruitment in Justice Shallow's Gloucestershire in Part II, Hal has, with, perhaps, a parallel degree of cynicism, to learn the bluff arts of military command. Falstaff, Shakespeare's amplest comic invention, squashes all endeavour; Hal, the playboy Prince, has occasionally to pause to remind us that he is in fact in earnest training for his future role as 'the mirror of all Christian kings'. Falstaff is warned of his, and Hal's, destiny, in one of the most carefully modulated exchanges in *I Henry IV*. In Act II, scene v the two men play an acting game which parodies an interview between the penitent Prince and his sorrowing father; when Falstaff in the part of Hal mounts a highly imaginative defence of the character of 'plump Jack', the real Hal royally responds to the challenge of banishing him with the blunt force of 'I do: I will'. The scene is suddenly interrupted by the sound of knocking, and it is for the actors to determine how pregnant is the potential pause, how potent is the moment of truth.

The England that contains Justice Shallow's orchard and the battlefield at Shrewsbury, Gad's Hill and the Jerusalem Chamber at Westminster, is a hierarchically ordered nation threatened on all levels by disorder. The English history plays consider how civil order is related to central government. If government is generally represented by the medieval concept of rule by a divinely appointed king from whom honour and justice spring, Shakespeare also suggests that king and subject are linked together by mutual responsibilities. It would be anachronistic to suggest that these responsibilities imply some kind of contract between ruler and ruled, but in certain plays, notably in *Henry V*, he seems to be stressing that a king can rule legitimately only with the assent of those whom he rules, be they nobles or commoners. Powerful noblemen break their feudal oaths in *Richard II*, and in 2 *Henry VI* insurgent peasants attempt to break feudalism itself, but throughout Shakespeare's works it is rulers who more often seem to fail in their moral, communal, and governmental responsibilities. The usurping Duke Frederick poisons relationships in *As You Like It*; Vincentio, the Duke of Vienna in *Measure for Measure*, admits that he has 'ever loved the life removed' and that he has for fourteen years neglected 'the needful bits and curbs to headstrong weeds'; Prospero, sometime Duke of Milan, confesses in *The Tempest* that he 'grew stranger' to his state by 'being transported | And rapt in secret studies'; in *Hamlet*, Claudius destroys his brother, marries his sister-in-law, assumes the throne, and introduces a rot into the state of Denmark; and in *Macbeth* a usurper and regicide proves as tyrannical and bloody a curse to Scotland as Richard III had to England. By looking beyond England, whether in the comic mode or the tragic, Shakespeare seems to have accepted, as the vast majority of his contemporaries did, that good government meant the rule of an assiduous and virtuous prince with a sanctioned claim to the throne.

It was only in the more austere Roman plays, dramas which offer a retrospect on governmental systems alien to those of most of sixteenth- and early seventeenth-century European states, that Shakespeare was obliged to confront alternatives to the rule of Christian princes. But if *Julius Caesar* (1599) and *Coriolanus* (c.1608) deal with historical alternatives, they also vividly reflect back on Shakespeare's present (corn riots, as an English audience of 1608 would readily have recognized, were not purely a Roman phenomenon). The compact Roman Republic of *Coriolanus* is riven by patrician arrogance and plebeian self-assertion; in *Julius Caesar* and *Antony and Cleopatra* a now tired republic commands an empire; it staggers on the brink of a lapse into imperial autocracy before beginning the long slide into the imperial decadence of *Titus Andronicus*. To most men and women of the Renaissance, the sweep of Roman history contained within it paramount examples of sober ideals, barely attainable splendours, and dire warnings. As Shakespeare represents that history in his four Roman plays it is the warnings against demagoguery and decadence that predominate. The same warnings have continued to resonate into the twentieth century.

Tragedy and Death

When the disconsolate Richard returns from Ireland to his troubled kingdom in the play to which Shakespeare gave the full title *The Tragedy of King Richard the Second*, he insists that no one speak to him of comfort. 'Let's talk of graves, of worms and epitaphs', he suggests before proceeding, in a homely and unregal manner, to sit on the ground and tell sad stories of the death of kings: 'How some have been deposed, some slain in war, | Some haunted by the ghosts they have deposed, | Some poisoned by their wives, some sleeping killed, | All murdered.' For Shakespeare and his contemporaries, as much as for their ancient Greek and Roman predecessors, the very nature of tragedy seemed to require that it explored the sad stories of kings, or at the very least of men and women dignified by royal blood or civil authority. An exemplary dramatic fall, one which stirred the emotions of pity and fear in lesser mortals, had to be a fall from a height of influence and honour. Shakespeare's tragedies deal almost exclusively with the destinies of kings and princes on whose fortunes depend those of the nations they rule. If neither Julius Caesar nor his noble murderers are of royal rank, Caesar at least aspires to it and, as the phenomena which accompany his murder appear to suggest, his greatness is supernaturally affirmed. Only Othello, the noble servant of the Most Serene

Republic of Venice, has a merely military rank, but, though his tragedy may ostensibly seem domestic, seventeenth-century audiences would have been well aware of the threat his downfall posed to Christian supremacy in Cyprus at a time of Turkish ascendancy over the Eastern Mediterranean.

As Kyd, Marlowe, and earlier sixteenth-century English dramatists had defined it on the stage, tragedy was reinforced by explicit enactments of the death of kings. The popularity of the revenge plays that developed from the example of *The Spanish Tragedy* also demonstrates that English audiences rejoiced in the representation of what Shakespeare's Horatio describes as 'carnal, bloody, and unnatural acts . . . accidental judgements, casual slaughters . . . [and] deaths put on by cunning and forced cause'. Although, as the sometimes vexed reputation of *Hamlet* (*c.*1599–1601) in the seventeenth and eighteenth centuries serves to suggest, such deliberate or casual slaughters on stage may not have been to the taste of neo-classical critics, they were integral to the kind of tragedy that Shakespeare accepted as normative. To think of a performance of *Hamlet* without its murders is as absurd an exercise as to contemplate excising the Prince's lengthy meditations on mortality from his soliloquies. Shakespeare's tragic world is uncertain, dangerous, and mortal, and the catastrophes to which all his tragic dramas inexorably move are sealed by the deaths of their protagonists.

It is possible that this dramatic emphasis on mortality reflected the violence of contemporary political life, both at home and abroad. If Protestant England claimed to be righteously indignant over the slaughter of French Huguenots on St Bartholomew's Day 1572, and if it sometimes dwelt pruriently on the seamy side of French, Italian, and Spanish court life, it was itself an uneasy society, haunted by ideas of treason and assassination. It was also ready enough both to extract information from suspects by torture and to execute those it deemed to be traitors according to the bloody ritual of public hanging, drawing, and quartering. The idea of murder as politically expedient may have seemed repugnant to the professionally self-righteous but assassination was by no means a remote or alien phenomenon (as the carefully staged trials of the so-called 'Gunpowder' plotters in 1605 brought home to contemporaries). The glancing references in *Macbeth* (*c.*1606) to the moral issues raised by this same Gunpowder Plot suggest how a representation of the hurly-burly of the politics of the Scottish past could be made to reverberate into the tangled British present. A historical tragedy written to flatter a Stuart king descended from both Banquo and Edward the Confessor it may be, but *Macbeth* also reflects a deep political unease in which, despite the hiatus between past and present, no monarch could find reassurance. The exploration of turbulence and distrust in the play is not limited to the images of blood and dismemberment with which it begins, nor is it given full expression in King Duncan's inability to find 'the mind's construction in the face'; it is rendered implicit in nature and explicit in the fatal visions, the brain-sickly thoughts, the butchery, the desperate defences, and the fearful isolation of Macbeth himself. Far more so than the sleepless Plantagenets of the history plays, Macbeth is a monarch haunted by personal desolation and by the extinction of royal ideals and of effective royal influence:

> My way of life
> Is fall'n into the sere, the yellow leaf,
> And that which should accompany old age,
> As honour, love, obedience, troops of friends,
> I must not look to have, but in their stead
> Curses, not loud but deep, mouth-honour, breath
> Which the poor heart would fain deny and dare not.

In *Macbeth* Shakespeare explores a monarch's despair at having to live with the consequences of his desperate and bloody appliances to the inherent political diseases of autocratic government.

The usurping Claudius in *Hamlet*, still clinging to 'those effects for which I did the murder—| My crown, mine own ambition and my queen', seems, despite his own soliloquy of ineffective penitence, to experience relatively little of Macbeth's heavy affliction of conscience. Claudius is Shakespeare's supremely politic king; manipulative, calculating, smooth, secretive, suspicious, and generally well-served by malleable courtiers. His Elsinore is characterized by its eavesdroppers, its note-takers and its double agents. It is not a place where innocence thrives. Elsinore forms a tortuous, patriarchal maze for Ophelia who fails both to negotiate its pitfalls and to understand the cynical logic of its twists and turns; it is a prison for Hamlet who multiplies its complexities while ostensibly attempting to purge them. Hamlet's public problem is how to avenge a political murder in a culture where private vengeance is politically and morally unacceptable; his equally pressing private problem is how to come to terms with the death of his father, with his uncle's accession, and, above all, with his mother's remarriage (and possible complicity in Claudius's crimes). The intertwined dilemmas posed by those problems render the Prince an unsteady and an ineffective revenger. *Hamlet* the drama confuses and complicates the clean lines of a 'revenge play' as soon as Hamlet the character begins to assume roles, to experiment with devices, and to debate issues which veer off from the central one. His meditations, one of which leads Horatio to suggest that he considers 'too curiously', confront him again and again with the fear not of judgement, but with the chill shiver of death and the prospect of a dream-haunted afterlife. The active life is waylaid by the idly contemplative, the confident Renaissance prince by the restless melancholic, the concept of man as the paragon of animals by the *memento mori*. Hamlet's most significant stage-props are a rapier and a skull. *Hamlet* ends with a certain moral neatness which compensates for the disordered heap of corpses which litters the stage. Its protagonist has proved himself ready both for his own contrived death and for the wild justice he brings down upon Claudius and Laertes. Nevertheless, his is an end which contrasts with the more resolute deaths of Shakespeare's other tragic heroes.

If throughout *Hamlet* suicide is seen either as forbidden by a canon of the Everlasting or as an untidy quietus for the unhinged Ophelia, in *Othello* and the Roman plays it is raised again to its pre-Christian, classical dignity. For many members of Shakespeare's first audiences, however, suicide remained a damnable act, a rash end to present woes or accumulated sins on earth (as in the case of Kyd's Isabella and Hieronimo), or a dark act of despair (as in the grave temptation of Spenser's Redcrosse). In *Romeo and Juliet* (*c.*1594–5) the defeated lovers rush into death as precipitously, as incomprehendingly, and as clumsily (if not as fulfillingly) as they had earlier embraced a passionate life. By contrast, in Shakespeare's two great mature love tragedies, *Othello* (1604) and *Antony and Cleopatra* (*c.*1606–7), suicide figures as a noble culmination rather than as an ignoble or despairing escape. For Antony, death by his own hand (albeit bungled) is seen as the proper response of a Roman general to military failure and as the only alternative to public disgrace. For Cleopatra, finally glorious in her robes of state, 'immortal longings' suggest the possibility of a final reunion with a transfigured and heroic husband. The asp's bite seems to her both 'a lover's pinch, | Which hurts and is desired' and a baby at her breast 'who sucks the nurse asleep'. Like Antony, Othello dies as a soldier intent on preserving what is left of his honour and his integrity. He may despair as a man who has been cruelly manipulated and as one whose soul has been caught by perdition, but he too knows what is required of him as a soldier who must follow through the consequences of his earlier ill-considered resolution. If Antony and Cleopatra revel in the chance of an immortal freedom from an empire regulated by the zealous Octavius, Othello, by contrast, dies claiming his part in an ordered Christian society where there are chains of command, records, and distinctions between the baptised and the heathen:

> I pray you in your letters,
> When you shall these unlucky deeds relate,
> Speak of me as I am. Nothing extenuate,
> Nor set down aught in malice. Then must you speak
> Of one that loved not wisely but too well,
> Of one not easily jealous but, being wrought,
> Perplexed in the extreme; of one whose hand,
> Like the base Indian, threw a pearl away
> Richer than all his tribe; of one whose subdued eyes,
> Albeit unused to the melting mood,
> Drops tears as fast as the Arabian trees
> Their medicinable gum. Set you down this,
> And say besides that in Aleppo once,
> Where a malignant and a turbaned Turk
> Beat a Venetian and traduced the state,
> I took by th' throat the circumcised dog
> And smote him thus.
>   *He stabs himself*

In a sense Othello both dictates his own epitaph and acts out the drama of his inevitable and violent end. Here the 'high Roman fashion' of death, of which his fellow-African Cleopatra speaks, is reasserted for modern times.

High Roman fashions and chivalric military codes are alike absent from the most disturbing, and most obviously revised of Shakespeare's major tragedies, *King Lear* (*c.*1605, printed 1608 with a substantially different text published in the 1623 Folio). *King Lear*, set in pre-Christian Britain, presents us with both a despairing suicide (that of the defeated lover and poisoner, Goneril) and an attempt at suicide (Gloucester's). The main tragic drive of the play derives, however, not from any consistent and inevitable movement towards the death of its main characters but from a series of expectations which Shakespeare systematically confounds or reverses. It is a pattern which would be essentially comic elsewhere in his work. The subversive comments of Lear's Fool, the adoption by Edgar of the role of a crazed beggar, and the fairy-tale-like improbability of the play's opening scenes all suggest how precipitously *King Lear* teeters on the edge of absurdist comedy. When the blinded Gloucester attempts to destroy himself by throwing himself over a cliff at Dover he merely ends up flat on his face (thanks to his son's contrivance). When the painfully chastened Lear seems about to be restored to his rights at the end of the play, Shakespeare, in a calculated reversal of the story provided by his sources, deprives him of Cordelia, of full control of his reasoning faculty, and, above all, of a conventional tragic dignity. In Act III the King madly rages against human ingratitude, exposed to the ravages of the weather like the 'poor naked wretches' who are the meanest of his former subjects. He enters in Act IV 'crowned with weeds and flowers', pronouncing himself 'every inch a king' to the kneeling Gloucester. In Act V he comes on to the stage for the last time bearing the dead body of his daughter, in a scene which proved unpalatable to theatre audiences between 1681 (when Nahum Tate's happy ending was first introduced) and 1838 (when the tragic actor W. C. Macready returned to Shakespeare's original). In the revised version of the play-text (published in the 1623 Folio) Lear's jerky expression suggests that he is torn between the conflicting emotions of agony ('Howl, howl, howl, howl!'), of tenderness ('Her voice was ever soft, | Gentle and low'), and of self-assertion ('I killed the slave that was a-hanging thee'). As he finally collapses, the body in his arms, he may have been forced to abandon the illusion that Cordelia is still breathing but he continues to confuse rage and pity, despair and a sense of natural injustice, perhaps even the dead Fool and the dead daughter:

> And my poor fool is hanged. No, no life.
> Why should a dog, a horse, a rat have life,
> And thou no breath at all? O, thou wilt come no more.
> Never, never, never.—Pray you, undo
> This button. Thank you, sir. O, O, O, O! (1608 text)

When it is recognized that the King has died, Kent's dual epitaphs emerge as scarcely consolatory ('Vex not his ghost. O, let him pass. He hates him | That would upon the rack of this tough world | Stretch him out longer', 'the wonder is he hath endured so long. | He but usurped his life'). *King Lear* offers little of the tidiness of reordering of most other tragic endings, still less of catharsis, resolution, or absolution. The villainous and the virtuous are silenced by death or distress, and the Duke of Albany, to whom the minimal summing up falls, can only insist that the survivors must 'Speak what we feel, not what we ought to say'.

Like the problematic *Troilus and Cressida* (*c.*1602) and the possibly collaborative *Timon of Athens* (*c.*1604), *King Lear* insistently explores the awkward, nasty, and uncomfortable aspects of the human condition rather than dignifying them with the paraphernalia, the elevated language, and the rituals demanded by received ideas of tragedy, whether ancient or modern. In significant ways, too, all three plays shift away from a discussion of the ideological, political, and social values of seventeenth-century Europe to a consideration of more alien and alienated worlds where all human values and all human relationships are called into question. Where a Macbeth or a Claudius had usurped a crown, the aged and enraged Lear seems finally to have usurped life itself; where a Hamlet, an Othello, or an Antony had departed with something approaching soldierly dignity, Lear, worn out by life and kingship, dies in a swoon, sadly sitting on the ground.

Women and Comedy

When the brainsick Lear refers to his daughter Cordelia's voice as 'ever soft, | Gentle and low, an excellent thing in women', he seems to be belatedly distinguishing her from the more obvious strident vocal company of her sisters, Goneril and Regan. To many critics of the eighteenth and nineteenth centuries, most of the broader sisterhood of the women of Shakespeare's histories and tragedies could be safely divided between the strident and the soft and between those who exhibited a distinctly 'unfeminine' aggression (such as Queen Margaret or Lady Macbeth) and those who were all too readily cast as passive female victims (such as Ophelia or Desdemona). Such distinctions are likely to seem grossly inadequate to twentieth-century readers, playgoers, and actors. If Shakespeare, in common with most of his contemporaries, tended to see women as defined and circumscribed in a patriarchal society by their roles as queens, wives, mothers, daughters, and lovers, his plays show that he was also capable of exploring both gender opposition and, more crucially, gender blurring. His women fall into neither 'types' nor 'stereotypes'. In his innovative romantic comedies in particular, where the roles of a Rosalind, a Beatrice, or a Viola would originally have been assigned to men, he allows that women both take crucial initiatives in male-dominated worlds and confuse distinctions between what might loosely be assumed to be 'male' and 'female' characteristics. In general, Shakespeare's sources for the histories and the tragedies obliged him to reflect on power struggles between men, struggles in which women were marginalized unless, like Lady Macbeth, they denied aspects of their femininity or, like Cleopatra, they were prepared to accentuate their physical allure in order to gain a limited political advantage. In the comedies, where happy denouements replace tragic ones and romantic and domestic alliances tend to supersede those engineered in the interests of state policy, negotiations between men and women begin to take place on something approaching an equal footing. Where in the tragedies the vivid independence of a Desdemona is stifled by the weight of male circumstance and the courage of Cordelia is ignored and disparaged, in the comedies women's integrity and intelligence do not merely shine, they briefly triumph.

The structural awkwardness and the many loose ends of what are probably Shakespeare's two earliest comedies, *The Two Gentlemen of Verona* (*c.*1587) and *The Taming of the Shrew* (*c.*1588), suggest a beginner's uncertainty about dramatic technique and form. Both plays also indicate the degree to which he was dramatizing the ambiguities of his age concerning the freedom of women to act and think independently in courtship and marriage. In the first, a woman dangerously resolves to prove her faith to an undeserving lover; in the second, a woman is brutally schooled in wifely duty by a husband who appears not to merit her service. As part of the contorted plot of *The Two Gentlemen of Verona* Julia disguises herself as a man in order to follow Proteus from Verona to Milan. Her action (common enough in the prose literature of the sixteenth century) is the first of Shakespeare's many theatrical experiments with the device of female cross-dressing, or, to be more precise, with the disconcerting nuances of a boy actor dressing as a boy while playing the role of a woman. However much Julia's romantic ploy may be related to the European carnival tradition of transvestism, it is one that the far more rumbustiously carnivalesque *The Taming of the Shrew* carefully eschews. The unromantic Katherina's 'taming' by the far from gentle Petruchio consists of a series of rough games, staged tantrums, and physical trials. Throughout, Katherina has to meet direct challenges to her assumed identity and to cope with the antics of a man whose volatility appears to be equally assumed. Finally both have to drop false identities and proclaim their mutual respect. Katherina's public response to her last test, in which she is called upon to affirm a kind of feudal submission to her husband's will ('Thy husband is thy lord, thy life, thy keeper, | Thy head, thy sovereign, one that cares for thee . . .'), has been seen by some as a properly cynical response to a hardened cynic. Nevertheless, Katherina's servile placing of her hands beneath Petruchio's foot is answered not by a kick, but by a raising from her knees and a kiss.

Throughout his career Shakespeare amplified, varied, and, at times, reversed the ambiguous gestures of his earliest experiments with comedy. The slick Roman symmetry of *The Comedy of Errors* (*c.*1589–94) is relieved by reflections on family and amatory relationships which almost slip into tenderness. The familial and matrimonial sulkiness of the Athenians with which A *Midsummer Night's Dream* (*c*.1595–6) opens is reflected in the far more acrimonious and threatening disputes of Oberon and Titania. The play begins with crossed purposes; it unwinds, ironically enough, with a tidiness enforced by the interference of that traditional embodiment of the malign disordering of human affairs, Puck; it ends with multiple marriages celebrated to the accompaniment of a superbly inept tragic entertainment and with the blessing of the once disruptive fairies. As the human lovers wake from their respective dreams in Act IV, each is discovered magically placed beside an unexpected but 'proper' partner, but it is the once rejected Helena who has the hazy wisdom to grasp that she has 'found Demetrius like a jewel, | Mine own and not mine own'. Love in *A Midsummer Night's Dream* is a matter of uncertain discovery; it both claims possession and is obliged to recognize distinctions, differences, individualities. Much the same is true of the discountenancing of the rash and possessive presumptions of the male lovers at the end of *Love's Labour's Lost* (*c*.1593–4). In a play shaped around role-playing, word-games, and rhetorical devices it is shockingly apt that at the end life should encounter death, that verbal posturings should be countered by 'Honest plain words', and that sentimental male pretensions of love should be squashed by the Princess's hard-headed insistence that they were received merely as 'bombast and as lining to the time'. When the King of Navarre protests that his proposal of marriage should be accepted at this 'latest minute of the hour', the Princess has the presence of mind to rebut him with the most refined and serious of all Shakespeare's put-downs: 'A time, methinks, too short | To make a world-without-end bargain in'. The play concludes with separations. Jack has not Jill, winter succeeds spring, and characters leave the stage 'severally' to live apart for a twelve month, perhaps for ever.

Although *The Merry Wives of Windsor* (*c*.1597) (which so inspired Verdi and his librettist, Boito) has tended to be overshadowed in the twentieth century by the popularity of the romantic comedies, its position in Shakespeare's comic *œuvre* is central in more than simply the chronological sense. Shakespeare re-introduces characters (Falstaff, Mistress Quickly, Pistol, Nym, and Shallow) from his *Henry IV* plays, but, by implication, he also transfers the setting from Plantagenet to late Tudor England. Its scene is a prosperous English town on the fringes of a royal castle and its park, not an imagined Illyria or an unlocated Arden; its characters are mercantile not noble, and its language is colloquial rather than lyrical. Despite this down-to-earth prosiness, the play allows for the triumph of romantic love over the well-intentioned schemes of parents and the ill-conceived ones of a would-be adulterer. Jack (Fenton) woos and wins his Jill (Anne Page), but Ford, Page, Caius, Slender, and Falstaff, all in their different ways, conspicuously fail in their designs. Although the Falstaff of *The Merry Wives of Windsor* may lack the bouncy resilience of the Falstaff of *I Henry IV*, his role as a self-deceived and preposterous wooer of married women is crucial to the presentation of sexual politics in the play. He is humiliatingly removed in a basket of dirty linen, compromised in women's clothing (as the 'fat woman of Brainford') and, finally, equipped with the horns traditionally associated with cuckoldry, he is tormented by women and by children disguised as fairies.

In the last scene of *The Merry Wives of Windsor* ruse is piled upon ruse, and exposure follows on exposure. It is not only Falstaff who is discountenanced, for both Slender and Caius, who assume that they have assignations with women in Windsor Forest, find themselves fobbed off instead with boys in female attire. Disguise and cross-dressing, schemes that explode upon themselves and contrived encounters also figure prominently in the so-called 'romantic' comedies of Shakespeare's middle career. In these plays, however, such festive fooling tends to be demoted to sub-plots while the pains, strains, and pleasures of young love become the central concerns. Essentially, too, the successful resolution of each play depends upon the resourcefulness of its woman protagonist. In *The Merchant of Venice* (*c.*1596–7) Portia, who at the beginning of the action bemoans the passivity posthumously imposed on her by her father ('the will of a living daughter curbed by the will of a dead father'), in Act IV assumes the robes of a male advocate and exercises her ingenious intellect in order to rescue Antonio from the dire conditions of Shylock's bond (though in her final dealings with Shylock she signally fails to exhibit the quality of mercy she had once advocated). In *As You Like It* (*c.*1599–1600) Rosalind, banished from her uncle's court, retires to the forest of Arden disguised as a youth named Ganymede. If the name she adopts has overtones of the epicene, the play-acting in which she indulges with Orlando, in order to 'cure' him of his romantic passion for the 'real' Rosalind, adds to the volatility of gender in the play. Rosalind/Ganymede assumes control not simply of Orlando's emotional development but, gradually, of the destinies of virtually all the temporary and permanent sojourners in Arden. Despite the ambiguity of her outward appearance, she is triumphantly the mistress of herself; controlled, sensible, self-analytical, yet neither cold nor phlegmatic. If at one moment she can unsentimentally anatomize human affection in a reproof to the love-sick Orlando ('men are April when they woo, December when they wed. Maids are May when they are maids, but the sky changes when they are wives'), in another she can turn to her cousin Celia and exclaim wonderingly: 'O coz, coz, coz, my pretty little coz, that thou didst know how many fathom deep I am in love. But it cannot be sounded. My affection hath an unknown bottom, like the Bay of Portugal.' Where Rosalind exercises benign authority in exile, the shipwrecked Viola of *Twelfth Night* (1601) is obliged to steer a middle way between the contradictions, the oppositions, and the displays of melancholy, spleen, and choler in the disconcerting world of Illyria. Her protective assumption of the role of a eunuch ('Cesario') effectively protects her from very little; Orsino flirts languorously, Olivia makes direct sexual advances, and the incompetent Sir Andrew Aguecheek insists on challenging her to a duel. It is her resourceful intelligence, and not her disguise, which preserves her both from the affectations of blinkered lovers and from the folly, hypocrisy, and cruelty that flourishes below stairs in Illyrian aristocratic households.

The disconcertions, tensions, and ambiguities of Illyria are to some degree mirrored in the more violent dislocations of Messina in *Much Ado About Nothing* (*c*.1598–9). They are painfully accentuated in the so-called 'problem' comedies, *All's Well That Ends Well* (*c*.1603) and *Measure for Measure* (1604). *Much Ado About Nothing* begins with references to martial conflict, but as its plot develops it does more than refine and limit that conflict to the battle of wits between Beatrice and Benedick; it is perilously fragmented by slander, acrimony, and dishonour and then rescrambled to allow for a somewhat insecure reconciliation in the last act. It is essentially a play about mutuality, not serenity. Its bitter-sweetness is echoed in Balthasar's song 'Sigh no more, ladies'; men are deceivers, and the much put-upon Hero seems condemned to sigh, but both its comic resolution and its comic energy ultimately turn on the transformation of the grating of Beatrice and Benedick (the blesser and the blessed) into an agreement between equal partners. The conversion of sounds of woe into 'hey, nonny, nonnies' is, however, far more uneasy in the concluding scenes of *All's Well That Ends Well* (with its sick king, its unattractive 'hero', and its long-suffering and determined heroine, Helena) and of *Measure for Measure* (with its problematic Duke, its hypocritical Angelo, and its prickly heroine, Isabella). Both plays rely on bed tricks so that spurned mistresses may claim lovers and both plays force couples into relationships rather than allow relationships to be forged by mutual assent. As its title suggests, *Measure for Measure* offers a series of juxtapositions rather than coalescences. Isabella's passionate and articulate defence of the concept of mercy in Act II is Shakespeare's most probing statement about the difficulty and consequences of judgement, but Isabella can be seen as arguing here as much from untried ideals as from an instinctive or acquired wisdom. Elsewhere, her idealism suggests a naïvety about herself and about the shortcomings of others. *Measure for Measure* is a play of dark corners, hazy margins, and attempts at rigid definition. It poses the necessity of passing moral judgement while demonstrating that all judgement is relative.

The internal 'problems' that are supposed to determine the nature of the 'problem' plays are largely the invention of late nineteenth- and early twentieth-century Shakespeare criticism. It was argued that because a play like *Measure for Measure* did not necessarily accord with the tidy romantic syntheses of a play such as *Twelfth Night*, Shakespeare was likely to have been distracted while writing it by some kind of (undetermined) personal crisis. Unease, uncertain or divided responses, and relative judgements shape all his plays, whether comic or tragic. The tendency to divide his dramatic works into groups and subgroups, with their own internal reflections and parallels, has also helped to determine the varied critical fortunes of Shakespeare's last plays—the four heterogeneous comedies *Pericles* (*c*.1607–8), *Cymbeline* (*c*.1610–11), *The Winter's Tale* (*c*.1609–10), and *The Tempest* (*c*.1610–11)—and the equally heterogeneous history play *Henry VIII* (sometimes also known as *All is True*, *c*.1612–13). Where some critics have seen evidence of harmony and spirituality, others have noticed only untidiness and tiredness; where some have insisted on Shakespeare's fresh experimentation, others have objected to a rehashing of moribund theatrical conventions; some recognize a new realism, others insist on a calculated retreat from realism.

Shakespeare's last plays effectively continue the irregular line of development of his earlier work by interfusing comic and tragic themes with a new intensity. More piquantly, they seem to affirm that in certain kinds of comedy, human happiness can be rescued from the jaws of despair. Imogen in *Cymbeline* and Hermione in *The Winter's Tale* are faced with personal and political crises and meet them with a mature and articulate dignity. Both the untidy and textually problematic *Pericles* (which the editors of the Folio left out of their collection) and the almost neo-classically neat *The Tempest* (to which these same editors gave pride of place) stress the intensity of a father–daughter relationship. *The Winter's Tale* moves jerkily between seasons, kingdoms, and generations, while the action of *The Tempest* takes place on one island in one afternoon. All the last plays require elaborate stage-machinery and all seem to have exploited the scenic effects available in the Blackfriars Theatre. All, in their distinct ways, contrast the sins and shortcomings of an older generation with the resurgent hopes represented by a new, and all balance the advances of death with enactments of rediscovery, rebirth, and resurrection. In each play treachery, calumny, and tyranny distort human and political relationships, and in each the humanist ideals of self-discipline and self-knowledge are represented as counters to public and private misgovernment.

In the last of his plays (probably written in collaboration with John Fletcher) Shakespeare returned to the 'matter' of England. In the often paradoxical political world of *Henry VIII* the true eminence of the King seems to rise as his former allies, friends, and counsellors fall. The play ends with the King benignly content with the prophecies of a glorious future for his infant daughter Elizabeth, but its course has suggested quite how vexed, deathly, and dangerous life could be at Henry's court. For Buckingham and, above all, for Wolsey a reversal of political fortunes, and an impending judicial end, occasion dignified confessional meditations. For Queen Katherine, rejected by the King for reasons of state, but sure and certain of her justification before God and man, the approach of death requires an act of reconciliation with her enemies. In accordance with the accepted rules of a Christian death-bed it also required an ordering of her earthly affairs. Katherine, blessed by a stately vision of bliss, quietly commands a funeral which will proclaim her personal integrity and her unusurped dignity:

> When I am dead, good wench,
> Let me be used with honour. Strew me over
> With maiden flowers, that all the world may know

> I was a chaste wife to my grave. Embalm me,
> Then lay me forth. Although unqueened, yet like
> A queen and daughter to a king inter me.

Queen Katherine dies peacefully in her bed, not raging against heaven or threatened by the ministers of hell. Significantly, too, she is neither condemned to the scaffold nor slaughtered on a battlefield, she is removed neither by poison nor by an assassin's dagger. For all its indeterminate mixture of history, tragedy, comedy, pageant, and spectacle, the once much-admired and now much-neglected *Henry VIII* also introduced the quiet death-bed to non-devotional literature. It both dignified a wronged woman and, perhaps more distinctively, it domesticated a queen.

Ben Jonson and the Comic Theatre

In the 'Induction on the Stage' to his London comedy *Bartholomew Fair* (acted 1614, published 1631) Ben(jamin) Jonson (1572/3–1637) gives to the actor playing his scrivener (copyist) the claim that the new play which will follow will be 'merry, and as full of noise as sport, made to delight all, and to offend none'. This Induction initiates the seepage between actor and non-actor and the interaction of illusion and reality on which the whole comedy is based. It also introduces some pointed side-swipes at the tastes of contemporary audiences. 'He that will swear *Jeronimo* or *Andronicus* are the best plays yet', the scrivener announces with reference to Kyd's *The Spanish Tragedy* and to Shakespeare's earliest and bloodiest tragedy, 'shall pass unexcepted at here as a man whose judgement shews it is constant, and hath stood still these five and twenty, or thirty years'. He deliberately exaggerates the datedness of the bombastic tragedies of the 1590s and implies that old fashions should now be laid to rest (though this may be an ironic suggestion given that the young Jonson was said to have acted the part of Hieronimo and had later written additional speeches for a revival of Kyd's play). The scrivener's subsequent comments on the theatrical vogue for tragi-comical mixed drama, of the kind evolved in Shakespeare's last phase, are, however, far less patronizingly indulgent. '*Tales*, *Tempests*, and such like drolleries' are disdained as indecorous; they are unreal, they offend against nature, and they are vulgarly marred by a 'concupiscence of jigs and dances'.

Shakespeare was, however, not alone in pandering to the public demand for romantic escapism and for happy resolutions to potentially tragic dramas of which Jonson complained. In the address 'to the Reader' prefaced to the Hellenic pastoral *The Faithful Shepherdess* (*c.*1608) John Fletcher (1579–1625) insisted that tragi-comedy was not so called because it intermixed mirth and murder, but because it eschewed death 'which is enough to make it no tragedy, yet brings some near to it, which is enough to make it no comedy'. A tragi-comedy represented the sufferings and joys of 'familiar people' and, despite

Sir Philip Sidney's strictures in *The Defence of Poesie*, it could happily inter-
mingle the elevated and the ordinary ('a God is as lawful in this as in a tragedy,
and mean people as in a comedy'). Fletcher, who in his close and successful
collaborations—notably with Francis Beaumont (1584–1616)—worked in a
variety of theatrical modes, had evolved a particular kind of play characterized
by its heterogeneous and sometimes startling combination of intrigue and
romance, of the amorous and the perilous, of the bucolic and the lyrical. His
tragi-comedies reflect back on the prose pastorals of Sidney and his Italian
models and they employ the formula of a happy denouement which implies
that even in an imperfect world, virtue could be perfectly rewarded. The plot
of Beaumont and Fletcher's *Philaster, or Love lies a-bleeding* (c.1609, published
1620) shows injustices reversed, disasters averted, and heirs restored to their
rights once assumed disguises and contrived misunderstandings have finally
been removed. In their *A King and No King* (1611, published 1619) King
Arbaces's incestuous passion for his supposed sister and his potentially tragic
plans for murder, rape, and suicide are somewhat arbitrarily, but necessarily,
dissipated by the timely revelation that he is in fact neither a king nor a brother.
Fletcher's collaboration with Shakespeare, *The Two Noble Kinsmen* (1613,
printed 1634), draws on Chaucer's Knight's Tale in order to retell a story of
knightly rivalries, vexed relationships, and sudden reversals. In his concluding
speech, however, Duke Theseus offers a distinctly un-Chaucerian meditation
on the whims of fortune which might appropriately stand at the end of any of
these tragi-comedies. For Theseus, the play's paradoxes and disconcertions can
be interpreted as reflections of the unpredictability of Fate and the timing
of heavenly justice: 'O you heavenly charmers, | What things you make of us!
For what we lack | We laugh, for what we have, are sorry; still | Are children
in some kind. Let us be thankful | for that which is . . .'.

Francis Beaumont's rattling burlesque, *The Knight of the Burning Pestle*
(c.1607, printed 1613) differs markedly from his tragi-comic collaborations
with Fletcher. It is set in modern London, not in an imagined Arcadian landscape, and it begins as the Prologue to a performance of a genteel play at the
Blackfriars Theatre is interrupted by an unruly citizen and his wife who
demand that the actors perform something more to their middle-brow taste.
Worthy London merchants, this uppity grocer claims, are mocked and irritated
by the courtly prejudices of most modern writers; proper subjects of drama,
he suggests, might better be found in the mercantile achievements of past and
present London. The grocer also wants a part in the play to be reserved for
his apprentice, the cocky amateur actor, Rafe. When the citizens get their way
and Rafe mounts the boards, chivalry and trade are forced first into an incongruous embrace and ultimately into an unconvincingly genial reconciliation.
Although it was not a success with its first audiences, *The Knight of the Burning
Pestle* vividly demonstrates the extent to which City manners and City characters had come to determine the subjects chosen by the London-based comic
dramatists of the late sixteenth and early seventeenth centuries.

Since its awkward beginnings in plays such as *Ralph Roister Doister*, non-romantic comedy had made rapid advances in theatrical sophistication and topical cross-reference. *The Old Wives' Tale* (*c.*1590, published 1595) is a dislocated medley of Plautian and modern English folk elements and an intermixture of the Roman and the rustic, presented by its author, George Peele (1556–96), as a satirical comment on escapist 'pastoral' fashions. Thomas Dekker's *The Shoemaker's Holiday, or A Pleasant Comedy of the Gentle Craft* (1599, published 1600) is both more shapely and more specifically a relocation of the ancient Roman urban comedy in commercial modern London. Dekker (?1570–1632), like Deloney before him, is equally specific in his presentation of honest toil and honourable trade as the keys to the health of a modern commonwealth. The play, set at the time of Henry V's French wars, stresses what many Elizabethan merchants would have taken as a self-evident, but none the less revolutionary, social truth, the equal dignity of the gentleman and the skilled craftsman. Simon Eyre, the hero of *The Shoemaker's Holiday*, rises to the essentially bourgeois dignity of the Lord Mayoralty of London but his daughter Rose marries a kinsman of the Earl of Lincoln. If, however, the King is prepared to recognize that 'love respects no blood', to Eyre the alliance between the court and trade is an unequal one. 'Those silken fellows are but painted images, outsides, outsides', he tries to insist to his socially mobile daughter, 'What? The Gentle Trade is a living for a man through Europe, through the world!'

Professional pride, the pushiness of the *arriviste*, and the comic conflict between generations and classes also figure in three of Thomas Middleton's London comedies, *A Mad World, My Masters* (*c.*1605–7, printed 1608), *A Trick to Catch the Old One* (1605, printed 1608), and *A Chaste Maid in Cheapside* (1611). For Middleton, however, social anomalies, new mercantile value-systems, and the equation of money and sex suggest the corruption of urban society. In each play foxes have to be outfoxed and the old who lack both spritely wit and integrity are successfully outwitted by the young. Ingenuity proves to be the best defence against arbitrary oppression. In *A Trick to Catch the Old One* Middleton (1580–1627) shows Theodorus Witgood (whose name implies that his quick intelligence is a divine gift) getting the better of two 'old ones', his usurious London uncle, Pecunius Lucre, and the miserly Walkadine Hoard. From the first he regains his lost inheritance, from the second a bride. If the plot of *A Chaste Maid in Cheapside* depends less on wit, it shows an equal concern with money, sex, and rank. A London goldsmith, appropriately named Yellowhammer, and his wife Maudline attempt to secure their new position in society by marrying off their daughter to Sir Walter Whorehound, a man of greater social, if not (as his name suggests) moral, standing. Moll Yellowhammer finally manages to trounce them by eloping with an impoverished gentleman of her own choice. At the same time, the Yellowhammers determine that their undergraduate son should be allied to a wealthy Welsh widow ('Yes, sure', Maudline insists, 'a huge heir in Wales, | At least to

nineteen mountains, | Besides her goods and cattell'). The widow, it unfortu-
nately transpires, is no more than Sir Walter's whore. Throughout the play
Middleton exposes pretension, false estimates, and idle expectations. His
middle-class Yellowhammers err in their vulgar snobberies (they have, for
example, sent a silver spoon to their son in Cambridge 'to eat his broth in the
hall amongst the gentlemen commoners') while his gentlemanly Whorehound
lacks both honour and scruples. The happy denouements of the plays may
allow for the triumph of young lovers, but they also revel in the discountenancing of pretenders, fools, and villains.

Philip Massinger (1583–1640), a regular collaborator of Fletcher's from
*c.*1616, moderated much of Middleton's harsh irony in his own later citizen
comedies by informing them with his own distinctly gentlemanly prejudices.
A New Way to Pay Old Debts (*c.*1625, published 1633) and, to a lesser extent,
The City Madam (1632, published 1658) follow the precedent of *A Trick to
Catch the Old One* in contrasting gentlemanly wit and prodigality with bourgeois hypocrisy and mean-spiritedness. In the long-popular *A New Way to Pay
Old Debts* the flamboyantly rapacious Sir Giles Overreach is tricked into restoring his nephew Wellborn's fortunes and reputation. The play is effectively
shaped around a struggle between the well-born and the ill-gotten. Wellborn's
restored social status is confirmed by his being given charge of a company of
soldiers; his new patron, Lord Lovell, marries Lady Allworth, while the tricked
parvenu Overreach is driven into a despairing madness and is forcibly removed
to Bedlam. The traditional order of things also triumphs in *The City Madam.*
Luke Frugal, given charge of his brother's extravagantly ambitious household
when that good-natured brother is supposed to have retired to a monastery,
proves as monstrous an oppressor as Shakespeare's Angelo (Massinger probably knew *Measure for Measure*). Luke serves his turn in bringing the family
back into line, however, and the true master is welcomed back as a deliverer
and an exposer of hypocrisy. For Sir John Frugal this restoration of order
implies that members of his family should henceforth know their place in the
social, sexual, and economic hierarchy, and his wife is told to 'instruct | Our
city dames, whom wealth makes proud, to move | In their own spheres, and
willingly to confess | . . . A distance 'twixt the city, and the court'. For
Massinger tidy comic endings seem to require a return to the status quo ante.
The patriarch reassumes command over his household, the parvenu defers to
the gentleman, and old money glitters more brightly than the new.

The urban comedies of Ben Jonson are at once more exuberant, more
aggressive, and more subversive than those of his contemporaries and imitators. However much his royal entertainments, his court masques, and the
poems he addressed to prominent aristocrats may express a deference to the
principles of monarchic rule and noble patronage, Jonson's plays reveal him to
be an unthinking respecter neither of persons nor of authority. His comedies
possess an extravagance of characterization coupled with an extraordinary
neatness of plotting. While his earlier plays ridicule the absurdities, anomalies,

and inconsistencies which he typifies as 'humours', the sharply crafted plays of the early 1600s deal more directly with power and manipulation. His protagonists glory in their native genius, but their ambitions, like those of the headstrong ancient builders of the Tower of Babel, are inherently flawed. Like the Babelites, Jonson's characters are confounded by language. In *The Alchemist* in particular, egocentricity, self-centredness, professional jargon, and private cant serve to preclude listening and responding; characters are effectively divided from each other by their distinctive voices, idiolects, and expressions. They can be lost for words or, more crucially, lost in words.

Jonson, who was much given to manifestos and declarations of literary intent, insisted in one of the entries in his various collection of notes and reflections, *Timber, or Discoveries Made upon Men and Manners* (published posthumously in 1640) that comedy had been considered by the Greeks to be equal in dignity to tragedy. Comic dramatists, he added, were held to be moral instructors 'no lesse than the Tragicks'. Modern theatre audiences, he complained, had consistently failed to grasp the point that 'the moving of laughter' was not essential to comedy whereas 'equity, truth, perspicuity, and candour' were. The Prologue to the second version of *Every Man in His Humour*, printed in the Folio volume of his works in 1616, equally represents an attempt to define the qualities of his own dramas in the face of debased popular taste. He claims to 'hate' the kind of play that makes 'a child now swaddled, to proceed Man, and then shoot up, in one beard and weed, | Past threescore years' and that which 'with three rusty swords' re-enacts 'York and Lancaster's long jars'. *His* plays will have no apologetic choruses, no scenic effects, and no ominous noises off. They will rather employ

> . . . deeds and language, such as men do use,
> And persons, such as comedy would choose,
> When she would show an image of the times,
> And sport with human follies not with crimes.
> Except we make them such, by loving still
> Our popular errors, when we know they're ill.
> I mean such errors as you'll all confess,
> By laughing at them, they deserve no less . . .

This is an attempt to announce the advent of a theatrical new age, an age which will dispose of artifice and substitute plain words, one which will subvert rather than confront, one which will allow that drama can represent a shared and deficient humanity rather than elevate and isolate the tragic hero.

Jonson's revision of *Every Man in His Humour* was in itself a signal to his readers of a personally engineered revolution. The first version of the play, in which Shakespeare is named in the cast list, was first performed in 1598 with a Florentine setting and Italian-sounding characters. In 1616 it re-emerged as an emphatically *London* play, its Lorenzos replaced by Knowells, its Musco by Brainworm, and its 'Bobadilla' translated into the extravagantly English Bobadill, a 'Paul's man', a lounging, professional *flâneur* in the once highly public space of the nave of St Paul's Cathedral. The 'English' *Every Man* does more than simply sport with human folly; it is a precise study of the kind of whimsical excess which Jonson believes disturbs the steady and reasoned development of human affairs. Excess also determines the nature of Jonson's most subtle, various, and energetic comedies, *Volpone* (1605–6, printed 1607), *Epicene, or the Silent Woman* (1609–10, printed 1616). *The Alchemist* (1610, printed 1612), and *Bartholomew Fair* (1614, printed 1631) *Epicene* is centred on the obsession of Morose, 'a gentleman that loves no noise', with silence. However ecologically sound his private campaign might seem to a twentieth-century audience, Morose is rendered absurd to a seventeenth-century one. He hates the essential sounds of city life, its bells, chatter, street-cries, cart-wheels, and occasional cannon. He seeks instead to withdraw from human society into the selfish security of his own company ('All discourses but mine own afflict me, they seem harsh, impertinent and irksome'). Morose emerges as an eccentric misanthropist who is fair game for those who expose his misanthropy to public scrutiny and ridicule. In order to spite his nephew, he marries himself to a 'silent woman', but his bride first turns out to be a nagging shrew and is ultimately revealed to be no bride at all, but a boy dressed as a girl. The comedy ends with a disturbing ambiguity, not with the tidy romance of a marriage but with a necessary divorce and with the financial justification of Morose's disinherited nephew, Sir Dauphine Eugenie (another 'well-born' heir).

The Alchemist centres not on the admirable tricker as the exposer of folly but on the professional trickster as the maker of fools. It begins with a noisy quarrel ('I fart at thee', 'I'll strip you', 'I'll gum your silks | With good strong water'), rapidly develops by setting a series of carefully engineered schemes in motion, gathers speed in the third act, and then seems to head towards an inevitable catastrophe which Jonson averts by letting the intrigue unwind rather than explode. The whole action of the play is confined to a house in Blackfriars, but as the original audience in the Blackfriars Theatre must have guessed, the play draws a larger London, including that of the audience's experience and expectations, into itself. When in the last act Subtle, the alchemist of the title, vanishes, he is left free to find more gulls in whatever larger London he escapes into (indeed his erstwhile assistant, Face, offers to send him a customer 'now and then, for old acquaintance'). In the course of the action Subtle and Face have managed to exploit an extraordinary range of urban suckers (Mammon the gourmandizing knight, Drugger the tobacco seller, Surly the gamester, and the self-righteous Puritans Tribulation Wholesome and his deacon, Ananias), but we are left at the end with the feeling that the next victim may be sitting next to us in the theatre. Jonson exploits similarly disconcerting effects in *Bartholomew Fair*, a play set in London's once great August Fair. The Fair, with its multi-purpose side-shows (such as Ursula's pig tent which serves as eating-house, privy, and brothel, where 'you may ha' your punk, and your pig in state, sir, both piping hot'), is in fact an unrestrained, carnivalesque city beyond the City. Those who attempt to restrain it, witness against it, or jeer at it, whether they be Justice Adam Overdo, the Puritan Zeal-of-the-Land Busy, or the two gallants, Quarlous and Winwife, are drawn willy-nilly into its reversals, ambiguities, surprises, and role changes. 'Remember you are but Adam, flesh and blood!', the floundering Overdo is counselled at the end of the play, 'You have your frailty; forget your other name of Overdo and invite us all to supper'. He can do nothing but accede.

Volpone, or The Fox is Jonson's most savage comedy. Despite its title and its Italianate menagerie of characters ('Fox', 'Flesh-fly', 'Vulture', 'Crow', 'Raven') it never seeks to reduce men to beasts or mere concepts. Its virtuous characters, Celia ('Heavenly') and Bonario ('Good'), may act like ciphers and may mouth moral platitudes, but they leave us wondering how else upright-ness might express itself in such a singularly naughty world. The Venice of *Volpone* is anything but serene. Its merchants are unscrupulous and self-seeking, its husbands mercenary and violent, its lawyers mendacious and corrupt, and even visitors to it mistake its dissimulation for sophistication. In Volpone's superbly modulated opening speech all values are reversed or thrown open to redefinition:

> Good morning to the day; and next my gold
> Open the shrine, that I may see my saint.
> [*Mosca draws a curtain, revealing piles of gold*]
> Hail the world's soul, and mine! More glad than is
> The teeming earth to see the longed-for sun
> Peep through the horns of the celestial Ram,
> Am I, to view thy splendour darkening his;
> That lying here, amongst my other hoards,
> Show'st like a flame by night, or like the day
> Struck out of chaos, when all darkness fled
> Unto the centre. O, thou son of Sol
> But brighter than thy father, let me kiss,
> With adoration, thee, and every relic
> Of sacred treasure in this blessed room.

Volpone flaunts his riches as did Venice in its prime, and like the city he glories 'more in the cunning purchase of my wealth | Than in the glad possession, since I gain no common way'. Nevertheless, he allows that gold overturns the metaphors of pagan legend and Christian Scripture alike; it usurps the splen-dours of nature and the joys of love and even renders hell 'with thee to boot' worth heaven. Volpone is no Marlovian outsider, no aspiring intellectual, no detached, clever upstart (unlike Subtle); he is an aristocratic insider with a par-ticular flair for exploiting the darker, passive side of mercantile acquisitiveness. He is, above all, a man of creative energy, one who splendidly acts out a series of roles (the plutocrat, the invalid, the mountebank, the musician, the poet, the lover) but one who is finally obliged by a court (which is only marginally less shifty than he is) to become the permanent invalid he once pretended to be. Venetian justice in *Volpone* is not the ideal held up in *The Merchant of Venice*.

But then Jonson the dramatist, unlike his 'beloved' Shakespeare, seems to have possessed a far greater tendency to distrust both romance and political ideals.

Jonson and the High Roman Fashion

Although Jonson did not necessarily trust ideals and idealists, he was certainly capable of adulating them if and when occasion demanded. 'Occasion' was generally the coincidence of aristocratic aspiration and aristocratic patronage in an age when aristocracy and an aristocratic culture mattered. Jonson, perhaps the most truly neo-Roman of all English writers of the Renaissance period, readily associated himself with Horace and associated the subjects of Horace's poetry with the ambiguities and anomalies of the reign of Augustus. The breadth of his classical reading was particularly evident in the printed form of the masque *Hymenaei* (originally performed at court in 1606 as part of the celebrations of the marital alliance between two upper-class families), for the extensive scholarly notes which supplement the text render it virtually an antiquarian treatise on Roman marriage customs. It was, however, with the poems collected as *Epigrammes* and *The Forrest* in the 1616 Folio that Jonson's direct debt to the Roman poets became most evident (the name of *The Forrest*, for example, translated the Latin word 'silva', both a forest and a collection). The *Epigrammes*, which Jonson considered 'the ripest fruit' of his studies, and which he claimed to value above his plays, contain pithy addresses to his Muse, to King James, to prominent noblemen and noblewomen, to literary friends, allies, and enemies, all expressed as rhymed English adaptations of the compact forms perfected in Latin by Juvenal and Horace. In epigrams 103 and 105, for example, Lady Mary Wroth is praised as the 'faire crowne' of her fair sex, as living up to her famous family and, most elegantly, as the reincarnation of the classical deities ('Madame, had all antiquitie beene lost, | All historic seal'd up, and fables crost; | That we had left us, nor by time, nor place | Least mention of a Nymph, a Muse, a Grace . . . Who could not but create them all from you?'). Lady Mary's husband, Sir Robert Wroth, is the recipient of a Horatian epistle, included in *The Forrest*, which contrasts the vices, sports, and entertainments of the city and the court with the alternative pleasures of country life. Instead of masques ('the short braverie of the night') Wroth can enjoy sound sleep or, from his bed, hear 'the loud stag speake'. He can delight in the ordered and fruitful progress of the seasons and 'live innocent' while others 'watch in guiltie armes, and stand | The furie of a rash command'. A similar evocation of refinement in gentlemanly retirement marks 'To Penshurst', an address to the country estate of Sir Robert Sidney (Mary Wroth's father). The poem's learned recalls of certain of Martial's epigrams and its replay of the anti-urban moralism which pervades Roman poetry of the first century AD help shape a tribute to the aristocratic values that Jonson chooses to see as eternal.

Penshurst is neither architecturally pretentious nor the expression of its owner's oppressive pride. Its park and its tenantry share an extraordinary fertility: fat carps run into nets, eels jump on land in front of fishermen, figs, grapes, and quinces mature in order, and the 'ripe daughters' of farming families come to the house bearing 'an embleme of themselves, in plum, or peare'. Above all, Jonson seems to find an especial joy in his own courteous reception at Penshurst:

> Where comes no guest, but is allow'd to eate,
> Without his feare, and of the lord's owne meate:
> Where the same beere, and bread, and self-same wine.
> That is his Lordships, shall be also mine.
> And I not faine to sit (as some, this day,
> At great mens tables) and yet dine away.

'To Penshurst' purposefully dwells on the idea of the open-handed generosity, the easy elegance, and the unaffected cultivation which Jonson saw as linking a modern aristocracy to the idealized patrician patrons of the ancient Roman poets.

In the eighty-ninth of his prose *Discoveries* ('Nobilium Ingenia') he offered a radically different analysis of the political characteristics of the ruling class. Some noblemen, he insists, serve their prince disinterestedly; others 'love their own ease' and out of vice, nature, or self-direction 'avoid business and care'; others still 'remove themselves upon craft and design' and these the prince should reckon 'in the list of his open enemies'. It is these contradictory inclinations to virtue, service, sloth, treachery, and conspiracy that he explores in his two Roman tragedies, *Sejanus his Fall* (1603, printed 1605) and *Catiline* (1611). Both plays rely heavily on classical dramatic precedent and on learned reference to Latin historians, orators, and poets, but both endeavour to do more than display Jonson's scholarly credentials. Both suggest vivid parallels between Roman corruption, treachery, and venality and the instability of the modern state. Jonson's first audiences may have remained unresponsive to the learned *Catiline* (obliging its author to defend his enterprise in the preface to its printed text), but few would have failed to recognize an analogy between the Catiline conspiracy in 63 BC and that of the Gunpowder Plot of AD 1605. As the more vivid *Sejanus* also suggests, Jonson readily recognized that if patrician virtue could be seen as an ideal linking the ancient and the modern orders, so ancient vice could find echoes in modern social disease. The tragedy centres on the devices and desires of Tiberius, a lazy, suspicious, unscrupulous Emperor determined to rule an increasingly sleazy Rome through the offices of the low-born favourite whom he has promoted to a position of power. Abetted by his master and 'rarefied' by the (literally) poisonous dowager Empress Livia, Sejanus attempts to crush all potential opposition by means of a singularly nasty mixture of threats, violence, fear, and murder. As with many of Jonson's comic sinners (who, in so many ways, stem from him), Sejanus aspires too highly and his schemes begin to totter. At the opening of Act V he triumphs in his genius and his influence:

> Swell, swell, my joys: and faint not to declare
> Yourselves, as ample, as your causes are.
> I did not live, till now; this is my first hour:
> Wherein I see my thoughts reached by my power.
> But this, and grip my wishes. Great, and high
> The world knows only two, that's Rome and I.
> My roof receives me not; 'tis air I tread:
> And, at each step, I feel my advanced head
> Knock out a star in heav'n! Reared to this height,
> All my desires seem modest, poor and slight,
> That did before sound impudent: 'tis place,
> Not blood, discerns the noble, and the base.
> Is there not something more, than to be Caesar?
> Must we rest there?

The play does not see this dangerous ambition as rooted solely in the unnatural advance of a commoner; it rather observes the social decay of Rome as stemming from the nature of its autocratic government and from the person of an Emperor determined to build a new world in his own image. Sejanus is destroyed because Tiberius finds him dispensable and because the master can manipulate a craven Senate more artfully than the servant. He dies passive and inarticulate, torn apart by a vengeful Roman mob, his body 'scattered, as he needs no grave, | Each little dust covers a little part: | So lies nowhere, and yet often buried'.

The rarely performed *Sejanus* is the only one of the Roman tragedies written by Shakespeare's contemporaries worthy to stand beside *Coriolanus* and *Antony and Cleopatra*. George Chapman's *Caesar and Pompey* (*c.*1599–1607, printed 1631), which impressively explores Roman stoicism through the witness and heroic suicide of Cato of Utica, has a slow dignity of expression but lacks a compensatory dramatic dynamism. Massinger's *The Roman Actor* (1626, printed 1629) moves away, like *Sejanus*, from the dying Roman republic to the decadence and uncertainties of imperial rule. The Emperor Domitian is as immoral and as dangerously arbitrary in his command as Jonson's Tiberius. The Rome that once fostered the virtues of a Lucrece and a Brutus, the Emperor is told, has 'nothing Roman left now, but in you | The lust of Tarquin'. The play is chiefly remarkable for its strenuous defence of theatre as a corrective to a lax or an oppressive political morality ('Actors may put in for as large a share | As all the sects of the philosophers. | They with cold pre- cepts (perhaps seldom read) | Deliver what an honourable thing | The active virtue is. But does that fire the blood . . . equal to that | Which is presented in our theatres?'). Paris, the Roman actor of the play's title, is to prove a martyr to his cause, dying, as his murderer Domitian cynically notes, 'in action'. Digressive as Paris's proud advocacy of his profession has seemed to some commentators, it long remained popular as an actor's manifesto. In its time it must have seemed as much a protest against historic immorality as it was a declaration in support of the modern stage against the Puritan intolerance which sought to close the theatres on moral grounds.

'Debauch'd and diversivolent': Men, Women, and Tragedy

Although most of the tragedies written for the London stage in the last decade of the sixteenth century and in the first thirty years of the seventeenth century were concerned with the fatal destinies of foreign emperors, kings, princes, or, at the very least, of noblemen, a handful of subsequently influential plays took English domestic mayhem and the fraught relations of middle-class husbands and wives as their subject. Certain of these plays, such as Jonson and Dekker's collaborative *The Lamentable Tragedy of the Page of Plymouth* (payment for which is recorded' in the 1590s) have not survived. Notable amongst the plays that have come down to us are three anonymous works, *The Tragedy of Mr Arden of Faversham* (printed 1592 and once, somewhat rashly, attributed to Shakespeare), *A Warning to Fair Women* (printed 1599), and *A Yorkshire Tragedy* (1608, with the yet more rash claim to Shakespearian authorship printed on its title-page). All three were based on real events, the sensational murders of husbands by adulterous wives or their lovers in the first two, and the terrible slaughter of his family by a deranged husband in the third. Thomas Arden, a prosperous Kentish landowner, was murdered in Faversham in 1551; the London merchant, George Sanders, whose lamentable death is re-enacted in *A Warning to Fair Women*, was stabbed in a wood near Woolwich in 1573. Both plays offer somewhat rushed and untidy accounts of murderous plans, fortuitous escapes, bloody dispatches, clumsy attempts at concealment, and final judicial retribution. Neither could be properly styled 'tragic' (though in both, distressed and oppressed women murderers are brought to a tearful penitence before their respective executions). If *A Warning to Fair Women* varies its glimpses of London bourgeois life with moralistic pageants and allegorical dumb-shows, *A Yorkshire Tragedy* tells a stark story starkly, barely pausing, with the exception of one soliloquy for the hair-tearing husband, to allow its characters to articulate the nature of their circumstances. All three plays offer a foretaste of the later development of domestic drama and of the horripilant prose and ballad narratives which marked the popular criminal literature of the late eighteenth and nineteenth centuries.

Thomas Heywood's *A Woman Killed with Kindness* (*c.*1603, printed 1607), though set in contemporary Yorkshire, has no obvious source in sensational fact. It does, however, make the most of a sensational fictional situation. Heywood (?1574–1641) opens his play with a wedding between a supposedly 'ideal' woman and a man proud of both his happiness and his social standing ('I am a gentleman, and by my birth | Companion with a king'). The two distinct strands of the plot rapidly degenerate into bloodshed, deception, and destruction (suggested in scene ii by a brawl and murder during a morning's hawking). Anne, the wife, finds herself in an adulterous maze that she rightly fears 'will prove the labyrinth of sin'. Frankford, the husband, who probes his impending domestic disaster by means of a card-game fraught with *doubles entendres* and dark suspicions, and who later discovers his wife in bed with her lover, finally 'kindly' banishes her from his house and children. 'A mild sentence', Anne laconically comments, though her exile results in a contrite death and ultimate forgiveness from her long-suffering husband. *A Woman Killed with Kindness* is a revenge play without revenge, one in which murderous impulses are controlled and dispelled. It is, nevertheless, like Heywood's second study of adultery, *The English Traveller* (*c*.1625), a play told from a male point of view, with an audience's sympathies purposefully directed away from 'deceiving' women to 'deceived' men. Heywood does, however, reveal a compensating sympathy with a spirited (if neither domestic nor adulterous) woman in the two parts of *The Fair Maid of the West; or, A Girl worth Gold* (Part One *c*.1600, Part Two *c*.1630). The two plays trace the story of Bess Bridges, a Plymouth tanner's daughter, who shows an extraordinary presence of mind both as an innkeeper and as the adventurous owner of a privateer. Bess is neither a blushingly patient innocent nor a brazen transvestite tart, but a resourceful, courageous, and generous heroine who strives for goals and who manages to win what she seeks.

Two spirited women of complementary temperament, but of opposing circumstances, distinguish Beaumont and Fletcher's high-flown, aristocratic, and neo-Greek drama *The Maid's Tragedy* (*c*.1610, printed 1619). Evadne, conveniently married off to Amintor, refuses to sleep with her new husband on their wedding night; it is neither prudery nor a vow of celibacy that moulds her decision ('A maidenhead, Amintor, | At my years?') but the fact that she is the king's mistress. Aspatia, the 'maid' of the title, who has been abandoned by the same Amintor, spends much of the first part of the play in Ariadne-like bewailings of her loss ('Suppose I stand upon the sea-beach now, | Mine arms thus, and mine hair blown with the wind, | Wild as that desert'). Both women transform their initial passivity into striking action. Aspatia disguises herself as her brother and provokes Amintor to a duel in which he fatally wounds her. Evadne kills the lecherous king by first tying him to his bed ('What pretty new device is this, Evadne? . . . By, by love. | This is a quaint one', he excitedly asks), and then stabbing him. The play ends with the death of Aspatia, with Evadne's suicide following her rejection by Amintor, and with Amintor killing himself beside the corpse of his first love ('Here's to be with thee, love!').

Lysippus, the successor to the throne at the sanguinary climax of *The Maid's Tragedy*, draws a moral conclusion from the events he has witnessed. 'On lustful kings, | Unlook'd-for, sudden deaths from heaven are sent', he proclaims. He then adds a second warning: 'Curst is he that is their instrument'. Lysippus's words might act as motto for any of the revenge plays that stemmed from Kyd's *The Spanish Tragedy* and as a comment on the shady, sinister,

libidinous worlds of those Jacobean dramas set in the palaces of Catholic
Europe. George Chapman's *Bussy D'Ambois* (*c.*1604, printed 1607), based on
the dangerous career of a protégé of the brother of Henry III of France, offers
a highly unflattering picture of the nastiness of the later sixteenth-century
French court. King Henry himself confesses that his own circle is tawdry compared to that of Queen Elizabeth in England:

> . . . as Courts should be th'abstracts of their kingdoms
> In all the beauty, state and worth they hold,
> So is hers, amply, and by her informed.
> The world is not contracted to a man
> With more proportion and expression
> Than in her Court, her kingdom. Our French Court
> Is a mere mirror of confusion to it.

Chapman (?1559–1634) is offering more than a golden retrospect on Elizabeth;
he is outlining one of the many juxtapositions on which his play is built. Bussy,
like so many of the marginalized malcontents who will follow him in the plays
of the 1600s, is a misfit in the discordant and corrupt courtly world in which
he moves. His opening soliloquy shifts restlessly between images of uncertain
Fortune and equally uncertain Virtue, images which echo Plutarch's *Moralia*
rather than the Homer with whose name Chapman's is most frequently associated (his translations of the *Iliad* and the *Odyssey*, the work that he 'was born
to do', appeared in 1616). Throughout the play Bussy stands quarrelsomely
alone, at times the cursed instrument of the mighty, at others the disinherited
outsider who vindicates no moral causes but his own. At the end, entrapped
and mortally wounded by the chief of his many enemies, he props himself up
on his sword and proclaims himself a Roman statue, already a monument to
his own future fame. Chapman's later tragedies, *The Revenge of Bussy D'Ambois*
(*c.*1610, printed 1613) and the two parts of *The Conspiracy and Tragedy of
Charles, Duke of Byron* (*c.*1607, printed 1608), return to the dark intrigues
of the French court and to historical characters flawed by the very grandeur
of their ambitions. The 'Senecal' Clermont D'Ambois, urged by Bussy's angry
ghost to avenge his brother, insists on an honourable course in gaining his ends
but finally finds himself unable to carry on living as 'the slave of power' amid
'all the horrors of the vicious time' and resolves to kill himself. Bussy may be
revenged, but the ultimate triumph belongs to a corrupt society. The central
character of *The Conspiracy . . . of Byron* is, by contrast, supremely confident
of his own independent distinction ('. . . men in themselves entire | March
safe with naked feet on coals of fire: | I build not outward, nor depend on
props'). When he excitedly intrigues against the order imposed by Henry IV,
as if he were testing his superior prowess, the King's justice catches him out
and condemns him. Byron, faced with an imminent death-sentence, oscillates
frenziedly between defiance and acceptance, between an insistence on his
justification and a terror of ultimate negation.

The ambivalent gestures of Chapman's plays are to some extent reflected in those of Jonson's sometime bitter enemy and later cordial friend, John Marston (1576–1634). When Jonson privately jested that 'Marston wrott his Father in Lawes preachings and his father in Law his Commedies' he was not necessarily poking fun at Marston's vocation (he followed his father-in-law into the Anglican priesthood in 1609). Jonson was, perhaps, voicing his unease at the moral censoriousness which, coupled with an indeterminacy of genre, marks much of Marston's work. This indeterminacy is particularly evident in the two-part play, *Antonio and Mellida*, written for a boys' company in *c*.1599 and printed in 1602. The first part explores the 'comic crosses of true love' in upper-class Italy; the second (sometimes known as *Antonio's Revenge*) deals far more darkly, in the manner of *Hamlet*, with tragic crosses, intrigues, ghosts, feigned madness and, above all, revenge. Marston's discordant moral vision is reflected in his equally discordant rhetoric. He echoes Senecan stoicism and Senecan bombast, but he adds to it his own distinct despondency and a verbal cacophony, jolting his audiences with tortuous phrasing, cumulative lists of words, and jerky neologisms. These devices are particularly evident in *The Malcontent* (printed 1602), a play variously (and uncertainly) typed by its critics as a satirical comedy, a tragi-comedy, and a tragedy. With its central character, the banished Duke of Genoa, Altofronto, disguised as Malevole (the malcontent of the title) the play veers disquietingly between snarling exposure of moral corruption and justifications of Malevole's pursuit of political justice. He spits out prose curses ('I'll come among you, you goatish-blooded toderers [*sic*], as gum into taffeta, to fret, to fret. I'll fall like a sponge into water, to suck up, to suck up') and his restlessness is expressed in equally agitated verse:

> I cannot sleep . . .
> The galley-slave, that all the toilsome day
> Tugs at his oar against the stubborn wave,
> Straining his rugged veins, snores fast;
> The stooping scythe-man that doth barb the field
> Thou mak'st wink sure. In night all creatures sleep;
> Only the malcontent, that 'gainst his fate
> Repines and quarrels—alas, he's goodman tell-clock;
> His sallow jaw-bones sink with wasting moan;
> Whilst others' beds are down, his pillow's stone.

Like Malevole, Marston seeks to make his moral point by fretting, by quarrelling, and by exaggerating the male and female disorders of an evil age until they appear as grotesque offences against heaven. His climb into a pulpit was perhaps only a short one.

The anonymous *The Revenger's Tragedy* (printed 1607) takes up many of Marston's themes and devices, distilling them into something more pungent. The play, formerly ascribed to Cyril Tourneur (?1575–1626), the author of *The Atheist's Tragedy* (printed 1611), has recently been more confidently recognized as the work of Thomas Middleton. *The Atheist's Tragedy* offers an exposure of the dangers of vice consequent upon freethinking (divinely checked when the atheistic villain, D'Amville, accidentally dashes his brains out while raising an axe to behead the virtuous Charlemont) and of the principle of revenge (which the ghost of Charlemont's father insists should be left 'unto the king of kings'). The moral demonstrations of *The Revenger's Tragedy* are equally graphic but, to most twentieth-century audiences, somewhat less risible. It is set in an extravagantly unpleasant but unspecified Italian court, but a disillusioned observer might just as easily have applied its many expressions of disgust with the ways of the princely world to the corruptions of Jacobean England. Not only is the play shaped by an irony akin to Jonson's, but the names of its characters, like those of *Volpone*, are effectively Italianate versions of the type-figures to be met with in the earlier English tradition of Morality plays. Its revenger, the brother of the wronged Castiza (chaste), is bluntly called Vindice; its nobly born villains are expressively named Lussurioso (lecherous), Spurio (the bastard), Ambitioso (ambitious), and Supervacuo (vain) and their followers rejoice in the names Nencio (fool) and Sordido (dodger). The play's discourse is built around frank statements of villainy, cynical assertions of self-justification, and quasi-proverbial maxims which characters employ ironically and sententiously. It is equally emblematic in its action. *The Revenger's Tragedy* is something of an animated *memento mori*, emphatically so when Vindice disposes of the libidinous Duke by contriving that he should kiss the poisoned skull of his murdered mistress. At the beginning of the play Vindice had appeared nursing this 'sallow picture of my poison'd love, | My study's ornament'; in Act III he reappears with the skull 'dressed up in tires' (a wig and women's clothes) and tells his brother that this emblem will both catch a sinner and stand as a warning against all human vanity:

> Does every proud and self-affecting dame
> Camphor her face for this? and grieve her maker
> In sinful baths of milk, when many an infant starves
> For her superfluous outside—all for this?

Vindice is a supremely inventive revenger, one who is overweeningly proud of his invention. As a man, however, he finally stands condemned by a reassertion of the human justice which had seemed so absent from the play. He sees his imminent execution as a last gesture of self-assertion ('are we not reveng'd? | Is there one enemy left alive amongst those? | 'Tis time to die when we ourselves are foes . . . We die after a nest of dukes'). Somehow Antonio's brief attempt to draw token religious and political consolation from the retributive death of the revengers ('Pray heaven their blood may wash away all treason!') echoes hollowly in this generally Godless, unjust, and sepulchral world.

In Middleton's two grimly chilling later tragedies, *Women Beware Women* (*c*.1621, printed 1657) and his collaboration with William Rowley (?1585–1626) *The Changeling* (1622, printed 1653), it is women who are first corrupted and then obliged to follow through the consequences of their corruption before being consumed by it. The two interwoven plots of *Women Beware Women* also show women trapped in spaces, often confined, locked and shuttered ones, contrived by men or by other women acting as willing agents of male power. Livia seduces her own niece into an adulterous relationship with her uncle and then works as the Duke of Florence's accomplice in his off-stage seduction of the married Bianca (she plays a distracting game of chess with Bianca's mother-in-law in which the references to black kings, lost pawns, and mating have a horrid duality). Despite her brutal ravishing, Bianca is no Lucrece. Brought up, she later claims, 'with many jealous eyes . . . that never thought they had me sure enough | But when they were upon me', she resolves never to use any daughter of her own so strictly, even though her prospective espousal of liberal parenthood broadens into permissiveness ('they will come to't | And fetch their falls a thousand mile about, | Where one would little think on't'). Sin, as Livia notes at the end of Act II, might taste 'at the first draught like wormwood-water', but when drunk again ''tis nectar ever after'. Moral licence and naked ambition drive both Livia and Bianca to enjoy the exercise of sexual, financial, and political power in a sordid, patriarchal society. Both are, however, to share in the exemplary and emblematic punishments meted out to the Duke's court during the performance of his marriage masque. A range of theatrical props (Cupid's arrows, Hymen's incense, Juno's flaming gold, and nuptial cups) prove fatal to actors and observers alike.

The intoxicating taste of what had once seemed forbidden fruits also marks the central intrigue of Middleton and Rowley's *The Changeling*. Beatrice-Joanna, the daughter of a Spanish grandee, escapes from an undesired marriage by hiring De Flores, whom she claims to find physically repulsive, to dispose of her fiancé. Her tidy plan does not work out as she had hoped. Instead of fleeing and leaving her to marry the man of her choice, De Flores insists that his price is her virginity. When she protests her modesty, he, with proper justice, responds: 'Push! You forget yourself! | A woman dipp'd in blood, and talk of modesty'. Throughout the intense and febrile scene in which De Flores confronts Beatrice-Joanna with their mutual complicity and interdependence, he systematically inverts each of her protective pretensions. Her last, kneeling, attempt to repulse him as a viper is answered by his embrace:

> Come, rise, and shroud your blushes in my bosom;
> Silence is one of pleasure's best receipts;
> Thy peace is wrought for ever in this yielding.
> 'Las, how the turtle pants! Thou'lt love anon
> What thou so fear'st and faint'st to venture on.

Having found herself 'undone . . . endlessly' she discovers that, willy-nilly, her loathing of De Flores has become love, her repulsion revelation, her physical revulsion physical rapture. What obsesses her now is how to deceive. *The Changeling* outdoes merely 'Gothic' perturbations. Few things in European culture written before the 1890s rival the power of this representation of antipathy realized as empathy and of the passionate release of an upper-class woman's repressions. Beatrice-Joanna's neuroses are, however, given both a context and a larger dimension in *The Changeling* by the 'comic' sub-plot (probably provided by Rowley). Trivial as the frenzied amatory intrigues of Antonio and Francisco may seem by comparison, their disguises as 'fools and madmen', in order to woo the young wife of the keeper of a madhouse, reflect back on the confinements, the mental disjunctions, and the violence of the main plot.

The dark fatalism, the satiric urgency, and the nervous fragmentation of character in Middleton's tragedies are further accentuated in those of John Webster (*c.*1578–*c.*1634). A collaborator of Dekker's and probably also of Rowley's, Heywood's, and Ford's, Webster had also expanded Marston's *The Malcontent* in 1604. His individual reputation rests, however, on two major works, *The White Devil* (*c.*1609–12, printed 1612) and *The Duchess of Malfi* (*c.*1613, printed 1623). As his address 'To the Reader' prefaced to *The White Devil* suggests, Webster saw himself as a modern dramatic poet aware of the example of the ancient tragedians and one who particularly 'cherish'd [a] good opinion of other men's worthy labours' (by which he meant the work of his contemporaries, Chapman, Jonson, Beaumont, Fletcher, Shakespeare, Dekker, and Heywood). Although the subjects of both of his tragedies are based on true, bloody, and recent occurrences in the shifty courts of Italy, Webster was an adept borrower of devices, effects, themes, and metaphors from his fellow English dramatists and a gifted, if idiosyncratic, remoulder of second-hand materials. If, as has been argued, he derived his representation of Cornelia's distraction in *The White Devil* from Ophelia's mad-scene in *Hamlet*, his paraphernalia of ghosts, dumb shows, and expedient retribution from revenge plays, and his two satirical Malcontents, Flamineo and Bosola, from Chapman and Marston, he yet managed to place his borrowings in strikingly novel and distinctive contexts.

As its title suggests, *The White Devil* is concerned with paradoxes, antitheses and with enforced dissimulation. When Vittoria Corombona attempts to protest at the quality of 'dissembling men', her brother Flamineo responds, 'We suck'd that, sister, | From women's breasts in our first infancy'. In Act V the same Machiavellian Flamineo offers a further, but far more pained, apology for the exercise of hypocrisy:

>   . . . I have liv'd
> Riotously ill, like some that live in court;
> And sometimes, when my face was full of smiles
> Have felt the maze of conscience in my breast.
> Oft gay and honour'd robes those tortures try,—
> We think cag'd birds sing, when indeed they cry.

The major characters in this fast-moving play rarely pause to explore or expound their conditions. They reveal themselves in flashes and in fragmentary confessions, or are defined in juxtaposition and conflict with other characters. When, for example, Vittoria is put on trial as a 'debauch'd and diversivolent [desiring strife] woman', she demands of the Cardinal who is her chief accuser 'Ha? whore—what's that?'. Once the Cardinal has offered a spluttering definition of the term, she has the gall to reply: 'This character scapes me'. When, later, her equally 'diversivolent' and murderous husband Bracciano faces her with old love-letters from Florence, the discourse seems to scurry from issue to issue and from startling metaphor to metaphor.

The verse, the action, and the situation of *The Duchess of Malfi* are generally less restless. The tragedy opens with references to the 'fix'd order' imposed on the French court by 'their judicious king'. Things prove to be far less well ordered in the courts of Italy. The widowed Duchess of Malfi commits what is seen by her villainous brothers as an unforgivable sin against the dignity of their blood by marrying her steward. These same brothers, Ferdinand, Duke of Calabria, and a Cardinal (who has failed to become Pope because 'he did bestow bribes so largely, and so impudently'), determine to destroy their sister, her husband, and their children. Ferdinand is possessed of an especially vicious and nasty mind. 'I would have their bodies | Burnt in a coal-pit', he declares in Act II, 'or dip the sheets they lie in, in pitch or sulphur, | Wrap them in't, and then light them like a match'. Somewhat more controlledly, but no less viciously, he outlines a more effective plan of psychological torture in Act IV:

> Damn her! that body of hers,
> While that my blood ran pure in't, was more worth
> Than that which thou wouldst comfort, call'd a soul—
> I will send her masques of common courtesans,
> Have her meat serv'd up by bawds and ruffians,
> And, 'cause she'll needs be mad, I am resolv'd
> To remove forth the common hospital
> All the mad-folk, and place them near her lodging;
> There let them practise together, sing, and dance,
> And act their gambols to th' full o'th' moon:
> If she can sleep the better for it, let her— . . .

The Duchess, like a prophetic female victim of the twentieth century's refinements of mental degradation, is gradually worn down by the yelps of lunatics and by waxworks supposedly representing her dead family. She is finally dispatched by executioners who enter bearing a coffin, cords, and a bell. She dies passively, mustering what dignity remains to her, meekly kneeling before her murderers and declaring 'heaven-gates are not so highly arch'd | As princes' palaces, they that enter there | Must go upon their knees'. The Duchess poses, like an assured and decorous martyr in a Renaissance painting, a lonely pattern of virtue in an otherwise dark, immoral, male, and seemingly irredeemable world.

The Duchess's husband's dying wish is that his son should 'fly the courts of princes'. This prayer could be echoed, and still remain unanswered, through the tragedies of John Ford (1586–*post* 1639) and James Shirley (1596–1666). Where the seventeenth-century English court, often under Jonson's tutelage, chose to see itself and its manners idealized in masques, Ford's and Shirley's plays, written for the commercial theatre rather than the court, continued the line of disturbing explorations of aristocratic corruption into the Caroline age. The cultivated Charles I, who became king in 1625, tended to favour the kind of courtly, formal drama that served as an instrument of state and accentuated the principles of order, divine harmony, and royal dignity that he espoused. A good number of his metropolitan subjects, however, continued to patronize the public theatres that presented plays which must have offended the highminded King as much as they outraged the increasingly censorious Puritan members of his Parliament.

The political and moral concerns of court theatre and public theatre were not necessarily as disparate as we might at first think. Ford's early poem *Christ's Bloody Sweat* (1613) is a reminder that he was not devoid of a sense of an urgent human need to respond to God's mercy. Indeed, the central characters in his later tragedies can be seen as moving in a Calvinistic world where, despite gestures of self-assertion, their destinies are inexorable and their souls preordained to damnation. Even in *The Broken Heart* (printed 1633), set in pagan Sparta, the disciplined values of an old military code continue to dominate the action, despite the jealousy, resentment, and pursuit of revenge which threaten to undermine the order of the state. In the third act of the play, the philosopher Tecnicus insists to his pupil Orgilus that honour consists 'not in a bare opinion' but exists as 'the reward of virtue . . . acquir'd | By justice or by valour, which for basis | Hath justice to uphold it'. Nevertheless, in *The Broken Heart*, and in the more celebrated *'Tis Pity She's a Whore* (also 1633), assertions of selfhood through the evolution of private moral codes stand opposed to an inherited social morality. Almost as a parody of Puritan individualism, Ford's leading characters, both male and female, define themselves by declaring war on received or traditional definitions of spiritual value. Most shockingly, Giovanni and Annabella, the incestuous brother and sister of *'Tis Pity She's a Whore*, insist on the rightness of their inverted passion regardless of the strictures of Church, family, and society. 'I have asked counsel of the holy church | Who tells me I may love you', Giovanni contortedly explains to his sister in Act I, 'and 'tis just, | That since I may, I should; and will, yes, will.' He has discovered a sanction which is no sanction and constructed a private moral theology out of feeling. Brother and sister recognize that their illicit love is eternally damnable, but, as Giovanni explains in Act V, this makes for a temporal and temporary paradise:

> O, the glory
> Of two united hearts like hers and mine!
> Let poring bookmen dream of other worlds;

My world and all of happiness is here,
And I'd not change it for the best to come;
A life of pleasure is Elysium.

This is Faustian daring and Faustian arrogance. Giovanni does not merely break a great social taboo, he finally compounds his sin against heaven by killing his sister, parading through a banqueting room with her heart fixed to his dagger, declaring that his act of murder sacrilegiously parallels the sacrifice of Christ and the eclipse which accompanied it ('The glory of my deed | Darken'd the midday sun, made noon as night').

Ford's *The Chronicle History of Perkin Warbeck; A Strange Truth* (printed 1634) attempted, as its Prologue admitted, to revive a genre that had become 'so out of fashion, so unfollow'd'. It did more than resurrect the Elizabethan history play; it returned forcefully to the old political problems of usurpation and good government, but it did so by contrasting the effective but 'usurping' King Henry VII, with a rival pretender to the throne who seriously believes that he is the true heir. Where Ford's sources tend to stress that Perkin Warbeck, the would-be king, was a fraudulent and deluded claimant, the Perkin of the play continues to assert his claim even in the teeth of defeat. He views his imprisonment in the Tower as a return to 'our childhood's dreadful nursery' and his imminent execution as 'A martyrdom of majesty'. Others may see him as a candidate for Bedlam but in his own serenely focused eyes he is an undoubted Prince.

The political disjunctions, contradictions, and disruptions which marked the troubled reign of Charles I overshadowed James Shirley's literary career. Ordained an Anglican priest in the early 1620s, Shirley appears to have resigned his orders on his (rumoured) conversion to Roman Catholicism. Having first established himself as a schoolmaster, from *c*.1625 he pursued a second successful career as a dramatist. Certain of his comedies, notably *Hyde Park* (1632, printed 1637), look forward to the gentlemanly smoothness of Restoration drama, while *The Triumph of Peace*, a particularly lavish masque written for the Inns of Court in 1634, shows him as an adept flatterer of the 'great king and queen, whose smile | Doth scatter blessings through this isle, | To make it best | And wonder of the rest'. By contrast, Shirley's most notable tragedies, *The Traitor* (1631, printed 1635) and *The Cardinal* (1641, printed 1652), both show courts troubled by dissent, lust, pride, and ambition. The murky Florence of *The Traitor* is ruled by a debauched Duke who is finally disposed of by his ambitious and scheming kinsman, Lorenzo. The Navarre of *The Cardinal* is more blessed in its ruler. It is, however, a kingdom destabilized by untrustworthy and self-seeking counsellors, notably the unscrupulous Cardinal of the title (in whom some commentators have seen elements of both Richelieu and Archbishop Laud). If, as is possible, Shirley was reflecting on the example of Shakespeare's *Henry VIII*, he would probably also have acknowledged a parallel between the ultimate authority of his King of Navarre and the English King who frees himself from the oppressive influence of yet another proud and political Cardinal, Wolsey. 'How much are kings abused by those they take to royal grace', Navarre muses, before adding a final emphatic maxim: *'None have more need of perspectives than kings.'*

The Cardinal is a royalist play which may, in part, be seen as a late, flickering contribution to the larger Renaissance humanist discourse on the principles of good government. It is also, in its somewhat stodgy way, the last of the revenge plays, if one largely shorn of Jacobean extravagance and Jacobean verve. When the theatres were shut by an Order of Parliament in 1642, Shirley was obliged to return to school-teaching and to the printing of his now unperformable playscripts. As an avowed royalist he was also later impeached and fined. Although he provided a relatively modest and tactful masque, entitled *Cupid and Death*, for Cromwell's official reception of the Portuguese ambassador in 1653, Shirley's career effectively belonged in the past. The writing of plays in the 1640s had become an intensely fraught political activity. If some contemporaries viewed the closure of the public theatres in 1642 as a temporary measure and as an expedient sop to Puritan opinion, it must have been obvious that the English state had declared itself antipathetic to the stage, when, five years later, a further parliamentary ordinance against acting was enforced. The traditions of acting and production evolved in the Shakespearian theatre had come to an abrupt end. Until London theatres reopened in 1660, plays were to be literature read, but not literature performed. By 1660, however, though old play-texts remained constant, plays in performance were subject to new theatrical fashions, new styles of acting, and new canons of taste which demanded often drastic revisions, additions, and excisions.

The English Renaissance, which had begun as an opening up to new European learning and to new European styles, ended as a restrictive puritanical assertion of national independence from European norms of government and aesthetics. The English Reformation, which had begun as an assertion of English nationhood under a monarch who saw himself as head, protector, and arbiter of a national Church, ended as a challenge to the idea of monarchy itself. In England the principles on which the Renaissance and the Reformation were based, and by means of which both developed, were, as its literature serves to demonstrate, inextricably intertwined.

4

Revolution and Restoration: Literature 1620–1690

ON the feast of the Epiphany (6 January) 1620, the year in which the Pilgrim Fathers set sail for America, Ben Jonson's masque *News from the New World Discovered in the Moon* was presented at court before King James I. The masque formed the climax to the celebration of the twelve days of Christmas and it offered to the King a fantastically contrived vision of his own greatness. Moon creatures, formed in the image of man, and 'animated, lightned, and heightened' by a rapt contemplation of royal virtues, descended from a frosty stage heaven, shook off their icicles, sang of the King's perfection, and danced to represent the harmony of his rule. Chief amongst the dancers was the King's heir, Charles, Prince of Wales. The contrast between the extravagant courtly theatre of the masque and the determined refugees from James's religious policies who were to establish Plymouth Plantation could not be more extreme. Those extremes characterize both the politics and the literature of the seventeenth century. The masque celebrated an ideal monarch whose merits could be studied, like the Bible, as 'the booke of all perfection'; the narrow Bible-centred Puritanism of the Pilgrims demanded a rejection of a cornerstone of James's idea of kingship, an integrated union of the English state with the English Church through the person of the King himself and the bishops appointed by him.

James's son, who succeeded to the throne as Charles I in 1625, was the first English monarch to have been born into the Church of England; he also proved to be its stoutest, and most extreme, defender. Charles's attempt to extend its ecclesiastical order and its liturgy to his northern Kingdom of Scotland began the long-drawn-out challenge to his authority which ended in his trial and execution and in the abolition of 'the Kingly Office' itself by the English Parliament. In December 1641 Charles had proclaimed the Church of England 'the most pure and agreeable to the Sacred Word of God of any religion now practised in the Christian World' and declared that, if martyrdom were required of him, he would be prepared to seal his profession of faith with his own blood. Charles and the chief instrument of his ecclesiastical policy,

Archbishop Laud, were both to end their lives on the scaffold after the failure
of their strenuous attempts to assert the principle of uniformity in the Church.
In no period of British history has the disparity between an ideal of political
and spiritual order and the reality of dissent and disorder been so destructive
of civil life and so productive of an expressive and often partisan literature.

That James I and his son should have so rejoiced in the art of the masque
is testimony to their desire to use symbolic theatre in order to celebrate their
belief in the divine appointment of earthly kings. For both, the union of the
Crowns of England and Scotland under the Stuarts betokened a restoration of
the primitive kingdom of the mythical Trojan, Brutus, from whom Britannia
had derived its name. For both, a policy of European neutrality, and a reconciliation with the old enemy, Spain, seemed to usher in a new era of peace,
prosperity, and concord in which the English court would outshine those of its
Habsburg, Bourbon, Gonzaga, and Medici rivals. Its festivals symbolically proclaimed the special providence that had brought Britain to its unique glory.
The first of Jonson's masques for James, *The Masque of Blacknesse* of 1605,
had proudly announced the distinctive destiny of 'this blest isle' which had
'wonne her ancient dignitie, and stile, | *A world divided from the world*'. For
Jonson and his royal patrons the masque form was a complex political statement of the highest order. Long before Wagner conceived of the idea of a
Gesamtkunstwerk (the total, or all-embracing, work of art) the masque was a
fusion of poetry, scene-painting, music, song, dance, stage-machinery, and
elaborate costumes. These spectacles, mounted but once, or at most three
times, were also awesomely expensive to produce. The court spent the then
phenomenal annual sum of £3,000–£4,000 on such entertainments and in 1634
James Shirley's *The Triumph of Peace* cost the Inns of Court no less than
£20,000 in an exorbitant attempt to counter Charles I's displeasure at the veiled
insult to his Queen published by one of their members.

The special feature of the masque, as opposed to the public theatre, lay in
its combination of amateur and professional actors, or, more precisely, in its
use of princely or aristocratic participants in the most prominent roles. Not
only was the entertainment centred on the monarch, and the audience drawn
exclusively from the most favoured members of the court, but the extravagantly costumed appearance of James's consort, Anne of Denmark, or of
Charles I and his wife, as dancers or as embodied virtues was viewed as a proper
extension of their nobility. The whole was deemed to be a stately, dramatic
exercise in ethics. Introducing his *Hymenaei; or the Solemnities of Masque and
Barriers at a Marriage* (1606) Jonson insisted that masque 'hath made the most
royall Princes, and greatest persons (who are commonly the personators of
these actions) not onely studious of riches, and magnificence in the outward
celebration, or shew (which rightly becomes them) but curious after the most
high, and heartie inventions, to furnish the inward parts'. The splendour
of outward representation ideally testified to an instinctive inward virtue.
Unmasked, or bereft of a symbolic costume, the courtier-actor emerged with

his or her courtly nobility aggrandized. That the masque demanded relatively little action was integral to its form. The involvement of Inigo Jones, the first British architect and designer to share the sophistication of his Italian counterparts, in the most lavish of the court entertainments meant that the sensational stage effects, such as the opening vistas, the ideal landscapes, or the glimpses of celestial perfection through a representation of sublime architecture, became triumphant visual statements of a mysterious interaction of earth and heaven.

Charles I's last masques—Thomas Carew's *Coelum Britannicum* (1634) and Sir William Davenant's *Britannia Triumphans* (1638), *Luminalia* (1638), and *Salmacida Spolia* (1640)—all offered dense allusions to the developing political storm. In Carew's fantasy the heroes of ancient Britain were joined by the King and Queen in what was both a perfected vision of a glorious future and a lavish attempt to dispel the rising criticism of the reign. *Salmacida Spolia*, contrived jointly by Davenant and Inigo Jones, stretched classical allusion even further. The fountain of Salmacis, supposed to reduce 'the barbarians . . . of fierce and cruel natures' to the 'sweetness of the Grecian customs', was loosely interpreted as an allusion to the King who 'out of his mercy and clemency . . . seekes to reduce tempestuous and turbulent natures into a sweet calm of civil concord'. Charles appeared attired as Philogenes (the 'lover of his people') whose 'secret wisdom' exorcised the forces of Discord. This 'wisdom' also enabled Philogenes to prove that he could govern 'a sullen age, | When it is harder far to cure | The People's folly than resist their rage'. The King—the Earl of Northumberland reported some two weeks before the entertainment was performed—was 'dayly so imployed about the Maske, as till that be over, we shall think of little ellse'. Charles was not necessarily fiddling as London smouldered around him. His fellow-actors included at least five members of the aristocracy who would soon actively support the opposition to his rule. *Salmacida Spolia* was both an expensive attempt to plaster over cracks and a final theatrical assertion of a divinely justified ideal of royal government.

The Advancement of Learning: Francis Bacon and the Authorized Version

Masques and Triumphs, Francis Bacon grudgingly noted in one of his *Essayes or Counsels, Civill and Morall* of 1625, 'are but Toyes, to come amongst such Serious Observations. But yet, since Princes will have such Things, it is better, they should be Graced with Elegancy, then Daubed with Cost.' The essay suggests that the rational Bacon (1561–1626) did not set much store by allegorical theatre, though he offers a list of practical recommendations designed to save both cost and human energy in its performance. By the 1620s Bacon was both an experienced and an unfortunately disgraced statesman. He no longer had a pressing obligation to flatter his sovereign or to nod honourably to the ceremonies of the court. In dedicating the first book of his *The Advancement of Learning* to King James I in 1605, however, he had laid the flattery on with a trowel in comparing the King to 'ancient Hermes', the possessor of a 'triplicity' of command. James, he avowed, had 'the power and fortune of a King, the knowledge and illumination of a Priest, and the learning and universality of a Philosopher'. Bacon's aim in 1605 seems to have been to encourage James to support 'some solid work, fixed memorial and immortal monument' worthy of so gifted a man and so glorious a reign. That 'solid work' would have been the promotion of a methodical enquiry into natural phenomena and a national investment in what we now call scientific research. In the dedication of his *Novum Organum* of 1620 he returned to his plea. 'You who resemble Solomon in so many things', James was told, 'would further follow his example in taking order for the collecting and perfecting of a natural and experimental history, true and severe.' James, a genuine if scarcely generous patron of the varieties of learning that suited his eclectic tastes, remained unmoved. Indeed, he is said to have remarked on receiving his copy of *Novum Organum* that it was like the peace of God, past all understanding.

The Advancement of Learning attempted to draw a distinction between two kinds of Truth, a theological Truth 'drawn from the word and oracles of God' and determined by faith, and a 'scientific' Truth based on the light of nature and the dictates of reason. Both, he freely conceded, possessed an equal intellectual validity. But if Bacon continued to exhibit an abiding concern with natural knowledge and with inductive reasoning, his work was not inconsistent with the pursuit of the occult. Nevertheless, in the first book he offered a defence of proper learning against misleading distortions, 'vanities', 'distempers', and 'peccant humours', before moving on to a critique of what he deemed to be the 'vain affectations' of those Renaissance humanists who had concentrated on rhetoric rather than matter, of the hidebound Aristotelianism of the universities, and of the delusions of alchemy and astrology. Throughout his work, Bacon is a great classifier, a forthright proponent of the innovative power of human reason, and a firm believer in a 'perpetual renovation' of knowledge. The theories of *The Advancement of Learning* were later reworked and expanded in its Latin version, *De Augmentis Scientiarum* of 1623, but both works should properly be seen as preliminaries to the larger overarching argument of the 'true directions concerning the interpretation of nature' contained in *Novum Organum* (the 'New Instrument' by which human understanding would be advanced). Here, in a weighty introductory preface, Bacon presents his 'Great Instauration', the laying of the intellectual foundations 'not of a sect or doctrine, but of human utility and power', and he insists on his own 'utmost endeavours towards restoring or cultivating a just and legitimate familiarity between the mind and things'. The *Novum Organum* argues in Latin for a new method of scientific thinking, free of the prejudices of the past and the received affectations of the present (characterized as the 'Idols' of the Tribe, the Cave, the Market Place, and the Theatre). The engraved title-page to its first part bore the image of two ships confidently sailing through the Pillars of Hercules and its message was reinforced by a Latin motto from the Book of Daniel: *Multi pertransibunt & augebitur scientia* ('many shall go to and fro and knowledge shall be increased'). Bacon's work marks a decisive rejection of the old ways of syllogistic deduction and a defence of the inductive investigation of nature. He has properly been hailed as the initiator of the modern scientific movement, a factor stressed by the posthumous honour accorded to him by the founders of the Royal Society in 1660.

Bacon's *Essayes*, first published as a group of ten 'religious Meditations' and 'Places of perswasion and disswasion' in 1597, and much augmented in both 1612 and 1625, reveal a similar clarity of thought and a parallel didacticism. They also indulge in the pithy aphoristic style which he had defended in principle in *The Advancement of Learning* as proper for the expression of tentative opinions or 'broken knowledges'. His title, *Essayes or Counsels*, derives from the usage and practice of Michel de Montaigne whose *Essais* had been translated into English by John Florio in 1603. Like the work of Montaigne, the first experiments of 1597 (such as the later much revised 'Of Studies') are best seen as short 'attempts' at presenting 'broken knowledges'. The texts of 1612, and the final fifty-eight essays of 1625, suggest a far greater confidence of expression in their continuous flow of argument, quotation, anecdote, conceit, and demonstration. His famous opening sentences, which immediately take up the subject of each essay, have an arresting drama: 'What is *Truth*; said jesting *Pilate*; And would not stay for an Answer'; '*Revenge* is a kinde of Wilde Justice; which the more Mans Nature runs to, the more ought Law to weed it out'; 'The Joyes of *Parents* are Secret; And so are ther Griefes, and Feares; They cannot utter the one; Nor they will not utter the other'; '*Suspicions* amongst Thoughts, are like Bats amongst Birds, they ever fly by Twilight'; '*Ambition* is like *Choler*; Which is an Humour, that maketh Men Active, Earnest, Full of Alacritie, and Stirring, if it be not stopped'. Bacon's subjects range from statecraft and social theory to personal morality and aesthetics. He offers advice on the construction of an elaborate mansion and its large 'Prince-like' gardens, he states the ideals of early colonialism (to avoid settling 'the Scumme of People, and Wicked Condemned Men' in potentially profitable plantations), and he speculates, with a degree of cynicism and calculation, on the uses of friendship (for confession), celibacy (to save money and to promote social advancement), and cunning (a 'Sinister or Crooked Wisdome' which pays off in politics). The essays are full of instances observed or reported during an active legal career closely associated with the royal court. It is possible that in noting that 'all Rising to *Great Place*, is by a winding Staire' Bacon was recalling something of his own rapid promotion and the murky circumstances of his disgrace amid the social, political, and architectural vagaries of an Elizabethan or Jacobean palace.

If James I had shown no real interest in Bacon's intellectual schemes, which culminated in the utopian proposal for a College of Science, 'Salomon's

House', envisaged in *The New Atlantis* of 1624, he was keen enough to prove himself a sound Defender of the Church of England, one well-versed in the true principles of theology and ecclesiology. Soon after he came to the throne he summoned a conference at Hampton Court of English bishops and their leading Puritan antagonists over which he presided personally. No compromise between the two sides was forthcoming, and James came down firmly on the episcopal side in enunciating the terse summary of his religious policy: 'No bishop, no king'. The one solid achievement of the 1604 Conference resulted from a Puritan proposal, made late in the day and warmly endorsed by the King, that there should be a new and broadly acceptable translation of the Bible into English. The resulting 'Authorized' or 'King James' version of 1611 was to become the single most influential work of English prose, if one whose underlying rhythms and variations are those of Hebrew prophecy and song and of Greek narrative. The dedication of the completed work to the King affirms the double aim of the new version. It was to provide a 'more exact Translation of the holy Scriptures into the *English Tongue*' by freshly considering the Hebrew and Greek originals and by drawing on the international scholarship of 'many worthy men who went before us'. It was also to offer a palpable defence against the criticisms of 'Popish Persons at home or abroad' and of 'selfe-conceited Brethren, who runne their owne wayes, and give liking unto nothing, but what is framed by themselves, and hammered on their Anvile'. The new Bible was intended to draw its English readers together as members of a national Church which was determined to demonstrate its credentials as a middle way between the extremes of Roman Catholicism and Genevan Calvinism. Some fifty-four translators worked in six groups, two centred in London and two each in the universities of Oxford and Cambridge. The drafts produced by these groups were then circulated and revised by a central committee. It was a remarkable achievement given the diversity of the translators who, with rare exceptions, were men known for their scholarly rather than their 'literary' distinction. The committees were able to draw substantially on the so-called 'Bishops' Bible', first published in 1568 and made compulsory in churches by order of Convocation in 1571, and they consulted its main rival, the popular, beautifully phrased, version known as the 'Geneva Bible' of 1560 (the first English version to introduce verse numeration). Any parallels to the extensive, Calvinistically inclined notes added to the 'Geneva Bible' were, however, excluded by the express command of the King. Substantial reference was also made to the great, but incomplete, translation of William Tyndale and to the supplementary work of Miles Coverdale.

Although the Authorized Version proclaimed itself to be 'Appointed to be read in Churches' no formal authorization was ever given to it. Its consistent dignity of expression, its memorable cadences, its felicitous, if limited, choice of vocabulary, and its general intelligibility meant, however, that it effectively displaced its rivals within the space of a generation. Its translations of certain familiar passages, such as the 40th chapter of Isaiah ('Comfort ye, comfort ye my people, saith your God . . .'), the 37th chapter of Ezekiel ('The hand of the Lord was upon me, and carried me out in the spirit of the Lord, and set me down in the midst of the valley which was full of bones . . .'), the 5th, 6th, and 7th chapters of the Gospel according to St Matthew (containing the Sermon on the Mount), the opening verses of St John's Gospel ('In the beginning was the Word, and the Word was with God, and the Word was God . . .'), or St Paul's famous account of Christian Love (I Corinthians 13, 'Though I speak with the tongues of men, and of angels, and have not charity, I am become as sounding brass, or a tinkling cymbal . . .') have often been integral to how English-speaking readers since 1611 have understood the majesty and simplicity of the Word of God. For some three and a half centuries it has formed a vital link between the divided English and Scottish Churches and the linguistically distinct English and Scottish nations. It has also been hallowed, memorized, quarried, cited, and echoed by a whole variety of Christian opinion wherever English came to be spoken. Despite its occasional mistranslations, its awkwardnesses, and its misreadings which have niggled subsequent scholars, it was not substantially revised until 1881–5. The Authorized Version triumphantly managed both to sum up and to embrace the best aspects of all the translations that had preceded it. No modern version has ever approached its richness and its resonance.

Andrewes and Donne

In 1618, as proof of his active interest in the theological basis of the religious divisions of Europe, James I sent a group of English churchmen to the great Synod of the Dutch Reformed Church convened at Dort (Dordrecht) in the Netherlands. Representatives from Lutheran Germany and from the Calvinist Churches of Switzerland and France were also invited. James's decision to send English observers stemmed not simply from his interest in the contentious subject of the Synod—the disruptions caused by the teaching of the unorthodox Dutch theologian Arminius—but also from a long-held desire for reconciliation between the Protestant powers of Europe. In the event, the revisionist doctrines of Arminius were condemned and his followers were dismissed from their official posts. The Synod of Dort had only a limited impact on the affairs of the English Church. For the many Calvinists within its body the reaffirmation of the doctrine of Predestination, which Arminius had questioned, and the return to the asperity of the strict discipline of the Reformed Church were welcome gestures. To certain prominent Anglicans, however, the Synod confirmed a deep-seated distaste for the extremes of Calvin's teaching and for the practice of the Genevan and Dutch Churches. It was against them that the word 'Arminian' was sneeringly, if inaccurately, employed in the increasingly vituperative debate between advocates of continued Reformation in the Church of England and those who tenaciously held to the ideal of the

Anglican compromise and to its twin pillars, both of them anathema to Puritans: episcopal government and liturgical worship.

In 1621, with some reluctance, James I appointed William Laud (1573–1645) to the see of St Davids. 'He hath a restless spirit and cannot see when matters are well', the King is said to have remarked, 'but loves to toss and change and to bring things to a pitch of reformation floating in his own brain'. Laud proved himself a vigorous and forthright defender of the Anglican position, both in written controversy with the Jesuit John Percy (known as 'Fisher the Jesuit') over the nature of 'Catholicity' and in his assaults on the supposed 'indiscipline' of Puritans within his own Church. Under Charles I his promotion was rapid. He became in turn Bishop of Bath and Wells in 1626 and of London in 1628 and in 1633 he was elevated to the archbishopric of Canterbury. As the would-be imposer of liturgical uniformity and as an encourager of a modestly baroque ritual and decoration within churches, he aroused intense hostility among his opponents, alienating both potential friends and convinced foes alike. His sporadic ruthlessness as an administrator and his close association with the King became one of the prime causes of active opposition to the policies of the court voiced within the House of Commons and beyond it. In 1641 he was impeached for high treason by a predominantly Puritan Parliament and imprisoned in the Tower of London. He was belatedly tried in 1644 and executed on Tower Hill in January 1645.

The 'Arminian' Laud's failure to impose an acceptable and lasting degree of uniformity on English and, by unhappy extension, on Scottish Church affairs stemmed from an intolerance of ecclesiastical and liturgical variety and from an underestimation of the popular strength of the extremes of British Protestantism in the first forty years of the seventeenth century. Laud was, however, merely the most visible, active, and consequently expungable figure in a period when embattled Anglicanism had embarked on a remarkable definition of certain aspects of its churchmanship and its equally distinctive spirituality. The day before his own execution in January 1649 Charles I earnestly recommended the three books that he had been reading in his final imprisonment to his daughter Elizabeth. The Princess was advised that Laud's defence of Anglican Catholicity against the strictures of 'Fisher the Jesuit', Richard Hooker's *Treatise on the Laws of Ecclesiastical Polity* (1594–7, 1648, 1662), and the *Sermons* of Lancelot Andrewes would 'ground [her] against Popery'. Richard Hooker (*c.* 1554–1600) had provided the Church of England with its most clearly argued theological and philosophical defence, one which justified episcopacy and which elaborated a theory of civil and ecclesiastical law based on a natural law whose 'seat is the bosom of God, her voice the harmony of the world'. He had also put forward the argument that the Church, though continuous with its primitive apostolic beginnings, was an organic, not a static institution which was bound to develop as times and circumstances changed. The works of Lancelot Andrewes (1555–1626) reveal an equally learned defence of the Catholic claims of the Church of England and a similar

antipathy to Puritan rigidity, particularly in matters concerned with the
absolute authority of the Scriptures.

Despite their intricate and meticulous analyses of Scriptural texts,
Andrewes's *XCVI Sermons* (1629) generally avoid specific controversy. Most
of these sermons were originally delivered at court on the great feast-days of
the Christian calendar. They speak to the attentive mind, not to the emotions;
to the quiet spirit, not to the troubled one. Andrewes argues exactingly, precisely, unemotionally, and vigorously, never relaxing his concentration on the
few words of the text, both in Latin and English, from which he steadily
extracts meaning. Few English writers have ever laid such stress on the *Logos*,
the word which Andrewes takes both as the literal Word of God and as the
central focus of his teaching. In the Christmas Day sermon of 1622, for
example, he develops a succession of ideas from St Luke's account of the
archangel's message to the shepherds, gradually defining concepts and extending the ramifications of the words 'Saviour', 'Christ', and 'Lord'. He imagines
a scene and then systematically establishes its physical and intellectual context.
In the Easter Day sermon of 1623, he carefully explores a series of related ideas
drawn from the prophet Isaiah's vision of a man in red-stained garments 'like
him that treadeth in the winepress'. Having suggested the prophet's hesitant
understanding of his vision ('Sees Him; but knowes him not: thinks Him
worthy the knowing; so thinking, and not knowing, is desirous to be instructed
concerning Him'), he proceeds to establish a pattern of fused metaphors of
Christ as the treader of the winepress, Christ as the victim, and Christ as the
provider of the sacramental cup. At its simplest, his text becomes a dialogue
between Isaiah and Christ, between the prophet and the prophesied. More
profoundly, he seeks a kernel of 'spiritual meaning that hath some life in it'
in which life and death, suffering and celebration are reconciled: 'He that
was trodden on before, gets up againe, and doth here tread upon and tread
down . . . The press He was trodden in, was His Cross and Passion. This which
he came out of this day, was in His descent and resurrection both proper to
this feast: one to Good Friday, the other to Easter-day.' The sermon serves as
an enactment of the mystery of the feast itself, passing from a rapt contemplation of the immolation of Christ to a triumphant acclamation of the
Resurrection which is affirmed in the act of communion.

In 1625 a week after the King's accession, John Donne (1573–1631), Dean
of St Paul's Cathedral, preached the first public sermon before the new King
Charles I. Prophetically, as some later thought, he chose as his text a verse from
Psalm 11, 'If the foundations be destroyed, what can the righteous do?' and he
expanded on a reference to Christian martyrdom by noting the fact that 'in the
Office and Service of a Martyr, the Church did use this Psalme'. It was also
before Charles in February 1631 that Donne so dramatically preached what
many of his audience took to be his own Funeral Sermon ('Death's Duell'),
having risen from his sick-bed for the purpose. It was, however, upon
Andrewes's sermons and not Donne's that Charles ultimately chose to

meditate. Donne, like Andrewes, divides his sermons into three parts: a preliminary explication of the chosen text, a confirmation and an illustration of its meaning, and an application of that meaning to its audience. But where Andrewes dwells scrupulously on explication, Donne stresses illustration and application. The former demands concentration; the latter commands attention.

Donne had no sympathy with the extempore preaching often favoured by Puritans. His first biographer and former parishioner, Izaak Walton (1593–1683), describes how the Dean researched his theme by consulting the works of the Church Fathers and then memorized the words of his sermon, preaching only with the assistance of notes. In preparing individual sermons for publication, or in 'reviewing' and writing out the eighty sermons that he left in fair copy when he died (published in 1640), Donne seems to have taken care to limit obviously rhetorical gestures. Nevertheless, his delight in verbal and stylistic flourish is real enough. In the 'Sermon of Valediction' preached at Lincoln's Inn before his departure for Germany in 1619 he tailored his multiple extrapolations from the text 'Remember now thy Creator in the daies of thy youth' to an audience likely to have been familiar with his own dissolute youth as a member of the Inn. His illustrative metaphors are always striking. In the same sermon he demanded of his audience: 'No man would present a lame horse, a disordered clock, a torn book to the king? . . . thy body is thy beast; and wilt thou present that to God, when it is lam'd and tir'd with excesse of wantonness? when thy clock, (the whole course of thy time) is disordered with passions, and perturbations; when thy book (the history of thy life,) is torn, a thousand sins of thine own torn out of thy memory, wilt thou then present thy self thus defac'd and mangled to almighty God?' In the sermon preached in St Paul's Cathedral in January 1626 he fancifully and rhythmically develops the idea suggested by his text (Psalm 53, verse 7) of the sheltering, brooding power of the wings of God: 'Particular mercies are feathers of his wings, and that prayer, Lord let thy mercy lighten upon us, as our trust is in thee, is our birdlime; particular mercies are that cloud of quails which hovered over the host of Israel, and that prayer, Lord let thy mercy lighten upon us, is our net to catch, our Gomer [container] to fill of those quails.' The final section of the St Paul's sermon is shaped around a modern metaphor, an extraordinary analogy between a flat map of the earth, divided into two hemispheres, and a visionary map of heaven divided into a hemisphere of joy and a hemisphere of glory. The joy of heaven can be known in this life, Donne asserts, much as the limits of the Old World were known before the discovery of America; just as God reserved the treasure of America 'for later discoveries', so, by extension, 'that hemisphere of heaven, which is the glory thereof' will be opened to human eyes by death and resurrection.

In common with most preachers of his time, both Catholic and Protestant, Donne seems to be fired more by a contemplation of sin, death, and judgement than by a prospect of a rejoicing earth imbued with the joys of heaven.

His last sermon, 'Death's Duell, or A Consolation to the Soule, against the Dying Life, and Living Death of the Body' (1631, published 1632), stresses the interconnection of life and death throughout human existence. 'Wee have a winding sheet in our Mothers wombe', he insisted to his courtly audience, 'which growes with us from our conception, and wee come into the world, bound up in that *winding sheet*, for wee come to *seeke a grave.*' Death, as all of Donne's contemporaries readily recognized, was not simply inevitable and all-pervasive, it was a familiar presence in an unstable, unhygienic, and disease-ridden world. The tolling of the passing bell for a dying parishioner was to Donne not simply a stimulus to pray for a troubled soul but a personal *memento mori*. His passionate calls to repentance in his last sermon emerge not simply from an awareness of the imminence of his own demise, but from a pressing sense of shared mortality: 'Our *criticall* day is *not* the *very day* of our *death*: but the whole course of our life. I thanke him that *prayes* for me when the *Bell* tolles, but I thank him much more that *Catechises* mee, or *preaches* mee, or *instructs mee how to live.*' The *Devotions Upon Emergent Occasions*, which Donne had written during a serious illness in 1623, had also dwelt upon the interconnection of the dying and those meditating upon death: 'who bends not his *eare* to any *bell*, which upon any occasion rings? but who can remove it from that *bell*, which is passing a *peece of himselfe* out of this world?' The meditation moves him to the now famous geographical metaphor of co-operant sympathy: 'No man is an *Iland*, intire of it selfe; every man is a peece of the *Continent*, a part of the *maine*; . . . any mans *death* diminishes *me*, because I am involved in *Mankinde.*'

In 1621, six years after he had been ordained to the priesthood, Donne had been offered the prestigious deanship of St Paul's. All avenues to his civil promotion had been blocked since the time of his secret marriage to the niece of his patron, Sir Thomas Egerton, and his dismissal from Egerton's service in 1601, but in no sense should his priestly vocation be viewed cynically. The intervening years were spent in a professional wilderness, watered by close study, an active involvement in religious controversy, and the composition of much of his devotional poetry. Nothing in Donne's intellectual and religious development can, however, be easily categorized. 'My first breeding and conversation', he remarked of himself in *Biathanatos* (his experimental apology for suicide, published posthumously in 1646), was 'with men of supressed and afflicted Religion, accustomed to the despite of death, and hungry of an imagin'd Martyrdome'. The enforced secrecy and introspection and the dangerous temptation to martyrdom in this Roman Catholic recusant background was probably accentuated in 1593 by the death in prison of his younger brother Henry, arrested for illegally harbouring a priest. Precisely how, when, and why he broke his allegiance to Rome cannot be determined, but though his decision to conform outwardly to the Church of England in the mid-1590s may have been influenced by a desire for an official career, his later Anglican apologetics suggest that his religious affiliation was also shaped by wide reading, by a deep fascination with religious controversy, and by a profound and consistent perturbation at the thought of death and judgement. Walton remarks of this period that Donne had 'betrothed himself to no Religion that might give him any other denomination than a Christian'. However much the older Donne lacerated himself with memories of a variously misspent youth, he was prepared in 1608 to see his worst and most distracting 'voluptuousness' as a 'Hydroptique immoderate desire of human learning and languages'. From the evidence of his various writings, religion was neither a refuge for him nor an escape from worldly contradictions and confusions; it was the centripetal force in his intellectual and spiritual involvement with mankind. In all his poetry, both amorous and devout, he intermixes orthodox religious imagery and allusions with metaphors derived from a variety of secular learning, both ancient and modern. Mental conflict for Donne was dynamic. The poet who saw himself in the nineteenth of his Holy Sonnets as vexed by the meeting of contraries had in his earlier *Paradoxes and Problemes* (published posthumously in 1633) revealed an intellectual engagement with paradox as a method of analysis. Discord, he noted, had its own creative energy: 'While I . . . feele the contrary repugnances and adverse fightings of the Elements in my body, my body increaseth; and whilst I differ from common opinions, by this discord the number of my Paradoxes encreaseth.' It was from the resolution of paradox in Christian theology that Donne derived a profound intellectual pleasure.

In a letter of *c.*1608 he turned from a discussion of religious controversies to a brief reference to his poetry. 'I doe not condemn in my self', he remarked, 'that I have given my wit such evaporations, as those, if they be free from prophaneness, or obscene provocations.' 'Wit', the free play of intelligence and a delight in intellectual games and cerebral point-scoring, characterizes all his most brilliant verse. Donne forges unities out of oppositions, ostensible contradictions, and imaginative contractions. In the 'Hymn to God My God, in My Sicknesse', for example, he plays with the idea that Adam's tree and Christ's cross might possibly have stood in the same place and that east and west *are* one on a flat map; he makes theological capital out of the homonymic qualities of 'Sun' and 'Son' in the second of the Divine Sonnets and in 'A Hymne to God the Father'; and in the 'Hymne to God' and the eighteenth and nineteenth elegies—'Loves Progress' and 'To His Mistris Going to Bed'—he variously compares the human body to a map, a landscape, or a continent. As his famous image of 'stiffe twin compasses' in 'A Valediction: Forbidding Mourning' also suggests, he was delighted by the serenity of a circle, an image of eternity, which has neither a beginning nor an end, but whose beginning *is* its end. He was fascinated both by the inheritance of ancient learning and by new advances in science and geography. He nods acknowledgement to the disruption of the old, tidy, intellectual, and theological world order brought about by the discoveries of Copernicus and Columbus, but he refers ambiguously to the imagined four corners of a round world in the seventh of his Holy Sonnets and he finds poetic use for the redundant Ptolemaic planetary system in his references to the spheres in 'The Extasie', 'A Valediction: Forbidding Mourning', and 'Goodfriday, 1613. Riding Westward'. The often heterodox and destabilized world of Donne's poetry is held together both by a transcendent and almighty Creator and by a God-like poet who shows his power by enforcing conjunctions and exploring correlatives and analogies.

There is, however, a steady note of scepticism in Donne's erotic verse, one often accentuated by the poet's projection of himself as a narrating, and sometimes dictating voice. The speculative, colloquial, and boisterous early *Satyres* (printed 1633) suggest a narrator caught up in the animated life of the streets and in the secrets of privy chambers (though Satyre III vividly explores the difficulty of discovering a true Church amid the conflicts of human opinion). The fifty-five various poems known as the *Songs and Sonets* (from the title under which they were first published in the edition of 1633) have never been satisfactorily dated. Some, including those that Donne may later have condemned for exhibiting an excess of 'prophaneness' and 'obscene provocation', had clearly achieved a considerable éclat through circulation in manuscript. Many of the poems affront readers with a brusque opening command—'Goe, and catche a falling starre'; 'For Godsake, hold your tongue, and let me love'; 'Stand still, and I will read to thee | A Lecture love, in Loves philosophy'— others have a conversational casualness or give an impression of interrupted business—'I wonder by my troth, what thou, and I | Did till we lov'd?'; 'Sweetest love, I doe not goe, | For wearinesses of thee'; 'So, so, breake off this last lamenting kisse'. The poems suggest a variety of often dramatic situations but they always present a speaker in immediate relation to a listener even though, as Donne puts it in 'The Extasie', the discourse can effectively be a 'dialogue of one'. They can vary in form from a neat, comic demonstration of the folly of resisting seduction (such as 'The Flea') to more sober attempts to justify seizing love's moment (such as 'A Lecture upon the Shadow'). In contrast to the Petrarchan tradition of love-poetry that he had inherited, Donne never attempts to deify or idealize the objects of his passion. In 'The Dreame' he does not try to pretend that his dream is chaste. In 'The Sunne Rising', where he responds to the challenge of Ovid, his celebration of eroticism takes the form of an irreverent address to the Sun who has dared to awake the sleeping lovers. It presents us with two outside worlds, one of petty activity and drudgery and another of wealth and power; but both are outclassed by love. The universe is contracted to the lovers' bed, the epicentre beyond which, in a line of abrupt and triumphant arrogance, we are told that 'Nothing else is'.

Throughout Donne's work, however, the real triumphs are those of Death and Resurrection. Some of the 'Songs and Sonets' ('The Apparition', 'The Will', and 'The Funerall' for example) make an easy, even jesting, play with mortality. Others suggest a far greater earnestness. Potential observers of the rapt lovers in 'The Extasie' might note 'small change' in the two when they will have 'to bodies gone'. 'A Valediction: Forbidding Mourning' opens with reference to the 'mild' death-beds of 'virtuous men' and proceeds by means of complex illustration to justify the idea of the enduring power of a rarefied love. In the two funeral elegies known as the 'Anniversaries', Donne contemplates the survival not of love but of virtue, or rather he contrasts an ideal of womanhood spiritualized in his 'Immortal mayd', Elizabeth Drury, against an 'anatomic' of a corrupted, incoherent and untidy world. It is with the darkness of the human condition in this world that the most vivid of Donne's Holy Sonnets are concerned. Most enact a double drama; they evoke a picture—of the end of the world (sonnets 7 and 13), of Death itself (sonnet 10), or of a distressed sinner fearful of his damnation (sonnets 5, 11, and 14)—but they also project the personality of a responsive speaker, one who seems to stand as a vulnerable representative of sinful humanity. Like the love-poems, Donne's religious verse insistently suggests an emotional relationship, that of the sinner to a loving but severe God. The narrator stands defiantly against Death (sonnet 10), but quakes before the prospect of judgement (sonnets 4, 7, and 9). In the extraordinary sonnet 14 ('Batter my heart, three person'd God') he balances a plea for a violent physical stirring of his passion against an evident intellectual pleasure in the display of theologically resolved paradoxes ('Take mee to you, imprison mee, for I | Except you'enthrall mee, never shall be free, | Nor ever chast, except you ravish mee'). A similar drama, matched by an equally energetic pursuit of analogues, is evident in two poems modelled on journeys, 'Goodfriday 1613. Riding Westward' and 'A Hymne to Christ, at the Authors last going into Germany'. The first contrasts the idea of a westerly ride away from a Christ who is crucified in the east with a vivid imaginative recall of Calvary, the site of the humiliation of God's greatness ('Could I behold those hands which span the Poles, | And tune all the spheares at once, peirc'd with those holes?'). The second meditates on the dangers of diplomatic mission in 1619 (the same that had provoked the 'Sermon of Valediction') by seeking parallels to, or 'emblems' for, his sea-voyage, his separation from friends and family, and the relationship between human and divine love. The argument culminates in the juxtaposition of three complementary ideas: 'Churches are best for Prayer, that have least light: | To see God only, I go out of sight: | And to scape stormy dayes, I chuse | An Everlasting night.'

Donne's last poem, 'A Hymne to God the Father', which almost mockingly puns on his name in the penultimate line of each stanza, was, like the sermon 'Death's Duell', to serve its author as a part of the ceremonial acting out of his final drama of self-projection and self-abnegation. This final, seemingly incongruous drama, which included the performance of a musical setting of the hymn by the choristers of St Paul's, centred on the contemplation of a picture of himself dressed in his winding sheet, emerging from a funerary urn as if summoned by the Last Trump. Donne had risen from his sick-bed to pose for the picture, standing, shrouded, on a wooden urn and facing towards the east from whence he expected his ultimate redemption to come. Such intertwining of humility with glory, of theatre with devotion, of the mortal body with its representation in art, of playfulness and seriousness, of rules and the bending of rules, are characteristic of the kind of international baroque art of which Donne's life and work form part. The suspicion of flamboyance which periodically surfaces in English art can be seen as emanating from the strains of puritanism and pragmatism, conservatism and compromise, which run through the national culture. Despite the contraries of Catholicism and Calvinism which meet in his life and work, such insular strains were largely alien to Donne.

'Metaphysical' Religious Poetry: Herbert, Crashaw, and Vaughan

The picturesque emotionalism of continental baroque art was a central feature of the Counter-Reformation crusade to win back the hearts and souls of those lost to the Roman Church by the fissures of the Reformation. Protestant England remained largely untouched by the more heady pictorial and architectural styles sponsored by the Pope's main agents in the campaign, the Jesuits, but, despite gestures of resistance and disapproval, a degree of Jesuit spirituality left its mark on English literature. The martyred missionary priest, Robert Southwell (?1561–95, canonized in 1970), managed to work secretly for nine perilous years in England before his execution; his books circulated far less secretly. The prose meditation, *Marie Magdalens Funeral Teares*, which was published in 1591, ran through some seven further editions by 1636, and the two collections of verse, *Saint Peters complaynt, with other Poems* and *Moeoniae: or, Certaine excellent Poems and Spiritual Hymnes*, both of which contain poems written during his three-year imprisonment, were printed in London in the year of his death. Southwell's poems were respected both by Roman Catholics and by Anglicans, the extraordinarily contrived Christmas meditation, 'The Burning Babe', being particularly admired by Ben Jonson. Donne, the author of the scurrilous anti-Jesuit tract *Ignatius his Conclave* of 1611 and who eight years later feared for his safety at the hands of 'such adversaries, as I cannot blame for hating me' when he travelled across Germany, was none the less influenced by the kind of meditative religious exercises recommended to the faithful by the founder of the Society of Jesus. St Ignatius Loyola's *Spiritual Exercises* had been approved by the Pope in 1548 as a manual of systematic devotion which employed sense impressions, the imagination, and the understanding as a means of prompting the spirit to consider the lapsed human and the glorious divine condition. The Ignatian method was not unique (it drew on late medieval precedents and it was adapted by later Spanish and French churchmen) but its currency was assured by the missionary and educational work undertaken by the Jesuits. The fact that such regulated guides to meditation could be used privately meant that they appealed, with varying degrees of excision, to secluded Recusants, devout Anglicans, and soul-searching Puritans alike.

A similar spiritual cross-fertilization is evident in the popularity of emblem books in seventeenth-century England. The emblem consisted of three inter-related parts—a motto, a symbolic picture, and an exposition—each of which suggested a different means of considering and apprehending a moral or religious idea. The form had had a certain currency as a learned, and generally secular, educational device in the sixteenth century, but its renewed application to private religious study and its intermixture of Latin motto, biblical quotation, engraved and ostensibly enigmatic picture, and English poem made for a widespread influence which readily cut across confessional barriers. Francis Quarles's *Emblemes, Divine and Morall* (1635) proved to be the most popular book of verse of its age. Quarles (1592–1644) and his engraver took and, where Protestant occasion demanded, adapted plates from Jesuit emblem books; only the disappointingly pedestrian accompanying poems were original. *Emblemes* and its successor *Hieroglyphicks of the Life of Man* (1638) demand that the reader interpret and gradually unwind an idea which is expressed epigrammatically, visually, and poetically. 'The embleme is but a silent parable', Quarles insisted in his address to the user of his books, and he goes on to suggest the importance of the linkage of word and picture: 'Before the knowledge of letters, God was knowne by Hieroglyphicks; And indeed, what are the Heavens, the Earth, nay every Creature, but Hieroglyphicks and Emblemes of his Glory?' The moral message is, however, predominantly one which stresses a conventionally Christian contempt for the world ('O what a crocodilian world is this | Compos'd of treach'ries, and insnaring wiles', 'O whither will this mad-brain world at last | Be driven? Where will her restless wheels arrive?'), and the pictures variously show children confusing a wasps' nest for a beehive in a globe, fools sucking at a huge earth-shaped breast, and a figure of vanity smoking a pipe while perched perilously on a tilting orb.

The intellectual demands made on a reader by an emblem book were paralleled by the wit, the imaginative picturing, the compression, the often cryptic expression, the play of paradoxes, and the juxtapositions of metaphor in the work of Donne and his immediate followers, the so-called 'metaphysical poets'. The use of the term 'metaphysical' in this context was first given critical currency by Samuel Johnson in the eighteenth century and it sprang from an unease, determined by 'classical' canons of taste, with the supposed contortions of the style and imagery of Donne and Cowley. Johnson had a particular distaste for the far-fetched or strained 'conceits' (witty and ingenious ideas) in which Donne's poetry abounds. This prejudice against the distinct 'metaphysical' style had earlier been shared by Quarles, who in 1629 complained of 'the tyranny of *strong lines*, which . . . are the meere itch of wit; under the colour of which many have ventured . . . to write *non-sense*'. The work of Donne's friend, admirer, and fellow-priest, George Herbert (1593–1633), possesses a restrained and contemplative rapture which is paralleled less by the extravagances of southern European baroque art than by the often enigmatic understatement of the paintings of his French contemporary, Georges de la

Tour. Herbert's own 'itch of wit' can none the less find its expression in playing with the shapes and sounds of words: he puns in his title to 'The Collar' and with the name 'Jesu' in the poem of that name; he teases letters in his 'Anagram of the Virgin Marie'; in 'Heaven' he exploits echo-effects as delightedly as did his Venetian musical contemporaries, and he gradually reduces words to form new ones in 'Paradise'. His relationship to the emblem book tradition is evident in his printing of certain of his poems as visual designs (the shapes of 'The Altar' and the sideways printed 'Easter Wings' make patterns which suggest their subjects). If he is a less frenetic and startling poet than Donne, he is a far more searching and inventive one than Quarles. The two poems called 'Jordan' (from the fount of their inspiration) describe the act of writing a sacred poetry which eschews a structural 'winding stair' and the 'curling with metaphors' of a 'plain intention'. As with his most influential models, the parables of Jesus, Herbert's illustrations of the central mysteries of God and his creation take the form of sharply observed but 'plain' stories drawn from, and illuminated by, everyday experience.

The elegance of Herbert's poetry is as much the result of art as it is an expression of a cultivated, but not forced, spiritual humility. He had been born into a distinguished and cultured noble family but his decision to take deacon's orders in 1626, and his ordination to the priesthood and appointment as rector of a country parish in 1630 struck many of his grand contemporaries as a deliberate turning of his back on secular ambition. According to Izaac Walton, Herbert responded to a friend who taxed him with taking 'too mean an employment, and too much below his birth' that 'the Domestick Servants of the King of Heaven, should be of the noblest Families on Earth'. He would, he insisted, make 'Humility lovely in the eyes of all men'. Herbert's work is permeated with reference to service and to Christ as the type of the suffering servant, but his poetry is equally informed by a gentlemanly grasp of the chivalric code of obligation. Society, as we glimpse it in this world and the next, is hierarchical and ordered, and the human response to God's love can be expressed in terms of an almost feudal obligation. In 'The Pearl', for example, the poet insists that he knows 'the wayes of Honour, what maintains | The quick returns of courtesie and wit'. In the first of the poems called 'Affliction' he describes a changing understanding of service to a liege-lord, a service which at first gives rich satisfaction ('Thy glorious household-stuffe did me entwine') and brings rewards ('thou gav'st me milk and sweetness; I had my wish and way'); as a process of disillusion sets in, the poem allows a sense of betrayal to surface, but this in turn is transformed by the final insistence on an obligation shaped not by duty but by the more pressing demands of love ('Ah my deare God! though I am clean forgot, | Let me not love thee, if I love thee not'). 'Redemption' describes a tenant's search for his 'rich Lord' only to find him mortally wounded amid 'a ragged noise and mirth | Of theeves and murderers'; the magnanimity of the Lord is proved in a dying gesture of assent to the tenant's request. In 'The Collar' the remarkable evocation of impatient resistance to service ends as the 'raving' protests subside in response to the steady call of Christ. The call to the '*Child*' (perhaps here both the disciple and a youth of gentle birth) evokes the willing reply '*My Lord*'.

Herbert's vocation as a priest of the Church of England, and his loyalty to its rituals, calendar, and discipline is central both to his prose study of the ideal country parson, *A Priest to the Temple* (published in *The Remaines of that Sweet Singer of the Temple George Herbert* in 1652), and to his Latin sequence *Musae Responsariae* (1633) (poems which assert the propriety of Anglican ceremonial and orders in the face of Puritan criticism). It is, however, in *The Temple*, the influential collection of his English poems published posthumously in 1633, that Herbert most fully expresses his aspirations, failures, and triumphs as a priest and as a believer. Sections of *The Temple* are shaped according to the spiritual rhythms and the ups and downs of religious experience. More significantly, the volume as a whole possesses both an architectonic and a ritual patterning which derives from the shape of an English parish church and from the festivals and fasts celebrated within its walls. The whole work is prefaced by a gnomic poetic expression of conventional moral advice to a young man. The title of this preliminary poem, 'The Church-Porch', serves as a reminder not only of a preparatory exercise before worship but also of the physical importance of the porch itself (once the setting of important sections of certain church services). The titles of poems in the body of the volume ('The Church') imply both a movement through the building noting its features ('The Altar', 'Church-Monuments', 'Church-lock and key', 'The Church-floore', 'The Windows') and the significance of its liturgical commemorations ('Good Friday', 'Easter', 'H. Baptisme', 'The H. Communion', 'Whitsunday', 'Sunday', 'Christmas'). Interspersed are meditations on Christian belief and the varied experience of the Christian life. The 'sacramental' poems have a particular importance. By means of repeated words and phrases 'Aaron' establishes a balanced contrast between the ceremonially vested Jewish priest and his spiritually defective modern Christian counterpart. The poem's debate is determined by an exploration of the import of the words 'Holiness to the Lord' engraved on Aaron's ceremonial mitre. It is only when Christ himself is recognized as the true sanctifier of the parish priest that all unworthiness falls away and the vested minister can properly present himself to his congregation, ready to celebrate the Holy Communion: 'Come people; Aaron's drest'. The theology and typology of eucharistic celebration are also explored in 'The Agonie' and the concluding poem of the volume, 'Love III'. 'The Agonie' takes as its central issue the human study of Sin and Love. The effect of Sin is revealed in an agonized Christ 'so wrung with pains, that all his hair, | His skinne, his garments bloudie be'. The very hyperbole here allows for the conceit on which the poem turns; Sin is a wine-press painfully proving the worth of Love and when in the concluding stanza the crucified Christ's blood flows from his side it is mystically perceived as sacramental wine: 'Love is that liquour sweet and most divine, | Which my God feels as bloud; but I, as wine'.

Bitterness is transubstantiated into sweetness. 'Love' takes the form of a colloquy in which the Lord, personified as Love, welcomes the sinner to his feast, insistently answering each protest of unworthiness with a gentle assertion of his grace:

> And know you not, sayes Love, who bore the blame?
> My deare, then I will serve.
> You must sit downe, sayes Love, and taste my meat:
> So I did sit and eat.

The uneasy guest and the would-be servant are entertained as equals.

Throughout *The Temple* the quakings of fear, the doubts, and the attempts at rebellion are subsumed in a quiet loyalty inspired by the love of a generous God. Restlessness, as seen in the deftly argued parable of free will, 'The Pulley', prompts the soul to seek heavenly comfort. In 'Affliction III' the very utterance of the heaved sigh '*O God!*' is interpreted as a barely recognized sign of redemption and as an admission of shared sorrow ('Thy life on earth was grief, and thou art still | Constant unto it'). Even the figure of Death, in the poem of that name, loses its skeletal terrors by being transformed by the sacrifice of Christ into something 'fair and full of grace, | Much in request, much sought for as a good'. Herbert's 'Prayer before Sermon', appended to *A Priest to the Temple*, addresses a God who embodies 'patience, and pity, and sweetness, and love', one who has exalted his mercy above all things and who has made salvation, not punishment, his glory.

According to Izaac Walton's account the dying Herbert entrusted the manuscript of his poems to his pious friend Nicholas Ferrar (1592–1637) who in 1625 had retired to his estate at Little Gidding in Huntingdonshire to establish a 'Little Colledge', or religious community of men and women, dedicated to the 'constant and methodical service of God'. Ferrar was instructed that he would find in *The Temple* 'a picture of the many Conflicts that have past betwixt God and my Soul' and he was allowed to choose whether to publish or burn the manuscript. As his short preface of 1633 indicates, he clearly recognized both the quality of the poems and their significance to the increasingly beleaguered discipline of the Church of England. Although his community impressed Charles I, it steadily provoked the hostility of those Puritans who criticized it as an 'Arminian Nunnery' and who in 1646 finally succeeded in breaking it up.

Richard Crashaw (1613–49) was, through his friendship with Ferrar, a regular visitor to and keeper of vigils at Little Gidding. He was the son of a particularly zealous Puritan 'Preacher of Gods worde' who had made himself conspicuous as an anti-Papist. Crashaw's own religious pilgrimage was to take him in an opposite direction to his father. As a student at Cambridge and later as a fellow of Peterhouse he closely associated himself with the extreme Laudian party in the University. Deprived of his fellowship after the college chapel, to which he had contributed fittings, was desecrated by Parliamentary Commissioners in 1643 he travelled abroad, eked out a precarious existence on the fringes of Queen Henrietta Maria's court in exile, became a convert to Roman Catholicism, and ended his short life as the holder of a small benefice at the Holy House at Loreto in Italy. His English poetry—collected as *Steps to the Temple: Sacred Poems, with other Delights of the Muses* (1646, considerably expanded 1648) and later as *Carmen Deo Nostro* (published in Paris in 1652)— clearly shows the nature of his religious inclinations, both Anglican and Roman. The Preface to his earlier volumes proclaims his allegiance to the English Church through reference to Lancelot Andrewes and through the claim that the poems were written as '*Stepps* for happy soules to climbe heaven by' under a 'roofe of Angels' at Little St Mary's Church in Cambridge; the 1652 volume more assiduously advertises the Catholic piety which had been only implicit before, and offers an apology, probably not Crashaw's own, for the 'Hymn to Saint Teresa' as 'having been writt when the author was yet among the protestants'. The frontispiece to the 1648 volume showed the faithful mounting steps to a chastely decorous English church; the 1652 edition is decorated throughout with lushly Catholic devotional images.

Although the title *Steps to the Temple* nods back to Herbert, and though the volume contains a particularly fulsome tribute to 'the Temple of Sacred Poems, sent to a Gentlewoman', Crashaw's stylistic and structural debt to his model is limited. Crashaw is the most decoratively baroque of the English seventeenth-century poets, both in the extravagance of his subject-matter and in his choice of metaphor. Where Donne is ingenious and paradoxical, or Herbert delicately and aptly novel, Crashaw propels traditional Christian images until they soar and explode like sky-rockets or inflates them until they burst like plump confections. His verse exhibits a fixation with the human body and with bodily fluids: tears gush from eyes, milk from breasts, blood from wounds, and at times the emissions become intermixed expressions of passionate emotion. The series of 'Divine Epigrams' suggests a particular fondness for miraculous or alchemical changes of substance: not only does water become wine, or wine blood, but tears are pearls and drops of blood rubies; the water of Christ's baptism 'is washt it selfe, in washing him'; the water with which Pilate washes his hands is 'Nothing but Teares; Each drop's a teare that weeps for her own wast'; the naked Lord on the cross is clothed by 'opening the purple wardrobe of thy side'; and the blood of the Holy Innocents is both blended with milk and translated heavenwards. A similar, surreal vision informs the triumphantly hyperbolic meditation on the Magdalen, 'The Weeper'. The tears of the penitent flow unceasingly; transformed into stars they form not simply a Milky Way in the heavens but a stream of cream from which 'a briske Cherub something sips | Whose soft influence | Adds sweetnesse to his sweetest lips'.

Crashaw's attraction to the history and the writings of the great Spanish mystic, Teresa of Avila, who was canonized in 1622, is a further reflection of his interest in highly charged religious emotion. In her spiritual autobiography Teresa had described the climax of her most celebrated vision of union with God in which she had become aware of the presence of an angel bearing a great golden spear tipped with fire; this he plunged several times into her heart. Teresa's amorous language in expressing her awareness of a 'gentle . . . wooing which takes place between God and the soul' clearly had its effect on Crashaw's luxuriant meditation first entitled 'In Memory of the Vertuous and Learned Lady Madre de Teresa that sought an early Martyrdome' and now generally known as 'A Hymn to Saint Teresa' from the abbreviation of its more explicitly Catholic title of 1652. The poem returns repeatedly to the idea of divine love as the wooer and arouser of the faithful soul; the 6-year-old seeking martyrdom is glimpsed as 'her weake breast heaves with strong desire', while the adult nun willingly opens herself as 'Loves victim' pierced not simply by a single seraphic dart, but exposed to a whole troop of armed Angels, 'Loves souldiers' who 'exercise their Archerie'. Teresa's vision of the spear reappears in a new guise in Crashaw's address to the Countess of Denbigh 'perswading her to Resolution in Religion' (in fact a plea to resolve herself into the Roman communion). The Countess is instructed to unfold herself like a flower in order to receive 'love's shower' which will fall like 'the wholesome dart', a 'healing shaft which heavn till now | Hath in love's quiver hid for you'. The most florid poetic expression of Crashaw's earlier Laudian ideal of worshipping the Lord in the beauty and dignity of holiness is the 'Hymn to the Name of Jesus'. This ceremonious paean to the 'Fair KING of NAMES' draws its impulses from a long tradition of devotion to the incarnate Word, both biblical and mystical. The poem insists on the daily renewal of worship through the reawakening of the mind and the senses, and it particularly stresses the importance of music, the 'household stuffe of Heavn on earth', as an accompaniment to praise. Crashaw's sensitivity to music, also evident in his richly adjectival representation of instrumental sound and bird-song in 'Musicks Duell' (an elaboration of a Latin poem by the Jesuit, Strada), is here expressed in his deliberate echoes of musical phrasing. The 'Hymn to the Name of Jesus' recognizes an interrelationship between natural and musical harmony in which the vocal human heart plays its part in an 'unbounded All-imbracing SONG', but it also requires the heart to open itself, even in agony, to the promptings of divine love. The martyr's love-death no longer requires a seraphic dart, for the 'Rackes & Torments' of the earthly persecutors of true religion force open the human breast and cleave the heart ready for the reception of the Heavenly fire. Pleasure and pain, orgasm and martyrdom, rape and resolution are yoked together by a lexical violence which seeks to express ultimate spiritual fulfilment.

Where Crashaw yearns to represent an interior mystical passion through sensual metaphors drawn from the exterior human world, Henry Vaughan (1621–95) returns to the chaster and more private world of George Herbert as a means of articulating an inner sense of wonder. The subtitle of Vaughan's

Silex Scintillans (1650, enlarged 1655), 'Sacred Poems and Private Ejaculations', is an exact echo of that of *The Temple*, and the Preface, dated 1654, refers to 'the blessed man, Mr *George Herbert*, whose holy *life* and *verse* gained many pious *converts*' (amongst whom Vaughan counted himself). Above all, one of the most Herbertian poems in the collection, 'The Match', represents a personal submission, artistically to a model poet and spiritually to that poet's God:

> Dear friend! whose holy, ever-living lines,
> > Have done much good
> > To many, and have checkt my blood,
> My fierce, wild blood that still heaves, and inclines,
> > But still is tam'd
> > By those bright fires which thee inflam'd;
> Here I joyn hands, and thrust my stubborn heart
> > Into thy *deed*.

Vaughan most differs from Herbert, however, in his consistent rather than incidental use of natural imagery and in his steady exploration of the revelation of God in his creation. As a loyal royalist and Anglican writing at the time of the triumph of republican arms and the imposition of an alien church order, he retired to rural seclusion in Wales. That this retirement was sympathetic to him is suggested by his translations from the Latin of the stoic meditations on the flux of worldly affairs of Boethius and the Polish Jesuit, Casimir Sarbiewski (published in *Olor Iscanus*, 'the Swan of Usk', in 1651). Vaughan's finest devotional poetry, contained in the two volumes of *Silex Scintillans*, does, however, suggest a quite individual vision of a pastoral paradise which had been glimpsed in childhood, but which once lost to the adult could be regained only through contemplation and revelation.

Despite its dominant mood of serenity, *Silex Scintillans* is periodically charged with a subversive energy directed against the new political and religious status quo imposed by Parliament. The poem 'Abel's Blood' ostensibly protests at the blood shed by the first murderer and, by implication, at the crucifixion of Christ, but the complaint 'What thunders shall those men arraign | Who cannot count those they have slain, | Who bathe not in a shallow flood, | But in a deep, wide sea of blood' seems also likely to be a barbed reference to a parliamentary army which had not only waged a civil war but then proceeded to execute the King, the earthly governor of the Church. In 'The World' the 'darksome States-man' who feeds on churches and altars may equally be a reference to Cromwell, and in 'The British Church' the soldiers who 'here | Cast in their lots again' seem to be rending the seamless robe that once was the Church. The references in the titles of poems to the major feast-days of the Prayer Book Calendar ('Christ's Nativity', 'Easter-day', 'Ascension-day', 'White Sunday', 'Trinity Sunday') are also an Anglican assertion of the propriety of marking particular festivals in opposition to an official ban. The uncertainties, insecurities, and redefinitions of the political world seem to have driven Vaughan in on himself and to an expression of an alternative spirituality. He looks less to a temple built with human hands than to open-air sanctuaries such as the tabernacles of the patriarchs of Israel. God is evident in numinous landscapes where angels discourse with men in sacred groves (in the poem 'Religion' the 'leaves thy spirit doth fan' are also the pages of the Bible). The true worship of God is expressed in a sense of harmony with observed Nature, the 'great *Chime* | And *Symphony* of nature' of 'The Morning-watch'. When in 'The Search' Christ is sought for at the sites associated with his earthly life, the pilgrim is bidden to look beyond the 'old elements or dust' and to find him in 'another world'. Vaughan seems to have responded particularly to the story of the patriarch Jacob, who had dreamed of an angelic ladder while resting on a stone pillow at Bethel, who had wrestled with an angel at Peniel, and at whose well at Sychar Jesus had spoken to the Samaritan woman of the water of life. Jacob's attributes—wells, fountains, stones, and angel-haunted groves—figure throughout his religious verse, notably in the extraordinary poem 'Regeneration', which Vaughan placed early in the first part of *Silex*. The poem traces an interrelationship of natural, biblical, and internal landscapes, the exploration of one leading inexorably to another as the spiritual pilgrim probes the mysterious workings of grace. The divine breath called for in the poem's last lines takes up yet another biblical reference, one that is explained by the quotation from the Song of Solomon appended to it: 'Arise O north, and come thou south-wind, and blow upon my garden, that the spices thereof may flow out.' The secluded garden of the soul is stirred and quickened by the spirit of life itself.

Silex Scintillans ('the sparkling flint') bears on its title-page an emblem of a flashing flint struck by a thunderbolt from the hand of God; the flint is shaped like a weeping or a bleeding heart and it flames as the lightning falls. Vaughan's emblem is variously explained; a Latin poem which prefaces the volume draws out Ezekiel's prophecy that God will 'take the stony heart out of their flesh, and will give them a heart of flesh', but the personal application of the idea to the poet is twofold. His own comment that 'Certaine Divine Raies break out of the Soul in adversity, like sparks of fire out of the afflicted flint' illuminates the dominant idea, but the actual choice of a flint was determined by a Latin pun on 'silex' and on the name of the ancient British tribe from which Vaughan claimed descent, the Silures. 'The Silurist', as the poet habitually styled himself, sees himself as made vocal by adversity. His Church and his political cause are devastated, and, as the nine untitled poems interspersed in his two volumes suggest, the death of friends has disturbed his peace of mind. These elegiac verses often suggest the dragging movement of time and the painful counting of its passage ('Each day is grown a dozen year, | And each houre, one'; 'Silence, and stealth of dayes!' tis now | Since thou art gone, | Twelve hundred houres'), but their mourning mood is variously checked; internal qualifications bring consolation and individual poems relate not only to each other but to the titled poems which surround them. The 'pearl' discovered in 'Silence and stealth of dayes' is Christ's 'pearl of great price' which outweighs all other value; the roots that sleep in the wintry soil of 'I walkt the other day' are to bring forth new life in an eternal spring; the sense of lonely exile in 'They are all gone into the world of light!' is transformed by the investigation of a series of conceits (death as a jewel shining in the night, an empty bird's nest, a dream of angels, a star confined in a tomb) which serve to 'disperse these mists, which blot and fill | My perspective'. The dispersal of gloom is elsewhere taken as a central metaphor for revelation: 'The Morning-watch' welcomes the floods of light as a foretaste of heaven; 'The Dawning' recognizes that dawn is 'the only time | That with thy glory doth best chime' and therefore the fittest time to meditate on the Second Coming; Eternity ostensibly glimpsed with such wonderful casualness in 'The World' is like 'a great *Ring* of pure and endless light' in which 'the world | And all her train were hurl'd'. When in 'The Night' Vaughan describes the nocturnal visit of Nicodemus to Jesus, he plays with a series of contrasts between light and darkness, waking and sleeping, education and oblivion. The poem centres on a pun and a paradox: at midnight Nicodemus sees both the Son and the Sun and his enlightenment consists of an insight into the mystery of God's 'deep, but dazling darkness'. It is a night into which Vaughan's poetry consistently peers.

Henry King's meditations on mortality and eternity lack the often electrifying originality of Vaughan's. As Dean of Rochester Cathedral in 1642, King (1592–1669) had had his library destroyed and his church pillaged by a rampaging gang of Puritan iconoclasts; in the same year he was appointed Bishop of Chichester only to be ejected from his see in 1643 (he was restored to it in 1660). As his somewhat florid 'Elegy upon the most Incomparable King Charles the First' of 1649 demonstrates, the nature of his political and religious loyalties was never in doubt. The 'Elegy' unequivocally sees Charles as a martyr enthroned in heaven while below him his former subjects are sundered from each other by 'that Bloody Cloud, | whose purple Mists Thy Murther'd Body Shroud'. Vengeance, King solemnly reminds his readers, is a prime prerogative of God, a factor which 'bids us our Sorrow by our Hope confine, | And reconcile our *Reason* to our *Faith*'. Much of King's verse is, however, secular in subject and unspecifically Christian in its imagery, though even his amorous poetry is haunted by a vague melancholy and an awareness of transience. Both the 'Midnight Meditation' and the much imitated stanza 'Sic Vita' (generally ascribed to him) stress the frailty of human life and human aspiration. Amongst his many elegies the tribute to his dead wife, 'The Exequy. To his Matchlesse never to be forgotten Freind', quite transcends the rest of his poetry in quality and poignancy. Although the poem scarcely sets out to forbid mourning, its interplay of images of books and libraries, of suns, stars, and seasons, and finally of battle ('My pulse like a soft Drum | Beats my approach, tells *Thee* I come') suggests something of King's debt to the 'valedictions' of John Donne.

Secular Verse: Courtiers and Cavaliers

In his poetic tribute to his 'worthy friend' George Sandys, Thomas Carew (1594/5–1640) contrasted his own 'unwasht Muse' to the hallowed temple frequented by Sandys's. Sandys (1578–1644), the author of a verse *Paraphrase upon the Psalmes of David* (1636), the translator of Hugo Grotius's sombre Latin tragedy, *Christ's Passion* (1640) and, somewhat less devoutly, of Ovid's *Metamorphoses* (1621–6), seemed to Carew to have set a standard against which his own secular poetry was impiously wanting. Carew's aspirations to turn to religious verse are, however, only modestly voiced in his poem: his 'restlesse Soule' may, perhaps, find itself tired with the pursuit of mortal beauty, and the same 'perhaps' conditions the idea that his soul may neither quench her thirst nor satisfy her appetite for things spiritual by contemplating the earthly. Prompted by Sandys's example he proposes that he may at some future point cease adoring God 'in moulds of Clay' and may turn instead to writing 'what his blest Sp'rt, not fond Love shall indite'. These remained largely unfulfilled ambitions. When Carew's *Poems* appeared in print in 1640 they were on the whole elegantly turned, witty, gentlemanlike love-lyrics. Some, such as the epitaphs to Lady Mary Wentworth and to Lady Mary Villiers, develop conceits appropriate to a meditation on untimely death; others, such as 'To my Friend G. N. from Wrest' and 'To Saxham', celebrate country-house hospitality in the manner of Jonson's 'To Penshurst', but the real substance of the volume lies in its variety of amorous addresses to, and reflections on, a fictional mistress known as Celia. These verses play with the supposed power of the poet to make and unmake a reputation for beauty; they neatly exploit a simple metaphor (such as the idea of excommunication in 'To my inconstant Mistris' or a parallel with an armed rebellion in the state in 'A deposition from Love'); or, as in the smooth 'Song', 'Ask me no more', they establish an indulgently erotic mood through a series of sensual images (roses, sun-rays, nightingales, stars, and, finally, the Phoenix in her 'spicy nest'). Carew's direct debt to the divergent examples of Jonson and Donne is evident more in the poems he addressed to both masters than in his own love-poetry. The 'Elegie upon the Death of the Deane of Pauls, Dr John Donne' is eloquent in its appreciation of the innovatory power of a poet whose 'brave Soule' had committed 'holy Rapes upon our Will' and it is enterprising in its own trawling for striking images. The poem, published in the edition of Donne's verse of 1633, darts between ideas of a quickening Promethean breath, a purging of the 'Muse's Garden' of its 'Pedantique weedes', a paying of the debts of a poetically bankrupt age, and a girding of 'Giant phansie' with the 'tough-thick-rib'd hoopes' of the 'stubborne' English language. It ends by proclaiming Donne's posthumous title to a 'universall Monarchy of wit'.

Carew served his struggling, temporal monarch, Charles I, in the military campaign against Scotland, the so-called first Bishops' War of 1639. His death in the following year prevented any further involvement in the increasingly polarized manœuvres of the King and of those in both England and Scotland determined to stand their ground against royal influence. Carew's younger acquaintances—fellow-courtiers and fellow-poets, Sir John Suckling (1609–42) and Richard Lovelace (1618–56/57)—were drawn to the King's party by ties of old loyalty and by a patrician relish for military adventure. Both men's verse exhibits the gentlemanly lightness of touch and the equally lax morality typical of 'Cavalier' poetry. Their politics (sexual as much as national) render both equally representative of the easy, confident, flirtatious, essentially unearnest world of courtly manners. Suckling's poetry, collected posthumously with his plays and letters as *Fragmenta Aurea* (1646), suggests an almost cynical impatience with ideals. 'Loving and Beloved', for example, even dares to equate kings with lovers, not for their glory, but because 'their chief art in reigne dissembling is'. The song 'Why so pale and wan fond lover?' dismissively concludes with the thought 'If of her self she will not love, | Nothing can make her: | The divil take her'. 'Sonnet ii' (though not a sonnet in the strict sense of the term) professes an indifference to defined ideas of female beauty; love is a sport, specific attractions are arbitrary, and it is appetite, not meat, which 'makes eating a delight'. When in 'Sonnet iii' an afterworld is imagined, it is a pagan Elysium where star-crossed lovers find their proper partners; even so, the risk of not achieving ultimate fulfilment prompts the poet to opt for a more immediate satisfaction with 'the Woman here'. Even the delightfully relaxed account of the ceremonies accompanying an aristocratic wedding, which purports to be told from the point of view of a country bumpkin ('A Ballad upon a Wedding'), ends with the commonsensical observation that the real pleasures of copulation are classless ('All that they had not done, they do't: | What that is, who can tell? | But I believe it was no more | Than thou and I have done before | With *Bridget,* and with *Nell*').

Richard Lovelace's lyrics, the majority of which were published in 1649 as *Lucasta; Epodes, Odes, Sonnets, Songs etc.,* convey a similar impression of smug male assurance in dallying with love and the emotions of women, but through them there echoes the alternative, but also exclusively male, martial urgency of the 1640s. The subdued tribute to Donne's 'A Valediction: Forbidding Mourning'—'To Lucasta going beyond the Seas'—has none of the sharp intellectual energy of the original, but 'To Lucasta, Going to the Warres' suggests a new valedictory exigency as it balances peace-time flattery against the summons of that 'new Mistresse', military honour. Lovelace can jest about male inconstancy in 'The Scrutinie' ('Have I not lov'd thee much and long, | A tedious twelve houres space?') and he can lovingly indulge in describing the feminine gestures that arouse him (Amarantha dishevelling her hair, Lucasta manipulating her fan, Gratiana dancing on a floor 'pav'd with broken hearts'), yet when, in his most famous lyric, he purports to write 'To Althea from Prison' he can blend and contrast ideas of love and loyalty, mental freedom and physical restriction, private victory and public defeat. Imprisoned by Parliament for presenting a petition from Kentish royalists demanding the restoration of the army to Charles I, Lovelace casts himself as a caged linnet singing of the 'sweetnes, Mercy, Majesty, | And glories of my KING'. His sublimity is conditioned by a sense of an interrelation of divine and human love:

> Stone Walls doe not a Prison make,
> Nor Iron bars a Cage;
> Minds innocent and quiet take
> That for an Hermitage;
> If I have freedom in my Love,
> And in my soul am free;
> Angels alone that sore above
> Injoy such Liberty.

The prison bursts when confronted by an inner conviction, much as in 'The Grasshopper' the winter of adversity, following the defeat of the royal cause, is reversed by a retreat into a private world warmed by an eternal summer of cultivated Cavalier friendships and loyalties.

To many eighteenth-century critics the work of Edmund Waller (1606–87) seemed to embody the metrical and verbal smoothness which ushered in the triumph of classical principles in English verse. Later in the seventeenth century John Dryden praised Waller's poetry for its model 'Excellence and Dignity'; it was Waller, he claimed, who 'first made Writing easily an Art' and who 'first shew'd us to conclude the Sense, most commonly in Distichs; which in the Verse of those before him, runs on for so many Lines together, that the Reader is out of Breath to overtake it'. This is something of an exaggeration, but the 'sweetness' of Waller's lyricism (notably in his famous 'Song', 'Goe Lovely Rose', and in his hyperbolically gallant 'On a Girdle'), and the shapeliness of his couplets were clearly aspects of his art which most pleased his immediate literary successors. Such praise of his easy art, and particularly of his limpid verses to Sacharissa, tend to blot out the political contortions of a literary career which stretched from the 1630s to the 1660s. The proposed dedication of the poems in his first volume to the Queen was tactfully dropped for its publication in 1645, though the volume contains effusive public reflections on such subjects proper to a loyal courtier as 'The Danger His Majesty (being Prince) Escaped in the Road at Saint Andero' (probably written as early as 1625), 'To the King on his Navy', and 'Upon his Majesty's repairing of St Paul's', as well as two addresses to the Queen which stress both her beauty and her fecundity. Waller joined the Queen in exile in 1643 following the failure of his botched plot to seize parliamentarian London in the name of the King (he was briefly imprisoned and heavily fined for his part in the plot, but seems to have bought his life by naming his accomplices to his captors). His return to republican England in 1651, as the result of an official pardon, was marked by an astutely tuned couplet celebration of Cromwell, 'A Panegyrick to my Lord Protector' (1655), in which Cromwell is praised for his political wisdom and for his military prowess and the new Commonwealth hailed as a pattern for Europe. Further timely, if less distinguished, essays in panegyric mark the new editions of the *Poems* published after the restoration of Charles II in 1660. 'To the King, upon his Majesty's happy Return' is a distinctly less enterprising piece of work than the eulogy of Cromwell, but Waller was able to defend himself against the King's expression of disappointment by replying, 'poets, Sire, succeed better in fiction than in truth'. His later loyal and royal addresses are singularly flabby. 'On St James's Park, as lately improv'd by his Majesty' sees the park as an Elysium whose beauty blots out the memories associated with the nearby House of Commons 'where all our ills were shap'd'; a birthday ode to the new Queen recalls her 'happy recovery from a dangerous sickness', and her praise of tea provided the occasion for a short sycophantic verse on the pleasure of the new beverage ('The Muse's friend, Tea, does our fancy aid').

The poetry of Abraham Cowley (1618–67), against which Dr Johnson directed much of his criticism of 'metaphysical' poetry, possesses little of the intellectual and verbal muscularity of Donne's verse and even less of its opposite, the empty, if much admired, musicality of Waller's. Cowley was a precocious poet, having written a verse romance on the subject of Pyramus and Thisbe at the age of 10 (published in his *Poetical Blossoms* of 1633), but it was with the outbreak of the Civil War and with his moves first to the King's headquarters in Oxford and, in 1644, to the Queen's court in Paris that he found a proper expression for his talent and an audience to appreciate it. The love-poems collected as *The Mistress* in 1647 suggest less of a pursuit of a particular beloved than a series of general attempts to amuse disconsolate lovers or to excuse unrequited or absent love. 'The Spring', which in many ways seems to prefigure wittily Andrew Marvell's preference for trees over human fellowship in 'The Garden', in fact steadily insists on the emptiness of nature without a loving companion to share in its pleasures. 'The Change', too, meditates on an exclusion of love which can be remedied only by the radical shift exemplified by a literal exchange of hearts. 'The Wish', however, seeks for a retreat from 'this busie world' to 'a *small House* and *large Garden*' accompanied by true friends, true books, and a '*Mistress* moderately fair'; this modest suburban dream is finally conditioned not by the ideal of separation from ambition but by the unspecific '*She* who is all the world, and can exclude | In *desarts Solitude*'. During his sojourn at Oxford, Cowley began his grand but ultimately unfinished project of an epic treatment of the dominant national subject of the times, *The Civil War* (Book I was published in 1679; Books II and III, once presumed lost, were edited and published only in 1973). It is a dutiful rather than an inspired work which extravagantly associates all heroic virtue with the royalist cause, all undoing with Parliament and the proliferating Puritan sects. Of necessity, *The Civil War* broke down as the King's cause and, with it, the ambitious fabric of the poem collapsed. A second uncompleted epic, 'Davideis', which awkwardly recognizes a shadowy reflection of the biblical struggles of Saul and David in those of Charles I and Cromwell, was published in the *Poems* of 1656. In the Preface to these *Poems* Cowley, who had returned to England in somewhat dubious circumstances in 1654, acknowledged both a submission to the conditions of 'the conqueror' and, with it, a need to 'lay down our pens as well as our arms'. Despite its opening claim that it will avoid a recall of 'those times and actions for which we have received a general amnesty as a favour from the victor', the volume contains some contentious material, notably the series of intellectually and lexically clumsy 'Pindaric Odes' (amongst which the address to 'Brutus' manages to fudge the issue of both Roman politics and Cromwellian parallels). The 1656 volume also contains Cowley's contrasting tributes to dead friends: the diffuse and rambling 'On the Death of Mr William Hervey' and the tenser, lusher, and more expressive appreciation of Crashaw ('*Poet* and *Saint*! To thee alone are given | The two most sacred *Names* of *Earth* and *Heaven*'). To a distinctly non-ecumenical age this latter poem proclaims both a need for a continuing reformation of English poetry by purging its pagan elements according to Christian principles and a tolerant admiration for Crashaw's example ('For even in *Error* sure no *Danger* is | When joyn'd with so much *Piety* as His').

Hesperides: or the Works both Humane & Divine of Robert Herrick Esq. of 1648 is divided into two: the first part, *Hesperides* proper, contains some of the most titillatingly erotic and overtly pagan verse in English; its second part, *His Noble Numbers,* has its own title-page and is separately paginated in order to mark off a series of religious poems from the 'unbaptized Rhimes' of the secular body of the volume. Despite their baptism, the poems in *His Noble Numbers* suggest that their author's imaginative engagement in expressions of literary piety was occasional rather than consistent. Herrick (1591–1674) was a well-educated parish priest from rural Devonshire who was ejected from his living in 1647 as a man assertively loyal to the old order in Church and State. Although, as far as we know, he had neither sought nor been offered the opportunity of serving his King as either a courtier or a soldier, his verse proves him to be the most expressively 'cavalier' of the seventeenth-century love-poets. He woos and flatters, philanders and warns, observes and compares, with little cerebration and even rarer earnestness. As a whole, *Hesperides* side-steps the confessional and political divisions of contemporary England. Its opening 'Argument' proclaims that its poet will 'sing' of brooks and blossoms, of spring and summer, of wooing and wedding; his court will be that of the Fairy King and Queen and his creed will be based on a somewhat indistinct hope of heaven. Its most weighty 'political' statement lies in its generous, tolerant, and profoundly anti-Puritan, treatment of sexuality.

Herrick's most effective religious verse expresses a childlike acceptance of faith and divine providence, though its innocence is quite distinct from the wondering mysticism of Vaughan. His 'A Thanksgiving to God, for his House' gratefully lists the simple comforts and rural blessings of a retired life, but it never attempts, as Herbert might have done, to move from the everyday to the theological. When Herrick speaks of heaven in 'The White Island: or place of the Blest', he imagines it as a floating island of happy blankness free of the 'teares and terrors' of this life, but neither here nor in his prayers for comfort in the 'Letanie, to the Holy Spirit' is there any suggestion of a quivering fear of judgement akin to Donne's. His evident delight in a white vision of a heaven characterized by candour and sincerity is, however, reflected in the air of inno-cent celebration that haunts much of his secular verse. The pleasures of the flesh as they are both spelled out and lovingly alluded to in *Hesperides* are threatened not by prurience or moral disapproval but by the cold winds of time and death. Young lovers, like the transient blossoms, the rosebuds, the tulips, or the daffodils of his best-known lyrics, need to 'make much of Time' in order to seize the brief moment of pleasure. The only immortality available on this side of heaven lies in the survival of poetry, as Herrick persistently reminds the Antheas and Julias to whom individual poems are addressed. Despite his resentment of a 'long and irksome banishment' in the 'dull confines of the drooping West', Herrick particularly relishes describing those rural cere-monies, such as May Day and Harvest Home, that uncomplicatedly link human and natural fertility, procreation, and fulfillment. This is not simply because he recognizes their pagan roots, or because he sees them as reflections of Greek and Roman pastorals, but because he allows them to be 'country matters' in the truest sense of the term. When Corinna goes a–Maying in the poem of that name, when the village girls dance 'like a Spring, | with Honysuckles crown'd' in 'To Meddows', or when the Earl of Westmorland is reminded of his obliga-tion to extend hospitality to his harvesters in 'The Hock-Cart', Herrick cele-brates expressions of unity which are part innocent ceremony, part knowing physical enactment. In his richly allusive marriage poem, 'A Nuptiall Song, or Epithalamie, on Sir Clipseby Crew and his Lady', he brings 'the youthfull Bridegroom, and the fragrant Bride' together at their 'proud | Plumpe Bed'

> . . . swelling like a cloud
> Tempting the too too modest; can
> You see it brusle like a Swan,
> And you be cold
> To meet it, when it woo's and seemes to fold
> The Armes to hugge you? throw, throw
> Your selves into the mighty over-flow
> Of that white Pride, and Drowne
> The night, with you, in floods of Downe.

It is a consummation which is devoutly, ceremonially, and sensuously to be wished.

When Herrick speaks of himself as a poet he either clings desperately to the traditional idea of verse outliving its maker or he evokes a picture of the pleasurable dissipation of male conviviality as a proper stimulus to poetry and an ideal setting for its recitation. In 'When he would have his verses read' he insists on the fitness of a time 'when that men have both well drunke, and fed'. This feeling for relaxed, alcohol-enhanced fellowship re-emerges in one of his tributes to his adored Ben Jonson ('An Ode for Him') where he imaginatively links himself to the metropolitan tavern-centred culture in which 'each Verse of thine | Out-did the meate, out-did the frolick wine'. These literary bac-chanals rise to their peak in the poem entitled 'To live merrily, and to trust to Good Verses' where, amid a 'golden pomp', Herrick purports to drink the health of the classical poets for whom he feels an especial sympathy and to whose literary company he aspires. The classical literary allusions of the poem partly reinforce the idea suggested by the volume's engraved title-page where the poet is represented as a hirsute bust, casually draped in the antique manner, and set in the midst of a cheerful pagan landscape. It is at once an Arcady where cupids play ring-a-roses, a Parnassus in which Hippocrene gushes, and the mythical western garden of the Hesperides where the plump golden apples of life are tended by nymphs.

Anatomies: Burton, Browne, and Hobbes

Despite the breadth of his own classical learning, reference, and allusion, Herrick appears to have had a frequent and creative recourse to Robert Burton's *The Anatomy of Melancholy* (1621, reissued, enlarged and revised 1624, 1628, 1632, 1638, and 1651). For Herrick, as much as for Lawrence Sterne in the eighteenth century and John Keats in the nineteenth, Burton's encyclopaedic treatise on psychology proved to be a mine of reworkable details, phrases, images, and anecdotes. Burton (1577–1640), a somewhat awkward, retiring, and donnish Oxford clergyman, drew on a mass of ancient and modern authority to produce what is part medical treatise and part vast com-monplace book. Apart from the Bible and other anonymous sources, Burton cites some 1,250 named authors, and his compendious argument evolves by means of an interlarding of science, philosophy, poetry, history, and divinity. Each page is, to many modern readers, disruptively littered with Latin quota-tions, some of considerable length. Within individual sentences opinions are established, qualified, or shaped by strings of complementary and suggestive words. The book's organizational principles, which have eluded many casual readers, are emphasized both by the full title of the work (*The Anatomy of Melancholy. What it is, With all the kinds, causes, symptomes, prognostickes, & severall cures of it. In three Partitions, with their severall Sections, members & subsections, Philosophically, Medicinally, Historically opened & cut up*) and by yet another of the complex iconographical title-pages in which the early seven-teenth century excelled. If the work is not always exactly coherent, it achieves what unity it possesses by an involved process of inclusion and through a multiplicity of demonstration and definition. The title-page, which is explained in an accompanying poem, is divided into ten panels, each of which

emblematically represents the symptoms or attributes of melancholy. A picture
of the Greek philosopher Democritus, seated under the sign of Saturn (the
'Lord of Melancholy'), is balanced on either side by representations of aspects
of 'Zelotopia' (jealousy) and by 'Solitudo' (solitariness). Beneath these stand
effigies of a young lovesick melancholic, an older and emaciated hypochon-
driac, a superstitious monk, and a shackled madman in rags. The page is completed by pictures of 'sovereign plants to purge the veins of melancholy, and
cheer the heart' and by a portrait of the author himself as 'Democritus Junior'.
It is 'Democritus Junior' who addresses the reader in a substantial Preface and
who offers glancing, self-deprecatory insights into his own temperament ('I
have lived a silent, sedentary, private life') and into the nature of his mind
('This roving humour . . . I have ever had, and like a ranging spaniel, that barks
at every bird he sees, leaving his game, I have followed all saving that which
I should . . . I have read many books, but to little purpose, for want of good
method'). It is precisely this disorganized learning, methodized into a treatise
which forms part of a larger historically based discourse on mania and
madness, that gives *The Anatomy of Melancholy* its continuing fascination. In
stressing the lapsed state of humankind, Burton equally recognizes the entangled and disordered nature of the human condition and the susceptibility
of the human mind to the unbalancing disease of melancholia. His book is an
attempt to distinguish and define the components of this confusion and constipation in human affairs, but a tidy scientific logic, Burton sometimes
manages to persuade us, cannot always be applied effectively to an untidy
subject.

   'In our study of Anatomy', Sir Thomas Browne noted in a digression on
the elusive nature of the soul in *Religio Medici*, 'there is a mass of mysterious
Philosophy, and such as reduced the very Heathens to Divinity'. Browne
(1605–82) writes as a well-informed and experimental physician who found his
religious faith confirmed by his scientific awe. *Religio Medici* ('the Religion
of a Doctor') was composed in the mid-1630s but was first published, without
Browne's authorization, in 1642; a revised edition, corrected by its author,
appeared in the following year. His lenient *apologia* for his belief and for his
allegiance to the Church of England had a particular currency in the 1640s,
but his book is notable more for its stylistic effects than for the originality of
its thought or the stringency and urgency of its argument. The devout doctor
poses more as a moralist than as a diagnostician, more as the man of common
sense than as the anatomist of the body or the soul. Browne, who had pursued
his medical studies in both Catholic and Protestant Europe, proves to be a prag-
matist in his attitude to the formularies of religion and he demonstrates an
exemplary tolerance of both Christian dissent and Christian diversity. He
admits to being 'of that Reformed new-cast Religion, wherein I dislike nothing
but the Name' because he sees Anglicanism as rooted in an apostolic tradition;
he admits having been moved to tears by continental Catholic devotion 'while
my consorts, blind with opposition and prejudice, have fallen into an excess of

scorn and laughter'; he can proclaim that 'there is no man more Paradoxical than my self', but he can later formulate the principle that 'no man can justly censure or condemn another, because indeed no man truly knows another'.

Browne's profession of open-mindedness is linked to the very nature of his discourse, one which both draws on a variety of received fact and opinion and echoes a Baconian insistence on the 'perpetual renovation' of knowledge. *Pseudodoxia Epidemica: or, Enquiries into Very many Received Tenents, And Commonly Presumed Truths* (1646, revised and augmented 1650, 1658, 1672), Browne's longest and most intellectually experimental work took its cue directly from Bacon's distinction between 'truths' determined by the exercise of human reason, and the 'vanities' and 'distempers' of pseudo-science and uninformed credulity (the book is sometimes known by the title *Vulgar Errors*). The treatise moves steadily, but never ponderously, from human to natural history, from theology to physiology, from the superstitious distortions of logic to the radiance of beliefs erected on 'the surer base of reason'. Browne's works of the 1650s, *Hydriotaphia, Urne Buriall; or, A Discourse of the Sepulchrall Urnes Lately found in Norfolk* and *The Garden of Cyrus; or, The Quincunciall Lozenge or Net-work Plantations of the Ancients, Artificially, Naturally, Mystically Considered* (both 1658), are essentially loose, archaeological studies which interrelate ancient custom, symbolism, a fascination with form and development, and a pervasive awareness of transience and mortality. *Hydriotaphia*, like Browne's posthumously published *To A Friend, Upon the Occasion of the Death of his Intimate Friend* (1690), suggests a particular concern with the phenomena of decay, death, and disposal in the ancient and modern worlds and with the significance of religious rites and religious comfort. The Christian weight of Browne's argument lies in his stress on the promise of a hereafter which eclipses the need for earthly commemoration or exposes the vanity of monumental masonry: '*Pyramids*, *Arches*, *Obelisks*, were but the irregularities of vainglory, and wilde enormities of ancient magnanimity. But the most magnanimous resolution rests in Christian Religion, which trampleth upon pride, and sits on the neck of ambition, humbly pursuing that infallible perpetuity, unto which all others must diminish their diameters, and be poorly seen in Angles of contingency.' Such architectural and geometrical metaphors are typical of the consistent tendency of Browne's mind to lose itself in a 'wingy' mystery, or, as he memorably puts it in *Religio Medici* 'to pursue my Reason to an *O altitudo*'.

The intellectual architecture of Thomas Hobbes's great philosophical tract *Leviathan, or The Matter, Forme, and Power of A Commonwealth Ecclesiastical and Civil* (1651) is, in an important sense, based on the passion for geometry that he discovered at the age of 40. 'Geometry', Hobbes (1588–1679) noted in the fourth chapter of the first part of his book, 'is the only science that it hath pleased God hitherto to bestow on mankind' and this 'only science' serves as an abstract model for the shaping of the other significations, or 'definitions', on which he bases his complex argument. As the impressive structure of his

thesis steadily rises, a reader grasps that it is built on a series of proved, packaged, and sealed logical propositions. Dissent, let alone qualification, is not
encouraged. Hobbes divides *Leviathan* into four parts; the first, 'Of Man',
attempts to define the nature and quality of human reasoning (as opposed to
'reason') largely in reaction to the contortions of the 'Aristotelity' which had
continued to dominate the English universities. When he extends his survey
to an exploration of human motivation, he consistently observes a rational
animal whose action is determined by aggression rather than by love, by acquisitiveness rather than by generosity, by self-interest rather than by any altruistic ideal. For Hobbes, the selfish pursuit of 'felicity' in which all human
beings engage essentially excludes benevolence.

Parts Two, Three, and Four proceed to develop this thesis into an examination of 'Civil Society', the commonwealth into which rational animals form
themselves for mutual security. In the opening chapter of Part Two ('Of the
Causes, Generation, and Definition of a Commonwealth') Hobbes finally
introduces the Leviathan of his title, 'that *mortal god*, to which we owe under
the *immortal God*, our peace and defence'. When he returns to the idea in
chapter 28 he further explains how 'the nature of man' has 'compelled him to
submit himself to government' and how that government can be likened to
'*Leviathan*, taking that comparison out of the two last verses of the one-and-
fortieth of *Job*; where God having set forth the great power of *Leviathan*, called
him, King of the Proud'. This mighty governor, or government, once constituted according to an agreed contract and given sovereignty, assumes absolute
power. He, or it, must not, according to Hobbes, brook opposition. In the subsequent chapter, the 'late troubles in England' emerge as a determining factor
in the argument concerning 'those things that weaken, or tend to the dissolution of a Commonwealth'. Neither the royalist nor the republican cause is particularly favoured (Hobbes himself had gone into exile in Paris and in 1647 had
been appointed tutor to the Prince of Wales, but in 1651 he had reconciled
himself to Cromwell's England). When, however, he expands on his belief that
a sovereign should not be subject to civil laws, or to the idea that too close a
study of Greek and Roman history suggests that 'regicide' can be glossed as
'tyrannicide' and therefore rendered respectable, he is clearly appealing to conservative royalist sympathies. His references to Julius Caesar as the 'popular'
man or 'potent subject' who threatens the status quo are somewhat more
ambiguous. In one sense they suggest a critical parallel to a usurping Cromwell
(whose panegyrists were much inclined to appeal to Roman precedent); in
another, they hint at the continuing threat to the Protector's own rule from
his erstwhile supporters. The danger from a 'popular' and ambitious rebel
is greater 'in a popular government, than in a monarchy', Hobbes explains,
'because an army is of so great force, and multitude, as it may easily be made
believe, they are the people'. *Leviathan* sets down a theory of an authoritarian
government which wields both spiritual and temporal power. In their time
Hobbes's arguments had little appeal to those radical Puritans who pleaded

particular inspiration and freedom of conscience as a defence against the State's insistence on uniformity and assent. Nevertheless, the strong strains of anti-clericalism and theological nonconformity that run through *Leviathan* offered equally little intellectual comfort to those devout Anglicans who prayed for a determined restoration of the old order in Church and State. Since the 1650s *Leviathan* has continued to vex the world rather than to divert it.

Political Prose of the Civil War Period

Hobbes's contention that governments were constituted by the demands of human security and that states were held together by a contract between the ruler and the ruled rather than immutably ordained by God was scarcely original. His emphatic restatement of the idea was, however, a reflection of the revolutionary times in which his *Leviathan* evolved. In the late 1640s and 1650s the debate about the shape and authority of the rapidly changing constitution of England was intensely partisan. A defeated king had been obliged to surrender what remained of his sovereignty to the parliamentary victors of the Civil War, though he never abandoned the belief that he had been placed on his throne by God and had exercised a sacred trust as monarch. Parliament was obliged by its victorious army to bring the King to trial on the charge of being 'a Tyrant, a Traitor and a Murderer, and a public enemy to the Commonwealth of England'. In October 1646 the episcopal structure of the Anglican Church had been formally dismantled; with one traditional pillar of the historic state removed, the 'Rump' Parliament proceeded in March 1649 to abolish two others, the monarchy and the House of Lords. In May of the same year the House of Commons affirmed that England should from henceforward be ruled as 'a Commonwealth and free state by the supreme authority of this nation, the representatives of the people in parliament'. Once the King and his cause had been disposed of, power remained with the effective brokers of Parliament, the commanders of the army, most of them gentlemen landowners. Oliver Cromwell, who later refused the offer of a supposedly defunct Crown, was proclaimed Lord Protector in December 1653. He made his impatience with truculent parliaments and with extra-parliamentary opposition to his rule perfectly plain. Despite the widespread, free and public debate about the nature of sovereignty and the potential for sustained constitutional development, the Cromwellian Commonwealth was not marked by radical social change or by any notable experiment in popular democracy. In republican England political changes, conducted in the name of the people, remained reshuffles of the ruling élite. The Commonwealth proved to be more intent on enforcing a relatively narrow idea of godly rule than on advancing the inheritance of the meek.

To the victors in the struggle against monarchical 'tyranny' the defeat of the King seemed to open the way to a just restructuring of institutions by men of

goodwill and energy. 'If God and a good cause give them Victory, the prosecution whereof for the most part, inevitably draws after it the alteration of
Lawes, change of Government, downfal of Princes and thir families', wrote
John Milton in 1649, 'then comes the task to those Worthies which are the
soule of that enterprize, to be swett and labour'd out amidst the throng and
noises of Vulgar and irrational men.' These 'Worthies', the new men at the
top, were consistently harried by 'irrational' opposition, an opposition which
came both from apologists for the old order and from those who sought further
to radicalize the new. The day after Charles I's hugger-mugger funeral at
Windsor in January 1649, the most effective of the many pieces of royalist
propaganda was published in London. *Eikon Basilike; the Pourtraicture of
His Sacred Majestie in his Solitudes and Sufferings* consisted of the supposed
meditations and prayers of the 'martyr' King. The volume, which probably
drew on authentic materials, has since been generally ascribed to John Gauden
(1605–62), a former sympathizer with Parliament and a future Bishop of
Worcester. Any doubts as to its true authorship failed to dent its impressive
sales and its widespread influence. Some forty-seven editions eventually
appeared and the impact of the book was directly felt by Anglican and devoutly
royalist readers well into the eighteenth century.

The political arguments of dissenting Puritans have belatedly attracted more
detailed and sympathetic interest, particularly amongst historians determined
to suggest a continuity in English radical thought or a primitive formulation
of socialist and libertarian ideology. When Hobbes insisted on the proper 'subjection of ecclesiastics to the commonwealth', in order to protect the civil
power against any dissolution of its authority, he appears to have been thinking not only of the temporal and spiritual claims of a Pope or of a state Church
but also of the challenge to authority presented by the individual conscience.
Hobbes foresaw his commonwealth tottering if it allowed assent to the twin
doctrines of Puritan dissenters: that '*whatsoever a man does against his conscience, is sin*' and that 'no man dare to obey the sovereign power, further than
it shall seem good in his own eyes'. The restless Protestant sectarians who had
so unsettled the uniform tidiness of Archbishop Laud's ecclesiastical vision
proved equally to be thorns in the side of Cromwell's generals. With the
Anglican order, which they had so long opposed, gone, disagreements over
authority and congregational discipline broke the tactical alliance between
Independents and Presbyterians. It was, however, the smaller sects and the
political groupings associated with them which seemed to threaten to disrupt
the state. Cromwell was particularly vexed by the rebellion of the 'Fifth
Monarchy Men', fanatical believers in the literal truth of the prophet Daniel's
vision of the advent of a Fifth and Universal Monarchy which would succeed
the four defunct ancient empires. They went beyond the Reformation
identification of the Pope with the Antichrist by asserting that the rejection
of papal authority marked the end of the lingering tyranny of Rome, and
prepared the way for the imminent coming of Christ as King. The relatively

conservative leaders of the Commonwealth did not prove to be willing ushers to the millennium or builders of a new social order either at home or abroad.

A more specifically English strain runs through the pamphlet literature of those radicals who held that the overthrow of Charles I had begun to undo the social and political evils of the Norman rather than the Roman Empire. With the removal of the lineal descendant of the Conqueror, England could again assert her native freedoms and throw off the yokes of a Norman aristocracy and Norman-imposed feudalism. This argument surfaces prominently in the vigorous debates held at Putney between representative officers of the parliamentary army in the late autumn of 1647. The debates arose from an attempt to keep the army united following the spread of Leveller politics and theology through its ranks. The Levellers, emboldened by God's evident hand in forging the new order, sought a fundamental rather than a cosmetic change in English society. *An Agreement of the People for a firme and present Peace, upon grounds of common-right*, which had been drawn up by 'agents' (elected representatives) of five regiments, was systematically invoked at Putney. This document demanded a more equal distribution of parliamentary constituencies, biennial elections, and an independent executive assembly which would control vital issues of civil, military, religious, and legal policy. Above all, it insisted on the *'native Rights'* of 'the noble and highly honoured . . . Free-born People of ENGLAND' and it sought to raise all male commoners to the full dignity of equal citizens by removing the property qualifications of voters. The record of the debates themselves (not published until the late nineteenth century) reveals the sharp differences between the cautious and essentially conservative General Henry Ireton (1611–51), and the articulate challenges of Colonel Thomas Rainborough (1610–48). Rainborough's memorable summary of his belief that 'the poorest he that is in England has a life to live as the greatest he' and his development of the idea that 'the poorest man in England is not at all bound in a strict sense to that government that he has not had a voice to put himself under' were interpreted by his opponents as an invitation to anarchy. To Rainborough they were expressions of a creed founded in natural and divine law. John Lilburne (1614–57), nicknamed 'Free-born John', was perhaps the most determined and contentious representative of the Leveller party. A seasoned antagonizer of bishops, Lilburne endured five separate periods of imprisonment as the various provoker of Episcopal, Presbyterian, parliamentary, and republican displeasure. In February 1649 he published an address to Parliament, a reiteration of Leveller demands coupled with a stinging attack on the Council of State's proposed legal moves against his party. *Englands New Chains Discovered: or The serious apprehensions of a part of the People, in behalf of the Commonwealth* accuses the Council of acting against the interests of a free nation by lumping together all opposition 'with such appellations as they knew did most distaste the People, such as Levellers, Jesuites, Anarchists, Royalists, names both contradictory in themselves and altogether groundlesse in relation to men so reputed; meerly relying for release thereof upon the easinesse and credulity of the People'. In his later apologia _The Just Defence of John Lilburn, against Such as Charge Him with Turbulency of Spirit_ (1653), he spiritedly contends that he had suffered in the past for 'the right, freedom, safety and well-being of every particular man, woman and child in England' as the would-be preserver of 'ancient laws and ancient rights'. For the future, he urges every democratic citizen 'continually to watch over the rights and liberties of his country, and to see that they are violated upon none, though the most vile and dissolute of men'.

The writings of William Walwyn (1600–80) and Gerrard Winstanley (?1609–76) stress the importance of brotherhood and the militant force of Christian love as a means of achieving a radical change in social relationships. Walwyn's pamphlet, _The Power of Love_ of 1643, is steeped in the prophetic utterance of the Bible, but it also represents an explosion of anger at the manifest contrasts between rich and poor, between outward vanity and the burning inner light of faith. Although he was himself a prosperous merchant of gentleman stock, Walwyn insists in his preliminary address 'To the Reader' that the moral reformer must note 'the whole body of religious people themselves, and in the very Churches . . . view them well, and see whether they have not this worlds goods . . . and the wants and distresses of the poore will testifie that the love of God they have not'. A related anger at the anomalies of class privilege and class deprivation surfaces in Walwyn's attack on those who suppose that all good learning stems from universities: 'And as for learning, as learning goes now adaies, what can any judicious man make of it, but as an Art to deceive and abuse the understandings of men, and to mislead them to their ruine? if it be not so, whence comes it that . . . University men throughout the Kingdome in great numbers are opposers of the welfare of the Commonwealth, and are pleaders for absurdities in government, arguers for tyranny, and corrupt the judgements of their neighbours?' Now that the Scriptures are in English, he insists, 'why may not one that understands English onely, both understand and declare the true meaning of them as well as an English Hebrician, or Grecian, or Roman whatsoever?'

The Leveller insistence on individual freedom and equality in social and religious life took a practical, but to many local landowners, a particularly objectionable turn in April 1649 with the establishment of a small and emphatically Christian co-operative community on former Crown Land at St George's Hill in Surrey. The members of this so-called 'Digger' community preferred to be known as 'True Levellers'. They were obliged to defend themselves before the Council of War in the following December by claiming that they were recovering what had been originally stolen from the common people of England by the ancestors of 'Charles our Norman oppressour'. The most articulate of these Diggers, Gerrard Winstanley, was also aware that he and his comrades were attempting to regain an ideal, a model of Eden governed not by property rights but by love. Winstanley's fiercely argued defence of his project, _A New-Yeers Gift Sent to the Parliament and Armie_ (1649), sees those who opposed the Diggers' scheme as perpetuators of the power of the king and defenders of the principles of an unredeemed creation. Towards its conclusion Winstanley's defence rises to an apocalyptic emphasis: 'Therefore, you rulers of England, be not ashamed nor afraid of Levellers. Hate them not. Christ comes to you riding upon these clouds. Look not upon other lands to be your pattern. All lands in the world lie under darkness. So does England yet, though the nearest to light and freedom of any other; therefore let no other land take your crown. You have set Christ upon his throne in England by your promises, engagements, oaths, and two acts of parliament . . . Put all these into sincere action, and you shall see the work is done, and you with others shall sing Hallelujah to him that sits upon the throne, and to the Lamb for evermore.' Just in case his vision has not had the desired impact on Parliament and its army, Winstanley adds a dire warning: 'If you do not, the Lamb shall show himself a lion and tear you in pieces for your most abominable, dissembling hypocrisy, and give your land to a people who better deserves it.' Neither Christ, the 'great Leveller', nor the new rulers of England (who were inclined to see themselves as Christ's deputies) moved to save the doomed Digger community.

James Harrington's analytical exploration of the basis of an ideal republic, *The Common-Wealth of Oceana* (1656), which was also conspicuously dedicated to Cromwell, had a far greater impact both on contemporaries and on the two centuries that followed. Harrington (1611–77) shared with the Diggers a belief that the key to all social progress lay in the ownership and management of land. If he never quite accepts the kind of protocommunism with which the Diggers experimented and if he rejects the easy but unhistorical linkage of the Norman Conquest to the advent of feudalism, he places a considerable stress on the relationship between the nature of government and the equable distribution of property. Harrington's argument is firmly based in history and in ancient and modern political theory, notably that of Machiavelli; it finds examples in Roman experience, draws parallels with modern Venice and, above all, traces the steady decline of feudalism in England and the concomitant challenge to the monarchic principle. When a strong nobility and a richly endowed Church possessed the land then monarchy flourished, but, after the dissolution of the monasteries and the redistribution of Church land amongst a new order of rising gentry, the power of the king was weakened. 'The dissolution of the late Monarchy', Harrington notes, 'was as natural as the death of a man.' Charles I had been faced with circumstances the true nature of which he had signally failed to recognize; once Parliament had been stirred into action the only thing which stood in the way of the destruction of the throne was the fact that the people were 'not apt to see their own strength'. His case for a new republican order rising out of the ashes of the old is based on the idea of a commonwealth constituted of equal powers in which landed property is perpetually redistributed amongst the many and not accumulated by a few. This 'equal Commonwealth' is ruled by three separated powers: an elected and meritocratic Senate 'debating and proposing', the people 'resolving', and an elected and rotating magistracy which also has control over a state religion. Oceana's constitutional development rests on the wisdom and determination of a victorious general, one 'Olphaeus Megalator', a thinly disguised Cromwellian clone. Harrington later propagated his ideas by presenting them in new dresses. His *The Art of Law-giving in three Books*, published after Cromwell's death in 1659, offers a more succinct account of historical development and a somewhat less fancifully Utopian project. Its urgent concern for the future of the Republic is evident in the despairing statement: 'England is now in such a condition that he who may be truly said to give her law shall never govern her; and he who will govern her shall never give her law.' The pamphlet dialogue *Valerius and Publicola, or the true Form of A Popular Commonwealth*, also of 1659, addresses the crisis caused by the dissolution of the Rump Parliament and the emergence of an army-dominated 'Committee of Public Safety' by reiterating the case for an enforced experimental change and by setting out the reasons against reestablishing the monarchy. Like Winstanley's equally pressing, if less sophisticated, pleas it fell on deaf military ears.

Milton

As a prose polemicist, John Milton (1608–74) was a masterly and at times vituperative defender of the various public causes he chose to espouse. In the early 1640s he produced five pamphlets attacking both the idea and the supposed enormities of English episcopacy; between 1643 and 1645 he published four tracts in favour of divorce, stemming from the unhappiness of his own marriage; in 1644 he offered his great defence of 'free' speech, *Areopagitica*, as a means of countering the licensing ordinance of a predominantly Presbyterian Parliament; following the execution of Charles I in 1649 he argued in both English and Latin for the propriety of bringing a tyrant to account and he attempted to undermine the success of *Eikon Basilike* by scathingly attacking its pretensions; in 1660, shortly before the restoration of the monarchy, he proposed in *The Readie and Easie Way to Establish a Free Commonwealth* the establishment of a 'Grand Councel of ablest men chosen by the people' as a means of safeguarding the unsteady republic. Of the anti-episcopal tracts, two, *The Reason of Church Government* and *An Apology for Smectymnuus* (both 1642), contain pertinent digressions on Milton's own life, education, and development. In the earlier tract he writes of his serene determination 'to lay up as the best treasure, and solace of a good old age . . . the honest liberty of free speech from my youth', and, with a self-assertive attempt to disarm protest, he adds, 'if I be either by disposition, or what other cause too inquisitive, or supositious of my self and my own doings, who can help it?' His intellectual credentials, he insists, had been proved by his ready acceptance into the high-minded salons of Italy during his travels of 1638–9, but despite his early success as a Latin stylist, he had subsequently resolved 'to be an interpreter & relater of the best and sagest things among mine own Citizens throughout this Iland in the mother dialect'. In *Of Reformation Touching Church Discipline*

(1641), however, he briskly lays out a general argument against the Anglican compromise based on a severely anti-episcopalian reading of English Reformation history. Bishops are blamed not simply with propping up an incompletely reformed church but, worse, with being the persecutors of the righteous; they have precipitated a war between England and Scotland ('dearest brothers in *Nature*, and in CHRIST') and their fury has forced 'faithfull, and free-born Englishmen, and good Christians' to forsake 'their dearest home, their friends and kindred' in order to find refuge in 'the savage deserts of *America*'.

Milton's controversial tracts on divorce attempt to justify the idea of a godly separation of those whom the Law and the Church insisted had been permanently joined together by God. 'No effect of tyranny can sit more heavy on the Commonwealth', he stresses, than that of 'this household unhappines', a strained and unfulfilling marriage. In *The Doctrine and Discipline of Divorce* (1643, revised 1644) he draws extensively on arguments from history, theology, and Scripture and he skirts round Christ's own explicit condemnation of divorce by flourishing a series of novel and convenient theological ideas. 'Unmeet consorts' make for a kind of chaos which stands against God's order in creation; Christ claimed that his yoke was easy and his burden light, therefore the burden of marriage law ought to reflect that ease; God, who offers liberty in his service, 'delights not to make a drudge of vertue, whose actions must be al elective & unconstrain'd'. The divorce tracts interlink a radical Puritan insistence on rethinking the implications of inherited moral laws with a distinctly personal irritation with received wisdom.

The greatest and most lastingly persuasive of Milton's pamphlets, *Areopagitica; A Speech of Mr John Milton for the Liberty of Unlicenc'd Printing, to the Parliament of England* (1644) argues for a far broader constitutional liberty. It pleads for an uninhibited exchange of ideas in a modern Protestant Commonwealth in the form of an ancient oration (the Areopagus had been the site of the meetings of the Council of State of ancient Athens). Despite the classical rhetorical form of his tract, Milton avoids Greek or Latin tags and laborious authoritative citations. When he protests that he cannot praise 'a fugitive and cloister'd vertue, unexercis'd & unbreath'd, that never sallies out and sees her adversary', he is also indirectly insisting on his Christian duty to speak out in English in the name of 'truth' (or at least his own idea of truth). He defines his aspirations by stressing the severe, logical beauty of his vision of liberty by contrasting it with the myopic fudges of his enemies (Roman, Laudian, and, by implication, Presbyterian censors). When he famously claims that books 'are not absolutely dead things, but doe contain a potencie of life in them to be as active as that soule was whose progeny they are', he opens up an extended, and highly charged, parallel between the unreformed Church's persecution of heretics and the attempted suppression of ideas in a Protestant state. Both are taken to be unlawful murder: 'As good almost kill a Man as kill a good Book; who kills a Man kills a reasonable creature, Gods Image; but hee who destroyes a good Booke, kills reason it selfe, kills the Image of God, as it were in the eye.' As he develops the idea, he subtly inflates the nature of this 'murder' from homicide to martyrdom, finally comparing the suppression of the entire issue of a book to a massacre of the human spirit ('whereof the execution ends not in the slaying of an elementall life, but strikes at that ethereal and fift essence, the breath of reason it selfe, slaies an immortality rather than a life'). At two crucial points in his discourse Milton assumes a patriotic register in order to both hector and flatter the parliamentary representatives of a rising and exemplary England, a nation 'not slow and dull, but of a quick, ingenious, and piercing spirit, acute to invent, suttle and sinewy to discours, not beneath the reach of any point the highest that human capacity can soar to'. For Parliament to deny such a nation its proper freedom, he asserts, would challenge the special revelation of God's liberty to 'his Englishmen'. When he returns to his grand national theme he again adopts an oratorical voice, part classical, part biblical in its inspiration: 'Methinks I see in my mind a noble and puissant Nation rousing herself like a strong man after sleep, and shaking her invincible locks: Methinks I see her as an Eagle muing her mighty youth, and kindling her undazl'd eyes at the full midday beam; purging and unscaling her long abused sight at the fountain itself of heav'nly radiance; while the whole noise of timorous and flocking birds, with those also that love the twilight, flutter about, amaz'd at what she means, and in their envious gabble would prognosticate a year of sects and schisms.'

Milton's grand vision floundered amid the evident divisions, schisms, and uncertainties of the England of the Interregnum. The 'timorous and flocking birds' had outstared the revolutionary eagle. Milton had explicitly affirmed his own republicanism in a series of pamphlets. *The Tenure of Kings and Magistrates*, published shortly after Charles I's execution in 1649, had argued that kings derived their authority solely from the people, and, as its full title indicated, it also attempted to prove '*that it is Lawfull, and hath been held so through all Ages, for any who have the Power, to call to account a Tyrant, or wicked King, and after due conviction, to depose, and put him to death; if the ordinary Magistrate have neglected, or deny'd to doe it. And that they, who of late, so much blame Deposing, are the Men that did it themselves*'. Yet more boldly, given the developing political situation, *The Readie and Easie Way to Establish a Free Commonwealth* (1660) adulated the achievements of the fragmenting English Republic and warned of a return of 'the old encroachments . . . upon our consciences' if an Anglican monarchy were restored. The 'good Old Cause' of the Republic would, he insists, be utterly undermined by kings who, 'never forgetting thir former ejection, will be sure to fortifie and arm themselves sufficiently for the future against all such attempts hereafter from the people'. As an alternative, Milton presents the case for a free and emphatically Protestant Commonwealth which would preserve both civil and religious liberty. Yet more daringly, he suggests that this commonwealth would ensure its freedoms by introducing a kind of federalism based on county assemblies subordinate to a national Parliament.

If Milton's career as a public apologist for the English Revolution effectively ended with the extinction of the Republic and the restoration of Charles II in May 1660, his career as a poet took on a new significance. His first collected volume of verse, the *Poems of Mr John Milton, both English and Latin, Compos'd at Several Times* (1645), had been the fruit of some fifteen years of experiment with English and Latin metres. It was published when the poet himself had written little new verse for five years and when he was aware, at the age of 36 that he was going blind. Although his publisher announced in the Preface to the volume that he hoped that Milton's work would have the popular success of Waller's recent collection, he proved to be unduly optimistic (Waller's went through three editions in 1645 alone; the reputation of Milton's was assured only by its belated reissue in 1673). As it was originally constituted in 1645 the *Poems* showed off the range and variety of Milton's achievement to date, from his adolescent paraphrases of the Psalms and his 'On the Morning of Christs Nativity' (written in 1629) to the 'Mask', now generally known as *Comus* (first published anonymously in 1637), and 'Lycidas' (which had been published under the signature 'J. M.' in a volume of tributes to Edward King in 1638). The poem placed prominently at the beginning of the volume, 'On the Morning of Christs Nativity', is an essay in devotional poetry parallel to Crashaw's 'A Hymne of the Nativity', but where Crashaw allows his wondering shepherds to observe the incarnate Word as a weeping infant, Milton concentrates on a wondrous divine sovereign whose birth extinguishes the power of the pagan gods and silences their oracles. The stress throughout is cosmic rather than human. In some senses Milton's Christ child, who was 'wont at Heav'n's high Councel-Table, | To sit the midst of Trinal Unity', is already the father to the man who will ride in majesty against the rebel Angels in *Paradise Lost* and who will coldly dumbfound Satan in *Paradise Regained*. The longest poem in the collection, *A Maske Presented at Ludlow Castle*, had been extensively revised by Milton from its performing version. Although the work originally stemmed from a fruitful working relationship between Milton, who had a fine ear for music, and his friend, the composer Henry Lawes, its emphasis in published versions fell on the word, not on music, dance, or spectacle. Yet *Comus* remains a later flowering of the forms evolved at court earlier in the century. It is in essence an occasional piece written for performance at the official residence of the newly appointed Lord President of Wales whom the attendant spirit praises as 'a noble Peer of mickle trust' whose 'temper'd awe' will direct the Welsh, an 'old and haughty Nation proud in Arms'. Its original actors included the Earl of Bridgewater's three children as the Lady and her two noble brothers and Lawes himself as 'the attendant Spirit afterwards in the habit of *Thyrsis*'. Sabrina the nymph who finally releases the Lady from her troubled enchantment by Comus in the 'drear Wood', is the spirit of the 'smooth Severn stream', the river that waters the western marches of England. The dissimulating Comus is neither the protagonist nor the anti-hero of the piece, but it is through him that Milton first establishes what proved to be a lasting professional interest in the nature and force of temptation and in the character and motivation of a tempter.

Although they are too neatly complementary to evoke the real lure of contrasting temptations, inclinations, and antipathies, 'L'Allegro' and 'Il Penseroso' are shaped as representations of opposed states of mind. Both are written in deft octosyllabic couplets. The first of the poems seeks to banish melancholy, the second to cultivate it; the first turns actively to public mirth, the second to the private pleasures of the *vita contemplativa*. Where 'L'Allegro' somewhat forcedly celebrates the rustic joys of 'Jest and youthfull Jollity, | Quips and Cranks, and Wanton Wiles', 'Il Penseroso' calls for the company of a 'pensive Nun, devout and pure, | Sober, stedfast, and demure'. Where the narrator of 'L'Allegro' professes to be drawn to comedy on the 'well-trod' modern stage, that of 'Il Penseroso' meditates alone by reading the 'Gorgeous Tragedy' of the ancients 'in som high lonely Towr'. The fact that the Puritan Milton should in the latter poem allow his narrator to seek out 'Cloysters pale', organs, choirs, and painted windows which cast 'a dimm religious light' suggests the degree to which he is conventionally reliant on the panoply of the old religion rather than on the clear and unfiltered light of reformed faith. By contrast, 'Lycidas', a monody bewailing the drowning of the pious scholar, Edward King, in 1637, is transfused with evocations of light and learning. The name 'Lycidas' (the 'best of pipers') is taken from the Greek bucolic poet, Theocritus, and distant but distinct echoes of classical pastoral poetry run through Milton's elegy. Its form, however, is that of an English adaptation of current Italian *canzone*, a form which gave Milton the freedom to vary both the structure of his verse paragraphs and the lengths of his lines. 'Lycidas' blends elements of the pagan and the Christian, and intermixes gods and saints, nymphs and angels. It mirrors the contemporary idea of revealed Christianity as an enlightened extension of aspects of pagan spirituality by moving from a grieving and almost stoic acceptance of loss to an assertion of a sure and certain hope of the Christian Resurrection. When Camus, the personification of the University of Cambridge, enters the poem at line 103 its frame of reference shifts easily enough towards modern learning and to modern Puritan polemics. Camus is closely followed by the figure of St Peter, the keeper of the keys of heaven and hell, who expresses not merely regret for the loss of the talented Cambridge graduate, King, but a deeper sadness for the state of the Church which he might nobly have served. Milton not only hijacks the first Pope to his cause, but makes him the mouthpiece for an attack on bad shepherds (Anglican prelates and 'corrupted Clergy') who fail both to feed 'the hungry Sheep', and to offer proper defence against the 'grim Woolf' (the Roman Church) who 'daily devours apace'. The closing sections of the poem transform the earlier evocation of mourning with an allusion to the might of the redeeming Christ 'that walk'd the waves'. Lycidas rises above the waters in which he once sank to be received into the 'blest Kingdoms meek of joy and love'. In the last lines the lamenting, uncouth (here 'unknown') shepherd who has been the narrator of the poem rises, twitches his 'blue' mantle (that is, no longer of mourning colour) and sets out to 'fresh Woods, and Pastures new'.

The 1645 edition of the *Poems* contains some ten sonnets, five of which are in Italian. The 1673 reissue added nine more, all composed between 1645 and 1658; three further, including 'To the Lord General Cromwell' of 1652, were published posthumously in 1694. If the Italian sonnets play with conventionally amorous ideas, those in English turn, for the most part, to private and political themes. Milton honours the dead wife of a friend, and pays public tribute to the talents of his sometime friends and associates Henry Lawes, Cyriack Skinner, and Edward Lawrence. More poignantly, he also takes up personal issues, notably the consequences of his blindness ('When I consider how my light is spent') and a vision, as through a glass darkly, of his dead second wife ('Methought I saw my late espoused Saint'). It is, however, in the explicitly political sonnets that his resonant, declamatory style moves him furthest from the ideas and the imagery of love. 'On the late Massacher in Piemont', for example, rings with religious indignation at the massacre of Waldensian Protestants by the Duke of Savoy in 1655 and demands divine retribution for such an offence against God's truth. A similar urgency echoes through the sonnet which Milton addressed to Cromwell ('our cheif of men') in May 1652. Its opening octave plays tribute to the Protector's 'faith & matchless Fortitude' and to his recent military successes, but its sestet shifts from adulation to a demand for renewed civil action. In returning to the religious issues that had long concerned him, Milton insists on the rights of dissenters to detach themselves from any established state Church which might attempt to bind 'our soules with secular chains'. The final couplet cleverly reverses a reference to Christ's parable of the hireling shepherd, who, unlike the good shepherd, runs away from the threatening wolf. Only Cromwell, it is implied, has the energy and determination to keep the pack of 'hireling wolves' at bay.

With the collapse of his hopes for the development of an earnest Protestant republic in 1660, Milton seems, of necessity, to have turned away from overtly political literature and to have redirected his creative urge into a long cultivated project for an English epic poem. His heroic poem might, he trusted, proclaim to the civilized world the coming of age of English literature. Milton assiduously prepared for the intellectual challenge he had posed himself, searching for both an appropriate subject and an epic style worthy of it. In the Latin poem 'Mansus' of 1638–9 he had considered the fitness of subjects drawn from national history, and in particular from Arthurian legend; in the early 1640s he noted down some twenty-eight further ideas including a heroic treatment of King Alfred whose exploits, he held, might stand comparison to those of Homer's Odysseus. At some point in the Civil War the idea of ancient kingly heroism must have seemed too coloured by the sins of modern monarchs to be a fit subject for epic celebration, though material assembled for these abortive projects was reshaped as the prose *History of Britain* (probably written in the late 1640s, published 1670), a volume which bemoans the failure of both Britons and Saxons to maintain and defend their ancient liberties.

The exploration of a more devastating and universal failure emerges in the project for a sacred tragic drama entitled 'Adam Unparadiz'd'. To what extent Milton had developed the scheme of this tragedy can no longer be ascertained but it would seem that certain elements of it served in the dramatic shaping of the providential theme of *Paradise Lost* (1667, revised 1674). As the poem's opening lines stress, he had moved from a meditation on the political disappointments visited on 'God's Englishmen' to an epic treatment of 'Man's First Disobedience . . . Death . . . woe . . . loss'. Earlier European epic poems had celebrated some kind of military success: Homer's *Iliad* traced the causes and progress of the Greek struggle against Troy; Virgil's *Aeneid* explored the origins and nature of Rome's imperial destiny; Tasso's *Gerusalemme Liberata* (1581) dealt heroically and romantically with the First Crusade; and Camoens's *Os Lusiadas* (1572) rejoiced in the past and present expansion of maritime Portugal. Milton, who was familiar with all these works, was ready to assume neither a nationalistic nor an optimistic stance in the scheme of *Paradise Lost*. His subject was the failure of humankind to live according to divine order and its slow but providential deliverance from the consequences of the Fall. The myth with which he chose to deal, and in which he believed literally, was, like many other parallel myths and folk-tales, an exploration of the moral consequences of disobedience. The discovery of the knowledge of good and evil is neither accidental nor happy. The central 'character', Adam, has no heroic destiny. Through his, and Eve's corruption all humankind is corrupted and, as both are finally obliged to understand, the spiritual struggle to regain Paradisal equity and equability extends through each generation of their descendants. In a profound sense Adam and Eve fall from the ideal into the human condition. The great theme of the poem is obedience to the behests implicit in the creative order of an omnipotent God. The will of God is imprinted in the harmony of nature, and the disaster of the Fall is as much ecological as it is moral. Despite the temptation presented by the poem itself to see the rebellion of Satan as a heroic gesture of liberation and the Fall of Adam as a species of gallantry towards his wife, *Paradise Lost* insistently attempts to assert to a reader the ultimate justness of a loving God's 'Eternal Providence'.

Although Milton plays with heroic parallels and allusions throughout the poem, in the case of Satan such references help to place both the fallen angel's sense of himself and the reader's sense of him. Satan is also negatively defined by his standing in antithesis to the accumulated ideas of Christian heroism which run through the poem. Elsewhere, echoes of older epics, such as the extended similes or the idioms derived from Greek and Latin, help to forge a new, sustained, variable, weighty, and to some extent artificial language appropriate to the poem's ambitious scheme. Even the structural parallels with the epic poems of Homer and Virgil, such as the battle in Heaven, the formal debates, and Satan's exploratory journey through Chaos, are given a new cosmic context. Milton deals with what are ostensibly incomprehensible perspectives stretching outwards and upwards in time and space, and his language, remote as it frequently is from everyday discourse, both challenges earth-bound concepts and relocates received images. In vastly elaborating the bald account of Adam's Fall in the Book of Genesis, he extends his viewpoint beyond the acts of Creation and Eden to an imaginative history of how the peccant angels fell from Heaven, how Satan evolved and perfected his scheme to mar Creation, and how God's promise of redemption will be realized. The structure of the poem breaks both with simple sequential chronology and with conventional perceptions of time and the measurement of time. Neither Adam nor any of the angels conceives of mortality, and though Adam knows days and nights in Eden, neither Heaven nor Hell recognizes such divisions. Light itself is described as more than simply the radiance of a sun on which Satan can land as if he were one of Galileo's sunspots (III. 588–90). If Hell is characterized by lightless penal flames and by 'darkness visible', Heaven blazes with inextinguishable divine effulgence which both is and is not conterminous with that of the sun. The blind poet addresses this light in his induction to Book III:

> Hail holy Light, offspring of Heav'n first-born,
> Or of th' Eternal Coeternal beam
> May I express thee unblam'd? since God is Light,
> And never but in unapproached Light
> Dwelt from Eternitie, dwelt then in thee,
> Bright effluence of bright essence increate
> Or hear'st thou rather pure Ethereal stream,
> Whose fountain who shall tell? . . .
>
> .   .   .   .
>
>   thee I revisit safe,
> And feel thy sovran vital Lamp; but thou
> Revisitst not these eyes, that roul in vain
> To find thy piercing ray, and find no dawn;
> So thick a drop serene hath quencht thir Orbs,
> Or dim suffusion veild.

The narrator dwells on his human disability in the face of the blazing perfection of an unseen, but imagined, Godhead; he can neither see in normal human terms, nor properly comprehend in Heavenly terms.

Milton's avoidance of precise definition here is typical of his acceptance of the limitations of human knowledge throughout his poem. In Book VIII Adam, who 'thirsts' for knowledge, is advised by the visiting archangel Raphael of the likely nature of his defective fumbling for 'scientific' truth:

> To ask or search I blame thee not, for Heav'n
> Is as the Book of God before thee set,
> Wherein to read his wondrous Works, and learn
> His Seasons, Hours, or Dayes, or Months, or Years:

> This to attain, whether Heav'n move or Earth,
> Imports not, if thou reckon right, the rest
> From Man or Angel the great Architect
> Did wisely to conceal, and not divulge
> His secrets to be scannd by them who ought
> Rather admire . . .

'Reckoning right' becomes an essential educational element in the working out of the narrative. *Paradise Lost* is primarily neither a didactic poem nor a piece of evangelical propaganda, but its impact on a reader depends on Milton's essentially Puritan insistence on a reader's unimpeded freedom of interpretation. Although the narrator prompts certain assumptions (that Satan and the fallen angels are mistaken in their belief that they can effectively fight back against Heaven, for example, or that God is both benevolent and omnipotent in his plan for creation), the epic voice never narrowly enforces meaning. A reader, like Adam, is at all times bidden to exercise the principle of 'rational liberty' and to explore and analyse the evolving pattern of moral and religious experience. The poem systematically disturbs the complacency about the myth it is retelling and re-presenting. The infernal debate in Book II, for example, poses contradictory questions about resistance and rebellion and it allows for the mental force of a sometimes specious, sometimes persuasive rhetoric (particularly that of Belial and Satan). By contrast, the seemingly awkward, austere and largely biblically-expressed externalization of the forethought of God in Book III presents a concise summary of biblical assumptions about the nature of the Godhead and a careful restatement of the theological significance of freewill in Heaven and Earth. The presentation of Paradise and its human inhabitants equally demands interpretation. Milton's narrative scrupulously suggests the nature of the gulf that separates an unfamiliar, seasonless, unfallen world of thornless roses and frisky beasts from the familiar one of tempests, frosts, shame, and bloodshed. The uncorrupted, temperate Adam and Eve 'innocently' express their sexual relations 'founded in reason, loyal, just, and pure' but the fallen pair are inwardly shaken by 'high passions, anger, hate | Mistrust, suspicion, discord'. Adam's final wisdom is not defined by his knowledge of the distinction between good and evil but by his willingness to accept obedience 'and love with fear the only God'. As the archangel Michael comfortingly instructs him, a proper combination of faith and good works will render him 'not loth | To leave this Paradise' and to possess instead 'A Paradise within thee, happier far'.

Paradise Lost attempts to uphold the virtues of patience not passivity, of enlightened learning not submissive ignorance. It shows us not simply Adam un-Paradised, but Adam possessed of true humanity: mortal, suffering, and seeking for both grace and liberty. It also sustains the probity of inner certainty, in terms both of Adam's insight and of a reader's freedom of judgement. From this idea of the primacy of conscience stems Adam's wounded reaction to the vision of future corruptions, tyrannies, and injustices presented to him by Michael in Books XI and XII. His and Eve's departure from Paradise is tearful, but it also offers the prospect of a 'subjected' world which is 'all before them' and in which they can choose their place of rest. Their choices, and those of their descendants, will, it is implied, be part of a greater quest to restore a Paradisal order in the fullness of time.

The consistency of Milton's achievement in *Paradise Lost* was not matched by what is ostensibly its successor, the four books of *Paradise Regain'd* of 1671. Despite its title, *Paradise Regain'd* does not assert the idea that the redemption of humankind hinges on Christ's resistance to temptation in the wilderness, though a Job-like patient submission to the will of God is clearly a dominant theme. Milton's interest in the withdrawn, meditative Christ at the beginning of his ministry had been hinted at in the parallel drawn in Book XI of *Paradise Lost* when Adam is led to the highest hill of Paradise from where a vast prospect opens:

> Not higher that Hill nor wider looking round,
> Whereon for different cause the Tempter set
> Our second *Adam* in the Wilderness,
> To shew him all Earth's Kingdoms and thir glory.

The 'second Adam' is here to reverse the cause of the Fall if not yet to undo its consequences. We are presented with a serious, scholarly, articulate, ethical, passionate, sinless Christ, but a cold one. Essentially, the poem lacks drama. Although the Christian reader of *Paradise Regain'd* knows the outcome of the encounter with Satan in the wilderness as much as he or she knew earlier that Adam and Eve would fall, a meeting of the incarnate, omnipotent, and omniscient God with his far from omnipotent opponent inevitably suggests an unequal struggle of wills and a foregone conclusion. The real interest of Milton's poem lies in its presentation of arguments, not in an exploration of personality or an imaginative speculation about the unknowable. Satan's intellectual and sensual assaults, and Christ's reasoned responses to them, juxtapose ideologies, ways of seeing, thinking, reading, interpreting, and believing. Satan asks less for submission than for compromise and to answer him Christ insists on the wisdom of understanding, a wisdom which locates and judges rather than deprecates and fudges.

Milton's tragedy *Samson Agonistes* was published with *Paradise Regain'd* in 1671 though its date of composition is uncertain. The tragedy takes as its subject the ruined and blinded Samson, the failed hero of Israel, taunted by his alien wife Dalila, the cause of his downfall, and scorned by Harapha, the representative of the victorious Philistines. Yet Samson's former failure to resist temptation also proves a fortunate fall. Herein lies the problem of its dating. The drama has been traditionally assumed to date from the period of Milton's own proscription and blindness and to be a further reflection on the mysteries of divine providence which casts down those who had once seemed champions of the national cause. Some critics have, however, been inclined to see it as a work of the late 1640s or early 1650s. Its subject is essentially appropriate to both phases in Milton's career for *Samson Agonistes* seeks to adapt the form of Greek tragedy to the needs of a Christian society and to equate a Hebrew moral to the faith of a Protestant elect. The drama closely follows both classical models and the prescriptions of classical critics. Unlike the English tragedies of Milton's immediate forebears and contemporaries, it adheres faithfully to the unities of time, place, and action, it places considerable weight on its Chorus of Danites, and it traces the growth in enlightenment of its protagonist. It differs from its models in that it is emphatically optimistic in its internal insistence that Christian tragedy is a contradiction in terms. Samson's slow enlightenment drives him not to despair but to a reconciliation to the benign purposes of God. His death is seen not as a purging but as a triumph in which the Chorus is finally brought to an awareness of the hero's 'dearly-bought revenge, yet glorious'. Samson's father Manoah proclaims the special nature of the sacrifice of his son:

> Nothing is here for tears, nothing to wail
> Or knock the brest, no weakness, no contempt,
> Dispraise or blame, nothing but well and fair,
> And what may quiet us in a death so noble.

Samson, as a type of Christ, prefigures the Messiah's redemptive death, mastering defeat through a submission to the will of God. True liberty, all of Milton's biblically based works imply, rests in a resolved and independent understanding of the nature of service.

Marvell

Three major poets, all secretaries to the republican government and all dressed in official mourning, walked behind Cromwell's coffin in the Lord Protector's magnificent funeral procession to Westminster Abbey in November 1658. The eldest, John Milton, had proved his loyalty to the doomed Commonwealth, a loyalty that he silently maintained. The youngest, John Dryden, later tactfully shifted his poetic ground away from tributes to Cromwell to celebrations of the returning Charles II. The loyalties of the third poet, Andrew Marvell (1621–78), appear to have been far more subtly ambiguous. Marvell had spent the early part of the Civil War travelling in The Netherlands, France, Italy, and Spain and it was during a second visit to France in 1656 that a visiting English royalist described him as a 'notable Italo-Machavillian'. The exact degree of Marvell's commitment to the divisive causes of his day will always be indeterminate; the acute political intelligence which permeates his poetry is not. In the Preface to the second part of his prose satire *The Rehearsal Transpros'd* (1673) he insisted that until 1657 he had 'not the remotest relation to publick matters' and that thereafter he had entered into an official employment which he considered 'the most innocent . . . toward his Majesties affairs of any in that usurped and irregular Government'. Despite this exculpatory insistence, it is evident that Marvell recognized in Cromwell the dynamic spirit of the age, the kind of decisive figure whom Machiavelli had seen as the shaper of political change.

Although Marvell's earliest published poems suggest an association with royalist literary circles, his support for the new Republic is plain enough in 'An Horatian Ode Upon Cromwell's Return from Ireland' of May 1650. Some surviving copies of Marvell's posthumously published *Miscellaneous Poems* (1681) contain versions of two further commendatory poems to the Lord Protector (though in most copies of the volume a censor, either official or private, has excluded them). All three poems celebrate a victorious general and a heroic instrument of God. 'The First Anniversary of the Government under his Highness the Lord Protector, 1655' recognizes an 'indefatigable' Cromwell who 'cuts his way still nearer to the Skyes, | Learning a Musique in the Region clear, | To tune this lower to that higher Sphere'. In 'A Poem upon the Death of His Late Highness the Lord Protector' (1658) the dead Cromwell is proclaimed not only to have outbraved King Arthur and outprayed King Edward the Confessor but also to have left a reputation which will increase with the passage of time 'when truth shall be allow'd, and faction cease'. The subtlest and most probing of these public poems is the earliest, Marvell's joint tribute to the literary example of Horace and to the extraordinary vitality of Cromwell. The 'Horatian Ode' sees its addressee in the complementary roles of the fulfiller of tradition and the breaker of moulds. Cromwell outclasses Roman precedent and he assumes the role of the Christian hero, the man made by the peculiar circumstances of modern times who will act according to the will of God. He brings not peace but a sword. At the opening of the poem a 'forward Youth' is stirred to turn from the arts of peace to those of war; at its close, military might is brought to bear not simply on rebellious Ireland and Scotland, but also, if God wills, on Catholic France and Italy (where Cromwell may yet equal the triumphs of Caesar and Hannibal). But at the centre of the ode Marvell places a careful tribute to Charles I as the representative of an honourable but dying order. Charles is a *'Royal Actor'*, playing his final part with proper decorum and bowing out of the historical scene. The King's 'bleeding Head' is seen not as a threat to the fledgling Republic but as a sacrifice prophetic of its 'happy Fate', akin to the legendary sign offered to the Roman architects who laid the foundations of the Capitol. Yet the new England holds more promise than ancient Rome. It has been set apart for a special destiny evident in the triumphs of an agent who remains a faithful servant to the policies of the Commonwealth and a falcon obedient to the parliamentary falconer.

The 'Horatian Ode' recognizes a Cromwell who, like the 'forward Youth', had forsaken rural retirement in favour of service in a just war. In June 1650 Cromwell's former commander-in-chief, Thomas, Lord Fairfax, resigned his parliamentary commission and withdrew from public life to his Yorkshire estates. Here at Nun Appleton Marvell joined him as tutor to his daughter. The poems which are generally assumed to date from this period reveal a concern with the interconnections of public and private life in a time of violent disruption. The four 'Mower' poems, for example, see death, disappointment, and 'common ruin' intruding into a rural Arcadia. More substantially, Marvell's lengthy tribute to his patron, 'Upon Appleton House: To My Lord Fairfax', is an adaptation of the mode established by Ben Jonson in his 'To Penshurst' fitted to new times. But where the narrator of Jonson's poem is confident, that of Marvell's is uneasy; the first observes the extravagant plenty stemming from peace and order, the second is aware that beyond the house's 'composition' there is war and the rumour of war. In Marvell's opening stanzas, Appleton House and its demesne are given a context which relates them to an ancestral past and to an uncertain but progressive future. At stanza 41, however, the scope broadens to refer to a greater garden, that of a ruined and fallen England, an Eden devastated by war ('What luckless Apple did we tast, | To make us Mortal, and Thee Wast?'). Fairfax's retirement, though admirable in itself, has deprived England of the gardener fittest to bring it to a new perfection. The glimpses of rural violence in the fields around the estate (mowers 'massacring' grass, for example) serve as metaphors of a more universal devastation. This confusion, and the play of paradoxes involved, seem to impose upon narrator and reader alike a need to read a given selection of signs in order to interpret the workings of providence. The end of the poem is typically ambiguous. There is a firm return to the ideal embodied by the house and its occupants as Fairfax's daughter is presented as the auspicious restorer of a limited earthly paradise, much as her father may still be to the country at large. But the enigmatic last stanza moves yet again into a realm of dislocation and upheaval as salmon-fishers pull their leather boats on to their heads and appear as strange tortoise-like representatives of a 'dark *Hemisphere*'.

Marvell's other poems of retreat into gardens are, despite their recalls of the fallen state of humankind, less ambiguous. 'Bermudas' refers to a providential 'accident' by means of which Puritan refugees from Laudian persecution make a landfall on a paradisal island in the New World. Here all Marvell's hopes of renewal, so readily associated with the word 'green', inform a hymn of praise written in the manner of a metrical psalm. There is a similar delight in rediscovering Eden in 'The Garden', a poem which opens with a flamboyant display of erudite wit; gardens, we are told, sustain the rewards of all ambition in that they are the source of the symbolic crowns once awarded to saints, soldiers, athletes, and poets; they contain the originals of traditional metaphors for, and expressions of, physical love; and they suggest that all passion ends in vegetable life (Apollo only chased Daphne, and Pan Syrinx, knowing that they would conveniently turn into plants). When the narratorial 'I' enters the poem in the fifth stanza, we are presented with an alternative vision, that of a fertile paradise where fruits offer themselves to be touched and tasted and where, as yet, the only fall results from the amorous outreaching of melon tendrils and the embraces of flowers. This, however, is neither Goblin Market nor the loquacious garden of *Alice in Wonderland*. The poem represents an attempt to recapture innocence through meditation and solitude. The creative mind finds the strength to 'annihilate' all existing creation into the freshness of 'a green Thought in a green shade' and the imagined world is seen as an exclusive paradise possessed by a solitary Adam. Only the references to time in the final stanza subtly suggest that seasonless Eden is separated from a corrupted and transient world by the consequences of a historic Fall.

Marvell's lyric poems are haunted by time and a tantalizing and sometimes disorienting sense of human failure. Like explicatory poems from an emblem book, 'On a Drop of Dew' and 'A Dialogue between the Soul and Body' contrast pictures of the 'restless' and 'unsecure' soul, longing for heaven, with those of the enclosing and complaining prison of the body. 'The Definition of Love' plays, in the manner of Donne, with paradoxes and images of frustration in dealing with a love 'begotten by despair | Upon Impossibility'. 'Young Love' and 'The Picture of little T. C. in a Prospect of Flowers' express a delight in the beauty of young girls, girls courted by an older poet or, in the case of 'little T. C.', wooed by Nature, but preserved from any consummation of love by the fact of their youth. Marvell's famous address 'To his Coy Mistress' is perhaps the finest of the many variations on the theme of *carpe diem* developed in English Renaissance poetry. It has a witty urgency which is both fantastic and millenarian:

> Had we but World enough and Time,
> This coyness Lady were no crime.
>
> .   .   .   .   .   .
>
>   I would
> Love you ten years before the Flood:
> And you should if you please refuse
> Till the conversion of the *Jews*.

The inclination of the Lady's heart may well be revealed by 'the last Age', but the narrator presses her to yield before the extinction of passion on the Day of Judgement. Time does not redeem, it destroys; its 'winged Charriot' rushes the lovers towards the prospect of 'Deserts of vast Eternity' and to a grave where the poet's song echoes in the vacancy. The last section attempts to counter these negatives with a reassertion of life and pleasure. Only here does the narrator insist that the lovers' energy can try to outpace or stop Time; by rolling their strength into a ball they can 'tear', like cannon-shot, through 'the Iron gates of Life', though what kind of serenity they will achieve once through these barriers remains indeterminate. 'To his Coy Mistress' both argues against and assaults resistance. It sees an unconsummated relationship standing fraily against a background of mortality, war, and the end of all things; it briefly, even desperately, holds out the possibility of a physical triumph against the all too evident encroachments of change and decay.

Pepys, Evelyn, and Seventeenth-Century Autobiographical Writing

As a 15-year-old schoolboy Samuel Pepys (1633–1703) had witnessed the execution of King Charles I at Whitehall. In an entry in his diary for 30 January 1663 he notes the official commemoration of the event in Restoration London with wry solemnity; the *Fast for the King's murther* was one which his household was forced to keep 'more than we would have done, having forgot to take any victuals into the house'. Pepys expressed his loyalty to the restored Crown by going to his parish church for the newly decreed service marking 'the Day of the Martyrdom of the Blessed King' and by hearing a sermon 'upon David's heart smiting him for cutting off the garment of Saule'. Pepys had begun his diary in January 1660 well aware of the rapid and momentous changes taking place in British politics; in May of that year he accompanied his patron, Lord Sandwich, on the voyage to bring over Charles II from the Netherlands, and in October he saw the 'first blood shed in revenge for the blood of the king' when the regicide Thomas Harrison was publicly hanged, drawn, and quartered at Charing Cross.

Pepys is not merely the most celebrated of the seventeenth-century diarists, he is also the most vivid and the most entertaining; but he is by no means a unique phenomenon. His century saw an increase in autobiographical writing which has sometimes been vulgarly accredited to a rise in 'bourgeois individualism' and to a concomitant interest in self-analysis and individual experience. It was a form of self-expression open to both men and women and it was one that later led on to experiments with fictional first-person narratives (such as those of Daniel Defoe), but it was not necessarily one that was confined to an urban middle class. Pepys's origins were certainly bourgeois, but his employment as Surveyor-General of the Admiralty victualling office opened up to him the world of court politics and aristocratic manners and his diary carefully records the distinctions between the tastes of 'Citizens' and those of the Restoration court. Two of the most avid chroniclers of themselves and their family connections, Lady Anne Clifford (1590–1676) and Margaret Cavendish, Duchess of Newcastle (1623–73), stemmed from, and married into, distinguished aristocratic families. The stimulus to record details of the world as it impinged on the individual consciousness appears primarily to have been religious rather than social. If confined to the literate, it was generally a classless phenomenon. Contemporary diarists and autobiographers seek to catalogue examples of divine providence, to count personal blessings, and even to present their financial accounts for God's scrutiny. Others recognize a pressing necessity to demonstrate the working-out of divine purpose in private and public history, either to prove the nature of new beginnings or to find evidence of the imminent end of time.

Lucy Hutchinson (b.1620), the wife of the regicide John Hutchinson, produced her *Memoirs of the Life of Colonel Hutchinson* (published 1806) as a justification of her husband's republican career and for the benefit of her children. Although she had contrived to save her husband's life at the time of the Restoration by writing a penitent letter to the Speaker of the House of Commons, her private memoir is far removed from a mood of penitence. It offers a vivid, shrewd, and plainly expressed picture of the life of an influential Puritan family during the Civil War, with an autobiographical 'Fragment' added to it. Lucy Hutchinson's account of herself suggests the innate strength and resourcefulness of a much-tried woman, one who in her young days 'had a melancholy negligence both of herself and others, as if she neither affected to please others, nor took notice of anything before her . . .'. This tendency to melancholy, perhaps the product of the severe limits imposed on women's action in a patriarchal society, is briefly reflected in Margaret Cavendish's *A True Relation of my Birth, Breeding and Life* which was added to the original edition of her stories *Natures Pictures* in 1656. Cavendish, who married the exiled Marquis (later Duke) of Newcastle in Paris in 1645, was a convinced royalist, a lady-in-waiting to Queen Henrietta Maria and, like her husband, an accomplished if essentially dilettante writer. She was, according to a distinctly unimpressed Pepys, known for the 'antic . . . extravagancies' of her appearance and remarkable only for the commonplaces she expressed on a visit to the Royal Society. Her *True Relation* suggests a more vivid and self-analytical character. She admits to being 'dull, fearful and bashful' in her youth, but the reverses of family circumstances during the Commonwealth rendered her, she proudly claims, 'fortune-proof'; she sees herself in exile as passing her time 'rather with scribbling than writing'; she had loved, she claims, 'extraordinarily and constantly, yet not fondly, but soberly and observingly'. A far greater mixture of love and pride, self-criticism and self-projection marks the career of Lady Anne Clifford, by her two marriages Countess of Dorset and Countess of Pembroke. She was also, by right of succession, the heir to vast estates in the north of England. It was for these disputed rights that she fought against the browbeating of her first husband, the specious arguments of lawyers, and the bullying of King James I. Her tenaciousness is evident in the surviving portions of the diary that she kept for the years 1616, 1617, and 1619 (published in 1923). In April 1617, for example, she records of her husband: 'Sometimes I had fair words from him and sometimes foul, but I took all patiently, and did strive to give him as much assurance of my love as I could possibly, yet I told him that I would never part with *Westmoreland* upon any condition whatever.' Elsewhere she notes of the two great houses of which she was mistress by marriage that 'the marble pillars of Knole in Kent and Wilton in Wiltshire were to me often times but the gay arbours of anguish'. Her diary also suggests the profound spiritual comfort she found in a disciplined Anglicanism and in an informed interest in literature. She refers to her reading of Chaucer and Sidney, but the range of her tastes is clearer in the Clifford family triptych, the 'Great Picture' she had had painted of herself and her immediate kin in the

1640s, where she appears surrounded by a select library which includes volumes of St Augustine, Spenser, Jonson, Donne, and Herbert.

Samuel Pepys's diary covers the years 1660–9, breaking off on 31 May 1669 with a mournful reflection on 'all the discomforts' that would accompany what he had reason to believe was the onset of blindness. He neither went blind, nor began another diary. The surviving six-volume manuscript, written in the shorthand he had learned as an undergraduate, was not transcribed until the early nineteenth century (a bowdlerized version was published in 1825, but a thorough transcription had to wait until 1970–83). The original editing was deemed to be necessary not because Pepys had used his shorthand, as was sometimes customary with his contemporaries, to record significant ideas in sermons (he records sleeping through many of the sermons he heard) but because he chose to present an account of what Coleridge was later memorably to call 'the mind in undress'. Pepys is sheepishly honest about his extramarital sexual diversions. In September 1663, for example, he records taking a Mrs Lane with him to Lambeth 'and there did' what I would with her but only the main thing, which she would not consent to, for which God be praised'. Later we find him describing his amorous adventures in a peculiar private language cobbled together from English, French, Italian, and Spanish: 'And so I walked to Herberts and there spent a little time avec la mosa, sin hazer algo con ella que kiss and tocar ses mamelles, que me haza la cosa a mi mismo con grand plaisir.' Pepys's 'undressed' mind is, however, far from simply self-indulgent or self-condemnatory. He writes a frank account of his daily affairs, noting the state of his health as much as that of the nation he serves, annually congratulating himself on his personal good fortune and thanking God for his advancement and that of the realm. The diary serves as an indispensable historical source largely because of the receptive and steady mind of its maker. His accounts of court and parliamentary intrigues and gossip, of the workings of the Admiralty administration, and of great public misfortunes, such as the Plague of 1665 and, most memorably, the Great Fire of London of 1666, are interspersed with sharp observations on food and dress, on servant problems and domestic comforts, on medical progress and novelty in poetry, on music (for which he had a passion) and manners (for which he had a sharp eye). Pepys had a particular relish for the repertory on offer in the newly opened London theatres, showing a preference for Jonson's comedies over those of Shakespeare: *A Midsummer Night's Dream*, acted at the King's Theatre in 1662, struck him as 'the most insipid ridiculous play that I ever saw in my life' (though he rejoiced at the innovative presence of 'handsome women' on the stage); two years later a performance of *Bartholomew Fair* at the same theatre provoked the sentiment that it was 'the best comedy in the world'; *Volpone* proved 'a most excellent play', but *Twelfth Night*, which he saw in 1663, was 'a silly play and not relating at all to the name or day'. His appreciation of Shakespeare's tragedies, both in performance and on the page, is, however, evident not simply in his comments on *Macbeth* ('a most excellent play for variety . . . one of the best plays for a stage') but also in his claim to be able to recite Hamlet's soliloquy 'To be or not to be' by heart.

Compared to Pepys's the diary of his friend John Evelyn (1620–1706) seems staid, self-consciously pious, even reserved. It is far more a formal record of the public events of what Evelyn's epitaph described as 'an age of extraordinary events, and revolutions' interspersed with informed reflections on the high culture and the scientific enterprise of the period. In his lifetime, and in the century following, Evelyn was known as a connoisseur, an amateur antiquarian and, above all, as the author of *Sylva: or a Discourse of Forest Trees* (1664), a scientific disquisition on the art of arboriculture and the cultivation of the informal garden. His diary, which was discovered in 1813 and published five years later, covers the years 1620–1706, from the reign of James I to that of Queen Anne. The first part, offering an account of his family, his youth, and an educational tour across Western Europe during the period of the Civil War, was written retrospectively in 1660; the second section dates from the early 1680s; only the third part, dealing with the years from 1684 onwards, is actually a contemporary diary. Evelyn emerges from his '*Kalendarium*', as he called it, as a man of illimitable curiosity. He has a keen eye for painting and sculpture, noting with pride his 'discovery' in 1671 of the talent of the woodcarver, Grinling Gibbons, 'in an Obscure place . . . neere a poore solitary thatched house'. Despite his admiration for the increasingly unfashionable architecture of the Middle Ages (he found Salisbury Cathedral 'the compleatest piece of Gotic Worke in Europe, taken in all its uniformitie'), he is convinced of the superiority of the ordered regularity of the classical style, admiring the Renaissance buildings of Rome as a young man and, later, the mastery of the 'incomparable' Sir Christopher Wren. His interest in the possibilities of the new science is manifold. He makes a point of witnessing operations for gallstone and for gangrene, studies the effects of torture on the human body, becomes an early member of the new Royal Society, and delights in Sir Thomas Browne's eclectic and somewhat fusty 'Cabinet of rarities'. Throughout, he professes an informed loyalty to the teachings and practices of the Church of England as opposed to the religious fragmentation imposed under the rule of the 'arch-rebell' Cromwell. When in 1685 the Catholic Duke of York, James II, succeeds Charles II on the throne, he confidently proclaims that 'the Doctrine of the Church of Eng: will never be extinguish'd, but remaine Visible though not Eminent, to the consummation of the World'. In his view of religion, as much as in his observation of things secular, Evelyn is well aware of the necessity of accommodation to the *Zeitgeist* of the latter half of the century, the new spirit, developed from the ideas of Bacon, of rational clarity and practical enquiry. If, on the one hand, a performance of *Hamlet* in 1662 seems to him to 'disgust this refined age', on the other an old priest preaching in the manner of Lancelot Andrewes in 1683 ('full of Logical divisions, in short and broken periods and latine sentences') seems quirkily old-fashioned to an ear grown accustomed to a 'plaine and practical' exposition. Plainness and practicality later proved to be the keynotes of a new sensibility.

Varieties of Religious Writing in the Restoration Period

When Charles II was restored to his throne in 1660 the Church of England was restored with him. Despite the fact that he had taken the Presbyterian Covenant in 1650 in an attempt to secure the support of Scottish Protestants and had followed the leanings towards Roman Catholicism of the Stuart court in exile, Charles attempted to maintain a double policy of support for the national Church and its bishops as an ideal of religious toleration. His attempts were always awkward. In the 'Declaration of Breda', prudently published immediately before his restoration, Charles had pronounced 'liberty to tender consciences' in matters of religion and in his two later 'Declarations of Indulgence' (1662, 1672) he reiterated the principle of tolerance towards Dissenters from the Church of England, both Roman and Protestant. Yet as 'Defender of the Faith' he faced sustained opposition to a policy of tolerance from an Anglican Parliament and from the newly reinstated and triumphalist bench of bishops. Both bodies were intent on enforcing uniformity in the guise of religious and social consolidation. The Corporation Act of 1661, for example, required all members of municipal corporations to declare that they had received the sacrament according to the rites of the state Church; the Act of Uniformity of 1662 reinforced the use of the Book of Common Prayer and required assent from all ordained ministers to its exclusive use; the Conventicle Act of 1664 declared illegal all dissident religious meetings in private houses; and finally the Test Act of 1673 required all holders of office under the Crown to conform to Anglican usages and beliefs. The one glory of these otherwise repressive Acts of Parliament was the final revision of the Book of Common Prayer. Apart from its lectionary based on the 1611 translation of the Bible and a new service in solemn commemoration of the 'martyred' Charles I (abandoned only in 1859), the 1662 Prayer Book confirmed the uses, translations, traditions, and innovations gradually evolved from historic sources since the time of Cranmer. It remained the unchallenged pillar of Anglican worship until the abortive, but essentially conservative, attempts at reform in 1928 and until the introduction of the flat, flabby, but arguably more flexible, 'Alternative Service Book' in 1965.

The imposition of the conditions of the Act of Uniformity on St Bartholomew's Day 1662 reminded one distinguished Puritan divine, Richard Baxter (1615–91), of the infamous massacre of Protestants in Paris in 1572. Baxter estimates in his memoirs, *Reliquiae Baxterianae* (1696), that some two thousand non-conforming ministers 'were silenced and cast out' by being deprived of their parishes and pulpits. The effects of Carolean legislation moulded the distinctive early radicalism of Nonconformity. They did more than confirm that English religious affairs were plural rather than uniform; they ultimately determined the nature and future role of dissent in British political life. Although Baxter had been appointed to a royal chaplaincy in 1660 and had been offered, but had declined, the bishopric of Hereford, he felt that he could conform neither to the definitions of the Prayer Book nor to the traditional conception of the rule of bishops in the Church. Baxter, who had been distressed by the sectarian schisms within Cromwell's army, was no proponent of narrow definitions or of theological nit-picking; he was, rather, an early advocate of basic ecumenism, a multiform union of Christian believers regardless of credal distinction. His benign influence ran through English Nonconformist thought in the eighteenth century and bore a hybrid fruit in the religious ideas of his Anglican admirer, Coleridge, in the nineteenth century. Baxter's moderate, reasonable ecumenical strain, one which he types in his autobiography as an inclination to 'reconciling principles', is evident both in his life and work. It had determined his deep suspicion of Cromwell's civil and religious policies and his distaste for fragmentary and disputatious Puritan sects; it also moulded his devotional writings, in particular, his once vastly popular treatise *The Saints' Everlasting Rest* (1650). In this treatise he writes of the operation of grace on the individual as a reasonable process, not as one of sudden inspiration or irrational personal conviction: 'Whatever the soul of man doth entertain must make its first entrance at the understanding; which must be satisfied first of its truth, and secondly of its goodness, before it find further admittance. If this porter be negligent, it will admit of anything that bears but the face of truth and goodness . . .'. Baxter is scarcely a coldly dispassionate writer, as his tribute to his dead wife *A Breviate of the Life of Margaret Baxter* written 'under the power of melting grief' in 1681 amply demonstrates, but his memoirs consistently point to the importance of temperate thoughtfulness. The battles over episcopacy in the reigns of both Charles I and Charles II were, he suggests, lost and won (depending on which side the arguer stood) due to an ignorance of the spirit of reconciliation and a rejection of 'true moderate healing terms . . . by them that stand on the higher ground, though accepted by them that are lower and cannot have what they will'.

Amid the diverse setbacks and persecutions of the latter part of his career Baxter came to recognize the true quality of the stand taken by the most troublesome of the mid-seventeenth-century 'sectaries', the Quakers. In the late 1650s he had seen them merely as Ranters 'turned from horrid profanenesse and blasphemy to a life of extreme austerity'. These 'Friends', as they were properly called, posed problems for the English magistracy under the regimes of both Cromwell and the restored Stuarts. To Evelyn in 1657 the humble, imprisoned Friends he visited in Ipswich seemed merely 'a new phanatique sect of dangerous Principles' and 'a Melancholy proud sort of people, and exceedingly ignorant'. Pepys describes an encounter between a would-be flippant Charles II and a forthright Quaker woman who remained determinedly silent until the King was prepared to be serious and then 'thou'd him all along', making her case by addressing him informally in the intimate second-person singular. The *Journal* of George Fox (1624–91), the founder of the Society of Friends and the first to formulate a doctrine of reliance on the 'Inner Light' of Christ, most clearly demonstrates why the uncompromising zeal of the early Quakers seemed so socially disruptive. After long wrackings of conscience, Fox came to recognize the peculiar nature of his calling in 1646. Prompted by the inner voice which he associated with the voice of God, he withdrew from worship in 'steeple-houses', the churches controlled by the 'priests' (both Anglican or Presbyterian) of whose teaching he disapproved, and began his own ministry as an itinerant preacher. The surviving manuscripts of Fox's *Journal*, which retrospectively describe his mission, appear to have been begun during one of his frequent terms of imprisonment in 1673 and were finished after his release in 1675. This self-justifying account of the acts of a latter-day apostle was published posthumously in 1694. At its opening Fox explains the origin of the nickname 'Quaker', a term first used by a Justice of the Peace at Derby 'because wee bid them tremble at the Word of God', but the substance of the work traces a series of challenges to the world. The account of the year 1651, for example, offers accounts of his preaching barefoot on market-day in Lichfield and proclaiming the doom of the unrepentant 'bloody citty', his berating of a Catholic who had the temerity to invite him home, and his refusal to speak in a painted church because 'the painted beast had a painted house'. In 1654 he writes to Cromwell as a 'Deare Friend' advising him to 'be still, and in the Councill of God stand . . . that thou mayst frustrate mens ends and calme mens spirits, and Crumble men under, and arise and stand up in the power of the Lord God, and the Lambes Authority'; in 1660 he writes with an equally presumptuous informality to Charles II, recommending him not to encourage 'Maygames with Fiddlers, drumms, trumpetts' and Maypoles 'with the Image of a Crowne on topp of them'. In 1669 he ventures to Catholic rural Ireland, in 1671 to the West Indies, and in 1672 to the eastern seaboard of North America. Throughout he stresses an absolute rightness of the divine nature of his calling and the new religious order he had introduced. 'Them that bee in Christ Jesus', he insists, 'are new Creatures: and in him all flesh is silent: but they that have the worde of the Lord and from the Lord may speake it freely as they are commanded.'

John Bunyan's autobiographical account of the awakening of his soul to sin, his conversion, and his later ministry in *Grace Abounding to the Chief of Sinners: Or a Brief and Faithful Relation of the Exceeding Mercy of God in Christ, to his poor Servant* (1666) to some degree mirrors Fox's. Both saw the delineation of their sufferings in the world, their awareness of their personal election, their vocation to preach the Gospel, and their perception of glory in the hereafter, not merely as a private process of self-examination but as a means of inspiriting the faithful. Both produced much of their finest work while enduring long terms of imprisonment as a direct result of their principled law-breaking and the accounts of both suggest a hard, uncompromising, proletarian zeal which is quite distinct from the melting, principled gentlemanly moderation of their fellow Puritan visionary, Baxter. Bunyan (1628–88), who was in fact no friend to Quakers, is intent on offering a picture of 'the merciful working of God upon my soul' and he describes a process of delivery both from worldly delights (such as dancing or bell-ringing) and from an acute and painful sense of sin (which early manifested itself in the form of nightmares and visions). He also stresses his conviction that he was called from his despair of salvation by a persistent inner voice: 'one morning when I was again at prayer and trembling under the fear of this, that no word of God could help me, that piece of a sentence darted in upon me, *My grace is sufficient* . . . And, O methought that every word was a mighty word unto me; as *my*, and *grace*, and *sufficient*, and *for thee*; they were then, and sometimes are still, far bigger than others be.' Bunyan is always careful with words, always alert to the expression of what he sees as the inspired word of God manifested to the world.

Bunyan's saturation in the Bible is particularly evident in his greatest and most lastingly influential work, *The Pilgrim's Progress from this World to That which is to come; Delivered under the Similitude of a Dream Wherein is Discovered The manner of his setting out, His Dangerous Journey; And safe Arrival at the Desired Country* (1678, Part II, 1684). It is a direct development from *Grace Abounding* in that it objectifies and universalizes what had been an account of a personal spiritual pilgrimage. It is also a startling departure from the earlier work in its allegorical illumination of spiritual experience, an allegory which draws on biblical images, on popular retellings of stories of righteous warfare, and on the kind of illustration offered in emblem books. As Bunyan claims in his verse 'Apology for his Book', he 'fell suddenly' into his allegory and as he worked ideas 'began to multiply | Like sparks that from the coals of fire do fly'. It remains a work of fiery immediacy; the language in which it is told is vivid, dignified, and straightforward and its narrative line is as direct and unbending as the narrow road to heaven pursued by Christian, Faithful, and Hopeful. The names of the compromised back-sliders the pilgrims encounter on their journey, as much as the words they utter, deftly suggest the real opposition to the forward progress of the elect; Mr Worldly-Wiseman counsels caution in taking the 'dangerous and troublesome way'; Formalist and Hypocrisy avoid the gate of conversion by taking a short cut and doing 'what they had custom for'; Talkative, the son of Saywell, and the dweller in Prating-row, talks glibly but fails to act on his words; the twelve jurymen at Vanity Fair (Mr Blind-man, Mr No-good, Mr Malice, Mr Love-lust, Mr Live-loose, Mr Heady, Mr High-mind, Mr Enmity, Mr Liar, Mr Cruelty, Mr Hate-light, and Mr Implacable) readily condemn Faithful to death in obedience to convention, ease, and precedent. Christian's journey from the City of Destruction to the Heavenly City is also beset by a darkness—outwardly represented by the Slough of Despond, the Castle of Giant Despair, and the Valley of the Shadow of Death—that is recognizable from the account of Bunyan's own inner tribulations in *Grace Abounding*. Christian's progress, accompanied at first by the martyred Faithful and latterly by the redeemed Hopeful, represents that of the individual believer blessed by the three theological virtues of faith, hope, and charity. He is also blessed with a gathering certainty of his election to eternal salvation and he forges a way forward aided simply by his understanding of Scriptural promises. Much as Milton allows in *Paradise Lost*, a reader's response to the narrative line of *The Pilgrim's Progress* depends on an individual's freedom to identify with the process of spiritual learning and ordinary heroism allotted to Christian. This process is extended in the second part to Christian's family, and above all to his wife Christiana, who accompanied by her champion and protector, Great-heart, retreads the road marked by memories of her husband's moral victories.

The original sales of *The Pilgrim's Progress* seem to have been matched by those of Bunyan's now largely forgotten tracts such as *A Few Sighs from Hell* (1658) and *Come and Welcome to Jesus Christ* (1678, reissued twelve times by 1720); later editions had a unique currency in ordinary and far from exclusively Puritan homes. More than a hundred years after it first appeared it was one of the very few books, apart from the Bible, owned and studied by relatively uneducated men and women such as the parents of the Reverend Patrick Brontë and those of George Eliot; later, it provided Thackeray with the title he had long sought for *Vanity Fair* and moulded important aspects of Dickens's very different pilgrimage narratives, *Oliver Twist* and *The Old Curiosity Shop*. None of Bunyan's later allegories ever rivalled its inventiveness and popular prestige. Both *The Life and Death of Mr Badman* (1680) and *The Holy War* (1682) share a considerable vitality of observation and moralistic comment. *Mr Badman* has often been thought of as an early experiment in realist fiction or, less helpfully, as a proto-novel. It takes the form of a spirited, but somewhat repugnant, question-and-answer dialogue between Mr Wiseman and Mr Attentive concerning the steady moral descent of a far from exceptional sinner, a small tradesman wallowing sordidly in petty lusts and animal pleasures and clearly on his way to the Infernal rather than the Celestial City. *The Holy War, Made by Shaddai upon Diabolus, For the Regaining of the Metropolis of the World. Or, The Losing and Taking Again of the Town of Mansoul* is less narrowly censorious and more vividly informed with the language of battle that Bunyan had doubtless picked up during his service with the armies of Parliament. It tells the story of the sieges and liberations of, and the attempted coups within, the city of Mansoul, the delight of its creator, Shaddai (God the Father). Mansoul is liberated after its betrayal to Diabolus (Satan) by Shaddai's son Emanuel, only for it to lapse twice again, partly in analogy to what Bunyan would have seen as the centuries of papal darkness. Emanuel's steadfast and undeterred deliveries of the citizens of Mansoul, and his trust in his worthy lieutenants (Lord Self-denial, Lord Wilbewill, Mr Godlyfear, Meditation, Conscience, and Understanding), look forward to a final, but as yet unrealized, judgement and a redemptive purging of all corruption. That apocalypse, Bunyan seems to be implying, was near at hand.

Innocence, so obviously lost in the fallen world of Bunyan's visions, manages to reassert its command in the work of Thomas Traherne (1637–74). Traherne was, like Fox and Bunyan, the son of poor parents; unlike them, he was sent to Oxford through the generosity of a well-off relative and unlike them he found in Anglicanism a framework within which he could develop and explore his extraordinary spiritual gifts. Under the Commonwealth he had served as the minister for a Herefordshire parish, but in 1660 he chose to be ordained priest under the newly restored Anglican dispensation. It was in Herefordshire in the 1660s that he became closely involved with the pious circle surrounding Susanna Hopton, a grouping less formal than that which had earlier flourished at Little Gidding, but one which shared many of its spiritual disciplines and aspirations. From his childhood Traherne seems to have experienced a mystical feeling for the unspoilt radiance of creation; at the age of 4, while sitting 'in a little Obscure Room in my Fathers poor House', he claims to have been prompted to a meditation on the goodness of God by 'a real Whispering Instinct of Nature'. In his early manhood he cultivated what he saw as the virtues of 'Profound Inspection, Reservation and Silence', writing in the third part of his *Centuries of Meditations* of a resolution to spend the period of his return in rural England 'in Search of Happiness, and to Satiat that burning Thirst which Nature had enkindled in me from my Youth'. With the exception of Vaughan, few writers of his period describe such an intense relationship with nature. It is possible that for both, the absence of the formal flow of the Anglican liturgy during the time of the Commonwealth intensified their experience of a God revealed as much in the multifariousness of the natural world as in sacramental worship within the walls of a church. Traherne's poems and rhapsodic prose of his *Centuries* (published from the surviving manuscripts in 1903 and 1908) retain a sense of a free, urgent, and far from Puritan, response to the wonder and infinity of God. For him the revolution in human affairs consisted of regaining and exploring the paradisal vision vouchsafed in childhood rather than in building an earthly Jerusalem in anticipation of the millennium. In his poem 'Innocence' he looks back to a time flooded with heavenly light as a way of looking forward:

> That Prospect was the Gate of Heav'n, that Day
> The anchient Light of Eden did convey
> Into my Soul: I was an Adam there,
>   A little Adam in a Sphere
>
> Of Joys! O there my Ravisht Sence
> Was entertaind in Paradice,
> And had a Sight of Innocence.
> All was beyond all Bound and Price.

A similar evocation of uncomplicated primal felicity pervades the poems 'Wonder' ('How like an Angel came I down! | How bright are all things here!') and 'The Rapture' ('Sweet Infancy! | O fire of Heaven! O sacred Light!').

Traherne's lyrics 'My spirit', 'The Circulation', and 'The Demonstration' offer a series of Neoplatonic reflections on the interrelationship of the delighted human soul and the intellectual perfection of God. 'The Demonstration' speaks, for example, of a God seeing, feeling, smelling, and living through his creatures: 'In them ten thousand Ways, | he all his Works again enjoys, | All things from Him to Him proceed | By them; Are His in them: As if indeed | His God head did it self exceed.'

In the 510 meditations which make up the *Centuries* (the incomplete fifth *Century* has only ten sections) Creation is seen as imbued with the light and presence of God. In the opening meditation the human soul is compared to an empty book, awaiting the imprint of the truth, the love, and the whispered counsels of its Maker. As a whole, the *Centuries* form a record of an intense spiritual communication with God, a process detached from the distractions of contemporary politics by which the alert soul advances to glory not by 'the Nois of Bloody Wars, and the Dethroning of Kings' but by the 'Gentle Ways of Peace and Lov'. Despite the occasional awareness of the pain of desertion, of the fading of light, or of 'a certain Want and Horror . . . beyond imagination' at the diminution of vision, Traherne generally expresses a rapt wonder and an unalloyed joy stimulated by the evidence of God's presence in the visible world. Traherne does not attempt to write in terms of what would later be termed 'Natural Theology', a demonstration of God and his workings through a close 'scientific' observation of nature, for he glimpses a bright world in which God is implicit rather than defined. 'You never Enjoy the World aright', Traherne insists in the twenty-ninth meditation of the first *Century*, 'till the Sea it self floweth in your Veins, till you are Clothed with the Heavens, and Crowned with the Stars'. This sense of union with Creation is presented as a vision vouchsafed by Heaven rather than as the achievements of an energetic proto-Romantic imagination. In the fifty-fifth meditation Traherne sees his experience as flowing freely in time and space and fused with that of the patriarchs and the prophets: 'When I walk with Enoch, and see his Translation, I am Transported with Him. The present Age is too little to contain it. I can visit Noah in His Ark, and swim upon the Waters of the Deluge . . . I can Enter into Aarons Tabernacle, and Admire the Mysteries of the Holy Place. I can Travail over the Land of Canaan, and see it overflowing with Milk and Hony.' He moves freely backwards and forwards through both biblical and personal history, both histories being records of providential direction. In the opening sections of the third *Century* he recalls 'those Pure and Virgin Apprehensions I had from the Womb, and that Divine Light wherewith I was born'. As a child he had seen the English rural world as 'New and Strange at the first, inexpressibly rare, and Delightfull, and Beautifull'; the cornfields are 'Orient and Immortal' and the dust and stones of the street appear 'as Precious as GOLD'. The vision fades not simply because the child loses his innocence, or takes on a pressing awareness of sin, but because custom, education, and quotidian usage intervene. To regain this lost paradise the soul must 'unlearn, and becom as it were a little Child again'; what has been glimpsed in the here is to be realized in the hereafter.

Private Histories and Public History: Aubrey, Sprat, and Clarendon

The Oxford antiquarian Anthony Wood (1632–95) somewhat ungenerously described one of his major sources of biographical information, John Aubrey (1626–97), as 'a pretender to antiquities . . . a shiftless person, roving and magotie-headed, and sometimes little better than crased'. Wood's *History and Antiquities of the University of Oxford* (1674, 1792–6) and his biographical dictionary of Oxford worthies, *Athenae Oxonienses* (1691–2), retain some curiosity value as once influential, if torpid, assemblages of information; Aubrey's work, by contrast, has an explorative freshness which stems from the very nature of its eccentric randomness. The only work that Aubrey himself saw through the press, *Miscellanies*, 'a Collection of Hermetic Philosophy' (1696), is in its way a pioneer essay in anthropology jumbled together with folklore, superstition, and occult learning. His other studies—observations on the topography, natural history, and antiquities of the counties of Surrey and Wiltshire and the pithily brief lives of British celebrities—remained in manuscript until their publication in subsequent centuries. Aubrey is now recognized as a major figure in the early history of British archaeology, but it is as an anecdotal biographer that he has achieved popular and posthumous celebrity. He wrote unmethodically or, as he put it himself, he set information down 'tumultuarily, as if tumbled out of a Sack', but more significantly as an enterprising biographer he recognized the importance of private history and the transitory nature of ephemeral and oral sources of information. ''Tis pitty that such minutes had not been taken 100 years since or more', he complained to Wood in 1680, 'for want thereof many worthy men's names and notions are swallowd-up in oblivion'. He relished unconsidered trifles, he collected gossip, and he haunted the funerals and the church monuments of friends and notable strangers alike. As a 9-year-old boy he claims to have been fascinated by a series of engravings of the elaborate funeral of Sir Philip Sidney; he was a pall-bearer at the obsequies of the satirist Samuel Butler and the anatomist William Harvey and he recalls the details of the dramatist Sir William Davenant's handsome walnut coffin; he is equally taken with the idea of an old woman living amongst the bones in the crypt at Hereford Cathedral and with the discovery of the pickled body of the humanist John Colet amidst the ruins of old St Paul's after the Great Fire. He had a nose for gossip and an ear for a telling expression. He notes, for example, that the mathematician Sir Jonas Moore cured his sciatica by 'boyling his Buttock' and that the Puritan controversialist William Prynne studied with a long quilt cap shading his eyes, having arranged to be interrupted every three hours by a servant bringing him a roll 'and a pott of Ale to refollicate his wasted spirits'. Aubrey's lives of Milton and Hobbes (he knew the latter well) are his most substantial and amongst his most lively. He apologizes for Milton's republicanism by asserting that he acted 'out of pure Zeale to the Liberty of Mankind', but he notes, on the evidence of John Dryden, that the poet's conversation was 'pleasant . . . but Satyricall' and that he pronounced the letter R 'very hard—a certain signe of a Satyricall Witt'. Of Hobbes's pleasure in geometry he recalls that he 'was wont to draw lines on his thigh and on the sheets, abed, and also multiply and divide'.

References throughout Aubrey's 'Brief Lives' suggest something of the honour accorded by learned contemporaries to the Royal Society, founded in London in the years of Charles II's restoration and awarded charters by its royal patron in 1662 and 1663. In his account of the life of the statistician Sir William Petty, for example, Aubrey records Sir William's suggestion that the Society should hold its annual elections on St Thomas's rather than St Andrew's Day, for the former saint had required evidence before he was prepared to believe. The Royal Society was both a club for like-minded enthusiasts and a partial realization of the progressive 'scientific' ideas fostered earlier in the century by Bacon. In its professed ambition of advancing learning in general, it attempted to gather together a broad range of thinkers, both professional and amateur, and to provide a focus for a variety of investigation and experiment. Its early members included those whose contribution to the history of science proved remarkable, such as Robert Boyle, Robert Hooke, and John Ray, and those who have since been chiefly remembered for their non-scientific work, such as the mathematician turned architect, Sir Christopher Wren, and the writers, Cowley, Evelyn, Waller, and Dryden. No clear distinction between scientific and humanistic knowledge, or between specialist spheres of human enterprise, was drawn until late in the nineteenth century. In his confident *The History of the Royal Society of London*, begun as early as 1663 and published in 1667, Thomas Sprat (1635–1713) attempted to define the role of empirical thought in 'this Learned and Inquisitive Age' and to defend the record of the '*Illustrious Company*', which has already laid such excellent Foundations of so much good to *Mankind*'. 'The increase of Experiments will be so far from hurting', he insists, 'that it will be many waies advantageous, above other Studies, to the wonted Courses of Education'. Natural Philosophy, Sprat maintained, was the key discipline of the new age; it both helped in the advance of industry and national prosperity and provided a reasoned prop to Anglican Christianity. Moreover, the very nature of pragmatic scientific enquiry was also antipathetic to the disruptive 'passions, and madness of that dismal Age' of the Civil War and the Republic.

As a practical statesman of the 1640s and the 1660s, and a loyal servant of the Crown, Edward Hyde, Earl of Clarendon (1609–74) recognized in the Restoration settlement a judicious return to a balanced constitution of the state in which order stemmed from an Anglican monarch obedient to the law. Like Sprat, he believed that empiricism and pragmatism should be preferred to idealism and to the tunnel-vision so characteristic of much Puritan radicalism. In common with Sprat's *History of the Royal Society*, Clarendon's *The True Historical Narrative of the Rebellion and Civil Wars in England* (begun in 1646, completed during his second exile in 1671–4, published 1702–4) demonstrates the extent to which certain dominant and devout English thinkers had moved away from the conviction that the Day of Judgement was at hand. Their *Histories* are not concerned with eschatology or with the impulse to restore an earthly paradise but with the idea of progressive development. For Sprat, God's purposes are revealed in the investigation of the laws of created nature. For Clarendon, the severe political disruptions of the mid-century provide monitory signals to the opening future and to those rebuilding the state according to historical principles. His *History* traces the breakdown of the institutions in which he most trusts and the progress of a 'rebellion' against duly ordained order. At its conclusion he briefly recognizes 'the merciful hand of God' in the 'miraculous restoration of the Crown, and the Church, and the just rights of Parliament' and he somewhat tentatively trusts that the providential process will continue: 'no nation under heaven can ever be more happy if God shall be pleased to add establishment and perpetuity to the blessings he then restored.' Although such royalist, conservative prejudices broadly determine the nature of his argument, he can be a sharp enough critic of those he once served or advised. Clarendon remains amongst the most observant of the many analysts of the character and policies of Charles I, praising real enough virtues and probing the all too disastrous shortcomings: 'He was, if ever any, the most worthy of the title of an honest man; so great a lover of justice, that no temptation could dispose him to a wrongful action, except it was so disguised to him that he believed it to be just . . . He was very punctual and regular in his devotions . . . and was so severe an exactor of gravity and reverence in all mention of religion, that he could never endure any light or profane word, with what sharpness of wit soever it was covered . . . His kingly virtues had some mixture and allay, that hindered them from shining in full lustre, and from producing those fruits they should have been attended with. He was not in his nature very bountiful, though he gave very much . . . He was very fearless in his person; but, in his riper years not very enterprising. He had an excellent understanding, but was not confident enough of it; which made him oftentimes change his own opinion for a worse, and follow the advice of men that did not judge so well as himself.' Although this last sentence expresses something of Clarendon's own impatience with his sometime master's inconsistency, he writes more in irritation than in anger. His clear, moderated, clausal style allows for an easy interplay of praise and dispraise, compliment and the withdrawal of compliment, statement and qualification. Clarendon's works were presented by his heirs to the University of Oxford and from the considerable profits earned by the publication of the *History* a new printing-house, named for the historian, was constructed. These profits testify to the degree of esteem in which the weight of Clarendon's opinions, his political assessments and, above all, his careful style were held by the generations that immediately succeeded him. They were generations that believed in the merits, principles, and inheritance of a very different revolution from that of the 1640s.

The Poetry of the Restoration Period: Rochester and Dryden

Charles I's famously happy, faithful, and fruitful marriage was not mirrored by that of his eldest son. If the first Charles's court was characterized by what Clarendon calls 'gravity and reverence in all mention of religion', the second Charles's was, despite its cloak of Anglican conformity, far more inclined to accept and enjoy sexual, religious, and verbal licence. The restored King, who had been schooled in a certain kind of elegant cynicism by his years in exile, set the tone of a cultured but libidinous court. The marked change of mood was evident not simply in the contrast between the personalities of two kings or between two types of court poetry but also in the reaction of certain influential patrons and writers against two older fashions: the dense, intellectual quirkiness of the school of Donne and the humourless, moral seriousness of Puritan writing and Puritan mores. The new ethos was one where sexual innuendo flourished. It was also one which stimulated and fostered the stricter disciplines of poetic satire, a satire which fed on the contradictions, the ironies, and the hypocrisies of society. Most of the verse written by Marvell after the Restoration, the verse that was most admired by his later contemporaries, was of a political or satirical character. 'Sharpness of wit', spiced with a degree of profanity or ribaldry, was as much to Charles II's taste as were cultivated indolence, ministerially abetted chicanery, and the distractions of his mistresses. One of his most prominent courtiers, John Wilmot, Earl of Rochester (1647–80), is famously said to have reacted to the King's announcement that he would tolerate a relaxed frankness amongst his intimates with the impromptu quatrain: 'We have a pritty witty king | Whose word no man relys on: | He never said a foolish thing, | And never did a wise one.' Unabashed, the King replied that though his words were his own it was his ministers who were responsible for his actions.

Rochester is the most subtle, brilliant, and scurrilous of the Restoration heirs to the poetry of Lovelace, Suckling, and Carew. In his work, and in that of less vitally intelligent poets such as Sir Charles Sedley (?1639–1701) and Charles Sackville, Earl of Dorset (1638–1706), Cavalier gallantry is rearticulated through the exercise of an indulgent world-weariness. As both his letters to his wife and the poems reveal, Rochester was capable of adjusting and interfusing the seeming anomalies of tenderness and cynicism, domesticity and debauchery, quick wit and meditative seriousness in his nature. Some of his periods of provincial exile from court were occasioned by his having overstepped the limits of royal tolerance (as when he satirically assaulted the King with such couplets as 'Nor are his high desires above his strength: | His sceptre and his prick are of a length' and 'Restless he rolls about from Whore to Whore, | A Merry Monarch scandalous and poor'); others were elective interludes of recuperation, study, and meditation. 'He loved to talk and write of speculative matters', wrote Bishop Burnet, the man who brought him to a death-bed reconciliation with Christianity, but as much of his poetry suggests, Rochester also delighted in the pleasures that dulled and unperplexed thought. In 'Upon Drinking in a Bowl' he proclaims Cupid and Bacchus his patron saints, washes his cares with wine, and turns to Love again. The songs 'An Age in her Embraces past', 'Absent from thee I languish still', and 'All my past Life is mine no more' hedonistically announce that soul is sense and attempt to hold on to what 'the present Moment' offers. A more distinctly speculative, but no less wittily sceptical, poet emerges in his address to the 'Great Negative', 'Upon Nothing'. It is a poem which plays with the theological concept of a Nothing from which Something emerges, but it is also haunted by a sense of futility and universal human hypocrisy and it finally sees Nothing as an unholy trinity of 'the great Man's Gratitude to his best Friend, | King's Promises, Whores Vows'. Rochester's finest exercise in the satirical mode, 'A Satyr against Mankind' (1675), returns to the idea of the basic falseness of all human pretension to honesty, virtue, wisdom, and valour, but it opens with a devastating undercutting of the great panjandrum of the age, human reason:

> Reason, an *Ignis fatuus* of the Mind,
> Which leaves the Light of Nature, Sense, behind.
> Pathless, and dangerous, wand'ring ways it takes,
> Through Errour's fenny Bogs, and thorny Brakes . . .

The deluded victim of this presumption to rationality first stumbles into doubts, is temporarily buoyed up by philosophy, and then finally and painfully recognizes the terrible error into which he has fallen:

> Then old Age, and Experience, hand in hand,
> Lead him to Death, and make him understand,
> After a Search so painful, and so long,
> That all his Life he has been in the wrong.

The poem presents human life as a jungle in which creatures prey on one another and in which fear is the dominant stimulus to action ('Meerly for safety, after Fame they thirst; | For all Men would be Cowards if they durst'). Unsurprisingly, Rochester seems to have felt a special affinity with his pet monkey. His portrait, now in the National Portrait Gallery in London, shows him crowning this monkey with a poet's laurels. In response, the monkey offers its master a mangled sheet of verses. Like much of Rochester's poetry it is a self-mocking artifice, at once cynical and provocative, flippant and serious.

Although poetic satire was a form cultivated by court wits, it was far from being an exclusively aristocratic property. Two highly esteemed satirists, John Oldham (1653–83) and Samuel Butler (1613–80), emerged from relative obscurity to assert their significance as professional, as opposed to amateur, poets. In the case of Oldham, who made a living as a schoolteacher and private tutor, literary fame came towards the end of a relatively short life and was largely assured by a succession of posthumous editions of his poems. Butler, the son of a Worcestershire farmer, achieved startling success only at the age of 49 with the publication of the first part of *Hudibras* in 1662. *Hudibras* (Part II of which appeared in 1663 and Part III in 1678) proved to be the most popular long poem of its day, quoted, cited, imitated, admired, and flattered by parody. The reputations of both poets have since suffered from this initial blaze of contemporary adulation and the failure of later audiences to be enthralled by their work. Although the names of the major characters in Butler's *Hudibras* are derived from Spenser's *Faerie Queene*, his mock-heroic, digressive narrative from Cervantes's *Don Quixote*, and much of his ironic tone from Rabelais's *Gargantua*, the prime objects of its satire are very much the products of the confused, divisive, post-revolutionary age. The poem's comically cumbersome octosyllabic couplets also allow for a considerable range of allusive comment on what Butler saw as the intellectual, political, and religious charlatanism of modern England. As a Baconian sceptic he was far more inclined to attack the prevalence of popular error and personal delusion than to hold up self-evident truths or ideals. *Hudibras* aphoristically glances at churchmen and statesmen pursuing strategies of power under the guise of Presbyterian or monarchical principle:

> To domineer and to controul
> Both o're the body and the soul,
> Is the most perfect *discipline*
> Of Church-rule, and by *right divine*.

If the varieties, obsessions, and peculiar rhetoric of English Puritanism prove to be the poem's main bugbear, and the petty theological divisions between the Presbyterian Sir Hudibras and his Independent squire, Ralpho, the initial focus of its satire, the introduction of the deluded astrologer Sidrophel in the second book and the reflection on the recent political disruption of the Civil War in the third serve to emphasize the breadth of Butler's satirical commentary.

Oldham, the son of a Puritan minister, is both a more disciplined and more directly classically rooted satirist. In the Preface to his imitation of Horace's *Ars Poetica*, for example, he aspires to put the Roman poet 'into a more modern dress, that is, by making him speak as if he were living and writing now'. Oldham's poetry looks back in order to attack the vices of the present; it reflects on precedent by insisting on a continuity in the expression of poetic indignation. The poems by which he was best known in his lifetime, the four vituperative *Satyrs upon the Jesuits* (1679–81), are unrelievedly angry denunciations of Jesuit machinations (a particularly hot issue in the wake of the exposure of the so-called 'Popish Plot' to assassinate Charles II in 1678). If scarcely ever a gentle poet, Oldham is certainly a subtler one in his later work such as the 'Satyr concerning Poetry', the 'Letter from the Country to a Friend in Town', or 'A Satyr address'd to a Friend that is about to leave the University, and come abroad in the World'. This last poem underlines the neglect and poverty which is the likely lot of a schoolmaster ('A Dancing-Master shall be better paid, | Tho he instructs the heels, and you the Head') and it also reflects on the blessings of 'a close obscure retreat', a small estate sufficient to support a private man's withdrawal from the irritations of work and public affairs. Here in an English equivalent of Horace's Sabine farm, 'free from Noise, and all ambitious ends', the poet aspires to 'Enjoy a few choice Books, and fewer Friends, | Lord of my self, accountable to none, | But to my Conscience, and my God alone'.

John Dryden's 'To the Memory of Mr Oldham' (1684) claims an affinitive sympathy between the two poets ('sure our Souls were near ally'd'). It also, somewhat unfairly, suggests that Oldham died before he had learned to purge his poetic style of 'harsh cadence', a ruggedness which Dryden held was not fully appropriate to satire. Dryden (1631–1700) uses his elegy to display his own versatility; it is an exercise in modulation, a smooth play with couplets and triplets, written in a pentameter which is subtly extended into an occasional hexameter and in couplets varied by a single effective triplet. Oldham is mourned both as a reflection of Virgil's Nisus, who slipped and failed to win a race, and as a poetic equivalent to Marcellus, the prematurely dead heir of the Emperor Augustus of whom much had been hoped. In both cases Dryden seems to be modestly projecting himself as the poet who has achieved the eminence denied to Oldham. As much of his criticism suggests, Dryden also seems to have seen himself as the heir to Milton's laurels. Nevertheless, his vision of Britain under the restored Stuarts is conditioned not by the idea of a stern republic outbraving the Roman, but by the example of the Imperial Rome of Augustus. In both periods the rule of an enlightened monarch could be seen as eclipsing the divisions of a preceding civil war. In the title of his elegy to Charles II, *Threnodia Augustalis* (1685), he glances at the parallel between the Emperor and the King while stressing the 'healing balm' of the Restoration and the maintenance of a distinctive brand of English liberty under the Stuart Crown ('Freedom which in no other Land will thrive | Freedom an *English* Subject's sole Prerogative'). This singular modern kingdom, Dryden maintained in the dedication to his tragedy *All For Love* (1678), required a disciplined poetry worthy of its heroic destiny and of its exalted place amongst the nations of Europe. The proper models for this poetry could only be Augustan. If his translation of *The Works of Virgil* (1697)—appearing at a time when Dryden's hopes for the Stuart dynasty had been dashed by the defeat and exile of James II—no longer exhibits a confidence in parallels between a dubious then and a triumphant now, his dedicatory essay still infers that patriotism demands an appropriate modern prosody and that 'A Heroick Poem, truly such', was 'undoubtedly the greatest Work which the Soul of Man is capable to perform'.

Though Dryden produced no heroic poem of his own, his quest for an English equivalent to Virgilian 'majesty in the midst of plainness' remained central to his patriotic mission as a poet. He continually strove for a Latinate precision, control, and clarity, but if his supreme poetic models were classical, his response to a select band of English writers suggests the degree to which he also saw himself as standing in a vernacular apostolic line. The Preface to his volume of translations—*Fables, Ancient and Modern* (1700)—stresses, for example, that he saw Chaucer as the prime figure in this canon (though his attempts at 'translating' certain of *The Canterbury Tales* into English 'as it is now refined' are far from distinguished tributes). This same Preface also declares a larger affinity in its assertion that poets have 'lineal descents and clans as well as families'. Spenser, he believes, 'insinuates that the soul of Chaucer was transfus'd into his body', while Milton 'has acknowledg'd to me that Spencer was his original'. Much of Dryden's most strenuous criticism appeared as prefaces to his own work but his most shapely critical manifesto, *Of Dramatic Poesie, An Essay* (1668), is a set piece written at a time of enforced theatrical inactivity during the Plague of 1665. It takes the form of a conversation between four characters in which the assertion of one is answered by the response of another; each character is allotted a formal speech, one defending ancient drama, another the modern; one proclaiming the virtues of French practice, another (Dryden's patriotic mouthpiece) the English. There is no real dialogue in the Platonic sense though there is a good deal of name-dropping and, latterly, of weighing the respective merits of Jonson, Fletcher, and Shakespeare. Jonson ('the most learned and judicious Writer which any Theater ever had') stands throughout as a touchstone of theatrical 'regularity', while the more 'natural' Shakespeare ('the man who of all Modern and perhaps Ancient Poets, had the largest and most comprehensive soul') is approvingly allowed the rank of an English Homer 'or Father of our Dramatick Poets'.

Three of the four disputants of *Of Dramatic Poesie* are typed as 'persons whom their witt and Quality have made known to all the Town'. The fourth, who seems to stand for Dryden himself, is clearly their social and intellectual equal. All are members of a court which the essay's dedication confidently proclaims to be 'the best and surest judge of writing'. This was possibly the last point in English history at which such a flattering observation might be regarded as having a ring of authenticity. Dryden was also amongst the last influential writers to have sought and won discriminating court patronage and advantageous royal promotion. On the death of his erstwhile dramatic collaborator, Sir William Davenant, in April 1668, he was appointed Poet Laureate and in 1670 he also obtained the post of Historiographer Royal. Throughout his career he seems to have projected himself as an official spokesman in poetry. His early public verse—the grotesque schoolboy elegy 'Upon the death of

Lord Hastings' (1649), the maturer tribute to the dead Cromwell (the *Heroique Stanzas Consecrated to the Glorious Memory of his Most Serene and Renowned Highness Oliver*) of 1659, and the two fulsome panegyrics addressed to Charles II (*Astraea Redux* of 1660 and *To His Sacred Majesty* of 1661—testifies to a desire to be a representative voice. The nimble 'historical' poem, *Annus Mirabilis, The Year of Wonders, 1666* (1667), is floridly dedicated 'to the Metropolis of Great Britain' both as a tribute to London's ordeal during the Great Fire and as a patriotic and emphatically royalist statement in the face of metropolitan resentment of the restored monarchy. In the poem it is the King's policies that serve to defeat the Dutch in war and the King's prayers that persuade Heaven to quell the flames.

Fourteen years elapsed between the composition of *Annus Mirabilis* and the publication in 1681 of the political satire *Absalom and Achitophel*. They were years spent actively in writing for the theatre, an experience which helped both to purge Dryden's verse of its early tendency to picturesqueness and to foster an interest in character and repartee. Dryden the satirist entertains through a witty intermixture of reasoned argument, refined technique, and invective. *Absalom and Achitophel* is a party poem, one designed to please friends by advancing their cause and to provoke enemies by ridiculing theirs. 'The true end of *Satyre*', he wrote in his preliminary declaration to his reader, 'is the amendment of Vices by correction'; the satirist himself is a physician prescribing 'harsh Remedies to an inveterate Disease', a disease affecting the body politic in which 'an Act of *Oblivion* were as necessary in a Hot, Distemper'd State, as an *Opiate* would be in a Raging Fever'. Dryden's reference here is specific. He wishes to memorialize and not to forgive the treasonable acts of Charles II's illegitimate son, the Duke of Monmouth, and his main abettor, the Earl of Shaftesbury, in attempting to exclude legally from the throne the King's proper successor, his brother, the Catholic Duke of York. The poem, which takes as its basis the biblical story of the rebellion of Absalom against his father David, is both a *histoire à clef* and a witty deflation of those, generally humourless, Protestants whose first recourse in argument was to refer to biblical precedent or justification. Dryden's narrative makes little direct appeal to the sacred but it does allow the radiance of divine pleasure to reflect from David to Charles and it opens with a witty deflection of any taint of adultery on Charles's part by insisting that it is set 'In pious times . . . Before *Polygamy* was made a sin'. The real joy of the poem lies in its exploration of forced parallels (Absalom and Monmouth, Achitophel and Shaftesbury, Saul and Cromwell, Pharaoh and Louis XIV of France, the Sanhedrin and Parliament, and the Jebusites—a name with a hint of 'Jesuit' about it—and English Catholics) and in its deftly scathing portraits, notably those of Shaftesbury, Buckingham (Zimri), and the Whig Sheriff of London, Bethel (Shimei). The aristocratic villains are introduced solemnly as if in a heroic poem; the less elevated, especially the shabby plotter Titus Oates (Corah), far more abusively ('Prodigious Actions may as well be done | By Weavers issue, as by Princes

Son'). Shaftesbury/Achitophel is cast as the Satanic tempter of the honourably
gullible Monmouth/Absalom; he holds out the prospect of personal glory and
public salvation, and he flatters the young man with perverted biblical images
pregnant with a sense of a divine mission:

> Auspicous Prince! At whose Nativity
> Some Royal Planet rul'd the Southern sky;
> Thy longing Countries Darling and Desire;
> Their cloudy Pillar, and their guardian Fire:
> .   .   .   .   .   .
>
> The Peoples Prayer, the glad Diviners Theam
> The Young-mens Vision, and the Old-mens Dream
> Thee *Saviour*, Thee, the Nations Vows confess;
> And never satisfi'd with seeing bless . . .

The poem, which has relatively little 'plot' in the strict sense of the term, is
structured around a series of vivid arguments and apologies. It closes with a
reasoned affirmation of intent from the 'Godlike' David, part a regretful
denunciation, part a defence of royal prerogative, part a restatement of an ideal
of constitutional balance. It is presented as a second Restoration with the
King's position approved, in late baroque pictorial fashion, by an assenting
God and a thundering firmament.

Shaftesbury's continued machinations against Charles's policy of support
for his Catholic brother stimulated two pale satirical reflections of *Absalom and
Achitophel*. The King himself is said to have provided the subject of Dryden's
The Medall: A Satyre Against Sedition (1682), a frontal attack on Shaftesbury's
character and on the motives of his party (the Whigs to whom the poem is
slyly dedicated). *The Second Part of Absalom and Achitophel* also of 1682 is
largely the work of Nahum Tate, but Dryden's contribution of some two
hundred lines of abuse, especially the sketches of the 'Heroically mad' Elkanah
Settle (Doeg) and of Thomas Shadwell (Og), have a vicious palpability about
them. Shadwell (?1642–92) became the object of Dryden's satire partly as a
result of his political affiliations, but more directly as a result of an increasingly unfriendly rivalry in the theatre (Shadwell's operatic adaptation of *The
Tempest*, *The Enchanted Isle* of 1674, was a particularly galling success).
Dryden's bitter distaste for the flippancy and shoddiness of Shadwell's work
as a poet reached its peak in the lampoon which he had begun in the late 1670s
but published only in 1682, *Mac Flecknoe, or A Satyr upon the True-Blew-
Protestant Poet, T.S.* It is a poem which advances beyond critical sniping to a
rage at the deathliness of human stupidity. Flecknoe, whom Dryden assumes
to be an Irishman, finds his true heir in a loquacious Celtic bard, the irre-
pressible (and non-Irish) Shadwell. The poem defines by negatives and dis-
crepancies; it undoes epic pretensions by playing with mock-heroic and it
purports to let dullness express itself while showing off the virtues of wit. The
elevated tone of its opening couplet crashes once Flecknoe emerges as a fatuous

Augustus seeking to settle his succession; Shadwell, the inadequate prince of a London slum, is enthroned bearing 'a mighty Mug of potent Ale' instead of an orb and, with a due sexual innuendo, a copy of his play *Love's Kingdom* instead of a sceptre as a symbol of his impotent claims to literary worth.

Dryden's two philosophico-religious poems of the 1680s, *Religio Laici, or A Laymans Faith* (1682) and *The Hind and the Panther* (1687), are public defences of the authority of a Church rather than, as they might have been in the hands of earlier seventeenth-century poets, explorations of the springs of devotion or private faith. In the Preface to the earlier poem Dryden describes himself as one who is 'naturally inclin'd to Scepticism in Philosophy' though one inclined to submit his theological opinions 'to my Mother Church'. The poem sees the Church of England as serenely fostering '*Common quiet*' in the face of attacks from Deists, Dissenters, and Papists and it blends within the form of a verse-epistle theological proposition with satirical exposition. Its striking opening image of human reason as a dim moon lighting the benighted soul is developed into an attack on those Deists who reject the Scripturally based teachings of Christianity. As it proceeds, the poem also attempts to demolish both Roman claims to infallible omniscience and the Puritan faith in individual inspiration, but it ultimately begs the vital question of religious authority. This question is emphatically answered in *The Hind and the Panther*, Dryden's longest poem, written after his reception into the Roman Catholic Church in 1685. It is a somewhat wordy and unworthy tribute to his new-found religious security, an allegorical defence of James II's attempts to achieve official toleration for Catholics in a predominantly Anglican culture and an attempt to prove the validity of Catholic claims to universal authority. It takes the form of a beast fable in which Quakers appear as hares, Presbyterians as wolves, Romans as hinds, and Anglicans as panthers. It is obliged to resort to the absurdity of a good-natured conversation about the mysteries of religion in which a hind actually attempts to *persuade* a panther, and to the incongruity of casting the Christian God as the nature god, Pan. Personal conviction and a certain political urgency coincided again in *Britannia Rediviva*, the propagandist public ode written to celebrate the birth of James II's heir in June 1688. Dryden's poem rejoices in the fact that the Stuart family has at last produced legitimate male issue and it attempts to brush aside the protests of 'th' ungrateful Rout' who both doubted that the child was truly the King's and were profoundly uneasy at the prospect of an assured Catholic succession to the throne.

The birth of James's son was not received with universal rejoicing in his kingdom, bringing as it did a long-drawn-out constitutional crisis to a head and immediately precipitating the overthrow of an alienated regime and with it the Poet Laureate's pious hopes. With the abrupt end to his official career in 1688, Dryden's sense of a patriotic mission for English poetry was forced to take a new and less overtly political turn. Apart from his translations and his libretto for Henry Purcell's extravagant 'Dramatick Opera' *King Arthur, or The British Worthy* (1691), two late lyric poems—*A Song for St Cecilia's Day, 1687*, and *Alexander's Feast; or the Power of Musique. An Ode, in Honour of St Cecilia's Day* (1697)—proved of particularly fruitful impact on the eighteenth century. Both poems contributed to the fashion for the irregular stanzas and verse paragraphs of the 'Cowleyan' Ode. More significantly, both later attracted the attention of Handel, anxious to prove his credentials as a composer resident in England and as a setter of English texts. If in *Britannia Rediviva* Dryden had produced the right words for what was soon seen as a wrong and intensely divisive cause, in his two St Cecilia *Odes* he provided the occasion for an extraordinary exploration of the potential of harmony.

Women's Writing and Women Writing in the Restoration Period

Dryden's ode 'To the Pious Memory of the Accomplisht Young Lady Mrs Anne Killigrew, Excellent in the two Sister-Arts of Poesie, and Painting' (1686) was, according to Dr Johnson, 'the noblest ode that our language has ever produced'. It was remarkable not simply for its intrinsic qualities but also for its celebration of an exceptional woman artist in a world largely dominated by patriarchal principles, prejudices, and images. Anne Killigrew (1660–85) had quietly earned a respect as a practitioner of what Dryden significantly styles 'sister arts' before her life was cut short by smallpox. She was the daughter of a well-connected royalist clergyman and the niece of the playwrights Thomas and Sir William Killigrew. To mention Anne in connection with her theatrical relatives and her famous obituarist is neither to belittle her art nor to reach out automatically for masculine comparisons but to establish her good fortune in being born into a cultured family, one which used its social influence in her favour and fostered the flowering of her talent. She served at court as a maid of honour in the cultured and sober household of Mary of Modena (the second wife of James II) where she was acquainted with other women of talent and ambition (notably Anne Finch, Countess of Winchilsea and Sarah Jennings, the future Duchess of Marlborough). If her 'accomplishment' as a mythological painter and portraitist has since been largely ignored, her poetry has properly gained a modest reputation. In her over-ambitious first poem, 'Alexandreis' (published in the posthumous collection of 1686), she prayed that her 'frozen style' might be warmed by 'Poetique fire'. That the prayer was answered is shown in her far more sophisticated address to the undemonstrative Mary of Modena ('To the Queen'), a poem which stresses the Queen's piety and virtue while appealing to heaven for a 'Prowess, that with Charms of Grace and Goodness' the poet might pay due honour to a queen suspected and unloved by the public at large.

   Killigrew's work is essentially that of an amateur, aware of the high culture of court circles surrounding her, but precluded from ever training her poetic voice to its proper pitch and fluency. The nagging self-doubt, evident in her defence of her work in 'Upon the saying that my Verses were made by another', is partly qualified by reference to the work of an earlier poet, one known to her admirers as 'the Matchless Orinda'. Katherine Philips (1631–64) seems to Killigrew to be the model of a woman writer accepted by her literary peers and the reading public alike ('What she did write, not only all allow'd, | But ev'ry Laurel, to her Laurel, bow'd!'). Philips, the well-educated daughter of a London merchant, at the age of 16 married into the Welsh gentry. Despite her husband's service as a Member of Parliament during the Commonwealth, Philips herself seems to have maintained certain royalist sympathies and to have won the respect of Henry Vaughan who in 1651 praised her work in *Olor Iscanus*. The *Poems. By the Incomparable, Mrs K.P.*, which first appeared in 1664 without the aggrieved author's permission, are marked by a celebration of female friendship. In her seclusion in Wales in the 1650s Philips drew round her a circle of like-minded women and cultivated particularly intense platonic and poetic relationships with Mary Aubrey ('Rosania') and Anne Owens (the 'Lucasia' to whom nearly half her verses are addressed). In April 1651 she writes in 'L'Amitie: To Mrs M. Awbrey' of two souls grown 'by an incomparable mixture, One', and with a Donne-like sense of the exclusivity of love in perilous times, she proclaims that 'sublim'd' lovers rise 'to pitty Kings, and Conquerours despise, | Since we that sacred union have engrost, | Which they and all the sullen world have lost'. In welcoming 'the excellent Mrs A.O.' into her little society Philips compares her circle to 'A Temple of divinity' which will attract pilgrims a thousand years hence. 'There's a religion in our Love', she declares in 'Friendship's Mysterys, to my dearest Lucasia', a poem set to music by Henry Lawes in 1655, and in contrasting the 'Apostasy' of Rosania to the steady friendship of Lucasia she resorts to a parallel with Elisha's succession to Elijah as the new friend takes up the mantle of Orinda's love. Philips's poems in memory of her dead infant son Hector (the 'Epitaph' and 'On the death of my first and dearest childe', both dated 1655) poignantly mourn a long-hoped-for child cut off before his proper time. Her best 'public' poetry tends to mark royal occasions: she laments the execution of Charles I, and anxiously anticipates the return of his son ('Hasten (great prince) unto thy British Isles | Or all thy subjects will become exiles; | To thee they flock'); she bemoans the passing of the much admired 'Winter Queen', Elizabeth of Bohemia, in 1662 ('this Queene's merit fame so far hath spread | That she rules still, though dispossesst and dead'); and she responds gracefully to the Duchess of York's request for examples of her work with a poem opening with the lines: 'To you, whose dignitie strikes us with awe, | And whose far greater judgment gives us law'. In her short lifetime Philips's main claim to fame was her successful rhymed-couplet translation of Corneille's tragedy *La Mort de Pompée*, performed in Dublin and London in 1663. At the time of her death she left incomplete a version of the same dramatist's *Horace* (completed by John Denham and acted in 1668). Both translations were printed in the posthumous collection *Poems. By the Most Deservedly Admired Mrs Katherine Philips. The Matchless Orinda* in 1667.

The acclaim accorded to Philips's work was a rare enough phenomenon in a period of markedly unequal opportunities for women writers. A prosody shaped by reference to ancient poetry and a universal insistence on the primacy of Latin and Greek in education left many women, to whom the public educational system was largely closed, without what was regarded as the essential basis for the development of a poet's craft. Although there were relatively few direct heirs to the remarkable generation of highly educated sixteenth-century aristocratic women, changing social and religious conditions in the 1640s and 1650s do seem to have forced open literary doors. Nevertheless, even the gifted Dorothy Osborne (1627–95) could complain in one of her celebrated letters to her fiancé in 1653 that the poems of Margaret Cavendish (which she was anxious to read) were somehow a literary aberrance, or, as she put it, an 'extravagance': 'Sure the poore woman is a little distracted, she could never bee soe rediculous else as to venture at writeing book's and in verse too.' The emergence of distinctive women's writing has all too frequently been ascribed in over-neat socio-historical terms to the rise of the bourgeoisie and bourgeois reading habits or to the impact of certain Protestant sects. The poems of the emigrant Puritan, Anne Bradstreet (*c*.1612–72), were clearly admired enough by certain of her American co-religionists to be sent to London for publication in 1650 as *The Tenth Muse Lately Sprung Up in America*. Quakerism too laid great stress on the equality of the spiritual experience and testimonies of women and encouraged the forthright witness of female Friends. Many of the most prominent women writers of the Restoration period would, however, have eschewed all connection with either the merchant class or with the still *déclassé* extremes of sectarian Puritanism. Women found their own voice, and made that voice respected, in the face of manifest disadvantage but not necessarily by confronting the intolerance of any given 'establishment'. The extraordinarily well-connected Margaret Cavendish herself partly disdained female pretensions to fashion rather than intellectual pursuits: 'Our sex takes so much delight in dressing and adorning themselves . . . and instead of turning over solid leaves, we turn our hair into curles, and our Sex is as ambitious to shew ourselves to the eyes of the world when finely drest, as Scholers do to express their learning to the ears of the world, when fully fraught with authors . . .' Most gentlewomen, whether or not they had a rudimentary education, were, like their middle-class sisters, primarily required to be efficient and skilled managers of their sometimes considerable households rather than bluestockings *manquées*. Piety and Christian observance were, however, never regarded as exclusively male preserves and the very emphasis on the niceties and complications of religious affiliation, which is so characteristic of seventeenth-century writing, inevitably influenced the expression of female spirituality. The upheavals of the Civil War and the Commonwealth seem also to have prepared the way for the more general acceptance of the authority of women's voices, not all of them conventionally pious or decorous. The impulse to speak out was as much Anglican and royalist as it was Dissenting and republican, as chaste as it was licentious.

To some of her twentieth-century cultural heirs the work of the pioneer feminist Mary Astell (1666–1731) has seemed enigmatic and contradictory in its impulses. Astell's best-known work, *A Serious Proposal to the Ladies for the advancement of their true and great interest* (1694), argues that unmarried women of the upper and middle classes should use their dowries to establish and endow women's 'seminaries', colleges which would serve both as educational institutions and as refuges for 'hunted heiresses' and the aged. The second part of *A Serious Proposal* (1697) advocates the importance to women's intellectual development of the kind of abstract reasoning too often regarded as an exclusively masculine pursuit, and her *Some Reflections on Marriage* (1700) warns women of the seriousness of committing themselves to the potential tyranny of a husband. The vast body of Astell's writing is not, however, exclusively concerned with women's prospects. She uses poetry primarily to express her religious hopes. 'Ambition' was first published in a collection of poems presented to her patron, Archbishop Sancroft, in 1684. It is a poem which asserts the spiritual rights of women but which scorns temporal ambition; it looks to the pleasures of retirement from the world but it also lays an emphatic claim to equality in the sight of both posterity and God. When in January 1688 she writes 'in emulation of Mr Cowley's Poem call'd The Motto' she pursues a series of brief meditations on worldly limitation as opposed to heavenly freedom. She acknowledges her divine calling, but modestly recognizes the restraints imposed on her mission by her gender:

> How shall I be a Peter or a Paul?
>   That to the Turk and Infidel,
>   I might the joyful tydings tell,
> And spare no labour to convert them all:
>   But ah my Sex denies me this,
>   And Marys privledge I cannot wish
> Yet hark I hear my dearest Saviour say,
> They are more blessed who his Word obey.

Astell seems to be thinking less of Cowley and more of that other confounded missionary and revolutionizer of women's lives, St Theresa. But Astell was no Papist. Her determined polemical support for the Church of England against the claims of Dissenters, in such conservative essays as *Moderation Truly Stated* and *A Fair Way with Dissenters and their Patrons* (both 1704), can be seen as integral to her claim to be a respected participant in the intellectual debates of her time.

Aphra Behn (1640–89) has long been claimed to have been the first professional woman writer in England. She was a professional not by inclination or choice, but of economic necessity. Like her less talented contemporary Delarivière Manley (1663–1724), Behn wrote fiction for easy domestic consumption and comedy as a proven way of making money in the theatre. If much was once made of the contrast between the reputations, styles, and *œuvres* of the upright 'Orinda' Philips and the notoriously immodest 'Astrea' Behn, the contrast was not consciously fostered by either party. Behn, of indeterminate social origins, seems to have had little formal education, but her experiences as a colonist in Surinam in the early 1660s almost certainly schooled her in the ways of a dissolute world more efficiently than any course in classical rhetoric or Roman history. Her facility in French is, however, evident in her translations of Fontenelle's *The History of Oracles* and *A Discovery of the New Worlds* in 1688 and, in the same year, of the romance *Agnes de Castro*. Behn's reputation as a poet loyally anxious to commemorate any given royal occasion was rivalled only by her considerable success with the London public as a dramatist. Her first play, *The Forc'd Marriage,* was produced at the Duke of York's Theatre in September 1670; seventeen further plays, the vast majority of them comedies, were acted and printed during her lifetime. Her comedies are generally energetic intrigues marked by sexually frank and witty banter between characters. There is little room for *gravitas* or learning. *The Feign'd Curtezans* (1679) (dedicated to Charles II's mistress, Nell Gwynn) revolves around the amatory negotiations of two wild local girls and two English gentlemen in Rome, an intrigue varied by distressed ex-fiancés and brothers and by the folly of Sir Signal Buffoon and his Puritan tutor, Mr Tickletext. Behn's antipathy to Puritanism and its political allies is particularly evident in the chaotic comedy *The Roundheads* (1681/2), a play in which the wives of prominent Puritan politicians are wooed by two cavaliers (Loveless and Freeman) and in which the interconnection between pimping and politicking occasionally hits its mark. Behn's most vividly successful achievement remains the first part of *The Rover* (1677), a play based on Thomas Killigrew's *Thomaso or The Wanderer* but replete with self-reference. Its dominant male characters, Belvile and Willmore, are the kind of exiled cavaliers that Behn must have known from her days in Surinam, men in whom she seems to have taken a distrustful pleasure; both are refugees from political failure in England who espouse the cause of philandery almost as a royalist protest against Puritan restraint. The flamboyant Willmore wins his true-love in time-honoured fashion by confounding the wishes of her father but in the process he breaks off his liaison with Angellica Bianca, a 'famous courtesan' who shares the playwright's initials. When Angellica confronts her faithless lover at the end of the play she attempts to stress the pain of her disillusion; she had once lovingly hoped to raise his soul 'above the vulgar', even to make him 'all soul . . . and soft and constant', but she has discovered that what she received in return was 'no more than dog lust . . . and so I fell | Like a long-worshipped idol at the last | Perceived a fraud, a cheat, a bauble'.

Angellica's picture of herself as a slave to the whims of a fickle male enforces Behn's constantly implied theme of the limited choices open to contemporary women. Permissiveness may offer a merry freedom to men, but that freedom too often relies on the servitude of the other sex. Although she generally draws back from defining and directly protesting against this servitude in her plays,

Behn's most famous novel, *Oroonoko, or the History of the Royal Slave* (1688), forms an early attack on what she perceives as the more distant colonial problem of human slavery, degradation, and suffering. *Oroonoko* is on one level a clumsy and romanticized account of the betrayal of an African prince into American slavery; on another it is an early attempt to insist on human dignity and to examine the redemptive force of love. Before his contrived fall, the hero is described as a man capable of 'reigning well, and of governing as wisely . . . as any Prince civilised in the most refined schools of humanity and learning, or the most illustrious courts', but it is through his love of 'the brave, the beautiful and the constant Imoinda' that he is inspired to rebel, to suffer silently the horrible consequences of his rebellion, and to assert his understanding of a morality which transcends that of his oppressors. As a writer who had acted out the roles of both colonizer and courtesan, Behn suggests that she possessed a proper insight into the meaning of oppression.

'Restoration' Drama

When the public theatres reopened in 1660, after eighteen years of official displeasure, a tradition needed to be re-established which was both responsive to the recent past and a reflection of new tastes and fashions. Two well-connected impresarios, both with roots in the courtly and theatrical past, effectively nursed the London stage into robust health. Sir William Davenant (1606–68), who was rumoured to be the godson and, even more preposterously, the bastard of Shakespeare, had established his credentials as a playwright and a librettist of court masques in the reign of Charles I. In 1656 he had managed to evade the government ban on theatrical performances by staging an opera, or 'Entertainment after the manner of the ancients', *The Siege of Rhodes*. This English opera, with music (now lost) by Henry Lawes, boasted 'a Representation by the Art of Prospective in Scenes and the Story sung in Recitative Musick' and included a timely musical debate between Diogenes and Aristophanes on the virtues and demerits of public amusements. Thomas Killigrew (1612–83), with Davenant a holder of one of the two royal patents granting a monopoly over London acting, had written, and had possibly seen performed, the bawdy, anti-romantic comedy *The Parson's Wedding* before the theatres were closed in 1642. It was, however, the innovations fostered by the more extravagant Davenant which appear to have led the way. The introduction of overtures, 'curtain tunes', instrumental interludes, and 'ayres' with unsung dialogue led in the early 1690s to some of Purcell's most interesting public commissions, but the very use of such music during scene-changes serves as an indicator of the vital changes in production introduced in the Restoration period. Davenant's theatres at Lincoln's Inn Fields and Dorset Garden and Killigrew's at Drury Lane were expensively designed, purpose-built, and covered. A proscenium arch with flat wings, painted shutters, and backcloth behind it allowed for complex illusions of space and distinct changes of scene. Above all, the actors who performed on a well-lit apron stage now included women, a result both of the break in the training of boys to play female roles and of the influence of continental practice.

The active patronage of King Charles II and his brother James, Duke of York, assured that the court attended performances mounted beyond its confines and open, at a somewhat steep cost of one to four shillings, to any who could afford admission. When Killigrew's company opened their first theatre (a converted tennis-court) in November 1660 with a performance of the first part of Shakespeare's *Henry IV*, they were looking back to an established 'classic' with a sound royalist theme. The plays of Shakespeare, Jonson, and Fletcher continued to hold their own, if sometimes after a process of cosmetic 'improvement'. Although the *Henry IV* plays, *Hamlet*, *Othello*, and *Julius Caesar* survived without major alteration, and attracted actors of the calibre of Thomas Betterton (1635–1710) (who was personally tutored in the part of Hamlet by Davenant who claimed' to have known the actor first instructed by Shakespeare himself), Davenant proved to be an efficient cobbler together of texts revised according to new canons of taste. His *The Law Against Lovers* (1661–2) ingeniously fused *Measure for Measure* with *Much Ado About Nothing* and his versions of *Macbeth* and *The Tempest* (the latter in collaboration with Dryden) allowed for musical and choreographic spectacle and for a quite excessive symmetry of plotting. Balletic witches and siblings for Miranda and Caliban apart, the most celebrated and enduring of the Restoration adaptations was Nahum Tate's *History of King Lear* of 1681. Tate (1652–1715), who claimed to have found the original tragedy 'a heap of jewels, unstrung and unpolish't', hamstrung his own version by omitting the Fool and by introducing a love-plot for Edgar and Cordelia and a happy ending in which Lear, Cordelia, and Gloucester all survive. In common with Colley Cibber's melodramatic simplification of *Richard III* it was performed, in preference to Shakespeare's original, until well into the nineteenth century.

The natural enough preoccupation of much Restoration tragedy with politics also took its cue from Shakespeare, if a Shakespeare recast in a severely Roman mould. Dryden's *All for Love: or, The World Well Lost* (1677) claims to imitate the style of 'the Divine *Shakespeare*' while radically rearranging the story of Antony and Cleopatra; and Thomas Otway's *The History and Fall of Caius Marius* (1680) loosely adapts elements of *Romeo and Juliet* in a charged Roman Republican setting. The steady dignity of Dryden's blank verse in *All for Love*, and his decorous tidying-up of Shakespeare's complexities of plot in conformity with neo-classical canons, are likely to strike its modern readers (and its occasional audiences) as more appealing than the ambitious and extravagant heroics of his earlier tragedies such as *Tyrannick Love, or, The Royal Martyr* (1669), *The Conquest of Granada* (1670), and *Aureng-Zebe* (1675). Dryden's fascination with the dilemmas of the great in antique or exotic settings is to some degree paralleled by that of Otway (1652–85). *Caius Marius*, like his far finer tragedies *Don Carlos, Prince of Spain* (1676), *The Orphan, or, The Unhappy Marriage* (1680), and *Venice Preserv'd, or A Plot Discover'd* (1682), originally served as vehicles for the tragic histrionics of the actor Thomas Betterton. All are high-flown and declamatory, showing suffering, emotional conflict, and intrigue shot through with mawkish sentiment. The situation of the noble Jaffeir, torn by opposed loyalties, in *Venice Preserv'd* is, however, handled with real panache, while its echoes of contemporary English plots and counterplots give it a particular urgency which has ensured its periodic revival.

The Shakespeare who served as an adaptable native model to the writers of tragedy in the 1660s, 1670s, and 1680s proved far less influential on those who evolved a new comic style. If much Restoration tragedy deals with foreign politics, the comedies of the period are concerned with English philandery. In a period of literary history notable, in aristocratic circles at least, for its rejection of solemnity and moral seriousness, the darker and more questioning side of Shakespeare's comedies and the earnest morality of Jonson's provided hints rather than patterns. Restoration comedy, like the satyr-plays of the ancients, reverses and debunks the heroics of contemporary tragedy. In *The Rehearsal* George Villiers, second Duke of Buckingham (1628–87), cleverly burlesqued the extremes of the heroic mode through a series of parodies. *The Rehearsal*, first produced in December 1671 and continuously adapted and flatteringly imitated in the eighteenth century, freely satirizes plays and playwrights, producers and actors, but its appeal to audiences must always have lain in a sneaking respect for the form it lambasts. The plays of Sir George Etherege (?1634–91) and William Wycherley (1641–1715) are far more characteristic of the hybrid, symmetrical, sexual comedy popular in the reign of Charles II. Both are masters of a comedy which accentuates the artificiality of the stage in order to mirror and comment on the sheen of the 'polished' society that produced it. Where contemporary tragedy can be heightened to a point of pompous absurdity, the comedy is frank and 'realistic'. Etherege's *The Comical Revenge: or Love in a Tub*, first performed at the Duke's Theatre in March 1664, was said to have 'got the Company more Reputation and Profit than any preceding Comedy'. It has a double plot in the earlier seventeenth-century manner: one, concerning the amatory rivalry of two gentlemen, is written in couplets; the other, dealing farcically with the antics of the playboy Sir Frederick Frollick and of his French valet, Dufoy, is both distinguished from it by its prose and partly mediated by the evident gentility of Sir Frederick. *She wou'd if she cou'd* (1668) is, as its suggestive title indicates, far more of a signal of what was to become the general current of contemporary comedy. Lady Cockwood, up from the country, frantically courts adultery despite her front of prudish respectability; Courtall and Freeman, both London libertines with names that indicate their predilections, ultimately find satisfaction in the arms of Sir Oliver Cockwood's younger kinswomen, Ariana and Gatty. The play presents its audience with two kinds of hypocrisy and double standards;

the pretentious and reprobate Cockwoods are unmasked, but the gallants triumph through an alternative deception which wins them witty, willing and, above all, young lovers. Older lovers, it is implied, are implicitly ridiculous while young women of good society are the proper prey of those young men who dare to angle for them. Etherege's funniest and best-crafted play, *The Man of Mode: or, Sir Fopling Flutter* (1676) brings this adulation of the successful philanderer to a dashing crescendo. Dorimant and Medley are, we assume, to be taken as models of merriment, cleverness, resilient 'good nature', and sexual irresistibility (or at least they see themselves as such); against them, Etherege pits a Frenchified fool, Sir Fopling Flutter, 'a person . . . of great acquir'd follies' who fails where they win, who sparkles like tinsel where they attempt to blaze like well-cut diamonds (albeit paste diamonds). Yet it is in the very intensity and control of Dorimant's charm that much of the power of the play lies. He is a sceptical, manipulative corrupter, but he is also a man capable of falling for Harriet Woodvil, a woman able to parry his wit and his manœuvres alike. *The Man of Mode* remains a quizzical and ambiguous play designed to divert a cynical world and to vex moralizing ones.

Wycherley's friend Dryden held that *The Plain-Dealer* (1676) 'obliged all honest and virtuous men, by one of the most bold, most general, and most useful satires which has ever been presented in the English theatre'. Despite Dryden's admiration of him as a satirist by inclination, Wycherley is rarely an earnest moralist. He is amused with, rather than scathing about, the dubious morals of society and he disconcerts more than he disturbs. He both enjoys and acknowledges the dangers of posturing. Wycherley's plays suggest that high society's cultivation of the superficial elevates wit and politeness above personal decency. The aimless confusions and *longueurs* of his first two comedies, *Love in a Wood, or, St James's Park* (1671) and *The Gentleman Dancing-Master* (1672), contrast vividly with the mastery of construction and situation evident in *The Country-Wife* of 1675. Although he cannot be called central to the plot, the play's major character, the sexual gourmand Horner, establishes its sardonic tone. If the emerging love of the honest Harcourt and the stubborn Alithia is ultimately blessed, and a series of fools, hypocrites, and gulls are ruthlessly ridiculed, it is Horner who after a triumphant campaign of debauchery (hidden by the ruse that he is impotent following an operation for the pox) escapes any kind of retribution. Other characters prate about their 'dear, dear, honour' while Horner, whose name is a sexually loaded pun on the word 'honour', both undermines pretence and exposes the pretenders to contempt. *The Plain-Dealer* of 1676, in part an adaptation of Molière's *Le Misanthrope*, is at once a more savage and more romantic play. Its ambiguous and world-hating protagonist, Manly, 'of an honest, surly, nice humour', has patriotically procured the command of a ship 'out of honour, not interest'. He is the 'plaindealer' who announces to the audience in the Prologue that he has been created to disconcert: 'I, only, act a part like none of you' | And yet you'll say, it is a fool's part too: | An honest man who, like you, never winks | At faults; but unlike you, speaks what he thinks.' Much hinges on the words 'plain' and 'honest' but rather than face the inevitability of the undeceived Manly's descent into a Timon-like rejection of the shams and deceptions of a parasitic society, Wycherley somewhat gratuitously delivers him into the arms of the chastely honest and abstract Fidelia. Although love does not exactly conquer all, reconciliation does, perhaps because Wycherley cannot really conceive of any viable or acceptable alternative.

With the death of Charles II in 1685 and the flight to France of James II in 1688, direct royal patronage of the stage diminished (though James's daughter and successor, Mary II, maintained a discriminating interest in the theatre). A generation of playwrights passed with the political regimes which fostered their wit, but both comedy and tragedy were set, even stuck, in smooth grooves. In the Preface to his tragi-comedy *Don Sebastian* of 1689/91 Dryden mourned that 'the Humours of Comedy were almost spent, that Love and Honor (the mistaken Topicks of Tragedy) were quite worn out, that the Theatres could not support their Charges, and that the Audience forsook them'. Because of these discouragements he felt condemned as a dramatist 'to dig in those exhausted Mines'. This same Dryden could, however, recognize that by 1694 one major new talent had emerged, one hailed in his poem 'To Mr Congreve' as the true heir to Etherege's 'Courtship' and to Wycherley's 'Satire, Wit, and Strength'. William Congreve (1670–1729) achieved a startling popular success with *The Old Batchelour* in 1691 and followed it in 1693 with *The Double-Dealer* and in 1695 with *Love for Love*. Congreve acquired his mastery through a combination of instinct and experience. Each of his early plays advances his technique and assimilates the lessons of his predecessors. If his Spanish tragedy *The Mourning Bride* of 1697 might seem aberrant to latter-day readers, its initial popularity is testified to by the familiarity of its opening line ('Music has charms to sooth a savage breast') and of its famous observation that 'Heav'n has no rage, like love to hatred turn'd, | Nor Hell a fury, like a woman scorn'd'. His last and most brilliant comedy, *The Way of the World* (1700), was by comparison a failure with its public. Little of the play, Congreve remarked in its Dedication, had been 'prepared for that general taste which now seems predominant in the pallats of our audience'. To some later commentators, however, it is the last and greatest play of the 'Restoration' period, the climax of the dramatic experiments of forty years and the comedy that uniquely allows for both true wit and genuine feeling, for social satire and for the establishment of marital alliances based on tenderness rather than convenience. The impact of the play depends both on the complex social and family interrelationships of the characters and on the discrepancies between what is publicly declared and what is privately acknowledged. The importance of definition is especially evident in the relationship between Mirabell and Millamant. In the famous 'proviso' scene in Act IV each lays down conditions to the other; though she has admitted to loving 'violently', she seeks a relationship which looks cold to the outside world ('let us be as strange as if we had been married a great while; and be as well bred as if we were not married at all'); he insists that she abhor the trivia that divert less intelligent women. Both determine to stand aside from the marital way of the world, and the way of much contemporary comedy, which the play's concluding couplets see as a 'mutual falsehood' and as 'marriage frauds' that are 'too oft paid in kind'.

The work of two of Congreve's far less subtle contemporaries serves to throw the quality of *The Way of the World* into further relief. Sir John Vanbrugh (1664–1726) is now far better known as a flamboyantly inventive architect than as a dramatist. His buildings are brilliant, balanced, whimsical, and weighty; his plays are merely brilliant and whimsical. Vanbrugh had a hand in some eleven plays, most of them collaborations or adaptations from the Spanish and the French. Only two, *The Relapse; or Virtue in Danger* (1696) and *The Provok'd Wife* (1697), are completely his. A third, *A Journey to London,* was finished by Colley Cibber and produced posthumously in 1728 under the title *The Provok'd Husband. The Relapse* is a somewhat conventional response to, and a continuation of, Cibber's far drabber comedy *Love's Last Shift.* In the original production at Drury Lane Cibber himself played Lord Foppington, the character to whom Vanbrugh allots his most effervescently witty and harsh lines. The discordant picture of marriage in *The Provok'd Wife* is relieved only by the suppleness of the colloquial comic dialogue in which the play abounds. The work of the Irishborn actor/playwright, George Farquhar (?1677–1707), is marked by a shift away from the London-oriented comedies of his predecessors into the fresh fields of the English provinces. *The Constant Couple, or a Trip to the Jubilee,* produced in 1699, was one of the theatrical hits of its day but like its sequel, *Sir Harry Wildair* (1701) it seems a slight, if sexually candid, piece of work compared to the long-popular *The Recruiting Officer* (1706) and *The Beaux' Stratagem* (1707). With the British victory at Blenheim of 1704 vividly impressed on the public mind, and with the military campaign against Louis XIV of France still being pursued, *The Recruiting Officer* had a particular contemporary currency. Despite its thin plot and the lightness of its intrigues, the play is tartly observant of the nastiness of a soldierly career and, in the resourceful Sergeant Kite, offers one of the finest comic roles in the English theatre tradition. *The Beaux' Stratagem* reveals an equally relaxed interplay of cynicism, realism, and romance. Its central male characters, Aimwell and Archer, both 'gentlemen of broken fortunes', are fortune-hunters rather than rakes and success in their chosen provincial careers is ultimately determined by the emergence of their natural virtue. At a crucial point in the action Aimwell is obliged to admit that he is 'unequal to the Task of Villain' having been won over to the uprightness of love by Dorinda's 'Mind and Person'. It is an admission that might have seemed merely a cynical device in a play of the 1670s. By 1707 it may well have been taken as indicative of honest geniality.

By the late 1690s, what the Victorian historian, Macaulay, later saw as the 'hard-heartedness' of 'Restoration' comedy was melting under the sun of benevolence. It was a form initially evolved to divert a jaded élite and to reflect on their manners and morals (or their spectacular lack of the latter). It was a form that flourished both because of the accuracy of the reflection and because of the cultivated artificiality of high society and the stage alike. When Dryden claimed that the new 'refinement' of conversation was a direct result of the influence of Charles II and his court, he was in part thinking of the new 'naturalism' of the stage. The King, he argued, had 'awakened the dull and heavy spirits of the English from their natural reservedness' and had loosened 'their stiff forms of conversation, and made them easy and pliant to each other in discourse'. The 'wit' of the period certainly follows the lead of the court in its 'hard-heartedness'. It is in part a revolution against moral seriousness and the kind of piety that is worn on the sleeve, in part an echo of a new respect for clarity and reason. The world of the seventeenth century had been turned upside down; crowns and mitres had been knocked off heads only to be restored in a world that looked more cynically and questioningly at all forms of authority. Many of the private convictions which had been revolutionary in the 1640s seemed reactionary in the 1680s. The drama of the 'Restoration' period ought, however, to be seen as an essential element in the literature of a revolutionary age. Unlike much of its satirical poetry the comedies of the last forty years of the seventeenth century have retained an immediacy, a subversiveness, and an ability to provoke the prejudices of audiences. If scarcely revolutionary in themselves, the plays of the period are a response to revolution and to the seventeenth century's experimental reversal of values. The comedies do not offer anything so pretentious as redefinitions but they do continue to irritate and laugh audiences into reaching out for definitions.

5

Eighteenth-Century Literature
1690–1780

ALEXANDER POPE'S epitaph for the monument erected to the memory of Sir
Isaac Newton in Westminster Abbey in 1731 succinctly proclaims the extraordinary intellectual virtue of the greatest scientific innovator of the age. A Latin
inscription witnesses to Newton's immortality, an immortality triply safe-
guarded by Time, Nature, and Heaven; a couplet in English, the sublime
confidence of which has served to provoke later generations, unequivocally
asserts that the systematized vision which he offered was divinely inspired.
'Nature and Nature's Laws lay hid in Night. | God said, *Let Newton be!* and
All was *Light*.' Pope's epitaph is more than a personal tribute to a great man;
it is a public statement displayed in a much frequented national church which
sums up the gratitude of a proud civilization. Newton (1642–1727), 'the
Miracle of the present Age' as Joseph Addison called him, had given his
eighteenth-century heirs a carefully reasoned theoretical framework on which
a whole range of additional theories could be hung. His *Principia* of 1687 and
his *Opticks* of 1704 suggested that there were indeed intelligible laws in nature
which could be demonstrated by physics and mathematics, and, moreover, that
the universe exhibited a magnificent symmetry and a mechanical certainty.
This universe, Newton had declared, could not have arisen 'out of a Chaos by
the mere Laws of Nature'; such a 'wonderful Uniformity in the Planetary
System' had to be the handiwork of an intelligent and benevolent Creator. To
the many eighteenth-century propagators of Newton's thought, the great
could be related to the less, the cosmic to the terrestrial, and the divine to the
human by means of a properly tutored understanding of the natural scheme
of things. By interpretation, Newton's heavens declared that there was order,
law, and indeed design in creation. Largely thanks to the propagandist work of
the Royal Society in London and European-wide advances in astronomy, mathematics, mechanics, physics, and optics, natural philosophy had shed the taint
of forbidden knowledge. Religious mystery could be enhanced, and sometimes
even replaced, by rational wonder. The revolution in scientific thought begun
by Copernicus 150 years earlier was to be fulfilled as popular enlightenment.

The ideal of universal law, order, and tidiness which could be extrapolated from Newtonian physics proved to have widespread ramifications, especially when pursued in conjunction with arguments derived from the reasoning of contemporary philosophers. John Locke (1632–1704) and his one-time pupil Anthony Ashley Cooper, third Earl of Shaftesbury (1671–1713), both provided an intellectual basis for easily digested theories of politics, religion, and aesthetics and for precepts pertaining to social happiness. Locke's epistemology and his crucial rejection of innate ideas in favour of the notion of knowledge based on external sensation and internal 'reflection' helped, it has been argued, to determine the tendency in many eighteenth-century writers to describe the observable world rather than offer a subjective interpretation of the workings of the psyche. For Locke, the mind was a *tabula rasa* at birth, a 'white Paper, void of all Characters, without any *Ideas*'. When he rhetorically demanded how the mind acquired 'all the materials of Reason and Knowledge', he answered succinctly, 'From *Experience*'. If at one point in his *Essay Concerning Human Understanding* (1690) Locke famously compares the mind to a Newtonian *camera obscura*, at another he employs a palatial metaphor to suggest that ideas are admitted to the brain through an ordered enfilade of state rooms which lead steadily to the Royal Presence, the senses and the nerves acting as 'Conduits, to convey them from without to their Audience in the Brain, the mind's Presence-room'. The discussion of language in Book III of the *Essay* centres on the premiss that words are signs not of things, but of ideas, and on the related insistence that language is the creation of a society the members of which consent to the fact that certain words stand for certain ideas. Common usage and mutual consent provide an acceptable authority for regulating the use of words in ordinary conversation (if not a precise enough one for philosophical discourse). Locke's influential explorations of a theory of government are related to this concept of social consent. His *Two Treatises of Government* (probably composed before 1682, but published to coincide with the success of the 'Glorious Revolution' in 1689/90) emphasize that civil societies are bonded together by enlightened self-interest and by the dual necessities of securing individual liberty and the protection of individual property rights. Government existed as a trust conferred upon it by the consent of citizens; if that trust were abused, or if power became arbitrary, then citizens, the true makers of laws, had a right to withdraw confidence and authority from their rulers. Locke's *Two Treatises* reveal him to be the direct heir to the political and constitutional debates of the seventeenth century. As the reasoning advocate of a 'mixed constitution', which interfused monarchy, oligarchy, and democracy, he was also, to some degree, the validating spirit of the British political compromise of the eighteenth century.

Locke's faith in the rights of the citizen enshrined in the rule of law, and in law as the product of consent, is in part reflected in the easier philosophical arguments of Shaftesbury. Both philosophers were proponents of religious toleration, and indeed of a rational Christianity based on common sense, virtuous action, and a perception of the nature of God through his creation rather than through revelation. To Shaftesbury the contemplation of the universe was 'the only means which cou'd establish the *sound Belief* of a Deity', and such 'sound Belief' in a blessed order could stand counter both to the Godless confusion of the atheists and the sin-infused, fallen world of orthodox Christianity. 'All Nature's Wonders serve to excite and perfect this idea of their *Author*', Shaftesbury wrote in his dialogue *The Moralists: A Philosophical Rhapsody* (1709), ''Tis here he suffers us to see, and even to converse with him, in a manner suitable to our Frailty; How glorious is it to contemplate him, in this noblest of his Works apparent to us, The *System* of *the bigger World*.' Shaftesbury's *Characteristicks of Men, Manners, Opinions, and Times* (1711, revised 1714), a collection which includes *The Moralists*, is insistent in its expressions of the divine perfection of nature and of the interconnection of aspects of creation according to observable laws; it is also explicit in its arguments proposing the essential goodness of the human element in creation. Humankind, naturally virtuous and naturally sociable, finds its true destiny in acknowledging a correspondence between the harmony and the proportion evident in the macrocosm and the individual spirit. A sociable morality, which suppresses such unnatural passions as tyranny or misanthropy, itself derives from a reasoned observation of '*the Order of the World it-self*'. Shaftesbury's optimistic view of innate human benevolence did not go unchallenged. In his *A Search into the Nature of Society*, added in 1723 to the second edition of *The Fable of the Bees: or Private Vices, Public Benefits*, the Dutch-born Bernard de Mandeville (1670–1733) bluntly complained that the 'boasted middle way, and the calm Virtues recommended in the Characteristicks, are good for nothing but to breed Drones'. To Mandeville, Shaftesbury's notions were 'a high compliment to human-kind . . . What a pity it is they are not true!' His moral system was, moreover, 'not much better than a Wild-Goose-Chase'. A far sounder picture of human society should be based not on flights of wild geese but, as his larger, controversial, and widely read *Fable* suggests, on a hive of bees, a mutual society which thrives because its individual members are acquisitive. This acquisitiveness, and a concomitant love of luxury, could, he indicated, be properly interpreted as a public benefit rather than as a private vice, selfishness and pride being the basis of commercial prosperity and therefore, ultimately, of social well-being.

   Locke's concept of a virtuous citizen as a man of 'large, sound, round-about sense', Shaftesbury's almost bland assertion that 'to philosophize is but to carry good breeding a step further', and the popular immediacy of Mandeville's *Fable* variously serve to suggest something of the contemporary esteem accorded to reasoned argument, good humour, and common sense as opposed to the disharmony of superstition, spleen, and 'enthusiasm'. These moral and social ideals are also reflected in the broader culture of the period, most notably in its music and its architecture. Classical proportion in eighteenth-century music, embodied in the discipline of sonata form and in the need for resolution within a closed or framed harmonic pattern, imposed a convention, acceptable to composer and audience alike, rather than a constricting strait-jacket of rules. 'Good breeding', in music as much as in the other arts, implied a shared education and shared expectations rather than an insistence on the personality or the eccentricities of the artist. In English architecture the principles derived from the study of ancient precedent and from the writings of the Roman theorist Vitruvius had dominated the style of the court since the time of Inigo Jones, but it was with the gradual triumph in the 1720s of the severer styles imitated from the works of the sixteenth-century Venetian architect, Palladio, that influential aristocratic patrons and the designers they employed found a common aesthetic language equally expressive of political and economic power and of the leisure and comfort to enjoy it. The linkage between what became an essentially Whig style and dominance of Whig politics is perhaps best evidenced in the dismissal of the ageing Tory, Sir Christopher Wren, from his official government post as Surveyor-General in 1718. Wren's dismissal effectively marks the end of the idiosyncratic English flirtation with the international baroque style. English Palladianism, with its emphasis on subdued good taste, balance, and a strict adherence to classical proportion, as opposed to exuberance, ebullience, and innovation, became the national style of the midcentury. The symmetry and order of English Palladianism, with its distant echoes of modern Venice and ancient Rome, became associated with the government of a liberal-minded oligarchy as opposed to royal autocracy. The baroque style suggested, on the one hand, the spiritual restlessness of earlier generations and, on the other, the suspect encroachments of continental tyranny in both Church and State. In its architecture, as much as in its politics and its literature, England took pride in being marked off from European norms and especially from those inspired by the centralizing tastes and the cultural and religious politics of Louis XIV of France.

English distaste for the policies of Louis XIV was not based purely on military and diplomatic opposition to French attempts to secure European hegemony or to the King's persecution of his Huguenot subjects; it was equally founded on the evolution of a distinctive theory of the government of Britain. By the 1680s it had become evident that the Restoration settlement had settled comparatively little in English and Scottish political life. James II, who had succeeded his brother as king in February 1685, managed, with a tactless ineptitude dangerously allied to religious arrogance, to alienate sections of influential opinion naturally loyal to the Crown. His attempts to secure toleration for non-Anglicans were received as an affront to the Church; his promotion of zealous Roman Catholics to positions of national and local power as an attempt to undermine the State. In June 1688 the birth of a son to the King precipitated events by provoking four Whig and three Tory peers to invite William of Orange to supplant his father-in-law and to deliver England from his royal oppression. On 5 November William landed at Torbay with a Dutch army, his fleet having been driven, it was fondly believed, by a divinely granted Protestant wind. William's rapid advance towards London was speeded by a ground swell of popular support in the shires through which he passed. King James's failure either to rally his forces or to take control of the immediate situation later led Gilbert Burnet, Bishop of Salisbury (1643–1715), to remark in his admixture of autobiography and anecdote, *The History of My Own Times*, that this was 'one of the strangest catastrophes that is in any history . . . A great king, with strong armies and mighty fleets, a great treasure and powerful allies, fell all at once'. James's escape from England at one o'clock in the morning on 11 December was deemed to mark the moment of his abdication of the throne. On 13 February 1689 William and his wife Mary, James's Anglican daughter, were declared joint sovereigns of England. The 'Revolution' had been bloodless; it was later also proclaimed 'Glorious'. The constitutional settlement which evolved in this period, and which was enshrined in the Bill of Rights of this same February, endured substantially unchallenged until 1829. A temporary expedient, designed to exclude James II and his immediate heirs from the throne and to secure a Protestant succession, was interpreted by generations of Whig commentators as a turning-point in the history of the British Constitution.

The Revolution and its subsequent legislation was designed to ensure the rule of law and the dominance of Parliament in England. In the northern kingdom in 1689 a Convention followed the English precedent in offering the Crown of Scotland jointly to William and Mary and in passing the Claim of Right. In 1701, however, when the Westminster Parliament voted for the Act of Settlement by which the English Crown was to pass to the House of Hanover, it was evident that Scotland would not automatically follow suit. The two kingdoms, united by Stuart inheritance but still divided by their distinct legal, religious, and parliamentary systems, remained mutually hostile. From 1705 onwards a terminal crisis in the relationship between the two nations and the two parliaments was averted only by a rare enough combination of diplomacy and vested interest on the part of the aristocratic agents of both sides. A Treaty of Union was drawn up which was extensively debated on both sides of the border in the winter of 1706–7 and on 1 May 1707 the 'Act for an Union of the Two Kingdoms of England and Scotland' came into effect. The Union made for the single kingdom of Great Britain with an agreed royal succession and a single national flag; it also united the parliaments into one and it opened 'to all subjects of the united kingdom . . . full freedom and intercourse of trade and navigation'. Scotland preserved her distinctive legal and religious traditions and won access to the lucrative trade with North America; England gained proper security on the island of Britain, free of the future threat of northern secession and of inconvenient or antagonistic alliances formed by its poorer neighbour. Thus an ideal of providential harmony, of co-operation, and of a political order reflecting that of nature seemed to many to be realized in the triumph of practical reason, liberal religion, and impartial law. Temperate kings would reign over a united nation in which individual liberty would be constitutionally guaranteed.

In many practical ways that ideal remained as much an illusion as it was a century before, more valid as propaganda or as an image of perfection than as an effective political or social fact. Real order proved to be as elusive in eighteenth-century Britain as in any other century. The intense political and religious passions of the Civil War may have gradually diminished but they were superseded by the equally fierce, if less bloody, antagonism of party and parliamentary faction. The years 1690–1725 are marked by some of the most urgent dialogue that the pursuit of high politics has thrown up in Britain and Ireland, and it was a dialogue which steadily drew committed writers into its vortex. Although Parliament passed a Toleration Act in 1689, 'their Majesties protestant subjects dissenting from the church of England' were, under certain conditions, freed from active persecution rather than actively 'tolerated'. Their Majesties' Roman Catholic subjects, unhappily regarded as the potentially treasonable tools of foreign powers, were still subjected to severe legal disabilities and, if not exactly harried, tended to retreat into political passivity. Such passivity does not, initially, characterize Anglican and Nonconformist apologists, as the divergent careers of Jonathan Swift and Daniel Defoe amply demonstrate. The fate of the talented hymn-writer and theologian, Thomas Ken (1637-1711), who persisted in maintaining his oath of loyalty to James II despite the change in regime, also suggests the force of the constitutional inter-relationship of Church and State. Deprived of his ecclesiastical office, in common with other nonjurors, Ken withdrew from public life, leaving the Church open to the increasing influence of a dominant political party rather than of the will of the sovereign. Despite often principled protests, the post-Revolutionary Church of England, becalmed by the arguments in favour of 'natural religion' propounded by the disciples of Locke and Shaftesbury, settled into a period of relative complacency as the willing spiritual arm of the Whig political machine.

As the two great Jacobite Rebellions of 1715 and 1745, the violence of the so-called Porteous Riots in Edinburgh in 1736, and the Gordon Riots in London in 1780 suggest, religious, political, or simply popular opposition to the status quo was not far below the surface. If the Edinburgh mob of 1736 demonstrated both a ready and anti-authoritarian sympathy with the gallantry of a convicted smuggler and, more worryingly to the Government, an antipathy to decisions made in London, the two risings in support of the exiled Stuarts provoked a more determined policy of repression. Both risings made clear the force of Scottish dissent from the new regime, but both also suggested the limited degree of disaffection present amongst the English gentry with Jacobite sympathies. Horace Walpole's letters of 1745, for example, exhibit by their unaccustomed brevity both an urgent, if temporary, concern over the threat of a combined Scots–French invasion and a genuine enough relief that the Pretender's army found neither an English rising in its favour nor that ill-led backwoodsmen could properly confront the professional army of a modern state. The failure of the Stuart cause in the eighteenth century became a matter of self-congratulation amongst those in England and Scotland who had invested in, or benefited from, the success of the Hanoverian dynasty. The incursion of rebellious Highland clansmen into Lowland Scotland and into the middle of England was a reminder of the existence of an alternative mode of government and of a distinct, if increasingly archaic, form of society.

The Gordon Riots, which devastated much of central London for a period of some six days in June 1780, provided culminating evidence of urban violence in the capital, the unreasoning violence of the dispossessed who had remained untouched by high-minded theories of order and symmetry. That the riots should have been occasioned by official moves to give relief to English Catholics also brought home the unabated force not only of bigotry but of 'enthusiasm'. The riots reinforced the steady awareness in eighteenth-century literature and painting that society, rather than being exclusively subject to orderly influence from above, was liable to disruption from below, and indeed that that disruption and anti-social behaviour remained endemic. It was not insignificant that, seventeen years after Captain Cook's first landfall on the unexplored eastern coast of Australia in 1770, the Government should feel pressed to colonize New South Wales by establishing a penal colony at Botany Bay for the convicted rejects of British society.

To see the culture of the period as exclusively a reflection of ideas of order and proportion is inevitably to see it partially, even distortedly. As the work of the most popular English painter of the age reveals, beauty did not lie solely in demonstrations of the grand style, in further refinements of classical precedent, or in an observation of nature according to Newtonian precepts. William Hogarth (1697–1764), who in 1745 painted an image of himself resting on volumes of Shakespeare, Milton, and Swift, saw himself as the pictorial heir to the dramatic, epic, and satiric tradition already established in English literature. In 1761 he added his own couplet to his satirical etching, *Time Smoking a Picture*: 'To Nature and your Self appeal, | Nor learn of others what to feel'. Hogarth's volume of aesthetic theory, *The Analysis of Beauty* (1753), had earlier attempted to define an equally personal concept of beauty according to a three-dimensional serpentine rhythm, arguing for the principle of intricacy in art. 'The active mind is ever bent to be employ'd', he wrote, 'Pursuing is the business of our lives; and even abstracted from any other view, gives pleasure.' This notion of 'pursuit' leads directly to a definition of intricacy or 'that peculiarity in the lines, which comprise it, that *leads the eye a wanton kind of chase*, and from the pleasure that it gives the mind, entitles it to the name of beautiful'. Hogarth's idea of 'intricacy', linked as it is to 'peculiarity' and 'wantonness' in the chase, manages to suggest a freer and less strictly regulated response to observed nature. The busy mind is stimulated by the diverse business of humanity, not simply by human pretensions to live out an elevated and rational image of universal order. Hogarth's most famous images—the narrative series showing the Harlot's and the Rake's progresses (1732, 1735) and the blighted marital relationship of *Marriage à la Mode* (1743)—achieved wide circulation by being distributed as engravings which, to cite a contemporary witness, 'captivated the Minds of most People persons of all ranks & conditions from the greatest Quality to the meanest'. These modern moralities show London fraught with temptation, indulgence, violence, murder, disease, and the consequences of selfishness; they chart declines not simply from prosperity to destitution but from innocence to depravity. When Hogarth shows us a paragon, as in the series of engravings charting the divergent fortunes of the idle and the industrious apprentices, he also hints at an immoderate degree of smugness on the part of his serene model of industry; when he paints criminals, as in his portrait of the triple murderess Sarah Malcolm in Newgate (1732/3), he can be as probing of the outward traits of character as when he considers the features of a worldly Whig bishop such as Hoadly of Winchester (1743). If Locke's *Two Treatises of Government* propose the ideal of a consenting civil society ruled by law, Hogarth's four depictions of a corrupt provincial election of 1754 observe both an inherent ludicrousness in the political process and the untidy energy of humanity. In the last picture, *Chairing the Member*, the newly elected Member of Parliament is both supported and effectively toppled by the vitality of embattled life swirling underneath his precarious chair.

Jonathan Swift

In a letter of December 1703 Jonathan Swift (1667–1745) described the activity of ten days of 'the highest and warmest reign of party and faction' that he had either known or read of. This particular period of fractious political and ecclesiastical manœuvring at the court of Queen Anne was concerned with the privileges and exclusive influence of the Established Church in national life, but it had had such a universal effect on the nation, Swift whimsically added, that even the dogs in the streets were 'much more contumelious and quarrelsome than usual'. Throughout his career Swift remained in part compelled, in part repelled by politics; he also remained fascinated by reflections of, and parallels to, human behaviour in the animal world. Swift was born in Dublin of newly settled English parents; he was educated according to Anglican principles in Ireland, and was ordained into the Irish Church in which he held benefices throughout his priesthood. He also consistently, but unsuccessfully, sought promotion in the better endowed sister-Church of England. If much of his propagandist writing is dedicated to the cause of Irish independence from English interference, and if he has also often been viewed as the quintessential voice of the eighteenth-century Protestant Ascendancy in Ireland, he seems steadily to have thought of himself as a stranger and an unhappy exile in the land of his birth. He was, however, equally awkward in identifying himself with England, or at least with what became the Whig mainstream of English politics in the latter half of his life. His writings—characterized throughout by a subtle ambiguity, by a troubled delight in oppositions and reversals, and by a play with alternative voices, personae, and perspectives—are intimately related to the deeply riven political, religious, and national issues of the Britain and Ireland of his time.

The severe disruption of Irish affairs attendant upon James II's attempt to rally Catholics to his cause in the summer of 1690 obliged Swift to seek refuge in England and it was in the house of the distinguished diplomat and essayist, Sir William Temple (1628–99), that he composed his effusively celebratory ode on the success of William III's expedition against James, the aftershocks of which still unsettle Irish history. Swift remained an adherent of the principles of the 'Glorious Revolution', convinced, as he expresses it in his poem, that William's 'fond enemy' had tried 'upon a rubbish heap of broken laws | To climb at victory | Without the footing of a cause'. If in 1702 he insistently declared himself still a defender of the cause of the Revolution, 'a lover of liberty' and much inclined to be 'what they called a Whig in politics', he laid equal stress on another principle of the post-1688 settlement, the supremacy of the Anglican Church. He was a High-Churchman, he told Lord Somers, and he could not conceive 'how anyone who wore the habit of a clergyman, could be otherwise'. These loyalties, like so much in Swift's career as a priest and a writer, steadily came into conflict with one another, driving him, without obvious incongruity, towards an espousal of English Toryism and the nascent nationalism of the new Irish Ascendancy. His spiritual and political adherence to Anglicanism is spelled out in a further product of his years in the service of Sir William Temple, the prose satire *A Tale of a Tub* (written in part perhaps *c.*1696, published in 1704). This story of the diverging tastes and opinions of three brothers who represent Roman Catholicism, Anglicanism, and Calvinistic Dissent, constantly seems to question its own shape through a use of multiple narrators and editors, through subversions, gaps, disjunctions, and long digressions on criticism, ancient and modern literature and, above all, madness. The core of the narrative, however, presents an effervescent attack on Catholic additions to, and Protestant detractions from, the fundamental doctrines of the Church, doctrines metaphorically expressed as a coat which the brothers alter according to the whims and fashions that they contortedly justify. The 'Anglican' brother, Martin, comes out, just, as the most vindicated of the three. The 'Author's Apology' prefaced to the work in 1709 attempts both to excuse its 'youthful sallies, which from the grave and wise may deserve a rebuke' and, far less tongue-in-cheek, to offer a clear celebration of the Church of England 'as the most perfect of all others in discipline and doctrine'.

This 'Author's Apology' concludes with the observation that 'as wit is the noblest and most useful gift of human nature, so humour is the most agreeable'. Swift's distinction between 'wit' and 'humour' is one which is too often glossed over by modern readers. It was a vital enough one in the eighteenth century. Johnson's *Dictionary* of 1755 defines 'wit' as both 'the intellect' and as 'quickness of fancy', attaching to this second definition a quotation from

Locke: 'Wit lying in the assemblage of ideas, and pulling these together with quickness and variety, wherein can be found any resemblance or congruity, thereby to make up pleasant pictures in the fancy.' For Johnson one pertinent definition of 'humour' entailed 'grotesque imagery, jocularity, merriment', and he illustrated this with a brief reference to Sir William Temple: 'In conversation humour is more than wit, easiness more than knowledge.' Swift had aspired to variety and to an intermixture of wit and humour, quickness of fancy and jocularity, both in *A Tale of a Tub* and in the satire on the pretensions of modern literature, *The Battle of the Books*, published with it in 1704. *The Battle of the Books* or, to give the allegorical squib its full title, *A Full and True Account of the Battel fought last Friday, Between the Antient and the Modern Books in St. James's Library*, originated as a complement to Temple's defence of classical literature as opposed to its modern vernacular rival. The real 'battle', fiercely fought over in the academies and salons of Europe, was once taken very seriously, not to say pompously, but Swift's allegory part ridicules, part supports the validity of the contention. In the midst of the dispute the animal-loving Æsop mediates between the claims of a pro-'modern' spider, who spins his dirty webs out of his own entrails, and a pro-'ancient' bee, who goes to nature in order to produce, in the now famous phrase, 'the two noblest of things . . . sweetness and light'. Although Æsop reaches a reasoned conclusion, his arbitration simply serves to heighten animosities. The consequent tumult spills over into a farcically confused disorder in which Aristotle tries to fire an arrow at Bacon and hits Descartes by mistake, and Virgil encounters his translator, Dryden, accoutred in a helmet nine times too large for his head. Dryden's attempts to soothe his opponent are diminished by the tenor of a voice which, 'suited to the visage', sounds 'weak and remote'. The published text of *The Battle of the Books*, purporting to be derived from a much-damaged manuscript, is broken up by *non sequiturs* and hiatuses and its end ends nothing, concluding as it does with an aborted new paragraph.

Swift's later satires play with the idea of a narrator who appears to have assumed a mask in order to strip masks from the men, the women, and the opinions which are the object of his attack. All draw more distinctly from his notion of 'wit' than they do from the ease of 'humour'. In a simple form, such as the early spoof, *Meditation on a Broomstick* (1710), he imitates the solemn style and manner of a primly pious moral essayist, but effectively undermines the tone of seriousness by the patent ridiculousness of the chosen subject (though the meditation is said to have taken in Lady Berkeley who, believing it was by her favourite author, Robert Boyle, remarked 'there is no knowing what useful lessons of instruction this wonderful man may draw from things apparently the most trivial'). The extraordinary force of *A Modest Proposal for preventing the Children of poor People in Ireland, from being a Burden to their parents or Country; and for making them beneficial to the Publick* (1729) stems, however, from the very reasonableness, arithmetical orderliness, and modesty of expression of what is effectively a monstrous proposal for the human consumption of the surplus infant population. The Irish dimension, which adds a special piquancy to the supposed argument of *A Modest Proposal*, reflects Swift's newly determined defence of Irish interests and sensibilities. *The Drapier's Letters* (1724) stem from a more obviously public and popular indignation at English indifference to Ireland. The five letters, purporting to be the work of 'M.B.', a Dublin draper, play on provincial pride and a specifically local grievance. The Draper's popularity with a wide cross-section of Irish opinion stemmed not simply from a general assent to his opposition to the relatively petty injustice which he addressed, but from a narrating voice which was carefully attuned to a broad audience: he is colloquial, mocking, denunciatory; he tellingly quotes Scripture as well as pertinent facts; he speaks in earnest and he occasionally rises to patriotic rhetoric when he knows that the rhetoric will hit home.

Swift's skill in selecting a voice appropriate to the form in which he is working is nowhere more evident than in his masterpiece *Travels Into Several Remote Nations of the World*, familiarly known as *Gulliver's Travels* (1726). Lemuel Gulliver is an English surgeon who rises to be a ship's captain; he is well-educated, proud of his national origins, and informed both professionally and politically, but he is essentially *l'homme moyen sensuel* and it is by means of his limitations that Swift scores his finest effects. In each of the four books into which his narrative is divided Gulliver is faced with the extraordinary. He copes efficiently, even bravely; he masters foreign languages and he observes and reports scrupulously, but he judges partially and, as his name implies, he is all too readily 'gulled'. He seems to be oblivious to the parallels between the pettiness of the affairs of Lilliput and Blefescu and those of Europe, and having stoutly defended the history, belligerence, and institutions of Great Britain to the king of Brobdingnag he seems unshaken by the king's trenchant conclusion that the bulk of Gulliver's compatriots appear to be 'the most pernicious race of little odious vermin that nature ever suffered to crawl upon the surface of the earth'. Gulliver is, however, both fascinated and shocked by ordure and the evidence of physical decay that he encounters. His tact in disposing of his own excreta in Lilliput and his practical (if offensive) means of extinguishing the fire in the royal palace have tended to be edited out of bowdlerized versions of the story, but his fastidious horror at the smell, skin, and hair of the Brobdingnagian maids of honour, and his alarm at the sign of a gigantic decapitation, are integral to his overall reaction to the disturbing magnification of the human form. In the third book he detachedly confronts both mental aberration and the terrible anguish of the Struldbruggs, condemned to an immortality of slow decay, a 'mortifying sight' which quells his 'keen appetite for perpetuity of life'. The first two voyages deal with physical disproportion; the episodic third largely with mental imbalance; the fourth serves both to replay themes of physical and mental disorder and to demand a reordering of all Gulliver's, and by extension, his readers' preconceptions. In the land of the Houyhnhnms it is clear from the beginning that Gulliver is unwilling to associate himself with the abominable humanity of the Yahoos by his constant reference to them in animal terms and by his all too evident disgust at their proximity to him. Nevertheless, his often desperate attempts to associate himself with real, if extraordinarily endowed, animals lead both to failure and to a mental state which can only be called aberrant. Though the Houyhnhnms have reason, stoic morality, sociability, and the outward signs of an advanced civilization based on qualities most admired by eighteenth-century theorists, they lack passion. In Lilliput or Brobdingnag Gulliver had quickly adjusted to the standards of the nations in which he found himself; in the land of the Houyhnhnms he passionately seeks to be considered an honorary horse rather than an honourable Yahoo, and it is this passion, a distorted, panicking reasonability, which leads to his final imbalance. In his voyage back to England he seems incapable of coming to terms with basic human goodness; at home he rejects human companionship and human relationships in favour of life in a stable where, he tells us, 'my horses understand me tolerably well'. Mind and body, reason and passion, seem to be angrily and disastrously disjointed.

Many commentators have wanted to see Book IV of *Gulliver's Travels* as a dark howl of rage against humankind, a howl which somehow echoes the gloom of Swift's own last years. His Latin epitaph in St Patrick's Cathedral in Dublin, composed by Swift himself, speaks of his final rest as relieving his heart from the laceration of 'savage indignation', but it also refers to 'one who strove with all his might to champion liberty'. To confuse Gulliver with his creator is to detract from Swift's greatness as a writer, a satirist, and a champion of liberty. The distaste for the human body and for female sexuality evident in the late scatological poems, such as 'The Lady's Dressing Room' (1730), 'A Beautiful Young Nymph Going To Bed', and 'Strephon and Chloe' (both 1731), may well be related to the intermingling of beauty and disease and the human and the animal form in Gulliver's experience but mere reflection does not make an equation. Swift's striving for liberty, unlike his Drapier's, is directed not purely at freeing Ireland from her temporary political oppressors but at opening the broad vista of real freedom, that of self-knowledge, independence, and responsibility to humanity as a whole. Swift's misanthropy (if such it be), unlike Gulliver's, is based, as he explained to Alexander Pope, on a 'hearty love' for individuals as distinguished from a general hatred for 'that animal called man'. That 'general hatred' stems from an indignation against a race which refuses to acknowledge the need for harmony, proportion, and a balance between its rational capacity and its animal instincts. A traditional theologian would also recognize that Swift, as an Augustinian, abhors all those human defects generally included under the definitions of sin as original, venial, and mortal. His picture of humankind suggests not simply the depravity inherent in the very nature of life after the Fall, but also the continuing indulgence in the consequences of the Fall unchecked by reasoned self-discipline, an altruistic morality, or divine grace. Swift's professed aim to vex the world rather than to divert it stems from a particularly demanding morality, one which is both more ancient and more excoriating than Locke's or Shaftesbury's pleasant faith in the ethics of rational sociability.

Pope and the Poetry of the Early Century

Swift's increasingly shrill denunciations of human self-satisfaction and self-confidence may seem ostensibly to stand apart from the scientific optimism of many of the literary propagandists of his time. His awareness of depravity and his urgent stress on a general human failure to live up to ideal norms of behaviour and to embody natural or divine harmony ought, however, to be seen as an integral part of the often rumbustious eighteenth-century satirical tradition. That tradition, which drew as much on Roman models as it did on the newly established authority of Dryden, reached its apogee in the poetry of Swift's friend, correspondent, and fellow outsider, Alexander Pope (1688–1744). But Pope's careful cultivation of poetic technique, his concern with precision and propriety, and his ambitious determination both to define and to refine the tastes and ideas of his age render him more than an exclusively satirical poet. His lifelong experimentation, his scrupulous revisions and recensions of his poems, his varied modes and forms, his 'imitations' and his translations steadily won him the broad respect of his influential contemporaries that his relatively humble Catholic origins initially denied him. His position in society and his vision of himself as an artist always remained paradoxical. Though he could complain as late as 1733 that 'Tories call me Whig, and Whigs a Tory', he seems to have moved into a firm sympathy with Tory politics because he found it congenial to stand to one side of the cultural mainstream. He used satire as his chief 'weapon' in a land full of what he saw as 'Hectors [bullies], Thieves, Supercargoes [merchants' agents], Sharpers and Directors', a land rife with political and economic exploitation. He railed against the corruptions of modern life and letters because he was goaded into speech by the shabbiness of his time-serving, second-rate rivals. Pope's satiric invectives are immediate responses to the almost universal acrimony of early eighteenth-century cultural discourse, but they consistently manage to outclass the often venomous provocations of his enemies, both real and imagined. Pope's poetry may be as splenetic as that of his rivals, but it has a range, a sophistication, an energy, and a precise delicacy which is quite unmatched by that of any other poet of his time.

Pope's career began with 'imitations' of those recent English writers whose work revealed a debt to the admired precedents of Greek and Roman poetry and which suggested 'the highest character for sense and learning'. If Milton's long shadow falls over all Pope's essays in, and variations on, the epic form, and if Dryden's carefully crafted couplets clearly inform much of Pope's apprentice-work, it was to the limpid poetry of Waller and Cowley that he first experimentally turned. He was not alone in looking to these particular models of Latinate chastity of diction and disciplined lyric form. Most prominent amongst the direct heirs of the Restoration court poets, and the one who rises most fluently above mere *vers de société*, is Matthew Prior (1664–1721). Prior's early collaborative satire on Dryden's *The Hind and the Panther*—*The Hind and the Panther Transvers'd to the Story of the Country Mouse and the City Mouse* (1687)—is a boisterous enough political poem, indicative both of a hostility towards 'drudge Dryden' and of a determined interest in current affairs (he later pursued a successful career as a diplomat). The long, gloomy, couplet soliloquy, 'Solomon on the Vanity of the World' (1718), on which Prior's reputation once rested, provoked even its erstwhile admirer, Dr Johnson, to confess, damningly, that 'tediousness is the most fatal of all faults'. It is, however, for his 'light' verse, for his wryly polished observations on love, and for his frank delineations of sexual approach, erotic negotiation, and amorous conciliation that Prior has been more recently admired. The gentle melancholy of 'To a Child of Quality of Five Years Old, the Author Supposed Forty' (*c.*1700), with its glances back to Marvell, is balanced by the bawdy narrative poems, 'Hans Carvel' (1701) and 'The Ladle' (1718), and by the pragmatic urbane analyses of sexual encounters presented in, for example, 'A Better Answer to Cloe Jealous' (1718) and 'An Ode' (1709). Prior's relaxed and almost colloquial elegy for his former housekeeper and mistress 'Jinny the Just' (written *c.*1708, but not published until 1907) celebrates the uncomplicated practicality of a working woman. It is an unfussy poem in triplets which mingles affection with sharp scrutiny, praise with a ready tolerance of idiosyncrasy—'With a just trim of virtue her soul was endued, | Not affectedly pious nor secretly lewd, | She cut even between the coquette and the prude'. 'Just' remains the operative word throughout the poem.

In advocating the use of a circumspect and refined diction in verse, a careful selection of metaphors, and a tidy couplet form in which the weight of the sentence often fell on the governing verb, the poets and critics of the early eighteenth century were attempting to prescribe a norm for poetry in English. When, for example, in 1704 Pope 'improved' on Chaucer's Merchant's Tale by paraphrasing, and when he 'versified' Donne's Satyres II and IV in 1713 (revised 1733), he was both looking back with a certain respect to earlier proponents of the couplet form and attempting to smooth out what he saw as the metrically awkward and lexically archaic. In both instances, he was also placing the paraphrased work of English poets beside his own couplet versions (or 'imitations') of poems by Homer, Ovid, and Horace. English vernacular poetry, he was implying, had come of age, purged alike of medieval archaism and 'metaphysical' quirkiness. The one mid-seventeenth-century poet, apart from Milton, whom Pope and his contemporaries unequivocally admired and actively imitated was Sir John Denham (1615–69). Denham, a vigorous supporter of Charles I during the Civil War, had not only saturated his pastoral meditation, *Cooper's Hill* (1642, 1688), with royalist sentiment but had also established what Dryden saw as 'the exact standard of good writing', a due obedience to decorum and a correctness of form, imagery, and vocabulary. *Cooper's Hill* set a pattern for loco-descriptive poetry in English, a poetry which celebrated place as much as politics, national associations as much as classical mythology. From his elevated viewpoint, the poet looks to the distant prospects of London and Windsor and down on the fields of Runnymede (where Magna Carta had been signed in 1215). Denham had, however, been concerned less with describing a landscape than with appealing to national sentiment and to patriotic good sense. The prospect from Cooper's Hill both inspires an advocacy of temperate kingship and melts into an Arcadian vision of a numinous England peopled with gods, demi-gods, nymphs, and tutelary spirits.

Denham's mode was much copied. His poem was quoted on the title-page of William Diaper's *Dryades: or, The Nymph's Prophecy* in 1713, and its structure clearly informs two further patriotic and local pastorals, Pope's own *Windsor-Forest* (1713) and John Dyer's *Grongar Hill* (1726). Diaper (1685–1717) is a far less dextrous craftsman than Pope, but his substantial and often extraordinary evocations of a subaqueous world of mermen in *Nereides: or, Sea-Eclogues* (1712), and his Virgilian prospect of an England rejoicing and prospering in the European peace which succeeded the Treaty of Utrecht of 1712 in *Dryades*, possess a formal, if sometimes artificial, charm. Pope's witty dismissal of an 'unhappy' Diaper (in the first version of *The Dunciad*) who 'searched for coral, but he gathered weeds' is less than generous (the couplet was deleted from all subsequent editions). Dyer's *Grongar Hill* is a work of particularly emphatic local piety, at once a panoramic tribute to his ancestral estate in Wales and a celebration of rural retirement. Dyer (1699–1757) is more concerned with the pleasures of a native landscape than with national politics, and his ascent of the hill overlooking the river Towy in order to survey the surrounding countryside inspires in him a sense of provincial contentment distinct from both the historic associations of the ruined castles he observes and the pursuit of power in the unseen, happily distant metropolis. Peace, he asserts at the end of the poem, 'treads | On the Meads, and Mountain-heads, | Along with Pleasure, close ally'd' and hears 'the Thrush, while all is still, | Within the Groves of Grongar Hill'. If the dispraise for Dyer's poetic investigation of the wool-trade in *The Fleece* of 1757 was once almost universal, it found a belated admirer in William Wordsworth.

Wordsworth was an equally convinced admirer of the work of Anne Finch, Countess of Winchilsea (1661–1720), a selection of whose verse had first appeared anonymously as *Miscellany Poems on Several Occasions, Written by a Lady* in 1713. Finch had found a comparable solace in retirement, albeit a retirement enforced on her by her husband's continued loyalty to the cause of James II. Her finest poetry stems from an appreciation of the seclusion of her Kentish estates and from a reasoned awareness of the distinctive role of an educated woman both within marriage and in a wider society. In writing of the natural beauty of her surroundings she aspired, she claimed, to 'soft and

Poeticall imaginings' akin to those of the 'mighty' Denham, trusting that her hand 'Might bid the Landskip, in strong numbers stand, | Fix all its charms, with a Poetick skill, | And raise its Fame above his Cooper's Hill'. As a writer determined to demonstrate that 'Women are Education and not Nature's Fools', she counters the stereotyping of women in poetry as sex-objects and mistresses by asserting the alternative dignity of married love. In 'The Spleen' she protests at the restrictions generally imposed upon women, restrictions flatteringly disguised as 'Good breeding, fashion, dancing, dressing, play', and she complains at the attitude of mind which insists that 'To write, or read, or think, or to enquire | Wou'd cloud our beauty, and exhaust our time'. Her poems of retreat seem to delight in a world where social restrictions and conventions become happily redundant. The 'Petition for an Absolute Retreat', for example, espouses the principle of a withdrawal into a shady, verdant privacy where 'unshaken Liberty' quietly triumphs. A similarly placid mood informs 'A Nocturnal Reverie', a poem which opens hauntingly with a reminiscence of the fifth act of *The Merchant of Venice* and which recalls, with precise satisfaction, the sounds and sensations of a summer night in a wooded garden with a working landscape beyond it. The night brings an undisturbed calm of mind 'Till Morning breaks, and All's confused again; | Our Cares, our Toils, our Clamours are renew'd, | Or Pleasures, seldom reach'd, again pursu'd'.

On one level, Pope's *Windsor-Forest* also rejoices in the diffuse spiritual permeation of a southern English landscape by the Olympian deities; on another, it moves far beyond an Arcadian vision to a painful recall of the English past and to various projections of a far happier military, commercial, and imperial future. The royal demesne is first seen as 'the Monarch's and the Muse's seats', a Parnassus enlarged by particular historical associations and modern royal influence, but its paradisal echoes are drowned by an evocation of the savage past, or, more particularly, by reference to the lust for hunting of the first builders of Windsor Castle, the Norman kings. Pope recalls an England laid waste by its invaders, and preyed upon by 'Savage beasts and Savage Laws' and 'Kings more furious and severe than they'. The carefully established contrast between these dead 'sportive Tyrants' (William I and William II) and the living, Stuart queen, Anne ('whose care ... protects the Sylvan Reign') may well be an indirect, Jacobite-inspired, hit at Anne's immediate predecessor, the unmentioned, 'usurping' modern invader, William III. Nevertheless, the vividly pictorial succeeding account of the pursuit of game in Anne's reign serves to suggest that hunting is now integral to the management of a working, fertile, and serene landscape. England is not only at peace with itself, but a greater destiny is opening to it. The last sections of the poem look forward to an energetic and triumphant exercise of power by the now united Britain, a power expressed in terms of a commercial hegemony in which trade replaces tribute and co-operation dispels subjection. It ends with a vision of a water-borne deluge of blessings in which the 'unbounded Thames shall flow for all

Mankind, | Whose nations enter with each swelling Tyde, | And Oceans join whom they did first divide'.

Pope's first popular success was a far less pictorial poem. *An Essay on Criticism* (1711) is an exercise in aphoristic verse discourse which presents criticism as a disciplined extension of common sense, clear-headedness, and neo-classical good manners. He adapted the mode in *An Essay on Man* (1733–4), an audacious attempt to illuminate and explain the premisses of contemporary moral philosophy in the form of popular and accessible verse. The four books that make up *An Essay on Man* variously explore the relationship of humankind to the Newtonian universe ('a mighty maze! but not without a plan') and they offer observations on human limitation, passion, intelligence, sociability, and the potential for happiness. Throughout the fabric of the poem, Pope lays an insistent, rhetorical stress on the concept of a pervasive order which links human beings to nature, creature to creature, and creature to Creator in a 'vast chain of being'. The epigrammatic quality of the verse has often, wrongly, led its detractors to suppose that the poem's tone is acquiescent and smug. If the now-celebrated, 'clear' summary of 'truth' with which the first epistle ends ('Whatever IS, is RIGHT') has all too frequently been condemned as an apology for philosophical and social complacency, this assertion has to be balanced against Pope's far from self-congratulatory observations on the dire effects of intellectual pride elsewhere in the poem. The perception of human ambiguity and human deficiency, neatly encapsulated in the description of man as 'The glory, jest, and riddle of the world', suggests the degree to which Pope the stringent satirist felt obliged to temper the confidence of Pope the optimistic, but often inadequate, philosopher.

The four *Moral Essays* of 1731–5 reveal a poet far less inclined to offer universal generalizations. The four Epistles are addressed to carefully selected figures; one of them, Martha Blount, was an intimate friend; the others, Lords Cobham, Bathurst, and Burlington, were prominent national figures or arbiters of taste. The Epistles are linked by a recurrent emphasis on the idea of balance, both within the personality and in public and artistic life. The first two poems deal with aspects of the passions, but in the third, addressed to Lord Bathurst, Pope shifts to an examination of the 'use of Riches' and in the splendidly inventive fourth Epistle to Burlington to a consideration of aesthetics. This last poem interrelates sense and expense, the rational harmony of the contemplative mind and architectural proportion. Burlington, the most gifted aristocratic proponent of Palladianism and a generous patron of the arts, is presented with a series of satiric vignettes which endeavour to expose the follies of excess. The central vignette is a fanciful account of a visit to the expensive vacuity of Timon's villa. 'Timon', whose name is derived from the Athenian voluptuary turned misanthrope, is a useful fiction. He is the flashy owner of a grandiose villa into which, as Pope sees it, moral and aesthetic errors are built. Its vast size, parallel to those of Wentworth Woodhouse in Yorkshire, and, perhaps more appositely, to Sir Robert Walpole's Houghton Hall in Norfolk and to the Duke of Chandos's Cannons in Middlesex, brings 'all Brobdignag [*sic*] before your thought'; its gardens, lakes, and terraces suggest unnatural waste and inefficient show; its vast and pompous interiors bespeak inconvenience. Pope's verbal and moral detailing are exact and telling. In its chapel, for example, a silver bell summons worshippers to the 'Pride of Prayer':

> Light quirks of Musick, broken or uneven,
> Make the soul dance upon a Jig to Heaven.
> On painted Cielings you devoutly stare,
> Where sprawl the Saints of Verrio or Laguerre
> On gilded clouds in fair expansion lie,
> And bring all Paradise before your eye.
> To rest, the Cushion and soft Dean invite,
> Who never mentions Hell to ears polite.

This pompous chapel, with its fashionable murals and its Handelian anthems, is quite up to date, but, as Pope subtly suggests by transposing the adjective 'soft' from the cushion to the obliging Dean, the values that it embodies have little Christian rigour. Timon's villa weighs heavily on its landscape, but, thanks to its very existence, its 'charitable Vanity' clothes the surrounding poor and feeds the hungry without actually intending to do so. Against Timon's example, Pope essentially poses the alternative principles of deliberation rather than accident, good taste and good sense, rather than waste and pretence. *An Epistle from Mr Pope to Dr Arbuthnot* (1735) equally catalogues a series of vexations and it attempts, with a new urgency, to define the nature of right action as opposed to wrong, good literature as against bad. The tone of the poem is initially more informal, but as it moves into embittered verbal assaults on personal and public enemies it develops into an indictment of a shabby and corrupt society from which the true artist remains detached and withdrawn. The *Epistle to Arbuthnot* splutters its protest with a controlled, disciplined, but none the less bitter wit. The specific objects of its attack, most notably Addison ('Atticus' who damns with faint praise, assents with civil leer 'and without sneering, teach[es] the rest to sneer') and Lord Hervey ('Sporus', a 'Bug with gilded wings' whose 'Eternal Smiles his Emptiness betray', and a Toad who 'half Froth, half Venom, spits himself abroad'), are perceived as symptoms of a general social and aesthetic malaise.

Pope's two most sustained narrative satires, *The Rape of the Lock* (1712, expanded 1714) and *The Dunciad* (1728, expanded and revised 1742–3), show the extent to which his savage verbal assaults on society and its shortcomings increased as both his reputation, and the objects of his acrimony, grew. *The Rape of the Lock*, ostensibly an undercutting of the 'dire Offence' which arose from 'trivial' things, takes on the weight of a criticism of the manners of aristocratic society as observed by an amused friend. His delight in domesticizing the epic and debunking the heroic is evident throughout. The mighty angels of *Paradise Lost* are diminished to the 'light *Militia* of the lower Sky', fluttering sylphs who complicate the amorous games played out by the human actors; the ceremonial arming of the heroes of Homer and Virgil is parodied in the description of Belinda at her dressing table, and the descent to the Cave of Spleen in Canto IV offers a sly and sexually knowing variation on classical visions of the Underworld. If, superficially, the poem undermines pomposity, on another level it serves to expose false or inverted values. It sees the relations between men and women reduced by social conventions to a battle in which beauty is a weapon and reputation merely a defence.

The Dunciad engages in a far less courtly battle for souls and minds, a battle with often equally trivial causes but with far more serious and universal consequences. The first version of the poem, in three books, established its antiheroic, mock-epic ambitions immediately by parodying in its own first phrase Dryden's translation of the opening line of Virgil's *Aeneid*. As completed by the addition of a further book and by a radical overhaul of the text in 1743, this parodic element was expanded by the introduction of an up-ended and debunked heroic triumph. The symbolic implications of an epic procession, shot through with those of the Lord Mayor of London's annual ceremonial progress from the City to Westminster, are overturned in a heterogeneous vision of the coronation of the goddess of Dullness, the patron of dunces and the destroyer of order and the intellect. The poem as a whole offers an apocalyptic vision of the dire consequences of the union of the shabby literary values of Grub Street, the money values of the City, and the corruption of the court and its ministers. If elsewhere in his verse Pope had attempted to uphold the ideals of reasonableness, good sense, and balance, here each ideal is overturned and the dunces come into their own. He is neither sparring with personal enemies, nor simply sporting with human folly; he is contemplating the threat of a final triumph of Chaos brought about by human ignorance and desuetude. Dullness is more than the 'Mother of Arrogance, and the Source of Pride', the genius of pride, selfishness, and stupidity, she is also the anti-*Logos*, the disorderer of a divinely tidy universe. The last lines of the poem shudder with horror at the prospective undoing of heaven and earth:

> *Religion* blushing veils her sacred fires,
> And unawares *Morality* expires.
> Nor *public* Flame, nor *private*, dares to shine;
> Nor *human* Spark is left, nor Glimpse *divine*!
> Lo! thy dread Empire, CHAOS! is restor'd;
> Light dies before thy uncreating word:
> Thy hand, great Anarch! lets the curtain fall;
> And Universal Darkness buries All.

In his earlier dialogue poem, the *Epilogue to the Satires* of 1738, Pope had responded to questions about his motivation as a satirist with the assertion that his provocation lay in the 'strong Antipathy of Good to Bad' and in his personal reaction to general affronts to 'Truth' and 'Virtue'. The fourth book of *The Dunciad* explores what to Pope and many of his contemporaries was the most provocative, antipathetic, and affronting of concepts, the wilful undoing of the Newtonian universe and the eclipse of rational light by the darkness of ignorance.

Thomson and Akenside: The Poetry of Nature and the Pleasures of the Imagination

When Isaac Newton died in 1727 James Thomson, already celebrated as the author of *Winter* and *Summer*, produced what is perhaps the finest of the numerous adulatory elegies written to the memory of the man who 'diffusive saw | The finished university of things | In all its order, magnitude and parts'. Thomson (1700–48), the son of a Scottish Presbyterian minister and a former student of divinity at Edinburgh University, had migrated to London in 1725. In the metropolis he had become a tutor at Watts's Academy, a popular disseminator of Newtonian science. His poetry consistently intermixed expressions of a delight in physics and optics, a pleasure in observing landscape, genial optimism, and the kind of vague but rational theology which drifts towards a creedless deism. Thomson is not a profound or original thinker. He is essentially an assimilator of current modes of thought, scientific, aesthetic, and philosophical, and a poet who found creative stimulus in a variety of received ways of observing both nature and society. *To the Memory of Sir Isaac Newton* exhibits a subdued rapture in contemplating natural law and offers a view of Newton's perceptions as outclassing the visions of both poets and philosophers. The body of Thomson's encyclopaedic, moralizing masterpiece, *The Seasons*, however, suggests a poet variously indebted to the model of the Latin pastoral, to the weight and rhythm of Milton's blank verse, to the social philosophy of that 'friend of man', Shaftesbury, and to the generally received theories of the so-called physico-theologians.

As is the case with many other long eighteenth-century poems, *The Seasons* grew in size and scope over some twenty years. It was systematically revised and reshaped over the same period. Its revisions reflect Thomson's growing awareness of an overall poetic design, a design expressive not simply of seasonal progression but also of a grander, overarching and all-inclusive natural order. *Winter*, first published as a poem of 405 lines in 1726, was expanded later in the same year and again in 1728, 1730, and 1744; the most substantial of the sections, *Summer*, of 1727, was steadily enlarged in the same years; *Spring* appeared in 1728 and, with the addition of Autumn, was republished with the earlier poems in a collected edition of 1730. The last edition of *The Seasons* published in Thomson's lifetime, that of 1746, which contains some 5,541 lines, proved hugely popular and, in its numerous translations, highly influential on other European literature (in a German version it formed the basis of Haydn's *Die Jahreszeiten* of 1801). The distinction of the poem was recognized as lying both in the diversity and didacticism of its meditations and in its relatively novel foregrounding of landscape. Thomson's particular response to landscape is conditioned both by his acute sensitivity to the effects of light (a sensitivity shaped by Newton's *Opticks*) and by his sense of the economic centrality of agriculture. The wonders of the divine order are implicit not simply in the detailed observations of the workings of nature and in imaginative evocations of diverse climates, contours, and tropics, but also in the frequent reference to the harmony established between human exploitation of the land and a divine plan for creation. Throughout *The Seasons* great emphasis is laid on the interrelationship, and not the conflict, of the interests of the country and the town; national prosperity is tied to pictures of agricultural well-being. Nature, the 'vast Lyceum', is a grand encircling theatre of education, but, as Thomson's frequent recourse to descriptions of happy, therapeutic walks in the rustic environs of London suggest, he is insistent on the co-operative functioning of civilization. London is in a sense framed by the working landscape from which its real fortunes are drawn. That working landscape is not simply that of the Home Counties, but includes all the fertile island of Britain.

As the opening section of *Autumn* stresses, human society has progressively evolved from a state of barbarity to one where it has become 'numerous, high, polite, | And happy', where there is a constructive balance of agrarian productivity and urban trade. Mercantile enterprise is confidently interpreted not as an interference with a natural organism but as the crowning achievement of the harmonious interaction of man and nature: 'All is the gift of Industry,— whate'er | Exalts, embellishes, and renders life | Delightful.' There is no room for noble savages in Thomson's landscapes; his retrospects and his prospects are equally conditioned by a sense of a modern civilization which is as inevitable as it is desirable. *Spring* concludes with a picture of a happy family compassed around by 'all various Nature pressing on the heart' and happily sustained by

> An elegant sufficiency, content,
> Retirement, rural quiet, friendship, books,
> Ease and alternate labour, useful life,
> Progressive virtue, and approving Heaven!

Thomson's choice of the adjectives 'polite', to describe human society, and 'elegant', attached to the idea of economic sufficiency, and his stress on retirement and the place of books in his account of family life indicate the degree to which he trusted to social as opposed to solitary virtue, to philosophy rather than to a creative impulse derived directly from nature. His responses to the natural world are related to the way it had been perceived by civilized and bookish observers. If the structure of the individual sections of *The Seasons* harks back to the intertwining of the pastoral, the patriotic, and the philosophical in Virgil's *Georgics* (the 'rural scenes, such as the Mantuan swain | Paints in the matchless harmony of song'), and if his idealization of individual figures in his landscapes remains both conventional and moral,

Thomson's wide-ranging reference and his evident interest in classification suggest his immediate debt to seventeenth- and eighteenth-century science. His frequent resort to periphrasis in, for example, differentiating between the 'wanderers of heaven' and the 'household feathery people' (wild and domesticated birds) or his references to the 'milky drove' (cows) and 'finny swarms' (herrings) should be seen both as a reflection of Latinate convention and, more importantly, as an attempt to suggest the place of each creature in the natural system. Similarly, the periodically expressed criticism of a supposed lack of method in each of *The Seasons* ignores the ordering principles dictated both by Thomson's reference to a tidy cosmic scheme and by the steadiness of his own tone. What might appear to be digressions concerning the extremes of the torrid zones of Africa and Asia in *Summer* or the excursive glimpse of Russian snows in *Winter*, in fact serve as contrived contrasts which point up the blessings of the temperate climate of north-western Europe. His paeans to philosophy and English learning and literature are attempts to place his own work in a national and international context; his play with colour and the effects of light are intended to reflect a vital force, and even the very order in which the poems were finally placed (from *Spring* to *Winter*) serves as an extended metaphor of transience and sequence in the created order. Newton's science had proclaimed the importance of sight as the basis of intellectual and imaginative speculation. Thomson's poetry stems from trained observation and a blend of the didactic and the descriptive. It offers a broad view of the ultimate rightness of things by exploring images of the vastness, the delicacy, and the multifariousness of the cosmos.

Mark Akenside's poetry generally lacks the fluid dignity of Thomson's. At its worst, his style can be pompous and sententious, and his most substantial work, *The Pleasures of Imagination* (1744, republished as *The Pleasures of the Imagination*) is, despite its title, more an essay in poetic grandiloquence than a persuasive discourse on creative visualization. Akenside (1721–70), a physician by profession, is at his best when he writes with restraint. His nocturnal ode 'To the Evening-Star' (published posthumously in 1772), though larded with classical epithet and allusion, has a certain elegant regularity and self-conscious serenity, qualities evident too in his modestly learned 'retirement' poem 'Inscription for a Grotto' (1758). *The Pleasures of Imagination* is a lengthy, discursive, and often rhapsodic celebration of the imaginative faculty. It moralizes more than it defines and it delights more in the 'complicated joy' derived from the contemplation of grandeur than it really attempts to unravel imaginative complexity. It parallels the philosophy of *An Essay on Criticism* and the inclusiveness of *The Seasons*, but it lacks the poetry of both. Nevertheless, the poem contains passages of real clarity and steady invention, notably in its excursion in the third book in which Akenside attempts to expound a series of ideas associated with poetic creation (lines 312–436) and when, in his fragmentary fourth book, he dwells nostalgically on his early memories of the valley of the Tyne 'when all alone, for many a summer's day | I wandered through your calm recesses, led | In silence by some powerful hand unseen'.

Other Pleasures of Imagination: Dennis, Addison, and Steele

The older critic, John Dennis (1657–1734), proved to be one of the prime irritants to Alexander Pope's spleen. In *An Essay on Criticism* Pope had generally alluded to 'Some [who] have at first for *Wits* then *Poets* past, | Turn'd *Criticks* next, and prov'd plain *Fools* at last', and had, more specifically, insulted Dennis under the name of Appius (one of the characters in his recent dramatic flop *Appius and Virginia*). Not one to take such comments placidly, Dennis replied with the equally provocative, but more unpleasantly personal, *Critical and Satirical Reflections upon a late Rhapsody call'd, An essay upon Criticism*. Pope took further revenge by adding a note to his own poem referring to 'a furious old Critic by profession, who upon no other provocation, wrote against this Essay and its author, in a manner perfectly lunatic'. The feud continued up to the time of the revised *Dunciad*. Such vituperative, tit-for-tat critical sparring was not untypical of the period. Regardless of Pope's venom, and despite serious temporary fluctuations in his reputation, Dennis the critic, if not Dennis the poet and dramatist, has remained modestly influential. He wrote with a blithe confidence in his own cleverness and in the correctness of the strict neoclassical principles he had espoused, but much of the continuing interest in his work lies in its novel concern with the nature of the Sublime (though Pope mocked his overuse of the word 'tremendous'). His essays on poetry, notably *The Advancement and Reformation of Modern Poetry* (1701) and *The Grounds of Criticism in Poetry* (1704), offer analyses of the processes of poetic creation and explore the idea of a creativity based in passion and emotion. Although Dennis insists that 'there is nothing in Nature that is great and beautiful without Rule and Order' he also speaks of the inspirational quality of 'delightful Horrour' and 'terrible Joy' and remarks that 'if the chief Thing in Poetry be Passion, why then, the chief Thing in great Poetry must be great Passion'. He was a convinced admirer of Milton and was one of the earliest writers to attempt a detailed, critical analysis of *Paradise Lost*. The *Three Letters on the Genius and Writings of Shakespeare* (1711) offer a more stilted, erratic, even blinkered, view of an admired poet. He is happy to attack the anomalies and the historical inconsistencies in Shakespeare's plays, and he is perturbed by what he sees as deficiencies in their 'design', but he none the less responds enthusiastically to the 'raising of terror' in the tragedies.

To Dennis's younger contemporary, Joseph Addison (1672–1719), writing in one of a series of essays on 'the Pleasures of the Imagination' published in *The Spectator* in the summer of 1712, Shakespeare's 'noble extravagance of fancy' thoroughly qualified him to touch the 'weak superstitious part of his reader's imagination'. Addison's criticism shows him to be fascinated by the 'very odd turn of thought required' for what Dryden had earlier styled 'the fairy way of writing', the delineation of imaginary or supernatural beings.

Although he classes 'the pleasures of the imagination' at a mid-point between the grosser 'pleasures of sense' and the refined 'pleasures of the understanding', he insists that his contemporaries should begin to question neo-classical critical prejudices and grant precedence to the workings of the imagination in the writer and the reader alike. He allows, for example, that the complementary insights of Newton and Locke had altered modern perceptions of the relationship between the observed object and the apprehension of the imagination. With Dennis, Addison grants that greatness in nature inspires greatness in art, but he goes on to suggest that though 'the works of Nature [are] more pleasant to the imagination than those of art' they are 'still more pleasant, the more they resemble those of art' and that, conversely, works of art are more pleasant 'the more they resemble those of Nature'. These interrelationships, Addison implies, are self-evident in an educated observation of creation. The imaginative faculty has been implanted in humankind by a loving Creator 'so that it is impossible for us to behold his works with coldness or indifference, and to survey so many beauties without a secret satisfaction and complacency'.

The 1712 essays on the imagination, and the notable series of Saturday essays on the genius of Milton of the same year, are attempts to refine public taste by offering short, reasoned, and accessible articles on ancient and modern literature. They also aim to interlink the study of literature with scientific theory, with recent developments in philosophical, political, and moral thought, and with the pervasive religious optimism of the period. Addison defines taste as 'that faculty of the soul, which discerns the beauties of an author with pleasure, and the imperfections with dislike'. In other words, 'taste' is the result of the refinement of a susceptible natural faculty. 'Conversation with men of a polite genius', he further affirms, 'is another method for improving our natural taste' and it was in the role of 'the polite genius', the embodiment of the refined spirit of the age, that he habitually cast himself. Addison, the self-appointed definer of cultural rules and cultural boundaries for a broad spectrum of society, consistently returned to the idea of inner assurance contained in his expression 'secret satisfaction and complacency'. This assurance was essentially religious in origin. It has all too readily been confused with an easy, spiritual smugness. Addison's is an amiable religion, dually founded on a sense of the just proportions of the observed world and on a projection of private justification. It elevates morality over faith and Newtonian physics over revelation; it prefers 'strong, steady, masculine piety' to the kind of 'enthusiasm' and 'zeal' which Addison all too readily related to the anti-social spiritual vices of 'Pride, Interest and Ill-nature'.

Addison was an insistent popular propagator of what he took to be 'the best ideas' of his time. In the tenth number of the highly influential daily journal, *The Spectator* (co-founded with Richard Steele in March 1711), he published what is virtually a manifesto of his aims: 'I shall be ambitious to have it said of me, that I have brought Philosophy out of Closets and Libraries, Schools and Colleges, to dwell in Clubs and Assemblies, at Tea-Tables, and in Coffee-Houses.' Clubs and' coffee-houses, both the subjects of *Spectator* essays, had proliferated in late seventeenth- and early eighteenth-century London. With the relative decline of both the court influence and a court culture they offered non-aristocratic male cliques an important focus for discussion and debate. These informal institutions never came to rival the salons of the French nobility as centres of intellectual life, nor did they ever serve to disseminate knowledge on the scale with which they were once credited, but their members did provide the kind of normative, influential model on which Addison and Steele based the assumed reader of their journals. The success of their assumption seemed proven in their calculation that each issue of *The Spectator* was reaching some 60,000 readers in London alone. 'Mr Spectator', who purportedly wrote these papers, was a man of broad education, well-travelled and politically alert. Around him there was gathered a small club representative of different aspects of modern English life, a club which included the Tory country squire (Sir Roger de Coverley), the rich, Whiggish, City merchant (Sir Andrew Freeport), the army officer (Captain Sentry), and the man-about-town (Will Honeycomb). Sir Roger's provincial idiosyncrasies are described with an amused tolerance intended both to divert a sophisticated London audience and gently to laugh eccentric Tory backwoodsmen out of their old-fashioned and benighted prejudices. The optimistic tone of the assumptions of 'Mr Spectator' is that of a thoroughgoing metropolitan supporter of the 'Glorious Revolution' settlement, though he rarely expresses a direct political opinion and generally prefers to avoid controversy. He interests himself in financial and international affairs, approvingly observing the actions and opinions of Sir Andrew Freeport at the Exchange and in his transactions in a London that has developed into 'a kind of emporium for the whole earth'. He is proudly patriotic, insularly confident about the opening future, and modestly progressive (though he tends to look down on women as frivolous, ostentatious, and ill-educated). Essentially he is Addison's ideal persona, the observant generalizer who seeks out the serenity of the middle way, the educated common man speaking directly to, and on behalf of, his less articulate fellows. He is the father of British journalism.

Addison's sometime fellow-student and later literary collaborator, the Dublin-born Sir Richard Steele (1672–1729), has often been unjustly relegated to a place in his shadow. Steele's professional life was complex, colourful, and often contradictory. If much that he wrote has failed to find a sympathetic audience in the twentieth century it is not for lack of variety. After a brief, but successful, career as a rakish officer in the Coldstream Guards he produced his worthy treatise, *The Christian Hero: An Argument proving that no Principles but those of Religion are Sufficient to make a great Man* (1701). The military life, he explained to his readers, was 'exposed to much Irregularity' and his principled tract was specifically designed to fix upon his own mind impressions of religion and virtue as opposed to 'a stronger Propensity towards unwarrantable Pleasures'. *The Christian Hero*, which steadily rejects stoicism in favour of Christian morality, found relatively little favour with Steele's unregenerate brother officers; its appearance had, he wryly noted, 'no good effect but that from which being thought no undelightful companion, he was soon reckoned a disagreeable fellow'. Perhaps stimulated by this social ostracism, a strain of missionary endeavour ran through much of his subsequent journalism. Steele's *The Tatler*, which ran from April 1709 to January 1711, announced itself as a journal that was 'principally intended for the Use of Politick Persons who are so publick-spirited as to neglect their own Affairs to look into Transactions of State'. It did not really live up to these ambitions, choosing instead, with Addison's help, to amuse readers with 'accounts of Gallantry, Pleasure and Entertainment'. The editor's literary persona, spokesman and earnest advocate of ethical propriety, Isaac Bickerstaff, was borrowed from Swift but in Steele's hands he becomes an admonisher of dissolute London, the checker of 'Rakes and Debauchees . . . Thoughtless Atheists and Illiterate Drunkards . . . Banterers, Biters, Swearers, and Twenty new-born Insects . . . the Men of Modern Wit'. As a contributor to *The Spectator*, Steele proved a censorious critic of the drama, putting down the moral excesses of the Restoration stage in favour of the soberer joys of Terence. It is scarcely surprising that Fielding's Parson Adams should have found Steele's own later comedies, such as the highly moral *The Conscious Lovers* (1722), 'almost sober enough for a sermon'.

Gay and the Drama of the Early Eighteenth Century

Of the scores of classical and modern tragedies, comedies, pastorals, burlesques, and adaptations of foreign plays written for the London stage in the first half of the eighteenth century only one, John Gay's *The Beggar's Opera*, has remained a standard repertory piece in the twentieth century. Although certain plays of the period retained both a high reputation as texts, and a popular appeal in performance, well into the Victorian age, their one-time fame has been virtually eclipsed by that of their predecessors, the sexually charged Restoration comedies, and by their immediate successors, the romantic comedies of Sheridan and Goldsmith. The dramatic work of Colley Cibber (1671–1757), the prime butt of Pope's satire in the fourth book of *The Dunciad*, forms something of a bridge between the licence of the Restoration stage and the soberer values advocated by Steele. Cibber's early plays may parallel those of Vanbrugh and Farquhar, but, as his *An Apology for the Life of Mr Colley Cibber, Comedian* insists in 1740, 'nothing is more liable to debase and corrupt the Minds of a People, than a licentious Theatre', a situation which, Cibber claimed, could be corrected only 'under a just, and proper Establishment' which would render it 'the School of Manners and of Virtue'. Largely through his example, first established in *Love's Last Shift* in 1696, a sentimental romantic comedy, shorn of harsh wit and rakishness, gradually emerged as an acceptable norm. Cibber's other comedies, notably *Love Makes A Man* (1700), *She Would and She Would Not* (1702), and *The Careless Husband* (1704), equally suggest a playwright determined to avoid coarseness and to proclaim the chastening merits of experience. His virtually unrecognizable adaptation of Molière's *Tartuffe—The Non-Juror* of 1717—is little more than an anti-Jacobite squib centred on the devilish plots of Dr Wolf. Cibber's tragedies, *Xerxes* (1699) and *Caesar in Ægypt* (1724), could be said to justify Pope's elevation of him to the throne of Dullness, but his once popular, if very loose, version of Shakespeare's *Richard III* (1700) suggests, by way of contrast, that he possessed a real grasp of melodramatic action.

Addison's once highly esteemed and financially successful venture into tragedy, *Cato* (1713), deals with the stoical principles of the Roman republican who determines to commit suicide rather than submit to the tyranny of the victorious Caesar. In the fourth-act crisis of the play, Cato prophesies that his son, sacrificed to the cause of the Republic, will not have died in vain: 'The firm patriot there, | Who made the welfare of mankind his care, | Though still by faction, vice and fortune cost, | Shall find the gen'rous labour was not lost.' This was precisely the kind of sentiment that assured the popularity of the play with those Whigs who sought historic justification for the Glorious Revolution that they had engineered in Britain. A similar proclamation of the patriotic virtue of liberty runs through Nicholas Rowe's tragedy *Tamerlane* (1701), a new interpretation of the triumphs of the all-conquering Tamerlane quite distinct from Marlowe's. Rowe (1674–1718) identifies his hero with the supposedly enlightened William III, casting him as a champion of liberty in opposition to the wicked machinations of Bajazet, all too readily recognizable as Louis XIV. Far more psychologically probing is Rowe's long-admired *The Fair Penitent* (1703), the story of the misfortunes of the 'false and fair' Calista and her seducer, the 'haughty, gallant, gay Lothario'. The play shifts away from the rhetorical flourishes and fustian declamations of established forms of heroic tragedy towards a greater delicacy of expression and a newly intimate exploration of complex and ambiguous relationships. This espousal of intimacy may well have been dictated by the more compact design of the new London theatres in which Rowe worked. Like his two later costume dramas, *Jane Shore* (1714) and *Lady Jane Grey* (1715), *The Fair Penitent* opened up heroic opportunities for a new generation of women actors and revealed a profound sympathy with historical women trapped in political or emotional situations over which they had little control. That Samuel Richardson should echo Calista's woes and Lothario's recklessness in his essentially bourgeois novel *Clarissa* (1747–9) is a tribute to Rowe's impact on the developing cultural consciousness of eighteenth-century women.

The comedies of Susanna Centlivre (?1670–1723) and George Lillo's domestic tragedy *The London Merchant, or the History of George Barnwell* (1731) suggest the degree to which the early eighteenth-century theatre responded to the values and preoccupations of the urban middle class as distinct from the manners and aspirations of an aristocratic or court culture. Centlivre had a notable professional success despite the dominance of the male playwright and the male impresario over the contemporary stage. Her sixteen full-length plays generally reveal an adroit grasp of stagecraft, character, and incident, but even the two fine late comedies, *The Wonder: A Woman Keeps a Secret* (1714) and *A Bold Stroke for a Wife* (1718), have received relatively little attention in the twentieth century. *A Bold Stroke* deals with the need for its heroine, Anne Lovely, to gain the consent of her four guardians to her marriage to Colonel Fainwell. The inventive Fainwell's impersonation of a preposterous Quaker preacher from Pennsylvania is finally exposed by the arrival of 'the real Simon Pure', an incident which gave a once-current phrase to the English language and established an archetype much exploited by later writers. George Lillo (1693–1739) created in *The London Merchant* a highly original, energetic, and dramatically powerful study of fatal obsession. George Barnwell, an apprentice to the London tradesman, Thorowgood, is seduced by a whore, and persuaded by her to rob his employer and finally to murder his own uncle. When the misdeeds of both are exposed, Barnwell earnestly repents, but his bolder, socially conscious accomplice goes to her death denouncing her accusers with the words: 'The judge who condemns the poor man for being a thief, had been a thief himself had he been poor—Thus you may go on deceiving and deceived, harassing, plaguing, and destroying one another. But women are your universal prey.' The play's urban victims, potential and real, are all endued with the kind of dramatic dignity associated elsewhere with noblemen. *The London Merchant's* celebration of bourgeois values, through the figure and sentiments of Thorowgood, and its moments of proto-feminist defiance, have an idiomatic directness which contrasts vividly with the rhythmical posturing of much contemporary heroic tragedy.

The work of John Gay (1685–1732) suggests a more general restlessness with inherited forms, heroic assumptions, and imposed classical rules. Gay's steady attraction to theatrical burlesque was probably accentuated by his close association with Swift and Pope in the informal grouping of the Scriblerus Club, a gathering of like-minded, and predominantly Tory, writers who were determined to debunk pretensions to 'false tastes in learning'. *Three Hours after Marriage*, a collaborative satire jointly written by Gay, Pope, and John Arbuthnot (1667–1735) in 1717, is rich in passages of *double entendre* and in caricature, both direct and indirect. Colley Cibber, who played Plotwell in the original production, is said to have only belatedly realized that his stage role was a comment on his own literary pretensions, while Sir Tremendous, whose plays raised 'the pity of the audience on the first night, and the terror of the author for the third . . . and have rais'd a sublimer passion, astonishment', was a dig at the old enemy, John Dennis. Gay's earlier comedy *The What D'Ye Call It: A Tragi-Comi-Pastoral Farce* (1715) had attempted to expose the falsity of heroic assumptions in drama both by mocking the diction of couplet tragedy and by suggesting the incongruity of the setting of its absurd play-within-a-play. *The Beggars Opera* of 1728 quite transcends the contrived silliness of these two earlier plays. Its continuing appeal to audiences may be due to its extensive borrowings of English folk and ballad tunes (originally introduced as a means of exposing the pomposity of contemporary Italian opera), but its real satiric bite lies in its exuberant reversal of political and moral values and in its undoing of conventional theatrical expectations. This so-called 'Newgate Pastoral', the theme of which was suggested to Gay by Swift, explores the corrupt ways of the criminal underworld while subversively suggesting parallels between them and the shady manœuvres of politicians. Incongruity thus becomes the key. If grand London society considered that its culture was enhanced by the posturing of operatic castrati, so Gay poked fun both at potent grandees and at the impotent objects of their admiration. To Gay's contemporaries, the character of the thief-taker Peachum (who is first observed 'sitting at a table, with a large Book of Accounts before him') stood both for the famous criminal Jonathan Wild and for that other arch-manipulator, the Whig Prime Minister, Walpole. The play consistently suggests embarrassing parallels between high life and low life. It represents the beggary, roguery, whoring, and thieving of the poor while implying that the same vices determine how power is manipulated by the ruling class. Power does not simply corrupt, it is seen as the stuff of corruption.

Gay's poetry has been comparatively neglected. *Rural Sports* of 1708 and *The Shepherd's Week* of 1714 suggest a writer experimenting both with the bucolic and with a burlesque commentary on Arcadian escapism and Arcadian moonshine (though he returned to Arcady in a more serious mood in his majority contribution to the libretto of Handel's *Acis and Galatea* of 1718). Gay's finest achievement in verse, *Trivia: or, The Art of Walking the Streets of London* (1716), abandons the pastoral in favour of a novel urban 'eclogue', a gentle reversal of the taste for rustic idylls. The three books of the poem abruptly shift rural conventions to the town and they wittily exploit the disjunction of a mannered verse and the essential indiscipline of London. They blend a lofty, Latinate solemnity of tone with detailed topographic observation. Trivia, the pretended goddess of the Highways, serves as a Muse leading the narrator through familiar mazes and hazards, from back lanes to thoroughfares, from day to night, from the underworld to the world of fashion, and back again to the raucous, untidy lives of tradesmen and hawkers.

Lady Mary Wortley Montagu

Until the closing decades of the twentieth century Lady Mary Wortley Montagu (*née* Pierrepont; 1689–1762) was chiefly celebrated by posterity as a pioneer of inoculation against smallpox. Lady Mary, who had herself been scarred by the disease, had carefully observed the technique of 'engrafting' in Turkey, had had her own children inoculated, and, once back in England, had, despite medical opposition, actively campaigned for the widespread adoption of the practice. The Turkish technique of 'engrafting' had also been described in her correspondence from Constantinople, written during the period of her husband's service as British ambassador to the Sublime Porte. This correspondence was published posthumously as her *Embassy Letters* in 1763. Since the appearance of the much amplified *Complete Letters* in the 1960s Lady Mary, who was an assiduous correspondent throughout her life, has an established reputation as one of the sharpest-witted and most polished of English letter-writers; she is also acknowledged to be a shrewd and innovative travel writer. Throughout her life Lady Mary was a determined self-improver, ever curious about new ideas and acute in her judgements of men, women, and manners. Even as a girl, as her earliest letters reveal, she rejoiced in the leisured seclusion that gave her the opportunity 'to passe whole days in reading'. As a precocious 13-year-old, having acquainted herself with a good deal of English poetry and drama, she taught herself the rudiments of Latin; a year later she assembled a manuscript album of her poetry, though she was prepared to plead for a prospective reader's indulgence of its shortcomings given that she was a woman who lacked 'any advantage of Education' and that 'all these was writ at the age of 14'. It is, however, her letters from her arduous journey across Europe to Constantinople, most of which were never actually dispatched to their addressees, that distinguish her as a writer. The letter form provided her with a means of frank self-expression. It also became a vehicle for shaping her vivid perceptions of people, politics, and events. Her correspondence shows her responding, with studied alacrity, to the rich, the strange, and the diverting. Writing of the Jesuit church in Cologne, for example, she claims to have found herself admiring 'the magnificence of the altars . . . and the enchassures of the relics' while murmuring at the same time, with due Protestant suspicion, at 'the profusion of Pearls, Diamonds and Rubies bestow'd on the adornment of rotten teeth, dirty rags, etc.'. Dropping such pious protests, she then whimsically digresses into coveting the pearl necklace decorating the bones of St Ursula and imagining the great silver image of St Christopher looking well in a cistern in her garden. At Adrianople, however, she begins to discover the fascination of the far greater 'otherness' of the Ottoman Empire. Here a hospitable and bibulous Turkish Bey proves to be delighted 'with the liberty of conversing with me' and she responds to his literary tastes with a new-found enthusiasm for oriental poetry ('I believe I really should learn to read Arabic'). It is, however, in Constantinople and its environs that she begins to revel in an idyllic way of life utterly distinguished from the English countryside in which she had been brought up:

The young Lads gennerally divert themselves with makeing Girlands for their favourite Lambs, which I have often seen painted and adorn'd with flowers, lying at their feet while they sung or play'd. It is not that they ever read Romances, but these are the Ancient Amusements here, and as natural to them as Cudgel playing and football to our British Swains, the softness and warmth of the Climate forbidding all rough Exercises, which were never so much as heard of amongst 'em, and naturally inspiring a Lazyness and aversion to labour, which the great Plenty indulges. These

Gardiners are the only happy race of Country people in Turkey. They furnish all the
City with Fruit and herbs, and seem to live very easily. They are most of 'em Greeks
and have little Houses in the midst of their Gardens where their Wives and daughters
take a Liberty not permitted in Town: I mean to go unveil'd . . . I no longer look upon
Theocritus as a Romantic Writer . . .

The dreamy pastoral of antiquity thus seems to this latter-day observer to be
realized in a modern market gardener's *douceur de la vie*. Like many of her aristocratic contemporaries, Lady Mary responded to those aspects of rural life
that reflected a received image of a simple country way of living which stood
in contrast to the civilized veneer of the Court. As she reveals elsewhere in her
correspondence, however, she was well acquainted with the sophistications of
courtly manners and more amused by, than averse to, the whims, vanities, and
ambitions of courtiers. Certainly, when she returned to England, her letters
took on a new edge. Sir Robert Walpole's England was decidely more venal
than it was Arcadian. As she remarked ironically to her friend Lady Mar in a
letter of June 1726, 'we insensibly begin to taste all the Joys of Arbitrary Power.
Politics are no more; no body pretends to wince or Kick under their Burdens,
but we go on cheerfully with our Bells at our ears, ornamented with Ribands
and highly contented with our present condition.' In this same letter, however,
Lady Mary recognized that she was not alone as a female epistolary observer
of modern upper-class life. She had been reading the account of the Court of
Louis XIV offered in recently published letters of Madame de Sévigné
(1626–96). 'Very pretty they are,' she remarked, 'but I assert without the least
vanity that mine will be full as entertaining 40 years hence.' At least one distinguished contemporary French critic, Voltaire, was prepared to agree with
her.

Defoe and the 'Rise' of the Novel

One theme in particular echoes through Daniel Defoe's great topographical
account *A Tour through the Whole Island of Great Britain* of 1724–6. That
theme is of pride in the steady and visible growth of the prosperity and well-
being of the newly united kingdom. When, for example, he arrives in Reading
he notes 'a very large and wealthy town, handsomely built, the inhabitants rich,
and driving a very great trade'; he finds Liverpool 'one of the wonders
of Britain' which still 'visibly increases both in wealth, people, business and
buildings'; Exeter is famous for its being 'full of gentry, and good company,
and yet full of trade and manufactures'; Leeds, too, is 'a large, wealthy and
populous town'; and Glasgow, since the Union of Scotland with England and
the consequent opening up of the Atlantic trade, has become 'the cleanest
and beautifullest and best built city in Britain, London excepted'. Defoe's
evident satisfaction at this evidence of national economic success is not

confined to the market towns of the south and the burgeoning manufacturing cities of the north, though it does tend to emphasize urban activity as opposed to agricultural enterprise. The view of London from its southern suburbs obliges him to seek for superlatives. London offers 'the most glorious sight without exception, that the whole world at present can show, or perhaps could ever show since the sacking of Rome in the European, and the burning the Temple of Jerusalem in the Asian part of the world'. As his *Tour* steadily reveals, Defoe is an informed, scrupulous, and sometimes boastful observer of an expanding nation, but he is systematically drawn back, both in imagination and in fact, to the magnet of his native London. London is his reference point and the gauge by which he measures the quality of the trade, the expanding merchant class, and the new architectural development of the provinces.

The claim made by successive generations of literary historians and critics that Defoe (1660–1725) is the first true master of the English novel has only limited validity. His prose fiction, produced in his late middle age, sprang from an experimental involvement in other literary forms, most notably the polemic pamphlet, the biography, the history and, latterly, the travel-book. His novels included elements of all of these forms. Nor was he the only begetter of a form which it is now recognized had a long succession of both male and female progenitors. He may, in *Robinson Crusoe* (probably his 412th work), have perfected an impression of realism by adapting Puritan self-confession narratives to suit the mode of a fictional moral tract, but he would in no sense have seen that he was pioneering a new art form. Nor would he necessarily have seen fiction as superior to, or distinct from, his essays in instructive biography such as his lives of Peter the Great and Duncan Campbell, the deaf and dumb conjuror. Defoe was merely mastering and exploiting a literary form of various and uncertain origins. He would probably not have recognized the kinship to his own fiction of *Crusoe*'s vast and diverse progeny.

That the art of prose fiction developed prodigiously in the years 1720–80, and that its potential as both instructor and entertainer was readily recognized by a new body of largely middle-class readers, are matters of little debate. Defoe's fascinated awareness of the increase in the population and the prosperity of Britain in the years following the 'Glorious Revolution' and the Act of Union can be related to his responsiveness to the immediate audience for his books. As a mercantile and manufacturing class grew, so, concomitantly, did literacy and leisure. The wives and daughters of tradesmen were rarely employed in any form of business; their marginally better educated sisters in the professional classes and the provincial gentry were equally likely to have a good deal of enforced leisure. Those readers who had been alienated from courtly styles either by an inherited Puritan earnestness or by the simple fact of their social class and education, proved particularly receptive to an easily assimilated, but morally serious, 'realist' literature. If heroic prejudices were gradually rejected in the theatre by self-assured metropolitan audiences permeated by commercial, professional, and ethical codes of value, so the English novel appears to have developed in response to a demand for a new kind of literature which emphasized the significance of private experience. It cannot be argued that the central characters in the novels of the first half of the century are drawn exclusively from the middle classes, but few are aristocrats and none are monarchs. Tyranny and murder are domesticated; usurpation is replaced by disputes over title-deeds, entails, and codicils; courtship and marriage become affairs of the heart not of the state, and the death-bed enters the English novel as death on the battlefield exits. Even the panoply of the funeral, a major concern of Richardson's dying Clarissa, is democratized.

Defoe's long experience of the vagaries of official censorship and the book-trade clearly stood him in good stead when he began a vigorous new phase in his career with *The Life and Strange Surprizing Adventures of Robinson Crusoe* in 1719. The earlier stages of his career are marked by abrupt twists and entanglements which took him from his respectable origins as a Presbyterian tradesman in London, through an active espousal of the doomed rebellion of the Duke of Monmouth and the more propitious cause of William of Orange, to employment as a government spy. His first literary success, *The True-Born Englishman* (1701), an anti-xenophobic plea for the acceptance of a foreign king and his Dutch friends, was overshadowed by the reaction to the transparently ironic pamphlet *The Shortest Way with the Dissenters* (1702). Having attempted to win sympathy for his Dissenting co-religionists, in a particularly volatile political atmosphere, with the hyperbolical argument that Dissenters should simply be exterminated, Defoe found himself the immediate object of state persecution. His pamphlet was publicly burned and its author imprisoned and exposed in the pillory. After a period as founder of, and chief contributor to, the thrice-weekly newspaper *The Review* (from 1704), he became an undercover agent for the Government, monitoring Scottish responses to the proposed Union. This Scottish episode provided material both for his *Tour* and for his *History of the Union* of 1709. *Robinson Crusoe* differs from most of Defoe's earlier works in that it represents private moral zeal rather than a public plea for reform; propaganda it may be, but its emphasis is on spiritual rather than on political justice. Robinson Crusoe 'of York, Mariner' gives over only some two-thirds of his narrative to his life on his desert island, but the account of those twenty-eight years forms the most compelling section of his memoirs. He is an ideal choice of narrator given the extraordinary nature of his experiences. Crusoe is 'of good family' and because of his sound education 'not bred to any trade'. His decision to go to sea is an act of rebellion, determined on in defiance to both his mother and his father, and from it he traces his withdrawal from grace and his embarkation on the slow, painful redemptive journey back to a state of grace. Although Crusoe's self-exploratory time on his island, his cultivation of the land and of his soul, and his later imposition of his codes of belief and action on Friday, have frequently been interpreted as a fictional enactment of the processes of European colonization, his story has both a particular and a more universal application. When his island is 'peopled' by Friday and by Friday's father and a Spanish sailor (both of them rescued from the cannibals) Crusoe thinks of himself as a king with 'an undoubted right of dominion', an 'absolute Lord and Law-giver'. As such, however, he establishes a principle which many contemporary Europeans would have regarded as offensively radical: a 'Liberty of Conscience' which tolerates pagan, Protestant, and Catholic alike. It was not a principle that was fully established in contemporary Britain. More significantly, Crusoe's earlier heroism is that of the ordinary human will pitted against an alien environment; as far as he can, he brings his surroundings under his rational and practical control not as a proto-colonist but as a lonely exile. He records his experiences and his achievements meticulously, even repetitively, because he is logging the nature of his moral survival. He is the methodical diarist delighted both by his own resourcefulness and by his awareness that a benign God helps those who help themselves.

Crusoe's *Further Adventures*, published later in the same year, do not live up to the promise of the earlier volume. Defoe's cultivated ease in exploiting the first-person narrative form, as an imitation either of a journal or of confessional memoirs, is, however, evident in the flood of fiction he published between 1720 and 1724. Both *The Fortunes and Misfortunes of the Famous Moll Flanders* (1722) and *The Fortunate Mistress* (generally known as *Roxana*) (1724) have much-abused, belatedly penitent, entrepreneurial women as narrators. Moll, born in prison, zestfully and practically recounts her dubious liaisons with husbands, lovers, and seducers, and her progress through thievery to transportation to Virginia and final financial and emotional happiness. Hers is a difficult, but none the less upward, social and moral progress which contrasts sharply with that of the *demi-mondaine* heroine of the Abbé Prévost's *Manon Lescaut* (1731). If Moll's memoirs somewhat awkwardly suggest a rather too meticulous retrospect on a period of personal disorder, those of Roxana reveal a duller process of self-description. Roxana declines from respectability, partly through the disgraceful treatment meted out to her by the men on whom she relies, partly through her own, highly selfish, sense of self-preservation. When she announces in her Preface that 'all imaginable Care has been taken to keep clear of Indecencies, and immodest Expressions' we sense not only the impact of her soundly Protestant penitence but also that her narrative might be disappointingly elusive and unspecific. The *Adventures of Captain Singleton* (1720) describes the career of a seafarer, initially possessed of 'no sense of virtue or religion', who becomes both mutineer and pirate before discovering the virtues of religion, honest money, and marriage. It is a restless and untidy book but its account of a fraught journey across central Africa gives it many of the qualities of an adventure story. Defoe's announcement in the Preface to *Moll Flanders* that 'The Fable is always made for the Moral, not the Moral for the Fable' equally applies to *The History of the Remarkable Life of the truly Honourable Colonel Jacque* (commonly called *Colonel Jack*) (1722). Jack's struggles as a child pickpocket in the disorienting and claustrophobic slums of London are described with an almost Hogarthian intensity, an intensity which is strangely dissipated as his experience of the world widens. Much of the problem lies in the narrator's apparent unease with the sins in which he indulges and the consequent pressure to mould the fable as evidence of the ultimate moral. Nevertheless, as Jack himself acknowledges at the end of his narrative, 'Perhaps, when I wrote these things down, I did not foresee that the Writings of our own Stories would be so much the fashion in *England*, or as agreeable to others to read, as I find Custom, and the Humour of the Times has caus'd it to be'. 'One private mean Person's Life', he adds, 'may be many ways made Useful, and Instructing to those who read them, if moral and religious Improvement, and Reflections are made by those that write them.'

Defoe's two remarkable 'historical' narratives can be said to have preempted, in some significant ways, the development of the nineteenth-century historical novel. Both *A Journal of the Plague Year* (1722) and *Memoirs of a Cavalier* (1724) are triumphs of the exercise of the historical imagination. The pretended author of the *Memoirs of a Cavalier*, Colonel Andrew Newport, is a gentleman officer, first in the German campaigns of the Swedish king, Gustavus Adolphus, during the Thirty Years War and latterly in the service of Charles I during the English Civil War. His descriptions of the siege and sack of Magdeburg and of the battles of Edgehill and Naseby are deliberate and often flatly descriptive (a proper failing, perhaps, in a soldier narrator), but a good deal of the interest of the narrative lies in the distinction Newport draws between his deep loyalty to the person of Gustavus Adolphus and the Protestant cause and his evident lack of fervour for the alliance of Church and King in England. As a rare enough gentleman narrator in Defoe's work, his moments of disillusion reveal him to be drawn more by the obligations of his class than by personal conviction. *A Journal of the Plague Year*, 'observations or memorials of the most remarkable occurrences, as well public as private, which happened in London during the last great visitation in 1665', purports to be written 'by a Citizen who continued all the while in London'. Though no one in Defoe's London realized it, the threat of the return of an epidemic of bubonic plague had largely receded in the eighteenth century. The book was nevertheless intended to serve both as a warning to the present and as an example of endurance and spiritual reassessment in the recent past. The constant citizen observes, records, and analyses; he is both ignorant of causes and disturbed by effects. His account is at once a series of anecdotes and an attempt at computation, but it also works as the narrative of an insider, and as the speculation of 'one private mean Person' faced with an incomprehensible public problem.

The citizen preaches Christian comfort and wonders at the nature of the divine visitation, but he also observes examples of Christian charity in some of his fellow-citizens and patently irreligious self-seeking in others. Despite its occasional randomness and the *longueurs* of its detailing, *The Journal of the Plague Year* remains a remarkable innovatory fictional experiment, an almost disconcerting interplay of voices and statistics, of facts and impressions.

The Mid-Century Novel:
Richardson, the Fieldings, Charlotte Lennox

The novels of Henry Fielding (1707–54) and Samuel Richardson (1689–1761), written in the 1740s, form what Richardson himself called 'a new species of writing'. They do not so much reject the autobiographical model established by Defoe as amplify and finally supersede it. Writing in *The Rambler* in 1750, Dr Johnson spoke of works of fiction which 'are such as exhibit life in its true state, diversified only by accidents that daily happen in the world, and influenced by passions and qualities which are really to be found in conversing with mankind'. The 'heroick romance', Johnson implied, was now dead and in its place there had sprung up a new prose fiction whose province was 'to bring about natural events by easy means, and to keep up curiosity without the help of wonder'. The fiction of the 1740s was ample both in its design and in its appeal. The phenomenal popularity of Richardson's work with readers at home and abroad is well attested. His *Pamela* (the first two volumes of which appeared in 1740) ran through six London editions in its first year of publication and was celebrated by parodies, by an early French translation and, in 1744, by a place on the Vatican's *Index* of prohibited books (where it remained until 1900). *Clarissa* (1747–9) also reached a large European audience in its edited French translation of 1751 (the work of the Abbé Prévost) and through versions in the German and Dutch languages. It was honoured by a fulsome eulogy from Diderot and by the unstinted praise of Rousseau. The ready availability of often expensive novels to the British reading public had been promoted in 1716 by the establishment in Edinburgh of the first circulating library, a move followed in London only in 1740. These circulating libraries, supported by subscribers, rapidly spread to most of the major towns of Britain in response to the needs of those who did not necessarily want to own books and of those who could not afford to do so. New literature in general, and novels in particular, circulated, for a moderate fee, amongst a wide range of readers and the popularity of a book with the customers of a library became, for some two subsequent centuries, a mark of true commercial success and a measure of its popular esteem. The libraries also helped to consolidate national taste by dissolving certain provincial and class distinctions in literature. When that great letter-writer, pioneer feminist, and intellectual snob, Lady Mary Wortley Montagu, remarked of *Pamela* that it had become 'the joy of chambermaids of all nations', she was not merely denigrating Richardson's achievement; she was also paying an indirect tribute to the classless appeal of a new art form.

Richardson came to fiction by an unpredictable route. He was a self-educated London tradesman with little practical knowledge of what would have been called at the time 'polite' society or of 'elegant' literature. He had been apprenticed at the age of 16 to a printer and had risen, by a steady application worthy of Hogarth's industrious apprentice, to two successive marriages to the daughters of former employers and, in 1753, to the Mastership of the Stationers' Company. He confessed in later life that as a boy he had stolen times for the improvement of his mind 'from the hours of Rest and Recreation' granted by a master who grudged them to him. He also took care to buy his own candles 'that I might not in the most trifling instance make my master a sufferer'. If his disclosure sounds more than a little Heepish, his claim to have been in correspondence with a gentleman, greatly his superior in degree, 'and ample of Fortunes, who had he lived, intended high things for me', offers clues as to the nature of Richardson's later fascination with class. In no sense, however, is he a social or moral iconoclast. As a printer and publisher in the 1730s he had been instrumental in the reissue of several of Defoe's works, but his own first publication *The Apprentice's Vade Mecum or Young Man's Pocket Companion* of 1733 is little more than a handbook of ethics for the aspirant lower middle class. The impetus to turn to fiction came, by his own admission, through a commission to write a further manual, a series of 'familiar letters' concerning the problems and circumstances of everyday life which could serve as models to prospective correspondents. Richardson provided ideal letters of consolation, excuses for not lending money, and formal recommendations for wet-nurses and chambermaids, but amongst them he included some seven letters developing the story of a virtuous servant-girl, embarrassed by the sexual attentions of her master, who finally succeeds in marrying her sometime persecutor. *Pamela; or Virtue Rewarded* sprang directly from this recall of the kind of true story likely to appeal to a self-made man with, what some might see as, a prurient concern with sexual rectitude. *Pamela* was not the first epistolary novel (there seem to have been some hundred earlier novels and stories told in the form of letters) but it proved the most influential. Pamela's story is told partly through long missives to her worthy parents and, when letters become difficult to send, partly through her recourse to her journal. Unlike Robinson Crusoe's, Colonel Jacque's, or Moll Flanders's ostensibly public and retrospectively instructive memoirs, Pamela's letters are private and immediate and a reader of them becomes something of an intruder into her confessions. The reward for Pamela's virtue is the respect, and ultimately the love, of her erstwhile employer, Mr B., but the slow process of the winning of this reward has, from the beginning, persuaded certain of her readers to see her as a calculating hypocrite and an upwardly mobile self-seeker well aware of the marital price of her virtue. These problems are only partly dispelled within a narrative charged with frustrated sexuality and with the mutual incomprehension of master and servant, man and woman. At a mid-point Pamela can complain to her parents that 'poor people are despised by the proud and rich' and that 'we were all on a footing originally: and many of those gentry, who brag of their ancient blood, would be glad to have it as wholesome and as *really* untainted as ours'. It is both a proclamation of democratic principle and an admission of deference. A similar ambiguity lies at the heart of her proud declaration to Mr B. in Letter XXIV that she is 'Pamela, indeed I am: indeed I am Pamela, *her own-self!*' Despite Richardson's concern with the independence of the individual throughout his work, and despite the moral ennoblement that Pamela finally receives, selfhood, in Richardson's first novel at least, is defined largely through what his heroine is not.

Similar charges cannot be brought against Richardson's masterpiece, the huge but meticulously shaped *Clarissa: or, The History of a Young Lady*. The novel has four major letter-writers, Clarissa Harlowe and her friend Anna Howe, Lovelace and his friend John Belford, and, beyond these four, a host of minor correspondents or note-writers, perceptive and myopic, involved and detached, fluent and semi-literate. *Clarissa* is not merely multi-voiced, it also exploits the narrative potential of multiple viewpoints. If this multiplicity might seem to threaten to explode all attempts at imposed order, Richardson counters this explosive potential with a deliberate chronological discipline. Anna Howe's short opening letter to Clarissa both expresses concern 'for the disturbances that have happened in your Family' and announces a major theme. Although the novel appears to begin *in medias res*, with the news of a duel and 'public talk' of the affair, Anna's letter, which is dated 10 January, is essentially the initiator of a 'private' expository process which stretches over nearly twelve months and which follows the cycle of the seasons. Clarissa is forced to escape from her home and from an unwanted marriage in spring; she is drugged and raped by her supposed 'deliverer', Lovelace, on Midsummer Night; she dies in December and her death is followed by the fatal wounding of Lovelace in a second duel.

The Harlowes are a successful landed family with recent connections to the City of London. The family is poised for further social promotion if the problem of the dowries of Clarissa and her elder sister can be disposed of; Clarissa's marriage to the physically repulsive, rich, if 'upstart', Mr Solmes therefore seems desirable to all except the prospective bride. Money, class, and competition thus lie at the heart of the manœuvres which serve gradually to isolate Clarissa from her self-seeking family; she is the object first of jealousy, then of personal and economic rancour, finally of active persecution. Her response is to assert her moral integrity as a defence against antipathy and marginalization. The novel's full title asserts that the story will show 'the Distresses that may attend the Misconduct both of Parents and Children, in Relation to Marriage'. This principle is returned to in the Preface (added later) where parents in general are cautioned against 'the undue exercise of their natural authority over their children in the great article of marriage' and, more significantly, women are warned against preferring a man of pleasure to a man of probity 'upon that dangerous but too commonly received notion that a reformed rake makes the best husband'. The novel consistently demonstrates how authority and power are misused, both by parents and lovers. Although Clarissa is the victim of parental strictures, sibling rivalry, and the physical and spiritual abuse of her lover, she emerges as a model of discretion and conscience and she endures her slow martyrdom with patience and intelligence.

She is the first great bourgeois heroine and the first female Protestant saint of fiction. Her seeming protector, her would-be lover, and her diabolically gifted antagonist, Lovelace, is a direct descendant of the aristocratic rakes of Restoration drama. He rejoices in plots, hunts, stratagems, and sieges and he clearly derives a satisfaction from his admission to Belford that 'I love, when I dig a pit, to have my prey tumble in with secure feet and open eyes: then a man can look down upon her, with an, *O-ho, charmer! how came you there?*' Each assault upon the captive Clarissa demands new invention and new ruses; he supposing that she really, if secretly, desires him; she slowly gaining the tragic awareness that she has partly brought ruin on herself. Richardson's skill also lies in his tense, essentially pre-Freudian, perception that attraction and repulsion are not polar opposites in the emotions. Clarissa confesses to Anna Howe that 'men of [Lovelace's] cast are the men that our sex do not *naturally* dislike' and that she could indeed have liked him 'above all men'. As she further acknowledges, 'like and dislike as reason bids us' is not easily practised. Clarissa's emotions as much as her body are violated by Lovelace. The letters which succeed her rape show her reduced to a traumatized incoherence, to anecdotal or fabular attempts to grasp at meaning, and a whole range of typographical devices, dashes, asterisks, and printer's flowers suggest the degree to which her manuscripts are disturbed. When after a long-drawn-out death her last hours and her pious last words are witnessed by the now penitent Belford, further textual disjunctures and lacunae indicate the intensity of his emotional involvement. Clarissa dies a Christian death, having rediscovered the meaning of her sufferings. The narrative, which had opened with Anna Howe's reference to a duel between Clarissa's brother James and Lovelace, comes full circle with a further duel in which Lovelace is mortally wounded. He dies painfully, pronouncing the words 'LET THIS EXPIATE!'

Richardson's third epistolary novel, *The History of Sir Charles Grandison* (1754), never satisfyingly emulates the tensions or sustains the anxieties so powerfully evoked in *Clarissa*. Its principal shortcoming lies in the character of its protagonist, the 'Good Man' about whom the novelist's friends had urged him to write. The novel begins promisingly with the world of high society opening to an *ingénue* (a theme which attracted Fanny Burney later in the century) but it is marred once the priggish virtue of Grandison breathes its petrifying breath over the narrative. The former *ingénue*, Harriet Byron, is rescued from an attempted abduction at the hands of yet another rake by the upright Sir Charles, and she in turn proves instrumental in lovingly delivering him from the complications of an amatory obligation to an Italian, and worse, Catholic, lady. Everything remains deadeningly proper. *Grandison*'s strengths lie in its relatively fast movement and in its occasionally successful social comedy but these are not merits which sufficiently redeem it in the eyes of its many detractors (though it was admired above Richardson's other novels by both Jane Austen and George Eliot).

Henry Fielding, an early and contemptuous detractor of *Pamela*, found himself so overwhelmed by *Clarissa* that he was obliged to write to Richardson in 1749 to express his enthusiasm for its fifth volume. 'Let the overflows of a Heart which you have filled brimful speak for me', he gushed without a hint of his customary irony, 'my compassion is often moved; but I think my admiration more.' In sharp contrast to the staid, bourgeois Richardson's, the gentlemanly Fielding's literary career had begun in the theatre with *Love in Several Masques* of 1728, had continued with two adaptations from Molière (*The Mock Doctor* and *The Miser*) and with a successful series of sharp comedies, notably *The Author's Farce*, which satirically depicts the mouldy world of hacks and booksellers, and the sensationally titled *Rape upon Rape; or, the Justice Caught in his own Trap* (both 1730). His exuberant burlesque *Tom Thumb: A Tragedy* (1730) (a revised version of which appeared as *The Tragedy of Tragedies* in 1731) plays ingeniously with the effects of parody, literary allusion, irregular blank verse, bathos, and the mannerisms of academic editing. Fielding's flirtation with the theatre came to an abrupt end in 1737 when his political satires *Pasquin* and *The Historical Register for 1736* provoked Walpole's Government into passing a Licensing Act which introduced official censorship and restricted London performances to two approved theatres.

Fielding had, however, learned much from his practical experience of the stage. His novels reveal a grasp of idiomatic speech and dialogue, a sound understanding of the patterning of incident and a relish for a well-established denouement. His delight in burlesque also influenced the first of his two antipathetic satires on *Pamela*, *An Apology for the Life of Mrs Shamela Andrews* of 1741. *Shamela* purports to set a record straight by exposing and refuting 'the many notorious Falsehoods and Misrepresentations' of the earlier novel; it also puts 'in a true and just Light' the 'matchless Arts' of a calculating female hypocrite. Shamela discourses on what she insistently and distortedly calls her 'Vartue', and proclaims that she is prepared to talk of 'honorable Designs till Suppertime'. Her employer and future husband, modestly referred to as Mr B. in the original, is exposed as the bearer of the name 'Booby', while the once sympathetic Parson Williams 'is represented in a manner something different from what he bears in *Pamela*'. *Shamela* systematically debunks both Richardson's moral sententiousness and the essentially subjective nature of his narrative.

When Fielding returned to the attack in *The Adventures of Joseph Andrews and his Friend, Mr Abraham Adams* in 1742 he rejected the inward-looking epistolary form in favour of a third-person narrative. His narrator is talkative, clubbable, knowing, and manipulative; he speaks urbanely, sharing jokes and educated allusions with the reader, shifting us into a world of sophisticated gentlemanly discourse quite alien to Richardson. Although *Joseph Andrews* begins as a parody of *Pamela*, by tracing the complications of the life of Pamela's brother in the service of another branch of the Booby family it rapidly transcends the parodic mood by experimenting with a new, neo-classical fictional form. In his Preface to the novel Fielding insisted that his was 'a kind of writing, which I do not remember to have seen hitherto attempted in our language' and he outlined the concept of 'a comic epic poem in prose'. His ambitions for prose romance were comprehensive; he proposed to take the wide range of character, incident, diction, and reference from the epic and to remould this material according to 'comic' rather than 'serious' principles. This stress on comedy made for a further insistence on the place of the 'ridiculous' in art. The true ridiculous, he affirmed, had a single source in a human affectation which proceeds from either vanity or hypocrisy. Prose fiction could successfully adopt a moral stance without resorting to the cant of a novel such as *Pamela;* it could, moreover, endeavour to laugh away faults rather than to preach against them. To justify his case, Fielding significantly referred to Ben Jonson, 'who of all men understood the Ridiculous the best' and who 'chiefly used the hypocritical affectation'. The implications of this prefatory theoretical discourse are explored in the subsequent narrative, or, more precisely, the two types of theoretical discourse, the epic and the comic, are interpolated within a single text. *Joseph Andrews* has, as its full title suggests, two heroes, the innocent Joseph and his equally innocent Christian protector, Parson Adams. Adams is a man of learning and good sense but he is 'as entirely ignorant of the ways of this world as an infant just entered into it could possibly be'. Joseph and Adams, cast out as wanderers, engage in an epic voyage of discovery during which they generally seem to encounter selfishness, villainy, and corruption. But the naughty world through which they pass is illuminated not simply by Adams's selflessness but also by the unexpected charity of the humble and meek. If the novel variously exposes hypocrisy, it also discovers simple honesty and ordinary generosity in the interstices of a corrupt society. It is a virtue that does not seek for a reward.

Fielding's *The Life of Jonathan Wild the Great*, published as the third volume of his *Miscellanies* in 1743, further ramifies the novelist's experimental interest in the force of the ridiculous as an exposer of the hypocritical. It also reasserts the essentially social, as opposed to private, weight of his moral insistence. The narrative is shaped around a simple recurrent biographical formula: a 'Great Man' brings 'all manner of mischief on mankind', whereas a 'good' man removes mischief; the 'great' man exploits society, the 'good' man enhances it. In low life, as much as in high life, the 'great' are held up as examples; thus, if the professional criminal and thief-taker Wild can be called 'great', so a 'great' man, such as the Prime Minister, Sir Robert Walpole, can be equated with a thief. The steady, anti-heroic stance of *Jonathan Wild the Great* exerted a profound influence over Fielding's most dedicated nineteenth-century admirer, Thackeray. In his longest and most articulate work, *The History of Tom Jones, a Foundling* (1749), however, Fielding returned to the ambiguities of 'goodness' and 'greatness' and to the latitudinarian Christian balance of faith and works that he had earlier considered in his characterization of Parson Adams. In one important regard, the moral of *Tom Jones* hovers around the aristocratic principle of the nobility of 'good nature', a liberality of spirits which the novelist observes is 'scarce ever seen in men of low birth and education'. The novel's often wayward hero is told by his noble guardian, Squire Allworthy, that he has 'much goodness, generosity and honour' in his temper but that in order to be happy he must add the further qualities of 'prudence and religion'. That Tom is of gentle birth, and therefore of instinctively 'gentle' manners, is the half-hidden premiss of the story, but to see *Tom Jones* as a reassertion of old, élitist social and moral codes is to misread it. Essentially, it argues for the need for a broad reform of society, an ethic emphasized through the narrator's reiterated declaration that he is describing humankind as a species not as a group of individuals. Where Richardson had sought to examine the inner life of his confessional correspondents, Fielding's narrator insists that he must generalize and observe the evidence of external human characteristics. His moral preoccupation is not with a single class or with the individual ideal, but with the definition of a human norm.

Tom Jones is Fielding's most meticulous response to the challenge of classical epic and his most considered comic redefinition of the role of the epic hero. That Tom and his 'good nature' will be finally justified by the shape of the narrative is a basic assumption of the comedy; that his journey towards justification, 'prudence and religion' will be complex is dependent on the very nature of the epic structure. The novel is divided into eighteen books, the first six of which establish Tom's supposed origins, his education, and the nature of his fall from grace; the second six trace his journey to London, a journey paralleled by that of his adored, but often estranged, Sophia; the last six bring all the characters together amid the confused and morally suspect life of the metropolis. The symmetry of the novel's construction is not, however, merely a modern prose version of Homeric or Virgilian form; it is a tidy neo-classical shape which can contain within it a whole series of comments on other eighteenth-century forms: the satire, the pastoral, the comedy, and the mock-heroic. It is also a reflection on the work of modern masters: Cervantes, Rabelais, Swift and, through a steady stream of visual reference, Hogarth. The whole is interspersed with 'pauses' in which the omniscient narrator expatiates on his methods, on literary criticism in general, on philosophy, or on 'little or nothing', but it is also varied with reflexive, interpolated stories, with recapitulations and echoes, and with unexpected reappearances of characters. It is a *tour-de-force* of patterning, an assertion of the ultimate tidiness and proportion of the universe, and a working-out of a representative human destiny. Tom remains resilient despite his misfortunes; he makes mistakes, he is misjudged, and he is plotted against, but his triumph is viewed as a moral vindication. For Richardson individual 'virtue', even selfhood, had too easily been equated with sexual purity. Fielding rejoices most in the representation of gentleman-like spontaneity, and as his narrative suggests, restraint is best acquired through experience, not imposed by the norms, laws, and codes to which his numerous hypocrites pay lip-service.

The benevolent figure of Squire Allworthy is believed to have been loosely based on Fielding's friend and sometime patron, Ralph Allen. It was to Allen that he dedicated his most sombre novel, *Amelia*, in 1752, announcing that the book was 'sincerely designed to promote the cause of virtue, and to expose some of the most glaring evils, as well public as private, which at present infest the country'. *Amelia* is a novel of married life which dispenses with the epic journey of his earlier fiction. It traces the fraught and uncertain career of Captain Billy Booth and the frequent distress and isolation of his prudent, constant, loving wife. It begins in a magistrate's court, descends to the squalid confinement of Newgate prison, and maintains an impression of the general oppressiveness and multiple temptations of London life. Only with the fortuitous final discovery that Amelia is an heiress does the couple manage to escape again to the purer pleasures and securities of country life. Despite its vivid depiction of urban tawdriness, its often savage exposure of trickery, tinsel, and vulgarity, and its suggestion of psychological intensity, it has always been Fielding's least loved work.

In 1744 Henry Fielding provided a short Preface to his sister Sarah's novel *The Adventures of David Simple in Search of a Real Friend* in which he reiterated many of the ideas he had already expressed in *Joseph Andrews*. It is unhelpful to see the novels of Sarah Fielding (1710–68) solely in relation to her brother's, for, though her characters may often seem thinly drawn, she is more keenly interested in feeling, more penetrating of motive, and generally more analytical of the nature of mutual attraction and friendship. *David Simple* and its sequel, *Volume the Last* (1753), consider both social naïvety and the equation of virtue and suffering. Having achieved a kind of emotional fulfilment at the end of the first part of his adventures, David faces financial loss, a devastating decline in all his hopes, and finally death in the second. Both stories show innocence exposing corruption and innocence tested; the second shows it crushed by circumstance and human malevolence. *The History of the Countess of Dellwyn* of 1759 somewhat melodramatically considers the equally tragic theme of the moral corruption of a marriage between an older husband and a young wife, but the far more optimistic *History of Ophelia* (1760) describes the ultimate vindication of its ingenuous heroine despite abduction and threatened seduction by an aristocratic rake.

Charlotte Lennox (?1729–1804), the well-educated daughter of an army officer, spent her childhood in North America, marrying a shiftless and impecunious husband in 1747. Having attempted, unsuccessfully, to launch herself on a career as an actress, she turned, like Sarah Fielding, to writing as a profession. Lennox produced some five novels, a string of translations from the French, and a pioneer study of Shakespeare's Italian sources. Her novels were directed primarily at a female audience as popular guides to manners and a morals. Her first, *The Life of Harriot Stuart* (1750), and her last, *Euphemia* (1790), toy with American settings, but her most sustained work, *The Female Quixote: or, the Adventures of Arabella* (1752), deals with an aristocratic

Englishwoman brought up in isolation on her father's country estate. Its heroine's often fantastic perceptions are moulded by her avid reading of romances (hence the novel's title); she exaggeratedly confuses highwaymen with chivalrous adventurers and, more worryingly, mistakes honest suitors for ravishers. The novel satirically exposes the dangers of empty-minded reading, but it ends in proclaiming the instructive virtues of 'an admirable Writer of our own Time'. That writer was Richardson.

Smollett and Sterne

'A novel is a large diffused picture, comprehending the characters of life, disposed in different groups, and exhibited in various attitudes for the purpose of an uniform plan, and general occurrence, to which every individual figure is subservient.' Tobias Smollett's theory of the novel, formulated, in the manner of Fielding, in a Preface to his proto-Gothic story *The Adventures of Ferdinand Count Fathom* (1753), is not always realized in the structures of his own fiction. The diffusion is certainly there, but clear evidence of a 'uniform plan' has often escaped his readers. When Smollett (1721–71) further insists that the 'propriety, probability, or success' may depend on the need for 'a principal personage to attract the attention, unite the incidents, unwind the clue to the labyrinth, and at last close the scene, by virtue of his own importance', he also seems to be sketching an ideal rather than summing up his own method. If Charlotte Lennox's Arabella receives distorted images of life from the predominantly seventeenth-century French romances that she devours, the Preface to Smollett's first novel, *The Adventures of Roderick Random* (1748), stresses that there was now a real distinction between the 'romance' (which owed its origin to 'ignorance, vanity and superstition') and the new fiction of his own day. Although he praises the brio and the plan of Alain-René Lesage's rambling picaresque narrative *Gil Blas* (1715–35), and indeed translated it into English in 1749, Smollett distances himself from Lesage's deviations from 'probability' and from his sudden transitions which 'prevent that generous indignation, which ought to animate the reader, against the sordid and vicious disposition of the world'. His own fiction adapted the picaresque tradition both to suit a modern English taste for realism and in order to describe a recognizably modern world. It was also full of an indignation that was more often righteous than 'generous'.

Roderick Random has as its hero a well-born and educated Scot exposed to the 'selfishness, envy, malice, and base indifference of mankind' in England and the wider world. Roderick is often aggressive and combative; he is affectionate and sexually inquisitive; he is also a victim who, through singularly devious paths, fights his way back to money and respectability. Despite being a wronged and disinherited heir and a stranger in his wanderings, he never emerges as the kind of rebel and romantic outsider that later novelists might have made of him. Much of the 'randomness' had of course been implied by the title, but the novel's true originality lies in its inclusion of scenes of modern warfare as clear alternatives to the fantasy battles of earlier romances. Having been press-ganged into the navy, and having experienced the foetid horrors of the lower decks of a British man-of-war, Roderick is present at the disastrous siege of Cartagena of 1741 and later in the story, as a soldier in the French army, he fights at Dettingen in 1743. In neither instance does Smollett spare his reader the nastier details of combat, details which as a former ship's surgeon he had known at first hand. *The Adventures of Peregrine Pickle* of 1751 contains in the figure of Commodore Hawser Trunnion a further, if wonderfully exaggerated, reflection on Smollett's naval experience. The novel is centred on a wandering hero who even as a boy has shown 'a certain oddity of disposition'. Peregrine maintains this oddity as an adult, exhibiting a violence, an imprudence, a phil-andering, a savage coldness, and an arrogance which both alienates sympathy and attracts retribution. At various times he is imprisoned in the Bastille in Paris and in the Fleet prison in London where he languishes as 'the hollow-eyed representative of distemper, indigence, and despair'. His repentance, which coincides with rescue from prison and an inheritance, allows for a happy marriage and retirement to the country beyond the pull of metropolitan temptation.

The interval between the composition of *Peregrine Pickle* and the publication of Smollett's most satisfying novel, *The Expedition of Humphry Clinker* (1771), was taken up with diverse literary projects, which vary from a medical treatise on the external use of water, to a translation of Cervantes' *Don Quixote*; it also included the completion of a four-volume *Complete History of England* and two uneven novels, *Ferdinand Count Fathom* and *The Life and Adventures of Sir Launcelot Greaves* (serialized 1760–1). *Humphry Clinker* is concerned with a family journey from the estates of Matthew Bramble in Wales, through western England to London, and then northwards to Smollett's native Scotland. It is told in a series of eighty-two letters, twenty-seven of which are by the elderly and often sarcastic Bramble himself (the title character, a servant acquired on the journey, does not appear until letter 28, and he will later be discovered to be Bramble's natural son). The letter form allowed both for an overlap in the accounts of the events, people, and places encountered during the journey and for a multiplicity of viewpoints and epistolary styles; it also helped shape the haphazardness of this particular 'large diffused picture'. Its topographical exactness and its sharp, if succinct, observation of social and geographical whims, particularly those of Bath, seem to have been calculated to appeal to an audience alert to the literary attractions of sentimental journeyings.

Laurence Sterne (1713–68) probably began his *A Sentimental Journey through France and Italy* in the summer of 1766 when he was still at work on the last volume of his vastly popular *Tristram Shandy*. It was not published until a month before his death in 1768. Whether or not the shadow of his impending demise hangs over the book has long been a matter of debate. There is little that could be called gloomy in it but there is a good deal of pathos, and its narrator, Mr Yorick, is much given to shedding sentimental tears. The 'grossness' of which some readers of *Tristram Shandy* had complained is diminished in favour of a new 'design' which, Sterne told a friend, was intended 'to teach us to love the world and our fellow creatures better than we do'. Many original readers would have agreed that the cultivation of sentiment, under the guidance of a witty country parson, might prove beneficial to the heart. At its best, *A Sentimental Journey is* a wonderfully various parody of the conventional travel-book. It deliberately never lives up to its full title. The journey ends in Lyons without ever nearing the French border with Italy; Yorick almost mischievously declines to see the sights of Calais and Paris, and the often whimsical narrative concludes startlingly and ambiguously with an abruptly broken sentence. It is essentially an episodic collection of sketches and interludes, selected so as to give an impression of artful randomness.

The narrative playfulness of *A Sentimental Journey* modestly extends something of the extraordinary invention of the nine volumes of *The Life and Opinions of Tristram Shandy, Gentleman*, published between 1759 and 1767. Of all eighteenth-century novels it is the one that is freest of insistent linearity, the one that makes the most daring bid to escape from the models established by epic or by history. It glances back to the anecdotal learning of Burton's *The Anatomy of Melancholy*, to the bawdy ebullience of Rabelais, and to the experimental games of Swift and the Scriblerians, but it is ultimately an unprecedented, and still unrivalled, experiment with form. Its organization lies in the consciousness of a narrator who fails in the first two volumes even to get himself born. When Tristram refers to Horace's idea of a history that proceeds *ab ovo*, from an obvious beginning, he begs 'Mr *Horace*'s pardon;—for in writing what I have set about, I shall confine myself neither to his rules, nor to any man's rules that ever lived'. Tristram's world is neither traditionally regulated nor a reflection or a representation of a tidy, ordered Newtonian universe. It is, rather, a pattern of comic ironies observed in the 'Shandean' manner which Sterne defines as 'civil, nonsensical, good-humoured'. *Tristram Shandy* does not lead its central character forward towards a crock of gold, to a heaven-made marriage or to an ideal retirement. No predetermined comic expectations are set up as they are in Fielding's fiction; everything remains provisional and the sense of an ending is consistently denied both in terms of single episodes and in the overall structure. In the twenty-second chapter of his first volume Tristram celebrates digressions as 'incontestably . . . the sunshine;—they are the life, the soul of reading'. He goes on, typically, to shift his image from the natural to the mechanical, comparing his narrative to a complex working machine: 'I have constructed the main work and the adventitious parts of it with such intersections, and have so complicated and involved the digressive and progressive movements, one wheel within another, that the whole machine, in general, has been kept a-going.' Everything—digressions, hiatuses, absences, lacunae, dashes, asterisks, and the famous black, blank, and marbled pages—is co-productive of the novel's peculiar energy and essential to its questioning of meaning. The title-pages of the first two volumes published in 1760 bore the epigraph derived from the Greek philosopher Epictetus: 'Not things, but opinions about things, trouble men.' *Tristram Shandy* suggests that all information is contingent, all interpretation relative. The very act of reading draws the reader into a participation in the creative process. If Smollett's novels have had a peculiarly fruitful influence on the development of the nineteenth-century novel, the impact of Sterne's liberation of narrative has been most fully appreciated in the twentieth century.

Sensibility, Sentimentality, Tears, and Graveyards

In 1749 Samuel Richardson's by now regular correspondent, Lady Bradshaugh, wrote to him asking: 'What, in your opinion, is the meaning of the word *sentimental*, so much in vogue among the polite . . . every thing clever and agreeable is comprehended in that word . . . I am frequently astonished to hear such a one is a *sentimental* man; we were a *sentimental* party. I have been taking a *sentimental* walk.' We do not have Richardson's reply to her question but he must surely have guessed that she already knew the answer. A year earlier Lady Bradshaugh had initiated the correspondence by writing pseudonymously to the novelist with the request that he save the 'divine Clarissa' from the threat of impending death and grant her a happy end with the penitent Lovelace. Despite being past what she termed her 'romantic time of life' Lady Bradshaugh blushingly admitted 'that if I was to die for it, I cannot help being fond of Lovelace'. Her tears over Clarissa and blushes over Lovelace are evidence of the emotional effect produced on early readers of Richardson's fiction; her wonder at the fashionable use of the word 'sentimental' equally testifies that such emotions were shared by others. The novelist himself had proclaimed that he had aimed to 'soften and mend the Heart' and he had stressed in *Grandison* that 'a feeling heart is a blessing that no one, who has it, would be without'. A literature that moved pity in its readers was viewed as morally instructive. A powerful evocation of feeling, or a shared compassion, it was held, made ultimately for a more humane society. Where Shaftesbury had proposed that benevolence be viewed as an expression of natural virtue, the fiction of Richardson and his sentimental successors could be seen as ducts for the emotional sympathy which bound a community together.

Dr Johnson's definition of 'sensibility' in his *Dictionary* as 'quickness of sensation', 'quickness of perception', and 'delicacy' indicates something of the new prominence of a balance of 'sense' and 'reason' in the mid-eighteenth-century understanding of the processes of perception. Whereas Johnson defined 'emotion' as, on the one hand, a 'disturbance of the mind', he also offered the alternative idea of it as a 'vehemence of passion' which could be either pleasing or painful. Provided excess was avoided, emotion and spontaneity were seen as necessary complements to reason and deliberation, not as oppositions to them. Two singularly lacrimose descendants of Sarah Fielding's *David Simple*—Henry Brooke's *The Fool of Quality* (1764–70) and Henry Mackenzie's *The Man of Feeling* (1771)—stress the importance of male emotion, as opposed to male rationality, in an often unfeeling world and a calculating society. Brooke (1703–83) presented his 'fool', Harry Clinton, as a product of a benign philosophical scheme of education, one which already shows the influence of Rousseau's *Émile* (1762); this education, which pre-serves rather than conditions his natural innocence, is both a buffer against the multiple misfortunes that befall him and a means of reconciling his aware-ness of human misery with his euphoric conviction of divine providence. Mackenzie's *The Man of Feeling* had an even greater currency. Its hero, Harley, is, like Clinton, a sentimental innocent who weeps uncontrolledly over the suc-cession of unfortunates he encounters. Mackenzie (1745–1831), who was much given to asterisks as a means of expressing inexpressible emotion, exposes the unworldly Harley to those who are victims of the world's callousness in order to test the flow of his gushing fount of human sympathy. Mackenzie's later story *Julia de Roubigné* (1777) deals with a yet more tragic vehemence of passion, an account of a fraught marital crisis crowned by the murder of a sup-posedly adulterous young wife by her despairing, but otherwise virtuous, husband. When Goethe's *Die Leiden des jungen Werthers* appeared in transla-tion in the 1770s, receptive English ground was already well watered with tears.

John Wesley (1703–91) devoutly recommended *The Fool of Quality* to his followers as an illustration of the 'religion of the heart'. Tears of remorse and of passionate joy were an essential feature of the great open-air missionary campaigns conducted by Wesley in the 1740s and 1750s. Despite the religious establishment's distrust of 'enthusiasm', this missionary work and the emer-gence of a separate Methodist Church had an immense impact on English, and, by extension, English-speaking, culture. Wesley's *Journal*, which began to appear in print as a devotional companion as early as 1739, animatedly charts a heroic progress through the island in defiance of ignorance, superstition, rain, mud, and hostile mobs. The first collection of psalms and hymns designed for the congregational singing which was an essential expression of Methodist religious emotion was published in Charleston, South Carolina, in 1737. Other, grander, collections of hymns 'for the use of the people called Methodists' rapidly began to circulate on both sides of the Atlantic, many of them the editorial work of Wesley himself and containing a wealth of popular and sentimental religious poetry designed for collective musical expression rather than for private reading. The finest hymns are the work of Wesley's brother Charles (1707–88), the author, amongst many hundreds of others, of 'Jesu, lover of my soul', 'O for a thousand tongues to sing My dear Redeemer's praise', 'Forth in thy name, O Lord, I go', 'Love divine, all loves excelling', and 'Christ, whose glory fills the skies'. Each moves towards a prevision of eternal bliss and ultimate fulfillment in heaven. The Wesley hymns suggest a poet ravished by divine love and also deeply affected by the idea of a bloody cleansing from sin; they rejoice in the light and the sufferings of Christ and shrink away in horror from the profound darkness of a life without redemption. Though many retain the currency of popular classics, the now more neglected hymns in these collections dwell with an almost embarrassing relish on backsliding, mutability, human transience, physical decay, and death.

The work of Edward Young (1683–1765) and Robert Blair (1699–1746) reflects much of the Wesleyan concern with mortality if little of its Christ-centred ecstasy. Neither is anything but orthodox in his expression of Christian hope, but the mood of the major poems of both writers is predominantly sombre, reflective, melancholic, and moral. Both have latterly been seen as central members of a loose grouping of writers known as the 'graveyard poets'. Young's *The Complaint: or, Night Thoughts on Life, Death and Immortality* was published serially from 1742 to 1745. It is a 10,000-line blank verse meditation on a death-saturated life, on death itself, and on resurrection and immortality. Young divides his poem into nine sections, or 'nights', each of which responds to atheistic emptiness or deistic vagueness by arguing for the evident power of God in nature and for the inherent promise of eternity. The darkness of the night, Young affirms, aids 'intellectual light'. Much of the argument takes the form of an urgent, largely one-sided, debate with an infidel youth called Lorenzo but the debate has little real direction, pattern, or conclusion despite the ever-present reminders of the frailty of life and the imminence of divine judgement. Blair's *The Grave* (1743) is a dramatic evocation of the horrors of corruption and of the solitude of death. It is at its most vivid when it conveys a sense of mystery or of terror, as in its eerie opening sketch of a schoolboy 'lightly tripping o'er the long flat stones' of a moonlit graveyard before flying from a 'horrid *Apparition*, tall and ghastly, | That walks at Dead of Night, or takes his Stand | O'er some new-open'd *Grave*'. Its passages of religious consolation seem perfunctory by comparison.

The most enduringly famous, fluent, and diversified of all 'graveyard' poems is Thomas Gray's 'Elegy written in a Country Church-Yard' (1751). Gray (1716–71) was by inclination and by cultivation withdrawn, vulnerable, and melancholic. His finest verse reflects a taste for meditation rather than action, for retired contemplation rather than for public jubilation. As the abandoned fragment of a tragedy *Agrippina* (1741–2) and the 'Ode on the Spring' (1742) suggest, Gray could at times be keenly observant of detail while lacking the tact and subtlety evident in his best work. The 'Ode on a Distant Prospect of Eton College', also of 1742, is, by contrast, only ponderous when it briefly describes the games played by the schoolboys, the 'little victims' who have no sense 'of ills to come'. The overall effect of the poem is of a recall of lost innocence which has delicacy uncloyed by self-indulgent nostalgia; the emotionally gasped 'ahs' of the second section ('Ah, happy hills, ah, pleasing shade . . . I feel the gales, that from ye blow, | A momentary bliss bestow'), however, seem to look directly forward to the plain lyricism of A. E. Housman at the end of the nineteenth century. When Gray addressed himself to the mock heroic in the 'Ode on the

Death of a Favourite Cat' (1748) he proved himself capable of both an equal delicacy of expression and a gentle, scholarly wit. The poem contains glancing reminiscences of Milton, Dryden, Pope, and Gay but it carries its learning lightly and moves with an easy, but distinctive, sophistication to its double proverbial moral conclusions ('A favourite has no friend'; 'Not all that tempts your wandering eyes | And heedless hearts is lawful prize; | Nor all that glisters gold').

Gray's 'Pindaric Odes'—'The Progress of Poesy' (1754) and 'The Bard' (1757)—show a different kind of ambition. They offer both a scholarly tribute to Greek poetic form and an experimental interest in a new kind of subject. Pindar's complex metric frameworks and his elaborate prosody had served as models to Cowley and Dryden, but Gray's Odes reveal a lyric poet experimenting both with an elevated mood and a weighty historical moral. 'The Progress of Poesy' traces a patriotic genealogy for English verse by suggesting a history of a poetic tradition that moves allusively from Greece and Rome to England, from Helicon, the watery inspiration of the Muses, to the inspired Shakespeare's Avon. Where the first Ode celebrates the continuity of poetry, 'The Bard' considers a discontinuity. The poem is based on the tradition that King Edward I, having ordered the extinction of the Bards of Wales, was confronted with a venerable survivor of the order who prophesies the end of the Plantagenets and the triumphant renewal of poetry under the Tudor dynasty (whose origins lay in Wales). Having delivered his prophecy, the Bard precipitates himself from the mountain top and plunges into 'endless night'. Gray boldly attempts to interfuse a Celtic tradition and an English inheritance within a classical framework. The modest sensationalism of the poem's setting, and the very weirdness of the Bard's incantatory curses, have often been seen as an anticipation of the Romantic fascination with the sublime.

His sense of tradition and of historical continuity found a more placid and contemplative expression in the famous 'Elegy written in a Country Church-Yard'. The Odes celebrate national literature, not national power or prosperity; the Elegy finally focuses on a solitary poet, a man of 'humble birth' and a stranger to national glory, to fortune, and to fame. The poem's broader meditation on the obscure destinies of the unknown and undistinguished villagers buried in the churchyard culminates in the celebrated comment on unfulfilled greatness; village Hampdens, mute inglorious Miltons, and guiltless Cromwells (all figures associated with the Republican cause) had both their talents and their potential crimes 'confined' by a lack of opportunity. Gray is not making a political protest on behalf of the meek or the downtrodden; he is merely siding with the passive placidity of rural rhythm and rustic verse:

> Far from the madding crowd's ignoble strife
> Their sober wishes never learned to stray;
> Along the cool sequestered vale of life
> They kept the noiseless tenor of their way.
>
> Yet even these bones from insult to protect
> Some frail memorial still erected nigh,

With uncouth rhymes and shapeless sculpture decked,
Implores the passing tribute of a sigh.

Thus the poetry of sophistication complements the unsophisticated rhymes on the grave-stones. The 'Elegy' intermixes the poetry of country retirement with a self-reflexive nocturnal musing on the egalitarian nature of mortality. The unnamed 'hoary-headed swain' of the end of the poem becomes the memorializer of an inconspicuous bard. He speaks not in 'uncouth rhymes', but in the smooth closing quatrains which form an epitaph, and renders the melancholy poet one with the dead villagers. Gray's brief prose epitaph for his mother's tomb in Stoke Poges churchyard notes that she was 'the tender careful mother of many children: one of whom had the misfortune to survive her'. It is a typically self-pitying comment, one accentuated by the fact that when Gray was himself buried in the same tomb no further reference was made to him on the stone. In sharp contrast, the monument later erected to his memory in Westminster Abbey, immediately under that to Milton, bore a far more assertive quatrain by his friend William Mason (1725–97): 'No more the Grecian Muse unrivall'd reigns, | To Britain let the Nations homage pay; | She felt a Homer's fire in Milton's strains, | A Pindar's rapture from the Lyre of GRAY.'

Gray's younger contemporary, William Collins (1721–59), began his literary career with the publication of his genteelly escapist schoolboy verses, the *Persian Eclogues*, in 1742. They are an early example of the growing fashion for the exotic, and particularly for the oriental. Despite Collins's whimsically expressed belief that 'elegancy and wildness of thought' characterized oriental poetry, the Persian settings and references are somewhat perfunctory and an English pastoral smoothness effectively counters any real leaning towards the 'wild'. The *Odes on Several Descriptive and Allegoric Subjects* of 1746 (dated 1747) reveal a more assured, if imitative, poet. Collins's debts to Milton, and to his 'L'Allegro' and 'Il Penseroso' in particular, are manifold, but in the most purely 'descriptive' of his own Odes, that to Evening, he achieved an intensely delicate evocation of landscape, established through a succession of distinct scenes and images. The 'Ode to Evening's unrhymed stanzas and its impression of relaxed quietness partly disguise the extent to which it is the achievement of careful art. Five of the twelve odes in the 1746 collection have a patriotic theme and the longest and liveliest of them, the 'Ode to Liberty', traces the descent of British freedom from classical roots to confident modern fulfillment. The extraordinary, but unfinished, 'Ode on the Popular Superstitions of the Highlands of Scotland, Considered as the Subject of Poetry' (1749–50, published 1788) deals with an issue of some urgent contemporary interest to those English readers who had recently found their cultural values rudely threatened by the incursion of wild Highlanders under the command of the Young Pretender. The wild Scotland of the poem is both 'Fancy's land . . . where still, 'tis said, the fairy people meet', and an imagined landscape filtered variously through travellers' descriptions, ballads, and

Macbeth. Collins's restlessness with received notions of literary decorum and proper subject-matter is evident in his clumsy title, but his rag-bag of a poem remains a fascinating experiment in opening up the range, style, and reference of contemporary poetry.

The Ballad, the Gothic, the Gaelic, and the Davidic

The three short essays on ballad literature published by Addison in *The Spectator* in May 1711 are a minor milestone in the revival of critical interest in popular and provincial literature. Addison centred his essays on an appreciation of the 'majestic simplicity' of 'Chevy Chase', a ballad probably produced in the fifteenth century on the then fraught border between England and Scotland. Despite his frequently forced parallels between the ballad and the epic sentiments of Homer and Virgil, Addison returns repeatedly to the directness of British ballad narrative, a 'plain simple copy of nature, destitute of all the helps and ornaments of art'. Similar, but more developed arguments inform two pioneer explorations of alternative literary traditions, Richard Hurd's *Letters on Chivalry and Romance* (1762) and Thomas Percy's great three-volume collection of ballad poetry, *Reliques of Ancient English Poetry* (1765). Both writers were scholarly bishops, the last of a line of prelates who were able to indulge in dilettantism without feeling pressurized to concentrate their intellectual energies on theology. Both men had been educated to appreciate classical principles, but both also reflect the shift towards a new and receptive poetic sensibility. Hurd (1720–1808) argued that medieval romance could be seen as a northern European reflection of Greek perceptions of heroism and that chivalry embodied a code of values as influential to a literary culture as those of the ancients. His *Letters* offer both a preliminary attempt to deconstruct the span of literature which he loosely labels as 'romance' and a more developed appreciation of the 'gothic' elements in the work of Spenser and Shakespeare. His description of the Gothic as a 'latent cause' in the 'workings of the human mind', and his belief that his own rational age had lost 'a world of fine fabling' suggest the rumblings of a real revolution in taste. Percy (1729–1811) possessed a yet more defined and exotic relish for literature outside, or alternative to, narrowly defined canons. He published a translation (from a Portuguese version) of the Chinese novel *Hau Kiou Choaan, or The Pleasing History* in 1761 and two years later he produced his *Five Pieces of Runic Poetry Translated from the Islandic Language*. His *Reliques*, largely based on a various seventeenth-century manuscript collection now known as 'The Percy Folio', reveal a careful scholar of a native tradition, but one prepared to tamper with texts as an editor and 'improver'. Percy's limitations as an editor derive from his awareness that 'in a polished age, like the present, . . . many of these reliques of antiquity will require great allowances to be made for them'; his distinction as a collector lies in his alertness to the fact that a plain mode of expression often possessed virtues beyond those which polish gives to the surface of civilization.

The contributions of James Macpherson (1736–96) and Thomas Chatterton (1752–70) to literature are essentially vicarious. Macpherson's pretence of having discovered and translated the works of the early Scottish Gaelic poet 'Ossian, the son of Fingal' created a widely received Romantic image of the primitive poet; Chatterton's publication of poems, supposedly by a medieval priest, Thomas Rowley, his relative lack of literary success, and his despairing suicide impressed an image of the suffering modern writer on the minds of the Romantic poets. Whereas Ossian was hailed as a master by Goethe, by Schiller, and (strangely enough) by Napoleon, and was depicted, parallel to Homer, as the Bard of the North on the proscenium arch of the rebuilt Covent Garden Theatre as late as 1858, Chatterton was to emerge as Wordsworth's 'marvellous Boy' in 1807, as the dedicatee of Keats's *Endymion* in 1818, and as the subject of Henry Wallis's painting of 1856 (for which George Meredith posed as the dead poet). Neither writer has had an enthusiastic body of readers since the nineteenth century. Some Gaelic ballad poetry is truly attributed to one 'Oisean', the son of the warrior Fionn, but Macpherson, who had only a limited command of Celtic languages, substantially invented both 'Ossian' and a corpus of works ascribed to him by cleverly adapting, re-creating, and expanding mere fragments of surviving verse. *Fingal, An Ancient Epic Poem in Six Books* was published in 1762 and a second epic, *Temora*, appeared, somewhat suspiciously, hard on its heels, a year later. Macpherson, who also produced an exceptionally stodgy prose version of the *Iliad* in 1763, gave a Homeric coherence and a classical solemnity to disparate ballad accounts of ancient Scottish feuds. Alert to current tastes, he also played with a whole gamut of sentiments, exploiting a new interest in primitive heroism and in the emotive associations of wild landscape. His fraud was not properly exposed until after his death. Chatterton's schoolboy fascination with the Middle Ages, fed by his reading of Chaucer, Percy's *Reliques* and, to a lesser degree, Ossian, produced an equally extraordinary fruit. Only one of his so-called 'Rowley' poems, the 'eclogue' 'Elinoure and Juga', was published in his short lifetime (a collected edition appeared posthumously in 1777). Despite his obvious borrowings, his deliberate use of archaic words picked out of dictionaries, and his anachronistic use of Elizabethan verse forms, Chatterton's mock medieval poems still have a certain flair which derives from an imagination utterly steeped in the artefacts and sounds of another age.

The work of Christopher Smart (1722–71) emerges from a sensibility rapt not by the national past but by a religious ecstasy (some might call it mania) which drove him to imitate and adapt the Hebrew psalmody of King David. His verse has a simple directness of expression, and an imaginative fluency even within the constraints of the traditional quatrains and the bald sing-song rhythms of the metrical psalm form. Much of Smart's work does, however, possess a real complexity. A *Song to David* of 1763, for example, celebrates the psalmist ('highest in the list of worthies' and 'the minister of praise at large') in sections arranged according to the mystic numbers three, four, and seven and their multiples. When it was reprinted in 1765 in the awkwardly titled *A Translation of the Psalms, &c Hymns and Spiritual Songs for the Fasts and Festivals &c*, the 'song' was surrounded by a considerable variety of metrical experiments with hymn-like forms. The hymn designed for the feast of St Philip and St James (anciently celebrated on 1 May) ecstatically contemplates a flowery, bird-haunted English spring, while those for the Nativity and Easter delight in a 'God all-bounteous, all-creative' who is expressed in the workings of nature and yet who mightily gives nature its meaning. Smart's most eccentric achievement, the fragmentary *Jubilate Agno* (*c.*1759–61, published 1939), was written in the period when the poet was confined in St Luke's Asylum in London. *Jubilate Agno* is an essentially private outpouring which cannot have been intended for use in public worship, but it retains the antiphonal, exhortatory shape of some liturgical canticles. Each sentence beginning with a 'Let' ('Let Shuah rejoice with Boa, which is the vocal serpent') finds a response in a parallel beginning with a 'For' ('For there are still serpents that can speak—God bless my head, my heart and my heel'). The poem interlinks Hebrew proper names with an international menagerie of animals, each presenting a distinct form of worship to its Creator. Sarah, for example, is bidden to rejoice with the redwing, Tobias to bless Charity with his dog ('who is faithful, vigilant, and a friend in poverty'), and Anna to bless God with the cat who, more obscurely, 'is worthy before the throne of grace, when he has trampled upon the idol in his prank'. Some of the versicles and their responses have a delightful oddity; others an elusive and probably personal bitterness; still others, particularly those pertaining to cats, an appreciative tenderness. Smart's work is by turns mystical and contemplative, idiosyncratic and hybrid, formal and obscure. Unlike the gloomy and now distant thunders of Macpherson and the adolescent lightning flashes of Chatterton, the full range of Smart's often bizarre but temperate poetry has found its most appreciative audience only since the appearance of *Jubilate Agno* nearly two hundred years after its composition.

Goldsmith and Sheridan: The New 'Comedy of Manners'

When Oliver Goldsmith (*c.*1730–74) dedicated his semi-autobiographical poem *The Traveller: or, A Prospect of Society* (1764) to his clergyman brother he praised his brother's choice of profession and his rejection of 'the field of Ambition, where the labourers are many, and the harvest not worth carrying away'. In this same dedication he also took the opportunity of disparaging the confused state of contemporary poetic theory and practice. The themes of a rejection of male ambition and a desire for tidiness and philosophic harmony run through the range of Goldsmith's literary work. He was not without ambition himself, as his varied experiments in literature, his professional application, and his often pressing need to write for money suggest, but what he wrote reveals a systematic attempt to condition restlessness and to come to equable terms with passion. The dedication to *The Traveller* objects to the contradictory and disordered critical voices currently raised in favour of 'blank verse, and Pindaric odes, chorusses, anapests and iambics, alliterative care and happy negligence'; the poem itself employs the already somewhat conservative couplet form and it preaches the vanity of searching the external world for a bliss 'which only centers in the mind'.

The Traveller glancingly retraces Goldsmith's own earlier wanderings through France, Switzerland, and Italy before a return to an England caught up with a pursuit of political liberty and with a related, but less socially desirable, commercial ambition. It presents an impression of a morally educational journey rather than a sentimental one. In its strange insistence on the depopulation both of Italian cities and, more emphatically, of the English countryside it also contains the germ of *The Deserted Village* (1770). Where the earlier poem sees emigration as a result of laws that 'grind the poor' enacted by rich, self-seeking, and powerful champions of liberty, *The Deserted Village* indirectly attacks the enclosure system (by which peasants were deprived of common land by successive Acts of Parliament) and more directly protests against the concentration of wealth in fewer and fewer hands and against the creation of a private 'luxury . . . curst by Heaven's decree'. 'Sweet Auburn', the 'loveliest village of the plain', has been destroyed by the effects of aristocratic, mercantile, or simply urban 'luxury'. Auburn is, however, unlocated (though some commentators have sought to place it in Goldsmith's native Ireland). Once a harmoniously working village which has now vanished, it seems bathed in the golden evening light of nostalgia. Most prominent amongst its lovingly recalled inhabitants is its spiritual guide and moral arbiter, a parish priest 'passing rich' on forty pounds a year, a man content to run his godly race remote alike from towns and from hopes of ecclesiastical preferment.

The figure of an unworldly priest recurs in both *The Citizen of the World* (1762) and the philosophical tale *The Vicar of Wakefield* (1766). The 'Man in Black', innocently observed by the 'Chinese Philosopher residing in London' of *The Citizen of the World,* is generous to a fault; he is exploited because of the very nature of his charity, but he proves to be no more gullible than the Chinese narrator he has taken under his wing. The device of using an alien innocent abroad as a commentator on the whims and hypocrisies of European society was scarcely new (it had been used by Addison in *The Spectator* and, more recently and more trenchantly, by Montesquieu in France), but Goldsmith's oriental sage, Lien Chi Altangi, appears to be as fascinated by his fellow innocents as he is by the vanity, dress, law, literature, and cocksure pomposity of his English hosts. The appropriately named Dr Primrose, the freshly innocent 'priest . . . husbandman . . . and father of a family' of *The Vicar of Wakefield*, shares something of Lien Chi Altangi's calm, gentle, even fastidious, detachment in the face of confusion. Primrose's circumstances are, however, both more dire and more personal and he bears them with a Job-like patience. As the recounter of the misfortunes which befall him and his family, he is also required to defuse emotionally charged situations by asserting the comfortable virtues of temperance and faith. The words 'prudent' and 'prudence' recur throughout his extraordinarily symmetrical narrative. It is a tragic story concerned with sensibility not with sensation, with pity not with terror, and carefully restrains the tearful emotions which had earlier been indulged by writers such as Brooke and Mackenzie. In the eighth chapter of his second volume, Dr Primrose compares himself to a legislator 'who had brought men from their native ferocity into friendship and obedience'. Although he never really asserts himself, and never seeks to pose as a political or domestic tyrant in his little republic, he none the less attempts to act as a moral persuader, firm in his belief in the benign workings of divine providence. Despite his frequent ineffectualness, Primrose is one of the blessed meek whose inheritance is ultimately allowed to be a well-ordered patch of earth.

'Our taste has gone back a whole century, Fletcher, Ben Johnson (*sic*), and all the plays of Shakespear, are the only things that go down', remarks a 'poor player' encountered by Dr Primrose on his travels. The player later asserts that in his experience 'Congreve and Farquhar have too much wit in them for the present taste'. Goldsmith's two shapely and commercially successful plays, *The Good-Natur'd Man* (1768) and *She Stoops to Conquer* (1773), only partially bear out the truth of the player's observation. In his 'Essay on the Theatre', also of 1773, Goldsmith himself had drawn a clear distinction between what he saw as 'laughing and sentimental comedy', that is between a satirical laughing away of faults and an emotional stimulus to sympathetic tears. If it is sometimes hard to recognize Goldsmith as a direct theatrical heir to either Jonson or Congreve, his plays suggest a more forthright moralist than do his poems and his fiction. He claims to have distrusted the kind of comedy which 'aims at touching our passions, instead of being truly pathetic'. Goldsmith's remarks in the 'Essay' are likely to have been directed, in part, against the plays of his contemporary Richard Cumberland (1732–1811), the author of the sentimental comedies *The West Indian* (1771) and *The Fashionable Lover* (1772). Cumberland was later caricatured by Richard Brinsley Sheridan as Sir Fretwell Plagiary in *The Critic* (1779). Goldsmith and his fellow Irishman, Sheridan (1751–1816), share a certain acerbity of wit and an ebullient criticism of affectation which is generally absent from the exploration of tearful neuroses by the proponents of sensibility. Both prefer the poignant to the passionate, the witty to the lacrimose. The plays of Goldsmith and Sheridan reveal a positive, but newly refined, pleasure in the devices, the amatory intrigues, and the exposures of the 'comedy of manners' perfected in the late seventeenth century. Goldsmith's comedies also suggest a writer more happy to expose the social shortcomings of a generous nature than does either *The Citizen of the World* or *The Vicar of Wakefield*. When he wrote *The Good-Natur'd Man* he confessed to being 'strongly prepossessed in favour of the poets of the last century' and his story of the testing and curing of a generously credulous hero by the devices of a sensible uncle gesture both back to Jonson and forward to a new kind of comedy of 'nature and humour'. *She Stoops to Conquer, or the Mistakes of a Night* is more complex, varied, and socially observant than its predecessor. Its 'bashful and reserved' central character, young Marlow, who only relaxes in the company of servants, is brought out of himself by the 'stooping' (in terms of class rather than sex) of a resourceful heroine, Miss Hardcastle, a 'stooping' dramatically complicated by a succession of misunderstandings and social *faux pas*.

Sheridan's comedies are equally full of action, reversal, confusion, and verbal wit. Like *She Stoops to Conquer*, they are also supremely *actable*. His first plays—*The Rivals*, the farce *St Patrick's Day*, and the 'comic opera' *The Duenna*—were all written in his early twenties and were all produced on stage in 1775 with a view to dazzling audiences with a new talent. *The Rivals*, in particular, harks back to the inherited conventions of the Restoration period, such as the booby squire and the father who requires 'absolute' obedience, but it also reveals a fresh and relatively chaste benignity. The play confronts the authority of an older generation with the success of the stratagems of its young lovers, but it also allows for an extraordinary linguistic variety which deftly embraces the inventive oaths of Bob Acres ('Odds blushes and blooms!', 'Odds triggers and flints!'), the inflated Irishisms of Sir Lucius O'Trigger, and, above all, the wonderful misapplications of Mrs Malaprop ('Sure, if I reprehend any thing in this world it is the use of my oracular tongue, and a nice derangement of epitaphs!'). If *The Trip to Scarborough* of 1777, a refashioning of Vanbrugh's *The Relapse*, reveals the extent to which Sheridan responded both to the attractions of a good plot and to the need to expunge what he recognized as indecorous expression and ambiguous motivation, *A School for Scandal* (also of 1777) reveals his own mastery of language and complex plotting. It is his most aphoristic and shapely play, one moved easily forward by its own exuberant momentum. What is basically a moral fable, playing in the manner of *Tom Jones* with the contrast between two brothers—Joseph Surface, a sentimental and sanctimonious villain, and Charles, a virtuous and generous libertine—is transformed by a clever exploitation of theatrical devices (such as the use of hidden eavesdroppers) into an unmasking of bluffs, prejudices, and disguises. It is, above all, a marvellously witty exposure of surfaces, of the affectations, petty hypocrisies, and peccadilloes which form the stuff of the 'scandal' bitchily relayed by characters called Snake (a writer and critic), Sneerwell, Candour, and Backbite. *The Critic: or, A Tragedy Rehearsed* of 1779, loosely developed from Buckingham's *The Rehearsal*, is a clever burlesque on the problem of producing a play and a satirical defence of Sheridan's own art against the hacks and detractors whom he considered to be unworthy rivals for public attention. After a modestly successful career as a politician and a parliamentary orator, he returned awkwardly to drama in 1799 with *Pizarro*, a drably orotund adaptation of Kotzebue's German tragedy. It was a disappointing gesture more characteristic of a politician given to wordy defences of the public good than of a playwright known for his verbal scintillation.

Though its first audiences cheered its noble expressions of patriotism at a time of national crisis, it can also be unflatteringly seen as something of a belated justification of the affectations of Joseph Surface.

Johnson and his Circle

When Samuel Johnson (1709–84) proposed the young Sheridan for membership of the informal group of writers and artists known as the Club, he proclaimed *The Rivals* and *The Duenna* 'the two best comedies of the age'. Prospective membership of the Club and Johnson's praise were perhaps the highest accolades that a young writer on the make could earn. The Club, later known as the Literary Club, had first been formed in 1764 at the suggestion of the painter, Sir Joshua Reynolds. Its nine original members included Goldsmith and Edmund Burke, and it was later expanded to involve, amongst others, Johnson's former pupil, the actor David Garrick (1717–79), Bishop Percy, and, above all, the disciple whose name is still most immediately linked with Johnson's, James Boswell (1740–95). The fact that such a club had formed itself around Johnson, and that the wider circle of his friendships and influence, less circumscribed by male clubbishness, included another anecdotal memorializer, Hester Thrale (later Piozzi) (1741–1821), and the novelist Fanny Burney, is tribute to his considerable reputation both as a senior man of letters and as a galvanizing force in contemporary literature and society. That reputation had been painstakingly and worthily established over many years. The sparsity of the young Johnson's financial resources had obliged him to leave Oxford without a degree in 1731 (his famous doctorates were awarded in 1765 by Trinity College, Dublin, and in 1775 by the University of Oxford). His early career as a schoolmaster and his later as a journalist on the fringes of Grub Street had at times hovered precariously near economic and emotional disaster. That Johnson readily recognized both the potential and the real perils of the life of a young writer in London is evident in his own *Life of Mr Richard Savage* (1744). That he was later prepared to denounce the evils inherent in a writer's dependence on the patronage of grandees rings through the letter he wrote to Lord Chesterfield in 1755 (published posthumously in 1790), a letter which refers to the seven years of Chesterfield's neglect and bitterly defines a 'Patron' as 'one who looks with unconcern on a Man struggling for Life in the Water and when he has reached the ground encumbers him with help'.

Johnson's various essays in poetry span his career. He had come to London in 1737 carrying with him his incomplete blank-verse tragedy *Irene*, a play performed twelve years later through the good offices of Garrick, but greeted with jeers by its original audience and with patronizing sneers by its first critics. Little has been done to enhance its reputation since. *London: A Poem* of 1738 has much more distinction. This verse satire, modelled on the splutteringly indignant third satire of Juvenal, reflects on London as a city destructive of artistic talent and of the physical and mental well-being of the artist. If there is a comic exaggeration in the disillusioned narrator's claim 'Prepare for Death, if here at Night you roam, | And sign your Will before you sup from Home', the poem also plays a dense English historical reference against a sombre view of 'these degen'rate Days' in which 'softer Smiles and subtler Art . . . sap the Principles, or taint the Heart'. *The Vanity of Human Wishes* in 1749 is also an 'imitation' of Juvenal (this time the tenth satire), but here Juvenal's acerbic laughter is tempered by a Christian stoicism which seeks to deflate human pride and to illustrate the folly of human aspiration. Johnson's interest in the moral art of biography is evident in his exploration of examples of blind confidence challenged by time or destiny: Cardinal Wolsey falls from his 'full-blown dignity'; imagined aspirants to knowledge, longevity, and beauty find themselves caught out by the inevitability of change and decay; and the once victorious Charles XII of Sweden meets defeat, exile, ignominy, and an obscure death:

> Hide, blushing Glory, hide *Pultowa*'s Day:
> The vanquish'd Hero leaves his broken Bands
> And shews his Miseries in distant Lands
> Condemn'd a needy Supplicant to wait
> While Ladies interpose, and Slaves debate.
> But did not Chance at length her Error mend?
> Did no subverted Empire mark his End?
> Did rival Monarchs give the fatal Wound?
> Or hostile Millions press him to the Ground?
> His Fall was destin'd to a barren Strand,
> A petty Fortress, and a dubious Hand;
> He left the Name, at which the World grew pale,
> To point a Moral, or adorn a Tale.

The poem's unrelenting exposition of the precariousness of secular hope as compared to patient submission to the will of God is conveyed through both an adjectival precision and a steadily reverberant rhythm. A related tribute to a far less elevated human victim, 'condemn'd to hope's delusive mine', was to re-emerge in the short, melancholy, quatrain elegy 'On the Death of Dr Robert Levet' of 1783.

Johnson's finest prose echoes the balanced and measured weight of his verse. In the wide range of his periodical journalism, in his criticism, and in his philosophical tale, *The History of Rasselas, Prince of Abyssinia* (1759), his long, shapely, supple, and deliberate sentences serve to shape the cogent development of an argument. *Rasselas* traces the wanderings of an African prince and his sister Nekayah as they escape from 'the soft vicissitudes of pleasure and repose' of the 'happy valley' in which they have been royally confined. The plot is minimal and incidental, but the tale presents a series of encounters, experiences, and discussions which serve as evaluations of the pursuit of human happiness. The extended discourse on the freedom to choose how to live allows both for the relative pessimism of the philosopher Imlac's conclusion that 'Human life is everywhere a state in which much is to be endured, and little to be enjoyed', and for the Princess Nekayah's insistence that in viewing the 'contrarieties of pleasure' it is vital? when faced with 'the blessings set before you', to 'make your choice, and be content'. Her sagacity is spiced with an appropriately oriental metaphor: 'No man can taste the fruits of autumn while he is delighting his scent with the flowers of spring: no man can, at the same time, fill his cup from the source and from the mouth of the Nile.' Despite the pithy proverbiality of its wisdom, the tale ends with a conclusion 'in which nothing is concluded' and its last short sentences lead back to the point at which the story began.

Johnson's syntactical skill at both granting and gradually withdrawing assent to an argument, a proposition, or an aspect of character has both impressed and irked readers of his essays and his criticism. He can be dogmatic, but he can also present an impression of intellectual equilibrium by conditioning or undoing an initial proposition through a series of dependent clauses or a clever use of parallelism and antithesis. His mastery of lexicographical skills, evident in the range and originality of his compendious *Dictionary of the English Language* (1755), also informs his stylistic play with definitions, his learned use of Latinate vocabulary, and his somewhat ponderous pleasure in the polysyllabic. The periodical essays published in the 200 issues of his own journal, *The Rambler*, between 1750 and 1752 introduce a wryly humorous, discursive, informed, moral narrator as opposed to the essentially middle-brow entertainer of *The Spectator*. Where Addison generalizes, Johnson seeks to give the impression of speaking from painfully acquired personal experience. *The Rambler* considers aspects of literature, biography, religion, philosophy, and ethics (notably in number 185 which debates the opposition of vengeance and the Christian duty of forgiveness). The *Idler* papers, contributed to the *Universal Chronicle* between 1758 and 1760, adopt a persona who is ostensibly both more genial and more facetious, but here too there is a steady underpull of sobriety. 'It would add much to human happiness', the Idler remarks in his seventy-third paper, 'if an art could be taught of forgetting all of which the remembrance is at once useless and afflictive, if that pain which never can end in pleasure could be driven totally away, that the mind might perform its functions without incumbrance, and the past might no longer encroach upon the present.'

Johnson's edition of Shakespeare, which he finally published in 1765, offered the public a substantial critical Preface, a carefully revised text, and extensive explanatory notes to each of the plays. If the emendations of, and revisions to, Shakespeare's text have not always elicited the assent of subsequent editors, the Preface and the notes remain landmarks in the development of textual and critical study. Johnson not only extended a scholarly tradition which had been established in the century, but gave readers a new standard of interpretation, one received, according to Boswell, 'with high approbation by the publick'. The

Preface's criticism is two-pronged; it seeks to consolidate Shakespeare's reputation as a national classic by rejecting the criticisms of those who had seen
him as defective in both learning and dramatic tact, and to project an image of
him as 'the poet of nature' who 'holds up to his readers a faithful mirrour of
manners and of life'. In developing this supra-classical and patriotic thesis,
Johnson singles out for praise elements, such as Shakespeare's admixture of
tragedy and comedy and his failure to adhere to the 'unities', which had earlier
been disparaged by neo-classical critics. Johnson's *ex cathedra* judgements, both
flattering and fault-finding, fall thick and fast. His critical annotations offer a
more sporadic, and more suddenly illuminating, form of comment. He may
often be prescriptive in his treatment of awkwardnesses, embarrassments, or
anomalies in Shakespeare's texts, but he unfailingly detects both particular
problems and particular felicities. He balances an acknowledgement of the
'mean, childish, and vulgar' passages of *Love's Labour's Lost* against a full
appreciation of the play's distinctively Shakespearian 'sparks of genius'; he
weighs the redeeming wit of the 'unimitated, unimitable' Falstaff against his
sins; he complains of 'too much bustle' in the first act of *Coriolanus* and too
little in the last; and he notes of the 'artful involutions of distinct interests' in
King Lear that they 'fill the mind with a perpetual tumult of indignation, pity,
and hope'.

Johnson's last great undertaking, the *Lives of the Poets*, appeared from 1779
to 1781 as 'Prefaces, Biographical and Critical' to a new edition of English
poets deemed by the book-trade to have achieved classic status. Johnson provided fifty-two such prefaces, all but two of which deal with poets of the late
seventeenth and eighteenth centuries. The model for the longer essays came
partly from his own early *Life* of Richard Savage, a study which combines a
sympathetic appreciation of the struggles of a young outsider with an irritation at Savage's inclination to be 'petulent and contemptuous'. The *Lives of
the Poets* intermix extended passages of literary criticism, biographical information (much of it acquired at first hand), and a limited delineation of a
cultural context. Johnson expresses himself with an epigrammatic authority
which can reveal an acute observation and an equally distinct intolerance.
In the life of Cowley, for example, he famously defines the wit of the
'Metaphysical' poets which had so vexed him: 'The most heterogeneous ideas
are yoked by violence together; nature and art are ransacked for illustrations,
comparisons, and allusions.' His otherwise adulatory and systematic study of
the canonical status of Milton can still complain about the poet's 'acrimonious
and surly' politics, a republicanism which was founded 'in an envious hatred
of greatness, and a sullen desire of independence'. It is in the essays on
Dryden, Swift, Addison, Thomson, and Pope, however, that Johnson offers
definitions of the leading characteristics of his age, of his immediate literary
inheritance, and of his own taste. 'Genius', the power which 'constitutes a
poet', he notes in his study of Pope, is 'that quality without which judgement
is cold and knowledge is inert; that energy which collects, combines, amplifies

and animates'. It is a definition which could very properly be applied to Johnson's own idiosyncratic genius.

Boswell's *The Life of Samuel Johnson* appeared in 1791. It projects the image of Johnson as the doyen of his age, generous, honest, compassionate, censorious, and devout; it avidly reports the words and the deeds of a public man, confident in his values and forthright in his opinions; but it also attempts to show a more troubled private man, one prone to self-examination and vexed by both religious gloom and divine hope. Some fifty years later the biography was to provide Thomas Carlyle with much of the material he required to claim Johnson as 'the Hero as Man of Letters', a new kind of hero who stood apart from the narrow confines of his time and who informed an essentially romantic awareness of the long sweep of cultural history. Johnson the humbly born outsider, the struggling young writer, the setter-aside of aristocratic patrons, and the maker of his own way in the world was to emerge, somewhat incongruously, as the challenger of what was seen as the smug, tidy, enclosed, and élitist values of an age that had set too much store by the power of human reason. To Carlyle, Johnson was not the summer-up of the virtues of his time, but the heroic redeemer of its faults. The decades that immediately succeeded Johnson's death in 1784 were to witness cataclysmic political and cultural change in Europe. The Revolution in France was to turn the world upside down again. It was to bring about not only a series of radical reassessments of the British constitutional settlement of 1688, but, perhaps more significantly, a profound re-estimate of a rational world-order and of a culture which drew its inspiration from a perception of divine symmetry.

6

The Literature of the Romantic Period 1780–1830

'MY temper is not very susceptible of enthusiasm, and the enthusiasm which I do not feel I have ever scorned to affect', Edward Gibbon noted of himself in his *Memoirs of My Life and Writings* (posthumously printed in 1827). Nevertheless, when Gibbon (1737–94) recalled his first sight of the city of Rome some twenty-five years after the event, he admitted to having been troubled by strong emotions which had agitated his mind and which had led to a sleepless night and to 'several days of intoxication' before he could bring himself 'to descend to a cool and minute investigation' of the historic objects that he had come to Rome to study. Gibbon, the greatest English historian of the eighteenth century and the supremely reasonable and sceptical product of the European Enlightenment, felt obliged to confess to the kind of 'enthusiasm' which he scorned. His emotional excitement on seeing Rome may also suggest the degree to which he was the product of a culture which had come, not simply to appreciate the significance of 'sensibility', but actively to indulge it.

To one enthusiastic later visitor to Italy, Shelley, Gibbon seemed in retrospect to be the possessor of a 'cold and unimpassioned spirit'. To another, Byron, swayed by the kaleidoscopic beauty of Italy and by the massive splendour of the Alps, Gibbon was one of the tutelary spirits of Lake Geneva, one who, with Voltaire and Rousseau, had 'sought and found, by dangerous roads, | A path to perpetuity of fame'. Gibbon's 'dangerous road' had led him, in his monumental *The Decline and Fall of the Roman Empire* (1776–88), to question both a providential reading of history and the assumption that modern Europe was singularly blessed in its inherited forms of government and religion. The principles on which his history is built may look back to the culture of the intellectual salons of pre-revolutionary Paris and to the world of the aristocratic Grand Tour, but they also hark forward to the ideals of republican restructuring which would haunt the nineteenth-century European mind. Although Gibbon would certainly have been unhappy at Byron's linking his name to those of the 'intolerant bigot', Voltaire, and to the self-absorbed social optimist, Rousseau, the influence of his iconoclastic rationality was to be felt in the work of a new generation of writers who often distrusted reason and who earnestly sought to redefine the intellectual and political assumptions of its fathers.

Gibbon showed little sympathy with those who saw the Revolution in France as a new dawn for humanity. His picture of ancient Rome, meticulously observed as it slid into its decadence, had been conditioned by an awareness of a past loss of power and prestige, not by a feeling for future social regeneration. Nor did the new France which emerged in the years following 1789 assume the status of a political paragon for a man who had charted an earlier loss of republican virtue and a decline into demagoguery, innovation, and bloodshed. An empire, which had lost its integrity and its self-confidence, and whose failure was accentuated by the emergent Christian Church, seemed unlikely to be rebuilt by a society intent on merely demolishing the political structures of the Middle Ages. Gibbon's history looked back to a lost era of civic duty, military and patriotic service, and to the principle of public participation in national affairs but it did not seek to predict how the ideals of a new generation of 'patriots' and 'active citizens' might be formed. If he despised the 'oriental' despotism and the compromising politics of the later Roman emperors, and if he readily recognized the false pride and the unsteady claims of their latter-day Christian successors, he preferred to pose troubling questions about the past rather than to espouse modern causes. The essential tolerance of the original *pax romana* appealed more than the prospect of a new political puritanism disguised as revolution. Gibbon's vast historical narrative was intended to grate on modern Christian sensibilities, not to inspire new cults of the Supreme Being; its organized antitheses and its ironic set pieces were meant to challenge modern assumptions about progressive development, not to knock kings off their thrones and heads from kings' necks.

To see *The Decline and Fall of the Roman Empire* as the consummation of Enlightenment reasoning and yet to view the work of Gibbon's contemporaries, such as William Blake and Ann Radcliffe, as somehow belonging to a new age and to a new sensibility is both incongruous and the result of an over-categorical reading of literary history. Any determined attempt to define this supposed 'incongruity' derives from what can be seen as a proleptic historicism, one that determines that culture moves in ways which fit easily into progressive patterns. The period 1780–1830 is more open to conflicting interpretation than most others. It is an age obviously moulded by the impact of the revolutionary upheaval in France, but if neutrality was difficult to maintain at the time, the avoidance of taking sides, or silence, or a withdrawal of commitment, ought not to be interpreted as an inability to read what we loosely deem to be the signs of the times or as a failure of a proper response to a predetermined political or cultural alignment. It was an age of 'Romanticism', but the complex definition of 'Romanticism', or of

'Romanticisms', could be variously ignored, challenged, subsumed, debated, or simply questioned by writers who were not necessarily swimming against a contemporary tide. A variety of ways of writing, thinking about, criticizing, and defining literature co-exist in any given age, but in this particular period the varieties are especially diverse and the distinctions notably sharp. Such distinctions were not, properly enough, those which were inevitably drawn by contemporaries.

The most persuasive, fluent, and antipathetic survey of the immediate consequences of the first stage of the French Revolution is Edmund Burke's tract *Reflections on the Revolution in France and on the Proceedings in Certain Societies in London Relative to that Event* (1790). As its long title suggests, these 'reflections' pertain to the uneasy state of political affairs on both sides of the Channel. Burke (1729–97), one of the most polished parliamentary orators of his day, was attempting to check and condition the libertarian optimism which had greeted the 'Declaration of the Rights of Man' (enthusiastically promulgated by the French National Assembly in August 1789). From his firmly British constitutional standpoint (though he was by birth and education an Irishman), Burke stressed a need for tradition rather than innovation, for gradualism rather than radicalism. Having once stoutly defended the principles of the American Revolution in Parliament (again from a constitutionalist, traditionalist standpoint), he now attempted to explain the dangers of espousing a faith in a radical new order of things. Commonsensical American rhetoric was acceptable; French philosophism and Rousseauistic sentimentality were abominable. Burke's *Reflections* argues for a 'spirit of rational liberty', the reasonableness of which he saw as grounded in the legal compromises of the 'Glorious Revolution' of 1688 and in the 'manly, moral, regulated liberty' assured by the English Bill of Rights. 'Metaphysical abstraction', such as was now determining policy in Paris, seemed contrary to the substantial 'ancestral freedoms' which he claimed were dear to English hearts. As Burke's sharpest contemporary critic, Thomas Paine, later observed, Burke is conservatively smug in his confident acceptance of the British constitutional status quo and in his belief in the 'perfectly adequate' representation of the British people in their existing Parliament. Nevertheless, his *Reflections* attempts to define a theory of government based on a reasoned fear of the disruption of revolutionary reform. 'Government', he argues, 'is a continuance of human wisdom to provide for human *wants*', wants that were answered by the fundamental right to a sound government which both fostered civil society and restrained human passion. Burke may, in his most memorable paragraphs, have mourned the extinction of chivalry in France, but his main recourse was not to the spirit of the Middle Ages but to the eighteenth-century concept of an equable political balance, a balance which he finds evident in the existing order of things in Britain.

Paine, Godwin, and the 'Jacobin' Novelists

Burke's attack on the 'metaphysical abstractions' on which the evolving Revolution in France was based, and his related challenge to British apologists for the French experiment, were readily taken up. Burke had extended his criticism to include comment on the Constitutional Society and the Revolution Society, both of them radical clubs supported largely by religious Nonconformists, men who saw themselves as direct heirs to the spirit of the seventeenth-century English Revolution and as victims of discriminatory laws. Prominent amongst members were the Unitarian minister, Richard Price (1723–91) (who had actually provoked Burke's riposte by preaching a sermon on the need to apply French lessons to Britain), and a fellow Unitarian, the chemist, Joseph Priestley (1733–1804) (who had his house wrecked by a Birmingham mob as a result of attempting to celebrate the anniversary of the Fall of the Bastille in 1791). Amongst the most committed of these radicals, in terms of both his writings and his actions, was the independent republican, Thomas Paine (1737–1809). Paine's support for both the American and the French Revolutions had made him friends in these revolutionary nations and powerful enemies at home (his books were burned by the Public Hangman, but, having been obliged to flee to Paris in 1792, he was granted the privilege of French citizenship). Paine's acclaim in Jacobin France was largely based on his reputation as the trouncer of the tyrant-loving Burke in his book *The Rights of Man* (1791, 1792). If his book lacks the elegance and the systematic argument of Burke's, its attack upholds a new faith in constitutionally defined rights and liberties and renders much of Burke's creaking pragmatism ridiculous. The 'poison' of Burke's 'horrid principles' is countered by a delineation of a despotism which extends beyond the person of a king into 'every office and department' whose petty reflections and abuses of royal power are founded on 'custom and usage'.

The circulation of *The Rights of Man* through a chain of British and Irish radical clubs openly sympathetic to France (and therefore increasingly hostile to the existing British Constitution) may well have reached hundreds of thousands. Paine's active political career in France was less propitious. It was while in prison (and under the shadow of the guillotine from which he was released only by the fall of Robespierre) that he completed what was once his most notorious work, *The Age of Reason* (1794–6). Here the 'age of Revolutions' bears a post-Voltairean and post-Jeffersonian fruit, one poisonous to Christianity and atheism alike. The 'Cult of the Supreme Being', propagated in Jacobin France, is developed with a no-nonsense English thrust quite free of Robespierre's posturing and ritualizing. Paine dedicated his tract to his 'fellow-citizens of the United States of America', but his blunt arguments have implications well beyond the Quaker libertarianism of Franklin or the nonsectarian aspirations of the American Constitution. Paine proclaims his theism and a faith in a broad egalitarian morality of 'doing justice, loving mercy, and endeavouring to make our fellow-creatures happy'. He rejects all forms of established, defined, or 'revealed' religion by treating the nature of 'revelation' as if it were little more than hearsay. Scriptural authority is disposed of with much the same verve. The books of the Old Testament are dismissed as a collection of 'obscene stories . . . voluptuous debaucheries . . . cruel and torturous executions and unrelenting vindictiveness'. The Gospels strike him as merely anecdotal mystifications. 'The Word of God', he proclaims in capital letters, 'IS THE CREATION WE BEHOLD', and God himself stands for 'moral truth' not 'mystery or obscurity'.

William Godwin (1756–1836), born into a strong Dissenting tradition, abandoned both his Calvinist theology and his Congregationalist ministry in 1783 and assumed the alternative career of journalist and pamphleteer. His interest in both the dissidence of Dissent and contemporary political developments led to his active participation in the debates of the Constitutional Society. In 1789 he formed part of the congregation that heard Richard Price's 'Discourse on the Love of our Country' and he was sufficiently provoked by Burke's response to it to begin work on what became his own treatise, the *Enquiry Concerning Political Justice* (1793). The *Enquiry* is Godwin's most systematic theoretical work. He views human happiness and social well-being as the sole purpose of existence, but unlike Rousseau (whose influence pervades the work) he looks forward to a gradual melting away of all government to be replaced by a new system of radical anarchy. A rigid adherence to the leading principle of reason is substituted for Rousseau's cult of sensibility and his innate religiosity. Law, government, property, inequality, and marriage would be abolished as part of a gradual process by which human perfectibility, conditioned by human reason, would transcend existing limitations and impediments to fulfilled happiness.

Godwin's revolutionary hatred of all forms of injustice, privilege, and political or religious despotism also informs his novel, *Things as They Are or, the Adventures of Caleb Williams* (1794), a narrative centred on the problems of class perception and the nature of oppression. Godwin is less concerned with the authority of the state and more with the relatively petty, but no less damaging, exercise of power by a privileged class. 'It is now known to philosophers', he remarks in his Preface to the novel, 'that the spirit and the character of government intrudes itself into every rank of society', a factor exemplified in the story by the pervasive tyranny of a landowner, the once well-meaning Falkland. Falkland's tentacles are observed catching at the novel's hero, Caleb Williams, at every turn. Imprisoned by one of his persecutor's many contrivances, Caleb exclaims against the false assumption that England has no Bastille: 'Is that a country of liberty where thousands languish in dungeons and fetters? Go, go, ignorant fool! and visit the scenes of our prisons! witness their unwholesomeness, their filth, the tyranny of their governors, the misery of their inmates!' Such rhetoric forms part of a series of counterblasts to the complacent upholders of the idea of the free-born Englishman. If Caleb fails finally to confront his persecutor in public, a failure which he regrets, he is no passive victim. His escapes from confinement, his disguises, wanderings, and abortive attempts to flee from England, give the novel something of the quality of an adventure story, but his understanding of his predicament, and his articulation of this understanding as a critique of the existing ills of society, give his narrative a truly radical bite. At the opening of his story the narrator identifies Falkland's attraction to the principles of chivalry. In concluding his memoirs, Caleb returns to the issue. Chivalry has, he claims, served to corrupt a noble mind and perverted 'the purest and most laudable intentions'. The survival, or worse, the revival of aristocratic codes, it is suggested, works both as a disguise to, and a justification of, class-oppression.

Mary Wollstonecraft's *Vindication of the Rights of Man* (1790) also forms a protest against Burke's nostalgia for the age of chivalry by ridiculing defunct, upper-class codes of behaviour. But her treatise goes beyond a mere attack on a system of aristocratic values which keep the greater proportion of humankind in subservience. For Wollstonecraft (1759–97), that greater part of humankind embraced the thraldom of women of all classes. Wollstonecraft was the most articulate of a small group of writers, all of them associated with Godwin's circle, who used fiction to propagate certain key aspects of the new revolutionary ideology. This group included two other women writers, Mary Hays (1760–1843), the author of *Memoirs of Emma Courtney* (1796), and Elizabeth Inchbald (1753–1821) whose novel *A Simple Story* appeared in 1791. Hays's Emma Courtney is 'a human being, loving virtue', but one 'enslaved by passion, liable to the mistaken weaknesses of our fragile nature', and hers is a story of unhappy and unrequited love and of a suffering accentuated by a character insufficiently disciplined by education. Hays's later work includes the six volumes of *Female Biography, or Memoirs of Illustrious and Celebrated Women of all Ages and Countries* (1803). Inchbald's *A Simple Story* scarcely reveals itself now as a work of political or sexual radicalism, concerned as it is with a quiescent English Roman Catholic family, but it does manage to assert the pressing need for women's education in order to respond to a stifling lack of fulfilment. Inchbald's later literary career included the novel *Nature and Art* (1796), two unperformed dramas set in revolutionary France, and a string of comedies, one of which, a version of Kotzebue's *Lovers' Vows* of 1798, is the play disastrously rehearsed in Jane Austen's *Mansfield Park*.

The modest fiction of Hays and Inchbald shows a concern with the inconsistencies, limitations, and shortcomings of a contemporary society, but neither writer possessed the fire and the outspoken feminist zeal apparent in Wollstonecraft's flawed, rancorous, polemical, and radically original novels. Both *Mary* (1788) and the unfinished *The Wrongs of Woman* (1798) deal with the evidence of a universal oppression of women by men. *Mary* is told in an unadorned, laconic, matter-of-fact way, a style which, despite its periodic recourse to irony, might almost be described as perfunctory. The narrative touches on a variety of issues which figure prominently in 'Romantic' literature, notably on the significance of the imagination, the nature of religious feeling, and the soul-expanding effects of travel, and it interestingly opposes the emotional security of female friendship to a loveless marriage and an unfulfilled love-affair, but it is ultimately a tragedy without real substance. *The Wrongs of Woman* is a far more persuasive polemic concerning the need for a public recognition of women's rights. It is also a more impressive, if equally restless, work of fiction. Its heroine, Maria, is in many ways a development from the suffering Mary. She is acutely sensitive to landscape and ambience, but her Rousseauistic musings are balanced by her rejection of intellectual passivity and the kind of decorous feeling in which Rousseau himself ('the Prometheus of sentiment') patronizingly limited women's perceptions. Maria is also alert to 'the present state of society and government' and to what she sees as the 'enslaved state of the labouring majority'. To her alertness she adds the experience of thraldom within a loveless marriage. The novel opens with her literal imprisonment in a rambling madhouse, Gothic both in its architecture and in its *frissons*. The unhappy state of her suffering sisters is brought home to her through the melancholy catalogue of male oppression that she hears from her fellow inmates. If Maria's spirits are temporarily raised by the contemplation of Italy and 'the heart-enlarging virtues of antiquity', it gradually becomes clear that she is most inspired by the new virtues of revolutionary France. The judge who systematically rejects her pleas for independence and for the enjoyment of her own fortune recognizes that her motivation is, to him, a gross parody of all demands for political change. 'We do not want French principles in public or private life', he asserts in the novel's last completed chapter, 'and, if women were allowed to plead their feeling, as an excuse or palliation of infidelity, it was opening a flood-gate for immorality'.

Wollstonecraft's most effective attempt to prize open the flood-gates remains her highly influential treatise *A Vindication of the Rights of Woman* (1792), an adaptation and remoulding of French revolutionary theory to the universal needs of women. It is dedicated to a French hero of the moment, the ex-Bishop and singularly devious statesman, Talleyrand. This dedication sets out the nub of the argument of the treatise as a whole: 'If woman be not prepared by education to become the companion of man, she will stop the progress of knowledge and virtue.' 'Who made man the exclusive judge', Wollstonecraft demands, 'if woman partake with him the gift of reason?' Her book is centred on these twin appeals to education and to reason: education to render the further subjection of women indefensible and reason applied to all future questions of gender. The relevance of her argument to contemporary political debate is carefully indicated by comparisons of the particular enslavement of humankind by tyrannical kings to the general enslavement of women by universally tyrannical men. In Louis XIV's France, she asserts in her fourth chapter, a nation and a sex were forced into a subjection which was disguised by a picturesque cloak of chivalric flattery. Similarly, in the ninth chapter, she complains of 'the pernicious effects which arise from the unnatural distinctions established in society', distinctions which divide nations into classes and ranks and which serve to deny both dignity and liberty to the suffering majority. The new order in France, she implies, has a vital relevance to all future attempts to define relationships between class and class, gender and gender.

Independent-minded women figure prominently in the novels of two further members of the Godwin circle, Robert Bage (1728–1801) and Thomas Holcroft (1745–1809). In the work of both writers, however, it is men who assume the burden of the fictional argument. Bage, a Midlands industrialist, wrote six novels, the last two of which, *Man as He Is* (1792) and *Hermsprong, or Man as He is Not* (1796), show the clearest evidence of the impact of revolutionary thought. Bage's earlier works are variously concerned with the prospects of regenerated humanity in communities freed of pretension and extravagance. In *Man as He Is*, however, he traces the moral growth of Sir George Paradyne, a young man torn between hedonism and earnest practicality, a practicality conditioned by experience of worthy manufacture in Birmingham. As *Hermsprong* also emphasizes, Bage is determined to uphold the propriety of hard work and the right use of earned wealth in opposition to inherited privilege. Essentially, he looks to a future, American-style property-owning democracy, the values of which will be determined by men of sense and not men of rank (though this premiss is partly undermined in *Hermsprong* by the final revelation that its supposedly 'savage' American hero is in fact an English aristocrat!). Bage is no sansculotte, but he does identify the ills of present society with its hierarchical composition and he also firmly recognizes that sexual egalitarianism must form a part of the process of human liberation.

Holcroft's *Anna St Ives* (1792) is a witty and various epistolary novel, one which shows its debts to Richardson in its scenes of confinement and in the threatened rape of its abducted title character. Anna is courted by two men, rivals contrasted by birth, station, and literary style. Frank Henley, the practically educated son of an upwardly-mobile gardener, expresses himself 'frankly'. Coke Clifton has a very different, rakish, inflated style which plays with Latin tags and affects a restless desperation. Clifton is, however, no Lovelace despite his emotional lurches between wrath and regret, convention and excess. Henley, of course, wins the battle for the intelligent Anna's hand. The novel's discursive development also allows for some pointed asides concerning the 'barbarity' of the Europe of the *ancien régime*. Holcroft's second revolutionary novel, *The Adventures of Hugh Trevor* (1794), was published in the year in which its author spent some eight weeks in Newgate prison on an indictment for high treason (he was acquitted without any charge being preferred). *Hugh Trevor* is a *Bildungsroman* which traces the unsteady fortunes of its narrator and a destiny which is almost Hardyan in its unhappiness. All occasions seem to inform against him, and his splenetic denunciations of the corruptions of the Church, the Law, and the State suggest a real bitterness founded on experience. Despite its occasional sensationalism (as when Hugh finds himself, by accident, in an anatomist's cadaver store) the novel provides a generally effective criticism of the body politic. Holcroft's plays, *Duplicity* (1781), *Love's Frailties* (1794), and the once popular *The Road to Ruin* (1792), are equally sprinkled with aspersions concerned with the injustice of a hierarchical society (appropriately enough, it was he who adapted Beaumarchais's *The Marriage of Figaro* for the English stage in 1784). His posthumously published memoirs (1816), which describe his early struggles against poverty and rejection, later moved Charles Dickens to express the hope that his own autobiography (had he ever finished it) might one day stand on the same shelf.

Gothic Fiction

'When danger or pain press too nearly', Edmund Burke argues in his *A Philosophical Enquiry into the Origin of Our Ideas of the Sublime and Beautiful* (1757), 'they are incapable of giving any delight and are simply terrible; but at certain distances, and with certain modifications, they may be, and they are delightful, as we every day experience.' Burke's reference to the everyday delights evoked by representations of danger and pain is not merely an expression of relief from discomfort, or a gratuitous satisfaction in feeling 'There but for the Grace of God go I', but a tribute to the power of mimetic art. Aristotle's identification of the power of tragedy as lying in its evocation of pity and fear, and in its effective purging of these emotions, is shifted by Burke into new aesthetic territory. Pain and terror, he suggests, 'are capable of producing delight'; this delight was not pleasurable, 'but a sort of delightful horror, a sort of tranquillity tinged with terror'. The sublime, the awareness of which produces 'the strongest emotion which the mind is capable of feeling', he relates to ideas of vastness, infinity, and astonishment. The sublime could be experienced in the contemplation of nature, especially wild and mountainous scenery, or in the study of architecture, notably in the appreciation of soaring medieval cathedrals and rugged castle ruins. Such stimuli were to become the stock-in-trade of English Romanticism.

Burke readily recognized that certain kinds of literature also evoked a sense of 'delightful horror'. He specifically cited the instance of Milton's *Paradise Lost*, but he was also evidently thinking of Shakespeare's tragedies. References to, citations from, and distinct structural and thematic echoes of the works of Shakespeare and Milton were heard throughout the late eighteenth- and early nineteenth-century fiction which has long been typed as 'Gothic'. The strain begins, self-consciously enough, with Horace Walpole's brief novella *The Castle of Otranto* of 1764. It flourished in the closing years of the century, but ripples of its impact, and significant aspects of its sensationalism, have continued to be felt in English literature from the time of the Brontës and Dickens until the present day. 'Delightful horror' was bred amid historic ruins and in historical settings. It prospered by means of steady reference to crags and chasms, to torture and terror, to necromancy, necrophilia, and the uneasily numinous. It rejoiced in hauntings, sudden death, dungeons, dreams, diablerie, phantasms, and prophecies. Gothic fiction was, and is, essentially a reaction against comfort and security, against political stability and commercial progress. Above all, it resists the rule of reason.

Horace Walpole (1717–94), the third surviving son of the Prime Minister, Sir Robert Walpole, began creating a mock castle for himself at Strawberry Hill on the western fringes of London in 1749, gradually filling his new residence with a choice, eclectic, and extraordinary collection of *objets d'art*. As its pretty name suggests, in no sense did Strawberry Hill attempt to evoke the defence-works or the sublime battlements of a genuine fortress. Nevertheless, its fancy, castellated domesticity, its fretted plaster vaults, and the catholicity of its contents, seem to have inspired something of the whimsy of *The Castle of Otranto*, a story which purports to be a 'translation' of an old Italian tale of improbable catastrophes in medieval Apulia. As a connoisseur and an antiquarian, Walpole remains a figure of considerable cultural importance (his *Anecdotes of Painting in England* of 1762–80 is still a prime source for the study of the early pictorial arts in Britain), but his Gothic *divertissement*, which he claimed had blended 'two kinds of romance, the ancient and the modern', is by comparison a slight work chiefly remarkable for the quite extraordinary variety of its literary progeny.

The Castle of Otranto was the direct inspiration of Clara Reeve's short tale *The Old English Baron* of 1777. Reeve (1729–1807) produced what to all intents and purposes is an engaging fairy-tale of chivalric virtue and unlawful disinheritance, with a ghost standing in for a fairy godmother as the justifier of the righteous. Ann Radcliffe's work is both more expansive and more serious in its implications. Radcliffe (1764–1823) was, as Sir Walter Scott later acknowledged, the true 'founder of a class or school' which led the way 'in a peculiar style of composition affecting powerfully the mind of the reader'. In an essay published posthumously in 1826, Radcliffe herself drew a distinction between the representation of terror and that of horror; terror, she claimed, 'expands the soul, and awakens the faculties to a high degree of life'; horror, by contrast, 'contracts, freezes, and nearly annihilates them'. It was terror, and not horror, that was the source of her own fictional sublime. Her fiction, which may seem to some readers relatively tame, is more closely related to Burke's notion of a 'tranquility tinged with terror' than to the supernatural sensationalism of the later Gothic novelists whose works have inspired the literary, and cinematic, 'horror' of the late nineteenth and twentieth centuries. Radcliffe's sensibility had been formed by the wild and perilous landscape paintings of Salvator Rosa and her sublime was centred on descriptions of imaginary scenery. It is to Salvator Rosa that she refers her readers in the third chapter of *The Mysteries of Udolpho* (1794) in her delineation of a scene of 'barrenness . . . interrupted by the spreading branches of the larch and cedar, which threw their gloom over the cliff, or athwart the torrent that rolled in the vale'. In *The Italian* (1797) her heroine, Ellena, is imprisoned in a convent the site of which overlooks a plain fringed with a 'vast chain of mountains, which seemed to form an insurmountable rampart to the rich landscape . . . Their towering and fantastic summits, crowding together into dusky air, like flames tapering to a point'. Such impressions of solemn or 'peculiar grandeur' serve both to elevate and to awe the spirits of Radcliffe's romantically susceptible heroines. Hers is an imagined Italy (she left England only once, to visit the Low Countries and the Rhineland), informed by impressions and powerful visual stereotypes. Both Emily in *The Mysteries of Udolpho* and Ellena in *The Italian* prove to be victims of long-drawn-out male threats, but they are threats accentuated by cultivated memories of *banditti*, feudal princes, Machiavels, and an encroachingly sinister Catholicism. Both heroines are decorous and sensible, and both find resource in their very reasonableness, but they also appreciate the sexual and moral dangers of their respective situations with a heightened and comple-mentary sensibility. At the opening of *Udolpho*, for example, Radcliffe is at pains to suggest the quality of Emily's education at the hands of her refined, nature-loving father, an instruction which has taught her 'to resist first impres-sions, and to acquire that steady dignity of mind, that can alone counter-balance the passions and bear us, as far as is compatible with our nature, above the reach of circumstances'.

In his various anthology *Literary Hours* of 1798 the minor essayist the Reverend Nathan Drake (1766–1836) praised Ann Radcliffe as 'the Shakespeare of Romance writers', a novelist who had the tact never to 'degen-erate into horror'. In his essay 'On Objects of Terror' Drake attempted to categorize such objects. Into a first category he placed 'those which owe their origin to the agency of superhuman beings, and form a part of every system of mythology'; into a second he put 'those which depend upon natural causes and events for their production'. An increasingly supernatural emphasis in Gothic fiction is evident in the work of Matthew Gregory Lewis (1775–1818) and Charles Robert Maturin (1782–1824), both of whom seem to have relished a degeneration into the world of horror. Lewis's *The Monk* of 1796 is set in a Capuchin friary in Madrid, a small world of repression, obsession, ambition, and intrigue which contrasts vividly with the calm reflection generally evident amongst the inmates of Radcliffe's convents. Ambrosio, the monk of the title, is seen steadily falling away from the false state of grace in which he begins and from his popular reputation as a saintly preacher. The novel lacks any real psychological depth in its investigation of a tormented soul, but it powerfully evokes, and semi-pornographically exploits, incidents and images which serve to suggest the labyrinthine nature of Ambrosio's buried life. Throughout the narrative structural play is made with hidden chambers, subterranean passages, and sealed vaults; underground life, like concealed passion, breaks threateningly into the open or serves to undermine all pretension to chaste sobriety. *The Monk* is prefaced with an epigraph from *Measure for Measure*, and it later echoes and transforms the monument scene from *Romeo and Juliet*, but Ambrosio's explosive escape from repression goes well beyond anything suggested by Shakespeare's Angelo, and his attempted rape in a charnel-house quite outdoes Juliet's horridest imaginings. The termination of Ambrosio's Faustian compact with the Devil results in his being physically and spiritually broken and with his agonizingly slow death described in self-indulgent detail ('Myriads of insects . . . fastened upon his sores, darted their stings into his body . . . and inflicted upon him tortures the most exquisite and insupportable. The Eagles of the rock tore his flesh piecemeal, and dug out his eye-balls with their crooked beaks'). What Lewis lacks in discretion and tact he makes up for in energetic verve and frenetic action. Desperate diseases are everywhere relieved by desperate appliances.

Charles Robert Maturin was a priest of the Church of Ireland, endued with a strongly Calvinist theology, who had found ecclesiastical promotion as elusive as literary and financial success. Before the publication of *Melmoth the Wanderer* in 1820 he had written one historical and two Irish-based novels, and had had his tragedy *Bertram* performed at Drury Lane thanks to the good offices of Scott and Byron. A feeling for the wild western reaches of Ireland, an acute appreciation of disappointment, and a gloomy sense of theological despair and incipient damnation inform *Melmoth*, a fiction shaped around a series of anguished attempts by its hero to shrug off the consequences of yet another diabolic compact. Melmoth seeks for more than sympathy for his situation; he needs to persuade a fellow-despairer to take his place. The effect of the novel is cumulative, built up as it is on narratives describing the unhappy destinies of the hero's potential substitutes and moving across both geographical space and historic time. The panoply of a deeply suspect Catholicism and the persecuting zeal of the Inquisition haunt the various stories as much as they had shaped the prejudices implicit throughout *The Monk*; the distinction of *Melmoth* lies in the variety and complexity of its psychology and in its examination of the grim isolation of its central character. In the Preface to his earlier novel *The Milesian Chief* (1812) Maturin had confessed: 'If I possess any talent, it is that of darkening the gloomy, and developing the sad; of painting life in extremes, and representing those struggles of passion when the soul trembles on the verge of the unlawful and the unhallowed.' Maturin's Wanderer is an archetype of northern European Romanticism, linked in the popular imagination with Byron's Childe Harold and Cain, with Goethe's Faust, with Dostoevsky's Raskolnikov, and with the legend of the Wandering Jew. He is also peculiarly the product of an increasingly restless and marginalized Anglo-Irish culture, troubled by the cultural oppositions of guilt and detachment, of rootlessness and disinheritance.

The unlawful and the unhallowed also figure prominently in a further, if somewhat less exotic, Calvinist novel, James Hogg's *The Private Memoirs and Confessions of a Justified Sinner* (1824). Hogg (1770–1835) was best known to his contemporaries as a rustic poet of the Scottish Borders, the 'Ettrick Shepherd' who had supplied Sir Walter Scott with folk-ballads and who had gradually established a reputation for himself as a writer of verse and occasional prose. His novel was originally published anonymously, as if it were the genuine evangelical confession promised by its baldly Protestant title, but his title-page ruse serves as a merely temporary disguise to the challenging innovation of the succeeding fiction. *The Private Memoirs and Confessions of a Justified Sinner* subverts the implications of the Calvinist theology of predestination by pushing to an extreme the antinomian idea that the Christian elect is set free by divine grace from the need to observe the moral law. Robert Wringhim, the 'justified sinner' of the title, draws his assurance of belonging to 'the community of the just upon earth' from the religious culture of his adopted father, but the perversion of his 'sanctification' is very much his own, worked out as it is with the prompting sophistry of a figure whom he identifies as his *alter ego*, Gil-Martin. Wringhim commits a series of 'justified' murders, beginning, in a fit of pious indignation, with that of a preacher whose doctrine he finds unsoundly flabby, before coming to the horrified awareness that his prompter is the Devil and that an eternal retribution awaits him. The narrative, divided between a third person 'editor' and Wringhim's own 'memoir', suggests that Wringhim's problem is more internal than external, more an unnatural fragmentation of the self and a psychopathic case-history than a conventionally 'Gothic' play with the supernatural.

The critical umbrella of the term 'Gothic' has been taken to cover a number of anomalous texts which allow both for a convergence and for a conflict of the natural and the supernatural. The contrast presented by William Beckford's oriental fantasy *Vathek* (1786) and Mary Shelley's proto-science fiction *Frankenstein* (1818) is particularly pointed. Neither novel is narrowly 'Gothic', dispensing as they both do with medieval trappings and the diabolic in favour of an investigation of esoteric or forbidden knowledge. Beckford (1759–1844), the heir to a phenomenal fortune, was able, like Walpole, to act out his fantasies in the architectural pleasure-domes he built for himself and amid the extraordinary collection of artefacts which he assembled. Like Fonthill Abbey and Lansdown Tower, his short, exotic romance *Vathek* (originally written in French) offered an escape from the plodding, orderly pleasures of the life of an eighteenth-century gentleman. The dissolute and disillusioned Arabian hero of the tale thirsts for power, both secular and material, and for a supernatural control over life and death, appetites which are sated only by entry into the caverns of the underworld, secret halls which belatedly force upon him the wisdom that his cravings are empty. Vathek and his hedonistic companions are finally condemned to lose the gift of hope and to 'wander in an eternity of unabating anguish . . . the punishment of unrestrained passions and atrocious deeds'. *Vathek* is a *Rasselas* bereft of much of its moral philosophy, a study of unhappy yearning and unfulfilment.

Frankenstein works on quite a different level. Mary Shelley (1797–1851), the daughter of Mary Wollstonecraft and William Godwin, and the wife of Percy Bysshe Shelley, conceived her novel as a *divertissement* during a wet summer in Switzerland with her husband and Byron. Talk in this literary circle had, according to the novelist's own introduction to her work, dwelt on philosophy and nature, on the origins and meaning of life, on the myth of Prometheus, and on the enterprise of modern science. The proposal that each member of the circle should write a 'ghost story' stimulated a sleepless night and a fertile, unconscious drift into 'terror' on Mary Shelley's part. *Frankenstein* is, however, more than simply a recall of her 'thrall of fear'; it is a morally probing exploration of responsibility and of the body of knowledge which we now call 'science'. The tendency amongst Byron's associates to push ideas to extremes, and to test sensation and experience, is here developed as a study of the consequences of experiment and of moving into the unknown. *Frankenstein* is also an imaginative expatiation of the principles of liberty and human rights so dear to the novelist's parents. The interconnected layers of the fiction lead from one variety of intellectual ambition to another, from the first-person account of the solitary explorer, Robert Walton, to the confessions of Dr Frankenstein (the 'modern Prometheus' of the subtitle) and of his unhappy creation. Like the legendary Prometheus, Frankenstein's enterprise is punished, but not by a jealous heaven; his suffering is brought upon him by a challenge to his authority on the part of the creature that he has rashly made. A parallel is drawn not only between classical myth and modern experiment, but also between the story of Frankenstein's miserable creature and that of Adam. This artificial man, like the ruined, questioning Adam, turns to accuse his creator with an acute and trained intelligence (he has also grasped the theological and educational implications of *Paradise Lost*, a recitation of which he has overheard). Like Adam he insists on both his loneliness and, later, his wretchedness. He also comes to recognize how much he has in common with Milton's Satan ('When I viewed the bliss of my protectors, the bitter gall of envy rose within me'). Envy, defeat, and unhappiness express themselves in a course of jealous destruction which he sees as vindicating his separate existence. The novel ends where it began in a wild and frozen polar landscape, a wasteland which both purges and purifies the human aberrations represented by Frankenstein and his flawed experiment. The shifting ice is not only effectively placeless, it also allows for the opening of new perspectives and uncertainties. *Frankenstein* is no meditation on historical, pictorial, or mythological terrors; its fascination and its power lie in its prophetic speculation.

Smith and Burney

The modern view of the range of late eighteenth-century fiction has for too long been conditioned by an appreciation of its extravagant and political aspects to the detriment of its romantic realism. The life and work of both

Charlotte Smith (1749–1806) and of Frances (Fanny) Burney (1752–1840) were directly touched by the French Revolution, but neither writer was to espouse radical causes in her fiction and Burney in particular increasingly emphasized the passivity of her female protagonists. The world may be viewed by both novelists as unstable and oppressive, it may stimulate Gothic sensibility or sentimental asides on war and revolution, but it is generally observed as providing an uncomfortable environment in which the moral maturity of men and women is tested and not found wanting. Fanny Burney's heroines enter society at an awkward age or in unfavourable circumstances and they are obliged to learn through mistakes, embarrassments, and reverses, but they are equally allowed to enjoy the love of an upright suitor and the ultimate prospect of a happy marriage. Virtue is rewarded by a slow process of learning how to recognize the correct amatory and social signals. Women in the fictions of both novelists are not so much threatened victims as dependants, sojourners in the shadow of energetic men, and decision-makers only in so far as they are presented with moral choices.

Charlotte Smith, herself the far from passive victim of a miserable marriage, wrote to make money to support her children. Her contemporary reputation was based largely on her poetry, notably the *Elegiac Sonnets, and other Essays* of 1784. In her verse she cultivates the figure of a melancholy narrator, a narrator sometimes literally modelled on Goethe's Werther, who is responsive to seasonal change but equally alert to a disjunction between nature's outward harmony and a private restlessness (the 'tyrant passion and corrosive care' of her 'Sonnet Written at the Close of Spring'). Her distinctive power as a poet lies in a combination of detailed observation and recurrent evocation of misery. Smith's novels are far less personal and emotional, concerned as they often are with money, inheritance, and the world of the country house. In *Emmeline* (1788) she makes play with the Gothic by initially confining her heroine, an 'orphan of the castle', in a rambling Pembrokeshire fortress and by allowing her to elude unwanted suitors by escaping down labyrinthine corridors. In *The Old Manor House* (1793) she deals once more with seclusion in a mansion, adding what prove to be unfounded suspicions of ghosts and poltergeists (the bumps in the night are made by smugglers who are effectively undermining the house's foundations). *The Old Manor House* is, despite its title, preoccupied with the dilemmas, the politics, and the sentiments of the present. The manor's owner, Mrs Rayland, dwells on her family's ancient chivalric pretensions, and, as an old-fashioned Tory, pours scorn on those whom she terms 'the Rebels of America'. Her young cousin, Orlando Somerive, discovers less narrow political definitions when fighting with the British army in North America, berating the miseries of army life and 'the folly of mankind' in proceeding with such a war. Neither Orlando's daring pacifism, nor the nefarious activities of the smugglers, ever take on a major thematic emphasis in a story essentially concerned with romantic love and a proper line of succession. In *Desmond* (1792) Smith had made a limited attempt to defend the liberal principles of the first stages of the French Revolution, but her disillusion with its bloody progress emerges in her long poem *The Emigrants* of 1793. In the poem, the subject of which derives from her active sympathy with, and support for, French refugees in England, she mourns 'with swimming eye' the desolation of 'the Temple, which they fondly hoped | Reason would raise to Liberty, destroyed | By ruffian hands'.

Fanny Burney's sympathies were never swayed towards the Revolution. As a sometime lady-in-waiting to Queen Charlotte, and as the future wife of the *émigré* General Alexandre d'Arblay, she noted in her Diary for 1792, for example, that 'the famous Tom Paine' was propagating 'his pernicious doctrines' in Suffolk. In her own county of Surrey she frequented 'a little colony of unfortunate . . . French noblesse' at Juniper Hall at Mickleham, a colony which contained her future husband and which gave her the opportunity of observing the complex amatory adventures of Germaine de Staël and her lovers Narbonne and Talleyrand (though Burney also admitted to being impressed by Mme de Staël's 'extraordinary intellect'). Her first novel, *Evelina, or the History of a Young Lady's Entrance into the World* (1778), describes an English society far removed from that of flirtatious Paris and its dangerous liaisons. Its heroine is a girl with 'a virtuous mind, a cultivated understanding, and a feeling heart', one who is initially ignorant of 'the forms, and manners, of the world'. What Evelina comes to learn is the value of decorum in fashionable society, but she also acquires a modest wisdom which transcends the limits of that society. Her letters to her clerical mentor, Mr Villars, reveal an occasionally witty discrimination as well as a protest against the ways of a world which both elevates and narrows the scope of women. She finally finds security as the wife of the worthy Lord Orville (a muted reflection of Richardson's Grandison).

Burney's more expansive later novels, *Cecilia, or Memoirs of an Heiress* (1782), *Camilla; or, a Picture of Youth* (1796), and *The Wanderer: or, Female Difficulties* (1814) all re-examine the motif of the *ingénue* entering the 'world'. *Cecilia* is a substantial development of the themes of *Evelina*, whose popular success had established Burney's reputation, but its satirical edge is far blunter and its assertion of moral conventions both more emphatic and more verbose. In *Camilla* the comedy is yet more subdued, and the critical ebullience, which had marked Evelina's observation of society, is more tacit so as to present a firmer defence of social values in the face of revolutionary questioning. Camilla is obliged to win respect for her innate virtue and for her selfhood, but her unsteady relationship with her priggish suitor cum mentor, Edgar Mandlebert, consists of a series of misunderstandings, surmountable obstacles, and tearful reconciliations. It is a sombre novel which hovers close to tragedy and which insistently presses home its moral message about the importance of good conduct. The fifth chapter consists largely of a 'Sermon' addressed to Camilla by her father Mr Tyrold. This sermon puts forward an ideal of female action and provides a counterblast to Mary Wollstonecraft's demands for education, equality, and independence by insisting on the vaguer notion that 'the temporal destiny of woman is enwrapt in still more impenetrable obscurity than that of man' and that 'the proper education of a female . . . is still to seek, still a problem beyond human solution'. Tyrold's Christian stress on patience, self-conquest, and good sense as the means of controlling 'passion' evidently received Burney's own assent, for she later allowed his sermon to be separately reprinted as part of a conduct book for young ladies. The distinction between the control of passion and its free expression, between the operation of sense and an indulgence in sensibility, provides the shape of *The Wanderer*, an investigation of the struggles of a disorientated and nameless refugee in England, a victim of French revolutionary persecution. Although by 1814, the year of the novel's belated publication, the Reign of Terror was long past, Burney was at pains to stress in her Preface that the 'stupendous iniquity and cruelty' of the period had left real enough scars. The unhappy wanderer, Juliet (known through most of the novel by her awkwardly acquired pseudonym 'Ellis'), is contrasted with an English enthusiast for revolutionary liberty, Elinor Joddrel, a girl 'inebriated . . . with the revolutionary beverage' and enthusiastically convinced that the epoch in which she lives 'lifts our minds from slavery and from nothingness, into play and vigour, and leaves us no longer, as heretofore, merely making believe that we are thinking beings'. Such high-minded confidence is shown to be misplaced; Elinor is both restless and reckless, unhappy in love and incapable of adjusting to the stodgy stability of upper middle-class English society. Burney's picture of that society is scarcely flattering, for it is variously seen as snobbish, selfish, insular, and cruel, but it is Juliet and her practical sense, cultivated under adversity, who finally triumphs and who profits from the unbroken English barriers of 'custom and experience, raised by the wisdom of foresight, and established, after trial, for public utility'. Such traditionalism and social conservatism is a keynote of the novel. *The Wanderer* is nevertheless implicitly marked by a genteel feminism which steadily emerges in Burney's careful delineation of the fortunes of her struggling, rejected, and often isolated heroine.

Cowper, Blake, and Burns

The conflicting, even contradictory, pulls of passivity and active commitment have often determined the subject-matter and mood of English poetry. This is as true of religious verse as of its political and secular counterparts. These tensions are especially evident in the late eighteenth and early nineteenth centuries, a period marked as much by evangelical religion as by international political engagement, by a moralizing spirituality as by a struggle for liberation. In some vital and effective ways, most notably in the battle against the slave-trade and, later, against colonial slavery itself, pious sentiment and moral conviction went hand in hand with campaigns for political action. In other cases, an insistent internalization of religious experience, and an emphasis on private and public morality, seemed to preclude a preoccupation with constitutional and legal reform. Whereas the various crises created by the evolving nature of French revolutionary politics presented a series of unre-solved dilemmas and inspiriting impulses to sympathetic English observers, a contrary impulse towards contemplation and withdrawal also tends to mould intellectual and religious life in the period. To regard the poetry of these years as dominated by novelty, liberty, and experiment is to distort it accord-ing to perceptions proleptically shaped by a fascination with a supposed progressive advance from a defined 'Romanticism' to 'Modernist' reaction against it.

No poet of the period better embodies these contradictory movements than William Cowper (1731–1800). Cowper was a man naturally subject to fits of depression, a trait accentuated by religious melancholia and informed with a strongly Calvinist sense of sin and potential damnation. Retirement from the pressures of work and of city life was enforced by his temperament and intel-lectually justified by recourse to an anti-urban, anti-courtly tradition dating back to the Latin poetry of Horace (to whose work he makes frequent refer-ence). But for Cowper, retirement never implied a dissociation of himself from secular concerns, nor was it conditioned by a desire for solitary contemplation. In the 'Verses supposed to be written by Alexander Selkirk, during his Abode in the Island of Juan Fernandez' he recoils with a conditional horror from the isolation of this 'monarch of all he surveys', the presumed original of Defoe's Robinson Crusoe. Selkirk's monarchy may deny him rivals, but it also entails a lack of 'society, friendship, and love', a loss which is balanced by a minimal assertion of divine mercy which 'reconciles man to his lot' in the final lines of the poem. Such reconciliation frequently informs Cowper's meditations on sin or misfortune, or on the general corruption of the world, but his poetry also allows for eruptions of anger at abuses and offences and for forceful denuncia-tions of oppression. Throughout his verse there echo diatribes against slavery and colonial intrusion into non-European societies. 'The Negro's Complaint' turns arguments about 'civilization' on their heads and finally demands proof of slave-traders that their 'human feelings' are in any way superior to those of the Africans they exploit (a similar sentiment shapes 'Pity Poor Africans'). In Cowper's most substantial poem, *The Task* (1784), his complaints range over colonial oppression, the condition of the poor at home, the corruption of London and its commercial enterprise, the conduct of war, and, supremely, unjust imprisonment. The fifth book of the poem, 'The Winter Morning Walk', moves from an opening description of a snow-covered landscape, to a meditation on the ice-palace built by the Empress Anna of Russia and reflections on the 'playthings' of despots, to a forceful advocacy of pacifism, but the book centres on an imagined picture of a prisoner in the Bastille, a victim of Bourbon tyranny. 'There's not an English heart', Cowper propheti-cally announces of the Bastille, 'that would not leap | To hear that ye were fall'n at last; to know | That ev'n our enemies, so oft employ'd | In forging chains for us, themselves were free.' Cowper's passion for liberty is not, however, confined to a political construct ('the cause of man'), for he is equally determined to insist on a liberty of conscience and worship and yet more on the service of God which brings perfect freedom ('liberty of heart deriv'd from Heav'n').

The structure of *The Task* is essentially discursive, using ideas of provincial retirement and the active contemplation of nature as a basis from which other meditations open up. It is not a shape which has appealed to the kind of modern reader conditioned by a demand for logical progression and a consequential process of argument. Cowper roots each book of his poem in his own natural surroundings and in the sequence of seasonal change, but as his choice of winter settings for three of his six books indicates, he also seeks to suggest the quality of contemplation both during a walk outdoors and in an evening's fireside assimilation of the day's thoughts and sensations. The arrival of the post and the daily newspaper described at the opening of Book IV ('The Winter Evening') allows for the secure consideration of a larger world-view, examined at 'a safe distance'.

> Now stir the fire, and close the shutters fast,
> Let fall the curtains, wheel the sofa round,
> And, while the bubbling and loud hissing urn
> Throws up a steamy column, and the cups,
> That cheer but not inebriate, wait on each,
> So let us welcome peaceful ev'ning in.

As so often in Cowper's work, a determined act of withdrawal from the world ushers in sober contemplation and peace of mind. The choice of blank verse, prompted, as was the poem's first title ('The Sofa') by Cowper's friend Lady Austen, also permits a general ease of telling and an echo of comfortable, refined, but relaxed, rhythms of speech. The work as a whole, he asserts, had one major tendency: 'to discountenance the modern enthusiasm after a London life, and to recommend rural ease and leisure, as friendly to the cause of piety and virtue.' Sophistication, urbane politicking, and noisy declaration are rejected in favour of a therapeutic absorption in the pleasures of stillness.

For Cowper, 'the cause of piety and virtue' demanded a response both to God and to humankind. His evangelical strictures on the wickedness of the world can be both political and intensely private, and his distinctive sensitivity to nature suggests an almost Franciscan awareness of a co-operative unity in creation. He recognizes in the fourth book of *The Task* that there is 'a soul in all things, and that soul is God' and that nature itself can be a name for an effect 'whose cause is God'. When he addresses his pet hare ('Epitaph on a Hare') or when he complains of the casual cruelty of a 'gentle swain' who has allowed a goldfinch to starve in its cage, he is essentially in the same frame of mind as when in *The Task* he views hunting as an unhappy consequence of the loss of Eden or when, seated on a felled tree, he contemplates the frailty of life ('The Poplar Field'). Cowper's shorter religious lyrics, included in the collection known as the *Olney Hymns* (1779), suggest a similarly delicate, if often tense, sensibility, one urged to express a public sentiment but constitutionally inclined to the form of the interior monologue. The *Olney Hymns* enjoyed a considerable popularity, passing through some twenty editions between 1779 and 1831. Their success with readers and singers alike is testimony both to the strength of evangelical piety in the period and to Cowper's particular evocation of an intimacy in responding to divine grace, a factor evident in the celebrated quatrain songs 'O for a closer walk with God' and 'Hark, my soul, it is the Lord'. His rarer assertions of congregational unity (such as 'Jesus, where'er thy people meet'), or of professions of public faith ('God moves in a mysterious way'), stand as more affirmatively communal statements.

Cowper's steady popularity contrasts strikingly with the obscurity in which William Blake worked, his most circulated works amongst his contemporaries being the *Songs of Innocence and of Experience* of which only some twenty-two copies of the first collection and twenty-seven of the combined volume were printed. Blake (1757–1827) died, according to one of his friends, singing 'Hallelujahs and songs of joy and triumph', impromptu songs which his wife described as being 'truly sublime in music and in verse' and performed with 'extatic energy'. If Blake's lyric verse can and ought to be seen as derived from a hymnological tradition in English verse, it has, perhaps fortunately, had only a limited impact on the subsequent compilers of congregational hymn-books. 'The Divine Image' has been awkwardly appropriated to certain hymnals, and 'Jerusalem' (the inductive preface to the poem *Milton*) has, in Sir Hubert Parry's setting, become celebrated as both a religious and a political rallying-call, but the very subtlety and elusive ambiguity of most of Blake's lyrics have generally denied them repetitive melodic musical settings and over exposure in narrow or sectarian contexts.

Blake, born into a Dissenting tradition (a tradition that sometimes encouraged extempore hymn-singing), remained a religious, political, and artistic radical throughout his life. From his childhood, when he claimed to have seen the prophet Ezekiel sitting under a tree, he insisted that he had been granted visions by God and that he could translate and interpret those visions as designs which interfused picture and word. Although the inspiration was visionary, the process by which these designs reached an audience was laborious. Blake, who had been trained as an engraver, would transfer the written text of a poem to an etched copper plate, accompanying it with appropriate illustration or decoration; when printed, the page was elaborately hand-coloured or, in some cases, actually printed in colour by a method of his own invention. Blake's works, if studied in their original configurations, interrelate image and text. The text does not simply follow a picture, nor does a picture solely represent a text; both demand interpretative or speculative readings.

Together they form a total text in which different signs prove to be co-operative, manifold, even contradictory.

Blake's literary sources and inspirations range from the Bible and the Bible-derived epic structures of Dante and Milton, to the moralizing children's poetry of Isaac Watts (1674–1748), the hymns of Charles Wesley, and the records of the eccentric Swedish visionary and mystic, Emanuel Swedenborg (1688–1772). Blake's work is in many ways both eclectic and syncretic. It is pervaded with the symbolism, imagery, and prophetic utterance of the Bible, but, as the poem *Milton* (1804) suggests, Blake also identifies himself both with the author of *Paradise Lost* and with the angels, both fallen and unfallen, who figure in Milton's narrative. It is Blake who, assuming a diabolic voice, declares in *The Marriage of Heaven and Hell* (1790–3) that Milton was 'a true poet and of the Devil's party without knowing it'. Despite his disillusion with Swedenborg's all-embracing 'Church of the New Jerusalem', and his parodies of the pompous declamatory style of Swedenborg's writings Blake remained fascinated with the celebration of 'contraries' and the opposed ways of feeling, seeing, and believing which he had originally evolved as a corrective to Swedenborgianism. In his complex, personal redefinitions of Swedenborg's cosmology, Blake approached more closely to the obscure mysticism of the seventeenth-century German theosophist Jakob Boehme (1575–1624) who had argued that God the Father was the undefinable matter of the universe, neither good nor evil, but containing the germs of both. This Godhead, according to Boehme, had two wills: one good, one evil; one loving, one wrathful. Though evil, as integral to the nature of God, was necessary, humankind could conquer on Earth, and ultimately assume the empty places of the fallen angels in Heaven, by faith in Christ. In his own prophetic books, Blake sees Heaven as forming part of a framework which must merge with the creative energy of Hell rather than stand in opposition to it. The 'doors of perception' are cleansed by an apocalyptic transformation of categories so that contraries meet in newly energetic formations. Thus the tigers and horses, the lions and lambs, the children and adults, the innocent and the experienced of Blake's symbolism ought to be perceived as integral elements in the dynamic of synthesis which he saw as implicit in creation.

The complex mythology and the heretical perversity of much of Blake's thought often runs counter to an easy appreciation, let alone an understanding, of his work as a whole. This, however, is far from true of the lyrics describing contrary states of feeling and seeing, published as the *Songs of Innocence* (1789) and linked with the *Songs of Experience* in 1794. The songs of both books are interrelated, not simply as reflecting oppositions, but as a series of shifting perceptions. The 'two contrary states of the human soul' of the work's sub-title form a kind of dialectic which suggests not only a falling away from Edenic innocence to experience, but also the possibility of progress towards a Christ-inspired 'higher' innocence and a future regain of paradise. Despite their hymn-like simplicity and their nursery-rhyme rhythms, the poems in both books assume ramifications from their contexts and their interrelationships.

The *Songs of Innocence* frequently suggest challenges to and corruptions of the innocent state; children are afraid of the dark, brute beasts threaten lambs, slavery imprisons the negro and a vile trade the little chimney-sweep. In 'Holy Thursday' a multitude of charity-children march in under 'the high dome of Pauls' in order to sing praises to God, but what on one level is a poem rejoicing in infant joy is, on another, a condemnation of regimentation, exploitation, and the smugness of 'the aged men, wise guardians of the poor'. The 'wisdom' of the old is generally equated with oppression in the *Songs of Experience*, poems with a far greater satirical, even sarcastic, edge. Parents, nurses, priests, and the calculating force of human reason serve to limit and confine what once was innocent. In 'London' the very shape of the city, with its 'charter'd' streets and river, marks its inhabitants with signs of weakness and woe and the 'mindforg'd manacles' tyrannize and terrorize its poor. Mental, spiritual, and intellectual distortion is also suggested by the moral pillaging of the 'invisible worm' which destroys the sensual beauty of the rose in 'The Sick Rose' and by the destructive force of repression in 'The Poison Tree' (a poem which was entitled 'Christian Forbearance' in Blake's manuscript):

> I was angry with my friend:
> I told my wrath, my wrath did end.
> I was angry with my foe:
> I told it not, my wrath did grow.
>
> And I waterd it in fears,
> Night & morning with my tears
> And I sunned it with smiles,
> And with soft deceitful wiles.
>
> And it grew both day and night.
> Till it bore an apple bright.
> And my foe beheld it shine,
> And he knew that it was mine
>
> And into my garden stole.
> When the night had veild the pole;
> In the morning glad I see
> My foe outstretchd beneath the tree.

'The Poison Tree' is both the forbidden tree of knowledge and a metaphor for repressed emotion, both an expression of the evils of a negative Christian hypocrisy and an exploration of the imperative and liberating power of Christian forgiveness. The 'Garden of Love' is also wrecked by a 'thou shalt not' in the shape of 'priests in black gowns' who have planted tombstones and who bind 'joys and desires' with briars. At the end of the *Songs of Experience*, the piper who had introduced the first sequence is superseded by an 'Ancient Bard' who sees the 'Present, Past and Future' and who seems to have moved beyond a past state of innocence into a present awareness of the Fall. But this same bard, as a poet, has heard the word of God. In his response to this divine voice he is aware that the fallen condition of humankind, exemplified by doubt, reason, disputes, and folly, need not be permanent. The daybreak with which the volume opens is darkened by the poems that follow, but in the final poem 'The Voice of the Ancient Bard' (transferred, significantly enough, from *Innocence* to *Experience*) another morning opens after a night of stumbling 'over the bones of the dead'. A new age of spiritual liberty and regeneration is perceived, the Kingdom of God received by those who have become again as little children.

Blake's proclamation of liberty takes many forms in his later mythological work, generally known as the Prophetic Books. The figure of Urizen, the bearded representative of a negative God of 'thou shalt nots', functions as the prime oppressor in *The First Book of Urizen* (1794). The fragmentary *The Book of Los* (1795) traces the indignant rebellion against Urizen by the energetic Los, but it is Orc, the lawless embodiment of revolution, who is seen as both rebel and oppressor. In *America: A Prophecy* (1793) Orc precipitates the action as the incarnate spirit of the revolutions in America and France; in its sequel, *Europe: A Prophecy*, Orc's mother Enitharmon both breeds revolution and checks it as a queenly repressor and stagnator who is ultimately dismayed by her son's descent into 'the vineyards of red France'. Blake's 'prophecies' have been subject to much critical interpretation, contortion, and distortion; they remain, however, singular, fascinating, elusive, and at times infuriating works. A prophet, Blake himself once noted, 'is a Seer, not an Arbitrary Dictator'. As he also remarks in his prose exposition of a now lost picture, *A Vision of the Last Judgement* (1810), 'Men are admitted into Heaven not because they have curbed & governd their Passions, or have No Passions, but because they have Cultivated their Understandings'. Blake's search for new patterns of religious symbolism and experience, and his creation of an experimental mythology, was, despite his later fascination with Dante's *Divine Comedy*, an essentially Protestant yearning for an imaginative faith free of dogmatic assertion. His insistent struggle to find metaphors of freedom was, despite the intensity of his own myth-making, an essentially antinomian expression of the heretical belief that Christians were set free by grace from the need to observe the old, restrictive, moral law. His anticipation of the dawning of a 'New Age' and of the concomitant regeneration of humanity has generated much sympathetic response in latter-day post-Christians, the myth-making of that other Protestant, W. B. Yeats, being notable amongst them.

Blake's passionate, visionary libertarianism contrasts starkly with the frankly secular democratic bent of the poetry of his Scots contemporary, Robert Burns (1759–96). Both poets were grounded in what Blake styled the 'book of liberty', the Bible, and both drew from its potentially revolutionary prophetic pronouncements, but Burns's egalitarian vision is effectively that of a Presbyterian tenant-farmer who suffered no fools gladly and who recognized something of the fulfilment of his ideal of human community in the classless brotherhood of Freemasonry. The 'heaven-taught ploughman', praised by the novelist

Henry Mackenzie (whose sentimental novel *The Man of Feeling* Burns much admired), was toasted by the Grand Lodge of Scotland in January 1787 as 'Caledonia's Bard'. Late eighteenth-century Scotland, having put the Jacobite rebellion behind it (in spite of a lingering national attachment to the romance of the Stuart cause and a proper sense of grievance at the nature of the suppression of the Highland risings), had generally prospered under the Union with England and the opening up of its trade with the English colonies. Edinburgh had steadily won itself a position as a leading educational, intellectual, and artistic centre of Europe. Coupled with this achievement was an often self-conscious redefinition of 'Scottishness' and a revival of serious interest in the Scots vernacular and in Scots traditions. Burns's first published volume, the *Poems, Chiefly in the Scottish Dialect*, of which 612 copies were published in the provincial town of Kilmarnock in 1786, found a responsive enough local and national audience, attuned to the literary use of the vernacular by the pioneering work of the poet and editor of earlier verse, Allan Ramsay (1686–1758), and by the verse of Robert Fergusson (1750–74). But, as Sir Walter Scott later noted, Burns had 'twenty times' the abilities of his predecessors.

Burns's poetry always remained close to its vital roots in the oral traditions of Scotland. His work as a collector, editor, and adaptor of folk-songs and popular airs eventually received European acclaim, but his keen ear for Scots vocabulary, idiom, and rhythm also enabled him to transform folk-song into a poetry of his own. What he acknowledged in his Commonplace Book as a 'degree of wild irregularity' in the songs of Ayrshire also stimulated him to imagine that 'it might be possible for a Scotch Poet, with a nice, judicious ear, to set compositions to many of our favourite airs'. Many of his most circulated songs were set to old tunes, notably 'Scots wha hae' of 1793, and 'O whistle an' I'll come to you, my lad' and 'The Birks of Aberfeldy', both published in the volumes of *The Scots Musical Museum* (1787–1803). Burns's aspirations as a distinctly national poet emerge most fully in his dialect poems. His verse in 'standard' English, even his musings on Scottish history and patriotism, is flat compared to his evocations of locality through the medium of local language. Much of his finest work is satirical or descriptive of the hardness of rural work, the uprightness of 'honest poverty', and the raucousness of country amusements. 'The Twa Dogs', which voices the opinions of two dogs—one (called Caesar) a rich man's, the other (called Luath) a ploughman's collie—concerning the respective lifestyles of their masters, stands in the tradition of Scots animal poems which dates back to Henryson, but it gives the tradition a new edge by exploiting the revolutionary questioning of class privilege:

> Our Laird gets in his racked rents,
> His coals, his kain [farm produce], and a' his stents [dues];
> He rises when he likes himsel';
> His flunkies answer at the bell;
> He ca's his coach; he ca's his horse

He draws a bonny silken purse
As lang's my tail . . .

.   .   .   .

Our whipper-in, wee blastit wonner [wonder]!
Poor worthless elf! it eats a dinner
Better than ony tenant man
His Honour has in a' the lan';
An' what poor cot-folk pit their painch [stomach] in,
I own its past my comprehension.

In 'The Holy Fair' and 'Holy Willie's Prayer', however, the satire is directed at exposing the double-standards which challenge the illusion of Presbyterian respectability and solemnity. 'Holy Willie', a Kirk Elder, is given a monologue expressive both of conventional moralizing piety and of a real, if only barely admitted, relish for the sins of the flesh (the poem was not included in published collections until after Burns's death). Burns's most celebrated long poem, the verse-tale 'Tam o' Shanter' (1791), contrasts the vividly sketched, welcoming interior of an inn with the unfriendly terrors of Tam's frenzied escape from a witches' coven. The contrast is rendered particularly striking by Burns's drolly ironic narrative manner.

Wordsworth

Burns's expression of human solidarity which could dispense with class distinction was substantially derived from his intimate understanding of the rural community from which he sprang. No poet of the period so effectively extended this grasp of rural communal relationships as did William Wordsworth (1770–1850). Wordsworth's admiration for Burns's achievement is evident both in the pilgrimage he made to Ayrshire in 1803 in search of sites associated with the poet and in a poem of his own addressed 'To the Sons of Burns after visiting their Father's Grave' ('Be independent, generous, brave! Your Father such example gave'). His real tribute to Burns's example lies, however, in his own poetry of place, of character, and of relationships. Although Wordsworth's contribution to *Lyrical Ballads* (1798) consisted chiefly of his use of ballad form and in remoulding its traditional subjects, he also strove, as he later argued in the celebrated Preface, to find an appropriate language. He had chosen to describe 'humble and rustic life', he claimed, because in that condition 'the essential passions of the heart find a better soil in which they can attain their maturity' and because they 'speak a plainer and more emphatic language'. Burns's vernacular poems drew their strength from the very vigour of a living dialect. For Wordsworth, no such alternative to 'standard' English seemed appropriate to poetry, however radical his desire to break with the artificialities of the tradition he had inherited from the poets of the eighteenth century. His viewpoint on 'humble and rustic life' may not be that of a ploughman, but it does nevertheless demand an expression of passions and values which stand apart from those of an exclusively aristocratic or urban civilization. It stands apart, too, from the language of the decorous shepherds of the pastoral tradition. Wordsworth's early poetry is radical not because it embodies revolutionary thought or theory, or because it voices the complaints of the poor, but because it attempts to shift a literary perspective away from what he saw as gentility and false sophistication. Burns's work may have suggested a precedent for this radicalism, but the very provinciality of its language militated against Wordsworth's professed ambition to begin a process of literary reform in the realization of which he might claim a place in a line of succession with Spenser, Shakespeare, and Milton.

In Book VIII of *The Excursion* (1814) Wordsworth records his impressions of a manufacturing district of northern England, 'a huge town, continuous and compact, | Hiding the face of earth for leagues . . . O'er which the smoke of unremitting fires | Hangs permanent'. It is against the physically ugly and socially challenging background of the rapid pace of the industrialization of much of Britain in the closing years of the eighteenth century that we must judge both his poetry and his ideas about what he aimed to achieve through his poetry. His birth and early education in the mountainous north-western counties of England which contain the Lake District gave him, he believed, a particularly acute sensitivity to wild nature and to the co-operative workings of humankind and nature. If he defined himself through his perception of the natural, as opposed to the mechanical, world around him, he tended also to order his political and social ideas according to the patterns of mutual responsibility he observed in rural as opposed to urban contexts. His early poetry (or at least the portion of it that he was prepared to print) is marked by protest against unnecessary or imposed suffering, injustice, incomprehension, and inhumanity, though he declined to publish his radical *Salisbury Plain* (begun in 1793) and gradually revised the revolutionary aspects out of *The Ruined Cottage* of 1797 until it appeared neutrally enough as Book I of *The Excursion* seventeen years later. In the last poem printed in the various editions of *Lyrical Ballads* (1798, 1800, 1802), 'Lines Written a few miles above Tintern Abbey, on revisiting the Banks of the Wye during a Tour, July 13, 1798', Wordsworth offers a self-justifying explanation of his partial retreat from politics. Here it is the sensations of remembered natural scenery, 'felt in the blood, and felt along the heart', that bring 'tranquil restoration' to a once troubled soul, and the recall of the 'still, sad music of humanity' that makes for a chastening and subduing of restlessness. The intensity of his expressed love of nature and its teachings seems to preclude other perceptions, particularly those related to the acute class division inherent in urban industrialization, in the related depopulation of the countryside, or, most pressingly, in the explosion of social questioning presented by the French Revolution. What Wordsworth elsewhere in his Preface to the *Lyrical Ballads* calls 'emotion recollected in tranquillity' is an emotion uniquely stimulated by nature and then related outwards, and

variously applied or illustrated, by moral and social incident. The understanding of society is essentially secondary to, and derivative from, the primary
and essential experience of a natural world still largely undamaged by human
mismanagement.

Although many of Wordsworth's contributions to *Lyrical Ballads* describe
tragic or unhappy incidents in an unadorned language appropriate to the ballad
form, other poems in the collection assert a happier, if passive, responsiveness
to place and to sensation. This passivity, expressed both in the form of dialogue (as in 'Expostulation and Reply') or as a further injunctive response to a
posed question ('The Tables Turned'), entails turning from books to nature as
the teacher and as the giver of an 'impulse from a vernal wood' that may teach
more 'than all the sages can'. 'Tintern Abbey', the longest poem, and the one
which most obviously eschews the simplicity of the ballad, both crowns the
collection and gives it a direction beyond the purely narrative; it moves from
a process of telling or listening implied by a poem such as 'The Thorn' (with
its insistent interplay of personal experience, speculation, and hearsay) into
introspection and meditation. But even here the solitary and secluded narrator implies a listener in the form of the friend (Coleridge) and the sister
(Dorothy) and the silent presence of a larger humanity represented by the
wreathes of smoke sent up from distant cottages. The responsive recall within
the poem of 'that best portion of a good man's life', his 'little, nameless
unremembered acts | Of kindness and of love', also allows for an interaction
of a personal morality and the larger tutelary power of landscape. Vision is
translatable into action.

Wordsworth's insistence on the morally educative influence of nature, and
on the interrelationship of a love of nature and a love of humanity, pervades
his long autobiographical poem *The Prelude*. This poem (first drafted in 1799,
expanded in 1805, revised at intervals until 1839, and finally published posthumously, with a title chosen by his widow, in 1850) records the 'growth of a
poet's mind' and it also attempts to shape certain crucial incidents in a poet's
life into an ideal pattern of self-representation. Its many revisions served to
change not only its narrative shape but also the impression it gives of how
Wordsworth chose to read his own imaginative history. If Keats, who did not
know *The Prelude*, was able to detect in Wordsworth's work the element of the
'egotistical sublime', this autobiographical experiment of necessity renders the
poet the hero of his own poetic life, or rather of the period of preparation for
self-expression in poetry. The 'fair seed-time' of the soul, the boy's childhood
in the Lake District 'foster'd alike by beauty and by fear', as much as his adolescent experiences in Cambridge, his sense of the teeming and overwhelming
confusion of London, and his initial exultation at the progress of the
Revolution in France are all shaped into an exploration of his destiny as a poet.
Despite its vivid accounts of action, of learning, and of secular speculation,
the poem constantly returns to the idea of the retired life where the imagination is at its freest and most creative and to the solitary figure, observant of his

surroundings because he is not distracted by company. The poem contains some of Wordsworth's most striking descriptive blank verse, notably the accounts in Book I which mimetically evoke the actions of rowing or of the smooth, sheer, exhilarating freedom of skating on a frozen lake:

> All shod with steel,
> We hissed along the polished ice in games
>
> . . . . . .
>
> So through the darkness and the cold we flew,
> And not a voice was idle; with the din,
> Meanwhile, the precipices rang aloud;
> The leafless trees and every icy crag
> Tinkled like iron; while the distant hills
> Into the tumult sent an alien sound
> Of melancholy not unnoticed, while the stars
> Eastward were sparkling clear, and in the west
> The orange sky of evening died away.
> Not seldom from the uproar I retired
> Into a silent bay, or sportively
> Glanced sideway, leaving the tumultuous throng,
> To cut across the image of a star
> That gleamed upon the ice . . .

The poem also periodically pauses to meditate, to assess, and to draw conclusions concerning what Wordsworth calls in Book II 'that universal power | And fitness in the latent qualities | And essences of things, by which the mind | Is mov'd by feelings of delight'.

The often ecstatic accounts of the awing grandeur of nature in *The Prelude*, the delicacy of occasional observation which informs poems such as 'To the Daisy', 'To the small Celandine', and 'I wander'd lonely as a Cloud' (all published in the 1807 collection, *Poems, in Two Volumes*), or the precise, incantatory recall of sight and sound in the 'Ode' ('Intimations of Immortality') with which that collection ends, all serve to suggest the extent to which Wordsworth's poetry had moved beyond the mere loco-description of his predecessors. His landscapes are no longer filtered through the Claude-glasses with which so many eighteenth-century seekers after the picturesque sought to order nature selectively, as if it were a painting. His representation of nature is dynamic, panoramic, variously lit, multitudinous, and shot through with the creative energy of God. The *banditti* and the displaced Italianate peasants of the painters and their literary disciples are superseded by English pedlars, leech-gatherers, farmers, labourers, and wanderers. *Michael; A Pastoral Poem*, published in 1800, which effectively undoes the fancies of the Arcadian pastoral and its English imitations, is carefully 'placed' in the poet's own Grasmere, beside 'the boisterous brook of Greenhead Ghyll', and it treats of a real shepherd (with a mind 'intense, and frugal, apt for all affairs'). Landscape in Wordsworth is at once useful and massive, historic and impersonal, peopled and empty, readable yet infinitely larger than its reader. In a sense *Michael* reads landscape archaeologically by interpreting signs and evolving a lost history from them. For his immediate successors, Wordsworth's work, like Scott's, re-created and revivified history. His redefinition of the proper subjects and objects of poetry, and his extraordinary lexical and metrical gift, derived in part from an awareness of the increasingly acute distinctions between urban and rural civilization, and between manual and mechanical labour, in his time. 'A multitude of causes unknown to former times', he wrote in 1800, 'are now acting with a combined force to blunt the discriminating powers of the mind.' His later impact on English culture, and on a century of English literature from the time of Carlyle to that of D. H. Lawrence, is incalculable. He effectively completed the process of breaking old prejudices and tastes and, by means of his pervasive influence, he moulded new ones.

Wordsworth's ambition to speak as 'a man speaking to men' implies not only a listener but a community of listeners. The solitary walker, or the poet who composed, according to Hazlitt, 'walking up and down a straight gravel walk, or in some spot where the continuity of his verse met with no collateral interruption', should not be seen as an isolated or self-centred speaker. Although one is sometimes left wondering to what extent his narrators actually *listen* to the people who talk to them, the interlocutors in his poetry are certainly not interrupters. The child in 'We are Seven', the leech-gatherer of 'Resolution and Independence', or the ragged soldier of Book IV of *The Prelude* are all engaged in conversation by a narrator, and the words of all three serve to alter and expand that narrator's perception. In Wordsworth's most obviously public declarations in poetry—the 'Sonnets dedicated to Liberty' published in the 1807 collection, or the vastly inferior (but equally earnest) historical sequences of 'Ecclesiastical Sonnets' of 1822–45—he addresses his fellow countrymen, and beyond them the world, in a consciously Miltonic tone. Milton, for him the embodiment of the spirit of English (as opposed to French revolutionary) liberty, was a model to whom he regularly turned in his desire to address a 'fit audience' If his sharpest early critics, such as Francis Jeffrey, the editor of the *Edinburgh Review*, viewed Wordsworth, Southey, and Coleridge as representatives of a '*sect* of poets . . . dissenters from the established systems in poetry and criticism' who constituted 'the most formidable conspiracy against sound judgement in matters poetical', the poet himself sought to assert both his sense of literary succession and his right to move from solitary contemplation to public statement. Milton, of whom 'England hath need' to give it 'manners, virtue, freedom, power', helped him to articulate national, political, and moral sentiments. The 'Sonnets dedicated to Liberty' range from meditations on the dire consequences of French policy abroad ('On the Extinction of the Venetian Republic', 'To Toussaint L'Ouverture', and 'Thought of a Briton on the Subjugation of Switzerland'), to equally troubled comparisons of a selfish and corrupt English present, to the nobler passions of the Civil War. Modern revolutions are read through past experience, modern disillusion through historic principle. The older, yet more conservative Wordsworth, distressed by threats to the Anglican settlement, turned to the ideas of succession and continuity in the 'Ecclesiastical Sonnets', a long sequence which occasionally flares into poetic life and which seeks to find a pattern of divine inspiration and benevolent progress. The Recluse readily assumed the role of public orator.

Coleridge, Southey, and Crabbe

Despite his strong sympathy with the ideas and achievements of the Revolution at the time of his sojourn in France in 1790, and despite the passionate radicalism of his unpublished 'Descriptive Sketches' of 1792 and the republican spirit of his unsent 'Letter to the Bishop of Llandaff', Wordsworth remained, to the general public at least, an uncommitted radical. The same could not be observed of his friends Samuel Taylor Coleridge (1772–1834) and Robert Southey (1774–1843). Both poets planned the foundation of an ideal commune, on Godwinian libertarian principles, on the banks of the Susquehanna, but this American 'Pantisocracy' resulted in little more substance than a pair of sonnets composed by Coleridge in 1794 ('I other climes | Where dawns, with hope serene, a brighter day | Than e'er saw Albion in her happiest times, | With mental eye exulting now explore'). The same year saw the publication in Cambridge of the historic drama *The Fall of Robespierre*, signed by Coleridge but in fact a collaboration with Southey who contributed the second and third acts. This attempt 'to imitate the empassioned and highly figurative language of the French orators, and to develop the characters of the chief actors on a vast stage of horrors' has never been realized in a theatre.

Most of Coleridge's early work is tinged by a similar radicalism and by an urge to proclaim a political cause. The 'Sonnets on Eminent Characters' contributed to the *Morning Chronicle* in December 1794 and January 1795 are clearly partisan, defining enemies to the cause (the Prime Minister, Pitt, a 'foul apostate from his father's fame', and two further political apostates, Burke and Sheridan, 'by the brainless mob ador'd') and radical friends at home (Priestley, Godwin, and Southey) and abroad (the American and Polish patriots Lafayette and Kosciusko). When disillusion with France set in the late 1790s, Coleridge viewed his own disaffection more as the end of a Wordsworthian educative process under the tutelage of true and 'Natural Liberty' than as apostasy. 'France: An Ode', published in 1798, distinguishes the 'spirit of divinest Liberty', which is to be found implicitly and explicitly in nature, from the false spirit in whose name the French now enslave their Swiss neighbours. France 'adulterous, blind, | And patriot only in pernicious toils' is a blasphemy. Coleridge had met Wordsworth at some point between August and late September 1795 when the former's political commitment was at its height and his denunciation of monarchy and aristocracy at its most fiery. For the next ten years the opinions of both worked co-operatively, coinciding initially in a revolutionary enthusiasm for change in society and literature and later in a compensatingly ready response to a nature charged with the glory and power of God. Whereas Coleridge helped Wordsworth to articulate his ideas, to examine their implications, and to explore unfamiliar intellectual territory (including a rejection of Godwinism), Wordsworth seems to have exhilarated Coleridge. In the period of their closest association, from the midsummer of 1797 to the end of 1798, Coleridge composed much of his best work, including the conversation poems 'This Lime-tree bower my Prison' and 'Frost at Midnight' and his two great visionary poems, 'The Ancient Mariner' and 'Kubla Khan'. The much bruited close collaboration of the two poets on joint projects was, however, never properly realized.

Coleridge's conversation poems show a distinct movement away from the public declamatory style of the sonnets to a new intimacy, from the Miltonic mode to the Cowperian. 'The Eolian Harp', written in August 1795, traces a speculative transition from a pantheistic awareness of 'Life within us and abroad | Which meets all motion and becomes its soul' to an expression of a firmer Christian faith that inwardly feels the presence of the 'Incomprehensible'. Both 'This Lime-tree bower my Prison' and 'Frost at Midnight' suggest a Wordsworthian sense of the transcendental reality of natural phenomena together with an ease of expression which approaches that of relaxed conversation. 'This Lime-tree bower', ostensibly an address to his schoolfriend Charles Lamb, interlinks human affection, a sense of joy in the detail of the natural world, and a profound awareness of its unity, a power that transcends both separation and temporary confinement. 'Frost at Midnight' opens with an echo of Cowper's solitary fireside meditations on a larger world beyond the cottage (Coleridge's 'abstruser musings'), but it also radically leaps backwards from present contentment to painful schoolboy memories of displacement and loneliness. The contrast of town and country, of rural companionship and urban isolation, is reinforced by a further leap, this time forward to the prospect of the poet's growing son blessed by Nature's benevolence:

> But *thou*, my babe! shalt wander like a breeze
> By lakes and sandy shores, beneath the crags
> Of ancient mountain, and beneath the clouds
> Which image in their bulk, both lakes and shores
> And mountain crags: so shalt thou see and hear
> The lovely shapes and sounds intelligible
> Of that eternal language, which thy God
> Utters, who from eternity doth teach
> Himself in all, and all things in himself.

In this blessed vision the influence of Wordsworth is most evident, suggesting the extent to which it is part of a larger discourse which also includes 'Tintern Abbey'.

Coleridge's most memorable contribution to *Lyrical Ballads*, and the most substantial product of his direct collaboration with Wordsworth, was 'The Rime of the Ancient Mariner'. The poem was planned jointly, with Wordsworth suggesting some of its most significant elements (though he contributed next to nothing to its actual composition). 'Our respective manners proved so widely different', Wordsworth later recalled, 'that it would have been quite presumptuous in me to do anything but separate from an undertaking upon which I could only have been a clog.' Despite its metrical and verbal debts to the simplicity of the traditional ballad form, 'The Ancient Mariner' is distinctly in Coleridge's manner. The poem takes the form of a voyage of discovery, both literally and figuratively, but it is also a psychodrama concerned with the guilt and expiation of a Cain-like figure, the arbitrary 'murderer' of an albatross which, we are told, appears through the fog 'as if it had been a Christian soul'. The poem defeats precise definition. The Mariner's experience is tangled and often bewildering; he is not a pilgrim who measures himself by definable spiritual milestones or who encounters and progressively overcomes obstacles; he is, rather, an outcast who witnesses an invisible action which interpenetrates the physical world. Despite its framework of Catholic Christian faith and ritual, the Mariner appears to discover a series of meanings concerning the interdependency of life, not merely the consequences of breaking taboos. His route back to the place from which he started requires suffering, but his pain is explored in the context of benevolence, and the truths he perceives stretch beyond mere religious formulae into an affirmation of universal harmony. 'Kubla Khan', written in the summer of 1797, derives much of its exotic imagery from Coleridge's wide reading of mythology, history, and comparative religion. The poem famously remains 'a fragment', because, as the poet explains in his prefatory note, he wrote it down immediately after waking from 'a profound sleep, at least of the external senses' in which he had composed 'two to three hundred lines' but was interrupted by a caller,' 'a person on business from Porlock'. This 'Vision in a Dream' remains a riddle, a pattern of vivid definitions amid a general lack of definition, expressed with a rhythmic forward drive which suggests a mind taken over by a process of semi-automatic composition. Coleridge's third visionary 'Gothic' poem, 'Christabel', was originally intended to be included in the second edition of *Lyrical Ballads* but was excluded partly because of Wordsworth's distaste for its strangeness and partly because of Coleridge's own 'indolence' in leaving the poem yet another substantial fragment. It is in many ways a complement to 'The Ancient Mariner', not simply because it too echoes the style of old ballads, but because it appears to link the nature of Christabel's experience of the powers of life and death to that of the Mariner. The poem is concerned with the attempted penetration of Christabel's psyche by the daemonic force represented by Geraldine, but it also allows for a balancing contrast of two powerful aspects of nature, the sympathetic and the energetic, and for a symbolic investigation of what Coleridge later called 'the terra incognita of our nature'.

'Dejection: An Ode', written in April 1802, opens with an epigraph from, and a reference to, the ballad of Sir Patrick Spence. It is the last and most despondent of Coleridge's conversation poems, marked as it is by an acknowledged failure of response to the phenomena of nature and by an expression of the decay of an imaginative joy fed by 'outward forms'. The poet's former 'shaping spirit of Imagination', suspended by various 'afflictions', seems to be no longer subject to external stimuli; the alternative inspiration, a recognition of inward vision, remains as yet a dim positive to set against a series of negatives. During the early 1800s as Coleridge became increasingly aware of the desiccation of his poetic inspiration and the dissipation of his 'visionary gleam' he grew compensatingly more interested in the processes and implications of critical theory, an intellectual exercise which ranged over literature and the workings of the mind to religion and the development of society. Despite the decline of his Pantisocratic ventures and his early revolutionary hopes, he continued to speculate around the central principle of his philosophy, the ultimate unity and indivisibility in Creation. Like Blake, he recognized contraries and complementary states of being; unlike him, he attempted to argue for interdependency, for wholeness, and for 'continuity . . . in self-consciousness' as the dynamic of human creativity. The 'shaping spirit' of 'Dejection' manifests itself throughout *Biographia Literaria* as the 'esemplastic' or unifying power of the Imagination. *Biographia Literaria* (1817) is a loosely shaped, digressive series of meditations on poetry, poets, and, above all, the nature of the poetic imagination. Its complex philosophy draws both from Coleridge's fruitful relationship with Wordsworth and from a wide range of European thinkers; it is both original and plagiaristic, prophetic and profoundly indebted to tradition, at once a personal apologia and a public discourse on metaphysics. Its most influential attempts at definition concern the distinction which Coleridge carefully draws in the thirteenth chapter between 'Fancy', which merely assembles and juxtaposes images and impressions without fusing them, and 'Imagination', which actively moulds, transforms, and strives to bring into unity what it perceives. What Coleridge sees as the 'primary Imagination' is, moreover, nothing less than 'a repetition in the finite mind of the eternal act of creation in the infinite I AM', a reflection of the working mind of the Creator himself. It is, however, through a discussion of the 'vital' 'secondary Imagination' that he most develops the contrast with Fancy for here he describes the mind creatively perceiving, growing, selecting, and shaping the stimuli of nature into new wholes.

In the fifteenth chapter of *Biographia Literaria* this definition of the creative imagination is exemplified in a study of Shakespeare's work, a subject to which Coleridge had already addressed himself in his *Lectures on Shakespeare* (delivered in 1808) and to which he frequently returned in the casually diffuse *Table Talk* (published posthumously in 1836). He remains, with Dr Johnson, one of the most observant and provocative critics of Shakespeare, one who acknowledges distinctive qualities and yet allows for shortcomings, one who is both 'genial' and 'reverential' yet who shrinks from bardolatry. While he readily acknowledges that 'no work of true genius dares want its appropriate form', the form of his own criticism is often sporadic and expressed in bursts of perceptive energy. It is tinged with the 'abstracting and generalizing habit over the practical' which he recognizes as the essential characteristic of Hamlet, a figure with whom the poet readily identified. Coleridge's later philosophical writing is preoccupied with religious issues, with the problem of belief and the joy of believing, with a morality concerned with inward impulses, and with an informed criticism of the Scriptures (he was amongst the first to appreciate the work of those German scholars whose research so shook the foundations of Victorian belief). The impact of his attempt to free Christianity from fundamentalism was not, however, generally appreciated by believers responsive to a culture imbued with Evangelicalism. *The Constitution of Church and State* (1829), the essay which brings to a climax his concern with dynamic unity, was also intended to form part of the national debate on reform. His vision of a Church doctrinally recharged and reinvigorated, and of religion itself as infinitely more than a social cement, is complemented by a new view of the state served and enhanced by a 'clerisy', those concerned primarily with education and spirituality. This clerisy would not be a disaffected intelligentsia, but a corporate body, integral to the proper workings of a co-operative nation state. As in all his later work, Coleridge attempts to bring together and not to diffuse, to develop tradition by a process of refertilization and not of deracination.

The arguments of Robert Southey's *The Book of the Church* (1825) and *Sir Thomas More* (1829) are similarly directed to the relationship between history and the present, between precedent and development, but both books lack Coleridge's political intelligence, originality, and integrity. To many of his younger and radical contemporaries, Southey appeared to have sold out to the Establishment in his contributions to the Tory *Quarterly Review* from 1809, in his acceptance of the post of Poet Laureate in 1813, and, above all in his toadying poem on the death of George III (which Byron mocked so devastatingly in his *The Vision of Judgement* in 1822). Southey's radical phase was as short-lived as those of Wordsworth and Coleridge, blossoming in the 1790s with his pro-revolutionary poem *Joan of Arc*, and with his plays *The Fall of Robespierre* and *Wat Tyler* (the latter published in 1817, much to his chagrin and embarrassment, when he had espoused quite different political causes). He nowhere reveals a talent parallel to that of the two friends with whom his name was originally linked under the pejorative description of a 'Lake Poet'. Despite the success of his ballad poems, such as 'The Inchcape Rock' and 'The Battle of Blenheim' (both once much loved by reciters), Southey's poetry, and particularly his ambitious long poems, such as his oriental verse epic *Thalaba the Destroyer* (1801), is beset with narrative dullness. What was once perceived as a radical plainness and frankness of style now suggests merely a flatness of expression which, at its worst, can approach the banal.

George Crabbe (1775–1832), though a near contemporary of Wordsworth and concerned like him with the relationship of character and rural environment, remained rooted in an earlier tradition of poetic representation and in established moral and religious prescriptions. His mentors were Pope, Goldsmith, and Johnson, and his generous and perceptive patron, Burke, introduced him to a London literary establishment attached to conservative norms in poetry. As a faithful and respected parish priest of humble origins (one who reminded Lord Chancellor Thurlow of Fielding's Parson Adams) he appears to have been more concerned with charity than with revolution, more with the relief and description of suffering than with political panaceas. Crabbe's essential conservatism is evident both in his tolerant analysis of human shortcomings—or of outsiders—in the context of stable communities and in his continued use of the kind of rhyming couplets which had provided the normative poetic form of the eighteenth century. His narrative style can be as relaxed as Cowper's, but his acceptance of the variety and flexibility of the couplet form, as evolved by Pope, allows for both antithesis and qualification, and for an expressive and variable use of the caesura to approximate to the rhythms of speech. Throughout his work, from the didactic satire *Inebriety* of 1775 and the work that made his reputation, *The Village* of 1783, to *The Borough* (1810) and *Tales of the Hall* (1819), Crabbe reveals himself as a determined anti-pastoralist, as a representer of an observable reality not as an imaginative idealist. This aspiration to present 'the real Picture of the Poor', as he puts it in *The Village*, also entailed the new moral necessity of painting 'the Cot | As Truth will paint it, and as Bards will not'. Village life, as represented in his work, is 'a life of pain'. His townscapes are dotted with human and architectural wreckage and haunted by the encroaching shadows of rejection, the poor house, and pauper burial. The poet whom Byron admired as 'Nature's sternest painter, yet the best' struck the far less sympathetic Hazlitt as merely a renderer of 'discoloured paintings of life' and as 'a misanthrope in verse . . . a Malthus turned metrical romancer'.

In *The Parish Register* (1807) Crabbe introduces as a narrator a country parson exploring 'the simple annals' of his parish poor, leafing through, and commenting on, entries in his register of births, marriages, and deaths. The three-part poem looks both back to Goldsmith's idealized representation of Auburn and forward to the interconnections between character and environment which were later developed in the novels of Sir Walter Scott. In the extraordinary study of 'Sir Eustace Grey', written in eight-line stanzas, he also explores the obsessed psyche of a hallucinating dreamer, an inmate of a madhouse who is troubled both by past guilt and by present religious mania. The poem illustrates Crabbe's skill in creating a poetry of mood, using dislocated images and details in order to suggest a mind whirled towards incoherence. Crabbe creates a related effect in his description of the isolation of Peter Grimes, perhaps the most impressive of the stories in *The Borough*. Grimes, an unhappy rebel against his rigid father, and a man known to be an abuser of the apprentices placed in his charge, is gradually driven out of his community to live in a boat on the dreary mud-flats where he views 'the lazy tide | In its hot slimy channels slowly glide'. If Grimes is the most notable of Crabbe's outsiders, both *The Borough* and the *Tales* of 1812 suggest a critical interest in those insiders who foster conventional moral and religious values, the unremarkable parish priests and their equally unremarkable curates, and magistrates such as the 'impetuous, warm and loud' Justice Bolt. In the first of the *Tales*, 'The Dumb Orators, or the Benefit of Society', Justice Bolt is shown as disconcerted and silenced by a group of free-thinkers, and then later as embarrassingly vocal in his triumph over a single supposed foe of order, the sceptical Hammond. In many ways, the poem allows for Hammond's moral victory as a representative of a free conscience faced with a blustering assertion of the status quo (albeit a status quo that Crabbe himself represented). Despite such gestures to religious and social questioning, the moral sensibility of Crabbe's narrative poetry is generally derived from a loyally Anglican understanding of the nature of society, its ranks, relationships, and responsibilities. The representation of nature in his poetry is likewise confined to a picture of a co-operative working environment, conditioned by the shifting moods and patterns of the sea. It offers a picture of a peopled landscape observed, as Coleridge was prepared to concede, with a 'power of a certain kind', yet constricted by what many of Crabbe's younger contemporaries saw damningly as 'an absolute defect of the high imagination'.

Austen, the 'Regional' Novel, and Scott

Wordsworth, goaded by the high poetic standing accorded to Crabbe by the critics of the great early nineteenth-century journals, consistently denigrated his rival's work. In one of his sharper asides he even ventured to compare Crabbe's poetry to Jane Austen's fiction. Though he admitted that her novels were 'an admirable copy of life', he nevertheless insisted that he could not be interested in 'productions of that kind' and, he protested, 'unless the truth of nature were presented to him clarified, as it were, by the pervading light of imagination, it had scarce any attraction in his eyes'. Wordsworth's comment suggests something of the breadth of the gulf which seemed to separate the new poetry from the staid, older fashion of a literature which aspired merely to represent nature by copying it. The idea of the transforming power of the imagination, which was to become so much a commonplace of subsequent criticism, cannot uniformly be applied to the literature of the English 'Romantic' period, nor can the absence of visionary gleams or pervading lights be now seen as crucially detrimental to a substantial portion of the poetry and the fiction of the period. Jane Austen (1775–1817) was, according to her first biographer, an admirer of Johnson in prose, Crabbe in verse, and Cowper in both; she 'thoroughly enjoyed' Crabbe's work and would sometimes say 'in jest' that if ever she married at all 'she could fancy being Mrs Crabbe'. Such conservative tastes in matrimony and literature should not be viewed as inconsistent either with Austen's own work or with the opinions of many of her original readers.

J. E. Austen-Leigh's memoir of his unmarried aunt assumes that she shared the feeling of 'moderate Toryism which prevailed in her family'. Austen's novels ostensibly suggest little active political commitment or deep involvement in national and international affairs. The class to which she belonged, and which her fiction almost exclusively describes, had largely remained unruffled and unthreatened by the ructions across the Channel, but the immediate aftermath of the French Revolution, the long-drawn-out conflict between Britain and France and the active risk of a French invasion, left few families untouched by the Napoleonic Empire and the domestic and foreign policies of the succession of repressive Tory governments. Although a well-connected cousin of the Austens had died on the scaffold in France, and although the novelist's two younger brothers served as officers in the navy in the great campaign against Napoleon, any discussion of revolutionary politics is eschewed and the war remains a relatively marginal (or at least, largely male) concern even in novels such as *Mansfield Park* and *Persuasion* which introduce naval officers as characters. The desperate domestic measures introduced by British governments to counter political dissent, notably the frequent suspensions of the Habeas Corpus Act (which secured the liberty of the citizen against arbitrary imprisonment) and the emergency legislation aimed against all kinds of 'sedition' (such as the enforcement of the Combination Acts), are passed over silently. The agricultural depression which left many farm labourers destitute and the widespread evidence of rural pauperism is glanced at only as the occasion of genteel charity or, as in the case of Lady Catherine de Bourgh in *Pride and Prejudice*, as an occasion for scolding the poor 'into harmony and plenty'. The vast advances in industrialization and imperial expansion, and the social earthquake consequent upon both, elicit mere allusions. The upper-middle-class world of Austen's fiction is seen as secure in its values, its privileges, and its snobberies. It is a society which defines itself very precisely in terms of land, money, and class and it accepts that rank is an essential guinea-stamp. Its awareness of geographical space is generally revealed only with reference to far-flung estates and to the incomes derived from them, and to forays into the fashionable society of London or Bath. Its attachment to nature and to natural scenery is expressed in transitory enthusiasms for picnics at Box Hill and trips to the seaside or for parkland disciplined and tidied up by landscape gardeners.

Jane Austen is far too subtle, challenging, and inventive a novelist to be usefully defined by negatives. Her work may seem to stand apart from the preoccupations of many of her literary contemporaries, but it remains very much of its time. It is, in many significant ways, defined in Christianly conservative, but not necessarily reactionary, terms against current radical enthusiasms. It should also be seen as standing in, and presenting variations on, an established fictional tradition. Where new writers who had espoused Jacobin libertarianism spoke of rights, Austen refers to duties; where they look for steady human improvement, she remains sceptical about the nature of the fallen human condition. The late eighteenth-century cultivation of sensibility and sentiment, and the new 'Romantic' insistence on the propriety of passion, are consistently countered in her novels by an ironic exposure of affectation and by a steady affirmation of the virtues of restraint. Austen chose her own literary limitations, not simply because she held that 'three or four families in a country village' were an ideal subject for the novel, but because her omissions were considered and deliberate. Her moral message is infused with an ideological insistence on the merits of good conduct, good manners, sound reason, and marriage as an admirable social institution. She never scorns love, but she balances its often disconcerting and disruptive nature with a firm advocacy of the complementary qualities of self-knowledge, self-discipline, and practicality. Her heroines can be as vivaciously intelligent as Elizabeth Bennet and as witty, egotistic, and independent as Emma Woodhouse, but both, like the essentially introspective Elinor Dashwood or the passive and self-effacing Fanny Price, are finally brought to mature judgement and, by proper extension, emotional fulfilment. The narrative line of *Sense and Sensibility* (1811), which balances maturity against impulsiveness, also systematically undermines the attractions of superficial glamour and contrasts conflicting value systems and ways of seeing. In the two other novels which were probably begun in the 1790s and later revised, *Northanger Abbey* (1818) and *Pride and Prejudice* (1813), first impressions, illusions, and subjective opinions or prejudices give way to detachment, balance, reasonableness and, more painfully, to humiliating reassessment. Mere cleverness, wit, or spontaneity, though admirable in themselves, are never allowed to triumph without being linked to some steadier moral assurance.

The scrupulous pattern of education that Austen requires of her major characters (both male and female) is also required of her readers. Those who merely seek to escape into a delicately placid and undemanding fictional world wilfully misread her novels. Throughout her work, but especially in her three later novels, *Mansfield Park* (1814), *Emma* (1816), and *Persuasion* (1818), she obliges readers to participate in the moral processes of disciplined learning, weighing, and judging, and in the gradual establishment of the principle that judgement is contingent upon understanding. This is not to imply that Austen is either priggish or stridently polemic (she is, it should go without saying, one of the most calculatingly amusing of all English novelists), but to suggest that her readers have to be constantly alert to her tone and to her supple narrative method. The relatively restricted world of her novels, and the social and physical confines of her settings, define the limits in which opinions are formed and within which her fools and snobs, her bores and gossips, her prudes and poseurs, must be both endured and accepted. The illusion of actuality which she so succinctly suggests also enforces a response to a society confident of its own codes and values. In *Emma*, for example, we follow the heroine in her often

wayward exploration of manipulations, misapprehensions, niceties, complacencies, and lapses in judgement, but we also see her finding a personal liberation within the enclosure of the society whose rules she learns to respect and
use. Austen's often astringent anti-romanticism is nowhere more evident than
in *Mansfield Park*, a novel centred on a heroine suffering from what she admits
are 'faults of ignorance and timidity', but also one who embodies, like the man
she finally marries, a Christian forbearance which can be seen as informing her
grasp of tact and decorum. If the values of the novel, most clearly expressed
in the embarrassments surrounding the play-acting which so offend Sir
Thomas Bertram, often seem to be at odds with twentieth-century preconceptions of character and social action, for Austen such values are projected as
essential to the happy development of human affairs. The relatively sombre
tone of *Persuasion* also emphasizes the importance of the process of learning
and judging through which all her heroines pass. Anne Elliot is not only
Austen's most astute literary critic (she finds it 'the misfortune of poetry, to be
seldom safely enjoyed by those who enjoyed it completely'), she is also her most
discriminating woman character, the one whose intelligence most effectively
balances the merits of conflicting opinions, ideas, impressions, and feelings. It
is against Anne's sunny 'domestic' virtues that the world in which she moves
so often seems shallow, worldly, petty, and vain. The freedom which all
Austen's lovers attain is a freedom of action and moral decision worked out,
not in a deceptively 'gracious' society, but in a post-lapsarian world often
unaware that it is in constant need of grace.

Susan Ferrier's work, which often explores related comic themes, generally
lacks Austen's economy and her intelligence. Ferrier (1782–1854) is also a distinctively Scottish writer whose novels seem raw and provincial beside her contemporary's confident urbanity. *Marriage* (1818) traces the responses to
matrimony of two generations of women, those of Lady Juliana, the rash
daughter of an Earl who elopes with a penniless Scots officer, and those of her
twin daughters, the one brought up in London society, the other trained in the
rougher, but honester, household of her Caledonian aunts. Ferrier plays
throughout with contradictory attitudes to love, ranging from the old Earl's
dismissal of the emotion as something 'now entirely confined to the *canaille*',
to a final awareness that a woman can indeed be 'beloved with all the truth and
ardour of a noble ingenuous mind, too upright to deceive others, too enlightened to deceive itself'. Despite the evidence to the contrary—the deceptions,
the semblances of affection, the elopements, and the adulteries—the novel ends
with the proclamation of a single 'happy Marriage'. Deceptions and semblances also run through the twists and turns of the plot of *The Inheritance*
(1824), a novel which suggests the emotional dangers of an over-reliance on
money as a determiner of the heart.

Ferrier's modest and often mocking use of the Scots dialect and of Scottish
traits is to some extent mirrored in the work of a more determinedly provincial novelist, John Galt (1779–1839). Galt, well aware of the importance of the
English market for fiction, was not, however, inclined to limit the circulation

of his novels to an exclusively Scottish audience by an excessive use of the vernacular. Scotland, which was beginning to enjoy and exploit the international celebrity brought to it by the success of the poetry of Burns and Scott, had in 1822 been the object of a state visit by its new king, George IV (a visit partly stage-managed, tartan and all, by Scott). The King who was not a popular figure in London, was the first sovereign of the Hanoverian dynasty to visit Edinburgh and this trip to 'the venerable home of [his] Royal Ancestors' proved to be a considerable public-relations success. Galt recalled his own homage to the King at Holyrood in the somewhat obsequious royal dedication of his most Scottish novel, *The Entail* (1822). *The Entail* is also Galt's most ambitious and carefully shaped work of fiction, darkened as it is by the tragedy which develops from the greed of Claud Walkinshaw and his determination to keep the estate of Kittlestonheugh together by entailing it on his male heirs. Galt was himself disinclined to refer to his three slightly earlier and more episodic works—*The Ayrshire Legatees* (1820-1), *Annals of the Parish* (1821), and the secular parallel to the *Annals*, *The Provost* (1822)—as novels, preferring to characterize them as 'theoretical histories of society, limited . . . necessarily to the events of a circumscribed locality'. This 'locality' is, in the case of the last two stories, a small town in western Scotland. In *Annals of the Parish* the minister of Dalmailing anecdotally traces the public and private history of his parish from the time of his induction in 1760 to his resignation in 1810. The second half of the narrative increasingly refers to the gathering pace of social and political change, from the construction of a cotton mill to the impact of international events on small-town perceptions. The minister, loyal equally to the Hanoverian throne and to the traditions of the Presbyterian Church, is troubled by the signs of dissent evident in the establishment of a schismatic chapel and in the seditious 'itch of jacobinism' which irritates the local mill workers. Where the minister accredits both bane and blessing to the workings of Providence, Provost James Pawkie (whose surname implies that he is 'sly') is confident of his own prowess as a self-made man and as the first citizen and chief landowner of Gudetown. As Coleridge, an admiring early reader of *The Provost*, acknowledged, the novel is masterly in its evocation of 'the unconscious, perfectly natural, Irony of Self-delusion', of a man 'cheating' himself into 'a happy state of constant Self-applause'.

Galt's royalism, and his ready acceptance of the historic fact of the Union with England, is paralleled from a quite distinct Irish angle in the work of Maria Edgeworth (1767–1849), a writer drawn by circumstance and experience to a depiction of the cultural divisions inherent in the land settled by her colonizing ancestors. Edgeworth had been born and educated in England and only returned to her father's Irish estates in 1782, the year in which the Irish Parliament won the right to legislate separately from the British Parliament. With her family she had been forced to flee from the abortive French invasion of 1798, and despite her father's initially spirited resistance to the Union with Great Britain, she, like him, acquiesced to its legal enforcement. Maria's understanding of Ireland was based on a firm, if partisan, grasp of history, both that of her family and that of the nation. She also possessed a ready enough sympathy with the oppressed Catholic majority and a complementary, but, to some modern perceptions, contradictory and Spenserian conviction of the superiority of English manners (Spenser's *View of the Present State of Ireland* is one of the works which affords Lord Colambre 'most satisfaction' in her novel, *The Absentee*). Her culture was that of the still secure Protestant Ascendancy and her hopes for the future, as embodied in her Irish novels, appear to be founded on the faith that the landowning aristocracy might regenerate both itself and the nation it still dominated.

If Edgeworth's early work—*Letters to Literary Ladies* (1795), *The Parent's Assistant* (1796–1800), and her collaboration with her father, *Practical Education* (1798)—reveals an applied Rousseauism and a relatively radical feminist concern with the inadequacy of contemporary women's education, any hint of Jacobinism in her thought was later qualified both by the Irish Rebellion of 1798 and by family pride (her distant cousin, the Abbé Edgeworth, had attended Louis XVI on the scaffold). Edgeworth's Irish novels form subtle, comic discourses on the present state of society and establish their arguments through an interplay of voices (including that of the author as editor and annotator), each supporting or subverting a social or cultural viewpoint. Although there is scant advocacy of independence or Catholic nationalism, *Castle Rackrent* (1800), *The Absentee* (1812), and *Ormond* (1817) all suggest the changing complexion of Ireland in the years immediately preceding and succeeding the Act of Union of 1801 and all explore the historic rifts in Irish society. All are concerned with succession and inheritance and all attempt to counter a potential alienation of the landowning class from its tenantry. *Castle Rackrent* is probably the first novel to represent society in a specific region and in a given historical period. It traces the varying and shaky fortunes of four generations of the Rackrent family, from the inheritance and conversion of Sir Patrick (né O'Shaughlin) to the failure of Sir Condy and his dislodgement by Jason Quirk, the son of the narrator, the Rackrents' steward. Thady Quirk's narrative gives the novel both its structure and much of its energy, but it is interestingly qualified by Edgeworth's pointed addition of a Glossary ('for the information of the *ignorant* English reader') which serves to interpret and condition both a way of speaking and a way of observing.

In common with a good deal of Anglo-Irish literature from the time of Swift onwards, *The Absentee* is in part written in a code which has to be interpreted by a knowing reader. Names, places, tastes, and glancing references suggest a system of signs related to the equally entangled history of Ireland. The novel is concerned with the return of Lord and Lady Clonbrony to their Irish estates and inheritance, a return manœuvred by their son, the perceptive and explorative Lord Colambre, who finally marries his probably Catholic cousin, Grace Nugent. Although initially concerned with the ready desertion of Ireland by an aristocracy drawn by the magnet of English fashion after the Union, the novel gradually establishes the necessity of return and the *mission civilisatrice* of those who have an obligation to mould Irish manners and mend Irish ills. Here, as in *Ormond*, Edgeworth evinces little admiration for the underlying Celtic civilization or for an alternative return to the idea of ancient Ireland, but she does suggest a new working-out of old antagonisms in her espousal of a progressive and civilized society. Count O'Halloran, the descendant of an exiled Jacobite ancestor and the holder of a foreign title, welcomes the English militia to Ireland and affirms that 'the two countries have the same interest' and that 'from the inhabitants discovering more of each other's good qualities . . . their esteem and affection for each other would increase, and rest upon the firm basis of mutual utility'. This 'mutual utility' also consists in the redis-covery of the land of their breeding, if not always of their birth, by the new generation of voluntary exiles, the 'absentees' of the novel's title. Their absence has driven their tenants to the state of a 'wretched, wretched people', bereft of 'hope and energy' and living in a village of squalid cabins which once formed 'a snug place, when my lady Clonbrony was at home to whitewash it'. The new Ireland may be exemplified as much by a pushy, vulgar, rising bourgeoisie as by the beggars who assault Colambre's eye as he lands in Dublin, but it is Edgeworth's advocacy of revival and the resuscitation of principle, example, leadership, and good management on the part of an increasingly disenchanted ruling class that give the novel its political edge and much of its historical significance.

In the Preface to *Castle Rackrent* Edgeworth had recognized the fluid rela-tionship between her fiction and the writing of history. In a way that prefigures Thackeray's suspicion of the elevation of fancy-dress heroes by historians, she states her preference for a history which looks beyond the 'splendid characters playing their parts on the great theatre of the world' and which begs to be admitted behind the scenes 'that we may take a nearer view of the actors and actresses'.

It was Edgeworth's ability both to puncture the pretensions of conventional historians and to establish a 'behind the scenes' picture of society in a state of flux which seems to have inspired Sir Walter Scott (1771–1832) to return to the unfinished and abandoned manuscript of *Waverley* in 1813. Her Irish novels, he later maintained, 'had gone so far to make the English familiar with the characters of their gay and kind-hearted neighbours of Ireland, that she may truly be said to have done more towards completing the Union than perhaps all the legislative enactments by which it has been followed up'. It is an ambitious claim, but no more so than Scott's own professed hope 'that some-thing might be attempted for my own country, of the same kind with that which Miss Edgeworth so fortunately achieved for Ireland—something which might introduce her natives to those of her sister kingdom in a more favourable light than they had been placed hitherto'. What Scott managed to achieve for Scotland was a far broader popular understanding of the distinctive nature of Scottish history and culture, its divisions and contradictions as much as its vitality. If he can at times be accused of having sanitized much in the Scottish tradition of dissent from English norms of government and civilization, he did manage to explore and to explain swathes of northern history ignored by English cultural imperialists and Scottish social progressives alike. In choosing to eschew the Scots dialect, both as a poet and as a novelist, he rendered his work acceptable to a wide audience likely to be alienated by a merely parochial self-assurance. By varying, examining, and imagining vital aspects of national history he also managed to present an analysis of a historical process at work. In drawing on, and adapting for the purposes of prose fiction, something of the method perfected by Shakespeare in his two *Henry IV* plays, and by intermixing politics and comedy with the fictional and the historical, Scott also shaped aspects of Scottish nationhood to suit his own Unionist and basically Tory ends. He both invented tradition and used it, and if he can be blamed on the one hand with exploiting an overtly romantic view of Scotland's past, he must also be allowed to have moved the British novel towards a new seriousness and a new critical respect. In developing the form beyond the fantastic excesses of the Gothic and beyond the embryonic shape moulded by Maria Edgeworth, Scott effectively created the nineteenth-century historical novel. His creation, fostered by the universal popularity of his work, was to have vast influence over European and American literature.

When he published *Waverley* anonymously in 1814 Scott already possessed a high reputation as the best-selling new poet of his age. Drawing on private research, on his considerable learning, and on memories of his youth spent in the Scottish Borders, he had published the influential collection of ballads, *Minstrelsy of the Scottish Border* (1802–3). The *Minstrelsy*, which went through five editions by 1812, interspersed previously uncollected folk-poetry with verse by the editor himself. Scott may have rigorously over-edited some of the original pieces, but his collection was a triumph of enterprise matched in importance only by Bishop Percy's *Reliques of Ancient English Poetry* (1765). His antiquarian enthusiasms marked his entire career as a writer and collector, but his early translations of Goethe and of German ballads, and an attachment to the history of the Borders, served to stimulate a narrative poetry of his own. *The Lay of the Last Minstrel* (1805) recounts the story of a family feud in the sixteenth century, replete with sorcery, alchemy, and metaphysical intervention. Scott's energetic, rushing metre, his varying line-length and wandering stress within the lines, and his highly effective introduction of shorter lyrics or songs into the narrative also mark three further long and involved verse tales: *Marmion: A Tale of Flodden Field* (1808), *The Lady of the Lake* (1810), and *Rokeby* (1813). These poems achieved an immediate celebrity and retained the high esteem of succeeding Victorian generations, even, despite their length, being learnt by heart. Their glamour has now faded and, despite occasional patches of still vivid colour, the passage of time has exposed them as threadbare in terms of their subjects and their style.

Scott's novels, an epoch-making phenomenon in their own time, retain more of their original impact on readers despite a relative decline in their critical and popular esteem. His initial, highly successful, impulse to concern himself with

Scottish affairs, and yet always to include the observation and experience of a pragmatic outsider (often an Englishman), links his first nine novels together. The shape and theme of *Waverley*, which is concerned with the gradual, often unwitting, involvement of a commonsensical English gentleman in the Jacobite rising of 1745 and his exposure to the thrilling but alien culture of the Highland clans, are subtly repeated, with significant variation, in *Guy Mannering* (1815), *Old Mortality* (1816), and *Rob Roy* (1817). It is cleverly reversed in *The Heart of Midlothian* (1818), a tale set in Edinburgh in the period of anti-government Porteous riots of 1736, by the device of Jeanie Deans's epic walk to London to plead for her sister's life and by the contrast drawn between the somewhat narrow puritanism of Jeanie and the sophisticated but worldly nature of the Hanoverian court. In all these novels Scott exposes his protagonists to conflicting ways of seeing, thinking, and acting; his Scotland is variously divided by factions—by Jacobites and Unionists, Covenanters and Episcopalians, Highland clansmen and urban Lowlanders—and in each he suggests an evolutionary clash of opposites, the gradual convergence of which opens up a progressive future. The fissures of Scottish history are allowed to point the way to a present in which Scotland's fortunes are inexorably bound up with those of liberal, duller, more homogeneous, shop-keeping England. The dialectic established by the narrative offers some kind of movement away from a mere nostalgia for the past and for past manners or factions. As Scott stresses in chapter 72 of *Waverley*, no European nation had changed so much between 1715 and 1815: 'The effects of the insurrection of 1745 . . . commenced this innovation. The gradual influx of wealth, and extension of commerce, have since united to render the present people of Scotland a class of beings as different from their grandfathers, as the existing English are from those of Queen Elizabeth's time.' In order to suggest the nature and the implications of change to his readers, Scott opens up the past by carefully establishing a picture of men and women moving naturally in a historic environment. His characters are no longer represented in the fancy dress of Gothic fiction; they are shown at ease with the objects, furniture, and attitudes of their proper times. Fictional heroes encounter historical ones and are allowed to find them wanting, both being subject to the narrator's own imaginative and ideological interpretation of their development. Equally significantly, the novels present character as being shaped and determined by environment, an environment which is as much local as it is temporal, and as subject to geography as it is to history. If Scott's real sympathies lie in recording the steady triumphalism of the dominant culture, he is still a tolerant and often persuasive memorializer of lost causes and lost tribes, of dissent and of the alternative perceptions of minorities marginalized by those who hold political and intellectual sway.

In 1820, with the publication of *Ivanhoe*, Scott's fiction took a fresh, but not always happy, direction in moving abruptly away from Scotland and from recent, even remembered, history. *Ivanhoe* and two further, and far weaker, stories set in the time of the Crusades, *The Talisman* and *The Betrothed* (both

1825), form a continuous discourse which questions the origins and usefulness of the medieval code of chivalry and military honour and distantly reflects on the survival of both into the age of the French Revolution. All three novels, however, require turgidly lengthy explications of historical detail and resort to an often highly artificial dialogue in order to establish the authenticity of their twelfth-century settings. It is a fustian dialogue which contrasts vividly with the far easier evocations of home-spun, local speech which enliven the Scottish fiction. Similar faults mar the otherwise lively pictures of Elizabethan England in *Kenilworth* (1821) and of the period of the Commonwealth in *Woodstock* (1826). *The Fortunes of Nigel* (1822) and *Quentin Durward* (1823), concerned respectively with the adventures of exiled Scottish knights at the courts of James I of England and Louis XI of France, are both vigorous variations on the idea of the upright innocent abroad making his way through mazes of corruption, but the finest of Scott's later works is probably *Redgauntlet* (1824), an investigation of the dying flame of Scottish Jacobitism seen from the divided perspective of two heroes, the phlegmatic Alan Fairford and the romantic Darsie Latimer. Sadly, illness and financial disaster overshadowed the novelist's last years and his still phenomenal output bears the marks of the strain, declining as it does into rambling, but often highly charged, experiments with material which even the polymathic Scott had not properly assimilated.

Byron, Shelley, and Keats

Despite the anonymity of the 'author of Waverley', a ruse which was maintained on the title-page of all of *Waverley*'s fictional successors, the 'secret' of Scott's authorship was a thoroughly open one. In January 1821 Byron, an unstinted admirer, claimed, without a glimmer of doubt as to their authorship, to have read 'all W. Scott's novels at least fifty times'. Scott was, he noted in his journal, the 'Scotch Fielding, as well as a great English poet', and, he characteristically added, '—wonderful man! I long to get drunk with him'. It was Byron, properly George Gordon, Lord Byron (1788–1824), who alone managed to eclipse Scott's primacy as the best-selling poet of the second decade of the nineteenth century, but he never attempted to rival him as a novelist. If the poetic eclipse was far from total, the appearance of the first two cantos of *Childe Harold* in 1812 gave Byron an immediate celebrity, or, as he famously remarked, 'I awoke one morning and found myself famous'. Byron, like Scott, struck the appreciative hordes of his original readers as the most articulate voice of the post-revolutionary era, the writer who most fluently expressed the spirit of the age, its discontents as well as its often frenetic energy. But if Scott was the insider explaining the evolution of the past into the present and reconciling historic contradictions, Byron was, by his own choice, the outsider, vexed and amused by the anomalies of his own time and culture. Byron's least effective poetry may be 'modern', theatrical, and extravagant, but his best work is generally rooted in an established satiric tradition in which, as he himself acknowledges, it was better to err with Pope than to shine in the company of the contemporary writers that he despised and often deliberately undervalued. His poetry is informed not by nature or by the contemplation of nature, but by public life and by recent history, by British politics and by the feverish European nationalisms stirred by the French Revolution. It ranges in its geographical settings from Russia to the Mediterranean, from Portugal to the Levant, and it moves easily between different modes of telling and feeling, from the self-explorative to the polemic, from the melancholic to the comic, from the mock-heroic to the passionately amorous, from the song to the epic. Byron the libertarian and Byron the libertine readily assumed the public role of a commentator on his times because he both relished his fame and enjoyed the later Romantic pose of being at odds with established society. His role-playing, both in his convoluted private life and in his poetry, had a profound impact on his fellow-artists throughout Europe, and the sullen, restless 'Byronic' hero took on an international currency as if all societies had universally conspired to complicate his destiny.

Byron's international celebrity helped to render his life a work of art which interrelated and interfused with his poetry and his plays. Despite this iconic status, in his own time and far beyond it, his verse is idiosyncratic. It is radical only in the sense that it exhibits a distinctively patrician individualism. If in 1820 he could blame 'the present deplorable state of English poetry' on 'the absurd and systematic depreciation of Pope', he never cast himself in the role of a latter-day spokesman for a received culture. He speaks instead as an outsider and an exile, an articulator of disdain rather than simply dissent. His first work, the precociously self-indulgent schoolboy exercises published in 1806 as *Fugitive Pieces*, was revised and expanded no less than three times. Its second transmogrification, *Hours of Idleness* (1807), was selected for a particularly scathing critical attack by the *Edinburgh Review*, an assault which in turn provided the impetus for Byron's explosive broadside against the accepted culture of his times, *English Bards and Scotch Reviewers* (1809). This verse satire, written in somewhat old-fashioned rhyming couplets, suggests a poet at odds with the present, with its literary innovators (such as 'turgid' Coleridge and 'simple' Wordsworth) as much as with the conservative literary establishment which he identified with the dogmatic Edinburgh reviewers. His praise, which is faint enough, is reserved for Scott and 'Monk' Lewis. Byron's departure from England in 1809 for an extended visit to Portugal, Spain, and the Levant signalled both a rejection of England and a determination to explore alternatives to insular attitudes. The multifarious impressions left by this tour provided the material out of which the first two cantos of *Childe Harold* were shaped. *Childe Harold*, expanded by two further cantos in 1816 and 1818, offers a view of the western Mediterranean scarred by war and of the 'sad relic' of

Greece decaying under Ottoman misrule, but it also introduces as a central observer and participant a splenetic aristocratic exile, 'sick at heart' and suffering strange pangs 'as if the memory of some deadly feud | Or disappointed passion lurk'd below'. The memories of feuds and passions in the poem were as much historic and public as they were present and private.

In the 1812 Preface to *Childe Harold* Byron quotes James Beattie's praise of the flexibility of the Spenserian stanza which Beattie (1735–1803) had used in his once celebrated poem, *The Minstrel* (1771, 1774). 'The style and stanza of Spenser', Beattie had remarked, could be 'either droll or pathetic, descriptive or sentimental, tender or satirical'. Such flexibility is evident neither in Beattie's own work nor especially in the often morose self-consciousness of *Childe Harold*. Nevertheless, Byron clearly aspired to experiment with a verse form which would allow for a variety of both expression and mood, for satire as much as for sentiment. He discovered such a form in the eight-line, eleven-syllable *ottava rima* of the Italian poets Tasso, Ariosto, and Pulci and he adapted it to his own English purposes by shortening the verse-line to ten syllables. In *Beppo* (1818) and in *Don Juan* (1819–24) he did more than simply relish the disciplined freedom that *ottava rima* gave to his verse; he also shifted his poetic focus away from Childe Harold's melancholy and incipient misanthropy. Taking leave of his 'sketch of a modern Timon', he proclaims to his readers in an 'Addition to the Preface' that it would have been 'more agreeable, and certainly more easy, to have drawn an amiable character'. Although the characters of privileged, intelligent, arrogant, and accursed heroes continue to fascinate him in his highly original and daring poetic dramas (notably in the two tragedies *Sardanapalus* and *The Two Foscari* and in his superb 'mystery' *Cain*, published together in 1821), *Don Juan* introduces a new kind of central character, one who is at once more passive and more vivacious. The scheme of *Don Juan* allows for colloquy and polyphony, the voice of the often cynically droll narrator being the dominant one. Byron's narrator casts himself as relaxed and speculative, digressive and discursive—'never straining hard to versify, | I rattle on exactly as I'd talk | With anybody in a ride or walk' (Canto XV, 19). The ease of telling is matched by the hero's indeterminate peripateticism, an often disrupted, circuitous wandering across the Mediterranean world ending in a movement northwards to the Russia of Catherine the Great and finally westwards to the amorously frivolous world of aristocratic London society from which Byron had attempted to distance himself. Byron's perhaps fanciful notion of dramatically ending his hero's career with a guillotining in Jacobin Paris was never realized. Juan's adventures and misadventures, and the narrator's worldly-wise commentary on them, serve to debunk a series of received ideas and perceptions ranging from the supposed glory of war and heroism to fidelity in love and oriental exoticism. Byron is also undermining the myth of a picturesque and educative journey across Europe, the Romantic idea of a splendidly benevolent, fostering nature, and the Rousseauistic faith in basic human goodness. These challenges are especially evident in his vivid

and varied description of a sea-storm and shipwreck and in the blackly comic
account of the cannibalism of the survivors in Canto II:

> The lots were made, and mark'd, and mix'd, and handed,
>   In silent horror, and their distribution
> Lull'd even the savage hunger which demanded,
>   Like the Promethean vulture, this pollution;
> None in particular had sought or plann'd it,
>   'Twas Nature gnaw'd them to this resolution,
> By which none were permitted to be neuter—
> And the lot fell on Juan's luckless tutor.
> He but requested to be bled to death:
>   The surgeon had his instruments, and bled
> Pedrillo, and so gently ebb'd his breath,
>   You hardly could perceive when he was dead.
> He died as born, a Catholic in faith,
>   Like most in the belief in which they're bred,
> And first a little crucifix he kiss'd
> And then held out his jugular and wrist.

The poem veers easily, and often comically, between extremes of suffering and
luxury, hunger and excess, longing and satiety, ignorance and knowingness,
shifting appearance and an equally shifting reality. Both the art and the artful-
ness of the narrator are frequently concealed under a pretence of purposeless-
ness and self-deprecation—"'tis my way, | Sometimes *with* and sometimes
without occasion | I write what's uppermost, without delay; | This narrative is
not meant for narration, | But a mere airy and fantastic basis, | To build up
common things with common places' (Canto XIV, 7). Byron's earnestness,
evident enough in his earlier poetry and in the urgently fluent lyric 'The Isles
of Greece' which he introduces into Canto III, is now steadily qualified, or, in
the case of the lyric, framed by comments on the supposed 'trimming' nature
of its imagined singer. The 'earnest' poet is reduced to the level of the despised,
time-serving, pliable Southey, the chief object of ridicule in *The Vision of
Judgement* (1821). Byron's poetry, like his letters and the surviving fragments of
his journals, emerges from an energetic restlessness tempered by an amused
detachment, not from a carefully formulated theory of literature, a determining
philosophy, or a desire to enhance and improve public taste. 'I have written', he
told his publisher in 1819, 'from the fullness of my mind, from passion—from
impulse—from many motives—but not for their [his public's] "sweet
voices".—I know the precise worth of public applause.'

Byron's friend and sometime companion in self-imposed exile, Percy Bysshe
Shelley (1792–1822), had an equally low view of 'public applause' and an
equally distinct distaste for the British Establishments, literary and political.
Unlike Byron's, his work derives from a consistent, if malleable, ideology, one
determined by a philosophical scepticism which questions its Platonic roots as
much as it steadily rejects Christian mythology and morality. Shelley's first

public diatribe against Christianity, the undergraduate pamphlet *The Necessity of Atheism*, so antagonized the authorities of University College at Oxford in 1811 that its author was expelled from the University. Although Shelley's rejection of 'revealed' religion and its dogmas remained a cardinal element in his thought, and though he systematically maintained his faith in the principle that 'every reflecting mind must allow that there is no proof of the existence of a Deity', his later work suggests both a steady qualification of arguments based purely on 'reason' and a search for the source of the mysterious 'Power' that he acknowledged to be implicit in wild nature and in the inspiration of poetry. This complex and intellectually demanding aspiration is paralleled by, and to some extent married to, Shelley's abiding interest in the politics of revolution and evolution and to the idea of a gradual and inevitable social awakening.

Shelley's political thought, informed as it is with experimental scientific theory and with the social ideas of his father-in-law Godwin, elucidates more than simply an opposition of liberty and tyranny; it explores future possibilities and not past defeats and, in attempting to adduce the nature of egalitarianism, it moves beyond the general disillusion resultant from the defeat of the ideals of the French Revolution. As Shelley wrote to Godwin in 1817, he felt himself 'formed . . . to apprehend minute & remote distinctions of feeling whether relative to external nature, or the living beings which surround us, & to communicate the conceptions which result from considering either the moral or the material universe as a whole'. He recognized the significance of details, but as a poet and a theorist of poetry and politics he tended to concentrate on 'wholes' and on the possibilities of new perceptions and new orders. The radicalism, which led him with an almost adolescent enthusiasm to espouse a whole range of worthy causes from Irish nationalism to vegetarianism, was more than simply a reaction against the conservative triumphalism which marked post-Napoleonic Europe and more than an instinctive rejection of the restrictive political, religious, and moral formulae of his aristocratic English background; it was at once the root and the fruit of his intellectual idealism. The direct and graphic quatrain poem, *The Mask of Anarchy* (1819), inspired by Shelley's disgust at the so-called 'Peterloo' massacre, is perhaps his most effective and unadorned statement of protest against contemporary British repression. Earlier, in *Queen Mab: A Philosophical Poem* (1813), he had moulded 'the fairies midwife', the dream-maker of Mercutio's speech in Shakespeare's *Romeo and Juliet*, into the midwife of a broader revolutionary dream and the instructor of the soul of Ianthe in the principles of historical change. 'Kings, priests, and statesmen', Ianthe learns, 'blast the human flower | Even in its tender bud; their influence darts | Like subtle poison through the bloodless veins | Of desolate society.' Society, consoled by a purgation of its historic oppressors, and the human spirit, freed from the taint of a despotic tradition, are finally allowed to see the prospect of following 'the gradual paths of an aspiring change'. Shelley's original notes to *Queen Mab* make explicit the particular aspects of the present tyranny which threaten the fairy vision of a regenerated future humanity.

Imperative hope also marks the epic poem originally entitled 'Laon and Cythna; or, The Revolution of the Golden City: A Vision of the Nineteenth Century' but discreetly and topically renamed *The Revolt of Islam* for its publication in 1818. The poem describes the doomed but heroic struggle for liberation of a brother and sister (originally also lovers) against the manifold oppressions of the Ottoman Empire; at the poem's conclusion the defeated and immolated revolutionaries take on the posthumous role of inspirers of a continuing and multilateral struggle. *The Revolt of Islam* is more than a condemnation of distant oriental despotism, for it reflects both on the temporary failure of the liberating impulse of the French Revolution and on the present state of Britain. It was written, Shelley insisted, 'in the view of kindling within the bosoms of my readers a virtuous enthusiasm for those doctrines of liberty and justice, that faith and hope in something good, which neither violence nor misrepresentation nor prejudice can ever totally extinguish among mankind'. Shelley's play with archetypes and with a syncretic mythological system by means of which he dramatizes a revolutionary process equally determines the structures of his two 'lyrical' dramas, both reworkings of, and developments from, Aeschylean models. Both *Prometheus Unbound* (1820) and *Hellas* (1822) show a diminution of theatrical action in favour of a dramatic representation of imaginative motivation (the 'lyric' as opposed to the 'dramatic', a distinction which Shelley possibly derived from the German critic, August von Schlegel), and both form substantial and intense verse discourses on the nature of liberation. *Hellas*, inspired by the Greek rebellion against its Ottoman rulers, prophesies 'upon the curtain of futurity' the triumph of the Greek cause 'as a portion of the cause of civilisation and social improvement' but it ends with a far from triumphant final chorus which foresees the possibility of a return of 'hate and death' and of a cyclical succession of bloody revolution upon bloody revolution. *Prometheus Unbound* is ostensibly more confident in its view of historical necessity for it links the idea of revolution more closely to the radical reordering of human vision and to the processes of perceiving, imagining, and articulating thought as speech. To some extent the characterization of Prometheus derives from the figure of Milton's Satan, whom Shelley, like Blake, saw as 'a moral being . . . far superior to his God', but his is essentially a heroic struggle concerned with more than self-vindication. Prometheus is seen battling against despair and arbitrary tyranny, and his achievement is presented as a liberation of both body and spirit and as a heightened state of consciousness which implies a wider liberation from enemies which are both internal and external. With the summary overthrow of Jupiter at the beginning of Act III, and the reunion of the unchained Prometheus with Asia, the final act of the drama is given over to lyrical celebration; the triumph of the revolution is marked by the triumph of song.

Shelley's often passionate discussions of poetry are closely related to his idea of the interconnection of the process of the liberation of the soul, the growth of altruism inspired by love, and the ultimate extermination of tyrants. In *Alastor; or, The Spirit of Solitude* (1816) he had presented an account of the quest of a young poet, led by idealism, who discovers 'the spirit of sweet human love' too late. The poem may also be a protest against the Wordsworthian egotism which Shelley so distrusted in *The Excursion*. In his Preface he outlines his scheme as showing 'the Poet's self-centred seclusion . . . avenged by the furies of an irresistible passion' and he adds that 'those who love not their fellow-beings, live unfruitful lives, and prepare for their old age a miserable grave'. He may have wilfully misread Wordsworth, but the protest against an indulgence in solitude derives much of its force from his unforgiving awareness of the older poet's retreat from political action into an alternative contemplation of nature. The idea of recoil and recuperation which informs much of Wordsworth's finest lyric poetry is certainly absent from Shelley's two searching, if ultimately ambiguous, meditations on the natural world, the 'Hymn to Intellectual Beauty' and 'Mont Blanc' (both 1816). In the latter poem, the mountain seems to command action against 'large codes of fraud and woe' rather than represent a silent, God-imbued check to human activity.

It is, however, in his essay *A Defence of Poetry* (written in 1821 and published posthumously in 1840) that Shelley most confidently proclaims the essentially social function of poetry and the prophetic role of the poet. His assertions, like Sidney's before him, are large, even at times outrageous, but his examination of the idea of political improvement as a criterion of literary value and his idea of poetry as a liberator of the individual moral sense carry considerable intellectual force. The argument of the *Defence* opens with the development of a distinction between the workings of the reason and the imagination, with the imagination seen as the synthesizer and the unifier which finds its highest expression in poetry. Shelley dismisses as 'a vulgar error' the distinction between poets and prose writers, and proceeds to dissolve divisions between poets, philosophers, and philosophic historians. Thus Shakespeare, Dante, and Milton emerge as 'philosophers of the very loftiest power' and Plato and Bacon, Herodotus and Plutarch are placed amongst the poets. Essentially, the essay seeks to demonstrate that poetry prefigures other modes of thought and anticipates the formulation of a social morality—'ethical science arranges the elements which poetry has created, and propounds schemes and proposes examples of civil and domestic life.' Love, 'or a going out of our own nature, and an identification of ourselves with the beautiful', is projected as the 'great secret of morals' and, by feeding the imagination, poetry 'administers to the effect by acting upon the cause'. Shelley's argument continues to circulate around these propositions; poetry enhances life, it exalts beauty, it transmutes all it touches, and it tells the truth by stripping 'the veil of familiarity from the world' and laying bare 'the naked and sleeping beauty which is the spirit of its forms'. The poet is priest and prophet to a world which can move beyond religion and magic; he is an 'unacknowledged legislator' for a future society which will learn to live without the restrictions of law; he is, above all, the liberator and the explorer. Shelley's projection of the poet as hero, as the leader and representative of society, is more than veiled self-aggrandizement, it is a reasonable assertion of the irrational power of the imagination against a purely utilitarian view of art.

Adonais (1821), Shelley's elegiac tribute to the dead Keats, pursues the idea of the poet as hero, here triumphant even in the face of death and 'awakened from the dream of life'. If Keats/Adonais is 'one with Nature' and has become 'transmitted effluence' which cannot die 'so long as fire outlives the parent spark', the earth-bound survivor yearns, almost suicidally, for a part in the same life-transcending immortality. The unfinished *The Triumph of Life*, derived metrically and thematically from Dante and Petrarch, suggests an alternative, if phantasmagoric, vision of life. The poem opens with a dawn and an ecstatic evocation of the sublime amid a mountainous landscape:

> Swift as a spirit hastening to his task
>   Of glory and of good, the Sun sprang forth
> Rejoicing in his splendour, and the mask
>
>   Of darkness fell from the awakened Earth.
> The smokeless altars of the mountain snows
>   Flamed above crimson clouds, and at the birth
>
> Of light, the Ocean's orison arose
>   To which the birds tempered their matin lay
> All flowers in field or forest which unclose
>
>   Their trembling eyelids to the kiss of day,
> Swinging their censers in the element,
>   With orient incense lit by the new ray
>
> Burned slow and inconsumably . . .

This initial celebration of energy and renewal is countered by the darkness of the narrator-poet's 'strange trance', a 'waking dream' of a haunted past and an allegory of death in which the processing participants appear fascinated by their mortality. When the poet recognizes and confronts the figure of Rousseau, the central questions of the poem are raised. Rousseau, in a self-indulgent probing of his own memories, describes too a circuitous process of forgetting and erasing which necessarily evades answers as to the meaning of life. When, finally, the bewildered poet demands 'Then what is Life?' no answer is forthcoming. The poem breaks off, and with it the search for responsive definitions of the inspiring 'Power' behind creation; the fallacy of an egotistic solitude has been exposed, but the offer of alternative assertion remains a hiatus.

John Keats (1795–1821), ever sensitive to criticism and ever open to the influence of other poets, both living and dead, was also extraordinarily able to assimilate and then to transform both criticism and influence. In 1817 he had declined to visit Shelley on the grounds that he preferred to keep his distance, fearing a too immediate challenge to his 'unfetterd [*sic*] Scope'. His development as a poet was rapid, particular, and individual and it was articulated in the bursts of energetic self-critical analysis in his letters. Keats's background and education denied him both the social advantages and the ready recourse to classical models shared by those contemporaries to whose work he most readily turned (though not always favourably)—Wordsworth and Coleridge, Scott, Byron, and Shelley. The enthusiasm which marks his discovery in 1816 of George Chapman's sixteenth-century translation of *The Iliad*, a discovery celebrated in one of his finest sonnets, is notable not simply for its sense of release from the limitations of Alexander Pope's couplet version, but also for the very fact that Homer's Greek was not directly open to him. Throughout his working life Keats had recourse to Lemprière's *Classical Dictionary* and not to a classical memory fostered at school or university. He was, however, extremely well read and his letters record a series of new, excited, and critical impressions formed by his explorations of English seventeenth-century drama, of Chaucer, Spenser, Milton, and Dryden, of Dante, Boccaccio, Ariosto, and Tasso (whose Italian he was beginning to master towards the end of his life) and, above all, of Shakespeare. It is to the example of Shakespeare that he habitually refers in his letters when he seeks to demonstrate a sudden insight into the nature of poetic creation, notably in 1817 in his definition of what he styles 'Negative Capability' ('when a man is capable of being in uncertainties, mysteries, doubts, without any irritable reaching after fact and reason') and in his attempt in October 1818 to distinguish between 'the Wordsworthian or egotistical sublime' and the 'poetical Character' that 'lives in gusto' and has 'as much delight in conceiving an Iago as an Imogen'.

In this same letter of 1818 Keats famously remarks that what shocks the virtuous philosopher 'delights the chameleon Poet'. The nature of this particular chameleon lay, for Keats, in its ability to assimilate impressions and temporarily, but totally, to identify with external objects, both animate and inanimate. He felt himself, he adds, 'a creature of impulse'. In some ways his development as a poet confirms his self-analysis, moving as he does from impulsive attraction to a dedicated absorption and adaptation of stimuli through a process of intellectualization and poetic articulation. He draws his immediate experience into his verse, finding metaphors in the natural world, in his responses to architecture, painting, and sculpture or in his magpie reading. His ambition to be counted worthy of a place in the English poetic tradition drove him as much into a succession of creative experiments with form and metre as into the high-flown essays in sub-Shakespearean historic drama so favoured by his contemporaries. To the end of his short career he seems to have experienced a dissatisfaction with his own achievement which stretched beyond its lack of public and critical appreciation; it was a disappointment which inspired the notions of self-denigration and disintegration implicit in his choice of epitaph: 'Here lies one whose name was writ in water'. The work contained in his first two volumes, the *Poems* of 1817 and *Endymion: A Poetic Romance* of 1818 was, in his own terms, transcended before it had made any impact on readers beyond the poet's own immediate circle. The 1817 collection contains much immature work, imitations of and reflections on *The*

Faerie Queene as much as the somewhat shapeless effusions 'Sleep and Poetry' and 'I Stood Tip-Toe Upon a Little Hill', both chiefly memorable for the minute observation crystallized in their delicate imagery. In *Endymion* Keats's consistent ambition to move beyond the lyrical to the narrative and the epic finds its first significant expression, but it is an experiment with which he had evidently become restless before he had completed it. The strengths of the poem are most often occasional and lie chiefly in the introduction of the lyrical hymns and songs which enhance the meandering narrative line. Although he was pained by the unfavourable reviews accorded to the poem, Keats himself readily recognized its shortcomings and what they had come to imply to him. 'I have written independently *without Judgment*', he writes in October 1818, 'I may write independently, & *with Judgment* hereafter . . . In Endymion, I leaped headlong into the Sea, and thereby have become better acquainted with the Soundings, the quicksands, & the rocks, than if I had stayed upon the green shore, and piped a silly pipe, and took tea & comfortable advice.—I was never afraid of failure; for I would sooner fail than not be among the greatest.'

Keats's *Lamia, Isabella, The Eve of St Agnes, and other Poems* was published in July 1820 when his mortal sickness had fully declared itself. The majority of the poems in the volume had been written in a period of fertile hyperactivity between the spring of 1818 and the early autumn of 1819. Apart from the three substantial narrative poems named in the title, the 'other poems' include the five odes which have since become his best-known works and the fragmentary *Hyperion* which he had abandoned in April 1819 and which was printed, as the publishers were obliged to acknowledge, 'contrary to the wish of the author'. The earliest of the narrative poems, 'Isabella; or, The Pot of Basil', was originally intended to form a contribution to a collection of versetales based on stories by Boccaccio. Keats's version of the story of two tragic lovers elaborates on the original by introducing a complex scheme of natural imagery, an interpolated social and moral commentary, and elements of the Gothic. It became in the poet's own opinion 'too smokeable . . . "A weak-sided poem" with an amusing sober-sadness about it'. 'The Eve of St Agnes', written some eight months later, shares a medieval setting with its predecessor but moves far beyond it in what it reveals of Keats's new mastery of dramatic and verbal effect and of narrative shape and tension. The poem is shaped around a series of intense contrasts, of cold and warmth, of dark and light, of hardness and softness, of noise and stillness, and, above all, of cruelty and love, but it is ultimately as ambiguous and uncertain as the superstition on which its heroine, Madeline, sets her hopes. As Madeline anxiously enters her chamber her taper flickers out and the moonlight falls on her through a stained-glass window:

> A casement high and triple-arched there was,
> All garlanded with carven imag'ries

> Of fruits and flowers, and bunches of knot-grass,
> And diamonded with panes of quaint device,
> Innumerable of stains and splendid dyes,
> As are the tiger-moth's deep-damasked wings;
> And in the midst, 'mong thousand heraldries,
> And twilight saints, and dim emblazonings,
> A shielded scutcheon blushed with blood of queens and kings.

The poem is emphatically concrete in the variety of its clustered, sensual suggestion, but both abrupt and elusive in its final wrench away from the lovers' escape 'into the storm' and its return to suggestions of sickness, death, and penitence. A far greater ambiguity marks the retelling of a classical haunting in 'Lamia', an ambiguity which begins with Keats's omission of the associations of vampirism with the figure of his half-serpent 'lamia' (according to Lemprière such monsters 'allured strangers . . . that they might devour them'). His serpent is beautiful, agonized by her transformation into a lover and enchanting rather than devouring. The narrative pits her against an aged, rational philosopher, Apollonius, in a competition for the attention of Lycius, but if Lycius is finally the victim of the piercing of the illusion on which his world becomes centred, the poem allows little sympathy with the reasoning dream-breaker. Lamia builds fairy palaces, Apollonius demolishes them; she fosters the imagination, his philosophy clips angel's wings and will 'conquer all mysteries by rule and line, | Empty the haunted air and gnomed mine— | Unweave a rainbow'. The poem does not manœuvre a reader into taking sides, but its juxtapositions of illusion and reality, of the ideal and the actual, of feeling and thought, remain tantalizingly unresolved.

A related debate about contraries informs the five odes included in the 1820 volume (a sixth, the 'Ode on Indolence', written in May 1819, was published posthumously in 1848 in a collection which also included a reprinting of Keats's most famous lyrical treatment of the idea of fairy enthralment, the ballad 'La Belle Dame Sans Merci'). The earliest of the odes in terms of composition, that to Psyche, has often been seen as an enactment of a ceremonial dedication of the Soul—'as distinguished from an Intelligence'—and as a variation on the idea of the world as 'the vale of Soul-making' which Keats outlined in a long letter of April 1819, a letter which also included a draft of the poem. The odes to a Nightingale and on Melancholy, both of which slightly vary the metrical structure evolved in the earlier poem, were composed in May 1819. The former takes as its subject the local presence of a nightingale, and the contrast of the 'full-throated ease' of its singing with the aching 'numbness' of the human observer, the rapt and meditative poet. The ode progresses through a series of precisely delicate evocations of opposed moods and ways of seeing, some elated, some depressed, but each serving to return the narrator to his 'sole self' and to his awareness of the temporary nature of the release from the unrelieved contemplation of temporal suffering which the bird's song has offered. The more succinct 'Ode on Melancholy' opens with a rejection of traditional, and gloomy, aids to reflection and moves to an exploration of the interrelationship of the sensations of joy and sorrow. The perception of the transience of beauty which haunts the poem also informs the speculations derived from the contemplation of the two scenes which decorate an imagined Attic vase in the 'Ode on a Grecian Urn', one showing bucolic lovers, the other a pagan sacrifice. Both scenes are frozen and silent, images taken out of time and rendered eternal only by the intervention of art. The image of the sacrifice, in particular, has something of the sculptural patterning and spatial imagination of Poussin:

> Who are these coming to the sacrifice?
>   To what green altar, O mysterious priest,
> Lead'st thou that heifer lowing at the skies,
>   And all her silken flanks with garlands dressed?
> What little town by river or sea shore,
>   Or mountain-built with peaceful citadel,
>   Is emptied of this folk, this pious morn?
> And, little town, thy streets for evermore
>   Will silent be; and not a soul to tell
>   Why thou art desolate, can e'er return.

The poem allows for the high compensations offered by art, but its vocabulary steadily suggests the loss, even the desolation, entailed in the 'teasing' process of contemplating eternity. The latest of the odes, 'To Autumn', was written in September 1819. Here the tensions, oppositions, and conflicting emotions are diminished amid a series of dense impressions of a season whose bounty contains both fulfilment and incipient decay, both an intensification of life and an inevitable, but natural, process of ageing and dying.

Keats's two extensive drafts of the fragmentary *Hyperion*—the second of which, known as *The Fall of Hyperion: A Dream*, was published only in 1856— confront the problems of transience, transition, defeat, and progressive revolutionary change in an attempt to retell the story of the resistance of the last of the Titans to the coming new order of the Gods. In his reconstruction of his poem in the second half of 1819 he attempted to reduce the pervasive influence of Milton on his own blank verse, both because he sought a more personal expression and because he was beginning to suspect Milton's aesthetic ('Miltonic verse cannot be written but in the vein of art—I wish to devote myself to another sensation'). But the remodelling also entailed a radical shift in perspective by allotting the main narration of the fall of the Titans to Moneta, the veiled priestess and prophetess encountered in a prefatory vision. This vision, Dantean rather than Miltonic in its inspiration, explores the idea of the influence of suffering on the imagination of a modern poet, requiring the visionary to experience pain and the 'giant agony of the world' before being vouchsafed an understanding of both the power and the limitation of art; Moneta's tale of the past, as it begins to emerge, serves to illuminate and reinforce what the poet has already partially discovered in his vision. *The Fall of Hyperion* begins with the clear distinction between dreaming 'fanatics', the representatives of and apologists for the Christianity which Keats had rejected, and the figure of the poet-prophet seeking a new cosmology. The poem does more than counter Milton's example with a pagan scheme, or adjust Dante to suit post-Christian arguments about the nature of evolution; it seeks to balance the darkness, the misery, the ruin, and the disillusion with the still uncertain hope that the suffering and responsive poet may yet find his voice. It is Keats's most triumphant declaration of his independent self-hood as a poet.

The 'Romantic' Essayists

In the closing months of 1817 *Blackwood's Edinburgh Magazine* began a series of venomous articles on what the magazine styled 'the Cockney School of Poetry'. In these articles the name and work of the London-based Keats was linked to that of his friend and former mentor James Henry Leigh Hunt (1784–1859). Both writers were taken to be representatives of a gauche and vulgar group of poets whose every gesture betrayed their 'low birth and low habits'. Though at the beginning of his literary career Keats had needed Hunt's timely encouragement, he rapidly outgrew Hunt's purely decorative influence on his verse. Hunt is an occasionally diverting poet and a florid translator (his version of Tasso's *Amyntas: A Tale of the Woods* (1820) was dedicated to Keats), but his work as a journalist and essayist, a central expression of one of the great ages of English journalism, is far more enterprising. Between 1808 and 1825 he acted as editor of the anti-Establishment periodical *The Examiner* which he had founded with his brother John. In 1813, as the consequence of an extremely uncomplimentary article on the Prince Regent, he was obliged for two years to continue his editorial work from a not uncomfortable prison cell. *The Examiner* provided a platform for William Hazlitt's theatre criticism and through its pages Hunt was instrumental in introducing the work of both Shelley and Keats to a wider readership. In the years 1819–21 Hunt also edited *The Indicator* and in 1822, with the collaboration of Byron and Shelley, established the short-lived *The Liberal*. His gossipy later volumes—*A Jar of Honey from Mount Hybla* (1848) and his study of Kensington, *The Old Court Suburb* (1855)—are scarcely worthy of his former literary and political radicalism (he was by this stage the recipient of a state pension), but his *Autobiography* (1850, revised edition 1859) manages to rekindle some of the old fire in its reminiscences of lost friends and lost causes. The book and its penurious and effusive author are now most commonly remembered through their influence on Dickens's slanderous portrait of Harold Skimpole in *Bleak House* (1852–3).

William Hazlitt (1778–1830) is, with Coleridge, the foremost literary critic of the age. Both men recognized the importance of journals in disseminating information and in reflecting on contemporary issues, and both successfully responded to, and profitably indulged, the growing metropolitan taste for public lectures. Both were also acquainted with modern German thought and both proved to be discriminating hierophants in the now international cult of Shakespeare. Hazlitt was particularly alert to the significance of art and the creative imagination amid the political demands and disappointments of the post-revolutionary era. Although an early disciple of Godwin's and a democrat by principle, he became, and remained, an equally determined idolizer of Napoleon. Napoleon, as the radical hero, the champion of progress, and the vigorous alternative to the negatives and vacuity of modern Britain, was the subject of Hazlitt's last major project, a biography published in 1828–30, and he perversely haunts the pages of the prose medley *Liber Amoris: or, The New Pygmalion* (1823), a scrapbook account of a fraught and unfulfilled adulterous affair.

It was, however, as a literary theorist and as a critic of Shakespeare and Elizabethan drama that Hazlitt most conspicuously influenced his own contemporaries. Keats, in particular, drew considerably from his reading of Hazlitt's An *Essay on the Principles of Human Action* (1805); he avidly studied *Characters of Shakespear's Plays* on its publication in 1817 and he attended the series of lectures on English poets delivered at the Surrey Institution in the opening months of 1818. *Characters of Shakespear's Plays* acknowledges a debt to the pioneer work of Schlegel, but the lectures are more often shaped by dissent from the English acting tradition and by vexation with earlier English critics, notably with the *ex cathedra* pronunciations of Dr Johnson. Johnson's prose in particular irritates him: 'He no sooner acknowledges the merits of his author in one line than the periodical revolution of his style carries the weight of his opinion completely over to the side of objection, thus keeping up a perpetual alternation of perfections and absurdities.' Hazlitt includes generous appreciations of the great actors he had seen (Mrs Siddons, Kemble, Kean), but he also distances himself from plays in performance. While freely admitting that *Richard III* may well 'belong to the theatre, rather than to the closet', he insists elsewhere in his lectures that he did not like to see Shakespeare acted and that performances of *A Midsummer Night's Dream* served only to convert 'a delightful fiction to a pantomime'. By way of contrast, he emphasizes Shakespeare's continuing political relevance. 'No reader of history can be a lover of kings', he notes in an aside in his account of *Henry VIII* and he discovers a 'store-house of political commonplaces' in *Coriolanus* which might save a student 'the trouble of reading Burke's Reflections or Paine's Rights of Man, or the Debates in both Houses of Parliament since the French Revolution or our own'. Hazlitt readily concedes that he prefers Shakespeare's tragedies to his comedies, but some of the most telling observations occur in the lectures on *The Merchant of Venice* (where he speaks sympathetically of Shylock as a 'good hater'), on *Measure for Measure* (which he finds 'a play as full of genius as it is of wisdom', if one lacking in 'passion'), and on *The Tempest* (where he recognizes the interconnection of all the parts of the play and in particular the fact that the drunkards 'share, in the disorder of their minds and bodies, in the tumult of the elements').

Hazlitt is an equally sharp and original critic of his literary and political contemporaries in the essays published as *The Spirit of the Age* in 1825. In this attempt to examine aspects of the *Zeitgeist* of a period that Hazlitt himself sees as 'an age of talkers, and not of doers', he deals with twenty-five prominent politicians, thinkers, and writers. He praises, discriminates, and, when the occasion suits, damns with an aphorism or an image. Jeremy Bentham 'turns wooden utensils' as a relaxation from thought 'and fancies he can turn men in the same manner'; Byron 'lounges with extravagance, and yawns so as to alarm the reader'; Cobbett wields not simply 'a true pen, but a great mutton fist'; while Crabbe's *The Borough* is 'done so to the life, that it seems almost like some sea-monster, crawled out of the neighbouring slime, and harbouring a breed of strange vermin, with a strong local scent of tar and bilge-water'. Hazlitt is supportively generous to the Godwin whom he sees as having 'sunk below the horizon' of public attention, even though his works are 'a standard in the history of intellect', and he is kind enough to the much-despised Southey by praising his prose works while deploring his 'political inconsistency'. The essay on Wordsworth forthrightly proclaims his centrality in modern English culture and his genius as 'a pure emanation of the Spirit of the Age'. Wordsworth's mind may well be 'obtuse', but, as Hazlitt explains, that is because 'it is not analytic, but synthetic; it is reflecting rather than theoretical'.

Hazlitt's short sketch of 'Elia', his friend Charles Lamb (1775–1834), acknowledges that Lamb had succeeded as a writer 'not by conforming to the *Spirit of the Age*, but in opposition to it'. Lamb the antiquarian, and Lamb the reflective exploiter of nostalgia had somehow turned his back on the issues of the day, preferring the byways of the past to the highways of the present. In his lectures on Shakespeare and the Elizabethan dramatists Hazlitt flatteringly highlights aspects of his friend's often cogent appreciation of classic English drama, citing notes and asides in Lamb's pioneer anthology *Specimens of English Dramatic Poets who lived about the Time of Shakespeare* (1808). This anthology extracts scenes and speeches from the work of writers neglected and unregarded at the time, but it also reveals often surprising judgements in a man noted for his 'gentleness' in his own circle. Lamb admits to enjoying Elizabethan and Jacobean drama 'beyond the diocese of strict conscience' and, although he finds Marlowe extravagantly offensive, he delights in Webster's ability 'to move a horror skilfully' and to 'wean and weary a life till it is ready to drop'. Elsewhere, in an essay 'On the Tragedies of Shakespeare', he notes of the happy ending contrived for the bastardized version of *King Lear* then current on the English stage: 'A happy ending!—as if the living martyrdom that Lear has gone through,—the flaying of his feelings alive, did not make a fair dismissal from the stage of life the only decorous thing for him.' It was, however, as 'Elia', the author of a series of essays mostly contributed to the *London Magazine*, that Lamb achieved a real rapport with contemporary readers and a reputation testified to by numerous subsequent reprints of the two original collections first published in 1823 and 1833. The essays cultivate a form and a style that Lamb admired in his seventeenth- and eighteenth-century mentors, Bacon, Browne, Walton, Fuller, Addison, and Steele. He plays with archaisms and with a familiar archness, but he superadds his own delight in whimsy, reminiscence, and digression. 'Elia' is self-evidently a Londoner, with a cockney's pleasure in London streets and institutions and an equally cockney attachment to a countryside situated at a convenient distance from the town, but he is rarely specifically topographical, preferring to culti-vate aspects of the autobiographical or merely a taste for charm and serendip-ity. The *Essays* were to find a distant echo in the general, short radio talks perfected in the mid-twentieth century by the likes of E. M. Forster and J. B. Priestley.

Thomas De Quincey (1785–1859) was obliged throughout his career to support himself and his family by contributing stories, essays, articles, and reviews to various prominent journals. His most celebrated and once notori-ous work, *The Confessions of an English Opium Eater*, appeared in two parts in the *London Magazine* in 1821 (it was subsequently revised and expanded in 1856). This study of addiction and hallucination, of the induction of dreams as much as of the impossibility of forgetting a personal past, moves far beyond a merely Gothic or Piranesian fascination with the dark and contorted architecture of the soul. It is a work of considerable psychological daring, prefiguring Freudian theories and preoccupations, as much as an intricate personal apologia which interweaves recollections of human kindness, night-marish recalls of childhood trauma, and an equivocating justification of drug-taking. The indulgent, feverish clarity of De Quincey's accounts of his own exploration of memory, imagination, and waking dream is related elsewhere in his work to his profound appreciation of the 'moral sublime' in Wordsworth's poetry and to sometimes startling critical insights into other literature. *Recollections of the Lakes and the Lake Poets* (1834–9) was written some twenty years after the period of his intimacy with Wordsworth, Coleridge, and Southey, and combines fulsomely admiring reminiscence with often seditious, malicious, or negative inferences about the less than sublime private short-comings of the individuals concerned. De Quincey's journalism, which is often marked by a wry humour, ranges from the study in black comedy, 'On Murder Considered as One of the Fine Arts' (1827) (which purports to be a lecture to the Society of Connoisseurs in Murder on the aesthetics of slaughter), to the remarkable fantasias on dreaming, *Suspiria de Profundis* (1845) and *The English Mail Coach* (1849). Both of these latter essays are highly digressive while at the same time justifications of digression. The short critical study, 'On the Knocking at the Gate in Macbeth' (1823), was originally one of a series of mis-cellaneous 'Notes from the Pocket-Book of a Late Opium Eater'. It has a logic quite lacking in De Quincey's more personal psychological explorations, moving as it does from an initial perplexity at the emotion aroused by the knocking at the gate, through a seeming digression, to a lucid answer to the opening question. It is none the less a characteristic work, both an explanation of emotional arousal and a perception of the nature of dramatic dynamism and opposition. The knocking at the gate is a crux, a moment of revelation in which murder and the murderer—'cut off by an immeasurable gulph from the ordinary tide and succession of human affairs'—is juxtaposed with a reassertion of human value.

Walter Savage Landor (1775–1864) was, like Thomas De Quincey and Thomas Love Peacock, one of those relatively rare early nineteenth-century writers who lived well into the Victorian era and who continued to make a mark on Victorian letters. Indeed, Landor was to be satirized in his friend Dickens's *Bleak House* (1852–3) as the incorrigibly irascible but generous-minded Lawrence Boythorn. Landor was never a conventionally minded man and his determined independence of thought and action rarely rendered him an easy man to work with. In 1808, in a fit of impetuosity, he enlisted in the Spanish army in order to join the struggle against his great bugbear Napoleon (having been promoted to the rank of colonel by the King of Spain, he later angrily resigned his commission in protest at the King's re-establishment of the Jesuit order). After an unhappy period as a Welsh landowner he sank to complaining that 'if drunkenness, idleness, mischief and revenge are the principal characteristics of the savage state, what nation . . . is so singularly tattooed with them as the Welsh?' Nonetheless, Landor's most celebrated work, the five volumes of *Imaginary Conversations* (1824–9) show little of this intemperance. These learned, speculative essays on philosophy, politics, and historical motivation were written during an extended period of self-imposed exile in Florence. They take the form of carefully orchestrated conversations between eminent historical figures ('Diogenes and Plato', 'Epicurus, Leontion and Ternissa', 'Epictetus and Seneca', 'Marcellus and Hannibal' amongst the ancients; 'Henry VIII and Anne Boleyn', 'Queen Elizabeth and Cecil', 'Andrew Marvel and Bishop Parker', 'Middleton and Magliabechi', 'Washington and Franklin', and 'Pitt and Canning' amongst the moderns). Although Landor had earlier tried his hand at writing for the theatre (the lame, unperformed verse tragedy *Count Julian* was printed in 1812, but the comedy *Charitable Dowager* failed to find both a stage and a publisher), the *Imaginary Conversations* have little that is dramatic about them. There is equally little attempt at characterization. The *Conversations* are more akin to symposia, the arguments of which develop, after a series of commonplace, introductory pleasantries, by means of deliberate and thoughtful exchanges between the conversers. There is, on occasion, room for pungency ('Barrow and Newton', for example, contains the memorable aphorism: 'Money is like muck; not good except it be spread'), but, generally, the exchanges suggest a thoughtful series of might-have-beens and might-yet-bes, both political and philosophical. At the end of 'Washington and Franklin', for example, the two elder statesmen speculate about the future of their nation. Will continuing economic development bring about a gradual dissolution of the Union? Franklin dismisses Washington's 'horrible prediction' of secession with the pious hope that the future citizens of the United States will have learned through 'long experience of their true interests, a certainty that they depend upon peace and concord . . . resolute to defend these advantages, the children of America are for ever free'. By contrast, Franklin predicts that the children of Europe must, for many years yet, 'thread the labyrinth and face the Minotaur'.

The seven compact novels of Thomas Love Peacock (1785–1866) satirically explore the ways in which philosophical or ideological stances sever his characters from ordinariness and from ordinary human communication. Peacock generally models his fictions on parodies of Socratic dialogues or Platonic symposia, withdrawing his thinly, but deftly, sketched characters into the relative luxury and seclusion of country houses where they have the leisure to make fools of themselves. Writing in 1836 on the nature of French comic romance, for which he had a particular relish, Peacock noted that there were 'two very distinct classes of comic fictions: one in which the characters are abstractions or embodied classifications, and the implied or embodied opinions the main matter of the work; another in which the characters are individuals, and the events and the action those of actual life'. His own satires tend to fall into the first category, based as they are on speech rather than action, on preoccupation and obsession rather than on psychology and motivation. Despite the historical setting of both *Maid Marion* (1822) and *The Misfortunes of Elphin* (1829), all the tales concern themselves with the ramifications of modern political, social, and aesthetic theory; history proves to be little more than a vehicle for witty discourses on the nature of government, on monarchy, and on the nature of revolutionary opposition to the powers that be. As Peacock himself remarks in a Preface to a collection of his first six novels in 1837, his first, *Headlong Hall*, had begun with the now defunct Holyhead Mail, and his latest, *Crotchet Castle*, had ended with an equally defunct 'Rotten Borough'. The books had taken up issues of the moment which the passage of time had rendered dated, but, he hoped, 'the classes of tastes, feelings and opinions, which were brought into play in these little tales remain substantially the same'. In many ways Peacock's own modest analysis of his work is at fault, for his novels are very much tied to the particular debates of the first two decades of the nineteenth century, and even his 'Victorian' tale of 1860–1, *Gryll Grange*, harks back to the mode, the debates, and the gourmandizing clergymen of his earlier fiction.

Peacock's intimacy with Shelley, and his acquaintance with the radical speculations of Shelley's circle, gave him an amused grasp of both a particular language and an innate inconsistency. His sceptical treatment of leading aspects of 'the Spirit of the Age' nevertheless extends beyond the whims of a radical chic into a general ridicule of the intellectual posturing of the first third of the nineteenth century. Shelley himself appears under various guises in Peacock's early stories, most notably as the crankily esoteric Scythrop Glowry in *Nightmare Abbey* (1818). He cast Coleridge as the transcendental

Mr Flosky in the same novel, as Moly Mystic in *Melincourt* (1817) and, belatedly, as Mr Skionar in *Crotchet Castle* (1831). The self-dramatizing Mr Cypress of *Nightmare Abbey* is a projection of Byron and the political renegades, Wordsworth and Southey, are caricatured in *Melincourt* as Mr Paperstamp and Mr Feathernest, names which suggest the nature of their profitable association with the State. *Melincourt* is ambitiously shaped around an abduction (indirectly derived from both *Clarissa* and *Anna St Ives*), but the plot is rendered farcical by the bizarre introduction of a flute-playing orang-utan as the heroine's gallant deliverer. 'Sir Oran Haut-ton', educated in all things except speech by the idealistic primitivist Mr Sylvan Forester, is also, thanks to his patron's purchase of a seat for him, a Member of Parliament. The rival claims of progress and regress, of reform and conservatism, of perfectibilians, deteriorationists, and statu-quoites variously figure in all the tales, but the contrived comic resolutions of the plots, the multiple marriages, the averted suicides, or simply the exposure of pretence, never effectively serve to resolve the ideological contradictions voiced by the characters. Peacock's last novel, *Gryll Grange*, partly concerns itself with the Victorian debate about the use and misuse of science but unlike most other mid-nineteenth-century novels it never comes down didactically on one side to the prejudice of another; in common with Peacock's other fiction it reveals a genial narrative pleasure in preposterous incident which works more on the level of entertaining diversion than as an ideological plot device.

Clare and Cobbett

Peacock's long life extended well into the Victorian period, in marked contrast to many of those whom he had satirized in his first six novels. Largely because the three major poets of the younger generation—Byron, Shelley, and Keats— were dead by the late 1820s, or because the work of Wordsworth, Coleridge, and Scott markedly declined in quality and imaginative energy as the writers grew older, it has often proved difficult to determine precise literary continuities and influences from the first to the second third of the century, and convenient therefore to cite the beginnings of new careers (notably those of Carlyle, Dickens, and Tennyson) as evidence of a fresh literary sensibility in the 1830s. Victorian preoccupations seem to supersede rather than to accentuate the concerns of the 1820s. A systematic argument over the nature of the gradualist parliamentary and social reform replaced an active involvement with, or a distaste for, revolutionary politics (though the disruptive fact of the French Revolution continued to haunt all Victorian political thinking). Relative constitutional stability at home served to enhance the reputation of a temperate monarchy against the foreign principles of republicanism and absolutism. The question of growing class-consciousness, and the acute divisions between the rich and the poor, loomed larger than the ideal of a society purged of a semi-feudal landed aristocracy. Social and cultural commentators from the time of Hazlitt onwards tended to agree that the nineteenth century was a period marked by radical readjustment and that the French Revolution and its immediate consequences had forced on Europe changes in sensibility and belief as significant as those of the sixteenth-century Reformation. The present seemed as marked off from the century that preceded it as absolutely as the Protestant Reformers drew distinctions between their own times and Catholic ages of darkness. The major difference lay in a clear distinction between the evangelical confidence of earlier Protestants and the deep-seated doubts and scruples which infect so many nineteenth-century thinkers. The new century was also witness to unprecedented shifts in social and technological experience, most notably the rapid acceleration of industrialization and urbanization, which seemed to many to demand fresh insights into human morality and renewed incentives to human action.

In their very different ways the work of two essentially rural writers, John Clare (1793–1864) and William Cobbett (1763–1835), heralds this period of reassessment and lost content. Clare, the son of a Northamptonshire labourer, and himself employed in various ill-paid agricultural jobs, was acutely aware of the changes brought about in the countryside by the extension of the estates of the gentry through the parliamentary Acts of Enclosure. He was also particularly sensitive to the relationship between landscape and human labour. Clare's *Poems Descriptive of Rural Life and Scenery*, which appeared in 1820 (thanks to an enterprising publisher aware of both Clare's talent and his own likely profit from it), found an immediate response from readers already accustomed to the vernacular of Burns and to the work of the English 'peasant poet', Robert Bloomfield (1766–1823). Bloomfield's *The Farmer's Boy* (illustrated with wood-engravings by Thomas Bewick) had sold 26,000 copies within three years of its publication in 1800. It is deeply indebted to Thomson's *Seasons*, though it observes nature from the distinctive perspective of a farm-worker. Unlike Bloomfield, Clare was determined not to have his own provincial voice manipulated into accents acceptable to upper-class or metropolitan tastes. 'I think vulgar names to the flowers best as I know no others', he told his publisher and pointed out on another occasion that 'Putting the Correct Language of the Gentleman into the mouth of a Simple Shepherd or Vulgar Ploughman is far from Natural'. In his best poetry Clare's language is neither tamed nor emasculated by gentility; it has a direct unfussiness rendered more exact by provincial words and turns of phrase. The practice of modern editors in returning to the quirks of grammar, punctuation, and spelling in the surviving manuscripts, rather than the over-tidied and expurgated original editions, has further reinforced the forthrightness of his verse.

Clare was never an untutored poet, for he learned readily and appreciatively from the work of other writers, as his poem to Cowper ('the poet of fields | Who found the muse on common ground') and his imitations of Byron attest, but he was always aware that his own experience of nature and his acute sense of locality gave him an individual voice. His often exquisitely detailed lyrics, popular with anthologists in both the nineteenth and the twentieth centuries, have often been allowed to eclipse the achievement of his longer poems, and particularly the satirical couplet poem, *The Parish* (published posthumously) and *The Shepherd's Calendar* (1827). Clare's meandering survey of village society in *The Parish* contains much sharp and critical observation of petty-minded oppression and petty oppressors, ranging from squires, farmers, magistrates, and overseers to village politicians and ranting sectarian preachers. As its subtitle—'the Progress of Cant'—implies, the poem charts the advance of a new, self-propagating rural order which has broken down old responsibilities and corrupted old manners. Throughout his work Clare hankers for a lost Eden, a golden world of agricultural co-operation and mutual respect as opposed to urban-based prejudices and snobberies and harsher economic regimentation. The old vicar, remembered in the central section of *The Parish*, is a figure from 'days gone bye | When pride and fashion did not rank so high', a man 'plain as his flock' and simple in his habits. Clare's Eden may be unlocated in a precise time past, but it is never a misty and sentimental pastoral. In the 'June' section of his masterpiece, *The Shepherd's Calendar*, a description of summer 'ale and songs and healths and merry ways' stirs the memory of a real community in a lost time of 'the old freedom that was living then | When masters made them merry wi their men | Whose coat was like his neighbors russet brown | And whose rude speech was vulgar as his clown'. Clare's poetry, for all its delight in the profuse variety of the natural world, is darkened not so much by reference to the cold, to leaking thatches, or to stark rural poverty and the threat of the workhouse, as by an awareness of, and variation on, the private and social ramifications of the Fall.

As William Cobbett's radical journalism developed after 1804 he increasingly found himself able to identify an English paradise and the precise date of its loss, even if his definition began as little more than a debating point. The largely self-educated Cobbett learned his politics through his personal experience of the corruptions of the ruling class and through a wide knowledge of the peopled, working landscape of England. He was a passionate patriot, but his patriotism, which embraced a dislike of Scots theorists as much as of foreign wickedness, derived from a deep faith in the virtues of the cottage economy and the old collaborative relationship between those who owned the land and those who worked it. His vision of a dying co-operative order and of radical resistance to the 'unnatural' advance of the machine and machine-oriented ways of thinking, which he consistently propagated through his vastly successful newspaper the *Political Register* (founded in 1802), served to influence the countryman Clare and to provoke the now metropolitan Coleridge (who in 1817 described Cobbett as a viper). Although he used London as his base, he insisted that he loathed the city's established social influence and its rapidly swelling physical proportions (he habitually uses the shorthand term 'the Wen'—the wart—to describe it); in his *Rural Rides*, which began to appear in the *Political Register* from 1821, he is vituperative about all the evidence of cockney 'tax-eaters' observed in his travels. *Rural Rides* reveals Cobbett at his most typical: arrogant, intolerant, and controversial on the one hand; observant, intelligent, and vigorous on the other. He confines his observations largely to the once rich agricultural lands of southern England—preferring them to the scant farmlands and the burgeoning industry of the North and the Midlands—but he makes them a vehicle both for a broad criticism of society and for often rapturous and detailed descriptions of the land, its people, and its agricultural and social archaeology. He can dismiss the new spa towns as resorts of 'the lame and the lazy, the gourmandizing and guzzling, the bilious and the nervous', but he can also wax lyrical over sights as various as that of industrial Sheffield at night ('Nothing can be conceived more grand or more terrific than the yellow waves of fire that incessantly issue from the top of these furnaces') or remains of Malmesbury Abbey.

At Malmesbury in 1826 Cobbett reiterated the theme which runs through much of his later work; the medieval church in the town was built by happy, free, and prosperous Englishmen, 'men who were not begotten by Pitt nor by Jubilee George'. The English of the nineteenth century are a fallen race, ruled by inferior men and possessed of a distorted view of their great historic inheritance. The Reformation, in dissolving and ruining the abbeys, destroyed more than an architectural fabric; it wrecked what Cobbett sees as a perfected and heroic society. His rhetorical insistence on this loss of grace is explicated in the series of pamphlet letters published between 1824 and 1827 and provocatively entitled *A History of the Protestant 'Reformation', in England and Ireland: Showing how that event has impoverished and degraded the main body of the People in those Countries*. The letters are addressed to 'all sensible and just Englishmen' and attempt to demonstrate how 'the happiest country, and the *greatest* country too, that Europe had ever seen' had fallen victim to the reforming vultures let loose by Henry VIII and Elizabeth I. Cobbett was no Catholic, but his apology for a lost Catholic Merry England is as passionate as his distaste for the 'bloody cruelty' of the 'master-butcher' Henry which reduced England to 'a great human slaughter-house', and the '*pauper* and *ripping-up* reign' of the tyrannous Elizabeth (or 'Betsy' as he prefers to call her). Cobbett's *Protestant 'Reformation'* is more than simply a lament, it is a rumbustious outflanking of modern self-congratulatory readings of national history. For all its distortions and inaccuracies the book popularly introduces the idea of a stark contrast between the illusion of a medieval co-operative state, in which the rural poor were nourished by a Catholic Church and a Catholic nobility alike, and the untidy modern world of sectarian Dissent, of poor-laws, game-laws, parliamentary commissions, urban slums, and impersonal industrialists whom Cobbett had earlier characterized as 'Seigneurs of the Twist, sovereigns of the Spinning Jenny, great

Yeomen of the Yarn'. If his battle to preserve a predominantly agricultural order of things was doomed by the advance of industrialization, his vision of a simpler, devouter, united nation continued to carry great political force as an alternative to the self-evident confusion of Victorian England.

7

High Victorian Literature 1830–1880

A GREAT deal of Victorian intellectual effort was spent in trying to hold together a universe which was exploding. It was an age of conflicting explanations and theories, of scientific and economic confidence and of social and spiritual pessimism, of a sharpened awareness of the inevitability of progress and of deep disquiet as to the nature of the present. Traditional solutions, universally acknowledged truths, and panaceas were generally discovered to be wanting, and the resultant philosophical and ideological tensions are evident in the literature of the period from Carlyle's diatribes of the 1830s and Dickens's social novels of the 1840s to Arnold's speculations of the 1870s and Morris's socialist prophecies of the 1880s, from the troubled early poetry of Tennyson to the often dazzled theology of Hopkins.

Like all ages it was an age of paradox, but the paradoxes of the mid-nineteenth century struck contemporaries as more stark and disturbing than those which had faced their ancestors. Despite the shocks to complacency occasioned by the 1851 religious census—which revealed that out of the now swollen population of 17,927,609 for England and Wales only 7,261,032 attended some kind of service on the census Sunday in March—there remained a high degree of Christian commitment. Even given the token nature of much of this commitment, religion remained a powerful force in Victorian life and literature. The census revealed that there were still large numbers who adhered to the increasing diversity of the Church of England, but the majority of them lived in the south and east of the island. In a burgeoning northern industrial city, such as Leeds, only 15 per cent of the population went to an Anglican church, while some 31 per cent attended a Dissenting chapel. Dissenters also formed a comfortable majority of Sunday worshippers in both Manchester and Birmingham, and in Wales they outnumbered Anglicans by four to one. In Scotland, where a similar census was held three years later, it was found, somewhat more encouragingly to the religious authorities, that just over 60 per cent of the population went to church. If the vast number of those who failed to attend public worship on the census Sundays were working-class men and women who easily found alternative and more agreeable ways of spending the one day of rest allowed to them, there were also, amongst the educated classes, deep and growing doubts as to the very doctrinal and historical bases of Christianity. These doubts were often dryly rooted in German biblical scholarship (known as the 'Higher Criticism'); they were fostered and emboldened by the appearance in 1859 of Charles Darwin's *On the Origin of Species by means of Natural Selection*, by the steady development of Darwin's theories by his disciples, and by an intellectual culture increasingly influenced by scientific materialism.

Mid-Victorian society was still held together by the cement of Christian moral teaching and constricted by the triumph of puritan sexual mores. It laid a particular stress on the virtues of monogamy and family life, but it was also publicly aware of flagrant moral anomalies throughout the social system. Although the supposed blessings of ordered family life were generally proclaimed to be paramount, many individual Victorians saw the family as an agent of oppression and as the chief vehicle of encompassing conformity. The period which saw the first real stirrings of the modern women's movement also received and revered the matronly model provided by Queen Victoria herself and acquiesced to the stereotype of virtuous womanhood propagated by many of its novelists and poets. It was not idly that Thackeray complained in his Preface to *Pendennis* in 1849 that 'since the author of Tom Jones was buried, no writer of fiction among us has been permitted to depict to his utmost power a MAN'. Many ladies, he claimed, had remonstrated with him because he had described a young man 'resisting and affected by temptation'. Thackeray did not actually use the words 'sex' and 'sexual temptation', but his readers would have known what he was talking about. Lest we assume too readily that Thackeray was a representative voice raised against English double standards, and against enforced limitations to his art, it is worth remembering that in the fourth chapter of Dickens's *David Copperfield* (which also appeared in 1849) David notes of the imaginative influence of his boyhood reading that he had 'been Tom Jones (a child's Tom Jones, a harmless creature) for a week together'. As David Copperfield seems anxious to point out, innocence too had its premium. It was, moreover, a tactful influence that most mid-Victorian novel readers seem to have appreciated.

The Victorian age had its continuities, its revivals, and its battles of styles in painting and architecture as much as in literature. It was as much an age in which the Greek, the Gothic, and the Italianate could vie with one another as advanced and inventive expressions of the *Zeitgeist* as it was an age of experimental engineering. It produced both the intricate Gothic of the new Palace of Westminster and the functional classical ironwork of the Great Exhibition pavilion (which the satirical magazine *Punch* dubbed the 'Crystal Palace'). As the Great Exhibition of 1851 proudly demonstrated, this was the age both of applied art and of the application of new technologies to all aspects of design and production. This first true 'machine age' reaped both the material benefits and the social advantages of the factory system and of vigorous, unrestrained capitalism. New urban prosperity, and industrial enterprise, gave the middle and working classes alike a variety of small domestic comforts and ornaments which were once confined only to the very rich. They also led to a domestic clutter and to an eclecticism which is, to an interesting degree, reflected in the careful delineation, organization, and association of objects in the work of contemporary novelists.

The years 1830–80 were years of British self-confidence and semi-isolationism in terms of European affairs, but the illusion of peace in the 1850s was broken by the disasters of the Indian Mutiny and by the incompetent bungling of the Crimean War. The domestic political scene saw the sacredness of the principles of liberty of conscience and the freedom of the individual enshrined in law and in the writings of Macaulay and Mill, but these principles most benefited middle-class men and were of little immediate relevance to the many women who were still denied proper education and property rights and to all the women who were excluded from the franchise. They were often of even less relevance to those amongst the poor whose only real freedom was the freedom to starve. In society as a whole they were challenged not by an interfering state but by the pressures exerted by a 'moral' majority and by the debilitating freedoms of poverty, homelessness, and hunger.

If upper- and middle-class Britain congratulated itself on avoiding the revolutionary upheavals that shook Europe in the late 1840s, it should not be presumed that this relative social and political stability was easily won or easily maintained. In many senses the Victorian age was ushered in by a series of moderate political reforms which were specifically designed to avert the tide of more radical change. In 1829 a sobbing George IV had signed the Act of Parliament granting civil rights to his Roman Catholic subjects in Great Britain and Ireland. The King was sobbing because he believed that he was breaking his coronation oath to protect the constitutional rights of the Church of England. The Catholic Emancipation Act had become inevitable not simply because many liberal-minded Englishmen believed tolerance to be a virtue, but because the Parliamentary Union of Great Britain and Ireland had left the latter kingdom largely disenfranchised. If the 1829 Act threw down a civil and religious challenge to the constitutional settlement of 1688, the challenge was extended by the pressure for far wider reform of the Constitution. In March 1831 a Reform Bill was unsuccessfully introduced into the House of Commons. After a general election, a second Bill was passed by the Commons in September, but was rejected by the House of Lords. Under the threat of widespread civil unrest, and with King William IV's offer to create new peers hanging over their heads, the Reform Act was finally passed by the Lords in June 1832. The City of London cast a bronze medal showing the kneeling figure of Liberty, with Magna Carta at her feet, presenting the new Act to Britannia in front of an altar inscribed with the names of its main proponents (including, somewhat incongruously, the King). The Reform Bill abolished the so-called 'Rotten Boroughs' (where scandalously few electors had lived) and redistributed constituencies in the important new towns (such as Manchester and Birmingham). It extended the franchise to all male householders rated at £10 and over and to £50 leaseholders (who were generally rural tenants). Although the bill doubled the electorate by including many more middle-class voters, it still left twenty-nine out of every thirty citizens without a constitutional voice. It supposedly reduced the number of 'Pocket Boroughs' (once exclusively controlled by aristocratic or landowning interest), but it left many parliamentary seats still firmly in the voluminous pockets of the aristocracy. The struggle for, and the modest consequences of, the Reform Bill were to preoccupy and amuse many subsequent writers. The corruptions of an old-style election are memorably witnessed by Mr Pickwick at the appropriately named Eatanswill; Sir Leicester Dedlock in *Bleak House* (set just before 1832) 'delivers in his own candidateship, as a kind of handsome wholesale order to be promptly executed', and treats two other seats that belong to him 'as retail orders of less importance, merely sending down the men'; George Eliot's Mr Brooke comically fails to be elected to the new Parliament in *Middlemarch* and in *Felix Holt* her 'radical' protagonist, somewhat more dourly, contemplates the social unrest, the divided loyalties, and the feverish popular pressure for continued reform in a Midlands town of the early 1830s.

Felix Holt, published in 1866, had a particular relevance to a new wave of reform which culminated in a second overhaul of the electoral system in 1867 (when seats were again redistributed, and, more significantly, a million urban working men were added to the electorate). The 1867 Reform Act (together with its successor of 1884, which enfranchised a further two million working-class labourers) was the indirect consequence of continued working-class pressure for democratic representation, pressure which had first become vocal with the drawing up of the 'People's Charter' in 1838. This Charter, its articulate framers, and its many determined supporters (the 'Chartists') emerged as a significant, and to many unsympathetic observers, worrying new force in British political life in the 1840s. Although, to an important degree, they were the heirs to the radical Dissent of the French Revolutionary era, they were to another the vanguard of a newly self-conscious and expanding industrial working class. The Chartists, with their determination to press for change from below, struck many early Victorians as perhaps the most vocal and disconcerting of the signs of the times.

'The Condition of England': Carlyle and Dickens

The disconcertions and anomalies of early Victorian Britain are nowhere more trenchantly examined than in the pamphlets, essays, lectures, and books of its most noisy and effective critic, Thomas Carlyle (1795–1881). Carlyle was a late product of the Scottish Enlightenment, and of the culture which had made the *Edinburgh Review* (founded in 1802) an intellectual force to be reckoned with beyond the borders of Scotland. The power and effect of his own writings do not, however, derive exclusively from the classical rationality of late eighteenth-century Edinburgh philosophy. Carlyle's fundamental debt to the rhythms and the confident, prophetic utterance of the Bible is profound, as is his sense of himself as a latter-day Jeremiah, endowed with the urgent accents of a Presbyterian pulpit. He was also exceptionally well read in modern German thought which was already exerting a powerful cerebral influence over the literatures of other European nations. His own *Life of Schiller* was published in the *London Magazine* in 1823–4 and his translation of Goethe's seminal novel *Wilhelm Meister's Apprenticeship* appeared in 1824.

When, in 1834, Carlyle settled in London he was seeking a broader metropolitan base, and a wider audience, for his increasingly urgent commentaries on the times. The year before his move he had begun the serialization in *Fraser's Magazine* of his perplexing fiction, *Sartor Resartus*, a work which combines a theorizing German central character with a mediating, and explicitly English, editor. Much earlier in his career he had aspired to a fiction which would speak 'with a tongue of fire—sharp, sarcastic, apparently unfeeling' but which would nevertheless convey the central precepts of his philosophy: energy, earnestness, and duty. *Sartor Resartus* ('The Tailor Retailored') realizes that ambition in the form of a reflexive discourse moulded around a learned study of the philosophy of clothes. Carlyle's English editor describes the nature of this tract as made up of two undemarcated parts and of 'multifarious sections and subdivisions' in which each part 'overlaps, and indents and indeed quite runs through the other'. It is like 'some mad banquet, wherein all courses had been confounded'. The style in which it is written embodies this 'labyrinthic combination' by intermixing German and English, by echoing earlier literature, and by playing games with meanings and with translations from one language to another. Like all Carlyle's styles it works through a process of amalgamation and assimilation. Although *Sartor Resartus* has its English precedents in Swift's *Battle of the Books* and Sterne's *Tristram Shandy*, it also looks uneasily forward to the experiments of James Joyce.

Sartor Resartus was more than simply game-playing. It also carried a message for the times in which it was written, a message which warned of the dangers of 'sham' in all its forms and which contrasted the undoing force of the 'Everlasting No' with the constructive imperative of the 'Everlasting Yea', an imperative which solves all contradiction. This 'Everlasting Yea' demands a submission to the will of God and an active commitment to work, though what Carlyle meant by 'God' and 'work' remained imprecise throughout his career (Nietzsche, for one, suspected that 'at bottom, Carlyle is an English atheist who makes it a point of honour not to be one'). This ultimate elusiveness does not appear to have diminished the effect of his writings upon his literary contemporaries. Those who responded to the urgency of his warnings in the 1830s and 1840s seem to have assented more to his analyses of historic and modern ills rather than to his vaguer proposals for future remedies. In the essay *Chartism* of 1839 he confronted the growing threat of class war posed by the new political articulacy of industrial workers. In so doing, he glanced back to the formative events of the French Revolution and to their dislocating effect on all Europe, an effect which was 'full of stern monition to all countries'. But for England the warning was specific: 'These Chartisms, Radicalisms, Reform Bill, Tithe Bill, and infinite other discrepancy, and acrid argument and jargon that there is yet to be, are *our* French Revolution: God grant that we, with our better methods, may be able to transact it by argument alone!' This essay begins by offering definitions of what Carlyle styles 'the Condition of England Question', definitions which derive from the observation of the state of a nation attempting to come to terms with its parliamentary and social reforms aimed at deflecting revolution.

As in everything he wrote, history provides Carlyle with a pattern of precedents; his evident dread is a process of repetition and of an equally threatening fracture of patterns and precedents. In the series of six lectures *On Heroes, Hero-Worship and the Heroic in History* (1841) he developed aspects of the thesis of *Sartor Resartus* by stressing that heroism manifested itself in a wide range of human activity and that the 'hero', whether king or prophet, poet or philosopher, was a challenger of convention and of sham and a reformer of the defunct and the empty. More significantly, the lectures outlined an idea of history which profoundly, if sometimes maladroitly, influenced the work of Carlyle's English successors. 'The History of the World', he insisted, 'is but the Biography of great men . . . Could we see *them*, we should get some glimpses into the very marrow of the world's history.' *Past and Present* (1843) juxtaposes the past—in the form of a highly sympathetic commentary on the recently published *Chronicle* of Jocelin of Brakelond which describes the achievements of the twelfth-century Abbot Samson of Bury St Edmunds—with the confusions and contradictions of the present. The form of the book both supports the Victorian medievalist idea of an organic, stratified, and securer social past and challenges it by acknowledging that modern industrialization and historical progress have utterly altered the nature of society and its institutions. Carlyle, like the pragmatic, 'heroic' Abbot Samson, has no place for sentimentalism or nostalgia. Despite the catalogue of modern ills described in the second half of *Past and Present*, and despite the satiric wit which sets up and demolishes the stock figures of Sir Jabesh Windbag and Plugson of Undershot, there remains room for a visionary optimism of the type indulged in elsewhere by 'prophetic' writers as diverse as Blake and D. H. Lawrence. At the conclusion, Carlyle reassembles and reshuffles the images and ideas he has developed through the narrative and looks forward to the sweeping away of the 'Sooty Hell of mutiny and savagery and despair' to allow for a benign heaven overarching the 'cunning mechanisms and tall chimney-steeples'. Even the world of the machine can be redeemed by human enterprise and confidence.

Carlyle's central and most sustained achievement is his great history of *The*

French Revolution (1837). The history opens with the death of Louis XV and with a scathing account of the deficiencies of French government, institutions, and culture under the *ancien régime* and it ends with Napoleon's bid for power as the Revolution declines into directionless anarchy. In a sense the 'hero' is set once again to sweep away sham, but the book is much more than a tribute to the heroic in history; it is, more significantly, a subtle and complex demonstration of the biographical approach to the writing of history. The biographies are rarely those of heroes or anti-heroes. Carlyle weaves and interweaves a variety of sources, notably biographical and autobiographical ones, but, with considerable novelty, he also exploits historical ephemera—letters, newspaper articles, pamphlets, broadsheets, and advertisements. His text is a remarkable amalgam, built around the evidence of a multiplicity of witnessing or interpreting voices, but moved forward by a dominant, didactic narrator. Words, phrases, and slogans, in English, French, and Latin, are played and replayed, turned on their heads, deflated, or suddenly charged with fresh energy. *The French Revolution* implicitly warns Victorian England of the nature, causes, and progress of civil disruption, but it also creates stylistic effects and presents carefully assembled, and highly individual, descriptions of characters and events which render it more than just obstreperous didacticism.

Carlyle's influence over an important group of early and mid-Victorian writers, notably Elizabeth Gaskell, Charles Kingsley, Alfred Tennyson, John Ruskin, and William Morris, is of great significance to the social direction of much of their work. But none of his contemporaries was as well versed in Carlyle's writings as was Charles Dickens (1812–70) and none transformed that influence as spectacularly. Dickens, who once rashly claimed to have read *The French Revolution* five hundred times, shows his discipleship naturally enough in his own revolutionary novel, *A Tale of Two Cities*, but echoes of Carlyle can also be heard in those of his novels which deal most directly with the 'Condition of England Question' (such as *Bleak House* or *Hard Times*) and in the most urgent of the Christmas Books of the so-called 'Hungry Forties', *The Chimes* (1844). Dickens learned, as did his literary contemporaries, to direct his fiction to a questioning of social priorities and inequalities, to a distrust of institutions, particularly defunct or malfunctioning ones, and to a pressing appeal for action and earnestness. If he cannot exactly be called a 'reforming' novelist, Dickens was prone to take up issues, and to campaign against what he saw as injustice or desuetude, using fiction as his vehicle. He was not alone in this in his own time, but his name continues to be popularly associated with good causes and with remedies for social abuses because his was quite the wittiest, the most persuasive, and the most influential voice. Dickens's success in propaganda lay not in the causes he espoused, in the changes of opinion he effected, or in the propriety or the logic of his arguments, but in the very nature of his writing and its appeal to an exceptionally broad spectrum of Victorian readers. He was faithful to the teaching, and to the general theological framework, of Christianity as a moral basis for his thought, his action and, above all, for his writing. Nevertheless, a critical awareness that there was something deeply wrong with the society in which he lived sharpened the nature of his fiction and gave it its distinct political edge. Like all great comic writers, Dickens allows humour to subvert assumptions, both general and particular. More significantly, the very vitality and variety of his comedy confronts, and to a degree subsumes, the potential anarchy he saw around him.

Dickens's novels are multifarious, digressive and generous. In an important way, they reflect the nature of Victorian urban society with all its conflicts and disharmonies, its eccentricities and its constrictions, its energy and its extraordinary fertility, both physical and intellectual. Whereas Dickens's fictional roots lie in the novels of Defoe, Fielding, Smollett and Goldsmith (as we know from the records of his own and of David Copperfield's early reading), he was uniquely equipped to transform eighteenth-century models into the fluid, urban fiction of a new age. His own first experiments, later republished as the *Sketches by 'Boz'* (1833–6, 1836–7), reveal a writer with an acute ear for speech, and for aberrations of speech, and with an equally acute observation of gesture and habit, of London streets and London interiors, of spontaneity and of misery. The *Sketches* are essentially anecdotal and descriptive. Dickens's first full-scale work of fiction, *The Posthumous Papers of the Pickwick Club* (1836–7) (generally known simply as *The Pickwick Papers*), suggests the degree to which he gradually, but easily, adapted from the small scale to a larger narrative sweep. The origins of *Pickwick* lie in a commission for a series of linked anecdotal stories concerning the members of a London club, to be published on a monthly basis accompanied by illustrations. The peregrinatory and exploratory nature of the club, as Dickens initially defined it, allows him to move his characters around England and into various comic encounters, but its 'plot' achieves greater direction once Pickwick becomes caught up in the snares of the law and is briefly confined to prison.

This darker side to Dickens's imagination is also reflected in *Oliver Twist*, the shorter, tighter novel he embarked on while he was still serializing *Pickwick*. In *Oliver Twist: or The Parish Boy's Progress* (1837–8) he again glances back to the eighteenth-century, or more specifically Hogarthian, precedents, but he was also reacting to two contemporary stimuli, the propagandizing of the supporters of the New Poor Law of 1834 and the popularity of fiction adulating the careers and adventures of criminals (the so-called 'Newgate Novels'). His attack on the effects of the workhouse system is confined to the novel's opening chapters, but its stark juxtapositions, and the very blackness of its comedy, succeeded in damning workhouse abuses in the popular imagination, if not in eliminating them from physical reality. The scene of Oliver Twist asking for more, so graphically caught by Dickens's illustrator, George Cruikshank, rapidly became, and has remained, the most familiar incident in any English novel. Oliver's adventures in London, and the opposition of the insecurities of criminal life to the comforts of bourgeois respectability, are again rendered through a series of sharp contrasts of scene, mood, and narrative style, an effect

Dickens himself compared to 'streaky bacon'. In *Nicholas Nickleby*, which was serialized between April 1838 and October 1839, Dickens again took a particular abuse as the focus of his story. The description of Dotheboys Hall exposes the exploitation of unwanted children in a bleak Yorkshire school, but the novel also attacks a do-nothing and snobbish aristocracy, the creaking inefficiency of Parliament, and the aggression of market capitalism. *Nicholas Nickleby* is an untidy novel, rambling, excursive, and occasionally interpolated with short stories which have no real bearing on the plot; its strengths lie essentially in its comedy and in its brilliantly eccentric characters. Dickens's introduction in chapter 22 of the seedy theatrical company run by Vincent Crummles allows him to express something of his own fascination with the nature, the whims, and the mentality of Victorian actors (a profession which he had once, very briefly, considered joining).

The monthly parts of *Nicholas Nickleby* sold vastly well, firmly establishing Dickens as the dominant novelist of his time and as an unrivalled literary phenomenon. At a banquet to celebrate the completion of the book the painter David Wilkie made a speech noting that there had been nothing comparable to him since the days of Richardson for 'in both cases people talked about the characters as if they were next-door neighbours or friends'. Letters, he claimed, had been written to the author imploring him not to kill Smike, much as Richardson had been begged to 'save Lovelace's soul alive'. Dickens relished, cultivated, and honoured the intimate relationship with his readers opened up to him by monthly, and occasionally weekly, serialization. In his earlier fiction he readily responded to the evident popularity of certain characters and he carefully attuned himself to what his public demanded, in terms both of sentiment and of comic and stylistic variety. He nevertheless appears to have retained a certain restlessness about the burgeoning nature of his career and as to the particular form his future novels should take. The somewhat awkward origins of *The Old Curiosity Shop*, first published in his anecdotal weekly magazine, *Master Humphrey's Clock*, in 1840, suggest something of this restlessness. The 'Master Humphrey' stories necessarily diminished as the pressing demand for a full-length story increased, but Dickens's control over a narrative inexorably following Little Nell to her rural death-bed rarely falters after the initial chapters. Little Nell's mortality, which so profoundly moved the first readers of the novel (including the lachrymose former editor of the *Edinburgh Review*, Francis Jeffrey, who had once damned Wordsworth's 'unlucky habit of debasing pathos with vulgarity'), gives direction, and a certain solemnity, to an extraordinarily diverse novel. Later readers have often, wrongly, balked at what has all too often been assumed to be Dickens's vulgar exploitation of sentimentality. *Barnaby Rudge*, which succeeded *The Old Curiosity Shop* in the pages of *Master Humphrey's Clock* in 1841, is amongst Dickens's most neglected works. It is a historical novel, set at the time of the Gordon Riots of 1780, which begins somewhat slowly and archly by establishing the concerns, origins, and obsessions of its characters; it comes vividly and distinctively to life once these same characters get caught up in the violent progress of the Riots. Some of its descriptive passages show a mastery of rhythm and image that he never excelled. Both *Martin Chuzzlewit* (1843–4) and *Dombey and Son* (1846–8) reveal the extent to which Dickens developed his mastery over the sprawling serial forms he and his readers enjoyed. *Martin Chuzzlewit* examines a wide range of selfishness, self-centredness, criminality, and exploitation, and allows for the title character's discovery that America contains as many shams, frauds, and delusions as does his native England. It did not, initially, please many American readers despite the real popularity Dickens discovered he had earned during his trip to the United States in 1842. *Dombey and Son* has an even greater degree of narrative tightness derived from thematic consistency and its almost symphonic use of motifs, repeated phrases, and images.

To those readers who prefer Dickens's darker, tidier, and less exuberant later fiction, *Dombey and Son* has often been seen as ushering in a new phase in his art. The use of semi-autobiographical material and the discipline imposed by the introduction of a first-person narrator in its immediate successor, *David Copperfield* (1849–50), suggest the extent to which he had moved away from the laxer, digressive, inclusive forms of *Pickwick* or *Nicholas Nickleby*. *David Copperfield* is central to Dickens's career in more than simply the chronological sense; its evocation of suffering derives directly from the novelist's acute awareness of his own boyhood reverses, but its wit, its detailed observation, and its description of the slow 'disciplining' of the heart give it a confident vitality and a progressive optimism which allow for the transmutation of tragedy. Although the novel examines a series of relationships and marriages, happy and unhappy, its satire and its treatment of social problems are marginal compared to those of the complex and demanding *Bleak House* of 1852–3. Here the use of a double narrative, one narrator employing the present, the other the past tense, helps create a sense of unfolding mystery, even confusion. The confusion itself reflects that of the main object of the novel's satire, the convoluted workings of the Court of Chancery, but the legal obliquity is in turn echoed and re-echoed in the words and actions of a succession of purblind characters muddling their way through a miry, fog-bound London. While private mysteries, lawsuits, and crimes are solved, the underlying problems of dirt, disease, and urban decay remain intractable.

Dickens uniquely transferred his concern with the modern condition of England out of London in his succinct and often bitter satire on the effects of the Industrial Revolution in northern England, *Hard Times* (1854). Private pasts, private secrets, illusions, and the corrupting power of possession equally haunt his most sombre novel, *Little Dorrit* (1855–7). It returns to the oppressive image, and the multiple ramifications, of a London debtors' prison, but it also has a broader European frame of reference. Two very different prisons, Newgate and the Bastille, dominate the first two books of *A Tale of Two Cities* (1859), set in London and Paris in the 1770s and 1780s. Its third section moves to revolutionary France and to the penal consequences of the overturn of old oppressions and the introduction of new ones. *A Tale of Two Cities* has Dickens's most carefully constructed plot, and, by means of its charged and very public historical setting, particularly successfully dramatizes personal dilemmas, divisions, and commitments.

The idea of the divided self marks all Dickens's late works. From 1858, when he began to give the series of public readings from his novels which so mark his last years, Dickens intensifies his 'particular relation (personally affectionate and like no other man's)' between himself and his public. He had always been a talented and passionate amateur actor and it is likely that this new-found professional role-playing on public platforms added to his existing fascination with double lives and masks. Sydney Carton's 'dead life' is answered by his final self-sacrifice, but the careers of his male-successors are not always as providentially blessed. Pip in *Great Expectations* (1860–1) is manipulated and gentrified and left empty; John Harmon in *Our Mutual Friend* (1864–5) is obliged to adopt the persona of a dead man; and, most disturbingly, the probably murderous John Jasper in *The Mystery of Edwin Drood* (1870) agonizes over the chasm between his respectable life as a cathedral choirman and his London-based opium addiction. Each of the three last novels differs from the others, each suggesting a new experimentation on Dickens's part. *Great Expectations* again uses a confessional, first-person narrator, but Pip is of a lower social class than David Copperfield and lacks his ebullience and resilience and his final reward consists merely of a muted semi-fulfilment. To many readers, however, it remains the most completely satisfying and haunting of Dickens's works. *Our Mutual Friend* seems ungainly by comparison. The London of the novel is dreary, dusty, and unredeemed and it is only in the exploratory independence of the four central characters that any future hope appears to rest. Nevertheless, it contains some of Dickens's most fluently inventive dialogue and some of his finest gestures towards the variety of comedy which is properly called 'black' (notably in his picture of Mr Venus's shop). The unfinished *The Mystery of Edwin Drood* would almost certainly have been a murder story, though the fragment which we have leaves both the murder and the potential murderer unspecific. It has consistently invited much speculation as to how Dickens would have proceeded with such a tantalizing narrative. Perhaps fortunately, most attempts to provide solutions have proved less than satisfying. In some ways it is appropriate that Dickens's last work should be an unfinishable, obsessive, mystery story. He remained to the end 'The Inimitable'.

Despite the specificity of his detailing and the acuteness of his observation of the outward traits of character, Dickens cannot be properly defined as a 'realist'. He rarely speculates about the workings of his characters' minds and consciences, but he is perhaps the finest delineator in English of mental aberration and he is the creator of a surprisingly varied line of murderers, self-tormentors, and Gothic villains. Above all, Dickens both recognized and exploited the relationship between character and environment, moulding them into a singular but always recognizable fictional world. Though he was neither born nor died in London, he made a protean, physical London, the greatest city of the nineteenth century, the centre of his work and its drab tangle of streets his major source of inspiration.

'Condition of England' Fiction

Dickens's *Hard Times* still remains the most vivid and familiar of the novels which deal with the social and industrial problems of mid-Victorian England but it was, in its time, neither unique nor necessarily the best informed. Dickens himself was well aware of the earnest propaganda disseminated by one of the most gifted of his women contemporaries, Harriet Martineau (1802–76), whom Carlyle had described as 'swathed like a mummy in Socinian and Political-Economy formulas'. Dickens may indeed have been provoked into writing *Oliver Twist* by her flatly factual, emphatically polemic sequence of tales, *Poor Law and Paupers Illustrated* (1833). Martineau was a highly educated and highly independent woman with a refined social conscience and a convincedly Utilitarian philosophy, but her best-selling early fiction, notably the twenty-three didactic stories uninvitingly grouped together under the title *Illustrations of Political Economy* (1832–4), lacks the substance of her occasionally penetrating novel *Deerbrook* (1839), and her fictional study of Toussaint L'Ouverture, *The Hour and the Man* (1841). She had, she claimed in 1855, long felt 'that it was one of the duties of my life to write my autobiography'. That dutiful call was finally answered by the posthumous appearance of the confident, self-justifying *Autobiography* of 1877. If scarcely a lovable work, it remains one of the pioneer classics of Victorian women's writing.

Martineau's innovative story 'A Manchester Strike' of 1832, one of the earlier *Illustrations of Political Economy*, prefigures some of the ideas and the open-minded tolerance of Elizabeth Gaskell's *Mary Barton*. Gaskell (1810–65) is still generally associated with industrial Manchester by her readers, though only two of her novels are actually set in the city. As Carlyle had recognized, Manchester was the urban phenomenon of the age; it was a 'prophetic city' in that it had pioneered the factory system and had harnessed and exploited huge amounts of human and physical energy; it was a 'sublime' city in that nothing really like it had been seen before. As Disraeli noted, without his tongue in his cheek, in *Coningsby* (1844): 'What Art was to the ancient world, Science is to the modern—the distinctive faculty . . . rightly understood, Manchester is as great a human exploit as Athens.' But the Manchester of the 1840s exposed the human problems of rapid industrialization as starkly as it embodied the commercial success of manufacture. Although she did not know his untranslated work, Elizabeth Gaskell observed the same divisions of class, labour, and quality of life as did Manchester's most exaggeratedly celebrated critic of the period, the expatriate German industrialist, Friedrich Engels. It was, however, under the aegis of Carlyle that Gaskell felt impelled to write her first 'Tale of Manchester Life', *Mary Barton* (1848). It was Carlyle who was quoted on its title-page and whose *Past and Present* was half-echoed in its opening sentences. *Mary Barton* dramatizes the urban ills of the late 1840s, an era marked by industrial conflict, by strikes and lock-outs, by low wages and enforced unemployment, by growing class-consciousness and by Chartist agitation which reached its climax in the year of the novel's publication. The strengths of *Mary Barton* lie not in its political analysis, or in its suggested resolution, but in its detailing, its observation and, above all, in its careful establishment of contrasted ways of living, working, and perceiving. It also powerfully exposes ignorance, on the part of prospective readers who knew (and know) nothing of conditions in Manchester's slums, and the ignorance of characters who are severed from one another's daily lives and concerns. In the novelist's own terms it achieved precisely the effect she wanted. 'Half the masters [mill owners] are bitterly angry with me', she wrote of her novel in 1848, '—half (and the best half)—are buying it to give to their work people's libraries'. When Gaskell returned to industrial fiction in *North and South* (1854–5) it was as a result of a commission from Dickens to write for his journal *Household Words*. Her second Manchester novel (in which the city appears as 'Milton-Northern'), is radically different from *Mary Barton* in that it views class-conflict from a new, politically optimistic, viewpoint, that of potential compromise. There was much contemporary justification for the optimism. *North and South* does not, however, compromise on social issues. As its title implies, it contrasts the snobberies, chivalries, and artificiality of the country gentry of the South of England with the distinctive energetic anti-gentlemanly world of self-made manufacturers of the North. Its highly perceptive heroine, Margaret Hale, may at first be shocked by a market economy which works 'as if commerce were everything and humanity nothing' but she is later impressed by a dinner at which Manchester men 'talked in desperate earnest,—not in the used-up style that wearied her so in the old London parties'. The novel also points to the independence of industrial workers, a pride in themselves which survives despite the appalling working and living conditions which they have to endure, which is contrasted to the subservience, acquiescence, and superstition of the rural poor.

Margaret Hale is intelligent, humane, wilful, and independent. She also achieves an active mastery over her situation which is denied to Gaskell's other central women characters. Miss Matty, the focus of the easy, rambling narratives of *Cranford* (1851–3), has social status and true gentility, but her moral standing is based on decency and respect within the limited community of a country town. In *Ruth* (1853), which treats the problem of the unmarried mother with delicacy and sympathy, Ruth is none the less required to endure a process of redemptive self-sacrifice in order to win back respect from society at large. Gaskell's two finest novels, *Sylvia's Lovers* (1863) and *Wives and*

Daughters (1864–6), both trace the growth and development of their contrasted heroines; Sylvia Robson, a farmer's daughter, is barely educated, self-willed, passionate, and fatally divided between resolution and equally heady irresolution; Molly Gibson, the daughter of a respected, widowed doctor, is obliged to face a series of domestic crises in which her initial insecurity gives way to a resourcefulness, growing maturity and poise which serve to distinguish her from her flighty step-sister. Sylvia's marriage proves disastrous; Molly's prospective alliance with Roger Hamley is a meeting of equals. *Sylvia's Lovers* is set at the time of the Napoleonic Wars and its plot hinges on the disappearance of a lover who is carried off by a press gang enforcing recruitment into the Navy. The representation of northern speech throughout the narrative serves to reinforce emphatically the precision of its local detailing, but the novel is given a larger scope by its constant reference to the disruption and violence of war and to the romantically dangerous draw of the sea. It is one of the finest of provincial novels, indebted to the model provided by the Waverley novels, but drawing out and subtly amplifying Scott's example. It explores the lives of humble people with a sympathy and delicate power which had rarely been seen before in English fiction. *Wives and Daughters*, by contrast, examines family relationships and social class from an amplified Trollopian perspective. It is made up of a series of interwoven stories, but it is also an ambitious, careful, and delicate psychological study of an often fraught household and its social connections. In 1860 Gaskell had written of *Framley Parsonage*, then being serialized in the *Cornhill Magazine*: 'I wish Mr Trollope would go on writing Framley Parsonage for ever. I don't see any reason why it should ever come to an end . . .'. Her pleasure in the slow and easy development of a largely uneventful plot and in the gradual interaction of upper-middle-class characters is evident in her own novel, also serialized in the *Cornhill* and abruptly concluded, but not left unresolved, by her untimely death.

Charles Kingsley (1819–75), a priest of the Church of England by vocation and ordination, and a determined preacher all his life, tended to use fiction as an extension of his secular and religious missions. In the late 1840s he had been sufficiently moved by Carlyle's imperatives to become actively involved in the Christian Socialist movement, established to wean Chartists away from the French-inspired, anti-clerical and often atheist Socialism into an alternative religious commitment to the reform of society. *Yeast: A Problem*, serialized in *Fraser's Magazine* in 1848, intersperses scenes describing rural degradation with a narrative discourse which entwines an advocacy of sanitary reform with dire warnings about the moral dangers of Roman Catholicism. Its successor, *Alton Locke: Tailor and Poet* (1850), is a far more impressive achievement. *Alton Locke* purports to be the autobiography of a working man, stung into Chartist protest by his experience of sweated labour, London poverty, and fever-haunted London slums, but finally persuaded of the fitness of the Christian Socialist cause. Kingsley's frank descriptions of the effects of a cholera epidemic in the slums are particularly powerful. His later novels, with the exception of *Two Years Ago* (1857), have historical settings and arguments tailored to appeal to modern sensibilities and modern sensitivities. The subtitle of *Hypatia* (1852–3), 'New Foes with an Old Face', underlines its religious relevance to Kingsley's contemporaries (the 'new foes' were clearly meant to be superstitious modern Catholics, successors to a dubious Catholic past). The story is set in an unhappily multicultural Alexandria in the fifth century AD and is ostensibly concerned with the decay of Hellenistic civilization in the face of an aggressive, and by no means sympathetic, monastic Christianity. Its contrasts of the empty Nubian desert and the confused culture of the city are effectively controlled, as are the novel's often compromised argument as to the necessary progress of enlightened religion, and its subdued, seemingly hollow, ending. *Westward Ho!* (1855) and *Hereward the Wake* (1866) are more bloodthirsty and untidy as narratives, suggesting the extent to which Kingsley had retreated into the cult of the hero as an explication of the historical process and into the worship of heroism as a literary creed.

Benjamin Disraeli, Earl of Beaconsfield (1804–81) was not the only British Prime Minister to have maintained an active literary career beyond his main political concerns (in 1953 Sir Winston Churchill was awarded the Nobel Prize for Literature for his work as a historian), but he remains the only one to have begun as an escapist society novelist and to have continued writing fiction until the year before his death. Disraeli's first novels—*Vivian Grey* (1826), *The Young Duke* (1831), *Contarini Fleming* (1832), and *Alroy* (1833)—are fantasies of high society which fall into the loose category of 'Silver-fork fiction' so cleverly satirized by Dickens in chapter 27 of *Nicholas Nickleby*. It was with the development of a serious interest in politics, and with his success in being elected a Member of Parliament in 1837 (after three failures), that Disraeli's fiction took a new, but equally speculative and fantastic, turn. The 1830s and 1840s were a period of political experiment and realignment following the passage of the Reform Bill. If little had actually changed in the nature of Parliament, in its system of patronage or in the social complexion of its members, the time was ripe for new political ideas and intellectual initiatives. The trilogy of novels written in the 1840s—*Coningsby: or The New Generation* (1844), *Sybil: or The Two Nations* (1845), *and Tancred: or the New Crusade* (1847)—indicate the degree to which Disraeli was determined to involve himself in extra-parliamentary debate and in the contemporary discussion of the nature and progress of industrial Britain. Each of the novels shows a real grasp of historical precedent and of modern social complexity, but the solutions he suggests are often paradoxical or simply wishful. Disraeli can both play with the 'Young England' dream of an anti-bourgeois alliance between the old landed aristocracy and the new working classes, and yet acknowledge and celebrate the political, economic, and cultural sway of the middle classes. The opinions of the super-sophisticated, multicultured Jew, Sidonia, who rides dashingly into *Coningsby* in a flash of lightning, in many ways provide the clue to the quality of Disraeli's own arguments. Sidonia is the romantic outsider who sees through things, offers speculative analyses, and suggests ways out. None of the programmes outlined in the novels was ever truly espoused by the practical, pragmatic, and sometimes flashy politician that Disraeli became. The two later novels, *Lothair* (1870) and *Endymion* (1880), show no advance in style or characterization but both reveal a sharp satire and a continuing investigation of political possibility and political improbability. *Lothair*, in particular, considers the overlap of religion and high politics and the relationship between English idealism and Italian nationalism, and shows the occasional flair that characterizes Disraeli's best earlier work. For the once and future Prime Minister of 1870, however, the pressure to deal in fiction with what the 1840s had seen as the 'Condition of England' was evidently less urgent.

Macaulay, Thackeray, and Trollope

The most persuasive and influential Victorian advocate of gradual political evolution, firmly rooted in national history, was Thomas Babbington Macaulay (1800–59), created Baron Macaulay in 1857. Macaulay first made his reputation through the essays on literature, history, and politics published in the *Edinburgh Review* between 1825 and 1844. These essays reveal a probing mind, with clearly defined tastes and antipathies. The same qualities mark the five volumes of his monumental *History of England* published between 1848 and 1861. The *History* had an immediate popular impact, selling three thousand copies of its first two volumes within ten days of their publication and thirteen thousand in four months. Its title has always been recognized as a misnomer, for Macaulay skims over medieval and Tudor history as a mere prelude to his real subject, the revolutions of the seventeenth century and, in particular, the origins and constitutional effects of the 'Glorious Revolution' of 1688. Perhaps as a result of the impact of the Waverley Novels (which Macaulay saw as having 'appropriated' something of the province of the historian) his volumes are as much concerned with the affairs of Scotland and Ireland as they are with England. The Scott whom Macaulay so jealously admired also influenced the manner in which grand evocations of 'local colour', sweeping set-piece description, and careful character analysis are redirected back into non-fictional narrative, or, as many readers might still have seen it, into the 'higher' art of history writing. As a narrative *The History of England* is compelling; its heroes and its villains are placed and defined and the larger life of the nation, working and creating beyond the court and the power brokers, is steadily adumbrated. Macaulay's pellucid style, balancing long clausal sentences with punchy short ones and rhetorically inviting reader participation in the explicatory process, demands assent to his overarching argument. That argument, which insists that the history of England was 'emphatically the history of progress . . . the history of a constant movement of the public mind, of a constant change in the institutions of a great society', powerfully served to reassure liberal Victorian England, and by extension, Scotland and Ireland, of the rightness of their historic evolution and of their constitutional singularity. It was an argument that opponents of the constitutional settlements of 1688 and 1832, and of the principles of Union and uniform cultural progress, were intended to dispute at their peril.

It had originally been Macaulay's larger intention to carry his *History* forward to the period of the French Revolution and to the Reform Bill. His death foreshortened the scheme. In 1863, shortly before his own death, William Makepeace Thackeray (1811–63) contemplated a continuation of the *History* into the reign of Queen Anne, but, perhaps typically, nothing was realized. Thackeray and Macaulay had earlier established cordial relations based on a mutual admiration of one another's books. The novelist's series of lectures, *The English Humourists of the Eighteenth Century* (1851), is coloured not only by Macaulayan Whiggism but also by shared literary predilections. Thackeray came relatively late to novel writing, having served a long and valuable apprenticeship as an essayist and an intensely amusing comic journalist writing under the various pseudonyms of James Yellowplush (who purports to be a footman), George Savage Fitz-Boodle (a London club-man), and Michael Angelo Titmarsh (an artist). From 1842 he had also actively contributed to the newly founded *Punch* where his most notable pieces included the series of short parodies of leading writers of the day *Punch's Prize Novelists* (including a devastating skit on Disraeli's *Coningsby*).

Thackeray's earliest fictional experiments define themselves beside the great precedent of Fielding and against the excesses of the modern 'Newgate School' of criminal literature, especially those perpetrated by Edward Bulwer-Lytton (1803–73) (whose truly dreadful, ponderous sentences he had wonderfully parodied in *Punch*) and William Harrison Ainsworth (1805–82). *Catherine* (1839–40) is a short anti-heroic tale in the manner of Fielding's *The Life of Jonathan Wild the Great*, a work which also provided something of a model for the more ambitious *The Luck of Barry Lyndon*, serialized in *Fraser's Magazine* in 1844 (revised in 1852 as *The Memoirs of Barry Lyndon*). Thackeray's narrator is an Irish adventurer who is obliged to join the army at the time of the Seven Years War, who deserts, and who manages to establish himself as a professional gambler in the courts and spas of Europe. His upward social mobility and his dramatic changes in fortune are marked by the uneasy shifts in his own name, the final form of which derives from his unhappy marriage to a wealthy aristocratic widow. Barry is, however, a congenital liar and his narrative is a cleverly sustained exercise in unreliability, occasionally corrected, or commented on, by an editor who adds an extra layer to the fictional games in which Thackeray habitually delighted. The novelist seems to have held *Barry Lyndon* in relatively little esteem, unlike the popular *Book of Snobs* 'By One of Themselves' which originally appeared in *Punch* in 1847 and was revised for republication in the following year. *The Book of Snobs* ranges satirically over upper- and middle-class society, shifting its viewpoint and its moral judgements, censoring, yet acknowledging the familiar addiction, even in the narrator himself, to the vices it observes.

Thackeray's facility for narrative disconcertion reached its zenith in the monthly-part serialization of *Vanity Fair* (1847–8). This 'Novel without a Hero' denies heroism to its characters and steadily questions all pretensions to vice and virtue. It playfully undercuts both military and civil greatness and it balances the unscrupulous ambitions of Becky Sharp, not with placid upright-ness, but with the asinine complacency of Amelia Sedley. Its only solidly 'good' character, the much put upon 'honest' William Dobbin, finally wins Amelia, the woman he has always loved, but it is an achievement which is gently squashed by a narrator who rhetorically, and knowingly, demands in the novel's closing sentence: 'Which of us is happy in this world? Which of us has his desire? or, having it, is satisfied?' *Vanity Fair* is a varied, stimulating, and chal-lenging work which is often as dark as it is funny. In it Thackeray allots to his narrator the complementary roles of showman and preacher, the one manipu-lating the puppets, the other drawing lessons from their often unpredictable and independent behaviour. The 'Manager of the Performance' of the novel's Preface self-deprecatingly announces that he has a general impression of things as 'more melancholy than mirthful'. Thackeray himself wrote to a friend in 1847 of having set himself up as a 'Satirical-Moralist' with a vast multitude of readers whom we not only amuse but teach'. 'A few years ago', he added, 'I should have sneered at the idea of setting up as a teacher at all . . . but I have got to believe in the business, and in many other things since then. And our profession seems to me to be as serious as the Parson's own.'

Thackeray's later, far more parsonic, novels have generally been denied the critical esteem which the twentieth century has accorded too exclusively to *Vanity Fair*. None of them has quite the same experimental ebullience and sharpness, and none expresses the same guarded fascination with the laxer morals of Regency England, but each in its way responds to particular aspects of mid-Victorian culture, to its earnestness as much as to the fascination with history, its sexual guardedness, and its prodigality. *The History of Pendennis* (1848–50) traces the development of a young gentleman by looking (as the sub-title suggests) at 'his fortunes and misfortunes, his friends and his greatest enemy'. The original paper covers to the monthly parts showed its protagonist torn between domestic virtue and the pleasures of the world, between a mater-nal brunette and a seductive blonde. Pen's 'greatest enemy' is himself, tempted by the ills to which adolescence and young manhood are heir—sexual awak-ening and exploration, laziness, indulgence, debt and immaturity. That he finally achieves success both in love and in the literary life is testimony both to a new geniality on Thackeray's part and to a Victorian seriousness (which is only partly tongue-in-cheek). Its successor, *The History of Henry Esmond* (1852), is a radically different work. Set largely in the reign of Queen Anne, and narrated by a melancholic, self-doubting, fitfully romantic aristocrat, it both pays tribute to the fiction of the previous century and offers distinctly nineteenth-century insights into the historical process. Like Scott before him, Thackeray intermixes the private and the public, but through his moody confessional, first-person narrator he allows for myopic perspectives and the expression of confused motives. The moral oppositions suggested by social pretences and a Jacobite Pretender to the throne, by honour and deception, by European war and London journalism, by shabby heroes and elusive lovers, by unsettling and divided England and an American Indian summer, make for a deeply disconcerting but profoundly fertile novel. In its final gestures of placid and passive withdrawal it not only qualifies the Whiggish confidence of Macaulay but also disturbs conventional Victorian notions of what might constitute a 'happy' ending.

The Newcomes of 1853–5, Thackeray's most obviously 'Victorian' novel, follows the vagaries of an extended genteel family (though there is a punning irony in his description of them in his subtitle as 'most respectable'). Only the upright Colonel Newcome, an Indian Army officer, bewildered by the ways of the world, maintains the virtues of true 'gentlemanliness' by which Thackeray and his class set such store (and which his many *déclassé* nineteenth-century contemporaries attempted both to refine and to redefine). In *The Virginians* (1857–9) the novelist returns to the destinies of the gentlemanly Esmond family in their Virginian retreat. The novel, which was partly inspired by Thackeray's visits to the United States in 1852–3 and 1855–6, re-examines the dilemmas posed by political division within a family in the period of the American Revolution. Despite its glancing, historically based, reflections on a nation approaching Civil War, and its evocation of the literary and fashionable worlds of eighteenth-century London, it is a broken-backed and often sentimental work, disappointing when set beside the intellectual stringency and narrative subtlety of *Henry Esmond*. *The Adventures of Philip* (which like *The Newcomes* purports to be told by Arthur Pendennis) loosely interconnects with its predecessors as if part of an expanding, loose family chronicle. It was first published serially in the *Cornhill Magazine* in 1861–2 during the brief period of Thackeray's editorship of one of the most innovative periodicals of its day. It must have been obvious, even to his most devoted admirers, that the scintillation of *Vanity Fair* was now elusive.

Anthony Trollope (1815–82) was Thackeray's most determined and consistent admirer amongst his fellow-novelists. From the evidence of his brief but antipathetic characterization of Dickens as 'Mr Popular Sentiment' in *The Warden* it is evident that Trollope distrusted that writer's campaigns, prejudices, and tear-jerkings; the fact that 'Mr Popular Sentiment' is in league with 'Dr Pessimist Anticant' (a side-swipe at Carlyle) suggests that he also disliked a noisily committed literature. Trollope is the most informed and observant political novelist in English, but his politics are those of parliamentary and ecclesiastical manœuvres and scandals, of country-house shuffles and re-shuffles, and of personalities in conflict and in mutual complement. When he describes himself in his often irritatingly misleading *Autobiography* (1875–6) as an advanced Conservative-Liberal he is not only using the new party terminology of the day, but attempting to point to his own aspiration to neutrality as a writer. Party politics fascinate him as an observer of human tribalism and ambition but particular policies and the high-minded pursuance of issues are of little consequence in novels which frequently touch on power and the delight in wielding power. When Trollope himself tried to enter Parliament, his campaign proved a disaster. When he developed the political career of his idealized gentlemanly power broker, Plantagenet Palliser, in *The Prime Minister* (1875–6) he revealed a thin-skinned but upright man whose ambition is merely to introduce a decimal currency. Power proves both elusive and hollow. What Trollope seems to have learned most from Thackeray is that heroes and ideals are constantly challengeable and that judgement is always conditional. He is a great political novelist precisely because, despite his outward easy-going tolerance, he distrusts both politics and politicians.

The *Autobiography* places an exaggerated stress on Trollope's supposedly miserable childhood. His humiliations, he argues, derived not simply from bad schooling but from parental neglect. His father, a barrister and unsuccessful farmer, struck him as a model failure, but his mother Frances (1780–1863), who had attempted to restore the family fortunes by writing professionally, seems to have inspired scant posthumous respect from her son. Frances Trollope's *Domestic Manners of the Americans* (1832) caused offence amongst American readers but amused a domestic audience sufficiently to make it a best-seller. It was, however, the subsequent stream of novels and travel-books, notable amongst them the socially conscious Manchester novel *The Life and Adventures of Michael Armstrong, the Factory Boy* of 1840, that appears to have offended her son sufficiently for him to have caricatured his mother as a genteel scribbler, Lady Carbury, in *The Way We Live Now* (1874–5). Frances Trollope's very efficiency, if not her style and her subjects, was something that did impress itself upon her son's imagination. Anthony's forty-seven novels, his travel books, his biographies, essays, and critical works, were produced with an enviable dedication to his craft and by means of a determined daily self-discipline and an addiction to routine. He was also capable of writing on shipboard, on trains, and in his club, while loyally attending to his duties as an official of the Post Office. If the *Autobiography* often appears to diminish the art of literature and to side-step questions of inspiration and authorial commitment, it asserts the alternative proprieties of the pleasures of the craft of fiction.

As Thackeray's fiction had developed novel from novel, so had the idea of somehow linking his stories together as a loose family saga, suggesting interconnections across time and place and relationships of blood, acquaintance, and resemblance. Little effectively came of the plan, but it is possible that it is from Thackeray's proposed example that Trollope took his cue for the sequences of novels which have later become known as the 'Barchester' and the 'Palliser' series. In these sequences connections can be both as strong as the continuation of the parliamentary and amatory career of Phineas Finn from one novel to another or as loose as the incorporation of *Doctor Thorne* (1858) into the Barchester cycle. Trollope's earliest works draw on his experience of, and affection for, modern Ireland, but after an unpropitious experiment with historical fiction in *La Vendée* (1850) he began what was to become the first of his novels set in a fictional English cathedral town and its surrounding countryside. *The Warden* (1855) is a short study of how the ripples of a local scandal broaden into a national issue and how an upright man becomes a victim of circumstances beyond his control. Its sequel, *Barchester Towers* (1857), centres not on Septimus Harding, the former Warden of Hiram's Hospital, but on the threat to the complacent security of the cathedral close presented by the advent of a new Bishop, and, moreover, of the Bishop's Evangelical wife, Mrs Proudie. It is one of Trollope's most successful comic observations of the political process at work, not on a national or a parliamentary scale, but as a series of petty ploys and manœuvres and as a clash of personalities. The upper clerics of these two novels figure prominently again in *The Last Chronicle of Barset* (1867), the novelist's personal favourite amongst his books and a conscious conclusion to a sequence. It suggests the effects of ageing, death, and ill-founded suspicion on an estabished community. *Doctor Thorne*, *Framley Parsonage* (1861), and *The Small House at Allington* (1862–4) concentrate less on clerical politics and more on secular match-making and on failures in love. All three move slowly and delicately, firmly rooted in genteel provinciality and in an England of rural backwaters and stable, traditional systems of value.

The so-called 'Palliser' novels, loosely centred on the family connections of the Duke of Omnium, involve a more metropolitan consciousness and a cosmopolitan culture. Political interests are largely peripheral to *Can You Forgive Her?* (1864–5) and to *The Eustace Diamonds* (1871–3), both serving to justify Trollope's self-deprecating authorial ambition to relieve parliamentary concerns by putting in 'love and intrigue, social incidents, with perhaps a dash of sport, for the sake of my readers'. Both *Phineas Finn* (1867–9) and *Phineas Redux* (1873–4) concentrate on the advances and setbacks in the political career of an Irish Member of Parliament, an outsider to the British Establishment but one who is variously the object of female flirtation and the victim of male jealousy and suspicion. The real sharpness, and occasional disillusion, inherent in Trollope's vision of society and its corruption is also evident in the complex ramifications of *The Way We Live Now* (1874–5). This novel fits into no 'series', but takes a broad, critical view of a nation caught up in deceit, decadence, and financial speculation. It is Trollope's most quizzically disconcerting work and his most distinctive tribute to a Thackerayan precedent.

The Brontë Sisters

Charlotte Brontë (1816–55) admired Thackeray quite as positively as Trollope. She saw his early satirical journalism and his first works of fiction as moral statements emanating from 'the first social regenerator of the day', and, provincially ignorant of the existence of Thackeray's insane wife, she somewhat gauchely dedicated the second edition of *Jane Eyre* to the none the less flattered fellow-author. Her own novels may lack the cultivated urbanity of *Vanity Fair* and the experimental role-playing of Thackeray's personae, but they are in no sense gauche or unsophisticated. Despite the intense privacy and relative seclusion of the Yorkshire parsonage from which her novels emerged, Charlotte Brontë shared with her sisters Emily (1818–48) and Anne (1820–49) a particularly informed, if somewhat detached, view of the wider world. As children, the three sisters had immersed themselves in the ideological debates publicized in the great journals of their time and in the late flickerings of European Romanticism. Their first collaborative fictions, the elaborate narratives concerned with the fantasy kingdoms of Angria and Gondal, are adaptations of, and variations on, oriental and Gothic extravaganzas heightened by modern political realities and personalities. In their adult fiction obvious escapism is diminished in the face of an oppressive, isolating present; the romanticism and the Gothicism are, however, creatively, forcefully, and sometimes threateningly, transmuted.

Charlotte Brontë's first mature novel, *The Professor*, was written in 1846, two years after she had returned from the Pensionnat Heger in Brussels where she had worked as a pupil-teacher. 'A first attempt', she later remarked of the novel in its Preface, 'it certainly was not, as the pen which wrote it had been previously worn a good deal in a practice of some years'. This reference back to the juvenilia and to the years of apprenticeship in fiction ('many a crude effort, destroyed almost as soon as composed') suggests the degree to which she felt that she was turning away from the 'ornamented and redundant' to the 'plain and homely'. Her choice of the word 'homely' here aptly suits the style and manner of her novel, though it tends to conflict with the Brussels setting and with the version of her own fraught and alien experience which she filters through the reminiscence of a male narrator. *The Professor* was rejected six times by publishers before it attracted the favourable notice of the literary adviser to the firm of Smith, Elder in July 1847. Although the story was held to be too colourless to sell independently, the literary promise it suggested inspired Smith, Elder to note encouragingly that the submission of another work of fiction from its pseudonymous author 'would meet with careful attention'. *The Professor* finally appeared posthumously in 1857, but the publishers' offer to consider a new novel was taken up by Charlotte with alacrity. The well-advanced manuscript of *Jane Eyre: An Autobiography* was completed within three weeks, dispatched to London, enthusiastically accepted, and published in October 1847.

Jane Eyre was, and remains, an extraordinary phenomenon: a totally assured, provocative, and compelling piece of realist fiction. To its first readers, and even its publishers, it seemed to have come from nowhere, being ascribed to the genderless figure of 'Currer Bell', the supposed 'editor' of an obviously female narrative. It has not lost its power to surprise and provoke. However much *Jane Eyre* has established itself as a 'classic' and popular love-story, it in fact insists on independence as forcefully as it recognizes the importance of sexual and marital interdependence. It recognizes the virtues of self-discipline and rejection as much as it tests the probity of passionate commitment. Primarily through the example and influence of Helen Burns, it deals with submission and Christian resolution, but it also allows for successive explosions of wrath, misery, and despair. Jane never quite dissolves the iron that entered her soul as an unloved and unjustly persecuted child, nor does she gladly suffer fools or readily love her persecutors. She may profess to forgive the dying Mrs Reed, but her narrative periodically burns with a sense of injustice which is as much sexual as it is religious and familial. 'Women are supposed to be very calm generally', she explains in her twelfth chapter, 'but women feel just as men feel; they need exercise for their faculties, and a field for their efforts as much as their brothers do; they suffer from too rigid a restraint, too absolute a stagnation, precisely as men would suffer.' Jane never stagnates. Her quest is to find a partner worthy of her intelligence, her judgemental wit, and her determined selfhood, one who will learn to respect her integrity (as Mr Rochester, in their first courtship, signally fails to do) and her determination (which St John Rivers misreads). Jane's rejection of an adulterous, bigamous, and perhaps glamorous relationship with Rochester, is complemented later in the novel by her firm rejection of the far more sombrely respectable prospect of life as a missionary's wife (a proposal that some Victorian Evangelical readers might have assumed would have opened up the yet more glorious prospect of her salvation). In both cases Jane follows the dictates of her refined conscience. She finds it her 'intolerable duty' to leave Thornfield Hall, and she does so by solemnly echoing the 'I do' of the Anglican Marriage Service in reply to Rochester's passionate question: 'Jane, do you mean to go one way in the world, and to let me go another?' When pressed by St John Rivers to accept him she is equally firm in her strangely insistent 'I will be your curate, if you like, but never your wife'. The serenity of the novel's conclusion (in which Jane and the widowed and maimed Rochester are reunited) is qualified by its final references to the sacrificial ministry of St John Rivers in India. The novel's last sentences enforce the co-existence of alternative duties and vocations. Jane has chosen secular happiness as a means of salvation; as her narrative has so often demonstrated, free will and the due exercise of a God-given conscience lie at the core of the divine scheme of things.

Shirley (1849) lacks the intensity and the compelling narrative direction of *Jane Eyre*. It is, in many ways, a 'Condition of England' novel, one which offers a bold retrospect on the Luddite agitation and machine-breaking that had characterized the politics of the industrial North in the early 1810s. This retrospect allows for a certain distancing and for an examination of period details and assumptions, many of them culled from the first-hand witness of the Reverend Patrick Brontë and his acquaintance. The main interest of the story derives from its particularly distinctive female characters, most notably that of Shirley Keeldar (whom Elizabeth Gaskell affirmed in her *Life of Charlotte Brontë* (1857) was a 'representation' of Emily Brontë). Some of the local and thematic material of *The Professor* was strikingly reshaped into a far finer novel, *Villette* (1853). *Villette* may avoid touching on 'topics of the day' in a limited political sense, but it deals directly and often painfully with the pressing issues of women's choice and women's employment. The novel's narrator, Lucy Snowe, is an autobiographer denied the scope, the certainties, and the happy personal resolution of Jane Eyre. She is priggish and frosty where Jane Eyre was bold and fiery. Her English Protestant isolation, and indeed alienation, is stressed by the novel's unlovely, urban Belgian setting, by its frequent recourse to French dialogue and terminology, and by its variously intrusive, inquisitive, flirtatious, and restrictive Catholic characters. Lucy's circumstances and her hyperactive conscience oblige her to assert her separateness and to insist on the superiority of her own personal, moral, and professional sensibility. Her confessions, both to the reader, and, awkwardly and desperately, to a Villette priest, are restless and self-absorbed and played against an equally uneasy, not to say suspicious, background. Lucy's growing love for a waspish Catholic, Paul Emmanuel, ultimately allows her glimmers of real emotional happiness and professional achievement, but the narrative ends with an Atlantic storm and a profound uncertainty as to whether her love will ever be fulfilled.

Anne Brontë's *Agnes Grey* was co-published with her sister Emily's *Wuthering Heights* in 1847. Its first grudging reviews were inevitably overshadowed by the often bemused notices given to Emily's novel. All three sisters had maintained the use of the non-specific pseudonyms they had chosen for the unsuccessful publication of the *Poems, by Currer, Ellis and Acton Bell* in 1846. This very non-specificity originally gave rise to suppositions about single authorship or of collaboration and, even since the nineteenth century, *Agnes Grey* has remained firmly in the shadow of the work of Charlotte and Emily. Its governess-narrator endures loss of status, humiliation, snobbery, and insult, but her account of herself is characterized by a calm sense of her own moral justification. It presents an impressively harrowing picture of the restrictions on contemporary middle-class women seeking the only respectable form of paid employment, but it lacks the fire and anger which blaze up in *The Tenant of Wildfell Hall* (1848). Anne Brontë's second novel describes the events surrounding a drastically unhappy marriage and the escape from that marriage by its heroine, Helen Graham. The story is told by means of a receding double narrative. It ends happily, but the graphic descriptions of the alcoholic Huntingdon's brutality provoked one early reviewer to complain of 'coarse and disgusting' language and another to deplore 'the tendency of the author to degrade passion into appetite'. To Charlotte Brontë, acting as her sister's literary executor, *The Tenant of Wildfell Hall* seemed barely 'desirable to preserve . . . the choice of subject in that work is a mistake'. This over-protective, censorious attitude may derive from an honest desire to cultivate the impression of Anne's 'meekness'; it may also, more revealingly, be an embarrassed response to the fact that Anne had based Huntingdon's language and behaviour on that of her singularly wayward brother, Branwell.

Charlotte proved to be an equally unsympathetic critic of Emily Brontë's *Wuthering Heights*. She stresses its 'faults' and, most revealingly, seeks for an appropriately local metaphor to explain its 'rusticity': 'It is rustic all through. It is moorish, and wild, and knotty as the root of heath.' This 'knottiness' does not necessarily refer to the quality that subsequent readers have most admired in *Wuthering Heights*, its extraordinary narrative complexity. It plays with shifts of time and perception by balancing the complementary, but not really concordant, viewpoints of two major and five minor narrators. It juxtaposes the worlds of Thrushcross Grange and Wuthering Heights; the passive gentility of the Lintons and the restless, classless energy of Heathcliff; the complacency of insiders and the disruptive intrusions of outsiders. Above all, it opposes freedom and restraint, love and pain, while holding all oppositions in a very specific geographical area, in a tight community, and within an exceptionally neat dynastic pattern. The exposed ancestral house of the title is, as the opening sentences suggest, 'so completely removed from the stir of society'; it is subject to 'pure, bracing, ventilation' and to a wind that slants 'a few stunted firs' and stretches 'a range of gaunt thorns'. Nature, and phenomena within and beyond nature, remain 'wuthering' and turbulent throughout the narrative. In its last chapter, the parish church may lie peacefully under a 'benign sky', but its glass has been broken by storms, its roof-slates hang jaggedly, and there are reports that the 'phantoms' of Heathcliff and a woman have been seen 'under t'Nab'. Despite 'the moths fluttering among the heath and harebells' the churchyard provokes images of 'unquiet slumbers, for the sleepers in that quiet earth'.

The phrase 'the quiet earth' is that of the prime narrator, the often impercipient, would-be misanthrope Lockwood. There is little 'quietness' either in the landscape or the society which he has observed. Both are marked by change, confusion, violence, and unpredictability. When Nelly Dean interposes as an alternative narrator, she speaks as an insider both to the family and to their environment, yet Nelly shifts not simply perspectives but loyalties and emotional alliances (Heathcliff accuses her of 'prying' and of 'idle curiosity'). It is she who conveys to us Catherine's stunning admission: 'My love for Heathcliff resembles the eternal rocks beneath—a source of little visible delight, but necessary. Nelly, I *am* Heathcliff—he's always in my mind—not as a pleasure to myself—but as my own being.' But it is Nelly, never an unqualified adherent of Heathcliff's, who feels constrained to add: 'I was out of patience with her folly.' Where Catherine feels like the unlovely, underlying rocks, Nelly is as sharp, deceptive, and inconsistent as the northern weather. Throughout the telling of the story, readers have to work to interpret the information and the impressions that the tellers choose to recount. The seeming randomness of events and associations and the arbitrariness of what and how we learn, fall into their proper place as readers explore the diverse and multilayered narrative through the very act of reading. If *Wuthering Heights* adjusts the conventional paraphernalia of the Gothic, its unquiet graves, its explosive passion, its illicit relationships, its wild landscapes, and its tempestuous climatic conditions, it remoulds them into an unconventional narrative shape that neither follows nor creates precedents. Despite its utterly assured mastery of form, it remains the most unconventional and demanding of all English novels.

Heathcliff's insistent claim that in opening Catherine's coffin he disturbed no one, but rather 'gave some ease to myself . . . I was tranquil. I dreamt I was sleeping the last sleep, by that sleeper, with my heart stopped, and my cheek frozen against hers', suggests the degree to which Emily Brontë strained to move beyond necrophiliac *frissons*. Her novel is an evocation of freedom, a strange, tranquil, and compelling freedom which also haunts her poetry. The themes of the soul set at liberty by death, or calmed by the contemplation of death within a natural scheme, figure notably in the song 'The linnet in the rocky dells' where the sounds of the moors 'soothe' those lying under the turf. Death may be a troubling severer in 'Cold in the earth', but in the lyric 'Shall earth no more inspire thee' a voice, perhaps from beyond the grave, or perhaps (as Charlotte Brontë believed) of 'the Genius of a solitary region', insists on the enduring and inspiring beauty of wild and empty landscape. Her final poem, 'No coward soul is mine', speaks of a God who is both internalized within the human creature and who is evident in the creation which he continues to foster. This transcendent God animates 'eternal years' and 'Pervades and broods above, | Changes, sustains, dissolves, creates and rears'. The lyrics, published from surviving manuscripts in the early years of the twentieth century, powerfully reinforce the mood of ecstatic intensity evident in the finest of the poems in the collaborative volume of 1846. Most of these poems date from the years 1837 and 1838. The landscapes recalled are vibrant both in summer and winter, in rain and cloud, or when lit by the last beams of 'the cold, bright sun'. It is a landscape which is both physical and visionary, both haunted and possessing:

> The night is darkening round me,
> The wild winds coldly blow;
> But a tyrant spell has bound me
> And I cannot, cannot go.

> The giant trees are bending
> Their bare boughs weighed with snow,
> And the storm is fast descending
> And yet I cannot go.

> Clouds beyond clouds above me,
> Wastes beyond wastes below;
> But nothing drear can move me;
> I will not, cannot go.

This acute, passionate attachment to place, one so akin to Catherine Earnshaw's self-identification with the rocks and the moorland, is not paralleled in the work of Emily's sisters. Anne's placid verse may reinforce the impression we have of a woman who was 'a very sincere and practical Christian' with a 'tinge of religious melancholy', but it is insipid in comparison. Even Charlotte's poetry, which occasionally flickers with the narrative assertiveness of her fiction, seems otherwise unexceptional and unadventurous.

Tennyson and the Pre-Raphaelite Poets

Arthur Hallam (1811–33), Alfred Tennyson's intimate friend and his most immediate early critic, recognized the extent to which Tennyson's early poetry was derived from the emotional norms evolved by the second generation of Romantics, and especially from Shelley and Keats. These norms were still far from universally accepted by early Victorian readers, as the unfavourable reviews of Tennyson's second volume of verse proved. A poetry 'of sensation rather than reflection', Hallam argued, had been created by those whose lives had consisted 'in those emotions, which are immediately consonant with sensation'. But for his own time, an age now dominated by the 'diffusion of machinery', Hallam looked for a new poetry which would express a 'decrease of *subjective* power . . . and a continual absorption of the higher feelings into the palpable interests of ordinary life'. The 'melancholy' which he saw as characteristic of modern literature turned 'the mind upon itself', where it sought relief 'in idiosyncrasies rather than community of interest'. Hallam's essay, which appeared in the *Englishman's Magazine* in August 1831, both publicly pressed the idea that Tennyson was the poet of the new age and privately served as a prompt to Tennyson to turn away from 'idiosyncrasy' towards an alternative interest in 'ordinary life' and 'community'. The process by which Tennyson became the most influential and admired poet of the Victorian era owed much to his intellectual and emotional debt to Hallam. It was a debt which was richly, but posthumously, repaid in *In Memoriam*.

Tennyson (1809–92) published three early volumes of verse, the last being dated 1833, the year of Hallam's untimely death in Vienna. The volumes published in 1830 and 1833 most clearly exhibit his quite extraordinary power, so much admired by Hallam, of embodying himself in characters, or moods of characters, and his 'vivid, picturesque delineation of objects, and the peculiar skill with which he holds all of them *fused* . . . in a medium of strong emotion'. That this emotion was still predominantly melancholic runs as a warning subtext through Hallam's criticism. Many of the poems, which include 'Mariana', 'The Kraken', 'The Ballad of Oriana', 'The Lady of Shalott', and 'The Lotos-Eaters', deal exquisitely with death-like states, or with death itself as a climactic and releasing experience. Emergence into a world of work, action, sensation, or merely unsettling emotion seems to threaten or destroy the cushioned retreats forged by art or guarded by sleep. The hypnotic echoes, the repetitions, and the subtle, often lulling lyricism of the poems also reinforce the impression they convey of a protective and isolating artifice.

Following Hallam's traumatic death, Tennyson retreated into a period of mourning in which he seems to have indulged in a painful purgative process which was both personal and professional. Many of the short lyrics which date from this extended period of bereavement were later shaped into the elegiac 'mechanic exercises' which make up the early sections of *In Memoriam* (1850). Other, less direct tributes to Hallam appeared after a period of public silence, in the two volumes of *Poems* published in 1841. This collection, which reprinted much of the earlier verse as well as revisions of certain key poems, also balanced the old mood of narcotic drowsiness with the urgent simplicity of a lyric such as 'Break, break, break':

> Break, break, break,
>   On thy cold grey stones, O Sea!
> And I would that my tongue could utter
>   The thoughts that arise in me.
>
> O well for the fisherman's boy,
>   That he shouts with his sister at play!
> O well for the sailor lad,
>   That he sings in his boat on the bay!
>
> And the stately ships go on
>   To their haven under the hill;
> But O for the touch of a vanish'd hand,
>   And the sound of a voice that is still!
>
> Break, break, break,
>   At the foot of thy crags, O sea!
> But the tender grace of a day that is dead
>   Will never come back to me.

This is no longer simply an expression of debilitating melancholy or an imagining of restless complacency; it is an evocation of a desperate sense of exclusion, by private grieving, from a working, rejoicing human community. Although Tennyson conspicuously placed 'Break, break, break' as the penultimate poem in his 1842 volumes, their overall negatives were also decisively qualified by a group of new poems which suggest a far more positive social direction in his art. 'St Simeon Stylites' rejects ascetic escapism; 'Ulysses' emphatically embraces the idea of progressive development ('but something ere the end, | Some work of noble note, may yet be done . . .'), and the significantly titled 'Morte d'Arthur' ushers in what proved an enduring fascination with cyclic movement and historic renewal ('The old order changeth, yielding place to new, | And God fulfills Himself in many ways . . .').

The Princess: A Medley (1847) suggests both the extent and the frailty of Tennyson's new commitment to a poetry of social purpose and communal concern. It is a deeply ambiguous and cautiously ambitious narrative poem, one which moves uncertainly from a present-day prologue to a story set in an undefined medieval past and which attempts to explore the pressing modern subject of women's higher education. Despite its persuasive endorsement of Princess Ida's experiment, Tennyson's poem is ultimately both noncommittal and compromised. It does, however, contain a series of superbly evocative, and dramatically effective, lyrics, two of them, 'Now sleeps the crimson petal' and 'Come down, O maid, from yonder mountain height', being amongst the most suggestively erotic poems of the nineteenth century. *In Memoriam A.H.H.* (1850) offers an utterly different view of love and education. It is a tribute to Hallam as friend and mentor which evokes both an enervating grief and an elevating grasp of an idea of spiritual and physical evolution. A shifting and developing perception of Hallam as a mortal victim and an immortal spiritual pioneer runs through the poem, but Tennyson also points its long, steadily ramified argument with recurrent images, with visits to specific places, and with seasonal and calendar events which suggest the movement and measurement of time. Time moves painfully for the mourner at the beginning of the poem, its passage through anniversaries, through Christmas and New Year being marked by comfortless recalls and anguished memorializing. But, as the second lyric ('Old Yew, which graspest at the stones . . .') powerfully suggests, nature has other rhythms, impersonal and unsympathetic:

> The seasons bring the flower again,
>   And bring the firstling to the flock;
>   And in the dusk of thee, the clock
> Beats out the little lives of men.

If, as here, Tennyson initially explores the notions of becoming 'incorporate' in the 'grasping' 'sullen' graveyard tree and of an impersonal time, these are views of growth and time which are not sustained by later perceptions. Tennyson's advanced and informed use of nineteenth-century scientific theory, theory which pertained to both the animal and the mineral universe, also broadens the poem's intellectual perspectives. In lyric 66, for example, a geological past in which 'A thousand types are gone' and in which 'dragons of the prime . . . tare each other in their slime' presents both a fearful retrospect on dinosaurs and a potentially disturbing prophecy of human viciousness and human futility. Answers may lie hidden behind 'veils', but they are also discovered in a now confident and active participation in the continuing evolutionary process which links the material to the spiritual, the animal to the divine. Hallam, like Christ, appears as a forerunner, an Adam transformed and resurrected, who quells the doubts associated in the poem with mortality and agnostic scientific theory. In lyric 123, for example, there is no longer a recoil from natural flux, from geological change, from death and decay:

There rolls the deep where grew the tree.
  O earth what changes hast thou seen!
  There where the long street roars, hath been
The stillness of the central sea.

The hills are shadows, and they flow
  From form to form and nothing stands;
  They melt like mist, the solid lands,
Like clouds they shape themselves and go.

But in my spirit will I dwell,
  And dream my dream, and hold it true;
  For tho' my lips may breathe adieu,
I cannot think the thing farewell.

God's time, and the realization of God's purposes in the human spirit as much as in the universe, have supervened. The poem's last gestures express a joyful acceptance of a far-off divine consummation in which evolution is clearly providential and the sense of God is mystically perceived in the totality of creation. Despite its climactic confidence, *In Memoriam* remains as much an exploration of doubts as it is an assertion of faith. It may insist on the benign inevitability of progress, but it also steadily acknowledges the stumbling nature of human advances in understanding. Most powerfully, it recognizes two conflicting validities, those of the reasoning mind, which comes to perceive ultimate purpose, and the agnosticism of the feelings, which continue to crave for present comfort.

In Memoriam, with its wide range of reference to modern thought and modern politics, suggests the extent to which Tennyson had moved away from his earlier self-absorption into the public realm. His appointment in 1850 as Poet Laureate, in succession to Wordsworth, struck many of his contemporaries as a fit confirmation of his stature. His first Laureate volume, *Maud: and Other Poems* (1855) contains reprints of two of his most famous public utterances of the early 1850s, the 'Ode on the Death of the Duke of Wellington' and his vigorous, rhythmical combination of protest and celebration, 'The Charge of the Light Brigade'. This last evocation of a magnificence *qui n'est pas la guerre* (as Marshal Bosquet described the charge), and of a blunder which provokes an act of useless heroism, is linked by subject to the title poem in the volume. *Maud*, originally subtitled 'The Madness', is one of the most inventive and distinctively original poems of the century. It is a love-poem which opens starkly with the words 'I hate'. It is shot through with violence, opprobrium, and failure. The excited, various, and sometimes lurching rhythms manage to convey both an exalted passion and a sense of incipient breakdown, while the passages of lyrical imagining are countered by equally telling diatribes against social injustice and anguished accounts of mental distress. The narrator's painful and guilty dilemma is resolved in his final espousal of a war which destroys 'the long, long canker of peace', the flaming of a flower beyond those of Maud's garden, 'the blood-red blossom' of the thin red line.

None of Tennyson's long later poems rivals the verbal energy of *Maud*. From 1859 he began to develop the great Arthurian cycle, *The Idylls of the King*. In revising and republishing the earlier 'Morte d'Arthur' in 1870 as 'The Passing of Arthur' he removed its original framework and offered it as the tenuously optimistic climax to a series of poems about the failure of an ideal. The *Idylls* express something of his own dismay at the opening future, with Arthur's court presented as a paradigm and its decay, due ultimately to sexual betrayal, as a guarded warning to modern idealists, libertarians and politicians alike. Gerard Manley Hopkins announced to a friend in 1864 that he had begun 'to *doubt* Tennyson' after reading *Enoch Arden and Other Poems* in 1864. His doubt centred on the problem of expression; gone was the poet's inventive 'language of inspiration' which being 'the gift of genius, raises him above himself'. The new self-indulgent, cultivatedly artificial, 'Parnassian' language, running in 'an intelligibly laid down path', did not 'sing in its flight'. The justice of Hopkins's observation has perhaps been proved by the relative neglect of Tennyson's later work in the twentieth century, a neglect which derives not necessarily from the subject-matter of the poems concerned but from their lexical complacency. The *Idylls* are, more often than not, boring.

The indulgent and artificial 'Parnassian' mode (as Hopkins styled it) was also very much in evidence in the so-called 'Pre-Raphaelite' poetry of the mid-century. The original Pre-Raphaelite Brotherhood of young, anti-Establishment painters (Dante Gabriel Rossetti, John Everett Millais, William Holman Hunt, F. G. Stephens, and James Collinson) and one sculptor (Thomas Woolner) had drawn up a scheme for revolutionizing the pictorial arts in 1848. The scheme entailed rejecting the norms of painting current since the late Renaissance in favour of what they insisted was the superior directness of expression of those artists who worked before the time of Raphael. Their tastes were not especially novel, despite their own determination to shock a complacent British art world. In England a revival of interest in medieval painting had gone hand in hand with an often strident appreciation of Gothic architecture and design, while in Germany the Nazarene painters had begun to cultivate an affinity with what they saw as the pure, untainted Christian art of the period before the Reformation. What was special about the Pre-Raphaelite revolution was its frequent reference to cultural heroes who were not exclusively painterly. Christ, as for the Nazarenes, stood at the pinnacle of human aspiration to the divine in art and life, but other exclusively Pre-Raphaelite heroes included Chaucer, Shakespeare, and, most radically, given his still unsteady reputation, Keats. These poets provided a stream of subjects for the young artists and their growing circle of associates. Chaucer and Gower stand admiringly by as John Wyclif reads his translation of the Scriptures in Ford Madox Brown's *The First Translation of the Bible into English* (1847–8) and Chaucer also assumes a central position in Brown's triptych showing *The Seeds and Fruits of English Poetry* (1845–51, 1853). Millais's *Ferdinand Lured by Ariel* (1850) takes an episode from *The Tempest*, and in 1853–4 Brown painted a sleeping King Lear comforted by an attendant Cordelia. Holman Hunt's *The Flight of Madeline and Porphyro* (1848) shows the final tableau of Keats's 'Eve of St Agnes' while Millais's *Isabella* (1848–9) takes as its subject a scene of tender love contrasted with sneering brotherly jealousy.

The group's short-lived journal, *The Germ*, an experimental amalgam of poetry, prose, and essay, also served to extend the range of their literary and pictorial predilections. Of the founder 'Brothers', only Dante Gabriel Rossetti (1828–82) has any claim to literary distinction, although the poetry of Thomas Woolner (1825–92), a contributor to *The Germ* and the author of the sequence *My Beautiful Lady* (1864), achieved some critical success at the time. Rossetti's poetry is essentially decorative and descriptive. In some of his landscape poems ('A Half-Way Pause', 'Autumn Idleness', or 'The Woodspurge', for example) he can colourfully suggest momentary experience and an intensity of vision, but the majority of his verses deal with his fascination with the female face and the female body. In his best-known poem 'The Blessed Damozel' Rossetti develops a fleshly but heavenly vision of a transfigured beloved from Dante's Beatrice, a figure who endlessly haunts his paintings. He idealizes women both sexually and spiritually, and with the exception of his strikingly earthy address to a woman of the streets in 'Jenny', he distances them as objects of desire, even worship. The sonnet sequence *The House of Life* bears certain parallels to the work of a fellow-contributor to *The Germ*, Coventry Patmore (1823–96), the author of the uxoriously adoring long poem, *The Angel in the House* (1854–63). Where Rossetti yearns for the supreme and often elusive mistress, Patmore idolizes his wife, tenderly incarcerating her in her domesticity.

Algernon Charles Swinburne (1837–1909) briefly formed part of the extraordinary household Rossetti assembled round himself at Chelsea, a menagerie of artists, artists' models, poets, and animals dedicated to extending the frontiers of art and experience. Swinburne remained an outsider and a rebel, despite the steady popularity of his weighty adjectival poetry, throughout his life. His early attraction to the cause of Italian unification was partly moulded by his acquaintance with Giuseppe Mazzini, the apostle of Italian Republicanism exiled in England. The *Songs before Sunrise* (1871) express a thrilled passion for the Risorgimento with a political conviction rare enough in English poetry. Swinburne proved equally radical in his assaults on received morality and Christian teaching. Throughout his work there runs a defined paganism and an instinctive libertarianism, shaped both by his profound understanding of the forms and styles of classical culture and by his distaste for Christian narrowness. His finest collection, the once notorious *Poems and Ballads* of 1866, reveals both the subtlety of his metrical echoes of and variations on Greek poetry and his power to disturb convention. His 'Hymn to Proserpine' purports to be spoken by the dying anti-Christian Roman Emperor Julian (nicknamed 'the Apostate' by his enemies) while the erotic 'Dolores' reverses the Catholic notion of the suffering Virgin by indulgently addressing 'a poisonous queen', a priestess desired for her power to inflict pain. Swinburne found his most receptive audience amongst the unconventional literary and moral rebels of the late century.

Rossetti's friend and artistic associate, William Morris (1834–96), was a rebel in quite another sense. Morris revolutionized English design (and attempted to revolutionize English politics) in the second half of the nineteenth century, but the same cannot be said of his contribution to literature. He saw poetry as an extension of craft and as a natural enhancement of the quality of life, but his own poetry is generally lifeless, derivative, and long-winded. He sought to create a popular narrative art akin to Chaucer's, and his most substantial work, *The Earthly Paradise* (1868–70), loosely intermixes retold tales from classical and northern sources, drawing in particular on the newly rediscovered Icelandic sagas. Unfortunately, Morris lacked Chaucer's wit and variety; nor was he ideally equipped to adapt the blunt plainness of his Old Norse originals successfully. He attempted to unmake much that he saw as false and artificial in the culture of his time, but his very sophistication militated against his avowedly folksy aspirations. In the late 1870s and early 1880s Morris was drawn first to Liberal and then to Socialist politics (he was amongst the first appreciative readers of Marx in England) and he translated his new commitment into an awkwardly jolly sing-song ballad poetry in such works as the 'Chants for Socialists' (1885). His most impressive works of this period are in prose, the two polemical fantasies *A Dream of John Ball* (1886–7) and *News from Nowhere* (1890). Both use the past to project an ideal into the future, the latter being a particularly forceful vision of a world which has freed itself from machines and from mechanical ways of thinking in order to release individual creativity.

The most distinguished of the poets associated with the Pre-Raphaelite movement is Christina Rossetti (1830–94), the younger sister of Dante Gabriel. Her earliest published poetry, in an escapist, dreamy sub-Tennysonian mode, appeared in the first number of *The Germ* in 1850, but her distinctive female voice is clearly heard in her first major collection, *Goblin Market and Other Poems* (1862). The title poem of the volume is an extraordinary achievement, accumulative in its imagery, rhymed and half-rhymed, at times languorous, at times aggressive, and always rhythmically restless. At its climax, the redemptive Lizzie is assaulted by the far from whimsical goblins who attempt to force her to eat their seductive fruit:

> Though the goblins cuffed her and caught her,
> Coaxed and fought her,
> Bullied and besought her,
> Scratched her, pinched her black as ink,
> Kicked and knocked her,
> Mauled and mocked her,
> Lizzie uttered not a word;
> Would not open lip from lip
> Lest they should cram a mouthful in:

> But laughed in heart to feel the drip
> Of juice that syrupped all her face,
> And lodged in dimples of her chin,
> And streaked her neck which quaked like curd.

The poem has something of the strangeness of the work of Lewis Carroll, but its nasty ramifications and its implied spiritual message stretch far beyond childhood and childish fears into the realm of sexual threat and female self-assertion. When Christina Rossetti wrote directly for children, as in her *Sing Song: A Nursery Rhyme Book* (1872), she exhibits a direct simplicity which is equally distinct from the knowingness of 'Goblin Market' and from the playful narrative inventiveness of Carroll. *The Prince's Progress and Other Poems*, which was published in 1866, subtly develops the use of alliteration and assonance both in its title-poem, an allegory which describes the unhappy uncertainty of emotional commitment, and in a sequence of lyric poems, secular and devotional. Further lyrics were added to a new collected edition of poems in 1875 and the ambitious *A Pageant and Other Poems*, which contains the religious sequence of Petrarchan sonnets 'Monna Innominata', appeared in 1881. Christina Rossetti's devotional poetry derives much from the powerful influence of Dante which was shared by all the younger members of her Anglo-Italian family (her sister Maria is the author of the pioneer English analysis *A Shadow of Dante* (1872), and in 1861 Dante Gabriel Rossetti had published his study *The Early Italian Poets*, later revised as *Dante and His Circle*) but her piety is also distinctly English. Her own intense Anglo-Catholicism readily responded to Anglican precedents, most notably that of George Herbert whose influence is particularly evident in the question-and-answer 'Up-Hill' and in the dialogue poem 'A Bruised Reed shall He not Break'. In the shorter poems which deal with secular relationships she explores emotional evasion and the failure of human sympathy as human alternatives to religious consolation and heavenly consummation. A tentative *eros* may supplant *agape*, but *eros* appears to have offered no certainty and little security in the past; the present and the future (even one which embraces death) seem to hold no more optimistic prospect. These themes are variously investigated throughout her writing career, almost mockingly in 'Promises Like Pie-Crust', elusively in 'Winter My Secret', ambiguously and mortally in the sonnet 'Remember'. In the short and even more ambiguous Song 'When I am Dead my Dearest' human love is treated with a take-it-or-leave-it quality which serves to qualify its Keatsian metaphors and suggestions. Keats's distant shadow also haunts 'Autumn Violets', a poem which anxiously reverses the idea of autumnal fulfilment. Love in middle age, Rossetti implies, is as forced and inappropriate as spring flowers (however sensuous) in autumn, the season when 'A grateful Ruth' should be grateful for the 'scanty corn' that she gleans. This, however, seems to be a Ruth with no generous Boaz hovering at the edge of the cornfield.

The Brownings

Elizabeth Barrett Browning's passionate outpourings of love-poetry in the *Sonnets from the Portuguese* (1850), addressed from a woman to a man, publicly recall a powerful, private emotional awakening. Despite the implications of the title, there are no Portuguese originals (the 'Portuguese' of the title being an esoteric reference to the sixteenth-century Portuguese poet Camoens and to Robert Browning's nickname for his wife). The sonnets were written during the courtship of the two poets, he junior to her both in years and in terms of publication, but her fourth poem expresses a deferential acceptance of the reversal of roles, she the senior now allowing that her 'cricket' merely chirps against his 'mandolin'. Since the time of their marriage Robert Browning's reputation has overshadowed that of his wife and it is only relatively recently that the real individuality, and quality, of the work of Elizabeth Barrett (1806–61) has been critically recognized. Her precocious early poetry, including a translation of Aeschylus' *Prometheus Bound* (1833) and the favourably received *The Seraphim and Other Poems* (1838), is relatively unadventurous compared to her later work. The translation of Aeschylus was, however, reworked for publication in the *Poems* of 1850, the volume that also contained the florid *Sonnets from the Portuguese*. Following their decision to live in Italy in 1846, both husband and wife responded variously to the history, the tradition, and the effervescent politics of a nation experiencing a painful evolution into a modern state. Where Robert Browning generally retreated into historical perspectives, Elizabeth Barrett Browning confronted contemporary issues (as she had earlier done with English social problems) in her sequence *Casa Guidi Windows* (1851). The poems may lack the republican commitment of Swinburne and the vivid questioning of Clough, but they boldly and intelligently confront Italian political flux and the often contradictory nature of nationalist aspirations. Barrett Browning's most substantial work in every sense is her long blank-verse 'novel' *Aurora Leigh: A Poem in Nine Books* (1856). Its verse may not be consistently inspired, and its encyclopaedic show of learning may sometimes clog both its imagery and its narrative line, but it remains a vital, highly original and outspoken feminist statement. *Aurora Leigh* traces two careers, one male, one female, one philanthropic, one artistic, and it allows for digression into other lives and other circumstances beyond the comfortable world of the heroine. Aurora's autobiography is written for her 'better self', as a poet exploring experience, inspiration, and independence, knowing that she must 'analyse, | Confront, and question'. It traces processes of self-liberation which are related to informed confrontation and informed questioning. In Book I, for example, Aurora first amusedly, then ecstatically, recalls her discovery of poetry:

> I had found the secret of a garret-room
> Piled high with cases in my father's name,
> Piled high, packed large,—where, creeping in and out
> Among the giant fossils of my past,
> Like some small nimble mouse between the ribs
> Of a mastodon, I nibbled here and there
> At this or that box, pulling through the gap,
> In heats of terror, haste, victorious joy,
> The first book first. And how I felt it beat
> Under my pillow, in the morning's dark,
> An hour before the sun would let me read!
> My books! At last because the time was ripe,
> I chanced upon the poets.
>   As the earth
> Plunges in fury, when the internal fires
> Have reached and pricked her heart . . .
>
>   .   .   .   .   .
>
>   —Thus, my soul,
> At poetry's divine first finger-touch,
> Let go conventions and sprang up surprised . . .

Poetry erupts volcanically and, like a geological rift, it releases 'elemental freedom', a freedom that Aurora here and elsewhere enthusiastically embraces. The poem ends confidently with a glimpsed vision of a new dawn reflecting its heroine's name, a new Day 'which should be builded out of heaven to God'.

Robert Browning's own verse 'novel', *The Ring and the Book* (1868–9), differs radically from his wife's. The viewpoint is multiple, the effect cumulative, and the narrative line, or lines, require exploration rather than mere imaginative sympathy or suspension of disbelief. Browning (1812–89) obliges his reader to play the role of an alert investigating magistrate, probing confessions and impressions and sifting a weight of contradictory evidence. *The Ring and the Book* is the culmination of his long poetic experiment with the dramatic monologue and of his fascination with the establishment of 'truth', a truth that can be both objective and subjective, external and experiential. In 1860 Browning had discovered the source for his poem, a collection of documents, bound together, concerning a sensational Roman murder trial of 1698. This chance find on a Florentine bookstall appealed to Browning's delight in exploring the self-justifying contortions of the minds of sinners and criminals; it also stimulated his intellectual and poetic curiosity. The finished poem is as layered as a texture of voices, each of the narratives qualifying and expanding on the one preceding it, each of his witnesses opening up freshly complex vistas and new questions.

The Ring and the Book appeared in four volumes over a period of as many months, thus signalling to its first readers its relationship to the contemporary serial novel. Browning's reputation as a major poet was already firmly established, based on what are still recognized as his four most important volumes of verse, *Dramatic Lyrics* (1842), *Dramatic Romances and Lyrics* (1845), *Men and Women* (1855), and *Dramatis Personae* (1864). As the titles of these volumes suggest, the nature of drama, or rather the characters of drama, served to stimulate Browning's most distinctive writing. In spite of his early ambition to write for the stage, and the modest success of his play *Strafford* (1837), his real penchant was for scenes and for monologues divorced from the theatre. The characters of his poetry do not necessarily have to interact with others, for the majority are overheard in self-revelatory, if scarcely truth-telling soliloquy. The situations he presents, however, require a reader's complicity. In the case of Fra Lippo Lippi, a compromised painter in holy orders forces his confession on those who discover him, 'at an alley's end | Where sportive ladies leave their doors ajar'. In 'My Last Duchess' participation is yet more uneasy. As the Duke of Ferrara gradually explains both himself and the select contents of his privy chamber, a reader is cast in the role of listening ambassador opening the preliminaries to the acquisition of the next duchess (the last one having been disposed of). The Duke's menace, like his cultivation, is established cumulatively:

> She thanked men,—good! but thanked
> Somehow—I know not how—as if she ranked
> My gift of a nine-hundred-years-old name
> With anybody's gift. Who'd stoop to blame
> This sort of trifling? . . .
>
> . . . . . .
>
> and I choose
> Never to stoop. O sir, she smiled, no doubt,
> Whene'er I passed her; but who passed without
> Much the same smile? This grew; I gave commands;
> Then all smiles stopped together.

In many instances Browning wrenches us into a troubled private history by making that history work itself out before us. It is the method of Sir Walter Scott returned to its proper origins in the drama of Shakespeare, and remoulded into single charged incidents recounted by single, expressive voices. Even when Browning's soliloquizers are not known historical figures, as in the instances of the unnamed monk in his Spanish cloister or of the Bishop ordering his tomb, he establishes a physical context through carefully selected details, references, or objects. None floats in the relatively unlocated realms of Tennyson's Ulysses and Tithonus. Each of the speaking voices is given an individual articulation, a turn of phrase, an emphasis, a pause, a reiteration, or an idiolect which serves to identify them. Significantly, most of them are connoisseurs (like the Duke), artists, musicians, thinkers or even, in the case of Mr Sludge the Medium, manipulators. A creativity, or at least an appreciation of the creative process, marks the individuality of each of them. Even Browning's theologians, from the worldly Bishop Bloughram and the earthy Caliban to the more spiritual Rabbi Ben Ezra and Johannes Agricola, speculate from a physical base in the world of the senses or from an appreciation of sensual experience.

Those poems of Browning's which dispense with an identified persona as narrator generally retain a conversational directness, even an easy familiarity between addresser and addressee. 'The Lost Leader', for example, may noisily explode in its vexation and may insist on a sharing of the indignation, but 'De Gustibus' gives a very different impression of emerging from quieter, amorous discourse shaped around the oppositions of England and Italy. 'Two in the Campagna' opens with a questioning voice reminiscent of Donne's, but it speaks of distinctness not union, of an agnosticism in love not of ideal convergence. The famous 'Home-Thoughts, from Abroad' opens with a gasped aspiration and refers possessively to 'my blossomed pear-tree' and to a 'you' who might think the thrush incapable of recapturing 'the first careless rapture'. The narrator of the children's poem 'The Pied Piper of Hamelin' talks of 'my ditty' and ends addressing 'Willy' on the virtues of keeping faith with pipers. Browning's most elusive and suggestive poem 'Childe Roland to the Dark Tower Came' has a first-person narrator who draws us into his quest by suggesting an eerily Gothic response to an already posed question:

> My first thought was, he lied in every word,
>   That hoary cripple, with malicious eye
>   Askance to watch the working of his lie
> On mine, and mouth scarce able to afford
> Suppression of the glee, that pursed and scored
>   Its edge, at one more victim gained thereby.

The poem takes its suggestive title from one of Edgar's songs in *King Lear*, but the line provides merely a footing on which Browning builds a complex fabric, vaguely medieval in its setting but ominous and disturbing in its precise evocation of horror ('—It may have been a water-rat I speared, | But, ugh! it sounded like a baby's shriek', 'Toads in a poisoned tank, | Or wild cats in a red-hot iron cage'). In a sense the poem circles back to its title as the knight blows his 'slughorn', announcing both his presence and his recognition of how and why he framed his journey. Unlike the narrators of Browning's other poems, the very strangeness of the knight and his quest preclude the familiar; a reader is alienated, not by a character, but by an impersonality and by receding layers of 'truth' and 'lying' which look forward to the experiments of the early twentieth-century Modernists.

The Drama, the Melodrama, and the 'Sensation' Novel

Robert Browning's tragedy *Strafford* had been conceived and written in the mid-1830s at the earnest request of the great actor William Charles Macready. Macready was a determined and intelligent pillar of the English stage, a committed reformer and performer of the Shakespearian repertoire as much as a patron of new national talent. *Strafford* pleased him, though he confessed on his first reading of the play that he had been 'too much carried away by the truth of character to observe the meanness of plot, and occasional obscurity'. It needed substantial revision before it reached the stage of the Covent Garden Theatre in April 1837. It has very rarely been performed since. Macready also directed, and took the leading roles in, other now-forgotten plays by Victorian writers whose reputations today are exclusively based on their work in other media. The most notable of these was the historical novelist Edward Bulwer-Lytton, who wrote *The Lady of Lyons; or, Love and Pride* for Macready in 1838, following it in 1839 with the tragedy *Richelieu*. Both dramas remained standard repertory pieces throughout the century, attracting actors of the standing of Charles Kean, Helen Faucit, and later Henry Irving and Ellen Terry to its star roles. Irving, the leading Shakespearian actor of the second half of the century, was also instrumental in the honourable, if unacclaimed, staging of Tennyson's sprawling verse-drama *Queen Mary* in 1876. In 1893, after the poet's death, Irving took the lead in the more favourably received *Becket*, the second of Tennyson's three epic dramas concerned with turning-points in English history. The shade of Shakespeare haunts the theatrical work of all those Victorian writers, from Bulwer-Lytton to Swinburne, who attempted to evolve a modern equivalent to his tragedies and history plays. The scrupulous, scholarly, elaborate, and often admirable productions of Shakespeare which so mark the history of the theatre in the nineteenth century tended to smother all serious imitation under the weight of fussy period costumes, archaeologically correct properties, and an appropriately fustian language.

The Victorian theatre evolved a far more fluid and inventive comic style than it did a tragic one. Although Charles Dickens dabbled unprofitably with burlesque in the mid-1830s, he clearly sensed that neither his talent nor his power to make money lay in that direction. Where the dialogue in his early sketches and novels is vivid, that in his plays is stilted and contrived; the conventions that he transforms in his fiction remain irredeemably conventional in his stage-works. Dickens's friend Douglas Jerrold (1803–57) proved a far more successful writer of comedy. His farce *Paul Pry* (1827) and his popular nautical melodrama *Black-Eyed Susan; or, All in the Downs* (1829) established his once considerable reputation, but Jerrold was increasingly drawn away from the theatre and from theatrical management by his commitment to journalism, and especially to *Punch* (founded in 1841). The only mid-Victorian dramatist to have found favour with twentieth-century producers and audiences, and thereby to have been rescued from the semi-oblivion of 'theatre history', is Dion Boucicault (1820–90). Boucicault's Irish roots are evident in his three witty admixtures of comedy, crime, nationalist politics, and love-interest, *The Colleen Bawn* (1860), *Arrah-na-Pogue* (1864) and *The Shaughraun* (1874). These brought the figure of the resilient 'stage Irishman' to the fore, quietening British fears of the new anti-British force of Fenianism and dulling the edge of much Nationalist aspiration (this same figure was rejected by the later playwrights associated with the Abbey Theatre in Dublin). Boucicault's earliest success was, however, the thoroughly English five-act comedy, *London Assurance* (1841), a play successfully derived in its plot, style, and setting from the models provided by Goldsmith and Sheridan. Boucicault was an unashamed plagiarist, cobbling together elements from existing plays (English and foreign), from history, from fiction, and from popular topics of the day to shape the 200-odd plays ascribed to him. The realistic domestic comedies of the almost equally prolific Thomas William Robertson (1829–71) remain comparatively neglected. Robertson came of a theatrical family, and like Pinero (who later represented him as Tom Wrench in *Trelawny of the 'Wells'*), intimately understood theatre life and theatre people (as his novel *David Garrick* of 1864 suggests). His best work, the six comedies presented at the Prince of Wales's Theatre between 1865 and 1870, also indicates the extent of his grasp of theatrical techniques. The plays, which include *Society* (1865), *Caste* (1867), and *School* (1869), proved innovatory in their rejection of bombast in favour of delicacy, observation, and an anti-sentimental presentation of love.

Bombast can still be most readily associated with the frequent excesses of Victorian melodrama, a form developed variously from a popular taste for spectacle, from folk-story and press reports, from accounts of criminal enterprise and criminal deviation, from Gothic and historical fiction, from continental romantic theatre and native romantic sentiment. Most melodramas were centred on fraught amatory interest and particularly on much-put-upon heroines. The influence of unsophisticated representations and misrepresentations of Shakespeare (of the kind that Dickens wonderfully describes in *Great Expectations*) was also considerable. Melodrama as an art form held sway over the popular imagination both as cheap fiction and as cheap theatre, but it also fed more would-be genteel and lofty forms. The absurdity of plots may have declined in the more prestigious theatres, the blood-curdling, the scenic sensationalism, the assertive patriotism, and the easy juxtapositions of good and evil seem rarely to have done so. Throughout the mid-century the novel fed the theatre and the theatre the novel, generally to the detriment of both. The fitfully impressive social and historical novelist and playwright Charles Reade (1814–84) adapted and readapted his prison story *It Is Never Too Late To Mend* (1856) for both media and in 1857 his novel *White Lies* became his play *The Double Marriage*. It has been estimated that there were some 750 Victorian stage adaptations of the novels of Sir Walter Scott, and even by 1850 the stories of Dickens had been dramatized some 240 times, a process which continued until well after his death (and continues in very different theatrical circumstances today). These dramatizations sometimes presumed to offer endings to stories before the novelist himself had completed his serialization and had decided on his own conclusion. Unlike some of his fellow-authors, Dickens seems to have accepted the process sanguinely, readily recognizing the uses of the additional popular éclat it brought him.

Dickens's collaborator in the maladroit melodrama which eventually served to inspire *A Tale of Two Cities* was his friend William Wilkie Collins (1824–89).

The Frozen Deep, set in England and in the Arctic wastes, has been very rarely performed since the mid-1850s and then only at the risk of making an audience wince at its parade of hearts on sleeves and dizzily heightened emotions. Collins was, however, serious about the theatre. In 1855 he had collaborated with Dickens over another play, *The Lighthouse*, and in 1867 they jointly produced an acting version of Dickens's short story *No Thoroughfare*. Collins also provided in 1862 his own stage version of his novel *No Name*.

Despite his often flat and unexpressive style, Collins possessed an extraordinary narrative gift, one ideally suited to his pioneering interest in the evolution of the detective story rather than to the more immediate denouements of the theatre. His novels actively appealed to the demand in the 1860s for what has become known as 'sensation fiction', stories centred on theft, deception, or murder and during the course of which the nature of the crime and the motives of the criminal are revealed. Such sensationalism can be related both to the popular taste for melodrama and to the influence of the criminal fiction of the French writer Eugène Sue and his English imitator G. W. M. Reynolds (1814–79). In Collins's case, however, there is a refinement of the narrative invention of his fiction which is generally absent from the work of his rivals. *The Woman in White*, which was first serialized in Dickens's Journal *All the Year Round* in 1860, treats of insanity, selfishness, and guilty secrets. It also has perhaps the most colourful and suave of all Victorian villains, an Italian exile mixed up in secret societies and suspicious oath-takings (who has the singularly disconcerting habit of playing with white mice as he talks). The story is told through a series of cleverly juxtaposed eye-witness accounts. The scrupulous plotting and the control of suspense are also evident in *No Name* (1860) and the much admired *Armadale* (1864–5), the latter suggesting both a refined use of tension and suspense in its original serial divisions in the *Cornhill Magazine* and a careful manipulation of the discovery of evidence. Collins's masterpiece, *The Moonstone* (1868) (also first serialized in *All the Year Round*), is a multiple narrative which subtly explores the nature of detection and the vagaries of memory and observation. Its oriental background and its play with the effects of opium on the consciousness contribute an element of the exotic to an otherwise severely disciplined and steadily plotted pursuit of the science of detection. Collins remains the first, and undoubtedly the greatest, of the many English masters of the detective story.

Mary Elizabeth Braddon (1835–1915) achieved immediate popular acclaim with her gripping, almost breathless novel *Lady Audley's Secret*, hurriedly written for serial publication in 1862. It is the story of an ambitious murderess intent on covering up both her crime and her earlier career. Lady Audley is a highly distinctive villain/heroine who, despite her beauty and her social grace, displays few of the idealized qualities, and none of the passivity, that many Victorian readers and most Victorian writers readily associated with women (and particularly with 'ladies'). None of Braddon's eighty other novels, mostly written in response to the appeal of her first success, ever created the same sensation or have ever since been accorded the same prestige. As a skilled cultivator of literary fashion Braddon was well aware that fashions both move on and become jaded. In her *The Doctor's Wife* (1864) (the plot of which is loosely modelled on that of Flaubert's *Madame Bovary*) she poked fun at a somewhat down-market 'sensation author', Sigismund Smith, who had produced 'about half a dozen highly-spiced fictions, which enjoyed an immense popularity amongst the classes who like their literature as they like their tobacco—very strong'. While remaining keenly alert to the market for 'sensation', she was, in her own prime, determined to distinguish the best of her own efforts from run-of-the-mill fiction which merely exploited that market. Her best work followed closely in the wake of the success of *Lady Audley's Secret* and shared much of its inventive energy and narrative verve. *Aurora Floyd*, a tale of bigamy, blackmail, and murder, was serialized in 1862–3 concurrently with *John Marchmont's Legacy*. The latter novel is particularly tautly constructed, with a series of unexpected contrivances and cliff-hanging twists to the plot which seem to oblige a reader to collude in the process of solving the central mystery.

Much of the Indian material that Wilkie Collins used with such effect in *The Moonstone* may well suggest a debt to the most remarkable fictional account of thuggism in British India, Philip Meadows Taylor's *Confessions of a Thug* (1839). It is a highly individual, and often exotically charged, crime novel which draws from Taylor's detailed knowledge of India and of the murderous cult of thuggee (or thagi) that the British administration had fought hard to suppress between 1810 and the early 1830s. Taylor (1808–76), who had worked for the Nizam of Hyderabad as an assistant superintendent of police, gives his vivid story the form of the supposed confessions of the captive leader of a band of thugs, Ameer Ali, to an unnamed British officer. Ameer Ali expresses few regrets for his career, glorying, as his calm interlocutor notes, 'in describing the minutest particulars of his victims, and the share he had in their destruction, with scarcely a symptom of remorse'. The central character's 'swagger' and his often arch language, an English rendering of a 'pure and fluent' Urdu 'a little affected by his knowledge of Persian', serve to enhance the novel's distinctive evocation of an 'otherness' both in Ali's culture and, to Victorian English eyes, in his decidedly alien religious morality.

The New Fiction of the 1860s: Meredith and Eliot

The early work of George Meredith (1828–1909) created a sensation of quite another order. His first novel, *The Ordeal of Richard Feverel*, was banned by Mudie's Circulating Library for its supposed moral offence, and his most substantial volume of poetry *Modern Love* (1862) tackled the still *risqué* subject of the disintegration of a marriage. *Modern Love* may have emerged from personal circumstances and a private crisis, but, as its very title implies, it also expressed a distinctive 'modernity' in the circumstances of marital breakdown and the incompatibility of unloving partners. The fifty 16-line poems initially record the failure of a relationship and the venom and irritation that has replaced passion. The tensions are strikingly evident from the very first of the poems:

> By this he knew she wept with waking eyes;
> That, at his hand's light quiver by her head,
> The strange low sobs that shook their common bed,
> Were called into her with a sharp surprise,
> And strangled mute, like little gaping snakes,
> Dreadfully venomous to him. She lay
> Stone-still, and the long darkness flowed away
> With muffled pulses . . .
>
> .   .   .   .   .   .
>
> Like sculptured effigies, they might be seen
> Upon their marriage-tomb, the sword between;
> Each wishing for the sword that severs all.

The hypocrisy of the public pretence that all is well is countered at a half-way point in poem 25 by reference to the franker moral decisions described in a French novel; thereafter husband and wife lead separate lives, he actively consoling himself with a mistress.

It is, however, as Meredith himself proclaims, the 'Comic Spirit' that generally rules in his novels, a comedy that informs his representation of human discourse and his analysis of character. Meredith's female characters have a particularly distinctive quality, ranging from the calculated social mobility of Evan's sisters in *Evan Harrington* (1860) to the impulsive, restless independence of Diana Warwick in *Diana of the Crossways* (1885). His fascination with political manœuvre as an extension of amatory interaction (evident enough in the treatment of Diana's affair with a young politician, Percy Dacier) is considered more fully in the complex contortions and ramifications of *Beauchamp's Career* (1874–5). An interest in the political tensions of contemporary Italy shaped both *Sandra Belloni* (1864) and its sequel *Vittoria* (1867). Meredith has long been most admired for the substantial dialogue scenes and the tense comedy of English upper-class manners in *The Egoist* (1879). His once startling free-thinking, free-ranging morality and his dense narrative style held a special appeal for those late nineteenth-century critics and readers who sought to break away from the supposed restrictions of mid-Victorian moral earnestness.

George Eliot (1819–80) is the most earnestly imperative and the most probingly intelligent of the great mid-Victorian novelists. Her seriousness was readily praised and acclaimed by the reviewers of her first published works of fiction, the three *Scenes of Clerical Life* (originally printed in *Blackwood's*

Magazine in 1857) and the greatly esteemed *Adam Bede* (1859). Queen Victoria read *Adam Bede* with such pleasure that she not only keenly recommended it to her royal relatives but also commissioned two paintings of scenes from the novel. On one level the appeal of the book lay in its detailed and sympathetic representation of a rural community in the recent past, a working community free of the confusions and contradictions of the industrial and urban present; it also allowed for a new kind of heroism, a heroic uprightness which emerged from the conditions and the morality of ordinary country life. Eliot was not escaping into a rural idyll, but remoulding the expressive provinciality of much of the best of Scott's work. Despite her deliberate, bluntly English, masculine pseudonym, and the ruse that her narrator had the tastes, opinions, and clothes of a man, Charles Dickens, for one, perceived that 'no man ever before had the art of making himself mentally so like a woman since the world began'. Acknowledging the quality of her work he later tried, unsuccessfully, to persuade the now firmly established 'George Eliot' to write a new novel for him for serialization in his *All the Year Round*. The identity of the gender of the author hiding behind the pseudonym had at first been kept a close secret as a means of maintaining a public distinction between a highly moral narrator and a woman who, according to the narrow standards of her time, was an outcast, an adulteress and a religious sceptic. 'George Eliot' won respect as a writer on the merits of her work alone. That respect gradually eclipsed the affront to public morality presented by the Godless Marian Evans.

Marian Evans (or, as she generally preferred to call herself in deference to her unsanctified 'marriage' to the already married G. H. Lewes, Marian Lewes) was no stranger to controversy when she published her first stories. Her gradual loss of an intense girlhood Evangelicalism had been stimulated by her reading of the German 'Higher Criticism' of the Bible. Her first published work was a translation of *The Life of Christ Critically Examined by Dr David Friedrich Strauss* in 1846, and the only work published under her own name is her English version of Ludwig Feuerbach's *The Essence of Christianity* of 1854. Her scrupulous and demanding process of self-education had included the study of religious history, of the ancient classics (she remained especially fond of the plays of Aeschylus and Sophocles), of philosophy (especially that of Spinoza), of modern science, and of pioneer works of continental sociology and politics (notably the work of Auguste Comte). Much of this learning touched her fiction, not only providing her with chapter epigraphs and narratorial reflections but also, and far more significantly, shaping the nature and arguments of her novels. Her political guardedness—some might call it a cautious conservatism—and her general avoidance of outspokenness on matters of faith, feminism, and sexual morality may at first sight seem to run counter to the radical commitments of her private life. Essentially, however, the patient and generally tolerant narrative voice of Eliot's novels advocates a slow, considered, and gradual evolution. This evolution would, she suggests, become evident first in terms of human perception and action; only latterly would its beneficial effects on society at large be felt. Eliot's narrative voice consequently calls not simply for a sympathetic intellectual and emotional response from readers, but, more insistently, for a flexible and demanding moral one.

In spite of the tragedy of Hetty Sorrel and the moral and social failure of Arthur Donnithorne, *Adam Bede* generally seeks to uphold the values of an old-fashioned, deferential, and stratified England. It explores a society on the edge of change, one potentially divided by war and industrialization, but one still held together by religion and class-interdependence. In *The Mill on the Floss* (1860), however, Eliot examines a very different pattern of loyalties and relationships. The novel shows provincial English society which, while it reinforces family values, serves to stifle aspiration and particularly its heroine's bids for personal liberation. Maggie Tulliver is both an aspirer and a victim; she is blessed with a singularly happy childhood, but becomes disoriented when the stable world around her, and her assumptions about it, are gradually demolished. Experience brings only a limited wisdom, and the deluge of the novel's ending offers a resolution in the form of a catastrophe which literally overwhelms its protagonist. The far more schematized *Silas Marner* (1861) transforms rustic tragedy into a more optimistic moral fable, albeit a fable which explores a series of dense ethical, social, and spiritual dilemmas.

Eliot's acute sense of historical conditioning and of progressive development, clearly evident in her historical novel *Romola* (1863), also determines the nature of the political discourse of the two novels set in the period of the 1832 Reform Bill. *Felix Holt, the Radical* (1866) is a highly sophisticated and analytical political novel, though one now far removed from the preoccupations of the 'Condition of England' fiction of the 1840s. It may evade the issue of the radicalism promised by its title, but it nevertheless presents a highly perceptive, retrospective view of popular agitation in an English country town and it both animates debates about conservative fears for the Constitution and observes the distinctly limited changes that the Reform Bill actually brought about. Eliot's studies of provincial life reached their apogee in the densely argued, carefully wrought *Middlemarch* (1871–2). The novel is built around a 'web' of individual destinies each of which is interwoven with others and closely related to the determining spirit of the age. Its setting in the years 1829–32, its patient delineation of aspects of contemporary economic, social, artistic, scientific, and religious life, and its vivid contrasts of public and private history (and particularly of the juxtaposition of the historic burden of Rome and the evolving modern history of an English town), all give it an ambitious, epic resonance that few other novels have rivalled.

The Prelude to *Middlemarch* opens with a reference to the 'history of man' and narrows immediately to the particular history of a remarkable woman, St Theresa. The sixteenth-century Theresa, we realize, had scope and an 'epos' which is denied to the central fictional character, the nineteenth-century Dorothea Brooke. Both women aspire to serve and to reform, but Dorothea is shown as lacking the 'coherent social faith and order which could perform the function of knowledge for the ardently willing soul'. At the end of her story her destiny is likened to a broken river, its might spent in channels 'which had no great name of earth'. Dorothea's historical impact depends, ironically, on 'unhistoric acts', nameless and unremembered, and yet making for 'the growing good of the world'. Despite its epic potential, *Middlemarch* deliberately undermines epic by stressing that women like Dorothea are constricted, diminished, and silenced by the social conditioning inherited by the nineteenth century. Good deeds have to substitute for great ones. The only true feminist heroine that Eliot created is Romola de' Bardi. Romola's world is that of Renaissance Florence and her rejection of the narrow obligations of the Church and the State are observed within a framework of lost Renaissance values (albeit a framework shot through with Comtean prejudices about the futures of both Church and State).

Historical fiction generally seems to have offered Eliot an enterprising freedom absent from the novels set in periods nearer to her own time and in or near the landscapes of her own birthplace (the same is true of her ambitious, but ungainly, narrative poem *The Spanish Gipsy* of 1868). *Romola* can seem over-learned, stiff-jointed, and stumblingly expressed, but it has an experimental daring which is also evident in her much-criticized Anglo-Jewish novel, *Daniel Deronda* (1876). It is her most truly cosmopolitan work, dealing not simply with a cultivated European world of artists and musicians but also with the contrast between the sensibilities of a pampered and limited English aristocracy and those of despised, but intense, Jewish outsiders. *Daniel Deronda* consistently looks at a culture in need of redefinitions. It represents a new and restless spiritual yearning in its characters and a yet vaguer sense of disturbance at the threatening ideological prospects opening for European civilization in the late 1870s (the implications of Darwinism being prominent among them). At the end of the novel, Gwendolen Harleth may also appear to be a broken river flowing several ways at once, but she lacks both Romola's determined purpose and Dorothea's moral resources. She is aware of the 'terrible moment' when 'the great movements of the world, the larger destinies of mankind . . . enter like an earthquake into their own lives'. Eliot's geological metaphor does not imply that it is a moment of liberation. Gwendolen's is a crisis resultant from 'feeling the pressure of a vast mysterious movement' whose mystery remains unsolved, perhaps unsolvable. That movement does more than 'dislodge' her from her egotistical supremacy in her own world; it painfully unites her with an inevitable and not always welcome progress into an uncertain future, a future in which the destinies of both women and men are to be destabilized by the universal cultural earthquake.

The 'Strange Disease of Modern Life': Mill, Arnold, Clough, and Ruskin

From the late 1860s onwards, the prospect of radical change to society and to its political constitution was viewed with increasing unease by liberal and conservative-minded Victorians alike. The Macaulayan confidence concerning the benefits of progress had not exactly evaporated, but it had certainly been unsettled by an increasing awareness of the more disturbing implications of intellectual and social development. If the dual threats of revolutionary upheaval and of the imminent collapse of institutions which had so haunted the 1840s had receded, so too had the economic optimism and the spirit of compromise which mark the middle decades of the century. Significantly, the high tide of Victorian liberalism contained within it the understanding that tides both wax and wane. Matthew Arnold claimed that he heard the 'melancholy, long withdrawing roar' of the sea of faith on Dover Beach in 1867; others pointed to what they saw as the equally melancholy evidence of the sapping of the political status quo and of the stable foundations of bourgeois culture. The publication of Charles Darwin's *On the Origin of Species by Means of Natural Selection* (1859) presented an argued rejoinder to long accepted beliefs about humankind and its place in the order of creation. As Darwin's arguments, and those of his more vocal disciples, gradually forced informed opinion to adapt to its challenges, a sense of dislocation infected established modes of thought. A steady stream of pessimism emerged in English letters, accentuating an existing scepticism and reaching its climax in the 1880s. Darwin had effectively scotched the idea that humankind stood at the pinnacle of the universe as the lord of creation and the master of all it surveyed; he had also effectively undermined easy assumptions as to the nature of progress. The theory of natural selection shook the religious faith of the susceptible; more significantly, it unsteadied a secular and materialist view of the future. Although a positive response to Darwin's ideas was far from universal, even amongst the educated, a fashionable 'modern' gloom and uncertainty hung over English intellectual life and the literature of ideas in the last quarter of the nineteenth century, concentrating earlier doubts and uncertainties and opening the way to new, not always welcome, experimentation.

Much of the political despondency was related to the supposed consequences of the extension of the franchise by the second Reform Bill of 1867. Although passed by a Conservative government in order to steal the thunder of its Liberal opponents, it was frequently presumed that the Bill opened the way to a future mass democracy and that the masses posed a threat to the present workings of democracy. George Eliot expressed her cautious support for an extended franchise for the educated in her 'Felix Holt's Address to Working Men', but she nevertheless urged restraint and an avoidance of class antagonism. John Stuart Mill (1806–73), the leading philosopher of liberalism of his day, had, by contrast, been an active supporter of Reform in the House of Commons and a steady advocate of the extension of democracy. Mill remains the most articulate and sympathetic apologist for the cause of individual liberty. His great essay *On Liberty* (1859) defines, for a bourgeois democracy, the principles of mutual tolerance, of the freedom of the citizen, and of the non-interference of government. It was written at a time when the British parliamentary system had virtually no parallels on mainland Europe and when constitutional guarantees of the liberty of the citizen were either non-existent or disregarded outside the spheres of influence of Britain and the United States. It also appealed to an anti-theoretical, anti-institutional streak in English culture. 'A State which dwarfs its men', Mill argues at the end of his essay, 'in order that they may be more docile instruments in its hands even for beneficial purposes—will find that with small men no great thing can really be accomplished.' As he also crucially acknowledges, the democratic process had in the future to include women (his pioneer study *The Subjection of Women* was published in 1869).

Mill had emerged from a narrow Utilitarian background and from a strict educational regime which had virtually denied him a normal boyhood. Like one of the forced 'mental green peas' of Dr Blimber's school in *Dombey and Son*, Mill had been set to learn Greek at the age of 3; by 8 he was well versed in the classics; at 12 he was studying Aristotle's *Logic* and at 13 he was pursuing a course in political economy. As his *Autobiography* (1873) reveals, this educational forcing deprived him of a defined spiritual aspiration; not only was he untouched by religion (anti-clericalism had been as prominent in his training as had a hatred of aristocratic privilege), he was also unaware of the Romantic stress upon the creative power of the Imagination. Mill's discovery of Wordsworth's poetry in the autumn of 1828 delivered him, he claimed, from a nervous crisis and opened to him 'the very culture of the feelings' for which he had darkly yearned. His awareness of the rational as well as of the emotional, of the calculated as much as of the sensual, feeds his theoretical work. It also directs his libertarian and tolerant convictions beyond a Benthamite insistence on usefulness and happiness to an insistence both on freedom and on the propriety of constitutional safeguards in a free society.

In his provocative tract *Culture and Anarchy* (1869), Matthew Arnold (1822–88) offered definitions of a different kind. Arnold's argument intermixes a post-Carlylean irony and an often heavy-handed wit; it reiterates phrases, terms, and embodied ideas; it offers its readers what purports to be an investigative moralism and it attempts to establish the nature of a broad and all-embracing notion of culture. The influence and the intellectual discipline of his remarkable father Thomas Arnold, the eminent headmaster of Rugby school in the 1820s and 1830s and the godfather of Victorian earnestness, can be felt throughout. Dr Arnold had reformed his school by means of a hierarchical system of moral responsibilities and by fostering in his pupils an awareness of mutual obligations and the promptings of hyperactive consciences. His system had produced a generation of restless, socially conscious boys forced into adult decision-making before their proper time and often exhausted by the process. Few, however, felt able to express a disillusion with the headmasterly influence of Arnold, as the lasting popular success of the boys' story *Tom Brown's Schooldays* (1857), written by one of his less than star pupils, Thomas Hughes (1822–96), serves to suggest. Dr Arnold's boys were induced to take upon themselves the weight of a life-long struggle between truth and falsehood and between Christian independence and the atheistic tyranny of the mob.

Culture and Anarchy playfully divides English society into three constituent classes: a 'Barbarian' aristocracy, a 'Philistine' bourgeoisie and an unlettered 'Populace'. None of these classes either sympathizes with, or upholds, a truly refined high culture which could withstand further decay in the political and religious order. Arnold selectively cites ideas from the European cultural tradition in order to determine the nature of a new social and moral cement which could serve to bond classes together and also provide a fulfilling spiritual ethos capable of superseding sectarian religion. The narrow strictures of an inherited 'Hebraism', particularly in the Puritan culture of English religious Nonconformity, needed the balance of the softer and sweeter arts of the ancient Greeks in order to shape a more tolerant and fluent civilization which could do away with classes, sects, and élites. The book's satire is particularly barbed in its attack on the shortcomings of the pragmatic, anti-idealistic English present; its vision of the future offers an escape into a bright world which has abolished the tyranny of the low-brow. The spirit of universal enlightenment and of personal integrity could, Arnold held, transform mass democracy. Nevertheless, his argument suggests an earnest authoritarianism which both despises and suspects popular culture. It lays down rules and claims that it offers freedom; it enforces peace by effectively suppressing the inconvenient and the disruptive.

Arnold recoils from vulgarity throughout his prose works (he complains, for example, that the problem with the English Romantic poets lay in their provinciality and lack of wide reading). Nevertheless, his essays on Wordsworth, Shelley, and Keats are models of their kind, probing and illuminating and defending their subjects even when Arnold himself seems more inclined to diminish them. His criticism of the culture and the institutions of his time emerges both from a professional interest in education (he was appointed an inspector of schools by the government in 1851 and worked hard at the job for some thirty-five years) and from his own practice as a poet and as a student of the European poetic tradition. He tends to hold up the intellectual, philosophical, and educational enterprise of France and Germany to the decided detriment of a mentally foggy England. More significantly, he fatally ignores the real energy of the literature of his English contemporaries. He rarely mentions the poetry of Tennyson and Browning, he glances narrowly and unhelpfully at that of his friend Clough, and he generally implies that Dickens's novels are little more than classics of philistinism.

'The true basis for the creative power's exercise', Arnold noted in his essay 'The Function of Criticism at the present Time', was the fact that a poet lived 'in a current of ideas in the highest degree animating and nourishing' to his creativity. At such epochs, he added, society was 'in the fullest measure, permeated by fresh thought, intelligent and alive'. Arnold held that his own age

manifestly demonstrated that English society lacked the proper degree of intellectual permeation, or rather that its confusions and uncertainties militated
against the achievement of an expressive modern poetry. His own five volumes
of verse, published between 1848 and 1867, explore many of the negatives that
he saw in the culture around him. The upright, God-centred struggle for truth
of Dr Arnold celebrated in the poem 'Rugby Chapel' (1857, published 1867)
still holds meaning in the 'hideous, and arid, and vile' modern world, but both
the headmaster and God seem since to have withdrawn into silence. If his criticism seeks to counter negatives, his poetry embraces them, worries over them,
and attempts to redirect them towards some glimmer of progressive hope.
Arnold was well aware of a discrepancy between what he felt he had to say and
what he aspired to express as a poet. His longest poem, *Empedocles on Etna*,
first published in 1852, quickly struck him as too imbued with 'modern feeling'
(despite its classical subject), too expressive of 'depression and overtension of
mind'. He suppressed the poem a year later and apologized for its absence from
a new edition of the poems in a long self-defensive Preface. He did not reprint
it until 1867 when both the spirit of the age and the decline of his inspiration
seemed to justify its reappearance in print.

Arnold's 1853 Preface to a sequence of poems, some new, some reprinted,
some altered, argues that *Empedocles* had failed to 'inspirit and rejoice' its
readers. As if in response, the volume included one of Arnold's most resolvedly
'joyful' longer poems, 'The Scholar Gipsy', a poem which celebrates the twin
freedoms of an Oxford student's escape from routine and a poet's attempt to
escape into a history unburdened by present confusions and uncertainties:

> O born in days when wits were fresh and clear,
>   And life ran gaily as the sparkling Thames;
>   Before this strange disease of modern life,
>   With its sick hurry, its divided aims,
>   Its heads o'ertax'd, its palsied hearts, was rife—
>   Fly hence, our contact fear!
>   Still fly, plunge deeper in the bowering wood!
>   Averse, as Dido did with gesture stern
>   From her false friend's approach in Hades turn,
>   Wave us away, and keep thy solitude.

The student's escape is into an unattached, gipsy rejection of the consequences
of the urban civilization of the nineteenth century (the Thames is still
'sparkling' as it had for Spenser and not the polluted sewer of Dickens's
novels). Like Virgil's Dido, he can spurn the representative of the progressive
and inevitable future because that restless future is not his. Arnold's essential
ambiguity about the present, and his poignant nostalgia for an easier and idealized past are also evident in his elegiac monody for the dead Clough, 'Thyrsis'
(1867). The poem returns to the same contours of the Oxfordshire landscape,
but now imbues them with reminiscences of the Greek and Roman pastoral

tradition which both Arnold and Clough had studied as schoolboys amid the old certainties of Rugby. 'Thyrsis' too is haunted by the 'stormy note of men contention-tost' and the restless soul of the dead poet is required to act as an inspirer, an elusive bringer of joy to a world which, despite its physical beauty, has lost its spiritual way. Arnold's determined, but none the less vague, directions to future progress, like his conjuration of the spirits of his father and of Clough, sound a note of desperate optimism. In the poem called 'The Future' (1853), the river of Time has swept humanity from mountain fastnesses to the grubby, industrialized plain of the nineteenth century, 'border'd by cities and hoarse | With a thousand cries'. The immediate prospect is only of 'blacker cities and louder din', and those on the river's 'flowing breast' will never see 'an ennobling sight, | Drink of the feeling of quiet again'. The poem ultimately offers a vision of a future oblivion, blissfully and vaguely lost in 'the murmurs and scents of the infinite Sea'. The capital 'S' for the sea here both suggests God's complicity and denies it. Arnold's image can be read both as implying something akin to a Tennysonian purpose in nature and as a passive drift into nothingness.

It is Arnold, rather than Arthur Hugh Clough, who was the true 'too quick despairer' of 'Thyrsis'. Where Arnold suggested the force of alienation, Clough strove for some kind of human and moral attachment; where Arnold sought to associate himself with the spirit of the times and then agonized over its defective joylessness, Clough detachedly accepted and exploited contradiction. Clough (1819–61) was described by another Rugby schoolfriend as having received 'into an unusually susceptible and eager mind the whole force of that electric shock which [Dr] Arnold communicated to all his better pupils'. Clough's later agnosticism retained a sometimes startling frankness and honesty; his disillusion was, however, generally shaped by a diffidence, a wit, and an acceptance of the failure of mission. He is a candid poet, rarely fretful but rarely confident; one who almost relishes the nature of doubt and the anarchy of multiple ways of seeing. In his greatest poem, the sequence of verse letters *Amours de Voyage* (1858), he announces its prospective irresolution in four brief epigraphs (in English, French, and Latin) which variously suggest self-absorption, self-doubt, the elusiveness of love, and the freedom of travel. The poems, written in hexameter, are expressed in a relaxed, conversational manner and tellingly detailed with snatches of travelogue, dialogue, and gestures of self-analysis on the parts of the various correspondents. They are set against the background of the disruptions of Italian politics, and particularly the brief establishment of a Roman Republic in 1848–9. Claude, Clough's male correspondent from Italy, seems bemused by human relationships and bewildered by the violence which intrudes both into his Roman sightseeing and into his English political assumptions. In the seventh letter to Canto II he describes the messy, almost casual murder of a priest by a Republican mob:

I was returning home from St Peter's; Murray, as usual
Under my arm, I remember; had crossed the St Angelo bridge; and
Moving towards the Condotti, had got to the first barricade, when
Gradually, still thinking of St Peter's, I became conscious
Of a sensation of movement opposing me,—tendency that way
(Such as one fancies may be in a stream when the wave of the tide is
Coming and not yet come,—a sort of poise and retention);
So I turned, and, before I turned, caught sight of stragglers
Heading a crowd, it is plain, that is coming behind that corner . . .

                    .   .   .   .

                                                and now the
Crowd is coming, has turned, has crossed the last barricade, is
Here at my side. In the middle they drag at something. What is it?
Ha! bare swords in the air, held up! There seem to be voices
Pleading and hands putting back; official, perhaps; but the swords are
Many, and bare in the air. In the air? They descend; they are smiting
Hewing, chopping—At what? In the air once more upstretched! And
Is it blood that's on them? Yes, certainly blood! Of whom, then?
Over whom is the cry of this furor of exultation?

Claude's conversational tone here, commas, dashes, questions, and all, allows
for a sense of incomprehending urgency. Elsewhere, his detachment becomes
almost mocking, variously shifting his tone from one of polite chit-chat to discussions of religion, from a disillusion with Roman monuments to sexual flirtation, from artistic discrimination to political nonchalance. As its title suggests,
Amours de Voyage is a love-poem, or rather it is a poem about casual love-
making and love-doubting. Its fragmentary nature and its revolutionary setting
establish an awareness of the transitory and arbitrary nature of human contact
and human experience, something which had been less successfully dealt with
in Clough's earlier narrative experiment *The Bothie of Tober na Vuolich* (1848).
Shifting perspectives and a fascination with religion and with the failure of the
religious impulse also mark Clough's best lyric verse, such as 'The New
Sinai' and 'Bethesda: A Sequel'. His real enough sympathy with the Italian
Risorgimento is clear in politically committed poems such as 'Peschiera' and
'Alteram Partem'; his playful, mildly provocative wit shines through his jests
about money, in 'Spectator ab Extra' (with its chorus 'How pleasant it is to
have money, heigh ho!'), and his commentary on moneyed middle-class
misinterpretations of the Ten Commandments in 'The Latest Decalogue'.
    Clough's poems were collected posthumously in 1862 and 1869 when the
impact of his religious and social agnosticism was heightened by sympathetic
echoes in the work of other distinctly 'modern' writers. From the 1860s
onwards the writing of the century's greatest art critic, John Ruskin
(1819–1900) assumed an equally challenging new edge. Ruskin's 'agnosticism',
if it can properly be described as such, consisted of a gradual rejection of the
narrow, strident Protestantism of his childhood and early manhood and in a

discovery of a puzzling multifariousness in the natural, industrial, spiritual, and human worlds. In 1860 he had begun publishing in the newly founded *Cornhill Magazine* a series of essays, entitled *Unto This Last*, concerning the economic and social integrity of mid-Victorian Britain, but the challenges he threw down to the readers of the journal proved offensive to middle-class palates and he was obliged to abort the series (the essays appeared in book form in 1862). The essays attempt to redefine value by moving beyond economic theory into moral speculation. Ruskin expresses himself with a bald, almost innocent, simplicity, steadily establishing his premises and drawing conclusions which demolish a complacent economic and social *laissez-faire*. His basis is firmly Christian, deriving much of its language and metaphoric power from the parables of Jesus, but his definitions were intended to apply not simply to an ancient agrarian economy, but to a modern industrial society blinded by acquisitiveness. Definitions of value, he insisted, must be related to whatever 'avails towards life'. The 'real science of political economy' as he defined it, had to be distinguished from an existing 'bastard' science of economics in order that it might teach nations both 'to desire and labour for the things that lead to life' and to 'scorn and destroy the things that lead to destruction'. Ruskin's moral teaching, like his art criticism, was not to be confined and defined by accepted dogmas, disciplines, and sectarian interpretations. *Unto This Last* applies basic Christianity to a mechanized and urban civilization that he increasingly found morally and aesthetically repugnant. It later became one of the pillars of a very English, untheoretical Socialism.

Ruskin's literary career consisted of a hugely expanding, but interconnected, series of experimental essays. He began in *Modern Painters* (1843, 1846, 1856, 1860) by ambitiously attempting to place the paintings of J. M. W. Turner in various contexts, most startlingly of all in relation to extensive and multifarious definitions of Truth, Beauty, Imagination, Representation, and Nature. The third volume of *Modern Painters* (1856) is broadly, typically, and somewhat disconcertingly, subtitled 'Of Many Things'. The vast learning and the range of literary references in *Modern Painters* still allows for substantial and carefully worked descriptive passages where Ruskin's wonderfully emotive mastery of a lucid style is most evident. The slow evolution of the often sprawling arguments of *Modern Painters* was interrupted in 1849 by the composition of an influential treatise on the art of building—*The Seven Lamps of Architecture*—and by the three volumes of *The Stones of Venice* (1851–3). Ruskin's work has sometimes been seen as a series of digressions from a central concern with painting, digressions which lead him into increasingly arcane and voluminous analysis. His books are better seen as complements to one another, growing organically from related roots, stems, and branches, but developed in particular ways. His concern with the problems of modern society, for instance, is always implicit in his dissections of historic experience and achievement; once it emerges explicitly, as in the famous chapter on 'The Nature of Gothic' in the second volume of *The Stones of Venice* (1853), he establishes certain leading ideas which he insistently develops in other essays, tracts, and lectures. His discussion of the triumph and decline of Venice links geography to geology, urban history to economic and social history, painting to religion, architecture to morality and to a perception of shape and colour. His Venice, though meticulously observed in its historic context, is always a paradigm for Victorian Britain. If its glory could potentially also be Britain's, so, he warns, could its decline into insignificance and its political extinction.

Ruskin's work requires multiple reading. Its encyclopaedic density is always related both to its complex structures and to its attempt to co-ordinate an often contradictory pattern of observations and understandings. His frenetic energy, his expository imagination, his exploration, and his attempts to hold a range of disparate elements together were, however, countered by the increasing strains of mental breakdown. From the 1870s his work is yet more miscellaneous, though often brilliant in the gestures which illuminate an increasing darkness and in an occasional clarity which balances a pervasive desperation. His digressive and evasive autobiography *Praeterita*, published serially between 1885 and 1889, marginalizes the painful elements in his experience and concentrates instead on formative traits and, above all, on his private and meticulous discovery of nature and art. His late prose has an extraordinary limpidity, rising to *crescendi* and melting away into contemplation. *Praeterita* suggests something of the force with which Ruskin helped his contemporaries to see and to analyse what they saw. He was ravished not simply by the Alps or by Turner's representations of the sublime, but by the delicate and the ostensibly inconsequential, by hoar frost and by the 'beautiful lines' of a small aspen tree against the blue sky near Fontainebleau, 'composed . . . by finer laws than any known of men'. He saw 'the thing itself' and communicated both a scientific enthusiasm and a semi-religious wonder to the vast and various body of his disciples.

The 'Second Spring' and Hopkins

In spite of the very public admissions of religious doubt, and the post-Darwinian accentuation of the so-called Victorian 'crisis of faith', the nineteenth century remained a profoundly religious age, a period when the faith of Britain's numerous, and often mutually antagonistic, Christian confessions still managed to touch all classes and moulded both their social morality and their patterns of thought. If a substantial body of conscience-stricken intellectuals found themselves bereft of a comfortable faith and persuaded of the validity of arguments against a revealed religion, a considerable swathe of the working classes was reconverted by the energy, conviction, and respectability of the numerous Nonconformist chapels and reclaimed by the rituals of the Anglican and Roman churches. Very few Dissenting ministers found favour with Victorian novelists, however, their zeal being frequently confused with cant, their Puritan heritage implying that they were sympathetic neither to the arts nor to the existing social order. Upwardly mobile Dissenters were supposedly notorious defectors to the Established Church, while the more vociferously eccentric of their ministers were caricatured as Dickens's Melchisedek Howlers, red-nosed Stigginses, and oily Chadbands. Only with Elizabeth Gaskell's patient Quakers and socially conscious Unitarians and George Eliot's Methodists do the Nonconformist faithful find sympathetic delineators. George Eliot is also the most scrupulous and fair observer of the social impact of the Anglican Evangelical movement of the early 1800s, a movement deriving much of its own spirituality and drive from the earlier example of Methodism. Her representation of the mission of the Reverend Edgar Tryon to the backsliding community of Milby, in the third and longest of her *Scenes of Clerical Life*, forms a striking contrast to the very different antipathy provoked by the arrival in Barchester of Trollope's crusading Mrs Proudie and her protégé, Obadiah Slope (it is evident that Trollope shares much of his characters' dyspeptic reaction to the disruptive innovators).

Trollope's Barchester novels also touch on the other Anglican revolution, the Catholic revival within the Church of England known from its place of origin in the early 1830s as the 'Oxford Movement'. The Oxford Movement redirected an old-fashioned High Churchmanship into new channels of spirituality and reform; it was both a reaction against State interference in religious affairs in the 'Age of Reform' and a revitalization of the spirit of the great sixteenth- and seventeenth-century divines, Hooker, Laud, Andrewes, Ferrar, Donne, Herbert, and Ken. It stimulated a new generation of hymn writers and poets, primarily John Keble (1792–1866), the author of the placid, but much reprinted, volume *The Christian Year* (1827) which offered meditations on the festivals of the Anglican church year. The new attention to liturgy and to liturgical celebration emphasized by the leaders of the Oxford Movement also encouraged the translation of Latin and Greek hymns, such as those of John Mason Neale (1818–66), and the considerable body of religious poetry of the pious Christina Rossetti (who was steadily and devoutly drawn to Anglican ritualism).

In terms of fiction, the Oxford Movement's most articulate and influential disciple was Charlotte Mary Yonge (1823–1901), the author of some 150 works and most notably of *The Heir of Redclyffe* (1853), *The Daisy Chain* (1856), *The Trial* (1863), and *The Clever Woman of the Family* (1865). *The Heir of Redclyffe*, morally centred on an exploration of the ideals of Christian chivalry, spiritual generosity, and self-sacrifice, proved to be one of the great best-sellers of the age, earning for itself a wide range of emotional and discriminating readers who were as likely to be officers serving in the Crimea as they were Pre-Raphaelites.

The dominant figure amongst the original leaders of the Oxford revival was John Henry Newman (1801–90), a theologian of great originality, an elaborately persuasive thinker, preacher, and essayist, an elegantly fluent composer of prose argument, a poet of occasional subtletly, and the author of two creakily propagandist novels. Newman's probingly scrupulous mind led him inevitably away from attempts to justify the Anglican compromise into the newly energetic Roman Catholic Church, a Church romantically emerging in England from three centuries of persecution and enforced obscurity (Newman referred in a sermon to its new status and to its revived hierarchy as a 'Second Spring'). His conversion, certainly the most notable, even notorious, in nineteenth-century England, seemed to assert the renewed strengths and attractions of dogmatic and ceremonial religion in an age characterized by scholarly questioning and secular doubt. Newman's laboured but witty description of the process of conversion in his Oxford novel *Loss and Gain* (1848) is balanced by the detailed, if often evasive, account of his life and character later presented in the autobiographical *Apologia Pro Vita Sua* (1864, 1865).

To Dickens, and other Victorian progressives, the assertiveness of the Oxford Movement and the magnetism of the revived Roman Church seemed to be dangerous examples of 'Ecclesiastical Dandyism', an undoing of national history and a self-indulgent withdrawal from more urgent modern concerns. The career of Gerard Manley Hopkins (1844–89) might certainly have suggested the impropriety of such a withdrawal had the nature of his twin vocations to the Jesuit priesthood and to poetry been more widely known to his contemporaries. His conversion to Roman Catholicism at Oxford, and his decision to enter the Society of Jesus in 1868, effectively cut him off from the mainstream of contemporary English life. The failure of his Jesuit superiors to recognize and encourage his idiosyncratic poetic talent also severed him from the body of prospective readers to which he most earnestly sought to appeal. He burned much of his early work on his ordination and took up poetry again only in 1875 with the startlingly radical 'The Wreck of the Deutschland', a poem which the editor of the Jesuit periodical, *The Month*, decided that he 'dared not print'. No representative edition of Hopkins's poetry appeared until 1918.

Hopkins was fortunate in the poet-friends with whom he corresponded, Richard Watson Dixon and Robert Bridges (1844–1930), the latter his literary executor and editor. These non-Jesuit correspondents were the recipients of the theories that he attempted to articulate and of the often extraordinary poems that were developed in relation to these experimental ideas. After 1918 his work found the wide receptive audience which it had earlier been denied, but Hopkins's experiments, like the culture from which they emerge, remain essentially of the nineteenth century. As his Journals reveal, he observed nature in painstaking detail, patiently examining flowers and leaves, intently noting the effects of light and shade, and delighting in the gradations of texture and colour. Given the stringency of his Jesuit surroundings, his immediate culture may have been one of aesthetic deprivation, but his habits of observation and recording had been long acquired. His attention to the exactness of things is indeed akin to that of the Pre-Raphaelite painters (if not to Pre-Raphaelite poets) and his methods of analysis indicate a scrupulous Ruskinian apprenticeship. Hopkins's intellectual disciplines certainly benefited from his study of theology, and in particular from his somewhat eccentric (given the prejudices of his teachers) pleasure in the thought of the thirteenth-century philosopher Duns Scotus ('who of all men most sways my spirits to peace'). His poetry may have been far too idiosyncratic to appeal to the somewhat saccharine tastes of his contemporary co-religionists, but his structures derive from highly disciplined and often traditional ways of thinking, seeing, translating, and writing.

Most of Hopkins's surviving poems are distinctly God-centred. His is a God who resolves contradictions as the fount of all that is and as the Creator who draws all the strands of Creation back to himself. Created nature is in itself immensely precious, for the glory and wonder of God is implicit in it. In 'Pied Beauty' Hopkins celebrates harmonized oppositions, dapples and 'all things counter, original, spare, strange' because they express the energy and vitality of the visible world, a world held together by a divine force which constantly regenerates it. Undoing, desolation, and the 'problem of pain' are, however, never eliminated from his most searching poems. At times it is humankind which mars the integrity of beauty by unfeelingly trampling 'the growing green', by felling the 'especial' sweetness of a line of poplars, or by caging skylarks, but Hopkins is never simply or naïvely 'green'. His poems also explore the presence of violence in the realm of the parahuman. Despite the wonder of it, the windhover's ecstatic swoop is none the less predatorial, breaking lines and straining words as it falls:

> I caught this morning morning's minion, king-
>   dom of daylights dauphin, dapple-dawn-drawn Falcon, in his riding
> Of the rolling level underneath him steady air, and striding
> High there, how he rung upon the rein of a wimpling wing
>
> In his ecstasy! then off, off forth on swing,
>   As a skate's heel sweeps smooth on a bow-bend: the hurl and gliding
>   Rebuffed the big wind. My heart in hiding
> Stirred for a bird,—the achieve of, the mastery of the thing.
>
> Brute beauty and valour and act, oh, air, pride, plume, here
>   Buckle! AND the fire that breaks from thee then, a billion
> Times told lovelier, more dangerous, O my chevalier!
>   No wonder of it: shéer plód makes plough down sillion
> Shine, and blue-bleak embers, ah my dear,
>   Fall, gall themselves, and gash gold-vermilion.

The windhover's beauty is 'brute', yet its 'brutality' is of the essence of its animal perfection. Hopkins's poem gasps at the wonder of a creature whose free movement and concentrated strength stir an awesome sense of the presence of the Creator-Redeemer (its subtitle directs it 'To Christ our Lord'). Elsewhere in his work, most notably in the complex theological frameworks of 'The Wreck of the Deutschland' and the parallel poem 'The Loss of the Eurydice', Hopkins ponders the mystery of human suffering by forging parallels with a paradoxical Christ, the Man of Sorrows and the Suffering Servant who is, at the same time, the Divine Judge and the Merciful Redeemer. He pulls dissolution into resolution by seeing patterns, not simply in the seasons or in the forms of nature, but also in religious imagery, in the observances of the Christian calendar, and in the ultimate meaning of the universe. The very intricacy of his verse is an attempt to express and record something of the multifariousness of the visible and aural world. The very 'difficulty' and the contortion of his poetry, its intellectual leaps and its violent 'metaphysical' yoking together of images, offer a momentary stasis and a fusion of divergent insights and impressions. Hopkins found order where other Victorians saw anarchy; he recognized purpose where many of his contemporaries began to despair over what they presumed was an increasingly meaningless fragmentation. Even in his dark, straining, disappointing, despairing last sonnets ('No worst, there is none', 'To seem the stranger lies my lot', 'I wake and feel the fell of dark, not day', 'Patience, hard thing!', 'My own heart let me have more pity on') there still remains the conviction that somehow a barely comprehended God comprehends all things.

Coda: Carroll and Lear

On 4 July 1862, a full year before Hopkins went up to Balliol College, Oxford, the Reverend Charles Lutwidge Dodgson (1832–98), a mathematics don at Christ Church, Oxford, began to tell the story which he provisionally entitled *Alice's Adventures Underground* to the children of Dean Liddell. The 'golden afternoon' of fond memory was, according to the meteorological records of the period, a 'cool and rather wet' day in Oxford, but the narrative that emerged from that damp picnic on the banks of the Thames plays throughout its course with reversals, projections, upheavals, and dreams. Lewis Carroll, the name under which Dodgson disguised himself for the publication in 1865 of the revised story, now renamed *Alice's Adventures in Wonderland*, had managed to transcend the dry reserve demanded by his clerical and educational position. After a period of scrupulous hesitation, in which he had looked for a vocation amid what he described in his diary as the propounded 'nostrums' and the negative 'Babel of voices' of mid-Victorian England, Dodgson had accepted the dull stability of life as a mathematics don and had been ordained a deacon in the Church of England. 'It is a *good* thing', his bishop had remarked, 'that many of our educators should be men in Holy Orders.' The author of *A Syllabus of Plain Algebraical Geometry* (1860), *Condensation of Determinants* (1866), and *Euclid and his Modern Rivals* (1879) appears to have remained untroubled by the scientific and religious controversies of his time, yet it is perhaps from a combination of a rapt delight in mathematical order and pattern and a perception of the workings of God in a shapely universe that the logic of his children's fantasies emerges. *Alice's Adventures in Wonderland*,

Through the Looking-Glass and What Alice Found There (1872), and *The Hunting of the Snark* (1876) have quite eclipsed Dodgson's professional scholarship, but all three suggest a pleasure in exploring nonsense because nonsense, like looking-glasses, offered an alternative way of viewing things. 'Lewis Carroll' recognizes the joy in disjunction, distortion, and displacement because they are mirror images of unity, shapeliness, and stability.

The emergence of an intelligent and whimsical children's literature was perhaps the most remarkable result of the revolution in sensibility which came to see children as distinct from adults rather than as adults-in-waiting. Essentially the work of both Carroll and of Edward Lear (1812–88) transformed adult assumptions by considering them through the eyes of children. Pomposity, pretension, and all conventional pieties have, therefore, to be radically rejudged and re-presented. This is not to say that Victorian children's literature rigorously excludes adult concerns, but that however gloomy and perplexing the grown-up world might seem to be, there remained a space in which the playful and the joyfully absurd could triumph. There is a wistful sadness about the work of both Carroll and Lear, both of them lonely and to some degree unfulfilled men, but neither dwells self-indulgently on the problems of the alienated adult self. For both, the recapture of childhood seems to offer release. Lear's world is full of terrors, errors, and misapprehensions (as his limericks vividly suggest) but the sing-song of his rhythms holds them (just) in their due place. If his longer poems ('The Owl and the Pussy Cat' and 'The Jumblies' of 1871 and 'The Dong with a Luminous Nose' of 1877) echo something of the nostalgic, elusive yearning of Tennyson, when Lear writes directly of himself (as in the lyric, 'How pleasant to know Mr Lear') his lightness of touch banishes melancholy almost as soon as it is evoked:

> 'How pleasant to know Mr Lear!'
> Who has written such volumes of stuff!
> Some think him ill-tempered and queer,
> But a few think him pleasant enough. . . .
>
> He weeps by the side of the ocean,
> He weeps on the top of the hill;
> He purchases pancakes and lotion,
> And chocolate shrimps from the mill.
>
> He reads but he cannot read Spanish,
> He cannot abide ginger-beer;
> Ere the days of his pilgrimage vanish,
> How pleasant to know Mr Lear!

For Lewis Carroll, poetry offered the opportunity to play rhythmically with the paradoxes and whimsically with philosophical propositions which clearly fascinated him in his professional life. This is evident not simply in his parodies of Isaac Watts, Southey, or Wordsworth or in his jesting at Old English verse (in 'Jabberwocky') but also in his stretchings of logic in *The Hunting of the Snark* (1876) and of sense in 'The Walrus and the Carpenter':

> The sun was shining on the sea,
>   Shining with all his might:
> He did his best to make
>   The billows smooth and bright—
> And this was odd, because it was
>   The middle of the night.

In Carroll's narratives paradox finds resolution once there has been assent to the idea of an ultimate and alternative order in which the findings of science, philosophy, and religion are not in conflict. The two Alice books have a commonsensical protagonist, a child insistent on the rightness of the values of middle-class society and of the elementary education that she takes with her into landscapes which warp, overturn, and subvert ordinary perception. Alice survives her nightmares perhaps because she is only partly aware that they are nightmares; her self-confidence gives her a mental clarity which can counter the games, the formulae, and the twisted syllogisms which confront her. When the universe periodically threatens to explode or dissolve around her, Alice the representative child is rendered a survivor both by her own earnest assurance and by the circumambient, often riddling logic of the narrative. Alice wakes from her dreams, or crosses back through the looking-glass into what child readers are led to assume is an emotionally, physically, and intellectually secure world. Its securities proved far less certain to the generation of newly mature writers whose work dominated the closing years of the nineteenth century.

8

Late Victorian and Edwardian Literature 1880–1920

On the title-page of his *Past and Present* of 1843 Thomas Carlyle had quoted Schiller's strident sentiment *'Ernst ist das Leben'* ('Life is earnest'). Some seven years later, in chapter 42 of *David Copperfield*, Dickens's hero expresses the opinion that 'there is no substitute for thorough-going, ardent, and sincere earnestness'. By the closing years of the nineteenth century such mid-Victorian moral confidence had begun to sound oppressively, even comically, outmoded. Oscar Wilde, for one, mocked at the very idea in the title of his 'Trivial Comedy for Serious People', *The Importance of Being Earnest* (1895) and it was scarcely casually that Samuel Butler selected Ernest as the Christian name of the intellectually and morally flabby hero of his *The Way of All Flesh* (1903). By the 1880s, when Butler was working on his novel, the virtues of old-fashioned earnestness—which entailed moral probity, religious orthodoxy, sexual reserve, hard work, and a confident belief in personal and historical progress—were open to question or had been supplanted by a new and more probing seriousness. In retrospect, the mid-Victorians looked both wrong, and, when their influence could be escaped, funny.

Although Queen Victoria, that embodiment of matronly uprightness, reigned until January 1901, and although the last years of her reign appeared to patriotic observers to mark the apogee of national and imperial glory, 'Victorian' values, beliefs, and standards of personal and social behaviour were already being challenged, sometimes angrily, by a new generation of intellectuals and writers. The literature of the last twenty years of the century engages in an extended and various discourse which attempts to re-evaluate the assumptions of the 1850s and 1860s and to work out the implications of new concepts of liberation and evolutionary development. If the writers of the first two-thirds of the century can be seen as struggling to come to terms with a multiplicity of impressions, convictions, facts, beliefs, and unbeliefs, their immediate successors reworked ideas and sought parallels, analogues, or images in contemporary scientific thought. They also agonized over disturbing new conclusions. When the instinctive Tess Durbeyfield voices a vague but ominous

dread of 'life in general' in Hardy's *Tess of the D'Urbervilles* (1891), her interlocutor, Angel Clare, perceives that she was 'expressing in her own native
phrases . . . feelings which might almost have been called those of the age—
the ache of modernism'. If this aching 'modernism' produced relatively little
experiment with new literary forms, it did seem to imply that inherited literary forms should be adapted to express what many writers assumed was a
general unease. The stress of novelty fell on messages, not on media. If the
bourgeois reader had to be shocked out of his or her complacency, as *Tess of
the D'Urbervilles* shocked some of its first readers, that shock of the new
seemed best administered through accepted and acceptable literary forms.
Conservatism of form did not, however, serve to blunt the frequent radicalism
of content.

The shift in literary tastes in the 1890s is suggested by the glance back to
the period offered in May Sinclair's novel *Mary Olivier* (1919). Sinclair points
to the contrast between the bookshelves of her would-be liberated heroine, who
reads Hardy, Meredith, and Kipling for stimulus, and those of her unadventurous mother who prefers to relax with the novels of Anthony Trollope. The
contrast between generations and attitudes is yet more pointed in George
Bernard Shaw's play *You Never Can Tell* (1896) where the liberal education of
an emancipated woman of the 1870s, an education based on studying Huxley,
Mill, and George Eliot, is wittily dismissed as now having nothing in it which
would 'prevent her marrying an archbishop'. It was not simply that certain
opinions had gone out of fashion, or had been discredited, but that late
Victorian readers tended to condition the idea of human progress with a prominent Darwinian question mark. Society itself was assumed to be developing
according to certain laws, but they were laws which threatened old, orderly
assumptions by introducing notions of flux, chance, and adaptation. The
movement for women's rights, and the emergence of the so-called 'New
Woman' (who, like Shaw's Mrs Clandon, rapidly became less new), was as
much a cultural norm as were the vituperative parliamentary debates over the
destinies of Ireland within or outside the United Kingdom and the extra-
parliamentary debates concerning the likelihood of a socialist future. After the
Reform Acts of 1867 and 1885, the extension of the franchise to a substantial
proportion of working-class men brought nearer the prospect of future mass-
politics, with the masses themselves determining the very nature of the commonwealth. The advent of popular democracy, and mass popular dissent,
seemed to many observers to entail the diminution of the function and ideology of British Liberalism. It also threatened to break the old consensus
politics of the mid-century. Socialism, shocking enough to Mrs Clandon,
struck propagandist and partisan writers such as Shaw and Wells as the true
liberating politics of the future. In 1894 even the often bland, and generally
unearnest, Oscar Wilde could voice the opinion that 'we are all of us more or
less socialists now-a-days'. In that 'more or less', however, lay the real dilemma
of the times.

The 'Agnostic' Fiction of the Late Century

English fiction in the last two decades of the nineteenth century has all too frequently been seen as dominated by the work of the subtle, demanding, expatriate American, Henry James (1843–1916), and by that of the novelist patronizingly dismissed by James as 'the good little Thomas Hardy'. The reality is both more complex and wide-ranging. James's increasingly elusive novels took time to find a discriminating and appreciative audience, while Hardy's far more popular, but rural and provincial, stories contrast strikingly with the predominantly urban, and indeed urbane, fiction of ideas which also marks the period. Mrs Humphry Ward's novel *Robert Elsmere* appeared in 1888 and sold 40,000 copies in Britain in its first year of publication (it sold some 100,000 more in America). These sales were stimulated by a series of vexed, dismayed reviews of the book, including one by the devout former Prime Minister, W. E. Gladstone. Mary Ward (1851–1920), still generally known to her readers by her married name, was the daughter of Dr Arnold's most wayward son Thomas and the niece of Matthew Arnold. The intellectual endeavour and aspiration of these earlier Arnolds saturate her work, but so does a distinct feminine and feminist bias and an equally individual, questioning spirit.

Robert Elsmere suggests that a chasm has opened up between the Christian earnestness of Dr Arnold's Rugby and those who resolutely search for a religion and a morality beyond the closed world of dogmatic Christianity. Its hero, an Anglican priest, becomes increasingly troubled by doubts occasioned by the German 'Higher Criticism', doubts which are reinforced by his acquaintance with the infidel local squire who has belatedly pursued his studies at the 'unextinguished hearth' of the University of Berlin. Elsmere's own deconversion is slow and deliberate. It follows a refusal merely to 'look after the poor and hold his tongue', and the novel traces both an intense intellectual struggle (which is largely confined to male characters) and a strained relationship with his loving, but loyally orthodox Christian wife. When he resigns his orders, Elsmere retains his dedication to the betterment of society by finding a new mission amongst the unchurched poor of the East End of London. His is a dedication to a demythologized Jesus and to a secular 'Church'. His 'New Brotherhood of Christ', a body which espouses the principles of ethical and social improvement, nevertheless steers well clear of socialism. As a child, Ward had been alerted to the personal and social ramifications of religious controversy by her father's periodic and painful driftings between the Roman Catholic and Anglican Churches. Her novel openly discusses the religious doubts which had remained merely implicit in Elizabeth Gaskell's *North and South* and the agnosticism which had formed the often unrecognized subtext of George Eliot's fiction, but its particular force and intelligence are very much part of a new, frank, if less optimistic, culture in which Mrs Ward is a central figure. Her later fiction includes the masterly study of the tensions between Catholicism and free-thinking, *Helbeck of Bannisdale* (1898), and *Marcella* (1894), the story of an idealistic, socialist heroine struggling with the dilemma posed by her love for an uncompromisingly Tory landowner. *Marcella* is a subtle, but ultimately ambivalent novel, one in which both love and philanthropy manage to share the ultimate victory.

The work of Samuel Butler (1835–1902) is also central to the cultural debates of the 1880s and 1890s, though Butler's best-known works, *Erewhon, Or Over the Range*, and *The Way of All Flesh*, were published respectively in 1872 and 1903. Despite his scholarly, if idiosyncratic, debates with Darwin and Darwinism (which dominate his output in the 1880s), Butler struck his contemporaries as *homo unius libri*, a man of one book. That book was his utopian fantasy *Erewhon* (its title being an anagram of 'nowhere'). It is a perplexing work, one which tends to define its terms of reference by means of negatives while relegating its positives to singularly dark corners. Its reflections back on High Victorian England remain open to various interpretation. Butler treats religion with a quizzical irreverence, rendering ridiculous the narrator's desire to convert to Christianity the natives of the country he discovered by exposing his zeal as half-hearted and his theology as decidedly quirky. Erewhon itself is no ideal alternative to England, for it is shown as an irritatingly, semi-lunatic nation where sickness is punished and crime cured, a land which lives without watches and machines and which dedicates its colleges of higher education exclusively to the study of hypothetics and 'Unreason'. Butler's posthumously published *The Way of All Flesh* offers an account of the family background and the education of Ernest Pontifex (the family being so named due to their habit of dogmatically laying down the law). The book both denounces narrow Victorian family values and attempts to stress the significance of social evolution and family influence (which had tended to be diminished by Darwinists). Its central character's struggle is to find personal integrity by escaping the browbeating of his elders, but the narrative often shows more signs of splenetic personal resentment on Butler's own part than it does of the conventional *Bildungsroman*. Ernest's career as a clergyman proves a disaster, for he is wrecked both by his own scruples and by the unscrupulousness of others. If he is not, strictly speaking, a sceptic, he emerges as a man who 'though he would not stand seeing the Christian religion made light of, he was not going to see it taken seriously'. *The Way of All Flesh* is at its sharpest and its most didactic when it evokes and damns the distorting, thwarting power of an inherited Victorian ideology which confuses theology with righteousness.

'Mark Rutherford', the name by which William Hale White (1831–1913) is still generally known, was equally concerned with a steady process of clerical and spiritual disillusionment. Hale White's background, unlike Butler's, was that of Dissent. He had trained as a Nonconformist minister, but had given up his ministry in 1854 and entered the civil service. *The Autobiography of Mark Rutherford* (1881) proclaims itself to be 'a record of weaknesses and failures' and it attempts to delineate a provincial minister's declining religious vocation and his consequent descent into melancholia and alcoholism. Its narrative is permeated by a barely suppressed emotionalism and by an acute self-distrust which propels its narrator towards loneliness and a restless exile in London. It is in the metropolis, in the household of a publisher (loosely based on George Eliot's former patron, John Chapman), that Rutherford encounters the kind of society that 'blessedly' heals him of his 'self-despisings'. Its sequel, somewhat inaptly entitled *Mark Rutherford's Deliverance* (1885), suggests a more positive commitment to the problems of a troubled social fabric in London, a city where bourgeois civilization is seen as 'a thin film or crust lying over a volcano'. Despite this Conradian perception, no real investigation of this volcanic situation is on offer; instead, Rutherford insists on an anti-socialist drift into theological, moral, and philosophical generalization. It is never a comfortable book, ending abruptly with the untimely death of its protagonist and with the intrusion of a memorializing 'Editor'. White's *The Revolution in Tanner's Lane* (1887) moves beyond individual clerical doubt to the broader, proletarian world of the articulate artisan and the Dissenting tradesman. It discusses, sometimes powerfully, the radical, political edge of early and mid-nineteenth-century Nonconformity, or rather the blunting of that edge by petty-bourgeois aspirations to gentility and respectability. What begins as an account of the continued rumblings of French revolutionary Republicanism in Regency England, ends with the construction of a new Independent Chapel in the Tanner's Lane of the 1840s. Ironically, this is the real 'revolution' implied by the novel's title, a revolution which has narrowed down from a European sphere to the small world of provincial Cowfold; from a religion which truly dissents, to one which reconstructs itself according to the Victorian social compromise.

Walter Pater's scepticism is of a different order. Pater (1839–94), a scholar by training and inclination and an Oxford University don by profession, provoked widespread public debate due to his supposed advocacy of aesthetic hedonism in his collection of essays, *Studies in the History of the Renaissance* (1873). Such was the subversive impact of the book that Pater was obliged to withdraw the now celebrated 'Conclusion' to his argument from its second edition, fearing that it might 'possibly mislead some of those young men into whose hands it might fall'. Into the hands of impressionable young men like Oscar Wilde and W. B. Yeats it assuredly did fall, though neither came to see its profound influence on him as 'misleading'. Pater advocates a refinement of sensation in pursuit of an ultimate truth in Art and Life and in order that an ecstasy of passionate response might be maintained. In the face of the transience of life, he suggests, the cultivation of the momentary appreciation of the beautiful, and therefore of the 'truthful', could serve to fire the spirit. 'Not the fruit of experience', Pater argues, 'but experience itself, is the end.' His book is a key to the cultivated aestheticism which dominated avant-garde culture in England in the 1890s. It is also one of the first serious experiments in art history, advancing beyond Ruskin's restrictive canons and burgeoning speculations into an analytical study of Renaissance painting. Pater was also amongst the first critics to point to the elusive smile of the Mona Lisa. *Studies in the History of the Renaissance* remains a triumphant assertion of style, a style which is dense and subtly shaped around relative clauses, phrases, and parentheses. It both offers an argument and withdraws from one, combining hesitancy and archness.

This hesitancy of expression is also evident in Pater's historical novel *Marius the Epicurean* (1885). On one level the novel seems to tell the story of the slow movement of a pagan Roman towards Christian conversion (thereby reversing the general tenor of contemporary accounts of deconversion); on another, it remains a distinctly provisional statement. The noble Marius is never in fact formally received into the Church; his is the culture of the humane and just Antonine emperors and his journey is always towards a moral coincidence with Christianity rather than to an immersion in it. Unlike Cardinal Newman's earlier *Callista* (1856), Pater's Christians have neither the best arguments nor the best tunes. Marius dies on the road to martyrdom, and the Church claims him as one of its own, but his personal faith is based, we learn, on 'one long unfolding of beauty and energy in things, upon the closing of which he might gratefully write his "*Vixi*"'. It is a Christianity unordered by theological overdistinctions and dogmatic insistences and a religion untroubled by the possibility of scholarly doubts. It is a numinous, poetic and metaphysical faith, an all-conquering creed lit by the hard, gem-like flame of the purely aesthetic.

'The Letter Killeth': Hardy, Gissing, and Moore

Thomas Hardy's fictional world is one that lacks the comfortable shapes and contours of the old theology. The Church of England is observed as still firmly rooted in a rural society, much as its buildings are part of the Wessex landscape, but its authority has been withdrawn and its physical structures are seen as now incapable of holding, framing, and interpreting a grand, but essentially discomforting, idea of the universe. Although Hardy (1840–1928) publicly fostered the impression, outlined in the second volume of his autobiography, that he was 'churchy', if not in an intellectual sense, 'but in so far as instincts and emotions ruled', there is little real evidence of this 'churchiness' in any of his novels beyond the early *Under the Greenwood Tree* (1872). His aesthetic appreciation of church architecture, fostered by his training as an architect, is steadily countered in his novels by the idea that the historic religion practised in churches is redundant. In *Far From the Madding Crowd* (1874) he contrasts the design of the great medieval barn, in which the sheep-shearing takes place, with those of a church and a castle in that 'the purpose which had dictated its original erection was the same to which it was still applied'. This is no mere reference to the liturgical changes of the Reformation, but an indication that the Christian religion as a whole has gone the way of feudalism. At the opening of his last novel, *Jude the Obscure* (1895), 'the ancient temple of the Christian divinities' (a contorted avoidance of the word 'church') has been replaced by a 'tall new building of modern Gothic design unfamiliar to English eyes' (in Hardy's eyes, a misguided and intrusive attempt to assert the vigorous continuity of the faith). Throughout *Jude* the Christian religion, and 'Christian' morality are variously seen as stultifying and irrelevant to the complexities of modern experience. Religion serves to complicate and further frustrate the destinies of the central characters (who are 'churchy' enough themselves to have made Gothic 'Christminster Cakes'). At the climactic point in the story two clergymen are overheard discussing where they should stand liturgically at the altar, at a time when a more immediate sacrifice has been offered in the form of Jude's children. 'Good God', the traumatized Jude exclaims, 'the eastward position, and all creation groaning'.

Hardy's reversal of St Paul's image of creation groaning in its birth pangs reflects his interest in geological theory and in the doubts cast on traditional interpretations of the origins of life by Charles Darwin. Hardy claimed to have been amongst the first readers of *The Origin of Species*, but much of what he learned from it appears to have rearticulated an older, peasant fatalism inherited from his Dorset forebears (the fatalism with which he later endowed Tess Durbeyfield). Darwin's vastly expanded chronology of life, his displacement of humankind from its proud assumption of superiority, and his arguments concerning natural selection and adaptation, seem merely to have confirmed Hardy's sense of a dispassionate, evolving universe and of a nature which had to be understood without recourse to the idea of a benevolent Creator. In certain ways, both his plots and the fates of his protagonists reflect these concerns. The immense process of evolution advances regardless of human bane and human blessing. Nature rarely fosters individual enlightenment and, seen in a proper perspective, it militates against any comforting belief in providence and in a sympathetic response between human beings and their environment. To Tess, 'as to not a few millions of others', Hardy remarks towards the end of *Tess of the D'Urbervilles*, there was a 'ghastly satire' in Wordsworth's confident lines: 'Not in utter nakedness | But trailing clouds of glory do we come'.

In Hardy's sprawling poetic drama, *The Dynasts* (1904–8), the petty delusions and ambitions of humankind are watched over by choric forces who, from their extended perspectives, undercut any assumption of heroic action. Napoleon achieves nothing, despite his illusion of his own greatness, and general human passivity is seen to be as worth while as any pretension to significant action. Nevertheless, the slow and painful progress of human history fascinated Hardy. History emerges in his work as a partial realization of 'universal consciousness' and as a process misunderstood both by conventional historians and by romantically speculative poets (such as Wordsworth). His most obviously 'historical' novel, *The Trumpet Major* (1880), seems ostensibly slight beside the grand sweep of *The Dynasts* (whose Napoleonic setting it shares), but it is amongst the most carefully *located* of all Hardy's novels and it presents a supremely delicate study of characters choosing and making the wrong choices. Elsewhere in his fiction, history, geology, geography, and astronomy variously serve as macrocosmic ramifications of the human microcosm represented by an intertwined knot of individual fates. The observation of the courses of the stars, coupled with an evocation of prehistory, runs tellingly through the extraordinary *Two on a Tower* (1882), while the looming presence of Egdon Heath acts as a shaper of consciousness in the far more dramatic and disturbing *The Return of the Native* (1878). The physical peculiarity of the Isle of Slingers (Portland Bill) conditions the odd twists of the plot of *The Well-Beloved* (1892, 1897), and in *The Woodlanders* (1887) Hintock Wood is presented as somehow expressive of the 'Unfulfilled Intention which makes life what it is'. The relics of older, pre-Christian civilizations also manage to work their impassive influence. Michael Henchard's tragedy is partly enacted against the background of a Roman amphitheatre and of the pre-Roman Maiden Castle (also the setting of the short story 'A Tryst at an Ancient Earthwork'). When Tess is arrested at dawn, lying 'upon an oblong slab' at Stonehenge, the weighty pictorial significance almost topples over into the improbably theatrical (or, at the very least, cinematic). In the highly eclectic *Jude the Obscure*, the 'city of light', the visionary Christminster, gradually emerges as a human artefact, older and mightier than the historic university for which Jude vainly yearns, and older and more significant than 'Christ' or 'minster'. The city's colleges exclude Jude as much by their architecture as by their narrow admissions policy, but the Fourways, Christminster's ancient central crossroads, 'teems' with an alternative life, 'stratified, with the shades of human groups, who had met there for tragedy, comedy, farce; real enactments of the intensest kind'. Here at the Fourways, history, like the underlying rocks, has its strata, and here Jude takes his place with dons and drabs, students and gownless artisans, as a living, suffering part of the larger 'Unconscious Will' of humanity.

Hardy's novels develop from relatively relaxed, straightforward expositions of 'tragedy, comedy, farce' to what some might see as the over-complex stratification of his later work. Both *Tess of the D'Urbervilles* and *Jude the Obscure* are concerned with characters wrenched from their roots and from the communities which might have sustained, or at least tolerated, their distinctiveness. Hardy's dislocations are, however, far from simply related to character and environment. Both novels also have a narratological density which interfuses literary and biblical citation, scientific reference and allusion, philosophical speculation, superstitious hints at the chthonic and folkloric, and dark, but tentative, suggestions of genetic conditioning and even animism. The fluent, but relatively stark and disciplined, lines of Greek tragedy are here fleshed out by a prose which often seems to aspire to the freer conditions of poetry. It was in poetry that Hardy found the ultimate expression of his instinctive ambiguity and his intellectual evasiveness. It was also in these two particular novels that his complex view of woman, as variously virgin and coquette, as endurer and *ingénue*, as actor and victim, culminates. The 1860s had witnessed the emergence of the so-called 'New Woman', educated, individualistic, but still unfulfilled by the very fact of her continued subservience to men. Through the whole range of his fiction, Hardy's women are neither metropolitan bluestockings nor university educated campaigners, yet they generally emerge as both more determined and more truly sophisticated than his male characters. They also range widely in terms of class and outlook. Tess Durbeyfield, the 'Pure Woman' of the novel's subtitle, has much of the passivity of an instinctive fatalist, but her native 'purity' is reinforced by a countering strength of will which ultimately defies male domination and bourgeois condemnation alike. Her bids for freedom are, however, all doomed. In *Jude the Obscure* Arabella Donn is presented as both crude and exploitative, but she is also singularly practical (in marked contrast to the other major characters) and a survivor against the odds. It is, however, on the complex and often self-contradictory character of Sue Bridehead that much critical attention, some of it incredulous, has been concentrated. D. H. Lawrence, for one, found her 'the production of the long selection by man of the woman in whom the female is subordinated and who therefore only seems to exist to be betrayed by their men'. Lawrence's animus appears to have been prompted by Sue's combination of fictionality and frigidity, and his narrowed perspective fails to respond to the real quality of Hardy's observation, to her intensity, her neuroticism, and her lurches between freethinking and obsessive religiosity. The deep ambiguity of her characterization in fact echoes the central ambiguity and difficulty of the novel in which she appears. Her final self-abasement before the cross in an Oxford church seems to sum up its critical exploration of the varieties of human delusion. *Jude the Obscure* suggests that it is not only the letter that killeth (as Hardy's quotation from St Paul puts it in the novel's subtitle), but that there remains a general human inability to grasp the implications of the modern spirit, a spirit which offers a painful, but more clear-sighted freedom.

Hardy's discussion of sexuality and sexual morality scandalized the professional Mrs Grundys of late Victorian England, including a Bishop of Wakefield who attempted to burn his copy of *Jude the Obscure* at his domestic fireside in midsummer. Hardy's provocative frankness was not, however, unique. There is a similar guarded openness, expressed with a pioneering zeal, in the work of the Irish writer George Moore (1852–1933). In the 1880s Moore launched a series of attacks on the censorship exercised on readers' behalfs by the great circulating libraries, principally Mudie's, which had placed a ban on his first two novels *A Modern Lover* (1883) and *A Mummer s Wife* (1885). Mudie's had pleaded the defence of the tender moral principles of the British matron; Moore appealed to the wider 'truth' of art. 'Literature and young girls', he wrote in the Preface to a translation of one of Émile Zola's novels, 'are irreconcilable elements, and the sooner we leave off trying to reconcile the better'. The result of earlier attempts at reconciliation, he claimed, had been a new school of criticism whose criterion was: 'would you or would you not give that book to your sister of sixteen to read?' Moore, who had spent the years 1873–80 largely in Paris, mixing widely with members of the French cultural avant-garde, saw himself as in the vanguard of a British struggle for freedom from an 'illiterate censorship' and for a new realism in fiction. His early novels were written very much under the shadow of Zola (indeed, he described himself as 'Zola's ricochet in England'), and in reaction to those 'flat and conventional' English novels which he thought lacked 'observation and analysis'. Moore's mature fiction, notably *A Drama in Muslin* (1886) and *Esther Waters* (1894) suggest French influences beyond that of Zola and probe distinctly native themes and social issues. *A Drama in Muslin* is set in an Ireland still dominated by the country houses of the Anglo-Irish Ascendancy and by a Viceregal court in Dublin Castle, but it also shows a nation troubled by the often exasperated protests of its landless peasants. The outspoken, provocative, and determinedly 'realist' *Esther Waters*, which also (scarcely surprisingly) suffered a ban imposed by Mudie's Library, has a working-class heroine, forced out of her home by a drunken stepfather and obliged to work as a servant at a racing stables in Sussex. Esther is seduced, made pregnant, and abandoned. Her grim experiences are compounded by the return of her former lover, by marriage, and by his ruinous penchant for gambling. Her final destitution is relieved by a return to the now decayed racing stables where Esther finds a modicum of happiness. Moore's stylized later work has little of the goading moral radicalism of *Esther Waters*. His retelling of the Gospels from the point of view of Joseph of Arimathea in *The Brook Kerith* (1916) caused a modest stir in its time, but his most memorable and popular work written in the twentieth century was his autobiographical comedy *Hail and Farewell* (1911–14), a trilogy which looks askance at contemporaries in the literary worlds of London and Dublin.

George Gissing (1857–1903) was equally determined to press home the significance of fictional 'realism' to English readers (though his literary tastes tended to be far less Frenchified). His steady, and at times incongruous, admiration for the work of Dickens seems at odds with the gloomy and disillusioned nature of his own fiction. Despite a brief flirtation with socialism and with socialist aspirations in his first novel *Workers in the Dawn* (1880), Gissing seems generally to have rejected social panaceas and anything resembling an optimistic prospect of a political dawn. Both *The Unclassed* (1884) and *Demos: A Story of English Socialism* (1886) suggest a considerable empathy with the urban poor and powerfully evoke the miseries and degradations of slum life, but both also portray popular radicals as self-deceived and self-seeking. 'I am no friend of the people', the narrator of *The Private Papers of Henry Ryecroft* (1903) announces, 'as a force, by which the tenor of the time is conditioned, they inspire me with distrust, with fear; as a visible multitude, they make me shrink aloof, and often move to abhorrence'. Such sentiments of 'fear' and 'abhorrence' elsewhere contribute to an impression of deep resentment and personal failure which haunts most of Gissing's fiction. It is the resentment of a middle-class outsider, an exile in a nether world, whose sympathies are drawn to those who have been denied a chance of prosperity and self-improvement, but Gissing's pervasive disillusion refuses to accept any new illusions, be they religious or philosophical, social or political.

Much of Gissing's most interesting and successful work is concerned with the emancipation of women and with the complexities and difficulties of the bohemian literary life. *The Odd Women* (1893) traces the history of three impoverished sisters who cling desperately to respectability in their shabby-genteel lodgings in London. The novel's subplot offers a striking contrast to the drab limitations of the sisters in the form of the independent career of Rhoda Nunn, a strong-minded woman whose professional skill and feminist advocacy give the book a firm hint of future benevolent change which is rare enough in Gissing's fictional world. The women writers of *New Grub Street* (1891) share with the novel's central male character, the impecunious Edwin Reardon, a discouraging awareness of bitterness, waste, and exploitation in contemporary literary London. The novel does, however, serve to reinforce Gissing's somewhat old-fashioned belief in the Romantic idea of the isolated, suffering artist (even though it scrupulously eschews all romantic affectation). It is not surprising, therefore, that Gissing should have found Dickens's picture of a happy, fulfilled, and prosperous David Copperfield both unconvincing and unappealing as an 'illustration of the artistic character'. His own literary men and women have no such worldly success, though they share something of Copperfield's childhood misery. Henry Ryecroft, for example, looks back on his cold, semi-starving past, and on his struggles to write in miserable garrets and ill-lit basements. Nevertheless, Ryecroft's retrospect is flooded with something akin to achieved happiness. 'I had nothing much to complain of except my poverty', he recalls, offering his readers a contrast between the squalid, foggy, hungry London of his past and the snug, rural retreat from which he writes. Gissing's ambiguities may not be as startling, vital, and illuminating as Hardy's but they do serve to suggest something of the dilemma of the English *fin-de-siècle* writer. As Ryecroft's 'private papers' indicate, the artist was not necessarily damned by retreating into placidity and compromise.

Mystery and History: Conan Doyle, Stoker, and Stevenson

In spite of the disquieting ripples of German philosophical and theological speculation, and the moral revisionism stimulated by the example of French realist fiction, late nineteenth-century English literature remained remarkably insular in its styles and preoccupations. Its predominant concerns were with English society and its ills, with English religion and its development, and with England's position within the United Kingdom and as the centre of a still expanding colonial and commercial Empire. There often seemed to be a full enough justification for this insularity, though not all the reasons behind the justifications were bred of success. 'Anglo-Saxondom' was still felt to matter to the exclusion of other cultures, an assumption which in part explains the growing oppositional vigour of Scottish and, in particular, Anglo-Irish literature in the period. But if England remained imperially central, it was a centre which did not hold with an absolute confidence. Horizons were, of necessity, broadening. The response to 'Greater Britain', as the Empire was sometimes fondly known, had generally been peripheral to the literature of the mid-century. In the late century it was emphatic, even though the emphasis was conditioned by disquiet. Unease, uncertainty, and a sense of strangeness haunt both the writing concerned with imperial expansion and much of the domestic discourse on social and political problems. Two contrasting movements, one outward to a wider world, and one inwards to a new social self-awareness, proved complementary. Both were responses to what Carlyle had earlier styled 'the Condition of England', a condition which now, perforce, embraced the conditions of Scotland, Wales, and Ireland as well as the colonies and the subject peoples of the Empire on which, it was proudly asserted, the sun never set.

In many interesting ways the preoccupation with social and spiritual ills, and the widespread awareness that ready answers to domestic problems were not to be found in conventional Christian teaching, made for a revival of interest in other religions, in scientific alternatives to religion, and in an anti-rational revival of Gothic extravagance. The post-Darwinian fascination with regression rather than with confident progress added a new *frisson* to the unhappy prospect of a human return to the bestial. Human destiny now seemed to have a frightening ambiguity which had been largely absent from the angelic prevision of Tennyson's *In Memoriam* and from the Whiggish progressivism of Macaulay. An obsession with crime, with anarchy, with decadence, with reversion, with the animal, or simply with the paraphernalia of horror can be seen running through the work of many of the key writers of the end of the century, writers as diverse in their styles and interests as Hardy, Wilde, Yeats, Conrad, Wells, and Stevenson.

The spectacular and sensational popular literature of crime, which had been a feature of mid-Victorian Britain, retained much of its currency in the late century (as the widespread speculation about the character and identity of Jack the Ripper might serve to suggest). The narrator of H. G. Wells's story *Tono Bungay* (1909) recalls the excitement of reading the street-literature of his youth in Kent in the 1880s: 'one saw there smudgy illustrated sheets, the *Police News* in particular, in which vilely-drawn pictures brought home to the dullest intelligence an interminable succession of squalid crimes, women murdered and put in boxes, buried under floors, old men bludgeoned at midnight by robbers, people thrust suddenly out of trains, happy lovers shot, vitrioled, and so forth by rivals.' This was, in part, the stuff of the cheap criminal fiction pioneered by G. W. M. Reynolds let alone of the darker sides of Dickens and

Wilkie Collins, but its ramifications in the 1880s and 1890s have left more lasting traces on the popular imagination. Sir Arthur Conan Doyle's story *A Study in Scarlet* introduced Sherlock Holmes to the reading public in 1887, but the vast success of Holmes, the super-perceptive scientific amateur who runs rings around plodding police detectives, really dates from the series of short stories published from 1891 in the *Strand Magazine*. Conan Doyle (1859–1930) resented being thought of solely as the creator of Holmes, but it was in these stories that he captured an impression of a foggy, disordered London, a city of mayhem, mystery, and murder, which will always continue to overshadow any larger view of his work. His historical fiction, in particular *Micah Clarke* (1889) and *The Exploits of Brigadier Gerard* (1896), or his Jules Verne-ish Professor Challenger stories such as *The Lost World* (1912), have great flair, but none of them has quite the brilliance of the accounts of Holmes's mind pitted against an international subclass of criminals and working in uneasy tandem with his slower-witted memorializer, Dr Watson.

Holmes reads signs and interprets them according to a process which combines logical deduction with leaps of the imagination. No such applied science can outwit the malevolent power released in England by a shipwreck at Whitby, described in Bram Stoker's *Dracula* (1897). Stoker (1847–1912), a Dubliner by birth and the personal manager to the great actor Sir Henry Irving, managed to combine in his remarkable novel a pronounced theatricality with something of the Irish Gothic of Maturin's *Melmoth the Wanderer*. *Dracula* is a masterpiece of horripilation. Its carefully wrought narrative intermixes diaries, letters, journals, and extracts from newspapers, suggesting a new kind of myth-making which moves beyond the moral dilemmas explored in *Frankenstein* into the realm of the parahuman and the purely superstitious. The novel is charged with sexuality—a perverted and exploitative sexuality—and with a pervasive sense of mental and spiritual disturbance. If the outward and visible signs of the Christian faith ultimately triumph over darkness, they often seem but token gestures designed to ward off a profound and recurrent spiritual malaise.

Robert Louis Stevenson (1850–94) was, despite his singular fascination with horror, a writer of a far greater variety and invention. Stevenson is one of a group of distinctively Scottish writers who flourished in the last years of the century and who used small-town settings, and the Scots vernacular, to reinforce a precise sense of Scottish place. If their roots lie in the work of Scott and Galt, this so-called 'Kailyard School' was also determinedly 'modern' (it also included J. M. Barrie, Ian Maclaren (1850–1907) and S. R. Crockett (1860–1914). Stevenson's work is far from parochial and indeed is often at its most remarkable when it is detached from Scotland or when it looks sideways, or retrospectively, at Scottish issues. The mystery story *The Strange Case of Dr Jekyll and Mr Hyde* (1886) is a case in point. It stands apart from the rest of his fiction, reaching back through its disparate, disbelieving narrative voices to a variety of English precedents, and yet, through its examination of the divided self, nodding to the great Scottish example of what can only be called

Calvinist Gothic, Hogg's *Confessions of a Justified Sinner*. Despite the Scots names of many of its characters, *Dr Jekyll and Mr Hyde* is set in England and centres on the horrid possession of a successful London physician. Stevenson wrote his uncanny story in an oddly placid exile, amid the villas of the English seaside, but the fact of his severance from Scotland and from urban life may well have provided the stimulus to his evident fascination with the widening gap between the respectable worlds of Jekyll and his *alter ego*, Hyde. It is a story of agonizingly disparate perceptions and actions which leads ultimately to Jekyll's suicide as the only effective release from the predatory Hyde.

It is, however, in his Scottish historical fiction that Stevenson's less speculatively fanciful imagination comes to the fore. Again there is an evident debt to tradition (in this case to Sir Walter Scott), and to a marked division between ways of seeing and acting (here between then and now). Gone is Scott's urge to find a historical and fictional compromise in order to justify the idea of progressive evolution. *Kidnapped* (1886) and its sequel *Catriona* (1893) are set in eighteenth-century Scotland, a nation riven by Jacobite divisions and older resentments, and both novels deal with deception, suspicion, injustice, and obligatory flight. Neither ends with any sense of achieved serenity and purpose or with any emphasis on historic justice or justification. *The Master of Ballantrae: A Winter's Tale* (1889), written in Stevenson's self-imposed exile in the South Seas, is narrated episodically by a family steward, Ephraim Mackellar, who, like the reader, is drawn into a duality of response to the central characters, two politically and emotionally divided brothers. The story, set yet again in the aftermath of the Jacobite rebellion of 1745, follows the twists and turns of an intensely fraught family relationship which has larger implications for the historic tensions within Scottish culture. Stevenson's romantic fascination with travel, with the dangerous side of things and with the exotic, evident enough in his famous boys' story *Treasure Island* (1883), culminated in his South Sea adventures *The Beach at Falesá* (1893) and *The Ebb Tide* (1894), both of which offer indictments of the malign effects of eighteenth-century colonialism as a new variation on piracy.

'Our Colonial Expansion': Kipling and Conrad

Rudyard Kipling (1865–1936), the apostrophizer of 'The White Man's Burden' (a poem addressed, incidentally, to the American imperial mission in the Philippines), has all too often been seen as the noisiest popular apologist for the climactic expansion of the British Empire. The closing years of the nineteenth century were marked by the European grab for Africa and by European rivalries as to which power could manage to grab most territory. Given its existing footholds, Britain did pretty well out of the enterprise, cementing it with effective influence over Egypt and, following Kitchener's victory at Omdurman in 1898, extending Anglo-Egyptian influence over the

Sudan. Though the wars against Boer settlers in South Africa were brought to an end in 1902 with an uneasy compromise over British influence in the colony, the wars themselves had by no means always gone Britain's way. For Kipling—assuming, as he periodically did, the voice of the ordinary British infantry, 'Tommy Atkins'—the African campaigns were more a matter of slog than of swashbuckling and Africa itself not so much a burden as a pain in the feet:

> We're foot—slog—slog—slog—sloggin' over Africa—
> Foot—foot—foot—foot—sloggin' over Africa—
> (Boots—boots—boots—boots—movin' up and down again!)
> There's no discharge in the war!

Kipling, born in Bombay, was, however, always more stimulated by the idea of the British imperial adventure in India than by the less romantic drive to acquire a colonial hegemony over Africa. He proved the most perceptive observer of the quirky anomalies of the British Raj in the relatively peaceful and prosperous period between the suppression of the Mutiny of 1857–8 and the growth of independence movements at the beginning of the twentieth century.

It would be difficult to describe Kipling as a cerebral writer. The social and moral dilemmas, the religious or irreligious scruples, and the alternative pulls of decadence and despair, which are evident in the work of his British-based contemporaries, seem at first sight to be quite absent from both his prose and his jingling, jingoistic verse. His work rapidly gained esteem both in Britain and in British India in the 1880s, and his particularly privileged place in English letters was internationally acknowledged in 1907 when he became the first British Nobel Laureate. Nevertheless, Kipling was in many ways an outsider, a colonial articulator of a commonsensical, almost proverbial, philosophy and a conservative upholder of the powers that be, but not a cultivator of the styles and codes of the London literary scene. The poet of 'If' and of the Jubilee poem 'Recessional' seems to sit uneasily in an anthology of the often effete poetry of the 1890s, and Kipling's deliberately 'plain' story-telling can seem flat, even coarse, beside the stylistic refinements of a Pater and a Wilde or the complex allusiveness of a James. His bluff, no-nonsense cruder side as a Cockney versifier is wittily summed up in Max Beerbohm's cartoon of a tweedy, drunken poet taking 'a bloomin' day aht, on the blasted 'eath, along with Britannia 'is gurl'.

Kipling is not, however, an untroubled apologist for the common man's idea of Empire and of the colonial races. His values may well be those of a world of masculine action, but he is also a writer who, at his best, is always alert to subtleties, to human weakness, to manipulation, vulnerability, and failure. India with its empty spaces and its densely overcrowded cities, its hill-stations and its hot deserts, its princely states and its cantonments, conditioned him; its ancient, mutually severed cultures fascinated, rather than overwhelmed him (as is the case with some other English writers). He retained the detachment of a European outsider, but he tried to see India from the inside, not as a curious interloper or as an obsessed neophyte. In his greatest literary achievement—the short stories which he began publishing in the mid-1880s—he demonstrated an extraordinary variety, tact, and vitality of tone; he moves from ghost-stories to tales of flirtation and adultery, from isolation to communal riot, and from the fear of death to the waste of life and talent. His 'soldiers three', Privates Mulvaney, Ortheris, and Learoyd, are pragmatic and stoical survivors, coping with the divergent promptings of the discipline of their regiment and the multiple confusions of India. A similar soldierly individualism marks the story 'The Man Who Would Be King', a clever and entertaining intermixture of freemasonry and unsanctioned extensions of the Pax Britannica.

Kipling may have wholeheartedly acquiesced to the idea of Empire and to the élite world of the British Babas of India, but he also points steadily and clearsightedly to both the merits and the demerits of the colonial regime. English children sent back 'home' for education suffer excruciatingly (as Kipling himself did) in his short story, 'Baa Baa Black Sheep', but none of his grown-up sahibs seem to exude the smug superiority of E. M. Forster's. They know that they cannot properly assimilate to native India, but they tend to recognize, as Kipling's Mrs Mallows puts it, that 'You can't focus anything in India'. His large-scale attempt at multifocusing, the novel *Kim* (1901), allows for many voices and conflicting traditions, exploring a fictional India through the cultural and geographical wanderings of its boy-hero, the orphan son of an Irish colour-sergeant. Kim awkwardly bridges the gap between rulers and ruled, serving both a Tibetan Lama as his disciple and the British Secret Service as a spy in the 'Great Game' which the sahibs are playing against the Russians to the north. The Lama, who expresses himself in an archaic, biblical English, is given an end to his spiritual search, but the end of Kipling's narrative leaves the destiny of his disciple much more ambiguous. *Kim* poses questions about identity and the problems of race, religion, isolation, loneliness, and courage. The Lama, who claims to see through actuality, believes that freedom lies in withdrawal. Kim may be left with the feeling that his more worldly soul is 'out of gear with its surroundings—a cog-wheel unconnected with any machinery', but he also senses, in a more practical and down-to-earth way, that 'Roads were meant to be walked on, houses to be lived in, cattle to be driven, fields to be tilled, and men and women to be talked to'. Despite the kaleidoscopic nature of Kipling's India, Kim at least finds something akin to a focus.

Joseph Conrad (1857–1924) was a different kind of outsider in search of integrity. Conrad, born in Poland the son of a prominent nationalist victim of Russian repression, was naturalized as a British citizen in 1886. If he did not in any truly treasonable sense betray his homeland, and if he rarely refers directly to the Poland he had left, a sense of betrayal nevertheless haunts his work. Conrad's career as an exile had begun and developed as a merchant seaman and it was as a writer of sea-stories set in the East Indies and the Pacific that he first attracted public attention. It was only with the appearance of his more obviously political fiction in the early years of the twentieth century that the true bent of his art became clear to a broad group of discriminating admirers. There is, however, no clear dividing line between his sea-stories and his land-stories, between tales set in European colonies and those set in an equally troubled and benighted Europe. Conrad's themes merely develop, broaden, and open up in the larger world beyond the confined, masculine world of the ship. In a dense late sea-story, *The Secret Sharer* (1909), the narrator speaks disarmingly of the 'great security of the sea as compared with the unrest of the land' and of a shipboard life which presents 'no disquieting problems'. The irony of the statement becomes obvious as this particular narrative develops, but no reader of Conrad's fiction, alert to his accounts of typhoons and tempests, of marine disasters and shipwrecks, could unprotestingly accept its validity. Nevertheless, there is a sense in which his descriptions of ship life suggest a relatively ordered society which is, by its very nature, prepared to face the challenges of an external and impersonal hostility. The ship also contains a small hierarchical society in which individual decision and responsibility take on the moral force of paramount virtue. In the sea-stories 'disquieting problems', frightful and utterly devastating as they may prove to be, do at least seem to find some kind of resolution, albeit a singularly fragile resolution.

Conrad's tales, concerned with the nature and effects of European imperialism, both economic and colonial, are of a different order to Kipling's. Conrad deals not with the multiple confrontations of India, but with the intrusion and interference of Europeans in the Pacific, in the East Indies, in South America, and in Africa. His colonizers are drawn from a variety of national backgrounds; most are disreputable, incomprehending, intolerant, and exploitative. The title character in *Lord Jim* (1900) may have proved himself a successful colonial agent and have earned himself the title of Tuan ('Lord') from his grateful subjects, but his organizing virtues are seen as countered by the lasting memory of the corruption of his predecessor and by the deception and ruthless European piracy of Gentleman Brown. In Conrad's work colonialism generally emerges as both brutal and brutalizing, alienating native and settler alike. Power is not simply corrupting, it is systematically open to abuse. In *An Outpost of Progress* (1898) 'progress' is an obvious misnomer. A newspaper from 'home' brightly discusses 'Our Colonial Expansion' (though Conrad does not locate the 'our') in terms of 'the rights and duties of civilization, of the sacredness of the civilizing work' and of 'the merits of those who went about bringing light and faith and commerce to the dark places of the earth'. There is little light. The story indicates that the 'darkness' corrupts both internally and externally, an idea which reaches its apogee in 'Heart of Darkness' (1899, 1902), a narrative which gradually unveils, layer by layer, an underlying horror. Imperialism is initially expounded as a variety of brutish idealism: 'The conquest of the earth, which mostly means taking it away from those who have a different complexion or slightly flatter noses than ourselves, is not a pretty thing when you look at it too much. What redeems it is the idea only. An idea at the back of it; not a sentimental pretence but an idea; and an unselfish belief in the idea.' The tale, as it unwinds, exposes the lack of such an 'idea' and the remoteness of any ideal from the colonial reality. There is no redemption from 'the buying and selling gang which bosses the rotten show'. *Nostromo* (1904) (a title which implies the presence of 'our man') is concerned with silver, insurrection, and external interference in an unstable South American republic. This particularly restless narrative has an uneasy edge to it, suggesting uncertain heroism, a tottering social order, and a corruption which is both imported and exportable.

Conrad's gentlemanly Polish background, and his diverse professional and intellectual interests, made for ambiguities which run through his life and work. Having been born an unwilling subject of the Russian Tsar, and having accepted exile from nationalist politics and his native language, he steadily explores and interrelates themes of guilt and dislocation. In *Under Western Eyes* (1911) he writes directly about the dangerous instabilities of society under the Russian autocracy, but his own antipathy to Russia and to things Russian renders it a somewhat wayward response to an obviously Dostoevskyan precedent. The novel's wondering narrator, an elderly English teacher of languages in Geneva, draws both on his experience of the exiled Russian student Kirylo Sidorovitch Razumov and on Razumov's diary. Razumov (whose name is derived from the Russian term 'son of reason') is a double exile in Switzerland; he has betrayed a revolutionary fellow-student to the Tsar's police, and, as his guilt remains concealed, he is acting out a lie of heroic virtue amongst a group of alienated expatriates. The narrator observes all with foreign, 'western' eyes, eyes which only partially grasp the import of Razumov's pressing need for confession and expiation. *The Secret Agent* (1907), in some ways a far more assured and far more disturbing novel, is also concerned with revolution and revolutionaries, unflatteringly observed in a murky, seedy, untidy London. In some telling ways *The Secret Agent* looks back both to Dickens (and to Dickens's policemen in particular) and to the 'sensation' fiction of the 1860s, but it also conveys a distinctly modern sense of alienation, disquiet, and dislocation. The central character, Verloc, an *agent provocateur* in the employ of a 'foreign' (but almost certainly Russian) embassy, is required by his ambassadorial handler to commit a terrorist act of 'shocking senselessness' and 'gratuitous blasphemy' by blowing up the Greenwich Meridian. Verloc may move in and out of anarchist circles, but even he is dumbfounded by the seeming absurdity of Mr Vladimir's carefully reasoned demand: 'There is learning—science. Any imbecile that has got an income believes in that. He does not know why, but he believes it matters somehow . . . All the damned professors are radicals at heart. Let them know that their great panjandrum has got to go, too, to make room for the Future of the Proletariat . . . Madness alone is truly terrifying, inasmuch as you cannot placate it either by threats, persuasion, or bribes . . . Since bombs are your means of expression, it would be really telling if one could throw a bomb into pure mathematics. But that is impossible . . . What do you think of having a go at astronomy?' The novel veers simultaneously towards farce and tragedy, and it is expressed in a terse matter-of-fact way which, like Mr Vladimir's colloquialisms, conveys a deep sense of linguistic unease beneath an ostensibly easy and complacent surface. The fragmenting, reiterated phrases '*An impenetrable mystery*' and '*This act of madness and despair*' which troublingly echo through its last pages take on something of the restless force of the self-consciously 'Modernist' texts that the book foreshadows.

'Our Theatre in the 90s': London and Dublin

Oscar Wilde (1854–1900) was a Dubliner distinguished by both his class and his education. He was also the son of a romantically inclined mother who dabbled in sentimental nationalist verse. Wilde himself only ever flirted fancifully with what was, in the 1880s, the particularly vexed and pressing question of Irish Home Rule. Having left Dublin to study at Oxford, he seems thereafter to have aspired to shine in England and, as far as was possible, to be the central figure in a fashionable metropolitan coterie of artists, writers, and wits. He also acted out the parts of a London socialite and of an amusingly provocative social critic. Underlying all Wilde's life and work (he readily acknowledged that there was an intimate relationship between the two) there were, however, both a seriousness and an acute, but amused, awareness that he *was* acting. Wilde's homosexuality, both covertly and overtly expressed in what he wrote during the 1890s, might at first have seemed little more than a gesture to an imported French *décadence*; after the terrible fall marked by his trial and imprisonment (a fall which in some ways he seems to have deliberately courted), the alienating bias of his art became manifest. The contrived style of much of his prose, the excessive elaboration of his poetry, and the aphoristic and paradoxical wit of his plays, are all subversive. They do more than reject mid-Victorian values in life and art in the name of aestheticism; they defiantly provoke a response to difference.

Amid a welter of affectation Wilde's essays suggest that he could, when it suited him, be a perceptive, rather than simply a naughty critic. He always questions institutions, moral imperatives, and social clichés; he rarely suffers fools gladly. From the refinedly outrageous lectures he gave to Colorado miners in the early 1880s (kitted out in velvet knee-breeches) to the calculatedly annoying challenges to conventional literary morality publicly expressed during his first trial, Wilde enjoyed his chosen roles as an aesthete and an iconoclast. His Platonic dialogue *The Decay of Lying* (1889) and the two parts of *The Critic as Artist* (1890) suggest something of the aphoristic dialogue of his later comedies (though his plays would rarely allow an authoritative voice to be so pointedly interrupted, or occasionally qualified, by a convenient stooge). The inspirer of these dialogues may have been Plato, but the sentiments are Pater's and the lexical virtuosity is characteristically Wilde's. He offers the kind of criticism which delights in snaring butterflies rather than breaking them on wheels. He can be memorably cruel (*Robert Elsmere* is squashed by the observation that it is Arnold's *Literature and Dogma* 'with the literature left out') and an initially flattering suggestion can be cleverly turned on its head ('Meredith is a prose Browning, and so is Browning'). Wilde's central arguments are, however, derived from an awareness that art is far more than a mere imitation of nature. 'A Truth in Art', he remarks in *The Truth of Masks* (1891), 'is that whose contradictory is also true'. In *The Decay of Lying* there is also a recurrent pleasure in insisting that 'the telling of beautiful untrue things, is the proper aim of Art'. Wilde's longest and most provocatively serious essay, *The Soul of Man under Socialism* (1891), does not argue primarily for a new social order or for a redistribution of property, but for a larger and expanding idea of freedom, a liberation from drudgery and the rule of machines. The future achievement of a socialist order offers the prospect of what Wilde candidly sums up elsewhere as 'enjoyment'.

Wilde's delight in provocation, and his exploration of alternative moral perspectives, mark his most important work of fiction, *The Picture of Dorian Gray* (1890). The novel's Preface presents a series of attitudinizing aphorisms about art and literature which end with the bald statement: 'All art is quite useless.' The narrative that follows is a melodramatic, Faustian demonstration of the notion that art and morality are quite divorced. It is, nevertheless, a text riven by internal contradictions and qualifications. Aestheticism is both damned and dangerously upheld; hedonism both indulged and disdained. *Dorian Gray* is a tragedy of sorts with the subtext of a morality play; its self-destructive, darkly sinning central character is at once a desperate suicide and a martyr. Wilde's stage tragedies have less interest and far less flair. His first play, *Vera: or, The Nihilists* (1880), suggests a pretty minimal mastery of theatre technique and an even thinner grasp of the Russian political realities which it attempts to dramatize. His blank-verse drama, *The Duchess of Padua* (written in Paris in 1883), never even reached the stage, while *A Florentine Tragedy*, begun in 1894 when Wilde was at the height of his powers, remained unfinished until 1897. Quite the most powerful and influential of his tragedies, *Salome*, was written in French and translated into English in 1894 by Wilde's lover, Lord Alfred Douglas. The play, which draws on the Bible account of the death of John the Baptist and on Flaubert's story *Herodias*, was not produced in England until 1931 (a victim both of its outrageous treatment of Bible history and of its author's reputation). The striking, overwrought imagery of *Salome*, and its shocking juxtapositions of repulsion and sexual desire, of death and orgasm, were particularly powerfully transformed in the German version which became the libretto of Richard Strauss's revolutionary opera of 1915.

Wilde's comedies of the 1890s have a far surer place in the theatre. *The Importance of Being Earnest* (1895) has indeed been accorded an unchallenged canonical status which is witnessed by its probably being the most quoted play in the English language after *Hamlet*. *Lady Windermere's Fan: A Play about a Good Woman* (1892) was Wilde's first supreme success on the London stage. It has distinct parallels with its comic successor, *A Woman of No Importance* (1893), in that it centres on the discovery of a dire secret and is at its most animated and conspicuously Wildean in the witty speeches of a dandified male aristocrat. Both plays have a noticeable feminist bias in that they stress the innate strength of their central female characters, a strength which draws on, and finally masters, a certain puritanism. In April 1895, at the time of Wilde's arrest, charged with illegal homosexual practices, both the carefully plotted *An Ideal Husband* (1895) and its successor *The Importance of Being Earnest* were playing to large London audiences. As the scandal developed, first Wilde's name was removed from the hoardings outside the theatres, then the runs of both plays were abruptly terminated. The real achievement of these plays lies neither in their temporary notoriety, nor really in their polished and anti-sentimental surfaces, but in their undercurrents of boredom, disillusion, alienation and, occasionally, real feeling. In both, despite their delightful evocations of flippancy and snobbery, and despite their abrupt shifts in attitudes and judgements, Wilde triumphed in capturing a fluid, intensely funny, mood of 'irresponsibility' which challenges all pretension except that of the artifice of the plays themselves.

Sir Arthur Wing Pinero's career had a steady professionalism about it which the more flamboyant Wilde's lacked. Pinero's dramatic challenges are based on convention rather than on the undercutting of convention. He had relatively little of Wilde's brilliance and none of his personal tragedy. Pinero (1855–1934) knew the theatre and its audiences intimately (he had worked as a professional actor in the 1870s and 1880s), and his admiration for the traditions and potential of his profession is affectionately displayed in his retrospect on the mid-Victorian stage, *Trelawny of the 'Wells'* (1898). *Trelawny* uses the theatre to speak about the theatre and actors to play actors; it both recognizes the artificiality of dramatic representation and affirms that the drama is a central expression of human value. It was, however, in his high-society dramas, most notably *The Second Mrs Tanqueray* (1893), that Pinero most boldly questioned both received conventions of sexual morality and standard theatrical representation of such conventions. Through the character and situation of Paula Tanqueray he also, somewhat tentatively, criticizes the secondary status of women and the assumptions made about women's roles in a male-dominated society. *The Second Mrs Tanqueray* remains a highly effective play despite, rather than because of, the melodramatic shock of Paula's climactic suicide.

Pinero's gestures towards a new sexual frankness suggest the degree to which the English theatre was edging towards the still dangerous openness of Ibsen. George Bernard Shaw, a far more fervent admirer of Ibsen than was Pinero, recorded that the initial London responses to the new drama in the late 1880s and early 1890s were vituperative. The first reviews of *Ghosts* outdid each other in bandying abusive terms such as 'morbid', 'putrid', 'literary carrion', and 'perilous nonsense'. By the time of the composition of the Preface to the second edition of Shaw's essay *The Quintessence of Ibsenism* in 1912 the dramatic climate had changed. As Shaw (1856–1950) insisted, Ibsen's work had helped stir the awareness in men 'that in killing women's souls they had killed their own' and had consequently 'appealed to the rising energy in the revolt of women against idealism'. Shaw's proposed collaboration on a play with Ibsen's English translator, William Archer, came to nothing, but the spirit of Ibsen, if not the letter, is evident throughout his own long career as a dramatist. It is perhaps most decisive in determining the line of men-mastering, no-nonsense, strong-willed women that he created. Nevertheless, much of Shaw's own instinct for dramatic action derives not from a new Nordic precedent but from the more established, but no less challenging, traditions of musical theatre and the Mozartian and Wagnerian opera in particular. *Man and Superman* (1905) acknowledges its debts to Mozart's *Don Giovanni*; and Wagner's innovatory music-dramas of the *Ring*-cycle were, Shaw explains in the *The Perfect Wagnerite* (1898), readily interpretable as analyses of modern rather than mythological realities. 'The dwarfs, giants and gods are dramatizations of the three main orders of men', he insists, the dwarfs representing 'the instinctive, predatory, lustful, greedy people'; the giants were 'the patient, toiling, stupid, respectful, money-worshipping people'; the gods 'the intellectual, moral, talented people who devise and administer States and Churches'. This Wagnerian scheme, further informed by a reading of Marxian theory and by Shaw's own wilful self-contradictoriness, shaped the criticism of slum-landlordism in his first play, *Widowers' Houses* (1892), but although imported ideas helped him to revolutionize the staid London theatre of the 1890s, Shaw was as much drawing from the native tradition as reacting against it. His dramatic criticism of 1895–8 may demonstrate his repudiation of the styles of acting and production still popular with audiences and impresarios, but it also stresses the extent to which his own bent was for comedy, a comedy which might develop less from the example of his fellow Irishman, Wilde, than from the novels of Dickens. 'To Ibsen', he wrote, 'from beginning to end, every human being is a sacrifice, whilst to Dickens he is a farce'. Though Shaw rarely used the devices of farce, he clearly continued to aspire to a dramatic reflection of Dickens's comic energy, social diversity, political observation, and subversive power to deflate pomposity.

Shaw remains the most inventively unpredictable, if scarcely the most delicate, playwright in the English tradition (it is harder to fit him into a specifically Irish tradition). His plays also reveal a forthright intellectual confidence which is lacking in much of the cautious, agnostic, depressive writing of his non-dramatic London contemporaries. Shaw presupposes that history can be illuminating, that the present can be vigorously reforming, and that the future (whether Darwinistically determined or not) will be exciting rather than exacting. His drama is not so much didactic as instructive; his arguments fuse elements of socialism, science, and philosophy in a way which continues to vex socialists, scientists, and philosophers; his dialogue can move easily, but disconcertingly, from broad comedy to anguish and declaration and back again to comedy; his protagonists have a vivid, if at times coarse, energy. His settings, like his preoccupations, may be predominantly those of the England of the turn of the twentieth century, but he continues to surprise, to nag, and to provoke at the turn of the twenty-first.

Shaw's early plays, *The Philanderer* and the far more assured *Mrs Warren's Profession* (both written in 1893), fell victims to the Lord Chamberlain's censorship and had to wait until the early 1900s for private productions (*Mrs Warren's Profession* received its licence for *public* performance only in the mid-1920s!). Of such official censorship Shaw complained in 1898 in the Preface to the published version of the two plays, classifying them, together with *Widowers' Houses*, as what he called 'Unpleasant Plays'. *Mrs Warren's Profession* boldly confronts two contemporary women's issues: the future professional careers of educated, would-be independent women, and the oldest profession, female prostitution. The arguments of the play suggest the propriety of both vocations, but its internal tensions derive from the juxtaposition of a liberated daughter, Vivie Warren, and her unashamed, brothel-keeping mother who sees 'the only way for a woman to provide for herself decently is for her to be good to some man that can afford to be good to her'. The play ends not with reconciliation, compromise or empty gestures of feminine solidarity, but with a slammed door and an isolated Vivie happily engrossed in her work. Shaw was justly proud of this 'unpleasant' play, but his discovery that, as he put it, 'the New Drama, in England at least, was a figment of the revolutionary imagination' virtually obliged him to write an alternative series of 'pleasant' plays for the commercial theatre. *Arms and the Man: An Anti-Romantic Comedy* (1894) sets out to subvert ideas of soldierly and masculine heroism in a fanciful Balkan setting; *Candida: A Mystery* (1897) turns Ibsen's *A Doll's House* upside down within the context of a Christian Socialist household; and the cleverly diverting *You Never Can Tell* (1899) allows for the happy, liberating victory of a new generation over the old.

In the opening years of the twentieth century Shaw's 'revolutionary imagination' began to realize its ambition to create a 'New Drama' on the stage of the Royal Court Theatre in London. In the seasons organized between 1904 and 1907 the Royal Court performed *John Bull's Other Island* (one of Shaw's rare direct treatments of Ireland and the Irish), *Man and Superman*, and *Major Barbara*. The 1905 production of *Man and Superman* daringly introduced an on-stage motor car in Act II, but omitted the vast, sprawling post-Nietzschean argument (or 'arias') of Act III (an act, set in an infernal afterlife, which transforms the play's characters into those of *Don Giovanni*). *Major Barbara* (also of 1905), which explores the conflict and the ultimate mutual assent of a strong-willed father and his equally strong-minded daughter, disturbed many of Shaw's socialist friends with its quizzical espousal of the idea of the future reconstruction of society by an energetic, highly-motivated, power-manipulating minority. Manipulation of a different order figures in *Pygmalion* (1913), ostensibly a withdrawal from politics and philosophy, but in fact a carefully worked study of the developing relationship between a 'creator' and his 'creation' (it possibly shares this 'grotesque' idea with Dickens's *Great Expectations*). Shaw's work written during and after the Great War both extends earlier styles and ideas and indirectly meditates on the cataclysm that the war represented. The wartime *Heartbreak House* (1920), described as a 'Fantasia in the Russian Manner on English Themes', plays in an unmistakably Shavian way with Chekhovian *ennui* and uncertainty. It also develops the theme, laid out earlier in *The Perfect Wagnerite*, of three contending orders of men (and women) finally destroying the 'predatory' burglar and the 'money-worshipping millionaire, Mangan, in a purgative Zeppelin raid. The god-like survivors are last seen in their Valhalla, looking forward to another explosive twilight. The real strengths of the play lie not in its symbolism, but in its powerful and subtle series of encounters between characters in which each in turn has to come to terms with disillusion and some kind of 'heartbreak'. For all its heavy-handedness *Saint Joan* (1923), celebrating (but scarcely in a churchy way) the recent canonization of the French military heroine, Joan of Arc, is an extraordinarily mobile, and versatile play. Its resourceful central character, far from appearing trapped by her visions, or by medieval or modern Catholicism, is presented as a remarkably self-aware, self-asserting woman. Joan is 'saintly' not in the sentimental sense, but by merit of the effect she has on others and in her willingness to give her life for the freedom opened up to her by her convictions.

Shaw's work for the Royal Court seasons of 1904–7 was paralleled by the contemporaneous appearance there of plays by two less strikingly talented English innovators, Harley Granville-Barker (1877–1946) and John Galsworthy (1867–1933). Granville-Barker, who had played Marchbanks in the 1900 production of *Candida*, and who later made a particular reputation for himself as a director of, and critical commentator on, Shakespeare, met with some success with *The Voysey Inheritance* in 1905, but had his play *Waste* (1907) banned by the censorious Lord Chamberlain. Galsworthy's best plays, like his famous sequence of novels, *The Forsyte Saga* (1906–22), are concerned with class-consciousness, and class conflict, a pressing theme in a period persuaded that it might well be on the brink of a social revolution. *The Silver Box* (1906) deals with the opposition of two families, one rich, one poor, their mutual alienation being complicated by the theft of the box of the title. Galsworthy's often stilted later plays tend to have stark, one-word titles expressive of their once urgent themes. *Strife* (1909), *Justice* (1910), and *Loyalties* (1922) are avowedly propagandist, using the bourgeois theatre to confront bourgeois audiences with the need to examine their social consciences. Each had its telling effect in its time, Winston Churchill, then Home Secretary, being so moved with the human suffering represented in *Justice* that he abolished solitary confinement in prisons. Galsworthy's evident compassion for the victims of an uncaring society, alas, often reeks of sentimentality; his political impartiality, admirable enough in its time perhaps, now seems awkward by the very nature of its uncomfortable fence-sitting.

In the plays of J(ames) M(atthew) Barrie, W(illiam) B(utler) Yeats and John Millington Synge a clear distinction emerges between the first, a Scottish writer resident in London and happy to work for the London stage (where he enjoyed a considerable success), and the two Irish playwrights who were determined to establish an alternative dramatic tradition in Dublin. Although Barrie (1860–1937) never severed his Scots roots, and although he steadily returned to Scottish themes and subjects in his work, he never seems to have aimed at evolving a distinctively 'national' style, let alone a nationalist theatre. His early fiction, notably in the essays and stories collected as *Auld Licht Idylls* (1888) and the novel, *The Little Minister* (1891), are provincial in their setting and vivid enough in their use of Scots speech and in their presentation of uniquely Scottish institutions (though when he dramatized *The Little Minister* for London audiences in 1897, he sacrificed much of the story's restlessness and darkness). Barrie's most interesting stage works exploit shifts in time and yet more radical changes of scene. *The Admirable Crichton* (1902) moves from the Mayfair drawing-room of Lord Loam to a desert island, where the sterling qualities of Loam's butler, Crichton, fully declare themselves. It is a play about class traits rather than class and, as Granville-Barker somewhat cruelly observed, it is eminently the work of 'a Scotsman living in luxurious, snobbish England'. The enduringly popular *Peter Pan* shifts from a Bloomsbury nursery to Never Land and centres on the essentially displaced figure of Peter, locked in his perpetual, escapist, mother-loving, sexless boyhood (the part has traditionally been played by a woman). Barrie's fascination with the power of myth and magic also shapes his *Dear Brutus* (1917) and the extraordinary *Mary Rose* (1920). The first play explores might-have-beens and the determining nature of the self, while the second hauntingly explores the mysterious disappearance and reappearance of its title character on a Hebridean island. It is an indeterminate and elusive play, intermixing Celtic Twilight with a good deal of Scotch Mist.

When in 1897 W. B. Yeats (1865–1939) was planning and determining the nature of an Irish theatrical renaissance, he wrote to the mother/father figure of the Celtic Revival, the Scottish writer 'Fiona Macleod' (the pseudonym of William Sharp (1855–1905)). His ambition, he told Sharp, was to achieve a 'poetical or legendary drama' which would have 'no realistic or elaborate, but only symbolic and decorative setting'. The acting, he added, 'should have an equivalent distance to that of the play from common realities'. Yeats's letter was an appeal to a fellow devotee of Celtic and occult alternatives to the drab materialism of modern English culture. It also marks a turning away from the 'common realities' of Ibsen's work and from Yeats's own earlier theatrical experiment, *The Countess Kathleen* (1892). This episodic, poetic drama, which combined folkloric elements with a nationalism fuelled by ancient and modern memories of injustice, had been chosen to inaugurate the Irish Literary Theatre in 1899 (the play was extensively revised in 1912). Yeats's original ambition had been to create a national dramatic style which would function on both a popular and a refinedly 'literary' level; as his ideas evolved, he shifted towards a concept of theatre which might draw from Irish traditions, both Celtic and Christian, and which might provide a focus for future national, and nationalist, aspiration. The acquisition of the Abbey Theatre in Dublin in 1904 gave Yeats and his associates (Lady Gregory, George Moore, and J. M. Synge) the base, if not the sympathetic audiences, that they required.

Yeats's sequence of plays concerned with the ancient hero Cuchulain began with *On Baile's Strand* in 1903. It was through this developing sequence that he began to explore the possibilities of an innovatory stage technique. The earlier plays have a certain stylization in which characters reflect abstract ideas and in which psychological 'realism' is broken down into oppositions, shadows, and reflections. A further breakthrough was initiated in 1913 by Ezra Pound's recommendation to him to study the 'distinguished, indirect, symbolic' patterns of Japanese Noh drama. The 'aristocratic' Noh also suggested to Yeats the possibilities of a freer symbolic and ritual drama, one that could harness and redirect the experimental methods already evolved by the innovative stage-designer Edward Gordon Craig (1872–1966). *At the Hawk's Well* (1916) moved away from direct reference to legend, and transfigured Cuchulain into a series of patterned words and symbols, a transfiguration emphasized by light effects and by the use of masks, dance, and the music of a drum, a gong, and a zither. The play's climax is a ritualistic dance. The two short late plays, *Purgatory* and *The Death of Cuchulain* (both 1939), suggest a further experimental move beyond Noh into bare stages, hauntings, and disconcerting shifts of time-perspective.

Synge's more conventionally shaped plays, written in the brief period between 1903 and the writer's death in 1909, create their singular effects through a language which struck its first Dublin audiences as 'strange'. Synge (1871–1909) too sought to minimize conventional action, but his stress fell less on ritual than on distinctive ways of speaking which echo the rhythms of the English of Western Ireland, a language moulded by an underlying Gaelic syntax and by the seepage of provincial Catholicism. Yeats's observation that Synge's English 'blurs definition, clear edges and everything that comes from the will' is particularly apposite to *Riders to the Sea* (1904), a short 'poetic' play which suggests the perennial failure of those who work with and on the sea. Character and action are subsumed in something approaching a choric flow which, through a series of reiterated similes, expresses a submissive fatalism. In *The Tinker's Wedding* (1903–7), *The Well of the Saints* (1905), and his masterpiece, *The Playboy of the Western World* (1907) Synge perfected a distinctively Irish comic form, one far removed from the stock Irishisms of Dion

Boucicault and English Victorian convention. If the plays reject the 'joyless and pallid words', which Synge regarded as symptomatic of the modern realism of Zola and Ibsen, they turn instead to the example of the London comedies of the seventeenth century and transform an essentially slick, urban dialogue into something both more lilting and wild. The remote Mayo coastline, on which *The Playboy of the Western World* is set, serves to confine an isolated rural community, one which is disturbed by the arrival of a fugitive, a supposed parricide. Words, and the illusion words create, dominate the action. Christy Mahon's prestige depends not upon a fulfilled deed but on his recounting of a deed which has failed to succeed; his final departure with his thrice 'resurrected' father is accompanied by a final, triumphant act of myth-making in which he declares that he goes away 'like a gallant captain with his heathen slave'. Nothing could be farther from the world of Oscar Wilde.

The Edwardian Age

To some nostalgic observers the short reign of King Edward VII (1901–1910) seemed like an autumnal idyll, an era of international peace, internal security, and relative prosperity. It was a period ushered in by the conclusion of the South African War in 1902 and by the consolidation of Britain's imperial possessions; to some it seemed to have symbolically closed, not with the end of the King's reign, but with the death of Captain Scott and his party in the Antarctic (having failed to reach the South Pole before the better organized Norwegian, Amundsen) in March 1912 and, a month later, with the terrible loss of life as the 'unsinkable' *Titanic* sank in the North Atlantic. For Thomas Hardy, the latter disaster had a horrible inevitability:

> And as the smart ship grew
> In stature grace and hue,
> In shadowy silent distance grew the Iceberg too.
>
> Alien they seemed to be:
> No mortal eye could see
> The intimate welding of their later history . . .

Scott's failure and death and the sinking of a great British passenger liner on its maiden voyage seemed somehow, darkly, to prepare the nation for what were to be yet greater checks to its pride and confidence during the war of 1914–18. Yet to look back on the Edwardian period as somehow cut off from what was to happen in 1914 is to misread history grossly. King Edward might have been happy with the popularly bestowed title of the 'Peacemaker', and even happier with the pomp and circumstance of State visits and intimate and avuncular chats with his numerous close relatives amongst the ruling dynasties of Europe, but in Britain at least policies were made by Cabinets not kings, and the drift of history was far from being in Britain's control.

Despite the reality of its international prestige and power, Britain's economic and military success was now relative. Its rate of economic growth was stagnating, especially when compared to those of the United States and Germany, and its much vaunted naval supremacy was being actively challenged by the rapid expansion of the Imperial German Navy. With the launch in 1906 of the *Dreadnought*, a revolutionary new type of 'all-big-gun' battleship, an armaments race began in earnest. If older types of battleship were now obsolete, Britain's aim of automatically outnumbering other naval powers became redundant (Germany laid down its own Dreadnought-type battleship, the *Nassau*, in 1907; the United States, France, and Japan rapidly followed suit). Military history was being 'welded' and those eyes that chose to see could readily recognize that a larger and more disastrous convergence beyond that of a ship and an iceberg was becoming inevitable.

The nation ruled by King Edward was far from consolidated and at peace with itself. The Irish question still festered, and though little political progress was made in the first decade of the twentieth century, when a third Home Rule Bill was introduced in Parliament in 1912 it aroused such determined opposition in Ulster that by 1914 Ireland seemed to be on the verge of civil war. Perhaps the most urgent political question of the Edwardian years was that of women's suffrage. The Women's Social and Political Union was formed in 1903 and between 1906 and 1914 the union undertook increasingly militant action to further its cause. Laws, some of them trivial, were broken, women were arrested, tried, imprisoned, and, most objectionably to public opinion, force-fed when on hunger strike. Though largely 'respectable' and middle class in inspiration, the suffragette movement was the first truly galvanizing force in the lives of a wide spectrum of British women for, as one activist later put it, it provided 'our education in that living identification of the self and with the corporate whole'. If war in 1914 put an end to organized suffrage agitation, it provided, through the significant contribution of women workers to the war-effort, the real catalyst to change. In March 1917 the Prime Minister himself moved the resolution of a bill which would include a limited franchise for women. The Representation of the People Act became law in February 1918 giving the vote to women over the age of 30 (the age qualification was reduced to 21 in 1928). It was, however, evident in all the parliaments of King Edward's reign that the old political status quo was beginning to fragment. In 1900 representatives from all the socialist groupings in Britain had set up the Labour Representation Committee with the professed aim of establishing 'a distinct Labour Group in Parliament'. In the election of 1906 some nineteen candidates supported by the LRC gained parliamentary seats and the new 'Labour Party' emerged, initially providing vital support for the social reforms embarked on by the governing Liberal Party. These reforms included in 1908 the introduction of old-age pensions (of 5 shillings a week for men of over 70) and in 1909 a so-called 'People's Budget' which proposed raising money to pay for both pensions and armaments from higher land taxes and death duties. When the Budget was rejected by the landowning interest represented by the

House of Lords, an extended constitutional crisis erupted. The crisis was only resolved by the Liberal election victory in 1910 and by the introduction of the Parliament Act which effectively deprived the Upper House of all power over money bills and limited its subsequent influence over all other legislation.

The 'golden age' of King Edward's reign was not always an illusion, but it was certainly a reality only for the relatively privileged. In some significant ways the early years of the twentieth century were marked by a triumphant Englishness, or at the very least by the confident swagger and independence of English architecture and English music. It was the age of 'the English house' and of a supremely sophisticated domestic style most readily associated with the name of Edwin Lutyens (though Lutyens was far from alone in perfecting it). It was also the age of the Garden City and of experiments with urban, sub-urban, and rural planning which have profoundly affected both how the English look at themselves and how foreigners look at the English. These architectural advances, which took Britain to the forefront of international innovation in design, also touched the lives of men and women of all classes. Their innate 'folksiness' was complemented by an eclectic and exultant revival of the baroque style which did not simply change the character of the centre of London but gave a touch of flamboyance to cities the length and breadth of the island. This flamboyance is also noticeable in the central works of the greatest British composer to emerge since the days of Purcell, Edward Elgar. Elgar's two symphonies of 1908 and 1911 have their moments of profound melancholy (the second symphony is dedicated to the memory of Edward VII), but they exude also a confident sense of the fact that English music had at last come of age. Whereas much of the energy of his composer contemporaries had been worthily directed towards the incorporation of national folk-music traditions into an orchestral mainstream, Elgar was, as he knew, a British music-maker with European roots and an emphatically European style. His work has a spaciousness which can variously be seen as a complement both to the rest-less, grandiloquent energy and to the introspective insecurities of Edwardian Britain.

The Edwardian Novel

In the mainstream English fiction of the early 1900s the religious doubts of the preceding twenty years, and the reaction against Victorian repression and social or familial oppression, are gradually marginalized. There remained a pervasive desire to articulate the unsaid and to give voice to formerly silent social groups—to women above all—and also to the often conventional, generally ignored petty bourgeoisie. The common man (and woman) briefly moved to centre stage before being ushered off again according to the élitist tastes of the Modernists. Although 'Modernist' writing, which has its roots in the early 1900s, looked to formal experiment, to verbal pyrotechnics, to synchronic play, and to the extraordinary in character and expression, more traditional writers, most notably Arnold Bennett and H. G. Wells, developed existing lines of story-telling and diachronic movement in order to delineate the 'ordinary'. To Arnold Bennett, writing in his disappointingly unadventurous study *The Author's Craft* (1914), the mind of the ideal novelist should be 'permeated and controlled by common sense'. This 'common sense' precluded a break with a received view of character and with the supposed stability of the narrative form. For both Bennett and Wells the acceptance of literary convention brought considerable popular and financial success (Bennett's *The Card* of 1911, for example, sold fifteen thousand copies within three years of publication). It also later entailed the overshadowing of their reputations by the canonical acceptance of the work of those of their younger contemporaries whose self-propagandizing had established 'Modernist' principles as the leading ideas of the new age.

As H. G. Wells generously acknowledged through the narrator of his *The New Machiavelli* (1911), there were hordes of men in 'the modern industrial world' who had 'raised themselves up from the general mass of untrained, uncultured poorish people in a hard industrious selfish struggle', but it was only in Arnold Bennett's novels that he had ever found a picture of them. These self-made, self-admiring small capitalists were now of a different breed from Dickens's Rouncewells and Gaskell's Thorntons, but they were generally despised by writers who rejected their enterprise, their vulgarity, and their belief in the virtue of work and reward. Bennett (1867–1931) is not habitually a fictional delineator of financial success, but he can be a meticulous analyst of the motives behind thrift, solidity, hard work, and public virtue. In this his models were, ironically enough, the great French anti-bourgeois writers Flaubert, Maupassant, and Zola rather than Dickens or Gaskell. His own affection for France and the French tradition gave him, as the Parisian episodes in *The Old Wives' Tale* suggest, a usefully detached perspective on his own birthplace, and the real focus of his fiction, the five drab towns of the Staffordshire Potteries.

Bennett's work oscillates interestingly between the poles of an insistent provinciality and domesticity and a taste for the exotic and the peregrinatory. Many of his novels either describe, or merely contain, a hotel, that temporary centre of a wanderer's life, that home-from-home that is never home. An over-written early work, *Grand Babylon Hotel* (1902), and a late documentary novel, *Imperial Palace* (1930), indicate something of the continuing force of his fascination, but the sections of *The Old Wives' Tale* dealing with Sophia Scales's Paris *Pension* and with the two sisters' sojourn at Buxton serve to ramify the idea of the hotel as a no man's land of comfort, tidiness, and impersonality. Bennett's finest fiction works through the establishment of contrasts, between situation and aspiration, between enclosure and flight, between endurance and escape, between security and insecurity. The sequence of three novels set in the Five Towns, *Clayhanger* (1910), *Hilda Lessways* (1911), and *These Twain*

(1916), are haunted by Darius Clayhanger's memories of the humiliation of the workhouse and by his son Edwin's attempts to escape from the cloying world of his father's respectable business. Bennett's masterpiece, *The Old Wives' Tale* (1908), traces the divergent fortunes of two sisters from the mid- to the late nineteenth century against the backgrounds of a slowly and unwillingly changing English industrial town and the turbulent Paris of the 1860s and 1870s. The small and provincial are counterbalanced by the metropolitan and the sophisticated, and generations conflict, converge, divide, and die. Bennett intricately relates his characters to the shaping topography, geography, class, and culture that surrounds them, but he always brings them back to acquired habit, the parochiality, and to plod. Similar qualities, exposed in a drab London setting, distinguish *Riceyman Steps* (1923). This post-First World War novel recalls physical and spiritual loss and wounding, but it centres on the limited ambitions and perceptions of a suburban bookseller, his wife, and his barely literate servant. The narrowness of the world Bennett describes is silently contrasted with that of the dusty and unopened books on the shelves of a shop whose contents are finally dispersed. Throughout the book the arbitrariness of commercial value is suggested (even down to a possessive attachment to the shop's dust) but its final pages allow for a questioning of literary value, of words on the page and the act of reading them. Without being a classic 'Modernist' text *Riceyman Steps* unobtrusively suggests many of the central experimental ideas of contemporary Modernism.

The work of H(erbert) G(eorge) Wells (1866–1946) has many parallels with that of the shop-keeping world of Bennett, but it has a far more evident political edge and a sometimes perversely 'scientific' programme. Wells is one of the few English writers to be well read in modern science and in the scientific method; he was also ambiguously persuaded both of the advantages of a socialistically and scientifically planned future and of the inherently anti-humanist bent of certain aspects of scientific progress. His science-fiction novels, *The Time Machine* (1895), *The Island of Dr Moreau* (1896), and *The War of the Worlds* (1898), still function as alarmist prophecies a century after their first publication. *The Island of Dr Moreau* is a chilling, almost Swiftian, fable of vivisection and genetic engineering. Moreau, a tyrannical exile on a Pacific island, is also a post-Darwinist Frankenstein, torturing and metamorphizing animals in his 'House of Pain' only to be destroyed as his horrid creations revert to their brutal types.

Wells's English social fiction contrasts starkly with such fantasies though even here science and men of science have leading roles. In *Tono Bungay* (1909) that role is divided between two Ponderevos: the small-town apothecary uncle who makes a fortune out of a spurious wonder-tonic, and the experimental nephew who re-establishes the lost family fortune by building battleships. Wells's socialism, a wayward, belligerent, and questioning socialism, also runs through his most demanding stories. In *Tono Bungay* the narrator moves between three Englands: the defunct, privileged world of the country house, the narrow perspectives of the draper's shop, and the heady exhilaration of market capitalism and invention. All three are found wanting, but he remains unpersuaded by an English brand of socialism which 'has always been a little bit too human, too set about with personalities and foolishness'. There is an individualism about Wells's arguments and the characters who mouth them which matches that of his sometime friend and Fabian socialist colleague, Shaw. In *Kipps: The Story of a Simple Soul* (1905) the critique of capital is more emphatic, and the socialist characters more sympathetic and influential, but the nation and the society observed in the book are seen as ruled by Stupidity 'like the leaden goddess of the Dunciad, like some fat, proud flunkey, like pride, like indolence, like all that is darkening and heavy and obstructive in life'. It is a stupidity which, it seems, no ideals can pierce. Even in the generally optimistic *The History of Mr Polly* (1910) the muddling nature of English society can be avoided only when the narrative endorses a fantasy of escape into a rural idyll. Wells's last major novel, before he retreated into writing the popular histories and digests of science with which he entertained his readers for thirty years, is *The New Machiavelli* of 1911. It is in part a personal testament, written from the point of view of a pragmatic Member of Parliament, as well as a perceptive account of parliamentary life in the early years of the twentieth century. Like *Ann Veronica* (1909) the book is forthright in its discussion of marriage and of women's rights, describing, very much from a male perspective, a 'gradual discovery of sex as a thing collectively portentous that I have to mingle with my statecraft if my picture is to be true'. It also contains sops for the supporters of women's suffrage, forcibly stating a case for the ceasing of 'this coddling and browbeating of women' and for the 'free and fearless' participation of women 'in the collective purpose of mankind'.

May Sinclair (1863–1946) became an active fighter for women's suffrage in 1908 and her fiction provided a useful vehicle for the expression of contemporary women's private and public aspirations. As an early reader of the theories of Sigmund Freud and his disciples, and as an admirer of what she recognized as the 'stream of consciousness' technique employed by Dorothy Richardson in her long sequence of novels *Pilgrimage*, Sinclair also investigated the new possibilities of women's 'psychological' fiction. *The Three Sisters* (1914) loosely parallels the story of the Brontë sisters but moves the period forward to the late nineteenth century and allows for amatory and marital complexities beyond that of a factual biography. Escape from the limiting life of a country parsonage also becomes a major thematic idea. A far more detailed study of individual repression and expression is provided in *Mary Olivier: A Life* (1919), a novel which traces the expanding consciousness of a middle-class girl, the youngest child in a family of boys. The opening of the story, which introduces the sharp sensory perceptions of a baby, bears a striking similarity to the technique used by Joyce in *A Portrait of the Artist as a Young Man* (1914–15). *Mary Olivier* deals subtly with the parent–child relationship, and especially with a daughter's strained love for her clinging, intellectually limited mother. It also movingly describes the slowly burgeoning career and reputation of a woman writer in literary London in the early years of the century.

E(dward) M(organ) Forster's six published novels are almost exclusively concerned with Edwardian middle-class perceptions and imperceptions. Forster (1879–1970), later a close associate of the so-called 'Bloomsbury Group', intermixes a sharp, observant, and sometimes bitter social comedy with didactic narrative insistence on the virtues of tolerance and human decency. His concern with the awakening of repressed sexuality, which was looked at from a heterosexual viewpoint in his first three novels—*Where Angels Fear to Tread* (1905), *The Longest Journey* (1907), and *A Room with a View* (1908)—was also treated in Forster's homosexual novel, *Maurice* (finished in 1914, but, on its author's insistence, published only after his death in 1971). *A Room with a View* contains some particularly trenchant observation of the smugness of English visitors to Florence before moving its major characters and their preoccupations back to the comfortable pretentiousness of Edwardian Surrey. It is essentially a love-story, but one shaped around reiterated contrasts between, on the one hand, English emotional repression and, on the other, the freedom of the spirit, suggested by the music of Beethoven, and the freedoms allowed to the passions by the far more 'civilized' Italians. Forster's relatively simple moral equations are explored with rather less subtlety in *Maurice*, a novel inspired, he explains in a 'Terminal Note' added to the manuscript in 1960, by his visits to the libertarian philosopher, Edward Carpenter (1844–1929), a 'Whitmannic poet whose nobility exceeded his strength'. *Maurice* is less a direct reflection of Carpenter's ideas than a nostalgic evocation of undergraduate friendship which steadily degenerates into fantasy when the hero's quest is satisfied by the nocturnal visitation of a young gamekeeper who appears through a fortuitously open window.

In its modest way *Maurice* offers a brave questioning of contemporary taboos (though they were no longer exactly taboos by the time of its publication). Its questioning of class-prejudices, class-assumptions, and local snobberies is, however, more half-hearted. This is a problem which also subtly besets *Howards End* (1910). Forster makes great, and often implied, narrative play with the novel's terse epigraph ('Only connect . . . '), forming and unforming a series of connections between characters and between what he sees as antipathetic cultures of business and the intellect. *Howards End* is carefully located in a society which lacks both confidence and spiritual idealism, but its narrative gestures often seem precariously agnostic rather than constructively connected (it contains a particularly awkward section which analyses Beethoven's Fifth Symphony in terms of dancing gnomes).

Forster's most ambitious and persuasive novel, *A Passage to India*, was published in 1924 following a period in which he had acted as secretary and companion to the Maharaja of Dewas Senior. The novel offers a distinctly less generous and complacent picture of the Raj and its British servants than had Kipling. The British form an élite, cut off by their ill-founded sense of racial, social, and cultural superiority from the multiple significance of the native civilizations of India, while maintaining the class-distinctions and petty snob-beries of 'home'. Throughout the story connections fail, doomed by race, class, colonialism, and religion. At the core of the novel Forster leaves a hiatus, a considered narrative gap in which an assault either happens, or doesn't happen, or is enacted by someone other than the man who is later accused of it. This hiatus takes on the force of a disjuncture which in turn enhances other dis-junctures, silences, and assaults on a reader's consciousness. Forster may at times appear to patronize his British and his Indian characters alike, and he may place too great a stress on humanism which is aspired to rather than real-ized, but *A Passage to India* contains a fluency of references and a far deeper questioning of the human muddle he saw around him than any other of his novels.

G(ilbert) K(eith) Chesterton's two 'Edwardian' novels, *The Napoleon of Notting Hill* (1904) and *The Man Who was Thursday: A Nightmare* (1908), have a narrative playfulness about them which is generally missing from the often glum political fiction of the period. Both are fantasies which lack substantial 'realist' characters and character psychologies. The first is set in the future, the second in an anarchic present. Both propose, withdraw, advocate, and under-mine social panaceas and easy political formulae. In *The Napoleon of Notting Hill* Chesterton's anti-centralist, anti-authoritarian, anti-theoretical prejudices serve to shape a utopian romance about an independent London ruled from an undistinguished inner suburb. Chesterton (1874–1936) produces a far more taxing and paradoxical fable in *The Man Who Was Thursday*. It is a story of London artists and London anarchists and it is cleverly made up of receding layers of deception and artifice; characters and roles prove to be as malleable as are the barriers between the diverse locations through which the plot moves (from leafy suburbia to secret hideaway to Leicester Square). The final solu-tion to the mystery posed by the narrative appears to lie in a coalescence of the Christian God with rampant human individualism. It is a disturbing and eccen-tric book, both drawing on tradition and traditionally told, but moving towards the fragmentation and narrative game-playing of those Modernists amongst whom the down-to-English-earth Chesterton would have found himself in odd company. His own literary tastes, as his sometimes perceptive, if over-neat and aphoristic, criticism shows, were finally rooted in mid-Victorian England (he produced a particularly good study of Dickens in 1906). His social prejudices, evident in his jolly later verse and his often presumptuous essays, were based on a nostalgic, Cobbett-like, vision of a lost, happy, Catholic England of beef, frothy beer, and good cheer.

The Poetry

To many contemporaries, the poetry of the 1880s and 1890s was dominated by the later work of those poets whose reputations had been made some thirty or forty years earlier. The prolific, if sometimes impenetrable, later verse of Browning and Tennyson continued to flow until their respective deaths in 1889 and 1892. On Tennyson's death, Queen Victoria, seeking advice on whom to appoint as the new Poet Laureate, was informed that Swinburne was the best living poet in her dominions (an opinion generally shared by the literary Establishment). Given Swinburne's notoriety, his appointment proved impossible to contemplate, though, as Oscar Wilde noted in *The Idler*: 'Mr Swinburne is already the Poet Laureate. The fact that his appointment to this high post has not been degraded by official confirmation renders his position all the more unassailable.' The job went to probably the worst candidate, the Tory rhymster Alfred Austin (1835–1913), a poet whose tenure of the laureateship was perhaps the dimmest and most risible in history.

The verse of the younger generation of poets was of a distinctly diverse kind, ranging from the often raucous balladry of Kipling to the effete, adjectival experiments of French-inspired decadents and the poised lyricism of the 'Rhymers' Club. Kipling's verse enjoyed a considerable popular success, particularly so as it appeared to give a voice to the otherwise inarticulate; to those supposed to be lacking in 'poetry' (that is, to ordinary soldiers and to the figures whom Chesterton later typed as 'the man on the Clapham omnibus'). Kipling used the role of a citizen-narrator in order to express what he took to be the appropriate middle-brow sentiments of the hour on such subjects as the old Queen's Jubilee ('Recessional'), the Empire ('The Ballad of East and West'), the trusty imperial subject ('Gunga Din'), or uppity women ('The Female of the Species' and 'The Ladies'). Wilde's verse, limited in scope and quality as it is, is also of an utterly different order, precise, refined, impressionistic, indeterminate. Lyrics such as 'Les Ballons' (1887) or 'Symphony in Yellow' (1889) suggest a poet wearing his sensibility, as well as his heart, upon his velvet sleeve and parading the notion that all beauty, common and uncommon, leaves him swooning. A completely different Wilde, one now vulnerable and protesting, emerges in *The Ballad of Reading Gaol* (1898).

> With slouch and swing around the ring
> We trod the Fools' Parade!
> We did not care: we knew we were
> The Devil's Own Brigade:
> And shaven head and feet of lead
> Make a merry masquerade.
>
> We tore the tarry rope to shreds
> With blunt and bleeding nails;
> We rubbed the doors, and scrubbed the floors,
> And cleaned the shining rails;
> And, rank by rank, we soaped the plank,
> And clattered with the pails.

If Wilde's term of imprisonment with hard labour nearly broke his spirit, it served at least to release from him a stark bluntness of expression.

A(lfred) E(dward) Housman (1859–1936) published only two volumes of verse in his lifetime (though a further 94 poems were published posthumously). Most of Housman's poetry is closely related to the form and the often tragic or elegiac mood of the traditional ballad. Housman himself maintained that he was also working under the influence of Shakespeare and of the *Volkslied* poetry of Heinrich Heine. The 63 poems assembled as the loose sequence entitled *A Shropshire Lad* (1896) show a scrupulous avoidance of richness and archness, though no attempt is made to represent them as the confessions of a rustic accustomed to his regional idiom. The poems are various in subject, setting, and speaker but they are linked by repeated themes (notably scenes of country wooing and events associated with soldiering) and by glancing references to Shropshire place-names and landscapes. Throughout Housman's work there is also a poignant sense of loss and lost illusions, the mood most famously caught in lyric 40 of *A Shropshire Lad*:

> Into my heart an air that kills
>   From yon far country blows:
> What are those blue remembered hills,
>   What spires, what farms are those?
>
> That is the land of lost content,
>   I see it shining plain,
> The happy highways where I went
>   And cannot come again.

The mood is not simply nostalgic. Love-making is interrupted by suicide, by murder, by death in battle, even by public execution (which is dwelt on in some detail). The generally heterosexual reference is shot through with a sublimated, but none the less fatalistic, homoeroticism which appears to render all emotional or sexual commitment unfulfilled, elusive, or ambiguous. In the extraordinary lyric 47 a male lover, 'the carpenter's son', dies on the gallows, he says, 'for love'. But this is no Christ. He dies futilely, advising other 'lads' and 'comrades' to adopt a 'shrewdness' in love. In lyric 42 a tempting, alluring 'merry guide', the embodiment of the pagan Hermes, leads the narrator onward 'with lips that brim with laughter', through a changing landscape. But he never responds. Housman, a Professor of Classics at London University, rusticizes and Anglicizes both his subjects and his sources, allotting a bucolic English voice to the Roman poet Terence (a voice 'friending' us 'in a dark and cloudy day') and translating Horace's celebrated *Diffugere nives* ('the snows are fled away') with a sad closing reference to the 'love of comrades'.

Charlotte Mew (1869–1928) was also troubled by images of unfulfilment, death, and burial. Mew's allusive short stories, the first of which appeared in 1894 in one of the celebrated 1890s anthologies, *The Yellow Book*, deal with defeat and with unrequited, but not always sexual, love. Her two volumes of verse which appeared in 1916 and 1929 suggest a new variety of perception and expression, much of it self-consciously impressionistic. As in the short stories, Mew's narrators are both male and female. The striking title poem of the first volume, *The Farmer's Bride*, has a rustic male speaker who incomprehendingly describes the failure of his marriage and the withdrawal of his bride into herself (the idea of mental aberration recurs in the poems 'Ken' and 'On the Asylum Road'). In other poems religion is both suspected and embraced, the need for a response to God in 'Madeleine in Church' being conditioned by a passionate exaltation of the transitory beauty of the world and of worldly things. The influence of Emily Brontë (on whose verse Mew published an essay in 1904), and of Christina Rossetti, is subtly transmuted both in her overtly religious lyrics and in those poems which suggest an elusive love or amatory betrayal.

The one major writer of an older generation whose poetry seemed to chart quite new territory in the opening years of the twentieth century was Thomas Hardy. Having ostensibly abandoned fiction after the public furore over *Jude the Obscure*, Hardy gave the impression of embarking on a new career as a prolific poet (his first volume appeared in 1898; his last in the year before his death). It would seem likely, however, that many of the poems in his first volume had been written much earlier. The agnosticism which so marks his novels takes on a new shaping power in the poetry, but the awkwardness, the strain, the conflicting perceptions and arguments, and the plethora of information in the late fiction are all controlled and disciplined within the succinct and varied verse forms that Hardy evolved. In the poem with which he nervously greeted the new century, 'The Darkling Thrush', landscape has its old impersonality, but it is shot through with suggestive hints of a strange anthropomorphism. 'Every spirit upon earth' seems to share a lack of fervour with the speaker. It is the lustily singing thrush that stirs spirits amid the 'growing gloom':

> So little cause for carolings
> Of such ecstatic sound
> Was written on terrestrial things
> Afar or nigh around,
> That I could think there trembled through
> His happy good-night air
> Some blessed Hope, whereof he knew
> And I was unaware.

The 'I' is left unaware, no longer dictating, undermining, or reinforcing impressions or interpretations. Hardy's poetry moves away from what in the fiction had seemed the pressing need to be literal or to offer explanation.

Much of the poetry in the early volumes recalls images, scenes, or incidents from a personal past and an immediate history which touches other histories, geographic, geological, architectural, and demographic. Love recalled is love lost, sometimes deliberately, sometimes perversely, and perception is frequently accompanied by a process of disillusion. Lovers meet ecstatically and part in misunderstanding or are sundered by incomprehending time. A great deal of critical and biographical attention has been focused on the elegiac poems of the period 1912–13 published in *Satires of Circumstance, Lyrics and Reveries* (1914). These poems in part celebrate, and in part expiate, the memory of the poet's first wife, Emma. Despite the volume's title (which embraces some earlier poems also published in it) the poetry of this period tends to reject the 'satiric' mode which Hardy himself acknowledged to be 'harsh'. Just as he returned physically to Cornwall to revisit spots where he had courted Emma forty years earlier, so there is a remaking of experience which is now conditioned by the awareness that so much has changed. The recalling voice, as in 'At Castle Boterel', is that of an older man but incidentals too, like the weather or the foliage, indicate the differences which divide then from now. In 'Under the Waterfall' (a poem shaped on the page to resemble the cascade it describes) the act of plunging an arm into cold water in a porcelain wash-basin brings back the memory of lovers picnicking beside a waterfall and losing a wineglass in the water:

> . . . There the glass still is.
> And, as said, if I thrust my arm below
> Cold water in basin or bowl, a throe
> From the past awakens a sense of that time . . .
>
> By night, by day, when it shines or lours,
> There lies intact that chalice of ours,
> And its presence adds to the rhyme of love
> Persistently sung by the fall above.
> No lip has touched it since his and mine
> In turns therefrom sipped lovers' wine.

The woman speaker's earlier use of the painful word 'throe' suggests that though the glass may have remained intact under the waterfall, the pledges once made in it have since been shattered. The water may sing continuously of a lost day of love, but the poem appears to recall the transience of love itself.

Hardy's huge and impressive expanse of lyric verse (all told, he wrote nearly a thousand poems) reveals an extraordinary metrical inventiveness and a technical mastery of a variety of forms. The style is plain, although there is a clear delight in the occasional deployment of lexical and phrasal obsolescence and in a play with localized 'Wessex' words which can serve to jolt a reader with the unexpected. An 'easy' reading can also be interrupted, challenged, or transformed by a word or idea which modifies what has been assumed or taken for granted. Commonplace meditations on mutability or time can be radically ramified by a fresh suggestion at mid-point in the poetic structure or by a closing stanza by means of which new connections are made or unmade. In 'The Phantom Horsewoman', for example, a reader is obliged to reconsider and reinterpret the meanings of 'phantom', of 'he' and 'she' and 'they' as the poem's perspectives shift. A later poem, 'During Wind and Rain', contrasts moments of fulfilment with the steady obliterations of human memory. Each human achievement, however simple or loving, is wrecked like summer blooms torn by an autumnal storm, and the echoed refrain which interrupts each stanza ('ah, no; the years O!') seems to express a wider, impersonal regret. At the climactic point the two visions coincide in a glimpse of a tombstone in the excoriating rain: 'Ah no; the years, the years; | Down their carved names the rain-drop ploughs.' Time is allowed one of his many triumphs.

The poetry of W. B. Yeats is rooted in a nineteenth-century tradition very different to Hardy's. Where Hardy frequently dwells on the cool disillusion of an informed agnostic and on the lost, but uncertain rapture of an elderly lover, Yeats attempts to assert the power of a mystical vision and an often passionate sexuality and sensuality. Hardy is a sceptical delineator of incident; Yeats a seeker of redefinitions, verbal as much as intellectual. Hardy attempts to suggest philosophical detachment in his poetry; Yeats presses for commitment, political and spiritual. Where Hardy is austere, Yeats implodes conflicting traditions and indicates, through a complex range of symbols, the outlines of new systems of thought and perception. Yeats, who refers to himself in 'Coole Park and Ballylee, 1931' as one of 'the last romantics' who had chosen 'for theme | Traditional sanctity and loveliness', continued to find a fresh vitality and variety in the potential explored by earlier generations of Romantics, projecting the mysticism of Blake and the symbolism of Rossetti into a newly suggestive poetry.

'I have desired', Yeats wrote in his essay *The Celtic Twilight* (1893), 'like every artist, to create a little world out of the beautiful, pleasant and significant things of this marred and clumsy world.' His early poetry, published in the volumes of 1889, 1893, and 1899, mixes post-Paterian aestheticism with a Celticism which is both nationalistic and escapist. As in the contemporary French culture of Maeterlinck and Debussy, Celtic legend offered an alternative way of seeing and representing the world, a non-classical, anti-urban, anti-mechanical, and anti-material intermixture of the physical and the metaphysical and of the sensual and the spiritual. Yeats's verse of the 1890s exploits a languorous repetition, learned from Tennyson and Swinburne, and calls for withdrawals into ideal landscapes, like that of Innisfree, or for driving with Fergus into 'the deep wood's shade'. The self-evident Irishness of these poems emerged from a context which, if thoroughly sympathetic to Celtic imaginings, was not itself exclusively Irish. The Rhymers' Club, whose members and meetings Yeats recalls in his *The Trembling of the Veil* (1922, incorporated in 1926 into *Autobiographies*), consisted of a loose gathering of friends with common interests and literary ambitions. To the honoured memory of Lionel Johnson (1867–1902) Yeats returned with affection throughout his own writing career. Johnson, a poet rhetorically inclined to explore Irish roots and the significance of his conversion to Roman Catholicism, can be both witty and delicate. Other members of the Club included Ernest Dowson (1867–1900) (the author of the haunting, non-committal 'Non sum qualis eram bonae sub regno Cynarae'), the gifted Scottish ballad poet John Davidson (1857–1909), and Arthur Symons (1865–1945). All are minor lyric poets whose significance is related to the particular *fin-de-siècle* context in which they worked rather than to English literature as a whole. The once influential Catholic apologist, Francis Thompson (1859–1907), the author of the ornate Swinburnian metaphorical poem, *The Hound of Heaven* (1893), made one appearance at the Club but never formally joined it. As Yeats later wrote: 'We read our poems to one another and talked criticism and drank a little wine. I sometimes say when I speak of the club, "We had such-and-such ideas, such-and-such a quarrel with the great Victorians, we set before us such-and-such aims", as though we had many philosophical ideas. I say this because I am ashamed to admit that I had these ideas and that whenever I began to talk of them a gloomy silence fell upon the room.' If Yeats here casts himself in the role of prime mover and bardic spokesman of a group of tavern wits, it is perhaps because he was aware, when he wrote the passage in 1922, that he was the survivor of an otherwise doomed generation and the one member whose art and ideas had developed and flourished.

The lullabies and the minstrelsy of faerie diminish in importance in the verse Yeats wrote after 1900. A suggestive poetry of vaguely perceived altern-ative visions gives way to a deeper speculation about love and the nature of the universe and to a political intensity inspired by an Ireland which had emerged from the haze of myth. The Ossianic is supplanted by the hermetic. Yeats always professed to see the world as in a state of perpetual flux. He also sug-gested that poets should share that flux by recognizing that poetic language was shaped and adapted by the shifting structures of culture and society. His translation of Jonathan Swift's Latin epitaph, worked into the poem of that name of 1933, dares the 'word-besotted traveller' to imitate a writer 'lacerated' by 'savage indignation'. The dare was taken up in the volumes entitled *The Wild Swans at Coole* (1919), *Michael Robartes and the Dancer* (1921), *The Tower* (1928), and *The Winding Stair and other Poems* (1933), volumes that contain poems which range in subject-matter from revolutionary politics to personal regret, from an evocation of an ideal past to prophecy, from private agonizing over the process of ageing to a celebration of cultural history. Yeats's progress as a poet can be compared to that of a man speaking in a succession of voices; his styles redefine his preoccupations and his images and they variously express the system of art and symbols that he announced in his highly speculative essay *A Vision* (1926, 1937).

Yeats opens the poem 'Vacillation', written in 1932, with the words 'Between extremities | Man runs his course'. The poem presents an argument framed by contraries and complements, dialogues between soul and heart and evoca-tions of the active, public domain of the soldier and the withdrawal of the meditating saint. Although he rejected much of the new philosophy of the cen-turies which his life spanned, the agnostic materialism of the nineteenth as much as the psychology, the physics, and the revolutionism of the twentieth, his later poetry proclaims the independence of the artist who creates and expounds a new spirituality. References to mythology and to Christianity, to

Homer and Dante, to Rome, Byzantium, or the quattrocento stand as points of reference within a new unity of vision which projects emblems of perfection and of the perfectibility of the soul. His visions are not always serene. In the tense sonnet, 'Leda and the Swan', for example—the rape of Leda by a superb, mastering bird—he transfers the sense of violation from the half-willing woman to the long-term consequences of the rape: the future ruin of Troy and the murder of Agamemnon:

> A sudden blow: the great wings beating still
> Above the staggering girl, her thighs caressed
> By the dark webs, her nape caught in his bill,
> He holds her helpless breast upon his breast.
>
> How can those terrified vague fingers push
> The feathered glory from her loosening thighs?
> And how can body, laid in that white rush,
> But feel the strange heart beating where it lies?
>
> A shudder in the loins engenders there
> The broken wall, the burning roof and tower
> And Agamemnon dead.
>   Being so caught up,
> So mastered by the brute blood of the air,
> Did she put on his knowledge with his power
> Before the indifferent beak could let her drop?

Sexist and phallocentric the poem may be, but for Yeats the enactment of the joining of the human and the divine transforms the intimate into the public, the woman's violation into a wider human tragedy. Other poems written in the 1920s share this divided vision of destiny and history. 'The Second Coming' suggests that a fearful revelation is at hand ('Things fall apart; the centre cannot hold; | Mere anarchy is loosed upon the world, | The blood-dimmed tide is loosed, and everywhere | The ceremony of innocence is drowned'). Alternatively the soul-making explored in 'The Tower' and 'Sailing to Byzantium' looks back either to an idealized Ireland or to the hieratic stillness of an iconic culture:

> O sages standing in God's holy fire
> As in the gold mosaic of a wall,
> Come from the holy fire, perne in a gyre,
> And be the singing-masters of my soul.
> Consume my heart away; sick with desire
> And fastened to a dying animal
> It knows not what it is; and gather me
> Into the artifice of eternity.

Where Yeats had begun his career assuming masks, he ended it fashioning masks for actors and dwelling on an art that had the potential to open up to eternity.

As an Irishman anxious to forge new loyalties, Yeats was famously detached from the British cause and British sympathies during the First World War. Unlike many of his class and religion in Ireland, he felt no moral obligation to be a combatant, nor was that obligation ever enforced by law (though conscription into the armed forces was introduced in Britain in January 1916, Ireland was exempted). When asked to write a war poem he later responded in a verse declaration that it was better 'in times like these | A poet's mouth be silent'. In 'An Irish Airman Foresees His Death' he produced a particularly impressive war poem, if one that expresses an indifference to other men's causes while still indulging in an exhilaration for 'this tumult in the clouds'. From the spring of 1916 he was properly preoccupied with the consequences of the 'terrible beauty' born of the Easter Rising in Dublin and not with the interminable slaughter on the Somme or at the Ypres Salient.

In editing *The Oxford Book of Modern Verse* in 1934 Yeats notoriously passed over the work of Wilfred Owen. For English poets, especially those younger than Yeats, the European War which began in the August of 1914 at first seemed an event to be spiritedly embraced. It could be greeted with youthful bravado and imperial confidence and celebrated with passionate pleas for the defence of the geographical entity of Britain in general and of a verdant England in particular. It is in many ways curious that a continuing avoidance of urban subject-matter in the English poetry of the opening years of the twentieth century projected a nostalgic view of an idealized landscape with the church clock stuck at ten to three. To the young men who fought in the trenches of the Western Front—poets, poetry readers, and those untouched by poetry alike—the war offered a ready enough excuse for the marginalization of domestic political problems. Men of the kidney of the pacifist, aristocratic, logician Bertrand Russell (1872–1970) were rare enough. Russell, who saw through self-justifying British 'War aims' as readily as he later saw through the specious intellectual justifications of Soviet Russia, was prepared to suffer for his pacifist convictions. The general patriotic enthusiasm of 1914 took time to waver; even longer to flounder. Feeling against the circumstances of the war, and a revulsion at its extraordinary waste, developed relatively late amongst a significant percentage of poets on active service. It was this singularly disillusioned verse which, despite Yeats's indifference, ultimately had a profound impact on the attitudes of later generations.

Edward Thomas, who was born in London in 1878, who enlisted in the Artists' Rifles in July 1915, and who was killed by a stray shell at the battle of Arras in April 1917, was a poet only for the last two and a half years of his life. The span of his work does, however, suggest a passionate feeling for the landscapes of southern England and an acute observation of the suffering occasioned by war, both at home and on the battlefield. It was as a result of conversations with the American poet Robert Frost that Thomas began to convert prose notes into poetry in 1914. Until that period he had subsisted as a critic for London journals and as a prose writer on nature in the tradition of the anti-London ruralist Richard Jefferies (1848–1887) (of whom Thomas published a biography in 1909). Thomas's journalism and prose essays have generally received less critical attention than his poetry. His editions of George Herbert (1908) and his appreciation of the newly published work of Thomas Traherne in *The South Country* (1909) suggest something of the formative influences on the plain diction, style, and rhythm of both his prose and his poetry. *The South Country* also testifies to a special sensitivity to topography and to the history which is implicit in a humanized landscape. 'In some places', he wrote, 'history has wrought like an earthquake, in others like an ant or mole; everywhere, permanently; so that if we but knew or cared, every swelling of the grass, every wavering line of hedge or path or road were an inscription, brief as an epitaph, in many languages and characters.' This sense of multiplicity, and of an ingrained past which must be read in nature, relates humankind to the phenomena of nature and indicates the extent to which Thomas's prose feeds into his belated outpourings of verse.

The landscapes of Thomas's poetry are often haunted by the ghosts of past occupants and users (both animal and human) and they contain the evidence of exploitation, work, and decay. In 'A Tale' (of which there exist two versions) there is an ambiguous contrast between the growing blue periwinkles and the broken fragments of blue china plates amid the ruins of a cottage. In one of the poems called 'Digging', two clay pipes, one a relic of a soldier of the time of Marlborough, the other the narrator's own, are 'let down . . . into the earth' as if their clay were that of human bodies joined in a common burial. Elsewhere time marks more roughly. In 'Blenheim Oranges' (the name of a variety of apple), an old house 'with grass growing instead | Of the footsteps of life' and a modern war which turns 'young men to dung' are yoked together with an awareness of loss which is both private and public, both present and historic. The war poem known by its first line, 'As the Team's Head-Brass', observes a ploughman and his team at work. Sporadic conversation develops between the ploughman and the narrator concerning the war and the consequent dearth of rural labour, but readers are made aware of other disjunctions. Conversation is interrupted each time the ploughman returns to his furrow and the war, somewhere over a horizon, suggests other, more drastic, breakings and severances:

> '. . . Have many gone
> From here?' 'Yes.' 'Many lost?' 'Yes, a good few.
> Only two teams work on the farm this year.
> One of my mates is dead. The second day
> In France they killed him. It was back in March,
> The very night of the blizzard, too. Now if
> He had stayed here we should have moved the tree.'
> 'And I should not have sat here. Everything
> Would have been different. For it would have been
> Another world.' 'Ay, and a better, though
> If we could see all all might seem good.' Then

> The lovers came out of the wood again:
> The horses started and for the last time
> I watched the clods crumble and topple over
> After the ploughshare and the stumbling team.

Thomas's sense of the encroachments of war in this poem is related to his evocations elsewhere of a transient and disappearing England, an England through which the poet passes, as in his much anthologized 'Adlestrop', merely as a traveller. The poems which deal directly with the Western Front treat death as the ultimate disrupter and destroyer of the already often violent co-operation of man and nature. A poem such as 'A Private' almost wryly notes the strangely abrupt distinction between a former ploughman, now lying dead in France, and his old habit of sleeping under English bushes when drunk. A very different address to death is suggested by 'Lights Out' where the military command of the title is translated into a journey through a dark wood 'where all must lose | Their way, however straight | Or winding'. The unnatural silence of the wood imposes a sense of loss, a loss not simply of direction but ultimately of the violated self.

Edward Thomas's poetry has only gradually won a wide audience for itself (the definitive edition of his verse appeared only in 1978); that of Rupert Brooke (1887–1915) had an immediate popular impact. It was an impact reinforced by Brooke's untimely death in the Mediterranean and by the iconic status accorded to his androgynous physical beauty. For some years after his death, Brooke's was perhaps the most reproduced image of a poet since Byron's. His pre-war poetry, most notably the cleverly urbane 'The Old Vicarage, Grantchester' of 1912, has a jesting and often colloquial nostalgia about it. The verse published posthumously in *1914 and Other Poems* (1915) including the five youthfully enthusiastic 'war sonnets' such as 'Peace', which thanks God for having 'matched us with His hour | And caught our youth, and wakened us from sleeping', and the famous 'The Soldier' ('If I should die . . .'), elicited from a fellow public-school poet the criticism 'he has clothed his attitude in fine words; but he has taken the sentimental attitude'. The critic was Charles Hamilton Sorley (1895–1915), later killed at the battle of Loos. Sorley died too young for his real individuality as a poet to have developed, but his *Marlborough and Other Poems* of 1916 ran through six editions in its first year of publication, evidence of the demand for, and response to, a certain kind of male war poetry in these years. The volume includes some striking sonnets addressed to Death, most impressively the poem beginning 'When you see Millions of the Mouthless Dead' which can be seen as anticipating the harsh disillusion of Sorley's poet successors.

In spite of the vast numbers of male combatants, and the stimulus to poetry represented by a community of soldiers and its enforced culture of male comradeship, the war and its aftermath also animated women's writing. Charlotte Mew's poem 'The Cenotaph' of 1919 was published in the second edition of her collection *The Farmer's Bride* in 1921. It is in many ways a typical memorial poem of its day, delicately apostrophizing a public, empty tomb as the focus of private mourning. The Cambridge poet Fredegond Shove's 'The Farmer' chillingly suggests the blighting of 'countless lives' amid the 'stillness, and long shivers, after death' and Margaret Postgate Cole's fine poems 'The Veteran', 'Afterwards', and 'Praematuri' centre on an acute awareness of the loss of youth and innocence and on the frightening sense of severance occasioned by the recall of the war's seemingly futile waste. Perhaps the most influential and personal of the women's books related to this dreadful period is Vera Brittain's once hugely popular memoir *Testament of Youth* (1933). Brittain (1893–1970), who served as a nurse during the war, interrupting her hard won studies at Oxford in order to do so, recalls not simply the ambitions and struggles of an educated woman, but also the tensions of waiting for news from the front and the profound emotional damage done to the bereaved by successive bereavements. The book contributed notably to an often pervasive mood of British pacifism in the troubled years immediately preceding the outbreak of the Second World War.

The two most influential autobiographies dealing with soldiers' experiences of the war were also published after a therapeutic and recuperative gap. Robert Graves's *Goodbye to All That* (1929) is experimental, quirky, and disrespectful of strict historical 'truth'. Siegfried Sassoon's trilogy—*Memoirs of a Fox-Hunting Man* (1928), *Memoirs of an Infantry Officer* (1930), and *Sherston's Progress* (1936)—written from the fictionalized point of view of 'George Sherston', records in its central volume Sassoon's celebrated 'A Soldier's Declaration'. This bold statement of July 1917 was made 'as an act of wilful defiance of military authority' because its author believed that the war was being 'deliberately prolonged by those who have the power to end it'. Sassoon also included a telling reference to the 'callous complacency' of the majority of men and women at home who had refused to comprehend the dire nature of conditions in the trenches. It was Graves who managed to persuade the War Office not to treat the Declaration as a disciplinary matter.

Sassoon's frustration and anger at the futility of the progress of the fighting is equally evident in his war poetry, poetry which emphasizes the chasm between those who make decisions, or accede to them, and those who suffer the consequences of them. He attacks not simply the Generals or the 'scarlet majors' of the poem 'Base Details', but also the incomprehending noncombatant civilians. Sassoon (1886–1967) vexedly and vividly suggests the unnaturalness (as it seemed) of life on leave from the front in 'Repression of the Experience', a simmering, restless piece which nervously gestures towards a breakdown of the mind and of the very structure of the poem. In 'Blighters', a music-hall entertainment provides a similar mockery of patriotism rather than any chance of relaxation, and in the ironic 'The Glory of Women' the speaker accuses those who unhelpfully cannot understand what is happening. Sassoon is at his succinct best as a poet in short, blunt lyrics; when he expands his themes, as in 'To any Dead Officer' or in the post-bellum 'To One who was with Me in the War', his ideas tend to become diffuse and his structures untidy. The bitter, satirical lyrics of 1917, such as 'The General' or the Kiplingesque 'Twelve Months After', have an iconoclastic pithiness. 'A Working Party', by contrast, allows for an elegiac memorializing of an unmemorable soldier 'accidentally' killed, and 'The Redeemer' makes play with the idea of transfiguration in an intermixture of religious and secular contexts. A soldier carrying wood is, while the light of a flare lasts, Christ-like; as the light fades, the soldier swears ('O Christ Almighty, now I'm stuck!'), surrendering his aura of the divine but retaining his suffering humanity. Sassoon's image, which has its roots in *Piers Plowman*, is also one which would be used to even more extraordinary effect by the only epic poet produced by the Great War, David Jones.

The war provided a disturbing context which forcibly transformed the often placid, elegiac, and unadorned poetry of the 1900s into a painfully observant record or a vehicle of protest. It is rarely an innovative poetry, however agonized its subjects or extraordinary its imagery. It is severely localized and the real individuality of certain war poets often shows up best when confined to anthologies of work by fellow-combatants. It is as idle to speculate as to how the work of the two most individual of these poets, Isaac Rosenberg (1890–1918) and Wilfred Owen (1893–1918), might have developed as it is to attempt to imagine Keats or Shelley as middle-aged Victorians. The two, temperamentally different and quite distinct in the traditions to which they responded, were both galvanized by their wartime experience. Rosenberg had certainly given indications of a radical poetic talent before 1914, but his poems of warfare, notably 'Break of Day in the Trenches', 'Louse Hunting', 'Returning, We Hear Larks', and 'Dead Man's Dump', suggest a kind of detached and curious fascination with the nature of war and with ravaged men and landscapes which is almost expressionist in its stark and often contrary energy. Rosenberg, who had drawn on Jewish history and mythology in much of his earlier experimental verse, remains explorative in his interest in the imagery he found around him in the desolation of the trenches. Death in 'Returning, We Hear Larks' is as natural and as dangerously deceptive as larks singing behind the battlefield:

> Death could drop from the dark
> As easily as song—
> But song only dropped,
> Like a blind man's dreams on the sand
> By dangerous tides,
> Like a girl's dark hair for she dreams no ruin lies there,
> Or her kisses where a serpent hides.

The larks seen this way, like the 'queer, sardonic rat' and the dropping poppies 'whose roots are in men's veins' in 'Break of Day in the Trenches', allow for an association of dissociated elements which looks forward to the early work of T. S. Eliot. Rosenberg's is a poetry of proto-Modernist fragmentation which discovers an objectivity in a world being physically pulled and blown apart.

Only four of Wilfred Owen's poems were published in his lifetime. His profound attraction to the work of Keats, and his debt to Keats's lushness, remain evident in one of these poems published in *Hydra,* the magazine edited by Owen during the late summer of 1917 when he was convalescing at Craiglockhart Hospital. 'Song of Songs' suggests little of the stark power that emerged in the poetry published posthumously in 1920 in an edition prepared by Sassoon, also a former fellow-patient at Craiglockhart. The finest of these war poems were written during an intense, creative period of eleven months which terminated in September 1918. Romantic exuberance no longer provided an appropriate literary model for what Owen now endeavoured to describe, though Keats's influence can still be inferred in the *Hyperion*-like vision of the unfinished 'Strange Meeting'. Owen also retained and experimented with other inherited forms and devices, notably the sonnet as in 'Anthem For Doomed Youth' and 'The Next War', and a fondness for rhyme which he developed, through half-rhyme, into para-rhyme in 'Strange Meeting' and the embittered 'Futility'. The sixteen-line 'The Parable of the Old Man and the Young' looks back, as Sassoon had done, to biblical precedent, but its real shape is determined not merely by its biblical echoes, or by its reference to modern warfare, but by its clever, disturbing, clinching, final couplet which turns the story of Abraham and Isaac on its head:

> So Abram rose, and crave the wood, and went
> And took the fire with him, and a knife.
> And as they sojourned both of them together,
> Isaac, the first-born spake, and said, My Father,
> Behold the preparations, fire and iron,
> But where the lamb for this burnt-offering?
> Then Abram bound the youth with belts and straps,
> And builded parapets and trenches there,
> And stretched forth the knife to slay his son.
> When lo! an angel called him out of heaven,
> Saying, Lay not thy hand upon the lad,
> Neither do anything to him. Behold,
> A ram, caught in a thicket by its horns;
> Offer the Ram of Pride instead of him.
> But the old man would not so, but slew his son,
> And half the seed of Europe, one by one.

There is a parallel anger at the sheer waste of human life in 'Futility', a poem which denies the reassuring Pauline associations between the stirring of seeds and the resurrection of the body. 'Dulce et Decorum Est' reverses Roman assumptions about patriotic sacrifice rather than comfortable Christian ones, by contrasting the ghastliness of death by mustard gas with the defunct

Horatian dignity which is damned as an 'old lie'. 'Strange Meeting', often conveniently interpreted as a knowing epitaph, pictures an escape from battle into 'some profound dull tunnel', a granite trench beyond a muddy trench, somehow a relic of 'titanic wars'. The poem moves to a meeting of enemies and to a mystic post-mortal reconciliation of two slaughtered soldiers:

> I am the enemy you killed, my friend.
> I knew you in this dark: for so you frowned
> Yesterday through me as you jabbed and killed.
> I parried; but my hands were loath and cold.
> Let us sleep now . . .

Owen was killed on 4 November 1918 before he had an opportunity to finish his poem. It was only a week before the Armistice which was to end 'the War to end Wars'.

In 1919 a 'Victory' medal was struck in Britain for presentation to all those soldiers who had survived what was described on its surface as 'The Great War for Civilization'. As the work of the war poets suggests, 'Civilization' had effectively floundered in the mire of the trenches or had been pitted and holed by the mechanisms and machines of modern military destruction. If Britain and the British Empire had emerged politically unscathed, the same was not true of the rest of combatant Europe, nor was it true of the minds and opinions of survivors or of those too young to fight. When the London-based American poet, Ezra Pound, wrote bitterly in *Hugh Selwyn Mauberley* (1920) of a human sacrifice in the name of 'an old bitch gone in the teeth | For a botched civilization', he was not merely summing up a hideous end of an era, he was also asserting the rights and privileges of a new literature which would attempt to sever itself from the traditions, and the 'traditional sanctities', of the old botched civilization.

9

Modernism and its Alternatives: Literature 1920–1945

WHEN the architect Sir Edwin Lutyens visited the battlefields of north-eastern France in July 1917 in order to investigate the need for permanent memorials to the vast numbers of British and Empire war-dead, he described in a tone of horrified amazement the strange interaction of man and nature he had witnessed. 'What humanity can endure and suffer is beyond belief', he told his wife, 'the battlefields—the obliteration of all human endeavour and achievement and the human achievement of destruction is bettered by the poppies and wild flowers that are as friendly to an unexploded shell as they are to the leg of a garden seat in Surrey.' For the moment, the only monument he could envisage as appropriate was 'a solid ball of bronze'. Lutyens's ambiguity concerning what he had seen as a non-combatant on the Western Front proved typical of the future reactions of those remembering or contemplating the wasteful devastation of the war. The post-war period was haunted by long memories, some tender, some angry, most sickening. According to the critic and poet Herbert Read, writing in *The Criterion* in 1930, it had taken more than a decade for ex-combatants to come to terms with what the war had meant to them and with 'the debris of its emotional conflicts' before they could begin to transform their experience into literature. Nevertheless, it was the incongruity implicit in the idea of the 'friendliness' of the unfeeling wild flowers noted by Lutyens, as much as that of the equally indifferent poppies, cornflowers, skylarks and rats of the poetry that had emerged from the war, that effectively marked the end of an art which had once reached for comforting or sympathetic images from nature. Stark and solid balls of bronze seemed a more appropriate tribute to those sacrificed to the unfeeling might of the machines devised and exploited by human ingenuity.

The feeling that a new start ought to be made, in politics and society as much as in art, was accentuated rather than initiated by the war and its immediate aftermath. When Virginia Woolf announced with a devastating flippancy that 'in or about December, 1910, human character changed', she was expressing what seemed by 1924 to be an accumulated sense of exhilaration at a variety of new beginnings and rejections of the past. Although she was referring back specifically to Samuel Butler's *The Way of All Flesh* as an early symptom of cultural questioning and to the plays of Shaw as a record of a continuing shift in attitudes, the intellectual élite who formed the first audience for Woolf's paper 'Mr Bennett and Mrs Brown' would probably have acknowledged the potent influence of other and wider European innovations. In November 1910 the eyes of London gallery-goers had been opened wide to the blazing colours and visual fragmentations of Cézanne, Van Gogh, and Gauguin at the exhibition organized by Roger Fry of 'Manet and the Post-Impressionists'. Although the Press had been vituperative and mocking in its criticism, and some visitors had laughed convulsively and shaken their umbrellas at the canvasses they found offensive, the exhibition's *succès de scandale* was to change the course of British painting in the twentieth century. In 1912 a second Post-Impressionist exhibition introduced the visual economies, the rethinkings of form, and the abstractions of Matisse, Picasso, Braque, and Derain to a London public. This second exhibition also included somewhat tamer pictures by English imitators, notably Duncan Grant and Virginia Woolf's sister Vanessa Bell, and a sprinkling of work by Russian artists.

A Russian contributor to the 1912 catalogue noted the significance of a new generation of national painters who had assimilated themselves 'to the popular art', rejoicing in its 'sincere directness' as a counterweight to what he saw as 'the over-refined and effeminate tastes' of the 'aesthetical gourmands' of St Petersburg. This comment related new Russian painting to the most familiar Western realization of the Slavic Renaissance, the seasons of ballet and opera organized in Paris and London by Diaghilev's company. Diaghilev's sensational contribution to the Coronation Gala programme at Covent Garden in 1911 had served to revolutionize English conceptions of dance and set design. On seeing Diaghilev's company in London, a gushingly enthusiastic Rupert Brooke wrote: 'They, if anything can, redeem our civilization. I'd give anything to be a ballet-designer.' It was not an ambition that Brooke was to realize, but the influence of the painters, designers, composers, and choreographers associated with Diaghilev's company remained remarkable. Besides ballets by Debussy, the second season of 1912 included the London première of Igor Stravinsky's *The Firebird*. It was followed in June 1913 by four performances of *The Rite of Spring*, a ballet which had been greeted with an orchestrated furore in Paris the month before. To ears unattuned to Orthodox liturgical chant and to Russian popular music, Stravinsky's aggressively repeated phrases and emphatic rhythms seemed like an excoriating exposure to something savagely primitive. To eyes accustomed to gently receding sylvan vistas as a frame for smooth and balanced balletic movement on the stage, the startling backdrops and the angularly athletic choreography jolted audiences into a new perception of theatrical kinetics. The very subjects of the new ballets commissioned by Diaghilev were seen as direct challenges to the vaunted 'refinement' and urbanity of inherited, aristocratic Western culture and to the emasculated nature of much of its own folk-tradition. Despite its reputation for being straitlaced and insular, pre-war London had cautiously emerged both as responsive to aesthetic novelty and as a focal point in the international dissemination of an art which seemed as distinctively 'modern' as it was innovative.

The outbreak of hostilities in August 1914 brought an abrupt if temporary end to easy international exchange and to expensive and overtly Germanic public displays in opera-houses. Even to non-combatants, to women, to middle-aged or unfit men, to exiled Americans, or to Irishmen unaffected by enforced conscription, the fabric of London intellectual life appeared to have deteriorated. To D. H. Lawrence, writing in 1923, the spirit of the old London collapsed in the winter of 1915–16: 'the city, in some way, perished, perished from being a heart of the world, and became a vortex of broken passions, lusts, hopes, fears and horrors.' Political dissent and debate too were suspended or at worst suppressed. The international General Strike, once seen as socialism's trump card to be played against a warmongering ruling class, failed to materialize in 1914 and Labour MPs were chosen to serve both in Lloyd George's War Cabinet and in minor governmental posts. The cause of women's suffrage, so actively pursued in the years up to 1914, was effectively silenced by the promise of future electoral reform (a promise partly redeemed in 1919). Even the subject of Irish Home Rule, the chief entanglement of domestic policy since the 1880s, was put on ice after the third reading of the Home Rule Bill in May 1914. It was violently kicked into life again by the six-day Easter Rising in Dublin in 1916. The 'Irish question', as with so many other suspended questions, was finally attended to in the context of a Europe which like Ireland had 'changed utterly' by the early 1920s. An Irish Free State, bereft of the six predominantly Protestant counties of Ulster, came into fudged being in 1921 and found itself immediately plunged into a brief but painful civil war.

By merit of its being deemed a 'domestic' concern of the victorious United Kingdom the problem of Ireland scarcely vexed the concentrated minds of the rulers of post-war Europe and America who met at Versailles in order to unravel the outstanding historical, geographical, religious, and racial knots in Central and Eastern Europe. In most cases severance proved quicker and more efficient than unravelling. Although there was no real hope of a return to the status quo ante, the treaties of Versailles and the Trianon proved only temporary compromises in the face of political circumstances moulded not simply by the disasters of war but also by the presumptions of the social and national revolutions the war had provoked. These new circumstances rarely left the politics, and by extension the literature, of the United Kingdom untouched. A sense of fragmentation, which was as much geographical and historical as it was cultural and psychological, haunted the experimental texts of the 1920s. The old continental empires had been convulsed and, in the case of Austria-Hungary and Turkey, posthumously dismembered. Humiliated Germany staggered from its attempts to establish a Marxist republic, to an unstable and impoverished 'bourgeois' democracy, and finally to a National Socialism intent on fulfilling what it claimed was the nation's unrealized European destiny. Above all, the October Revolution of 1917 had changed once arch-conservative Russia to a bright shade of red. It had also shifted the ground and the rules of all post-war political discussion.

The beleaguered Bolshevik state, first assaulted by armed Western intervention, then wracked by civil war and the destructive manœuvres of international capital, emerged for many post-war intellectuals as the model progressive society. In 1935 the veteran English collectivists and socialists, Sidney (1859–1947) and Beatrice Webb (1858–1943), subtitled their flattering study of Soviet Communism with the question 'A New Civilisation?'. In later editions the question mark was dropped. Respected British socialists such as H. G. Wells and Bernard Shaw returned from fact-finding missions to Soviet Russia in the 1930s and airily assented to the idea that they had seen the working future of humankind. Most conveniently avoided contemplating the fate of the Russian intelligentsia and the manifest suffering of uprooted, regimented, and forcibly collectivized peasants. To many British writers of the younger generation, the failure of the Western 'bourgeois democracies' to address the problems of poverty at home, and the problems of the explosive anti-democratic energies of Italian, German, and Spanish Fascism abroad, seemed further to expose Communist Russia as the only antidote to political despair. Fellow-travelling became the order of the day. It generally entailed keeping one bright eye on the goals at the end of the broad highway and a blind one on the deeds of one's travelling companions.

The optimism of 'progressive' British intellectuals about the vaunted achievements of the first 'Workers' State' was formed not simply by Soviet propaganda but by a pained awareness of the manifestly poor working and living conditions of a large percentage of their fellow-countrymen and women. The Britain to which demobbed troops returned in 1918 and 1919 proved not to be the 'Land fit for Heroes' promised by the wartime Prime Minister, David Lloyd George. Despite the social reforms initiated by pre-war Liberal governments, the condition of the industrial and agricultural poor, and of the unemployed, often contrasted as starkly with that of the rich as it had in mid-Victorian Britain. The peculiarly British brand of socialist thought and experiment, which had so marked the literature of the late nineteenth and early twentieth centuries, also served to determine the policies and electoral success of the Labour Party in the 1920s. That the party so stoutly resisted Marxist and Communist influence, and thereby alienated many young and more head-strong radicals, was an immediate result of its origins in quirky native ideologies and untheoretical traditions. A minority Labour Government was formed after the General Election of 1923 but fell only ten months later. Its impact on both the old order and the new was more symbolic than effective. In October 1924 the Government was profoundly shaken by the publication of a letter, supposedly from the Bolshevik Zinoviev, exhorting 'the masses of the British proletariat' to bestir themselves against the very sort of compromise the

Labour Party itself represented. A month later Labour defeat in a General Election brought the Conservatives back to power.

The General Strike of May 1926, which collapsed after nine days, demonstrated the failure of organized labour to topple, or even shake, a resolute and unsympathetic Government. The Government's propaganda victory was partly due to its successful control of the media, including, for the first time radio broadcasting. Continuing economic depression and rising unemployment nevertheless helped to ensure both that Labour was able to form a second Government between 1929 and 1931, and that Labour's reforming zeal floundered. There was relatively little any democratic government seemed to be able to do to reverse the devastating effects of the economic depression on heavy industry. Waste Lands seared themselves into more than simply the literary imagination. 'When the industry of a town has been killed', the trade unionist and politician Ellen Wilkinson wrote in her propagandist study of Jarrow, *The Town that was Murdered* (1939), 'it seems as difficult to apply artificial respiration as on a human corpse'.

Although the fate of Jarrow seemed to socialists like Wilkinson (1891–1947) to exemplify the inhuman shortcomings of the inherited capitalist order, it should not be assumed that British literature of the 1920s and 1930s was exclusively dominated by images of decay and instability or by a language of fragmentation and reformulation. The sometimes bright, sometimes troubled, new horizons opened by international cultural innovation were, however, rarely concordant with the working lives and domestic diversions of the vast mass of the British population. In his pithy essay 'Art and Life' (1917), republished as the first paper in his influential *Vision and Design* in 1920, Roger Fry (1866–1934) had argued that 'the correspondence between art and life which we so habitually assume is not at all constant and requires much correction before it can be trusted'. If Fry's argument sets out initially to counter the idea of art as photographic representation, it ends by announcing that 'the artist of the new movement is moving into a sphere more and more remote from that of the ordinary man' and that 'in proportion as art becomes purer the number of people to whom it appeals gets less'. Much of Fry's artistic mission consisted of attacks on the narrow perceptions of the now socially and intellectually emancipated lower-middle class. It was a class now served by new middlebrow newspapers such as the *Daily Mail* (founded 1896), *Daily Mirror* (the first newspaper devoted exclusively to women's interests, founded 1903), and the *Daily Express* (founded 1900 and developed into a journal of substantial influence and circulation under the proprietorship of Lord Beaverbrook in the 1920s). In the opinion of such newspapers and their readers, a broad national 'culture' and a sense of participation in all elements of national life were no longer the exclusive preserve of an educated or privileged élite. Popular newspapers helped secure their position as moulders of social opinion by sponsoring easily assimilated history books, illustrated commemorative volumes, reissued classic novels, dictionaries and, above all, moderately priced encyclopaedias. 'I know what I like' and 'I know how to see through what I have been told to like' became interchangeable and variable propositions according to class, education, and purchasing power. It was an aspect of freedom and cultural multiplicity which was rarely acceptable to an aesthetic and political avant-garde.

However disconcerting it may have seemed to highbrow opinion, the triumph of the middlebrow was successfully fostered by technological innovation. In many ways the British middle classes, and those who aspired to modest middle-class status and respectability, did well out of the inter-war period. The evolution of the detached and semi-detached villa by countless speculative builders seemed to offer the promise of a better and cleaner life in the expanding outer suburbs of those British cities which remained unaffected by the Depression. Lines of fussy, historically referential but unpretentious 'semis' spread out along arterial roads and sprawled over former farmland and the abandoned gardens of the demolished mansions of earlier and richer suburbanites. The construction of these suburbs was an enterprise as socially significant in its way as the building of the medieval cathedrals or the country houses of the Georgian aristocracy (if one rarely as aesthetically satisfying). They also gave, and still give, ordinary people a much-desired quality of life: a garden back and front, conveniently sized rooms, and a suburban ambience detached from the supposed annoyances of the town. With the advent of the wireless in the 1920s (the British Broadcasting Company merged into the British Broadcasting Corporation in 1926) a vital aspect of popular entertainment shifted classlessly away from the public domain and into the domestic, from the theatre and the ballroom to the parlour and the kitchen. The first music broadcast by the new Corporation on New Year's Day 1926 was the insistently democratic song 'The more we are together the merrier we'll be'. Programming decisions determined that dance music vied with the classical and the big band with the orchestra. Actors, music-hall artistes, novelists, journalists, and poets cemented their reputations by directly addressing audiences unimagined by their predecessors. Even the reserved King George V cultivated a newly intimate relationship with his people through the medium of cheery Christmas messages broadcast to the Empire (his wayward successor, Edward VIII, however, used the radio in December 1936 to announce his abdication from the throne).

With the brief advent of television in the late 1930s (an experiment terminated by the Second World War) a further dimension was added to home entertainment for those who could afford it. Television eventually diminished both the glory and the audiences of by far the most popular form of diversion in the 1930s, the cinema. The construction throughout Britain of the great 'picture-palaces' set the seal on the success of a form of entertainment that appealed equally to the middle and working classes. The achievement of the art of the cinema, and particularly the American cinema, had no real precedent. Its subjects, and the often fantastic buildings in which films were shown, looked both backwards and forwards. Audiences were imaginatively projected back to Imperial Rome and to Medieval Europe; they escaped into dreams of grand hotels and streamlined art deco apartments and, in the case of films like the admirable British film-version of H. G. Wells's *Things to Come* (1936), they glimpsed a disturbing but ultimately happy future. The efforts of both the Hollywood studios and, later, of their less well-endowed British shadows, also conditioned the popular perception of certain literary 'classics' for both good and ill. *The Barretts of Wimpole Street* of 1934, for example, wove fictional strands around the story of the elopement of Robert Browning and Elizabeth Barrett. The 1931 version of *Frankenstein* distorted Mary Shelley's plot and her central characters out of recognizable shape, while William Wyler's *Wuthering Heights* of 1939 rendered Emily Brontë's novel little more than a vehicle for the high-flown talents of Merle Oberon and Laurence Olivier. Olivier also starred in the 1940 adaptation of *Pride and Prejudice* (for which Aldous Huxley helped provide a screenplay). Both Shakespeare and Dickens were, however, better served by still celebrated versions by Max Reinhardt of *A Midsummer Night's Dream* (1935), by Olivier of *Henry V* (1945) and *Hamlet* (1948) (both with the director in the title-role), by George Cukor of *David Copperfield* (1935, with W. C. Fields as Micawber), and by David Lean of *Great Expectations* (1946) and *Oliver Twist* (1948). In a separate category stands the cinematic involvement of living British writers, notably the collaboration of Noël Coward with David Lean in the ever-so-British wartime heroics of *In Which We Serve* (1942), Coward's script for the delicate tear-jerker *Brief Encounter* (1945), and Terence Rattigan and Graham Greene's screenplay for John Boulting's film of Greene's novel *Brighton Rock* (1947).

The cultural perspective offered by the cinema, and by a director's freedom to depart from the limitations of a given text, serves as a reminder of the twentieth century's growing awareness of the instability of the relationship between the viewer and the viewed object, the reader and the text, the past and the present. Questionings of received ideas of form haunt the critical writings of the early Modernists. Debates about tradition and the rejection of tradition, about the use and interpretation of history, and about the very survival and value of the written word have taken on a renewed urgency as Modernism evolved into a variety of post-Modernisms. Any overview of the literature of a given historical period is, however, further conditioned by the awareness of often radically different perspectives between then and now. As with the years 1780–1830, to see one single mood, genre, style, or ideology as dominant in the Britain of the inter-war period serves to distort its real multiplicity. It is equally confusing to trust the opinions of contemporaries, from whatever side they come, without questioning them. When, for example, the middlebrow *Illustrated London News* published a 'Silver Jubilee Record Number' in 1935 to celebrate twenty-five years of the reign of George V, its retrospect on 'Writers of the Present Reign' diverged radically from the prospects for a new 'Georgian' literature earlier set out in Virginia Woolf's two essays 'Modern Fiction' (1919) and 'Mr Bennett and Mrs Brown' (1924). Where Woolf had divided her 'Edwardians' (Bennett, Wells, and Galsworthy) from her 'Georgians' (Eliot, Forster, Lawrence, and, somewhat reluctantly, Joyce), *Illustrated London News* commissioned a brief survey of modern letters from G. K. Chesterton and illustrated it with photographs of writers selected, one presumes, by the issue's editor. Chesterton skirted as carefully as he could around the evident disjunctures within his subject. He was evidently happier with the work of an older generation (Hardy, Shaw, Yeats) and even with the 'high note in normal English versification' of younger conservative poets (Alfred Noyes, John Drinkwater, Lascelles Abercrombie, and Humbert Wolfe) than he was with the fictional 'mud-slinging' of Aldous Huxley and with the poetry of Pound and Eliot (whom he sees as representing an unwelcome American innovation). Chesterton managed, with some reserve, to admire the novels of Woolf and Vita Sackville-West, and he found himself able to draw an over-neat contrast between Lawrence and Huxley ('Lawrence tried to escape through the body, and Huxley through the brain; but it is doubtful if either of them did escape'). More starkly out of step with what has become the received opinion of later generations are the twenty-two vignette-photographs of writers which illustrate the essay. Lytton Strachey appears as 'biographer and historian', but his name is somewhat incongruously linked to those of Hilaire Belloc and the now forgotten historians Sir Julian Corbett and Viscount Morley. Mrs Humphry Ward (d. 1920) rubs shoulders with Katherine Mansfield (d. 1923) but they are joined by a decidedly rum 'representative' selection of once popular novelists and essayists: Israel Zangwill, Mary Webb, Robert Hichens, W. J. Locke, 'F. Anstey', A. E. W. Mason, Sir Arthur Quiller-Couch, and E. F. Benson. Apart from W. B. Yeats the reputations of the four other selected poets (Alice Meynell, Robert Bridges, Stephen Phillips, and Sir William Watson) have slumped disastrously. To readers with sensibilities moulded by books which have since been deemed to be characteristic of the early 1930s—Eliot's *Ash Wednesday* (1930) and *Burnt Norton* (1935), Woolf's *The Waves* (1931), Huxley's *Brave New World* (1932), and Auden's *Poems* (1930) and *The Orators* (1932)—the *Illustrated London News*'s canon looks stillborn. It may still be possible that posterity will find Ezra Pound's insistence on new beginnings and a new kind of post-war writing misguided, but it seems unlikely. What the age 'demanded' when the guns fell silent in November 1918 still seems to us to have called forth a particularly influential form of rearticulation.

'Bloomsbury' and beyond: Strachey, Woolf, and Mansfield

When the narrator of Evelyn Waugh's novel *Brideshead Revisited* goes up to Oxford as an undergraduate in 1922 he decorates his college rooms with objects indicative of his 'advanced' but essentially derivative taste. Charles Ryder hangs up a reproduction of Van Gogh's *Sunflowers*, a painting which had been shown at the first Post-Impressionist exhibition, and he displays a screen painted by Roger Fry that he has acquired at the closing sale at Fry's pioneering Omega Workshops (a byword for the clumsily experimental interior design of the period). He also shows off a collection of books which he later embarrassedly describes as 'meagre and commonplace'. These books include volumes of *Georgian Poetry* (the last in the series of which had just appeared), once popular and mildly sensational novels by Compton Mackenzie (1883–1972) and Norman Douglas (1868–1952), Roger Fry's *Vision and Design* of 1920 and Lytton Strachey's *Eminent Victorians* of 1918. These last two volumes, issued in a similar popular format in the early 1920s, are the clearest signals of the extent to which the young Ryder has been influenced by the canons of taste enunciated by the group of writers and artists who have come to be known as the 'Bloomsbury Group'.

'Bloomsbury' was never a formal grouping. Its origins lay in male friendships in late nineteenth-century Cambridge; in the early 1900s it found a focus in the Gordon Square house of the children of Leslie Stephen in unfashionable Bloomsbury; it was only with the formation of the 'Memoir Club' in 1920 that it loosely defined the limits of its friendships, relationships, and sympathies. The 'Memoir Club' originally centred on Leslie Stephen's two daughters Virginia and Vanessa, their husbands Leonard Woolf and Clive Bell, and their friends and neighbours Desmond and Molly MacCarthy, Duncan Grant, E. M. Forster, Roger Fry, and John Maynard Keynes. The group was linked by what Clive Bell later called 'a taste for discussion in pursuit of truth and a contempt for conventional ways of thinking and feeling, contempt for conventional morals if you will'. Their discussions combined tolerant agnosticism with cultural dogmatism, progressive rationality with social snobbery, practical jokes with refined self-advertisement. When in 1928 Bell (1881–1964) attempted to define 'Civilization' (in a book of that name) he identified an aggrandized Bloomsbury ideal in the *douceur de vivre* and witty iconoclasm of the France of the Enlightenment (though, as Virginia Woolf commented, 'in the end it turns out that civilization is a lunch party at No 50 Gordon Square'). To its friends 'Bloomsbury' offered a prevision of a relaxed, permissive, and élitist future; to its enemies, like the once patronized and later estranged D. H. Lawrence, it was a tight little world peopled by upper-middle-class 'black beetles'.

The prime 'Bloomsbury' text, Lytton Strachey's *Eminent Victorians*, suggests that it is easier to see what the group did not represent than what it did. Strachey's book struck a sympathetic chord with both his friends and the public at large. *Eminent Victorians* (1918), a collection of four succinct biographies of Cardinal Manning, Florence Nightingale, Thomas Arnold, and General Gordon, seemed to many readers to deliver the necessary *coup de grâce* to the false ideals and empty heroism of the nineteenth century. These were principles which seemed to have been tried on the Western Front and found disastrously wanting. Strachey (1880–1932) does not so much mock his subjects as let them damn themselves in the eyes of their more enlightened successors. He works not by frontal assault but by means of the sapping innuendo and the carefully placed, explosive epigram. His models, like Bell's, are the Voltairean conversationalists of the Paris salons of the eighteenth century, not the earnest Carlylean lecturers of Victorian London. When, for example, he speculates about Florence Nightingale's conception of God he jests that 'she felt towards Him as she might have felt towards a glorified sanitary engineer'. In a review written in 1909 Strachey had endorsed the idea that 'the first duty of a great historian is to be an artist'. As his later studies of *Queen Victoria* (1921) and of *Elizabeth and Essex* (1928) suggest, Strachey was neither a great historian nor, ultimately, a great biographer, but he was undoubtedly an innovative craftsman. The 'art' of biography has never been quite the same since. It is not simply that he was an iconoclast; he was the master of a prose of elegant disenchantment. His age, if it did not always cultivate elegance, readily understood disenchantment.

Strachey's biographies challenged the conventional wisdom of interpretation. They sprang, like the disparate essays assembled in Roger Fry's *Vision and Design*, from an urge to establish a new way of seeing and observing which was distinct from the stuffy pieties of the Victorians. Fry's title carefully avoids the word 'form', but it is that word, linked to the crucially qualifying adjective 'significant', which weaves, by direct reference and by implication, in and out of the twenty-five short essays. Although *Vision and Design* is primarily dedicated to reconsiderations of painting and sculpture, the implications of its theoretical formulations for the experimental fiction of Virginia Woolf are considerable. In his 'Essay in Aesthetics' Fry distinguishes between 'instinctive reactions to sensible objects' and the peculiarly human faculty of 'calling up again . . . the echo of past experiences' in the imagination. The 'whole consciousness', he argues, 'may be focussed upon the perceptive and the emotional aspects of the experience' and thus produced in the imaginative life 'a different set of values, and a different kind of perception'. As the 'chief organ of the imaginative life' Art works by a set of values distinct from those of pure representation. When he specifically returns to his argument in the book's final 'Retrospect' Fry offers a further definition of the term 'significant form' as 'something other than agreeable arrangements of form, harmonious patterns, and the like'. A work of art possessing this elusive, and seemingly indefinable quality implies, he asserts, 'the effort on the part of the artist to bend to our emotional understanding by means of his passionate conviction some intractable material which is alien to our spirit'.

Virginia Woolf's criticism distils and reapplies Bell's and Fry's aesthetic ideas as a means of arguing for the potential freedom of the novel from commonly received understandings of plot, time, and identity. In discussing the revision of traditional modes of representation in her essay 'Modern Fiction', Woolf (1882–1941) insists that each day 'the mind receives a myriad of impressions—trivial, fantastic, evanescent, or engraved with the sharpness of steel'. The novelist, attempting to work with this 'incessant shower of innumerable atoms', is forced to recognize that 'if he could base his work upon his own feeling and not upon convention', there would be no plot, no comedy, no tragedy, no love interest or catastrophe 'in the accepted style'. The task of the future novelist, Woolf therefore suggests, is to convey an impression of the 'luminous halo' of life—'this varying, this unknown and uncircumscribed spirit'—with as little mixture of the 'alien and external' as possible. What Woolf seeks to defend in her essays is not necessarily a new range of subjects for the novel, but new ways of rendering and designing the novel. She does more than present a challenge to the received idea of realism; she reaches out to a new aesthetic of realism. Essentially, she defines her own work, and that of contemporaries, such as Lawrence and Joyce, against the example of the Edwardian 'materialists' (and Arnold Bennett in particular) who, to her mind, laid too great a stress on 'the fabric of things'. Not only did they weigh their fiction down with a plethora of external detail, they too readily accepted the constraints of conventional obedience to 'plot' and sequential development. Much as Roger Fry had seen the liberated artist 'bending' intractable material into significance, Woolf insists that the twentieth-century novelist could evolve a new fictional form out of a representation of the 'myriad impressions' which daily impose themselves on the human consciousness.

As Virginia Woolf's fictional style developed beyond the relatively conventional parameters of *The Voyage Out* (1915) to the experimental representations of consciousness in *Mrs Dalloway* (1925), *To the Lighthouse* (1927), and *The Waves* (1931), specific characterization recedes and the detailed exploration of the individual identity tends to melt into a larger and freer expression. The discontinuities, fragmentations, and disintegrations which her avant-garde artistic contemporaries observed in both the external and the spiritual world become focused for Woolf in the idea, noted in her diary in 1924, of character 'dissipated into shreds'. Her novels attempt both to 'dissipate' character and to reintegrate human experience within an aesthetic shape or 'form'. She seeks to represent the nature of transient sensation, or of conscious and unconscious mental activity, and then to relate it outwards to a more universal awareness of pattern and rhythm. The momentary reaction, the impermanent emotion, the ephemeral stimulus, the random suggestion, and the dissociated thought are effectively 'bent' into a stylistic relationship to something coherent and structured. A 'coherence in things' is what Mrs Ramsay recognizes in a visionary, and quasi-religious, moment of peace in *To the Lighthouse* as 'a stability . . . something . . . immune from change'. The supposedly random picture of the temporal in Woolf's later fiction is also informed and 'interpreted' by the invocation of the permanent and the universal, much as the 'arbitrary' in nature was 'interpreted' with reference to post-Darwinian science, or the complexities of the human psyche unravelled by the application of newly fashionable Freudian theory. Although her characters may often

seem to be dissolved into little more than ciphers, what they come to signify
is part of a complex iconographic discourse. In the instances of *To the
Lighthouse* and *The Waves* the glancing insights into the identities of characters are complemented by larger symbols (a flickering lighthouse or moving
water) which are allowed to be both temporary and permanent, both 'real' and
resonant, both constant and fluctuating. The fictional whole thus becomes a
normative expression of certain Modernist themes and modes. Woolf's particular preoccupation with time is closely related to her manifest interest in
flux, a dissolution or dissipation of distinctions within a fluid pattern of change
and decay, which she recognizes in nature and science as much as in the human
psyche. Her universe, though effectively Godless, is not one deprived of
imposed meaning and patterning. Her narratives are variously punctuated by
clock-readings and clock-soundings, by the measurement of tides and the alti-
tude of the sun, by history and archaeology, by ageing and dying. Whereas in
her longest novel, *The Years* (1937), she stresses the nature of a local awareness of the sequential passage of time from the 1880s to the 1930s, and explores
the consequences and processes of waiting, learning, and ageing, she elsewhere
shapes her fiction by means of the larger consciousness of a narrator alert both
to historical callibration of time and, more significantly, to an imaginative
freedom from time.

The informing presence of women characters with an aesthetic propensity,
or of particular women artists, serves to moderate and condition the larger
ambitions of the narratives in which they appear. Although Virginia Woolf
rarely directly echoes the insistent narrative voice of a George Eliot, her own
work does reflect what she recognized in her pioneer essay on Eliot (1925) as
a tendency to introduce characters who stand for 'that troubled spirit, that
exacting and questioning and baffled presence' of the novelist herself. If
neither Lily Briscoe nor Miss La Trobe possesses the cultural significance of
a Romola or a Dorothea, both are allowed, as amateur artists, to act out the
ordering dilemma of the professional. In the final part of *To the Lighthouse* the
'weight' of Lily Briscoe's painting seems to be poised as she explores the elusive
nature of mass and form: 'Beautiful and bright it should be on the surface,
feathery and evanescent, one colour melting into another like the colours on a
butterfly's wing; but beneath the fabric must be clamped together with bolts
of iron.' A similar 'visionary' insight temporarily enlightens the amateur
author of the historical pageant around which *Between the Acts* (1941) is
shaped. Miss La Trobe watches entranced as butterflies (traditional images of
the human soul) 'gluttonously absorb' the rich colours of the fancy dress
strewn on the grass; the possibility of a completer art briefly dawns on her,
only to fall apart again. In both novels women's sensibility (and sensitivity)
contrasts with the factual 'materialism' of a world dominated by the kind of
men who 'negotiated treaties, ruled India, controlled finance' or who insist,
as Colonel Mayhew does in *Between the Acts*, that no picture of history is
complete without reference to the British Army. The Mrs Ramsays, the Lily

Briscoes, and the Miss La Trobes dream their brief dreams or are vouchsafed momentary 'epiphanies'; the men are often left content with a limited grasp, and presumed control, of the physical world.

Virginia Woolf's most complete, but ambiguous, representation of the life of a woman character's mind in *Mrs Dalloway* is also her most thorough experiment with the new technique of interior monologue. The novel plays subtly with the problem of an identity which is both multiple and singular, both public and private, and it gradually insists on the mutual dependence and opposition of the perceptions of Clarissa Dalloway and the shell-shocked ramblings of a victim of the war, Septimus Warren Smith. *Mrs Dalloway* reveals both the particular originality of Woolf's fictional mode and the more general limitations of her social vision. When she returns to the problem of a dissipated identity in her extraordinary tribute to the English aristocracy, *Orlando* (1928), she seems to seek both to dissolve and define character in a fanciful concoction of English history and shifting gender. The book is in part a sentimental tribute to the personal flair and ancestral fixation of her aristocratic friend and fellow-writer, Victoria ('Vita') Sackville-West (1892–1962), in part an exploration of a 'masculine' freedom traditionally denied to women. If Woolf's depiction of the society of her time is as blinkered as that of E. M. Forster by upper-middle-class snobberies and would-be liberalisms, the historical perspective which determined her feminism made for a far more distinctive clarity of argument. In the essay 'Street Haunting' (published in 1942) she writes of the pleasures of a London *flâneuse* who discovers as the front door shuts that the shell-like nature of domestic withdrawal is broken open 'and there is left of all these wrinkles and roughnesses a central oyster of perceptiveness, an enormous eye'. Almost the opposite process is delineated in the study *A Room of One's Own* (1929), where the existence of a private space, and of a private income, is seen as a prerequisite for the development of a woman writer's creativity. *A Room of One's Own* is, however, far more than an insistent plea for privacy, leisure, and education; it is a proclamation that women's writing has nearly come of age. It meditates on the pervasiveness of women as the subjects of poetry and on their absence from history; it plays as fancifully as the narrator of *Orlando* might with the domestic fate of a woman Shakespeare, but above all it pays tribute to those English novelists, from Aphra Behn to George Eliot, who established a tradition of women's writing. 'Masterpieces are not single and solitary births', she insisted, 'they are the outcome of many years of thinking in common, of thinking by the body of the people, so that the experience of the mass is behind the single voice.' It is in this tradition that Virginia Woolf most earnestly sought to see herself, a tradition which to her would eventually force open a way for the woman writer to see human beings 'not always in relation to each other but in relation to reality; and to the sky, too, and the trees or whatever it may be in themselves'.

Woolf's 'significant forms', shaped from glancing insights and carefully placed and iterated details, are to some degree echoed in the work of her New

Zealand-born contemporary, Katherine Mansfield (the pseudonym of Kathleen Mansfield Beauchamp, 1888–1923). If Mansfield's success with reviewers and readers seems to have stimulated Woolf's jealousy rather than critical generosity (Woolf generally found Mansfield 'inscrutable'), both writers can be seen as developing the post-impressionist principle of suggestiveness and rhythm from a distinctively feminine point of view. Mansfield worked determinedly on a small scale, concentrating on carefully pointed, delicately elusive short stories. Her succinct narratives, collected as *In a German Pension* (1911), *Bliss, and other Stories* (1920), and *The Garden Party, and other Stories* (1922), are brief triumphs of style, a style which serves both to suggest a pervasive atmosphere and to establish a series of evanescent sensations (creaks, yawns, draughts, cries, footfalls, bird-calls, and cats' miaows). Where *In a German Pension* conveys a fastidious dislike of Teutonic manners and mannerisms (though Mansfield declined to have the volume reprinted during the Great War), her later stories move towards a greater technical mastery and to a larger world-view. She draws significantly on the landscapes and flora of her native New Zealand (in, for example, 'The Aloe'), she attempts to explore the responses of a wide spectrum of social types, and, by means of a style which takes on a yet more shimmering elusiveness, she endeavours to describe the mysterious 'diversity of life . . . Death included'. Her own untimely death from tuberculosis cut short a remarkably innovative career.

Richardson and Lawrence

The phrase 'stream of consciousness' was coined in 1890 by the American philosopher and psychologist William James (1842–1910) as a description of the flow of thought within the waking human mind. It was a phrase much used and abused in the criticism of the new fiction of the 1920s and 1930s, and particularly with reference to the work of Virginia Woolf, in an effort to come to terms with a literature which boldly attempted to replicate or represent the flux of thought and feeling within a character without resorting to objective description or to conventional dialogue. The technique had been first pioneered in France, notably by Édouard Dujardin in *Les Lauriers sont coupés* of 1888 and later by Marcel Proust whose vast serial novel, collectively known as *A la recherche du temps perdu* (1913–27), had a vast impact on Britain both in its original French and in the fine translation of 1922–31, retitled (with an intrusively nodding reference to Shakespeare) *Remembrance of Things Past*. The phrase 'stream of consciousness' had, however, first been adapted to literary-critical usage in 1918 by May Sinclair in an essay on Dorothy Richardson's attempt to eliminate 'the wise all-knowing author' from her novel sequence *Pilgrimage*. To Richardson herself, 'stream of consciousness' seemed a narrowly clumsy misnomer. 'In deploring the comparison of consciousness with a stream', she later wrote, 'and suggesting that fountain would be a more appropriate metaphor, I do not recognise the latter as a suitable label for the work appearing early in the century'. For Richardson (1873–1957) the novel of the period merely reflected a move away from 'Romance' to what she saw as a distinctive kind of 'Realism' which had dispensed with the old constrictions of 'plot', 'climax', and 'conclusion'.

Richardson's *Pilgrimage* is a sequence of twelve novels published between 1915 and 1938, with the posthumous addition of a thirteenth volume in 1967. The novelist latterly insisted that each volume was effectively only a chapter of the whole and that *Pilgrimage* should be read as a single sequence. Her originality lay not merely in the shape and scope of her huge undertaking but in her determination to forge a technique expressive of an explicitly female consciousness, a style which stood in antithesis both to a received 'masculine' tradition and to new male-dominated experiments in literature. Since most realist novelists happened to be men, Richardson wrote in the Preface to the 1938 Collected Edition, she found herself faced with the choice 'between following one of her regiments and attempting to produce a feminine equivalent of the current masculine realism'. 'Feminine prose', she further insisted, 'should properly be unpunctuated, moving from point to point without formal obstructions'. Her sentences are unanchored either by strict syntax or by formal reference to an exterior world; they fragment, drift, dissolve, and form themselves into new, ambiguous, and suggestive shapes. They allow for a representation of free association, for open-endedness, and for a perpetually varied interaction of the liberating inner consciousness (which Richardson particularly associated with the female) with an external world (whose control she saw as traditionally male). The eschewal of 'formal obstructions' in both her style and her overall structures has, however, often rendered her an unapproachable, demanding, and 'difficult' writer. When Virginia Woolf argued in 1923 that Richardson had invented a sentence 'of a more elastic fibre than the old' she perforce added, in a disdainful put-down, that it was a woman's sentence 'only in the sense that it is used to describe a woman's mind by a writer who is neither proud nor afraid of anything she may discover in the psychology of her sex'. Unlike Woolf, Richardson does not offer a fiction of fortuitous shapes, of patterns, of images, or of manipulated events. Not only is her chronology fluid, her narrative seems to repudiate linear development in order to allow for a reader's freedom of engagement with her implied thematic structures. It is not a freedom that all readers have relished.

The self-proclaimed apostle of new literary and moral freedoms, D(avid) H(erbert) Lawrence (1885–1930), had little time for Richardson's, Joyce's, and Proust's narrative experiments. They were, he facetiously observed in his essay 'Surgery for the Novel—or a Bomb?' in 1923, 'death-rattles' to which the novelists themselves were listening 'trying to discover whether the intervals are minor thirds or major fourths'. Some convulsion or cataclysm, he insisted, was still needed to get the 'serious' novel out of its self-consciousness and to force it 'to tackle new propositions without using abstractions'. The purged novel form had to present readers with 'new, really new feelings, a whole new line of new emotion, which will get us out of the emotional rut'. Lawrence's apostolic mission, loudly announced in a series of essays in the 1920s, was both to break open fictional doors and to nag readers and writers into passing through them. He was utterly persuaded that his mission as a novelist and as a critic of the novel was of the most elevated, most radical, and most urgent order. In the essay 'Morality and the Novel' (1925), he saw the twentieth-century novel as 'the highest example of subtle interrelatedness that man has discovered' and he confidently declared that if a novel revealed 'true and vivid relationships' it was a moral work; if the novelist *honoured* the relationship in itself, his work automatically took on greatness. In 'Why the Novel Matters' (also of 1925) Lawrence proclaimed the novelist to be superior to the saint, the scientist, the philosopher, and the poet. Other artists and thinkers had merely analysed parts of experience; the novelist, by contrast, dealt with life as a whole. 'Life with a capital L', the fully vibrant human organism, formed the peak of an energetic hierarchy: 'All things that are alive are amazing. All things that are dead are subsidiary to the living. Better a live dog than a dead lion. But better a live lion than a live dog. *C'est la vie.*' 'Man alive', feeling, experiencing, learning, and integrating, was the central concern of the supreme human achievement—the novel.

   D. H. Lawrence's utter confidence in his art is rooted, like his language, in the evangelical earnestness of the biblical prophets and visionaries and in that of their English Nonconformist successors. If Lawrence rejected the outward forms and the intellectual formularies of Christianity, he retained a vivid interest in its underlying mysteries, tropes, and patterns. He secularizes both the idea of a brooding Holy Spirit and the interrelationships of life and death, death and resurrection; he sexualizes the biblical language of possession and enthusiasm and he forges Christian images and metaphors into new and often shockingly gaudy shapes (a factor which particularly determines the nature of Lawrence's erotic fantasy about the resurrected Christ, *The Man who Died* (1927–8)). Above all, he seeks to propound a Modernist theology of the fulfilled and fully integrated personality. It is a theology which relies less on the death of God than on the advent of a Godless prophet, Freud. Lawrence's new philosophy, like Freudian psychology, is centred on the concept of a welling, subterranean male consciousness and on the liberation of sexuality from inherited social repression. In his two most Freud-inspired tracts, *Psychoanalysis and the Unconscious* (1921) and *Fantasia of the Unconscious* (1922) he also attempts to reach out to new definitions (though, admittedly, often rhetorical ones) of the essential dynamism of the personality. These essays extend the ideological and critical base for his own later fiction which had been set out in the 'Study of Thomas Hardy' (written in 1914). This essay is only marginally an appreciation of Hardy. It is often astute about Hardy's aesthetic predilections and reiterations, but it is more of an allusive exploration of the quirks and twists of Lawrence's mind (and particularly his view of women) than an exposition of Hardy's art. At its core lies an attempt to distinguish between notions of essential maleness and essential femaleness. The unsteady argument is developed by means of an interfusion of theological, mystical, pseudo-scientific, literary, and art-historical reference. It concludes with a contemplation of what Lawrence sees, as an 'antinomy' between the principles of 'Law and Love', or, put more crudely, between female 'inertia' and male 'movement'. This 'antinomy', he proposes, will progressively give way to a kind of fusion of wills and personalities in which Man, as the embodiment of Love, and Woman, as the embodiment of Law, will form the two complementary parts of a living human whole. It is in the exploration of erotic complementariness, in a sexual and spiritual coming together and in a vital expansion of shared consciousness, that Lawrence seeks to bed his nascent future for the human race. His post-war novels formed the Sibylline books from which he trusted the moral direction of the future might be spelled.

Lawrence's first fictions are less oracular. They are rooted both in what he later saw as the provisionality of his own early sexual experience and in his East Midlands working-class background. He was amongst the first English novelists to have profited from the effects of the late-Victorian Education Acts which enforced the provision of free elementary education for the poor; he was amongst the last to have benefited from a provincial self-helping, hymn-singing, richly Bible-centred Chapel-culture. Throughout his work, too, the mechanical rhythms, the monotonies, and the deprivations (both economic and spiritual) of industrial England are contrasted with vivid evocations of a working countryside that survives, if scarcely competes, with its machine-scarred urban counterpart. For Lawrence, the direct inheritor of Romantic prejudices against machines, the rural admonishes the industrial much as the instinctual takes precedence over the intellectual. In the semi-autobiographical *Sons and Lovers* (1913) the contrasts around which the novel is built are not simply those of ill-matched parents, of clinging mothers and releasing lovers, but also those of town and country, mining and farming, working and walking. At the opening of *The Rainbow* (1915) the Brangwen family farm, divided from the sprawling mining village by a canal, seems to be on 'the safe side of civilization' and the male members of the family are mystically linked by a 'blood-intimacy' to the fertility of the soil they till and to that of the animals they tend. The controlling images and the reiterated metaphors of both *The Rainbow* and of its successor, *Women in Love* (1920), stress a distinction between nature and anti-nature, between freedom and control, between instinct and will. In *Women in Love* Gerald Crich, the son of a colliery owner and the efficient masterer both of his men and of animal resistance, conceives of a world in which 'the will of man was the determining factor', where 'Man was the arch-god of earth' with a will that was 'the absolute, the only absolute'. As his fiction develops Lawrence increasingly associates true human freedom with the untamed and often unacknowledged might of nature rather than with a repressive will. Those who are seen to 'do the dirty on life' by denying their unconscious, natural or sexual energies bring about personal or symbolic dis-asters. Ursula Brangwen confronting apocalyptic horses at the end of *The Rainbow* or Rupert Birkin walking naked through the long grass at Breadalby in *Women in Love* are enriched, intense, ecstatic, and resurrected. By contrast, Gerald Crich wills his unbending life to an end in an Alpine snowdrift and a flood fortuitously purges the bitter and stuffy hypocrisies of the world of *The Virgin and the Gipsy* (1926).

The central achievements of Lawrence's career as a novelist, *The Rainbow* and *Women in Love*, reflect and echo what are assumed to be natural or psy-chical rhythms and currents. Certain passages in both novels (such as in the pressurized description of Lincoln Cathedral in the former or the car journey in the chapter called 'Excurse' in the latter) may burst unwelcomely into adjec-tival over-ripeness or may simply provoke derision, but the overall effect of the two novels is richly episodic, carefully wrought, and cumulative. *The Rainbow* deals with the evolving perceptions of three generations of a single family. Its 'sequel' *Women in Love*, which first outgrew then grew out of the originally arched scheme for a single novel, spans a far more contained period of time. In it Lawrence abandoned regular narrative linearity and shaped his fiction instead around certain charged, symbolic, even epiphanic incidents. The novel's central characters move easily through the stratified English society of the early years of the twentieth century, encountering industrial workers and industrial magnates, the inhabitants of arty-crafty cottages and cultured country mansions, the clienteles of effete London cafés, Southwell tea-shops, and Swiss skiing hostels. *Women in Love* opens with an unanswered question about marriage and ends with an unanswerable speculation about relationships beyond both the marital and the narrowly heterosexual. It explores a world which is fragmenting from a lack of coherence, but it neither looks nostalgi-cally back to a lost pre-industrial 'blood-intimacy' nor confidently forward to a new social order. In chapter 26 ('A Chair') Birkin and Ursula briefly con-template the prospect of an earth made safe for popular democracy and inher-ited by 'the meek' but they also recognize that it will not be their place. 'Then what are we going to do?' Ursula asks, 'We're not like them—are we? We're not the meek?' 'We've got to live in the chinks they leave us', Birkin replies.

When, in his novels of the later 1920s, Lawrence begins to ground his often ill-defined ideas of human liberation in a discourse which is both political and psycho-sexual, his writing is both more awkward and more problematical. Birkin's 'chinks' are prised open to provide an adequate *Lebensraum* for a newly enlightened and emboldened élite. Both *Kangaroo* (1923) and *The Plumed Serpent* (1926) explore a revitalized social ethic beyond the kind of socialism which Lawrence sees as offering a materialistic and flabby democracy to the 'meek'. Neither book has an English setting and neither has much time for defunct English niceties or socialistic panaceas. *Kangaroo* flirtatiously contem-plates the rise and the failure of an Australian proto-fascism based on male-bonding; *The Plumed Serpent*, set amidst the revolutionary fluidity of Mexico, dwells on the regenerative and redemptive potentiality of an Aztec blood-cult of dark gods and phallic power. Both novels are symptomatic of Lawrence's rejection of his roots and of his restless search for new landscapes and new bases for social relationships. This restlessness is more adventurously, more personally, and somewhat less dangerously explored in the series of travel-books written in his post-war *Wanderjahre: Sea and Sardinia* (1921), *Mornings in Mexico* (1927), and *Etruscan Places* (1932). Each traces a different affinity and a distinct fascination. His final large-scale fictional experiment, *Lady Chatterley's Lover*, emphatically returned to an England crushed and emasculated by the war. It is an ambitious work which inveighs against materialism, intellectualism, and priggism while lovingly delineating the worship of Priapus and composing poetic liturgies to accompany copulation. *Lady Chatterley's Lover* was not published in an unexpurgated form until 1960 and only then after a failed prosecution under the Obscene Publications Act of 1959. In a sense the book's uncensored reappearance belatedly ushered in a new literary decade, one in which Lawrence's literary reputation and his moral influence reached their zenith.

Old and New Writing: Practitioners, Promoters, and the 'Little Magazines'

'The essence of poetry with us in this age of stark and unlovely actualities', D. H. Lawrence wrote in 1916, 'is a stark directness without a shadow of a lie, or a shadow of deflection anywhere.' Such 'stark, bare, rocky directness of statement', Lawrence believed, constituted the only true poetic expression in an age marked by a disillusion with outmoded forms and by the cultural fragmentation imposed by the war. Lawrence was the only English-born poet of Modernist leanings who had published verse before 1914 to survive that war. His verse has always been difficult to classify. His poetry appeared both in the influential, but essentially conservative, volumes, of *Georgian Poetry* and in far more radical company in two of the anthologies entitled *Some Imagist Poets* (1915, 1916). His distinctively 'direct' and intense poetry sits somewhat uneasily beside the shapely, rhymed realism of the Georgians but, given that its subjects are most frequently derived from an observation of nature, it is not really out of place. Writing to Edward Marsh (1872–1953), the editor of *Georgian Poetry*, in 1913 Lawrence insisted that it was not the 'obvious form' or the subject that made poetry but the 'hidden *emotional* pattern'. His patterning, he explained, was not likely to appeal immediately to ears conditioned by the smooth traditions of late-Romanticism against which he had declared war. Later, in the Foreword to his volume *Pansies* (1929) he argues for a form that conveyed the tightness of thought; 'a real thought', he suggests, 'a single thought, not an argument, can only exist easily in verse', and, in what reads almost like perverse admission of personal culpability, he confesses that 'there is a didactic element about prose thoughts which makes them repellent, slightly bullying'.

Much of Lawrence's best poetry, concentrated, stark and unrhymed, appeared in the volume *Birds, Beasts and Flowers* in 1923. In the poem 'Figs', for example, he offers an analysis of a fruit which veers suggestively between the culinary, the botanical, the symbolical, and the sexual ('Fig, fruit of the female mystery, covert and inward'). Elsewhere in the volume, analysis is subsumed in an attempt on the poet's part to feel himself into the life of an animal or to identify with the intensity of life he observes in growing and moving things. Each poem represents an attempt to become familiar with, but never to domesticate, the exotic. He associates himself with the cypresses of Tuscany which seem to hold the dark secret of the dead Etruscans ('Dusky, slim marrow-thought of slender, flickering men of Etruria, | Whom Rome called vicious') ('Cypresses'), while wild cyclamens observed in a Sicilian dawn have a vivid particularity of their own, appearing 'like delicate very-young greyhound bitches | Half-yawning at the open, inexperienced | Vista of day, | Folding back their soundless petalled ears' ('Sicilian Cyclamens'). A male tortoise screaming as it mounts a female ('Tortoise Shout') seems to stand for all life that cries out either in pain or in ecstasy while a Sydney kangaroo, watching with 'eternal, cocked wistfulness', is taken as representative of the distinctive quality of Australian nature, both human and animal. In 'Snake', the transfixed poet watches, with an emotion that confuses honour, fear, gratitude, and mystery, as a snake drinks at his water-trough. When he frightens away the snake by throwing a log at it, the thrill is superseded by a new sense of guilt which is at once 'literary' and primitive and profound:

> And I thought of the albatross,
> And I wished he would come back, my snake.
> For he seemed to me again like a king,
> Like a king in exile, uncrowned in the underworld,
> Now due to be crowned again.

> And so, I missed my chance with one of the lords
> Of life.
> And I have something to expiate;
> A pettiness.

It would be wrong to confuse a cultivated simplicity with the merely petty in the work of two of Lawrence's most enduringly popular 'Georgian' contemporaries. Nevertheless, by comparison with the challenge of Lawrence's exhilarating energy much of even the best verse of John Masefield (1878–1967) and Walter de la Mare (1873–1956) seems merely unaffectedly dextrous. Despite the prominence of his work in the volumes of *Georgian Poetry*, a good deal of de la Mare's poetry, notably the volumes entitled *Peacock Pie* (1913), *Tom Tiddler's Ground* (1932), and *This Year: Next Year* (1937), was written specifically for children. His appealingly direct and fluent songlike manner still provides young readers with an ideally unpretentious introduction to the virtues of rhyme and rhythm. The best of Masefield's verse is haunted by the variety, wildness, and desolation of the sea; it is also occasionally marked by the inflections and peculiarities of sea-language. Two lyrics which first appeared in his volumes of 1902 and 1910, 'Sea Fever' ('I must go down to the sea again . . .') and 'Cargoes' ('Quinquireme of Nineveh from distant Ophir . . .'), remain amongst the most commonly cited and anthologized poems of the century. Neither Masefield's longer narrative poems, such as *The Everlasting Mercy* (1910) and the anti-blood sport *Reynard the Fox* (1919), nor the many bland lyrics which proclaim the virtues of the open road have the easy swing and the elegance of the early work. Masefield's *Collected Poems* of 1923, however, proved hugely popular with readers. It reached its twelfth edition in 1930, the year in which he was appointed Poet Laureate in succession to the equally unadventurous Robert Bridges (1844–1930).

It was largely through what have since become known as the 'little magazines' that the Modernist revolution in poetry was announced, carried forward, and propagated. It is by the very success of that revolution that we now inevitably judge the poetic achievement of the 1920s and 1930s. An educated audience, impatient with inherited conventions, was ready for change. If the audience was relatively small, 'advanced' in its opinions and predominantly young, its enthusiasms and perceptions steadily established new critical norms which came to be applied far beyond the predilections of a coterie. The appearance of T. S. Eliot's *The Waste Land* in the first issue of the quarterly magazine *The Criterion* (circulation 600) in October 1922 struck many as forcefully expressing the disordered and irregular nature of the modern condition in a language that was indisputably 'modern'. When the poem was published separately, initially in issues of one thousand, it gained in esteem and notoriety. In their Preface to the undergraduate volume of *Oxford Poetry 1926*, for example, Charles Plumb and W. H. Auden boldly pronounced that 'if it is a natural preference to inhabit a room with casements opening upon Fairyland, one at least of them should open upon the Waste Land'. In the same year Evelyn Waugh purchased Eliot's *Poems, 1909–1925* in Oxford and found them 'marvellously good but very hard to understand', adding that there was 'a most impressive flavour of the major prophets about them'. This was not an opinion shared by Waugh's father, the critic and publisher Arthur Waugh. Eliot's poetry, he held, offered a salutary example which reflected that of the ancients: 'It was a classic custom in the family hall, when a feast was at its height, to display a drunken slave amongst the sons of the household, to the end that they, being ashamed at the ignominious folly of his gesticulations, might determine never to be tempted into such a pitiable condition themselves.'

Arthur Waugh's outrage was not confined to Eliot. According to his son he had earlier been equally shocked by the 1916 anthology of *Some Imagist Poets*. The existence of the Imagists (or, as he first put it, the 'Imagistes') had been announced in a London tea-shop in 1912 to two startled fellow-poets by Ezra

Pound. Pound (1885–1972) had arrived in London from the United States in April 1909 and he made the metropolis the centre of his energizing activities for the following eleven years. They were years of crucial importance to the future of English, and to some extent American, poetry. Pound was as discerning as he was arrogant, as stimulating to fellow-writers as he was discriminating about their work, though he later seemed to the equally restless radical Percy Wyndham Lewis (1882–1957) merely a 'fire-eating propagandist' whose utterances 'were not accompanied by any very experimental efforts in his particular medium'. Lewis, the co-editor of *Blast, the Review of the Great English Vortex* (1914–15), scarcely rendered Pound proper justice after the collapse of their co-operative relationship. Their concerns had also veered apart, those of Lewis towards painting and prose, those of Pound towards a highly complex referential poetry (a poetry that Lewis improperly saw as looking backwards rather than forwards to 'the new burst of art in progress'). The two numbers of *Blast* had ambitiously attempted to forge together the interests and advances of writers, theorizers, and artists but its ultimate achievement is more strictly visual and typographical than 'literary'. It made loud but often empty revolutionary noises about there being no 'Verbotens' and about despising and ignoring 'this impure Present' but it grated nerves more than it shook foundations. Lewis's career beyond *Blast* is marked by some startlingly dynamic paintings and by a series of angry, edgy texts. His most innovative novel, *Tarr* (1918), is set in an artist-dominated Paris in which a frantic bohemianism has assumed a political and sexual arrogance in the face of bourgeois 'sentimentalism'. It is written in what Lewis described as a 'jagged prose', one in which he had attempted to eliminate 'anything less essential than a noun or a verb'. Ezra Pound remarked in 1920 that *Tarr* was 'the most vigorous and volcanic English novel of our time' and its author 'the rarest of phenomena, an Englishman who has achieved the triumph of being also a European'. Despite the sustained wit of Lewis's staccato sentences his later, far more parochially 'English' novel, *The Apes of God* (1930) reads like a satirical guide to the negatives and short-comings of artistic London in the 1920s (it is particularly acerbic about Bloomsbury). *The Revenge for Love* (1937), which begins in Civil War Spain, is by contrast an unsteady but scathing attack on the political (and particularly Marxist) deceptions of the 1930s. The three completed novels of a planned four-part sequence, *The Human Age*, began in 1928 with *The Childermass* but was resumed again only in 1955 with the publication of the grandly conceived sub-religious discourses, *Monstre Gai* and *Malign Fiesta*. Lewis's most considered, if jumpy, political and artistic manifesto *The Art of Being Ruled* (1926) argues that society had been inevitably revolutionized by mechanical change and that both change and revolution ought to be embraced by the artist. When he moves on to address the problem of a distinction between an artistic or intellectual élite and an indifferent mass he writes with considerable panache though, as ever, he tends to knock down Aunt Sallies with as much verve as he quixotically assaults windmills. He also determinedly abandons the use of certain capital letters as a gesture against the inherited privileging of certain words and titles. *The Art of Being Ruled* glances forward to a time when 'Everyman' will be loosed from the chains of poverty by a new absolutist state, a state which would do away with old niceties, economic injustices and inefficiencies. 'Can this poor man be the loser', he asks, 'has he *anything* to lose?—by his rulers shedding the pickwickian masks, the socialist noses, the kindly liberal twinkles of the european egalitarian masquerade?' In many ways Lewis's slide towards a lonely kind of Fascism in the late 1930s was inevitable.

Lewis's tendency to refer to whimsical ideas as 'pickwickian' was picked up by Richard Aldington (1892–1962) when he looked back in his autobiography of 1941 to Pound's confident announcement of the existence of 'Imagism'. Poems by Aldington and his American wife Hilda Doolittle ('H.D.') were published with brief notes ambiguously explaining that the Imagists were 'a group of ardent Hellenists who are pursuing interesting experiments in *vers libre*'. Precise definitions of the new poetry remained as vague, though an insistence on the 'principle of liberty' implicit in the irregular rhythms of *vers libre* remained constant. The Imagists were not Symbolists, Pound later insisted; where the Symbolists had dealt in 'association'—'in a sort of allusion, almost of allegory'—the images of the Imagists had 'a variable significance like the signs a, b, and x in algebra. Pound was also emphatic that 'the author must use his *image* because he sees it or feels, *not* because he thinks he can use it to back up some creed or some system of ethics'. This loose emphasis opened the way to the inclusion of a considerable variety of poets and poetic techniques in the Imagist anthologies. *Des Imagistes* of 1914 printed poems by Aldington, H. D., Pound, and James Joyce; the three later volumes entitled *Some Imagist Poets* (1915, 1916, 1917) introduced work by Ford Madox Ford and D. H. Lawrence. All these anthologies, which ultimately determined the future of American literature more than they did English, also contained seminal poems by the American poets Amy Lowell, John Gould Fletcher, Marianne Moore, and William Carlos Williams.

Since the 1920s, Aldington has been remembered more as a remarkably perceptive assistant editor of the periodical *The Egoist* (1914–17), as the controversial biographer of his sometime friend, D. H. Lawrence (1950), and as a sharply observant novelist than as a poet. In 1916 he had enlisted in the Infantry and his profound unsettlement as a result of the war is reflected in the often brilliant cynicism of his first novel *Death of a Hero* (1929), which deals with both the frustrations of pre-war English society and 'the false ideals, the unintelligent ideas . . . the humbug, the hypocrisy, the stupidity' of those who waged the war. Its 'hero', George Winterbourne, resists the dullness of convention with a kind of angry paganism, but as its poetic 'Epilogue' implies, the final mood of the novel is shaped by 'an agony of helpless grief and pity'. The disillusion which continues to condition his two later novels, *The Colonel's Daughter* (1931) and *All Men are Enemies* (1933), is somewhat dissipated in comparison.

For a short period in the 1920s Aldington worked as an assistant to a fellow ex-combatant, and already experienced novelist, Ford Madox Ford. Ford (born Ford Hermann Hueffer) (1873–1939), the grandson of the painter Ford Madox Brown, began his literary career in 1896 with a biography of his grandfather and developed his fictional style through a close association with Joseph Conrad (including collaboration on the novels *The Inheritors* of 1901 and *Romance* of 1903). *The Fifth Queen*, his decoratively ornate trilogy of historical novels about Catherine Howard, the unhappy wife of Henry VIII, appeared between 1907 and 1908. In the latter year he founded the *English Review*, a pioneer journal which published new work by established writers such as Hardy, James, Bennett, and Wells, and which also boldly printed poems by Lawrence for the first time. Ford's own series of polemical essays on the state of the novel (later republished as *The Critical Attitude* in 1911) also appeared in its pages. These essays contrast what Ford sees as the 'temperamentally British novel', a 'loose, amorphous, genial and easy-going thing' which had been almost casually evolved by Fielding, Dickens, Thackeray, and Trollope, with the tighter, more self-consciously artful form developed in France. Ford praises both James and Conrad for their 'great attention to their Art' and it is as a development of their techniques that his own fictional masterpiece, *The Good Soldier: A Tale of Passion* of 1915, can best be appreciated. Although the first part of the story (provisionally entitled 'The Saddest Story' appeared in *Blast* in June 1914, its fascination with Conradian shifts in time and perceptions of betrayal and its Jamesian concern with the subtleties of overlapping relationships and emotions mark it as essentially pre-Modernist in technique. At times, however, its ambiguous American relater, John Dowell, reveals a knowing awareness of the arbitrary nature of his narration before attempting to console himself 'with thinking that this is a real story and that, after all, real stories are probably told best in the way a person telling a story would tell them'. *The Good Soldier* doubtless seemed an appropriate title for a novel which finally appeared in wartime. Ford's exploration behind the disciplined and gentlemanly façade of his title character was to a limited extent continued in his post-war tetralogy *Parade's End*. The four novels, *Some Do Not . . .* (1924), *No More Parades* (1925), *A Man Could Stand Up* (1926), and *Last Post* (1928), are concerned with the gradual break-up of the traditional squirearchical values of Christopher Tietjens, an unhappy lover, a largely unsuccessful soldier, and a rootless, passive, and neurotic survivor after 1918. The very fact of Tietjens's post-war career as a restorer of antiques suggests the extent to which he is still trying to make sense of a battered old world which is now essentially fragmented.

Eliot, Firbank, and the Sitwells

'When I wrote a poem called *The Waste Land*', T. S. Eliot noted in 1931, 'some of the more approving critics said that I had expressed the "disillusionment of a generation", which is nonsense.' 'I may', he continued, 'have expressed for them their own illusion of being disillusioned, but that did not form part of my intention.' T(homas) S(tearns) Eliot (1888–1965) the most important and influential English poet of his own and of the two subsequent generations, did not write *The Waste Land* (1922) as an Englishman. He was, like his friend and early mentor Ezra Pound ('*il miglior fabbro*', 'the better craftsman', of the dedication to *The Waste Land*), an American resident in London. Unlike Pound, he had studied and found employment in England and in 1927 he took out British citizenship and was received into the Church of England. It was as the devout Anglo-Catholic author of the essay *Thoughts After Lambeth* (a reflection on the resolutions of the 1930 Lambeth Conference of Anglican Bishops) that Eliot proclaimed the 'nonsense' of the belief that his major poem had expressed the disillusionment of a generation.

If the body of Eliot's work can be claimed as much for 'English' as for 'American' literature it is because of the distinctively cisatlantic pointing that marks it (in his essay on William Blake, for example, he addresses his 'fellow' English readers). Although much of his topography, vocabulary, and awareness of public history and culture are self-consciously British, Eliot's literary roots were cosmopolitan. As a student at Harvard between 1906 and 1914 he had become acquainted with an eclectic range of philosophical, historical, and literary scholarship. In Paris in 1911 he attended lectures by Henri Bergson, practised French conversation with Henri Alain-Fournier, and encountered the monarchist Catholic journalism of Charles Maurras. At Harvard in 1908 he had been sufficiently fired by Arthur Symons's account of recent French poetry in *The Symbolist Movement in Literature* (1899) to send off to Paris for the poems of Jules Laforgue (1860–87). Through Laforgue he had discovered the attractions of a reticent, ironic, clever, and referential poetry, a poetry often cast in the form of free-verse dramatic monologues in which a wry persona expresses himself rather than acts out the private emotions of his creator. The influence of the brittle Laforgue, though crucial in moulding Eliot's early style, was transient; that of Baudelaire and Dante proved more lasting and more haunting. In Baudelaire's poetry he recognized what he described in 1930 as an elevation of 'imagery of the sordid life of a great metropolis . . . to the *first intensity*', an elevation which 'created a mode of release and expression for other men'. Baudelaire remained for him the great inventor of a *modern* poetry because his verse and language seemed 'the nearest thing to a complete renovation that we have experienced'. In Dante, by contrast, he found a medieval spiritual and a poetic authority which seemed to him to address the modern condition directly. Dante's verse, he reiterated throughout his career, was both scrupulously disciplined and easily intelligible. 'The thought may be obscure', he proclaimed in an essay of 1929, 'but the word is lucid, or rather translucent'. Speaking in 1950 he insisted that Dante's 'universality' provided any later poet with a constant reminder 'of the obligation to explore, to find words for the inarticulate, to capture those feelings which people can hardly even feel, because they have no words for them'. When in *Ash-Wednesday* (1930) and *Four Quartets* (1935–42) Eliot attempted to explore 'beyond the frontiers of ordinary consciousness', his immediate prompting and much of his reference was Dantean.

Eliot's Harvard doctoral thesis, left unexamined due to his prolonged absence in wartime England, was concerned with experience and the objects of knowledge in the work of the Oxford philosopher F. H. Bradley (1846–1924) (he published the manuscript in 1964 as *Knowledge and Experience in the Philosophy of F. H. Bradley*). Eliot later affirmed that his own prose style was closely formed on that of the subject of his dissertation, but something of Bradley's intellectual influence can also be indirectly felt in the concerns of the broad range of his writing. Although he disarmingly claimed in 1964 to be no longer able to understand much of his own argument, his emphasis on Bradley's interest in the relationship of the subjective consciousness with the objective world, and particularly on Bradley's notion of the correlation of the individual mind with a larger, single comprehensive consciousness, can be linked to Eliot's persistent interest in individual and external patterns of order. If in one sense he reinterpreted Bradley's idea of a comprehensive consciousness as a responsive God, in another he consistently sought to relate individual perception to a larger human tradition. Eliot's critical essays attempt to define and prescribe traditions which are historical, religious, moral, and, above all, literary. In one of his earliest and most celebrated, 'Tradition and the Individual Talent' (1917), he argues that 'no poet, no artist of any art, has his complete meaning alone'. He is equally insistent that personal emotions, provoked by particular events in a poet's life, do not make for 'remarkable or interesting' poetry. In its relation to a larger tradition, poetry is not 'a turning loose of emotion, but an escape from emotion; it is not the expression of personality, but an escape from personality'. In the series of lectures given at Harvard in 1932 and 1933 entitled *The Use of Poetry and the Use of Criticism* he defined the 'auditory imagination' of a poet as 'the feeling for syllable and rhythm' which penetrated 'far below the conscious levels of thought and feeling . . . sinking to the most primitive and forgotten, returning to the origin and bringing something back, seeking the beginning in the end'. Earlier in his influential study of 'The Metaphysical Poets' of 1921 he justified the contortions of John Donne's poetic thought by insisting that when a poet's mind is perfectly equipped for its work 'it is constantly amalgamating disparate experience'. The ordinary man's experience, Eliot argued, is 'chaotic, irregular, fragmentary'; the 'ordinary man' falls in love, or reads Spinoza, and these experiences have nothing to do with each other, or with the noise of the typewriter or the smell of cooking, but for the poet like Donne 'these experiences are always forming new wholes'. Eliot's attraction to the intellectual and lexical dexterity of 'Metaphysical' poetry would seem to have derived from a temperamental sympathy with a worldview which rejoiced in complex patterning and which perceived a divine order beyond the physical evidence of disorder. Throughout,

Eliot shapes his literary tradition around those writers whom he sees as feeding his particular concept of 'Modernism'. Shakespeare, Jonson, Middleton, Webster, Andrewes, Marvell, Dryden (just) and Dickens (glancingly) pass muster to join the company of Virgil, Dante, and Baudelaire; Milton fails the test aesthetically, Blake intellectually, Swinburne morally. In his discussion of two earlier critics whose stature he grudgingly acknowledges, Eliot sees the Coleridge of *Biographia Literaria* merely as a writer who had found a vocation as 'a ruined man' and Matthew Arnold as little more than an 'undergraduate' in philosophy and theology and a 'Philistine' in religion. When he treats his older contemporaries he finds much to admire in the mystical Yeats but dismisses the agnostic Hardy as 'an interesting example of a powerful personality uncurbed by any institutional attachment or by submission to any objective beliefs'.

Eliot's juvenilia, belatedly collected under the title *Poems Written in Early Youth* in 1950 (reissued posthumously in 1967), contains examples of hearty student graduation songs as much as quizzical tributes to Laforgue. Two poems in particular, 'Nocturne' of 1909 (a wry undoing of Romeo's *grand serieux* wooing of Juliet) and the unpublished and experimental 'The Death of Saint Narcissus' of *c.*1911 (whose opening lines were incorporated into *The Waste Land*), look directly forward to the work which first brought Eliot to wider public notice. His 'apprenticeship' proved to be remarkably fertile. When he showed 'The Love Song of J. Alfred Prufrock' (also of *c.*1911) to Ezra Pound in 1914, Pound announced he had found an American poet who had 'actually trained himself *and* modernized himself *on his own*' (that is, without Pound's generally benign interference). The poem was published in the Chicago magazine *Poetry* in 1915 and appeared again, due to Pound's shaping influence, in Eliot's first important collection *Prufrock and Other Observations* in 1917. The twelve poems in the collection include 'Portrait of a Lady', like 'Prufrock' an exquisitely poised account of uneasy social intercourse, bleakly restless evocations of urban landscape (such as the musically entitled 'Preludes' and 'Rhapsody on a Windy Night'), and the character sketches 'Aunt Helen', 'Cousin Nancy', and 'Mr Apollinax' (this last a sharply imaginative remaking of an encounter with Bertrand Russell at an academic tea-party at Harvard). The poems are specifically American and often precisely Bostonian (including the nods to the example and the titles of Henry James). 'The Love Song of J. Alfred Prufrock' sets the tone of the whole volume with its play with politeness and failures of comprehension, with surfaces and hints of subcutaneous despair. Prufrock carefully presents himself as modestly fashionable and sociable but he also reveals an acute self-consciousness about the opinions of others ('They will say: "How his hair is growing thin"' 'They will say: "But how his arms and legs are thin!"'). He indulges in the social niceties represented by 'the cups, the marmalade, the tea' but is aware of the impossibility of saying what he means while being 'formulated' like a butterfly 'sprawling on a pin'. It was in many ways fitting that this disconcerting and subtly evasive monologue should be placed first in all the collections of his verse published in Eliot's lifetime.

The nuances of a broader tradition which help shape the tone of 'Prufrock' (Dante, Michaelangelo, Shakespeare, Dostoevsky, the Bible) became more emphatic in Eliot's *Poems* printed in London in 1919 by Virginia and Leonard Woolf's Hogarth Press. The volume contained 'Gerontion' (an old man's monologue burdened with an ominous perception of divinity) and four poems in French (one of which, 'Dans le Restaurant', was also later fed into *The Waste Land*), but its overall character was most determined by the seven short quatrain poems. The temporary shift away from *vers libre* allowed both for a new sharpness, even slickness, and for a new variety of tone. In 'The Hippopotamus' Eliot comments satirically on the claims and pretensions of 'the True Church'; in 'Whispers of Immortality' he edgily contrasts the 'anguish of the marrow | The ague of the skeleton' in the work of Webster and Donne with the 'promise of pneumatic bliss' offered by an uncorseted Russian girl; in 'Burbank with a Baedaeker: Bleistein with a Cigar' he unflatteringly, even prudishly, observes the sexual adventures of American tourists against a backdrop of a decaying Venice derived variously from Canaletto, Shakespeare, and Jonson. The effects of incongruity, historical anomaly, and densely amalgamated reference are perhaps most successfully exploited in 'Sweeney Among the Nightingales'. The 'Nightingales' of the title are at once the prostitutes amongst whom the unlovely Sweeney amuses himself and the song-birds which 'sang within the bloody wood' | When Agamemnon cried aloud | And let their liquid siftings fall | To stain the stiff dishonoured shroud'. It is not only the murdered Agamemnon who is dishonoured; the whole inheritance of history, tradition, and historical literature seems soiled by the shabby commonplaces and compromises of the modern world.

The epigraphs to the *Poems*, derived from Shakespeare, Beaumont and Fletcher, Villon, St Paul, Marlowe, and Aeschylus, serve to alert readers to Eliot's fascination with order and fragmentation, with the survival of tradition and the collapse of tradition. The last section of *The Waste Land* ends with a series of quotations which are, if anything, yet more abstruse. In the midst of these echoes Eliot places his own line: 'These fragments I have shored against my ruins'. Is his poem therefore to be seen retrospectively as a series of fragments? Or does he intend that these jerky half-quotations from Dante, the *Pervigilium Veneris*, Tennyson, Nerval, Kyd, and the Upanishads somehow shore up a tottering ruin that was Western civilization? Or is he suggesting that a poet needs the shield of tradition as a defence against a hostile and encroaching world? The poem remains fragmentary and ambiguous to many of its readers. The original draft (published in 1971) was severely edited by Ezra Pound, and we are left with five interrelated sections, each with a separate title. This final shape, with a long introductory section, a terse fourth one, and a long meditative conclusion, was one that Eliot repeated in each of his *Four Quartets*. What unity the poem has is based on the reiterated idea of the exploration of a desert which is both physical ('where the sun beats, | And the dead tree gives no shelter') and figuratively urban (as in its references to the 'falling towers' of Jerusalem, Athens, Alexandria, Vienna and, above all, London). Baudelaire's 'fourmillante cité, cité pleine de rêves' is here a specific but 'unreal' London where bemused crowds flow over London Bridge, where there are recognizable streets, churches and hotels and suburbs called Greenwich, Richmond, and Kew. London accrues the cultural resonance not simply of its own Elizabethan and Dickensian pasts, of Baudelaire's Paris and Saint Augustine's Carthage, but also of the decayed metropolises of the Jewish and Greek Empires; like them all, it shares in corruption. Eliot delves into this corruption like an archaeologist exploring the layered detritus of broken civilizations. The urban wasteland also assumes a mythical identity as a landscape in which a quest for healing, fertility, power, and meaning is pursued. This 'quest' is both Arthurian (with occasional Wagnerian emphases) and anthropological (in its glances at the theories of Jessie L. Weston and Sir James Frazer). The most striking effects in *The Waste Land* are achieved through the play of jarring juxtaposition, inconsistency of perception, multiplicity of narration, and fluidity of time and place. These juxtapositions, inconsistencies, multiplicities, and fluxes are as much visual as lexical. The extended image of a woman drawing out her hair in the final section of the poem is, for example, disconcertingly surreal:

> A woman drew her long black hair out tight
> And fiddled whisper music on those strings
> And bats with baby faces in the violet light
> Whistled, and beat their wings
> And crawled head downward down a blackened wall
> And upside down in air were towers
> Tolling reminiscent bells, that kept the hours
> And voices singing out of empty cisterns and exhausted wells.

In passages like this *The Waste Land* challenges preconceptions as to the nature and effect of poetry by demanding redefinitions.

Eliot created a series of similarly surreal pictures in *Ash-Wednesday*. The six sections of this poem are, however, given an almost liturgical character by the reiterated echoes of the prayers and metaphors of Anglo-Catholicism (or, more precisely, of Catholic spirituality with a distinct English accent). The ambiguity of *Ash-Wednesday* is related less to the question of whether or not some kind of God might actually respond than to an open wonder at the epiphanies of a Christian God. It is a poem centred on the idea of 'quickening', of a painful awakening of the spirit in the midst of a mysterious landscape haunted by female figures (all of them types of the Virgin Mary). A parallel concern with the quality and pain of revelation runs through the three most successful of the 'Ariel Poems', poems published, as Eliot later explained, 'as a kind of Christmas card'. 'Journey of the Magi' (1927) and 'A Song for Simeon' (1928) are both concerned with literal epiphanies, experiences of the infant Christ which disturb or disorient aged eyewitnesses. 'Marina' (1930), which explores the awed rediscovery of his lost daughter by Shakespeare's Pericles, though more obviously secular in its subject, reaches out to the half-grasped mystery of 'grace dissolved in place'.

The intermixture of the secular, the topographical, and the mystical also determined the themes of Eliot's last major poems, 'Burnt Norton' (1935) and its related successors, 'East Coker' (1940), 'The Dry Salvages' (1941), and 'Little Gidding' (1942)—published together as *Four Quartets* in 1943. As their joint title implies, their form, their lyricism, and their relative intimacy of communication, are akin to the effect of chamber music. Although the five sections of each of the poems look back to the form of *The Waste Land*, they also suggest a move away from the jars and abrupt shifts of tone of the earlier poem towards a more consistent classicality (albeit the vaulting classicality of Beethoven's late string quartets). Gone are the clashing multiple speakers, the juxtaposed scenes, and the disparate or outlandish quotations; in their stead is a smoother narrative surface inlaid polyphonically with hints of other voices. Each poem in the opening of its fifth section ponders the signification of words, and the difficulty of building words into poetry. In 'Burnt Norton', for example,

> words strain
> Crack and sometimes break, under the burden,
> Under the tension, slip, slide, perish,
> Decay with imprecision, will not stay in place,
> Will not stay still.

In 'East Coker' military metaphors, appropriate to 1940, are employed to describe a poet's lexical battle against the yet unformulated:

> And so each venture
> Is a new beginning, a raid on the inarticulate
> With shabby equipment always deteriorating
> In the general mess of imprecision of feeling,
> Undisciplined squads of emotion.

Although each of the poems is related to a specific place, the ancestral significance of the village of East Coker and the religious-historical associations of the chapel at Little Gidding were given a particular urgency by the threat of wartime dissolution and destruction. The houses in East Coker, 'rise and fall, crumble, are extended', | Are removed, destroyed, restored'. In 'Little Gidding', where in an epiphanic moment history seems to be 'now and England', the idea of change and decay is reinforced by veiled references to the *Blitzkrieg*. From the uneasy, smoky silence after a London air raid, 'after the dark dove with the flickering tongue | Had passed below the horizon of his homing' there emerges the 'familiar compound ghost' of a poet. The ghost is both Dantean and Yeatsian, historical and ahistorical, an individual voice and the compounding of many voices. His voice speaks of 'the rending pain of re-enactment', a pain which also informs the references to the divisions of seventeenth-century politics, religion, and literature which Eliot associates with the disruption of Nicholas Ferrar's community at Little Gidding. This inherited pain of human sinfulness, the poem proclaims, is assuaged only by a redemption from time and by a renewal and transfiguration of history 'in another pattern'.

The mystical longing to be free from time and the perception of eternity in moments of vision which run thematically through *Four Quartets* also characterizes the experience of Archbishop Becket in the hieratic drama, *Murder in the Cathedral* (1935). It is the most successful, if the least experimental, of Eliot's six verse-dramas largely because of the ritual formality of its structure and the set-piece neo-classical confrontations between Becket, his tempters, and his murderers. Its forerunner, the church pageant *The Rock* (1934), is, by comparison, arch in its verse, lifeless in its dialogue, and embarrassingly clumsy in its presentation of society. Both plays stemmed from Eliot's long-held ambition to renew poetic drama by exploring what he recognized as 'a kind of doubleness in the action, as if it took place on two planes at once'. When in *The Family Reunion* (1939) he attempted to inject the modern middle-class, 'well-made' West End play with a portentous dose of Aeschylean doom, the effect was verbally dense rather than theatrically exhilarating. The verse 'comedies', *The Cocktail Party* (1950), *The Confidential Clerk* (1954), and *The Elder Statesman* (1959), were politely received in their time but, largely due to their somewhat laboured attempts to interfuse Greek myths with modern types and conditions, have met with only limited success on the stage since. All of them lack the jerky energy and effervescence which gives the unfinished *Sweeney Agonistes* its individuality. This fragment of 'an Aristophanic Melodrama', toyed with from the mid-1920s and published unperformed in 1932, to some extent parallels Yeats's contemporary experiments with ritual, masks, dance, and music (though Eliot consulted Arnold Bennett with reference to its potential dramatic impact). It is shot through with the syncopated rhythms of jazz and the bravura skittishness of the English music-hall (which Eliot so admired), and combines incantatory choruses with witty but nervous dialogue. It is an ambiguous, restless, death-haunted attempt to create a new drama appropriate to a broken and essentially iconoclastic age. Its inventiveness was not fully appreciated until a new age of theatrical experiment began in the late 1950s.

The dissonant clash of avant-garde applause and conservative disapproval which greeted the work of T. S. Eliot and James Joyce in the 1920s was to some degree symptomatic of an age that was acutely uncertain of its cultural bearings. Although their writings are essentially more frivolous in style and intent, the novels of Ronald Firbank (1886–1926) and the early poetry of Edith Sitwell (1887–1964) also typify the often simply naughty 'Modernist' interplay of tradition and individual talent. Both writers set out to provoke tight bourgeois literary conventions and to explore the creative potential of the impressionistic verbal mosaic. Firbank's last five completed novels—*Valmouth* (1919), *Santal* (1921), *The Flower beneath the Foot* (1923), *Sorrow in Sunlight* (known as *Prancing Nigger* in America) (1924), and *Concerning the Eccentricities of Cardinal Pirelli* (1926)—share a cosmopolitan brevity, a poised wit, and a camply decorative prose style. Each has a contrived surface which serves both to conceal and to reveal perfumed waves of eroticism. In *Valmouth* the residents of an ostensibly prim English watering-place are manipulated, both physically and mentally, by a black masseuse, Mrs Yajnavalkya (who first appears 'wreathed in smiles . . . a sheeny handkerchief rolled round and round her head, a loud-dyed petticoat and a tartan shawl'). In *Cardinal Pirelli* a Spanish prelate, accused of unmentionable vices and unbecoming peccadilloes (including making the sign of the cross with his left foot at meals) is forced by official disapproval into a far from chaste exile from his diocese. Firbank's effects depend upon an almost baroque play with lush adjectives, metaphors, and a provocative incongruity.

Edith Sitwell's poems for the musical entertainment *Façade* (1922) struck the audiences at its first public performances in 1923 as equally provocative and inordinately flippant. Her enterprise in planning *Façade* with the composer William Walton was actively abetted by her younger brothers Osbert (1892–1969) and Sacheverell (1897–1988), the former a future poet, librettist, and novelist of some flair, the latter an innovative art-historian, essayist, and travel-writer. Osbert Sitwell records in *Laughter in the Next Room* (1949), the fourth volume of his autobiography, that the *Façade* poems were written as exact complements to Walton's settings: 'neither music nor words were to be treated or taken as a separate entity—and thus . . . able to reach for once that unattainable land . . . full of meaning and of nuances, analogies and images'. The eighteen lyrics were exercises in rhythm, rhyme, assonance, and dissonance, skittishly varied in style and mood, and replete with arcane reference. They were recited by the poet herself through a Sengerphone (an advanced kind of megaphone) placed against a hole in a painted canvas curtain, a device which, in an exaggeratedly Eliotic manner, eliminated the personality of the reciter. Edith Sitwell's ultimate achievement as a writer and propagandist extended far beyond the early notoriety of *Façade*. As a determined opponent of the romantic ruralism of the volumes of *Georgian Poetry* she had earlier published her own anthology, *Wheels* (1916–21), the 1919 edition of which published six of Wilfred Owen's war poems for the first time. Her own autumnal outpouring of verse, notably that collected in the volumes *Street Songs* (1942), *Green Song* (1944), and *The Song of the Cold* (1945), reflects not simply her interest in history and her religious devotion but also the uncertainties of the period of the Second World War. In 'Still Falls the Rain', subtitled 'The Raids, 1940. Night and Dawn', she sees Christ recrucified 'each day, each night'; in 'Anne Boleyn's Song' she gives the condemned queen a vision of the embraces of a new king, 'Old amorous Death . . . acclimatised to my coldness'; in 'Harvest' her narrator proclaims herself 'an old woman whose heart is like the Sun', a theme taken up again in the poem simply called 'An Old Woman' ('I, an old woman in the light of the sun, | Wait for my Wanderer'). Although there is a clear debt to Eliot's later verse, Sitwell's poems with their reiterated images of juvenescence and senescence, of dark and light, and of the passion of Christ, are quite distinctly the product of an explorative feminine sensibility. Towards the end of her life she continued to act out the role of the eccentric artist, flamboyant in her dress and manner, much courted by painters, photographers, and interviewers, and always prepared to be oracular. Taken as a whole, the three Sitwells' contribution to twentieth-century British literature is far more than a history of patronage or élitist self-publicity but it is perhaps only in Edith's verse that a distinct and continually challenging note emerges.

Joyce

If T. S. Eliot recognized any true literary kinship amongst his contemporaries it was not with the likes of the Sitwells but with the Irish novelist James Joyce (1882–1941). In 1918 he proclaimed Joyce 'the best living prose writer' and a year later he described the 'Scylla and Charybdis' section of *Ulysses* as 'almost the finest I have read: I have lived on it ever since I read it', though he felt obliged to add that he had found it 'uphill and exasperating work trying to impose Joyce on such "intellectual" people, or people whose opinion carries weight as I know, in London'. Joyce too had found the struggle to get his works accepted by publishers and public alike an uphill one. His confrontations with official and unofficial censors were especially frustrating. The manuscript of his collection of twelve stories, *Dubliners*, finished in 1905, was rejected by its prospective London publishers after a period of protracted uncertainty. In 1909 it was submitted to a Dublin firm; publication was postponed in 1910 and in 1912 the type was broken up by the printers due to a fear of libel action from local tradesmen mentioned in the text (Joyce got his own back in the rumbustious broadside 'Gas from a Burner'). With the addition of three further stories the volume finally appeared in 1914. *Ulysses*, composed in three different cities, was published in Paris in 1922 in a limited edition; after the confiscation of subsequent editions, on pornographic grounds, by customs officers in Britain and America it was not made legally available in the United States until 1933 and was printed in an unlimited edition in London only in 1937. Joyce's relationship with Eliot as his publisher proved infinitely easier. In 1931 Eliot contracted to publish *Finnegans Wake* through the firm of Faber and Faber of which he was a director (he had already issued a section of the 'work in progress'). In order to introduce Joyce's work to the elusive 'general' reader, rather than simply to an intellectual coterie, Faber produced a short selection of his prose, edited by Eliot, in 1942.

The title of Joyce's somewhat mechanical and Ibsenesque play *Exiles* (written in 1914, but published and performed in 1918) is a key word in the writer's own career. His play is set in Dublin and is concerned in part with the conflicting emotions of his central character about his homeland. Should he remain loyal to Ireland and attempt to open up its culture to a broader Europeanism? Or would Ireland ultimately enforce upon him a Swiftian estrangement? For Joyce himself, and for his chief mouthpiece in fiction, Stephen Dedalus, a European exile was the only solution, an exile from 'home and friends' which could provide the right circumstances in which, as Stephen extravagantly puts it, to 'forge in the smithy of my soul the uncreated conscience of my race'. Joyce did not, significantly enough, choose London or New York over Dublin; instead, he moved away from an English-speaking environment to a succession of notably cosmopolitan and polyglot European cities. *Dubliners* was written in Trieste, Italian in population but still the main port of Austria-Hungary. *A Portrait of the Artist as a Young Man* is signed at the end 'Dublin, 1904. Trieste, 1914', *Ulysses* 'Trieste–Zurich–Paris 1914–1921', and *Finnegans Wake* 'Paris 1922–1939'. Despite the frustrations and limitations of the Ireland he happily left behind him, Joyce's loyalty to his native city was expressed, and steadily more complexly explored, in each of his prose works.

In September 1905 Joyce sent his brother Stanislas a list of questions from Trieste concerning details of Dublin life and customs which he needed for the stories on which he was working. In the same letter he explained that his collection would be based on a particular sequence. Three of the *Dubliners* stories would deal with childhood, three with adolescence, three with mature life, and three with public life. When he wrote in October to his prospective London publisher, he repeated the justification for his volume which he had previously articulated to Stanislas. No writer, he argued, had yet presented Dublin to the world; it had been a European capital for 'thousands of years'; it was supposed to be the second city of the British Empire and was nearly three times as big as Venice (so often the focus of classic English texts). In a further letter of May 1906 he insisted that he was writing 'a chapter of the moral history' of his country and that he had chosen Dublin not for its animation but because it seemed to him 'the centre of paralysis'. This idea of cultural 'paralysis' is stressed in the opening of the first story, 'The Sisters'. There is a reference in the first line to the priest's fatal stroke and later in the first paragraph the narrator repeats the word as he gazes up nightly at a window in the priest's house. Throughout the collection Dublin seems trapped by the mundane, the quotidian, and the historic. Its citizens are observed as bound up in private concerns and incapable of properly judging or quantifying their experience. Some are disillusioned, others lose vocations and illusions, others are graceless (both figuratively and spiritually). Any perspective is provided by the detached artist-narrator, observing, shaping his narratives but not offering judgement. In the haunting tenth story, 'Clay', the ungainly, ageing Maria loses a slice of plum cake on a tram. It is only through the shape of the complete narrative that the seemingly inconsequential loss is given a contextual perspective. At the close of the story, Maria's vulnerability is further exposed by her unconscious 'mistake' of singing 'in a tiny quavering voice' the Balfe song superstitiously held to foretell mortality, 'I Dreamt that I Dwelt in Marble Halls'. The various flat and conspicuously 'ordinary' details of the story are forged into a new whole, the nuances shaped into initially unperceived meanings, and the neutral tones assume hues as readers deduce significances. Only in the long last story, 'The Dead', does Joyce's baldly undemonstrative prose style, one he described as possessing the quality of 'scrupulous meanness', assume a greater luxury. The dominant figure of the literate and articulate Gabriel Conroy in this the last of the stories to be added to the collection shifts their general concern away from the uneducated and the narrow-minded. The quality of the family party he attends is established by snatches of conversation, exchanged politenesses, familiar memories, popular quotations and songs. By means of these fragments Joyce deftly draws together and re-echoes themes from earlier stories. He particularly allows for a sharp exchange between Gabriel and the insular Miss Ivors concerning the nationalist tensions of contemporary Ireland. Gabriel— who reviews English books and takes holidays in France and Belgium in preference to learning the Irish language in the western reaches of his own country—is accused of being a 'West Briton' (an Irishman content not to undo the Union with Great Britain). 'Irish', Gabriel insists, in a significant pre-echo of Stephen Dedalus, 'is not my language'. The issue, though seemingly forgotten amid the enforced accord of the party, re-emerges in its final paragraphs. Gabriel, temporarily alienated from his wife by her recall of memories of the song of a dead suitor from the Celtic West of Ireland, muses in his hotel room as snow falls in the city and unites it to the whole white island stretching westwards beyond it. The snow seems to join the living and the dead, the romantically lost and the practical present, but it does more than stir memory and desire; it offers a momentary vision of a release from time and from purely temporal and mundane preoccupations.

Before he had begun work on *Dubliners* Joyce had set down a series of what he styled 'Epiphanies' in his notebooks for 1903 and 1904. These short prose sketches vary from the drab and domestic to the dreamlike, but each is shaped around a moment of revelation related to, but rarely as emphatic as Gabriel's. In *Stephen Hero* (the discursive preliminary version of *A Portrait of the Artist* which was published from his fragmentary manuscript in 1944) Joyce gives his hero a definition of an epiphany as 'a sudden spiritual manifestation, whether in the vulgarity of speech or of gesture or a memorable phase of the mind itself'. These 'most delicate and evanescent of moments' seem to transform the commonplace into the special as tiny transfigurations worked without the operation of the divine. Joyce's use of theological terminology here and elsewhere in his definitions of his working methods is typical of the product of an exacting Jesuit education at school and university (he later compared the writing of *Ulysses* to the mystery of the Mass). With the exception of the converts Newman and Hopkins, Joyce is the first major writer in English since the Reformation to have been 'supersaturated' in specifically Roman Catholic teaching. Although Stephen Dedalus's admiration for Newman's prose style becomes a contentious issue in *A Portrait of the Artist as a Young Man* (1916) it is the eucharistic theology of Thomas Aquinas that most determines the complex aesthetics that Stephen expounds. Although his faith is replaced by scrupulous doubt, Stephen retains an insistent Jesuit authoritarianism in his arguments about definitions of beauty. As the latter stages of the story affirm, Stephen assumes a new priesthood, that of the artist. In a crucial sense, he also fulfils the implications of his pointedly un-Irish name. He is Daedalus, the builder of Cretan mazes and the ingenious feathered escaper from islands. It is to this symbolic artist, the 'old father, old artificer', that Stephen finally dedicates himself. But if the second half of *A Portrait of the Artist as a Young Man* is taken up with debate and definition, its opening sections attempt to describe, in an extraordinarily original manner, the growth of an artist's mind. There was obviously nothing new about the fictional autobiography, especially the kind that dealt with the emotional and intellectual development of a prospective writer. Its last conventional fling came in 1915 with W(illiam) Somerset Maugham's hugely popular account of a lonely boy's metamorphosis into responsive adulthood in *Of Human Bondage*. Where Maugham (1874–1965) ploddingly adapts formulas which would have been familiar enough to readers of *David Copperfield*, Joyce challenges received ideas of literary decorum. He plays even in his opening sentences with fairy-tale phraseology, nursery-rhyme rhythms and baby-talk and he deftly suggests how an infant's experience is shaped by sensual stimuli (Stephen hears a story; he smells his mother and the oil-sheet on his bed; he tastes lemon platt (a kind of children's sweet); he feels warm and wet). The narrative moves him forward from being the passive feeler, hearer, and observer to being the doer, reader, writer, and maker. It later seeks to express the process of Stephen's adolescent exploration of his personality and the flexibility of his mind. Above all, it describes him trying out the poses of the would-be priest, the lover, and the intellectual before finally breaking the narrative into a series of diary entries as the potential artist prepares himself for flight.

In *Ulysses*, once conceived of as a story for *Dubliners*, a troubled Stephen Dedalus has returned to his birthplace, to his circle of intellectual friends, and to the dangerously outstretched tentacles of his family. *Portrait* was focused on a single personality; *Ulysses*, by contrast, has a multiple focus. Stephen's refined perceptions are played against the earthier preoccupations of an *homme moyen sensuel*—the Dublin Jew, Leopold Bloom—and the consciousness of both is finally contrasted with that of Bloom's wife, Molly. The thought and actions of all three are interwoven with the diverse life of Dublin on a single day, 16 June 1904. Characters cross and recross the city (though Molly remains seemingly marginalized in her bed; she sleeps, entertains a lover, and ultimately moves centre-stage as she muses on her life and loves in an extraordinarily unpunctuated monologue). When Stephen and Bloom finally encounter one another, and drunkenly discover a brief intimacy, they have taken separate voyages of exploration through the city. Underneath each of the eighteen extended episodes around which the novel is built lies a Homeric precedent. Bloom is a latter-day Odysseus/Ulysses; Stephen his lost son Telemachus; Molly his Penelope. Mr Deasy, the opinionated Protestant schoolmaster with whom Stephen has an uneasy morning interview, corresponds to Nestor; Bloom's attendance at Paddy Dignam's funeral has overtones of the Homeric descent to Hades; the fantasizing Gerty MacDowell, whose sighting on the beach sexually stimulates Bloom, is a Nausicaa; and the xenophobic 'Citizen' in Barney Kiernan's is a type of the blinded giant, Cyclops. Beyond the explorations of the fluid consciousnesses of his major characters, and beyond the Homeric underpinning, Joyce ingeniously attempts to expand certain of the later episodes into experiments with form. In the 'Wandering Rocks' sequence, for example, the peregrinatory Father Conmee links together a series of brief scenes by crossing Dublin by a route meticulously plotted and timed by Joyce (with the aid of maps and of his Dublin-based brother) and by finally coinciding with a vice-regal cavalcade (representing a meeting of the Roman and the British domination of Ireland). In the 'Sirens' episode an attempt is made to reflect the musical form of a fugue and in the 'Oxen of the Sun' (set in the Holles Street maternity hospital) an extended pastiche of English prose style, from its beginnings to the present, parallels the embryonic development of a child in the womb. *Ulysses* is, however, far more than the self-referential series of echoes or the cryptogrammatic integration of puns, acrostics, and dense literary and historical allusion which its successor, *Finnegans Wake*, threatens to become. It rarely needs to be exactly untangled before it communicates. It is eminently *readable* rather than narrowly *studiable*. Reading *Ulysses* is a process of refamiliarization with a variety of adapted styles, modes, and techniques. In one sense, it stretches fictional realism almost to a point of absurdity, for example, in the 'Ithaca' section by subjecting Bloom, Stephen, and the objects in their immediate ambience to a process of forensic listing (Joyce himself called it a 'mathematical catechism'). In another, it consistently attempts to observe more intimately and precisely than any earlier novel. It follows the extraordinary vagaries of Bloom's mind as he shops, lusts, cooks, eats, relieves himself in the privy, and goes about his business. Whereas Stephen is preoccupied both with guilt over his failure to pray at his mother's death-bed and with intellectual speculation, Bloom's far less organized mind regularly throws up snippets of phrases and memories from a private past and from an observed world. His mind unsystematically returns to half-understood Hebrew and English words, to the smell of soap, to memories of his dead son, to an advertisement for Plumtree's Potted Meat, and to the jingling brass bed quoits which signal his wife's adultery. From these reiterations, repetitions, and variations Joyce gradually weaves a fabric which is at once startling and familiar, superbly comic and cerebral, rumbustious and refined. It mixes the music-hall with the opera house, the cliché with a disquisition on *Hamlet*, the 'fine tang of faintly scented urine' from mutton kidneys with the progress of European

civilization. If the contortedly encyclopaedic vision of *Finnegans Wake* determinedly shunts the modern literary experiment into a siding, *Ulysses* continues
to realize narrative vitality as exuberant as the God-like 'Hooray! Ay!
Whrrwhee' in Mr Deasy's school playground and as confident as Molly
Bloom's concluding 'Yes'.

Inter-War Drama:
O'Casey, Coward, Priestley, and Sherriff

The innovations of 'Modernism' or, more precisely, the dramatic experiments
of the leading 'Modernists', touched the English theatrical mainstream in the
twenty years between the two world wars only indirectly. Joyce's *Exiles* was
rejected by the normally progressive Stage Society in London and had to await
a first performance, in a German translation, at Munich in 1919. Eliot's
Sweeney Agonistes, published in 1932, was, somewhat bizarrely, given its first
performance a year later by the women students of Vassar College in the
United States. His *Murder in the Cathedral* was first acted in 1935 not in a
London theatre but in the chapter house of Canterbury Cathedral. Of D. H.
Lawrence's three remarkable, if somewhat static, explorations of working–class
life—*A Collier's Friday Night* (written *c.*1909 and published 1934), *The
Daughter-in-Law* (1912), and *The Widowing of Mrs Holroyd* (1914)—only the
last received a London performance, under the auspices of the Stage Society
in 1926. This performance belatedly provoked George Bernard Shaw to write
that its 'torrent of profuse yet vivid dialogue' made his own seem 'archaic in
comparison'. Even the redoubtable Shaw's most challenging late plays,
Heartbreak House (1919) and *Saint Joan* (1924), received their premières in
New York (though highly successful London productions of both followed
within months).

The three best-known plays of Shaw's younger compatriot, Sean O'Casey
(1880–1964), were shaped by the new Irish theatrical environment rather than
by the demands of the more conventional London Establishment. O'Casey
(born 'John Casey', and, at the peak of his association with the nationalist
Gaelic League, known as 'Sean O Cathasaigh') was the last of the major early
twentieth-century Irish playwrights to be associated with the Abbey Theatre
in Dublin. A poor Protestant Dubliner by birth, he wrote about what he knew
best—the sounds, the rhetoric, the prejudices, the frustrations, and the
manners of tenement dwellers of the slums of the Irish capital. Unlike his
Abbey predecessors he was not prepared to romanticize Ireland or to fantasize
about either its past or its bloody present. Nor was he inclined to 'poeticize'
the vigorously rhythmical language of the Dublin poor. *The Shadow of a
Gunman* (performed in Dublin in 1923 and in London in 1925) is set in a back
room in 'Hilljoy' Square at the time of the 'Black and Tan' repression in 1920.
The action of *Juno and the Paycock* (Dublin, 1924; London 1925) also takes

place in a single room in a two-room tenancy, though the period has moved forward to the time of the Irish Civil War in 1922. *The Plough and the Stars*, which provoked nationalist riots at the Abbey in 1926 but was more placidly received at the Fortune Theatre in London in the same year, describes the prelude to the eruption of the Easter Rising and the disjunctions of the Rising itself in 1916. Its action takes place in and around the Clitheroes' rooms 'in a fine old Georgian house struggling for its life against the assaults of time, and the more savage assaults of its tenants'. Despite the exemplary nature of O'Casey's nationalist credentials, in none of these three plays does he offer apologies for the troubles of Ireland, or take sides with its oppressors or its supposed liberators. The poor are seen as caught up in a struggle which disrupts their lives rather than enhances or transfigures them. They are never dumb victims, but their very garrulousness reveals them as incomprehending and unwilling sufferers for someone else's cause. All three plays are characterized by their author as tragedies, but in all three the shadow and the reality of death is relieved by a wit which is as instinctive as it is irreverent. This ambiguity is to some degree exemplified in *Juno and the Paycock* in Jack Boyle's blusteringly reiterated reflection that 'the whole worl's in a state o'chassis'. In *The Shadow of a Gunman* the theme of deception and self-deception, taken up from Synge's rural *Playboy of the Western World* (1907), is played ironically back in a revolutionary, urban setting. The play's title is itself ambiguous. Gunmen on both sides overshadow the characters, but *the* gunman of the play is a sham. It is not this supposed warrior, the 'poet and poltroon' Donal Davoren, who dies violently but the girl who looks upon him as a hero, the 'Helen of Troy come to live in a tenement', Minnie Powell. The conflict between bravado and bravery and between swaggering and fighting also determines the complex interactions of *The Plough and the Stars*. The assaulted tenement is both partially detached from the political struggle taking place beyond its walls and inextricably bound up in its confusions, injustices, and bloody accidents (again it is a woman, the otherwise impressively resilient Bessie Burgess, who is the victim). When O'Casey's experimental comment on the First World War, the 'Tragi-Comedy' *The Silver Tassie*, was rejected by the Abbey Theatre, O'Casey found a London theatre for its première in 1928 (he himself had already moved to England two years earlier). With Charles Laughton in the lead role and with scenery for the stylized expressionism of Act II designed by the painter Augustus John, *The Silver Tassie* seemed set to launch the dramatist on a new phase in his career. Its accentuated paradoxes, and the jerky contrast between the naturalism of its first and fourth acts and the exposed alienation of its middle two, in reality merely formed a prelude to the uncertainty, the awkwardness, and the socialist rhetoric of his later work. Neither *Red Roses for Me* (1943) nor the gesturing anti-clerical, anti-capitalist analyses of modern Ireland, *Cock-a-Doodle Dandy* (1949) and *The Bishop's Bonfire* (1955), managed to recall the tense, unsentimental energy of his Abbey plays.

The work of the most representative English dramatist of the period, Noël Coward (1899–1973), contrasts vividly with that of O'Casey. Coward combined the talents of actor, composer, librettist, playwright, and poseur and his long career allowed each aspect a more than ample expression. After uncertain theatrical beginnings in the immediately post-war years he achieved a double *succès de scandale* in 1924 with *The Vortex*, a high-flown exploration of the condition of a drug-addict tormented by his slovenly mother's adulteries, and the equally melodramatic *The Rat Trap*, a study of the miserable marriage of a playwright and his novelist-wife. In what must have seemed to audiences an abrupt change of style, in 1925 Coward produced *Hay Fever*. This elegantly malicious comedy, in which absurdity meets incomprehension, exposes both the eccentric, self-centred rudeness of the Bliss family and the bafflement of their conservative guests. His subsequent smartly packaged excursions into Ruritania—*The Queen was in the Parlour* (1926), *The Marquise* (1927), and the musical comedy *Bitter Sweet* (1929)—though vastly well-received in their time, effectively looked back nostalgically to the lost enchantments of the Edwardian theatre. In his three major plays of the early 1930s, however, Coward glanced freshly at the problems of the immediate past and the increasingly uneasy present. The elaborately staged *Cavalcade* (1931) traces the fortunes and opinions of the Marryot family in twenty-one short scenes covering the years 1899–1930, and includes episodes set variously in drawing-rooms, theatres, bar parlours, railway stations, and even on board the *Titanic*. It concludes with two contrasting scenes, the first of which shows its now aged central characters toasting the future in the hope that 'this country of ours, which we love so much, will find dignity and greatness and peace again'. The second, called 'Twentieth Century Blues', takes place in a nightclub and intermixes a song about 'chaos and confusion', popular dance, wounded war-veterans making baskets, and the cacophonous sounds of loudspeakers, jazz-bands, and aeroplane propellers. The 'angular and strange' effect that Coward sought at the end of *Cavalcade* is minimally reflected in the dialogue of his two comic studies of fraught marital relationships, *Private Lives* (1930) and *Design for Living* (1933), though, alas, neither play ultimately fulfils the psychological promise of the situations Coward wittily establishes. The limited ambitions of both were summed up in 1931 in their author's insistence that 'the primary and dominant object of the theatre is to amuse people, not to reform or edify them'. His last great success, *Blithe Spirit*, written in five days in 1941, ran for 1,997 performances in the West End of London (a record for a non-musical play in its time) as well as touring the provinces. It offered an essential escape from the preoccupations of the 'Home Front' in the Second World War, though it included, through the ethereal presence of Elvira and the spiritual interference of Madame Arcati, the reassurance to families parted by the war that death did not necessarily mark the end of a relationship.

J(ohn) B(oynton) Priestley (1894–1984), like Coward one of the most familiar and popular figures in the realm of propagandist entertainment during the

Second World War, established his reputation as a novelist with *The Good Companions* (1929) and *Angel Pavement* (1930). The first, an account of the vagaries of the life of a travelling theatrical troupe, was successfully dramatized (with the aid of Edward Knoblock) in 1931. It opened the floodgates to Priestley's career as a dramatist in his own right, a career which ultimately included more than forty plays. His stance as a no-nonsense populist and professional Yorkshireman, so self-consciously cultivated in his wartime radio broadcasts (published under the confident titles *Britain Speaks* (1940) and *All England Listened* (1968)), belied his genuine sophistication and dedication as an artist and critic. His best-remembered and most commonly revived plays, *Time and the Conways* (1937), *When We Are Married* (1938), and the mystery *An Inspector Calls* (1947), show a mastery of the conventional 'well-made' form and a tolerant sporting with human folly. The two comedies in particular tend to reinforce the virtues of common sense and stolidity rather than to challenge preconceptions as to the nature of society or the role of the theatre.

R(obert) C(edric) Sherriff's distinctly unreassuring dramatic account of life in the trenches of the First World War in *Journey's End* was translated from the Apollo Theatre (where it had been produced in December 1928 by the Stage Society) to the Savoy in January 1929. It ran for 594 performances before transferring to yet another West End theatre. Sherriff (1896–1975) never wrote anything more striking (though he had some later success in the theatre and with screenplays for the film-director Alexander Korda). *Journey's End* combines realism with the kind of restraint which is expressive of far more than the stiff-upper-lip heroics of idealized British officers. Its novelty lay in its stark portrayal of male relationships strained by an uncomfortable intimacy with discomfort, psychological dissolution, and death. It brought a frank representation of wastage and violence to the London theatre which served as effectively as Wilfred Owen's posthumously published poetry to stir unreconciled and unhappy emotions in ex-soldiers and to exemplify the pity of war to those who had not been required to fight.

Retrospect and Historical Memory: Graves, Jones, and Powys

The success of *Journey's End* on the London stage in 1929 coincided with the publication of the English translation of Erich Maria Remarque's powerful and phenomenally popular anti-war novel *All Quiet on the Western Front (Im Westen nichts neues)*. Writing in *The Criterion* in 1930 the poet, critic, and ex-combatant Herbert Read (1893–1968) argued that the human mind had 'a faculty for dismissing the debris of its emotional conflicts' and that only now, after a significant hiatus, did veterans feel ready 'for the spiritual awakening and *All Quiet* was the touch that released this particular mental spring'. As Read's three poems (published together in 1933 as *The End of a War*) themselves suggest, the 1930s were remarkable for a variety of delayed retrospects on the 'Great' War. These retrospects were shaped as memoirs, as novels, as collections of verse, and as experimental interfusions of verse and prose. As with the novels of Aldington and Ford and Siegfried Sassoon's fictionalized autobiography, completed in 1936, Robert Graves (1895–1985) felt prompted to public confession and evaluation. In his highly coloured autobiography, *Goodbye to All That* (1929, partly revised 1957), Graves describes a sense of alienation from post-war student life in Oxford which he shared with his friend and former fellow officer, the poet Edmund Blunden (1896–1974). Everything in their delayed studies was 'translated into trench-warfare terms' and Graves was apt to find the lectures he attended interrupted by 'a sudden very clear experience of men on the march up the Bethune–La Bassee road'. It was, however, through his Oxford acquaintance with one of the rare 'heroic' figures to emerge from the war, T(homas) E(dward) Lawrence (1888–1935), that Graves may have begun to recognize the fictional potential of feeling along an extended chain of connection between the present and the experience of the remoter past. The already 'legendary' Lawrence, deeply drawn to the continuities and raw grandeurs of Arab culture, was at work on his romantic account of his desert campaigns which he published, for private circulation, as *The Seven Pillars of Wisdom* in 1926, and which was posthumously released to a highly receptive wider public in 1935.

By his own account, Graves had begun to write his own autobiography in 1916 in the form of a novel, though he was obliged to 're-translate it into history' for *Goodbye to All That*. The processes of translating and intermixing also determined the nature of his string of popular first-person historical novels which began in 1934 with *I, Claudius*. His choice of narrator was striking. Tiberius Claudius Drusus Nero Germanicus, the future Emperor of the Romans and the successful colonizer of Britain, may be cast as an idiosyncratic and decidedly unheroic autobiographer, but he remains the central actor in the evolution of a large historical drama. Most historical fiction, from the time of Scott onwards, had employed observant, passive, fictional protagonists who stood on the sidelines of history. Although his attempts at valour are chiefly notable for their extreme discretion, birth and accident determine that the historical Claudius must fulfil his recorded destiny as Emperor. His is essentially a sordid, upper-class family history rather than an analysis of the growing pains of post-Republican Roman society, but it is animated with philosophical reflection and with a series of highly entertaining grotesqueries (notably the portraits of the Empress Livia and of her protégé Caligula). *I, Claudius* and its successor, *Claudius the God, and his wife Messalina* (also 1934), repackaged Roman history for an age which had begun to witness the decline of classical studies but which, conversely, had seen the rise of a new, imperially ambitious Italian autocrat, Benito Mussolini. None of Graves's subsequent historical fictions had quite the flair and modern relevance of his first.

The military career of David Jones (1895–1974), and the consequent Roman bias of the literature that eventually emerged from it, were quite distinct from

Graves's. Jones, born in London of a Welsh father and an English mother, remained fascinated by his divided British inheritance. He was a cockney Welshman who, despite his love of its sounds and its literature, never fully mastered the Welsh language. After studying at the Camberwell School of Art, Jones joined the Royal Welch Fusiliers and served as a private soldier in the trenches on the Western Front. It was this view from the ranks, partly refocused after his reception into the Roman Catholic Church in 1921, which determined the intimacy, the nervous intensity and peculiarly Latinate reference of his subsequent poetry (he remained an equally intense and experimental painter). Jones began work on his epic of suffering and comradeship, *In Parenthesis*, in 1927. It was not published until 1937 and was latterly reprinted with an appreciative 'Note of Introduction' by T. S. Eliot. Its title refers both to a private history which had become, as Jones saw it, 'a kind of space between', and to an escape from the 'brackets' of the 1914–18 war. *In Parenthesis* is divided into seven parts, each of which intermixes and combines the various registers of terse military commands, profane army slang, Welsh tags, cockney phrasing, reportage, description, extended prose meditation, and the striking fragmentation of prose into a dense and allusive poetry. Throughout, Jones sees his patient modern soldiers, Private John Ball and Private Watkin, the one the Saxon Londoner and the other the Celtic Briton, as bearing in their bodies 'the genuine tradition of the Island of Britain'. It was a tradition which he saw as moulded in turn by the popular vigour of Welsh and English comic literature, and the modern music-hall. But his soldiers have also unconsciously inherited a line of recorded history stretching back to the ancient meeting of Roman and Celt, a meeting finally cemented in the Latin Christianization of the colony of Britain. They move through a confused khaki world of reveilles, mud, mustard-gas, barbed wire, and bomb-craters, but it is also a world haunted by the ghosts of Welsh heroes and Roman legionaries. Out of the twisted debris of all battles, ancient and modern, Jones painstakingly assembled a diverse and often dazzling work of art, part *objet trouvé*, part collage, part expressionist construction.

The fragmentary archaeological poetry perfected by Eliot in the 1920s clearly left its imprint on Jones's slowly produced work. His longest poem, *Anathemata* (1952), in part a tribute to his native London, interweaves the legendary history of Britain with the complexly layered history and prehistory of Europe, tying the island to the Continent by threads that are both Celtic and Teutonic, both Imperial Roman and Roman Catholic. Celtic, Latin, and Germanic concepts jostle each other when, for example, he considers the anonymous prehistoric sculptor of the so-called Willendorf Venus (a buxom Celtic figure found near the Danube):

> Who were his *gens*-men or had he no *Hausname* yet
> no *nomen* for his *fecit*-mark
> > > > the Master of the Venus?
> whose man-hands god-handled the Willendorf stone
> > before they unbound the last glaciation

> for the Uhland Father to be-ribbon *die blaue Donau*
> with his Vanabride blue.
> O long before they lateen'd her Ister
> or Romanitas manned her gender'd stream.
> O Europa!

Anathemata is shot through with modernist effect, Modernist fragmentation, and modernist difficulty, but, as with Joyce's later work, it is ordered by an artistic sensibility which is essentially theological. When in a late poem, *The Tribune's Visitation* (1958, 1969), he returned to the idea of a Welsh soldier, he described not a muddy private on the Western Front, but a conscripted Celt in the Roman army witnessing the passion of Christ. For Jones, history was a process of conflations and synchronies out of which poetry was painfully squeezed.

A quite distinct variety of conflation and synchrony haunts John Cowper Powys's vast and idiosyncratic novel *A Glastonbury Romance* (1932). Powys (1872–1963) daringly attempts to persuade his readers of the existence of a 'reservoir of world magic' and a 'residue of unused power' centred on the nipple-shaped Tor and the ruined abbey at Glastonbury in Somerset, a site identified in medieval times with manifestations of the Holy Grail and aspects of the legends of King Arthur. The novel loosely interlinks an ancient, Aryan mysticism with a post-Freudian and post-Lawrentian quest for identity and self-discovery and it seeks to delineate the points at which magic touches, and occasionally transfigures, an evolving and assertive sexuality. 'The ecstatic quiver of that great cosmic ripple we call Sex', Powys's narrator notes, 'runs through the whole universe and functions in every organism independent of external objects of desire!' There is both a wonderful concreteness and an elusive strangeness about Powys's writing at its best, but at its worst his unwieldy novel looms like a foggy isthmus of psychological and social realism in a warmly seductive sea of new-age gobbledegook.

'Society' and Society:
The New Novelists of the 1920s and 1930s

To the upper- and middle-class generations that either avoided or missed combat in the First World War, the often flippant 1920s and the far gloomier 1930s were less a time for retrospects than an age that seemed like a springboard to an uncertain future. The uncertainties were built into an often sardonic, questioning, terse, and jerky new fiction. The poet Stephen Spender (1909–95) describes his boyhood and adolescence in his autobiography *World Within World* (1951) as a period of growing up 'in an atmosphere of belief in progress curiously mingled with apprehension'. His senior, William Gerhardie (originally Gerhardi) (1895–1977), who spent much of the war as a junior attaché in the British Embassy in Petrograd, viewed the 1920s as a decade in which inhibitions were broken down. 'Young people', he wrote in his comically subversive history of the first half of the twentieth century *God's Fifth Column* (1981), 'disillusioned by inconsistencies of avowed ideals with palpable results, as exemplified by the behaviour of their parents, discovered a style of life for themselves which allied mature superciliousness about their elders with an insistence on the advantages of young years and limbs'. A sense of disillusion and an amused superciliousness runs through Gerhardie's two first, and best, novels, *Futility: A Novel on Russian Themes* (1922) and *The Polyglots* (1925). Gerhardie, who had been born of British parents in Imperial St Petersburg, was well attuned to things Russian (he published a pioneer study of Chekhov in 1923 and a sharply observant history of the Romanov tsars in 1940). *Futility* is a sub-Chekhovian essay in absurdity, aimlessness, and non-communication set against the background of the Russian revolutions of 1917. There is a parallel series of diverse fictional manœuvres between comedy and tragedy in *The Polyglots*, whose setting moves panoramically from Japan, to Harbin in Manchuria, to Shanghai before ending up in the drizzling rain of England. The novel's narrator, the capriciously named Georges Hamlet Alexander Diabologh, is a polyglot English outsider, detached both from the displaced and disparate collection of refugees from Russia he encounters in the East and from the English with whom he is never properly at home. Despite the confusion of tongues and manners that the novel implies, Diabologh accepts the English language as his medium and uses it to create what he sees as an Anglo-Saxon 'world of assumed restraint' as opposed to a 'Maupassantian . . . candour'. 'The novel', he also remarks, 'is a cumbersome medium for depicting real people.' Diabologh's narrative is frequently threatened with dissolution by confusions of identity, trivialities, seeming inconsequences, and soliloquies (his middle name is not 'Hamlet' by accident). In a sense it enacts the disintegration which is its subject.

Henry Green (1905–73), the pseudonym of Henry Vincent Yorke, was the son of a wealthy Birmingham industrialist. For Green, writing in his 'self-portrait' *Pack my Bag* in the midst of another war in 1940, the domestic circumstances in which he found himself during the war of 1914–18 had opened up disorienting vistas. The family house at Tewkesbury had become a convalescent home for wounded officers, one of whom attempted to commit suicide. The event, coupled with the death of an elder brother at school and 'the lists of the dead each day in every paper', reinforced an acute awareness of mortality. Perhaps as significant was the opportunity provided to learn what he called 'the half-tones of class' and to experience 'those narrow, deep and echoing gulfs which must be bridged'. In *Party Going* (1939) Green's seemingly unpromising subject is the four-hour delay experienced by a young and smart set of party-goers. Little enough actually happens. Fog forbids departure by train and the group resort to the station hotel from whence they can look down on the masses of less privileged travellers below them, the 'thousands of Smiths, thousands of Alberts, hundreds of Marys, woven tight as any office carpet'. 'What targets', someone later remarks, 'what targets for a bomb'.

In *Party Going* the few are divided from the thousands, but they are also glimpsed as incomprehendingly surrounded by the evidence of death and decay. Not only does the order of society seem fragile when the topic of an air raid is raised (a very present threat in 1939), but the external gloom of the fog and the sudden illness of Miss Fellowes (who has inexplicably picked up a dead pigeon as the novel opens) serve to cast glancing shadows over the generally trivial gossip of the young travellers. Social class, and the problems attendant on class divisions, figure too in Green's below-stairs vista on country-house life in neutral Ireland, *Loving* (1945), but his most impressive achievement remains the neutral study of the commonplaces of Birmingham factory life, *Living* (1929). For this, his second novel, he evolved a startlingly abbreviated narrative style, a style which eliminates definite articles and adjectives, which experiments with verbless sentences, and which allows for the flatness of much colloquial discourse. It was a style modelled, by his own account, on the reflection of Arabic in the prose of the Victorian traveller C. M. Doughty (1843–1926) (Doughty's *Travels in Arabia Deserta* had been republished in 1921 with an introduction by T. E. Lawrence). There is nothing exotic about *Living*. As Dupret, the son of the factory-owner, walks through the artisan streets he remarks on their air of 'terrible respectability on too little money' and on a way of life that consists for all classes of the monotonies of being born, of going to school, of working, of being married, of bearing children, and of dying. 'What had you before you died?', he ponders, 'Grandchildren? The satisfaction of breeding the glorious Anglo Saxon breed?' This monotony is briefly relieved by the exploited Lily Gates's attempted escape to Canada with Bert Jones. The couple's elopement only takes them as far as Liverpool and their journey is marked by Lily's dim awareness that 'while she expected to be happy she was not and Mr Jones could only think of what they would do in Liverpool'. Lily returns, almost as arbitrarily as she left, to the routines of her life in Birmingham.

Living was praised in its time for its evocation of the rhythms, repetitions, and deprivations of industrial life. An equally original, but far wider ranging, representation of working-class life and working-class perception appears in Lewis Grassic Gibbon's remarkable trilogy, *Sunset Song* (1932), *Cloud Howe* (1933), and *Grey Granite* (1934), known collectively as *A Scots Quair* (its title is a proletarian echo of King James I of Scotland's *The Kingis Quair* of *c*.1423). Gibbon, the pen-name of James Leslie Mitchell (1901–35), uses the thread of the life of Chris Guthrie and her three marriages to draw his three independently shaped novels together. Chris's marriages and widowhoods occasion her movement from a farm in the north-east Lowlands first to a small-town manse and then to a boarding-house in a city. She endures the death of her farmer husband in the First World War and watches as the iron enters the soul of the Scottish working classes during the period of the General Strike, the Depression, and the Hunger Marches of the 1930s. The novels are distinctive not so much for their attempt to root private and public history in a Marxist understanding of class struggle as for their return to the matter and the speech of Scotland. For Gibbon, the assertively Scottish novel of the twentieth century should be expressed in a tempered version of the Scots vernacular that his characters speak, a language which for them is embedded in 'the smell of the earth . . . and the sweetness of the Scottish land and skies'. The predominantly rural *Sunset Song* opens with an evocation of place which is at once mythical and sub-medieval, legendary and historical: 'Kinraddie lands had been won by a Norman childe . . . in the days of William the Lyon, when gryphons and such-like beasts still roamed the Scots countryside and folk would waken in their beds to hear the children screaming, with a great wolf-beast, come through the hide window, tearing at their throats.' The violence implicit in this opening is reflected not only in the sharp divisions between the possessors and the dispossessed examined in the subsequent narratives, but also in the death in battle of Chris's husband Ewan with which the first volume concludes. The widow at first refuses to recognize that her husband could have been sacrificed for anything so irrelevant to him as somebody else's war: 'He wasn't dead, he could never have died or been killed for nothing at all, far away from her over the sea, what matter to him their War and their fighting, their King and their country? Kinraddie was his land, Blawearie his, he was never dead for those things of no concern, he'd the crops to put in and the loch to drain and her to come back to.' Chris's awareness of her particular place and of her local identity is reinforced in the 'Epilude' to *Sunset Song* by the inclusion of the music to 'The Flowers of the Forest' (originally a lament for the fallen Scots in the disastrous battle of Flodden fought against the English in 1513). The melody, played on the pipes as the village's War Memorial stone is unveiled, had earlier seemed to Chris to hold in it not simply sadness of mourning but the accumulated history of her nation.

In the latter stages of *Grey Granite* Chris's Communist son Ewan is fired by the idea that he is himself History: 'A Hell of a thing to be History!—not a student, a historian, a tinkling reformer, but LIVING HISTORY ONESELF. . .'. In the novels of Ivy Compton-Burnett (1884–1969) the pervasive detachment from public events might be said to render such an idea marginal, illusory, even irrelevant. Nevertheless the eighteen novels she wrote after disowning her first published work, *Dolores* (1911), describe an enclosed, circumscribed, and dying historical world, drab in its consistency. The variations between the novels are relatively small, though none precisely mirrors its predecessors. Each is concerned with a small upper-middle-class group of characters in the period antecedent to the First World War. The most common setting is a large if shabby country house, the most common grouping is the late Victorian extended family. The small society Compton-Burnett observes does not consider itself oppressive or exploited, but in each novel a complex series of oppressions and exploitations emerge. As a selection of her titles suggest (*Pastors and Masters* (1925), *Brothers and Sisters* (1929), *Men and Wives* (1931), *A House and its Head* (1935), *Parents and Children* (1941), *Manservant and*

Maidservant (1947), and *A Father and his Fate* (1957)) she concentrates on relationships which imply power on the one side and submission and humiliation
on the other. Power is exercised by genteel bullies largely for reasons of
personal vanity; it is these respectable oppressors who inflict an exquisite and
protracted mental suffering on their equally genteel victims. Men readily take
on dictatorial roles while women and, above all, children, represent an
exploited class (though the positions and oppressions are reversible). There is
little room for kindness, warmth, and affection. 'Dear, dear, the miniature
world of the family!', the eldest daughter in *Parents and Children* remarks, 'All
the emotions of mankind seem to find a place in it.' At the beginning of *A
Father and his Fate* the father, Miles Mowbray, serenely expounds the principle that his three unmarried daughters have the life they ought to have: 'A
life in the family home, with the protection and provision that is fit for them.
What more could they want?' When his nephew questions his judgement, the
offended Mowbray insists that he is not a tyrant and that his house is not a
torture chamber. 'Then it is different from many houses', his nephew retorts.
Compton-Burnett's style is as austere as her subjects are, though it often suggests a brittle sense of humour generally denied to her characters. Her effects
are achieved through conversation which is simple, undramatic, and determined by the flat good manners of a polite and often repressed society. It is,
however, through these flat, claustrophobic dialogues that there emerge the
deceptions, frauds, and the often melodramatic surprises on which the novels
turn. Crimes, imagined and realized, await exposure, and murders, committed
or contrived, serve to satisfy the demands either of vengeance or of selfishness.
Compton-Burnett's fictional style can be an acquired taste, requiring as it does
a susceptibility educated to respond to her distinctive but subdued acidity.

Bright Young Things and Brave New Worlds: Wodehouse, Waugh, and Huxley

The eccentricities, oddities, fogyisms, fads, and fashions of inter-war upper-
class England are nowhere better charted than in P. G. Wodehouse's mockery
of them. Between 1902 and the end of his life P(elham) G(renville) Wodehouse
(1881–1975) published over 120 volumes of novels and short stories. He first
introduced his most famous characters, Bertie Wooster and his man Jeeves, in
an unremarkable story in the collection *The Man with Two Left Feet and Other
Stories* in 1917. The modest collection itself is notable for its variety of narrators, which range from a dog to a London waiter, and amongst them the
Wooster narrative sits snugly and companionably. When, however, in 1919
Wodehouse began to explore further the potential of the disarmingly dim
Bertie as a narrator and his relationship to the resourceful Jeeves in *My Man
Jeeves*, he took the classic master–servant partnerships of literature into a new
era. Here was a Samuel Pickwick and a Sam Weller advanced both in fortune

and in class into the Jazz Age. Wodehouse's art lay in telling a simple and amusing story simply and amusingly. He once described his method of writing as 'making a sort of musical comedy without music and ignoring real life altogether'. Although Wodehouse's is a genuinely escapist fiction, it neither truly ignores 'real' life nor suggests an ignorance of the political and social currents of its time. It identifies likely disturbers of the public peace in the guise of aunts and flapper feminists, gangsters and *arrivistes*, cranks and enthusiasts, mindless bachelor members of the Drones Club and thuggish followers of the Fascist Black Shorts movement, and it systematically deflates them all.

Despite the fun, there is far less geniality in the early fiction of Evelyn Waugh (1903–66). There is a menace even in the titles of his first four novels, *Decline and Fall* (1928), *Vile Bodies* (1930), *Black Mischief* (1932), and *A Handful of Dust* (1934). *Decline and Fall*, with its Gibbonian suggestions of a society in decay, traces the disastrous career of the innocent Paul Pennyfeather, a failed undergraduate, a failing schoolmaster, and the exploited lover of the highly corrupt Margot Beste-Chetwynde (the future Margot Metroland). Sentenced to a term at the Egdon Heath Penal Settlement (a Dartmoor in the midst of Hardy country) thanks to Margot's white-slaving activities, Paul endures his fate patiently. 'Anyone who has been to an English public school', the narrator wryly remarks, 'will always feel comparatively at home in prison.' Throughout both *Decline and Fall* and *Vile Bodies*, the accumulated evidence of depravity is balanced by a comedy that sports not simply with human folly but with crime, injustice, and even potential horror. As with Ben Jonson's equally savage comedies or with Dickens's comic inflations, venality embraces vulgarity and the ridiculous frolics with the rapacious. In *Vile Bodies* the devaluation of received standards is typified by the filming of a preposterous life of John Wesley in which Wesley and Whitefield fight a duel for the love of Selina, Countess of Huntingdon. 'This is going to make film history', the director announces, 'We're recording extracts from Wesley's sermons and we're singing all his own hymns.' *Black Mischief*, set in the tottering African kingdom of Azania, intermixes farcical representations of the Emperor's birth-control campaign ('Through Sterility to Culture') with rum accounts of civil war, corruption, and mayhem which were imaginative expansions on the circumstances Waugh himself had witnessed in Ethiopia. He had initially described his African journey in the travel-book *Remote People* in 1931; he returned to Ethiopia during the Italian invasion, publishing an account of his experiences as a journalist in *Waugh in Abyssinia* in 1936 and a fictional enlargement on them in *Scoop* in 1938 (the novel is also a pointed satire on a popular newspaper industry dominated by the opinionated Lord Copper). By far the finest, and the most refinedly cruel, of the early novels is *A Handful of Dust*. The novel's title, amplified in its epigraph, reveals Waugh's debt to the bleakness of *The Waste Land*. Although it is quintessentially a commentary on 'the way we live now', it also glances back, both in terms of form and in reference, to the moral strictures on the decay of social responsibility in the works of Dickens and Trollope. *A Handful of Dust* explores the painful collapse of the illusions and complacencies of a rural feudalism, represented by Tony Last (whose name may reflect the passing orders of Bulwer-Lytton's titles), and it exposes the surface values and the cynicism of the thoroughly modern and essentially metropolitan 'bright young things'. It moves between a seedy Arthurian-Victorian country house, to glib London clubs and smart apartments, to a Brighton hotel, and to the uncharted equatorial forests of South America, each of them significant re-presentations of aspects of Eliot's poem. Literally and figuratively it centres on the idea of divorce, a divorce between old and new values and divorce as the legal end to marriage which was very much an aspect of upper-class social relationships at the time of its publication. The novel ends with the rootless and defeated Tony Last trapped in the jungle by the calculating, halfcrazed Mr Todd who forces him to read and reread Dickens's novels aloud to him: 'Your head aches does it not . . . We will not have any Dickens today . . . but tomorrow, and the day after that, and the day after that. Let us read *Little Dorrit* again. There are passages in that book I can never hear without the temptation to weep.' Without itself being insistently 'Modernist', *A Handful of Dust* is shaped around some of the most troubling juxtapositions, fragmentations, and allusions in English literature.

Brideshead Revisited: The Sacred and Profane Memories of Captain Charles Ryder (1945) reworks and reconsiders the thematic tensions of *A Handful of Dust* in the context of Britain in the Second World War. Here again was the romantic country house (though now baroque rather than Gothic) and here again was the clash of tradition with the modern fragmentations of the family and of society. What has shifted is Waugh's narrative perspective. Where the earlier novel was referential, *Brideshead* is essentially reverential. Waugh's narrator, Charles Ryder, is both the central actor in the plot and the far from detached observer and recorder of its action. It is Ryder who is required both to observe and to translate his experience from an agnostic negativity into a series of barely grasped Catholic positives. The harsh outlines of the ironies and unresolved oppositions of Waugh's earlier fiction now seem blurred by a dim religious light. Although Ryder's retrospect traces the effective decline of an aristocratic family, the final extension of his memories into the present allows for the momentary triumph of the ancient and the continuous over the modern and the ephemeral, of the flickering of a sanctuary lamp over the middle-brow popularism that Ryder identifies as 'Hooperism'. Despite its overall mood of nostalgia, *Brideshead* remains a more open and subtle novel than its critics often allow. When in the latter part of his career the convert Waugh adopted the role of amateur apologist for Roman Catholic teaching, as he did in his historical novel *Helena* (1950) and in his biographies of Edmund Campion (1935) and Ronald Knox (1959), his universal sense of the ridiculous tended to desert him and to be superseded by a pompous and exclusive piety. The old detached and dust-haunted Waugh blazed into satiric life one more time, however, in the short fantasia on the eccentricities of Californian funerary practices, *The Loved One* (1948). Otherwise the tone of his late fiction seems to have been determined by an often agonized Augustinian awareness of sin and human failure. The ambitious *Sword of Honour* trilogy (*Men at Arms* (1952), *Officers and Gentlemen* (1955), and *Unconditional Surrender* (1961)) traces the disappointments of another Catholic patrician, Guy Crouchback, as an army officer muddling through a decidedly un-heroic and often pathetic series of experiences during the Second World War. Though it is a far cry from the ideals of chivalric patriotism that he initially seeks to embody, Crouchback's basic decency emerges as a spot of civilized brightness in what Waugh portrays as an increasingly dismal world.

In a review of Waugh's *Vile Bodies* in the *Daily Sketch* in January 1930 Rebecca West recognized that the novel had 'a very considerable value as a further stage in the contemporary literature of disillusionment' and that it followed in a new tradition, first established by *The Waste Land* and continued by Aldous Huxley's novels *Crome Yellow* (1921), *Antic Hay* (1923), and *Those Barren Leaves* (1925). Waugh rarely appreciated comparisons between his work and that of Huxley (1894–1963). He found *Point Counter Point* (1928) a rehash of *Antic Hay* with 'all the same social uncertainties, bored lovemaking . . . [and] odd pages of conversation and biology'. There are, however, certain obvious parallels between the satirical pictures of the self-conscious pursuit of modernity by a young, smart set in the work of both novelists in the 1920s. Thereafter, their styles and subjects diverge radically. As the derivations of Huxley's titles from phrases of Shakespeare, Bacon, Milton, and Marvell imply, he was, like Waugh, self-consciously 'literary'. Unlike Waugh, he initially shaped his novels on the model of the densely conversational, country-house symposia of Thomas Love Peacock; as his experiments with form became more elaborate, so did his tendency to explore ideas at the expense of action. *Point Counter Point* is particularly intricately constructed. As suggested by its title, it attempts to investigate an analogy with musical counterpoint by offering glimpses of diverse experience which seem to be observed simultaneously. Huxley's 'musicalization of fiction . . . on a large scale, in the construction' is explained by one of his characters, Philip Quarles, a novelist-within-the-novel: 'A theme is stated, then developed, pushed out of shape, imperceptibly deformed, until, though still recognizably the same, it has become different . . . All you need is a sufficiency of characters and parallel, contrapuntal plots.' The ingenuity of the constructive concept is generally more impressive than the final achievement. The novel is notable for its sympathetic portrait of D. H. Lawrence as Mark Rampion, but it was Lawrence himself who remarked on its theme of the 'slow suicide of inertia'. Despite the sensationalism of the famous scene in *Eyeless in Gaza* (1936) in which a dead dog drops from an aeroplane and bloodily explodes on a flat roof where the hero is making love, the unchronological shifts in time and perspective around which the novel is built tend to fascinate rather than engage by their immediacy.

Huxley's most celebrated book, the Utopian, or rather Dystopian, fantasy *Brave New World* (1932), is essentially the projection of an idea that might have been debated at a Peacockian house-party to which a latter-day Mary Shelley had been bidden. The novel's germ can be precisely located within Huxley's own work in Mr Scogan's evocation of a scientific future in *Crome Yellow*, a future in which 'impersonal generation will take the place of Nature's hideous system'. 'In vast state incubators', Scogan continues, 'rows upon rows of gravid bottles will supply the world with the population it requires. The family system will disappear; society, sapped at its very base, will have to find new foundations; and Eros, beautifully and irresponsibly free, will flit like a gay butterfly from flower to flower'. Huxley, as a grandson of Darwin's defender, Thomas Henry Huxley, and a descendant of the Arnolds, might have been expected to have inherited a distinct family bias towards the idea of progress. Where, however, T. H. Huxley had sought to sap the biblical foundations of Victorian religious faith by arguing for rationalism and modern science, his grandson offered a challenge to scientific optimism about the future by presenting a case for individual freedom rooted in literature and religion (the monitory Savage of his tale moulds his opposition to Utopia on ideas derived from Shakespeare). When Huxley earlier described his experiences of India in the travel-book *Jesting Pilate* (1926), he had recognized the advantages that the example of Henry Ford offered over that of the Buddha: 'One is all for religion', he wrote, 'until one visits a really religious country. Then one is all for drains, machinery and the minimum wage.' In *Brave New World*, where the calendar is dated AF (after Ford), and the revolutionary thinkers of the modern age (Darwin, Marx, Helmholtz, Freud, Lenin, and even Mussolini) have left their mark on the names of the newly hatched élite of Alphas, the advantage begins to swing back to a religion which attempts to embrace and explore the problem of pain. The Savage seeks the admittedly narrow freedom to be unhappy rather than to escape into an induced, tidy, and controlled *soma* dream. Huxley was intellectually projecting himself beyond the political and social preoccupations of the 1930s towards a technologically engineered future. When he reconsidered the book for a new Foreword in 1946 he acknowledged that an immediate 'failure of foresight' had meant that he had omitted all reference to nuclear fission; more vitally, he saw that the European world that had emerged from the Second World War was already conditioned by science and the State to accept a 'horror' that could be upon us within a single century, 'that is, if we refrain from blowing ourselves to smithereens in the interval'. Although the brave world of the Seventh Century AF was to have rid itself of a sense of guilt, it was precisely to the 'savage', uneasy and unliberated consciences of the twentieth century that Huxley was addressing his book.

The Auden Circle

'We young writers of the middle 'twenties', Christopher Isherwood wrote in his partly fictionalized autobiography *Lions and Shadows* (1938), 'were all suffering, more or less subconsciously, from a feeling of shame that we hadn't been old enough to take part in the European war.' For Isherwood (1904–86), and for the group of writers and artists who shared his political ideology (and often his sexual inclinations too), this subconscious 'shame' determined the degree of relish with which they embraced the crusading militancy and social-ism in the 1930s. Socialism, generally with a strongly Marxist hue, appeared to be the leading vehicle for social, sexual, and literary emancipation. Although they had missed a European war, they were of a generation that recognized that siding with the Left in a class-war might bring about a purging of the inherited guilt of the upper and middle classes. As faith declined in the 'God of Battles', who had been so over-invoked during the Great War, the vacuum was filled by an evangelizing mission to change society and to foster the demo-cratic millennium. The much vaunted successes of Soviet Communism, which offered so blatant a contrast to the regimes of Hitler and Mussolini and their connivance in destabilizing the reformist Republican Government of Spain, seemed to be the paradigm of a future society. When in 1936 General Franco's Nationalist army invaded the Spanish mainland, the battle lines effectively stretched far beyond the Iberian peninsula.

A year after war broke out in Spain the *Left Review* (founded 1934) pub-lished its pamphlet, *Authors Take Sides on the Spanish Civil War*, the result of a survey of 149 writers out of which 127 proclaimed themselves 'FOR' the Spanish Republic. Taking sides, or rather forming ranks with the Left, seemed to many young English writers to be the order of the day. 'It became possible to see the Fascist-anti-Fascist struggle as a real conflict of ideas . . . To write about Fascism was . . . to write about the experience which had usurped the place of more personal ones', Stephen Spender (1909–95) reflected in *World Within World* in 1951. To confirm his notion of the conjunction of ideas and externalized experience he quoted twenty-nine lines of Wordsworth's *The Prelude*. The young writers of 1937, he claimed, had found themselves in a 'parallel situation' to that of Wordsworth in 1791; they felt that 'their duty was to survive and bear witness'. 'The strongest appeal of the Communist Party', Louis MacNeice reflected in 1941, 'was that it demanded sacrifice; you had to sink your ego.' Younger poets such as Spender and Cecil Day-Lewis (1904–72) and their less talented fellows, Randall Swingler (1909–67), John Cornford (1915–36), 'Christopher Caudwell' (Christopher St John Sprigg) (1907–37), and Sylvia Townsend Warner (1893–1978), joined the Communist Party after reading the signs of the times in a Marxist light. A further degree of solidar-ity was expressed by those who went out to beleaguered Republican Spain. Cornford and Caudwell fought with the International Brigade and were killed in action; Spender and MacNeice (1907–63) made investigative visits to Barcelona, Madrid, and the front line; even W. H. Auden, whose flirtation with Marxism was beginning to diminish, left for Barcelona in January 1937. Having had his services as an ambulance driver refused and having instead made token propaganda broadcasts (in English) for the Republican cause, he returned to England in early March.

When W(ystan) H(ugh) Auden (1907–73) left for Spain he had been hailed by the Communist *Daily Worker* as 'the most famous of the younger English poets . . . and a leading figure in the anti-Fascist movement'. Auden's rise to fame had been rapid. His distinctive qualities had forcibly struck fellow under-graduate poets at Oxford, but his wider reputation had to wait on T. S. Eliot's publication of his 'charade' 'Paid on Both Sides' in the January 1930 issue of *The Criterion* and of his *Poems* in the September of the same year. His repu-tation was cemented by the appearance of *The Orators: An English Study* in 1932 and by the collection *Look Stranger!* in 1936. The *Daily Worker* had also reminded its readers of the critical success of the play *The Dog Beneath the Skin*, produced by the Group Theatre in London in 1935. *The Dog Beneath the Skin*, written with Christopher Isherwood, was but one of a series of significant collaborations between Auden and his friends, collaborations which suggest his prominence in experimental artistic life in Britain in the 1930s. He worked again with Isherwood on the dramatic parable of power and will, *The Ascent of F6* (1936, performed 1937 with incidental music by Benjamin Britten) and on the less well-received *On the Frontier* (performed in Cambridge in 1938 with incidental music by Britten, and transferred to London in 1939). Auden had already established a working relationship with Britten at the GPO film unit (which produced the famous *Night Mail* in 1935); he selected texts for Britten's song cycle *Our Hunting Fathers* in 1936; his poems, together with those of Randall Swingler, were quarried for the *Ballad of Heroes* in 1939 (written in honour of those who had been killed in Spain); and he provided the composer with a libretto for the improbable opera of American lumberjack life, *Paul Bunyan*, in 1941. A trek across Iceland with Louis MacNeice in 1936 led to the 'travel-book' *Letters from Iceland* (1937), a volume remarkable more for its poetry than for its photographic illustrations (which have the amateur air of holiday snaps).

His collaborative experiments with drama apart, Isherwood is likely to be remembered for his two most individual works of fiction, *Mr Norris Changes Trains* and *Goodbye To Berlin* (1939). Both draw on his experiences of living and teaching in the uncorseted, anything-goes Berlin of the years 1929–33. At the end of *Lions and Shadows* ('An Education in the Twenties') the narrator's decision to go to Germany seems almost arbitrary. He had been urged, he says, to see Berlin by 'Hugh Weston' (Wystan Auden), but as Isherwood later revealed in his third-person study of himself, *Christopher and His Kind* (1977), the real motive for the visit was the perception that 'Berlin meant boys'. Neither of the Berlin books is explicitly homosexual, though in both a whole variety of sexual tastes, whims, and deviations are touched upon, all of them openly catered for at the clubs, bars, and nude beaches of Weimar Germany. Isherwood's Berlin is decadent, economically depressed, politically volatile, but for his narrator, artistically exhilarating. In *Mr Norris* the explosive mood of the city is suggested by its discourse, a language which is as 'inflated . . . beyond recall' as the Deutschmark: 'The vocabulary of newspaper invective (traitor, Versailles-lackey, murder-swine, Marx-crook, Hitler-swamp, Red-pest) had come to resemble, through excessive use, the formal phraseology of politeness employed by the Chinese. The word *Liebe*, soaring from the Goethe standard, was no longer worth a whore's kiss.' Against a shifting, and often shifty background, Isherwood's narrator in the sex sections of *Goodbye To Berlin* himself shifts between identities. He is variously addressed as 'Herr Issyvoo', 'Christoph', and 'Herr Christoph'. As the 'Herr Issyvoo' of the first section claims: 'I am a camera with its shutter open . . . Some day, all this will have to be developed, carefully printed and fixed.' The camera metaphor applies both to still photography and to the newer techniques of the documentary cinema (Isherwood probably knew Walter Ruttmann's inventive celebration of urban life in *Berlin: Die Symphonie der Grossstadt* of 1927). Isherwood sought to write a plain and objective prose which would fix an image of observed reality. In line with the picturesquely phrased condemnation of the 'bourgeois' élitism of Joyce and Proust at the Soviet Writers' Congress in Moscow in 1934 (the proceedings of which were published in English as *Problems in Soviet Literature* in 1935), Isherwood eschews an elaborate prosody in favour of an easily assimilated lucidity. As one alert to the techniques of Freudian therapy, he also conveys the impression of tolerance and sympathetic understanding (though tolerance and sympathy rapidly evaporate when he describes encounters with the Nazi party). In January 1939 Isherwood left Europe with Auden for the United States. While Auden settled on the East Coast, Isherwood (who became an American citizen in 1946) gravitated naturally towards the West. His fictionalized account of working with an exiled Austrian film-director, *Prater Violet* (1946), suggests that he had already imaginatively served an apprenticeship for his sporadic future employment as a Hollywood screen-writer.

Stephen Spender shrewdly remarked of Isherwood, with reference to the period they spent together in Berlin, that 'Christopher, so far from being the self-effacing spectator he depicts in his novels, was really the centre of his characters, and neither could they exist without him or he without them'. Spender's own art never makes a pretence of detachment. His early volumes, *Twenty Poems* (1930), *Poems* (1933), and *The Still Centre* (1939), intermix public, political, and private verse. He adulates the Romantic hero in 'Beethoven's Death Mask' and he un-Romantically analyses himself in 'What I Expected'; he attempts to empathize with van der Lubbe, the Dutchman accused by the Nazis of setting fire to the Reichstag, and rejoices in 'the black statement of pistons' and 'the luminous self possession' of a steam train in 'The Express'. His awareness of the cultural anomalies and conflicts of class interest in inter-war Britain shine through his 'An Elementary School Classroom in a Slum', and his sense of historical injustice determines the evocation of the voices of Victorian slum-children in 'A Footnote (from Marx's Chapter, *The Working Day*)'. It is, however, in the poems that rose out of his experience of the Spanish Civil War that Spender achieves his most effective balance of personal response and public engagement. In 'Two Armies' and 'Ultima Ratio Regum' he recognizes the erotic implications of the intimacy of huddled, sleeping soldiers ('a common suffering | Whitens the air with breath and makes both one | As though these enemies slept in each other's arms') and of a boy's corpse ('He was a better target for a kiss'). He assembles a mosaic of impressions of defeat in 'Fall of a City' and plays, both informally and earnestly, with the sense of an already fragmentary 'I' threatened with physical dissolution in 'Thoughts During an Air Raid' ('Of course, the entire effort is to put myself | Outside the ordinary range | Of what are called statistics'). In attempting to explain why, despite his support for the Spanish Republican cause, the poems in *The Still Centre* had not struck a more heroic note, Spender asserts in his Foreword 'that a poet can only write about what is true to his own experience, not about what he would like to be true to his experience'. The poem that most accurately captures his failure to convey a sense of the heroic at the 'still centre' both of the war and of the poet's consciousness is 'Port Bou'. The narrator sits 'at the exact centre' of the town, 'solitary as a target, | Where nothing moves against a background of cardboard houses | Except the disgraceful skirring dogs'. He feels himself to be neither at one with the embattled townspeople nor identified with the dogs, neither disillusioned nor capable of maintaining the illusion of courage. This ruminative inconclusiveness, coupled with a new evocation of the destructive energy of battle, also determines the mood of Spender's poems of the Second World War, notably 'Air Raid across the bay at Plymouth' and the fine picture of blitzed London in 'Epilogue to a Human Drama'. His later work, with its increasing stress on private emotions and relationships, suggests the degree to which he had retreated from his short-lived attempt to marry Liberalism and Marxism.

A sonnet published by Cecil Day-Lewis in *Left Review* in 1934 begins clumsily with the lines 'Yes, why do we all, seeing a communist, feel small?'. Its clumsiness derives from both its deliberate echo of Hopkins's 'Yes, why do we all seeing of a soldier, bless him?' and from the nature of its subject. It was not a poem that Day-Lewis chose to include in his *Collected Poems* of 1954 nor was it the kind of public verse that he would have seen as enhancing his official reputation as Poet Laureate (to which post he was appointed in 1968). Much of Day-Lewis's most distinctive early verse is, however, inescapably enthusiastic about the prospect of a Marxist transformation of society. In section 32 of *The Magnetic Mountain* of 1933, for example, he announces to those 'that love England' that they 'need fight in the dark no more' for they 'shall be leaders when zero hour is signalled . . . and welders of a new world'. In its original form, the volume *A Time to Dance* (1935) moved from the heroic celebration in its title poem of the pioneer airmen, Parer and M'Intosh (those 'haughty champions'), to a series of poems describing a seething and depressed England (including the sardonic poem later named 'A Carol', a lullaby which ends with the words 'Thy mother is crying, | Thy dad's on the dole: | Two shillings a week is | The price of a soul'). The time to dance, 'An Address to Death' asserts, is now and 'in the rhythm of comrades'. The same volume also contained two somewhat more ambiguous poems, 'The Conflict' and 'In Me Two Worlds'. The first pictures a poet singing 'on a tilting deck' in a sea-storm in order to 'keep men's courage up'. Is this the floundering ship of capitalism? Or is the Party itself losing impetus with one comrade worrying about who is steering? The poet sees himself as one 'between two massing powers . . . whom neutrality cannot save', but when he encouragingly speaks of the rallying force of 'the red advance of life', the surge of blood might as well be a blush as a declaration of solidarity with socialist progress. In 'In Me Two Worlds' he sees his body as a 'moving point of dust | Where past and future meet' and as a battlefield where 'the armies of the dead' meet their antagonists, 'the men to come', in an 'inveterate feud'. This feud is to be fought out not in clear day-light of dialectical materialism but in 'my senses' darkened fields'. In some ways we are back with Matthew Arnold's ignorant armies clashing by night. Day-Lewis's volumes *Overtures to Death* (1938) and *Poems in Wartime* (1940) signalled that he, like Spender, had begun to retreat from confident Marxist analyses as the Second World War approached. The faded elegance of a nineteenth-century terrace in 'Regency Houses' may be a metaphor for con-demned bourgeois society, but the poem goes on to evoke a different melan-choly, the disillusion of those who 'in younger days, | Hoping too much, tried on | The habit of perfection' and who have now 'learnt how it betrays | Our shrinking flesh'.

Much of Day-Lewis's later career was taken up with translations of Virgil, a poet who had oscillated between public celebrations of a national mission and a delight in bucolic retreat. A version of *The Georgics* appeared in 1940 and was followed in 1952 by *The Aeneid* and in 1963 by *The Eclogues*. Louis MacNeice, a poet of a very different disposition, was as a student and teacher of Greek and Roman literature equally attentive to the classical tradition which fed his own poetic preoccupations. At the beginning of his career he published a series of verse dialogues with the title 'eclogue' ('Eclogue for Christmas', 'Eclogue by a Five-barred Gate', 'Eclogue from Iceland', and 'Eclogue between the Motherless'). In 1936 he produced an often colloquial and distinctly unheroic verse translation of Aeschylus's the *Agamemnon*. Unlike Day-Lewis, MacNeice seems never to have fallen for the idea of feeling small when faced with a working-class Communist or to have embraced simple solutions to what he saw as complex historical, social, and political problems. 'My sympathies are Left. On paper and in my soul', he wrote, 'But not in my heart or my guts.' In the poem 'Snow', published in the *Poems* of 1935, he describes the world as 'crazier and more of it than we think, | Incorrigibly plural. I peel and por-tion | A tangerine and spit the pips and feel | The drunkenness of things being various'. 'Your thoughts make shape like snow', he tells a Communist in a short lyric from the same collection, 'Consult the barometer— | The poise is perfect but maintained | For one day only.' He concludes the poem 'Entirely', pub-lished in the collection *Plant and Phantom* in 1941, with the unblinkered assumption that 'In brute reality there is no | Road that is right entirely'.

MacNeice was an Ulsterman by birth and tradition, the son of a vicar of the fortress town of Carrickfergus who rose to the episcopate of the Church of Ireland. The geography and the folklore of Ireland haunt his verse, but there is a firm lack of commitment to any political or religious Establishment, whether Protestant or Catholic, whether Unionist or Nationalist. When he writes affectionately of Carrickfergus in the poem of that name, he describes his sense of exclusion from 'the candles of the Irish poor' yet he also implies a clear detachment from Protestant Ulster's involvement in the First World War. The quality of MacNeice's scepticism, and of his refusal to accept the 'jejune dichotomies' that he mentions in 'The Cromlech', was determined by an intellectual exploration which looked beyond Irish confines. He fluctuates between a God of discipline and a God of liberty, between divided vocations to the ascetic and the sensual in 'Stylite' and in 'London Rain', the latter evoking a wet London which is a place where 'God and No-God | Play at pitch and toss'. In the charmlike 'Prayer Before Birth' (published in *Springboard* in 1944) he asks for the spirit of delight and for freedom from those 'who would freeze my | humanity, would dragoon me into a lethal automaton | would make me a cog in a machine'. When he returns to an Ireland in wartime in the poem 'Neutrality' (published in the same collection), he recognizes a parallel between the geographical entity and 'the neutral island in the heart of man', both ostensibly non-committed, but both internally vexed by 'fermenting rivers' and 'intricacies of gloom and glint'.

MacNeice's landscape and townscape poems provide a focus for his preoccupation with ambiguity and for his divided literary loyalty between Ireland and England. In his unfinished autobiography, *The Strings are False* (1965), he describes his enthusiasm as a schoolboy in Wiltshire for *The Waste Land*, an enthusiasm which expressed itself in paddling a hired canoe 'beneath the gas works, a fine place . . . for reading Webster'. This feeling for incongruity and for urban unloveliness emerges in the poem 'Birmingham' of 1934, a tribute to the city in which MacNeice taught after his graduation from Oxford. 'Birmingham' is made up of a series of fragmentary impressions of railway cuttings, of cars, of factories, and of half-timbered suburban houses with 'lips pressed | So tightly and eyes staring at the traffic through bleary hews | And only a six-inch grip of the racing earth in their concrete claws'. In 'Woods', published in *Holes in the Sky* in 1948, he acknowledges a distinction between his father's relish for empty Irish moorland and his own for the woodlands of the 'tame' English landscape. The woods are romantically 'packed with birds and ghosts' but they are not like the wilds of Mayo, 'they are assured | Of their place by men; reprieved from the neolithic night | By gamekeepers or by Herrick's girls at play'. A similar feel for a lush and varied English West Country, an archaeological landscape haunted by historical and literary associations, shapes *Wessex Guidebook*, published in MacNeice's last volume *The Burning Perch* (1963). The land is historically endowed with memories of Roman emperors and English kings, but it is also a place where the local measurement of time is erased by villagers who forget the church clock 'in deference to Big Ben'. The indifference of Time to men, and of men to history in the last stanza takes on a deliberate and appropriately Hardyan tone:

> But hindmost, topmost, those illiterate seasons
> Still smoke their pipes in swallow-hole and hide-out
> As scornful of the tractor and the jet
> As of the Roman road, or axe of flint,
> Forgotten by the mass of human beings
> Whom they, the Seasons, need not even forget
> Since, though they fostered man, they never loved him.

MacNeice recognized his own contradictions as an artist in the external manifestations of human history, in smokestacks as much as in ploughmarks. The remarkable thematic consistency of his poetry emerges from a process of questioning and balancing those contradictions.

When W. H. Auden paid posthumous tribute to MacNeice he remarked on his friend's pleasure in 'language, in country landscapes, in city streets and parks, in birds beasts and flowers, in nice clothes, good conversation, good food, good drink, and in what he called "the tangles"'. These transient, temporal pleasures, tangles and all, are reflected in Auden's own verse. Auden, whose precocity of talent was evident in his first volume of 1930, is, however, a far more affirmative poet. The nature of his affirmation shifted as he gradually moved, in charted stages, from a Marxist alignment to a Christian one. When he removed himself to the United States in 1939 and took out US citizenship in 1946 he regarded both as decisive breaks with his personal, political, and literary pasts (though he returned to Britain at the end of his life). In his middle age he became a determined pruner and reviser of what he had come to regard as the excesses and infelicities of his poetic youth, first tampering with, then declining to reprint certain published poems. The most notable of these revisions and suppressions concern the poem 'September 1, 1939', a work which he later disdained as 'a hangover from the U.K.' and one 'infected with an incurable dishonesty'. 'September 1, 1939' was specifically transatlantic both in its setting ('I sit in one of the dives | On Fifty-Second Street') and in its first appearance in the American journal *New Republic*, but it strains to undo a tangle which is essentially European. The date of its title is that of Hitler's invasion of Poland, two days before the consequent precipitation of Britain into the Second World War; the focus of its argument lies, however, in a declaration of independence from the 'State' and of an alternate dependence on human relationships ('We must love one another or die . . . May I, composed like them | Of Eros and of dust . . . Show an affirming flame'). Having left his native island, Auden, the inveterate commender of islands, was now attempting to proclaim himself part of a continent.

It is possible that what Auden later recognized as the 'incurable dishonesty' of the poem lay in its very attempt to deny the significance of the insular. 'The whole talent, the whole genius of Auden', Stephen Spender remarked in 1970, 'has been never to be a central figure. He's a central figure on the margin.' That 'margin' is perhaps best typified by Auden's fondness for the role of an observer of islands. In this role he explores geographical and spiritual detachment from the mainland or the mass and, as his later interest in the Christian existentialism of Kierkegaard also suggests, he allows individual freedoms to take precedence over the demands of the community. The *Poems* of 1930 (which were revised, expanded, and excised in 1933) reflect, if not on islands, at least on a landscape of alienation peopled by strangers. This alienation is derived from a Marxist perception of the decay of late capitalist society, from a Freudian approach to psychic disorder, and from a relation of both to the imagined landscapes of *The Waste Land*. All human relationships evoked in the poems are conditioned by the reiterated imagery of invasions, conquests, sentries, spies, and frontiers. As Auden's verse developed in the later 1930s, however, geography took on a fresh significance. The title of the 1936 volume, *Look, Stranger!*, derived by its publishers from the opening line of one of the most sharply focused poems in the collection, was rejected by Auden who insisted that *On this Island* be substituted for the American edition. The poem (later renamed 'Seascape') from which both titles derive is concerned with perspectives; it distinguishes the 'far off' from a 'stable here', but it also leaves a reader of the poems that surround it free to interpret how its insistent direction, 'Look', be applied. Auden may cast himself as a 'lover of islands' in his maritime address to Isherwood, 'Journey to Iceland' of 1937, but his view of Iceland is tentative, escapist, and half-idealized. Following the evaporation of Auden's Marxist enthusiasm for communal action in the 1940s, a continental pull slackens, insular responses predominate, and 'unreality' becomes an emphatically acceptable norm in the sequence of meditations on Shakespeare's *The Tempest—The Sea and the Mirror* (1945). On Prospero's island, in contrast to all its earlier foreshadowings in Auden's verse, 'flesh and mind | Are delivered from mistrust' and Ariel, the 'unanxious one', is bidden to entrance and rebuke 'the raging heart | With a smoother song | Than this rough world'. In an even later celebration of islands in the fifth of the 'Bucolics' (published in *The Shield of Achilles* in 1955) the shore of a 'lake turned inside out' seems 'cosy' to the individual who fascinatedly rejoices in 'that class | Whose only member is Me'.

Auden's gradual eschewal of a narrowly political sympathy with the demands of a present community are countered by new, creative, though sometimes quirky responses to the 'old masters' (poets, painters, thinkers, and composers). In the various critical essays later collected as *The Dyer's Hand* (1962) and *Forewords and Afterwords* (1973) he can be both infuriating and incisive. The inherited literary tradition equally marks his poetry. The 'Letter to Lord Byron', published in *Letters from Iceland* in 1937, suggests a real relish for the 'something light and easy' (and the ultimate seriousness) of *Don Juan* (a text which Auden had taken with him to 'humourless' Iceland). Reworkings and rethinkings of an inherited tradition were especially evident in the verse that emerged in his first American years. In '*Musée des Beaux Arts*', for example, Auden identifies suffering and 'its human position' as a key concern of art (though in the Brueghel painting of the fall of Icarus to which the poem refers 'everything turns away | Quite leisurely from the disaster'). The two elegies to W. B. Yeats and Sigmund Freud (both of 1939 and both written in the tradition of Milton's *Lycidas*) celebrate continuity as much as they mourn the departed and the condition of the age. Yeats's words 'are modified in the guts of the living' and 'persuade us to rejoice' even in 'a rapture of distress', while Freud, the 'rational voice' and the demystifier of the human condition, provides the wisdom that 'to be free | Is often to be lonely'. Much of Auden's later work continues the process of bouncing tangentially and experimentally from works of art. His responses to Shakespeare in *The Sea and the Mirror*, to Hogarth in the libretto for *The Rake's Progress*, which he and Chester Kallman provided for Stravinsky in 1951, and to Mozart in his free translation (also with Kallman) of Schickaneder's libretto to *The Magic Flute* (1957), all reveal an interfusion of the bawdy, the commonplace, the unexpected, the evanescent, the magical, and the philosophical.

In spite of his withdrawal from the politics of community into the philosophy (and theology) of individualism, Auden spoke with a public, if reticent, voice. A good deal of his most assured verse emerges from his discovering for himself what Eliot had called an 'objective correlative', that is 'a set of objects, a situation, a chain of events' which become the formula for '*particular*' emotion. For Auden the imagining or contriving of a landscape serves as a reification of a psychological state or premiss. When in 'In Praise of Limestone' he reflected on *karst* contours, he sought to typify his own unpredictability, his elusiveness, even his fondness for change and changing things. Here is a limestone landscape which draws 'we the inconstant ones', one shaped by a rock which dissolves in water and which produces 'a secret system of caves and conduits'. The argument of the poem is made up of trickles of thought which seem to appear and disappear as a speaking voice rises and falls. The worried, heterogeneous, and contrived scenery of the *Poems* of 1930 is abandoned for a landscape which is now literally subverted, subverting, and unpredictable. It is a place where joy surprises and where Eros and Agape, human and divine Love, achieve a conditional but ultimate victory in the imagination:

> In so far as we have to look forward
> To death as a fact, no doubt we are right: but if
> Sins can be forgiven, if bodies rise from the dead
> These modifications of matter into
> Innocent athletes and gesticulating fountains,
> Made solely for pleasure, make a further point:
> The blessed will not care what angle they are regarded from,
> Having nothing to hide. Dear, I know nothing of
> Either, but when I try to imagine a faultless love
> Or the life to come, what I hear is the murmur
> Of underground streams, what I see is a limestone landscape.

Subversion and unpredictability, which had once so troubled Auden's fellow-poets of the 1930s, are now taken as evidence of the divine; the temporal seems to be dissolvable in the eternal, thisness in otherness, the material in the mystical.

'Rotten Elements':
MacDiarmid, Upward, Koestler, and Orwell

It was not surprising that the Scottish poet Hugh MacDiarmid (the pseudonym of Christopher Murray Grieve, 1892–1978) should have so admired the national emblem of Scotland. His life, work, and opinions were consistently as prickly as a thistle. MacDiarmid is the finest and most original of the writers who revived and invigorated an explicitly Scottish poetry in the mid-twentieth century. Having spent his early years as an active supporter of the Labour Party, in 1928 he became a founder member of the Scottish National Party and in 1934 a member of the Communist Party (he was expelled four years later, but perversely rejoined it, when so many others had left after the suppression of the Hungarian Revolution, in 1957). Despite, or perhaps because of, the internationalism of his Marxist vision, MacDiarmid was both passionately attached to Scotland and equally passionately disparaging of England and all it stood for (in his latter years he dreamed of a future Celtic Workers Republic embracing Cornwall, Wales, Ireland, and Scotland). He saw his own identity as a socialist and a poet as defined by a Scottish culture purged of its bourgeois anglicization. His most vigorous verse is written in a synthetic vocabulary forged from the vernacular of south-west Scotland and the distinctive archaisms he found in a dictionary of the Middle Scots Tongue. Collections and selections of his poetry have generally, and of necessity, been supplemented with glossaries. In his most celebrated poem, *A Drunk Man looks at the Thistle* (1926), MacDiarmid speaks in an authorial note of a logic of drunkenness, a logic which seems to allow for the poem's variety, sporadic inconsistency, and phantasmagoria within the framework of an extended dramatic monologue. It is on the acerbic and lyrical Scots poems contained in the volumes published in the 1930s (*First Hymn to Lenin and Other Poems* of 1931, *Scots Unbound and Other Poems* of 1932, *Stony Limits and Other Poems* of 1934, and *Second Hymn to Lenin and Other Poems* of 1935) that MacDiarmid's reputation will ultimately rest (his longer, later poems in English are singularly drab by comparison). The argumentative 'First Hymn to Lenin' challenges with its immediacy and with its uncompromising Marxist-Leninist evangelism:

> Christ said: 'Save ye become bairns again.'
> Bairnly eneuch [childish enough] the feck [most] o' us ha' been!
> Your work needs men and its worst foes are juist
> The traitors wha through a' history ha' gi'en
> The dope that's gar'd the mass o' folk pay heed
> 　　And bide [stay] bairns indeed.

As necessary, and insignificant, as death
Wi' a its agonies in the cosmos still
The Cheka's horrors are in their degree;
And'll end suner! What maitters 't wha we kill
To lessen that foulest murder that deprives
Maist men o' real lives?

This justification of Lenin's terror and his secret police also has a logic, the horrid logic of a man temporarily drunk on revolutionary politics. MacDiarmid may have been repelled by the poverty and deprivation of industrial Scotland during the Depression, but his ideological enthusiasms, like Dunbar's four hundred years earlier, may strike latter-day readers as deliberately provocative rather than considered and refined. A very different mood haunts the lyric 'Lourd in my Hert' of 1934 as a heavy-hearted poet contemplates 'the state of Scotland' in the midst of a 'dour winter' when it is 'scarce grey licht at noon'. As a light breaks in the East (the capital letter suggests that this 'east' is centred in Moscow) there is an urge to cry 'the dawn, the dawn', but the poem ends with the disillusioned: 'But ah |—It's just mair snaw!'

The English Marxist, Edward Upward (b. 1903), had little of MacDiarmid's prickly Scots obstreperousness and little of his provocative, imaginative energy. 'A modern fantasy cannot tell the truth', Upward proclaims in his 'Sketch for a Marxist Interpretation of Literature' published in C. Day-Lewis's collection of essays entitled *The Mind in Chains* (1937). Fantasy, Upward explains, implies 'a retreat from the real world into the world of imagination, and though such a retreat may have been practicable and desirable in a more leisured and less profoundly disturbed age than our own it is becoming increasingly impracticable today'. Upward, the dedicatee of Isherwood's first novel, and the addressee of Ode III of Auden's *The Orators*, shared with his middle-class English friends a sure and certain hope in the prospect of a socialist new order of things. 'A writer today who wishes to produce the best work he is capable of producing', he insisted in 1937, 'must first of all become a socialist in his practical life, must go over to the progressive side of the class conflict.' Despite these doctrinaire 'musts', and despite his once ardent espousal of the orthodoxies of the Communist Party, Upward too had his doubts about the exclusive validity of the party-lines on life and literature. His short novel *Journey to the Border* (1938) traces the growing determination of a singularly guilt-ridden and neurotic private tutor to 'get in touch with the workers' movement', a gesture which is seen as marking a break with his earlier allegiances, thoughts, and feelings. The long-term error of judgement that the hero makes becomes the theme of Upward's 'thesis' trilogy collectively known as *The Spiral Ascent*. The three novels, *In the Thirties* (1962), *The Rotten Elements* (1969) and *No Home but the Struggle* (1977), drably recount a series of ideological dilemmas, tergiversations, and intellectual shufflings on the part of the socialist poet, Alan Sebrill. As the second and third volumes explore, Sebrill finds it increasingly hard to reconcile an 'opportunist' party line with what he sees as his personal and artistic integrity. He becomes what his erstwhile comrades dismiss as a 'rotten element'. The corrosive force of this 'rot' also fascinated two less stilted, and far more 'deviationist' novelists of the 1940s, Arthur Koestler (1905–83) and George Orwell, the pen-name of Eric Arthur Blair (1903–50).

Koestler's contribution to R. H. Crossman's symposium, *The God That Failed: Six Studies in Communism* (1950) was entitled 'Confessions of a Tight-rope Walker'. A year after the publication of his wittily detached and self-critical essay Koestler returned to the subject of his journey into Communism and his exit from it in the first volume of his autobiography, *Arrow in the Blue.* 'In 1931', he claimed, 'we lived under the fascist threat, but we saw an inspiring alternative in Russia. In 1951 we live under the Russian threat, but there is no inspiring alternative in sight; we are forced to fall back on the threadbare values of the past.' Throughout his career as writer Koestler walked intellectual tightropes, nimbly balancing himself while recognizing the dangers of the abysses which opened up beneath him. An essential part of his daring lay in the fact that the English in which he wrote most of his books was not his native tongue (he was born into a polyglot Jewish family in Budapest, educated in Vienna, and produced his masterpiece, *Darkness at Noon*, in German). A Communist journalist and observer of the Spanish Civil War, he was arrested as a spy when Republican Málaga fell into the hands of General Franco, condemned to death, and ultimately released in exchange for a Nationalist prisoner. These experiences are recounted in his *Spanish Testament* (published by the Left Book Club in 1937), whose last section, 'Dialogue With Death', nurtured the account of the arrest, examination, and self-questioning of the veteran Revolutionary, Nicholas Salmanovitch Rubashov, in *Darkness at Noon* (1940). Although set in an unspecified European dictatorship and originally written in German, Koestler's novel in fact offers the most subtle, economical, and intelligent analysis of the contortions of Stalinist thought composed in England. It is a novel concerned with the structures, uses, and corruptions of power. When it considers the exercise of control, it seeks to liberate the 'I' from the 'We' and the 'They' and to free the individual from enforced fraternalism with the 'masses'. As Rubashov awaits execution, he defines for himself 'the grammatical fiction' by which the Party has disposed of the 'I': 'The infinite was a politically suspect quantity, the 'I' a suspect quality. The Party did not recognise its existence. The definition of the individual was: a multitude of one million divided by one million.' But Rubashov, as the now isolated, traduced, publicly vilified, and disillusioned individual, attempts to work out the personal and social consequences of this 'grammatical fiction'. Premisses of 'unimpeachable truth' have led to a result which appears to him completely absurd. It dawns on him that for forty years the masses have been driven through the desert 'with threats and promises, with imaginary terrors and imaginary rewards. But where was the Promised Land?'

The idea of a Promised Land, the Mosaic vision of which was denied to Rubashov, occurs again in Koestler's two interesting, if less satisfying, novels of the 1940s, *Arrival and Departure* (1943) and *Thieves in the Night* (1946). The former returns to a grim European dictatorship (now again a Fascist one) and to the slow disillusion of a middle-class revolutionary, but it finally offers a patriotic glimmer of hope in that its hero determines to continue his resistance to Fascism by travelling to embattled Britain rather than withdrawing as a refugee to neutral America. *Thieves in the Night* is set in Palestine as the British mandate draws to an end and as the battle lines between Jew and Arab are established. It lets a plague fall on both houses while offering a carefully observed picture of the tensions within a secular, but essentially alien and intrusive kibbutz. Koestler returned to the problem of what he saw as the inherent contradictions within Soviet Communism in the volume of essays *The Yogi and the Commissar* of 1945 but the concerns of much of his later prose owe more to the mysticism of the Yogi than to the over-defined ideology of Marxism-Leninism. His *The Sleepwalkers: A History of Man's Changing Vision of the Universe* (1959) ambitiously and provocatively attempts to draw together scientific and philosophical theories and to insist that 'our hypnotic enslavement to the numerical aspects of reality has dulled our perception of non-quantitative moral values'. Koestler's latter-day speculations about parapsychology and the paranormal, outlined in *The Ghost in the Machine* (1967) and *The Roots of Coincidence* (1972), suggest that even as an old man he still rejoiced in the precarious role of an intellectual tightrope walker.

George Orwell shared with Koestler a profound disillusion with Soviet Communism. Both recognized, as many of their blinkered liberal colleagues refused to do, that Stalin had betrayed a human ideal and had in the process of his betrayal exposed a fallacy at the heart of that ideal. In an essay of 1947 entitled 'Why I Write' Orwell insisted that every line he had written since 1936 had been written 'directly or indirectly, *against* totalitarianism and *for* democratic socialism' and that where he lacked '*political* purpose' he wrote lifeless books and 'humbug generally'. His early novels, *Burmese Days* (1934), *A Clergyman's Daughter* (1935), and *Keep the Aspidistra Flying* (1936), offer little more than fictional analyses of the narrownesses and idiocies of the British at home and abroad, as smug imperialists and even smugger domestic tyrants. It was as an investigative social journalist that Orwell's true distinctiveness as a writer emerged. He is an acute observer and a generalizer, an open-eyed crosser of class boundaries and a delineator of essentially English fudges and compromises (compromises which sometimes infuriate him, sometimes amuse him, sometimes rejoice his heart). Even in *Down and Out in Paris and London* (1933), his account of eking out a dire life in ill-paid jobs and common lodging-houses, he manages to delight in an England of 'bathrooms, armchairs, mint sauce, new potatoes properly cooked, brown bread, marmalade, [and] beer made with hops'. The main subject of both *Down and Out in Paris and London* and *The Road to Wigan Pier* (1937) is not, however, a comfortable and familiar England but a singularly uncomfortable and unfamiliar one. Orwell does more than puncture assumptions by exploiting easy contrasts between the rich and the poor; he attempts to describe the slums by slumming it and to write about the disinherited by disinheriting himself. The clothes he dons in order to learn about London tramps have 'a gracelessness, a patina of antique filth, quite different from mere shabbiness', and after an excruciating night in a lodging-house in the Waterloo Road he ruefully, but somewhat unscientifically, notes that 'bugs are much commoner in south than north London'. When he goes north in search of details of an urban life scarred by unemployment and poverty, he is repelled by the untidy ugliness of industrialism 'so frightful and so arresting that you are obliged, as it were, to come to terms with it', and yet he adulates the 'easy completeness, the perfect symmetry . . . of a working-class interior' with mother and father on each side of the fire and the children and the dog in the middle. It is, he adds tellingly, 'a good place to be in, provided that you can be not only in it but sufficiently *of* it to be taken for granted'.

At the close of 1936 Orwell left for Spain to fight for the Republican cause. His account of his experiences in *Homage to Catalonia* (1938) and the essay 'Looking Back on the Spanish War' (1943) reveal that what he chiefly discovered in Spain was personal discomfort and political disillusionment. *Homage to Catalonia* ends with his escape not from victorious Fascists but from persecution at the hands of one of the warring factions into which the Spanish Left had split. Orwell's book has always provoked those who insist on a rigid division of history into right causes defended by heroes and wrong causes supported by villains. 'I have the most evil memories of Spain', he wrote in 1938, 'but I have very few bad memories of Spaniards.' Looking back in 1943, he criticizes both those intellectual pacifists who hold to a theory that 'war is all corpses and latrines and never leads to any good result' and those who would dismiss as sentimental his contention that 'a man holding up his trousers isn't a "Fascist", he is visibly a fellow-creature, similar to yourself, and you don't feel like shooting at him'. *Animal Farm* (1945), Orwell's satire on the manifest failure of Communist ideals in Russia, vexed its targets sufficiently to bring about a ban on its publication in the Soviet Union and its satellites until after the revolutions of the late 1980s. The fable may sentimentalize working-class strength and good nature (as characterized by the carthorse, Boxer) but there was a fine appositeness in Orwell's choice of pigs as the vanguard and the undoing of the animals' revolution. Pigs may at times look suspiciously human (despite their four legs), they may traditionally be associated with greed and laziness, but they are also proverbially supposed to be incapable of flight. Their revolution remains earthbound, their aspirations all too like those of their enemies. The corruptions and distortions of language which serve Napoleon's dictatorial ends in *Animal Farm* became a particular concern of Orwell's last years. In the essay 'politics and the English Language' of 1946 he recognized that 'if thought corrupts language, language can also corrupt thought' and argued for a plain English 'as an instrument for expressing and not for concealing or preventing thought'. The idea that political language 'is designed to make lies sound truthful and murder respectable' is substantiated in the Party slogans picked out on the façade of the Ministry of Truth in *Nineteen Eighty-four* (1949): 'WAR IS PEACE'; 'FREEDOM IS SLAVERY'; 'IGNORANCE IS STRENGTH'. In *Nineteen Eighty-four* Stalin's Russia blends with bomb-scarred post-war Britain, Kafka's dark fantasies of incomprehension and impersonal oppression with Koestler's nightmares of totalitarian logic and Huxley's dystopian vision of an ordered scientific future. Purges and vaporizations have become 'a necessary part of the mechanics of government' and the Party's prospective Newspeak dictionary will not simply cut the official language 'down to the bone', but also serve to 'narrow the range of thought'. The Party's aim, O'Brien explains to Winston Smith, is to create a world where there are no emotions except fear, rage, triumph, and self-abasement; the 'intoxication of power' will remain, a 'thrill of victory' which is expressed in an excited mental picture of 'a boot stamping on a human face—for ever'. In Dickens's *Our Mutual Friend* the nature of a self-seeking, individualist society obsessed by the power of money is typified by the phrase 'scrunch or be scrunched'. For Orwell, who was amongst the first modern critics to take Dickens's fiction seriously, the scrunching has become the prerogative of a Party which has relieved the individual of responsibility and which enforces acquiescence. His 'modern fantasy' does not suggest a retreat from the real world but a monitory response to what he readily recognized was a 'profoundly disturbed age'.

Looking at Britain at War

One of the most striking and popular visual images to emerge from wartime Britain was John Armstrong's modestly surreal painting *Can Spring be far Behind?* of 1940. Armstrong, who was employed with Henry Moore, Graham Sutherland, Paul Nash, and John Piper as an Official War Artist, drew an outsize tulip sprouting from the bombed ruins of houses and factories set against a purplish early morning sky. His poetic title, derived from Shelley's 'Ode to the West Wind', enforces the idea of a spring of hope succeeding a winter of destruction. Unlike the battles of the First World War, the bombing raids of the Second World War brought death and dissolution to what was known as 'the Home Front'. The *Luftwaffe* campaigns of 1940 and 1941 left a good deal of Britain's industrial and cultural heritage in ruins, but the shells of buildings and the piles of rubble, which by 1945 had spread over the whole of Europe, took on a certain suggestive power. Domestic interiors exposed as façades collapsed, camouflaged factories, doors distended by sandbags, bodies huddled in bomb-shelters, corpses distorted by hunger or pain, and human faces preposterously hidden by gas masks had confounded life and art, vision and reality. If the churned moonscapes and the twisted metal of the Western Front had seemed to insist on a new kind of responsive art, the artists who confronted the violent fragmentations, waste lands, and unforeseen juxtapositions of the Second World War were to some degree already equipped with a post-impressionist and post-Eliotic vocabulary with which to articulate their reactions.

The impression of a shifting relationship between objects and concepts, and a Freudian stress on the significance of the unconscious, had become particular features of the publicity generated by the rise of the Surrealist movement. The international exhibition of the work of the Surrealists held in London in June 1936 had included the work of some sixty-eight artists, fourteen of them British. The near suffocation of Salvador Dali as, kitted out in a diving suit, he inaudibly addressed an audience, may have pointed to the extravagantly absurdist side of the movement, but the stress certain critics laid on native prefigurings of Surrealism partly explains why British opinion appears to have been far less provoked by the novelty of the new forms than it had been by Fry's Post-Impressionist exhibition of 1910. As Herbert Read pointed out in drawing a distinction between a 'classical art' which appealed to the intellect and a 'romantic art' which drew on 'irrational revelations' and 'surprising incoherencies', Surrealism could effectively look back to the work of Blake and Lewis Carroll, to Fuseli and Gillray, and find a reflection of itself. Nightmares and daydreams, distortions and distensions, snarks and mock-turtles, shoes and ships and sealing-wax were already part of an established verbal and pictorial tradition. Amongst the most determined of the British apologists for the brief blaze of surreal experiment in the late 1930s was the poet David Gascoyne (b. 1916). Gascoyne's *A Short Survey of Surrealism* appeared in 1935; his often obsessively odd collections of poems, *Man's Life is His Meat* in 1936 and *Hölderlin's Madness* in 1938. 'The Very Image' (addressed to the Belgian painter René Magritte) opens with a verbal evocation of 'An image of my grandmother | her head appearing upside-down upon a cloud | the cloud transfixed on the steeple | of a deserted railway-station | far away'; 'Figure in a Landscape', with its nods to the iterations of Eliot, enacts a kind of ritual awakening; 'The Seventh Dream is the Dream of Isis' (which dispenses with capital letters and, apart from two almost arbitrary full stops, with punctuation) restlessly intermixes the extraordinary, the challenging, and the unapologetically silly ('and the wings of private airplanes look like shoeleather | shoeleather on which pentagrams have been drawn | shoeleather covered with vomitings of hedgehogs | shoeleather used for decorating wedding-cakes'). Perhaps in response to genuinely urgent times, Gascoyne's wartime poems deviate into a certain kind of logical sense. His 'Farewell Chorus' (signed 'New Year 1940') greets the sphinx of 'the Forties' with the assertion that 'we see certain truths now' when 'each lonely consciousness' mirrors 'War's world . . . without end'. 'Walking at Whitsun', written at the time of the invasions of Belgium, the Netherlands, and France in May 1940, wonders at the 'anguish' which makes the English landscape seem 'Inhuman as the jungle, and unreal | Its peace' and it veers finally towards uneasy thoughts of helmets, ruins and 'invading steel'.

The association of the work of the Anglo-Welsh poet, Dylan Thomas, with a lush kind of Surrealism has more often been assumed than proved. As his ambitious and uneven first volume, *18 Poems* (1934), suggests, Thomas (1914–53) had begun to mould an extravagant and pulsatingly rhetorical style before he became aware of the imported innovations of international Surrealist writing. He was, however, decidedly a poet who thought in images. If there is a kinship evident in Thomas's verse it is with the 'difficulty', the emotionalism, the lyric intensity, and the metaphysical speculation (though not the intellectual rigour) of the school of Donne. It is Donne's 'Death's Duell' which is cited in the title of Thomas's volume *Deaths and Entrances* of 1946 ('our very *birth* and entrance into this life, is *exitus a morte*, an *issue from death*') and it is Donne's ghost that broods over the poem written in memory of Thomas's aunt, Ann Jones. 'In Memory of Ann Jones', published in *The Map of Love* in 1939, is, however, specifically Welsh in terms of its local reference and in the claims that Thomas makes for himself as 'Ann's bard on a raised hearth'. In considering the coffined corpse laid out in the farmhouse parlour it evokes a memory of a gush of love in the past (Ann's 'fountain heart once fell in puddles | Round the parched worlds of Wales and drowned each sun') and it yearns for a future, universal release from death as the 'stuffed fox' which decorates the room miraculously cries 'Love', and the once 'stale', and now 'strutting', fern lays 'seeds on the back sill'. The 'sensual strut', to which Thomas refers in the poem 'Twenty-four Years Remind the Tears of My Eyes', somehow typifies the confident, loose-limbed swing of much of his verse, and it is to the thematic interweaving of the turbulent pulses of nature and the stillness of death that his poetry steadily returns. In the Vaughan-like 'Fern Hill', the celebration of his youth 'easy under the apple boughs', he repeats the words 'green' and 'golden' as part of an incantatory recall of a golden age of innocence where the knowledge of death is kept at a distance. 'Poem in October', written in his 'thirtieth year to heaven', also re-enacts the scenes and freedoms of childhood before summer turns to autumn, the sun to showers. It is, however, in the sequence of wartime poems published in *Deaths and Entrances* that Thomas most impressively detaches himself from the flood of private reminiscence and addresses the idea of Death touching the Resurrection. The poems are explicitly, even noisily, Christian. The three stanzas of the volume's title poem each begin with the line 'On almost the incendiary eve', an apocalyptic linking of incendiary bombs and fire-storms with an impending Armageddon. 'Ceremony After a Fire Raid' and 'A Refusal to Mourn the Death, by Fire, of a Child in London' grieve and refuse to grieve. The first sees destruction enthusiastically translated into reconstitution ('And the dust shall sing like a bird | As the grains blow, as your death grows, through our heart'). The second, with its cold title which seems to demand explanation, is an ecstatic reflection on the promised Resurrection, if one in which the poet seems almost to be carried away by the unstoppably hypnotic music of his own voice:

Deep with the first dead lies London's daughter,
Robed in the long friends,
The grains beyond age, the dark veins of her mother,
Secret by the unmourning water
Of the rising Thames.
After the first death, there is no other.

Although in the intriguingly entitled sonnet, 'Among those Killed in the Dawn Raid was a Man aged a Hundred', Thomas again rejoices in images of a surreal rebirth ('The morning is flying on the wings of his age | And a hundred storks perch on the sun's right hand'), his most celebrated late poem, 'Do not go gentle', withdraws into a more personal and protesting anxiety in which 'rage, against the dying of the light' intrudes itself between death and ecstasy.

The work of two soldier poets, Sidney Keyes (1922–43) and Keith Douglas (1920–44), both of whom died in the war, is far less pictorially apocalyptic than Thomas's. Both were the sons of army officers and both discovered that a new kind of war poetry, quite distinct from that of the First World War, was wrenched out of them by the distinct nature of the new conflict. Douglas, in particular, felt that the weight of an earlier tradition had initially tended to dumbfound a new generation. 'The hardships, pain and boredom; the behaviour of the living and the appearance of the dead', he wrote from Tunisia in May 1943, 'were so accurately described by the poets of the Great War that every day on the battlefields of the western desert . . . their poems are illustrated.' A new imagery, related to a new landscape of war and to a far less dissenting ideology of battle, seemed gradually to impose itself. The poems that Keyes wrote during the early stages of the war look back to ancestral forms for refreshment. The ideas of a chain of experience interlinking writer and writer, and of humanity swept up in great creating nature, seem to have held a particular attraction for him in a time of unnatural change. His 'Cervières' of September 1940 addresses the French owners of a cherry orchard ravaged by birds and threatened by an invader who will take more than cherries. The poem's didactic expression of hope lies in its insistence on a natural sequence: the birds may drop the cherry stones and create new trees elsewhere; so, by analogy, the temporary defeat of human dreams may bear an incalculable future fruit. Keyes's meditation on 'Europe's Prisoners' of May 1941, somewhat airily trusts, as Wordsworth's sonnet to Toussaint L'Ouverture does, in the ultimate triumph of freedom and justice ('at last the courage they have learned | Shall burst the walls and overturn the world'). Wordsworth, in the sonnet that Keyes addressed to him in 1941, lives on 'a boy again' in a 'noisy glen', and the dead novelist in the 'Elegy for Mrs Virginia Woolf' becomes a single stream of consciousness with the watery element that drowned her ('Colours and currents tend her; no more vex | Her river-mind our towns and broken skies'). When, however, Keyes faced what by 1942 was the inevitability of his calling in the poem 'War Poet', he recognized himself as 'the man who groped for words and found | An arrow in my hand'. Although he hankers for the support of 'the immortals' in the poem 'Advice for a Journey', he acknowledges that those who remain 'too young | For explorers' are obliged to explore war without any hope of finding 'Canaan, or any golden mountain'. A similar bleakness shapes his Eliotic response to the desert in 'The Wilderness'. Here is a land without the civilized comforts of cultivation, water, and the dream of love, but here he purports to accept the knowledge that 'I am no lover, but destroyer . . . content to face the destroying sun.'

The lonely landscapes of Keith Douglas's desert poems are equally indebted to the examples of Eliot, Auden, and the Surrealists (he was himself a vivid pen-sketcher of the peculiar contortions and dislocations of wrecked bodies and machines). *Alamein to Zem Zem* (1946), Douglas's posthumously published diary account of his service in the desert campaign, remains one of the most vivid, lucid, and clear-headed prose documents of the war. His desert is a place of 'indeterminate landscapes of moods and smells' against which dance 'black and bright incidents', yet, he declares, his war offers 'things to excite financiers and parliamentarians—but not to excite a poet or a painter or a doctor'. In the poem 'Desert Flowers', in part a tribute to the painter-poet Isaac Rosenberg, he looks down from the angle of a pilot or an angel 'on some eccentric chart', a plain dotted with 'useless furniture . . . squashed dead or still entire, stunned | Like beetles'. In 'Cairo Jag' he returns from leave to a world where 'the vegetation is of iron | dead tanks, gun barrels split like celery | the metal brambles have no flowers or berries | and there are all sorts of manure'. When he attempts to describe a dead German soldier in the poem 'Vergissmeinnicht' he sees 'the dust upon the paper eye | and the burst stomach like a cave'. If he lacks the bitterness and disillusion of the First World War poets, he shares their sense of futility and their interrogation of the concept of heroism. The colonel who jokes with troops in 'Gallantry' may fail to see that the real jokers are the bullets and the shell splinters that kill his men; the bugle sounding reveille in 'The Trumpet' may seem to lie when it hints that 'war is sweet', but in the carefully ambiguous poem 'Aristocrats' of 1943 Douglas allows for the congruent jostling of noble carelessness and plain stupidity. 'How can I live among this gentle | obsolescent breed of heroes and not weep?' the poet asks when faced, as a note on his manuscript explains, with the death of an officer who had left money in his will to the Beaufort Hunt and who instructed that the incumbent of a Church living in his gift should be a man 'who approves of hunting, shooting, and all manly sports, which are the backbone of the nation'. The final stanza ambivalently struggles to suggest an answer:

> The plains were their cricket pitch
> and in the mountains the tremendous drop fences
> brought down some of the runners. Here then
> under the stones and earth they dispose themselves,
> I think with their famous unconcern.
> It is not gunfire I hear but a hunting horn.

The aristocratic dead 'dispose themselves' as elegantly as the heroes of romance, seeming to die according to the dictates of form and good manners. Yet the horn that finally drowns the guns might be as much Roland's Olivant as it is that of a hunting squire.

Alun Lewis (1915–44), born and educated in Wales, rarely poses in his poetry as a specifically Welsh poet-at-war (the peacetime lyrics 'The Mountain over Aberdare' and 'The Rhondda', and the wartime 'Destruction' and 'A Welsh Night' are exceptional). Of all the distinctive soldier writers of the Second World War, Lewis is the most assertively civilian. Despite its military title, his often reprinted first volume, *Raiders' Dawn* (1942), pays tribute to another unwilling soldier, Edward Thomas, and to the English landscapes most associated with him. The much anthologized 'All Day It Has Rained . . .' evokes the tedium of life in an encampment in 'the skirmishing fine rain | And the wind that made the canvas heave and flap'. It ends with a sweet-sour, inconsequent-consequential recall:

> And I can remember nothing dearer or more to my heart
> Than the children I watched in the woods on Saturday
> Shaking down burning chestnuts for the schoolyard's merry play,
> Or the shaggy patient dog who followed me
> By Sheet and Steep and up the wooded scree
> To Shoulder o' Mutton where Edward Thomas brooded long
> On death and beauty—till a bullet stopped his song.

Lewis's own brooding was prophetic. His second volume of poems, *Ha! Ha! Among the Trumpets*, was published posthumously in 1945 (he was killed accidentally in Burma 'by a pistol shot'). Although the volume's striking title derives from the description of a war-horse in the thirty-ninth chapter of the Book of Job, there is little of the war-horse's exhilaration ('he paweth in the valley, and rejoiceth in his strength: he goeth on to meet the armed men') in the poems themselves. Lewis arranged his volume (subtitled 'poems in transit') in three parts: the first variously describing a tense, waiting England, the second the voyage to the East, the third India. It is in the third section that his particular interest in landscape is revealed as he uncomfortably comes to terms with the alien contours, the harsh light, and the dry wastes of India (in, for example, 'The Mahratta Ghats', 'Indian Day', and 'Observation Post: Forward Area'). 'I'm as restless and fidgety as a man on a deserted platform . . . India! What a test of a man', he wrote in one of his last letters home. His best poems marvellously suggest this reluctant, deracinated, restlessness.

Faced with the demand that writers 'speak up in freedom's cause', C. Day-Lewis asked himself: 'Where are the War Poets?' In a resultant poem he arrived at the compromised conclusion that the best that an artist could do in the Second World War was to 'defend the bad against the worst'. Day-Lewis, like many others, may have been troubled by the uneasy compromises of those German artists who had accepted, but not necessarily endorsed, the National

Socialist regime. The question of a British artist's response to the Second World War, and to the concomitant threat of a dissolution of inherited cultural values, was frequently raised in the years 1939–45 and the idea of a co-operative struggle which united all classes against an external enemy was actively exploited by Government propaganda. Few established artists, even the famously 'detached' ones, remained untouched by the mood of embattled Britain. 'Now and in England' seemed like a historical imperative. Creativity both embraced and countered the evidence of destruction.

In one of the most strikingly affirmative and original novels of the war years, Joyce Cary's *The Horse's Mouth* (1944), an artist-hero paints a mural of the Creation on a threatened wall. Cary (1888–1957) allows the last word to his ageing, unconventional, unsentimental, Blake-obsessed painter-narrator, Gulley Jimson. Jimson has painted the wall in a state of indifference to its prospective demolition, to rumours of war, and to the approach of his own death. On his death-bed he both thanks God for 'that indefinable something' which is, for him, 'the final beauty of a wall', and he equates prayer with a full and lusty enjoyment of life. His picture, a wry footnote to the novel explains, proved to be as impermanent as his wall. For Cary and his hero, however, the very act of making was in itself a gesture against the abomination of desolation.

10

Post-War and Post-Modern Literature

WHEN the Second World War ended in Europe in the summer of 1945, much of Britain was in ruins. Quite literally in ruins. Its devastated industrial cities were not exactly the heaps of rubble that appalled post-war visitors to Germany. (Stephen Spender, for one, spoke of the 'astonishing and total change, that incalculable shift from a soaring to a sinking motion which distinguishes a dead body' that disturbed him when revisiting Hamburg), but British cities as diverse in character as Glasgow, Coventry, Canterbury, Bristol, Exeter, and Portsmouth had been torn apart by bombs. London, in particular, had been universally pitted and scarred and was now marked by absences where familiar landmarks had once stood. Whole districts were in ruins and most streets somehow bore the signs of blast, shrapnel, fire-bombs, or high explosives. Although its greater monuments, such as St Paul's, had survived largely intact, the cathedral itself now rose hauntingly and, to some imaginative observers, resolutely above the shells of churches and blasted office buildings. This broken London of bricks, façades, and dangerously exposed basements can now be only recognized from paintings and photographs and from the cinematic exploitation of bomb-sites in films such as the two early comedies made at the famous Ealing Studios, Charles Crichton's rowdy *Hue and Cry* (1947) and Harry Cornelius's farce *Passport to Pimlico* (1949).

This landscape of ruins must also be recognized as forming an integral part of much of the literature of the late 1940s and the early 1950s. It was a landscape which provided a metaphor for broken lives and spirits, and, in some remoter and less-defined sense, for the ruin of Great Britain itself. It was also a ruin-scape that could sometimes surprise its observers with joy. In 1953 Rose Macaulay (1881–1958) ended her highly romantic and impressively wide-ranging survey, *Pleasure of Ruins* with 'A Note on New Ruins', a note which briefly balanced a fascination with the 'catastrophic tipsy chaos' of a British bomb-site against her earlier explorations of the historic wrecks of Greek and Roman cities, of jungle-swamped Inca and Buddhist temples, and of ivy-mantled Gothic abbeys. Three years before the appearance of *Pleasure of Ruins*,

Macaulay's novel *The World my Wilderness* had focused on outsiders and exiles, all of them 'displaced' persons, finding the ruins of London a solace and a refuge. Her London, as her choice of words indicates, is both distinctly post-War and post-Eliotic: 'Here you belong; you cannot get away, you do not wish to get away, for this is the maquis that lies about the margins of the wrecked world, and here your feet are set . . . "Where are the roots that clutch, what branches grow out of this stony rubbish? Son of man, you cannot say, or guess . . ." But you can say, you can guess, that it is you yourself, your own roots, that clutch the stony rubbish, the branches of your own being that grow from it and nowhere else.' Macaulay's quotation from *The Waste Land* serves to re-inforce the view commonly held by artists and writers of the period that the strange juxtapositions of flowers and dust, of unexpected, wild gardens and shattered, empty houses, and of the familiar seen in an unfamiliarly surreal way through a broken wall had somehow been prepared for by Modernist experiments with fragmentation.

Amongst writers whose reputation had been established well before 1945, Macaulay was far from alone in seeing the immediately post-war period as one which required the reassembling of fragments of meaning (she was herself to return to a landscape of classical ruins and to jarring private experience in her novel *The Towers of Trebizond* in 1956). The Second World War had provided an additional means of focus for the fiction of Anglo-Irish novelist, Elizabeth Bowen (1899–1973). Throughout her earlier work, most notably in her novel *The Last September* (1929) and her memoir *Bowen's Court* (1942), she had explored the tensions implicit in the history of her landed family and the divided loyalties of the increasingly dispossessed Protestant Ascendancy in Ireland. When she wrote of England in the 1930s, as she did with supreme assurance in her most Jamesian novel, *The Death of the Heart* (1938), she took as her theme the loss of innocence in the face of shallow sophistication and the flashy glamour of metropolitan values. The sometimes painful rift between the perceptions of children and those of adults was re-examined very differently in her penultimate novel, *The Little Girls* (1964). It was, however, in the wartime collections of short stories, *Look at all those Roses* (1941) and *The Demon Lover* (1945), and, above all, in her novel *The Heat of the Day* (1949) that Bowen exploited the fictional potential of an upper-class Irish woman's perception of the British 'Home Front'. In all her fiction Bowen displays a finely tuned stylistic tact in deploying and using detail, a tact evident in her evocations of London and Londoners changing, adjusting, and adapting under the impact of the Blitz. In *The Heat of the Day*, for example, she establishes that the lovers, Stella Rodney and the invalided Robert Kelway, have met in the 'heady autumn of the first London air raids' and that Stella puts down her failure to notice Robert's limp 'to the general rocking of London and one's own mind'. It is a period of morning mists 'charred by the smoke from ruins', of evenings marked by a 'darkening glassy tenseness' while waiting for the air raid sirens, and of 'an acridity on the tongue and the nostrils . . . as the singed dust settled'. Robert's disabilty, the urban unease, the strangeness, and the headiness all have their place in a narrative from which it gradually emerges that Robert is an enemy spy, a betrayer both of an allegiance to Britain (which the Anglo-Irish Stella and her soldier son Roderick maintain) and of the partly bemused, partly detached Stella herself.

Betrayal, the unwinding and rewinding of the skeins of history, and an insistently feminine viewpoint also mark the wartime and post-war books of Rebecca West (the pen-name of Cecily Isabel Fairfield, 1892–1983). West, whose Anglo-Irish father had settled first in London and later in Edinburgh, meticulously reassembled and fictionalized certain aspects of her cultured, eccentric, and unsettled childhood in *The Fountain Overflows* (1956), a novel whose first-person narrator tells the story with a subtle combination of adult knowingness and a sense of lost, or never-achieved, content. Rebecca West adopted her pen-name at the age of 19, at the time of her espousal of the campaign for women's suffrage, from the strong-willed character in Ibsen's *Rosmersholm*. As she announced in 1941, however, her excitement with Ibsen's frankness and intellectual enterprise was temporary ('As I grew older I began to realize that Ibsen cried out for ideas for the same reason that men call out for water, because he had not got any'). Nevertheless, she neither lost the belief that 'it is ideas that make the world go round' nor abandoned her determined, outspoken, practical, and thoughtful feminism. Her remarkable first novel, *The Return of the Soldier* (1918), looks at the problem of the human ruins left by the First World War from the point of view of the women who are obliged to pick up, and come to terms with, the pieces. Thereafter, most challengingly in *Harriet Hume: A London Fantasy* (1929), she experimented with a form that can best be described as mannered whimsy (she later modestly claimed that she had written the novel in order to find out why she loved London).

It is, however, through the non-fiction and the journalism of the 1930s and 1940s that West's intelligence shines most radiantly. In 1933 she wrote a short biography of St Augustine which intermixes an antipathy to Augustine's introspective, life-denying, masculine, doctrinal narrowness with a real appreciation of the taut, and equally masculine, 'modernity' of the author of the *Confessions* ('One perceives the barbaric vitality which needed to be disciplined and acquainted with mildness, but which itself framed the discipline, so that in the end, though violence bent its neck to mildness, the proceedings were violent'). Her most searching work of non-fiction also emerges from a keen sense of the complex interrelationships of human beings with their historical environments. The two-volume study *Black Lamb and Grey Falcon: The Record of a Journey through Yugoslavia* (1941) is far more than a pre-war travel book; it is a vehicle for a dense and digressive discourse on European history which grows into an elegy for the Yugoslav national experiment then floundering under the impact of military occupation and a redrawing of its internal borders by the German Reich (the book reads yet more poignantly following Yugoslavia's slide into bloody dissolution in the 1990s). West can write both provocatively ('It is sometimes very hard to tell the difference between history and the smell of a skunk') and capriciously (she describes a baroque church in Dubrovnik as 'a captive balloon filled with infinity'), but she always returns to what history and historical artefacts imply for those who have to make sense of them amid the painful, destabilizing realities of the twentieth century. The intense ideological and political distortions of the Second World War were imaginatively explored in a series of articles on the Nuremberg trials of 1946 (republished in 1955 as *A Train of Powder*) and in her broad political analysis of the implications of the trial of the British traitor, William Joyce, in *The Meaning of Treason* (1949) (reworked, with additional material referring to the British spy-scandals of the 1960s, in 1965). This non-fictional enterprise shaped the argument of West's searching historical novel about the ideological divisions of pre-revolutionary Russia, *The Birds Fall Down* (1966). It is a book which seeks to respond to the political issues raised variously by Dostoevsky, Conrad, Kropotkin, and Lenin as they impinge upon the consciousness of an Anglo-Russian girl of the 1910s and as they are filtered through the intelligence of a woman writer of the 1960s. *The Birds Fall Down* remains one of the most stimulating novels of the latter half of the century.

Neither Bowen nor West responded in any profound way to the experiments with form and technique pioneered by the Modernist writers who were very nearly their contemporaries. Both appear to have accepted that their art was rooted in an older tradition and that, by means of a steady adaptation of this tradition, they could address a wide audience. Neither of them, however, ever rivalled the popular acclaim accorded to the work of Graham Greene (1904–91). 'For a writer, success is always temporary', Greene wrote in his autobiographical memoir *A Sort of Life* (1977). 'Success', he added with a characteristic note of pessimism, 'is only a delayed failure'. By the mid-1960s, when his novel *The Comedians* was published, he was able to command sales of some 60,000 copies in hardback alone (this was at a time when more 'experimental' work by less established contemporaries would probably have had a print-run of only 1,600 copies). Even though something of the commercial success of *The Comedians* can be put down to the international scandal it provoked (the Haitian Government brought a case against it in France, claiming that it had damaged the Republic's tourist trade), Greene was already by far the best known and most respected British novelist of his generation. Something of his international esteem can be put down to what at the time might have seemed the 'un-English' prejudices which were patently evident in his work. He was a devout anti-imperialist (resenting the new American imperialism as much as he despised the crumbling edifice of the British Empire). He was also a semi-devout, but believing, Roman Catholic. Greene, who later claimed to have been powerfully drawn to Africa by reading Rider Haggard's *King Solomon's Mines* as a boy, had, after a singularly unhappy and suicidal adolescence, been received into the Roman Church in 1926. The themes of a colonially wounded world beyond Europe, a gloomy sense of sin and moral unworthiness, and a commitment to outsiders and rebels, haunt his subsequent work.

Greene had published his first work of fiction, a short story, at the age of 16. In all, he wrote twenty-six novels and nine volumes of short stories. His first novel, *The Man Within* (1929), bore as its epigraph a quotation from Sir Thomas Browne: 'There is another man within me that is angry with me.' Many of his later protagonists reflected this two-sidedness, complicated by a seedy and dangerous self-destructiveness. The Catholic boy-gangster, Pinkie, in Greene's eighth novel *Brighton Rock* (1938) is not only fascinated by the concept of 'Hell, Flames and damnation' but seemingly intent on courting his own eternal destruction in the face of 'the appalling strangeness of the mercy of God'. Taken with his painful account of the career of a whisky-priest in anti-clerical Mexico in *The Power and the Glory* (1940), Greene seemed to many observers to have emerged as Britain's answer to the ambiguous, knotted, but affirmatively Catholic fiction of his French contemporaries, Mauriac and Bernanos. The angry, self-destructive, 'other man' was, however, to oblige Greene's fiction to move in a more distinctively agnostic direction. It may be significant that the phrase 'whisky-priest' is Greene's most obvious gift to the English language. *The Power and the Glory* was as much about doubt and failure as it was about faith (the novel was condemned as 'paradoxical' by the Holy Office which ought, given the nature of Christian doctrine, to have known better). The Catholic Christianity of Greene's novels, if that is what it can properly be called, seems most often to resemble a single ray of heavenly hope which glances over dark abysses of human depravity, despair, decay, and pain. To Greene's characters, God and his Church seem to be as distant as they are evidently 'appallingly strange'.

As with Bowen's novels, the Second World War sharpened certain of Greene's fictional perspectives and preoccupations. Certainly, what is generally agreed to be his finest work appeared between 1940 and 1951. The novels of this period modulate between troubled and disorienting topographies, each one of which seems to reflect the untidy frustration of another. The twilit, blitzed London of *The Ministry of Fear* (1943) and *The End of the Affair* (1951) opens up into the violently restless Mexico of *The Power and the Glory*; the precarious, 'smashed, dreary' and partly subterranean Vienna of *The Third Man* (1950) parallels the flyblown, rat-infested, war-blighted West African colony of *The Heart of the Matter* (1948). Most of the key characters in these stories are Catholics; all of them are ruins, or at best ruinous. Scobie, the suicidal protagonist of *The Heart of the Matter*, accuses God of 'forcing decisions on people' and blames the Church for having all the answers ('we Catholics are damned by our knowledge'). In *The Third Man*, a short novel which coexists with its more brilliant variant, the film-script that Greene wrote for the director Carol Reed in 1949, Catholic Vienna is wrecked, divided, and guilt-ridden, but then so are its citizens, its displaced refugees, and its military occupiers. It is scarcely surprising that its sewers, rather than its palaces, figure so prominently in the story. None of

Greene's sleazier and more ostensibly political later novels (*The Quiet American* of 1955 is set in Vietnam, its successor, *Our Man in Havana*, in Cuba) has quite the same edgy power or quite the same success in matching compromised and seedy people to compromising and mouldy places.

In the phantasmagoric world of *The Ministry of Fear*, the tormented Arthur Rowe recognizes the extent to which the man and the hour have coincided ('I'm hiding underground, and up above the Germans are methodically smashing London to bits all around me . . . It sounds like a thriller'). Rowe's frenetic hallucination contrasts markedly with the far more subdued and matter-of-fact references to wartime Britain in Anthony Powell's sequence of twelve novels known collectively as *A Dance to the Music of Time*. At the opening of the eighth volume, *The Soldier's Art* (1966), Powell's wryly observant but adaptable narrator, Nicholas Jenkins, buys an army officer's greatcoat in a London outfitters. It is a shop which also supplies theatrical costumes and there are two headless tailor's dummies in the fitting-room, one costumed as Harlequin, the other dressed in the scarlet uniform of an infantry regiment: 'allegorical figures, so it seemed, symbolising dualisms . . . Civil and Military . . . Work and Play . . . Detachment and Involvement . . . Tragedy and Comedy . . . War and Peace . . . Life and Death . . .'. Jenkins, the officer-narrator, sets the amused and dualistic tone for his war. He is a keen, detached observer of surfaces, but he is also alert to the fact that they only partly conceal the murkier, and even tragic, undercurrents in private and public histories. Jenkins's blitzed London is as memorable for its continuities as it is for its absences, for its specific locations as much as for its occasional dislocations.

Powell's *A Dance to the Music of Time* is neither a fictionalized war memoir, nor a prose elegy for the decline and fall of a ruling class. However, as a chronicle of British upper-middle-class life, set between the 1920s and the 1950s, it necessarily takes the disasters, disillusions, inconveniences, and changes of a society and its war in its leisurely and measured stride. Powell (b. 1905) had opened his first volume, *A Question of Upbringing* (1951), with the image of workmen warming themselves in the street amid flurries of snow. The image is in no sense 'timeless', but it is somehow allowed to float as if obedient to a broader concept of time than that measured by clocks and calendars. Powell's narrator makes this clear when he refers to the Poussin painting (in the Wallace Collection) from which the sequence takes its title: 'classical projections, and something in the physical attitudes of the men themselves as they turned from the fire, suddenly suggested Poussin's scene in which the Seasons, hand in hand and facing outward, tread in rhythm to the notes of the lyre that the winged and naked greybeard plays. The image of Time brought thoughts of mortality . . .'. As he closes the last novel in the sequence (*Hearing Secret Harmonies*, 1975), Jenkins quotes a meditation on human mutability from Burton's *The Anatomy of Melancholy* before returning glancingly to the classical rhythms of the Poussin painting ('even the formal measure of the Seasons seemed suspended in the wintry silence'). Time may suddenly seem to be suspended by eternity, but it is art, Jenkins's melancholy, oblique art, which seems to have imposed its own order on a series of fragments. *A Dance to the Music of Time* has sometimes been compared to Proust's *A la recherche du temps perdu*. It could, with rather more justice, be seen as rooted in the tidy, intricate English ironies of Jane Austen's fiction and in the seemingly more leisured and spacious tensions of Anthony Trollope's chronicles. Above all, and perhaps most unexpectedly, it expansively reflects Powell's professed delight in the gossip, the rumour, and the randomness of John Aubrey's *Brief Lives*.

Dividing and Ruling: Britain in the 1950s

One sometimes gets the impression that the Second World War was Britain's last great communal experience. Certainly, neither the readjustments demanded by the steady loss of an overseas Empire nor the equally radical challenges presented by a belated entry into the European Community seem to have rivalled the prominence in the popular imagination of Britain at war. Having been instructed by one of Winston Churchill's most memorable rhetorical flourishes that the Battle of Britain in 1940 marked 'their finest hour', many Britons seem to have since forgotten that Churchill was referring not simply to the embattled United Kingdom but to 'the British Empire and its Commonwealth'. In the immediately post-war years, the Empire melted into the larger concept of the 'Commonwealth', a loosely associated fellowship of independent former colonies dominated by Britain's closest wartime allies, the old, white Dominions of Canada, Australia, New Zealand, and South Africa. The acceptance by the post-war Labour Government that India should be granted its independence and that the sub-continent should be divided into two separate self-governing countries inevitably brought about the broadening of this concept of a 'Commonwealth of Nations'. In June 1947 King George VI formally abandoned his inherited title of 'Emperor of India' as a necessary prelude to India's assumption of self-determination in August. In May 1953 his daughter, Elizabeth II, formally expressed herself content with the compensatory royal title of 'Head of the Commonwealth'.

   Official propaganda greeted the subsequent granting of independence to former colonies in Africa, Asia, the West Indies, and the Pacific as successful examples of Britain's enlightened policy towards those it had once sought to educate in the principles of good government and fair play. Rather than leaving Britain without a role (as it was glibly supposed to have done), the loss of the Empire was probably deeply resented only by those members of the upper and middle classes who had once felt called to serve it as colonial governors, civil servants, district administrators, and law officers. Its gradual disappearance, together with that of its somewhat exclusive employment opportunities, was steadily compensated for by Britain's gain of a new cultural diversity following the immigration of a large body of workers, both professional and unskilled, from the Indian sub-continent and the West Indies. The British psyche had been wounded only when the last twilit days of the imperial dream became nightmarish (as in the bloody communal violence which attended the division of India in 1947 and the expiry of the British mandate in Palestine in May 1948). The 1950s were marked not solely by immigration but also by the deaths of conscripted British soldiers fighting against Communist insurgents in Malaya, the Mau Mau in Kenya, and EOKA guerrillas in Cyprus. Perhaps the most notable example of the failure of the imperial muscle and of the imperial will was the Anglo-French military débâcle at Suez in November 1956 following the nationalization of the Canal by the Egyptian Government. The Conservative Government's inept intervention, in the face of a radically changing pattern of international relations, was readily interpreted by many jaded observers at home as looking more like carelessness than misfortune.

It was a post-war Labour Government which, in the face of Winston Churchill's impotent dismay, had brought in the legislation which gave India its independence. This same government, led by Clement Attlee, had been elected with a clear majority in 1945 (Labour had received some 47 per cent of the vote, though some 20 per cent of the nation had declined to involve itself in the democratic process). Labour's mandate for the domestic reforms it attempted to introduce was based on a widespread popular acceptance that the war, the war economy, and wartime propaganda had prepared the way for social change. An Act passed in 1944 had already radically reorganized state-aided education by raising the school-leaving age and subdividing the system into primary, secondary, and further educational stages. It also, for the first time, provided the opportunity of a free, if selective, academic education at grammar schools irrespective of a pupil's social background. The incoming government was pledged to nationalize the railways and the coal and steel industries. It was also pledged to speed the advent of what had been hailed during the war as the 'Welfare State' (as opposed to Hitler's 'warfare state'). The 1948 National Assistance Act formally abolished the old, despised Poor Law, but the Welfare State's cornerstone was the new National Health Service Act of 1946 which required that by 5 July 1948 free medical treatment should be available to all citizens.

An air of optimism, which was not generally shared by the Conservative Opposition, fostered the idea that Britain was rebuilding itself in a new, socially responsive economic dawn. The mood had earlier been summed up in a stylishly illustrated pamphlet issued in the election year of 1945 and ambitiously entitled *Design for Britain*. 'The Aeroplane has not only given us a new vision', it blandly announced, 'but a new chance by blasting away centres of cities so that we can rebuild them with a new plan designed for the swift flow of modern traffic, for the play of light and air, inspiring to look at and live in.' This hopeful mood was also exemplified in the decision made by the Labour government in 1947 to commemorate the centenary of the Great Exhibition of 1851 by celebrating 'the British contributions to world civilisation in the arts of peace'. This scheme, brought to its final realization by the Conservative Government elected in 1951, was the Festival of Britain. The main Festival site was an area of bombed land on the south bank of the river Thames in London. Out of the dereliction rose an architect-designed simulacrum of the brave new world. London got a new concert-hall as a permanent memorial to the Festival's somewhat lofty view of the nation's culture, though airy, temporary pavilions on the south bank had proudly shown off examples of new school equipment and domestic furniture and illustrated modern advances in public health, industrial production, invention, and exploration. A pavilion called 'The Lion and the Unicorn' had also attempted to define the 'British character' by endeavouring to represent 'two of the main qualities of the national character: on the one hand, realism and strength, on the other fantasy, independence and imagination'. 'If on leaving this Pavilion', the official guide-book whimsically announced, 'the visitor from overseas concludes that he is still not much the wiser about the British national character, it might console him to know that the British people are themselves very much in the dark about it.'

The optimism implicit in the Festival of Britain was not exactly forced, but it was clearly designed to cheer up a dreary and deprived nation, one drained by the sacrifices which had been required of it by the effort of fighting the war. It had, however, been a 'People's War', one which had forcibly suppressed distinctions between classes, genders, and races through military conscription, a planned economy, the recruitment of women's labour, and the rationing of food and luxury goods. The victory, as much as the misery, had been shared by everyone. This was the loathsome future Britain, with its earth inherited by Hoopers, that Evelyn Waugh saw coming into being in *Brideshead Revisited* (1945). This was the drab, egalitarian Britain which found an exaggerated echo in the world of Oceania in George Orwell's *Nineteen Eighty-four* (1949). This was the Welfare Britain, with its citizens cared for from the cradle to the grave, that the post-war Labour government nobly attempted to forge into a united nation by the exercise of benign state planning. This too was the innocent world of the exemplary and improbable film comedy *Holiday Camp* (1948), a delightfully naïve film in which the diverse social classes of Mr Attlee's Britain are seen mixing easily amid the obligatory but frugal cheer of a seaside holiday camp. It was an orderly and conformist Britain that was also ripe for further change, not all of it disciplined or planned.

The New Theatre

It was assumed at the time, and it continues to be assumed, that John Osborne's play *Look Back in Anger*, which opened at the Royal Court Theatre in London on 8 May 1956, marked either a 'revolution' or a 'watershed' in the history of the modern British theatre. The play certainly shocked its first audiences, as well as some of its more perceptive critics, into responsive attention. It is also sometimes claimed that the play single-handedly provoked theatre managers and theatre companies out of their complacent faith in the middle-class virtues of 'the well-made play' and into a response to a new kind of drama which grappled with 'the issues of the day'. Osborne's play was revolutionary neither in its form nor in its politics; it was, however, by the standards of its time, alarming in its rancour, its language, and its setting. After *Look Back in Anger*, out went the country drawing-room with its platitudes and its sherry; in came the provincial bed-sitter with its noisy abuse and its ironing-board. The accepted theatrical illusion of a neat, stratified, and deferential society was superseded by dramatic representations of untidy, antagonistic, and disenchanted groups of characters grating on one another's, and society's, nerves. The social class of these characters may not have changed, but their social assumptions and their conversation had.

The transformation of the English theatre in the late 1950s and early 1960s was both more gradual and more truly radical than can be explained by focusing on a single production or on the work of a single playwright. Before 1956 British drama, and the London stage in particular, had been far more open to new influences, both from home and abroad, than is often supposed. The theatre could, and did, fall back on its inherited tradition of plays and acting styles, notably in its rethinkings of Shakespeare and in its revivals of more recent English, Irish, and European dramas. Although the record-breaking run of Agatha Christie's *The Mousetrap* at the Ambassadors Theatre may tell us something about the resilience of certain theatrical conventions and styles (the play opened in November 1952 and is still going strong in the 1990s), it does little to illustrate the real challenges that a discriminating theatre-goer might have discovered in the London theatres of the late 1940s and early 1950s. The repertoires of West End theatres and their provincial counterparts may, for the most part, have been selected so as not to offend the sensibilities of audiences happy with a pattern of light-hearted banter divided into three acts by two generous bar-intervals, but that does not tell the whole story. The work of two native playwrights, Christopher Fry (b. 1907) and Terence Rattigan (1911–77), belies the accusation of theatrical blandness with which some literary historians have damned the immediate post-war period. Since the 1960s, however, the dramatic achievement of both writers has been commonly belittled as irredeemably genteel. Fry's attempt to revive the fortunes of poetic drama both derived from, and was contemporary with, T. S. Eliot's later experiments in the same genre. Like Eliot, Fry saw poetry as the vehicle for a re-exploration of religious mystery in the theatre; unlike him, he never quite found a voice or a subject which satisfactorily echoed the essentially agnostic prosiness of modern life and thought. He put his considerable international critical success in the early 1950s down to what he saw as a reaction against 'surface realism' in the theatre, with its 'sparse, spare, cut-and-dried language', and to a post-war world which longed again for a poetry of 'richness and reaffirmation'. With hindsight, it now seems that his hopes of re-creating an Elizabethan ambience, in which 'the accent of living' was placed firmly on 'the adventuring soul', proved as ephemeral as his once inflated reputation. Nevertheless, the original commercial success of the comedies *A Phoenix too Frequent* (1946), *The Lady's Not For Burning* (1948), and *Venus Observed* (1950) and of the church pageant *A Sleep of Prisoners* (1951) (performed throughout England as part of the Festival of Britain), cannot be put down solely to the excellence of their original casts. At its worst, Fry's verse can seem mannered, arch, and effete; at its best, it enables him to distance his dramatic discourse from 'surface realism' in order to play with the effects of alienation, of the unexpected, and of metaphysical oddity.

Rattigan is a far more impressive dramatist. He was neither an innovator nor a particularly cerebral writer, but he was a profound sympathizer with the cause of the victims of what he saw as the tyrannous hypocrisies, the double standards, and the emotional coldness of 'respectable' British society. Although his first theatrical success, *French Without Tears* (which ran for 1,039 performances in 1936), made few real demands on either the emotions or the intellect, his equally 'well-made' post-war plays took up the themes of vulnerability and victimization. The upper-class Rattigan's sympathy with the wounded outsider, and with the insider compromised by his or her emotional choices, can certainly be related to his own discreet homosexuality (discreet in the sense that he made no parade of it, though he later acted as an appreciative and generous champion of Joe Orton). In *The Winslow Boy* (1946), a middle-class father determines to play by constitutional rules in battling against the oppressive weight of the British Establishment. In *The Deep Blue Sea* (1952), however, an equally middle-class character, the wife of a judge, determinedly breaks social rules by having a passionate affair with a bluff, down-at-heel RAF officer and by desperately attempting suicide. If this is not quite the world of *Look Back in Anger*, the play is set in a furnished flat which has 'an air of dinginess, even of squalor, heightened by the fact that it has, like its immediately blitzed neighbourhood, so obviously "come down in the world"'. People and places which have come down in the world also figure in the pair of one-act plays, *Separate Tables* (1954), set in the ironically named Beauregard Private Hotel near Bournemouth. The second play of the two, 'Table Number Seven', highlights the complementary emotions of two of the Beauregard's 'guests', a repressed girl and a bogus major who has been found guilty of molesting women in a local cinema. It exposes a communal pretence to 'virtue' which is far more damaging to society than the major's assumption of respectability, but it also affirms the possibility of a new strength emerging from the dismantling of protective illusions.

In the early 1950s Christopher Fry enhanced his already considerable reputation by translating into English two plays by Jean Anouilh (*Invitation au château* in 1950 and *L'Alouette* in 1955) and one by Jean Giraudoux (*La Guerre de Troie n'aura pas lieu* also in 1955). The London staging of all three translations bears witness to the fact that the British theatre was not as insular as it is sometimes made out to be. The new French drama, which so impressed post-war visitors to Paris by its energy, sophistication, and political directness, had a sustained impact on supposedly unreconstructed British audiences (Anouilh's *Antigone* and Sartre's *Huis Clos* had been performed in 1946 and Camus's *Caligula* in 1948). Even though the influential critic, John Lehmann (1907–87), had wondered in 1946 whether or not 'a vigorous theatre can exist on the cerebral subtleties of *Huis Clos* and *Caligula* alone', the much vaunted intellectuality of Paris did not prove completely alien to London. Nor did the sometimes shocking vitality of the new American drama. Tennessee Williams's *The Glass Menagerie* (1945) was produced in 1948 and *A Streetcar Named Desire* (1947) in 1949 (with Vivien Leigh as Blanche du Bois). *Cat on a Hot Tin Roof* (1955), having been refused a licence by the Lord Chamberlain in 1958, had, however, to be privately performed under the auspices of a 'theatre club'. Less controversially, Arthur Miller's *Death of a Salesman* (1949) appeared at the Phoenix Theatre in 1949, his *The Crucible* (1952) at the Bristol Old Vic in 1954, and his *A View from the Bridge* (1955) at the Comedy Theatre in London in October 1956. Perhaps the most striking theatrical event of all was the visit to London of the Berliner Ensemble in August 1956, some two weeks after the death of its founder, Bertolt Brecht. The company brought with them their celebrated productions (in German) of Brecht's *Mother Courage*, *The Caucasian Chalk Circle*, and his lesser-known adaptation of Farquhar's *The Recruiting Officer—Pauken und Trompeten*. Brecht's work, which proved so influential over a new generation of British playwrights, was, up to that time, little known to British theatre audiences (though there had been an amateur production of *Galileo* in Birmingham in 1947 and a professional staging of *Mother Courage* in Barnstaple in 1955).

With benefit of hindsight, it is arguable that by far the most significant 'foreign' novelty to be performed in London in the years immediately preceding the appearance of *Look Back in Anger* was Samuel Beckett's *Waiting for Godot*. The play opened to largely dismayed reviews at the small Arts Theatre in August 1955, but reports of the sensation it had caused in Paris two years earlier, coupled with a real enough and discriminating curiosity, allowed it to transfer for a longer run at the Criterion Theatre a month later. The success of *Waiting for Godot* in London cannot simply be put down to a yearning for innovation on the part of a theatre-going intelligentsia; the play also contained distinct echoes of a truly 'alternative', but often despised, British theatrical tradition, that of music-hall comedy. In Beckett's hands, however, that tradition had been transformed by a sparse, but none the less definite, musicality and by a dialogue rich in literary resonance. Beckett (1906–89), born near Dublin, educated (like Wilde before him) at Portora Royal School and at Trinity College, and since 1937 permanently resident in Paris, cannot be slickly or imperially fitted into a narrowly 'English' tradition of English writing and English theatre. He was an English-speaking, Protestant Irishman, and, as the full range of his work demonstrates, his highly literate, cricket-playing, Bible-reading, Irish background had a profound bearing on what and how he wrote. Having worked closely with James Joyce and his international circle in Paris in the late 1920s, Beckett also remained part of a polyglot and polyphonic world of literary innovation. His earliest publications (which, apart from his work as a translator and a novelist, include an essay on Joyce and a study of Proust) also testify to his espousal of a Modernism which transcended frontiers and what were often presumed to be the impassible barriers between languages. Beckett continued to work in both English and French, with French often taking precedence over his native tongue. His work, however, ceased to be tied to a monoglot environment once it had undergone the scrupulous linguistic metamorphosis which mark his own acts of translation (his puns, for example, are often exclusively and inspiredly English).

Although his trilogy of novels, *Molloy* and *Malone Meurt* (1951) and *L'Innommable* (1953), had established Beckett as amongst the most discussed and respected of the avant-garde Parisian writers of the early 1950s, it was *Godot* (also originally written in French) that gave him a wide international reputation. That reputation was cemented by his later work for the theatre, notably the plays known by their English titles as *Endgame* (1957), *Krapp's Last Tape* (1960), and *Happy Days* (1962). He also wrote innovatively for the radio (*All that Fall* of 1957, *Embers* of 1959, *Words and Music* of 1962, and *Cascando* of 1963) and for BBC television (*Eh, Joe* of 1965 and *Ghost Trio* of 1977). His one foray into the cinema, *Film* (a complex 'script' designed as a tribute to Buster Keaton in 1964), was remarkable not simply for its nods to a cinematic comedy rooted in music-hall and for its visual puns on the philosophical ideas of being and seeing but also for its silence broken only by the sound of a voice saying 'sssh'.

Beckett was consistent in his use of drama as an extension of his wider interest in the gaps, the jumps, and the lurches which characterize the functioning and the malfunctioning of the human mind. In his plays—as much as in his novels—ideas, phrases, images, and minds overlap; voices both interrupt and inherit trains of thought begun elsewhere or nowhere and separate consciousnesses both impede and impress themselves on one another. Beckett's dialogue, for which *Waiting for Godot* is particularly remarkable, is the most energetic, densely layered, and supple written by any twentieth-century playwright; his comedy, whether visual, verbal, ritual, or even, at times, slapstick is amongst the most subtle and surprising. The set of *Waiting for Godot* may, for example, require simply the suggestion of 'a country road' and 'a tree'; *Endgame* may take place in a 'bare interior'; and the designer of *Happy Days* may be instructed to aim for a 'maximum of simplicity and symmetry' in the representation of an 'expanse of scorched grass rising centre to low mound', but the static baldness of Beckett's visual statements serves both to counterpoise and complement the animation of his verbal ones. When Beckett uses blindness, as he does with Hamm in *Endgame*, he suggests that one kind of deprivation may alert audiences to the force of alternative ways of perceiving. When, by con-trast, he uses silence, as in *Film* and the mime play *Act without Words II* (1967), he seems to be directing his audiences to explore the value of new sensory and physical formulations. Beckett never plays with minimalism and reductionism simply for the sake of the *aesthetic* effects he could achieve. In parallel to the work of certain Modernist architects and composers, if without their puritan frugality, he was exploring the radical potential of the idea that 'less is more'.

Time-present, as Beckett represents it in his plays, is broken, inconsistent, and inconsequential. Nevertheless, in each play he allows for the intrusion of a past which is oppressively rich in the larger inconsistencies of private and public history. *Krapp's Last Tape* and the two far sparser late plays, *Footfalls* and *That Time* (both 1976), make much out of the involuntary, untidy, quirky, and even ghost-haunted memories of the old. These memories negate linear concepts of time and of ageing as much as they disturb old assumptions about 'plot'. The structural principles on which he built both his plays and his novels can be related back to the pattern of ideas explored in 1931 in the dense criti-cal essay on Proust. When, for example, he insists on Proust's 'contempt for a literature that "describes"', or when he affirms that 'there is no escape from yesterday because yesterday has deformed us, or been deformed by us', or when he describes 'the attempt to communicate where no communication is pos-sible' as 'merely a simian vulgarity, or horribly comic', it is possible to recog-nize the extent to which his theatrical innovation was rooted both in a literary precedent and in a coherent Modernist philosophical statement. Beckett con-tinued to be fascinated by what he saw as Proust's concern with the protective significance of habit: 'Habit is a compromise effected between the individual and his environment, or between the individual and his own organic eccen-tricities, the guarantee of a dull inviolability, the lightning-conductor of his existence.' His own dramatic repetitions and iterations, his persistent echoes and footfalls, emerge not from a negative view of human existence, but from an acceptance of 'dull inviolability' as a positive, if minimally progressive, force. As his inviolable and unsentimental Krapp also seems to have discov-ered, a path forward lay in exploring the resonances of the circumambient darkness.

Although Beckett gradually came to be recognized as the most important dramatist writing in English in the latter half of the twentieth century, his work initially struck many early critics as emerging from a largely foreign tradition of symbolic and philosophically based drama. If the purely British shock waves radiating from John Osborne's *Look Back in Anger* in 1956 need to be accounted for, it was because Osborne's work was more obviously a response to, as much as a reaction against, an established native theatrical tradition. His was the rebellion of an insider. Osborne (1929–94) had served his apprenticeship as an actor in provincial touring companies and his plays show an appreciation both of the craftsmanship that went into the making of the respectable 'well-made play' and of the art that allowed a Wilde, a Shaw, a Coward, and a Rattigan to transcend conventions while exploiting them. Osborne's sometimes painful witticisms can be as carefully and devastatingly placed as are those of Wilde and Coward, his confrontations and surprises can be as telling as those of Rattigan, his invectives and monologues can be as provocative as Shaw's. However, the origins of Osborne's style do not lie exclusively in what was once known as 'the legitimate theatre' but are also found in the noisier, often impromptu and far more various world of vaudeville. Where Beckett's debts to an inherited tradition of music-hall lie in his appreciation of dead-pan humour and careful timing, Osborne's are revealed in his love of the outrageous, of the suggestive and, above all, of loud-mouthed repartee. It was a debt acknowledged in his forceful juxtaposition of a shabby and increasingly outdated type of theatre with a faded and redundant British imperialism in *The Entertainer* (1957).

Look Back in Anger introduced the noisiest of what contemporary journalists dubbed the 'angry young men' to theatre audiences. Osborne's hero, Jimmy Porter, is 25 and 'a disconcerting mixture of sincerity and cheerful malice, of tenderness and freebooting; restless, importunate, full of pride, a combination which alienates the sensitive and insensitive alike'. He was for the 1950s what the restless, idealistic, public-school misfits had been to the 1930s (Porter's father, we learn, had fought in Spain, but Porter himself is neither an idealist nor an ex-public schoolboy). He is, as his wife's friend Alison recognizes, 'born out of his time'. He is a revolutionary without a revolution, or, to put it in terms readily grasped in the 1950s, he is a rebel without a cause. He fulminates against the crumbling authority of what he identifies as Establishment values; his wife's middle-class and ex-Indian army parents; his Sandhurst-educated, Member of Parliament brother-in-law (characterized as 'the platitude from outer space'); bishops and church bells; the intellectually pretentious Sunday newspapers; English music (Vaughan Williams) and English literature (Shakespeare, Eliot, and 'Auntie Wordsworth'). Nevertheless, Jimmy Porter is the protagonist in an otherwise affirmative play, one in which love and loyalty are tested and are found, despite the strains, not to be wanting. He may be a new type of character, classless, restless, and aimless, but his dramatic context was largely conventional. When a middle-aged Jimmy Porter returned to the stage in Osborne's play *Déjà Vu* in 1992, the force of those dramatic and philosophical conventions became self-evident.

In many ways Osborne's most impressive 'angry young man' is the title character in his historical play *Luther* (1961). When Martin utters his classic avowal of personal integrity—'Here I stand; God help me; I can do no more. Amen'— we sense that it has been refined by his latent anger: anger with his parents, his Church, and even with the demands of his God. Osborne's Martin may periodically clutch his bowels in agonies of constipation, and he may have flashes of theological insight in the latrine, but he is the quintessential spiritual Protestant, the lonely rebel whom God has graced with a cause. In *Inadmissible Evidence* (1964) Osborne asked for a location 'where a dream takes place . . .

a site of helplessness, of oppression and polemic', in essence an office-cum-courtroom in which an angry, sex-obsessed, middle-aged solicitor lurches rhetorically towards a private and professional breakdown. In the first volume of his pungently observant, and equally pungently spiteful, autobiography, *A Better Class of Person* (1981), Osborne observed of himself as a schoolboy that he already had a gift for smoking out 'the prigs, hedgers and dissemblers' and that he had a complementary talent to vex rather than to entertain, a talent 'not to amuse but to dissent, although I possibly thought I could do both'. The anger, the dissent, the vexatiousness, the protest, and the theatricality of Osborne's characters has always been an extension of his perception of himself.

The New Novelists of the 1950s

Samuel Beckett's trilogy, published together in London in 1959 under the English titles *Molloy*, *Malone Dies*, and *The Unnamable*, was in every sense the most radically innovative fictional statement of the 1950s. The edition bore the announcement that the three novels had been 'translated from the original French by the author'. Beckett's pre-war fiction in English—the episodic novel *A Dream of Fair to Middling Women* (written in 1932, but published post-humously in 1992), the ten interconnected stories derived from it and given the title *More Pricks than Kicks* (1934), and the novel *Murphy* (1938)—had responded with a gauche confidence to the challenge of Joyce's experimental 'work in progress', *Finnegans Wake*. The titles of the first two of his pre-war works (one being loosely adapted from Chaucer, the other bawdily punning on a phrase of St Paul's) also suggest the degree to which Beckett was self-consciously attempting to regenerate and re-energize the literary traditions of his native language. *Murphy* is the most substantial of the three. Its solitary title character, who 'sat it out, as though he were free, in a mew in West Brompton', is an Irishman in London, precisely placed in time and space (it is Thursday, 12 September 1935 and he has an unbroken view from his window to the north-west). His 'mew' (a bird-coop, originally one designed for moult-ing falcons) is condemned (we presume as unfit for human habitation) and Murphy must contemplate the upheaval of removal ('Soon he would have to buckle to and start eating, drinking, sleeping and putting his clothes on and off, in quite alien surroundings'). Ostensibly, *Murphy* is constructed around the drab rituals and the vacuous repetitions of a largely inert life passed in a confined urban space. More profoundly, it seeks to represent a man's energetic inner life which finds its own repetitive rhythms and patterns and its own time-scheme distinct from those of the outside world.

When Beckett returned to fiction after the Second World War, he opted for the discipline of writing in French rather than in English. He also chose the form of a fluid monologue, a positively gushing 'stream of consciousness', rather than that of a third-person narrative. *Molloy* (written in 1947, published in Paris in 1951, and subsequently translated into English in 1955) shares a deliberate ambiguity of telling with its two successors. Each of the ageing narrators in the trilogy habitually contradicts himself, stumbles over the contortions of his syntax, and is obliged to pause in order to reflect on precisely how he has to express himself or on what he feels pressed to say. Both the flow of narrative and the language employed threaten to break under the strain. Beginnings are vexed or subverted, tenses shift between past and present, and what seem to be digressions or interpolations assume a vital momentum. *Molloy* (the very title of which may possibly, with the addition of one simple vowel, glance back to Joyce's superlatively fluid consciousness, Molly) is built around two self-explorative consciousnesses, the one seeking the other. Much as the disabled Molloy melts disconcertingly into his complementary other half, the self-abused, decayed Moran, in the first novel, so both Molloy and Moran are subsumed in the other compulsive story-tellers of the trilogy, Malone and the isolated, unnamed narrator of *The Unnamable*. The last anguished and lachrymose teller recognizes the extent to which he has assimilated and now disowns the experiences of his narrative forebears: 'All these Murphys, Molloys and Malones do not fool me. They have made me waste my time, suffer for nothing . . . I thought I was right in enlisting these sufferers in my pains. I was wrong. They never suffered my pains, their pains are nothing, compared to mine, a mere tittle of mine, the tittle I thought I could put from me, in order to witness it . . . these creatures have never been, only I and this black void have ever been.' Whereas Murphy sits it out 'as though he were free', this man of sorrows, the Unnamable, wrenches phrases from himself in his isolation and probes the implications of the perception that he is neither truly alone nor free of a larger humanity ('the little murmur of unconsenting man, to murmur what it is their humanity stifles'). The trilogy ends with an ultimate contradiction in terms: 'in silence you don't know, you must go on. I can't go on. I'll go on.'

Beckett's experiments with narrative form and with the disintegration of narrative form had few immediate echoes in the more popular fiction of the 1950s. The one British writer of the period who keenly responded to the idea of creating an avowedly 'Modernist' fiction, and whose experiments were enthusiastically received by a wide public, was Lawrence Durrell (1912–90). Durrell was born in India of parents whose families had made the subcontinent their home for several generations. Although he became briefly acclimatized to bohemian (as opposed to 'respectable') England in the early 1930s, Durrell found what he regarded as his spiritual home in the Mediterranean, moving first to Corfu and then, after the German invasion of Greece, to Egypt. As a young man he also responded to the liberating influence of two modern writers in particular, D. H. Lawrence (with whom he shared an antipathy to British reserve as much as to British rain) and the Paris-based American novelist Henry Miller (with whom he embarked on a long correspondence). Miller's influence can be felt on Durrell's *The Black Book: an Agon*, 'a savage charcoal sketch of spiritual and sexual etiolation', which was privately printed in Paris in 1938 (its overt eroticism precluded its publication in Britain until 1973). In 1944, as Press Officer of the British Information Office in Egypt, Durrell was posted to Alexandria, the city of 'five races, five languages, a dozen creeds' which inspired the four novels of his 'Alexandria Quartet'—*Justine* (1957), *Balthazar, Mountolive* (both 1958), and *Clea* (1960). Durrell's dusty, sweaty, multi-layered Alexandria, a city he described in *Balthazar* as 'half-imagined (yet wholly real), [which] begins and ends in us', is a phantasmagoric, Eliotic place in which men and women dissolve into one another and ancient splendours melt into modern inconveniences. The city's real and imagined disconnections provide the setting for a series of interlocked fictions describing interconnected, unfulfilling love-affairs. The narrator, Darley, is both a self-conscious, self-referential teller and an incorporator of the narrative voices of other tellers, notably that of a fellow-writer, Pursewarden. In one of the 'work-points'—sentences, ideas, and occasionally poems or translations seemingly discarded from the main narrative of *Justine* and then appended to it as a kind of afterthought—Pursewarden's 'n-dimensional novel' is described by its author as having a forward narrative momentum which is 'counter-sprung by references backwards in time, giving the impression of a book which is not travelling from a to b but standing above time and turning slowly on its own axis to comprehend the whole pattern'. Readers are doubtless meant to read Darley's actual narrative as somehow shadowing Pursewarden's speculative one. The Alexandria Quartet, in common with Durrell's yet more ambitious 'Avignon Quintet'—*Monsieur* (1974), *Livia* (1978), *Constance* (1982), *Sebastian* (1983), and *Quincx* (1985)—attempts to break down preconceptions of time as much as it assaults inherited prejudices in favour of fictional realism. Durrell's literary reputation, so buoyant in the breezy, liberal climate of the early 1960s, tended to sag thereafter. Where his contemporary, Beckett, was economical, he was prodigal; where Beckett saw the force of scrupulous compression, he indulged in a passion for words which is more often libertine than it is liberating.

William Golding's first and most enduringly popular novel, *Lord of the Flies* (1954), gives a surer indication of his continuing concern with moral allegory than it does of his subsequent experiments with fictional form. Golding (1911–93) set the novel on a desert island on which a marooned party of boys from an English cathedral choir-school gradually falls away from the genteel civilization that has so far shaped it and regresses into dirt, barbarism, and murder. The island is cut off both from the disciplined harmony of the boys' musical background and from a disharmonious world of grown-ups at war. The novel is shaped intellectually by an intermixture of the Christian concept of original sin, a post-Darwinist and post-Wellsian pessimism, and a systematic undoing of R. M. Ballantyne's adventure story of plucky and resourceful boys, *The Coral Island* (1857). At the end of the story an officer from the warship that rescues the boys dejectedly remarks, 'I should have thought that a pack of

British boys . . . would have been able to put up a better show than that'. The sudden shift of viewpoint and the dejection were re-explored, with subtle variations and darker ramifications, in each of Golding's subsequent novels. As the range of his fiction shows, Golding emerged as a major successor to an established line of Modernist mythopoeists. Unlike Yeats, Eliot, Joyce, or Jones, however, he was not content with a reanimation of ancient myth; he was intent on overturning and superseding a variety of modern rationalist formulations and on replacing them with charged, unorthodox moral shapes. It is not just British boys who reveal their innate depravity, but the whole human race. *The Inheritors* (1955) moves back into an anthropological, rather than an Adamic, prehistory in which the talented, if thoroughly nasty and brutish, progenitors of *Homo sapiens* exterminate their gentler, simpler-minded Neanderthal precursors. The dense, difficult *Pincher Martin* (1956) has as its greedy egotistical 'hero' a drowned sailor, lost from a torpedoed destroyer, whose body is rolled by the Atlantic. But the 'Pincher' is also a survivor, one whose consciousness tries desperately to hold on to its fragmented identity in a watery purgatory. This identity attaches itself to an imagined rock, one that Martin names 'Rockall', and one which he also recognizes in its rhymed naval transmogrification as 'Buggerall' (a hellish nothing). Golding experimented with a similar metaphorical structure in *Free Fall* (1959), a tortuous exploration of free will and fallen humanity in relation to the scientific idea of the unrestrained movement of a body under the force of gravity. The subject of *The Spire* of 1964 was both more concrete and more elusive. Jocelin, the ambitious Dean of an unnamed English cathedral at an unspecified point in the Middle Ages, is a fallen man obsessed with raising a tall stone spire above his cathedral. His obsession is determined by a serpentine knot of motives—architectural, theological, visionary, psychological, sexual, self-deprecating, and self-aggrandizing. Jocelin both achieves his desire and fails in it; he builds an awe-inspiring structure on shaky foundations, but he is also forced to experience its maiming; he erects an airy reflection of heavenly glory, but he is also obliged to recognize the hot, distracting force of the phallus; he periodically escapes upwards, with a vertiginous thrill, into a Gothic fretwork, but he is held earthbound by the overloaded, creaking pillars that have to support his aspiration. Finally struck down by a mortal paralysis, and attended by a priest known as Father Adam, the dying Jocelin struggles to find the meaning of his life's work, a meaning which gradually forms itself around the metaphoric core of the lost earthly paradise: 'In the tide, flying like a bluebird, struggling, shouting, screaming to leave behind the words of magic and incomprehension—*It's like the appletree!*'

Golding's *The Pyramid* (1967) was followed by what appeared to be an abstention from fiction, an abstention broken in 1979 by *Darkness Visible*. All Golding's opening scenes, suggestions, and sentences are disconcertingly striking. None is more so than that of *Darkness Visible*, a compelling evocation of an intense fire-storm in the London Blitz out of which walks a fearfully burned child: 'He was naked and the miles of light lit him variously . . . The brightness of his left side was not an effect of light. The burn was even more visible on the left side of his head.' From the terrible beauty of this beginning there develops an intense and sometimes confusing exploration of the polarities of redemptive saintliness and destructive malignity, of disinterested love and calculated terrorism. The four novels published since *Darkness Visible*—*Rites of Passage* (1980), its sequels *Close Quarters* (1987) and *Fire Down Below* (1989), and *The Paper Men* (1984)—have extended what can be seen as an established rhythm of contrasted sea-stories and land-stories all of which are concerned with extremity and isolation. The most successful is *Rites of Passage*, the first volume of a sea-trilogy set on a decayed man-of-war bound for Australia in the opening years of the nineteenth century. Its cocky, journal-writing narrator, Edmund Talbot, is alerted to the problems of 'too much understanding' but can himself comprehend little of 'all that is monstrous under the sun'. Talbot, like all Golding's central characters, is rawly exposed both to his darker self and to the grinding despair of one of his fellow-passengers. Although Golding's work has sometimes been compared to that of Conrad, it is often closer in spirit, and in its aspirations to the condition of poetry, to that of Eliot. Each of Golding's male protagonists seems obliged to re-articulate the agonized, incomprehending, unspecific question of *Gerontion*: 'After such knowledge, what forgiveness?'

As his novels of the 1950s suggest, Angus Wilson (1913–91) seems to have been intent on restoring Victorian narrative styles to English fiction in opposition to what he saw as the errant experimentalism of the Modernists. In contrast to the slim, even anorexic, shapes accepted by his contemporaries, he steadily swelled the physical shape of the novel back to something approaching its nineteenth-century proportions. As a means of emphasizing where his artistic loyalties lay, he published a fine, but decidedly untheoretical, study of Émile Zola in 1952 (thoroughly revised in 1965); in 1970 he added an observant, semi-biographical, critical introduction to Dickens and in 1977 an essay on Kipling. Wilson recognized in Dickens a writer who combined 'art and entertainment' and whose works made up a 'complete whole—the World of Charles Dickens'. In 1961 he also proclaimed his continuing confidence in the 'God's eye view', the omniscient narrative stance of many of the Victorian novelists that he admired. Although some critics have attempted to draw parallels between Wilson's own work and that of Zola, Dickens, and even George Eliot, the parallels cannot really be sustained. He was, it is true, a convinced realist who occasionally indulged in grotesquerie and fantasy and a finely tuned comic writer who habitually allowed for the intrusions of tragedy and cruelty, but the world of his own novels is idiosyncratic and decidedly that of the mid-twentieth century. Wilson, who began his literary career with two volumes of short stories, *The Wrong Set* (1949) and *Such Darling Dodos* (1950), had a talent more developed for creating scenes, set pieces, and characters than for the spruce and ordered fictional shapes that defined themselves against what Henry James had dismissed as 'loose baggy monsters'. Wilson's novels, from his first,

Hemlock and After (1952) to his last, *Setting the World on Fire* (1980), are essentially comedies of manners in which the comedy winces, sometimes gratuitously, with pain. As an observer and mimic, Wilson also had an exceptionally sharp ear and eye for the whims, voices, vogues, pretensions, and pomposities of his time. He had a particularly fastidious distaste for the kind of social gatherings which represent what he called in his essay *The Wild Garden, or Speaking of Writing* (1963) 'the hell of the human failure to communicate', where the damned are 'the social climbers, those wanting to be loved, the unloved women who push people around, the organization men who fall to pieces when they are alone'. His two most 'traditional' novels, *Anglo-Saxon Attitudes* (1956) and *The Middle Age of Mrs Eliot* (1958), are also probably his surest comments on the cultural, social, and sexual tensions of a period struggling to come to terms with the conflicting claims of tradition and novelty. *Anglo-Saxon Attitudes* is especially adept in its panoramic movement from scene to scene and in its gradual establishment of connections between a disparate number of characters. Wilson beds his novel in an archaeological fraud (perpetrated in 1912 before the narrative begins) whose ramifications return to darken the present of Gerald Middleton, an ageing historian. *Late Call* (1964) also introduces the idea of historical determination (its opening 'Prologue' is set in 1911) but it narrows the scope of its plot to an account of the alienation of the retired Sylvia Calvert amid the affected liberalism and the engineered environment of one of the 'New Towns' (social experiments much promoted by government planners in the late 1950s). The latter part of Wilson's career was marked by an increasing experimentalism, not all of it successful. *Late Call* is notable for its deliberate use of pastiche and its undercutting of cliché; *Old Men at the Zoo* (1961, but set in an 'utterly improbable' 1970–3) for its juxtapositions of men and beasts against a background of 'wars, domestic and foreign'; *No Laughing Matter* (1967) for its long time-span (1912–67), for its parodies, and for its introduction of scenes presented as if they were written for the stage. Neither the capricious *As If By Magic* (1973) nor the yet wilder *Setting the World on Fire* (1980), however, exhibit quite the vivacious panache of Wilson's earlier work.

Iris Murdoch (1919–99) was, in the early part of her career, to remain equally faithful to traditional fictional shapes. Unlike Wilson, however, she underpinned her novels with arguments derived from a scrupulous investigation of the problems posed by moral philosophy. This underpinning has been consistently enhanced by a series of independent philosophical studies, notably *Sartre, Romantic Rationalist* (1953), *The Sovereignty of Good* (1970), and *Metaphysics as a Guide to Morals* (1992). If Murdoch was amongst the earliest readers to respond positively to Beckett's fiction (she read *Murphy* as an undergraduate at Oxford and paid homage to it in her own first published novel, *Under the Net*, in 1954), her only work of fiction which can be said to draw directly from Beckett's example is *Bruno's Dream* (1969), a study of the atrophying consciousness of an old man. Murdoch sketched the nature of her own philosophical and literary standpoint in an article entitled 'Against Dryness' in 1961. 'We live in a scientific and anti-metaphysical age', she argued, an age in which 'we have been left with far too shallow and flimsy an idea of human personality' and in which the connection between art and the moral life had languished 'because we are losing our sense of form and structure in the moral world itself'. The problem with much modern writing, as she saw it, lay in 'our tendency to produce works which are either crystalline or journalistic'; writers needed to turn away from 'the dry symbol, the bogus individual, the false whole, towards the real impenetrable human person'. Against the 'consolations of form, the clean crystalline work, the simplified fantasy-myth', writers should pit 'the destructive power of the now so unfashionable naturalistic idea of character'.

None of Murdoch's own novels could remotely be called 'dry', despite the determining concern with ethical dilemmas that each betrays. All of them are carefully patterned, though the rules of the obscure game which decide these patterns often seem to be broken, reformed, and realigned by the very nature of the freedom which she allows her characters. Jake Donaghue, the male narrator of *Under the Net*, both resists and creates theoretical patterns with words which, like nets, entrap and constrain perceptions of a larger and expanding reality. As a range of novels from *The Flight from the Enchanter* (1955) to *The Sea, The Sea* (1978) and *The Philosopher's Pupil* (1983) suggest, those characters who attempt to impose nets, theories, mystical enchantments, 'artistic' arrangements, or restrictive myths upon reality must themselves adapt to a world which of necessity eludes predetermined human systems of control. In *The Bell* (1958) and *A Fairly Honourable Defeat* (1970) the loss or fragmentation of objects also seems to suggest why established patterns of relationships between characters must themselves be removed and reordered. As Rupert warns in the latter novel, 'some general view . . . makes you blind to obvious immediate things in human life'. In some senses, Murdoch's fascination with spiritually gifted outsiders, androgynes, and foreigners (particularly East Europeans) further emphasizes the fictional significance she places on indeterminacy, difference, and strangeness. *The Bell*, set in a lay religious community established in a country mansion near to a convent of enclosed nuns, begins with a fragmenting marriage and gradually explores the emotional, sexual, and moral tensions which force the community itself to break up and re-form. The convent bell, from which the novel takes its title, bears the inscription '*Vox ego sum Amoris*' ('I am the voice of Love'); it is at once an aesthetic focus and a disturbing catalyst, an ideal and a breaker of ideals. It proves to be less of a link back to a restrictive and legendary past, than an announcer of new freedoms and the rightness of new contingencies. As the Abbess, one of Murdoch's first spiritually gifted outsiders, has announced, 'all our failures are failures in love'. New contingencies also determine the nature and the structure of what remains Murdoch's most experimental novel, *The Black Prince* (1973). Its narrator, Bradley Pearson, a novelist, both tells the story and, in a sense, is the story. 'Art', he remarks, 'is the telling of truth, and is the only available method for telling certain truths. Yet how almost impossibly difficult it is not to let the marvels of the instrument itself interfere with the task to which it is dedicated.' *The Black Prince* is, on one level, a contrived intellectual thriller; on another it is an equally contrived multiple and untrustworthy narrative. It opens with two Forewords, the first by a supposed editor, Loxias (whose name is derived from the Greek word for 'oblique'); the second by Pearson himself. As the narrative line develops, so do different ways of approaching and understanding 'truth' and 'reality'. It ends with six separate, disparate and, to some degree, conflicting Postscripts, four of them written by different members of what Murdoch describes as her 'dramatis personae'. The use of this theatrical term serves as a deliberate reminder of the Shakespearian echoes and connections with which the narrative has played and with which it finally fragments ('Art tells the only truth that ultimately matters. It is the light by which human things can be mended. And after art there is, let me assure you, nothing'). If Loxias, the supposed editor of the manuscript, is here echoing Pearson's own sentiments, he is also playing a Horatio to a dead Hamlet, an uncloaked Prospero, deprived of his charms, asking for the indulgence of an audience.

Muriel Spark (b. 1918), a Catholic convert of Jewish descent and Scottish birth, shares with Murdoch and Golding a pressing commitment to moral issues and to their relation to fictional form. Her first novel, *The Comforters* (1957), is concerned with a neurotic woman writer, Caroline Rose, having to come to terms with her new-found Catholicism, with her hallucinations, and with her God-like status as a creator. Rose, is not merely working on a study of contemporary fiction entitled *Form in the Modern Novel* (and having particular difficulty with the chapter on realism), she has also resolved to write a novel about writing a novel. Spark has been as consistently fascinated by the narrative problems posed by self-consciously literary texts as she has been preoccupied with the theological problem of evil. As the opening paragraph of her autobiography, *Curriculum Vitae* (1992), serves to suggest, she has been equally determined to explore the potential of light to dispel darkness and to illuminate the creatures, the thoughts, the motives, and the sins that dwell in darkness.

It is not insignificant that in 1951, before she had embarked on her own career as a novelist, Spark published a critical reassessment of the work of Mary Shelley under the title *Child of Light*. Her own early novels marked new advances in the often distinctively British exploration of the Gothic. If, on one level, she revealed herself as the Scots heir to the tradition of Burns, Hogg, and Stevenson, on another, hers is a Gothic enlivened by a decidedly post-Calvinist glee. *Memento Mori* (1959), which was recommended to readers as a 'brilliant and singularly gruesome achievement' by Evelyn Waugh, is concerned with a diverse group of London geriatrics who receive anonymous telephone calls telling them to remember the inevitable fact of their impending deaths. Spark's title recalls the skulls and funerary desk ornaments favoured by baroque meditators on mortality, but her own narrative is wry, blunt, and provocatively funny. She ends the novel with dry medical case histories as one of her characters, paralysed by a stroke, searches through his mind, 'as through a card-index', for the causes of his friends' mortal sicknesses: 'Lettie Colston, he recited to himself, comminuted fractures of the skull; Godfrey Colston, hypostatic pneumonia; Charmian Colston, uraemia; Jean Taylor, myocardial degeneration; Tempest Sidebottome, carcinoma of the bronchus; Guy Leet, arteriosclerosis; Henry Mortimer, coronary thrombosis . . .'. His litany is broken by the third-person narrator turning to a separate meditation, one that finally turns on the reader with the words of a children's catechism: 'Jean Taylor lingered for a time, employing her pain to magnify the Lord, and meditating sometimes confidently upon Death, the first of the four last things to be ever remembered.' The Gothic of *The Ballad of Peckham Rye* (1960) and *The Prime of Miss Jean Brodie* (1961) is quite distinct in its comic chill. Both novels are, in their different ways, concerned with possession: the first with necromancy in a south London suburb in the 1950s, the second with the peculiar exercise of psychological power in an Edinburgh girls' school in the 1930s. Miss Brodie's superbly poised and precisely defined moral sway over her favourite pupils is compared by one of her protégées to that of 'the God of Calvin'; the narrator, however, suggests a more deflationary contemporary parallel, based on Miss Brodie's fondness for pointing out the common Latin root of the words 'educate' and 'Duce': 'Mussolini stood on a platform like a gym teacher or a Guides mistress . . . the Brodie set was Miss Brodie's fascisti.'

The dispassionate, sometimes ironic, sometimes disingenuous tone of Spark's narrators helps her to create a sense of discordance between the aberrance of what happens and its cool, precise delineation. This is particularly true of her 'metaphysical shocker', *The Driver's Seat* (1970), a carefully ordered, even meticulous, present-tense account of a woman with a death-wish who plots the circumstances of her own violent murder. The novel undermines easy assumptions about cause and effect as much as it challenges ideas of authorial authority and control. If *Not to Disturb* (1971)—with its opening quotation from *The Duchess of Malfi*, its foul weather, and its 'zestful' aristocratic cretin imprisoned in a wing of a Swiss château—is Gothic in the traditional sense of the term, Spark's *The Abbess of Crewe* (1974), a brusque investigation of an upper-crust English convent, completely avoids the prurience traditionally inspirational to earlier Gothic novelists. The convent is ruled by an Abbess adept in exploiting all the technological and propagandist skills of the twentieth century in order to manipulate her sisters into compliance with her will. She not only appreciates the state of the art, she is also, like so many of Spark's protagonists, something of an artist herself. 'Scenarios', the Abbess tells the nuns, 'are an art-form . . . based on facts. A good scenario is a garble. A bad one is a bungle. They need not be plausible, only hypnotic, like all good art.' Throughout the narrative, she has revealed a remarkable taste for secular literature (Machiavelli jostles with a wide range of poetry). At the end, when she meets her Watergate, she gives orders 'for the selection and orchestration of the transcripts of her tape-recordings'. At certain points in the transcripts she includes the explanatory instruction 'Poetry deleted'. It is distinctly more elegant, but no less politic, than the phrase it echoes, Richard Nixon's 'Expletive deleted'.

The novels of L(eslie) P(oles) Hartley offer a distinctively oblique retrospect on an uneasy England from the point of view of the mid-century. Hartley (1895–1972), a product of the leisured middle classes, was in many ways a social insider who chose to explore the awkwardnesses, the vulnerability, and the disillusionment of the outsiders who are the central characters in his novels. His trilogy *Eustace and Hilda* (originally published as *The Shrimp and the Anemone* (1944), *The Sixth Heaven* (1946) and *Eustace and Hilda* (1947)) deals delicately with the contiguous worlds of a brother and his elder sister as those worlds diverge, expand, and painfully contract again. *The Hireling* (1957) edgily explores the class tensions inherent in the relationship between a lonely upper-class widow and the cynical, story-telling driver of her hired car. But it was with the carefully crafted *The Go-Between* of 1953 that Hartley's unease with his century became most manifest. The novel is narrated by a man who recalls, with an imaginative vigour, the period of his loss of innocence and of his sense of well-being as a 12-year-old boy in the hot summer of 1900. Leo, who had once so enthusiastically anticipated both his thirteenth birthday and the new century in which it fell, now looks back on fifty odd years as emotionally scarred and alienated as he is. As his narrative shows, he, the undeceived, is also able to marvel at the self-deceived who seem so effectively to have peopled his century.

Any critical overview of (Clarence) Malcolm Lowry's achievement as a writer will always be dominated by his masterpiece, *Under the Volcano* (1947). Lowry (1909–57) set his novel in Mexico on the macabre festival of the 'Day of the Dead' in November 1939. Over it brood the volcanic mountains of the title, the political restlessness of the 1930s, and the rumbling imminence of the Second World War. It opens with an allusion to Dante, and develops, through a series of flashbacks and twists of time and perspective, into a disturbing, but haunting, study of a self-destructiveness that is more internal than infernal. The torrid volcanic landscapes, the seemingly confused perceptions, and the often uneasy social relationships represented in the narrative are variously evoked by means of dense literary and mythological reference. Lowry himself aptly used the term 'delirious consciousness' to describe the state of mind of his major narrator, the British ex-consul Geoffrey Firmin. In a long letter of January 1946 the novelist defended the elusive complexity of his work to his publisher by referring to it as 'a kind of symphony . . . a kind of opera . . . It is hot music.' He went on to explain that his book was also concerned with the 'forces in man which cause him to be terrified of himself . . . with his remorse, with his ceaseless struggling towards the light under the weight of the past, and with his doom'. Despite the pervasive suggestions of an alcoholic haze, the ostensible randomness in its narrators, and the extended prose reveries, *Under the Volcano* remains one of the most scrupulously controlled and polished narratives of the century. Lowry's posthumous publications, most of them completed from untidy and sometimes incomplete manuscripts, include the collection of interrelated stories *Hear Us O Lord from Heaven thy Dwelling Place* (1961), the novel *Dark as the Grave Wherein my Friend is Laid* (1968), and the novella *October Ferry to Gabriola* (1970).

'Fields we do not know': Bunting and Larkin

Basil Bunting (1900–85) has proved one of the most difficult to 'place' of the major English poets of the twentieth century. He is certainly one of its most determinedly 'provincial', proud of his Northumbrian roots and culture and insistent in his use of northern words and in his echoes of northern speech rhythms (a note to *Briggflatts* insists that 'southrons [southerners] would maul the music of many lines' in the poem). He is at the same time one of the most sophisticated openers up of English Modernism, one attuned to an international recasting of literary forms and one whose work is informed by the contours of non-native landscapes (in Bunting's case particularly by his extended sojourns in Italy and Iran; he worked as a British spy in the latter country in the 1950s). He was one of a very select group of inter-war writers approved of by Ezra Pound, who in 1938 had jointly dedicated his *Guide to Kulchur* to him and Louis Zukofsky as 'strugglers in the desert'. His total output as a poet remains relatively slim, however. Bunting's first volume of poetry *Redimiculum Matellarum* was published in Milan in 1930 at the time of his closest association with Pound, but it was not until the appearance of his long poem *Briggflatts* in 1966 (followed by his *Collected Poems* in 1968) that he attracted due recognition and a wider audience for his sometimes elusive, often complexly referential, work.

In a sense Bunting's work can be characterized by the idea of rediscovery. Like that of David Jones, his poetry re-explores historical and personal pasts, interweaving archaeology and landscape, memory and a burgeoning and reawakened sensibility. Unlike the chaste, God-haunted Jones, Bunting rejoices in his sexual identity, an identity associated in *Briggflatts* with the recurrent phallic emblem of the slow-worm. He also delights in the conjunctions of times and places, and it is to the well-remembered fells and exposed sea-coasts of north-eastern England that the poem returns with a sense of exact, happy, even mystical, recall in which earthly shapes are caught up in celestial patterns:

> Shepherds follow the links,
> sweet turf studded with thrift;
> fell-born men of precise instep
> leading demure dogs

> from Tweed and Till and Teviotdale,
> with hair combed back from the muzzle,
> dogs from Redesdale and Coquetdale
> taught by Wilson or Telfer.
> Their teeth are white as birch,
> slow under black fringe
> of silent accurate lips.
> The ewes are heavy with lamb.
> Snow lies bright on Hedgehope
> and tacky mud about Till
> where the fells have stepped aside
> and the river praises itself,
> silence by silence sits
> and Then is diffused in Now.

Bunting's sharp detailing has reminded some of his readers of Wordsworth's, but the sensibility which determines that detailing is distinctively Modernist.

Philip Larkin's work, which so characterized the mainstream of English poetry in the 1950s and 1960s, stands in marked contrast to that of Bunting. Larkin's novel *Jill* (1946) is set in an Oxford from which Arnold's 'last enchantments of the Middle Age' and Waugh's *douceur de la vie* have been banished by the make-do-and-mend mentality of the Second World War. 'Life in college was austere', Larkin wrote in the introduction he added to the novel in 1963, 'Its pre-war pattern had been dispersed, in some instances permanently. Everyone paid the same fees . . . and ate the same meals . . . At an age when self-importance would have been normal, events cut us ruthlessly down to size.' *Jill* is remarkable not simply for its picture of an Oxford forced into a dispirited egalitarianism by the war, but also for its introduction of what became a common theme in the literature of the 1950s and 1960s, the awkward self-consciousness of provincial, lower-middle-class England and the upward mobility of a grammar-school educated intelligentsia. Although Larkin (1922–85) was not of the generation which benefited most from the provisions of the 1944 Education Act, he was typical of a new breed of articulate university graduate. As the key poet of the post-war decades he was also to chart other social and cultural changes with a sardonic percipience. Larkin was the most significant of a loose group of writers known in the early 1950s as 'the Movement', a group assumed by those who disliked what it stood for to be the typical product of wartime planning and the Welfare State. Evelyn Waugh, not unexpectedly, complained in 1955 of a 'new wave of philistinism with which we are threatened by these grim young people coming off the assembly lines in their hundreds every year and finding employment as critics, even as poets and novelists'. 'The Movement', which also included the novelist Kingsley Amis (1922–95), the poet and critic Donald Davie (1922–95), and the poet and novelist John Wain (1925–94), was united not so much by its class origins or by its beer-drinking, pipe-smoking, and jazz-appreciating friendships, but by a sensibility shaped by a shared antipathy to the cultural pretensions of Bohemia and Bloomsbury and to what it saw as the élitism of much Modernist writing. It would be preposterous to cast the self-effacing Larkin as a proto-type of the 'angry young man' of the late 1950s, but his was a distinctive and to some degree representative new voice.

The six volumes of verse that Larkin published in his lifetime were all modest in size. His first, *The North Ship*, appeared in 1945; it was succeeded by *XX Poems* (published in a tiny edition in 1951), by a slim pamphlet containing five further poems in 1954, and in 1955 by the volume that first made his name as a poet, *The Less Deceived*. His earliest published poem, 'Winter Nocturne' (printed in his school magazine in 1938), clearly shows the influence of Yeats, an influence, 'as pervasive as garlic', which Larkin claimed could also be felt in the poems in *The North Ship*. From the mid 1940s, however, he discovered a new model of poetic restraint in Hardy. It is Hardy's example which seems to inform even the title of *The Less Deceived*. Much of Larkin's subsequent poetry was to bypass Modernist experiment and high-flown language in favour of traditional metrical forms and a precise and plain diction. The two later collections, *The Whitsun Weddings* (1964) and *High Windows* (1974), point not simply to the sharpness of Larkin's ear for the inflexions of his own age, but also to a new and, at the time, deliberately provocative frankness. As the selection of his *Letters* published in 1992 reveals, Larkin had a private penchant for what was once coyly described as 'four-letter words'. If this vocabulary had only minimally entered the 'polite' literary mainstream before, Larkin's long-established admiration for Lawrence's *Lady Chatterley's Lover* may partly explain the plain speaking of certain of the poems published in *High Windows*. The language of the title poem stresses its contemporaneity: 'When I see a couple of kids | And guess he's fucking her and she's | Taking pills or wearing a diaphragm, | I know this is paradise | Everyone old has dreamed of all their lives'. 'Annus Mirabilis', an old man's sing-song ballad, sees the paperback publication of Lawrence's book as part of a wider shift in popular culture and manners: 'Sexual intercourse began | In nineteen sixty-three | (Which was rather late for me)— | Between the end of the *Chatterley* ban | And the Beatles' first LP.' What has since become Larkin's most quoted line ('They fuck you up, your mum and dad') opens 'This Be The Verse', a poem which at first sight appears to be a neat summary of Freudian theory and Hardyan pessimism, but one which moves into an intensely private disillusion: 'Man hands on misery to man. | It deepens like a coastal shelf. | Get out as early as you can, | And don't have any kids yourself.'

When he was asked by an interviewer in 1979 if he had felt like an outsider as a child, Larkin stressed that he had been fond enough of his parents even though 'they were rather awkward people and not very good at being happy'. 'These things rub off', he added ruefully. There is little exhilaration in Larkin's verse. Human history and human experience, as he observes them, provide few occasions for rejoicing. If he recognizes that certain inherited characteristics do indeed 'rub off', he nevertheless sees himself as alienated from both an uncomfortable past and a cheerless, Godless present. In 'I remember, I remember' a series of negatives undoes the fond sentimentality of Thomas Hood's poem of the same name. In a later poem, 'To the Sea', Larkin looks back far more gaily to the seasides of his parents' courtship and of his own boyhood, but the line expressive of the continuities that the poem recalls ('Still going on, all of it, still going on') scarcely suggests a sense of liberation in or from time. The snapshots in 'Lines on a Young Lady's Photograph Album' record 'dull days as dull, and hold-it smiles as frauds' and stir a sense of alienation from 'a past that no one now can share'. Larkin's present, a late 1950s present in the poems 'The Whitsun Weddings' and 'Afternoons', is that of an England of false cheer, cheap fashions, joyless wedding parties, drab recreation grounds, and 'estatefuls' of washing. His accounts of the past are marked by an awareness of a gulf fixed between then and now by death and ageing. In 'MCMXIV', a joint tribute to the art of Wilfred Owen and to the deceptions of photography, he describes an 'innocent' group of young recruits, 'grinning as if it were all | An August Bank Holiday lark', about to be bloodied by the Great War. The country church in 'Church Going' is inspected with an 'awkward reverence' by a 'bored, uninformed' post-Christian narrator who frets at the prospect of a future in which religion will have shrunk to a prevalent fear of death. In what is perhaps his most delicate and lyrical poem, however, history and time, an unease at the prospect of death and an uncertain glimmer of human hope are fused together into a new whole. 'An Arundel Tomb' describes a medieval funerary monument to a husband and wife who are shown lying side by side and hand in hand. The 'lengths and breadths of time' have not only marred the sculptural image, but have also served to alter the way in which all images are read and interpreted:

> Snow fell, undated. Light
> Each summer thronged the glass. A bright
> Litter of birdcalls strewed the same
> Bone-riddled ground. And up the paths
> The endless altered people came,
>
> Washing at their identity.
> Now, helpless in the hollow of
> An unarmorial age, a trough
> Of smoke in slow suspended skeins
> Above their scrap of history,
> Only an attitude remains:
>
> Time has transfigured them into
> Untruth. The stone fidelity
> They hardly meant has come to be
> Their final blazon, and to prove

Our almost-instinct almost true:
What will survive of us is love.

The Audenesque confidence of the last line is deliberately qualified by the two preceding 'almosts'. The provisionality is essentially Larkin's own.

'A dry distress': Poetry beside and beyond Larkin

John Betjeman (1906–84), whose poetry, almost uniquely amongst his contemporaries, Larkin professed to admire heartily, dealt with English tradition, English religion, and English melancholy in a distinctively un-Larkinesque manner. By the 1960s Betjeman's work was selling phenomenally well (his *Collected Poems*, first published in 1958, sold 90,000 copies within two years). His was a popular success based not simply on easily comprehensible, generously rhymed, and meticulously scanned verse, but also on a calculated projection of himself as a celebrity. He adopted an enthusiastic, if somewhat bumbling persona for himself on television (though he consistently proved to be an intelligent and inventive performer, and, as the collection of prose *Coming Home* (1997) suggests, an adept critic of architecture and a sensitive apologist for Poetry). Middle-brow readers also welcomed his somewhat unproductive tenure as Poet Laureate from 1972. Although Betjeman claimed in his gushy, blank-verse autobiography *Summoned by Bells* (1960) to have presented a volume of his schoolboy poems to 'the American master, Mr Eliot', his later verse never revealed much of a response to Eliot's metrical, intellectual, and lexical novelty. He did, however, share Eliot's Anglo-Catholicism and something of his feeling for national history and it was a fusion of religious and historical sentiment with the associations of certain buildings and places which made for the elements in Betjeman's most effective verse. His collection *Old Lights for New Chancels* (1940) opens with eighteen specifically topographical poems and ends with a 'Miscellaneous' section which includes his wry study of an upper-class woman at prayer, 'In Westminster Abbey'. His later volumes, *A Few Late Chrysanthemums* (1954), *High and Low* (1966), and *A Nip in the Air* (1972), suggest a poet further refining the techniques and forms he had evolved in the 1940s rather than one capable of surprising his readers. But then, most of Betjeman's readers, Larkin included, did not read him for surprises.

Stevie (Florence Margaret) Smith (1902–71) also won herself a wide, young, and sometimes unexpected audience in the 1960s. Smith, whose *Novel on Yellow Paper* (1936, reissued 1969) and two volumes of verse—*A Good Time was Had By All* (1937) and *Tender Only to One* (1938) (both illustrated by her own, straggly, naïve drawings)—had received relatively little attention in their time, achieved a belated celebrity in 1957 with her new collection *Not Waving But Drowning* (whose title poem proved her most popular). She cemented her reputation with a series of distinctive, incantatory public readings, with her *Selected Poems* (1962), and with a new volume, *The Frog Prince*, in 1966. A *Collected Poems* appeared posthumously in 1975. She made a barbed, ostensibly simple poetry out of the kind of subjects and expressions which other poets might have rejected as unconsidered trifles. She remained sentimentally attached to the Church of England while denouncing its doctrines and its priests; she immersed herself in mortality while whimsically greeting Death as a 'gentle friend' and dwelling, almost gaily, on the effects of physical and mental decay. The drowning man, whose gesturing is misunderstood in 'Not Waving but Drowning', moans that he was 'much too far out all my life' and Death in 'Do Take Muriel Out' is pressed to take the lonely Muriel on a last outing ('She will not complain | When you dance her over the blasted heath'). Smith wrote two poems with the Elizabethan title 'Come Death'. Both avoid echoes of Elizabethan melancholy and of the fraught mortal ambiguities of John Donne. The first, published in 1938, expresses a longing for extinction with an admixture of archaism and easy modern frankness ('Who would not rather die | And quiet lie | Beneath the sod | With or without a god?'). The second, written in the poet's final illness, has a far more lyrical form and a far more punchy simplicity:

> I feel ill. What can the matter be?
> I'd ask God to have pity on me,
> But I turn to the one I know and say:
> Come, Death, and carry me away.
>
> Ah me, sweet Death, you are the only god
> Who comes as a servant when he is called, you know,
> Listen then to this sound I make, it is sharp,
> Come Death. Do not be slow.

The poet of the younger generation who, in his striking first volume of poetry at least, most obviously owed a debt to Larkin is Douglas Dunn (b. 1942). The first part of *Terry Street* (1969) consists of a sequence of eighteen poems dealing with working-class life in a terrace in Hull (where Dunn had studied as a mature student; as a librarian he was later to work with Larkin at the University Library). What seemed to have set *Terry Street* apart from much of the other verse of its time was its 'gritty' realism ('In small backyards old men's long underwear | Drips from sagging clotheslines'). But this was more than a poetic meditation on kitchen sinks in back-to-backs, for the volume resonates with a tender lyricism and a carefully precise observation such as the moment when the men of the street seem to the poet to be like mysterious and invisible gods—'a pantheon of boots and overalls. | . . . They quicken their step at the smell of cooking, | They hold up their children and sing to them.' Dunn's later collections (notably *Barbarians* of 1979 and *St Kilda's Parliament* of 1981) indicate a far greater variety of tone and subject matter, as well as a new concern with formal verse structures, but the impulse to elegiac lyricism remains consistent. His *Elegies* of 1985 offer an extraordinarily delicate recall of, and tribute to, his dead wife. In *Northlight* of 1988, however, Dunn's native Scottishness (barely visible in *Terry Street*) dominates the tone and the subjects of the poetry. The volume contains a fine, appropriately off-hand tribute to Larkin, 'December's Door' ('And now I can't repay the debt I owe, | A withered leaf, a dry distress. | Sorrow's vernacular, its minimum, | A leaf brought in on someone's shoe | Gatecrashed the church in muffled Cottingham, | Being's late gift, its secret value | A matter of downtrodden poetry'), but it is most memorable for its sharp recalls of charged Scottish locations. 'Abernethy', for example, opens with gusts of wind, cold light, and the layering of local history:

> Air-psalters and pages of stone
> Inscribed and Caledonian
> Under these leaf-libraries where
> Melodious lost literature
> Remembers itself! A white
> Dove climbs on its Columban flight
> In the botanic radiance
> Northlight's late druidic rinse
> Lapping against time and earth
> In this root view of Fife and Perth.
> A thousand years of briars enclose
> A wild and matrilinear rose
> Whose house began before the oak
> First felt the axeman's stroke.
> An unrecorded Kentigern
> Disturbs a prehistoric fern
> And hours from the Pictavian clock
> Measure the lives of land and rock
> And miles before the pedlared road
> Winds of Iona and to God.

Dunn's is a verse which manages to incarnate both individual memory and human history in light and leaves and air as much as in bricks and mortar.

The 'New Morality': The 1960s and 1970s

When Philip Larkin located the stirrings of a sexual revolution in the 'annus mirabilis' of 1963, he was not simply hitting on a convenient rhyme for that other newish phenomenon, the 'LP'. Larkin had long admired what was probably the most influential novel of the British 1960s, the belatedly published *Lady Chatterley's Lover*, and he later expressed an appreciation of what he recognized as 'the first advance in popular music since the War', the songs of the Beatles. The unequivocal 'Not Guilty' verdict at the conclusion of the trial of

Penguin Books in 1960—after their publication of a paperback version of Lawrence's banned novel—seemed to Larkin, and to other contemporary observers, to be a liberating sign of the times. So, in a different sense, was the release of the Beatles' first album three years later. The *Lady Chatterley* verdict represented a breaking of the shackles of official censorship and public prudery; the Beatles' record expressed the energy of a new popular music, one that had appropriated the vitality of American styles and added a new lyricism and a home-grown romanticism. At the trial, *Lady Chatterley's Lover* had been defended against charges of obscenity by a succession of witnesses drawn from the literary, critical, and clerical establishment, but, despite the fact that it sold over two million copies in the year following its publication, the novel struck many of its readers as representative of an essentially high-brow, 'literary' tradition. The Beatles' music was, by contrast, patently not high-brow. It erupted from below, both socially and harmonically, and it offended against canons approved by right- and left-wing arbiters of taste alike. Not only Beethoven had to roll over: so did Bartok and Britten, Modern and Traditional Jazz, and the kind of folk-music regarded by its earnest *aficionados* as the authentic voice of the downtrodden. The music of the Beatles and other groups of the time was not simply an added stimulus to some amorphous 'cult of youth', but was itself a part of the vanguard of a new youth culture. This dissenting, anarchic, constantly shifting youth culture, which had been preliminarily delineated by Colin MacInnes (1914–76) in his novels *City of Spades* (1957) and *Absolute Beginners* (1959), was galvanically energized in the 1960s.

The decade was often hailed, though not universally welcomed, as the era of the 'New Morality'. It was certainly the era of the female contraceptive known popularly since 1960 simply as 'the pill'. In 1956 the influential theatre critic and baiter of Mrs Grundy, Kenneth Tynan (1927–80), had described Jimmy Porter's 'casual promiscuity' as typical enough of the sexual behaviour of post-war youth. A somewhat more flamboyant, rather than simply 'casual', promiscuity had been cultivated by the hero of Ian Fleming's popular James Bond novels, published between 1953 and 1964 and translated to the screen from 1962. But the 'New Morality', as it came to be defined, was not simply to do with promiscuity, the pill, and 'macho' male values. It was in part a reflection of a post-Freudian openness about sexual relationships and in part a post-Lawrentian attempt to sanctify sexuality. At the *Lady Chatterley* trial, John Robinson, the suffragan Bishop of Woolwich, had declared that Lawrence had portrayed 'the sex relation' as 'in a real sense an act of holy communion' and had exhibited a 'quite astonishing sensitivity to the beauty and value of all organic relationships'. Three years later, this same bishop announced in his contentious little book, *Honest to God*, that the doctrine that marriages were made in heaven was little more than 'the metaphysic of a pre-scientific age'. For Robinson, all of the Church's traditional moral teachings had to be scrutinized in accordance with the fashionable intellectual 'isms' of the age, and those that failed the test had to be jettisoned as so much redundant mumbo-jumbo. In the same year, the BBC's Reith Lecturer, Professor George Carstairs, announced that popular morality was a wasteland 'littered with the debris of broken convictions' because of the emergent concept of sexual relationships 'as a source of pleasure'. If the 1960s did not exactly mark the discovery of the pleasures of sexual intercourse, the decade proved memorable not simply for its legislative liberalization (birth-control and divorce were facilitated; abortion and adult male homosexual acts were legalized) but also for the gradual establishment of new moral, political, and cultural discourses.

The debates of the 1960s were, to a considerable degree, refocused by the consequent theoretical formulations of the 1970s and 1980s. They were also conditioned by the national and international political issues of the decade itself. In 1962 the temperature of the 'Cold War' was dangerously raised as a result of the crisis over the siting of Soviet missiles in Cuba. Britain, insistent both on the significance of its 'independent' nuclear deterrent and on the wider security offered by NATO, was obliged to stand by and watch as the United States and the Soviet Union uneasily defused the crisis before lumbering into others. Britain proved to be impotent also in the face of the Soviet invasions of Hungary in 1956 and Czechoslovakia in 1968, and attempted to avoid all direct involvement in the escalating American campaign in Vietnam. Although successive British governments remained firmly committed both to the use of nuclear weapons and to the NATO alliance, the appeal of the Campaign for Nuclear Disarmament (founded in 1957) pointed to a popular revulsion at the prospect of a nuclear war and a resurgence of idealist pacifism amongst the young. In 1959 some 50,000 people, including the aristocratic dissident, Bertrand Russell, and the theatrical one, John Osborne, attended the culminating protest rally in London after a march from Aldermaston in Berkshire. These Easter marches became something of a national institution in the early 1960s. In 1962 the American Embassy in Grosvenor Square in London was the focus of a 'Hands Off Cuba' rally organized by the anti-nuclear 'Committee of 100'. In 1966 and, yet more spectacularly, in the spring and summer of 1968 the Embassy drew far larger numbers of protectors against the war in Vietnam. To those who matured in, or who were matured by, 1968, the evidence of world-wide disaffection seemed to suggest that radical political change might not just be possible but imminent. A new generation, impatient with the fudges, compromises, and sins of their elders, felt they might be as much the forgers of a new social order as they were already the beneficiaries of a new moral one. For the 'New Left' authors of the 1968 *May Day Manifesto*, distributed by Penguin Books and edited by the socialist literary critic and novelist Raymond Williams (1921–88), 'the years immediately ahead' seemed likely to be 'confusing and testing', but there remained the real hope that what they defined as the 'active socialism of the immediately coming generation' would help shape 'the political structure of the rest of the century' rather than merely revise 'the forms which now embody the past and confuse recognition of the present'. Even to those to whom, through age, temperament, or lack of opportunity, the events of 1968 signified little, it was none the less a year which served to focus minds. When Lindsay Anderson's surreal cinematic study of a machine-gun-toting public-schoolboy revolution, *if . . .* , was released in the following year, it struck many sympathetic chords.

In terms of other international commitments and the long-term political destinies, the 1960s were notable for the attempts of British governments to negotiate a belated entry into the European Economic Community. Although the first two attempts were rebuffed by General de Gaulle and a French veto, the prospect of closer European involvement was not necessarily greeted with unadulterated enthusiasm on the part of the British electorate. In a symposium organized by the magazine *Encounter* in December 1962 some hundred 'writers, scholars and intellectuals' were asked to express an opinion about what was styled the 'Britain and Europe debate'. The replies received revealed deep divisions and often irrational prejudices parallel to those evident in the nation at large. T. S. Eliot declared that he was 'strongly in favour of close cultural relations with the countries of Western Europe', but E. M. Forster remained equivocal; W. H. Auden hoped that Britain would join the Community, but opined that that would not make her part of Europe, 'because Europe no longer exists'; Graham Greene, writing, he announced, 'as a materialist', was merely 'inclined' in Europe's favour; Arthur Koestler, referring back to an article he had written in 1950, pressed for the idea of a supranational federation, while Kingsley Amis claimed to be very disturbed by any future surrender of sovereignty; Iris Murdoch urged longer reflection because 'joining Europe' had such a dangerously romantic appeal to 'many naïve hearts'; Angus Wilson admitted to being 'filled with suspicion' and John Osborne proclaimed a faith in Britain's going it alone and making 'a small start on the socialist revolution by slinging away our defence expenditure'. Harold Pinter bluntly announced: 'I have no interest in the matter and do not care what happens.' Little enough did happen for some nine years. Together with the Republic of Ireland and Denmark, Britain became a full member of the European Community on 1 January 1973, a decision later confirmed by a referendum. Debates about the ramifications of these decisions for national sovereignty have continued just as divisively into the 1990s.

In 1957 the Conservative Prime Minister, Harold Macmillan, had blandly declared that Britain had 'never had it so good'. The relative prosperity of Britain in the late 1950s and 1960s may have been insecurely based on illusions of an economic renewal and a more equable distribution of wealth, but such economic optimism both propped up successive Conservative administrations and helped support the dream of a technological revolution sponsored by the Labour Government that supplanted them in 1966. Although the emphatically working-class fiction of Alan Sillitoe (b. 1928) offers little comfort to any Conservative, his first novel, *Saturday Night and Sunday Morning* (1958), confirmed that the living and working conditions of many working people had improved beyond measure (even though their real freedom of action had not).

Although Sillitoe's promiscuous protagonist, a Nottingham factory worker, may angrily recognize that his social and economic horizons remain severely restricted, his father believes that a decent wage, a holiday, and a television set have transformed his life. The 1960s and 1970s did not merely see wide-scale slum clearance and the reconstruction of swathes of industrial Britain in accordance with the high-rise architectural principles of the Modern Movement, they also offered new opportunities for travel and home entertainment. What had once seemed unaffordable luxuries, such as continental holidays and televisions and stereos, were gradually transformed into virtual necessities. Social deprivation and homelessness may not have been abolished, but they seemed less noticeable and were consequently less addressed as pressing problems. The material prosperity and consumerism of the 1960s and 1970s led directly to the relative complacency of the Thatcherite 1980s. The 'New Morality' and 'You've never had it so good' did not begin to sound really hollow until the frugal, AIDS-haunted 1990s.

Female and Male Reformulations: Fiction in the 1960s and 1970s

The broadening of women's perspectives and women's opportunities proved the most radical and substantial of the social changes of the 1960s. Not only had the 'New Morality' begun to challenge received perceptions of gender, sexuality, and marriage, but new patterns in women's employment, and particularly professional employment, had steadily emerged since the end of the Second World War. Germaine Greer's lively and largely untheoretical book, *The Female Eunuch* (1970, reissued in paperback in 1971 and later translated into twelve languages), provided a stimulus to the development of a newly outspoken and often provocative feminism in the period. For Greer (b. 1939), the campaigns of genteel suffragettes had represented the 'first feminist wave'; her own book, she claimed, formed part of a second wave which was already evident in the fact that 'ungenteel middle-class women are calling for revolution'. Greer's phrase may possibly echo the perception of one of the male characters in Doris Lessing's novel, *The Golden Notebook* (1962): 'The Russian revolution, the Chinese revolution—they're nothing at all. The real revolution is, women against men.' For both Greer and Lessing (b. 1919) that revolution began with a heightened alertness to the narrow representations of women's roles, and women's consciousness, in society and its literature.

Lessing had begun her career as a writer with novels concerned with the growth of political awareness amongst native blacks and white settlers in colonial East Africa. Her five-volume sequence *Children of Violence* (1952–69) deals with the developing political commitment, and the later political disillusion, of Martha Quest. Martha is carefully 'placed' at the beginning of the first novel as 'adolescent, and therefore bound to be unhappy; British, and therefore

uneasy and defensive; in the fourth decade of the twentieth century, and therefore inescapably beset with problems of race and class; female, and obliged to
repudiate the shackled women of the past'. Martha learns her radicalism in
colonial Africa, but she is also forced by circumstances to unlearn the Stalinist
assumptions she makes about world revolution. In the last, and most experimental, volume in the sequence, *The Four-Gated City* (1969), set initially amid
the fragmented political aspirations of British anti-nuclear campaigners,
Martha recognizes that there are few protesters 'whose lives did not have a
great gulf in them into which all civilization had vanished, temporarily at least'.
The novel ends with a projection forward to the years 1995 and 2000 after a
devastating atomic war. Martha discovers a hope for the future on a remote
Scottish island where a group of mutant children has had its mental powers
enhanced, and its social vision reintegrated, by the effects of radiation. In many
ways, *The Four-Gated City* marks the beginning of Lessing's exploration of
what she has called 'inner space fiction', a fiction that has systematically moved
away from conventional realism. It was, however, with her central work of
fiction, *The Golden Notebook*, that she first began to relate the concept of
mental fragmentation to the disintegration of fictional form. The novel is
shaped around the series of notebooks, Black, Red, Yellow, and Blue, kept by
a woman writer, Anna Wulf, as a means of separating and analysing different
aspects of her life. The notebooks seem to present her with a means of ordering her life according to neat categories, both private and public, but Anna's
evolving perceptions of herself finally dictate that her attempts at categoriza-
tion break down, not into new patterns but into an inevitable and welcome
formlessness. *The Golden Notebook* is in many ways a traditional narrative subjected to a process of disordering. It can be seen both as a wayward development of the kind of nineteenth-century realist fiction admired by Marxist
critics (including Lessing herself) and as an attempt to come to terms with an
intelligent woman's sense of private and public diffusion. Anna herself realizes that she is incapable of writing the only kind of novel which interests her,
'a book powered with an intellectual or moral passion strong enough to create
order, to create a new way of looking at life'. Her awareness is accompanied by
the conviction that this diffusion is a symptom not of social, mental, or ideological disease, but of personal liberation. Anna had once struggled with the
'banal commonplace' that 'women's emotions are all still fitted for a kind of
society that no longer exists'; the narrative shaped around her bid for freedom
gradually allows her the perception of the new, if still insecure, value that is
to be found in the fact of a woman's creativity.

Insecurities also haunt Jean Rhys's *Wide Sargasso Sea* (1966), in part a
rethinking of Mr Rochester's account of his courtship and marriage as given
in *Jane Eyre*. Rhys (1894–1979) transfers the scene of her novel away from
Charlotte Brontë's damp England to the lusher, more tempestuous West Indies
of her own childhood (she was born in Dominica). She also radically alters
perspectives. Her four earlier novels, published between 1928 and 1939 and set

in the lax, anything-goes world of European bohemians, had dealt with women determined to explore the implications of their sexuality and, ultimately, with women adrift and women exploited. In *Wide Sargasso Sea*, however, these themes were replayed with a new intensity and savagery. In a narrative divided between Rochester and his Creole wife-to-be, Antoinette Bertha Cosway, Rhys explores the nature of loneliness, exploitation, and victimization. The novel interlocks the corrupt and uneasy society of the post-emancipation Caribbean, its decaying plantations, its exotic, untrimmed gardens, its ghosts, and its tropical storms, with the onset of Bertha's mental turbulence. 'I think of my revenge and hurricanes', she writes, 'Words rush through my head (deeds too). Words. Pity is one of them. It gives me no rest.' The last section, set in the draughty attics of Thornfield Hall, ends with Bertha's unsteady awareness of what she has to do with the flickering candle that she has stolen.

Rhys's career contrasts vividly with that of the outwardly far more conventional Barbara Pym (1913–80). Like Rhys, Pym had to wait until the end of her life for real literary success. Her first novels, *Some Tame Gazelle* (1950), *Excellent Women* (1952), *Jane and Prudence* (1953), and *Less than Angels* (1955), culminated with *A Glass of Blessings* (1958). All proclaim the virtues of restraint, good behaviour, and feminine resilience, but *A Glass of Blessings* is particularly effective in its representation of the shortcomings of disingenuousness and of the lack of scope of women of a certain generation. The novel's comedy depends upon the misapprehensions and the conventional pieties of its slightly bored, fondly imaginative, dully married narrator. Pym's fiction is generally set in a small world of middle-class families and middle-aged spinsters, a world shaped by its topography of shops, tea-rooms, and Anglo-Catholic churches and ordered by rituals of sherry and gossip. Publishers of the 1960s, working under the assumption that readers would prefer accounts of up-market philandering in Hampstead, down-market adultery in Huddersfield, and downright fornication in Cumbria to Pym's sharp delineations of suburban gentility, rejected her subsequent submissions. The situation changed in 1977, largely thanks to Larkin's determined advocacy. The revival of her fortunes as a writer was marked by the appearance of two new novels, by the reprinting of her work of the 1950s, and, posthumously, by the publication of fiction she herself had set aside or abandoned. The finest of her later novels, *Quartet in Autumn* (1978), departs slightly from her established social patterns but not from the delicate representation of obscure lives in which she excelled. The 'quartet' of the title, two men and two women who work together in a London office, is observed as it divides, briefly celebrates, and privately decays. The novel's last sentence, with its reference to a life that 'still held infinite possibilities for change', has an irony which does not smother its pathos.

Angela Carter's fiction presents its readers with a world of magic and theatre in which there *is* an infinite possibility for change. Her's is an extravagance just held in check by the splendid artifice of her prose. Carter (1940–92) reinvented the fairy-tale for a knowing adult public, infusing her narratives with macabre fantasy and erotic comedy. Although she could scarcely be described as a pornographer herself, she recognized in her deft and suggestive essay, *The Sadeian Woman: An Exercise in Cultural History* (1979), that pornographic fantasy too would have its legitimate place in literature once it could be moulded to the service of women and once women had ceased to be considered as mere commodities. Carter is rarely a polemical writer, but as her novel *The Passion of New Eve* (1977) and her two volumes of Gothic stories, *Fireworks* (1974) and *The Bloody Chamber* (1979), suggest, she can startle by the very vividness of her renegotiations of the elements that have shaped traditional accounts of male–female relationships. When she describes the central (male) character in *The Infernal Desire Machines of Doctor Hoffman* as being divided between 'a barren yet harmonious calm and a fertile yet cacophonous tempest' and between 'the drab colourless world' and 'the fragile marginalia of our dreams', she suggests something of her own narrative attraction to the sonorities and colours of the margins of the imagination. This is particularly evident in her two major theatrical novels, *Nights at the Circus* (1984) and *Wise Children* (1991), both of them set in the golden age of escapist entertainment, the late nineteenth and early twentieth centuries. Fevvers, the cockney bird-woman of *Nights at the Circus*, has been hatched, like the offspring of Leda and Jove, from an egg; at the age of puberty she has also, miraculously, sprouted wings ('as my titties swelled before, so these feathered appendages of mine swelled behind'). After a foster-childhood spent in a Whitechapel brothel, Fevvers becomes a star of the London music-hall and the imperial circus in St Petersburg; she survives an attempt at seduction by a Russian Grand Duke ('his voice glutinous with tumescence'), and she ends married to an American journalist in the wastes of Siberia where she, literally, has the last laugh when her new husband discovers that she is not 'the only fully-feathered intacta in the history of the world'. Carter's last novel, *Wise Children*, dwells on the glossy careers of theatrical twins, both dancers, and the illegitimate offspring of an eminent Shakespearian actor, a pillar of the 'legitimate' theatre. The narrative is in part an autobiographical quest to justify this Shakespearian descent, in part an exploration of sisterhood and interchangeable identity. It is also a *tour de force* of ventriloquism. Carter's narrating twin is chatty, digressive, and theatrically camp, but her voice also creates and subverts. She forges links between 'theatre' and 'literature' and she threatens to undermine neat gender definitions. 'It's every woman's tragedy', says one middle-aged twin to the other as they make up for a party, 'that after a certain age, she looks like a female impersonator'. 'What's every man's tragedy then?' asks the other. 'That *he* doesn't, Oscar', comes the pat post-Wildean reply. Carter was no man's fool. Nor was she any woman's.

In comparison to the work of their women contemporaries, the novels of John Fowles (b. 1926) and Anthony Burgess (1917–93) can seem strained, contrived, and forced. Fowles's *The Collector* (1963) is a post-Freudian fantasy, a first-person narrative supposedly written by a repressed, butterfly-collecting clerk who, having won the football pools, kidnaps (or collects) the sophisticated art-student whom he has admired from a distance. Fowles has continued to be fascinated by repression and by what he tends to see as its happy antithesis, the release of sexual energy which can be equated with personal liberation. In *Mantissa* (1982), this espousal of the cause of psychic and sexual liberation wastes itself in an explosive, self-indulgent erotic fantasy; in *The Magus* (1966, revised 1977), it is intricately translated into an omnifarious masque and a pro-liferating orgy of mythology and literature. In Fowles's most popular and admired novel, *The French Lieutenant's Woman* (1969), the juxtapositions of repression and release serve to dictate not just the novel's argument, but its narrative shape as well. The novel's narrator looks back, somewhat smugly, from the moral and narrative redefinitions of the 1960s, 'the age of Alain Robbe-Grillet and Roland Barthes', to the narrower determinants of doing and telling in the 1860s. He both appreciates the art of the Victorian novel and feels infinitely superior to it. His central characters, a Darwinian palaeontolo-gist, Charles Smithson, and the supposedly abandoned mistress of the French lieutenant, Sarah Woodruff, play out his theme for him. Both seek to break 'iron certainties', the social, moral, and religious conventions of their day, much as the narrator consistently endeavours to remind us of his presence and of his very present power. Sarah tricks and eludes Charles, just as the narra-tor rejoices in his own tricksy elusiveness. He admits in his thirteenth chapter (typically choosing what has always been regarded as a dangerous number) that he 'stands next to God', but insists that liberal modern novelists 'are no longer the gods of the Victorian image, omniscient and decreeing; but in the new theo-logical image, with freedom our first principle, not authority'. God-like to the end, he offers his readers a trinity of possible conclusions to the narrative; one conventionally happy; one unconventionally happy; the last uncertain and open. In the final chapter a 'rather foppish and Frenchified' figure, with 'more than a touch of the successful impresario about him', adjusts his watch and seems to obliterate the second possible ending. This impresario drives 'briskly' away, supposedly leaving Charles to his freedom and his doubts, but he remains a god who has declined to stop interfering.

Anthony Burgess's narrators tend to be just as knowing as Fowles's, but they are far less tricksy, cocky, and manipulative. Kenneth Toomey, the autobio-graphical narrator of *Earthly Powers* (1980), loves effects. His 'It was the after-noon of my eighty-first birthday, and I was in bed with my catamite when Ali announced that the archbishop had come to see me' is perhaps the most strik-ing opening sentence in modern English literature. But he also loves 'cunning' and 'contrivance' and he knows the power of popular story-telling. Toomey, a Catholic, a homosexual, and a successful writer, bestrides the twentieth century without seeking the status of a colossus. He travels across the five continents; he finds himself close to 'Hitler . . . Mussolini and the rest of the terrible people this terrible century's thrown up'; he strikes up acquaintances with

Joyce, Wyndham Lewis, Ford Madox Ford, and Kipling; and he finds himself the brother-in-law of a saintly, sybaritic (and fictional) Pope. As so often in Burgess's earlier work, *Earthly Powers* is an entertaining exploration of moral antinomy. In his futuristic fantasy, *The Wanting Seed* (1962), he had somewhat slickly proposed that human moral history could be seen as evolving cyclically, swinging between Augustinian ages ('Gusphases', in which the concept of original sin is paramount), 'Interphases', and Pelagian ages ('Pelaphases', in which liberal humanism triumphs). Burgess's preoccupation with the theology and sociology of sin also determines the argument of his most brilliant and experimental novel, *A Clockwork Orange* (also of 1962). It is a sharply anti-utopian vision of the technological future, told from the point of view of Alex, a 15-year-old delinquent who fantasizes about rape, assault, and murder while listening to Mozart. It also throws down two distinct challenges to its readers. When, in Part 2 of the novel, Alex is brain-washed into conformity ('committed to socially acceptable acts, a little machine capable only of good') it questions the sentimentally framed ideals of freedom and social responsibility which were dear to the liberal 1960s. Secondly, and perhaps more disconcertingly, Burgess renders his narrator sympathetic by contrasting his geniality and vitality with the numb, soullessness of the society which has produced his reaction. Moreover, Burgess seems to make his readers complicit in what Alex thinks and does by obliging them to share in his lexical rebellion and his lexical excitement. Alex expresses himself in 'nadsat', a Russian-rooted argot, which is abbreviated, aggressive, rich, and strange ('Then we slooshied the sirens and knew the millicents were coming with pooshkas ... That weepy little devotchka had told them, no doubt, there being a box for calling rozzes not too far behind the Muni Power Plant'). If Burgess's work as a whole does not manage to rival the epic vitality of Joyce's, *A Clockwork Orange* does at least shift something of Joyce's linguistic ingenuity into the age of subcultures.

In some ways the most 'typical' (at least in the sociological sense) of the English novelists of the 1960s and 1970s is Margaret Drabble (b. 1939). Her first novel, *A Summer Bird-Cage* (1963), is a first-person narrative describing the gossipy, sexually liberated, party-going worlds of a university-educated woman and her married sister. *Jerusalem the Golden* (1967) is a far more assured, and far less jerky, account of another woman-graduate, this time a girl growing out of the cultural and moral narrowness of her northern background and opening up to what we are led to believe are the sophistications of high-brow London (including its bohemian male adulterers). Of her novels of the 1970s, perhaps the most artful and suggestive is *The Ice Age* (1977), a novel centred not on a woman exploring the process of her social liberation, but on a series of interlinked relationships all of which humourlessly suggest something of the shabby and disappointed state of contemporary England. Drabble touches on corrupt property-developers and IRA bombs, on broken marriages and the alienations of upward social mobility, on rural withdrawal and on what was then the 'other world' of Eastern Europe (if awkwardly glimpsed as Walachia, 'the most obscure and mysterious of the Communist states', a benighted country where one of the characters cannot buy sanitary towels). Each novel's setting seems to imprison its, sometimes willing, occupants. The process of negotiating a release is, as so often in Drabble's work, a precarious and unsatisfying one. Her England is not so much a promised land as a focus of redundant promises.

Drama since the 1950s

After more than sixty years of proposals, high hopes, and false starts, Britain finally got its National Theatre in July 1962. More precisely, it got an official announcement that a National Theatre was to come into being. A Board was established and in October 1963 a National Theatre Company presented its inaugural production of *Hamlet* in the cramped, but venerable, surroundings of the Old Vic (the Company was not able to move the relatively short distance to its partially completed new building on the south bank of the Thames until March 1976). Since its inception, the National Theatre (from 1988, the Royal National Theatre) has always had serious rivals, in terms of both prestige and innovation. In the 1960s and 1970s Britain's other subsidized 'national' theatre, the Royal Shakespeare Company, established an enviable record of experiment (though it has since largely concentrated on the work of Shakespeare and his contemporaries). For a remarkable, if relatively brief, period, which began with the formation of the English Stage Company in 1956, one commercial theatre, the Royal Court, also seemed to lead the way in encouraging, commissioning, and presenting the work of new dramatists, both native and foreign. In their different ways, all three companies engineered a London-based theatrical revolution.

Although the National Theatre had called on the services of the unconventional Kenneth Tynan as its literary adviser, its choice of plays and directors was initially somewhat cautious. The Royal Shakespeare Company, by contrast, startled audiences out of any sense of stability and complacency with four particularly celebrated productions by the director, Peter Brook (b. 1925): a much admired and starkly Beckettian *King Lear* in 1962; a version of the German dramatist, Peter Weiss's, play known colloquially as the *Marat/Sade* in 1964; and, following Brook's exploratory 'Theatre of Cruelty Season', the experimental Artaudian commentary on the Vietnam war, *US*, in 1966. Perhaps most stunning and provocative of all was his complete rethinking of *A Midsummer Night's Dream* in 1970, a rethinking which swept away fairyland glades and gauzes and boldly substituted dazzling light, erotic gestures, and perilous acrobatics. When Brook declared that his production of the *Marat/Sade* had been designed to 'crack the spectator on the jaw, then douse him with ice-cold water, then force him to assess intelligently what has happened to him, then give him a kick in the balls, then bring him back to his senses again', he was stating an extremist principle of what has come to be known as 'director's theatre' (though it was a principle which could be said to have determined many of the effects of the 'political' theatre of the 1970s). It was not a principle on which the Royal Court generally worked. Its intellectual assaults were of a different, though not necessarily more subtle, order.

John Arden (b. 1930) was in many ways typical of a new generation of playwrights launched at the Royal Court: provocative, argumentative, brusque, and Anglo-Brechtian. Arden's *Live Like Pigs* (1958), a play about the resettlement of gypsies in a housing-estate, explores anti-social behaviour. It leaves the firm impression that 'respectability' and its official guardians, the police, were ultimately far more damaging to society than the unconventional mores of the play's gypsies. Arden's most celebrated and punchy play, *Serjeant Musgrave's Dance* (1959), addresses its anti-militaristic theme with a combination of Brechtian exposition and music-hall routines (dance, song, and monologue). Although the play grew out of contemporary circumstances (army conscripts, recruited under the system known euphemistically as 'National Service', had recently suffered casualties in the campaign in Cyprus), its setting is loosely Victorian. Its red military tunics, its black bibles, its narrow logic, and its unresolved social tensions are all designed to disconcert audiences and to raise questions about the principles of duty, rigidity, and order. When Arden reworked his play in 1972 as *Serjeant Musgrave Dances On* he gave it a far more overt and direct political message, one focused on the engagement of British troops in Ulster. *Serjeant Musgrave Dances On* may have grown out of Arden's steady questioning of British political, legal, military, and imperial traditions in plays such as *Left-Handed Liberty* (1965), *The Hero Rises Up* (1968), and *The Island of the Mighty* (1972), but it seems like a crude piece of *agitprop* in comparison to the rigorous scepticism of his earlier work.

Arnold Wesker's *Chips with Everything*, performed at the Royal Court in 1962, is also concerned with National Service, though in this instance with a fictional expansion on Wesker's own experience in the RAF. The play contains remarkable moments of concerted physical action by the group of recruits (notably a raid on a coke store), but it ultimately suggests that, despite official pretensions to the contrary, conscription was no leveller and no social panacea. Wesker (b. 1932) had earlier shown himself capable of creating a virtuoso visual theatre in his representation of alternating periods of action and inaction in a restaurant in *The Kitchen* (1959). Both kitchen and camp serve as metaphors for an unfair and hierarchical society in which the disadvantaged are forced to fall back on their chief resource, their proletarian vitality and their innate capacity for feeling. In his most substantial work, the so-called 'Trilogy' (*Chicken Soup with Barley* of 1958, *Roots* of 1959, and *I'm Talking about Jerusalem* of 1960), Wesker manages to relate his intense respect for working-class community to a social, historical, and political perspective stretching from the anti-Fascist protests of the Jewish East End in 1936 to the failure of a project to establish a new Jerusalem and a new idealist-socialist lifestyle in the Norfolk of the late 1950s. In all three plays, Wesker conveys an acute sense of place by capturing distinctive ways of speaking (both London Jewish and rural East Anglian) and representing the distinctive rhythms of urban and rural domesticity. In 1958 he announced that he would like to write plays not simply 'for the class of people who acknowledge plays to be a legitimate form of expression', but also for 'the bus driver, the housewife, the miner and the Teddy Boy [the type of adolescent who in the 1950s affected a fashion for vaguely Edwardian clothes]'. With this aim in mind, and with the high-minded hope of forging links between the arts, socialist action, and society at large, Wesker founded Centre 42 in 1960–1. The substantial Trade Union involvement that Wesker required was not forthcoming, but the project failed largely because popular taste proved to be more resistant to his ideals than he had expected. Centre 42 aimed at creating the conditions in which old-fashioned sweetness and light could filter down. It was checked by an upsurge of a new 'alternative' and genuinely popular culture and it foundered. With it, sank the urgency of Wesker's dramatic enterprise.

By far the most original, flexible, and challenging of the new dramatists of the late 1950s, Harold Pinter (b. 1930), was, like Wesker, the son of an East End Jewish tailor. Unlike him, however, he was an actor by training and profession. All Pinter's plays suggest a sure sense of the dramatic effect of pacing, pausing, and timing. Despite his determined protest against National Service as an 18-year-old, and despite his two brushes with the law as a conscientious objector, his early plays generally eschew direct political engagement and comment. They open up instead a world of seeming inconsequentiality, tangential communication, dislocated relationships, and undefined threats. Many of the dramatic *non sequiturs* of Pinter's first four plays—*The Room*, *The Dumb Waiter*, *The Birthday Party* (all written in 1957), and *The Caretaker* (written in 1959 and performed in the following year)—indicate how positive was his response to the impact of *Waiting for Godot*; their distinctive air of menace, however, suggests the influence of Kafka and the patterning of their dialogue a debt to the poetry and early drama of Eliot. In all four plays Pinter also reveals himself to be a master of a colloquial, vapidly repetitive, London English, one adept at varying the idioms of his characters' speech to striking and sometimes disturbing effect. In the most polyphonic of the early plays, *The Birthday Party*, he intrudes seemingly incongruous clichés about cricket and Sunday School teachers into Goldberg's volubly Jewish dialogue and he softens McCann's edgy bitterness with Irish sentimentality. Both characters threaten, and finally break, the inarticulate Stanley with a monstrous, staccato barrage of unanswerable questions and half-associated ideas: 'You need a long convalescence.' | 'A change of air.' | 'Somewhere over the rainbow.' | 'Where angels fear to tread.' | 'Exactly.' | 'You're in a rut.' |

'You look anaemic.' | 'Rheumatic.' | 'Myopic.' | 'Epileptic.' | 'You're on the verge.' | 'You're a dead duck.' | 'But we can save you.' | 'From a worse state.'

The Homecoming, first performed by the Royal Shakespeare Company in 1964, marks something of a turning-point in his career. Though the play opens familiarly enough in an undistinguished room in a north London house and with a one-sided conversation, an indifferent exchange of insults, and an ostensibly comic reference to an advertisement for flannel vests, it steadily veers away from comedy. Everything in the play is unspecific. The rhythms of Max's speech ('One of the loves of my life, Epsom?') suggest that the family may be Jewish, but nothing definite is made of the fact. More significantly, there appears to be a family tradition of unfaithful women, for parallels are loosely established between the dead but adulterous mother and her living daughter-in-law, Ruth, whom the male members of the family treat as if she were a whore. There are also often inexplicit frictions between generations and between the uneducated stop-at-homes and the homecoming son, Teddy, a professor at an American university. *The Homecoming* leaves a residual sense of sourness and negativity. Its most notable successors, *Old Times* (1971), *No Man's Land* (1975), and *Betrayal* (1978), all extend its calculated uncertainty and its (now gentrified) hints of menace and ominousness. All of them are distinguished by their teasing play with the disjunctions of memory and with unstable human relationships. *Old Times* presents its audience with an open triangle, defined not only by its characters, two women and a man, but also by silences, indeterminacies, and receding planes of telling and listening. In *No Man's Land*, two elderly men, and two younger ones, seem to shift in relationship to one another; they know and do not know; they remember and obliterate memory. *Betrayal*, cleverly based on a series of retrogressions, deals, ostensibly realistically, with middle-class adultery in literary London (though its reiterated ideas, words, and phrases reveal how artificially it is patterned). Since *One for the Road* (1984), Pinter's plays have shifted away from developed representations of uncertainty towards a far more terse and more overtly political drama. Both *One for the Road* and *Mountain Language* (1988) are insistently concerned with language and with acts of interrogation. As in *The Birthday Party*, language is seen as the means by which power can be exercised and as something that can be defined and manipulated to suit the ends of those who actually hold power. Nevertheless, the two plays focus on individuals threatened no longer by an unspecified menace, as Stanley was, but by the palpable oppression of (unnamed) modern states. Where Pinter's earlier work had allowed for indeterminacy, his latest work seems to have surrendered to an insistent demand for moral definition. The ideas of 'them' and 'us', which were once open, subtle, fluid categories, have been replaced by a rigid partisanship. The publication in 1998 of Pinter's own selection of his non-dramatic work, *Various Voices: Prose, Poetry, Politics 1948–1998*, has, in its very 'variety', helped to identify how, when, and why the playwright has chosen to articulate his creativity, his excitements, and his political incentives.

'If I ever hear you accuse the police of using violence on a prisoner in custody again', Inspector Truscott announces in Joe Orton's *Loot* (1966), 'I'll take you down to the station and beat the eyes out of your head.' As all his plays suggest, Orton (1933–67) has quite as refined a sense of the potential of the state, its institutions, and its human instruments to oppress the citizen as has Pinter. He had good reason to distrust the political system under which he lived, and, by extension, all systems of authority and control. He was an active, not to say promiscuous, homosexual in a period when homosexual acts between consenting males were still regarded as a criminal offence. He was himself brutally murdered by his long-term companion, and erstwhile collaborator, Kenneth Halliwell. In 1962 Orton and Halliwell had been prosecuted on the relatively trivial charge of stealing and defacing library books and sent to prison by a particularly authoritarian magistrate. Orton the artist fought back against authority with the two weapons he wielded most efficiently: anarchic comedy and priapic energy.

The five major comedies that Orton completed before his untimely death— *Entertaining Mr Sloane* (1964), *Loot* (1966, published 1967), *The Ruffian on the Stair*, *The Erpingham Camp* (both 1967), and *What the Butler Saw* (1969)— were calculated to outrage. When, in whimsical mood, he took to writing to the press and to theatre managers under the *nom de plume* of Edna Welthorpe (Mrs), he was parodying the kind of bourgeois respectability against which he had long defined himself. But what Edna described as his 'nauseating work' and his 'endless parade of mental and physical perversion' were not just symptomatic expressions of the liberal 1960s, but gestures of protest extrapolated from a long and perfectly respectable comic tradition. Orton never simply hid behind jokes. His comedy served not simply to expose the folly of the fool, the double standards of the hypocrite, or the unbalanced humours of everyman, but to disrupt the very status quo. Pompous asses though they may be, Orton's villains, such as Erpingham, are no fools. Caught out though they may be, Orton's fools, such as Drs Rance and Prentice, are no innocents. Exploited, abused, and tormented though they may be, Orton's innocents, such as McLeavy, are no wronged paragons. In *The Erpingham Camp*, the camp's owner may dream a vulgarian's dream of a future England sprouting 'Entertainment Centres' from coast to coast, but, as the play makes clear, Erpingham is as much in the business of social control as are the posturing psychiatrists, Rance and Prentice, and his sordid camp is as much a metaphor for an over-organized and explosively revolutionary state as is the private clinic of *What the Butler Saw*. Revolutions may be waylaid by guile and incompetence, but in no sense can the meek inherit Orton's earth. As McLeavy is dragged away by the police in *Loot*, he first protests his innocence and then wildly exclaims: 'Oh, what a terrible thing to happen to a man who's been kissed by the Pope.' In none of Orton's plays can innocence ever be a defence. For a man to be obliged to exit in the arms of police officers while recalling another man's kiss sounds more like carelessness than pathos.

Orton does not simply exploit the traditional forms of comedy and farce, but also dangerously transforms them. He takes an anarchist's delight in fostering disorder, but none at all in seeing why order can or ought to reassert itself. When he gestures to a Pinterian inconsequentiality at the opening of *The Ruffian on the Stair* he adds a *double entendre* of his own by giving Mike an appointment with a man in the toilet at King's Cross station. Even when he uses the conventional embarrassments of farce—its undressings, its incongruous dressings, and its cross-dressings—he manages to render them not merely suggestive but distinctly suspicious. Kath's removal of Sloane's trousers in *Entertaining Mr Sloane* is accompanied by the knowing declaration: 'I've been doing my washing today and I haven't a stitch on . . . I'm in the rude under this dress. I tell you because you're bound to have noticed . . .'. Alternatively, when Mrs Prentice finds her husband holding a woman's dress in *What the Butler Saw*, she first asks whether he had taken up transvestism and then adds: 'I'd no idea our marriage teetered on the edge of fashion.' Orton is at his most consistently *risqué* in the topsy-turvey world of *Loot*, a play in which the Oedipal jostles with the necrophilic and in which the old buttresses of social order—love, medicine, religion, and law—are systematically sapped. Here, as in all Orton's work, moral floors dissolve leaving a space which is both amoral and, by extension, apolitical. If some of his critics po-facedly condemn him for never exploring the consequences of the social questions he raises, it should be allowed that the very velocity of his verbal comedy never really allows him to stay for answers.

Where Orton's comedy is explosive, untidy, and unresolved, that of Tom Stoppard (born in Czechoslovakia in 1937) is implosive, symmetrical, and logical. Where Orton disorders the traditional elements of farce, Stoppard takes a fresh delight in the kind of theatrical clockwork that was perfected by Feydeau. Unlike Orton or Feydeau, however, Stoppard seems to take a deep intellectual pleasure in parallels, coincidences, and convergences that extends beyond a purely theatrical relish. In an age which has exhibited a fascination with the often extraordinary patternings of mathematical and metaphysical theory, he has emerged as an almost exemplary artist, one with an appeal to the pragmatic and the speculative alike. At their most brilliant, his plays are carefully plotted, logical mystery tours which systematically find their ends in their beginnings. *Rosencrantz and Guildenstern are Dead*, which opened at the National Theatre in April 1967 (the year following its first, amateur, presentation at the Edinburgh Festival), begins, according to its stage direction, with 'two ELIZABETHANS passing the time in a place without any visible character'. This is *Hamlet* playfully reread according to Einsteinian laws, Eliotic negatives, and Beckettian principles. Everything is rendered relative. The perspective is changed, time is fragmented, the Prince is marginalized, and two coin-spinning attendant lords are obliged to take on the weight of a tragedy which they neither understand nor dignify. *Rosencrantz and Guildenstern are Dead* deheroizes, but, despite its frantically comic surfaces, it never expels the impending sense of death implied in its title. Shakespeare's toadying gentlemen are transformed into two prosy commoners endowed with twentieth-century sensibilities, men trapped by their costumes, their language, and their characterless setting. Their tragedy, if tragedy it is, lies in their awareness of convergence, concurrence, and consequence: 'Wheels have been set in motion, and they have their own pace, to which we are . . . condemned. Each move is dictated by the previous one—that is the meaning of order. If we start being arbitrary it'll just be a shambles . . .'. However arbitrary life might appear to be, logic is relentless and the pre-existent and inescapable pattern of *Hamlet* determines that Rosencrantz's and Guildenstern's strutting and fretting must end, like real life, with death.

Much of Stoppard's subsequent drama introduces characters who are as much out of their intellectual and social depths as are Rosencrantz and Guildenstern. In the short radio play, *If You're Glad I'll be Frank* (1966), a bemused husband desperately tries to reclaim his wife who has become subsumed into a speaking clock. In *The Real Inspector Hound* (1968), a superbly poised parody of an English detective story, two theatre critics find themselves absorbed into a play and a murder which they assumed they had come to observe. In *Jumpers* (produced by the National Theatre in 1972) a moral philosopher preparing a lecture on the existence of God, and on the related problem of the objectivity of good and evil, is confronted by the murder of an acrobat at a party in his own home. As its title so succinctly and riddlingly suggests, *Jumpers* is about intellectual gymnastics, the making of mental and moral jumps and the construction of an unsteady philosophical architecture; it is also a *tour de force* of plotting. Henry Carr, the somewhat dim-witted central figure of what is perhaps Stoppard's most sustainedly witty and inventive play, *Travesties* (1974), is equally overwhelmed by the events in which he becomes involved. The play begins with a historical footnote (the real Carr, British Consul in Zurich, had taken James Joyce to court, claiming reimbursement for the cost of a pair of trousers worn in an amateur production of *The Importance of Being Earnest* performed in Zurich in March 1918), and a historical coincidence (Joyce, Lenin, and the Dadaist poet, Tristan Tzara, all used Zurich as a refuge from the First World War), but it develops into a complex, totally speculative, extrapolation of political and literary history. Stoppard shapes his own play around echoes, parodies, and inversions of Wilde's comedy and, to a lesser extent, of Joyce's *Ulysses*. None of his later plays has quite the same confident verve. His excursions into explicitly political drama—with the unwieldy script for actors and symphony orchestra, *Every Good Boy Deserves Favour* (1977), and the clever television play, *Professional Foul* (1978)—demonstrate an (at the time) unfashionable concern with persecution of intellectuals by the thuggishly illiberal Communist regimes of Eastern Europe. *Hapgood* (1988), with its carefully deployed twins, its double-takes, and its spies who explain the particle theory of light, does, however, suggest something of a return to his old whimsy, albeit a singularly menacing whimsy.

Stoppard's most subtle and allusive later play is *Arcadia* (1994), a brilliant fusion of complementary oppositions. The play is set in a room in a country house which remains constant for scenes set in Byron's England and in Stoppard's own time, while its language shifts easily from a staidly elegant Regency English to a more raucous and casual modern register. It is structured on a steady, progressive, and revelatory argument rather than on the cerebral fits and starts which characterized his earlier work. In 1998 *Arcadia* was accorded the singular honour of being the first play by a living foreign play-wright to be produced in translation at the Salle Richelieu at the Comédie Française. The shapely *The Invention of Love*, a study of conflicting strands in the life and culture of A. E. Housman, was first produced at the Royal National Theatre in London in 1997. It is in many ways a less challenging and more contrived play than *Arcadia* if one as surely marked by Stoppard's delight in conjuncture and convergence. Stoppard's complex, demanding, and ambitious trilogy *The Coast of Utopia* was first performed at the Royal National Theatre in London in the summer of 2002 (a production in Russian was mounted by the Moscow Arts Theatre in the autumn of the following year). The three plays, *Voyage*, *Shipwreck*, and *Salvage*, are set between the years 1834 and 1868 and move in setting from an aristocratic estate in provincial Russia, to Moscow, to Germany, to heady revolutionary Paris in 1848, to mid-Victorian London, and finally to neutral Switzerland. The plays are nuanced by a philosophical speculation typical of Stoppard's work and, more subtly, by the Russian liter-ary tradition and the culture that invented the word 'intelligentsia'. Stoppard's subject is the influence of Romantic idealism on backward Russia ('the Caliban of Europe') and the erratic development of revolutionary and utopian social-ist ideas amongst exiles from the stultifying social, cultural, and political con-servatism of the tsars. Thus they meditate on the way in which the political dilemmas of a 'backward' nineteeenth-century state fostered a revolution which in turn bore on the thought and the politics of the twentieth century. Stoppard's central character is the radical exile Alexander Herzen, a thinker who, having espoused the idea of Russian populism, finds himself at odds both with contemporary European liberalism and with the idea of the purposeful march of history towards the kind of utopia defined by Karl Marx. Throughout the trilogy the 'voyaging' Herzen is variously seen asserting his vision of a regenerated, populist Russian state against the irony and detach-ment of Turgenev, the strident anarchism of Bakunin, and the monolithic determinism of Marx (all of them characters in the plays). 'We have to open men's eyes and not tear them out,' Herzen declares in his final speech in *Salvage*, ' . . . and if we see differently, it's all right, we don't have to kill the myopic in our myopia . . . We have to bring what's good along with us.' The plays offer audiences a series of debating points but, unlike the history with which they deal, they seem to resolve nothing.

Whimsy, intellectual gymnastics, and symmetry are not qualities that most audiences would readily associate with the work of Edward Bond (b. 1934). Bond has always rigorously cultivated plainness in both expression and design. His career began at the Royal Court Theatre with versions of plays by, and exercises in the manner of Brecht, and it is to the radical, didactic German tradition that he has remained faithful. If he later proclaimed that, in contrast to Brecht, he considered it necessary 'to disturb an audience emotionally' by finding ways to make what he called the 'aggro-effect' more complete, it has generally been to the bald agonies of Büchner and to the psychological aggression of Wedekind that he has looked. *The Pope's Wedding* (1962) and *Saved* (1965), the first of his own plays to be performed, both concentrate on a *Woyzeck*-like inarticulacy and on an inherited lexical and emotional poverty in English working-class life which finds a natural expression in violence. In *Saved* an unloved, unwanted baby is, almost gratuitously, stoned to death by a gang of grunting youths ('Right in the lug 'ole', 'Get its 'ooter', 'An its slasher'). Bond shows violence as the inescapable consequence of the brutalization of the working class in an uncaring, stratified, industrial society. In the authorial note prefaced to the play he nevertheless speaks of *Saved* as 'irresponsibly optimistic', as a work which suggests the survival of innate goodness despite 'upbringing and environment' and despite the ostensible failure of inherited patterns of religion and morality. The lapidation, he provocatively insists, was a 'typical English understatement' compared to the 'strategic' wartime bombing of German cities and to 'the emotional deprivation of most of our children'. If, for writers such as Greene, Golding, Spark, and Burgess, the violence with which Bond habitually deals is rooted in the concept of original sin, for Bond himself that concept needed to be redefined as 'a doctrine of natural aggression', one determined by a manifestly unjust society. In *Narrow Road to the Deep North* (1968), *Lear* (1971), *Bingo* (1974), and *The Fool* (1976) anger and violence are seen not merely as the only means of self-expression open to the socially deprived but also as the engine of social change, both for good and for ill. These plays are concerned with power and the corruptions of power, and are all equally concerned with the stance of the artist who is faced with the evidence of such corruptions. In *Narrow Road*, the poet, Basho, a would-be detached idealist, is seen as indirectly responsible for the atrocities the play describes (his responsibility becomes far more direct in the 1978 revision of the play as *The Bundle*). In *Bingo*, Shakespeare, in his complacent bourgeois retirement, is complicit in the economic oppression of the poor, active in the emotional oppression of the women members of his family, but silent when it comes to effective social protest. In *The Fool: Scenes of Bread and Love*, John Clare, the working-class poet whose class anger is real enough, is forced into frustrated compromise and madness because he cannot find the ideological weapons with which to fight his oppressors. In the most emotionally challenging of Bond's plays, *Lear*, he not only drastically revises the King Lear story but also re-engages with Shakespeare's themes of blindness, madness, and the exercise of power. There is little room for what might conventionally or comfortingly be seen as 'poetry' or 'tragedy'. Bond's version is remarkable for its brutally stilted language, for its extravagant and unremitting representation of violence, and for its messy, clinical dissection of human nastiness. When Lear witnesses the autopsy performed on the body of one of his dead daughters, he declares that he has never seen anything so beautiful: 'If I had known this beauty and patience and care, how I would have loved her.' In Bond's *Lear*, love, like political and moral clear-sightedness, always remains a might-have-been.

'May 1968 was crucial', Howard Brenton wrote in an article published in 1975, 'It was a great watershed and directly affected me . . . [it] disinherited my generation in two ways. First it destroyed any remaining affection for official culture . . . it also destroyed the notions of personal freedom, anarchist political action.' For Brenton (b. 1942) the generation which matured in 1968, a generation 'dreaming of a beautiful utopia' was kicked, 'kicked awake and not dead'. The new, radical drama of the 1970s and 1980s, with which Brenton, Trevor Griffiths (b. 1935), David Hare (b. 1947), and David Edgar (b. 1948) were prominently associated, was essentially the product of the assimilated political and cultural lessons of the Parisian *événements* of May 1968. For Edgar, writing in 1979, the implications of what had happened in Paris were just as plain: 'Revolutionary politics was seen as being much less about the organisation of the working class at the point of production, and much more about the disruption of bourgeois ideology at the point of consumption.' Despite largely token attempts to take a new type of polemic drama to the factory floor, and despite the development of small, experimental theatre-groups and workshops, much of the new dramatic energy of the Left was specifically, but no less provocatively, addressed to a relatively élite, bourgeois audience and performed in relatively conventional theatre buildings. In 1976, when Brenton had begun to establish himself at the National Theatre, he proclaimed that he would rather have his plays presented to 900 people 'who may hate what I'm saying than to fifty of the converted'. Bourgeois ideology was indeed being challenged at its 'point of consumption', but, given the generally imperturbable quality of London audiences in the period, it was only minimally disrupted. Much of the political drama of the 1970s and 1980s was founded on the assumptions that rotten capitalist society was on the brink of collapse and that there was a widening division between 'them' (the surprisingly elastic ruling class which hung on to its inherited power with increasing cynicism) and 'us' (the ruled, for whom proper enlightenment preceded liberation). This perception of a deeply divided society was accentuated in the spring of 1979 by the Conservative victory in the General Election and by the twelve-year Prime Ministerial regime of Margaret Thatcher. The early Thatcher years were remarkable for the uniformity of theatrical protest against Government policies, philosophies, and philistinism (albeit a protest often voiced in state subsidized theatres). As Hare's *The Great Exhibition* (1972) and

Griffiths's *The Party* (1973) had already suggested, resistance to 'Thatcherism' went hand in hand with a sense of disillusion with the earlier compromises of the Labour Party and with the tendency to bickering and in-fighting amongst the British political Left.

Generally, the political drama of the period worked from a basis of Marxist theory informed by the example of 1968, but it rarely addressed problems beyond those of the local difficulties which beset post-imperial little-England. Much of it now seems distinctly time-locked. References to Ireland and to the troubles of Ulster were legion, but neither subtle nor especially direct (Brenton's *The Romans in Britain* of 1980 is a case in point). The world at large, and Europe in particular, tended to be glimpsed through carefully angled binoculars (as the somewhat conventional assumptions about the nature of Soviet influence in Eastern Europe in plays such as Edgar's *Maydays* of 1983 suggest). The implicit parallel between the manipulation of information in the Soviet Union and the corrupt control of the British press by an ambitious and unscrupulous newspaper tycoon in Hare and Brenton's collaborative play *Pravda: A Fleet Street Comedy* (produced at the National Theatre in 1985) is ultimately as slick as its criticism of capitalism is melodramatic. Hare's subtlety as a dramatist and a political analyst is more evident in *Plenty* (also produced at the National Theatre in 1978). *Plenty* (which was filmed in 1985) is a study of an intelligent and corrupted woman, a former undercover agent in wartime France who has pursued a career in advertising in post-war Britain ('In France . . . I told such glittering lies. But where's the fun in lying for a living? . . . Sold out. Is that the phrase?'). His interest in character, and in how characters shape and are shaped by the institutions to which they give their loyalty, also determined the often elusive texture of *Racing Demon*, an amused, almost Trollopian, study of how power is manipulated by the smug hierarchy of the Church of England. Trevor Griffiths, always adept at articulating debate, if rarely given to comedy, made one supremely successful and ambitious stab at exploring the political nature of humour in the play *Comedians* (1975). Although the play ingeniously outlines a sociopolitical thesis, it also allows for a singular variety of demonstration and exemplification. The retired comic, who has taught a class of aspiring comedians at a Manchester night school, devoutly insists that a true joke 'has more to do than release tension, it has to *liberate* the will and the desire, it has to *change the situation*', but his tuition is effectively subverted by the theatrical agent who favours those who support the status quo by retaining old racial and sexual stereotypes. The strength of Griffiths's play lies in its creative tensions and in its representation of a battle of wits in which no holds are barred.

Caryl Churchill's work has been equally rooted in opposition to a social system based on exploitation. Unlike her male counterparts, however, Churchill (b. 1938) has recognized an equation between the traditional power exercised by capitalists and the universal subjection of women. Her woman characters emerge as the victims of a culture which has regarded them merely as commodities or which has conditioned them to submit to masculine social rules. Her plays have systematically thrown down challenges either by reversing conventional representations of male and female behaviour (as in the Ortonian *Owners* of 1972) or by drawing disconcerting parallels between colonial and sexual oppression (as in *Cloud Nine* of 1979, with its ostensibly farcical shifts of gender and racial roles). In the multilayered *Top Girls* (1982) Churchill explores the superficial 'liberation' of women in the Thatcherite 1980s by contrasting the lifestyle of Marlene, a pushy, urban, woman executive, with that of her articulate, rural, stay-at-home sister. More pointedly, the first act of the play puts Marlene's supposed success in the context of the careers of other 'top girls', historical women who either became famous by usurping male roles (Pope Joan, and the Victorian explorer, Isabella Bird) or remained obedient to male-imposed stereotypes (the Japanese courtesan, Lady Nijo, and Patient Griselda). All except Dull Gret, a figure taken from a painting by Brueghel whom Brecht had apotheosized as the representative of peasant rebellion, have ultimately submitted and been sacrificed. The women rarely seem to understand how much their circumstances and experience overlap, though Gret, the uneducated rebel who later reappears as Marlene's rejected daughter, seems to offer an angrier, vaguer, but more genuinely radical kind of liberation. Churchill's cultivated talent for documentary *pièces d'occasion* achieved considerable commercial success with the apocalyptic and, at the time highly topical, study of the effects of stock market deregulation in the City of London, *Serious Money* (1987). More remarkable was *Mad Forest: A Play from Romania* (1990), the outcome of her work with a group of British drama students in Bucharest in the immediate aftermath of the Romanian revolution. It is a powerful and demanding study of competing truths and half-truths, perspectives and distortions, aspirations and disillusionments. Churchill's two interrelated short plays *Blue Heart* were produced in 1997. The first, *Heart's Desire*, is cleverly and often wittily based on a series of false starts and unexpected variations, while the second, *Blue Kettle*, disconcerts both through its gradual breakdown of language and through the deceptions and self-deceptions of the characters. Both plays seem to waylay dramatic catastrophe while allowing for the disruptions inherent in the idea of catastrophe.

The most distinctive and sharp-witted new woman playwright to emerge in the late 1990s is Shelagh Stephenson (b. 1955). Stephenson, whose early work was, like so much inventive and original work of the second half of the century, broadcast as radio plays by the BBC, wrote her first stage play *The Memory of Water* for the Hampstead Theatre in London in 1996. *The Memory of Water*, which explores the tensions and the convergent memories of three sisters reunited in their mother's seaside house on the eve of her funeral, is a remarkable achievement, tense, witty (sometimes outrageously so), and consistently tender. Stephenson's later plays, *Ancient Lights* (2000) and *Mappa Mundi* (premiered at the Royal National Theatre in 2002), share the wit, delicacy, and the often playful delight in recall of *The Memory of Water* but they lack something of its persuasive solidity.

Probably the most intelligent, challenging, and humane of the political playwrights who established a reputation in the 1970s and 1980s is the most senior, Brian Friel (b. 1929), an Irishman who has written almost exclusively about and for Ireland. *Philadelphia, Here I Come* (1964), written after he had abandoned his chosen career as a schoolmaster, deals with a young man's decision to escape from the frustrations of village life in County Donegal by emigrating to America, but it does so by presenting a would-be emigrant's dilemma through two actors who separately represent his public and private consciousnesses. *The Freedom of the City* (produced in 1973) is set in a dangerous Londonderry in 1970 as British troops attempt to disperse Catholic civil-rights marchers, three of whom take temporary refuge in the assertively Unionist mayor's parlour in the Guildhall. This same Guildhall has figured prominently in Friel's subsequent career as the prime venue for the productions of Field Day, a small touring theatre company which has had the distinction not only of transferring productions to London theatres but, far more importantly, of winning financial and popular support from both sides of the Irish border. The Field Day company has premièred two of Friel's most remarkably revisionist plays, *Translations* (its première production in 1980) and *Making History* in 1988. *Translations* opens in a hedge-school in an Irish-speaking community in the 1830s. Although the play's medium is English, it is built around an implied clash of languages (English, Irish, Latin, Greek), around attempts to find a common means of communication, and around juxtapositions of cultures. On one level, the British Army surveyors, working on the Ordnance Survey map of Ireland, are intruders who impose their fudged and alien nomenclature on pre-existent ways of seeing and naming; on another, they are the representatives of disinterested scientific advance, jumping the West of Ireland into European conformity. The play's ramifications are relevant to virtually every territory over which tribes, aspirant colonizers, and recalcitrant natives have disputed and claimed as their unique possession. *Making History*, by contrast, explores how the writing of history imposes ordered arguments, narrative patterns, and convenient interpretation on essentially disordered and inconclusive material. Friel's questioning of assumptions, manners, and inherited prejudices is also evident in his subtlest and densest play, *Dancing at Lughnasa* (premièred at the Abbey Theatre in Dublin in 1990, and presented at the National Theatre in London later in the same year). The play's narrator, an adult looking back on and re-enacting his boyhood in a Donegal cottage, is faced with a series of confusions and half-truths, but *Dancing at Lughnasa* as a whole deals with far more than the altered perceptions of maturity. Its supposed date, 1936, removes it from simply nationalist preoccupations, but places it squarely on the margins of other conflicts: a Spanish civil war which causes Irish Catholics to lean instinctively towards Franco, and Irish involvement in Catholic missionary work in Africa. The play does not simply question the inward-looking, self-protecting values of a tightly knit family, it also exposes the ostensibly Catholicized culture of rural Ireland to direct parallels with despised 'pagan' Africa. Its delicacy, sympathy, and lexical richness render it comparable to the plays of Synge. Its multiple layers of reference, its political tensions, and its open-endedness render recent English attempts to write either about Ireland or about the rural working class patronizingly crude by comparison.

Friel's brief, but hauntingly subtle, postscript to Chekhov, *Afterplay*, was premiered in Dublin in 2002. The play brings together Sonya Serebriakova from *Uncle Vanya* and Andrei Prozorov from *The Three Sisters* in a seedy café in Moscow in the 1920s. Both characters are now middle-aged and both are displaced and unfulfilled. They have an immediate rapport. We never really know whether or not the Russian Revolution has taken place or, if it has, what precise impact it has had on the circumstances of the two characters. There is certainly no evidence of a commitment to the 'new' society. Friel describes them as being unable to escape their origins and confesses that had he created them 'in the first place' he would have felt free to reshape them as he had wished: 'But they are not mine alone. I am something less than a parent but I know I am something more than a foster parent.' As with the original Chekhov plays, *Afterplay* shows us characters trapped in a situation the solution to which is always elusive. For Friel, as for Chekhov, solutions do not lie in easy formulae and glib resolutions.

Broad as has been the theatrical appeal of most of the dramatists discussed so far, none has been able to match the popular success and the prolific output of Alan Ayckbourn (b. 1939), who in 1976 managed to have five plays running simultaneously in London. Ayckbourn's success has been based not simply on his sure ear for ordinary conversation or on his sharp observation of the whims, vices, irrationalities, and snobberies of precisely the kind of people who come to see his plays, but on his ability to amuse and provoke without giving offence. He has few ideological axes to grind. Some of his rapport with the public at large can also be put down to the fact that his plays have become central to the repertoires of the numerous middle-brow, amateur theatrical companies which operate in a long and honourable (if generally non-innovative) English tradition.

Despite Ayckbourn's prominence on both professional and amateur stages, his work, like that of many other living and dead dramatists, has reached a mass audience only through the medium of television. Though it has often been despised as a vulgar and largely commonplace form of entertainment and though it has sometimes been disparaged as a mere popularizer, British television has consistently attracted creative talent. Whereas the London stage was remarkable in the 1980s for adaptations of classic novels—notably Edgar's dramatization of *Nicholas Nickleby*, produced by the Royal Shakespeare

Company in 1980, and the extraordinarily effective version of Laclos's *Les Liaisons dangereuses*, adapted for the same company by Christopher Hampton (b. 1946) in 1987—the tradition of high quality adaptation had been kept vigorously alive in the 1950s, 1960s, and 1970s both by the BBC and by commercial television companies. Though some critics have always deplored the idea of translating prose fiction into drama, it ought to be conceded that modern television companies were only continuing practices actively espoused by the theatrical contemporaries of Scott and Dickens. New serialized versions of novels by Dickens (originally a serial novelist, of course) and Jane Austen were the classic staples of early television, their evident appeal to viewers encouraging now celebrated, sometimes lushly visualized, adaptations of works by Galsworthy (*The Forsyte Saga*, BBC 1969), Trollope, Graves, and Waugh. These versions have had an extraordinary success outside Britain, notably so in America and when they were shown on Soviet and Eastern European state television. Both the BBC and Independent television have proved enterprising patrons of more run-of-the-mill, but none the less thoughtful and socially responsive, serials in the form of vastly popular, long-running soap-operas, the most established of which is Granada Television's *Coronation Street* (which began in December 1960).

It is, however, as a patron of new drama that British television has performed an invaluable service to working writers and to their prospective audiences. Although at one stage the BBC prudishly decided that Osborne's *Look Back in Anger* was 'not suitable for a television audience' (the play was, however, transmitted by Granada), it later made honourable amends by commissioning new work by Beckett, Pinter, and Stoppard. Nevertheless, television's most solid contribution to artistic innovation has been through the evolution of a specific kind of drama shaped by the special resources of the medium. This innovation has been especially associated with Alan Bennett (b. 1934) and Dennis Potter (1935–94). Bennett, who has also maintained an active involvement with the theatre (his play *The Madness of George III* was produced by the National Theatre in 1991), has been adept at working with particular actors and particular themes. His *An Englishman Abroad* (BBC 1983), a piquant re-creation of the brief encounter in Moscow of the British spy, Guy Burgess, with the actress Coral Browne (who appeared in the production), uses both small and large spaces, cramped rooms and suggestions of Moscow theatres, streets, and churches. His series of monologues, *Talking Heads* (BBC 1990), however, concentrated on intimacy, on suggestive camera angles, and, above all, on physiognomies, glances, and revelatory turns of phrase. A second series of *Talking Heads* was broadcast in 1998. Potter is far more exclusively associated with television. His *Alice*, a version of Lewis Carroll's stories, was the first of a series of relatively shocking 'Wednesday Plays' broadcast by the BBC from December 1962, and his paired dramas about the career of an upwardly mobile Member of Parliament (*Vote, Vote, Vote for Nigel Barton* and *Stand Up, Nigel*

Barton, both 1965) suggested a quite new, far from deferential response to Establishment politics. Potter's later works—notably the six-part drama *Pennies from Heaven* (1978), the intense evocation of childhood disaster (in which the children's parts were played by ungainly adults), *Blue Remembered Hills* (1979), and the supremely ingenious intermixture of music, fantasy, sex, crime, and physical disease, *The Singing Detective* (1989)—suggest how profoundly television has been able to contribute to a still developing dramatic literature.

Other Humps: British and Irish Poetry from the 1960s

The considerable span of the poetry of Ted (Edward James) Hughes (1930–98) plays wolfish, unfriendly, but ultimately, and to some readers surprisingly, tender games with mortality. Hughes's first two volumes, *The Hawk in the Rain* (1957) and *Lupercal* (1960), express a rapt fascination with animal energy and independence and an awareness of the affinities between animal and human life, between human aspirations to freedom and power and the instinctive animal achievement of both. A caged jaguar in a zoo, 'on a short fierce fuse', is compared to a solitary visionary pacing his cell. A macaw in 'a cage of wire ribs | The size of a man's head' is provoked into 'conflagration and frenzy' by a little girl's caresses and tantrums. The intense physicality of 'The Bull Moses' is recalled in the 'warm weight of his breathing, | The ammoniac reek of his litter, the hotly-tongued | Mash of his cud', but the bull's gait as he is returned to his stall suggests that he was not named 'Moses' idly: 'something deliberate in his leisure, some beheld future | Founding in his quiet.' Hughes's otter 'brings the legend of himself', his pikes swim in a pond 'as deep as England', and his 'terrifying' thrushes, with their 'single-mind-sized skulls', possess an 'automatic purpose' parallel to that of a Mozart or to 'the shark's mouth | That hungers down the blood-smell even to a leak of its own | Side and devouring of itself'. Strikingly, Hughes compares his own creative purpose to a vulpine visitation in 'The Thought Fox'. The poem opens with an insistent act of imagination and with a 'blank page'. The fox approaches with stealth:

> Cold, delicately as the dark snow,
> A fox's nose touches twig, leaf;
> Two eyes serve a movement, that now
> And again now, and now, and now
>
> Sets neat prints in the snow,
> Between trees . . .
>
> Across clearings, an eye,
> A widening deepening greenness,
> Brilliantly concentratedly,
> Coming about its own business

> Till, with a sudden sharp hot stink of fox
> It enters the dark hole of the head.
> The window is starless still; the clock ticks,
> The page is printed.

When, in his most anthologized poem. 'Hawk Roosting', Hughes represents the consciousness of an animal, the hawk expresses its animal single-mindedness with an unmistakably human arrogance ('There is no sophistry in my body: | My manners are tearing off heads'). Hughes's language seems more taut in the interspersed prose and verse of *Wodwo* (1967) (a volume named from the wild men of the woods of *Sir Gawain and the Green Knight*), but his earlier experiments with the violent meshes of animal and human sense culminate in the gnomic sequence of poems *Crow: From the Life and Songs of the Crow* (1970, amplified 1972). Crow is a survivor, a blackly comic speculator about the inadequacy of the old definitions of the relationship of the Creator to his Creation, and the weaver of new myths about a God who sometimes sleeps and who occasionally perversely co-operates in the negatives of his adversaries. Crow himself plays pranks, refuses to learn the word 'love', and re-enacts aspects of the stories of Adam, Oedipus, Ulysses, and Hamlet. The poems intertwine and redefine established ideas by means of brash assertions and intense, even brutal stabs at meaning.

None of Hughes's subsequent volumes seemed to possess the same abrupt intensity until the appearance of his *Tales from Ovid: Twenty-four Passages from the Metamorphoses* (1997). Ovid's poem provides a story-line and a focus, for here Hughes's old fascination with violence and the strange fusion of the wild and the human takes on a new, sensuously charged power. There is also a fresh precision derived from the discipline of translation (or, in this case, metamorphosis, from Latin to English). Myrrha's transformation from woman in labour to a gnarled and weeping tree has a particularly agonized force about it:

> The earth gripped both her ankles as she prayed.
> Roots forced from beneath her toenails, they burrowed
> Among deep stones to the bedrock. She swayed,
>
> Living statuary on a tree's foundations.
> In that moment, her bones became grained wood,
> Their marrow pith,
>
> Her blood sap, her arms boughs, her fingers twigs,
> Her skin rough bark. And already
> The gnarling crust has coffined her swollen womb.
>
> It swarms over her breasts. It warps upwards
> Reaching for her eyes as she bows
> Eagerly into it, hurrying the burial
>
> Of her face and her hair under thick-webbed bark.
> Now all her feeling has gone into wood, with her body.
> Yet she weeps,

The warm drops ooze from her rind.
These tears are still treasured.
To this day they are known by her name—Myrrh.

Just as remarkable in their way is the sequence of poems celebrating the sometimes fraught, sometimes transfiguring love between Hughes and his first wife,
Sylvia Plath, who committed suicide in 1963. *Birthday Letters* (1998) describes
a continuing relationship with a restless wife and fellow poet through memory
and a precise recall of what was lost, what gained, and what survived. Shortly
before his own death Hughes wrote to a friend that he had once thought of the
poems as 'unpublishably raw and unguarded, simply too vulnerable'. The publication of the poems, he said, had given him a 'sensation of inner liberation—
a huge sudden possibility of new inner experience'. The wound and the
wounding, like the agonies of those transformed in the *Tales from Ovid*, had
also opened the way for a newly demanding, introspective, and often unexpected poetry, a poetry of readjustment.

Hughes's sly verse grew out of the distinctive dialect of his native West
Yorkshire, a dialect which the poet himself saw as connecting him 'directly and
in my most intimate self to Middle English poetry'. A quite distinct alertness to place and to the ramifications of local and historical speech is evident
in the work of Geoffrey Hill (born at Bromsgrove in the West Midlands in
1932). Although it can be equally bloody, Hill's England is far less demonic,
lonely, and wild than Hughes's. Where Hughes uses instinct and myth to
feel himself into a poetic space beyond recorded history, Hill has consistently
sifted through archaeological strata and explored human landmarks and
human residues. His particular fascination with English medieval history was
evident in his first volume *For the Unfallen* (1959), though the sonnet 'Re-
quiem for the Plantagenet Kings', with its overarching concept of 'caved
chantries, set in trust | With well-dressed alabaster and proved spurs', is
juxtaposed with two 'Formal Elegies' (again sonnets) for the Jews of Europe
slaughtered in the 1940s by those who believed that they had superseded
dynasties and elegies alike. All three poems are about the propriety of
requiems and elegies and about how human memories are formed and conditioned. *King Log* (1968), which opens with a poem about poetic choices
and evasions ('Ovid in the Third Reich'), also contains 'Funeral Music', a
sequence of eight unrhymed, fourteen-line poems written in commemoration
of three noblemen beheaded during the Wars of the Roses. Hill's 'essay'
on the sequence, published as an appendix to the volume, describes it as an
attempt to suggest 'a florid grim music broken by grunts and shrieks'. The
first poem, which recalls the dying command of John Tiptoft that he should
be decapitated in three strokes 'in honour of the Trinity', plays decorative vanity against ritual decorum, judicial murder against echoes of heavenly
order:

Processionals in the exemplary cave,
Benediction of shadows. Pomfret. London.
The voice fragrant with mannered humility,
With an equable contempt for this world,
'In honorem Trinitatis'. Crash. The head
Struck down into a meaty conduit of blood.
So these dispose themselves to receive each
Pentecostal blow from axe or seraph,
Spattering block-straw with mortal residue.
Psalteries whine through the empyrean . . .

This is the violent, sticky, unstable political world of Shakespeare's histories, but the fierce polyphony that Hill evolves from the 'grunts and shrieks' of the fifteenth century is decidedly his own. The thirty *Mercian Hymns* (1971) eschew the tortured lyricism of 'Funeral Music' in favour of a prosy, Modernist play with anachronism and incongruity. The hymns are a tribute to the great Anglo-Saxon king Offa, who ruled over the Midlands kingdom of Mercia in the late eighth century, and a celebration of Hill's own history. His Offa is king of then and now, at once the 'King of the perennial holly-groves' and the 'overlord of the M5'; a man who is proud to be the friend of Charlemagne and one who rules a land of gasholders, car parks, and charabancs. Past and present coexist and fluidly inform one another, easily so in the ninth poem (the account of a family funeral) and somewhat more restlessly in the twenty-fifth (which interlocks John Ruskin's complaints about the miserable conditions in which women nail-workers worked in the nineteenth century with the experience of his own grandmother 'whose childhood and prime womanhood were spent in the nailer's darg'). In the twentieth hymn the fanciful names of modern suburban villas are also, far less innocently, the names of the battles which determined the destinies of early England. Clashes of colour replace clashes of culture:

Primeval heathland spattered with the bones of mice
    and birds; where adders basked and bees made
    provision, mantling the inner walls of their burh:

Coiled entrenched England: brickwork and paintwork
    stalwart above hacked marl. The clashing primary
    colours—'Ethandune', 'Catraeth', 'Maldon',
    'Pengwern'. Steel against yew and privet. Fresh
    dynasties of smiths.

The smiths are both Offa's craftsmen and the modern inheritors of the commonest of British surnames. In his later volumes, *Tenebrae* (1978) and *The Mystery of the Charity of Charles Péguy* (1983), Hill moved beyond the matter of Britain towards a wider exploration of the problems of pain and death. In the 'Lachrimae' poems included in *Tenebrae* he returned to the densely worked

sonnet forms of his earlier work (though with reference to Renaissance spirituality and music), but in his extended tribute to the nationalist Catholicism
of Péguy, Hill investigates a new landscape, that of the war-torn fields of an
uneasy France. *The Triumph of Love* (1999), is made up of a varied series of
150 lyrics, at times jauntily flippant, at times ironic, even splenetic, at others
disarmingly hymn-like and meditative. Hill's customary themes—history, war,
the Holocaust, Midlands' landscape, music, poetry, faith and unfaith—are
revisited with glancing but often dense reference to the literature and the
echoing voices of the past. In the last lines of the antepenultimate lyric
(CXLVIII) he stabs at a definition of poetry which might serve to describe
much of his own achievement:

> What
> ought a poem to be? Answer, *a sad*
> *and angry consolation*. What is
> the poem? What figures? Say
> *a sad and angry consolation*. That's
> beautiful. Once more? *A sad and angry*
> *consolation*.

In a lecture given in 1976, and reprinted in his collection of essays
Preoccupations (1980), the Irish poet Seamus Heaney (b. 1939) traced a 'defensive love of their territory' through the work of Larkin, Hughes, and Hill, a
love 'which was once shared only by those poets whom we might call colonial'.
Heaney counts himself amongst the 'colonials', but, as other essays in the
volume suggest, he is fully aware of the doubleness and division of his
inheritance. 'I speak and write in English', he noted in an article written in
1972, 'but do not altogether share the preoccupations and perspectives of
an Englishman . . . and the English tradition is not ultimately home. I live
off another hump as well.' That other 'hump' is Ireland, or more particularly
the rural Ulster which figures so delicately, richly, and painfully in his
verse. His Irish inheritance is multiple. Heaney's *Death of a Naturalist* (1966)
and *Door into the Dark* (1969) wonderingly recall and reconstruct a
familiar childhood landscape peopled by farmers (both Catholic and
Protestant), labourers, and fishermen. In *Wintering Out* (1972) and its two successor volumes, *North* (1975) and *Field Work* (1979), Heaney broods less on a
private, remembered landscape and more on an island full of 'comfortless
noises', the Northern Ireland of the 'troubles'. His 'hump' is now a place in
which successive strata of history continue to determine the perceptions of the
present. In 'Tinder', flints, 'cold beads of history and home', serve to spark
recall of a prehistoric past. In 'Mossbawn: Two Poems in Dedication'—the
memorial lyrics which preface Heaney's most obviously 'political' volume,
North—he extends his perspective from his father's farm to include a larger,
troubled Ulster and the relationship of the distinctive history of that province
to the long and contentious history of Ireland as a whole. Part I of the volume

opens with 'Antaeus' (a reference to the giant whose strength came from touching his mother, the earth). It is followed by 'Belderg', a poem in which history emerges from the soil as 'quernstones out of a bog' and is implicit in the very name of the Heaney farm, 'Mossbawn' ('He crossed my old home's music | With older strains of Norse . . . I could derive | A forked root from that ground | And make *bawn* an English fort, | A planter's walled-in mound | Or else find sanctuary | And think of it as Irish'). These four strains, the prehistoric, the Gaelic, the Norse, and the English, continue to haunt and open up the volume as a whole. Although many of the poems deal directly with the present, with 'neighbourly murder', with Orange drums 'like giant tumours', and with blasted streets where 'the gelignite's a common sound effect', Heaney also sees the rifts in Irish life as rooted in a long history of occupation and imperial influence. 'Freedman' acknowledges parallels to ancient Roman slavery in subjugation to the culture of the Roman Church ('I was under that thumb too like all my caste'), but 'Viking Dublin: Trial Pieces', 'Bone Dreams', and 'Punishment' variously recognize the prefigurations of modern anxieties which are contained in Ireland's archaeological and linguistic subsoil. 'Bone Dreams' and the volume's title poem see 'dictions' and 'past philology and kennings' as an inheritance which obliges an Irish poet to come to terms with the Teutonic roots of the imperial language, English. In 'North', a sharply focused glance back to Viking Ireland, and to Norse enterprise and Norse ruthlessness, leads into a reflection on how a poet can use a language buried, like an alien treasure, in his native soil. A voice, associated with 'violence and epiphany', but, like some Viking longship, 'buoyant with hindsight', offers the advice:

> 'Lie down
> in the word-hoard, burrow
> in the coil and gleam
> of your furrowed brain.
>
> Compose in darkness.
> Expect aurora borealis
> in the long foray
> but no cascade of light.
>
> Keep your eye clear
> as the bleb of the icicle,
> trust the feel of what nubbed treasure
> your hands have known.

This is no retreat into the historical memory but a discovery of a poetic potential as liberating as Yeats's 'terrible beauty'. The Scandinavian burial mound, with its recalls of *Beowulf* (a poem which has continued to fascinate Heaney) and Sutton Hoo, offers an epiphanic transcendence of history. Heaney, who was awarded the Nobel Prize for Literature in 1995, has continued his explorations of landscape, language, and memory in the volumes published since *Field Work*—*Station Island* (1984), *The Haw Lantern* (1987), *Seeing Things* (1991), and *The Spirit Level* (1996)—though the verse in each suggests a new chastity of expression when compared with the sensuous early poetry and the sharp crystallizations of *North*. 'Postscript', the last poem printed in *The Spirit Level*, returns with a fresh exhilaration to the empty, Atlantic-buffeted west coast of Ireland:

> And some time make the time to drive out west
> Into County Clare, along the Flaggy Shore,
> In September or October, when the wind
> And the light are working off each other
> So that the ocean on one side is wild
> With foam and glitter, and inland among stones
> The surface of a slate-grey lake is lit
> By the earthed lightning of a flock of swans,
> Their feathers roughed and ruffling, white on white,
> Their fully grown headstrong-looking heads
> Tucked or cresting or busy underwater.
> Useless to think you'll park and capture it
> More thoroughly. You are neither here nor there,
> A hurry through which known and strange things pass
> As big soft buffetings come at the car sideways
> And catch the heart off guard and blow it open.

Heaney's fellow Ulsterman Derek Mahon (born in Belfast in 1941) shares with him a sense of an Ireland which can open up, through history and arte-facts, into a larger European cultural identity. Mahon's first volume of verse, *Night-Crossing*, which appeared in 1968, was marked as were its successors, *Lives* (1972), *The Snow Party* (1975), *The Hunt by Night* (1982), and *Antarctica* (1985), by a quiet wit and an intellectual sophistication. His work is cosmo-politan both in its broad reference and in its subject matter, often suggesting an affinity with that of Louis MacNeice in its sense of the nuances of places and things (the poem 'In Carrowdore Churchyard' recognizes a parallel between MacNeice's resting place and the dead poet's 'play of shadow' and 'humane perspective'). Irish places figure prominently enough in Mahon's work ('Glengormley', 'Day Trip to Donegal', 'A Disused Shed in Co. Wexford', 'North Wind: Portrush'), and memories of the narrowness of his God-fearing Protestant roots show in the distaste for a remembered Belfast Sunday epitomized by 'the | dank churches, the empty streets, | the shipyard silence, the tied-up swings' ('Ecclesiastes'), but he is often at his most eloquent when he sees Ireland mirrored, or even transfigured, in new and sometimes surprising contexts. This is wonderfully caught in 'Courtyard in Delft', a tribute to the meticulous representation of commonplace, well-swept bour-geois houses in the paintings of Pieter de Hooch:

That girl with her back to us who waits
For her man to come home for his tea
Will wait till the paint disintegrates
And ruined dikes admit the esurient sea;
Yet this is life too, and the cracked
Out-house door a verifiable fact
As vividly mnemonic as the sunlit
Railings that front the houses opposite.

I lived there as a boy and know the coal
Glittering in its shed, late-afternoon
Lambency informing the deal table,
The ceiling cradled in a radiant spoon.
I must by lying low in a room there,
A strange child with a taste for verse,
While my hard-nosed companions dream of fire
And sword upon parched veldt and fields of wind-swept gorse.

There is no such thing as 'timelessness' here. The placid Protestant courtyard, and the dreamy, poetic Protestant child may seem to be detached from Calvinist militancy (whether Dutch, Boer, or Orange and Irish) but, as the poem acknowledges, in certain charged places fire and sword, and avowals of 'No Surrender', lurk menacingly on the margins of quotidian decency and respectability.

The verse of the prolific English poet and translator Tony Harrison (b. 1937) has also consistently investigated the significance of native sounds, lurking native dangers, and native roots. Harrison, born and educated in Leeds, and resident in Newcastle, has, despite his frequent references to a wider world beyond Britain, emerged as an emphatically urban poet. More particularly, he is a poet of the industrial North of England who has explored the cultural rift that divides his educated adult eloquence and acquired 'sophistication' from the abrupt reticence of his working-class boyhood. He introduces *The School of Eloquence* (1978) with two quotations, the first (from which his own title derives) from E. P. Thompson's *The Making of the English Working Classes* (1963), the other from Milton's Latin poem *ad Patrem* ('To his Father'). To these quotations he adds 'Heredity', a short prefatory lyric of his own:

How you became a poet's a mystery!
Wherever did you get your talent from?
I say: I had two uncles, Joe and Harry—
one was a stammerer, the other dumb.

Harrison's own poetry gushes with a joy of release from impediments to speech. At times his adjectives, his metaphors, and his classical references seem to tumble over each other as prodigally as do Keats's. At others, and notably in his striking translations of the *Oresteia* and of plays by Molière, Racine, and Hugo, he writes with an expressive immediacy. This is particularly true of his versions of the medieval religious plays published in 1985 as *The Mysteries*, versions which are firmly rerooted in Harrison's own gritty Yorkshire English and in the continuing culture of the North. His urban poems, however, tend to look at cities from oblique angles. His Durham is culturally trisected as 'University, Cathedral, Gaol'; his York is contracted to a malodorous telephone kiosk; his Leeds is untidy, sooty, and war-scarred; his Newcastle, so exotically celebrated in 'Newcastle is Peru' (1970), is the city of the 'sluggish Tyne meandering through | the staithes and shipyards of Peru' where 'commerce and contraceptives glide | and circle of the turning tide'. Harrison's long quatrain poem *v* (1985) draws together many of the recurrent themes of his verse. As its abbreviated title (*v* for *versus*) suggests, it is a poem of contentions. It moves from the Leeds graveyard where his parents are buried, through an imagined dialogue with the inarticulate skinheads who have defaced the headstones with obscene graffiti, to a brief pondering of local demographic changes, and, finally, to 'Home, home to my woman, where the fire's lit'. As so often in his work, coal, coal dust, and coal fires represent the tangible fibres of working-class England, its pressed seams of meaning, its securities, and its distinctive but combustible values.

Fin de siècle: Some Notes on Late-Century Prose

'Each moment seems more urgent than all preceding ones,' the journalist Malcolm Muggeridge wrote in his neglected study *The Thirties* (1940), 'each generation of men are convinced that their difficulties and achievements are unparalleled'. The temptation to define the circumstances of the last decade of the twentieth century as unparalleled remains, as does the inclination of any given generation to see its cultural achievement as more significant and lasting than might its descendants. Official divisions of time into decades and centuries are arbitrary, of course, and, as with regnal dates, they have little operative effect on what is written or who writes it. Yet we continue to place great, but often casual, emphases on decades and centuries and in the Christian (or post-Christian) world much will be made of the end of a millennium. At such a juncture, looking back at where we have come from may prove to be more healthy than predicting how the present will influence the future. It would be presumptuous to attempt to draw any firm or precise conclusions as to the state of English literature in the last decade of the twentieth century, the last ten years of the second Christian millennium. Assuming the privilege of a historian, it is possible to suggest loose parallels, not necessarily with Muggeridge's 1930s, but with two other last decades, the closing years of the eighteenth and the nineteenth centuries, and thereby to observe that it would probably be foolish to attempt to be either categorical or prophetic. Our present, as Muggeridge observed, makes us myopic as well as arrogant. How literature might, or will, have developed twenty or thirty years hence is the business of the writers who will make it develop, not of prescriptive critics. In common with the 1790s and the 1890s, the 1990s look set to be a decade of uncertainties and redefinitions, and, yet more, of false starts, blind alleys, reiterations, and tired reaffirmations. There are certain periods (the 1830s was one; the 1930s another) when the *Zeitgeist* declared itself; but there are many others when contemporaries singularly miss the point about what will really matter to later generations in how they thought, acted, and wrote. While it was clear to the men and women of the 1790s that the period would have to come to terms with the political implications of the French Revolution, relatively few contemporary British critics and readers clearly identified what now seem to us the leading literary spirits of the time. The British and Irish 1890s were dominated by already established writers, but, with the exception of W. B. Yeats, very few of the new, young, and supposedly avant-garde writers of the decade did in fact determine how the Modernist revolution of the early twentieth century would be realized. Nor did they manage to influence the development of the non-Modernist Edwardian novel. What seemed, and seem, to be leading cultural lines lead nowhere. What strikes some observers as conservative may in fact be radical. What looks like a byway may be a high road. What assertive and high-minded critics insist is a contemporary canon of excellence, formed by particular perceptions of unparalleled 'difficulties and achievements', is nearly always wrong, sometimes spectacularly so.

What is certain is that the literature of the late 1990s lacks the tutelary presence of a major writer or writers. But literature flourishes none the less. British writing could be said to be living off the accrued fat of the twentieth-century past. The novel at least has little of the intellectual bite of recent work produced in the Americas. It also seems to be taking its time in assimilating the import of the substantial changes that have taken place in the world since the end of the Cold War, since the fragmentation of the Soviet Empire and its former satellites, and since the resurgence of Islam and the redefinitions of Orthodox and Catholic Europe. It may claim to have taken post-colonialism in its politically correct stride and it may have awkwardly flirted with the notion of 'multiculturalism', but it will have to learn the true significance of other histories and other ways of telling stories. The 'plural' Britain which has existed since the constitutional changes of the 1830s should more readily have learned its lessons. Despite the United Kingdom's prominent place in the European Union and despite the significance of the English language both to Europe and to the world as a whole, English literature still shows a marked tendency to be insular and to dwell on a narrow view of the past. The resurgence of a sense of Scottish identity in the 1980s and 1990s has not necessarily stimulated a literature north of the border which could be seen as either 'liberated' or non-insular in its rejection of the polite parameters of 'Englishness'. Although the recent novel in both England and Scotland likes playing games with narrative, and with the idea of narrative, it has relatively few grand ideas and rather fewer epic pretensions. Rarely, too, does it have much sense of literary style. As old assumptions go, as old ideologies turn rancid, as old borders are superseded, as some nations tear themselves apart or as others attempt to live in unprecedented intimacy with one another, so a future English literature might respond with new forms, sounds, subjects, and preoccupations. But then it might not. Stuffy, smug little-Englandism (or little-Scotlandism) would, however, seem unlikely to be capable of nourishing the embryonic writing of the twenty-first century.

In the 1990s the novel has remained the most accessible, the most discussed, the most promoted, and the most sponsored literary form. Literary prizes, such as the annual Booker Prize, founded in 1969 on the model of the French Prix Goncourt, have helped to stimulate an interest in new fiction which cannot be anything but healthy (even though many of the prize novels have not truly justified the temporary prestige they thus acquired, and many fine novels have been overlooked, or deliberately ignored, by the prize juries concerned). Judging from the work of new, or newish, novelists over the past fifteen years, the forms and subjects of the late twentieth century remain plural but conservative despite, or perhaps because of, the plethora of contemporary narrative theory. What some critics chose to identify under the catch-all term of 'post-Modernism' seems to have entailed both a return to the basic challenges posed by the pioneer experimentalists of the early century, and, by extension, a degree of subversion of the very assumptions upon which traditional and early-Modernist fictional forms were based. The novel has properly reflected 'modernity', the changes in how we think, move, and have our modern being, and the fragmentation and chaos which are supposed to characterize contemporary life. It has also had to readapt, modify, and question the Modernist insistence on new, or multiple, kinds of meaning. It has often shown itself to be singularly awkward and inept in these adaptations.

The 'campus fiction' of the 1970s and 1980s may still prove to have life in it. These novels, set in universities and colleges or dealing with wayward academics let loose on the wider world, both reflected American models and developed the line established in British fiction by Larkin's *Jill* (1946). Larkin was the dedicatee of Kingsley Amis's *Lucky Jim* (1954), a comic account of a would-be radical lecturer's floundering attempts at resistance to the culture of a provincial university, a culture which proves itself to be both earnestly pretentious and complacent. In *One Fat Englishman* (1963) Amis turned to a British visitor's experiences in an American college. While 'lucky' Jim Dixon had been a typical enough 'angry young man' and the portly Roger Micheldene the model of the kind of Englishman who grimly kicks against the pricks of the American way of life, in the hands of three slightly less manic writers the 'campus novel' of the 1970s served to reflect the academic ambitions and the academic tensions of the rapidly expanding world of higher education in the period. Tom Sharpe (b. 1928) proved to be the most vivacious *farceur* amongst them, extravagantly tripping up the good intentions of a technical college lecturer in *Wilt* (1976) and its sequels *The Wilt Alternative* (1979) and *Wilt on High* (1985) and literally exploding the unresolved frictions within a corrupt Cambridge college and its members in *Porterhouse Blue* (1974). Malcolm Bradbury (b. 1932) has shown himself to be a writer who is less concerned with fads and diversions than with façades and distortions. Bradbury's *The History Man* (1975) is a study of a smugly radical sociologist at a new university, one who has published books which are 'in consort with the times' and whose slickly packaged analyses are seen as symptomatic of what often passed for social criticism in the years following 1968 ('to understand [his radical transformation], Howard, always a keen explainer, always explains, you need to know a little Marx, a little Freud, and a little social history'). The texture of Bradbury's *Rates of Exchange* (1983) is less abrasive. The book, together with its witty fellow-traveller, the spoof guide book *Why Come to Slaka* (1986), offers a telling account of the profound ambiguities, inconveniences and mendacities of travelling in the unreconstructed Communist east of Europe before the fall of the Berlin wall. Bradbury's novel makes extensive and clever play with ideas of disparity and exchange (his central character, Petworth, on a British Council lecture tour in 'Slaka', is 'an expert on real, imaginary and symbolic exchanges among skin-bound organisms working on the linguistic interface, which is what linguists call you and me'). When one persistent Slakan asks Petworth if he knows a 'campus-writer Brodge' most of Bradbury's readers would have recognized the distortion as a yoking together of his own name with that of a fellow professor of literature, David Lodge (b. 1935). Lodge's novels *Changing Places: A Tale of Two Campuses* (1975), *Small World: An Academic Romance* (1984), and *Nice Work* (1988) are all loosely centred on the University of Rummidge. Where the first two novels deal with academic misunderstanding and intellectual crossed wires, the third explores the non-communication between representatives of Rummidge's university Arts faculty and its city's industry. Nevertheless, all three novels are self-consciously *literary* in the sense that they seek both to explore the implications of literary theory and to prod inherited narrative shapes into new life. Where *Small World* reinvigorates mediaeval concepts of pilgrimage and quest (shooting them through with a final Wildean contrivance), *Nice Work* takes up the themes and compromises of Gaskell's *North and South* and genially allows characters alienated by circumstances and prejudices to formulate a new basis for understanding. *Nice Work* deals with a British university suffering from cuts in its resources and staggering under the burden of the Benthamite ethics and calibrations imposed on it by central government. It is just possible that those same insistent economic, pedagogic, and structural reforms, which continued into the late 1980s and 1990s, have served irrevocably to change the once relatively leisurely and benign (though not always tolerant) culture of academe. As with the very phenomenon of academics who find sufficient time to write fiction, so the 'campus novel' may strike future readers as a quaintly telling period piece.

Broadly speaking, more recent British fiction can be seen as having explored four particular areas of interest: it has, sometimes outrageously, continued the development of the well-established Anglo-Scottish Gothic tradition into a new kind of urban fiction; it has sought a newly distinct expression of issues of gender and sexuality; it has tried out new varieties of historical writing; and it has begun to widen its horizons to include writers and subjects stemming from the old colonial Empire and from a wider world. All four areas have overlapped, been interwoven, and been allowed to inform one another. The neo-Gothic, so brilliantly engineered to suit her feminist ends by Angela Carter, has been taken up, in their very individual ways, by two distinctly urban, but distinctly dissimilar writers—Ian McEwan (b. 1948) and Alasdair Gray (b. 1934). McEwan's cultivatedly precise narrative *The Cement Garden* (1978) is the account of the private disposal of a corpse under domestic cement, a cement which reflects the drab uniformity of a London of concrete tower blocks standing 'on wide aprons of cracked asphalt where weeds were pushing through'. It established a disconcerting but chaste narrative manner on which McEwan has subsequently built in his *The Comfort of Strangers* (1981), *Black Dogs* (1992), and *Amsterdam* (1998), a somewhat diagrammatic and dispiriting study of euthanasia. In the sophisticated and often witty *Atonement* (2001), however, McEwan explored the consequences of an imaginative child's speculations and experiments. Although set in the 1930s, the novel glances back to Jane Austen. It not only uses the idea of an unperformed play, it also raises dark questions hinted at in its opening citation of a passage from *Northanger Abbey*. Gray's two most ambitious novels, *Lanark: A life in Four Books* (1981) and *Poor Things* (1992), fantastically re-imagine Glasgow. Both novels draw from the English and Scots Gothic traditions, the former acknowledging its multiple debts to the Modernists, the latter elaborately replaying themes from Mary Shelley and James Hogg against a backdrop of Scottish medicine and art. A very different Scottish experiment is evident in the violent, hallucinatory world of Irvine Welsh's *Trainspotting* (1993). Welsh (b. 1958) has a youthful cult following largely based on the verbal and vernacular freneticism of his novel and on its exaggerated impressions of a reeling Edinburgh drug culture. His later work retains an evident relish in shaking, even insulting, his readers into responding, but lacks the comic flair of his first novel. The cosmopolitan, but equally urban fiction of Martin Amis seems staid by comparison. Amis (b. 1949), the author of the ambitious *Money: A Suicide Note* (1986), the acclaimed *London Fields* (1989), and *Time's Arrow* (1991), is perhaps the most self-consciously 'American' writer of his generation. Amis has been fascinated by the distortions and tergiversations of city life, and he has cleverly intellectualized the kind of patterns so easily established in the 1940s by Raymond Chandler, and, as *Time's Arrow* shows, he can play artfully with narrative time. Nevertheless, despite their substance, his novels can also suggest a certain slickness and a triumph of structure over content.

Jeanette Winterson (b. 1959) began her career in 1985 with *Oranges Are Not the Only Fruit*, a witty, bitingly perceptive study of a provincial childhood passed within the narrow, women-dominated confines of an evangelical

Christian sect. It was also an avowedly lesbian novel of escape into a more open kind of gynocentrism. She has experimented since with two fantastic, quasi-historical novels, *The Passion* (1987) and *Sexing the Cherry* (1989), both of which fuse elements of the male and the female, the past and the present, and with a clever, non-gender-specific love-story *Written on the Body* (1992), an exploration of a loved woman's body which combines an intense, would-be poetic passion with clinical exactitude. *The Virgin in the Garden* (1978) and *Possession* (1990), the two most substantial and demanding novels of A(ntonia) S(usan) Byatt (b. 1936), also play with shifting perceptions of the past and the present and with the interrelationship of verse and prose. *The Virgin in the Garden* is set in 1953, the year of the coronation of Elizabeth II, and around the performance of a celebratory verse-drama concerned with the Virgin Queen, Elizabeth I. *Possession* alternates accounts of the modern researches of two young academics with a vivid, gently assembled, reconstruction of the once secret love-affair of the objects of their academic research, two Victorian poets. Byatt's imitations of the work of these imagined poets (loosely based, we suppose, on Robert Browning and Christina Rossetti) constitute one of the most sophisticated achievements of recent fiction.

Avowedly 'gay' fiction has been less impressive in its ambitions, its persuasiveness, and its general appeal (certainly so when compared to its transatlantic equivalent). The work of Alan Hollinghurst (b. 1954) has an extraordinary verbal poise and a chastity of expression which contrasts with its often overcharged, and deliberately indulgent, eroticism. His first novel, *The Swimming Pool Library* (1988), was much praised for its innovative daring by its first critics, but his second, *The Folding Star* (1994), is a far more refined, and haunting, achievement both in terms of its evocations of landscape and seascape and in its enigmatic and often elusive account of an obsessive pursuit. *The Spell* (1998) is far less compelling. Of novelists who have dealt delicately, but frankly, with HIV and AIDS two stand out for their sensitivity and their literary tact: Adam Mars-Jones (b. 1954) and the Irish writer Colm Tóibín (b. 1955). As Tóibín noted in an essay published in 2001, 'the gay past in writing is sometimes explicit and sometimes hidden, while the gay present is, for the most part, only explicit'. A painful aspect of this new explicitness is manifest in both writers' accounts of the physical embarrassments caused by the AIDS virus and the torments and steady decay of its victims. Tóibín's work is, however, far from narrowly death-haunted; it is, rather, characterized by its use of memory, both personal and historical, both private and public. *The Story of the Night* (1996) is concerned with the dilemmas faced by a homosexual man in the ambiguous and often fraught world of Argentina in the years following the Falklands War. His painfully beautiful *The Blackwater Lightship* (1999) is, however, confined to Ireland and particularly to the coastline of County Wexford (which had earlier figured in *The Heather Blazing* of 1992). *The Blackwater Lightship* explores how the steady physical decay of a brother forces some kind of reconciliation between a mother and a daughter long alienated from one another. Perhaps the most subtle and well-designed recent study of homoerotic obsession is Neil Bartlett's *Mr Clive & Mr Page* (1996). Bartlett (b. 1958) has made his career in the theatre, as a director and playwright, but his novel, set in a repressed, and characteristically reserved, London of the 1920s and 1950s, interconnects events, places, and people which seem initially to be severed one from another by time, environment, and class. It has a subtle mystery which partly derives from the cautious uncertainties and evasiveness of its narrator.

A similar meticulous ingenuity and alertness to the strangeness of the past is evident in Charles Palliser's historical novel *The Quincunx* (1989). Palliser (b. 1945) has scrupulously recreated a Victorian narrative, shaping it according to a precise fivefold pattern. In some senses it is a connoisseur's book, but like Umberto Eco's *The Name of the Rose* (which it resembles to some degree) it has also appealed broadly to *aficionados* of the mystery story and to unreconstructed admirers of tidy and resolved plots. Palliser's second historical novel, *The Unburied* (1999), set in a cathedral city, returns to the idea of an evolving Victorian mystery but interweaves it with an older and equally dark murder story. With its cast-list of feuding clerics, disgruntled artisans, investigative academics, and unexplained phenomena it looks back self-consciously to the dangerously haunted and wintry worlds of M. R. James (1862–1936), the minor master of the English ghost-story. The new historical novel, of which *The Quincunx* and *The Unburied* are relatively conservative examples, has also flourished in the hands of Peter Ackroyd (b. 1949), the author of, amongst other novels, *The Last Testament of Oscar Wilde* (1983), *Hawksmoor* (1985), *Chatterton* (1987), and *Dan Leno and the Limehouse Golem* (1994), and of biographies of T. S. Eliot (1984), Dickens (1990), and Blake (1996). Ackroyd has proved himself a particularly impressive ventriloquist, echoing the inflexions of the dying Wilde in the earlier novel and imagining confessional voices of the seventeenth, eighteenth, and nineteenth centuries in the three later ones. The finest of the four, *Hawksmoor*, cleverly juxtaposes then and now, exploring the career of a murderously necromantic church architect of the 1690s (who is *not* called Hawksmoor, despite his passing resemblance to the real and innocent architect of that name) and the latter-day detective work of a policeman (who *is* called Hawksmoor). The idea of juxtaposing supposedly contradictory narratives, each of which explores a historical murder mystery from a different angle, has been taken up with real learning and panache by Iain Pears (b. 1955) in his *An Instance of the Fingerpost* (1998). The resolution of the narrative, set in late seventeenth-century Oxford, finally hinges on the explorative Baconian mind of the antiquarian Anthony Wood, though what Wood disentangles proves to be an amalgam of state secrets, spiritual mysteries, and human accidents.

There is little that could be described as accidental in Matthew Kneale's compelling study of the human effects of British colonialism in Tasmania in the early and middle years of the nineteenth century, *English Passengers* (2000).

Kneale (b. 1960) deftly deploys a variety of narrators including an earnestly naive clergyman in search of the site of the Garden of Eden, a Manx sea-captain, and a determined theorist of British racial superiority. But the most persuasive of these narrators is Peevay, a native Tasmanian who bears testimony to the steady extermination of his race in a quirky English sprinkled with archaisms, strangenesses, and swear words ('Once when I was small and always running hither and thither, and all the world was puzzles to confound, I got myself that little surprise. Even now that bugger does stir tenderest feelings deep inside my breast. Other fellows might lose their way after that ruination, never to find it after, but not me. I did endure'). Kneale's fascination with language is equally evident in his appending of an Anglo-Manx glossary at the end of his narrative. The most ambitious sequence of late twentieth-century historical novels remains Patrick O'Brian's series of naval stories set between 1800 and 1815. The twenty volumes, sometimes known by the shorthand term 'the Aubrey–Maturin novels', are so named from its contrasted principal characters, the highly professional naval officer Jack Aubrey, and his friend the secretive doctor–spy Stephen Maturin. The sequence began in 1970 with *Master and Commander* and continued until the publication of *Blue at the Mizzen* in 1999. O'Brian (1914–2000), who was born Richard Patrick Russ, seems personally to have delighted in the elusiveness which so characterizes Dr Maturin. His novels, which combine elements of the swashbuckling adventure story with careful research and an acute observation of humankind in a particularly charged historical context, acquired something akin to cult status towards the end of his writing career. O'Brian's novels do much more than imaginatively re-create a lost world of square-rigged men-of-war; they explore ambitions and ever-present dangers, tangled motives and matters of honour, and, above all, the singularity of life at sea.

A quite different blend of ingenuity, literary detective work, and biographical reconstruction is evident in Julian Barnes's wry search for an elusive fellow-novelist in *Flaubert's Parrot* (1984). Barnes (b. 1946) plays with his careful, but somewhat bemused, narrator's obsession with fact as much as he delightfully toys with the fictional form that evolves under Flaubert's indirect tutelage ('I thought of writing books myself once. I had the ideas; I even made notes. But I was a doctor, married with children. You can only do one thing well: Flaubert knew that . . . The unwritten books? They aren't a cause for resentment. There are too many books already. Besides, I remember the end of *L'Education senti-mentale* . . .'). Graham Swift's perspective in his subtle, thoughtful novel *Waterland* (1983) is less drawn out but quite as decidedly historical. Swift's learnedly digressive narrator is a history teacher in a London school threatened with the extinction of his subject by a 'progressive' headmaster. He is also a reassembler of an agonized private and familial past, a past rooted in the East Anglian fens. There is no escaping existence, he writes, 'even if we miss the grand repertoire of history, we yet imitate it in miniature and endorse, in miniature, its longing for presence, for feature, for purpose, for content'. For

Swift (b. 1949) historic occasions conspire and combine just as surely as his ubiquitous watercourses feed into one another and carry the flotsam of evidence down towards the sea. Pat Barker's *Regeneration* trilogy (*Regeneration* (1991), *The Eye in the Door* (1993), and *The Ghost Road* (1995)) suggests a return to the 'classic' mode of historical fiction, intermixing real historical figures (Robert Graves, Siegfried Sassoon, Wilfred Owen, and their sympathic doctor W. H. R. Rivers) with invented ones (notably the working-class officer Billy Prior). Barker (b. 1943) shows her real originality, however, in her investigation of the emotional trauma experienced by soldiers on the Western Front during the First World War, both through an account of their treatment by Rivers, and by a description of the tangled and self-deceiving affairs of Billy Prior. The novels speak of enforced loneliness in a world in which comradeship and male-bonding often seem to be the only means of holding together a violently fragmenting experience. Barker's 'coda' to the trilogy *Another World* (1998) is far less satisfactory, though it again recognizes, as so much other literature in late twentieth-century Britain recognizes, the centrality of the Great War to the mood and manners of the century. As the central character contemplates the monument to the 'Missing of the Somme' at Thiepval he is repelled by it and then considers further: 'If, as Nick believed, you should go to the past, looking not for messages or warnings, but simply to be humbled by the weight of human experience that has preceded the brief flicker of your own few days, then Thiepval succeeded brilliantly.'

The history of the fragmented, and still fragmenting, former British Empire has held a notable fascination for other recent novelists. Victorian India has in particular attracted the restorer of the boy's adventure story for adult readers, George Macdonald Fraser (b. 1925). Three of the ten raffish volumes of the so-called 'Flashman Papers', dealing with the supposed career of the ex-villain of *Tom Brown's Schooldays* (the first of which appeared in 1969; the latest in 1994), have dealt variously with the Afghan war of 1842, with the British acquisition of the Punjab, and with the Mutiny of 1857. Far less provocatively schoolboyish is J(ames) G(ordan) Farrell's *The Siege of Krishnapur* (1973), an account of British common sense, British eccentricity, and British arrogance in a besieged and crumbling Residency during the Mutiny (or Sepoy Rebellion). Farrell (1935–79) offers a chronicle of events as seen from the perspective of the rulers and not the rebels, but it allows the flickering debates of the characters to illuminate the 'perplexing' question of the imperial mission and of British pretensions to cultural superiority. 'Things are not yet perfect, of course,' Farrell's Collector sighs. 'All the same, I should go so far as to say that in the long run a superior civilization such as ours is irresistible. By combining our advances in science and morality we have so obviously found the best way of doing things. Truth cannot be resisted!' But, as a round shot hits the roof, he is obliged to add: 'Er, that's to say, not successfully.' Farrell's flailing description of a peculiarly Anglican religious controversy in Victorian Simla in his unfinished *The Hill Station* (1981) has little of the verve of his earlier novel. The ultimate failures of British rule in, and, more significantly, of British attitudes to, India had earlier been yet more impressively explored in Paul Scott's four novels known collectively as the 'Raj Quartet' (*The Jewel in the Crown* of 1966, *The Day of the Scorpion* of 1968, *The Towers of Silence* of 1971, and *A Division of the Spoils* of 1975). Scott (1920–78) deals broadly with India during the Second World War and with its uneasy progress towards independence and partition, but his concentration on the complex, interconnecting careers of certain key characters also allows him gradually to establish an elaborate jigsaw, whose logic is only fully revealed once the picture is completed in the concluding volume. Scott's last novel, *Staying On* (1977), deals with two ageing minor characters from the earlier sequence, both of them social misfits, who have decided to eke out a living on an army pension and who are obliged to adjust to the circumstances of the (to them) disconcertingly new, independent India.

Quite the most striking and inventive single novel to discuss India's transition from Raj to Republic is Salman Rushdie's *Midnight's Children* (1981). Rushdie, born of a Muslim family in Bombay in 1947 and educated in England, deals phantasmagorically with a rising generation of Indians, born as midnight on 15 August 1947 ushers in independence and with it a new era of communal tension. Rushdie's central character, Saleem Sinai, is 'handcuffed to history', peculiarly endowed with a series of accentuated perceptions which allow him to explore his family's and his nation's twentieth-century destiny. 'Reality is a question of perspective,' he writes, 'the further you get from the past, the more concrete and plausible it seems—but as you approach the present, it inevitably seems more and more incredible.' Rushdie's own 'handcuffing' to history rendered him an especially effective, sensitive, and observant commentator on India for non-Indian readers. As the bitterly divided reception of his *The Satanic Verses* (1988) has shown, however, he has found himself handcuffed in a very different way. The novel offers its readers a further phantasmagoria, but now one with an international and multicultural dimension in which time and destiny, good and evil, the secular and the religious, the material and the spiritual are dangerously and inventively interfused. This interfusion has been read by many Muslims as deliberate confusion and as wilful blasphemy. In contrast, Rushdie's *The Moor's Last Sigh* (1995) is apparently more lighthearted in its tone and subject, playing wittily as it does with family history and cultural conjunctions (rather than clashes) within a pattern of kinship. Rushdie is, however, far from alone in his awareness of how non-European and multicultural awareness can shift the sometimes narrow temporal and intellectual perspectives of European, and specifically British literature. Timothy Mo, born in Hong Kong in 1950 of an English mother and a Cantonese father, has deftly described the closed, protective, alienated, and opportunistic society of the London Chinese in *Sour Sweet* (1983). More ambitiously, in the panoramic *An Insular Possession* (1986), he attempted to explore the beginnings of Britain's last surviving major outpost of Empire,

Hong Kong, as a trading colony following the shabby so-called 'Opium War' of 1839–42 (Hong Kong was reunited to China in 1997). Quite distinct, and far less easily or glibly characterized as 'post-colonial', is the work of the Japanese-born Kazuo Ishiguro (b. 1954), whose novel *An Artist of the Floating World* (1986) is a delicate fictional study of an ageing painter's awareness of, and detachment from, the political development of twentieth-century Japan (the 'floating world' of his title being a happy, and nicely ambiguous, translation of the Japanese term for the nineteenth-century wood-block prints so much admired by Europeans). When Ishiguro writes directly about Britain, as he does in his finely observed study of class and deference *The Remains of the Day* (1989), he manages to ask equally delicate, carefully framed, but none the less demanding cultural questions. The novel's retrospective butler–narrator, Stevens, sees the country houses in which he once worked as the 'hub' around which 'the world was a wheel'. 'It was the aspiration of all those of us with professional ambition', Stevens remarks, 'to work our way as close to this hub as we were each of us capable.' *The Remains of the Day* suggests how deference and tact manage to distort a perspective which is at once present and historical. Ishiguro's *When We Were Orphans* (2000) is an occasionally gripping account of a London detective's belated quest to find the parents and the world he lost as Shanghai fell to Japanese troops in the 1930s. As ever in Ishiguro's work, explanations often seem elusive and unenhancing.

Perhaps the most revealingly successful of the 'newly emergent' novelists of the 1990s has been Louis de Bernières (b. 1954). His three vivid, cruelly witty, and imaginatively titled novels set in a fictional South American country, *The War of Don Emmanuel's Nether Parts* (1990), *Señor Vivo and the Coca Lord* (1991), and *The Troublesome Offspring of Cardinal Guzman* (1992), all suggest a debt to the 'magic realism' associated with the work of Gabriel García Márquez. But it was with his *Captain Corelli's Mandolin* (1994) that de Bernières attracted a wide public to his fiction. His sensuously detailed and wonderfully tactile novel, set on the Greek island of Cephallonia during the period of its occupation by the Italians during the Second World War, has in many, perhaps unexpected, ways restored, even reinvented the love-story. It is a chaste enough love-story in twentieth-century terms, but one imbued with other unexpected late twentieth-century elements: clarity, joy, dignity, selflessness, and heroism.

The deep uncertainty of the late twentieth century and early twenty-first century about the nature and quality of its literary culture has become depressingly evident in the spate of questionnaires and surveys, commissions and committees, all of which have attempted either to draw up lists of 'classics' or to determine what is the 'book of the century'. In January 1997 a chain of British booksellers and an independent television channel announced the results of a survey in which some 25,000 people had been asked to assist in drawing up a list of the 100 best books of the century. No particular criteria for how the word 'best' might possibly be defined seem to have been used and, as a consequence, the final list looked both singularly arbitrary and distressingly predictable. There were a great number of children's books, a sprinkling of non-fiction, and a high percentage of autobiography. There was no poetry and no drama. Of the 'top ten' books four were North American and one South American in origin; two were by George Orwell, and one (*Ulysses*) was by James Joyce. Nevertheless, *Ulysses* in fourth place was ranked lower than Tolkien's *The Lord of the Rings* and was only five places above Irvine Welsh's recently published *Trainspotting*. A year later the Government's 'Millennium Commission' joined forces with a publisher in a project to give 250 works of literature to 4,500 schools in Britain. It was obviously an attempt to redress the balance in favour of the 'classics'. The 250 works were drawn from world literature, but again British and Irish writers dominate the selection and even here the choice seems determined by a certain degree of political correctness, or, at the very least, political convenience. The only poet writing after Keats is W. B. Yeats; the only dramatist writing after Shakespeare is Oscar Wilde, and the only post-Second World War novelists are Orwell, Waugh, Beckett, and Salman Rushdie (with *Midnight's Children*). In 1998 the BBC bravely, but again arbitrarily, selected 100 'seminal artistic works' for a radio series called *The Centurions*. Only ten of the international 100 works of art were by women and of these three were novelists (Woolf's *The Waves*, Murdoch's *Under the Net*, and Lessing's *The Golden Notebook*). What really marked the selection, however, was not its presumed masculine bias, but its tendency to see the 'seminal' as the equivalent to 'Modern'. The year 1999 has seen the choice of Shakespeare as the 'British Personality of the Millennium' by listeners to a popular news programme and the publication of a series of essays by forty-seven 'esteemed writers, journalists, publishers and critics' in an attempt to define the nature of a 'classic'. When the contributors' definitions were boiled down to make a list of 'essential classics for the next hundred years', it appeared that there was no drama and very little which passed for poetry. This is especially disturbing given consistent innovation evident in the British theatre and the flourishing state of poetry in late twentieth-century Britain and Ireland. One great narrative poem, *Paradise Lost*, just about gained its place on the list, but in competition with the choice of two works by A. A. Milne and of three novels each by Martin Amis, Angela Carter, and Salman Rushdie (though Dickens managed five and Joyce four!). What remains revealing is that, despite the fact that it appeared in the first quarter of the twentieth century, *Ulysses* was regularly selected as the greatest 'classic' novel of that century (though one contributor admitted that she could not get through it and another was prepared to dismiss it as 'simplistic tosh').

What this delight in list-making indicates is the generally low state of cultural appreciation and criticism in modern Britain. What passes for high culture is all too often the result of a short memory and a low concentration span. Both dismal states of mind have been encouraged by a decline in the standard of journalism at precisely the period when journalists, in radio and television as much as in the press, have assumed a powerful influence in forming and exploiting public opinion. It would be idle to suggest that there could be a return to the demands presented to readers by the great periodicals of the nineteenth century, but it is difficult not to mourn what we have lost. Too much has been squandered in the name of easy-reading and easy-listening. Axe-grinding passes for sharp intelligence, prejudice for discrimination, glibness for wit, and mutual flattery in a closed party circuit for the life of the literary salon. A great deal of the enterprise of journalist–critics in the late twentieth century resembles that of sextons who dig graves for literary reputations, clear up round the tombs of the dead, tend dung heaps, and (to use Dickens's memorable phrase) make hay of the flesh that is grass. Perhaps the condition of modern 'Literary London' differs very little from that which presaged the triumph of Alexander Pope's 'great anarch' at the end of *The Dunciad*, and perhaps again the impending darkness will lift. We can only look forward to new dawns.

What remains encouraging, despite the depredations of those whose influence ought to be better used, is the general health and variety of the literature of the British Isles. Not only are more 'classics' available in accessible form than ever before, but the flourishing sales of Austen, the Brontës, Dickens, Eliot, Hardy, and Woolf testify to the continuance of a discriminating and demanding reading public. Contemporary writing and contemporary publishers can only benefit from the competition. If Shakespeare is chosen as the representative Briton of the millennium, and *Ulysses* is regularly selected as the novel of the century, it can only be hoped that the twenty-first century will rise to the challenge presented by the extraordinary richness of the inherited literary past.

CHRONOLOGY

EVENTS

1170 Murder of Becket

1189 Death of Henry II

1204 Loss of Normandy
1215 Magna Carta

1221–4 Arrival of Dominican and
Franciscan friars in England

1314 Battle of Bannockburn
1327 Accession of Edward III
1337 Beginning of Hundred Years
War
*c.*1343 Birth of Chaucer
*c.*1344 Order of Garter founded
1346 Battle of Crécy
1348 First occurrence of the Black
Death in England

1377 Death of Edward III; accession
of Richard II
1381 The Peasants' Revolt
1384 Death of Wyclif

1394 Birth of Charles d'Orléans and
James I of Scotland
1399 Deposition of Richard II; accession of Henry IV
1400 Death of Chaucer; murder of
Richard II
1408 Death of Gower

1413 Death of Henry IV; accession of
Henry V
1415 Battle of Agincourt

LITERARY WORKS

1184–6 Andreas Capellanus, *De amore*
*c.*1188 Gervase, *History of Canterbury*

*c.*1200 *The Owl and the Nightingale*;
Laȝamon, *Brut*; Jocelin of Brakelond, *Chronicle*

*c.*1220 *Ancrene Riwle*

*c.*1225 *King Horn*
*c.*1275 Guillaume de Lorris, *Roman de la
rose*

*c.*1370 Chaucer, *Book of the Duchess*
*c.*1377 Langland, *Piers Plowman* (B Text)

*c.*1385 Chaucer, *Troilus and Criseyde*
*c.*1387 Chaucer begins *The Canterbury
Tales*
1390 Gower, *Confessio Amantis*

*c.*1400 Sole surviving MS of *Sir Gawain*,
Pearl, *Cleanness*, and *Patience*

1411–12 Hoccleve, *The Regiment of
Princes*

EVENTS

LITERARY WORKS

1535 Thomas More executed

1536 Anne Boleyn executed; William Tyndale burned in the Netherlands; union of England and Wales

1536–9 Dissolution of the Monasteries

1540 Institution of the Society of Jesus; fall and execution of Thomas Cromwell

1545 Council of Trent opens

1547 Death of Henry VIII; accession of Edward VI

1549 Act of Uniformity

1549 Book of Common Prayer

1553 Death of Edward VI; accession of Mary

1555–6 Executions of Cranmer, Ridley, and Latimer

1557 Tottel's edition of *Songes and Sonettes* ('Tottel's Miscellany') Surrey's translation of *Aeneid*, II and IV

1558 Loss of Calais; death of Mary; accession of Elizabeth I

1560 'Geneva' Bible

1561 Hoby's translation of Castiglione's *The Courtyer*

1563 Foxe, *Actes and Monuments*

1568 Bishops' Bible

1570 Excommunication of Elizabeth

1570 Ascham, *The Scholemaster*

1571 Battle of Lepanto

1577 Drake begins his circumnavigation

1577 Sidney, 'Old' *Arcadia*; Holinshed, *Chronicles*

1578 Lyly, *Euphues*

1579 Spenser, *Shepheardes Calender*

1581–6 Sidney, *Astrophil and Stella* (1581–3); *Defence of Poesie* (c.1582); 'New' *Arcadia*

1586 Death of Sidney at Zutphen

1587 Execution of Mary Queen of Scots; opening of Rose Theatre

1587 Camden, *Britannia*

1588 Defeat of Spanish Armada

1588–92 Shakespeare's early plays including *1,2,3 Henry VI, Taming of the Shrew, Love's Labours Lost, Richard III*

1589 Puttenham, *Arte of English Poesie*

1590 Spenser, *Faerie Queene* (I–III); Lodge, *Rosalynde*

EVENTS	LITERARY WORKS
	1592 Kyd, *The Spanish Tragedy*; Daniel, *Delia*
	1593 Marlowe, *Hero and Leander*; Shakespeare, *Venus and Adonis*; Drayton, *Idea*; Hooker, *Laws of Ecclesiastical Polity* (I–IV)
	1594 Shakespeare, *Sonnets*
	1594–1600 Shakespeare, plays including *Midsummer Night's Dream*; *1, 2 Henry IV*; *As You Like It*; *Merry Wives of Windsor*; *Julius Caesar*
	1595 Daniel, *Civil Wars* (I–IV); Spenser, *Amoretti*; *Epithalamion*
	1596 Spenser, *Faerie Queene* (I–VI); Davies, *Orchestra*
	1597 Bacon, *Essays*
	1598 Chapman-Marlowe, *Hero and Leander*; Stow, *Survey of London*; Jonson, first version of *Everyman in His Humour*
1599 Globe Theatre opened	1599 Daniel, *Poetical Essays*; Nashe, *Lenten Stuffe*
1601 Essex rebellion	1601–4 Shakespeare plays including *Hamlet*, *Twelfth Night*, *Measure for Measure*
1603 Death of Elizabeth; accession of James VI as James I; union of the crowns of England and Scotland	1603 Jonson, *Sejanus*
	1604–8 Shakespeare plays including *Othello*, *King Lear*, *Macbeth*, *Antony and Cleopatra*, *Coriolanus*
1605 Gunpowder plot; Jonson's first court masque with Inigo Jones	1605 Bacon, *Advancement of Learning*
1606 Charter granted to Virginia Company	
	1608–13 Shakespeare's last plays including *Tempest*, *Winter's Tale*, *Henry VIII*
	1611 'Authorized' version of Bible
1613 Globe Theatre burned	c.1613 Webster, *The White Devil*
1616 Death of Shakespeare	1616 Ben Jonson, *Works*
1618 Execution of Ralegh; beginning of Thirty Years War	
1620 Pilgrim Fathers sail for America	
1621 Donne appointed Dean of St Pauls	1621 Burton, *Anatomy of Melancholy*; Mary Wroth, *Urania*
	1622 Middleton, *The Changeling*
	1623 First Folio of Shakespeare

EVENTS	LITERARY WORKS
1625 Death of James I; accession of Charles I	1625 *Purchas his Pilgrimes*
1629 Charles I begins personal rule with dissolution of Parliament	1629 Andrewes, *XCVI Sermons*
1633 Laud appointed Archbishop of Canterbury	1633 Donne, *Poems*; Herbert, *The Temple*; Ford, *'Tis Pity She's a Whore*
	1634 Milton, *Comus* performed
	1635 Quarles, *Emblems*
	1637 Milton, *Lycidas*
1640 Long Parliament summoned	
1642 King attempts to arrest the five members; raises royal standard at Nottingham beginning Civil War; theatres closed by order of Parliament	
1644 Victory of Parliamentary Army at Marston Moor	1644 Milton, *Areopagitica*
1645 Execution of Laud; victory of Parliamentary Army at Naseby	
1646 Charles surrenders to Scots	1646 Crashaw, *Steps to the Temple*
1647 Putney debates	1647 Cowley, *The Mistress*
	1648 Herrick, *Hesperides*
1649 Trial and execution of Charles I	1649 Lovelace, *Lucasta*
1649–52 Cromwell's campaigns in Ireland and Scotland	
	1650 Marvell, 'An Horation Ode'; Vaughan, *Silex Scintillans*
	1651 Hobbes, *Leviathan*
1653 Cromwell becomes Lord Protector	
	1656 Harrington, *Oceana*
1658 Death of Cromwell; Richard Cromwell succeeds his father	
1659 Richard Cromwell overthrown by army; recall of Rump Parliament	
1660 Restoration of Charles II; re-opening of theatres	1660 Dryden, *Astraea Redux*; Pepys begins his diary
1662 Restoration of Church of England and final revision of Book of Common Prayer; Royal Society receives its charter	
	1664 Katherine Philips, *Poems*
1665 Plague in London	

EVENTS

LITERARY WORKS

1666 City of London destroyed by the Great Fire

1667 Dryden, *Annus Mirabilis*; Milton, *Paradise Lost*

1671 Milton, *Paradise Regain'd*

1675 Rochester, 'A Satyre against Mankind'; Wycherley, *The Country Wife*

1677 Dryden, *All for Love*; Behn, *The Rover*

1678 Bunyan, *The Pilgrim's Progress* (Part I)

1680 Rochester, *Poems*

1681 Lord Shaftesbury tried for High Treason: acquitted

1681 Marvell, *Miscellaneous Poems* (posthumously published); Dryden, *Absolom & Achitophel*

1685 Death of Charles II; accession of James II; Duke of Monmouth's rebellion crushed at Sedgemoor

1687 Newton, *Principia*

1688 'Glorious Revolution'; James II flees; William III and Mary II succeed

1690 Locke, *Essay Concerning Human Understanding*

1694 Death of Mary

1695 Congreve, *Love for Love*

1700 Congreve, *The Way of the World*

1701 War of Spanish Succession; Great Britain allied against France

1702 Death of William III; accession of Anne

1702–3 Clarendon, *History of the Rebellion*

1704 Marlborough's victory at Blenheim

1704 Swift, *The Battle of the Books* and *A Tale of a Tub*

1706 Farquhar, *The Recruiting Officer*

1707 Act of Union between England and Scotland

1707 Farquhar, *The Beaux Stratagem*

1709 Steele (and others), *The Tatler*

1711 Shaftesbury, *Characteristicks*

1711–12 *The Spectator*

1712 Pope, *The Rape of the Lock*

1713 Peace of Utrecht ends War of Spanish Succession

1713 Anne Finch, *Miscellany Poems*

1714 Death of Anne; George I, Elector of Hanover, succeeds

EVENTS	LITERARY WORKS
1715 Jacobite Rebellion in favour of James Edward (the 'Old Pretender')	
	1717 Pope, *Works*
	1719 Defoe, *Robinson Crusoe*
1721 Walpole forms ministry	
	1722 Defoe, *Moll Flanders* and *Journal of the Plague Year*
	1726 Swift, *Gulliver's Travels*; Thomson, *Winter*
1727 Death of George I; accession of George II; Walpole retains power; death of Newton	
	1728 Gay, *Beggars Opera*; Pope, *Dunciad* (1st version)
	1733 Pope, *Essay on Man*
	1738 Johnson, *London*
	1739 Charles Wesley, first collection of hymns
1740 War of Austrian Succession begins	1740 Richardson, *Pamela*
1742 Fall of Walpole	1742 Fielding, *Joseph Andrews*
	1743 Pope, *The Dunciad* (final version)
	1744 Sarah Fielding, *David Simple*
1745 Second Jacobite Rebellion led by Charles Edward (the 'Young Pretender')	
	1747–9 Richardson, *Clarissa*
1748 Peace of Aix-la-Chapelle ends War of Austrian Succession	1748 Smollett, *Roderick Random*
	1749 Fielding, *Tom Jones*
	1750–2 Johnson, *The Rambler*
	1751 Smollett, *Peregrine Pickle*
	1752 Lennox, *The Female Quixote*
	1754 Richardson, *Grandison*
	1755 Johnson, *Dictionary*
1756 Beginning of Seven Years War	
1757 Conquest of India begins under General Clive	1757 Burke, *A Philosophical Enquiry into the Origin of our Ideas of the Sublime and Beautiful*
1759 Wolfe takes Quebec	1759 Johnson, *Rasselas*
	1759–67 Sterne, *Tristram Shandy*
1760 Death of George II; accession of George III	

EVENTS

LITERARY WORKS

1763 Peace of Paris ends Seven Years War; British gains in India and North America

1764 Walpole, *The Castle of Otranto*
1765 Percy, *Reliques*
1766 Goldsmith, *The Vicar of Wakefield*
1768 Sterne, *A Sentimental Journey*

1770 Lord North, Prime Minister; suicide of Chatterton

1770 Goldsmith, *The Deserted Village*

1773 Goldsmith, *She Stoops to Conquer*
1775 Sheridan, *The Rivals*

1776 American Declaration of Independence

1776–88 Gibbon, *Decline and Fall of the Roman Empire*
1777 Sheridan, *School for Scandal*; Reeve, *The Old English Baron*
1778 Burney, *Evelina*
1779–81 Johnson, *The Lives of the Poets*

1780 Gordon Riots
1781 British forces defeated by Americans at Yorktown

1781 Sheridan, *The Critic*

1783 Independence of American Colonies recognized by Peace of Paris
1784 James Watt invents the steam engine
1785 Edmund Cartwright invents the power loom

1785 Cowper, *The Task*

1786 Beckford, *Vathek*; Burns, *Poems, Chiefly in the Scottish Dialect*

1787 Association for the Abolition of the Slave Trade founded

1788 Wollstonecraft, *Mary*

1789 French Revolution; Fall of Bastille; Declaration of the Rights of Man

1789 Blake, *Songs of Innocence*

1790 Burke, *Reflections on the Revolution in France*; Blake, *The Marriage of Heaven and Hell*

1791 Flight of Louis XVI

1791 Boswell, *Life of Samuel Johnson*; Paine, *The Rights of Man* (Part I)

1792 Siege of Tuileries; September Massacres

1792 Wollstonecraft, *A Vindication of the Rights of Woman*; Holcroft, *Anna St Ives*

1793 Execution of Louis XVI; Reign of Terror; Britain and France at war

1793 Blake, *America*; Godwin, *Political Justice*; Smith, *The Old Manor*

1794 Executions of Danton and Robespierre; Habeas Corpus Act suspended in Britain; Holcroft acquitted of treason charge

1795 Directory established in France; Speenhamland system of poor relief

1796 Bonaparte's Italian campaign

1798 Nelson's victory at Battle of the Nile; rebellion in Ireland

1799 Napoleon, First Consul

1800 Act of Union with Ireland

1801 Union of British and Irish Parliaments; Habeas Corpus Act again suspended

1802 Peace of Amiens

1803 Renewal of war against France

1804 Napoleon, Emperor of France

1805 Nelson's victory at Trafalgar

1807 Abolition of the slave trade in the British Empire

1808 Peninsular War begins

1811 Prince of Wales becomes Regent; Luddite riots

1812 French retreat from Moscow

1814 Abdication of Napoleon; restoration of Louis XVIII; Stephenson's steam locomotive

1815 Battle of Waterloo

1794 Blake, *Songs of Experience*; Godwin, *Caleb Williams*; Radcliffe, *The Mysteries of Udolpho*; Holcroft, *Hugh Trevor*

1796 Burney, *Camilla*; Bage, *Hermsprong*; Lewis, *The Monk*

1798 Wordsworth and Coleridge, *Lyrical Ballads*; Wollstonecraft, *The Wrongs of Woman*

1800 Edgeworth, *Castle Rackrent*

1802 Scott, *Minstrelsy of the Scottish Border*; foundation of the *Edinburgh Review*; Cobbett begins his *Political Register*

1804 Blake, *Milton*

1805 Scott, *The Lay of the Last Minstrel*; Wordsworth at work on a version of *The Prelude*

1807 Wordsworth, *Poems*

1808 Scott, *Marmion*; Hunt, *The Examiner*

1809 Byron, *English Bards and Scotch Reviewers*; foundation of the *Quarterly Review*

1810 Crabbe, *The Borough*; Scott, *The Lady of the Lake*

1811 Austen, *Sense and Sensibility*

1812 Crabbe, *Tales*; Byron, *Childe Harold's Pilgrimage*; Edgeworth, *The Absentee*

1813 Austen, *Pride and Prejudice*; Shelley, *Queen Mab*

1814 Wordsworth, *The Excursion*; Byron, *The Corsair*; Austen, *Mansfield Park*; Scott, *Waverley*; Burney, *The Wanderer*

1815 Wordsworth, *Poems*; Scott, *Guy Mannering*

EVENTS	LITERARY WORKS
	1816 Coleridge, *Christabel* and *Kubla Khan*; Shelley, *Alastor*; Austen, *Emma*; Scott, *The Antiquary* and *Old Mortality*; Peacock, *Headlong Hall*
1817 Habeas Corpus Act suspended	1817 Coleridge, *Biographia Literaria*; Byron, *Manfred*; Keats, *Poems*; Hazlitt, *The Characters of Shakespeare's Plays*; foundation of *Blackwood's Edinburgh Magazine*
1818 Habeas Corpus Act restored	1818 Austen, *Northanger Abbey* and *Persuasion*; Keats, *Endymion*; Scott, *Rob Roy* and *The Heart of Midlothian*; Mary Shelley, *Frankenstein*; Hazlitt, *Lectures on the English Poets*; Ferrier, *Marriage*
1819 Peterloo massacre	1819 Crabbe, *Tales of the Hall*; Byron, *Don Juan*; Scott, *The Bride of Lammermoor*
1820 Death of George III; accession of George IV	1820 Shelley, *Prometheus Unbound*; Keats, *Lamia, Isabella, The Eve of St Agnes and Other Poems*; Clare, *Poems Descriptive of Rural Life*; Scott, *Ivanhoe*; Lamb, *Essays of Elia* begun; Cobbett, *Rural Rides* begun; Maturin, *Melmoth the Wanderer*
1821 Greek War of Independence	1821 Byron, *Cain*; Shelley, *Adonais*; Clare, *The Village Minstrel*; De Quincey, *Confessions of an English Opium Eater*; Galt, *Annals of the Parish*
	1822 Wordsworth, *Ecclesiastical Sketches*; Byron, *The Vision of Judgement*; Galt, *The Entail*
1824 National Gallery opened; death of Byron in Greece	1824 Scott, *Redgauntlet*; Hogg, *Private Confessions of a Justified Sinner*; foundation of the *Westminster Review*
1825 Financial crisis; opening of Stockton and Darlington Railway	1825 Hazlitt, *The Spirit of the Age*; publication of Pepys's diary
	1827 Clare, *The Shepherd's Calendar*; Keble, *The Christian Year*
1828 Repeal of Test and Corporation Acts	
1829 Catholic Emancipation Act	
1830 Death of George IV; accession of William IV; opening of Manchester and Liverpool railway	1830 Tennyson, *Poems, Chiefly Lyrical*

EVENTS

LITERARY WORKS

1831 Unsuccessful introduction of Reform Bills; riots in Bristol and elsewhere

1832 Reform Act; Death of Scott

1833 Abolition of Slavery; Keble's Assize sermon

1834 New Poor Law; burning of Houses of Parliament; Fox Talbot's first photograph

1835 Municipal Reform Act

1832 Tennyson, *Poems* (dated 1833)

1833 Carlyle, *Sartor Resartus*

1835 Browning, *Paracelesus*

1836 Dickens, *Sketches by 'Boz'* and the first number of *Pickwick Papers* (1836–7)

1837 Death of William IV; accession of Victoria

1838 'People's Charter' published; London-Birmingham Railway opened

1839 Penny Postage Act

1840 Opium War; new Houses of Parliament begun; first presentation of People's Charter to Parliament

1837 Carlyle, *The French Revolution*; Dickens, *Oliver Twist*

1838 Dickens, *Nicholas Nickleby*

1839 Carlyle, *Chartism*

1840 Dickens, *The Old Curiosity Shop* and *Barnaby Rudge* (1840–1); Browning, *Sordello*

1841 Carlyle, *On Heroes and Hero Worship*; Newman, *Tract XC*; foundation of *Punch*

1842 Chartist riots; second presentation of Charter to Parliament; Copyright Act

1843 Theatre Regulations Bill (monopoly removed from Covent Garden and Drury Lane theatres)

1844 Royal Commission on Health in Towns

1845 Failure of Irish potato crop

1846 Famine in Ireland; repeal of Corn Laws

1847 Ten Hours Act

1842 Tennyson, *Poems*; Browning, *Dramatic Lyrics*

1843 Macaulay, *Essays*; Carlyle, *Past and Present*; Ruskin, *Modern Painters* (vol. i); Dickens, *A Christmas Carol*

1844 Disraeli, *Coningsby*; Thackeray, *Barry Lyndon*

1845 Disraeli, *Sybil*; Browning, *Dramatic Romances and Lyrics*

1846–8 Dickens, *Dombey and Son*

1847 Tennyson, *The Princess*; Charlotte Brontë, *Jane Eyre*; Emily Brontë, *Wuthering Heights*; Anne Brontë, *Agnes Grey*; Thackeray, *Vanity Fair* (1847–8)

EVENTS

LITERARY WORKS

1848 Chartist demonstration in London (third presentation of Charter); Public Health Act; foundation of Pre-Raphaelite Brotherhood; revolutions in France, Germany, Poland, Hungary, and Italy; Second Republic proclaimed in France; Roman Republic

1848 Gaskell, *Mary Barton*; Anne Brontë, *The Tenant of Wildfell Hall*; Thackeray, *Pendennis* (1848–9)

1849 Charlotte Brontë, *Shirley*; Ruskin, *Seven Lamps of Architecture*; Dickens, *David Copperfield* (1849–50); Macaulay, *History of England*

1850 'Papal Aggression' (following reestablishment of Roman Catholic hierarchy in England)

1850 Tennyson, *In Memoriam AHH*; Carlyle, *Latter-Day Pamphlets*; E. B. Browning, *Sonnets from the Portuguese*; Kingsley, *Alton Locke*

1851 Great Exhibition; Louis Napoleon's *coup d'état*

1851 Gaskell, *Cranford*, Ruskin, *The Stones of Venice* (1851–3)

1852 Death of the Duke of Wellington

1852 Thackeray, *Henry Esmond*; Arnold, *Empedocles on Etna*; Dickens, *Bleak House* (1852–3)

1853 Charlotte Brontë, *Villette*; Gaskell, *Ruth*; Arnold, *Poems*

1854 Crimean War breaks out; Battles of Alma, Inkerman, and Balaclava (with the Charge of the Light Brigade); Preston cotton spinners strike; Working Man's College opened

1854 Dickens, *Hard Times*; Thackeray, *The Newcomes* (1854–5)

1855 Fall of Sebastopol; Metropolitan Board of Works established; repeal of Stamp Duty on newspapers

1855 Tennyson, *Maud*; Kingsley, *Westward Ho!*; Browning, *Men and Women*; Gaskell, *North and South*; Trollope, *The Warden*; Dickens, *Little Dorritt* (1855–7)

1856 Peace of Paris (ending Crimean War)

1857 Indian Mutiny

1857 E. B. Browning, *Aurora Leigh*; Trollope, *Barchester Towers*; Gaskell, *The Life of Charlotte Brontë*; Eliot, *Scenes of Clerical Life*; Thackeray, *The Virginians*

1858 Peace in India; India transferred to British Crown

1858 Clough, *Amours de Voyage*; Carlyle, *Frederick the Great*

1859 Dickens, *A Tale of Two Cities*; Eliot, *Adam Bede*; Meredith, *The Ordeal of Richard Feverel*; Mill, *On Liberty*; Darwin, *The Origin of Species*; Tennyson, *The Idylls of the King* (1859–72)

1860 Garibaldi's campaign in Sicily and Naples

1860 Eliot, *The Mill on the Floss*; Collins, *The Woman in White*; Ruskin, *Unto This Last*; Dickens, *Great Expectations*

1861 Victor Emanuel, King of United Italy; outbreak of American Civil War, death of Prince Consort

1861 Eliot, *Silas Marner*; Trollope, *Framley Parsonage*

1862 C. Rossetti, *Goblin Market*; Meredith, *Modern Love*; Eliot, *Romola* (1862–3); Braddon, *Lady Audley's Secret*

1863 'Cotton Famine' in Lancashire

1863 Gaskell, *Sylvia's Lovers*

1864 Geneva Convention

1864 Gaskell, *Wives and Daughters*; Newman, *Apologia pro vita sua*; Dickens, *Our Mutual Friend* (1864–5)

1865 Suppression of Jamaican rebellion by Governor Eyre; assassination of Lincoln

1865 Arnold, *Essays in Criticism*; Swinburne, *Atalanta in Calydon*; Carroll, *Alice in Wonderland*

1866 Austro-Prussian War

1866 Eliot, *Felix Holt*; Swinburne, *Poems and Ballads*

1867 Representation of the People Act (second Reform Bill)

1867 Arnold, *New Poems*; Trollope, *The Last Chronicle of Barset*

1868 Collins, *The Moonstone*; Browning, *The Ring and the Book* (1868–9); Morris, *The Earthly Paradise* (1868–70)

1869 First Vatican Council

1869 Trollope, *Phineas Finn*; Mill, *The Subjection of Women*

1870 Married Woman's Property Act; Franco-Prussian War; Forster's Education Act; Papal States incorporated into Kingdom of Italy; death of Dickens

1870 Dickens, *Edwin Drood*; D. G. Rossetti, *Poems*

1871 Paris Commune

1871 Lear, *The Owl and the Pussy Cat*

1871–2 Eliot, *Middlemarch*

1872 Carroll, *Through the Looking-Glass*; Butler, *Erewhon*; Hardy, *Under the Greenwood Tree*

EVENTS

LITERARY WORKS

1873 Arnold, *Literature and Dogma*; Mill, *Autobiography*; Pater, *Studies in the History of the Renaissance*; Trollope, *The Way We Live Now* (1873–4)

1874 Hardy, *Far From the Madding Crowd*

1875 Agricultural Depression

1876 Eliot, *Daniel Deronda*

1877 Victoria proclaimed Empress of India

1878 Congress of Berlin

1878 Hardy, *The Return of the Native*

1879 Meredith, *The Egoist*

1880 Gladstone, Prime Minister

1880 Hardy, *The Trumpet Major*

1881 Death of Disraeli

1881 White, *Mark Rutherford's Autobiography*

1882 Hardy, *Two on a Tower*

1885 Radio waves discovered; internal combustion engine invented

1885 Pater, *Marius the Epicurean*; Meredith, *Diana of the Crossways*

1886 Gladstone's first Home Rule Bill for Ireland defeated

1886 Moore, *A Drama in Muslin*; Stevenson, *Kidnapped* and *Dr Jekyll and Mr Hyde*; Gissing, *Demos*

1887 Victoria's Golden Jubilee

1887 White, *Revolution in Tanner's Lane*; Doyle, first Holmes story published in the *Strand Magazine*

1888 Kipling, *Plain Tales from the Hills*; Ward, *Robert Elsmere*

1889 Yeats, *The Wanderings of Oisin*; Stevenson, *The Master of Ballantrae*

1890 Parnell falls as leader of Irish Home Rule Party after being cited in the O'Shea divorce case

1890 Kipling, *Barrack Room Ballads*

1891 Hardy, *Tess of the D'Urbervilles*; Gissing, *New Grub Street*

1892 Shaw, *Widowers' Houses*; Yeats, *The Countess Cathleen*

1893 Second Home Rule Bill rejected by the House of Lords

1893 Pinero, *The Second Mrs Tanqueray*; Shaw, *Mrs Warren's Profession*

1894 Ward, *Marcella*; Moore, *Esther Waters*

1895 X-rays discovered

1895 Wilde, *The Importance of Being Earnest* and *An Ideal Husband*; Wells, *The Time Machine*

1896 Wireless telegraphy invented

1896 Hardy, *Jude the Obscure*; Housman, *A Shropshire Lad*; Shaw, *You Never Can Tell*

EVENTS	LITERARY WORKS
1897 Victoria's Diamond Jubilee	1897 Stoker, *Dracula*
	1898 Hardy, *Wessex Poems*
1899–1902 Boer War	
1900 Relief on Mafeking	1900 Conrad, *Lord Jim*
1901 Death of Victoria; accession of Edward VII	1901 Kipling, *Kim*
	1902 Bennett, *Anna of the Five Towns*
1903 First aeroplane flight; foundation of Women's Social and Political Union	1903 Butler, *The Way of All Flesh*; Gissing, *Henry Ryecroft*
1904 Franco-British Entente	1904 Conrad, *Nostromo*; Hardy, *The Dynasts* (1904–8)
	1905 Shaw, *Major Barbara* and *Man and Superman*; Wells, *Kipps*
1906 Liberal government elected; launch of HMS *Dreadnought*	
1907 Anglo-Russian Entente	1907 Synge, *The Playboy of the Western World*; Conrad, *The Secret Agent*
1908 Old Age Pensions Act; Elgar's first symphony	1908 Bennett, *The Old Wives' Tale*; Forster, *A Room with a View*; Chesterton, *The Man Who Was Thursday*
1909 'People's Budget'; English channel flown	1909 Wells, *Tono Bungay*
1910 Death of Edward VII; accession of George V; first Post-Impressionist Exhibition	1910 Bennett, *Clayhanger*; Forster, *Howards End*
1911 National Insurance Act	1911 Conrad, *Under Western Eyes*; Wells, *The New Machiavelli*
1912 Second Post-Impressionist Exhibition; Home Rule Bill rejected by Lords; sinking of SS *Titanic*; death of Scott in the Antarctic	
1913 Second rejection of Home Rule Bill by Lords	1913 Lawrence, *Sons and Lovers*
1914 Home Rule Bill passed by Parliament; Britain declares war on Central Powers (4 Aug.)	1914 Lewis, *Blast*; Joyce, *Dubliners*; Yeats, *Responsibilities*; Hardy, *Satires of Circumstances*
1915 Second battle of Ypres; sinking of SS *Lusitania*	1915 Ford, *The Good Soldier*; Woolf, *The Voyage Out*; Lawrence, *The Rainbow*; Brooke, *1914 and Other Poems*; Richardson, *Pointed Roofs*
1916 First Battle of the Somme; Gallipoli Campaign; Easter Rising in Dublin	1916 Joyce, *Portrait of the Artist as a Young Man*

EVENTS	LITERARY WORKS
1917 Third Battle of Ypres (Passchendaele); T. E. Lawrence's campaigns in Arabia; Revolution in Russia (Feb., Oct.)	1917 Eliot, *Prufrock and Other Observations*
1918 Second battle of the Somme; final German offensive collapses; Armistice with Germany (11 Nov.); Franchise Act granting the vote to women over 30	1918 Lewis, *Tarr*; Hopkins, *Poems*; Strachey, *Eminent Victorians*
1919 Treaty of Versailles; Atlantic flown	1919 Sinclair, *Mary Olivier*
	1920 Owen, *Poems*; Lawrence, *Women in Love*; Shaw, *Heartbreak House*; Fry, *Vision and Design*
1921 Establishment of Irish Free State	1921 Huxley, *Crome Yellow*
1922 Fascist government in Italy	1922 Eliot, *The Waste Land*; Joyce, *Ulysses*; Lawrence, *Fantasia of the Unconscious*
	1923 Huxley, *Antic Hay*; Shaw, *St Joan*; Bennett, *Riceyman Steps*
1924 First Labour Government	1924 Forster, *A Passage to India*; O'Casey, *Juno and the Paycock*; Coward, *The Vortex*
	1925 Woolf, *Mrs Dalloway*; Gerhardie, *The Polyglots*
1926 General Strike	1926 MacDiarmid, *A Drunk Man looks at the Thistle*
	1927 Woolf, *To the Lighthouse*
1928 Death of Hardy	1928 Yeats, *The Tower*; Lawrence, *Lady Chatterley's Lover*; Waugh, *Decline and Fall*; Sherriff, *Journey's End*
	1929 Aldington, *Death of a Hero*; Green, *Living*
1930 World economic depression	1930 Auden, *Poems*, Eliot, *Ash Wednesday*; Waugh, *Vile Bodies*; Coward, *Private Lives*
1931 National Government formed	1931 Woolf, *The Waves*
	1932 Huxley, *Brave New World*; Gibbon, *Sunset Song* (first part of *A Scots Quair*)
1933 Hitler becomes Chancellor of Germany	1933 Orwell, *Down and Out in Paris and London*
	1934 Eliot, 'Burnt Norton'; Waugh, *A Handful of Dust*; Graves, *I, Claudius*; Beckett, *More Pricks than Kicks*

	EVENTS		LITERARY WORKS
1935	George V's Silver Jubilee	1935	Isherwood, *Mr Norris Changes Trains* and *Lions and Shadows*; Auden and Isherwood; *The Dog Beneath the Skin*; Eliot, *Murder in the Cathedral*
1936	Death of George V; accession of Edward VIII; abdication crisis; accession of George VI; Civil War breaks out in Spain; first of the Moscow show trials	1936	Auden, *Look Stranger!*
		1937	Auden and MacNeice, *Letters from Iceland*; Jones, *In Parenthesis*; Orwell, *The Road to Wigan Pier*
1938	German *Anschluss* with Austria; Munich agreement; dismemberment of Czechoslovakia	1938	Beckett, *Murphy*; Bowen, *The Death of the Heart*; Orwell, *Homage to Catalonia*; Greene, *Brighton Rock*
1939	End of Civil War in Spain; Russo-German pact; Germany invades Poland (Sept.); Britain and France declare war on Germany	1939	MacNeice, *Autumn Journal*; Green, *Party Going*; Isherwood, *Goodbye to Berlin*; Eliot, *The Family Reunion*
1940	Germany invades north-west Europe; fall of France; evacuation of British troops at Dunkirk; beginning of the 'blitz'	1940	Auden, *New Year Letter*; Eliot, 'East Coker'; Greene, *The Power and the Glory*; Koestler, *Darkness at Noon*
1941	Germany invades Russia; Japanese destroy US Fleet at Pearl Harbor	1941	Eliot 'The Dry Salvages'; Woolf, *Between the Acts*; Coward, *Blithe Spirit*
1942	Fall of Singapore; British victory in North Africa at El Alamein	1942	Eliot, 'Little Gidding'
1943	Allied invasion of Italy	1943	Greene, *The Ministry of Fear*
1944	Allied landings in Normandy ('D Day'); liberation of Paris	1944	Cary, *The Horse's Mouth*
1945	Surrender of Germany; atom bombs dropped on Hiroshima and Nagasaki; Labour Government elected	1945	Green, *Loving*; Orwell, *Animal Farm*; Waugh, *Brideshead Revisited*; Larkin, *The North Ship*
1946	Nuremberg Trials end; nationalization of coal industry; foundation of National Health Service	1946	Larkin, *Jill*; Rattigan, *The Winslow Boy*; Thomas, *Deaths and Entrances*
1947	Independence of India and Pakistan	1947	Compton-Burnett, *Manservant and Maidservant*
1948	Berlin Air Lift; 'cold war' at its height	1948	Greene, *The Heart of the Matter*; Fry, *The Lady's not for Burning*
		1949	Bowen, *The Heat of the Day*; Orwell, *Nineteen Eighty-four*; Eliot, *The Cocktail Party*

EVENTS	LITERARY WORKS
1950 Labour returned at election with reduced majority	1950 Auden, *Collected Shorter Poems*; Beckett, *Molloy* (first volume of trilogy)
1951 Conservative victory at General Election; Festival of Britain	1951 Douglas, *Collected Poems*; Powell, *A Question of Upbringing* (first volume of *A Dance to the Music of Time*)
1952 Death of George VI; accession of Elizabeth II	1952 Jones, *Anathemata*; Rattigan, *The Deep Blue Sea*; Wilson, *Hemlock and After*
	1954 Rattigan, *Separate Tables*; Golding, *Lord of the Flies*; Amis, *Lucky Jim*
	1955 Larkin, *The Less Deceived*; Golding, *The Inheritors*; Beckett, *Waiting for Godot* (first British performance)
1956 Egypt nationalizes Suez Canal; Britain and France intervene and are obliged to withdraw; Soviet invasion of Hungary	1956 Golding, *Pincher Martin*; Wilson, *Anglo-Saxon Attitudes*; Osborne, *Look Back in Anger*
1957 CND formed	1957 Hughes, *The Hawk in the Rain*; Spark, *The Comforters*; Durrell, *Justine*; Osborne, *The Entertainer*
	1958 Pym, *A Glass of Blessings*; Betjeman, *Collected Poems*; Pinter, *The Birthday Party*; Murdoch, *The Bell*
	1959 Spark, *Memento Mori*; Wesker, *Roots*; Golding, *Free Fall*; Arden, *Serjeant Musgrave's Dance*
1960 Unexpurgated text of *Lady Chatterley's Lover* published after obscenity trial	1960 Hughes, *Lupercal*; Pinter, *The Caretaker*; Beckett, *Krapp's Last Tape*; Spark, *The Ballad of Peckham Rye*
	1961 Osborne, *Luther*; Spark, *The Prime of Miss Jean Brodie*
1962 Establishment of the National Theatre	1962 Beckett, *Happy Days*; Wilson, *Late Call*; Lessing, *The Golden Notebook*; Burgess, *A Clockwork Orange*
	1963 Amis, *One Fat Englishman*; Fowles, *The Collector*
	1964 Orton, *Entertaining Mr Sloane*; Larkin, *The Whitsun Weddings*; Golding, *The Spire*; Osborne, *Inadmissible Evidence*; Pinter, *The Homecoming*
	1965 Bond, *Saved*

EVENTS	LITERARY WORKS
	1966 Heaney, *Death of a Naturalist*; Rhys, *Wide Sargasso Sea*; West, *The Birds Fall Down*; Scott, *The Jewel in the Crown*; Stoppard, *Rosencrantz and Guildenstern are Dead*
1967 Legalization, within limits, of homosexuality and abortion	1967 Orton, *Loot* and *The Erpingham Camp*; Hughes, *Wodwo*
1968 Événements in Paris; Soviet invasion of Czechoslovakia; 'Troubles' begin in Northern Ireland	1968 Stoppard, *The Real Inspector Hound*; Hill, *King Log*
1969 Abolition of capital punishment	1969 Heaney, *Door into the Dark*; Orton, *What the Butler Saw*; Fowles, *The French Lieutenant's Woman*
1970 Age of majority reduced from 21 to 18	1970 Hughes, *Crow*
	1971 Hill, *Mercian Hymns*; Bond, *Lear*; Pinter, *Old Times*; Spark, *Not to Disturb*
	1972 Stoppard, *Jumpers*
1973 United Kingdom enters European Economic Community	1973 Beckett, *Not I*; Murdoch, *The Black Prince*
	1974 Spark, *The Abbess of Crewe*; Beckett, *That Time*; Larkin, *High Windows*; Stoppard, *Travesties*
	1975 Heaney, *North*; Pinter, *No Man's Land*; Griffiths, *Comedians*; Bradbury, *The History Man*
	1977 Stoppard, *Professional Foul*; Drabble, *The Ice Age*; Pym, *Quartet in Autumn*
	1978 Pinter, *Betrayal*; Murdoch, *The Sea, The Sea*; Byatt, *The Virgin in the Garden*; Hill, *Tenebrae*
1979 Election of Margaret Thatcher's Conservative Government	1979 Golding, *Darkness Visible*; Heaney, *Field Work*
	1980 Golding, *Rites of Passage*; Burgess, *Earthly Powers*; Friel, *Translations*
	1981 Rushdie, *Midnight's Children*
	1982 Churchill, *Top Girls*
	1983 Swift, *Waterland*
	1984 Heaney, *Station Island*; Carter, *Nights at the Circus*
	1985 Hare and Brenton, *Pravda*; Ackroyd, *Hawksmoor*

EVENTS

LITERARY WORKS

1988 Pinter, *Mountain Language*;
Stoppard, *Hapgood*

1989 Revolutions in Eastern Europe
topple Communist regimes

1990 Fall of Margaret Thatcher

1990 Friel, *Dancing at Lughnasa*; Byatt,
Possession

1991 Carter, *Wise Children*

1994 Stoppard, *Arcadia*

1997 Election of Labour Government;
return of Hong Kong to China

1997 Hughes, *Tales from Ovid*;
Stoppard, *The Invention of
Love*

1998 Hughes, *Birthday Letters*

1999 Hill, *The Triumph of Love*

2001 '9.11': Terrorist attacks on
New York and Washington DC

2001 McEwan, *Atonement*

2002 Stoppard, *The Coast of Utopia*

GUIDE TO FURTHER READING

I. OLD ENGLISH LITERATURE

General

Calder, D. G., *et al.*, *Sources and Analogues of Old English Poetry*, 2 vols. (Cambridge, 1976, 1983). (Volume I gives Latin texts in translation, Volume II Germanic and Celtic texts; both volumes give valuable suggestions for further reading.)

Godden, Malcolm, and Lapidge, Michael (eds.), *The Cambridge Companion to Old English Literature* (Cambridge, 1991).

Greenfield, S. B., and Calder, D. G., *A New Critical History of Old English Literature* (New York, 1986).

Mitchell, Bruce, *An Invitation to Old English and Anglo-Saxon England* (Oxford, 1995).

Raw, Barbara, *The Art and Background of Old English Poetry* (London, 1978).

Shippey, T. A., *Old English Verse* (London, 1972).

Swanton, Michael, *English Literature before Chaucer* (London, 1987).

Szarmach, Paul (ed.), *Sources of Anglo-Saxon Culture* (Kalamazoo, Mich., 1986).

Wrenn, C. L., *A Study of Old English Literature* (London, 1967).

Historical

Blair, Peter Hunter, *An Introduction to Anglo-Saxon England*, 2nd edn. (Cambridge, 1977).

Blair, Peter Hunter, *The World of Bede* (Cambridge, 1970).

Bonner, Gerald (ed.), *Famulus Christi: Studies in Commemoration of the Thirteenth Century of the Birth of the Venerable Bede* (London, 1976).

Campbell, James (ed.), *The Anglo-Saxons* (Oxford, 1982).

Collingwood, R. G., and Myers, J. N. L., *Roman Britain and the English Settlement* (Oxford, 1937).

Dodwell, C. R., *Anglo-Saxon Art* (Manchester, 1982).

Frere, S. S., *Britannia: A History of Roman Britain*, 2nd edn. (London, 1978).

Loyn, H. R., *The Making of the English Nation: From the Anglo-Saxons to Edward I* (London, 1991).

Mayr-Harting, Henry, *The Coming of Christianity to Anglo-Saxon England* (London, 1972).

Stenton, F. M., *Anglo-Saxon England*, 3rd edn. (Oxford, 1971).

Whitelock, Dorothy, *The Beginnings of English Society*, Pelican History of England II (Harmondsworth, 1952).

Ælfric and Wulfstan

Gatch, M. McC., *Preaching and Theology in Anglo-Saxon England: Ælfric and Wulfstan* (Toronto, 1977).

Szarmach, Paul, and Hupper, B. F. (eds.), *The Old English Homily and its Backgrounds* (Albany, NY, 1978).

Beowulf

Bonjour, Adrien, *The Digressions in 'Beowulf'* (Oxford, 1965).
Chase, Colin (ed.), *The Dating of 'Beowulf'* (Toronto, 1981).
Irving, E. B., *Rereading 'Beowulf'* (Philadelphia, 1989).
Jones, Gwyn, *Kings, 'Beasts' and Heroes* (Oxford, 1972).
Niles, J. D., *Beowulf: The Poem and its Tradition* (Cambridge, Mass., 1983).

The Battle of Maldon and the Elegies

Bessinger, J. B., and Kahrl, S. J., *Essential Articles for the Study of Old English Poetry* (Hamden, Conn., 1968).
Green, Martin (ed.), *The Old English Elegies: New Essays in Criticism and Research* (London, 1983).
Scragg, D. G. (ed.), *The Battle of Maldon* (Oxford, 1991).

The Biblical Poems and *The Dream of the Rood*

Bennett, J. A. W., *Poetry of the Passion* (Oxford, 1981). (The first chapter deals with *The Dream of the Rood*.)
Calder, D. G., *Cynewulf* (Boston, 1981).

2. MEDIEVAL LITERATURE 1066–1510

General

Auerbach, Erich, *Mimesis: The Representation of Reality in Western Literature*, trans. W. R. Trask (New York, 1957).
Bennett, J. A. W., *Middle English Literature*, The Oxford History of English Literature I.2, ed. Douglas Gray (Oxford, 1986).
Bolton, W. F. (ed.), *The Middle Ages*, Sphere History of Literature in the English Language I (London, 1970).
Burrow, J. A., *Essays on Medieval Literature* (Oxford, 1984).
Burrow, J. A., *Medieval Writers and their Work: Middle English Literature and its Background, 1100–1500* (Oxford, 1982).
Chaytor, H. J., *From Script to Print: An Introduction to Medieval Literature* (Cambridge, 1945).
Curtius, E. R., *European Literature and the Latin Middle Ages*, trans. W. R. Trask (London, 1953).
Daiches, David, and Thorlby, A. K. (eds.), *The Medieval World* (London, 1973).
Edwards, A. S. G. (ed.), *Middle English Prose: A Critical Guide to Major Authors and Genres* (New Brunswick, NJ, 1984).
Ford, Boris (ed.), *Medieval Literature, Part One: Chaucer and the Alliterative Tradition*, The New Pelican Guide to English Literature I (Harmondsworth, 1982).
Ford, Boris (ed.), *Medieval Literature, Part Two: The European Inheritance*, The New Pelican Guide to English Literature I (Harmondsworth, 1983).
Gradon, Pamela, *Form and Style in Early English Literature* (London, 1971).
Lewis, C. S., *The Discarded Image* (Cambridge, 1964).

Marks, Richard, and Williamson, Paul, *Gothic: Art for England 1400–1547* (London, 2003).

Minnis, A. J., and Scott, A. B. (eds.), *Medieval Literary Theory and Criticism, c.1100–1375: The Commentary Tradition* (Oxford, 1988).

Pearsall, Derek, *Old English and Middle English Poetry*, Routledge History of English Poetry I (London, 1977).

Pearsall, Derek, and Salter, Elizabeth, *Landscapes and Seasons of the Medieval World* (London, 1973).

Salter, Elizabeth, *English and International: Studies in the Literature, Art and Patronage of Medieval England*, ed. Derek Pearsall and Nicolette Zeeman (Cambridge, 1988).

Spearing, A. C., *Medieval Dream Poetry* (Cambridge, 1976).

Turville-Peter, Thorlac, *The Alliterative Revival* (Cambridge, 1977).

Vinaver, Eugene, *The Rise of Romance* (Oxford, 1971).

Wallare, David, *The Cambridge History of Medieval Literature* (Cambridge, 1999).

Wilson, R. M., *The Lost Literature of Medieval England*, 2nd edn. (London, 1970).

Historical: 1066–c.1300

Benson, Robert L., and Constable, Giles (eds.), *Renaissance and Renewal in the Twelfth Century* (Oxford, 1982).

Chibnall, Marjorie, *Anglo-Norman England* (Oxford, 1986).

Clanchy, M. T., *England and its Rulers, 1066–1272* (London, 1983).

Clanchy, M. T., *From Memory to Written Record: England 1066–1307* (London, 1979).

Loyn, H. R., *The Making of the English Nation: From the Anglo-Saxons to Edward I* (London, 1991).

Southern, R. W., *The Making of the Middle Ages* (London, 1953).

Southern, R. W., *Western Society and the Church in the Middle Ages*, Pelican History of the Church II (Harmondsworth, 1970).

Stenton, Doris Mary, *English Society in the Early Middle Ages*, Pelican History of England III, 4th edn. (Harmondsworth, 1965).

Stenton, F. M., *The First Century of English Feudalism*, 2nd edn. (Oxford, 1961).

Historical: The Later Middle Ages

Bennett, H. S., *The Pastons and their England* (Cambridge, 1922).

Keen, Maurice, *England in the Later Middle Ages* (London, 1973).

Lander, J. R., *The Wars of the Roses* (London, 1990).

McFarlane, R. B., *Lancastrian Kings and Lollard Knights* (Oxford, 1972).

McFarlane, R. B., *The Nobility of Later Medieval England* (Oxford, 1973).

Myers, A. R., *England in the Late Middle Ages*, Pelican History of England IV, 8th edn. (Harmondsworth, 1971).

Scattergood, V. J., and Sherborne, J. W. (eds.), *English Court Culture in the Later Middle Ages* (London, 1983).

Scattergood, V. J., *Politics and Poetry in the Fifteenth Century* (London, 1971).

Ziegler, Philip, *The Black Death* (Harmondsworth, 1970).

Early Middle English Literature

Dobson, E. J., *The Origins of 'Ancrene Wisse'* (Oxford, 1976).

Georgianna, Linda, *The Solitary Self: Individuality in the 'Ancrene Wisse'* (Cambridge, Mass., 1981).

Hume, Kathryn, *'The Owl and the Nightingale': The Poem and its Critics* (Toronto, 1975).
Le Saux, Françoise, *Laȝamon's 'Brut': The Poem and its Sources* (Cambridge, 1989).
Tatlock, J. S. P., *The Legendary History of Britain* (Berkeley and Los Angeles, 1950).
Wilson, R. M., *Early Middle English Literature*, 3rd edn. (London, 1968).

Later Middle English Literature

Burrow, J. A., *Ricardian Poetry* (London, 1971).
Medcalf, Stephen (ed.), *The Later Middle Ages* (London, 1981).

Chivalry and 'Courtly' Love

Barber, Richard, *The Knight and Chivalry* (Harlow, 1970).
Coss, Peter, *The Knight in Medieval England* (Stroud, 1993).
Keen, Maurice, *Chivalry* (New Haven, 1984).
Lewis, C. S., *The Allegory of Love* (Oxford, 1936).
Loomis, R. S., *Arthurian Literature in the Middle Ages* (Oxford, 1959).
Riley-Smith, Jonathan, *The Crusades: A Short History* (London, 1987).
Topsfield, L. T., *Chretien de Troyes: A Study of the Arthurian Romances* (Cambridge, 1981).
Walsh, P. G. (ed.), *Andreas Capellanus on Love* (London, 1982).

English Romance and the Gawain-*Poet*

Barron, W. R. J., *'Trawthe' and Treason: The Sin of Gawain Reconsidered* (Manchester, 1980).
Bishop, Ian, *'Pearl' in its Setting* (Oxford, 1968).
Brewer, Elisabeth, *'Sir Gawain and the Green Knight': Sources and Analogues*, 2nd edn. (Cambridge, 1992).
Burrow, J. A., *A Reading of 'Sir Gawain and the Green Knight'* (London, 1965).
Kean, P. M., *The Pearl: An Interpretation* (London, 1967).
Mehl, Dieter, *The Middle English Romances of the Thirteenth and Fourteenth Centuries* (London, 1969).
Spearing, A. C., *The 'Gawain' Poet* (Cambridge, 1970).
Stevens, John, *Medieval Romance* (London, 1973).
Vinaver, Eugene, *The Rise of Romance* (Oxford, 1961).

Langland's Piers Plowman

Aers, David, *'Piers Plowman' and Christian Allegory* (London, 1975).
Alford, John (ed.), *A Companion to 'Piers Plowman'* (Berkeley, 1988).
Baldwin, Anna, *The Theme of Government in 'Piers Plowman'* (Cambridge, 1981).
Frank, Robert, W., *'Piers Plowman' and the Scheme of Salvation* (New Haven, 1957).
Godden, Malcolm, *The Making of 'Piers Plowman'* (London, 1990).
Judson, Allen B., *The Ethical Poetic of the Later Middle Ages: A Decorum of Convenient Distinction* (London, 1982).
Schmidt, A. V. C., *The Clerkly Maker: Langland's Poetic Art* (Cambridge, 1987).

Simpson, James, *'Piers Plowman': An Introduction to the B-Text* (London, 1990).
Stokes, Myra, *Justice and Mercy in 'Piers Plowman'* (London, 1984).

Geoffrey Chaucer

Bishop, Ian, *'Troilus and Criseyde': A Critical Study* (Bristol, 1985).
Boitani, Piero, and Mann, Jill (eds.), *The Cambridge Chaucer Companion* (Cambridge, 1986).
Brewer, D. S. (ed.), *Geoffrey Chaucer* (London, 1974).
Burnley, J. D., *Chaucer's Language and the Philosophers' Tradition* (Cambridge, 1980).
Burnley, J. D., *A Guide to Chaucer's Language* (London, 1983); republished as *The Language of Chaucer* (London, 1989).
Cooper, Helen, *The Canterbury Tales*, Oxford Guides to Chaucer (Oxford, 1989).
Mann, Jill, *Geoffrey Chaucer* (London, 1991).
Miller, R. P., *Chaucer: Sources and Backgrounds* (New York, 1977).
Minnis, A. J., *The Shorter Poems*, Oxford Guides to Chaucer (Oxford, 1995).
Muscatine, Charles, *Chaucer and the French Tradition* (Berkeley, 1957).
Pearsall, D. A., *The Canterbury Tales* (London, 1986).
Windeatt, B. A., *Chaucer's Dream Poetry: Sources and Analogues* (Cambridge, 1982).
Windeatt, B. A., *Troilus and Criseyde*, Oxford Guides to Chaucer (Oxford, 1992).

Gower, Lydgate, Hoccleve, and Margery Kempe

Burrow, J. A., *Thomas Hoccleve* (Aldershot, 1994).
Ebin, Lois, *John Lydgate* (Boston, 1985).
Fisher, John H., *John Gower: Moral Philosopher and Friend of Chaucer* (New York, 1964).
Hirsch, John C., *The Revelations of Margery Kempe* (Leiden, 1989).
Minnis, A. J. (ed.), *Gower's 'Confessio Amantis': Responses and Reassessments* (Cambridge, 1983).
Pearsall, D. A., *John Lydgate* (London, 1970).
Yeager, R. F., *Gower's Poetic* (Cambridge, 1990).

Poetry in Scotland in the Fifteenth Century

Bawcutt, Priscilla, *Gavin Douglas* (Edinburgh, 1976).
Bawcutt, Priscilla, *Dunbar the Makar* (Oxford, 1992).
Gray, Douglas, *Robert Henryson* (Leiden, 1979).
Kinsley, James, *Scottish Poetry: A Critical Survey* (London, 1955).
Kratzmann, Greg, *Anglo-Scottish Literary Relations 1450–1550* (Cambridge, 1980).
Ross, Ian Simpson, *William Dunbar*, Medieval and Renaissance Authors Series (Leiden, 1981).

Late Medieval Drama

Kolve, V. A., *The Play Called Corpus Christi* (Stanford, Calif., 1966).
Tydeman, William, *English Medieval Theatre 1400–1500* (London, 1986).
Wickham, Glynne, *The Medieval Theatre* (London, 1974).
Woolf, Rosemary, *The English Mystery Plays* (London, 1972).

Late Medieval Religious Writing

Aers, David, *Community, Gender and Individual Identity: English Writing 1360–1430* (London, 1988).

Glascoe, Marion (ed.), *The Medieval Mystical Tradition in England: Proceedings of the Exeter Symposium*, 5 vols. (I–II: Exeter, 1980–2; III–V: Cambridge, 1984–92).

Hodgson, Phyllis, *Three Fourteenth-Century English Mystics* (London, 1967).

Hudson, Anne, *Lollards and their Books* (London, 1985).

Hudson, Anne, *The Premature Reformation: Wycliffite Texts and Lollard History* (Oxford, 1988).

Kenny, Anthony, *Wyclif* (Oxford, 1988).

Kenny, Anthony, *Wyclif in his Times* (Oxford, 1986).

Knowles, David, *The English Mystical Tradition* (London, 1964).

Owst, G. R., *Literature and Pulpit in Medieval England,* 2nd edn. (Oxford, 1961).

Riehle, Wolfgang, *The Middle English Mystics*, trans. Bernard Standring (London, 1967).

Spencer, H. Leith, *English Preaching in the Late Middle Ages* (Oxford, 1993).

Watson, Nicholas, *Richard Rolle and the Invention of Authority* (Cambridge, 1991).

Malory and Caxton

Brewer, D. S., and Takamiya, T. (eds.), *Aspects of Malory* (Cambridge, 1981).

Field, P. J. C., *Romance and Chronicle: A Study of Malory's Prose Style* (London, 1971).

Lambert, Mark, *Malory: Style and Vision in the Morte Darthur* (New Haven, 1975).

Riddy, Felicity, *Sir Thomas Malory* (Leiden, 1987).

Vinaver, Eugene, *Malory* (Oxford, 1929).

Blake, N. F., *Caxton and his World* (London, 1969).

Eisenstein, Elizabeth, *The Printing Press as an Agent of Change* (Cambridge, 1979).

3. RENAISSANCE AND REFORMATION: LITERATURE 1510–1620

General and Historical

Ashton, Robert, *The City and the Court 1603–1643* (Cambridge, 1979).

Bevington, David M., *From 'Mankind' to Marlow* (London, 1962).

Bowers, Fredson, *Elizabethan Revenge Tragedy 1587–1642* (Princeton, 1940).

Bowle, John, *Charles I: A Biography* (Boston, 1975).

Bradbrook, M. C., *Themes and Conventions of Elizabethan Tragedy*, 2nd edn. (Cambridge, 1980).

Braunmuller, A. R., and Hattaway, Michael (eds.), *The Cambridge Companion to English Renaissance Drama* (Cambridge, 1990).

Briggs, Julia, *This Stage-Play World: English Literature and its Background, 1580–1625* (Oxford, 1983).

Butler, Martin, *Theatre and Crisis, 1632–42* (Cambridge, 1984).

Clare, Janet, *'Art made tongue-tied by authority': Elizabethan and Jacobean Dramatic Censorship* (Manchester, 1990).

Clark, Sandra, *The Elizabethan Pamphleteers 1580–1640* (London, 1983).

Clemen, Wolfgang, *The Development of Shakespeare's Imagery*, rev. edn. (London, 1977).

Cressy, David, *Literacy and the Social Order: Reading and Writing in Tudor and Stuart England* (Cambridge, 1980).

Davis, Walter R., *Idea and Act in Elizabethan Fiction* (Princeton, 1969).

Duffy, Eamon, *The Stripping of the Altars: Traditional Religion in England 1400–1580* (New Haven, 1992).

Evans, G. Blakemore, *Elizabethan-Jacobean Drama* (London, 1987).

Farley-Hills, David, *Shakespeare and the Rival Playwrights 1600–1606* (London, 1990).

Fraser, Antonia, *The Weaker Vessel: Woman's Lot in Seventeenth Century England* (London, 1984).

Gibbons, Brian, *Jacobean City Comedy*, 2nd edn. (London, 1980).

Grady, Hugh, *The Modernist Shakespeare: Critical Texts in a Material World* (Oxford, 1991).

Grundy, Joan, *The Spenserian Poets: A Study in Elizabethan and Jacobean Poetry* (London, 1969).

Gurr, Andrew, *The Shakespearean Playing Companies* (Oxford, 1996).

Gurr, Andrew, *Playgoing in Shakespeare's London* (Cambridge, 1987).

Gurr, Andrew, *The Shakespearean Stage, 1574–1642* (Cambridge, 1980).

Hattaway, Michael, *Elizabethan Popular Theatre* (London, 1982).

Hill, Christopher, *Society and Puritanism in Pre-Revolutionary England* (London, 1964).

Honigmann, E. A. J., *Shakespeare: The Lost Years* (Manchester, 1985).

Honigmann, E. A. J. (ed.), *Shakespeare and his Contemporaries* (Manchester, 1986).

Hussey, S. S., *The Literary Language of Shakespeare* (London, 1982).

Kerrigan, William, and Braden, George, *The Idea of the Renaissance* (Baltimore, 1989).

Leggatt, Alexander, *Citizen Comedy in the Age of Shakespeare* (Toronto, 1973).

Leggatt, Alexander, *English Drama: Shakespeare to the Restoration 1590–1660* (London, 1988).

Lever, J. W., *The Elizabethan Love Sonnet*, 2nd edn. (London, 1966).

Lever, J. W., *The Tragedy of State: A Study in Jacobean Drama* (London, 1971).

Lindley, David (ed.), *The Court Masque* (Manchester, 1984).

Lomax, Marion, *Stage Images and Traditions: Shakespeare to Ford* (Cambridge, 1987).

McAlindon, T., *English Renaissance Tragedy* (Basingstoke, 1986).

McGrath, Alister E., *Reformation Thought: An Introduction* (Oxford, 1988).

Margolies, David, *Novel and Society in Elizabethan England* (London, 1985).

Marotti, Arthur, *Manuscript, Print and the English Literature Lyric* (London, 1995).

Marsden, Jean I. (ed.), *The Appropriation of Shakespeare: Post-Renaissance Reconstructions of the Works and the Myth* (Hemel Hempstead, 1991).

Mason, H. A., *Humanism and Poetry in the Early Tudor Period* (London, 1959).

Norbrook, David, *Poetry and Politics in the English Renaissance* (London, 1984).

Ornstein, Robert, *The Moral Vision of Jacobean Tragedy* (Madison, 1960).

Parry, Graham, *The Golden Age Restor'd: The Culture of the Stuart Court, 1603–42* (Manchester, 1981).

Pooley, Roger, *English Prose of the Seventeenth Century, 1590–1700* (London, 1992).

Rhodes, Neil, and Sawday, Jonathan, *The Renaissance Computer: Knowledge Technology in the First Age of Print* (London, 2000).

Ribner, Irving, *The English History Play in the Age of Shakespeare* (Princeton, 1957).

Salzman, Paul, *English Prose Fiction 1558–1700: A Critical History* (Oxford, 1985).

Schoenbaum, Samuel, *William Shakespeare: A Documentary Life* (Oxford, 1975).

Sharpe, J. A., *Early Modern England: A Social History 1550–1760* (London, 1987).

Shell, Alison, *Catholicism, Controversy and the English Literary Imagination* (Cambridge, 1999).

Sinfield, Alan, *Literature in Protestant England, 1560–1660* (London, 1983).

Thomas, Keith, *Religion and the Decline of Magic: Studies in Popular Beliefs in Sixteenth and Seventeenth Century England* (London, 1971).

Waller, Gary, *English Poetry of the Sixteenth Century*, 2nd edn. (London, 1993).

Wells, Stanley (ed.), *The Cambridge Companion to Shakespeare Studies* (Cambridge, 1986).

Wells, Stanley (ed.), *Shakespeare: A Bibliographical Guide*, new edn. (Oxford, 1990).

Willson, David Harris, *King James IV and I* (London, 1956).

Wrightson, Keith, *English Society 1580–1680* (London, 1982).

Ways of Reading

Barbour, Reid, *Deciphering Elizabethan Fiction* (London, 1993).

Bate, Jonathan, *The Genius of Shakespeare* (London, 1997).

Belsey, Catherine, *The Subject of Tragedy: Identity and Difference in Renaissance Drama* (London, 1985).

Bloom, Harold, *Shakespeare: The Invention of the Human* (London, 1999).

Charney, Maurice (ed.), *'Bad' Shakespeare: Revaluations of the Shakespeare Canon* (London, 1988).

Dollimore, Jonathan, and Sinfield, Alan (eds.), *Political Shakespeare: New Essays in Cultural Materialism* (Manchester, 1985).

Dollimore, Jonathan, *Radical Tragedy: Religion, Ideology and Power in the Drama of Shakespeare and his Contemporaries*, 2nd edn. (New York, 1989).

Doran, Madeleine, *Endeavours of Art: A Study of Form in Elizabethan Drama* (Madison, 1954).

Duncan-Jones, Katherine, *Ungentle Shakespeare: Scenes from his Life* (London, 2001).

Dusinberre, Juliet, *Shakespeare and the Nature of Womankind* (London, 1975).

Eagleton, Terry, *Sweet Violence: A Study of the Tragic* (London, 2000).

Evans, Malcolm, *Signifying Nothing: Truth's True Contents in Shakespeare's Texts*, 2nd edn. (Hemel Hempstead, 1989).

French, Marilyn, *Shakespeare's Division of Experience* (London, 1982).

Glenz, Carolyn Ruth Swift, Greene, Gayle, and Neely, Carol Thomas (eds.), *The Woman's Part: Feminist Criticism of Shakespeare* (Urbana, Ill., 1980).

Goldberg, J., *James I and the Politics of Literature* (Baltimore, 1983).

de Grazia, Margareta, and Wells, Stanley (eds.), *The Cambridge Companion to Shakespeare* (Cambridge, 2001).

Greenblatt, Stephen, *Renaissance Self-Fashioning* (Chicago, 1980).

Greenblatt, Stephen, *Shakespearean Negotiations: The Circulation of Social Energy in Renaissance England* (Oxford, 1988).

Honan, Park, *Shakespeare: A Life* (Oxford, 1998).

Jardine, Lisa, *Still Harping on Daughters: Women and Drama in the Age of Shakespeare*, 2nd edn. (Hemel Hempstead, 1989).

Kermode, Frank, *Shakespeare's Language* (London, 2000).

Levin, Richard, *New Readings vs. Old Plays: Recent Trends in the Reinterpretation of English Renaissance Drama* (Chicago, 1979).

McLuskie, Kathleen, *Renaissance Dramatists* (Hemel Hempstead, 1989).

Tennenhouse, Leonard, *Power on Display: The Politics of Shakespeare's Genres* (London, 1986).

Vickers, Brian, *Appropriating Shakespeare: Contemporary Critical Quarrels* (London, 1993).

Wayne, Valerie (ed.), *The Matter of Difference: Materialist Feminist Criticism of Shakespeare* (Hemel Hempstead, 1991).

Wharton, T. F., *Moral Experiment in Jacobean Drama* (Basingstoke, 1988).

Woodbridge, Linda, *Woman and the English Renaissance: Literature and the Nature of Womenkind, 1540–1620* (Urbana, Ill., 1985).

Zimmerman, Susan (ed.), *Erotic Politics: Desire on the Renaissance Stage* (London, 1992).

Skelton, Wyatt, and Surrey

Fish, Stanley, *John Skelton's Poetry* (New Haven, 1965).

Greenblatt, Stephen, *Renaissance Self-Fashioning* (Chicago, 1980).

Muir, Kenneth, *Life and Letters of Sir Thomas Wyatt* (Liverpool, 1963).

Thomson, Patricia, *Sir Thomas Wyatt and his Background* (1964).

Howard, Henry, Earl of Surrey, *Poems*, ed. Emrys Jones (Oxford, 1964).

More, Elyot, and Ascham

Logan, George M., *The Meaning of More's 'Utopia'* (Princeton, 1983).

Hexter, J. H., *More's 'Utopia': The Biography of an Idea* (New York, 1952).

Lehmberg, S. E., *Sir Thomas Elyot, Tudor Humanist* (London, 1960).

Major, John M., *Sir Thomas Elyot and Renaissance Humanism* (Lincoln, Nebr., 1964).

Sidney and Puttenham

Buxton, John, *Sir Philip Sidney and the English Renaissance*, 3rd edn. (London, 1987).

Duncan-Jones, Katherine, *Sir Philip Sidney: Courtier Poet* (London, 1991).

Hamilton, A. C., *Sir Philip Sidney: A Study of his Life and Works* (Cambridge, 1977).

Kay, D. (ed.), *Sir Philip Sidney: An Anthology of Modern Criticism* (Oxford, 1987).

Stillman, Robert E., *Sidney's Poetic Justice: 'The Old Arcadia', its Eclogues, and Renaissance Pastoral Traditions* (London, 1986).

Lyly, Nashe, Deloney, Greene

Hunter, G. K., *John Lyly: The Humanist as Courtier* (London, 1962).

Saccio, Peter, *The Court Comedies of John Lyly* (Princeton, 1969).

Hibbard, G. R., *Thomas Nashe: A Critical Introduction* (London, 1962).

Hutson, Lorna, *Thomas Nashe in Context* (Oxford, 1980).

Ralegh and Spenser

Greenblatt, Stephen, *Sir Walter Raleigh: The Renaissance Man and his Roles* (New Haven, 1973).

Bayley, Peter, *Edmund Spenser, Prince of Poets* (London, 1971).

Bernard, John D., *Pastoralism in the Poetry of Edmund Spenser* (Cambridge, 1989).

Evans, Maurice, *Spenser's Anatomy of Heroism: A Commentary on 'The Faerie Queene'* (Cambridge, 1970).

Freeman, Rosemary, *'The Faerie Queene': A Companion for Readers* (London, 1970).

Hankins, John Erskine, *Source and Meaning in Spenser's Allegory: A Study of 'The Faerie Queene'* (Oxford, 1971).

Hume, A., *Edmund Spenser, Protestant Poet* (Cambridge, 1984).

Miller, David Lee, *The Poem's Two Bodies: The Poetics of the 1590 'Faerie Queene'* (Princeton, 1988).

Kyd and Marlowe

Barber, C. L., *Creating Elizabethan Tragedy: The Theatre of Marlowe and Kyd* (Chicago, 1988).

Healy, Thomas, *Christopher Marlowe* (London, 1995).

Levin, Harry, *Christopher Marlowe: The Overreacher* (London, 1961).

Sales, Roger, *Christopher Marlowe* (London, 1991).

Steane, J. B., *Marlowe: A Critical Study* (Cambridge, 1964).

Shakespeare: Poems

Dubrow, Heather, *Captive Victors: Shakespeare's Narrative Poems and Sonnets* (Ithaca, NY, 1987).

Martin, Philip, *Shakespeare's Sonnets: Self, Love and Art* (Cambridge, 1972).

Muir, Kenneth, *Shakespeare's Sonnets* (London, 1979).

Vendler, Helen, *The Art of Shakespeare's Sonnets* (London, 1997).

Winny, James, *The Master–Mistress: A Study of Shakespeare's Sonnets* (London, 1968).

Shakespeare: Histories

Champion, Larry S., *Perspectives in Shakespeare's English Histories* (Athens, Ga., 1980).

Leggatt, Alexander, *Shakespeare's Political Drama: The History Plays and the Roman Plays* (London, 1988).

Miola, Robert S., *Shakespeare's Rome* (Cambridge, 1983).

Ornstein, Robert, *A Kingdom for a Stage: The Achievement of Shakespeare's History Plays* (Cambridge, Mass., 1972).

Reese, M. M., *The Cease of Majesty: A Study of Shakespeare's History Plays* (London, 1961).

Siegel, Paul N., *Shakespeare's English and Roman History Plays: A Marxist Approach* (Cranbury, NJ, 1986).

Thayer, C. G., *Shakespearean Politics: Government and Misgovernment in the Great Histories* (Athens, Oh., 1983).

Traversi, Derek, *Shakespeare: The Roman Plays* (London, 1963).

Watson, Donald G., *Shakespeare's Early History Plays: Politics at Play on the Elizabethan Stage* (London, 1990).

Wilders, John, *The Lost Garden: A View of Shakespeare's English and Roman History Plays* (London, 1978).

Wilson, J. Dover, *The Fortunes of Falstaff* (Cambridge, 1943).

Shakespeare: Tragedies

Bayley, John, *Shakespeare and Tragedy* (London, 1981).

Bradley, A. C., *Shakespearean Tragedy*, 2nd edn. (London, 1905).

Brooke, Nicholas, *Shakespeare's Early Tragedies* (London, 1968).

Danby, John F., *Shakespeare's Doctrine of Nature: A Study of 'King Lear'* (London, 1948).

Dodsworth, Martin, *Hamlet Closely Observed* (London, 1985).

Drakakis, John (ed.), *Shakespearean Tragedy* (London, 1992).

Elliott, Martin, *Shakespeare's Invention of Othello* (Basingstoke, 1988).

Evans, Bertrand, *Shakespeare's Tragic Practice* (Oxford, 1979).

Everett, Barbara, *Young Hamlet: Essays on Shakespeare's Tragedies* (Oxford, 1989).

Honigmann, E. A. J., *Shakespeare: Seven Tragedies* (London, 1976).

McEachern, Claire (ed.), *The Cambridge Companion to Shakespearean Tragedy* (Cambridge, 2002).

Margolies, David, *Monsters of the Deep: Social Dissolution in Shakespeare's Tragedies* (Manchester, 1992).

Mehl, Dieter, *Shakespeare's Tragedies: An Introduction* (Cambridge, 1986).

Wilson, J. Dover, *What Happens in 'Hamlet'*, 3rd edn. (Cambridge, 1951).

Shakespeare: Comedies

Barber, C. L., *Shakespeare's Festive Comedy* (Princeton, 1959).

Felperin, Howard, *Shakespearian Romance* (Princeton, 1972).

Leggatt, Alexander, *Shakespeare's Comedy of Love* (London, 1974).

Leggatt, Alexander (ed.), *The Cambridge Companion to Shakespearean Comedy* (Cambridge, 2002).

Lewis, Anthony J., *The Love Story in Shakespearean Comedy* (Lexington, Mass., 1992).

Miles, Rosalind, *The Problem of 'Measure for Measure': A Historical Investigation* (London, 1976).

Nevo, Ruth, *Comic Transformations in Shakespeare* (London, 1980).

Thomas, Vivian, *The Moral Universe of Shakespeare's Problem Plays* (London, 1987).

Young, D., *The Heart's Forest: A Study of Shakespeare's Pastoral Plays* (New Haven, CT, 1972).

Jonson

Barton, Anne, *Ben Jonson, Dramatist* (Cambridge, 1984).

Clark, Ira, *The Moral Art of Philip Massinger* (London, 1993).

Dutton, Richard, *Ben Jonson: To the First Folio* (Cambridge, 1983).

Gibbons, Brian, *Jacobean City Comedy*, 2nd edn. (London, 1990).

Leggatt, Alexander, *Ben Jonson: His Vision and Art* (London, 1981).

Orgel, Stephen, *The Jonsonian Masque* (Cambridge, Mass., 1965).

Riggs, D., *Ben Jonson* (Cambridge, Mass., 1989).

Womack, Peter, *Ben Jonson* (Oxford, 1986).

Heywood, Beaumont and Fletcher, Chapman, Marston, Middleton, Tourneur, Webster, Ford, Shirley

Bliss, Lee, *Francis Beaumont* (Boston, 1987).

Clark, Sandra, *The Plays of Beaumont and Fletcher: Sexual Themes and Dramatic Representation* (Hemel Hempstead, 1994).

Finkelpearl, P. J., *Court and Country Politics in the Plays of Beaumont and Fletcher* (Princeton, 1990).

Holmes, David M., *The Art of Thomas Middleton* (Oxford, 1970).

Kerrigan, John, *Revenge Tragedy: Aeschylus to Armageddon* (Oxford, 1996).

Leech, Clifford, *The John Fletcher Plays* (London, 1962).

Scott, Michael, *John Marston's Plays: Themes, Structure and Performances* (Basingstoke, 1985).

Bromham, A. H., and Bruzzi, Zara, *The Changeling and the Years of Crisis, 1619–1624* (London, 1990).

Heinemann, Margot, *Puritanism and Theatre: Thomas Middleton and Opposition Drama under the Early Stuarts* (Cambridge, 1980).

Rowe, G. E., *Thomas Middleton and the New Comedy Tradition* (Lincoln, Nebr., 1979).

Bliss, Lee, *The World's Perspective: John Webster and the Jacobean Drama* (Brighton, 1983).

Pearson, Jacqueline, *Tragedy and Tragicomedy in the Plays of John Webster* (Manchester, 1980).

Farr, Dorothy M., *John Ford and the Caroline Theatre* (London, 1979).

Huebert, Ronald, *John Ford: Baroque English Dramatist* (Montreal, 1977).

Stavig, Mark, *John Ford and the Traditional Moral Order* (Madison, 1968).

Wymer, Rowland, *Webster and Ford* (Basingstoke, 1995).

4. REVOLUTION AND RESTORATION: LITERATURE 1620–1690

General and Historical

Austin, Frances, *The Language of the Metaphysical Poets* (Basingstoke, 1992).

Bennett, Joan, *Five Metaphysical Poets: Donne, Herbert, Vaughan, Crashaw, Marvell* (Cambridge, 1964).

Bevis, Richard W., *English Drama: Restoration and Eighteenth Century, 1660–1789* (London: 1988).

Birdsall, Virginia Ogden, *Wild Civility: The English Comic Spirit on the Restoration Stage* (London, 1970).

Brown, John Russell, and Harris, Bernard (eds.), *Restoration Theatre* (London, 1965).

Corns, Thomas N. (ed.), *The Cambridge Companion to English Poetry: Donne to Marvell* (Cambridge, 1993).

Donaldson, Ian, *The World Upside-Down: Comedy from Jonson to Fielding* (Oxford, 1970).

Fujimura, Thomas H., *The Restoration Comedy of Wit* (Princeton, 1952).

Hill, Christopher, *God's Englishman: Oliver Cromwell and the English Revolution* (Harmondsworth, 1970).

Hill, Christopher, *Milton and the English Revolution* (New York, 1977).

Hill, Christopher, *A Turbulent, Seditious and Factious People: John Bunyan and his Church, 1628–1688* (Oxford, 1989).

Hill, Christopher, *The World Turned Upside Down: Radical Ideas during the English Revolution* (Harmondsworth, 1972).

Holland, Norman N., *The First Modern Comedies: The Significance of Etherege, Wycherley and Congreve* (Cambridge, Mass., 1959).

Holland, Peter, *The Ornament of Action: Text and Performance in Restoration Comedy* (Cambridge, 1979).

Hume, Robert D., *The Development of English Drama in the Late Seventeenth Century* (Oxford, 1976).

Loftis, John, *Comedy and Society from Congreve to Fielding* (Stanford, Calif., 1959).

McKeon, Michael, *The Origins of the English Novel, 1600–1740* (Baltimore, 1987).

Miner, Earl, *The Cavalier Mode from Jonson to Cotton* (Princeton, 1971).

Miner, Earl, *Seventeenth-Century Imagery: Essays on Uses of Figurative Language from Donne to Farquhar* (Berkeley, 1971).

Muir, Kenneth, *The Comedy of Manners* (London, 1970).

Parfitt, George, *English Poetry of the Seventeenth Century* (London, 1985).

Parry, Graham, *Seventeenth-Century Poetry: The Social Context* (London, 1985).

Patrides, C. A., and Waddington, R. B. (eds.), *The Age of Milton: Backgrounds to 17th-Century Literature* (Manchester, 1980).

Pooley, Roger, *English Prose of the Seventeenth Century, 1590–1700* (London, 1992).

Powell, Jocelyn, *Restoration Theatre Production* (London, 1984).

Smith, Nigel, *Perfection Proclaimed: Language and Literature in English Radical Religion* (Oxford, 1989).

Willey, Basil, *The Seventeenth-Century Background: Studies in the Thought of the Age in Relation to Poetry and Religion* (London, 1934).

Ways of Reading

Brooks, Cleanth, *Historical Evidence and the Reading of Seventeenth-Century Poetry* (Columbia, 1991).

Erskine-Hill, Howard, *Poetry and the Realm of Politics: Shakespeare to Dryden* (Oxford, 1996).

Bacon

Jardine, Lisa, *Francis Bacon: Discovery and the Art of Discourse* (Cambridge, 1974).

Jardine, Lisa, and Stewart, Alan, *Hostage to Fortune: The Troubled Life of Francis Bacon 1561–1626* (London, 1998).

Vickers, Brian, *Francis Bacon and Renaissance Prose* (Cambridge, 1968).

Andrewes and Donne

Bald, R. C., *John Donne: A Life* (Oxford, 1970).

Carey, John, *John Donne: Life, Mind and Art* (London, 1981).

Edwards, David L., *John Donne: Man of Flesh and Spirit* (London, 2001).

Kermode, Frank, *John Donne* (London, 1971).

Leishman, J. B., *The Monarch of Wit: An Analytical and Comparative Study of the Poetry of John Donne*, 6th edn. (London, 1962).
Sanders, Wilbur, *John Donne's Poetry* (Cambridge, 1971).

Herbert, Crashaw, and Vaughan

Tuve, Rosemond, *A Reading of George Herbert* (London, 1952).
Fish, Stanley, *The Living Temple: George Herbert and Catechizing* (Berkeley, 1978).
Hodgkins, Christopher, *Authority, Church and Society in George Herbert* (London, 1993).
Schoenfeldt, Michael C., *Prayer and Power: George Herbert and Renaissance Courtship* (Chicago, 1991).
Vendler, H., *The Poetry of George Herbert* (Cambridge, Mass., 1975).
Healy, Thomas F., *Richard Crashaw* (Leiden, 1986).
Thomas, Noel Kennedy, *Henry Vaughan: Poet of Revelation* (Worthing, 1986).

Burton, Browne, Hobbes

Babb, Lawrence, *Sanity in Bedlam: A Study of Robert Burton's 'Anatomy of Melancholy'* (East Lansing, Mich., 1959).
Fox, Ruth A., *The Tangled Chain: The Structure of Disorder in 'The Anatomy of Melancholy'* (Berkeley, 1976).
Bennett, Joan, *Sir Thomas Browne* (Cambridge, 1962).
Huntley, Frank Livingstone, *Sir Thomas Browne: A Biographical and Critical Study* (Ann Arbor, 1962).
Patrides, C. A. (ed.), *Approaches to Sir Thomas Browne* (Columbia, 1982).
Brown, Keith (ed.), *Hobbes Studies* (Oxford, 1965).
McNeilly, F. S., *The Anatomy of 'Leviathan'* (London, 1968).
Mintz, Samuel I., *The Hunting of Leviathan: Seventeenth-Century Reactions to the Materialism and Moral Philosophy of Thomas Hobbes* (Cambridge, 1962).
Skinner, Quentin, *Reason and Rhetoric in the Age of Hobbes* (Cambridge, 1996).
Watkins, J. W. N., *Hobbes's System of Ideas* (London, 1965).

Milton

Bennett, Joan S., *Reviving Liberty: Radical Christian Humanism in Milton's Great Poems* (Cambridge, Mass., 1989).
Blamires, Harry, *Milton's Creation: A Guide through 'Paradise Lost'* (London, 1971).
Danielson, Dennis, *The Cambridge Companion to Milton* (Cambridge, 1989).
Empson, William, *Milton's God* (Cambridge, 1981).
Gregory, E. R., *Milton and the Muses* (Tuscaloosa, Ala., 1989).
Grossmann, Marshall, *'Authors to Themselves': Milton and the Revelation of History* (Cambridge, 1987).
Milner, Andrew, *John Milton and the English Revolution* (London, 1981).
Potter, Lois, *A Preface to Milton*, new edn. (Harlow, 1971).

Marvell

Chernaik, Warren, *The Poet's Time: Politics and Religion in the Work of Andrew Marvell* (Cambridge, 1983).

Legouis, Pierre, *Andrew Marvell: Poet, Puritan, Patriot*, 2nd edn. (Oxford, 1968).
Leishman, J. B., *The Art of Marvell's Poetry*, 2nd edn. (London, 1968).
Patrides, C. A. (ed.), *Approaches to Marvell* (London, 1978).
Rees, Christine, *The Judgement of Marvell* (London, 1989).
Summers, Claude J., and Pebworth, T.-L. (eds.), *On the Celebrated and Neglected Poems of Andrew Marvell* (London, 1992).
Wilcher, R., *Andrew Marvell* (Cambridge, 1985).

Bunyan

Colmer, Robert G. (ed.), *Bunyan in our Time* (Columbus, Oh., 1990).
Newey, Vincent (ed.), *'Pilgrim's Progress': Critical and Historical Views* (Liverpool, 1980).
Sim, Stuart, *Negotiations with Paradox: Narrative Practice and Narrative Form in Bunyan and Defoe* (Hemel Hempstead, 1990).

Aubrey

Hunter, Michael, *John Aubrey and the Realm of Learning* (London, 1975).
Powell, Anthony, *John Aubrey and his Friends* (London, 1963).

Rochester and Dryden

Greene, Graham, *Lord Rochester's Monkey* (Harmondsworth, 1992).
Treglown, Jeremy (ed.), *Rochester's Letters* (Oxford, 1980).
Treglown, Jeremy (ed.), *Spirit of Wit: Reconsiderations of Rochester* (Oxford, 1982).
Brady, Jennifer, *Literary Transmission and Authority: Dryden and Other Writers* (Cambridge, 1993).
Hammond, Paul, *John Dryden: A Literary Life* (London, 1991).
Hill, Geoffrey, *The Enemy's Country: Words, Contexture and Other Circumstances of Language* (Oxford, 1991).
Hopkins, David, *John Dryden* (Cambridge, 1986).
King, Bruce, *Dryden's Mind and Art* (Edinburgh, 1969).
Kinsley, Helen, *Dryden: The Critical Heritage* (London: 1971).
Winn, James Anderson, *John Dryden and his World* (New Haven, 1987).

Behn

Duffy, Maureen, *The Passionate Shepherdess* (London, 1977).
Todd, Janet, *The Secret Life of Aphra Behn* (London, 1997).

Etherege, Wycherley, Congreve, Vanbrugh, Farquhar

Bracher, Frederick (ed.), *Letters of Sir George Etherege* (Berkeley, 1974).
Underwood, Dale, *Etherege and the Seventeenth-Century Comedy of Manners* (New Haven, 1957).
Zimbardo, Rose A., *Wycherley's Drama: A Link in the Development of English Satire* (London, 1965).

Morris, Brian (ed.), *William Congreve* (London, 1970).
Novak, Maximilian, *William Congreve* (New York, 1971).
Williams, Aubrey, *An Approach to Congreve* (New Haven, 1979).
Whistler, Laurence, *Sir John Vanbrugh: Architect and Dramatist, 1664–1726* (London, 1938).
James, Eugene Nelson, *The Development of George Farquhar as a Comic Dramatist* (The Hague, 1972).
Rothstein, Eric, *George Farquhar* (New York, 1967).

5. EIGHTEENTH-CENTURY LITERATURE 1690–1780

General and Historical

Barrell, John, *The Political Theory of Painting from Reynolds to Hazlitt* (New York, 1986).
Bermingham, Ann, *Landscape and Ideology: The English Rustic Tradition 1740–1860* (Berkeley, 1986).
Brewer, John, *The Sinews of Power: War, Money and the English State 1688–1783* (London, 1989).
Brewer, John, *The Pleasures of the Imagination* (London, 1997).
Broadie, Alexander (ed.), *The Cambridge Companion to the Scottish Enlightenment* (Cambridge, 2003).
Clark, J. C. D., *English Society 1660–1832: Religion, Ideology and Politics during the Ancien Regime* (Cambridge, 2000).
Colley, Linda, *Britons: Forging the Nation 1707–1837* (London, 1994).
Colley, Linda, *Captives: Britain, Empire and the World 1660–1850* (London, 2002).
Erskine-Hill, Howard, *The Augustan Idea in English Literature* (London, 1983).
Langford, Paul, *A Polite and Commercial People: England 1727–1783* (Oxford, 1989).
McKendrick, Neil, Brewer, John, and Plumb, J. H., *The Birth of a Consumer Society: The Commercialization of Eighteenth-Century England* (London, 1982).
Porter, Roy, *English Society in the Eighteenth Century* (London, 1982).
Rogers, Pat (ed.), *The Eighteenth Century* (New York, 1978).
Rogers, Pat, *Literature and Popular Culture in Eighteenth-Century England* (Totowa, NJ, 1985).
Sambrook, James, *The Eighteenth-Century: The Intellectual and Cultural Context of English Literature 1700–1789* (London, 1986).
Speck, W. A., *Society and Literature in England 1700–60* (Dublin, 1983).
Turbeville, A. S., *Johnson's England* (Oxford, 1952).
Weinbrot, Howard, *Britannia's Issue: The Rise of British Literature from Dryden to Ossian* (Cambridge, 1993).
Willey, Basil, *The Eighteenth-Century Background: Studies in Nature in the Thought of the Period* (London, 1940).

Ways of Reading

Adorno, Theodor, and Horkheimer, Max, trans., Cumming, John, *The Dialectic of Enlightenment* (London, 1979).

Black, Jeremy (ed.), *Britain in the Age of Walpole* (Basingstoke, 1984).

Bond, D. D., and McLeod, W. R., *Newsletters to Newspapers: Eighteenth-Century Journalism* (Morgantown, W. Va., 1977).

Copley, Stephen (ed.), *Literature and the Social Order in Eighteenth-Century England* (London, 1984).

Cranfield, G. A., *A Handlist of English Provincial Newspapers and Periodicals* (Cambridge, 1952).

Downie, J. A., *Robert Harley and the Press: Propaganda and Public Opinion in the Age of Swift and Defoe* (Cambridge, 1979).

Goldgar, Bertrand, *Walpole and the Wits: The Relation of Politics to Literature, 1722–1742* (Lincoln, Nebr., 1976).

Guest, Harriet, *Small Change: Women, Learning and Patriotism 1750–1810* (Chicago, 2000).

Israel, Jonathan, *Radical Enlightenment: Philosophy and the Making of Modernity 1650–1750* (Oxford, 2001).

Jones, Vivien, *Women in the Eighteenth-Century: Constructions of Femininity* (London: 1990).

Mayo, R. D., *The English Novel in the Magazines 1740–1815* (Evanston, Ill., 1962).

Nussbaum, Felicity, and Brown, Laura (eds.), *The New Eighteenth Century: Theory, Politics, English Literature* (London, 1987).

Raven, James, Small, Helen, and Tadmor, Naomi (eds.), *The Practice and Representation of Reading in England* (Cambridge, 1996).

Varma, D. P., *The Evergreen Tree of Diabolical Knowledge* (Washington, 1972).

Pope and Swift

Fairer, David, *Pope's Imagination* (Manchester, 1984).

Fairer, David (ed.), *Pope: New Contexts* (London, 1990).

Mack, Maynard, *Pope: A Life* (New Haven, 1985).

Rumbold, Valerie, *Women's Place in Pope's World* (Cambridge, 1989).

Thomas, Claudia N., *Alexander Pope and Eighteenth-Century Women Readers* (Carbondale, Ill., 1994).

DePorte, Michael V., *Nightmares and Hobbyhorses: Swift, Sterne and Augustan Ideas of Madness* (San Marino, Calif., 1974).

Ehrenpreis, Irvin, *Swift*, 3 vols. (London, 1962–83).

Elion, Daniel, *Factions Fictions: Ideological Closure in Swift's Satire* (Newark, Del., 1991).

Flynn, Carol Houlihan, *The Body in Swift and Defoe* (Cambridge, 1990).

Higgins, Ian, *Swift's Politics: A Study in Disaffection* (Cambridge, 1994).

Foot, Michael, *The Pen and the Sword* (London, 1957).

Pollak, Ellen, *The Poetics of Sexual Myth: Gender and Ideology in the Verse of Swift and Pope* (Chicago, 1985).

Prose: Addison, Steele, and The Spectator

Bloom, Edward, *Addison and Steele: The Critical Heritage* (London, 1980).

Ketcham, Michael G., *Transparent Designs: Reading, Performance and Form in the Spectator Papers* (Athens, Ga., 1985).

Shevelow, Kathryn, *Women and Print Culture: The Construction of Femininity in the Early Periodical* (London, 1989).

Drama

Ellis, Frank H., *Sentimental Comedy: Theory and Practice* (Cambridge, 1991).
Richards, Kenneth, and Thomson, Peter (eds.), *The Eighteenth-Century English Stage* (London, 1972).
Straub, Kristina, *Sexual Suspects: Eighteenth-Century Players and Sexual Ideology* (Princeton, 1992).

The Novel

Armstrong, Nancy, *Desire and Domestic Fiction: A Political History of the Novel* (Oxford, 1987).
Ballaster, Ros, *Seductive Forms: Women's Amatory Fiction from 1684–1740* (Oxford, 1992).
Castle, Terry, *Masquerade and Civilisation* (London, 1986).
Day, Robert Adams, *Told in Letters: Epistolary Fiction before Richardson* (Ann Arbor, 1966).
Green, Katherine Sobba, *The Courtship Novel 1740–1820: A Feminized Genre* (Lexington, Mass., 1991).
Kay, Carol, *Political Constructions: Defoe, Richardson and Fielding in Relation to Hobbes, Hume and Burke* (Ithaca, NY, 1988).
McKeon, Michael, *The Origins of the English Novel 1600–1740* (Baltimore, 1987).
Miller, Nancy K., *The Heroine's Text: Reading in the French and English Novels, 1722–1782* (New York, 1980).
Mullan, John, *Sentiment and Sociability: The Language of Feeling in the Eighteenth Century* (Oxford, 1988).
Richetti, John, *The Cambridge Companion to the Eighteenth Century Novel* (Cambridge, 1996).
Richetti, John, *The English Novel in History 1700–1780* (London, 1999).
Spencer, Jane, *The Rise of the Woman Novelist from Aphra Behn to Jane Austen* (Oxford, 1982).
Tompkins, J. M. S., *The Popular Novel in England 1770–1800* (London, 1932).

Lady Mary Wortley Montagu

Grundy, Isobel, *Mary Wortley Montagu* (Oxford, 1999).
Halsband, Robert (ed.), *The Letters of Lady Mary Wortley Montagu*, 3 vols. (Oxford, 1965–7).
Lowenthal, Cynthia, *Lady Mary Wortley Montagu and the Eighteenth-Century Familiar Letter* (Athens, Ga., 1994).

Defoe, Richardson, Fielding

Backscheider, Paula R., *Daniel Defoe: His Life* (London, 1989).
Earle, Peter, *The World of Defoe* (London, 1976).

Rogers, Pat (ed.), *Daniel Defoe: The Critical Heritage* (London, 1972).
Doody, Margaret Ann, *A Natural Passion: A Study of the Novels of Samuel Richardson* (Oxford, 1974).
Doody, Margaret Ann, and Sabor, Peter (eds.), *Samuel Richardson: Tercentenary Essays* (Cambridge, 1989).
Eagleton, Terry, *The Rape of Clarissa* (Oxford, 1982).
Harris, Jocelyn, *Samuel Richardson* (Cambridge, 1987).
Keymer, Tom, *Richardson's Clarissa and the Eighteenth-Century Reader* (Cambridge, 1992).
Sale, William, *Samuel Richardson: Master Printer* (Ithaca, 1950).
Goldberg, Rita, *Sex and Enlightenment: Women in Richardson and Defoe* (Cambridge, 1984).
Battestin, Martin C., and Battestin, Ruth, *Henry Fielding: A Life* (London, 1989).
Rawson, Claude, *Henry Fielding and the Augustan Ideal under Stress* (London, 1972).
Smallwood, Angela J., *Fielding and Women* (London, 1989).
Watt, Ian, *The Rise of the Novel: Studies in Defoe, Richardson, Fielding* (Harmondsworth, 1957).

Lennox, Smollet, Sterne

Basker, James, G., *Tobias Smollet, Critic and Journalist* (Newark, Del., 1988).
Cash, Arthur H., *Laurence Sterne: The Early and Middle Years* (London, 1975).
Cash, Arthur H., *Laurence Sterne: The Later Years* (London, 1986).
Conrad, Peter, *Shandyism: The Character of Romantic Irony* (Oxford, 1978).
Fluchère, Henri, *Laurence Stern: From Tristram to Yorick* (Oxford, 1965).
Kelly, Lionel (ed.), *Tobias Smollett: The Critical Heritage* (London, 1987).
Lanham, Richard A., *Tristram Shandy: The Games of Pleasure* (Los Angeles, 1973).
Ross, Ian Campbell, *Laurence Sterne: A Life* (Oxford, 2001).
Rousseau, G. S., and Boucé, P. G. (eds.), *Tobias Smollett: Bicentennial Essays Presented to Lewis M. Knapp* (Oxford, 1971).

The Novel of Sentiment

Brissenden, R. F., *Virtue in Distress* (London, 1974).
Jones, Chris, *Radical Sensibility: Literature and Ideas in the 1790s* (London, 1993).
Markham, Ellis, *The Politics of Sensibility: Race, Gender and Commerce in the Sentimental Novel* (Cambridge, 1996).
Mullan, John, *Sentiment and Sociability: The Language of Feeling in the Eighteenth Century* (Oxford, 1988).
Todd, Janet, *Sensibility: An Introduction* (London, 1986).

Poetry

Battestin, Martin C., *The Providence of Wit: Aspects of Form in Augustan Literature and Arts* (Oxford, 1974).
Doody, Margaret Ann, *The Daring Muse: Augustan Poetry Reconsidered* (Cambridge, 1985).
Erskine-Hill, Howard, *The Poetry of Opposition and Revolution: Dryden to Wordsworth* (Oxford, 1996).

Jack, Ian, *Augustan Satire: Intention and Idiom in English Poetry 1660–1750* (Oxford, 1978).
Trickett, Rachel, *The Honest Muse: A Study in Augustan Verse* (Oxford, 1967).

Drama: Gay, Goldsmith, and Sheridan

Nokes, David, *John Gay: A Profession of Friendship. A Critical Biography* (Oxford, 1995).
Winton, Calhoun, *John Gay and the London Theatre* (Lexington, Ky., 1993).
Rousseau, G. S. (ed.), *Goldsmith: The Critical Heritage* (London, 1974).
Ayling, Stanley, *A Portrait of Sheridan* (London, 1985).
Loftis, John, *Sheridan and the Drama of Georgian England* (Oxford, 1976).
Worth, Katharine, *Sheridan and Goldsmith* (London, 1992).

Samuel Johnson and his Circle

Bate, Walter Jackson, *The Achievement of Samuel Johnson* (Oxford, 1955).
Grundy, Isobel, *Samuel Johnson and the Scale of Greatness* (Leicester, 1986).
Hudson, Nicholas, *Samuel Johnson and Eighteenth-Century Thought* (Oxford, 1988).
Rogers, Pat, *Samuel Johnson* (Oxford, 1993).

Hester Thrale and Frances Burney ('The Bluestockings')

Hyde, Mary, *The Thrales of Streatham Park* (Cambridge, Mass., 1977).
McCarthy, William, *Hester Thrale Piozzi: Portrait of a Literary Woman* (Chapel Hill, NC, 1985).
Myers, Sylvia Harckstark, *The Bluestocking Circle: Women, Friendship and the Life of the Mind in Eighteenth-Century England* (Oxford, 1990).

6. THE LITERATURE OF THE ROMANTIC PERIOD 1780–1830

General and Historical

Barrell, John, *The Dark Side of Landscape: The Rural Poor in English Painting 1730–1840* (Cambridge, 1980).
Butler, Marilyn, *Romantics, Rebels and Reactionaries: English Literature and its Background 1760–1830* (Oxford, 1981).
Cobban, Alfred (ed.), *The Debate on the French Revolution* (London, 1950).
Connell, Philip, *Romanticism, Economics and the Question of 'Culture'* (Oxford, 2001).
Crossley, Ceri, and Small, Ian (eds.), *The French Revolution and British Culture* (Oxford, 1989).
Curran, Stuart (ed.), *The Cambridge Companion to British Romanticism* (Cambridge, 1993).
Deane, Seamus, *The French Revolution and Enlightenment in England 1789–1832* (Cambridge, Mass., 1988).
Emsley, Clive, *British Society and the French Wars 1793–1815* (London, 1979).
Hobsbawm, E. J., *The Age of Revolution 1789–1848* (London, 1962).

Honour, Hugh, *Neo-Classicism* (Harmondsworth, 1968).

Honour, Hugh, *Romanticism* (Harmondsworth, 1979).

Wordsworth, Jonathan, Jaye, Michael C., and Woof, Robert (eds.), *William Wordsworth and the Age of English Romanticism* (New Brunswick, NJ, 1987).

Ways of Reading

Abrams, M. H., *The Mirror and the Lamp: Romantic Theory and the Critical Tradition* (Oxford, 1953).

Abrams, M. H., *Natural Supernaturalism: Tradition and Revolution in Romantic Literature* (London, 1971).

Barrell, John, *Poetry, Language and Politics* (Manchester, 1988).

Bate, Jonathan, *Shakespeare and the English Romantic Imagination* (Oxford, 1986).

Bloom, Harold, *The Visionary Company: A Reading of English Romantic Poetry* (Ithaca, NY, 1961).

Brinton, Crane, *The Political Ideas of the English Romanticists* (1926, repr. Ann Arbor, Mich., 1966).

Cave, Richard Allen (ed.), *The Romantic Theatre: An International Symposium* (Gerrards Cross, 1986).

Chase, Cynthia (ed.), *Romanticism* (London, 1993).

Clive, John, *Scotch Reviewers: The 'Edinburgh Review', 1802–1815* (Cambridge, Mass., 1957).

Copley, Stephen, and Whale, John (eds.), *Beyond Romanticism: New Approaches to Texts and Contexts 1780–1832* (London, 1992).

Day, Aidan, *Romanticism* (London, 1996).

Ferguson, Frances, *Solitude and the Sublime* (London, 1992).

Jack, Ian, *English Literature 1815–1832*, Oxford History of English Literature, vol. xii (Oxford, 1963).

Johnson, Claudia L., *Equivocal Beings: Politics, Gender and Sentimentality in the 1790s: Wollstonecraft, Radcliffe, Burney, Austen* (London, 1996).

Kelly, Gary, *English Fiction of the Romantic Period 1789–1830* (London, Wis., 1989).

Kiely, Robert, *The Romantic Novel in England* (Cambridge, Mass., 1972).

Klancher, John, *The Making of English Reading Audiences 1790–1832* (Madison, Wis., 1987).

McGann, Jerome, *The Poetics of Sensibility: A Revolution in Literary Style* (Oxford, 1996).

McGann, Jerome, *The Romantic Ideology: A Critical Investigation* (Chicago, 1983).

Murphy, Peter T., *Poetry as an Occupation and an Art in Britain 1760–1830* (Cambridge, 1993).

O'Neill, Michael (ed.), *Literature of the Romantic Period: A Bibliographic Guide* (Oxford, 1998) (for fuller bibliographies by the major Romantic poets and novelists).

Reiman, Donald H., *The Romantics Reviewed: Contemporary Reviews of English Romantic Writers*, 9 vols. (New York, 1972).

Ryan, Robert M., *The Romantic Reformation: Religious Politics, 1789–1824* (Cambridge, 1997).

Siskin, Clifford, *The Work of Writing: Literature and Social Change in Britain 1700–1830* (London, 1998).

Todd, Janet (ed.), A *Dictionary of British and American Women Writers 1600–1800* (London, 1987).
Watson, J. R., *English Poetry of the Romantic Period 1789–1830*, 2nd edn. (London, 1992).

Gibbon and Burke

Bowerstock, G. W., Clive, John, and Graubard, Stephen R. (eds.), *Edward Gibbon and 'The Decline and Fall of the Roman Empire'* (Cambridge, Mass., 1977).
Cobban, Alfred, *Edmund Burke and the Revolt against the Eighteenth Century* (London, 1929, 2nd edn. 1960).
Gossmann, Lionel, *The Empire Unpossess'd: An Essay on Gibbon's 'Decline and Fall'* (Cambridge, 1981).
Furniss, Tom, *Edmund Burke's Aesthetic Ideology: Language, Gender and Political Economy in Revolution* (Cambridge, 1993).
Langford, P., *et al.* (eds.), *The Writings and Speeches of Edmund Burke*, 12 vols. to date (Oxford, 1981–). (The best text of *A Philosophical Enquiry into the Origin of Our Ideas of the Sublime and the Beautiful* is that edited by Adam Philips (Oxford, 1990).)
O'Brien, Conor Cruise, *The Great Melody: A Thematic Biography and Commented Anthology of Edmund Burke* (London, 1992).
Mehta, Uday Singh, *Liberalism and Empire: A Study in Nineteenth-Century British Liberal Thought* (Chicago, 1999).

Paine, Godwin, and the 'Jacobin' Novelists

Butler, Marilyn, *Jane Austen and the War of Ideas* (Oxford, 1975).
Clemit, Pamela, *The Godwinian Novel: The Rational Fictions of Godwin, Brockden Brown, Mary Shelley* (Oxford, 1993).
Kelly, Gary, *The English Jacobin Novel 1780–1805* (Oxford, 1976).
Marshall, Peter H., *William Godwin* (New Haven, 1984).
Mellor, Anne K., *Mary Shelley: Her Life, her Fiction, her Monsters* (London, 1988).
Flexner, Eleanor, *Mary Wollstonecraft: A Biography* (New York, 1972).
Paine, Thomas, *The Rights of Man*, ed. Henry Collins (Harmondsworth, 1969).
The Complete Writings of Thomas Paine, ed. Philip S. Foner (New York, 1945).
St Clair, William, *The Godwins and the Shelleys: The Biography of a Family* (London, 1989).
Taylor, Barbara, *Mary Wollstonecraft and the Feminist Imagination* (Cambridge, 2003).
Tomalin, Claire, *The Life and Death of Mary Wollstonecraft* (London, 1974).
Wardle, R. M., *Godwin and Mary: The Letters of William Godwin and Mary Wollstonecraft* (Lawrence, Kan., 1967) (suppl. by the same editor's *Collected Letters of Mary Wollstonecraft* (Ithaca, New York, 1979)).

A Vindication of the Rights of Woman is edited, with an introduction dealing with Wollstonecraft's reading, by Carol Poston (New York, 1976). The best edition of *Mary* and *The Wrongs of Woman* is Gary Kelly's (Oxford, 1976, repr. in the Oxford World's Classics series).

Bage's *Hermsprong* (ed. Peter Faulkner) is available in the World's Classics series. Holcroft's *Anna St. Ives* (ed. Peter Faulkner, 1970), and *Hugh Trevor* (ed. Seamus

Deane, 1973), and Inchbald's *A Simple Story* (ed. J. M. S. Tompkins, 1967) were reprinted in excellent editions in the Oxford English Novels series and are now available in the Oxford World's Classics series.

Gothic Fiction

Kilgour, Maggie, *The Rise of the Gothic Novel* (London, 1995).

Miles, Robert, *Gothic Writing 1750–1820: A Genealogy* (London, 1994).

Sedgwick, Eve Kosofsky, *The Coherence of Gothic Conventions* (London, 1986).

Summers, Montague, *The Gothic Quest: A History of the Gothic Novel* (London, 1938, repr. New York, 1964).

Watt, James, *Contesting the Gothic: Fiction, Genre and Cultural Conflict, 1764–1832* (Cambridge, 1999).

Cottom, Daniel, *The Civilized Imagination: A Study of Ann Radcliffe, Jane Austen and Sir Walter Scott* (Cambridge, 1985).

Lees-Milne, James, *William Beckford* (London, 1976).

Gifford, D., *James Hogg* (Edinburgh, 1976).

Irwin, J. J., *M. G. 'Monk' Lewis* (Boston, 1976).

Kramer, Dale, *Charles Robert Maturin* (New York, 1973).

Poovey, Mary, *The Proper Lady and the Woman Writer: Ideology as Style in the Works of Mary Wollstonecraft, Mary Shelley, and Jane Austen* (Chicago, 1984).

Walpole's *The Castle of Otranto* (ed. W. S. Lewis, 1964, 1969), Reeve's *The Old English Baron* (ed. James Trainer, 1967), Radcliffe's *The Mysteries of Udolpho* (ed. Bonamy Dobree, 1966) and *The Italian* (ed. Frederick Garber, 1968), Beckford's *Vathek* (ed. Roger Lonsdale, 1970), Maturin's *Melmoth the Wanderer* (ed. Douglas Grant, 1968), Lewis's *The Monk* (ed. Howard Anderson, 1973), Hogg's *The Private Memoirs and Confessions of a Justified Sinner* (ed. John Carey, 1971), and Shelley's *Frankenstein* (ed. M. K. Joseph, 1969) were all published in the Oxford English Novels series. They are all now available as Oxford World's Classics.

Smith and Burney

Hemlow, Joyce, *The History of Fanny Burney* (Oxford, 1958).

Burney's *Journals and Letters* (ed. Joyce Hemlow *et al.*, 7 vols. (Oxford, 1972–8)) remain an indispensable source. Smith's *The Old Manor House* and Burney's *Evelina, Cecilia,* and *The Wanderer* are all available in the Oxford World's Classics series.

Cowper, Blake, and Burns

Newey, Vincent, *Cowper's Poetry: A Critical Study and Reassessment* (Liverpool, 1982).

An edition of Cowper's *Poems* (ed. John D. Bond and Charles Ryskamp, vol. i (Oxford, 1980)) is proceeding. His *Letters and Private Papers* (ed. James King and Charles Ryskamp) were published in 5 vols. (Oxford, 1979–86).

Ackroyd, Peter, *Blake* (London, 1996).

Bindman, David, *The Complete Graphic Works of William Blake* (London, 1977).

Erdman, David V., *Blake: Prophet against Empire: A Poet's Interpretation of the History of his Own Times* (Princeton, 1954, 3rd edn. 1977).

Frye, Northrop, *Fearful Symmetry: A Study of William Blake* (Princeton, 1947).
Paley, Morton D., *Energy and the Imagination: A Study of the Development of Blake's Thought* (Oxford, 1970).

Good texts of Blake's poems are provided in *The Poems of William Blake* (ed. W. H. Stevenson and David V. Erdman (London, 1971)), *The Complete Poetry and Prose of William Blake* (ed. David V. Erdman, rev. edn. (Berkeley and Los Angeles, 1982)) and *William Blake: Poetry and Design* (ed. Mary Lynn Johnson and John E. Grant (New York, 1979)). This last also contains a selection of critical assessments.

Law, Donald A., *Burns* (Edinburgh, 1986).

James Kinsley's edition of *The Poems and Songs of Robert Burns* (3 vol., Oxford, 1968) is complemented by Donald A. Low's well-annotated edition of *The Kilmarnock Poems* (London, 1985).

Wordsworth

Baron, Michael, *Language and Relationship in Wordsworth's Writing* (London, 1995).
Gill, Stephen, *William Wordsworth: A Life* (Oxford, 1989).
Jacobus, Mary, *Tradition and Experiment in Wordsworth's 'Lyrical Ballads'* (Oxford, 1976).
Moorman, Mary, *William Wordsworth: A Biography*, 2 vols. (Oxford, 1957, 1965).

Wordsworth's *Prose Works* have been edited by J. B. Owen and Jane Worthington Smyser (3 vols., Oxford, 1974). His *Poetical Works* were edited in 5 vols. (1940–9) by Ernest de Selincourt and Helen Darbishire (rev. edn. 1952–9). The most useful annotated edition of *The Prelude* remains that edited by Jonathan Wordsworth, M. H. Abrams, and Stephen Gill (New York, 1979). The indispensable *The Letters of William and Dorothy Wordsworth* (2nd edn., 8 vols., Oxford, 1969–93) was edited by Mary Moorman, Chester L. Shaver, and Alan G. Hill.

Coleridge, Southey, and Crabbe

Beer, John, *Coleridge's Poetic Intelligence* (London, 1977).
Beer, John (ed.), *Coleridge's Variety: Bicentenary Studies* (London, 1974).
Brett, R. L. (ed.), *S. T. Coleridge* (London, 1971).
Fulford, T. J., and Paley, Morton D. (eds.), *Coleridge's Visionary Languages: Essays in Honour of John Beer* (Cambridge, 1993).
Holmes, Richard, *Coleridge: Early Visions* (London, 1989).
Holmes, Richard, *Coleridge: Darker Reflections* (London, 1998).
Leask, Nigel, *The Politics of Imagination in Coleridge's Thought* (Basingstoke, 1988).

The standard edition of Coleridge's verse remains that edited by Ernest H. Coleridge (2 vols., Oxford, 1912). Coleridge's *Collected Works* (12 vols., London, 1971–92) has appeared under various editorships. His *Collected Letters* (6 vols., Oxford, 1956–71) were edited by Earl Leslie Griggs. The *Biographia Literaria* (2 vols., Princeton, 1983) was edited by James Engell and W. Jackson Bate.

Carnall, G., *Robert Southey and his Age* (Oxford, 1960).
Madden, Lionel (ed.), *Robert Southey: The Critical Heritage* (London, 1972).
New, Peter, *George Crabbe's Poetry* (London, 1976).

Lucas, John (ed.), *A Selection from George Crabbe* (London, 1967).
Pollard, Arthur, *Crabbe: The Critical Heritage* (London, 1972).

Austen, the 'Regional' Novel, and Scott

Butler, Marilyn, *Jane Austen and the War of Ideas* (Oxford, 1975).
Cope, Edward (ed.), *The Cambridge Companion to Jane Austen* (Cambridge, 1997).
Hardy, Barbara, *A Reading of Jane Austen* (London, 1975).
Nokes, David, *Jane Austen: A Life* (London, 1997).
Roberts, Warren, *Jane Austen and the French Revolution* (New York, 1979).
Southam, B. C., *Jane Austen's Literary Manuscripts: A Study of the Novelist's Development through the Surviving Papers* (Oxford, 1964).
Southam, B. C. (ed.), *Jane Austen: The Critical Heritage* (London, 1967).

Austen's letters were published as *Jane Austen's Letters to her Sister Cassandra and Others* (ed. R. W. Chapman (2nd edn. Oxford, 1959)). Excellent textual editions of her novels appeared under various editorships in the Oxford English Novels series. These texts are now available in the World's Classics series.

Parker, W. M., *Susan Ferrier and John Galt* (London, 1965).

Ferrier's *Marriage* (ed. Herbert Foltinek) was published in the Oxford English Novels series in 1971. It is available as a World's Classic.

Gordon, Ian A., *John Galt: The Life of a Writer* (London, 1972).
Scott, P. H., *John Galt* (Edinburgh, 1985).

Galt's *Annals of the Parish* and *The Provost* were edited in the Oxford English Novels series (1967, 1973) and are available as World's Classics.

Butler, Marilyn, *Maria Edgeworth: A Literary Biography* (Oxford, 1972).

Edgeworth's *Letters from England 1813–44* (ed. Christina Colvin (Oxford, 1971)) provide a personal and social context from which her novels emerged. *Castle Rackrent* (ed. G. Watson, 1964) is available, with other Edgeworth novels, in the Oxford World's Classics series.

Brown, David, *Walter Scott and the Historical Imagination* (London, 1979).
Lascelles, Mary, *The Story-Teller Retrieves the Past: Historical Fiction and Fictitious History in the Art of Scott, Stevenson, Kipling and Some Others* (Oxford, 1980).
McMaster, Graham, *Scott and Society* (Cambridge, 1981).
Robertson, Fiona, *Legitimate Histories: Scott, Gothic and the Authorities of Fiction* (Oxford, 1994).
Sanders, Andrew, *The Victorian Historical Novel 1840–1880* (London, 1978).
Sutherland, John, *The Life of Walter Scott* (Oxford, 1995).

Scott's *Letters* (ed. H. J. C. Grierson) appeared in 12 vols. (Oxford, 1932–7). J. C. Corson's accompanying *Notes and Index to . . . The Letters of Sir Walter Scott* was published in 1979. Scott's *Journal* (ed. W. E. K. Anderson) was published in 1972 (Oxford).

Byron, Shelley, and Keats

Lansdown, Richard, *Byron's Historical Dramas* (Oxford, 1992).
MacCarthy, Fiona, *Byron: Life and Legend* (London, 2002).
McGann, Jerome J., *'Don Juan' in Context* (London, 1976).

Marchand, Leslie A., *Byron: A Biography*, 3 vols. (London, 1958).
Rutherford, Andrew, *Byron: A Critical Study* (Edinburgh, 1961).

The best edition of Byron's *Complete Poetical Works* is that edited by Jerome J. McGann (3 vols., Oxford, 1980–1). Leslie A. Marchand's edition of Byron's *Letters and Journals* was published in 12 vols. (London, 1973–82).

Clark, Timothy, *Embodying Revolution: The Figure of the Poet in Shelley* (Oxford, 1989)
Dawson, P. M. S., *The Unacknowledged Legislator: Shelley and Politics* (Oxford, 1980).
MacNiece, Gerald, *Shelley and the Revolutionary Idea* (Cambridge, Mass., 1969).
O'Neill, Michael, *Percy Bysshe Shelley: A Literary Life* (Basingstoke, 1989).
O'Neill, Michael, *The Human Mind's Imaginings: Conflict and Achievement in Shelley's Poetry* (Oxford, 1989).
Webb, Timothy, *Shelley: A Voice not Understood* (Manchester, 1977).

The text of Shelley's poems remains a contentious issue. The editions by R. Ingpen and W. E. Peck (10 vols., London, 1965) and T. Hutchinson (rev. by G. M. Matthews (London, 1970)) are to some degree supplemented by the work of N. Rogers, whose edition began to appear in 1972 (Oxford). *The Prose Works of Percy Bysshe Shelley* (ed. E. B. Murray) began publication in collected form in 1993 (Oxford). F. L. Jones's 2-vol. *The Letters of Percy Bysshe Shelley* was published in 1964 (Oxford).

Bate, W. J., *John Keats* (Cambridge, Mass., 1963).
Gittings, Robert, *John Keats* (London, 1968).
Jack, Ian, *Keats and the Mirror of Art* (Oxford, 1971).
Ricks, Christopher, *Keats and Embarrassment* (Oxford, 1974).
Roe, Nicholas (ed.), *Keats and History* (Cambridge, 1995).

The best editions of Keat's *Poetical Works* are those by Miriam Alott (London, 1970) and Jack Stillinger (Cambridge, Mass., 1978). The standard edition of Keats's *Letters* is that by H. E. Rollins (2 vols., Cambridge, Mass., 1958). Rollins is also the editor of *The Keats Circle: Letters and Papers (1816–1879)* (Cambridge, Mass., 1965).

The 'Romantic' Essayists

Cafarelli, Annette Wheeler, *Prose in the Age of Poets: Romanticism and Biographical Narrative from Johnson to De Quincey* (Philadelphia, 1990).
Bate, Jonathan (ed.), *The Romantics on Shakespeare* (Harmondsworth, 1992).
Bloom, Harold, *William Hazlitt* (New York, 1986).
Jones, Stanley, *Hazlitt: A Life* (Oxford, 1989).
Park, R., *Hazlitt and the Spirit of the Age* (Oxford, 1971).
Paulin, Tom, *The Day-Star of Liberty: William Hazlitt's Radical Style* (London, 1998).

Lamb's *Letters* (together with those of his sister Mary Anne Lamb) were edited in 3 vols. by E. W. Mars (London, 1976–7).

Butler, Marilyn, *Peacock Displayed: A Satirist in his Context* (London, 1979).

The best edition of Peacock's *Headlong Hall* and *Gryll Grange* is that available in the Oxford World's Classics series.

Hanley, Keith (ed.), *Walter Savage Landor: Selected Poetry and Prose* (Manchester, 1981).
Proudfit, Charles L. (ed.) *Landor as Critic* (London, 1979).
Super, R. H., *Walter Savage Landor: A Biography* (New York, 1954).

Clare and Cobbett

Brownlow, T., *John Clare and the Picturesque Landscape* (Oxford, 1983).

Haughton, Hugh, Philips, Adam, and Summerfield, Geoffrey (eds.), *John Clare in Context* (Cambridge, 1994).

Storey, Mark (ed.), *The Letters of John Clare* (Oxford, 1985).

The best edition of Clare's *Later Poems* is that prepared by Eric Robinson and David Powell (2 vols., Oxford, 1984). Further volumes in this series are to appear. Clare's *Prose* was edited by J. W. and Anne Tibble (London, 1951).

Sambrook, James, *William Cobbett* (London, 1973).

Spater, George, *William Cobbett: The Poor Man's Friend*, 2 vols. (Cambridge, 1982).

Williams, Raymond, *William Cobbett* (Oxford, 1983).

The edition of *Rural Rides* prepared in 1930 by G. D. H. and M. Cole remains standard despite its limitations.

7. HIGH VICTORIAN LITERATURE 1830–1880

General and Historical

Altick, Richard D., *Victorian People and Ideas* (New York, 1973).

Ashton, Rosemary, *The German Idea: Four English Writers and the Reception of German Thought 1800–1860* (Cambridge, 1980).

Beer, Gillian, *Darwin's Plots: Evolutionary Narrative in Darwin, George Eliot and Nineteenth-Century Fiction* (London, 1983).

Briggs, Asa, *Victorian Cities* (London, 1963).

Brock, Michael, *The Great Reform Act* (London, 1973).

Chadwick, Owen, *The Victorian Church*, 2 vols. (London, 1966).

DeLaura, David J. (ed.), *Victorian Prose: A Guide to Research* (New York, 1973).

Faverty, Frederic E. (ed.), *The Victorian Poets: A Guide to Research* (Cambridge, Mass., 1956; 2nd edn. 1968).

Flint, Kate, *The Victorians and the Visual Imagination* (Cambridge, 2000).

Ford, G. H. (ed.), *Victorian Fiction: A Second Guide to Research* (New York, 1978).

Gill, Stephen, *Wordsworth and the Victorians* (Oxford, 1998).

Gilmour, Robin, *The Victorian Period: The Intellectual and Cultural Context of English Literature 1830–1890* (London, 1993).

Hilton, Boyd, *The Age of Atonement: The Influence of Evangelicalism on Social and Economic Thought* (Oxford, 1988).

Hoppen, K. Theodore, *The Mid-Victorian Generation 1846–1886* (Oxford, 1998).

Houghton, W. E., *The Victorian Frame of Mind 1830–1870* (New Haven, 1957).

Knoepflmacher, U. C., and Tennyson, G. B. (eds.), *Nature and the Victorian Imagination* (Berkeley, 1977).

Mason, Michael, *The Making of Victorian Sexuality* (Oxford, 1994).

Mason, Michael, *The Making of Victorian Sexual Attitudes* (Oxford, 1994).

Shattock, Joanne, and Wolff, Michael (eds.), *The Victorian Periodical Press: Samplings and Soundings* (Leicester, 1982).

Thompson, F. M. L., *The Rise of Respectable Society: A Social History of Victorian Britain, 1830–1900* (London, 1988).

Williams, Raymond, *Culture and Society 1780–1950* (London, 1958).
Woodward, E. L., *The Age of Reform, 1815–1870*, 2nd edn. (Oxford, 1962).

Ways of Reading

Armstrong, Isobel, *Victorian Poetry: Poetry, Poetics and Politics* (London, 1993).
Armstrong, Isobel, and Bristow, Joseph, with Sharrock, Clara (eds.), *Nineteenth Century Women Poets: An Oxford Anthology* (Oxford, 1996).
Ball, Patricia M., *The Heart's Events: The Victorian Poetry of Relationships* (London, 1976).
Booth, M. R., *English Melodrama* (London, 1965).
Booth, M. R. (ed.), *English Plays of the Nineteenth Century*, 6 vols. (Oxford, 1969–76). (The valuable introductions to these volumes were reprinted as *Prefaces to English Nineteenth-Century Theatre* (Manchester, 1980).)
Griffiths, Eric, *The Printed Voice of Victorian Poetry* (Oxford, 1989).
Gross, John, *The Rise and Fall of the Man of Letters: Aspects of Literary Life since 1800* (London, 1969).
Horsman, Alan, *The Victorian Novel*, vol. xiii of The Oxford History of English Literature (Oxford, 1990).
Leighton, Angela, *Victorian Women Poets: Writing against the Heart* (Hemel Hempstead, 1992).
Richards, Bernard, *English Poetry of the Victorian Period 1830–1890* (London, 1988).
Sanders, Andrew, *The Victorian Historical Novel 1840–1880* (London, 1978).
Sedgwick, Eve Kosofsky, *Between Men: English Literature and Male Homosocial Desire* (New York, 1989).
Sutherland, John, *Victorian Novelists and Publishers* (London, 1976).
Sutherland, John, *The Longman Companion to Victorian Fiction* (London, 1988).
Tillotson, Kathleen, *Novels of the Eighteen-Forties* (London, 1954).
Wheeler, Michael, *English Fiction of the Victorian Period* (London, 1985; 2nd edn. 1994).

Carlyle and Dickens

Heffer, Simon, *Moral Desperado: A Life of Thomas Carlyle* (London, 1995).
Le Quesne, A. L., *Carlyle* (Oxford, 1982); repr. in *Victorian Thinkers: Carlyle, Ruskin, Arnold, Morris* (Oxford, 1993).
Ackroyd, Peter, *Dickens* (London, 1990).
Butt, John, and Tillotson, Kathleen, *Dickens at Work* (London, 1957).
Carey, John, *The Violent Effigy: A Study of Dickens' Imagination* (London, 1973; 2nd edn. 1991).
Collins, Philip (ed.), *Dickens: The Critical Heritage* (London, 1971).
Collins, Philip, *Dickens and Crime* (London, 1962).
Flint, Kate, *New Readings: Dickens* (Brighton, 1986).
Hollington, Michael (ed.), *Charles Dickens: Critical Assessments*, 4 vols. (New York, 1995).
Sanders, Andrew, *Charles Dickens: Resurrectionist* (London, 1982).
Sanders, Andrew, *Dickens and the Spirit of the Age* (Oxford, 1999).
Sanders, Andrew, *Charles Dickens* (Oxford, 2003).
Schlicke, Paul (ed.), *The Oxford Companion to Dickens* (Oxford, 1999).

Slater, Michael, *Dickens and Women* (London, 1983).

Dickens's letters have been edited as *Pilgrim Edition of the Letters of Charles Dickens* (12 vols., Oxford, 1965–2002). The Clarendon Press at Oxford is also publishing the standard scholarly edition of the text of Dickens's novels. These texts are republished in the paperback World's Classics series, a series which generally provides the best editions available to students. The paperback Everyman edition of Dickens (1993–) also has excellent introductions and notes. A selected edition of Dickens's journalism (ed. Michael Slater) was published in 4 vols. by Dent (1994–2000).

Gaskell, Kingsley, and Disraeli

Chapple, J. A. V., and Pollard, Arthur (eds.), *The Letters of Mrs Gaskell* (Manchester, 1966).
Chapple, John, *Elizabeth Gaskell: The Early Years* (Manchester, 1997).
Easson, Angus, *Elizabeth Gaskell* (London, 1979).
Uglow, Jenny, *Elizabeth Gaskell: A Habit of Stories* (London, 1993).
Blake, Robert, *Disraeli* (London, 1966).
Braun, Thom, *Disraeli the Novelist* (London, 1981).
Flint, Kate, *Elizabeth Gaskell* (Plymouth, 1995).
Schwarz, D. R., *Disraeli's Fiction* (London, 1979).
Smith, Sheila M., *The Other Nation: The Poor in English Novels of the 1840s and 1850s* (Oxford, 1980).

Macaulay, Thackeray, and Trollope

Burrow, J. W., *A Liberal Descent: Victorian Historians and the English Past* (Cambridge, 1981).
Hardy, Barbara, *The Exposure of Luxury: Radical Themes in Thackeray* (London, 1972).
Pearson, Richard, *W. M. Thackeray and the Mediated Text: Writing for the Periodicals in the Mid-Nineteenth Century* (Aldershot, 2000).
Peters, Catherine, *Thackeray's Universe: Shifting Worlds of Imagination and Reality* (London, 1987).
Ray, Gordon N., *Thackeray: The Uses of Adversity 1811–1846* (London, 1955).
Ray, Gordon N., *Thackeray: The Age of Wisdom 1847–1863* (London, 1958).
Sutherland, J. A., *Thackeray at Work* (London, 1974).

Thackeray's *Letters and Private Papers* were published in 4 vols. (London, 1945–6), edited by Gordon N. Ray. Two supplementary volumes (ed. Edgar F. Harden) were published in New York in 1995.

Edwards, P. D., *Anthony Trollope: His Art and Scope* (Hassocks, 1978).
Hall, N. John, *Trollope: A Biography* (Oxford, 1991).
Halperin, John, *Trollope and Politics: A Study of the Pallisers and Others* (London, 1977).
Letwin, S. R., *The Gentleman in Trollope: Individuality and Moral Conduct* (London, 1982).
Sanders, Andrew, *Anthony Trollope* (Plymouth, 1998).
Wall, Stephen, *Trollope and Character* (London, 1988).

Trollope's *Letters* have been edited in 2 vols. by N. John Hall (Stanford, Calif., 1983).

The Brontë Sisters

Alexander, Christine, and Sellars, Jane, *The Art of the Brontës* (Cambridge, 1995).
Barker, Juliet, *The Brontës* (London, 1994).
Gaskell, Elizabeth, *The Life of Charlotte Brontë* (London, 1857).
Gerin, Winifred, *Charlotte Brontë: The Evolution of Genius* (Oxford, 1967).
Gerin, Winifred, *Emily Brontë: A Biography* (Oxford, 1971).
Shuttleworth, Sally, *Charlotte Brontë and Victorian Psychology* (Cambridge, 1996).

The vast amount of published material concerning the Brontës can best be investigated with the help of R. W. Crump's *Charlotte and Emily Brontë, 1846–1915: A Reference Guide* (Boston, 1982), *1916–1954* (1985), and *1955–1983* (1986). The novels of all three sisters have been published by the Clarendon Press. These edited texts, with additional annotation, are reprinted in the World's Classics series. The first volume of Charlotte's *Letters* (ed. Margaret Smith) was published by Oxford in 1995.

Tennyson and the Pre-Raphaelite Poets

Martin, R. B., *Tennyson: The Unquiet Heart* (Oxford, 1980).
Ormond, Leonee, *Alfred Tennyson: A Literary Life* (London, 1993).
Ricks, Christopher, *Tennyson* (London, 1972; rev. edn. 1989).
Sinfield, Alan, *Alfred Tennyson* (Oxford, 1986).

Tennyson's *Letters* (ed. C. Y. Lang and Edgar J. Shannon) were published in 3 vols. (Oxford, 1981–90). The standard edition of the *Poems* is that by Christopher Ricks, 2nd edn., 3 vols. (London, 1987).

Rees, Joan, *The Poetry of Dante Gabriel Rossetti: Modes of Self Expression* (Cambridge, 1981).

D. G. Rossetti's *Letters* (ed. Oswald Doughty and John Robert Wahl) were published in 4 vols. (Oxford, 1965–7).

Marsh, Jan, *Christina Rossetti: A Literary Biography* (London, 1994).

Christina Rossetti's *Complete Poems*, ed. R. W. Crump, 3 vols. (Baton Rouge, La., 1979–90) provides the best text, though selections of her verse are readily available. Her *Family Letters*, ed. W. M. Rossetti, were published in 1908.

Henderson, Philip, *Swinburne: The Portrait of a Poet* (London, 1974).

Swinburne's *Letters* (ed. Cecil Y. Lang) were published in 6 vols. (New Haven, 1960).

Faulkner, Peter, *Against the Age: An Introduction to William Morris* (London, 1980).
MacCarthy, Fiona, *William Morris: A Life for Our Time* (London, 1994).
Stansky, Peter, *Morris* (Oxford, 1983; repr. in *Victorian Thinkers*, Oxford, 1993).
Thompson, E. P., *William Morris: Romantic to Revolutionary* (London, 1955; rev. edn. 1977).

The Brownings

Margaret Reynolds's edition of *Aurora Leigh* (Columbus, Oh., 1992) is exemplary. Her text has been reprinted in a Norton Critical Edition (New York, 1995). The *Letters of Elizabeth Barrett Browning to Mary Russell Mitford 1836–1854*, ed. Meredith B. Raymond and Mary Rose Sullivan (Baylor University, The Browning Institute and Wellesley College, 1983) provides a vital insight into E.B.B.'s mind.

Armstrong, Isobel, *Robert Browning* (London, 1974).

Browning's poetry is the focus of editorial attention from three presses, but the 2 vols. of Browning in the Longman Annotated Poets series, ed. John Woolford and Daniel Karlin (London, 1991), probably provide the most usable text and annotation. The Penguin editions of *The Poems* (ed. John Pettigrew and Thomas J. Collins, 2 vols. (Harmondsworth, 1981)) and of *The Ring and the Book* (ed. R. D. Altick, 1971) remain exceptionally useful.

The Drama, the Melodrama, and the 'Sensation' Novel

For the Drama and the Melodrama, see the books listed above in the 'Ways of Reading' section.

Edwards, P. D., *Some Mid-Victorian Thrillers: The Sensation Novel: Its Friends and Foes* (St Lucia, Queensland, 1971).
Hughes, W., *The Maniac in the Cellar: Sensation Novels of the 1860s* (Princeton, 1980).
Lonoff, S., *Wilkie Collins and his Victorian Readers* (New York, 1982).
Ousby, Ian, *Bloodhounds of Heaven: The Detective in Fiction from Godwin to Conan Doyle* (Cambridge, Mass., 1976).
Page, Norman (ed.), *Wilkie Collins: The Critical Heritage* (London, 1974).
Peters, Catherine, *The King of Inventors: A Life of Wilkie Collins* (London, 1991).
Showalter, Elaine, *A Literature of their Own: British Woman Writers from Brontë to Lessing* (Princeton, 1977).
Wolff, R. L., *Sensational Victorian: The Life and Fiction of M. E. Braddon* (New York, 1979).

Meredith and George Eliot

Beer, Gillian, *Meredith: A Change of Masks: A Study of the Novels* (Cambridge, 1970).

Meredith's *Notebooks* have been edited by Gillian Beer and Margaret Harris (Salzburg, 1983). His *Poems*, ed. Phillis B. Bartlett, were published in 2 vols. (New Haven, 1978).

Ashton, Rosemary, *George Eliot: A Life* (London, 1996).
Beer, Gillian, *George Eliot* (Brighton, 1986).
Haight, Gordon S., *George Eliot: A Biography* (Oxford, 1968).
Hardy, Barbara, *The Novels of George Eliot* (London, 1959).
Levine, George (ed.), *An Annotated Critical Bibliography of George Eliot* (Brighton, 1988).
Shuttleworth, Sally, *George Eliot and Nineteenth-Century Science: The Make-Believe of a Beginning* (Cambridge, 1984).
Uglow, Jennifer, *George Eliot* (London, 1987).

The best scholarly texts of Eliot's novels are those appearing in the Clarendon Edition. These texts are reprinted, with additional notes, in the Oxford World's Classics series. Eliot's *Letters* (ed. G. S. Haight) appeared in 9 vols. (New Haven, 1954–78).

Mill, Arnold, Clough, and Ruskin

Cowling, Maurice, *Mill and Liberalism*, 2nd edn. (Cambridge, 1990).
Thomas, William, *John Stuart Mill* (Oxford, 1987; repr. in *Great Political Thinkers*, Oxford, 1992).

Collini, Stefan, *Arnold* (Oxford, 1988; repr. in *Victorian Thinkers*, Oxford 1993).
Culler, A. Dwight, *Imaginative Reason: The Poetry of Matthew Arnold* (New Haven, 1966).
Honan, Park, *Matthew Arnold: A Life* (London, 1981).

The standard edition of Arnold's *Poems* is that by Kenneth Allott (2nd edn. rev. Miriam Allott (London, 1979)). Arnold's complete prose works (ed. R. H. Super) are published in 11 vols. (Ann Arbor, 1960–77).

Biswas, Robindra Kumor, *Arthur Hugh Clough* (Oxford, 1972).
Kenny, Anthony, *God and Two Poets: Arthur Hugh Clough and Gerard Manley Hopkins* (London, 1988).
Cook, E. T., *The Life of Ruskin*, 2 vols. (London, 1911).
Hilton, Timothy, *Ruskin: The Early Years* (London, 1985).
Hilton, Timothy, *John Ruskin: The Later Years* (New Haven, 2000).
Hunt, John Dixon, and Holland, F. M. (eds.), *The Ruskin Polygon: Essays on the Imagination of John Ruskin* (Manchester, 1982).
Landow, George P., *Ruskin* (Oxford, 1985; repr. in *Victorian Thinkers*, Oxford, 1993).
Landow, George P., *The Aesthetic and Critical Theories of John Ruskin* (Princeton, 1971).
Leon, Derrick, *Ruskin the Great Victorian* (London, 1949).

Ruskin's *Works* (ed. E. T. Cook and Alexander Wedderburn) are published in 39 vols. (London, 1903–12).

Newman and Hopkins

Wolff, Robert Lee, *Gains and Losses: Novels of Faith and Doubt in Victorian England* (London, 1977).
Ker, Ian, *John Henry Newman: A Biography* (Oxford, 1988).

Newman's *Letters and Diaries* (ed. C. S. Dessain *et al.*) began to appear in 1961; 31 vols. are projected.

Bergonzi, Bernard, *Gerard Manley Hopkins* (London, 1977).
Martin, Robert Bernard, *Gerard Manley Hopkins: A Very Private Life* (London, 1991).
White, Norman, *Hopkins: A Literary Biography* (Oxford, 1992).

The standard edition of Hopkins's *Poetical Works* is that edited by Norman H. MacKenzie (Oxford, 1990). *The Journals and Papers of Gerard Manley Hopkins* were edited by Humphry House and Graham Storey (Oxford, 1959).

Carroll and Lear

Hudson, Derek, *Lewis Carroll: An Illustrated Biography* (London, 1954; rev. edn. 1977).
Gardner, Martin, *The Annotated Alice* (London, 1965; rev. edn. 1970).

Carroll's *Letters* (ed. M. N. Cohen and R. L. Green) were published in 2 vols. (New York, 1979).

Noakes, Vivien, *Edward Lear: The Life of a Wanderer* (London, 1968).

8. LATE VICTORIAN AND EDWARDIAN LITERATURE 1880–1920

General and Historical

Budd, Susan, *Varieties of Unbelief: Atheists and Agnostics in English Society 1850–1900* (London, 1977).

Chadwick, Owen, *The Secularisation of the European Mind in the Nineteenth Century* (Cambridge, 1975).

Hobsbawm, Eric, *The Age of Empire 1875–1914* (London, 1987).

Hollis, P., *Women in Public: the Women's Movement 1850–1900* (London, 1979).

Hynes, Samuel, *The Edwardian Turn of Mind* (London, 1968).

Mason, Michael, *The Making of Victorian Sexual Attitudes* (Oxford, 1994).

Perkins, Harold, *The Rise of Professional Society: England since 1880* (London, 1989).

Tate, Trudi, *Modernism: History and the First World War* (Manchester, 1998).

Wiener, Martin J., *English Culture and the Decline of the Industrial Spirit 1850–1980* (Cambridge, Mass., 1981).

Ways of Reading

Batchelor, John, *The Edwardian Novelists* (London, 1982).

Bloom, Harold (ed.), *Walter Pater* (New York, 1985).

Ellmann, Richard (ed.), *Edwardians and Late Victorians* (New York, 1960).

Hewitt, Douglas, *English Fiction of the Early Modern Period 1890–1940* (London, 1988).

Hibberd, Dominic, *The First World War* (London, 1990).

Hynes, Samuel, *The Edwardian Turn of Mind* (Princeton, 1968).

Kemp, Sandra, Mitchell, Charlotte, and Trotter, David, *Edwardian Fiction: An Oxford Companion* (Oxford, 1997).

Knoepflmacher, U. C., *Religious Humanism and the Victorian Novel* (Princeton, 1965).

Ledger, Sally, and McCracken, Scott (eds.), *Cultural Politics at the Fin de Siècle* (Cambridge, 1995).

Morton, Peter, *The Vital Science: Biology and the Literary Imagination 1860–1900* (London, 1984).

Pittock, Murry G., *Spectrum of Decadence: The Literature of the 1890s* (London, 1993).

Sandison, Alan, *The Wheel of Empire: A Study of the Imperial Idea in Some Late Nineteenth Century and Early Twentieth-Century Fiction* (London, 1967).

Showalter, Elaine, *Social Anarchy: Gender and Culture at the Fin de Siècle* (London, 1990).

The 'Agnostic' Fiction of the Late Century

Cunningham, Valentine, *Everywhere Spoken Against: Dissent in the Victorian Novel* (Oxford, 1975).

Sutherland, John, *Mrs Humphry Ward: Eminent Victorian Pre-Eminent Edwardian* (Oxford, 1990).

Ashton, Rosemary (ed.), *Robert Elsmere* (Oxford, 1980).

Furbank, P. N., *Samuel Butler* (Cambridge, 1948).

Willey, Basil, *Darwin and Butler: Two Versions of Evolution* (London, 1960).

Maclean, Catherine Macdonald, *Mark Rutherford: A Biography of William Hale White* (London, 1955).

Seiler, R. M., *Walter Pater: The Critical Heritage* (London, 1980).
Bullen, J. B., *The Myth of the Renaissance in Nineteenth-Century Writing* (Oxford, 1994).
Small, Ian (ed.), *Marius the Epicurean* (Oxford, 1986).
Dodd, Philip, *Walter Pater and the Imaginary Sense of Fact* (London, 1981).
Raby, Peter, *Samuel Butler* (London, 1991).

Hardy, Gissing, and Moore

Bullen, J. B., *The Expressive Eye: Fiction and Perception in the Work of Thomas Hardy* (Oxford, 1986).
Gatrell, Simon, *Hardy and the Proper Study of Mankind* (London, 1993).
Gregor, Ian, *The Great Web: Hardy's Major Fiction* (London, 1974).
Grundy, Isobel, *Hardy and the Sister Arts* (London, 1979).
Hardy, F. E., *The Early Years of Thomas Hardy, 1840–1891* (London, 1928).
Hardy, F. E., *The Later Years of Thomas Hardy, 1892–1928* (London, 1930).
Ingham, Patricia, *Thomas Hardy* (Oxford, 2003).
Miller, J. Hillis, *Thomas Hardy: Distance and Desire* (London, 1970).
Millgate, Michael, *Thomas Hardy: A Biography* (Oxford, 1982).
Millgate, Michael, *Thomas Hardy: His Career as a Novelist* (London, 1971).
Pinion, J. B., *Hardy the Writer: Surveys and Assessments* (Basingstoke, 1990).
Purdy, Richard Little, and Millgate, Michael (eds.), *The Collected Letters of Thomas Hardy*, 7 vols. (Oxford, 1978–88). Hardy's *Literary Notebooks* have been edited by Lennart A. Bjork, 2 vols. (London, 1985).
Seymour-Smith, Martin, *Hardy* (London, 1994) (the latest biography).
Halperin, John, *Gissing: A Life in Books* (Oxford, 1982).
Poole, Adrian, *Gissing in Context* (London, 1975).
Tindall, Gillian, *The Born Exile: George Gissing* (London, 1974).
Cave, Richard Allen, *A Study of the Novels of George Moore* (Gerrard's Cross, 1978).

Conan Doyle, Stoker, and Stevenson

Ousby, Ian, *Bloodhounds of Heaven: The Detective in English Fiction from Godwin to Doyle* (Cambridge, Mass., 1976).
Calder, Jenni (ed.), *Stevenson and Victorian Scotland* (Edinburgh, 1981).
Daiches, David, *Stevenson and the Art of Fiction* (New York, 1951).
Hennessy, John Pope, *Robert Louis Stevenson* (London, 1974).
Noble, Andrew, *Robert Louis Stevenson* (London, 1983).

Stevenson's *Letters* (ed. Sidney Colvin) were published in 2 vols. in 1899. A revised edition in 4 vols. appeared in 1911. Editions of four of Stevenson novels (ed. Emma Lettley) are available in the Oxford World's Classics series.

Kipling and Conrad

Brantlinger, Patrick, *Rule of Darkness: British Literature and Imperialism 1830–1914* (London, 1988).
Gilmour, David, *The Long Recessional: The Imperial Life of Rudyard Kipling* (London, 2002).
Wilson, Angus, *The Strange Ride of Rudyard Kipling* (London, 1977).

Batchelor, John, *The Life of Joseph Conrad: A Critical Biography* (Oxford, 1994).

Karl, Frederick R., *Joseph Conrad: The Three Lives. A Biography* (London, 1979).

Guerard, Albert, *Conrad the Novelist* (Cambridge, Mass., 1958).

Najder, Zdzislaw, *Joseph Conrad: A Chronicle* (London, 1983).

Sherry, Norman, *Conrad's Eastern World* (Cambridge, 1966).

Sherry, Norman, *Conrad's Western World* (Cambridge, 1971).

Sherry, Norman (ed.), *Joseph Conrad: A Commemoration* (London, 1976).

Watt, Ian, *Conrad in the Nineteenth Century* (London, 1980).

Three vols. of Conrad's *Collected Letters* (ed. Frederick J. Karl and Laurence Davies) have so far appeared (Cambridge, 1983–8).

'Our Theatre in the 90s': London and Dublin

Nicoll, Allardyce, *English Drama 1900–1930: The Beginnings of the Modern Period* (Cambridge, 1973).

Nicoll, Allardyce, *A History of English Drama, v: Late Nineteenth Century Drama* (Cambridge, 1959).

Worth, Katherine, *The Irish Drama of Europe from Yeats to Beckett* (London, 1978).

Dollimore, Jonathan, *Sexual Dissidence: Augustine to Wilde, Freud to Foucault* (Oxford, 1991).

Ellmann, Richard, *Oscar Wilde* (London, 1987).

Garelick, Rhonda, K., *Rising Star: Dandyism, Gender and Performance in the Fin de Siècle* (Princeton, 1998).

Raby, Peter, *Oscar Wilde* (Cambridge, 1988).

Raby, Peter (ed.), *The Cambridge Companion to Oscar Wilde* (Cambridge, 1997).

Sloan, John, *Oscar Wilde* (Oxford, 2003).

Stokes, John, *Oscar Wilde: Myths, Miracles and Imitations* (Cambridge, 1996).

Worth, Katherine, *Oscar Wilde* (London, 1983).

Wilde's *Letters* were edited by Rupert Hart-Davies (London, 1962). A supplementary volume, *More Letters of Oscar Wilde*, was published in 1985 (Oxford).

Dawick, John, *Pinero: A Theatrical Life* (Niwot, Colo., 1993).

George Rowell's edition of Pinero's *Plays* (Cambridge, 1986) remains standard.

Holroyd, Michael, *Bernard Shaw: The Search for Love* (London, 1988).

Holroyd, Michael, *Bernard Shaw: The Pursuit of Power* (London, 1989).

Meisel, M., *Shaw and the Nineteenth-Century Theatre* (Princeton, 1963).

Weintraub, Rodelle (ed.), *Fabian Feminist: Bernard Shaw and Woman* (University Park, Pa., 1977).

Wisenthal, J. L., *Shaw's Sense of History* (Oxford, 1988).

Shaw's *Collected Letters* (ed. Dan H. Laurence) have appeared in 3 vols. (London, 1972–88).

Rose, Jacqueline, *The Case of Peter Pan: The Impossibility of Children's Fiction*, rev. edn. (London, 1992).

Ormond, Leonee, *J. M. Barrie* (Edinburgh, 1987).

O'Driscoll, Robert, and Reynolds, Lorna, *Yeats and his Theatre* (London, 1975).

Taylor, Richard, *The Drama of W. B. Yeats: Irish Myth and Japanese No* (New Haven, 1976).

Ure, Peter, *Yeats the Playwright: A Commentary on Character and Design in the Major Plays* (London, 1963).
Greene, Nicholas, *Synge: A Critical Study of the Plays* (London, 1975).
King, M. C., *The Drama of John Middleton Synge* (London, 1985).

Synge's *Collected Works*, 4 vols. (Oxford, 1962–8) were edited under the supervision of Robin Skelton.

The Edwardian Novel

Drabble, Margaret, *Bennett* (London, 1974).
Lucas, John, *Arnold Bennett: A Study of his Fiction* (London, 1974).

Bennett's *Journals 1896–1928* were edited in 3 vols. by N. Flower (London, 1932–3). His *Letters* (ed. J. G. Hepburn) were published in 2 vols. (London, 1966, 1968).

Batchelor, John, *H. G. Wells* (London, 1985).
Haynes, R. D., *H. G. Wells: Discoverer of the Future* (London, 1980).
Kemp, Peter, *H. G. Wells and the Culminating Ape: Biological Themes and Imaginative Obsessions* (London, 1982).
Boll, Theophilus E. M., *Miss May Sinclair: Novelist* (Rutherford, NJ, 1973).
Beer, J. B., *The Achievement of Forster* (London, 1962).
Cavaliero, Glen, *A Reading of E. M. Forster* (London, 1979).
Das, G. K., and Beer, John (eds.), *E. M. Forster: A Human Exploration* (London, 1979).
Furbank, P. N., *E. M. Forster: A Life: The Growth of the Novelist 1879–1914* (London, 1977).
Furbank, P. N., *E. M. Forster: A Life: Polycrates' Ring 1914–1970* (London, 1978).

The Poetry

Bayley, John, *Housman's Poems* (Oxford, 1992).
Page, Norman, *A. E. Housman: A Critical Biography* (London, 1983).

Christopher Ricks's edition of Housman's *Collected Poems and Selected Prose* (Harmondsworth, 1988) offers a fine introduction and annotation.

Warner, Val (ed.), *Charlotte Mew: Collected Poems and Prose* (London, 1982).
Davie, Donald, *Thomas Hardy and British Poetry* (London, 1973).
Hynes, Samuel, *The Pattern of Hardy's Poetry* (Chapel Hill, NC, 1961).
Taylor, Dennis, *Hardy's Poetry: 1860–1928* (London, 1981).

The standard editions of Hardy's poetry are the Variorum Edition edited by James Gibson (London, 1979) and the continuing edition of *The Complete Poetical Works* by Samuel Hynes (vol. i, Oxford, 1982).

Donoghue, Denis, and Mulryne, J. R., *An Honoured Guest* (London, 1965).
Ellmann, Richard, *Yeats: The Man and the Masks* (London, 1949).
Foster, Roy, *W. B. Yeats: A Life*, i: *The Apprentice image 1865–1914* (Oxford, 1997).
Foster, Roy, *W. B. Yeats: A Life*, ii: *The Arch-Poet* (Oxford, 2003).
Jeffares, A. Norman, *W. B. Yeats: Man and Poet*, 2nd edn. (London, 1962).
Jeffares, A. Norman, *A Commentary on the Collected Poems of W. B. Yeats* (Folkestone, 1984).

Jeffares, A. Norman, and Cross, C. G. W. (eds.), *In Excited Reverie: A Centenary Tribute to W. B. Yeats* (London, 1965).

Macrae, Alasdair D. F., *W. B. Yeats: A Literary Life* (London, 1995).

Yeats's *Collected Letters* have begun to appear from the Clarendon Press under the general editorship of John Kelly (vol. i, ed. John Kelly, associate editor Eric Domville, 1986; vol. iii, ed. John Kelly and Ronald Schuchard, 1993; vol. ii, ed. Warwick Gould, John Kelly, and Deirdre Toomey, 1996).

Bergonzi, Bernard, *Heroes' Twilight: A Study of the Literature of the Great War* (London, 1965).

Fussell, Paul, *The Great War and Modern Memory* (Oxford, 1975).

Silkin, John, *Out of Battle: The Poetry of the Great War* (London, 1972).

Cooke, William, *Edward Thomas: A Critical Biography* (London, 1970).

Farjeon, Elinor, *Edward Thomas: The Last Four Years* (London, 1958).

Thomas, R. George, *Edward Thomas: A Portrait* (Oxford, 1985).

The standard edition of Thomas's verse is the *Collected Poems*, ed. R. George Thomas (Oxford, 1978).

Hassall, Christopher, *Rupert Brooke: A Biography* (London, 1964).

The Poetical Works of Rupert Brooke were edited in 1970 by Geoffrey Keynes.

Thorpe, Michael, *Siegfried Sassoon: A Critical Study* (Oxford, 1966).

Sassoon's *War Poems* (London, 1983) and his *Diaries 1915–1918* (London, 1983) were both edited by Rupert Hart-Davies.

Liddiard, Jean, *Isaac Rosenberg: The Half Used Life* (London, 1975).

Isaac Rosenberg's *Collected Works* (ed. Gordon Bottomley and Denys Harding) were published in 1937 (reissued London, 1979).

Owen, Harold, *Journey from Obscurity*, 3 vols. (London, 1963–5).

Stallworthy, Jon, *Wilfred Owen: A Biography* (London, 1974).

Owen's *Complete Poems and Fragments* (ed. Jon Stallworthy) were published in 1983. His *Collected Letters* (ed. Dominic Hibberd) were published in 1973.

The best anthologies of the poetry and other writings of the Great War are Brian Gardner (ed.), *Up to the Line of Death: The War Poets, 1914–1918* (London, 1964), I. M. Parsons (ed.), *Men Who March Away: Poems of the First World War* (London, 1965), Jon Silkin (ed.), *The Penguin Book of First World War Poetry* (Harmondsworth, 1979), Martin Taylor (ed.), *Lads: Love Poetry of the Trenches* (London, 1989), Catherine Kirby (ed.), *Scars Upon My Heart: Women's Poetry and Prose of the First World War* (London, 1981), and Margaret Kamester and Jo Vellacott (eds.), *Militarism versus Feminism: Writings on Women and War* (London, 1987).

9. MODERNISM AND ITS ALTERNATIVES: LITERATURE 1920–1945

General and Historical

Blyth, Ronald, *The Age of Illusion: Glimpses of Britain between the Wars, 1919–1940* (London, 1963; reissued Oxford, 1983).

Blyth, Ronald, *The Impact of Hitler: British Politics and British Policy 1933–1940* (Cambridge, 1975).

Crossman, Richard (ed.), *The God that Failed: Six Studies in Communism* (London, 1950).
Muggeridge, Malcolm, *The Thirties, 1930–1940, in Great Britain* (London, 1940).
Stevenson, John, *Social Conditions in Britain between the Wars* (Harmondsworth, 1977).
Stevenson, John, *British Society 1914–45* (Harmondsworth, 1984).
Taylor, A. J. P., *English History 1914–1945* (Oxford, 1965).

Ways of Reading

Armstrong, Tim, *Modernism, Technology and the Body: A Cultural History* (Cambridge, 1998).
Bell, Michael (ed.), *The Context of Modern Literature 1900–1930* (London, 1980).
Bergonzi, Bernard, *Reading the Thirties: Texts and Contexts* (London, 1978).
Bradbury, Malcolm, *The Social Context of Modern English Literature* (Oxford, 1971).
Bradbury, Malcolm, and McFarlane, J., *Modernism* (Harmondsworth, 1976, 1983).
Carey, John, *The Intellectuals and the Masses: Pride and Prejudice among the Literary Intelligentsia 1880–1939* (London, 1992).
Chothia, Jean, *English Drama of the Early Modern Period 1890–1940* (London, 1996).
Cunningham, Valentine, *British Writers of the Thirties* (Oxford, 1988).
Faulkner, Peter, *Modernism* (London, 1977).
Faulkner, Peter, *A Modernist Reader: Modernism in England 1910–1930* (London, 1986).
Fussell, Paul, *The Great War and Modern Memory* (Oxford, 1975).
Green, Martin, *Children of the Sun: A Narrative of 'Decadence' in England after 1918* (London, 1977).
Hewison, Robert, *Under Siege: Literary Life in London 1939–45* (London, 1977).
Hewitt, Douglas, *English Fiction of the Early Modern Period 1890–1940* (London, 1988).
Hynes, Samuel, *The Auden Generation: Literature and Politics in England in the 1930s* (London, 1976).
Kenner, Hugh, *The Pound Era* (London, 1977).
Levenson, Michael, *The Cambridge Companion to Modernism* (Cambridge, 1999).
Lucas, John, *Modern English Poetry: From Hardy to Hughes* (London, 1986).
Lucas, John, *The 1930s: A Challenge to Orthodoxy* (London, 1978).
Smith, Stan, *The Origins of Modernism: Eliot, Pound, Yeats* (London, 1994).
Spender, Stephen, *The Struggle of the Modern* (London, 1963).
Waugh, Patricia, *Revolutions of the Word: Intellectual Contexts for the Study of Modern Literature* (London, 1997).

Strachey, Woolf, and Mansfield

Bell, Quentin, *Bloomsbury* (London, 1968).
Johnstone, J. K., *The Bloomsbury Group* (London, 1954).
Edel, Leon, *Bloomsbury: A House of Lions* (London, 1979).
Holroyd, Michael, *Lytton Strachey*, 2 vols. (London, 1967–8).
Bell, Quentin, *Virginia Woolf: A Biography*, i: *Virginia Stephen* (London, 1972).
Bell, Quentin, *Virginia Woolf: A Biography*, ii: *Mrs Woolf* (London, 1972).
Clements, P., and Grundy, Isobel (eds.), *Virginia Woolf: New Critical Essays* (London, 1983).

Lee, Hermione, *The Novels of Virginia Woolf* (London, 1977).

McLaurin, A., *Virginia Woolf: The Echoes Enslaved* (London, 1973).

Woolf's *Diary* (ed. Anne Olivier Bell) was published in 5 vols. (London, 1977–82). *The Flight of the Mind: The Letters of Virginia Woolf* was edited in 6 vols. by Nigel Nicolson and J. Trautmann (London, 1975–80). *The Essays of Virginia Woolf 1904–1918* was edited by Andrew McNeillie in 2 vols. (London, 1986).

Alpers, Antony, *Katherine Mansfield: A Biography* (New York, 1980).

Bowlby, Rachel, *Virginia Woolf: Feminist Destinations*, 2nd edn. (London, 1997).

Fullbrook, Katherine, *Katherine Mansfield* (Brighton, 1986).

Lee, Hermione, *Virginia Woolf: A Biography* (London, 1996).

Richardson and Lawrence

Edel, Leon, *The Modern Psychological Novel* (New York, 1964).

Fromm, Gloria Gilkin, *Richardson: A Biography* (Urbana, Ill., 1977).

Staley, T. F., *Richardson* (Boston, 1976).

Watts, Carol, *Dorothy Richardson* (London, 1994).

Bell, Michael, *D. H. Lawrence: Language and Being* (Cambridge, 1991).

Black, Michael, *D. H. Lawrence: The Early Novels* (London, 1986).

Leavis, F. R., *D. H. Lawrence: Novelist* (London, 1955).

Meyers, Jeffery, *D. H. Lawrence: A Biography* (London, 1990).

Moynahan, Julian, *The Deed of Life: The Novels and Tales of D. H. Lawrence* (Princeton, 1963).

Nehls, Edward, *D. H. Lawrence: A Composite Biography*, 3 vols. (Madison, 1957–9).

Widdowson, Peter (ed.), *D. H. Lawrence* (London, 1988).

Lawrence's *Letters* have been published in 7 vols. under the editorship of J. T. Boulton and others (Cambridge, 1979–93). These volumes form part of the Cambridge edition of *The Works of D. H. Lawrence*, which has produced admirable texts of Lawrence's novels, tales, and essays under various editors.

Masefield, Aldington, Lewis, Ford

Smith, Constance Babbington, *John Masefield* (London, 1978).

Meyers, Jeffrey, *The Enemy: A Biography of Wyndham Lewis* (London, 1980).

Materer, Timothy, *Vortex: Pound, Eliot and Lewis* (London, 1979).

Wyndham Lewis's *Letters* (ed. W. K. Rose) were published in 1963.

Green, Robert, *Ford Madox Ford: Prose and Politics* (Cambridge, 1981).

Mizener, Arthur, *The Saddest Story: A Biography of Ford Madox Ford* (London, 1971).

Eliot, Firbank, and the Sitwells

Ackroyd, Peter, *T. S. Eliot* (London, 1984).

Ellis, Steve, *The English Eliot: Design, Language and Landscape in 'Four Quartets'* (London, 1991).

Gardner, Helen, *The Composition of 'Four Quartets'* (London, 1978).

Gordon, Lyndall, *Eliot's Early Years* (London, 1977).
Gordon, Lyndall, *Eliots' New Life* (London, 1988).
Kenner, Hugh, *The Invisible Poet: T. S. Eliot* (London, 1960).
Smith, C. Grover, *T. S. Eliot's Poetry and Plays* (London, 1974).

Valerie Eliot's edition of *'The Waste Land': A Facsimile and Transcript of the Original Drafts* (London, 1971) is an essential companion to a reading of the poem. The first volume of Eliot's *Letters* (ed. Valerie Eliot) was published in 1988.

Benkovitz, Miriam J., *Ronald Firbank: A Biography* (London, 1969).
Glendinning, Victoria, *Edith Sitwell: A Unicorn among Lions* (London, 1981).
Skipwith, Joanna (ed.), *The Sitwells* (London, 1994) (catalogue of the exhibition *The Sitwells and the Arts of the 1920s and 1930s*).

Joyce

As a guide through the full extent of Joycean exegesis, Thomas F. Staley's *An Annotated Critical Bibliography of James Joyce* (Hemel Hempstead, 1989) is very useful.

Attridge, Derek (ed.), *The Cambridge Companion to Joyce* (Cambridge, 1990).
Benstock, S. and B., *Who's he when he's at Home: A James Joyce Directory* (Urbana, Ill., 1980).
Blamires, Harry, *The New Bloomsday Book* (London, 1988).
Budgen, Frank, *James Joyce and the Making of 'Ulysses'* (London, 1934).
Ellmann, Richard, *James Joyce* (Oxford, 1959; rev. edn. 1982).
Fairhall, James, *James Joyce and the Question of History* (Cambridge, 1993).
Gifford, Don, *Ulysses Annotated: Notes for James Joyce's 'Ulysses'* (rev. edn. Berkeley, Calif., 1988).
Gilbert, Stuart, *Joyce's 'Ulysses'* (London, 1930).
Kenner, Hugh, *Joyce's Dublin* (London, 1955).
Kenner, Hugh, *Joyce's Voices* (London, 1978).

The best and fullest modern edition of *Ulysses* is the *Critical and Synoptic Edition*, ed. Hans Walter Gabler, Wolfhard Steppe, and Claus Melchior, 3 vols. (New York, 1984). *The Letters of James Joyce* have appeared in 3 vols. (vol. i, ed. Stuart Gilbert, New York, 1957, vols. ii and iii, ed. Richard Ellmann, New York, 1966). As a guide through the full extent of Joycean exegesis, Thomas F. Staley's *An Annotated Critical Bibliography of James Joyce* (Hemel Hempstead, 1989) is very useful.

Inter-War Drama

Krause, David, and Lowery, Robert G. (eds.), *Sean O'Casey: Centenary Essays* (Gerrards Cross, 1980).
Simmons, James, *Sean O'Casey* (London, 1983).

O'Casey's *Letters*, ed. David Krause, have been published in 2 vols. (London, 1975; New York, 1980).

Graves and Jones

Seymour-Smith, Martin, *Robert Graves: His Life and Work* (London, 1982).

A selection of Graves's letters of 1914–46 has appeared ed. Paul O'Prey as *In Broken Images* (London, 1982).

Blamires, David, *David Jones: Artist and Writer* (Manchester, 1971).
Hague, Rene, *A Commentary on 'The Anathemata' of David Jones* (Wellingborough, 1977).
Hooker, Jeremy, *David Jones: An Exploratory Study of the Writings* (London, 1975).

The New Novelists of the 1920s and 1930s

Davies, Dido, *William Gerhardie: A Biography* (Oxford, 1990).
Mengham, Rod, *The Idiom of the Time: The Writings of Henry Green* (London, 1982).
Campbell, Ian, *Lewis Grassic Gibbon* (Edinburgh, 1985).
Munro, I. S., *Leslie Mitchell: Lewis Grassic Gibbon* (Edinburgh, 1966).
Spurling, Hilary, *Ivy when Young: The Early Life of Compton-Burnett* (London, 1974).
Spurling, Hilary, *Secrets of a Woman's Heart: The Later Life* (London, 1984).

Wodehouse, Waugh, and Huxley

Myers, William, *Evelyn Waugh and the Problem of Evil* (London, 2001).
Stannard, Martin, *Evelyn Waugh: The Early Years, 1903–1939* (London, 1986).
Stannard, Martin, *Evelyn Waugh: No Abiding City: 1939–1966* (London, 1992).
Stannard, Martin, *Evelyn Waugh: The Critical Heritage* (London, 1984).

Waugh's *Letters* (ed. Mark Amory) and his *Diaries* (ed. Michael Davie), published in London, appeared in 1980 and 1976 respectively.

Baker, R. S., *The Dark Historical Page: Social Satire and Historicism in the Novels of Aldous Huxley, 1921–1939* (London, 1982).
Bedford, Sybille, *Aldous Huxley*, 2 vols. (London, 1973–4).
Bowering, Peter, *Aldous Huxley: A Study of the Major Novels* (London, 1969).

Huxley's *Letters* (ed. Grover Smith) were published in 1969 (London, 1969).

The Auden Circle

Boly, John R., *Reading Auden: The Returns of Caliban* (London, 1991).
Carpenter, Humphrey, *W. H. Auden: A Biography* (London, 1981).
Fuller, John, *W. H. Auden: A Commentary* (London, 1998).
Smith, Stan, *W. H. Auden* (Oxford, 1985).
Finney, Brian, *Christopher Isherwood: A Critical Biography* (London, 1979).
Day-Lewis, Sean, *C. Day-Lewis: An English Literary Life* (London, 1980).
Longley, Edna, *Louis MacNeice: A Study* (London, 1988).
McDonald, Peter, *Louis MacNeice: The Poet in his Contexts* (Oxford, 1991).
Hecht, Anthony, *The Hidden Law: The Poetry of W. H. Auden* (London, 1993).
Mendelson, Edward, *Early Auden* (London, 1981).
Bucknell, Katherine (ed.), *Christopher Isherwood: Diaries*, i: *1939–1960* (London, 1996) (more volumes to follow).

MacDiarmid, Upward, Koestler, and Orwell

Bold, Alan, *MacDiarmid: The Terrible Crystal* (London, 1983).
Law, T. S., and Berwick, Thurso, *The Socialist Poems of Hugh MacDiarmid* (London, 1978).

Alan Bold's edition of *The Letters of Hugh MacDiarmid* appeared in 1984 (Athens, Ga, 1984).

Crick, Bernard, *George Orwell: A Life* (London, 1980).

Sandison, Alan, *The Last Man in Europe: An Essay on George Orwell* (London, 1974).

Slater, Ian, *Orwell: The Road to Airstrip One* (New York, 1985).

Williams, Raymond, *Orwell* (London, 1971).

The Writers of the Second World War

Fussell, Paul, *Wartime: Understanding and Behavior in the Second World War* (New York, 1989).

Ackerman, John, *A Dylan Thomas Companion: Life, Poetry and Prose* (Basingstoke, 1991).

Bold, Alan (ed.), *Dylan Thomas: Craft or Sullen Art* (London, 1990).

Davies, Walford, *Dylan Thomas* (Milton Keynes, 1986).

Ferris, Paul, *Dylan Thomas: A Biography* (London, 1977).

Graham, Desmond, *Keith Douglas 1920–1944: A Biography* (London, 1974).

Scammell, William, *Keith Douglas: A Study* (London, 1988).

Alun Lewis Special Number of *Poetry Wales*, 10/3 (1975).

Pikoulis, John, *Alun Lewis: A Life* (Bridgend, 1984).

10. POST-WAR AND POST-MODERN LITERATURE

General and Historical

Addison, Paul, *The Road to 1945: British Politics and the Second World War*, rev. edn. (London, 1994).

Allsop, Kenneth, *The Angry Decade: A Survey of the Cultural Revolt of the 1950s* (London, 1958).

Calvocoressi, Peter, *The British Experience 1945–75* (London, 1978).

Hewison, Robert, *In Anger: Culture in the Cold War 1945–60* (London, 1981).

Hewison, Robert, *Too Much: Art and Society in the Sixties, 1960–75* (London, 1986).

Marwick, Arthur, *British Society since 1945* (London, 1982).

Sinfield, Alan, *Literature, Politics and Culture in Postwar Britain* (London, 1989).

Sked, Alan, and Cook, Chris, *Post-War Britain: A Political History* (London, 1979).

Vansittart, Peter, *In the Fifties* (London, 1995).

Waugh, Patricia, *Harvest of the Sixties: English Literature and its Background 1960–1990* (Oxford, 1995).

Ways of Reading

Bigsby, C. W. E., *Contemporary English Drama* (London, 1981).

Bradbury, Malcolm, *The Modern British Novel* (London, 1993).

Bradbury, Malcolm (ed.), *The Novel Today: Contemporary Writers on Modern Fiction* (Glasgow, 1977).

Corcoran, Neil, *English Poetry since 1940* (London, 1993).

Davie, Donald, *Under Briggflatts: A History of English Poetry in Great Britain 1960–1988* (Manchester, 1989).

Haffenden, John, *Poets in Conversation* (London, 1981).

Hayman, Ronald, *British Theatre since 1955: A Reassessment* (Oxford, 1979).

Jones, Peter, and Schmidt, Michael (eds.), *British Poetry since 1970: A Critical Survey* (Manchester, 1980).

Lodge, David, *The Modes of Modern Writing: Metaphor, Metonymy and the Typology of Modern Literature* (London, 1977).

Lucas, John, *Modern English Poetry: From Hardy to Hughes* (London, 1986).

Morrison, Blake, *The Movement: English Poetry and Fiction of the 1950s* (Oxford, 1980).

Picot, Edward, *Outcasts from Eden: Ideas of British Landscape in British Poetry since 1945* (Liverpool, 1996).

Raby, David Ian, *English Drama since 1940* (London, 2003).

Stevenson, Randall, *The British Novel since the Thirties: An Introduction* (London, 1986).

Taylor, John Russell, *Anger and After: A Guide to the New British Drama* (London, 1962).

Taylor, John Russell, *The Second Wave* (London, 1971).

Thwaite, Anthony, *Poetry Today: A Critical Guide to British Poetry 1960–1984* (London, 1985).

Trotter, David, *The Making of the Reader: Language and Subjectivity in Modern American, British and Irish Poetry* (London, 1984).

Worth, Katherine, *Revolutions in Modern English Drama* (London, 1973).

Rattigan

Wansell, Geoffrey, *Terence Rattigan: A Biography* (London, 1995).

Beckett

Bloom, Harold (ed.), *Samuel Beckett* (New York, 1985).

Butler, Lance St John, *Samuel Beckett and the Meaning of Being: A Study in Ontological Parable* (London, 1984).

Connor, Steven, *Samuel Beckett: Repetition, Theory and Text* (Oxford, 1988).

Harmon, Maurice (ed.), *No Author Served Better: The Correspondence of Samuel Beckett and Alan Schneider* (Cambridge, Mass., 1998).

Kenner, Hugh, *A Reader's Guide to Samuel Beckett* (London, 1973).

Knowlson, James, *Damned to Fame: The Life of Samuel Beckett* (London, 1996).

Pilling, John (ed.), *The Cambridge Companion to Samuel Beckett* (Cambridge, 1994).

Ricks, Christopher, *Beckett's Dying Words* (Oxford, 1993).

Worth, Katherine, *Beckett the Shape Changer: A Symposium* (London, 1975).

Bunting and Betjeman

Makin, Peter, *Bunting: The Shaping of his Verse* (Oxford, 1992).

Lycett Green, Candida (ed.), *John Betjeman: Letters*, i: *1926–1951* (London, 1994); ii: *1951–1986* (London, 1995).

Lycett Green, Candida (ed.), *John Betjeman: Coming Home: An Anthology of Prose* (London, 1997).

Osborne

Osborne, John, *A Better Class of Person: An Autobiography 1926–1956* (London, 1981).
Osborne, John, *Almost a Gentleman: An Autobiography 1955–1966* (London, 1991).
Trussler, Simon, *The Plays of John Osborne: An Assessment* (London, 1969).

Durrell

Fraser, G. S., *Lawrence Durrell: A Study* (London, 1968).

Golding

Carey, John (ed.), *William Golding: A Tribute on his 75th Birthday* (London, 1986).
McCarron, Kevin, *William Golding* (London, 1994).
Page, Norman (ed.), *William Golding: Novels 1954–67* (London, 1985).

Wilson

Drabble, Margaret, *Angus Wilson: A Biography* (London, 1995).
Faulkner, Peter, *Angus Wilson: Mimic and Moralist* (London, 1980).
Wilson, Angus, *The Wild Garden, or, Speaking of Writing* (London, 1963).

Murdoch

Bayley, John, *Iris: A Memoir of Iris Murdoch* (London, 1998).
Byatt, A. S., *Degrees of Freedom: The Novels of Iris Murdoch* (London, 1965).
Conradi, Peter J., *Iris Murdoch: The Saint and the Artist* (London, 1986).
Conradi, Peter J., *Iris Murdoch: A Life* (London, 2001).
Todd, Richard, *Iris Murdoch* (London, 1984).

Spark

Spark, Muriel, *Curriculum Vitae: Autobiography* (London, 1992).
Bold, Alan, *Muriel Spark* (London, 1986).
Page, Norman, *Muriel Spark* (London, 1990).

Lowry

Bowker, Gordon, *Pursued by Furies: A Life of Malcolm Lowry* (London, 1993).
Breit, Harvey, and Lowry, Marjorie Bonner (eds.), *Malcolm Lowry: Selected Letters* (London, 1967).
Gabral, Jan, *Inside the Volcano: My Life with Malcolm Lowry* (London, 2000).

'Fields we do not know': Bunting and Larkin

Makin, Peter, *Bunting: The Shaping of his Verse* (Oxford, 1992).
Thwaite, Anthony, *Selected Letters of Philip Larkin 1940–1985* (London, 1992).
Motion, Andrew, *Philip Larkin* (London, 1982).

Hartley, George (ed.), *Philip Larkin 1922–1985: A Tribute* (London, 1988).
Thwaite, Anthony (ed.), *Larkin at Sixty* (London, 1982).

Smith

Spalding, Frances, *Stevie Smith: A Critical Biography* (London, 1988).
Stemlicht, Sanford (ed.), *In Search of Stevie Smith* (London, 1991).

Hughes

Gifford, Terry, and Roberts, Neil, *Ted Hughes: A Critical Study* (London, 1981).
Sagar, Keith, *The Art of Ted Hughes* (Cambridge, 1975; rev. edn. 1978).
Sagar, Keith (ed.), *The Achievement of Ted Hughes* (Manchester, 1983).
Wagner, Erica, *Ariel's Gift: A Commentary on Birthday Letters by Ted Hughes* (London, 2000).
West, Thomas, *Ted Hughes* (London, 1985).

Hill

Hart, Henry, *The Poetry of Geoffrey Hill* (Carbondale, Ill., 1986).
Hill, Geoffrey, *The Lords of Limit: Essays on Literature and Ideas* (London, 1984).
Hill, Geoffrey, *The Enemy's Country: Words, Contexture and Other Circumstances of Language* (London, 1991).
Robinson, Peter (ed.), *Geoffrey Hill: Essays on his Work* (Milton Keynes, 1985).
Sherry, Vincent, *The Uncommon Tongue: The Poetry and Criticism of Geoffrey Hill* (Ann Arbor, Mich., 1987).

Heaney

Heaney, Seamus, *Preoccupations: Selected Prose 1968–1978* (London, 1980).
Corcoran, Neil, *Seamus Heaney* (London, 1986).
Curtis, Tony (ed.), *The Art of Seamus Heaney* (Bridgend, 1982).
Morrison, Blake, *Seamus Heaney* (London, 1982).

Harrison

Astley, Neil (ed.), *Tony Harrison* (Newcastle-upon-Tyne, 1991).

Lessing

Maslen, Elizabeth, *Doris Lessing* (London, 1994).
Sage, Lorna, *Doris Lessing* (London, 1983).
Sprague, Claire (ed.), *In Pursuit of Doris Lessing: Nine Nations Reading* (New York, 1990).

Rhys

James, Louis, *Jean Rhys* (London, 1978).
Staley, Thomas F., *Jean Rhys: A Critical Study* (London, 1979).

Carter

Gamble, Sarah, *Angela Carter: Writing from the Front Line* (Edinburgh, 1997).
Sage, Lorna, *Angela Carter* (London, 1994).

Fowles

Conradi, Peter, *John Fowles* (London, 1982).

Arden

Arden, John, *To Present the Pretence: Essays on the Theatre and its Public* (London, 1977).
Gray, Frances, *John Arden* (London, 1982).

Wesker

Wesker, Arnold, *As Much As I Dare: An Autobiography 1932–1959* (London, 1994).

Pinter

Almansi, G., and Henderson, S., *Harold Pinter* (London, 1983).
Bold, A., *Harold Pinter: You Never Heard Such Silence* (London, 1984).
Gussow, Mel, *Conversations with Pinter* (London, 1994).
Hayman, Ronald, *Harold Pinter* (London, 1968).

Orton

The Orton Diaries, ed. John Lahr (London, 1986).
Bigsby, C. W. E., *Joe Orton* (London, 1982).
Lahr, John, *Prick Up Your Ears: The Biography of Joe Orton* (London, 1978).

Stoppard

Cahn, Victor L., *Beyond Absurdity: The Plays of Tom Stoppard* (London, 1979).
Gussow, Mel, *Conversations with Stoppard* (London, 1995).
Hunter, Jim, *Tom Stoppard's Plays* (London, 1982).
Kelly, Katherine E., *Tom Stoppard and the Craft of Comedy: Medium and Genre at Play* (Ann Arbor, Mich., 1991).
Nadel, Ira, *DoubleAct: A Life of Tom Stoppard* (London, 2002).

Bond

Hoy, Malcolm, and Roberts, Philip, *Bond: A Study of his Plays* (London, 1980).

Hare

Homden, Carol, *The Plays of David Hare* (Cambridge, 1995).

Churchill

Kritzer, Amelia Howe, *The Plays of Caryl Churchill: Theatre of Empowerment* (London, 1991).

Friel

Andrews, Elmer, *The Art of Brian Friel: Neither Reality nor Dreams* (New York, 1995).
Dantanus, Ulf, *Brian Friel: A Study* (London, 1988).

Ayckbourn

Watson, Ian, *Conversations with Ayckbourn* (London, 1981).

Potter

Cook, John R., *Dennis Potter: A Life on Screen* (Manchester, 1995).
Fuller, Graham (ed.), *Potter on Potter* (London, 1993).
Gilbert, W. Stephen, *Fight and Kick and Bite: The Life and Work of Dennis Potter* (London, 1995).

INDEX

H